THE STUDY OF SOCIETY

An Integrated Anthology

Consulting Editor
CHARLES H. PAGE
University of Massachusetts

RANDOM HOUSE   NEW YORK

THE STUDY OF SOCIETY
An Integrated Anthology

SECOND EDITION

EDITED, WITH INTRODUCTIONS, BY **PETER I. ROSE** *Smith College*

FOR MY PARENTS, Aaron and Lillian Rose

PREFACE
to the second edition

Sociology Texts and the Teaching of Sociology

There are two main approaches to the teaching of introductory sociology. Each has advantages; each has limitations.

The first and most popular approach is that in which the instructor centers his course around a basic textbook which all students are required to read. Since the fundamental *raison d'être* of a textbook is to provide its readers with basic grounding in the essential concepts of the discipline, most writers tend to follow a relatively similar format—though the character of presentation and the quality of discussion do vary greatly from one book of this type to another.

In addition to what one might call the "conventional text," there are those rare volumes which occasionally appear that are something more than a detailed elaboration of basic concepts. They are better described as representing creative syntheses of sociological ideas.

Finally, of late, some textbook writers—cataloguers and synthesizers alike—have included in their books brief excerpts from the works of others in order to embellish or illustrate the points they are making. In many cases, instructors using textbooks have come to favor the latter type (or, at least, the idea of a text with readings), but often find themselves and their students dissatisfied with the abridged nature of the inserted presentations. Increasingly they have begun to ask students to purchase a book of readings to be used in conjunction with the core volume. Courses using texts and "readers" are frequently more interesting and stimulating than those which rely solely on a single textbook (whether a "cookbook," "creative synthesis," or "primer-cum-adaptations").

The second approach to the introduction of sociology is less widely used and, until recently, has been confined mainly to those colleges where contact between student and teacher is more intimate and informal and where library facilities are better suited to extensive "reserve room" reading. In such settings, instructors assign original material or journal articles to students for classroom discussion. When lectures are held, they are usually used to set the conceptual stage for the analysis of certain issues or problems or to highlight matters raised in the material being read. Many instructors in the small colleges eschew the textbook approach altogether, not only because of the greater access they have to library facilities, but also because they prefer not to constrain their students with the fetters of a single author(ity).

The large numbers of students enrolled in introductory courses in most institutions have tended to prevent course directors from entertaining the idea of library-based courses—even when they can see decided pedagogic merit in them. They claim, and with good reason, that their schools are simply ill-equipped to handle them. They also add that, since, in many cases, new instructors are assigned to teach the basic course, they must rely on the framework provided by a text rather than devising their own plan. While understandable, the situation is often lamentable. Too frequently the ingenuity of teachers is stifled, having a deleterious effect on classroom performance and, sometimes, on subsequent scholarship. In some instances, instructors and teaching assistants find their chores neither challenging nor rewarding and turn away (or are turned away) from teaching—especially the teaching of the introductory course—very early in their careers. The implications of this are manifold.

If the widely-used, text-centered approach is unsatisfactory for many students and teachers, and, if the nontext, library-based approach is out of the reach of most, there is an apparent need for another method of teaching introductory sociology. The original version of *The Study of Society: An Integrated Anthology* offered one such departure. It attempted to provide the student-reader (and his instructor) with a series of complementary and, often, interrelated articles on the principal areas of sociological inquiry. Many used the volume as a supplement to a basic textbook, while others found it valuable as a core volume. Those who used it as a core reported using lecture time as an opportunity to provide the idea and form to the material, to develop their own "oral" text. It was primarily, though not exclusively, for the latter group of instructors that the volume was originally conceived and published.

The Revised Version of The Study of Society

This book, like the original version mentioned above, is a collection of previously published essays and articles dealing with the major areas of sociological inquiry. In keeping with the spirit of providing an *integrated* approach—to meet the requirements of various sorts of teachers—the selections were again chosen to provide the student of contemporary sociology with a comprehensive overview of the nature of the discipline and a series of concrete illustrations of what sociologists have learned about their subject matter and how they have gone about studying it.

Convinced by numerous readers that the basic format of the original version was sound and useful, few "structural" alterations were made in this new edition. The flow of the Second Edition is much the same as the first and the material presented is partitioned into roughly the same compartments (although, in several cases, the labels have been slightly changed). The book begins with papers on the sociological approach. These are followed by a section in which the basic concepts of society and culture are explicated and the process of socialization is explained and illustrated. The third part of the book deals with small groups and large organizations and the characteristics of communities in a variety of social settings.

From the introductory (or "background") sections on society and culture, and social organization, the reader moves on to the ways in which societies (and communities) are stratified and their members categorically differentiated. Then, in Part V, the separable characteristics and functions of the principal social institutions (including familial, economic, political, educational, and religious systems) are discussed.

The original volume ended with a single part on "Continuity and Change." Here, instead, there are two parts. The first includes essays on the enforcement and violation of norms and on deviance; the latter deals with demographic trends, cultural moods, and social movements. The last part ends with three papers on changing times: one on the sounds of protest, one on the character of black nationalism, and the last on rebellious students.

While the entire last part in the book is new, it is not the only place where new material is offered. Changes have been made in every section and forty-five percent of the essays presented here are different from what was included before.

The rationale for making so many changes in content, if not in form, is based upon many things. Not least important was the reaction of colleagues and readers (including many student-readers) who suggested the substitution of one piece for another or recommended the inclusion of several papers in an area, like demography, which had not been dealt with in the original volume. In addition to considering and weighing the many solicited and unsolicited comments, a file was kept in which the editor put articles that might, one day, be useful in revising the book. Altogether, what is included here is the result of a combination of factors which, hopefully, will offer students an even better choice of material—however their courses are designed.

One last note on content: Most of the selections in the Second Edition, like those in the original one, are concerned with sociology in general or American society in particular. There are two reasons for the seemingly ethnocentric bias. First, although sociology was born in Europe, it has grown to maturity in the United States. An overwhelmingly-high proportion of important sociological research has been conducted in this country (or by American-trained sociologists abroad), especially since World War II, the period with which this book—and most courses—is most concerned. Second, since it is assumed that the majority who will read and use this book are students in American universities, a strong case can be made for exploring things close to home. One of the oldest shibboleths of sociology is that "things are seldom what they seem." Critical examination of the society in which we live will serve to attest to the veracity of this generalization. In saying this, however, the reader is cautioned to bear in mind the following caveat: this book is not designed merely to provide a portrait of American life or a baseline against which to compare our ways with those of others (though a quick perusal of the Contents will indicate that such might well be a latent feature of *The Study of Society*). Whatever else it may be, the primary purpose of this book is to provide readers with a basic understanding of sociological principles and perspectives—and to do so in a lively, interesting, and challenging way. If, by reading the selections included here, one is better able to comprehend the nature of sociology, then all who contributed to the preparation of this collection will have been amply rewarded.

Acknowledgments

In the preface to the first edition of this work I wrote that

Like all editors of anthologies, I owe a deep debt of gratitude to the original authors for allowing me to share their work with others. Each has graciously granted permission to use his selection and all join with me in hoping that *The Study of Society* will serve its intended purposes.

I am particularly appreciative of the advice and counsel of my editor, Charles H. Page, and my colleague, Ely Chinoy. And once again, I wish to acknowledge the forbearance of a faculty wife, Hedy.

The sentiments—all of them—expressed then still hold today.

PETER I. ROSE

Truro, Massachusetts

CONTENTS

PART FIVE

SELECTED SOCIAL INSTITUTIONS

PART SIX

CONFORMITY AND DEVIANCE

PART ONE
THE SOCIOLOGICAL
APPROACH

The perspectives,
principles and problems
of sociological inquiry

In 1837, Auguste Comte coined the word "sociology" (literally, the science of society), placed his new discipline at the acme of a hierarchy of the sciences, and ascribed to the sociologist the position of high priest in a future "Positive State." In the new society which Comte envisioned, the sociologist would represent the supreme embodiment of rational man. As the "positive philosopher" *par excellence,* he would be responsible for systematically improving the lot of those still constrained by the fetters of the traditional order.

Comte's intellectual heirs, the modern sociologists, have a far less grandiose image of their own self-importance and no illusions about their field being the queen of all the sciences. Yet, most continue to hold to the belief that sociology does provide a special frame of reference or "angle of vision" that not only enables one to stand outside his own milieu and explore the fads and foibles of social life, but allows him to see much farther because of it. Comte himself had said *voir pour prévoir* (to see in order to foresee) and *prévoir pour pouvoir* (to foresee in order to control). Sociologists continue to hold the view that the study of shared, patterned, human relationships should serve a dual purpose: sociology for the sake of understanding; and, understanding for the sake of providing solutions to the problems that beset man and his world.

Comte did more than give sociology a name and a purpose—he outlined a three-tiered approach to the study of society, a study that may be at once theoretical, empirical, and practical. The theoretical aspect pertains to abstract generalizations about the origins, structures, and functions of the various elements of social life, and a search for universal laws; the empirical aspect is concerned with what one might actually learn from observation, comparison, and experimentation; and, the practical aspect emphasizes the direct or indirect application to social conditions of theoretical assumptions and research findings.

Although from the beginning a debate has ensued over the proper amount of "weight" to ascribe to each dimension (the temper of the times and the temperaments of practitioners playing significant roles in the weighting process), there is substantial agreement that these themes have circumscribed and will continue to circumscribe the sociological endeavor.

The readings in this introductory section of *The Study of Society* clearly indicate the persisting relevance of the Comtean legacy and illustrate what is meant by the sociological approach. The first selection, by the late C. Wright Mills, sets the stage by explaining what sociology should be. Peter Berger's essay defines those special qualities which allow one to say that "sociology is a form of consciousness." Robert K. Merton offers a critical assessment of the interconnections between social research and sociological theory. Talcott Parsons presents a brief but cogent summary of the past, present, and future of sociology and its relation to the world which serves as its laboratory. In the last essay, originally called "The Functional Approach to Social Problems," Melvin M. Tumin raises some important questions about the values of sociologists and their orientations toward certain social patterns and processes.

1. THE SOCIOLOGICAL IMAGINATION

C. WRIGHT MILLS

When he died in 1962, C. Wright Mills was one of America's foremost—and most controversial—sociologists and social critics. His perceptive commentaries on American society are widely read and debated by social scientists, students, and laymen alike.

It was Mills' contention that to fully comprehend the life of an individual or the history of a society, one must understand both. To be able to do this is to possess what he called a sociological imagination. *Like his intellectual forebears, the classical social analysts of the nineteenth century, Mills implied that only through the intermeshing of "social statics" (the study of the structures and functions of given societies and their subdivisions) and "social dynamics" (the analysis of continuities and changes) can private troubles and public issues be understood and dealt with.*

Arguing that "no social study that does not come back to the problems of biography, of history and of their intersections within a society has completed its intellectual journey," Mills' essay sets the stage for our examination of the nature of sociological inquiry. It is a fitting introduction to The Study of Society.

At the time of his death C. Wright Mills was Professor of Sociology at Columbia University. Mills was the author and coauthor of many books including The New Men of Power *(1948),* The Puerto Rican Journey, *with Clarence Senior and Rose K. Goldsen (1950),* White Collar *(1951),* Character and Social Structure, *with Hans*

Gerth (1953), The Power Elite *(1956),* The Causes of World War III *(1958),* The Sociological Imagination *(1959),* Images of Man *(1960), and* Listen, Yankee: The Revolution in Cuba *(1960). A collection of his essays, edited by Irving L. Horowitz, is titled* Power, Politics, and People *(1963).*

Nowadays men often feel that their private lives are a series of traps. They sense that within their everyday worlds, they cannot overcome their troubles, and in this feeling, they are often quite correct: What ordinary men are directly aware of and what they try to do are bounded by the private orbits in which they live; their visions and their powers are limited to the close-up scenes of job, family, neighborhood; in other milieux, they move vicariously and remain spectators. And the more aware they become, however vaguely, of ambitions and of threats which transcend their immediate locales, the more trapped they seem to feel.

Underlying this sense of being trapped are seemingly impersonal changes in the very structure of continent-wide societies. The facts of contemporary history are also facts about the success and the failure of individual men and women. When a society is industrialized, a peasant becomes a worker; a feudal lord is liquidated or becomes a businessman. When classes rise or fall, a man is employed or unemployed; when the rate of investment goes up or down, a man takes new heart or goes broke. When wars happen, an insurance salesman becomes a rocket launcher; a store clerk, a radar man; a wife lives alone; a child grows up without a father. Neither the life of an individual nor the history of a society can be understood without understanding both.

Yet men do not usually define the troubles they endure in terms of historical change and institutional contradiction. The well-being they enjoy, they do not usually impute to the big ups and downs of the societies in which they live. Seldom aware of the intricate connection between the patterns of their own lives and the course of world history, ordinary men do not usually know what this connection means for the kinds of men they are becoming and for the kinds of history-making in which they might take part. They do not possess the quality of mind essential to grasp the interplay of man and society, of biography and history, of self and world. They cannot cope with their personal troubles in such ways as to control the structural transformations that usually lie behind them.

Surely it is no wonder. In what period have so many men been so totally exposed at so fast a pace to such earthquakes of change? That Americans have not known such catastrophic changes as have the men and women of other societies is due to historical facts that are now quickly becoming "merely history." The history that now affects every man is world history. Within this scene and this period, in the course of a single generation, one sixth of mankind is transformed from all that is feudal and backward into all that is modern, advanced, and fearful. Political colonies are freed; new and less visible forms of imperialism installed. Revolutions occur; men feel the intimate grip of new kinds of authority. Totalitarian societies rise, and are smashed to bits—or succeed fabulously. After two centuries of ascendancy, capitalism is shown up as only one way to make society into an industrial apparatus. After two centuries of hope, even formal democracy is restricted to a quite small portion of mankind. Everywhere in the underdeveloped world, ancient ways of life are broken up and vague expectations become urgent demands. Everywhere in the overdeveloped world, the means of authority and of violence become total in scope and bureaucratic in form. Humanity itself now lies before us, the super-nation at either pole concentrating its most co-ordinated and massive efforts upon the preparation of World War Three.

The very shaping of history now outpaces the ability of men to orient themselves in accordance with cherished values. And which values? Even when they do not panic, men often sense that older ways of feeling and thinking have collapsed and that newer beginnings are ambiguous to the point of moral stasis. Is it any wonder that ordinary men feel they cannot cope with the larger worlds with which they are so suddenly confronted? That they cannot understand the meaning of their epoch for their own lives? That—in defense of selfhood—they become morally insensible, trying to remain altogether private men? Is it any wonder that they come to be possessed by a sense of the trap?

It is not only information that they need—in this Age of Fact, information often dominates their attention and overwhelms their capacities to assimilate it. It is not only the skills of reason that they need—although their struggles to acquire these often exhaust their limited moral energy.

What they need, and what they feel they need, is a quality of mind that will help them to use information and to develop reason in order to achieve lucid summations of what is going on in the world and of what may be happening within themselves. It is this quality, I am going to contend, that journalists and scholars, artists and publics, scientists and editors are coming to expect of what may be called the *sociological* imagination.

–1–

The sociological imagination enables its possessor to understand the larger historical scene in terms of its meaning for the inner life and the external career of a variety of individuals. It enables him to take into account how individuals, in the welter of their daily experience, often become falsely conscious of their social positions. Within that welter, the framework of modern society is sought, and within that framework the psychologies of a variety of men and women are formulated. By such means the personal uneasiness of individuals is focused upon explicit troubles and the indifference of publics is transformed into involvement with public issues.

The first fruit of this imagination—and the first lesson of the social science that embodies it—is the idea that the individual can understand his own experience and gauge his own fate only by locating himself within his period, that he can know his own chances in life only by becoming aware of those of all individuals in his circumstances. In many ways it is a terrible lesson; in many ways a magnificent one. We do not know the limits of man's capacities for supreme effort or willing degradation, for agony or glee, for pleasurable brutality or the sweetness of reason. But in our time we have come to know that the limits of "human nature" are frighteningly broad. We have come to know that every individual lives, from one generation to the next, in some society; that he lives out a biography, and that he lives it out within some historical sequence. By the fact of his living he contributes, however minutely, to the shaping of this society and to the course of its history, even as he is made by society and by its historical push and shove.

The sociological imagination enables us to grasp history and biography and the relations between the two within society. That is its task and its promise. To recognize this task and this promise is the mark of the classic social analyst. It is characteristic of Herbert Spencer—turgid, polysyllabic, comprehensive; of E. A. Ross—graceful, muckraking, upright; of Auguste Comte and Emile Durkheim; of the intricate and subtle Karl Mannheim. It is the quality of all that is intellectually excellent in Karl Marx; it is the clue to Thorstein Veblen's brilliant and ironic insight, to Joseph Schumpeter's many-sided constructions of reality; it is the basis of the psychological sweep of W. E. H. Lecky no less than of the profundity and clarity of Max Weber. And it is the signal of what is best in contemporary studies of man and society.

No social study that does not come back to the problems of biography, of history and of their intersections within a society has completed its intellectual journey. Whatever the specific problems of the classic social analysts, however limited or however broad the features of social reality they have examined, those who have been imaginatively aware of the promise of their work have consistently asked three sorts of questions:

1. What is the structure of this particular society as a whole? What are its essential components, and how are they related to one another? How does it differ from other varieties of social order? Within it, what is the meaning of any particular feature for its continuance and for its change?
2. Where does this society stand in human history? What are the mechanics by which it is changing? What is its place within and its meaning for the development of humanity as a whole? How does any particular feature we are examining affect, and how is it affected by, the historical period in which it moves? And this period—what are its essential features? How does it differ from other periods? What are its characteristic ways of history-making?
3. What varieties of men and women now prevail in this society and in this period? And what varieties are coming to prevail? In what ways are they selected and formed, liberated and repressed, made sensitive and blunted? What kinds of "human nature" are revealed in the conduct and character we observe in this society in this period? And what is the meaning for "human nature" of

each and every feature of the society we are examining?

Whether the point of interest is a great power state or a minor literary mood, a family, a prison, a creed—these are the kinds of questions the best social analysts have asked. They are the intellectual pivots of classic studies of man in society—and they are the questions inevitably raised by any mind possessing the sociological imagination. For that imagination is the capacity to shift from one perspective to another —from the political to the psychological; from examination of a single family to comparative assessment of the national budgets of the world; from the theological school to the military establishment; from considerations of an oil industry to studies of contemporary poetry. It is the capacity to range from the most impersonal and remote transformations to the most intimate features of the human self—and to see the relations between the two. Back of its use there is always the urge to know the social and historical meaning of the individual in the society and in the period in which he has his quality and his being.

That, in brief, is why it is by means of the sociological imagination that men now hope to grasp what is going on in the world, and to understand what is happening in themselves as minute points of the intersections of biography and history within society. In large part, contemporary man's self-conscious view of himself as at least an outsider, if not a permanent stranger, rests upon an absorbed realization of social relativity and of the transformative power of history. The sociological imagination is the most fruitful form of this self-consciousness. By its use men whose mentalities have swept only a series of limited orbits often come to feel as if suddenly awakened in a house with which they had only supposed themselves to be familiar. Correctly or incorrectly, they often come to feel that they can now provide themselves with adequate summations, cohesive assessments, comprehensive orientations. Older decisions that once appeared sound now seem to them products of a mind unaccountably dense. Their capacity for astonishment is made lively again. They acquire a new way of thinking, they experience a transvaluation of values: in a word, by their reflection and by their sensibility, they realize the cultural meaning of the social sciences.

–2–

Perhaps the most fruitful distinction with which the sociological imagination works is between "the personal troubles of milieu" and "the public issues of social structure." This distinction is an essential tool of the sociological imagination and a feature of all classic work in social science.

Troubles occur within the character of the individual and within the range of his immediate relations with others; they have to do with his self and with those limited areas of social life of which he is directly and personally aware. Accordingly, the statement and the resolution of troubles properly lie within the individual as a biographical entity and within the scope of his immediate milieu—the social setting that is directly open to his personal experience and to some extent his willful activity. A trouble is a private matter: values cherished by an individual are felt by him to be threatened.

Issues have to do with matters that transcend these local environments of the individual and the range of his inner life. They have to do with the organization of many such milieux into the institutions of an historical society as a whole, with the ways in which various milieux overlap and interpenetrate to form the larger structure of social and historical life. An issue is a public matter: some value cherished by publics is felt to be threatened. Often there is a debate about what that value really is and about what it is that really threatens it.

This debate is often without focus if only because it is the very nature of an issue, unlike even widespread trouble, that it cannot very well be defined in terms of the immediate and everyday environments of ordinary men. An issue, in fact, often involves a crisis in institutional arrangements, and often too it involves what Marxists call "contradictions" or "antagonisms."

In these terms, consider unemployment. When, in a city of 100,000 only one man is unemployed, that is his personal trouble, and for its relief we properly look to the character of the man, his skills and his immediate opportunities. But when in a nation of 50 million employees, 15 million men are unemployed, that is an issue, and we may not hope to find its solution within the range of opportunities open to any one individual. The very structure of opportunities has collapsed. Both the correct statement of the problem and the range of possible solutions require us to consider the economic and political institutions of the society, and not merely the personal situation and character of a scatter of individuals.

Consider war. The personal problem of war, when it occurs, may be how to survive it or how to die in it with honor; how to make money out of it; how to climb into the higher safety of the military apparatus; or how to contribute to the war's termination. In short, according to one's values, to find a set of milieux and within it to survive the war or make one's death in it meaningful. But the structural issues of war have to do with its causes; with what types of men it throws up into command; with its effects upon economic and political, family and religious institutions, with the unorganized irresponsibility of a world of nation-states.

Consider marriage. Inside a marriage a man and a woman may experience personal troubles, but when the divorce rate during the first four years of marriage is

250 out of every 1,000 attempts, this is an indication of a structural issue having to do with the institutions of marriage and the family and other institutions that bear upon them.

Or consider the metropolis—the horrible, beautiful, ugly, magnificent sprawl of the great city. For many upper-class people, the personal solution to "the problem of the city" is to have an apartment with private garage under it in the heart of the city, and forty miles out, a house by Henry Hill, garden by Garrett Eckbo, on a hundred acres of private land. In these two controlled environments—with a small staff at each end and a private helicopter connection—most people could solve many of the problems of personal milieux caused by the facts of the city. But all this, however splendid, does not solve the public issues that the structural fact of the city poses. What should be done with this wonderful monstrosity? Break it all up into scattered units, combining residence and work? Refurbish it as it stands? Or, after evacuation, dynamite it and build new cities according to new plans in new places? What should those plans be? And who is to decide and to accomplish whatever choice is made? These are structural issues; to confront them and to solve them requires us to consider political and economic issues that affect innumerable milieux.

In so far as an economy is so arranged that slumps occur, the problem of unemployment becomes incapable of personal solution. In so far as war is inherent in the nation-state system and in the uneven industrialization of the world, the ordinary individual in his restricted milieu will be powerless—with or without psychiatric aid —to solve the troubles this system or lack of system imposes upon him. In so far as the family as an institution turns women into darling little slaves and men into their chief providers and unweaned dependents, the problem of a satisfactory marriage remains incapable of purely private solution. In so far as the overdeveloped megalopolis and the overdeveloped automobile are built-in features of the overdeveloped society, the issues of urban living will not be solved by personal ingenuity and private wealth.

What we experience in various and specific milieux, I have noted, is often caused by structural changes. Accordingly, to understand the changes of many personal milieux we are required to look beyond them. And the number and variety of such structural changes increase as the institutions within which we live become more embracing and more intricately connected with one another. To be aware of the idea of social structure and to use it with sensibility is to be capable of tracing such linkages among a great variety of milieux. To be able to do that is to possess the sociological imagination.

–3–

What are the major issues for publics and the key troubles of private individuals in our time? To formulate issues and troubles, we must ask what values are cherished yet threatened, and what values are cherished and supported, by the characterizing trends of our period. In the case both of threat and of support we must ask what salient contradictions of structure may be involved.

When people cherish some set of values and do not feel any threat to them, they experience *well-being*. When they cherish values but *do* feel them to be threatened, they experience a crisis—either as a personal trouble or as a public issue. And if all their values seem involved, they feel the total threat of panic.

But suppose people are neither aware of any cherished values nor experience any threat? That is the experience of *indifference*, which, if it seems to involve all their values, becomes apathy. Suppose, finally, they are unaware of any cherished values, but still are very much aware of a threat?

That is the experience of *uneasiness,* of anxiety, which, if it is total enough, becomes a deadly unspecified malaise.

Ours is a time of uneasiness and indifference—not yet formulated in such ways as to permit the work of reason and the play of sensibility. Instead of troubles—defined in terms of values and threats—there is often the misery of vague uneasiness; instead of explicit issues there is often merely the beat feeling that all is somehow not right. Neither the values threatened nor whatever threatens them has been stated; in short, they have not been carried to the point of decision. Much less have they been formulated as problems of social science.

In the 'thirties there was little doubt—except among certain deluded business circles that there was an economic issue which was also a pack of personal troubles. In these arguments about "the crisis of capitalism," the formulations of Marx and the many unacknowledged re-formulations of his work probably set the leading terms of the issue, and some men came to understand their personal troubles in these terms. The values threatened were plain to see and cherished by all; the structural contradictions that threatened them also seemed plain. Both were widely and deeply experienced. It was a political age.

But the values threatened in the era after World War Two are often neither widely acknowledged as values nor widely felt to be threatened. Much private uneasiness goes unformulated; much public malaise and many decisions of enormous structural relevance never become public issues. For those who accept such inherited values as reason and freedom, it is the uneasiness itself that is the trouble; it is the indifference itself that is the issue. And it is this condition, of uneasiness and indifference, that is the signal feature of our period.

All this is so striking that it is often interpreted by observers as a shift in the very kinds of problems that need now to be formulated. We are frequently told that the problems of our decade, or even the crises of our period, have shifted from the external realm of economics and now have to do with the quality of individual life—in fact with the question of whether there is soon going to be anything that can properly be called individual life. Not child labor but comic books, not poverty but mass leisure, are at the center of concern. Many great public issues as well as many private troubles are described in terms of "the psychiatric"—often, it seems, in a pathetic attempt to avoid the large issues and problems of modern society. Often this statement seems to rest upon a provincial narrowing of interest to the Western societies, or even to the United States—thus ignoring two-thirds of mankind; often, too, it arbitrarily divorces the individual life from the larger institutions within which that life is enacted, and which on occasion bear upon it more grievously than do the intimate environments of childhood.

Problems of leisure, for example, cannot even be stated without considering problems of work. Family troubles over comic books cannot be formulated as problems without considering the plight of the contemporary family in its new relations with the newer institutions of the social structure. Neither leisure nor its debilitating uses can be understood as problems without recognition of the extent to which malaise and indifference now form the social and personal climate of contemporary American society. In this climate, no problems of "the private life" can be stated and solved without recognition of the crisis of ambition that is part of the very career of men at work in the incorporated economy.

It is true, as psychoanalysts continually point out, that people do often have "the increasing sense of being moved by obscure forces within themselves which they are unable to define." But it is *not* true, as Ernest Jones asserted, that "man's chief enemy and danger is his own unruly nature and the dark forces pent up within him." On the contrary: "Man's chief danger" today lies in the unruly forces of contemporary society itself, with its alienating methods of production, its enveloping techniques of political domination, its international anarchy—in a word, its pervasive transformations of the very "nature" of man and the conditions and aims of his life.

It is now the social scientist's foremost political and intellectual task—for here the two coincide—to make clear the elements of contemporary uneasiness and indifference. It is the central demand made upon him by other cultural workmen—by physical scientists and artists, by the intellectual community in general. It is because of this task and these demands, I believe, that the social sciences are becoming the common denominator of our cultural period, and the sociological imagination our most needed quality of mind.

–4–

In every intellectual age some one style of reflection tends to become a common denominator of cultural life. Nowadays, it is true, many intellectual fads are widely taken up before they are dropped for new ones in the course of a year or two. Such enthusiasms may add spice to cultural play, but leave little or no intellectual trace. That is not true of such ways of thinking as "Newtonian physics" or "Darwinian biology." Each of these intellectual universes became an influence that reached far beyond any special sphere of idea and imagery. In terms of them, or in terms derived from them, unknown scholars as well as fashionable commentators came to re-focus their observations and re-formulate their concerns.

During the modern era, physical and biological science has been the major common denominator of serious reflection and popular metaphysics in Western societies. "The technique of the laboratory" has been the accepted mode of procedure and the source of intellectual security. That is one meaning of the idea of an intellectual common denominator: men can state their strongest convictions in its terms; other terms and other styles of reflection seem mere vehicles of escape and obscurity.

That a common denominator prevails does not of course mean that no other styles of thought or modes of sensibility exist. But it does mean that more general intellectual interests tend to slide into this area, to be formulated there most sharply, and when so formulated, to be thought somehow to have reached, if not a solution, at least a profitable way of being carried along.

The sociological imagination is becoming, I believe, the major common denominator of our cultural life and its signal feature. This quality of mind is found in the social and psychological sciences, but it goes far beyond these studies as we now know them. Its acquisition by individuals and by the cultural community at large is slow and often fumbling; many social scientists are themselves quite unaware of it. They do not seem to know that the use of this imagination is central to the best work that they might do, that by failing to develop and to use it they are failing to meet the cultural expectations that are coming to be demanded of them and that the classic traditions of their several disciplines make available to them.

Yet in factual and moral concerns, in literary work and in political analysis, the qualities of this imagination are regularly demanded. In a great variety of expressions, they have become central features of intellectual endeavor and cultural sensibility. Leading critics exemplify these qualities as do serious journalists—in fact the work of both is often judged in these terms. Popular categories of criticism—high, middle, and low-brow, for example—are now at least as much sociological as aesthetic. Novelists—whose serious work embodies the most widespread definitions of human reality—frequently possess this imagination, and do much to meet the demand for it. By means of it, orientation to the present as history is sought. As images of "human nature" become more problematic, an increasing need is felt to pay closer yet more imaginative attention to the social routines and catastrophes which reveal (and which shape) man's nature in this time of civil unrest and ideological conflict. Although fashion is often revealed by attempts to use it, the sociological imagination is not merely a fashion. It is a quality of mind that seems most dramatically to promise an understanding of the intimate realities of ourselves in connection with larger social realities. It is not merely one quality of mind among the contemporary range of cultural sensibilities—it is *the* quality whose wider and more adroit use offers the promise that all such sensibilities—and in fact, human reason itself—will come to play a greater role in human affairs.

The cultural meaning of physical science—the major older common denominator—is becoming doubtful. As an intellectual style, physical science is coming to be thought by many as somehow inadequate. The adequacy of scientific styles of thought and feeling, imagination and sensibility, has of course from their beginnings been subject to religious doubt and theological controversy, but our scientific grandfathers and fathers beat down such religious doubts. The current doubts are secular, humanistic—and often quite confused. Recent developments in physical science—with its technological climax in the H-bomb and the means of carrying it about the earth—have not been experienced as a solution to any problems widely known and deeply pondered by larger intellectual communities and cultural publics. These developments have been correctly seen as a result of highly specialized inquiry, and improperly felt to be wonderfully mysterious. They have raised more problems—both intellectual and moral— than they have solved, and the problems they have raised lie almost entirely in the

area of social not physical affairs. The obvious conquest of nature, the overcoming of scarcity, is felt by men of the overdeveloped societies to be virtually complete. And now in these societies, science —the chief instrument of this conquest— is felt to be footloose, aimless, and in need of re-appraisal.

The modern esteem for science has long been merely assumed, but now the technological ethos and the kind of engineering imagination associated with science are more likely to be frightening and ambiguous than hopeful and progressive. Of course this is not all there is to "science," but it is feared that this could become all that there is to it. The felt need to re-appraise physical science reflects the need for a new common denominator. It is the human meaning and the social role of science, its military and commercial issue, its political significance that are undergoing confused re-appraisal. Scientific developments of weaponry may lead to the "necessity" for world political re-arrangements— but such "necessity" is not felt to be solvable by physical science itself.

Much that has passed for "science" is now felt to be dubious philosophy; much that is held to be "real science" is often felt to provide only confused fragments of the realities among which men live. Men of science, it is widely felt, no longer try to picture reality as a whole or to present a true outline of human destiny. Moreover, "science" seems to many less a creative ethos and a manner of orientation than a set of Science Machines, operated by technicians and controlled by economic and military men who neither embody nor understand science as ethos and orientation. In the meantime, philosophers who speak in the name of science often transform it into "scientism," making out its experience to be identical with human experience, and claiming that only by its method can the problems of life be solved. With all this, many cultural workmen have come to feel that "science" is a false and pretentious Messiah, or at the very least a highly ambiguous element in modern civilization.

But there are, in C. P. Snow's phrase, "two cultures": the scientific and the humanistic. Whether as history or drama, as biography, poetry or fiction, the essence of the humanistic culture has been literature. Yet it is now frequently suggested that serious literature has in many ways become a minor art. If this is so, it is not merely because of the development of mass publics and mass media of communication, and all that these mean for serious literary production. It is also owing to the very quality of the history of our times and the kinds of need men of sensibility feel to grasp that quality.

What fiction, what journalism, what artistic endeavor can compete with the historical reality and political facts of our time? What dramatic vision of hell can compete with the events of twentieth-century war? What moral denunciations can measure up to the moral insensibility of men in the agonies of primary accumulation? It is social and historical reality that men want to know, and often they do not find contemporary literature an adequate means for knowing it. They yearn for facts, they search for their meanings, they want "a big picture" in which they can believe and within which they can come to understand themselves. They want orienting values too, and suitable ways of feeling and styles of emotion and vocabularies of motive. And they do not readily find these in the literature of today. It does not matter whether or not these qualities *are* to be found there; what matters is that men do not often find them there.

In the past, literary men as critics and historians made notes on England and on journeys to America. They tried to characterize societies as wholes, and to discern their moral meanings. Were Tocqueville or Taine alive today, would they not be sociologists? Asking this question about Taine, a reviewer in *The Times* (London) suggests:

Taine always saw man primarily as a social animal and society as a collection of groups: he could observe minutely, was a tireless field worker and possessed a quality . . . particularly valuable for perceiving relationships between social phenomena—the quality of springliness. He was too interested in the present to be a good historian, too much of a theorist to try his hand as a novelist, and he thought of literature too much as documents in the culture of an age or country to achieve first class status as a critic . . . His work on English literature is less about English literature than a commentary on the morality of English society and a vehicle for his positivism. He is a social theorist before all else.[1]

That he remained a "literary man" rather than a "social scientist" testifies perhaps to the domination of much nineteenth-century social science by the zealous search for "laws" presumably comparable to those imagined to be found by natural scientists. In the absence of an adequate social science, critics and novelists, dramatists and poets have been the major, and often the only, formulators of private troubles and even of public issues. Art does express such feelings and often focuses them—at its best with dramatic sharpness—but still not with the intellectual clarity required for their understanding or relief today. Art does not and cannot formulate these feelings as problems containing the troubles and issues men must now confront if they are to overcome their uneasiness and indifference and the intractable miseries to which these lead. The artist, indeed, does not often try to do this. Moreover, the serious artist is himself in much trouble, and could well do with some intellectual and cultural aid from a social science made sprightly by the sociological imagination.

–5–

. . .

At any given moment, of course, "social science"[2] consists of what duly recognized social scientists are doing—but all of them are by no means doing the same thing, in fact not even the same sort of thing. Social science is also what social scientists of the past have done—but different students choose to construct and to recall different traditions in their discipline. When I speak of "the promise of social science," I hope it is clear that I mean the promise as I see it.

Just now, among social scientists, there is widespread uneasiness, both intellectual and moral, about the direction their chosen studies seem to be taking. This uneasiness, as well as the unfortunate tendencies that contribute to it, are, I suppose, part of a general malaise of contemporary intellectual life. Yet perhaps the uneasiness is more acute among social scientists, if only because of the larger promise that has guided much earlier work in their fields, the nature of the subjects with which they deal, and the urgent need for significant work today.

Not everyone shares this uneasiness, but the fact that many do not is itself a cause for further uneasiness among those who are alert to the promise and honest enough to admit the pretentious mediocrity of much current effort. It is, quite frankly, my hope to increase this uneasiness, to define some of its sources, to help transform it into a specific urge to realize the promise of social science, to clear the ground for new beginnings: in short, to indicate some of the tasks at hand and the means available for doing the work that must now be done.

Of late the conception of social science I hold has not been ascendant. My conception stands opposed to social science as a set of bureaucratic techniques which inhibit social inquiry by "methodological" pretensions, which congest such work by obscurantist conceptions, or which trivialize it by concern with minor problems unconnected with publicly relevant issues. These inhibitions, obscurities, and trivialities have created a crisis in the social studies today without suggesting, in the least, a way out of that crisis.

Some social scientists stress the need for "research teams of technicians," others for the primacy of the individual scholar. Some expend great energy upon refinements of methods and techniques of investigation; others think the scholarly ways of the intellectual craftsmen are being abandoned and ought now to be rehabilitated. Some go about their work in accordance with a rigid set of mechanical procedures; others seek to develop, to invite, and to use the sociological imagination. Some—being addicts of the high formalism of "theory" —associate and disassociate concepts in what seems to others a curious manner; these others urge the elaboration of terms only when it is clear that it enlarges the scope of sensibility and furthers the reach of reasoning. Some narrowly study only small-scale milieux, in the hope of "building up" to conceptions of larger structures; others examine social structures in which they try "to locate" many smaller milieux. Some, neglecting comparative studies altogether, study only one small community in one society at a time; others in a fully comparative way work directly on the national social structures of the world. Some confine their exact research to very short-run sequences of human affairs; others are concerned with issues which are only apparent in long historical perspective. Some specialize their work according to academic departments; others, drawing upon all departments, specialize according to topic or problem, regardless of where these lie academically. Some confront the variety of history, biography, society; others do not.

Such contrasts, and many others of similar kind, are not necessarily true alternatives, although in the heat of statesman-like controversy or the lazy safety of specialization they are often taken to be. At this point I merely state them in inchoate form. . . .

In brief, I believe that what may be called classic social analysis is a definable and usable set of traditions; that its essential feature is the concern with historical social structures; and that its problems are of direct relevance to urgent public issues and insistent human troubles. I also believe that there are now great obstacles in the way of this tradition's continuing—both within the social sciences and in their academic and political settings—but that nevertheless the qualities of mind that constitute it are becoming a common denominator of our general cultural life and that, however vaguely and in however a confusing variety of disguises, they are coming to be felt as a need.

Many practitioners of social science, especially in America, seem to me curiously reluctant to take up the challenge that now confronts them. Many in fact abdicate the intellectual and the political tasks of social analysis; others no doubt are simply not up to the role for which they are nevertheless being cast. At times they seem almost deliberately to have brought forth old ruses and developed new timidities. Yet despite this reluctance, intellectual as well as public attention is now so obviously upon the social worlds which they presumably study that it must be agreed that they are uniquely confronted with an opportunity. In this opportunity there is revealed the intellectual promise of the social sciences, the cultural uses of the sociological imagination, and the political meaning of studies of man and society.

NOTES

1. *Times Literary Supplement,* November 15, 1957.

2. I feel the need to say that I much prefer the phrase, "the social studies" to "the social sciences"—not because I do not like physical scientists (on the contrary, I do, very much), but because the word "science" has acquired great prestige and rather imprecise meaning. I do not feel any need to kidnap the prestige or to make the meaning even less precise by using it as a philosophical metaphor. Yet I suspect that if I wrote about "the social studies," readers would think only of high school civics, which of all fields of human learning is the one with which I most wish to avoid association. "The Behavioral Sciences" is simply impossible; it was thought up, I suppose, as a propaganda device to get money for social research from Foundations and Congressmen who confuse "social science" with "socialism." The best term would include history (and psychology, so far as it is concerned with human beings), and should be as non-controversial as possible, for we should argue *with* terms, not fight *over* them. Perhaps "the human disciplines" would do. But never mind. With the hope of not being too widely misunderstood, I bow to convention and use the more standard "social sciences."

One other point: I hope my colleagues will accept the term "sociological imagination." Political scientists who have read my manuscript suggest "the political imagination"; anthropologists, "the anthropological imagination"—and so on. The term matters less than the idea. By use of it, I do not of course want to suggest merely the academic discipline of "sociology." Much of what the phrase means to me is not at all expressed by sociologists. In England, for example, sociology as an academic discipline is still somewhat marginal, yet in much English journalism, fiction, and above all history, the sociological imagination is very well developed indeed. The case is similar for France: both the confusion and the audacity of French reflection since World War Two rest upon its feeling for the sociological features of man's fate in our time, yet these trends are carried by men of letters rather than by professional sociologists. Nevertheless, I use "sociological imagination" because: 1) every cobbler thinks leather is the only thing, and for better or worse, I am a sociologist; 2) I do believe that historically the quality of mind has been more frequently and more vividly displayed by classic sociologists than by other social scientists; 3) since I am going to examine critically a number of curious sociological schools, I need a counter term on which to stand. [*Editor's note:* In *The Sociological Imagination,* C. Wright Mills criticizes what he sees as the foibles of certain sociological "schools" in the United States.]

2. SOCIOLOGY AS A FORM OF CONSCIOUSNESS

PETER L. BERGER

In this essay, Peter L. Berger briefly describes the social climate and intellectual tradition out of which sociology emerged as a discipline. To Berger, sociology is a form of consciousness, a particular angle of vision involving both theoretical perspectives and methodological procedures that allow the practitioner to "see through" the façades of the social order. The sociological approach permits the intensive analysis of the formal and informal components of political organization and community power, of religious expression and systems of belief, of economic and family life.

To Berger, the sociological frame of reference embodies four leit motifs: *1) the debunking motif, the tendency to look behind the scenes and uncover the latent as well as the manifest functions of social acts; 2) the theme of unrespectability, the concern with "the other side" of social life, with deviance as well as conformity to the status quo; 3) the idea of relativism, the notion that moral and political and philosophical beliefs are varied, that there is no single truth, that there exists a wide variety of ways of living and working and "being," and, finally, 4) the cosmopolitan motif, the desire to avoid the parochialism that inhibits objective appraisal.*

Peter L. Berger is Professor of Sociology in the graduate faculty of The New School for Social Research. He is the author of The Noise of Solemn Assemblies *(1961),* The Sacred Canopy *(1967),* A Rumor of Angels *(1969), coauthor of* The Social Construction of Reality *(1966), and author of* Invitation to Sociology: A Humanistic Perspective *(1963) from which this selection was chosen.*

.　　.　　.

The peculiarity of sociological perspective becomes clear with some reflection concerning the meaning of the term "society," a term that refers to the object *par excellence* of the discipline. Like most terms used by sociologists, this one is derived from common usage, where its meaning is imprecise. Sometimes it means a particular band of people (as in "Society for the Prevention of Cruelty to Animals"), sometimes only those people endowed with great prestige or privilege (as in "Boston society ladies"), and on other occasions it is simply used to denote company of any sort (for example, "he greatly suffered in those years for lack of society"). There are other, less frequent meanings as well. The sociologist uses the term in a more precise sense, though, of course, there are differences in usage within the discipline itself. The sociologist thinks of "society" as denoting a large complex of human relationships, or to put it in more technical language, as referring to a system of interaction. The word "large" is difficult to specify quantitatively in this context. The sociologist may speak of a "society" including millions of human beings (say, "American society"), but he may also use the term to refer to a numerically much smaller collectivity (say, "the society of sophomores on this campus"). Two people chatting on a street corner will hardly con-

15

stitute a "society," but three people stranded on an island certainly will. The applicability of the concept, then, cannot be decided on quantitative grounds alone. It rather applies when a complex of relationships is sufficiently succinct to be analyzed by itself, understood as an autonomous entity, set against others of the same kind.

The adjective "social" must be similarly sharpened for sociological use. In common speech it may denote, once more, a number of different things—the informal quality of a certain gathering ("this is a social meeting—let's not discuss business"), an altruistic attitude on somebody's part ("he had a strong social concern in his job"), or, more generally, anything derived from contact with other people ("a social disease"). The sociologist will use the term more narrowly and more precisely to refer to the quality of interaction, interrelationship, mutuality. Thus two men chatting on a street corner do not constitute a "society," but what transpires between them is certainly "social." "Society" consists of a complex of such "social" events. As to the exact definition of the "social," it is difficult to improve on Max Weber's definition of a "social" situation as one in which people orient their actions towards one another. The web of meanings, expectations and conduct resulting from such mutual orientation is the stuff of sociological analysis.

Yet this refinement of terminology is not enough to show up the distinctiveness of the sociological angle of vision. We may get closer by comparing the latter with the perspective of other disciplines concerned with human actions. The economist, for example, is concerned with the analyses of processes that occur in society and that can be described as social. These processes have to do with the basic problem of economic activity—the allocation of scarce goods and services within a society. The economist will be concerned with these processes in terms of the way in which

they carry out, or fail to carry out, this function. The sociologist, in looking at the same processes, will naturally have to take into consideration their economic purpose. But his distinctive interest is not necessarily related to this purpose as such. He will be interested in a variety of human relationships and interactions that may occur here and that may be quite irrelevant to the economic goals in question. Thus economic activity involves relationships of power, prestige, prejudice or even play that can be analyzed with only marginal reference to the properly economic function of the activity.

The sociologist finds his subject matter present in all human activities, but not all aspects of these activities constitute this subject matter. Social interaction is not some specialized sector of what men do with each other. It is rather a certain aspect of all these doings. Another way of putting this is by saying that the sociologist carries on a special sort of abstraction. The social, as an object of inquiry, is not a segregated field of human activity. Rather (to borrow a phrase from Lutheran sacramental theology) it is present "in, with and under" many different fields of such activity. The sociologist does not look at phenomena that nobody else is aware of. But he looks at the same phenomena in a different way.

As a further example we could take the perspective of the lawyer. Here we actually find a point of view much broader in scope than that of the economist. Almost any human activity can, at one time or another, fall within the province of the lawyer. This, indeed, is the fascination of the law. Again, we find here a very special procedure of abstraction. From the immense wealth and variety of human deportment the lawyer selects those aspects that are pertinent (or, as he would say, "material") to his very particular frame of reference. As anyone who has ever been involved in a lawsuit well knows, the criteria of what is relevant or irrelevant legally will often greatly surprise the principals in the case in question. This need not concern us here. We would rather observe that the legal frame of reference consists of a number of carefully defined models of human activity. Thus we have clear models of obligation, responsibility or wrongdoing. Definite conditions have to prevail before any empirical act can be subsumed under one of these headings, and these conditions are laid down by statutes or precedent. When these conditions are not met, the act in question is legally irrelevant. The expertise of the lawyer consists of knowing the rules by which these models are constructed. He knows, within his frame of reference, when a business contract is binding, when the driver of an automobile may be held to be negligent, or when rape has taken place.

The sociologist may look at these same phenomena, but his frame of reference will be quite different. Most importantly, his perspective on these phenomena cannot be derived from statutes or precedent. His interest in the human relationships occurring in a business transaction has no bearing on the legal validity of contracts signed, just as sociologically interesting deviance in sexual behavior may not be capable of being subsumed under some particular legal heading. From the lawyer's point of view, the sociologist's inquiry is extraneous to the legal frame of reference. One might say that, with reference to the conceptual edifice of the law, the sociologist's activity is subterranean in character. The lawyer is concerned with what may be called the official conception of the situation. The sociologist often deals with very unofficial conceptions indeed. For the lawyer the essential thing to understand is how the law looks upon a certain type of criminal. For the sociologist it is equally important to see how the criminal looks at the law.

To ask sociological questions, then, presupposes that one is interested in looking some distance beyond the commonly accepted or officially defined goals of human actions. It presupposes a certain awareness that human events have different levels of meaning, some of which are hidden from the consciousness of everyday life. It may even presuppose a measure of suspicion about the way in which human events are officially interpreted by the authorities, be they political, juridical or religious in character. If one is willing to go as far as that, it would seem evident that not all historical circumstances are equally favorable for the development of sociological perspective.

It would appear plausible, in consequence, that sociological thought would have the best chance to develop in historical circumstances marked by severe jolts to the self-conception, especially the official and authoritative and generally accepted self-conception, of a culture. It is only in such circumstances that perceptive men are likely to be motivated to think beyond the assertions of this self-conception and, as a result, question the authorities. Albert Salomon has argued cogently that the concept of "society," in its modern sociological sense, could emerge only as the normative structures of Christendom and later of the *ancien régime* were collapsing. We can, then, again conceive of "society" as the hidden fabric of an edifice, the outside facade of which hides that fabric from the common view. In medieval Christendom, "society" was rendered invisible by the imposing religiopolitical facade that constituted the common world of European man. As Salomon pointed out, the more secular political facade of the absolute state performed the same function after the Reformation had broken up the unity of Christendom. It was with the disintegration of the absolute state that the underlying frame of "society" came into view— that is, a world of motives and forces that could not be understood in terms of the official interpretations of social reality. Sociological perspective can then be understood in terms of such phrases as "seeing through," "looking behind," very much as such phrases would be employed in common speech—"seeing through his game," "looking behind the scenes"—in other words, "being up on all the tricks."

We will not be far off if we see sociological thought as part of what Nietzsche called "the art of mistrust." Now, it would be a gross oversimplification to think that this art has existed only in modern times. "Seeing through" things is probably a pretty general function of intelligence, even in very primitive societies. The American anthropologist Paul Radin has provided us with a vivid description of the skeptic as a human type in primitive culture. We also have evidence from civilizations other than that of the modern West, bearing witness to forms of consciousness that could well be called protosociological. We could point, for instance, to Herodotus or to Ibn-Khaldun. There are even texts from ancient Egypt evincing a profound disenchantment with a political and social order that has acquired the reputation of having been one of the most cohesive in human history. However, with the beginning of the modern era in the West this form of consciousness intensifies, becomes concentrated and systematized, marks the thought of an increasing number of perceptive men. This is not the place to discuss in detail the prehistory of sociological thought, a discussion in which we owe very much to Salomon. Nor would we even give here an intellectual table of ancestors for sociology, showing its connections with Machiavelli, Erasmus, Bacon, seventeenth-century philosophy and eighteenth-century *belles-lettres*—this has been done elsewhere and by others much more qualified than this writer. Suffice it to stress once more that sociological thought marks the fruition of a number of intellectual developments that have a very specific location in modern Western history.

Let us return instead to the proposition that sociological perspective involves a process of "seeing through" the facades of social structures. We could think of this in terms of a common experience of people living in large cities. One of the fascinations of a large city is the immense variety of human activities taking place behind the seemingly anonymous and endlessly undifferentiated rows of houses. A person who lives in such a city will time and again experience surprise or even shock as he discovers the strange pursuits that some men engage in quite unobtrusively in houses that, from the outside, look like all the others on a certain street. Having had this experience once or twice, one will repeatedly find oneself walking down a street, perhaps late in the evening, and wondering what may be going on under the bright lights showing through a line of drawn curtains. An ordinary family engaged in pleasant talk with guests? A scene of desperation amid illness or death? Or a scene of debauched pleasures? Perhaps a strange cult or a dangerous conspiracy? The facades of the houses cannot tell us, proclaiming nothing but an architectural conformity to the tastes of some group or class that may not even inhabit the street any longer. The social mysteries lie behind the facades. The wish to penetrate to these mysteries is an analogon to sociological curiosity. In some cities that are suddenly struck by calamity this wish may be abruptly realized. Those who have experienced wartime bombings know of the sudden encounters with unsuspected (and sometimes unimaginable) fellow tenants in the air-raid shelter of one's apartment building. Or they can recollect the startling morning sight of a house hit by a bomb during the night, neatly sliced in half, the facade torn away and the previously hidden interior mercilessly revealed in the daylight. But in most cities that one may normally live in, the facades must be penetrated by one's own inquisitive intrusions. Similarly, there are historical situations in which the facades of society are violently torn apart and all but the most incurious are forced to see that there was a reality behind the facades all along. Usually this does not happen and the facades continue to confront us with seemingly rocklike permanence. The perception of the reality behind the facades then demands a considerable intellectual effort.

A few examples of the way in which sociology "looks behind" the facades of social structures might serve to make our argument clearer. Take, for instance, the political organization of a community. If one wants to find out how a modern American city is governed, it is very easy to get the official information about this subject. The city will have a charter, operating under the laws of the state. With some advice from informed individuals, one may look up various statutes that define the constitution of the city. Thus one may find out that this particular community has a city-manager form of administration, or that party affiliations do not appear on the ballot in municipal elections, or that the city government participates in a regional water district. In similar fashion, with the help of some newspaper reading, one may find out the officially recognized political problems of the community. One may read that the city plans to annex a certain suburban area, or that there has been a change in the zoning ordinances to facilitate industrial development in another area, or even that one of the members of the city council has been accused of using his office for personal gain. All such matters still occur on the, as it were, visible, official or public level of political life. However, it would be an exceedingly naive person who would believe that this kind of information gives him a rounded picture of the political reality of that community. The sociologist will want to know above all the constituency of the "informal power structure" (as it has been called by Floyd Hunter, an American sociologist interested in such studies), which is a configuration of men and their power that cannot be found in any statutes, and probably cannot be read about in the newspapers. The political scientist or the legal expert might find it very interesting to compare the city charter with the constitutions of other similar communities. The sociologist will be far more concerned with discovering the way in which powerful vested interests influence or even control the actions of officials elected under the charter. These vested interests will not be found in city hall, but rather in the executive suites of corporations that may not even be located in that community, in the private mansions of a handful of powerful men, perhaps in the offices of certain labor unions or even, in some instances, in the headquarters of criminal organizations. When the sociologist concerns himself with power, he will "look behind" the official mechanisms that are supposed to regulate power in the community. This does not necessarily mean that he will regard the official mechanisms as totally ineffective or their legal definition as totally illusionary. But at the very least he will insist that there is another level of reality to be investigated in the particular system of power. In some cases he might conclude that to look for real power in the publicly recognized places is quite delusional.

Take another example. Protestant denominations in this country differ widely in their so-called "polity," that is, the officially defined way in which the denomination is run. One may speak of an episcopal, a presbyterian or a congregational "polity" (meaning by this not the denominations called by these names, but the forms of ecclesiastical government that various denominations share—for instance, the episcopal form shared by Episcopalians and Methodists, the congregational by Congregationalists and Baptists). In nearly all cases, the "polity" of a denomination is the result of a long historical development and is based on a theological rationale over which the doctrinal experts continue to quarrel. Yet a sociologist interested in studying the government of American denominations would do well not to arrest himself too long at these official definitions. He will soon find that the real questions of power and organization have little to do with "polity" in the theological sense. He will discover that the basic form of organization in all denominations of any size is bureaucratic. The logic of administrative behavior is determined by bureaucratic processes, only very rarely by the workings of an episcopal or a congregational point of view. The sociological investigator will then quickly "see through" the mass of confusing terminology denoting officeholders in the ecclesiastical bureaucracy and correctly identify those who hold executive power, no matter whether they be called "bishops," or "stated clerks" or "synod presidents." Understanding denominational organization as belonging to the much larger species of bureaucracy, the sociologist will then be able to grasp the processes that occur in the organization, to observe the internal and external pressures brought to bear on those who are theoretically in charge. In other words, behind the facade of an "episcopal polity" the sociologist will perceive the workings of a bureaucratic apparatus that is not terribly different in the Methodist Church, an agency of the Federal government, General Motors or the United Automobile Workers.

Or take an example from economic life. The personnel manager of an industrial plant will take delight in preparing brightly colored charts that show the table of organization that is supposed to administer the production process. Every man has his place, every person in the organization knows from whom he receives his orders and to whom he must transmit them, every work team has its assigned role in the great drama of production. In reality things rarely work this way—and every good personnel manager knows this. Superimposed on the official blueprint of the organization is a much subtler, much less visible network of human groups, with their loyalties, prejudices, antipathies and (most important) codes of behavior. Industrial sociology is full of data on the operations of this informal network, which always exists in varying degrees of accommoda-

tion and conflict with the official system. Very much the same coexistence of formal and informal organization is to be found wherever large numbers of men work together or live together under a system of discipline—military organizations, prisons, hospitals, schools, going back to the mysterious leagues that children form among themselves and that their parents only rarely discern. Once more, the sociologist will seek to penetrate the smoke screen of the official versions of reality (those of the foreman, the officer, the teacher) and try to grasp the signals that come from the "underworld" (those of the worker, the enlisted man, the schoolboy).

Let us take one further example. In Western countries, and especially in America, it is assumed that men and women marry because they are in love. There is a broadly based popular mythology about the character of love as a violent, irresistible emotion that strikes where it will, a mystery that is the goal of most young people and often of the not-so-young as well. As soon as one investigates, however, which people actually marry each other, one finds that the lightning-shaft of Cupid seems to be guided rather strongly within very definite channels of class, income, education, racial and religious background. If one then investigates a little further into the behavior that is engaged in prior to marriage under the rather misleading euphemism of "courtship," one finds channels of interaction that are often rigid to the point of ritual. The suspicion begins to dawn on one that, most of the time, it is not so much the emotion of love that creates a certain kind of relationship, but that carefully predefined and often planned relationships eventually generate the desired emotion. In other words, when certain conditions are met or have been constructed, one allows oneself "to fall in love." The sociologist investigating our patterns of "courtship" and marriage soon discovers a complex web of motives related in many ways to the entire institutional structure within which an individual lives his life—class, career, economic ambition, aspirations of power and prestige. The miracle of love now begins to look somewhat synthetic. Again, this need not mean in any given instance that the sociologist will declare the romantic interpretation to be an illusion. But, once more, he will look beyond the immediately given and publicly approved interpretations. Contemplating a couple that in its turn is contemplating the moon, the sociologist need not feel constrained to deny the emotional impact of the scene thus illuminated. But he will observe the machinery that went into the construction of the scene in its nonlunar aspects—the status index of the automobile from which the contemplation occurs, the canons of taste and tactics that determine the costume of the contemplators, the many ways in which language and demeanor place them socially, thus the social location and intentionality of the entire enterprise.

It may have become clear at this point that the problems that will interest the sociologist are not necessarily what other people may call "problems." The way in which public officials and newspapers (and, alas, some college textbooks in sociology) speak about "social problems" serves to obscure this fact. People commonly speak of a "social problem" when something in society does not work the way it is supposed to according to the official interpretations. They then expect the sociologist to study the "problem" as they have defined it and perhaps even to come up with a "solution" that will take care of the matter to their own satisfaction. It is important, against this sort of expectation, to understand that a sociological problem is something quite different from a "social problem" in this sense. For example, it is naive to concentrate on crime as a "problem" because law-enforcement agencies so define it, or on divorce because that is a "problem" to the moralists of marriage. Even more clearly, the "problem" of the foreman to get his men to work more efficiently or of the line

officer to get his troops to charge the enemy more enthusiastically need not be problematic at all to the sociologist (leaving out of consideration for the moment the probable fact that the sociologist asked to study such "problems" is employed by the corporation or the army). The sociological problem is always the understanding of what goes on here in terms of social interaction. Thus the sociological problem is not so much why some things "go wrong" from the viewpoint of the authorities and the management of the social scene, but how the whole system works in the first place, what are its presuppositions and by what means it is held together. The fundamental sociological problem is not crime but the law, not divorce but marriage, not racial discrimination but racially defined stratification, not revolution but government.

This point can be explicated further by an example. Take a settlement house in a lower-class slum district trying to wean away teen-agers from the publicly disapproved activities of a juvenile gang. The frame of reference within which social workers and police officers define the "problems" of this situation is constituted by the world of middle-class, respectable, publicly approved values. It is a "problem" if teen-agers drive around in stolen automobiles, and it is a "solution" if instead they will play group games in the settlement house. But if one changes the frame of reference and looks at the situation from the viewpoint of the leaders of the juvenile gang, the "problems" are defined in reverse order. It is a "problem" for the solidarity of the gang if its members are seduced away from those activities that lend prestige to the gang within its own social world, and it would be a "solution" if the social workers went way the hell back uptown where they came from. What is a "problem" to one social system is the normal routine of things to the other system, and vice versa. Loyalty and disloyalty, solidarity and deviance, are defined in contradictory terms by the representatives of the two systems. Now, the sociologist may, in terms of his own values, regard the world of middle-class respectability as more desirable and therefore want to come to the assistance of the settlement house, which is its missionary outpost *in partibus infidelium*. This, however, does not justify the identification of the director's headaches with what are "problems" sociologically. The "problems" that the sociologist will want to solve concern an understanding of the entire social situation, the values and modes of action in *both* systems, and the way in which the two systems coexist in space and time. Indeed, this very ability to look at a situation from the vantage points of competing systems of interpretation is, as we shall see more clearly later on, one of the hallmarks of sociological consciousness.

We would contend, then, that there is a debunking motif inherent in sociological consciousness. The sociologist will be driven time and again, by the very logic of his discipline, to debunk the social systems he is studying. This unmasking tendency need not necessarily be due to the sociologist's temperament or inclinations. Indeed, it may happen that the sociologist, who as an individual may be of a conciliatory disposition and quite disinclined to disturb the comfortable assumptions on which he rests his own social existence, is nevertheless compelled by what he is doing to fly in the face of what those around him take for granted. In other words, we would contend that the roots of the debunking motif in sociology are not psychological but methodological. The sociological frame of reference, with its built-in procedure of looking for levels of reality other than those given in the official interpretations of society, carries with it a logical imperative to unmask the pretensions and the propaganda by which men cloak their actions with each other. This unmasking imperative is one of the characteristics of sociology particularly at home in the temper of the modern era.

The debunking tendency in sociological thought can be illustrated by a variety of developments within the field. For example, one of the major themes in Weber's sociology is that of the unintended, unforeseen consequences of human actions in society. Weber's most famous work, *The Protestant Ethic and the Spirit of Capitalism,* in which he demonstrated the relationship between certain consequences of Protestant values and the development of the capitalist ethos, has often been misunderstood by critics precisely because they missed this theme. Such critics have pointed out that the Protestant thinkers quoted by Weber never intended their teachings to be applied so as to produce the specific economic results in question. Specifically, Weber argued that the Calvinist doctrine of predestination led people to behave in what he called an "inner-worldly ascetic" way, that is, in a manner that concerns itself intensively, systematically and selflessly with the affairs of this world, especially with economic affairs. Weber's critics have then pointed out that nothing was further from the mind of Calvin and the other leaders of the Calvinist Reformation. But Weber never maintained that Calvinist thought *intended* to produce these economic action patterns. On the contrary, he knew very well that the intentions were drastically different. The consequences took place regardless of intentions. In other words, Weber's work (and not only the famous part of it just mentioned) gives us a vivid picture of the *irony* of human actions. Weber's sociology thus provides us with a radical antithesis to any views that understand history as the realization of ideas or as the fruit of the deliberate efforts of individuals or collectivities. This does not mean at all that ideas are not important. It does mean that the outcome of ideas is commonly very different from what those who had the ideas in the first place planned or hoped. Such a consciousness of the ironic aspect of history is sobering, a strong antidote to all kinds of revolutionary utopianism.

The debunking tendency of sociology is

implicit in all sociological theories that emphasize the autonomous character of social processes. For instance, Émile Durkheim, the founder of the most important school in French sociology, emphasized that society was a reality *sui generis,* that is, a reality that could not be reduced to psychological or other factors on different levels of analysis. The effect of this insistence has been a sovereign disregard for individually intended motives and meanings in Durkheim's study of various phenomena. This is perhaps most sharply revealed in his well-known study of suicide, in the work of that title, where individual intentions of those who commit or try to commit suicide are completely left out of the analysis in favor of statistics concerning various social characteristics of these individuals. In the Durkheimian perspective, to live in society means to exist under the domination of society's logic. Very often men act by this logic without knowing it. To discover this inner dynamic of society, therefore, the sociologist must frequently disregard the answers that the social actors themselves would give to his questions and look for explanations that are hidden from their own awareness. This essentially Durkheimian approach has been carried over into the theoretical approach now called functionalism. In functional analysis society is analyzed in terms of its own workings as a system, workings that are often obscure or opaque to those acting within the system. The contemporary American sociologist Robert Merton has expressed this approach well in his concepts of "manifest" and "latent" functions. The former are the conscious and deliberate functions of social processes, the latter the unconscious and unintended ones. Thus the "manifest" function of antigambling legislation may be to suppress gambling, its "latent" function to create an illegal empire for the gambling syndicates. Or Christian missions in parts of Africa "manifestly" tried to convert Africans to Christianity, "latently" helped to destroy the indigenous tribal cultures and thus provided an important impetus towards rapid social transformation. Or the control of the Communist Party over all sectors of social life in Russia "manifestly" was to assure the continued dominance of the revolutionary ethos, "latently" created a new class of comfortable bureaucrats uncannily bourgeois in its aspirations and increasingly disinclined toward the self-denial of Bolshevik dedication. Or the "manifest" function of many voluntary associations in America is sociability and public service, the "latent" function to attach status indices to those permitted to belong to such associations.

The concept of "ideology," a central one in some sociological theories, could serve as another illustration of the debunking tendency discussed. Sociologists speak of "ideology" in discussing views that serve to rationalize the vested interests of some group. Very frequently such views systematically distort social reality in much the same way that an individual may neurotically deny, deform or reinterpret aspects of his life that are inconvenient to him. The important approach of the Italian sociologist Vilfredo Pareto has a central place for this perspective and the concept of "ideology" is essential for the approach called the "sociology of knowledge." In such analyses the ideas by which men explain their actions are unmasked as self-deception, sales talk, the kind of "sincerity" that David Riesman has aptly described as the state of mind of a man who habitually believes his own propaganda. In this way, we can speak of "ideology" when we analyze the belief of many American physicians that standards of health will decline if the fee-for-service method of payment is abolished, or the conviction of many undertakers that inexpensive funerals show lack of affection for the departed, or the definition of their activity by quizmasters on television as "education." The self-image of the insurance salesman as a fatherly adviser to young families, of the burlesque stripper as an artist, of the propagandist as a communications expert, of the hangman as a public servant—all these notions are not only individual assuagements of guilt or status anxiety, but constitute the official self-interpretations of entire social groups, obligatory for their members on pain of excommunication. In uncovering the social functionality of ideological pretensions the sociologist will try not to resemble those historians of whom Marx said that every corner grocer is superior to them in knowing the difference between what a man is and what he claims to be. The debunking motif of sociology lies in this penetration of verbal smoke screens to the unadmitted and often unpleasant mainsprings of action.

It has been suggested above that sociological consciousness is likely to arise when the commonly accepted or authoritatively stated interpretations of society become shaky. As we have already said, there is a good case for thinking of the origins of sociology in France (the mother country of the discipline) in terms of an effort to cope intellectually with the consequences of the French Revolution, not only of the one great cataclysm of 1789 but of what De Tocqueville called the continuing Revolution of the nineteenth century. In the French case it is not difficult to perceive sociology against the background of the rapid transformations of modern society, the collapse of facades, the deflation of old creeds and the upsurge of frightening new forces on the social scene. In Germany, the other European country in which an important sociological movement arose in the nineteenth century, the matter has a rather different appearance. If one may quote Marx once more, the Germans had a tendency to carry on in professors' studies the revolutions that the French performed on the barricades. At least one of these academic roots of revolution, perhaps the most important one, may be sought in the broadly based movement of thought that came to be called "historicism." This is not the place to go

into the full story of this movement. Suffice it to say that it represents an attempt to deal philosophically with the overwhelming sense of the relativity of all values in history. This awareness of relativity was an almost necessary outcome of the immense accumulation of German historical scholarship in every conceivable field. Sociological thought was at least partly grounded in the need to bring order and intelligibility to the impression of chaos that this array of historical knowledge made on some observers. Needless to stress, however, the society of the German sociologist was changing all around him just as was that of his French colleague, as Germany rushed towards industrial power and nationhood in the second half of the nineteenth century. We shall not pursue these questions, though. If we turn to America, the country in which sociology came to receive its most widespread acceptance, we find once more a different set of circumstances, though again against a background of rapid and profound social change. In looking at this American development we can detect another motif of sociology, closely related to that of debunking but not identical with it—its fascination with the unrespectable view of society.

In at least every Western society it is possible to distinguish between respectable and unrespectable sectors. In that respect American society is not in a unique position. But American respectability has a particularly pervasive quality about it. This may be ascribed in part, perhaps, to the lingering aftereffects of the Puritan way of life. More probably it has to do with the predominant role played by the bourgeoisie in shaping American culture. Be this as it may in terms of historical causation, it is not difficult to look at social phenomena in America and place them readily in one of these two sectors. We can perceive the official, respectable America represented symbolically by the Chamber of Commerce, the churches, the schools and other centers of civic ritual. But facing this world of respectability is an "other America," present in every town of any size, an America that has other symbols and that speaks another language. The language is probably its safest identification tag. It is the language of the poolroom and the poker game, of bars, brothels and army barracks. But it is also the language that breaks out with a sigh of relief between two salesmen having a drink in the parlor car as their train races past clean little Midwestern villages on a Sunday morning, with clean little villagers trooping into the whitewashed sanctuaries. It is the language that is suppressed in the company of ladies and clergymen, owing its life mainly to oral transmission from one generation of Huckleberry Finns to another (though in recent years the language has found literary deposition in some books designed to thrill ladies and clergymen). The "other America" that speaks this language can be found wherever people are excluded, or exclude themselves, from the world of middle-class propriety. We find it in those sections of the working class that have not yet proceeded too far on the road of *embourgeoisement,* in slums, shantytowns and those parts of cities that urban sociologists have called "areas of transition." We find it expressed powerfully in the world of the American Negro. We also come on it in the subworlds of those who have, for one reason or another, withdrawn voluntarily from Main Street and Madison Avenue—in the worlds of hipsters, homosexuals, hoboes and other "marginal men," those worlds that are kept safely out of sight on the streets where the nice people live, work and amuse themselves *en famille* (though these worlds may on some occasions be rather convenient for the male of the species "nice people"—precisely on occasions when he happily finds himself *sans famille*).

American sociology, accepted early both in academic circles and by those concerned with welfare activities, was from the beginning associated with the "official America," with the world of policy makers in community and nation. Sociology today retains this respectable affiliation in university, business and government. The appellation hardly induces eyebrows to be raised, except the eyebrows of such Southern racists sufficiently literate to have read the footnotes of the desegregation decision of 1954. However, we would contend that there has been an important undercurrent in American sociology, relating it to that "other America" of dirty language and disenchanted attitudes, that state of mind that refuses to be impressed, moved or befuddled by the official ideologies.

This unrespectable perspective on the American scene can be seen most clearly in the figure of Thorstein Veblen, one of the early important sociologists in America. His biography itself constitutes an exercise in marginality: a difficult, querulous character; born on a Norwegian farm on the Wisconsin frontier; acquiring English as a foreign language; involved all his life with morally and politically suspect individuals; an academic migrant; an inveterate seducer of other people's women. The perspective on America gained from this angle of vision can be found in the unmasking satire that runs like a purple thread through Veblen's work, most famously in his *Theory of the Leisure Class,* that merciless look from the underside at the pretensions of the American *haute bourgeoisie.* Veblen's view of society can be understood most easily as a series of non-Rotarian insights—his understanding of "conspicuous consumption" as against the middle-class enthusiasm for the "finer things," his analysis of economic processes in terms of manipulation and waste as against the American productivity ethos, his understanding of the machinations of real estate speculation as against the American community ideology, most bitterly his description of academic life (in *The Higher Learning in America*) in terms of fraud and flatulence as against the American cult of education. We are not associating ourselves here with a certain neo-Veblenism that has become fashionable with some younger American sociologists, nor arguing that Veblen was a giant in the development of the field. We are only pointing to his irreverent curiosity and clear-sightedness as marks of a perspective coming from those places in the culture in which one gets up to shave about noon on Sundays. Nor are we arguing that clear-sightedness is a general trait of unrespectability. Stupidity and sluggishness of thought are probably distributed quite fairly throughout the social spectrum. But where there is intelligence and where it manages to free itself from the goggles of respectability, we can expect a clearer view of society than in those cases where the oratorical imagery is taken for real life.

A number of developments in empirical studies in American sociology furnish evidence of this same fascination with the unrespectable view of society. For example, looking back at the powerful development of urban studies undertaken at the University of Chicago in the 1920s we are struck by the apparently irresistible attraction to the seamier sides of city life upon these researchers. The advice to his students of Robert Park, the most important figure in this development, to the effect that they should get their hands dirty with research often enough meant quite literally an intense interest in all the things that North Shore residents would call "dirty." We sense in many of these studies the excitement of discovering the picaresque undersides of the metropolis—studies of slum life, of the melancholy world of rooming houses, of Skid Row, of the worlds of crime and prostitution. One of the offshoots of this so-called "Chicago school" has been the sociological study of occupations, due very largely to the pi-

oneering work of Everett Hughes and his students. Here also we find a fascination with every possible world in which human beings live and make a living, not only with the worlds of the respectable occupations, but with those of the taxi dancer, the apartment-house janitor, the professional boxer or the jazz musician. The same tendency can be discovered in the course of American community studies following in the wake of the famous *Middletown* studies of Robert and Helen Lynd. Inevitably these studies had to bypass the official versions of community life, to look at the social reality of the community not only from the perspective of city hall but also from that of the city jail. Such sociological procedure is *ipso facto* a refutation of the respectable presupposition that only certain views of the world are to be taken seriously.

We would not want to give an exaggerated impression of the effect of such investigations on the consciousness of sociologists. We are well aware of the elements of muckraking and romanticism inherent in some of this. We also know that many sociologists participate as fully in the respectable *Weltanschauung* as all the other PTA members on their block. Nevertheless, we would maintain that sociological consciousness predisposes one towards an awareness of worlds other than that of middle-class respectability, an awareness which already carries within itself the seeds of intellectual unrespectability. In the second *Middletown* study the Lynds have given a classic analysis of the mind of middle-class America in their series of "of course statements"—that is, statements that represent a consensus so strong that the answer to any question concerning them will habitually be prefaced with the words "of course." "Is our economy one of free enterprise?" "Of course!" "Are all our important decisions arrived at through the democratic process?" "Of course!" "Is monogamy the natural form of marriage?" "Of course!" The sociologist, however conservative and conformist he may be in his private life, knows that there are serious questions to be raised about every one of these "of course statements." In this knowledge alone he is brought to the threshold of unrespectability.

This unrespectable motif of sociological consciousness need not imply a revolutionary attitude. We would even go further than that and express the opinion that sociological understanding is inimical to revolutionary ideologies, not because it has some sort of conservative bias, but because it sees not only through the illusions of the present *status quo* but also through the illusionary expectations concerning possible futures, such expectations being the customary spiritual nourishment of the revolutionary. This nonrevolutionary and moderating soberness of sociology we would value quite highly. More regrettable, from the viewpoint of one's values, is the fact that sociological understanding by itself does not necessarily lead to a greater tolerance with respect to the foibles of mankind. It is possible to view social reality with compassion or with cynicism, both attitudes being compatible with clear-sightedness. But whether he can bring himself to human sympathy with the phenomena he is studying or not, the sociologist will in some measure be detached from the taken-for-granted postures of his society. Unrespectability, whatever its ramifications in the emotions and the will, must remain a constant possibility in the sociologist's mind. It may be segregated from the rest of his life, overlaid by the routine mental states of everyday existence, even denied ideologically. Total respectability of thought, however, will invariably mean the death of sociology. This is one of the reasons why genuine sociology disappears promptly from the scene in totalitarian countries, as is well illustrated in the instance of Nazi Germany. By implication, sociological understanding is always potentially dangerous to the minds of policemen and other guardians of public order, since it will always tend to relativize the claim to absolute rightness upon which such minds like to rest.

Before concluding, we would look once more on this phenomenon of relativization that we have already touched upon a few times. We would now say explicitly that sociology is so much in tune with the temper of the modern era precisely because it represents the consciousness of a world in which values have been radically relativized. This relativization has become so much part of our everyday imagination that it is difficult for us to grasp fully how closed and absolutely binding the world views of other cultures have been and in some places still are. The American sociologist Daniel Lerner, in his study of the contemporary Middle East (*The Passing of Traditional Society*), has given us a vivid portrait of what "modernity" means as an altogether new kind of consciousness in those countries. For the traditional mind one is what one is, where one is, and cannot even imagine how one could be anything different. The modern mind, by contrast, is mobile, participates vicariously in the lives of others differently located from oneself, easily imagines itself changing occupation or residence. Thus Lerner found that some of the illiterate respondents to his questionnaires could only respond with laughter to the question as to what they would do if they were in the position of their rulers and would not even consider the question as to the circumstances under which they would be willing to leave their native village. Another way of putting this would be to say that traditional societies assign definite and permanent identities to their members. In modern society identity itself is uncertain and in flux. One does not really know what is expected of one as a ruler, as a parent, as a cultivated person, or as one who is sexually normal. Typically, one then requires various experts to tell one. The book club editor tells us what culture is, the interior designer what taste we ought to have, and the psychoanalyst who we are. To live in modern society means to live at the center of a kaleidoscope of ever-changing roles.

Again, we must forego the temptation of enlarging on this point, since it would take us rather far afield from our argument into a general discussion of the social psychology of modern existence. We would rather stress the intellectual aspect of this situation, since it is in that aspect that we would see an important dimension of sociological consciousness. The unprecedented rate of geographical and social mobility in modern society means that one becomes exposed to an unprecedented variety of ways of looking at the world. The insights into other cultures that one might gather by travel are brought into one's own living room through the mass media. Someone once defined urbane sophistication as being the capacity to remain quite unperturbed upon seeing in front of one's house a man dressed in a turban and a loincloth, a snake coiled around his neck, beating a tom-tom as he leads a leashed tiger down the street. No doubt there are degrees to such sophistication, but a measure of it is acquired by every child who watches television. No doubt also this sophistication is commonly only superficial and does not extend to any real grappling with alternate ways of life. Nevertheless, the immensely broadened possibility of travel, in person and through the imagination, implies at least potentially the awareness that one's own culture, including its basic values, is relative in space and time. Social mobility, that is, the movement from one social stratum to another, augments this relativizing effect. Wherever industrialization occurs, a new dynamism is injected into the social system. Masses of people begin to change their social position, in groups or as individuals. And usually this change is in an "upward" direction. With this movement an individual's biography often involves a considerable journey not only through a variety of

social groups but through the intellectual universes that are, so to speak, attached to these groups. Thus the Baptist mail clerk who used to read the *Reader's Digest* becomes an Episcopalian junior executive who reads *The New Yorker,* or the faculty wife whose husband becomes department chairman may graduate from the best-seller list to Proust or Kafka.

In view of this overall fluidity of world views in modern society it should not surprise us that our age has been characterized as one of conversion. Nor should it be surprising that intellectuals especially have been prone to change their world views radically and with amazing frequency. The intellectual attraction of strongly presented, theoretically closed systems of thought such as Catholicism or Communism has been frequently commented upon. Psychoanalysis, in all its forms, can be understood as an institutionalized mechanism of conversion, in which the individual changes not only his view of himself but of the world in general. The popularity of a multitude of new cults and creeds, presented in different degrees of intellectual refinement depending upon the educational level of their clientele, is another manifestation of this proneness to conversion of our contemporaries. It almost seems as if modern man, and especially modern educated man, is in a perpetual state of doubt about the nature of himself and of the universe in which he lives. In other words, the awareness of relativity, which probably in all ages of history has been the possession of a small group of intellectuals, today appears as a broad cultural fact reaching far down into the lower reaches of the social system.

We do not want to give the impression that this sense of relativity and the resulting proneness to change one's entire *Weltanschauung* are manifestations of intellectual or emotional immaturity. Certainly one should not take with too much seriousness some representatives of this pattern. Nevertheless, we would contend that an essentially similar pattern becomes almost a destiny in even the most serious intellectual enterprises. It is impossible to exist with full awareness in the modern world without realizing that moral, political and philosophical commitments are relative, that, in Pascal's words, what is truth on one side of the Pyrenees is error on the other. Intensive occupation with the more fully elaborated meaning systems available in our time gives one a truly frightening understanding of the way in which these systems can provide a total interpretation of reality, within which will be included an interpretation of the alternate systems and of the ways of passing from one system to another. Catholicism may have a theory of Communism, but Communism returns the compliment and will produce a theory of Catholicism. To the Catholic thinker the Communist lives in a dark world of materialist delusion about the real meaning of life. To the Communist his Catholic adversary is helplessly caught in the "false consciousness" of a bourgeois mentality. To the psychoanalyst both Catholic and Communist may simply be acting out on the intellectual level the unconscious impulses that really move them. And psychoanalysis may be to the Catholic an escape from the reality of sin and to the Communist an avoidance of the realities of society. This means that the individual's choice of viewpoint will determine the way in which he looks back upon his own biography. American prisoners of war "brainwashed" by the Chinese Communists completely changed their viewpoints on social and political matters. To those that returned to America this change represented a sort of illness brought on by outward pressure, as a convalescent may look back on a delirious dream. But to their former captors this changed consciousness represents a brief glimmer of true understanding between long periods of ignorance. And to those prisoners who decided not to return, their conversion may still appear as the decisive passage from darkness to light.

Instead of speaking of conversion (a term with religiously charged connotations) we would prefer to use the more neutral term of "alternation" to describe this phenomenon. The intellectual situation just described brings with it the possibility that an individual may alternate back and forth between logically contradictory meaning systems. Each time, the meaning system he enters provides him with an interpretation of his existence and of his world, including in this interpretation an explanation of the meaning system he has abandoned. Also, the meaning system provides him with tools to combat his own doubts. Catholic confessional discipline, Communist "autocriticism" and the psychoanalytic techniques of coping with "resistance" all fulfill the same purpose of preventing alternation out of the particular meaning system, allowing the individual to interpret his own doubts in terms derived from the system itself, thus keeping him within it. On lower levels of sophistication there will also be various means employed to cut off questions that might threaten the individual's allegiance to the system, means that one can see at work in the dialectical acrobatics of even such relatively unsophisticated groups as Jehovah's Witnesses or Black Muslims.

If one resists the temptation, however, to accept such dialectics, and is willing to face squarely the experience of relativity brought on by the phenomenon of alternation, then one comes into possession of yet another crucial dimension of sociological consciousness—the awareness that not only identities but ideas are relative to specific social locations. Suffice it to say that this relativizing motif is another of the fundamental driving forces of the sociological enterprise.

We have tried to outline the dimensions of sociological consciousness through the analysis of three motifs—those of debunking, unrespectability and relativizing. To these three we would, finally, add a fourth one, much less far-reaching in its implications but useful in rounding out our picture—the cosmopolitan motif. Going back to very ancient times, it was in cities that there developed an openness to the world, to other ways of thinking and acting. Whether we think of Athens or Alexandria, of medieval Paris or Renaissance Florence, or of the turbulent urban centers of modern history, we can identify a certain cosmopolitan consciousness that was especially characteristic of city culture. The individual, then, who is not only urban but urbane is one who, however passionately he may be attached to his own city, roams through the whole wide world in his intellectual voyages. His mind, if not his body and his emotions, is at home wherever there are other men who think. We would submit that socio-logical consciousness is marked by the same kind of cosmopolitanism. This is why a narrow parochialism in its focus of interest is always a danger signal for the sociological venture (a danger signal that, unfortunately, we would hoist over quite a few sociological studies in America today). The sociological perspective is a broad, open, emancipated vista on human life. The sociologist, at his best, is a man with a taste for other lands, inwardly open to the measureless richness of human possibilities, eager for new horizons and new worlds of human meaning. It probably requires no additional elaboration to make the point that this type of man can play a particularly useful part in the course of events today.

3. RESEARCH AND SOCIOLOGICAL THEORY

ROBERT K. MERTON

Here, Robert K. Merton discusses the bearing of empirical research on sociological theory. Claiming that research goes far beyond the passive roles of verifying and testing theory, he specifies four active roles that it plays in the analytical process.

The first of these is the serendipity pattern, the part played by the occurrence of "an unanticipated, anomalous and strategic datum" that exerts "pressure for initiating theory." The second is the recasting of theory based upon new information uncovered by the persistent review of previously neglected data. The third is the refocusing of theoretic interest owing to new innovations in methodological procedures. The last is the role played by empirical research for the clarification of concepts. Each of these roles is illustrated by Merton from a wide range of examples drawn from relevant sociological and anthropological studies.

Robert K. Merton is Giddings Professor of Sociology at Columbia University and Associate Director of the Bureau of Applied Social Research. One of America's best known sociologists, he is the author of Mass Persuasion (*1946*), Social Theory and Social Structure (*1949; revised 1957*), On the Shoulders of Giants: A Shandian Postscript (*1965*), *and* Science, Technology and Society in Seventeenth Century England (*1968*), *and coeditor of a number of volumes including* Continuities in Social Research: Studies in the Scope and Method of "The American Soldier" (*1950*), Reader in Bureaucracy (*1952*), The Student Physician (*1957*), Sociology Today (*1959*), *and* Contemporary Social Problems (*1961; revised 1966*).

History has a certain gift for outmoding stereotypes. This can be seen, for example, in the historical development of sociology. The stereotype of the social theorist high in the empyrean of pure ideas uncontaminated by mundane facts is fast becoming no less outmoded than the stereotype of the social researcher equipped with questionnaire and pencil and hot on the chase of the isolated and meaningless statistic. For in building the mansion of sociology during the last decades, theorist and empiricist have learned to work together. What is more, they have learned to talk to one another in the process. At times, this means only that a sociologist has learned to talk to himself since increasingly the same man has taken up both theory and research. Specialization and integration have developed hand in hand. All this has led not only to the realization that theory and empirical research *should* interact but to the result that they *do* interact.

As a consequence, there is decreasing need for accounts of the relations between theory and research to be wholly programmatic in character. A growing body of theoretically oriented research makes it progressively possible to discuss with

Reprinted from the *American Sociological Review,* **13** (1948), 505–515, by permission of the author and the American Sociological Association.

profit the actual relations between the two. And, as we all know, there has been no scarcity of such discussions. Journals abound with them. They generally center on the role of theory in research, setting forth, often with admirable lucidity, the functions of theory in the initiation, design and prosecution of empirical inquiry. But since this is not a one-way relationship, since the two *inter*act, it may be useful to examine the other direction of the relationship: the role of empirical research in the development of social theory. That is the purpose of this paper.

The Theoretic Functions of Research

With a few conspicuous exceptions, recent sociological discussions have assigned but one major function to empirical research: "testing" or "verification" of hypotheses. The model for the proper way of performing this function is as familiar as it is clear. The investigator begins with a hunch or hypothesis, from this he draws various inferences and these, in turn, are subjected to empirical test which confirms or refutes the hypothesis.[1] But this is a logical model, and so fails, of course, to describe much of what actually occurs in fruitful investigation. It presents a set of logical norms, not a description of the research experience. And, as logicians are well aware, in purifying the experience, the logical model may also distort it. Like other such models, it abstracts from the temporal sequence of events. It exaggerates the creative role of explicit theory just as it minimizes the creative role of observation. For research is not merely logic tempered with observation. It has its psychological as well as its logical dimensions, although one would scarcely suspect this from the logically rigorous sequence in which research is usually reported.[2] It is both the psychological and logical pressures of research upon social theory which we seek to trace.

It is my central thesis that empirical research goes far beyond the passive role of verifying and testing theory: it does more than confirm or refute hypotheses. Research plays an active role: it performs at least four major functions which help shape the development of theory. It *initiates*, it *reformulates*, it *deflects* and *clarifies* theory.[3]

The serendipity pattern

[*The unanticipated, anomalous and strategic datum exerts a pressure for initiating theory.*] Under certain conditions, a research finding gives rise to social theory. In a previous paper, this was all too briefly expressed as follows: "Fruitful empirical research not only tests theoretically derived hypotheses; it also originates new hypotheses. This might be termed the 'serendipity' component of research, *i.e.*, the discovery, by chance or sagacity, of valid results which were not sought for."[4]

The serendipity pattern refers to the fairly common experience of observing an *unanticipated, anomalous and strategic* datum which becomes the occasion for developing a new theory or for extending an existing theory. Each of these elements of the pattern can be readily described. The datum is, first of all, unanticipated. A research directed toward the test of one hypothesis yields a fortuitous by-product, an unexpected observation which bears upon theories not in question when the research was begun.

Secondly, the observation is anomalous, surprising,[5] either because it seems inconsistent with prevailing theory or with other established facts. In either case, the seeming inconsistency provokes curiosity; it stimulates the investigator to "make sense of the datum," to fit it into a broader frame of knowledge. He explores further. He makes fresh observations. He draws inferences from the observations, inferences depending largely, of course, upon his general theoretic orientation.

The more he is steeped in the data, the greater the likelihood that he will hit upon a fruitful direction of inquiry. In the fortunate circumstance that his new hunch proves justified, the anomalous datum leads ultimately to a new or extended theory. The curiosity stimulated by the anomalous datum is temporarily appeased.

And thirdly, in noting that the unexpected fact must be "strategic," *i.e.,* that it must permit of implications which bear upon generalized theory, we are, of course, referring rather to what the observer brings to the datum than to the datum itself. For it obviously requires a theoretically sensitized observer to detect the universal in the particular. After all, men had for centuries noticed such "trivial" occurrences as slips of the tongue, slips of the pen, typographical errors, and lapses of memory, but it required the theoretic sensitivity of a Freud to see these as strategic data through which he could extend his theory of repression and symptomatic acts.

The serendipity pattern, then, involves the unanticipated, anomalous and strategic datum which exerts pressure upon the investigator for a new direction of inquiry which extends theory. Instances of serendipity have occurred in many disciplines, but I should like to draw upon a current sociological research for illustration. In the course of our research into the social organization of Craftown,[6] a suburban housing community of some 700 families, largely of working-class status, we observed that a large proportion of residents were affiliated with more civic, political and other voluntary organizations than had been the case in their previous places of residence. Quite incidentally, we noted further that this increase in group participation had occurred also among the parents of infants and young children. This finding was rather inconsistent with commonsense knowledge. For it is well known that, particularly on the lower economic levels, youngsters usually tie parents down and preclude their taking active part in organized group life outside the home. But Craftown parents themselves readily explained their behavior. "Oh, there's no real problem about getting out in the evenings," said one mother who belonged to several organizations. "It's easy to find teen-agers around here to take care of the kids. There are so many more teen-agers around here than where I used to live."

The explanation appears adequate enough and would have quieted the investigator's curiosity, had it not been for one disturbing datum: like most new housing communities, Craftown actually has a very small proportion of adolescents— only 3.7%, for example, in the 15–19 year age group. What is more, the majority of the adults, 63%, are under 34 years of age, so that their children include an exceptionally large proportion of infants and youngsters. Thus, far from there being many adolescents to look after the younger children in Craftown, quite the contrary is true: the ratio of adolescents to children under ten years of age is 1:10, whereas in the communities of origin, the ratio hovers about 1:1.5.[7]

We were at once confronted, then, by an anomalous fact which was certainly no part of our original program of observation. This should be emphasized. We manifestly did not enter and indeed could not have entered upon the field research in Craftown with a hypothesis bearing an illusory belief in the abundance of teen-age supervisors of children. Here was an observation both unanticipated and anomalous. Was it also strategic? We did not prejudge its "intrinsic" importance. It seemed no more and no less trivial than Freud's observation during the last war (in which he had two sons at the front) that he had mis-read a newspaper headline, "Die *Feinde* vor Görz" (The *Enemy* before Görz), as "Der *Friede* von Görz" (The *Peace* of Görz). Freud took a trivial incident and converted it into a strategic fact. Unless the observed discrepancy between the subjective impressions of Craftown residents and the objective facts could undergo a somewhat similar transformation it had best be ignored, for it plainly had little "social significance."

What first made this illusion a peculiarly intriguing instance of a general theoretic problem was the difficulty of explaining it as merely the calculated handiwork of vested-interests engaged in spreading a contrary-to-fact belief. Generally, when the sociologist with a conceptual scheme stemming from utilitarian theory observes a patently untrue social belief, he will look for special groups in whose interest it is to invent and spread this belief. The cry of "propaganda!" is often mistaken for a theoretically sound analysis.[8] But this is clearly out of the question in the present instance: there are plainly no special-interest groups seeking to misrepresent the age-distribution of Craftown. What, then, was the source of this social illusion?

Various other theories suggested points of departure. There was Marx's postulate that it is men's "social existence which determines their consciousness." There was Durkheim's theorem that social images ("collective representations") in some fashion reflect a social reality although "it does not follow that the reality which is its foundation conforms objectively to the idea which believers have of it." There was Sherif's thesis that "social factors" provide a framework for selective perceptions and judgments in relatively unstructured situations. There was the prevailing view in the sociology of knowledge that social location determines the perspectives entering into perception, beliefs and ideas. But suggestive as these general orientations[9] were, they did not directly suggest *which* features of "social existence," *which* aspects of the "social reality," *which* "social factors," *which* "social location" may have determined this seemingly fallacious belief.

The clue was inadvertently provided by further interviews with residents. In the words of an active participant in Craftown affairs, herself the mother of two children under six years of age:

My husband and I get out together much more. You see, there are more people around to mind the children. *You feel more confident about having some thirteen- or fourteen-year-old in here when you know most of the people. If you're in a big city, you don't feel so easy about having someone who's almost a stranger come in.*

This clearly suggests that the sociological roots of the "illusion" are to be found in the structure of community relations in which Craftown residents are enmeshed. The belief is an unwitting reflection, not of the statistical reality, but of the community cohesion. It is not that there are objectively more adolescents in Craftown, but more who are *intimately known* and who, therefore, *exist socially* for parents seeking aid in child supervision. Most Craftown residents having lately come from an urban setting now find themselves in a community in which proximity has developed into reciprocal intimacies. The illusion expresses the perspective of people for whom adolescents as potential child-care aides "exist" only if they are well-known and therefore merit confidence. In short, perception was a function of confidence and confidence, in turn, was a function of social cohesion.[10]

From the sociological viewpoint, then, this unanticipated finding fits into and extends the theory that "social perception" is the product of a social framework. It develops further the "psychology of social norms,"[11] for it is not merely an instance of individuals assimilating particular norms, judgments, and standards from other members of the community. The social perception is, rather, a by-product, a derivative, of the structure of human relations.

This is perhaps sufficient to illustrate the operation of the serendipity pattern: an unexpected and anomalous finding elicited the investigator's curiosity, and conducted him along an unpremeditated bypath which led to a fresh hypothesis.

The recasting of theory

[*New data exert pressure for the elaboration of a conceptual scheme.*] But it is not only through the anomalous fact that empirical research invites the extension of theory. It does so also through the repeated observation of hitherto neglected facts. When an existing conceptual scheme commonly applied to a given subject-matter does not adequately take these facts into account, research presses insistently for its reformulation. It leads to the introduction of variables which have not been systematically included in the scheme of analysis. Here, be it noted, it is . not that the data are anomalous or unexpected or incompatible with existing theory; it is merely that they have not been considered pertinent. Whereas the serendipity pattern centers in an apparent inconsistency which presses for resolution, the reformulation pattern centers in the hitherto neglected but relevant fact which presses for an extension of the conceptual scheme.

Examples of this in the history of social science are far from limited. Thus it was a series of fresh empirical facts which led Malinowski to incorporate new elements into a theory of magic. It was his Trobrianders, of course, who gave him the clue to the distinctive feature of his theory. When these islanders fished in the inner lagoon by the reliable method of poisoning, an abundant catch was assured and danger was absent. Neither uncertainty nor uncontrollable hazards were involved. And here, Malinowski noted, magic was not practiced. But in the open-sea fishing, with the uncertain yield and its often grave dangers, the rituals of magic flourished. Stemming from these pregnant observations was his theory that magical belief arises to bridge the uncertainties in man's practical pursuits, to fortify confidence, to reduce anxieties, to open up avenues of escape from the seeming impasse. Magic was construed as a supplementary technique for reaching practical objectives. It was these empirical facts which suggested the incorporation of new dimensions into earlier theories of magic —particularly the relations of magic to the fortuitous, the dangerous and the uncontrollable. It was not that these facts were *inconsistent* with previous theories; it was simply that these conceptual schemes had not taken them adequately into account. Nor was Malinowski testing a preconceived hypothesis—he was developing an enlarged and improved theory on the basis of suggestive empirical data.

For another example of this pressure of empirical data for the recasting of a specific theory we turn closer home. The investigation dealt with a single dramatic instance of mass persuasion: broadcasting at repeated intervals over a span of eighteen hours, Kate Smith, a radio star, sold large quantities of war bonds in the course of the day. It is not my intention to report fully on the dynamics of this case of mass persuasion; [12] for present purposes, we are concerned only with the implications of two facts which emerged from the study.

First of all, in the course of intensive interviews many of our informants—New Yorkers who had pledged a bond to Smith —expressed a thorough disenchantment with the world of advertising, commercials and propaganda. They felt themselves the object of manipulation—and resented it. They objected to being the target for advertising which cajoles, insists and terrorizes. They objected to being engulfed in waves of propaganda proposing opinions and actions not in their own best interests. They expressed dismay over what is in effect a pattern of *pseudo-Gemeinschaft*—subtle methods of salesmanship in which there is the feigning of personal concern with the client in order to manipulate him the better. As one small businessman phrased it, "In my own business, I can see how a lot of people in their business deals will make some kind of gesture of friendliness, sincerity and so forth, much of which is phony." Drawn from a highly competitive, segmented metropolitan society, our informants were describing a climate of reciprocal distrust, of *anomie,* in which common values have been submerged in the welter of private interests. Society was experienced as an arena for rival frauds. There was small belief in the disinterestedness of conduct.

In contrast to all this was the second fact: we found that the persuasiveness of the Smith bond-drive among these same informants largely rested upon their firm belief in the integrity and sincerity of Smith. And much the same was found to be true in a polling interview with a larger cross-section sample of almost a thousand New Yorkers. Fully 80% asserted that in her all-day marathon drives, Smith was *exclusively* concerned with promoting the sale of war bonds, whereas only 17% felt that she was *also* interested in publicity for herself, and a negligible 3% believed she was *primarily* concerned with the re-sulting publicity.

This emphasis on her sincerity is all the more striking as a problem for research in the molding of reputations because she herself appeared on at least six commer-cially sponsored radio programs each week. But although she is engaged in ap-parently the same promotional activities as others, she was viewed by the majority of our informants as the direct antithesis of all that these other announcers and stars represent. In the words of one devo-tee, "She's sincere and *she really means anything* she ever says. It isn't just sittin' up there and talkin' and gettin' paid for it. She's different from what other people are."

Why this overwhelming belief in Smith's sincerity? To be sure, the same society which produces a sense of aliena-tion and estrangement generates in many a craving for reassurance, an acute will to believe, a flight into faith. But why does Smith become the object of this faith for so many otherwise distrustful people? Why is she seen as genuine by those who seek redemption from the spurious? Why are her motives believed to rise above avarice, and ambition and pride of class? What are the social-psychological sources of this image of Smith as sincerity incar-nate?

Among the several sources, we wish to examine here the one which bears most directly upon a theory of mass persuasion. The clue is provided by the fact that a larger proportion of those who heard the Smith marathon war-bond drive are con-vinced of her disinterested patriotism than of those who did not. This appears to indicate that the marathon bond-drive en-hanced public belief in her sincerity. But we must recognize the possibility that her devoted fans, for whom her sincerity was unquestioned, would be more likely to have heard the marathon broadcasts. Therefore, to determine whether the mar-athon did in fact extend this belief, we must compare regular listeners to her pro-grams with those who are not her fans. Within each group, a significantly larger proportion of people who heard the mara-thon are convinced of Smith's exclusive concern with patriotic purpose. This is as true for her devoted fans as for those who did not listen to her regular programs at all. In other words, we have caught for a moment, as with a candid camera, a snap-shot of Smith's reputation of sincerity in the process of being even further en-hanced. We have frozen in mid-course the process of building a reputation.

But if the marathon increased the belief in Smith's sincerity, how did this come about? It is at this point that our intensive interviews, with their often ingenuous and revealing details, permit us to interpret the statistical results of the poll. The mara-thon had all the atmosphere of deter-mined, resolute endeavor under tremen-dous difficulties. Some could detect signs of strain—and courageous persistence. "Her voice was not quite so strong later, but she stuck it out like a good soldier," says a discerning housewife. Others projected themselves into the vividly imagined situation of fatigue and brave exertion. Solicitous reports by her coadjutor, Ted Collins, reinforced the empathic concern for the strain to which Smith was subjecting herself. "I felt, I can't stand this any longer," recalls one informant. "Mr. Collins' statement about her being exhausted affected me so much that I just couldn't bear it." The marathon took on the attributes of a sacrificial ritual.

In short, it was not so much what Smith *said* as what she *did* which served to validate her sincerity. It was the presumed stress and strain of an eighteen-hour series of broadcasts, it was the deed not the word which furnished the indubitable proof. Listeners might question whether she were not unduly dramatizing herself, but they could not escape the incontrovertible evidence that she was devoting the entire day to the task. Appraising the direct testimony of Smith's behavior, another informant explains that "she was on all day and the others weren't. So it seemed that she was sacrificing more and was more sincere." Viewed as a process of persuasion, the marathon converted initial feelings of scepticism and distrust among listeners into at first a reluctant, and later, a full-fledged acceptance of Smith's integrity. The successive broadcasts served as a fulfillment in action of a promise in words. The words were reinforced by things she has actually done. The currency of talk was accepted because it is backed by the gold of conduct. The gold reserve, moreover, need not even approximate the amount of currency it can support.

This empirical study suggests that propaganda-of-the-deed may be effective among the very people who are distrustful of propaganda-of-the-word. Where there is social disorganization, *anomie,* conflicting values, we find propaganditis reaching epidemic proportions. Any statement of value is likely to be discounted as "mere propaganda." Exhortations are suspect.

But the propaganda of the deed elicits more confidence. Members of the audience are largely permitted to draw their conclusions from the action—they are less likely to feel manipulated. When the propagandist's deed and his words symbolically coincide, it stimulates belief in his sincerity. Further research must determine whether this propaganda pattern is significantly more effective in societies suffering from *anomie* than in those which are more fully integrated. But not unlike the Malinowski case-in-point, this may illustrate the role of research in suggesting new variables to be incorporated into a specific theory.

The refocusing of theoretic interest

[*New methods of empirical research exert pressure for new foci of theoretic interest.*] To this point we have considered the impact of research upon the development of particular theories. But empirical research also affects more general trends in the development of theory. This occurs chiefly through the invention of research procedures which tend to shift the foci of theoretic interest to the growing points of research.

The reasons for this are on the whole evident. After all, sound theory thrives only on a rich diet of pertinent facts and newly invented procedures help provide the ingredients of this diet. The new, and often previously unavailable, data stimulate fresh hypotheses. Moreover, theorists find that their hypotheses can be put to immediate test in those spheres where appropriate research techniques have been designed. It is no longer necessary for them to wait upon data as they happen to turn up—researches directed to the verification of hypotheses can be instituted at once. The flow of relevant data thus increases the tempo of advance in certain spheres of theory whereas in others, theory stagnates for want of adequate observations. Attention shifts accordingly.

In noting that new centers of theoretic

interest have followed upon the invention of research procedures, we do not imply that these alone played a decisive role.[13] The growing interest in the theory of propaganda as an instrument of social control, for example, is in large part a response to the changing historical situation, with its conflict of major ideological systems; new technologies of mass communication which have opened up new avenues for propaganda; and the rich research treasuries provided by business and government interested in this new weapon of war, both declared and undeclared. But this shift is also a by-product of accumulated facts made available through such newly developed, and confessedly crude, procedures as content-analysis, the panel technique and the focused interview.

Examples of this impact in the recent history of social theory are numerous but we have time to mention only a few. Thus, the increasing concern with the theory of character and personality formation in relation to social structure became marked after the introduction of new projective methods; the Rorschach test, the thematic apperception test, play techniques and story completions being among the most familiar. So, too, the sociometric techniques of Moreno and others, and fresh advances in the technique of the "passive interview" have revived interest in the theory of interpersonal relations. Stemming from such techniques as well is the trend toward what might be called the "rediscovery of the primary group," particularly in the shape of theoretic concern with informal social structures as mediating between the individual and large formal organizations. This interest has found expression in an entire literature on the role and structure of the informal group, for example, in factory social systems, bureaucracy and political organizations. Similarly, we may anticipate that the recent introduction of the panel technique —the repeated interviewing of the same group of informants—will in due course more sharply focus the attention of social

psychologists upon the theory of attitude formation, decisions among alternative choices, factors in political participation and determinants of behavior in cases of conflicting role demands, to mention a few types of problems to which this technique is especially adapted.

Perhaps the most direct impact of research procedures upon theory has resulted from the *creation* of sociological statistics organized in terms of theoretically pertinent categories. Talcott Parsons has observed that numerical data are scientifically important only when they can be fitted into analytical categories and that "a great deal of current research is producing facts in a form which cannot be utilized by any current generalized analytical scheme." [14] These well-deserved strictures of a scant decade ago are proving progressively less applicable. In the past, the sociologist has largely had to deal with *pre-collected series* of statistics usually assembled for nonsociological purposes and, therefore, not set forth in categories directly pertinent to any given theoretical system. As a result, at least so far as quantitative facts are concerned, the theorist was compelled to work with makeshift data bearing only a tangential relevance to his problems. This not only left a wide margin for error—consider the crude indices of social cohesion upon which Durkheim had to rely—but it also meant that theory had to wait upon the incidental and, at times, almost accidental availability of relevant data. It could not march rapidly ahead. This picture has now begun to change.

No longer does the theorist depend almost exclusively upon the consensus of administrative boards or social welfare agencies for his quantitative data. Tarde's programmatic sketch [15] a half century ago of the need for statistics in social psychology, particularly those dealing with attitudes, opinions and sentiments, has become a half-fulfilled promise. So, too, investigators of community organization are creating statistics on class structure, associational behavior, and clique formations, and this has left its mark on theoretic interests. Ethnic studies are beginning to provide quantitative data which are re-orienting the theorist. It is safe to suppose that the enormous accumulation of sociological materials during the war —notably by the Research Branch of the Information and Education Division of the War Department—materials which are in part the result of new research techniques, will intensify interest in the theory of group morale, propaganda and leadership. But it is perhaps needless to multiply examples.

What we have said does not mean that the piling up of statistics of itself advances theory; it does mean that theoretic interest tends to shift to those areas in which there is an abundance of *pertinent* statistical data. Moreover, we are merely calling attention to this shift of focus, not evaluating it. It may very well be that it sometimes deflects attention to problems which, in a theoretic or humanistic sense, are "unimportant"; it may divert attention from problems with larger implications onto those for which there is the promise of immediate solutions. Failing a detailed study, it is difficult to come to any overall assessment of this point. But the pattern itself seems clear enough in sociology as in other disciplines: as new and previously unobtainable data become available through the use of new techniques, theorists turn their analytical eye upon the implications of these data and bring about new directions of inquiry.

The clarification of concepts

[*Empirical research exerts pressure for clear concepts.*] A good part of the work called "theorizing" is taken up with the clarification of concepts—and rightly so. It is in this matter of clearly defined concepts that social science research is not infrequently defective. Research activated by a major interest in methodology may be centered on the *design* of establishing causal relations without due regard for analyzing the variables involved in the inquiry. This methodological empiricism, as the design of inquiry without correlative concern with the clarification of substantive variables may be called, characterizes a large part of current research. Thus, in a series of effectively designed experiments, Chapin finds that "the rehousing of slum families in a public housing project results in improvement of the living conditions and the social life of these families." [16] Or through controlled experiments, psychologists search out the effects of foster home placement upon children's performances in intelligence tests.[17] Or, again through experimental inquiry, researchers seek to determine whether a propaganda film has achieved its purpose of improving attitudes toward the British. These several cases, and they are representative of a large amount of research which has advanced social science method, have in common the fact that the empirical variables are not analyzed in terms of their conceptual elements.[18] As Rebecca West, with her characteristic lucidity, put this general problem of methodological empiricism, one might "know that A and B and C were linked by certain causal connexions, but he would never apprehend with any exactitude the nature of A or B or C." In consequence, these researches further the procedures of inquiry, but their findings do not enter into the repository of cumulative social science theory.

But in general, the clarification of concepts, commonly considered a province peculiar to the theorist, is a frequent result of empirical research. Research sensitive to its own needs cannot avoid this pressure for conceptual clarification. *For a basic requirement of research is that the concepts, the variables, be defined with sufficient clarity to enable the research to proceed,* a requirement easily and unwittingly not met in the kind of discursive exposition which is often miscalled "sociological theory."

The clarification of concepts ordinarily

enters into empirical research in the shape of establishing *indices* of the variables under consideration. In non-research speculations, it is possible to talk loosely about "morale" or "social cohesion" without any clear conceptions of what is entailed by these terms, but they *must* be clarified if the researcher is to go about his business of systematically observing instances of low and high morale, of social cohesion or cleavage. If he is not to be blocked at the outset, he must devise indices which are observable, fairly precise and meticulously clear. The entire movement of thought which was christened "operationalism" is only one conspicuous case of the researcher demanding that concepts be defined clearly enough for him to go to work.

This has been typically recognized by those sociologists who combine a theoretic orientation with systematic empirical research. Durkheim, for example, despite the fact that his terminology and indices now appear crude and debatable, clearly perceived the need for devising indices of his concepts. Repeatedly, he asserted that "it is necessary . . . to substitute for the internal fact which escapes us an external fact that symbolizes it and to study the former through the latter." [19] The index, or sign of the conceptualized item, stands ideally in a one-to-one correlation with what it signifies (and the difficulty of establishing this relation is of course one of the critical problems of research). Since the index and its object are so related, one may ask for the grounds on which one is taken as the index and the other as the indexed variable. As Durkheim implied and as Susanne Langer has indicated anew, the index is that one of the correlated pair which is perceptible and the other, harder or impossible to perceive, is theoretically relevant. [20] Thus, attitude scales make available indices of otherwise not discriminable attitudes, just as ecological statistics represent indices of diverse social structures in a given area.

What often appears as a tendency in research for quantification (through the development of scales) can thus be seen as a special case of attempting to clarify concepts sufficiently to permit the conduct of empirical investigation. The development of valid and observable indices becomes central to the use of concepts in the prosecution of research. A final illustration will indicate how research presses for the clarification of ancient sociological concepts which, on the plane of discursive exposition, have remained ill-defined and unclarified.

A conception basic to sociology holds that individuals have multiple social roles and tend to organize their behavior in terms of the structurally defined expectations assigned to each role. Further, it is said, the less integrated the society, the more often will individuals be subject to the strain of incompatible social roles. Type-cases are numerous and familiar: the Catholic Communist subjected to conflicting pressures from party and church, the marginal man suffering the pulls of conflicting societies, the professional woman torn between the demands of family and career. Every sociological textbook abounds with illustrations of incompatible demands made of the multiselved person.

Perhaps because it has been largely confined to discursive interpretations and has seldom been made the focus of systematic research, this central problem of conflicting roles has yet to be materially clarified and advanced beyond the point reached decades ago. Thomas and Znaniecki long since indicated that conflicts between social roles *can* be reduced by conventionalization and by role-segmentation (by assigning each set of role-demands to different situations). [21] And others have noted that frequent conflict between roles is dysfunctional for the society as well as for the individual. But all this leaves many salient problems untouched: on which grounds does one predict the behavior of persons subject to conflicting roles? And when a decision must be made, which role (or which group solidarity) takes precedence? Under which conditions does one or another prove controlling? On the plane of discursive thought, it has been suggested that the role with which the individual identifies most fully will prove dominant, thus banishing the problem through a tautological pseudo-solution. Or, the problem of seeking to predict behavior consequent to incompatibility of roles, a research problem requiring operational clarification of the concepts of solidarity, conflict, role-demands and situation, has been evaded by observing that conflicts of roles typically ensue in frustration.

More recently, empirical research has pressed for clarification of the key concepts involved in this problem. Indices of conflicting group pressures have been devised and the resultant behavior observed in specified situations. Thus, as a beginning in this direction, it has been shown that in a concrete decision-situation, such as voting, individuals subject to these cross-pressures respond by delaying their vote-decision. And, under conditions yet to be determined, they seek to reduce the conflict by escaping from the field of conflict: they "lose interest" in the political campaign. Finally, there is the intimation in these data that in cases of cross-pressures upon the voter, it is socio-economic position which is typically controlling.[22]

However this may be, the essential point is that, in this instance as in others, the very requirements of empirical research have been instrumental in clarifying received concepts. The process of empirical inquiry raises conceptual issues which may long go undetected in theoretic inquiry.

There remain, then, a few concluding remarks. My discussion has been devoted exclusively to four impacts of research upon the development of social theory: the initiation, reformulation, refocusing and clarification of theory. Doubtless there are others. Doubtless, too, the emphasis of this paper lends itself to misunderstanding. It may be inferred that some invidious distinction has been drawn at the expense of theory and the theorist. That has not been my intention. I have suggested only that an explicitly formulated theory does not invariably precede empirical inquiry, that as a matter of plain fact the theorist is not inevitably the lamp lighting the way to new observations. The sequence is often reversed. Nor is it enough to say that research and theory must be married if sociology is to bear legitimate fruit. They must not only exchange solemn vows—they must know how to carry on from there. Their reciprocal roles must be clearly defined. This paper is a brief essay toward that definition.

NOTES

1. See, for example, the procedural review of Stouffer's "Theory of intervening opportunities" by G. A. Lundberg, "What are Sociological Problems?" *American Sociological Review,* 6 (1941), 357–359.

2. See R. K. Merton, "Science, Population and Society," *The Scientific Monthly,* 44 (1937), 170–171; the apposite discussion by Jean Piaget, *Judgment and Reasoning in the Child,* London, 1929, Chaps. V, IX, and comment by William H. George, *The Scientist in Action,* London, 1936, p. 153. "A piece of research does not progress in the way it is 'written up' for publication."

3. The fourth function, clarification, will be elaborated in a complementary paper by Paul F. Lazarsfeld.

4. R. K. Merton, "Sociological Theory," *American Journal of Sociology,* 50 (1945), 469 n. Interestingly enough, the same outlandish term "serendipity" which has had little currency since it was coined by Horace Walpole in 1754 has also been used to refer to this component of research by the physiologist Walter B. Cannon. See his *The Way of an Investigator,* New

York: W. W. Norton, 1945, Chap. VI, in which he sets forth numerous instances of serendipity in several fields of science.

5. Charles Sanders Pierce had long before noticed the strategic role of the "surprising fact" in his account of what he called "abduction," that is, the initiation and entertaining of a hypothesis as a step in inference. See his *Collected Papers,* Cambridge, Mass.: Harvard University Press, 1931–35, VI, 522–528.

6. Drawn from continuing studies in the Sociology and Social Psychology of Housing, under a grant from the Lavanburg Foundation.

7. Essentially the same discrepancies in age distribution between Craftown and communities of origin are found if we compare proportions of children under ten with those between ten and nineteen. If we make children under five the basis for comparison, the disproportions are even more marked.

8. To be sure, vested interests often do spread untrue propaganda and this may reinforce mass illusions. But the vested-interest or priestly-lie theories of fallacious folk beliefs do not always constitute the most productive point of departure nor do they go far toward explaining the bases of acceptance or rejection of the beliefs. The present case in point, trivial though it is in any practical sense, is theoretically significant in showing anew the limitations of a utilitarian scheme of analysis.

9. For the differences between "theory" and "general orientations," see Merton, "Sociological Theory," p. 464.

10. Schedule data from the study provide corroborative evidence. In view of the exceptionally high proportion of young children, it is striking that 54 per cent of their parents affirm that it is "easier in Craftown to get people to look after our children when we want to go out" than it was in other places where they have lived; only 21 per cent say it is harder and the remaining 25 per cent feel there is no difference. Those who come from the larger urban communities are more likely to report greater ease in obtaining assistance in Craftown. Moreover, as we would expect from the hypothesis, those residents who are more closely geared in with Craftown, who identify themselves most fully with it, are more likely to believe it easier to find such aid; 61 per cent of these do so as against 50 per cent of those who identify with other communities, whereas only 12 per cent find it more difficult in comparison with 26 per cent of the latter group.

11. Muzafer Sherif's book by this title should be cited as basic in the field, although it tends to have a somewhat limited conception of "social factors," *The Psychology of Social Norms,* New York: Harper, 1936.

12. R. K. Merton, M. Fiske and A. Curtis, *Mass Persuasion,* New York: Harper, 1946.

13. It is perhaps needless to add that these procedures, instruments and apparatus are in turn dependent upon prior theory. But this does not alter their stimulating effect upon the further development of theory. Cf. Merton, "Sociological Theory," 463n.

14. Talcott Parsons, "The Role of Theory in Social Research," *American Sociological Review,* 3 (1938), 19; cf. his *Structure of Social Action,* New York: McGraw-Hill, 1937, pp. 328–329 n. ". . . in the social field most available statistical information is on a level which cannot be made to fit directly into the categories of analytical theory."

15. Gabriel Tarde, *Essais et mélanges sociologiques,* Paris, 1895, pp. 230–270.

16. F. S. Chapin, "The effects of slum clearance and rehousing on family and community relationships in Minneapolis," *American Journal of Sociology,* 43 (1938), 744–763.

17. R. R. Sears, "Child Psychology," in Wayne Dennis (ed.), *Current Trends in Psychology,* Pennsylvania: University of Pittsburgh Press, 1947, pp. 55–56. Sears' comments on this type of research state the general problem admirably.

18. However crude they may be, procedures such as the focused interview are expressly designed as aids for detecting possibly relevant variables in an initially undifferentiated situation. See R. K. Merton and P. L. Kendall, "The Focused Interview," *American Journal of Sociology,* 51 (1946), 541–557.

19. Émile Durkheim, *Division of Labor in Society,* New York: Macmillan, 1933, p. 66; also his *Les règles de la méthode sociologique,* Paris, 1895, pp. 55–58; *Le Suicide,* Paris, 1930,

pp. 356 and *passim.* Cf. R. K. Merton, "Durkheim's Division of Labor in Society," *American Journal of Sociology,* 40 (1934), esp. 326–327 which touches on the problem of indices.

20. Susanne K. Langer, *Philosophy in a New Key,* New York: Penguin Books, 1948, pp. 46–47.

21. W. I. Thomas and F. Znaniecki, *The Polish Peasant,* New York: Knopf, 1927, pp. 1866–1870, 1888, 1899 ff.

22. P. F. Lazarsfeld, Bernard Berelson and Hazel Gaudet, *The People's Choice,* New York: Duell, Sloan & Pearce, 1944, Chapter VI.

4. SOCIOLOGY AS A PROFESSION

TALCOTT PARSONS

Originally published as a report to the members of the American Sociological Association, this paper was intended to be used as a vehicle for raising questions about the problems facing sociology as a profession. To this end, Talcott Parsons, America's foremost sociological theorist, traced the history of sociology in Europe and the United States, specified those issues that continue to be relevant to the sociologist's view of his profession and his particular role in it, and discussed the relationship between sociology and the wider culture of which it is a part. His synoptic review considers the origins of scientific sociology built on a foundation provided by the social and intellectual climate of nineteenth-century Europe.

While many of America's early sociologists followed the teachings of Comte and Spencer, Parsons shows how others eschewed the macroscopic perspectives of their European counterparts, choosing to concentrate attention on more practical matters. Although such a turn temporarily impeded the growth of theory, it did serve to enhance the development of empirical techniques, abetting the institutionalization of sociology as a profession. The paper concludes with a discussion of sociology's contribution to contemporary thought patterns and its applied functions in a society that increasingly looks to the sociologist for information about and answers to pertinent social questions.

Talcott Parsons is Professor of Sociology in the Department of Social Relations at Harvard University. He is the author of The Structure of Social Action (*1937*), Essays in Sociological Theory (*1949*), The Social System (*1951*), Structure and Process in Modern Societies (*1960*), The Large Scale Society as a Social System (*1964*), Social Structure and Personality (*1964*), Societies: Evolutionary and Comparative Perspectives (*1966*), Sociological Theory and Modern Society (*1967*), *and coauthor of* Working Papers in the Theory of Action (*1953*), Family, Socialization and Interaction Process (*1955*), *and* Economy and Society (*1956*). *Professor Parsons is also coeditor of a translation of* Max Weber: The Theory of Social and Economic Organization (*1947*) *and coeditor of* Toward a General Theory of Action (*1951*), Theories of Society (*1961*), *and* The Negro American (*1966*).

. . .

In contrast to a predominantly applied profession like medicine, sociology is universally conceived as a scientific discipline which is *primarily* dedicated to the advancement and transmission of empirical knowledge in its field and *secondarily* to the communication of such knowledge to nonmembers and its utilization in practical affairs. The central agency for performance of these functions is clearly a body of professionally competent person-

Reprinted from the *American Sociological Review*, **24** (1959), 547–559. Reprinted by permission of the author and the American Sociological Association.

nel who have been trained in the mastery of the subject matter and the techniques of its advancement and use, and who have been socialized into the professional role, accepting certain responsibilities and enjoying certain privileges, in the society.

Given the clear centrality of the profession's organization about a scientific discipline, the first set of problems to be raised involves the state of the discipline as a cultural complex itself and as part of a larger one. This set of problems can in turn be broken down into four questions. The most central of these concerns the extent to which the canons of scientific adequacy and objectivity have come to be established as the working code of the profession in dealing with a defined intellectual subject matter. The second concerns the present clarity of the differentiation from the relation to neighboring scientific disciplines, so that we can speak with a certain definiteness about what, as distinct from other scientists, a sociologist does. The third question concerns the differentiation of sociology as a science from sociological "practice" or application to such problems as the welfare of various categories of handicapped or disturbed people, the efficiency of workers in industry, and so on, and its proper relation to this applied field. Finally, there is the problem of sociology's differentiation as a scientific discipline from the relation to the non-scientific aspects of the general culture, such as philosophy, religion, literature, and the arts, as well as the general *Weltanschauung*.

While these four problem areas are directly related to sociol*ogy* as a discipline within the culture, it is equally important to consider the corresponding set of problems which faces sociol*ogists* individually and collectively functioning in American society. In doing so, I would give unequivocal primacy to the sociologist's role as *scientist*. This is to say that I conceive the first obligation of sociology as a profession to be the promotion of the discipline:

on the one hand, through the investigations carried out by its members, and, on the other, through the "investment" of their capacities and energies in the training of others who will subsequently carry on this function. But this central function cannot be carried on in a social vacuum; in our type of society it is inherently linked with certain other functions which the profession cannot and should not evade.

The first of these is what may be called "citizenship" in the world of scientists and other culturally-oriented groups. This concerns the place of sociologists in universities and the responsibilities they carry outside their own departments, but also their relations with other intellectual groups—notably in neighboring disciplines—in the society at large. A second important social function carries the responsibility for facilitating the use of sociological knowledge for the practical interests of the society—the whole field of "applied" sociology. Finally, sociologists contribute to their society's general "definition of the situation." As experts in some sense in the interpretation of social events, they necessarily exercise a certain indirect influence, most conspicuously through teaching their subject to students who are not likely to become professionals in the field—a "general education" function. To their influence through formal teaching is added the influence exerted by sociologists through writing, lecturing, and other channels on the general "intellectual" concerns of the day. In the nature of the case, the more firmly sociology becomes established in the universities, the more important these three secondary social functions will become.

In this paper my main interest is to discuss the ways in which the profession of sociologist fits into the social structure, not how sociology as a discipline fits into the cultural setting. But these two topics are so closely intertwined empirically that in discussing either the other must continually be kept in mind. Precisely because of this intimate interrelationship, it is necessary to sketch the situation of the discipline as a background for discussing the profession itself.

The Situation of Sociology as a Discipline

In the perspective of history, any high-level scientific knowledge of human social behavior is a very recent phenomenon, having been achieved, with such antecedent developments as those in economic theory and in statistics, largely in the present century. In this brief period, sociology has advanced with seemingly great rapidity. But cultural growth is so complex and the time so short that it almost goes without saying that the development of sociology stands at present in an early stage.

Given this situation, it is not surprising that the differentiation between social science, on the one hand, and the most closely related non- or partially-scientific components of the general culture, on the other hand, is recent, incomplete, and unstable. I refer to the differentiation of social science from both "social philosophy" and "social problems." A field of science cannot be institutionalized until a relatively clear orientation to its own investigative problems has been worked out which is not dominated by either of these two socially important but predominantly non-scientific bases of concern. The third problem of differentiation, then, refers to the place of sociology within the corpus of scientific disciplines, above all those dealing with human behavior. A brief discussion of each of these three problems of differentiation seems to be in order.

First, with respect to the most general differentiation of social science from the philosophical matrix in which it had earlier been embedded, we may speak of a religious, a philosophical, and a more generally scientific aspect of this matrix. The relative predominance of these aspects partly corresponds with principal phases of Western intellectual history.

In the earliest of these phases, the differentiation of secular social thought from religious apologetics was brought about, becoming a considerable movement only in the 17th century. The primary emphasis in this first major secular phase was political in a broad and diffuse sense, dealing with secular society as a political organized "state" contrasting with the church. Once this step had been taken, a differentiation of substantive specialities within the field could gradually develop.

Not until the late 18th century did the field of economics begin clearly to emerge from this diffuse political matrix, with Adam Smith as the first highly eminent writer leading up to the classical economics. The focus of political theory tended to become considerably narrower, centering on the phenomena of government in the increasingly differentiated type of society of the time. Thus, along with history, which refused to identify itself with any particular focus of substantive interest, in the 19th century the broad frames of reference were laid out for political science and for economics.

This intellectual situation provided the main setting for the emergence of sociology along one of its main paths, namely the treatment of those more macroscopic aspects of society that were not adequately accounted for in the utilitarian tradition which had gained such prominence in political theory and in economics. With Comte as the most important precursor and Marx pointing up the problem of the status of "economic factors," Durkheim and Weber in Europe were the great theoretical tone-setters of the new sociological approach, being greatly preoccupied with the assessment of the institutional framework within which modern economic processes took place, and which were independent in certain ways of the operations of political organization. They were also oriented to the "collectivist" mode of thought stemming from Rousseau and from German idealism, which provided the major point of reference for their critiques of utilitarianism.[1] In general, they looked to the "ideal" as contrasted with "material" factors for the key concepts—such as values and institutionalized norms—of their analyses.

Within the "scientific" aspect of the philosophical matrix of social thought, referred to above, the phase given impetus by Darwinian biology in the second half of the 19th century had particular relevance to sociology. Spencer and the American evolutionists Sumner and Ward in particular derive from this background and its complex interrelations with utilitarianism and positivistic rationalism. But in addition to their influence on the emergence of sociology, the concept of evolution and the broad framework of the relation between competition and cooperation, laissez faire and planning, also provided the intellectual matrix from which grew anthropology in Great Britain, and which underlies much of the development of modern psychology. Of course, psychology, by way of Freud, also traces back in a complex manner to medical biology; and anthropology, especially as influenced in this country by Franz Boas, was infused by German idealist-historicist thinking. In the United States the "social psychology" of C. H. Cooley and G. H. Mead was an important bridge between these intellectual currents.

In very schematic terms, these are the main Western intellectual trends in the developmental background of the present social sciences. It can be readily seen that the lines which distinguish them from each other are far from being very sharply drawn. From the viewpoint of the more macroscopic disciplines like political science and economics, sociology has often been treated as a residual category or as a more or less "imperialistic" summation of all knowledge about society. In Germany in particular it has tended to be identified with the philosophy of history, the main difference being sociology's greater claim to empirical standing. There has been an increasingly clear focus, however, on phenomena of values and norms and their relation to personality, independently of technical concerns, particularly of economics.

Within the complex more closely associated with Darwinian biology, there are also difficult borderline problems *vis-à-vis* both anthropology and psychology. The earlier anthropological concentration on the study of non-literate peoples helped to postpone consideration of such questions, but more recently the distinction between sociology and anthropology has become less conspicuous. It is not an easy question whether the relative emphases on "culture," as made by many American anthropologists, and on social systems, as stressed by at least some sociologists, is an adequate working basis for a differentiation of the two disciplines. Psychology, however, seems clearly to focus on the study of analytically distinct components of behavior imputable to the "individual." But since virtually all human behavior is concretely both individual and social (and also cultural), here there are also formidable difficulties in drawing clear analytical lines; hence the ambiguous position of social psychology.

It seems to be in the nature of such a complex of scientific disciplines that, first, in studying empirical phenomena, any analytical classification crosscuts common sense classifications. Thus economics cannot be the theory of "business" in a simple sense, political theory the theory of "government," or psychology the theory of individual behavior, any more than physiology studies living organisms only and chemistry only lifeless matter. Secondly, the line cannot be drawn altogether clearly between the scientific components of this complex of disciplines and their non-scientific philosophical matrix. Such issues as positivism and the possible ontological status of the individual in the utilitarian frame of reference, for example, cannot be fully excluded from theoretical discussion in the social sciences.

These intellectual problems, which are unlikely to be easily and quickly settled, have an important bearing on the position and behavior of the professional groups involved in them. They are sources of strain both within and between disciplines. The social sciences have come to form a "family" which is well enough structured for certain working purposes, but which still leaves many areas of indeterminacy and of potential and sometimes open conflict. It may well be that only a minority of members of the relevant professional groups actively concern themselves with these problems at any given time—undoubtedly a desirable situation—but this does not justify treating the problems themselves as trivial in their implications for the professional situation.

I have suggested that the historical process by which the social science disciplines have come to be differentiated is so closely intertwined with the process by which they have gradually emerged from a more philosophical matrix that a single treatment of both trends has been necessary. Turning to the third problem of differentiation, between scientific disciplines and prescriptions for practical action, perhaps the most striking fact is the very near recency of any clear differentiation. Both political and economic theory throughout their formative periods were directly concerned with prescribing public policy and did not seriously attempt to separate even conceptually the bases of empirical generalization from the evaluative basis of policy recommendation. Marxism is a particularly important example of an economic theory that attempts no such distinction, and indeed denies its legitimacy. Max Weber was probably the first major theorist to assert the fundamental importance of carefully distinguishing between problems of scientific generalization and those of evaluation and policy, and to work out a clear methodological basis for the distinction. It is virtually only within the last generation that acceptance of this distinction has come to be generally diffused within the social science professions, and it is still quite incomplete. The strong positivistic component in the philosophical matrix underlying the social sciences has been one of the major impediments to such acceptance.

One feature of the history of American sociology, which differs from the European (especially Continental), is important in the present-day situation. European social sciences generally and sociology in particular had been primarily concerned with a highly macroscopic interpretation of society's development.[2] Hence the prominence of such general rubrics as capitalism and socialism. In the United States, however, there was considerably less concern with macroscopic interpretation.[3] The broad outline of the society and its major values were more apt to be taken for granted, with the emphasis given to particular "social problems." There was a deep concern with how actual situations deviated from values, which were above all the values of liberal Protestantism in the era when the "social gospel" was particularly prominent. Here problems associated with slums, rural life, immigration, and Negro-White relations were at the center of attention.

This kind of interest helps to explain why American sociology has been far less concerned with the borderline of philosophy than has European. It could become separated from political theory and economics more readily since these two disciplines tended to take a macroscopic view of society. Under these circumstances, the most serious problem of differentiation for American sociology has stemmed from its applied interests. In its earlier period sociology was closely identified with religiously defined ethical obligations and with philanthropy, which became institutionalized in certain aspects of community service and social work. Thus many early American sociologists were trained in the ministry, and several university departments combined sociology and social work. However, a rather early and sometimes sharp reaction developed against the latter association,[4] often resulting in the separation of the two fields, notably at the University of Chicago and later at Harvard.

Although the problem of differentiation from applied interests was particularly acute in the American case, concentration on less macroscopic problems had a special advantage. This emphasis encouraged the development of a variety of techniques for empirical research, for example, participant observation, the use of personal documents, interviewing, and questionnaire methods. That this rapid technical development coincided with a similar growth in statistics was highly important. In the general American climate of interest in empirical matters, this technical emphasis, much more pronounced than in Europe, helped significantly to speed the development of sociology as an empirical science.

It is also important that the more microscopic emphasis of American sociology brought it into relatively close touch with psychology, particularly in the overlapping field of social psychology, and with anthropology, particularly in the study of small communities, which were the first major objects in modern society of anthropological study. Both psychology and anthropology were fields which, in different ways, were very active in developing detailed empirical research. The Continental European type of sociology would have had much more difficulty in becoming an integral part of the more general trend of empirical research than this has actually been the case in the United States. It would be hard to exaggerate the importance of a strong tradition of empirical research in bringing about the differentiation between sociology as a scientific discipline and its application to social policy.

In sum, within the last generation or so sociology has reached what is, perhaps, a first level of maturity as a scientific discipline. Although the process of differentiation is far from complete and there remain many indistinct borderline areas, sociology, along with the other social sciences, has become relatively differentiated from the philosophical matrix. It has, again with a good deal of indistinctness, achieved a fairly clearly defined place in the general cluster of scientific disciplines which deal with human behavior. It has also been disentangled from the earlier simple identification with specific practical goals in the society, to become an independent, relatively "pure" discipline with a research and theoretical tradition of its own. As we have seen, however, each of these borderlines is still highly problematical, and the unclarity of the cultural lines is a focus of strain at each point. I would say that the problem of ideological contamination is the most urgent one *vis-à-vis* the philosophical background; that of interdisciplinary imperialisms and conflict in relations with sister disciplines; and the problem of full commitment to pure research and training, not the formulation of social policy, *vis-à-vis* the applied front.

The Institutionalization of Sociology in the Universities

Keeping in mind these intellectual highlights, I turn to a sketch of the institutionalization of the profession in the structure of our society. According to the conception of sociology as a scientific discipline, it is evident that the central point of its institutionalization should be university faculties of arts and sciences. Here sociology established a fairly secure foothold at an early stage, and has greatly extended it since. Clearly strategic for its development was sociology's introduction around the turn of the century in the new Faculty of Political Science at Columbia University and at the University of Chicago. These two departments, each led by a man of such stature as to play a leadership role in faculty affairs—Franklin H. Giddings and Albion W. Small, respectively—have served as the most important training grounds for the second generation of American sociologists, especially those with a strong orientation to establishment of the field as a scientific discipline, and have populated many of the important posts throughout the country. A notable early offshoot of Columbia, for example, was the introduction of sociology at the University of North Carolina under the leadership of Howard W. Odum. The story, of course, has not been without its vicissitudes. Certainly Columbia and Chicago have been the most consistently successful centers of sociology from the formative years, though each has had its ups and downs. But until very recently the early initiative of Ward (late in his career) at Brown University did not lead to a comparable development there, and the Yale tradition established much earlier by Sumner long remained under his successor largely insulated from the rest of the profession.

More generally, it is of the first importance that in this country training in sociology was established concomitantly with professional training in the other social sciences. Even though the emergence of sociology *as a discipline* has lagged somewhat behind the other social sciences, for reasons suggested above, sociology *as a profession* has not had to surmount alone the difficult barrier of gaining full university status.

Another notable feature of the development of sociology in American universities was its strength, in a decisive period, in the Middle West. Here the University of Chicago did not stand alone, but bore a very close relation to the Wisconsin of Ross and Gillin, the Michigan of Cooley, the Illinois of Hayes, and the Minnesota of Vincent and somewhat later, of Chapin. This expansion may have been related to the religio-ethical complex in that part of the country, noted above. In any event, the main pattern established in the Middle West, as well as in the East, was that of departments heavily committed to the pursuit of sociological research and of training competent and committed professionals.

The last generation has seen a diffusion of this professional pattern throughout the country's major universities. Among the several important steps in this further development have been sociology's establishment at Harvard in 1931, under the chairmanship of Sorokin, and its expansion in 1946; its development at Cornell, under the leadership of Leonard S. Cottrell, Jr., building on a foundation of rural sociology under the direction of Dwight Sanderson; and the great expansion within very recent years at Berkeley, California, building partly on Teggart's historical study of social institutions.

Now for the first time, sociology has come to be recognized as one of the regular disciplines in every major university in the United States—with Johns Hopkins finally completing the roster. Only in a few elite colleges of liberal arts—for example, Amherst, Williams, and Swarthmore—has this development still failed to occur. This situation stands in sharp contrast to that in Europe, where the total number of chairs constitutes a rather small fraction of the American, with as yet only minimal recognition of sociology at Oxford and Cambridge and, on the Continent, with only about one half of the universities north of the Alps showing some interest.*

If the conception of sociology as a profession organized about a scientific discipline be accepted, the importance of the broad development in the United States can scarcely be exaggerated. A secure position in university faculties of course is the structural base from which a scientifically oriented profession can most effectively

---

* [*Editor's note:* Recently, Amherst, Swarthmore, Williams, Oxford, and Cambridge have begun to offer programs in Sociology.]

operate. Sociology is thus completely involved in the situation confronting the scientific professions generally, and the social sciences particularly, in American society. Yet no other base of operations could be so advantageous for sociology's further development as a discipline and its eventual influence in the society.

If this position is to be firmly consolidated, it is crucial to have an adequate supply of able and properly trained personnel. People who entered the field in its earliest phase had highly diverse backgrounds, including the ministry, social work, journalism, and business. And their training was only minimally technical. The early expansion of the profession probably took place rather too rapidly; in the first decades of this century there were more positions available than there were trained people to occupy them, and hence a considerable influx of people without adequate professional qualification. It took time to get training programs established within the university framework.

In the last generation, however, this situation has greatly improved. The output of professionally qualified personnel has steadily increased, both through growing numbers being turned out by the same graduate schools and by new graduate training programs. For example, in the three years 1936–1938, the average number of new Ph.D. degrees reported to the *American Journal of Sociology* was 45 a year, compared to an annual average of 133 for the period 1955–1957. These degrees were granted by about 18 departments in the earlier period, and by about 35 departments in the recent period.

However, graduate training programs have come increasingly to include apprenticeship in empirical investigations within the framework of ongoing research programs. Some of these programs have been financed by grants to individual faculty members from foundations, or more recently, from the government; some are more formally organized through such devices as Columbia's Bureau of Applied Social Research; and some are carried on by such university-based survey research organizations as the National Opinion Research Center. Whatever the varying patterns of organization, these research facilities have added enormously to the promotion of the profession's two fundamental functions—the advancement of its own discipline and the training of its core personnel. Certainly this development could not have occurred without substantial advance both in research techniques and in theoretical sophistication. It is one of the clearest indications of the discipline's gradual coming of age.

As a result of this steady increase in the quantity and quality of graduate training programs, sociology in recent years has reached, I believe, the stage of professionalization where it no longer depends so heavily on the contributions of a few outstanding individuals, a seemingly inevitable feature of the earliest stage of a profession's development. We have instead a growing body of solidly trained and competent people who provide in the aggregate a *cumulative* development of knowledge on which their successors can build and which is the most important hallmark of a relatively mature science.

Sociology's central operating base in university faculties raises the important problem of the place of sociology relative to its sister disciplines in these faculties. As noted above, there are many points at which, in terms of intellectual content, the borderlines are unclear. Although many of these borderline problems lack clear substantive and organizational definition, the situation seems to be fairly satisfactory. From the point of view of the profession's institutionalization in the academic community, there are two conspicuous encouraging facts about the current situation. First, sociology as a "subject" has gained generally acknowledged academic "citizenship," as we have seen. Second, although there are cases in which sociology is organizationally combined with other disciplines—sometimes with the economics-political science complex, sometimes with psychology or anthropology or both—there is no threatening uniformity of the pattern in which this occurs.

Sociology's middle position in relation to the other "behavioral sciences" is clearly a highly strategic one. The professional group is in no danger of being absorbed into any of its neighbors; moreover it offers something essential to each of them. To economists and political scientists, for instance, it provides a better understanding of "institutional" factors than their own disciplines make readily available. To psychologists it contributes a focus on "social" factors not readily reducible to individual terms. *Vis-à-vis* anthropology, the line is not so clear, but perhaps without seeming invidious one may say that anthropologists, having derived so much of their experience from the study of relatively undifferentiated societies, can use some help in the analysis of structurally complex modern societies, a field in which sociologists have a certain "head start."

With respect to the familiar question of sociology's place in the "pecking order" of academic disciplines, we may note that (given the crudity of such a rating system) within the last generation sociology has risen substantially in relative prestige. I interpret this rise to be a consequence of its relative strengthening in all four of the variables which were distinguished at the beginning of this paper.

A final point concerning the relation of sociology to its sister disciplines concerns the increasing participation of sociologists in interdisciplinary research projects. One major type of interdisciplinary venture is the "area" study, but there is a variety of other types such as studies of organizations and local community situations. These projects provide an important setting in which the nature of the participating disciplines can become better defined.

I have briefly outlined the general strengthening of sociology's position as a scientific discipline, its establishment in university faculties, and the development of its research and training functions; and touched upon the contributions it can make to its sister disciplines. Two other main developments remain to be reviewed. Anticipating the subsequent discussion somewhat, it may first be said that sociology's contribution to our society's ideological "definition of the situation" has greatly increased in importance in recent years. The frequency with which the term "sociology" appears in popular discussions, albeit often with dubious technical justification, is an index of this situation. Secondly, although sociologists are still well behind their economist, political scientist, and psychologist colleagues, the change over the past twenty years in the extent to which they have won a place in the world of practical affairs is unmistakable. The upshot of this whole shift, to which no one factor has predominantly contributed, is that sociology may perhaps be said to have graduated from being the least respectable of the social science disciplines to being the most controversial.

Sociology's Contribution to Contemporary Ideology

An important index of the relationship which has been developing between changes in the society itself and the place of the social science professions within it is that the term sociology is coming increasingly to be a central symbol in the popular ideological preoccupations of our time. In this respect, perhaps we may say that, ideologically, a "sociological era" has begun to emerge, following an "economic" and, more recently, a "psychological" era.

Not only was the industrial economy the great new phenomenon from the latter 19th well into this century; intellectually economic theory of varying kinds provided the terms for defining the character of that period. Schools of thought ranged from the most orthodox laissez-faire capitalism through varying shades of liberalism and reformism to radical socialism, eventually crystallizing in Marxism; but underlying all these views was a common set of assumptions about the critical character of "economic factors." This ideological era, the last major phase of which was the New Deal period, was undoubtedly intimately connected with the process by which economics as a science came to be established in the academic world. The salience of economics as an ideological focus has now greatly subsided, although of course it continues to play an important role in various issues of public policy. The economic era was succeeded, in a considerably less "massive" form, by the psychological era. This shift, which came to a head in the 1930s, was signalled by the growing concern with the role of rational *versus* "irrational" factors in the motivation of the individual. Similarly, it was closely associated with the rapid development of psychology as a scientific discipline.

While the economic era of ideology was related to the *fact* of industrialization, the psychological era has been related to industrialization's *consequences* for the individual. If the psychological movement challenged the adequacy of simpler-minded economic interpretations of human behavior, however, it became apparent that the understanding of the complexities and changes of our large-scale society and its "mass" phenomena require more than analysis of individual conduct. The new ideological era, which has overlapped with the psychological one, can be described as a kind of dialectic between a psychological focus of interest in the individual and a sociological focus of interest in the society. Inevitably the problem of constraints on individual freedom is a central theme in this complex. This seems to be the background of contemporary concern with the problem of "conformity." Note the striking difference between the emphasis in this case and what it was in the era of economic ideological primacy, when the essential problem—often posed

as productivity *versus* equality—was to find a basis for adequate "satisfaction of wants." Certainly, in a sense, the conformity problem is peculiar to an "affluent society."

The emergence of this broad ideological preoccupation has affected the status of the sociological profession because now the sociologist is beginning to be defined by a much broader public as an expert on intellectual problems of public concern. The fact that his expertise is viewed with a large measure of ambivalence does not detract from the significance of this point. Although the extrapolation of trends is dangerous business, it seems justified to suggest a probable connection between the emergence of this sociological focus of ideological preoccupation and the consolidation of the sociological profession within the society. If this be the case, it is clearly a major harbinger of opportunity. At the same time it is a basis for stressing the urgency of certain problems of our own position and the way in which it is likely to develop.

There is an intimate connection between the growing ideological significance of sociology and what in many respects is its oldest function, namely the teaching of college undergraduates, the large majority of whom do not expect to become professional social scientists. Clearly this teaching function has always been one of the principal responsibilities of the profession and still is. It is primarily a general education function, helping to orient the student to aspects of the world in which he lives. Naturally the character of this function has changed, with change both in the society itself and in sociology as a discipline. The more technical the discipline becomes, the greater the problem of its adaptation to general education purposes.

The problem of the relation between the profession's research and training functions at the graduate level and the undergraduate educational function presents formidable complications. It is difficult to know the porportion of sociologists in academic positions mainly engaged in each of these functions. Those serving on the faculties of liberal arts colleges with only minimal or no graduate programs are primarily involved in general education. Yet in the universities there is generally a shading off, and many faculty members devote a substantial portion of their energy to undergraduate teaching. Such shading off is undoubtedly desirable, because undergraduate · work in sociology is continuous with graduate work, and also because it feeds into professional training in the neighboring disciplines. The so-called "university college" exposes its undergraduates to the influence of those who are pursuing research directly on the frontiers of their fields, thus providing opportunity for observing the actual process of culture building, rather than merely receiving the end "product."

Nevertheless there are important problems in integrating the two teaching functions. Since graduate training has come to be so highly oriented to the training of research and graduate school personnel, there has been a strong tendency for the undergraduate teaching function (where it is not merged with the graduate) to be carried out by personnel who have not been selected for careers of high professional prestige. Moreover, with increasing professionalization, the new Ph.D. who accepts a college teaching job finds it increasingly difficult to transfer to a university department. This growing rigidity of career lines has probably been accentuated by the enormous expansion of organized research facilities, so that a man who works in a university research setting early in his career has opportunities to accumulate a research record which, in competition for the higher level university appointments, cannot be matched by the man who has carried a heavy load of undergraduate teaching in an atmosphere where little research is going on—although their capabilities may be equal. There is, therefore, a tendency to make the college teacher a kind of second class citizen of the profession's academic branch.

To be sure, this is a problem shared by other academic disciplines and is in no way peculiar to sociology. But the situation may be aggravated by the recent expansion of opportunities for sociologists in other professional faculties and in non-academic fields. Thus the time seems to be approaching when we should give serious consideration to the establishment of special training programs for prospective college teachers. The profession's undergraduate teaching function is too important to be allowed to deteriorate by default.

Undergraduate teaching itself is undergoing an important shift in emphasis which increases its importance in relation to the problems of the profession. During the earlier period, the primary appeal of sociology to undergraduates lay in "social problems," including not only crime and poverty, but also such problem areas as marriage and the family. Now, even in these areas, the emphasis seems to have shifted from the problem of how to cope with clear-cut "evils" in the society, to the type of concern I have called ideological. Instead of taking for granted a clear definition of what needs to be done in our society, concern centers about what kind of a society it is, where it is going and the like. The most important consequence of this shift is to bring the undergraduate teaching of sociology much more closely into relation with the major general intellectual preoccupations of our society.

This shift imposes a heavy responsibility on sociologists. An ideology is precisely a meeting ground between a society's value-commitments and its empirical scientific culture. In the nature of the case powerful pressures come into conflict with standards of scientific objectivity. The emergence of sociology into a central position in the focus of ideological preoccupation means that it must serve as a primary guardian of the scientific tradition, counteracting the many tendencies to introduce biases and distortions. It must do this in a situation where its own technical resources are only partially adequate to the task, where the only honest professional answer to many questions is "we don't know," even though would-be sociologists loudly proclaim their pseudo-solutions of many problems.

Some scientific purists would advocate dealing with this situation by total withdrawal, by avoiding all connection with this wider public forum of discussion. This is feasible and often justifiable for certain purely technical specialists. For the profession as a whole, however, it is an impossible position to take. A publicly salient participation of the profession in these discussions is bound to occur somehow or other, and it is of crucial interest to the profession that enough highly competent and professionally responsible persons should be heard. This consideration applies not least to the function of teaching and writing for undergraduates.

The Applied Function

The fourth principal area of the profession's involvement in the structure of the society I have called the applied function. As noted, this interest was particularly prominent in sociology's early phase, especially in the social problems field, but was followed by a rather sharp withdrawal in favor of building up the central academic core of the discipline. More recently, however, there has been a notable return to applied interests over a far broader front than before. The turning point probably lay in the attempt to mobilize social science talent for military purposes in World War II, a movement in which sociology played an appreciable though far from leading part. Developments in such fields as industrial sociology and market research have also given impetus to the steady expansion of the applied function.

During the early development of a new discipline having practical possibilities, it is common for its own professional personnel directly to undertake these practical functions, and in some professions this pattern continues and expands. Chemistry perhaps is the profession in which this pattern is most prominent; a large proportion of those with Ph.D.s in chemistry do applied technological work for industry and government, probably outnumbering the chemical engineers. A similar pattern marks the recent growth of sociology and will probably continue to do so, most importantly perhaps in industrial organization, governmental organization, especially the armed services; opinion and attitude research; and various types of social agencies concerned with criminology, health, and the like. As yet, however, by far the largest proportion of sociologists with the Ph.D.—about 86 per cent—are employed by colleges and universities, exceeded in this respect only by history, literature, and other humanities, while a significantly smaller proportion of holders of the Ph.D. in political science and economics are so employed (76 and 69 per cent, respectively).[5]

An important and rapidly expanding bridge between non-academic and academic employment is the consultant role in various non-academic organizations. This ranges from a relatively individualized service to particular clients to a considerable amount of "conferencing" where groups of professionals, often interdisciplinary in composition, are called on to help clarify a practical problem area.

A critical difference between the development of applied functions in sociology and psychology is the lesser importance in the former of anything like "practice," in the sense of individual service for a fee. The employers of sociologists, on both full time and consulting bases, are more likely to be organizations such as business firms, governmental units, social agencies, and research offices, which as such are unlikely to need the same kind of protection against charlatanism or other exploitation needed by an individual employing professional services. Hence the sociological profession is more likely to be able to minimize the complicated problems of legal certification, licensing, or both, in which the psychologists have recently become heavily involved.[6]

A new pattern of application has recently emerged, however, in which sociologists participate along with specialists in other "basic sciences" in research and training for a range of applied professions. Historically the closest affiliation of sociology with an applied profession was that with social work. When sociology withdrew from this activity social work formed a primary alliance with psychiatry. Only recently has the relationship been reestablished, primarily through the participation of sociologists both in the training of graduate social work students and in research bearing on social work.[7]

The primary break-through of the new pattern has occurred in the field of health, especially mental health. After the overwhelming predominance, during the first quarter of the century, of the definition of "scientific" medicine as "organic" medicine, the emergence of concern with psychological and social factors in illness and health has been a dramatic development. Within this framework, sociologists perhaps have come to take the lead more than any other "behavioral" scientists, in collaboration and friendly rivalry with the anthropologists, and apparently drawing ahead of the psychologists, although the latter constitute numerically and organizationally a more powerful group. This seems to be largely because sociology is uninvolved in claims to control the therapy of individual patients. The sociologist helps with problems that impinge on medicine and public health, but his functions cannot be seen as practice in the traditional medical sense. Hence sociology is not viewed as a threat to the psychiatric treatment of patients in the same way as is clinical psychology.

It is now well known that appointments in medical and public health organizations of various sorts constitute one of the major fields of employment for sociologists, probably the largest single field ex-cept for the central teaching-research occupation. The character of these openings varies greatly, perhaps qualitatively the most important type being appointment to faculty posts in medical schools and schools of public health. The trend is certainly toward the inclusion of sociology among the basic sciences underlying the practice of medicine, and thus toward the incorporation of sociologists, along with other behavioral scientists, in an organizational status parallel to that of physiologists, biochemists, biophysicists, bacteriologists, and so on.

The health field, however, is only one of several applied areas in which this new pattern is emerging. Although not as yet on so large a scale, the same trend is observable in the relation of the social sciences generally, and sociology in particular, to schools of business and public administration, of education, of law, and even of divinity. Perhaps the furthest advancement along these lines so far is in business schools—the most important precursor of this development having been the linkage between rural sociology and colleges of agriculture. The two most important branches of sociology to business schools are of course industrial sociology and survey research. Probably the field in which sociology's role is most likely to grow rapidly in the near future is education, not least because of our society's present urgent need for expansion and improvement of educational facilities. The penetration of the social sciences into the field of law has been rather slow—notwithstanding such assertions as Dean Griswold's that law itself is a social science;[8] but it may be expected to accelerate and to be substantial in the long run.

Public funds have been very important in this general development. Funds available through the land-grant colleges and the agricultural experimental stations gave rural sociology considerable prominence a generation ago, and the Department of Agriculture, along with the Bureau of the Census, was the first agency of the Federal government in which social scientists gained a firm foothold. The role of the National Institute of Health in the development of social sciences in that area is well known. One reason for predicting a major development of the social sciences in relation to education is the expectation that federal activities will greatly expand in this field and that financial aid to training and research in the relevant professions will play a major part in this expansion.

This movement has been brought about not only by the various professional schools themselves and by the availability of public funds, but has been greatly aided in particular by the Russell Sage Foundation, which has acted as a catalyst in encouraging awareness among sociologists and the applied professionals of the relevance of each others' skills. As Donald Young pointed out in 1955: "Reference has been made to the needs of the practicing professions for social science data and techniques. . . . It would be a pity not to respond to their need and not to take advantage of the opportunity to test our 'wares'—to identify their deficiencies and to consider where to attempt to improve them." He also posed the question of "whether the aim should be the development of practicing sociologists to take direct responsibility for determination of policy, operation of action programs, and work with clients presenting personal problems; or whether the purpose should be the development of consultants or middlemen to work closely with the applied professions already established." [9]

I believe myself that it is of the highest importance to the development of sociology that its relation to a whole series of applied functions be *mediated* through the professional schools which train practitioners in these functions and which form centers for "action research" aimed at yielding directly practical results. In a highly differentiated society where applied science is rapidly increasing in importance in the social as well as the natural science fields, such schools are the most appropriate point of articulation between a scientific profession and the many urgent practical social needs. In general it is sounder that the primary responsibilities for implementation should be borne by members of the applied professions rather than by scientists as such. The existence of such a mediating structure provides a highly important protection of the scientific profession's central function against many types of diversionary pressures.

The expanding pattern of relationship with the applied professions presents an urgent problem to the sociological profession: we must try to ensure that the sociologists who are employed in these contexts meet very high standards of ability, training, and professional responsibility. In view of the rapidly expanding demand for sociologists' services, this is clearly going to be a very difficult requirement to meet.

Channels of Publication

One important facility on which a profession must depend consists of channels for publishing its research results and teaching materials, both in journals and in book form. In launching and developing the field of sociology, it was of the first importance that the *American Journal of Sociology* was established so early by the University of Chicago department under Small, and that in due course still other organs were established. By the time (1936) the *American Sociological Review* was started, there was urgent need for an additional journal, and now the range of such outlets is still widening.

It is not so easy for the profession itself to control book publishing opportunities. University presses of course have played an important part, but for a long period sociology was caught in a kind of vicious circle in which, due to the urgency of teaching needs and the limited library facilities at the undergraduate level, elementary textbooks were overemphasized, at the expense of more substantial studies. With the maturing of the field, this situation has greatly improved in recent years. The market for substantial books has widened and the output of publishable research has increased; in addition, classics in the field are being translated and reprinted, reaching a much wider public than before. The Free Press in particular has greatly increased the availability of sociological literature and has demonstrated to other publishing houses that serious non-textbook publications in sociology have a wide market.

The Organized Profession

The review of the problems facing the sociological profession concludes with a brief consideration of its own organization in professional associations. The founders of sociology in the United States took steps very early to organize the American Sociological Society, and there has been a clear continuity of responsible leadership ever since. A generation later several regional societies were established. Today there are various other specialized groups, affiliated with the national Society, such as the Rural Sociological Society and the Society for the Study of Social Problems, each having a journal of its own.

As is usual with such enterprises, in its early years the national organization was managed informally by a member of the profession who, as Secretary, carried on most of the routine business as a voluntary contribution. But by about 1948–1950, the Society had so expanded in membership and in range of activities that a major reorganization was undertaken, resulting in the establishment of a central Office under the direction of a paid Executive Officer. Since that time the membership has more than doubled and the activities of the office have expanded enormously.[10]

As emphasized above, the main anchorage of a scientific profession in a modern society must be the universities, which alone can provide the setting for the profession's primary teaching and research functions. At the same time, the importance of strong, well-managed professional associations should not be underestimated. Through their meetings, publications, and various other channels they form the most important single type of medium through which sociologists over the country communicate with one another. Furthermore they provide a means for concerted action in promoting interests and discharging responsibilities of the profession.

A professional association differs in ideal type from a trade union in that it is not so much an "interest group" as an agency for facilitating the development of its professional field and a guardian of the technical and ethical standards of its personnel. Its criteria of membership constitute an important symbol in this respect. At the same time, sociologists, of all professional groups, should be aware of their social and cultural involvement in all of the major respects noted above. The professional association can be especially helpful in mediating our "citizenship" relations to neighboring disciplines as well as to the public at large. And perhaps most urgent now is the function of the professional association in relation to the applied fields. Here, where conflicts of interest are likely to develop between disciplines and between academic and non-academic groups, perhaps a working code of relationships particularly needs to be worked out. For example, a current practical problem is posed by the ways in which civil service job descriptions specify disciplinary titles, so that any particular group of "-ologists" may need to protect its interests by keeping the Civil Service Commission informed about the scope of the profession. This and other problems have been made the special concern of the Society's recently-formed Committee on the Profession, which will address itself to a broad range of matters concerning not only the technical development of sociology but also the place of sociologists in our society.

Summary and Conclusion

This review yields a fairly clear picture. Sociology is a profession centered about a growing scientific discipline which, within the last decade or so, has reached a new level of maturity and has come to occupy an increasingly strategic place in the cluster of social sciences. The latter have acquired in this century a position in the society never before accorded to them. The technical basis of sociology has developed enormously in the last generation, with a far deeper and broader battery of research technology than before and a substantial improvement of its theory. The output of superior research results has greatly expanded at the same time that its average quality has substantially improved.

As a profession, its central working base in the universities has been greatly extended and consolidated; now every major American university has made a place for sociology. The number of professionally trained new personnel is about three times the figure of twenty years ago, and will certainly increase. Sociology has moved into a central place in current broad intellectual preoccupations. The involvement of sociologists in practical functions has greatly expanded. At least prominent beginnings have been made in establishing it as a basic science underlying a whole range of applied professions. The various professional associations have been greatly expanded and strengthened. On every essential front there has been growth and, I think, improvement.

If this be an accurate picture, it is highly gratifying, perhaps especially for those who entered the profession when its situation was much less promising. But at the same time the current state of affairs presents a number of serious difficulties

and dangers which call not for complacent relaxation but for intensified effort. In conclusion, I suggest several areas in which particularly urgent problems seem to lie ahead.

1) It should never be forgotten that the central task of a scientific profession is the development of its discipline and the training of its successors in carrying on that function. Increasing involvement in popular ideological discussions and in applied functions *could* readily divert attention from these functions, although of course here there need be no intense conflict. Highly qualified manpower in sociology is bound to remain scarce for a long time, since demand is apparently running well ahead of even the steadily increasing supply. In my opinion, our first priority should be the staffing of university departments with the ablest persons and the facilitation of their research on as "pure" a level as possible.

2) Some adjustment of the relations between sociology and its neighboring disciplines has occurred, but there remain many unsettled problems. The detailed solution of these must develop mostly in terms of research, of professional writings, and of the highly variegated relationships that sociologists, individually and in small groups, form with other social scientists. Here and there a problem may become a focus of action by the organized profession, but it is highly important that there should be no retreat into a disciplinary parochialism. Perhaps most important of all is the establishment and maintenance of good interdisciplinary contacts in the universities, although such enterprises as the Center for Advanced Study in the Behavioral Sciences also contribute greatly to good interdisciplinary relations.

3) Sociologists as a profession should prepare themselves for increased pressure stemming from the involvement of sociology in ideological controversy. Precisely because their subject is more in the public eye, it will be exposed to more distortion and misunderstanding than before. It is

their responsibility to maintain high standards of scientific competence and objectivity. Some will have to serve as mediators between the profession and the public, on occasion entering the forum of discussion on their own initiative. Retreat of the whole profession into technical preoccupations could be dangerous in the long run, especially since this situation is very closely linked with undergraduate teaching, in which lies so much of the discipline's strength.

4) We must look to further expansion of the applied functions and cope with the problems which arise here. I think that a great deal of effort should be devoted to promoting what has been called the basic science pattern of relation to many of these functions, even though this clearly means diverting an appreciable fraction of our valuable personnel. At the same time, there will be many sociologists who enter more directly into applied activities. The crea-

tion of codes for professional proper ways of organizing such participation will, I believe, constitute one major task of our professional associations, a task closely related to the protection of sociologists' interests as these are threatened more frequently with the increase in this participation.

In sum, it seems likely that the problems facing our profession in the coming years will center on the temptations and complications which set in with relative, though incomplete success. Sociology is becoming "important." Let us hope that this accomplishment will not divert us from the main task and at the same time that we take due account of the responsibilities and opportunities presented by our growing involvement in the larger social setting. Primary concentration on the science itself is not incompatible with good citizenship in the scientific community and in the general society. The great challenge is to maintain the proper balances.

NOTES

1. For a fuller discussion, see "The General Interpretation of Action," Introduction to Part I, Section A of *Theories of Society*, Glencoe, Ill.: Free Press, 1960, coedited with E. A. Shils, K. D. Naegele, and J. R. Pitts.

2. See, e.g., Karl Mannheim, "German Sociology (1918–1933)," *Politica*, 1 (1934), 12–33.

3. For perhaps the fullest historical account available, see Howard W. Odum, *American Sociology: The Story of Sociology in the United States through 1950*, New York: Longmans, Green, 1951.

4. Cf. Robert C. Angell, "A Research Basis for Welfare Practice," *Social Work Journal*, 35 (1954), 145 ff.

5. According to a 1952 survey reported in "Personnel Resources in the Social Sciences and Humanities," U. S. Bureau of Labor Statistics Bulletin #1169, Table A-17, pp. 94–96. The differences are even more striking among those holding a Master's degree: of sociology Masters, 69.1 per cent were employed in colleges or universities, but only 36.8 per cent of those in political science and 46.3 per cent of those in economics were so employed. It is suggestive in this connection that a more up-to-date survey of graduate students, not yet published by N.O.R.C., shows a smaller proportion (68 per cent) of sociologist-anthropologist Ph.D. candidates intending to enter academic life. By comparison, the proportions of candidates with this intention in some other fields are: English, 82 per cent; political science, 49 per cent; economics, 48 per cent; psychology, 42 per cent; chemistry, 39 per cent. (Personal communication from James A. Davis, National Opinion Research Center.)

6. In this case the problem stems mainly from the rapid expansion of practice in clinical psychology and the ambiguities of its relation to the practice of psychiatry. As a defense against the medical claim to a monopoly on legitimate psychotherapy, the psychologists have adopted a policy in favor of legal certification, to be implemented by certifying not functions as such but the use of the title "psychologist." This has impinged on the interests of sociologists because the certification of the title in the terms spelled out in some statutes would exclude social psychologists with sociological training and affiliation from certification and hence from performing various applied functions. This issue is currently the object of complex negotiation

between the two professional associations. But it is clear that certification of the title of an academic discipline in order to define legitimate applied practice seems to involve serious complications both for the discipline itself and for those closely related to it in the scientific community.

7. Angell, *op. cit.*

8. Erwin N. Griswold, "Law Schools and Human Relations," Tyrrell Williams Lecture delivered at the Law School of Washington University, St. Louis, April 19, 1955 (mimeo.), p. 6.

9. Donald Young, "Sociology and the Practicing Professions," *American Sociological Review,* 20 (1955), 646.

10. The pattern of membership of the Society is of interest. For the first decade it did not exceed about 500. Then, following World War I, it reached a plateau between 1,000 and 1,500 which was not exceeded until after World War II. By the time of the reorganization in 1948–1950, it had risen to about 2,500. In 1951 more stringent qualifications for active membership were introduced, but even so, by 1958 it reached 5,783, of whom approximately 2,600 were active members. Source: Official Reports and Proceedings, as published annually in the official journal of the Society.

5. VARYING PERSPECTIVES

MELVIN M. TUMIN

In the previous essay Talcott Parsons, a leading "functional analyst," presented his views of the past, present and future of sociology. Here Melvin M. Tumin raises some serious questions about the type of sociology Professor Parsons has represented.

Tumin also provokes reflection on the work of those sociologists (perhaps most sociologists) who "seem to be almost uniformly against poverty, mental illness, and racial discrimination . . . somewhat less than uniformly against war, and in some important senses . . . are for such things as divorce, adultery, prostitution, crime, delinquency, and interracial disorders."

Melvin M. Tumin, Professor of Sociology and Anthropology at Princeton University, is the author and editor of many books on social stratification and intergroup relations. Included among his works are Caste in a Peasant Society *(1952)*, Desegregation *(1958)*, Social Class and Social Change in Puerto Rico *(1960)*, An Inventory and Evaluation of Research on American Anti-Semitism *(1960)*, *and* Social Stratification: The Forms and Functions of Inequality *(1967)*.

It has been the steady fate of twentieth-century sociology to be deeply involved in matters of the highest relevance for policy, and often intentionally so. Our most recent involvements, however, have been matters of mixed blessings. For, while we have been handsomely supported in important and useful works, we have not altogether avoided some of the less benign features of affluence. One cannot easily shrug off, for instance, the moral and aesthetic pinch one feels at the fact that we prosper anew with each fresh wave of crime, delinquency, divorce, mental illness, and poverty.

It is surely not visionary to predict that in the next several decades the services of sociologists will be sought with even greater frequency by all kinds of governmental and private agencies. If portents are not altogether misleading, the next twenty years are likely to be known as the sociological decades. It may be more difficult to recruit sociologists to work for one rather than another administration. I am confident, however, that we shall find some satisfactory rationale for continuing to apply for and accept governmental funds for research on the problems of interest to us, and I have no less confidence that such funds will be available in fairly satisfactory amounts, no matter who is in the White House.

If these allegations prove true, it follows that an increasing number of sociologists will self-consciously orient their scientific work on the basis of significant value commitments. It is equally probable, however, that in the next two decades we shall also witness the most profound refinement and elaboration of scientific method in sociology. The number of sociologists able to employ sophisticated devices for analysis and measurement of so-

Reprinted from *Social Problems*, **12**, 4 (1965), 379–388, by permission of the author and The Society for the Study of Social Problems. This article was originally entitled "The Functionalist Approach to Social Problems."

cial phenomena in scientifically rigorous ways is likely to reach an all-time high, both absolutely and proportionately.

While it may at first strike us as disturbing that sociology should be approaching a period when it will become both more satisfactorily scientific and more consequentially political than it has ever been before, it is a happy coincidence that our dominant approach to social phenomena —namely, functional analysis—is in some ways ideally suited for just such a period. For a functionalist approach permits the investigator to take certain ends or interests or system-states as given, and to analyze the consequences—supportive and destructive—of any given set of practices for those ends, interests, or system-states. In the process, one may, without apparent penalty, narrow one's focus of attention so that only certain lines of consequence for certain actors are highlighted while others are ignored. This has the dual result of permitting scientific work to generate certain apparent value implications without really doing so, and, simultaneously, to carry real value implications without apparently doing so.

This two-sided role of functionalist science *vis-à-vis* social values is an important feature in view of the fact that there has developed among sociologists in recent years a substantial consensus around certain quite explicit value commitments. The functionalist approach has made the growth of these value commitments comfortably possible without impeding the concomitant development of rigor in the scientific procedures.

Now, functional analysis has come in for a good deal of scrutiny in the last ten years in the sociological journals. Some have contended it is a specific and unique form of sociological analysis, while others have insisted it is coterminous with all of sociological analysis. Some, too, have claimed that functionalism is essentially teleological and mystical, while others have denied these allegations and have shown how functional analysis can be free

of any such teleologies and can be scientifically rigorous. Other students have alleged that functional analysis is really a form of causal analysis, while their opponents have insisted that it is very difficult to go from a functionalist proposition to a causal proposition, unless one adds certain assumptions about human motives or evolutionary selection. Still other sociologists have tried to show how functional analysis is essentially conservative or reactionary in its political orientation, while their adversaries have denied that it has any inherent political orientation at all. Finally, significant disputes have arisen as to whether functional analysis can be used to deal with problems of social change or whether such analysis limits the sociologist alone to studying structures, statics, and the *status quo*.

You will all recognize these as references to matters raised explicitly or implicitly by such sociologists as Kingsley Davis, Wilbert Moore, Talcott Parsons, Robert Merton, Dennis Wrong, Ronald Dore, Harry Bredemeier, Walter Buckley, Francesca Cancion, and others; and [I am sure all here] will know of the contributions of the distinguished philosophers Carl Hempel and Ernest Nagel to these questions regarding functionalism.

If, as Kingsley Davis suggested, it was shrewd of Merton to show how the existence of contradictory claims regarding the political orientation of functionalism justified our concluding that it was neither conservative nor liberal, I am hard pressed to know what would be the shrewd conclusion to draw from all these opposing claims pro and con functionalism. The interesting thing is that, like schools of philosophy, they all sound right when one reads them, but they all sound wrong when one reads their critics.

There are two features of functionalist method, however, that have not received as much attention as they merit in these recent debates. The first is a set of difficulties for sociology as a science which functional analysis presents; the second is the variability of the values to which most of us have become committed. I want to look at each of these in turn.

Functionalism becomes most interesting —to sociologist and layman alike—when it is used as a means for determining the extent to which a given event or custom (or attitude, or practice, or law, or whatever) helps to maintain a system intact or works against the maintenance of the system, however that system may be defined. It seems to hold the highest promise when so conceived—a promise of scientific rigor and neutrality. Nothing need be said about the desirability or undesirability of the system; indeed, nothing *may* be said if functionalism, so conceived, is to be scientifically neutral.

The disturbing thing about functionalism, and maybe about all sociological analysis, is that there is one crucial thing we don't yet know how to do: devise a sensible, scientifically neutral arithmetic by which we can add up the so-called eufunctions and dysfunctions of any given set of practices and arrive at some meaningful over-all number or symbol which would specify the net extent to which the system under question was being maintained or destroyed. We can and do make a series of sequential but essentially unconnected statements about the consequences of actions—and some *have* to be "eufunctional" and some *have* to be "dysfunctional"; there is no way out of that. But an over-all summation of such mixed partial effects is out of our reach now— and may be inherently impossible.

Take, as an example, crime. The dysfunctions—their targets and their relative "amounts"—are roughly determinable. And while Durkheimian sophistication is often required to spell out and make convincing the eufunction of crime, simple observation of the persisting recidivism in the normal crime careers of some of our fellow citizens reveals an imposing array of the eufunctions of crime for criminals. Even for those who are caught and pun-

ished, crime may be eufunctional, and often is.

Other examples readily come to mind. Every young sociologist learns, for instance, what attention he can command by being sophisticated about the positive functions of prostitution, adultery, premarital sexual intercourse, divorce, and related practices. The interesting thing, of course, is that these claims for the positive functions of practices that are generally morally condemned are absolutely correct, if sensibly specified and limited.

But, on balance, what can one say about the total impact—eupacts and dyspacts (why not coin some terms while we're about it?)—of such practices. On the net balance, are they supportive or destructive of that system; and of which system? And how could one test the truth of any such claim? Notice, for instance, that no single institutional arrangement has enjoyed so much published disputation regarding its positive and negative functions as the phenomenon of social inequality. A number of us have variously taken turns reminding our antagonists of either eufunctions or dysfunctions they have overlooked. But in the end we come out where we started, namely, with a preference—supported by data, of course, but data that have been weighted and added according to our preferences. And there are no rules to determine which is the better or more correct method of toting up the diverse effects.

Now we can look at a second shortcoming of so-called functional analysis. We have just assumed it is possible, sometimes easily, sometimes with greater difficulty, to identify separate lines of consequences of various practices as either eupactful or dyspactful for a system which is taken as a "given." But that assumption needs to be examined more carefully, for there is, I think, an inherent tendency in functional analysis to close down one's observations too quickly. Let me give an example. Suppose we are analyzing the structure and function of a gang of delinquent boys. We find they have dramatic initiation ceremonies. With our newly acquired sophistication about such matters, we see that these ceremonies help to smooth the integration of new members into the group, solidify consensus, reawaken flagging commitments of old members, and generally distribute higher morale throughout the membership. Naturally, we would be led to assert that these ceremonies are eufunctional for the continuity and vigorous conduct of the gang and its affairs. Since we have taken the gang as the system, and, therefore, as our "given," we tend, naturally, not to go much further in the analysis. But suppose this reinvigoration of the group leads it to excesses of delinquent behavior into which it would not have been tempted if it had not been so reinvigorated, and suppose these excesses provide just that margin of outrage to the norm-minded community needed to incite a serious crackdown. What, then, of the so-called eufunctions of the initiation ceremonies, if in heightening group morale and consensus and unity they lead the group to engage in self-defeating and destroying actions? My point is that we do not often go on to look at the longer and larger and delayed consequences of actions, and we do not do so for two reasons: (1) The rules of functional analysis are pretty rigorously insistent that we delimit and specify the system to whose support or destruction we are referring our analysis. (2) Typically, moreover, we have *not* designed studies to watch the changing impact over time of various occurrences, events, and practices. Our analysis is not geared to historical waiting and depth. And so we often speak too easily and too quickly. For instance, is the emergence of a fairly rock-ribbed conservative trend in politics, such as is exemplified by Goldwater, positively or negatively functional for American democracy? Suppose there is backlash against the backlash in the near future,

and a reinvigoration of liberalism? Suppose this in turn generates a third party force? Suppose this leads to a real fractionating of political power, with strategic minorities coming to play even more dominant roles? How, then, will we assess the long range effects of the Goldwater party?

Examples such as these point up a painful dilemma. The strength of functional analysis presumably lies in its ability to do skilled dissection and analysis of the ways in which social actions interplay in a network of interdependence within a given system, and thus presumably clarify in some as yet unnamed way "why" the practices are present. In short, there is some presumed *unique* strength in the *ahistoricity* of the analytic method. But now we find that it is precisely this ahistoricity which makes our analyses often of such dubious value. And even worse, it is future history rather than past history that we seem to need to control. And how do we do that?

Let me briefly mention two other problems presented by functional analysis. The first of these can be stated simply as follows: using functional analysis, sociologists have no way of making relevant, competent scientific statements about any *system* taken as a *whole*. If we are in trouble, as we are, because we cannot sensibly add up the diversities of eupacts and dyspacts of various substructures within any given system, we are in even worse trouble when it comes to assessing a system as a whole. We simply have not developed a method or language adequate to total system comparison. Our only "out" is to take the system which we first used as a "given" and place it in a context of a larger system of which it is a sub-unit and ask questions about its positive and negative contributions to that larger system. Thus, we do reasonably well in considering, functionally, the sub-units of national state aggregates; but when we get to the level of nation-state aggregation, or go on to multi-national systems, we are simply unable to say things that couldn't just as well be said by anybody else. One has only to listen to the usual comparisons of, say, America with England or France to realize that one might just as well hold these conversations with untrained fellow tourists in the bar of the S.S. *Rotterdam*.

I believe the difficulty just stated is inherent in functional analysis taken in its best and most generous terms.

The second difficulty has to do with the internal pressure of functionalism to find a rationale for all things. Of course, all things have reasons for coming into being and other reasons for persisting. But to say this is to say nothing. For it is clear that some social events are much more deterministically generated by a given system, while others can be seen as system-bound and determined only in the loosest sense. I am trying to suggest that a great deal of what we do in any given day simply is irrelevant and unnecessary from the point of view of system maintenance. It is a frill or a fringe benefit, or deficit of the system; it is garbage or junk from the point of view of system-requirements. It may be esthetically gratifying, or neurotically compulsive, or luxuriously enjoyable; but those are very different kinds of reasons for the existence of practices than the reasons we might offer for the existence of a division of labor. Functionalism —and maybe that means sociology in general as presently practiced, in whatever version—is inadequate to this problem. Either we must learn to ignore the junk and garbage and frills and fringes; or we must find a meaningful place for them in our system of analysis, especially if they are features by which we are often most dramatically characterised, such as the state of our creative arts. At the moment, all we can do is be uneasy about these things because we neither ignore them nor find a place for them.

I now want to turn from this first set of problems presented by functional analysis and consider a second set of problems to which only sparse attention has been paid

in recent discussions of functionalism. These problems concern the relationships between functional analysis as a method, on the one hand, and our variable value commitments, on the other, specifically, our variable attitudes toward different "social problems." Here one must be avowedly more impressionistic.

Why is it, one must ask, that while we, i.e., practicing sociologists, seem to be almost uniformly against poverty, mental illness, and racial discrimination, we are somewhat less than uniformly against war, and in some important senses, we are *for* such things as divorce, adultery, prostitution, crime, delinquency, and interracial disorders.

When I say we are "for" or "against" any of these, I mean several things.

First, sociologists who work and report on problems of poverty, mental illness, and racial discrimination couldn't be clearer about their implied condemnation of these phenomena. These are social abominations to be done away with as quickly as possible.

By contrast, the sociological profession as a whole is much more ambivalent about war, and some sociologists have even made reputations as cold-war warriors, counselling very important persons lodged in the highest reaches of the Establishment. The implication here is also clear: war is sometimes good, or at least necessary.

By further contrast, sociological analyses of such matters as divorce, delinquency, crime, prostitution, and adultery often show either a cool detachment and implied lack of concern about the problematic aspects of these phenomena ordinarily attributed to them by the laymen of our society; or sociologists tend to display an almost whimsical kind of affection, guided by a thoroughly sympathetic understanding of how people could get involved in these normally disapproved patterns of behavior. Sometimes the attitude is not only "Well, what could you expect, given the situation of these people and the structure of society," but also includes a kind of militant applause for these types of reactions to the implied malfunctioning of the society.

A second indication of variable attitudes toward social problems is revealed in the informal judgments we tend to make about the expectability of the incidences and rates of these problematic phenomena. We write as if there were no good grounds on which to expect *any* poverty or racial discrimination—there are no ineluctable cultural compulsions in these directions, we imply. By contrast, we are somewhat tentatively expectant of a discernible incidence of mental disorder; and we tend to see recurring wars as quite expectable. And when it comes to divorce, adultery, delinquency, crime, prostitution, and racial protests, we often imply that, sociologically speaking, we are a lucky society to experience only as little of these matters as we do. We often add wisely that there is probably a lot more of these things than is ever recorded—except divorce, of course, and here we count "unhappy marriage" as the equivalent of divorce.

Third, and most relevantly here, we reveal our variable attitudes toward a range of social problems by the kinds of so-called functional analyses we do of these problems. Mental illness, racial discrimination, and poverty have no positive functions for anyone, judging by most sociological writings; or, if they do, then clearly the persons or interest blocs who do profit from these problems are villainous. Above all, no good can be identified for the system as a whole. By contrast, some wars are often seen at least as better than some peaceful alternatives; and in considering such phenomena as delinquency, divorce, adultery, prostitution, and crime, we have become very adroit at identifying positive functions for actors, interest blocs, and the society as a whole.

In sum, our so-called scientific analyses tend often to lean heavily on the side of negative functions in the case of some problem phenomena; range around a balance of positive and negative functions in the case of other phenomena; and lean heavily toward the other pole of positive functions in the case of still other problems.

Why should this be so? There is little, if anything, in the scientific findings *per se* that would suggest that these variable one-sidednesses in our analyses are justified. That all of these phenomena have both positive and negative functions is quite clear. There is no difficulty, for instance, in spelling out certain benign consequences of poverty, especially if one is indifferent to his moral standing in the community. One could, for example, mention the positive functions for wealthy people of the poverty of others; or the availability of cheap services and labor; or the disparate power quotients that some can enjoy; or the feelings of well-being that do-gooders and philanthropists can secure; or the political strength of party programs that pay attention to poverty; or the smug euphoria that reports of our poverty bring to Americanophobic Europeans.

So, too, one can even talk about the positive functions for the *system as a whole* of a quotient of poverty that can function as a rallying point for general social conscience and can energize ameliorative concern that might otherwise lie dormant. It does not take much imagination to do this kind of thing. Ever since Durkheim showed us how some crime is positively functional for the rest of society, it has not taken much sensitivity or cleverness to extrapolate to other phenomena and do the same thing.

Since, then, we can identify both positive and negative consequences or functions for all the social problems we face, the only possible justification for favoring some problems above others would lie in the net *balance* of positive and negative consequences. But we have shown earlier that we have no techniques available to us for adding up the pluses and minuses and coming out with some meaningful over-all calculation or quotient of net effect. We have no way, in short, of saying whether, on balance, the society is threatened more by the totality of mental illness and its consequences than by the totality of delinquency and its consequences. If we cannot do so, then we cannot scientifically justify our tendency to stress the negative aspects of some phenomena and the positive aspects of others.

So, it is not in the scientific findings themselves that we will discover why our biases are so variously distributed. Nor will we find the reason in the relative difficulty and ease of analysis of these problems. They are all relatively equally susceptible to clever or banal, mediocre or insightful analyses.

Nor can one find in the historical span of the problems any good grounds for feeling so differently about them. Poverty has been with us for as long as prostitution and adultery; and while it may be true that it required official certification by a presidential office to establish poverty as a legitimate focus of interest and attention, that would only account for the novelty of the interest and not the type of interest expressed.

I want to offer a number of hypotheses as to why some problems seem more baleful than others. We have spoken of the senselessness and needlessness of certain problems. Poverty doesn't make any sense; mental illness doesn't; racial discrimination doesn't—not by any tolerable moral standards accepted in our community. There are no good grounds for poverty, especially when there is so much wealth. Mental illness may serve many positive functions ancillary to the main body of identified negative functions, but there is no acceptable ground for putting up with it. This is, I think, how the public conscience runs among sociologists.

But this conscience needs accounting for.

The reason our analyses run the way

they do, I think, has to do with a part of functional analysis once again—namely, the doctrine of functional equivalents. Simply, I mean that the possible functional equivalents of the disapproved phenomena either are nonexistent or are even more repulsive than the actual problems themselves, while, by contrast, the functional equivalents of the more approved phenomena are themselves either as tolerable and acceptable as the phenomena, or even morally praiseworthy.

What, for instance, is the functional equivalent of mental disorder? If we pretend to know that mental illness functions to help the victim to get out of an intolerable situation, then some other forms of escape are the functional equivalents; and we don't approve of these escapes any more than we do of the illness itself.

One has to be careful, of course, with the doctrine of functional equivalents. For one must always ask: functionally equivalent for whom? It is one thing to ask what could serve the same functions for poverty-stricken people as poverty—and that would be an idiotic question—but it is not idiotic to ask what could substitute for poverty in the total culture that would have the same effects on the culture as poverty. For here one can think of such things as rigorous caste structures; or other forms of extreme status deprivations; or totalitarian power structures that would yield many of the same functions. As I noted before, these functional equivalents are even less tolerable than the actual manifestations.

By contrast, the functional equivalents of the more approved problems often have very strong positive connotations. Thus, one equivalent of delinquency is the expression of independence of adult norms and stuffiness. So, too, prostitution can be seen, and often is seen, as a symbolic rejection of intolerable sexual standards of the bourgeoisie, and an implicit denunciation of commercialized sale of sex hiding under the guise of marriage.

Or, divorce and adultery are simply evil-sounding terms for expressions of spirit that rise above the ordinary limitations of unjustified normative restraints. These may by hyperbolic ways of stating these matters—but the essential truth, or claim for it at least, is evidently there and quite plain to be seen.

In effect, then, I am contending we like some problems more than others because we don't think they're really problems. And we don't think they are really problems because we see them as indirect expressions of laudable human spirit and verve and honesty or straightforwardness breaking through the hypocritical bounds of our ordinary norms. For these reasons, I suggest, we tacitly applaud some of these problems by insisting on revealing a large proportion of positive functions these actions serve for a number of actors with whom we identify, and tacitly deny importance to the negative functions they play for other actors with whom we have not very much sympathy, or for the system as a whole, which we hold blameworthy in the first place.

A second source of our variable attitudes toward problems is also connected intimately with functional analysis. I suggest that most of us have been pressed against our own political inclinations to play the role of neutral social scientist, committed to withholding value judgments in those roles. Functional analysis does not make possible an over-all critical evaluation of our society. But our own inner selves will out, whether we like it or not. And so we employ functional analysis in such a way as to permit ourselves to be both sociologists and concerned citizens. What, in fact, we do is deliver ourselves of our over-all evaluations of our society by emphasizing the positive aspects of certain phenomena and the negative aspects of others. Our cultivated but repressed tendencies toward informed muckraking, our views of ourselves as conscientious citizens, which our neutral sociological roles do not permit us to indulge: these are given expression by the way in which we slant our work. So we give short shrift to poverty, mental illness, and racial discrimination; we are sophisticatedly ambivalent about war; and we portray our sympathies for the downtrodden in our analyses of crime and delinquency. In our own minds, we add up all these un-addible things and see ourselves as giving public vent to our condemnation of our society's malfunctionings. In short, we let people know where we stand on our society as a system and not simply what we know about it.

A third reason why we bias our functional analyses has to do with the process of identification. The victims of mental illness, poverty, and racial discrimination are not the least bit appealing, at least not by any sort of ordinary standards. It takes quite an effort, I suggest, for most people really to identify with the poor, the Negro, or the mentally sick in our society. Understand them, yes; and sympathize, yes; and want to help, yes; but *identify?* No. For that means actively thinking of ourselves as poor or Negro or mad. And not many of us are built to be able to take on those nightmares.

One might even suggest that the victims of these social outrages generate in us a certain amount of moral despisal which we recognize as cruelty, and about which we feel guilty; we handle our guilt by converting it into professed outrage at the society which throws up such victims.

By contrast, the actors in delinquency, crime, adultery, and divorce often tend to command our positive sympathies because, I suggest, they are doing things many of us would like to be able to do. Mitty-like, we dream about doing them, but never manage to get to them. And while it is probably rare for a male sociologist to dream affectionately about being a prostitute, or to wish he could be one, the kind of total situation in which the relative sexual freedom of the prostitute would be the prevailing norm is surely one about which many of us must often fantasize. Even the more pleasant aspects of taking drugs and of intoxication are probably quite within our scope of positive identification.

A fourth dynamic that may shape our attitudes toward social problems lies in the distinction between cause and symptom. As sociologists, we tend to see crime and delinquency and such other phenomena as symptoms of deep-lying disorders of the social system—of poverty, for instance. We are reluctant to condemn such symptomatic behaviors, especially if we see them as naturally arising out of the basic disorders over which the "deviant" actors or victims have little or no control. In some senses, indeed, we tend to impute certain "healthy" attributes to these symptomatic reactions to inadequacies and inequities in the social system. In much the same way we invest racial demonstrations with positive functionality, seeing such demonstrations as natural reactions to racial discrimination and as "healthier" modes of reaction than the historically traditional subservience of the "oppressed" groups. (We recognize that this line of reasoning will not apply to the attitudes we express toward mental illness, but that is no reason not to consider its relevance for the other phenomena just discussed.)

A fifth and final possible source of our variable attitudes toward social problems has to do with our judgment of the relative importance of the various problems. I suggest that we are relatively off-handed about crime and delinquency and prostitution and divorce, partly because we believe that they don't really matter very much—that they really don't disturb any important social values and don't really gum up the social works to any significant degree. This attitude is perhaps most obvious in the case of divorce, which we rarely deplore because we feel it is not only natural and expectable but a rather good institution, all things considered. Our tendency to press for far more liberal divorce laws is evidence in point. Our informal and perhaps unjustified sneers at marriage counselling also testify to our endorsement of the importance of the freedom to divorce.

If there is any credence to be given to these five suggested reasons for variable attitudes toward problems, then it is clear our functional analyses, attuned to these desires and preferences, are slanted in most unscientific ways. While some of our biasing sentiments match those of the rest of the community, by and large, as sociologists we tend to be less "square" about these matters than most other segments of the community. We stand in between the morally disapproving sections of the community, on the one hand, and the actual participants in the problems themselves, on the other.

I have indicated the intimate connection between so-called scientific sociology and a range of non- or unscientific elements that guide and condition that activity in important ways. I wish further to suggest, finally, that this kind of close interplay of values and science, or of sentiment and science, is probably most difficult to avoid. Perhaps it is altogether unavoidable, so long as functional analysis is our dominant mode of approach to social problems. Whether we *should avoid* these unscientific predilections and prefigurings of our scientific activity is quite another question. But it is interesting to note that a major function of functionalism for sociologists is that it minimizes role strain for them as they seek simultaneously to play the parts of both concerned citizens and neutral, value-free scientists. In an era when both these roles have high salience for a group of professionals, a general approach which reduces the potentially great role strain is not without virtue.

SUGGESTIONS FOR FURTHER READING
on *The Sociological Approach*

CHINOY, ELY. *Society*. Revised edition. New York: Random House, 1967. A clear and concise introduction to the field of sociology.

DEUTSCH, STEVEN E., and JOHN HOWARD, eds. *Where It's At*. New York: Harper and Row, 1970. A new reader offering radical perspectives in sociology.

GOULDNER, ALVIN W., and S. M. MILLER, eds. *Applied Sociology*. New York: Free Press, 1965. Thirty-five papers on the practical application of sociological principles, methods, and findings.

HINKLE, ROSCOE C., and GISELA J. HINKLE. *The Development of Modern Sociology*. New York: Random House, 1954. A short history of American sociology and its European antecedents.

MADGE, JOHN. *The Origins of Scientific Sociology*. New York: Free Press, 1962. Summaries and critiques of twelve major sociological studies.

MERTON, ROBERT K. *Social Theory and Social Structure*. Revised and enlarged edition. Glencoe, Ill.: Free Press, 1957. Nineteen essays by one of America's foremost sociologists in which the relationship between theory and research is clearly elucidated.

MILLS, C. WRIGHT. *The Sociological Imagination*. New York: Oxford University Press, 1959. A critique of contemporary sociology and a proposal for a return to classical social analysis.

NISBET, ROBERT A. *The Social Bond*. New York: Random House, 1970. A new and stimulating introduction to the field of sociology by one of America's finest writers.

NISBET, ROBERT A. *The Sociological Tradition*. New York: Basic Books, 1966. Origins of ideas and perspectives on community, authority, status, the sacred, and alienation.

PARSONS, TALCOTT. *The Structure of Social Action*. Glencoe, Ill.: Free Press, 1949. A study of the contributions of European sociologists to the "voluntaristic theory of social action."

THOMLINSON, RALPH. *Sociological Concepts and Research*. New York: Random House, 1965. A discussion of the acquisition, analysis, and interpretation of sociological information.

TIMASHEFF, NICHOLAS. *Sociological Theory: Its Nature and Growth*. Revised edition. New York: Random House, 1967. An introduction to the backgrounds of modern sociological theory.

TRUZZI, MARCELLO, ed. *Sociology and Everyday Life*. Englewood Cliffs, N.J.: Prentice-Hall, 1968. A "hip" reader. Social life as seen from the point of view of the actors.

VIDICH, ARTHUR J., and JOSEPH BENSMAN, eds. *Sociology on Trial*. Englewood Cliffs, N.J.: Prentice-Hall, 1963. Critical essays on contemporary American sociology.

PART TWO
SOCIETY, CULTURE, AND
THE INDIVIDUAL

The explicit and implicit ways
of men and how they are
learned and shared

Erich Fromm has written that man is "the only animal that can be bored, that can be discontented, that can feel evicted from paradise. Man is the only animal for whom his own existence is a problem that he has to solve and from which he cannot escape. . . ."

The way in which each individual comes to terms with these uniquely human problems, and with many others, depends in large measure upon the dictates of the milieu in which he is born and nurtured, and the thoughts, sentiments, and actions of those responsible for his socialization. Man alone possesses culture—and it possesses him.

It is often said that one begins life as a *tabula rasa,* a clean slate, on which the relevant aspects of "human-ness" are to be inscribed. The simile is somewhat misleading. The slate is never really clean, for each child enters the world already possessed of a dual heritage—one biological, the other social. To a very great extent, the roles he will be expected to play, the rules to which he will be asked to conform, the ideas that he will be required to accept, and even the kinds of social relationships that he will enjoy are predetermined by his parents' place in the social hierarchy and the cultural background from which he springs. In no known society are individuals born absolutely free and equal. One's social heredity, or culture, is there when one enters the scene; it defines the tolerance limits of accepted and expected behavior; it serves as a potential guide for social conduct.

Of course, particular cultural norms and values and the manner in which they are taught and learned vary widely from one society to another and, in many cases, within societies as well. For example, for some it seems only "natural" that there is but one God who knows innermost thoughts and feelings and to whom they will someday be accountable; for others such a notion is incomprehensible. For some a patriarchal family system is the only kind imaginable, while others can only conceive of a society with parental authority vested in the mother. Some people "know" that only squat and obese women are beautiful, while others prefer their women to be tall and lanky.

Each individual has a tendency to view the world through his own culture-bound perspective and many, understandably, believe that their ways are best. Recognition of such ethnocentrism is essential for understanding the mysteries of social life in distant places and foreign climes. Yet, one need not go far afield to see the extent to which socialization sets limits on perception and culture delineates conduct. Our heterogeneous society is marked by variant "styles of life"—including different religious beliefs, sexual mores, child-rearing practices, and social attitudes—all of which seem right and proper to those who have learned to accept them as their own.

The concepts of "society" and "culture" are basic to any understanding of why men act, react, and interact as they do in particular settings. In the first section of Part Two, Ely Chinoy illustrates why many sociologists consider these two words to be the master concepts. Chinoy's essay is followed by Gertrude Jaeger and Philip Selznick's examination of the possibilities of a rapprochement between the way in which social scientists and humanists have defined and used the culture concept. Edward T. Hall then offers a clear expression of the manners in which cultures provide the expressive symbols which guide behavior.

Harry C. Bredemeier and Richard Stephenson offer a framework by which sociologists might utilize the culture concept analytically. Dennis H. Wrong has a different view. He suggests that sociologists have an "oversocialized conception of man."

In the first essay of the second section, Joseph Bensman and Bernard Rosenberg offer the student an introduction to the notion of socialization, explaining the linkage between society, culture, and human behavior. The study of continuities and discontinuities in "cultural conditioning" offers a clear case of this linkage. So, in a different sense, do responses to pain. These patterns are discussed in papers by Ruth Benedict, and Mark Zborowski, respectively.

The last two essays in this section deal with adult socialization and the meaning of specialized professional roles. First, Howard Becker and Blanche Geer describe their study of "The Fate of Idealism in Medical School," then Edward Wakin and Joseph Scheuer consider some of the problems inherent in being a nun in America today.

The Basic Concepts

6. SOCIETY AND CULTURE

ELY CHINOY

"Culture," wrote Edward B. Tylor in 1871, "is that complex whole which includes knowledge, belief, art, morals, law, custom and any other capabilities and habits acquired by man as a member of society." Tylor recognized that the aspects of social life are learned and shared, two of the most important variables necessary to comprehend the nature of human endeavor in any society. His definition remains a classic to this day.

Here Ely Chinoy indicates the way in which sociologists continue to use the master concepts of culture and society and the "satellite" concepts of institutions and roles and social organizations. His essay provides the groundwork for further study.

Ely Chinoy is Mary Huggins Gamble Professor of Sociology and Anthropology at Smith College. A well-known authority on industrial sociology, he is the author of Automobile Workers and the American Dream *(1955),* Society: An Introduction to Sociology *(1961; revised 1967), and* Sociological Perspective *(1968) from which this essay was selected.*

Patterned Behavior and Collective Life

Sociology begins with two basic facts: The behavior of human beings shows regular and recurrent patterns, and human beings are social animals and not isolated creatures.

The fundamental events of birth, death, and marriage, the private details of bathing, eating, and love-making, the public occurrences of vote-getting and producing or selling goods, and the myriad other activities in which men engage usually follow recognizable patterns. We often lose sight of the repetitive nature of most social action, however, for when we observe those persons around us we are more likely to notice their idiosyncrasies and personal quirks than their similarities. But if we compare ourselves with Frenchmen or Japanese or Trobriand Islanders we find ourselves saying: We do it this way; they do it that way. Charles Horton Cooley, one of America's first important sociologists, once observed:

Is it not the case that the nearer a thing is to our habit of thought the more clearly we see the individual . . . ? The principle is much the same as that which makes all [Chinese] look pretty much alike to us: we see the type because it is so different from what we are used to, but only one who lives within it can fully perceive the differences among individuals.[1]

In studying ourselves as we might study the Chinese or any other society different from our own, we abstract the recurrent features of behavior from the unique. When men respond to a personal introduction with a standardized phrase— "How do you do?"—the intonation, the tone, the volume may vary, but the verbal formulation remains the same. Some people shake hands energetically, with a strong grasp, while others have a limp and flabby handshake; these personal differences have significance in the social interchange which takes place, but they do not deny the existence of the patterned form of behavior which recurs when people meet.

The repeated aspects of human action are the basis for any social science. Without ascertainable patterns there could be no science, for generalization would be impossible. Sociology is distinguished from economics, political science, and psychology by the particular patterns it studies and how it looks at them. Those

features of behavior upon which sociology focuses its attention are derived from the second basic fact upon which the discipline rests—the social character of human life.

"Man," wrote Aristotle more than two thousand years ago, "is naturally a political animal [in modern terms the word usually translated as *political* might more appropriately be translated as *social*] and . . . whosoever is naturally and not artificially unfit for society must be either inferior or superior to men." Adam Ferguson, an eighteenth-century Scottish moral philosopher, once observed in terms which are still appropriate: "Both the earliest and the latest accounts collected from every quarter of the earth, represent mankind as assembled in troops and companies; . . . [a fact which] must be admitted as the foundation of all our reasoning relative to man." [2] There are records of human beings who somehow manage to survive with little care or without normal association with other humans, but such cases of "feral man," as they are called, and of abused and rejected children show few of the characteristics normally attributed to man.[3]

In attempting to account for the apparent regularities of human action and the facts of collective life, sociologists have developed two concepts, *society* and *culture*, which may be considered basic to sociological investigation. Each of these terms has a long history. *Society* derives initially from attempts made during the sixteenth and seventeenth centuries to differentiate the state from the totality of social organization, although systematic analysis of the nature of society came only with the emergence of sociology. The term *culture* gained initial currency in Germany in the eighteenth century, was first used in anthropology by Edward Tylor, an English scholar, in 1871, and has come to be widely used in sociological discourse only in the twentieth century.[4] Both terms have been variously employed, and there is as yet no complete consensus as to their meaning. Despite this variation —or perhaps because of it—they can serve to define and suggest in a general fashion the nature and limits of the subject matter of sociology. It should be noted, however, that the phenomena to which culture and society refer do not exist independently of one another. Although we can distinguish between them analytically, human society cannot exist without culture, and culture exists only within society.

Society

Despite its importance there is no clear-cut agreement as to the meaning of *society,* even among social scientists or, more particularly, sociologists, some of whom have labeled their discipline the "science of society." "In the long history of the literature dealing with the life of human beings in groups," Gladys Bryson has commented, "perhaps no word offers less precision in usage than the word 'society.' " [5] We cannot therefore suggest a definition to which all, or perhaps even most, sociologists would give assent. Nor is there anything to be gained by adding another to the already imposing array of alternatives. Instead we can best carry forward our analysis by exploring the various meanings which have been given to the term and by examining briefly the uses to which they are put. As we pointed out earlier, conceptual differences often mean that people are looking at, or at least emphasizing, different aspects of the same phenomenon.

In its most general usage, society refers merely to the basic fact of human association. For example, the term has been employed

in the widest sense to include every kind and degree of relationship entered into by men, whether these relations be organized or unorganized, direct or indirect, conscious or unconscious, cooperative or antagonistic. It includes the whole tissue of human relations

and is without a boundary or assignable limits. Of amorphous structure itself, it gives rise to numerous, specific, overlapping and interconnected societies, but is not exhausted by them. [6]

This conception of society, which seems on occasion to encompass all of humanity, or mankind at large, serves chiefly to focus our attention upon a broad range of phenomena central to the analysis of human behavior, namely the varied and multiform relationships into which men necessarily enter in the course of group life.

The concept of *social relationship* is based upon the fact that human behavior is oriented in innumerable ways to other persons. Not only do men live together and share common opinions, values, beliefs, and customs, they also continually interact, responding to one another and shaping their behavior in relation to the behavior and expectations of others. The lover's effort to please the object of his affections, the politician's attempts to win the support of the electorate, the soldier's obedience to the orders of his commanding officer—these constitute familiar examples of behavior oriented to the expectations, desires, and wishes, whether real or imagined, of others. Action may be modeled on that of someone else; the child imitates his father, the teen-ager apes her favorite movie star. Behavior may be calculated to elicit responses from others, as in the child's effort to gain parental approval, or the actor's attempt to move his audience. It may be based on expectations as to how others will behave —for example, the boxer's feint before delivering a blow or the doctor's technique in reporting his diagnosis to a patient.

Interaction, however, is not one-sided, as these illustrations may suggest. The electorate responds in some fashion to the politician's actions, and he may then alter his methods or persist in his strategy, with further consequences in the attitudes and behavior of voters. The officer's behavior will be affected by the manner in which his men obey his orders. Courtship is not merely a case of hunter and hunted; to change the metaphor, two can and do play the game as well as one. Interaction, as the word itself suggests, is not a momentary occurrence, not a single response to a single stimulus; it is a persisting process of action and reaction.

A social relationship may be said to exist when individuals or groups possess reciprocal expectations concerning the other's behavior so that they tend to act in relatively patterned ways. To phrase the point differently, a social relationship consists of a pattern of human interaction. Parents and children respond to each other in more or less regular ways, based upon mutual expectations. The patterned interactions of student and teacher, policeman and automobile driver, salesman and buyer, worker and employer, doctor and patient, constitute social relationships of various kinds. From one point of view, then, society is the "web of social relationships."

Society, as the "whole tissue" or "whole complex scheme" of social relationships, can be distinguished from those specific societies in which men group themselves. The emphasis in some definitions of a society, however, is frequently upon the persons rather than upon the structure of relationships. Georg Simmel, one of the founders of modern sociology, considered a society to be "a number of individuals connected by interaction," [7] while the anthropologist Ralph Linton identified a society as "any group of people who have lived and worked together long enough to get themselves organized and to think of themselves as a social unit with well-defined limits." [8] This view of a society, although of value in directing attention to the network of relationships which hold together specific aggregations of people, is too general to be very useful. As thus defined, society could include any of the multiplicity of groups found among men. It could refer to "Society," members of the upper class whose doings are reported in newspaper "society pages." It could encompass organizations of many kinds: the Society of Friends, the Society for the Advancement of Management, the American Ethnological Society, as well as the endless array of clubs, lodges, fraternities, criminal groups, and professional organizations. It could include families, kinship groups, and clusters of friends. Although some writers do use "society" to refer to any kind of group, this term usually denotes a special kind of social unit.

Society, then, is that group within which men can live a total common life, rather than an organization limited to some specific purpose or purposes. From this point of view a society consists not only of individuals related to one another, but also of interconnected and overlapping groups. Thus, American society comprises 200 million or more individuals (in 1967) tied together in a complex network of relations, of approximately 49 million families (increasing by about .5 million families per year), of the multiplicity of urban and rural communities, religious denominations and sects, political parties, races and ethnic groups, social and economic classes, unions, business and veterans organizations, and the infinite variety of other voluntary organizations into which the population is divided. On the other hand, a simple society such as that of the Andaman Islands west of Burma consisted before the arrival of Europeans of a small population organized primarily into tribes, local groups, and families. The society of India includes the various religious groups, the innumerable castes and the "outcastes," the different races, the many tribes, the economic and political aggregates and organizations, and so on.

In any society smaller groups may be found within larger ones, and individuals simultaneously belong to various groups. Ethnic groups and social classes give rise to voluntary associations, cliques and factions emerge in political parties and other groups, families belong to country clubs and churches and engage in neighborly activities. Each person may participate in a family, a peer group, a business enterprise, or a union or professional organization. A society, then, can be analyzed in terms of its constituent groups and their relations to one another.

Culture

Each society possesses a way of life or, in our terminology, a *culture,* that defines appropriate or required modes of thinking, acting, and feeling. Culture, as thus used in sociological inquiry, has a much wider meaning than it is usually given. In conventional discourse, it refers to the "higher" things in life—painting, music, sculpture, philosophy; the adjective *cultured* stands close to cultivated or refined. In sociology culture refers to the totality of what is learned by individuals as members of society. Tylor's old (1871) but still widely cited definition indicates its scope: "Culture is that complex whole which includes knowledge, belief, art, morals, law, custom, and any other capabilities acquired by man as a member of society." The technique of brushing one's teeth, the Ten Commandments, the rules of baseball or cricket or hopscotch, the procedures for choosing a president or prime minister or members of the Supreme Soviet are as much a part of culture as the latest volume of avant-garde poetry, Beethoven's Ninth Symphony, or the *Analects* of Confucius.

Regularities of behavior do not in themselves constitute culture. They occur in large part because men possess culture, because they have common standards of good and bad, right and wrong, appropriate and inappropriate, and possess similar attitudes and share a fund of knowledge about the environment—social, biological, and physical—in which they live. Culture, George Murdock has noted, is to a large extent "ideational": it refers to the standards, beliefs, and attitudes in terms of which people act.

Recognition of the ubiquity and significance of culture, Ralph Linton has pointed out, is "one of the most important scientific developments of modern times." He continues:

It has been said that the last thing which a dweller in the deep sea would be likely to discover would be water. He would become conscious of its existence only if some accident brought him to the surface and introduced him to air. Man, throughout most of his history, has been only vaguely conscious of the existence of culture and has owed even this consciousness to contrasts between the customs of his own society and those of some other with which he happened to be brought into contact. The ability to see the culture of one's own society as a whole, to evaluate its patterns and appreciate their implications, calls for a degree of objectivity which is rarely if ever achieved.[9]

Because our culture is so much a part of us we take it for granted, frequently assuming that it is a normal, inevitable, and inherent characteristic of all mankind. Anthropologists have often reported that when they ask members of small preliterate groups why they act in some particular fashion they receive an answer which amounts to "That's just the way it's done" or "It's customary." "When Captain Cook asked the chiefs of Tahiti why they ate apart and alone, they simply replied, 'Because it is right.' "[10] Habituated to their own way of life, men frequently can conceive of no other. Among Americans, the expression "It's just human nature" is a characteristic explanation for many actions—competing for fame and power, profit-seeking, marrying for love or for money. Yet this "explanation," which by seemingly explaining everything explains nothing, is itself a manifestation of the ethnocentrism of Americans.

The importance of culture lies in the fact that it provides the knowledge and the techniques that enable man to survive, both physically and socially, and to master and control, insofar as it is possible, the world around him. Man seems to possess few if any instinctive skills and no instinctive knowledge which might enable him to sustain himself, either singly or in groups. The salmon's return from the sea to spawn and die in fresh water, the annual migration of birds from one part of the world to another, the nest-building of the mud wasp, and the complex living patterns of ants and bees are all inherited forms of behavior which seem to appear automatically at the appropriate times. They are not learned from parents or from other members of the species. Man, on the other hand, survives by virtue of what he learns.

Man is not, however, the only animal that learns to act instead of responding automatically to stimuli. Dogs can be taught a good deal and can learn from experience, as can horses and cats, monkeys and apes, and rats and white mice. But by virtue of his greater brain power and his capacity for language, man can learn more and therefore possesses greater flexibility of action than other animals. He can transmit a great deal of what he learns to others, including his young, and he can in part control the world around him— even to the point of transforming much of it. Man is the only animal to possess culture; indeed, this is one of the crucial distinctions between man and other animals.

Of central importance in the definition of culture is the fact that it is both *learned* and *shared*. Men, we have said, do not inherit their habits and beliefs, their skills and knowledge; they acquire them during the course of their lives. What they learn comes from the groups into which they are born and in which they live. The habits acquired by an infant are likely to be patterned on those of its family and of other persons close at hand. (Not all habits reflect customs or culture, however, for some are merely personal idiosyncrasies.) In an endless number of ways—via explicit instruction, the application of punishment and the offering of rewards, identification with elders and imitation of their behavior—each generation learns from its predecessors. Behavior which is universal,

though not learned, or is peculiar to the individual, is not part of culture. (Both unlearned behavior, such as reflexes, and personal idiosyncrasies may, however, be influenced or modified by culture. Indeed, except for biological peculiarities, individual aberrations are defined by their relationship to, or deviation from, cultural patterns.)

The learned and shared character of culture has led to its occasional identification as the "superorganic" or as man's "social heritage." The former term, used by Herbert Spencer, emphasizes the relative independence of culture from the realm of biology and its distinctive quality as a product of social life. "Social heritage" calls attention to culture's historical character and therefore to the possibilities of growth and change; it suggests the need for analyzing and understanding its temporal dimensions.

The Components of Culture

Culture is clearly so inclusive a concept that its principal components should be identified, labeled, analyzed, and related to one another. These components can be grouped roughly in three large categories: institutions, the rules or norms which govern behavior; ideas, that is, knowledge and belief of all varieties—moral, theological, philosophical, scientific, technological, historical, sociological, and so on; and the material products or artifacts which men produce and use in the course of their collective lives.

Institutions

We shall define institutions as *"normative* patterns which define what are felt to be . . . proper, legitimate, or expected modes of action or of social relationship."[11] Such norms or rules pervade all areas of social life: how one eats and what one eats, how one dresses, decorates oneself, responds to others, how one looks after children or the aged, and how one behaves in the presence of members of the opposite sex. Not all behavior conforms to rules, either explicit or implicit, but most actions of any individual reflect the presence of some accepted standards of behavior which he has learned from others and which in some measure he shares with them.

The concept of institution, like that of culture, has been variously defined, and the definition given above, which we shall use, represents only one of several alternatives. Because the other uses of the term appear frequently in sociological literature, it is necessary to detour briefly in order to note these other meanings, even though we shall try to be consistent in our own usage. Earlier definitions, which have been steadily refined or clarified, included not only normative patterns, but also what we shall identify later as groups and as social organization. We still find occasionally in sociological literature (and frequently in everyday discourse) an organized group of individuals referred to as an institution: Harvard College, for example, or the Republican Party. This usage coincides with the early definition by William Graham Sumner: "An institution consists of a concept (idea, notion, doctrine, interest) and a structure. The structure is a framework, or apparatus, or perhaps only a number of functionaries set to cooperate in prescribed ways at a certain conjuncture. The structure holds the concept and furnishes instrumentalities for bringing it into the world of facts and action in a way to serve the interests of men in society." [12] Both the norms *and* the group are included in this definition of an institution. There is an increasing measure of agreement that the term should be used only to refer to patterns of approved or sanctioned behavior, and that other terms should be used to denote the organizational aspects of such behavior and the group of persons involved.

Instead of limiting *institution* to specific social norms or rules—the Ten Commandments, laws against murder or burglary, business practices, or conventions governing daily social intercourse—some writers view an institution as a set of interrelated norms, a "normative system" centered around some type of human activity or some major problem of man in society such as providing subsistence and shelter (property, building techniques, "free enterprise"), caring for children (parenthood, the family), or maintaining order and harmony (the state). [13]

Whether one chooses this encompassing definition or the more limited one used in this volume is largely a semantic problem; there is no inherent correctness in either, and both refer to aspects of social life that are important and require analysis. The definition adopted here provides a generic concept for the variety of norms that govern social behavior: folkway, *mos* (the plural form, *mores,* is conventionally used), custom, convention, fashion, etiquette, law. The definition of *institution* as a "normative system" emphasizes the fact that the multiplicity of rules which govern the actions of men in society are tied together in a more or less organized fashion. There are, however, various ways of identifying (conceptualizing) these systems of norms—as clusters of rules that indicate how persons in particular positions in society, doctors or parents, for example, should act; as bodies of norms that organize the relations of people to one another in social groups; or in terms of their contribution to the performance of socially necessary or important tasks such as educating children or cultivating the soil.

One basic distinction among institutions is that between *folkways* and *mores,* concepts first employed by the pioneer American sociologist William Graham Sumner. A folkway is merely the conventional practice, accepted as appropriate but not insisted upon. The person who does not follow the rule may be looked upon as eccentric or merely as a staunch individualist who refuses to be bound by convention. The occasional man who objects to the irrationality of men's clothing, for example, and refuses under any circumstances to wear a tie is ignoring one of our folkways.

Mores are those norms, or institutions, which are morally strongly sanctioned. Conformity is enforced in various ways, and failure to conform elicits moral disapproval and frequently positive action. Examples are readily available: thou shalt not kill, thou shalt not steal, thou shalt love thy father and mother. Mores are looked upon as essential to the well-being of the group.

The line between folkways and mores is not always easy to draw. Clearly there is a kind of continuum, ranging from those conventions or customs that are loosely observed to those which are most insistently enforced. The rules governing modesty in dress or the consumption of wine and whiskey, for example, may be difficult to categorize. They elicit some moral disapproval if ignored or violated, but clearly do not carry the same moral sanction as adultery, theft, or murder. Moreover, there are wide differences in the attitudes of various social groups toward these rules.

Despite the absence of a sharp dividing line between them, the concepts of folkways and mores possess considerable heuristic value. They focus attention upon significant dimensions or aspects of social norms, the moral sanction attached to them, and the extent to which they are considered to be essential to social well-being.

A second dimension of institutions emerges from the contrast between *customs* and *laws*. The former comprise "long-established usage," those practices that have gradually become accepted as appropriate modes of behavior: the routines of work or leisure, the conventions of warfare, the rituals of religious observance, the etiquette governing social relationships. Customs are sanctioned by tradition and sustained by the pressures of group opinion. Laws, on the other hand, are rules enacted by those who exercise political power and they are enforced through the machinery of the state. They may or may not have the sanction of tradition. They are characteristic of complex societies with well-developed political systems; in those simple societies without distinctive political institutions and recognized sources of political authority law appears, if at all, only in embryonic form. In such simple societies behavior is regulated chiefly by custom, new rules are likely to emerge gradually rather than by formal enactment, and enforcement is not assigned to specific persons operating through a recognized governmental machinery.

The distinction between customs and laws cuts across folkways and mores. Some customs have the moral sanctions characteristic of the mores, while others are more or less casually accepted conventions. Similarly, some laws are supported by strong moral sentiments—thou shalt not kill—while others may virtually lack any moral support, except for whatever attitudes and sentiments sustain conformity with the law in general. Many laws regulating business practice fall into this latter category.

The line between custom and law, like that between folkways and mores, is not always easily drawn, particularly in simpler societies, in which the political structure from which law emerges and through which it is enforced is only partially developed. Even in more complex societies, like our own, the relations between law and custom are frequently complex and distinction between them difficult to draw. Some customary rules may be embodied in law, Sunday blue laws, for example, whose legal character has sometimes persisted after the customs which gave rise to legislative enactment have changed. Conversely, politically enacted rules may eventually gain an extra-legal, traditional sanction, a process which is clearly apparent in the history of American attitudes toward and sentiments about the Constitution. In addition, laws frequently acquire a barnaclelike accretion of customary practice which is as strongly enforced as though it were written into the law; witness the complex array of conventions and traditional practices governing the actions of Congress.

The concepts of custom and law do not encompass all forms of social norms. There are many institutions that do not seem to fit into either category, despite their apparent inclusiveness. The operating procedures of corporations and the rules of voluntary organizations such as the League of Women Voters, the National Association of Manufacturers, and the American Medical Association are, with some exceptions, neither sanctioned by tradition nor enforced by the state.

Despite these difficulties the conceptual distinction between law and custom does call attention to important differences in the origins of institutions and in the methods by which they are enforced. There are *crescive* institutions, to use another term drawn from Sumner, which, like Topsy, just grow, and those that are enacted and formally born at a given time. Clearly a different explanation will be required for the origin of a crescive than for an enacted institution, although the latter includes both laws and those formal rules promulgated by officials of nonpolitical organizations. The methods of enforcement may be largely informal, confined to the demands of tradition and the more or less subtly—or obviously—expressed opinions of others, or may be limited to the formal machinery of government, or may, to varying degrees, combine both mechanisms.

These categories for the analysis of institutions do not exhaust the complexity or variety of social norms, or their various aspects or dimensions. For the rules which govern behavior include the transitory standards of fad and fashion, the symbolic rituals of religious and patriotic observance, and the ceremonies which mark significant occasions. They include further the rules of scientific procedure sanctioned neither by tradition nor by legislative enactment, but only by the rationally based consensus of scientists and the empirically tested methods of rational economic enterprise, although all these rational norms may, of course, contain traditional or customary elements.

Institutions, we have said, account, in their many forms, for much of the regularity of behavior that we observe; it is because men possess these learned and shared standards that their actions seem to be alike, or at least similar. This statement, however, may suggest a degree of conformity that typically does not exist. Norms vary in the degree of conformity that they require, depending in some measure upon the nature of the approved or interdicted behavior. One cannot be just a little bit of a murderer. On the other hand, the amount of time which college students may be expected, or required, to devote to their studies may vary widely. The rules of dress, etiquette, and speech may be couched in such general terms that some variety will be expected within the limits set by the culture. In many cases, that is to say, the norms prescribe a range of behavior or set the limits beyond which it would be inappropriate or wrong to stray.

Even when the institution is precisely defined, the actual behavior of men and women is likely to vary around the norm from virtual nonconformity to elaborate overconformity. In many colleges and universities, for example, students are expected to devote two hours to study for each hour spent in class, or about thirty hours each week for a student carrying fifteen hours of class work. It is probably safe to say that most students do not meet this requirement; the actual time spent may vary from none to forty or fifty or even sixty hours per week, with an average probably somewhat less than thirty. Any analysis of institutions and behavior and the relations obtaining between them must therefore take into account the fact that both the definition of social norms and the description of actual conduct often refer to a range of behavior around some central tendency.

It is, of course, obvious that many institutions are often ignored in practice, that men break the Ten Commandments, do not give their seats to women in public conveyances, and doctor their income-tax returns. They defy the sex mores, disregard conventions governing work and play, and ignore the requirements of fashion. Indeed, the starting place for much sociological inquiry has been the effort to account for socially deviant activities—crime, delinquency, divorce, suicide—rather than for conventional behavior.

The fact that men do ignore or violate social norms indicates that conformity too cannot be taken for granted and must also be explained. When one accounts for patterned behavior by reference to cultural definitions of proper or expected behavior, one has taken only the first step in sociological analysis. Institutions are not self-enforcing, and it is necessary to discover why men conform to social rules, as well as ascertaining how institutions arise and what circumstances account for their persistence and for the changes that take place in them. In part, of course, men conform to social norms because they are taught to do so; they learn the customs and conventions of their culture as they are brought up and educated. In part, they conform because of sanctions, pressures, and controls which are institutionalized and built into the structure of society.

Ideas: beliefs, knowledge, and values

The second major component of culture, *ideas,* encompasses a varied and complex array of social phenomena. It includes the beliefs men hold about themselves and the social, biological, and physical world in which they live, and about their relations to one another, to society and nature, and to such other beings and forces as they may discover, accept, or conjure up. It embraces the whole vast body of ideas by which men account for their observation and experience—folklore, legends, proverbs, theology, science, philosophy, practical know-how—and which they take into account or rely upon in choosing alternative lines of action. It encompasses the forms in which men express their feelings about themselves and others and their responses, emotional and aesthetic, to the world around them.

In addition to cognitive and expressive ideas, men also learn and share the values by which they live, the standards and ideals by which they define their goals, select a course of action, and judge themselves and others: success, rationality, honor, courage, patriotism, loyalty, efficiency. These values are not specific rules for action but general precepts to which men give their allegiance and about which they are likely to have strong feelings. They represent as well the shared attitudes of approval and disapproval, the judgments of good or bad, desirable or undesirable, toward specific persons, things, situations, and events.

The term *value,* however, is sometimes used for the *objects* or *situations* which are defined as good, proper, desirable, worthwhile: for money, wives, jewelry, success, power, fame, rather than for shared sentiments or judgments. Values then acquire their character by virtue of men's judgments but are distinguished from them. It is this distinction that Robert M. MacIver emphasizes in differentiating between attitudes and interests, between the *"subjective* reactions, states of consciousness within the individual human being, with relation to *objects"* and the objects themselves.[14] Values, as things to which men assign desirability or importance, may then be beliefs or institutions, as well as the third general component of culture, material objects. The views men express as to the nature of God, or of man or society itself, may be subscribed to so intensely that they become objects of value; men may possess as strong an interest in their belief in God or their commitment to some scientific doctrine as they do in money or power. "For a vested interest in understanding," John K. Galbraith writes, "is more preciously guarded than any other treasure." [15] Similarly, institutions acquire value in men's eyes, and certainly many of the material objects created by men become the locus of approval or disapproval, desire or envy.

That men should evaluate their property, their laws and customs, ideas, and even themselves and others is perhaps inevitable as they make the choices inherent in social life. Viewing the same phenomenon from different conceptual perspectives —as instruments of production, rules governing behavior, or beliefs orienting man to nature and society, on the one hand, and as objects of value on the other—is not necessarily a source of confusion; it is rather a means for widening our vision and increasing our understanding.

The ideas men share—cognitive, expressive, and evaluative—consist of a body of symbols through which they can communicate with one another. Communication is a fundamental social process, for it is only through the exchange of ideas that organized social life is possible. What distinguishes man from other creatures is the development of a symbolic language that goes beyond crude signs or signals which can convey only limited information or serve as direct stimuli to action. While other animals communicate through gestures and a relatively simple assortment of sounds, only man has evolved a language which can express abstract ideas and the complexities of emotional or aesthetic response. As the philosopher Ernst Cassirer has pointed out, what transformed Helen Keller from a blind deaf-mute capable only of very limited participation in social life into a fully human being was the flash of insight that words stood for things, that "everything has a name." [16] Symbolic language is both a basic constituent of culture and that

which makes its elaboration and cumulation possible.

Some writers would confine the term *culture* only to the body of ideas, the symbols that men share and through which they exchange meaningful communication, thus distinguishing it from the system or structure of social relationships. This definition can be very useful and appears to be gaining substantial currency among sociologists. It enables one to distinguish between symbolic systems—language, beliefs, knowledge, and expressive forms—and their interrelations in contrast to the organized pattern of interaction among individuals and groups. [17]

Material culture

The third major component of culture is perhaps the easiest to define. It consists of those material things that men create and use, ranging from the primitive instruments of prehistoric man to the most advanced machinery of modern man. It includes the stone ax and the electronic computer, the outrigger canoe of the Polynesians and the luxury liner, the teepee of the Indians and the skyscraper of the modern city.

To identify these material objects as elements of culture without reference to their nonmaterial concomitants, however, can easily be misleading. When we refer to such objects we are apt to take for granted their uses, their value, and the requisite practical or theoretical knowhow. Yet machines or tools obviously are hardly useful unless their owners possess the knowledge and skill needed to operate or apply them. The same objects may be put to many alternative uses. Rings, for example, may be worn on one's fingers, arms, or legs, or may be put through one's lips, nose, or ears; all these uses may be found among the peoples of the world. The Quonset huts so familiar to World War II veterans as barracks or office quarters have been subsequently used as homes, garages, storage buildings, barns, factories, and roadside hot-dog stands. In William Morris's Utopian novel, *News from Nowhere,* the Houses of Parliament are reduced to storage houses for dung.

With different uses, of course, go different evaluations and meanings. Paintings may be treasured and displayed or hidden in the attic, seen as great artistic achievements or the scribblings of eccentrics. Automobiles may be visible symbols of social standing or merely practical utilities which provide transportation. Two crossed pieces of wood may be a religious symbol or fuel to be burned in order to keep warm. The division between ideas—knowledge, values, traditional beliefs—and material culture, though often useful, is therefore in a sense quite arbitrary, for to describe cultural artifacts fully it is necessary to know their uses, the attitudes taken toward them, and the body of knowledge and skills needed to produce them.

The Organization of Culture

It has been necessary, in this description of the components of culture, to refer several times to the complex relationships which exist among the several elements that make up the whole, between institutions and values, for example, or between values and artifacts. These relationships constitute one significant focus of sociological analysis. This analysis may remain at the level of culture in general, or, more frequently, it can be directed toward *a* culture, the cluster or system of institutions, values, beliefs, and objects possessed by a particular group of people. Thus we may consider separately American culture, the culture of India, of the Trobriand Islanders of the Western Pacific, and of the many separate tribes, peoples, and nations of the world. It is only by comparing these specific cultures that we may eventually enlarge our understanding of culture in general.

The components of any particular cul-

ture are not randomly assorted, but form a more or less coherent whole. Institutions such as marriage, for example, must be seen in relation to the values that men and women pursue in family life, norms governing the division of labor, and the general values concerning the place of men and women and the rights of individuals. The structure of the culture—its organizing principles and the relations among the parts—is therefore relevant to an understanding of any specific cultural pattern.

The components of any culture, as well as the culture as a whole, can be thought of as consisting of more or less independent systems, each with its own structure or organization. There is in the mores, Sumner pointed out, "a strain toward consistency," and a similar tendency is to be found throughout the culture and within its components—institutions, values, expressive symbols, bodies of knowledge, technological systems. There is nothing automatic about these tendencies; they emerge because men characteristically try to reduce the tension or conflict generated by contradictory or competing demands or ideas, and to maintain some order in their relations with one another.

Role and Status

By establishing rules that govern behavior and values by which men judge their own actions and those of others, culture also defines the pattern of social interaction that binds men together in an organized social life. Of central importance in analyzing social interaction are the concepts of *role* and *status*. These concepts provide a link between the analysis of *society* and of *culture,* and are of considerable value in establishing the relationships between the individual and his culture and society.

The concepts of role and status derive from certain basic observations about the nature of institutions. As one considers the variety of social norms or standards of behavior it is apparent that relatively few of them apply universally to all people. Some apply only to limited groups, others only to one person. Some apply in one context in which an individual happens to be; others apply in different contexts. We find these points illustrated by one of our basic and presumably universal mores: thou shalt not kill. The person who commits murder is guilty of the most serious crime in the whole criminal calendar. If caught he may be subject to the extreme penalty, or at least to the maximum possible penalty. But this rule does not apply to certain people under specified circumstances. The policeman in pursuit of his duty, the public executioner carrying out the edict of a legally constituted court, the soldier in battle, even on occasion the husband betrayed—these may kill another person or persons without being subject to criticism or sanction. Nor do we define such killings as murder; our verbal distinctions reveal our social values. The central fact in these illustrations is that the rule does not apply to people who occupy certain *positions* in society. The terms used in our illustrations—policemen, public executioner, soldier, husband—refer to such positions, or, in sociological terms, *statuses*. Each of these statuses carries with it a set of rules or norms which prescribe how the person who occupies it should or should not behave under particular circumstances. That cluster of norms we call a *role*. Status and role are thus two sides of a single coin. Status is a socially identified position; role is the pattern of behavior expected or required of persons who occupy a particular status.

The concept of role is, of course, not new, as illustrated by Shakespeare's oft-quoted lines:

All the world's a stage,
And all the men and women merely players:
They have their exits and their entrances;
And one man in his time plays many parts,
His acts being seven ages.

These ages or, to use our modern and less poetic vocabulary, roles, included the infant, schoolboy, lover, soldier, "justice," "pantaloon," and lastly "second childishness."

The long ancestry of the idea of social role does not necessarily mean, however, that the concept has been systematically used in the past. One will frequently find that some concept can be traced back to Biblical or classical sources, or to the writings of philosophers or poets or novelists. Our earlier citations of Aristotle and of Adam Ferguson give evidence that many basic ideas have been available for a very long time, a fact that has sometimes given rise to the argument that sociology frequently offers nothing more than familiar knowledge in a new package. What is new about the concept of role, or of many other modern concepts which embody older ideas, is the attempt to organize knowledge systematically, to test ideas against an accumulation of evidence, and to further knowledge by pushing beyond the original perceptions. The atomic theory of matter, it has been pointed out, probably was first formulated by Democritus, but the ancient Greeks possessed no science of physics which enabled them to split the atom. That men play "many parts" is familiar, but the systematic analysis of the relations among them, the processes by which they are acquired and learned, the "strains" that may exist among the roles one plays, and the relationships between roles and personality provide fresh insight into behavior. Science consists not merely of acute and penetrating observations (as the social sciences are sometimes viewed) but of orderly and cumulative development of knowledge. It entails the integration of findings so that they do not remain the random perceptions of wise men, sometimes erroneous and sometimes only partly true, but become firmly established scientific lore available to all.

Nonetheless we can use Shakespeare's theatrical image to develop and explain the concepts of role and status. Theatrical roles performed by "players" exist independently of the individuals, who must learn their lines and acquire the appropriate gestures and manners. Social roles are also learned as men and women acquire the culture of their group, although roles may become so much a part of the individual personality that they are played without awareness of their social character. (It is interesting to note that professional actors have long argued about the extent to which they must "live" their parts in order to perform them well.[18] Roles are not people; they are the parts played on the social stage, and they can be analyzed separately just as the drama can be considered apart from the performance and the performers.

The elements of a social role are both obvious and subtle. We know, for example, what a teacher is supposed to do in his professional role: to transmit to his students some kind of information or skill, and to follow more or less acceptable and understood methods of doing so. But in some communities a teacher also has been expected to avoid tobacco and liquor, and female teachers are not expected to wear slacks in public. In a study of the sex roles of college women it was reported that many of them "played dumb," belittled their intellectual achievements, and submitted to male leadership and authority when on dates because they felt that this was what men expected of them.[19] In an investigation of local union leadership in the United Automobile Workers it was discovered that union officers were expected to give no evidence of personal ambition. "The worst that can be said of a union leader is that he is an 'opportunist,' or that he is 'ambitious.' "[20]

As these illustrations suggest, many features of a social role are only implicit. As social actors men become aware of some of the rules which govern their behavior only when others disregard them or when the question of ignoring or violating them comes up. An important task of sociology is to discover not only the obvious and explicit norms which define and regulate men's actions but also those which usually remain hidden beneath the surface.

Men can be said to play or perform social roles; they fill or occupy statuses. Status is a kind of social identification tag which places people in relation to others and which also always implies some kind of role. Each man occupies many statuses and plays many roles. A man is a husband or bachelor or widower, a business executive or factory worker or professional, a Catholic or Protestant or Jew. He is a community leader or an ordinary citizen, a baseball fan, an avid fisherman, an amateur photographer. Each of these identifications constitutes a status and carries with it expectations of behavior, however precisely or vaguely defined, however rigidly or loosely enforced.

How a person behaves, therefore, depends in large part upon the particular position in which he finds himself—or in which he would like to be—and the role expectations that go with it. For example, a teacher is expected to disregard the sex of his students in assigning or evaluating their academic work. (The occasional teacher-student marriage indicates that sometimes the teacher has failed to ignore the sex of at least one of his students or, more likely, that teacher and student have encountered one another outside the classroom where they could disregard their academic roles and behave as male and female—although these are also socially defined roles and not merely biologically shaped patterns of behavior.) The tight-fisted businessman who is very generous in his contributions to charity and the hard-boiled racketeer who treats his wife, children, and aged mother with love and affection are not necessarily illustrative of hypocrisy or split personality, nor is the Indian warrior who carefully protected his loved ones by joyfully removing the scalps of his enemies. They are all behaving at different times in ways appropriate to the particular statuses they happen to be occupying and the roles they are playing. When a man refuses to raise the wages of his employees or sets out ruthlessly to take business away from his competitor, perhaps even to drive him out of business, he is acting as a businessman; in responding to an appeal from some charity he is behaving as a respected and influential member of the local community. The racketeer may shed his "business" role when he crosses his threshold in the evening.

The importance of social roles lies not only in the extent to which they regulate behavior, but also in the fact that they enable men to predict the actions of others and therefore to fashion their own actions accordingly. Social relationships therefore exist between or among the roles played by members of a society. These relationships are not only indirectly defined by values which provide general standards of behavior—courtesy, respect, obedience—but also by specific institutional prescriptions which indicate how occupants of defined statuses are expected to behave toward one another. Judges are not supposed to give preference to a litigant in a court on the basis of his age, sex, religion, wealth, or color (unless such preference is legally defined). Children are expected to follow their parents' rules as to when they go to bed, whether or not they can go out to play, and what they should eat for dinner. Men should tip their hats to women, walk on the outside of the sidewalk when accompanying women, and rise when a woman enters the room.

As our illustrations may suggest, roles and statuses are built upon various kinds of foundations. Certain biological facts provide the basis for differentiating some roles and statuses. In every society different roles are built upon the facts of age and sex. We distinguish, for example, infant, child, adolescent, adults of different varieties—young adults, the middle-aged, the old. In every society men and women occupy distinct positions and are expected

to behave differently, even to vary in character and personality, although societies differ widely in their definitions of sexual roles. Other biological features are sometimes, though not universally, seized upon as the basis for distinct statuses and roles. In Western society, as Talcott Parsons has shown in some detail, the ill person occupies a definite position which permits, encourages, and even requires certain kinds of behavior.[21]

But most roles and statuses emerge from the process of collective living itself. There is always some economic division of labor which entails the differentiation of positions and duties. As men deal with problems of maintaining order and harmony in society there develop distinct political roles and statuses: congressman, M.P., commissar, mayor, party chairman, precinct captain, judge. Religious practices and beliefs provide other grounds for social differentiation: priest, monk, nun, bishop, minister, deacon, rabbi. As societies grow larger and more complex, new positions and new expectations of behavior emerge: movie star, astronaut, probation officer, nursery school teacher, computer programmer, propagandist, atomic physicist, go-fors (errand boys for theatrical producers and directors), beatniks, *tummlers* (social directors in Catskill Mountain resorts—a "versatile *jongleur,* who performed frenetically around the clock and twice as fast on rainy days to keep restive guests from checking out" [22]), and countless others.

Among the many statuses men may come to occupy, we may distinguish those which are *ascribed* and those which are *achieved.* An ascribed status derives from attributes over which a person has no control—age, sex, or color, for example—or from membership in a group to which he is assigned by others—family, religion, nationality. On the basis of an ascribed status he is expected to acquire and perform certain roles. An achieved status is entered upon by some direct or positive action: One must get married in order to become a husband or wife, secure a majority of votes cast to become a Congressman, or graduate from medical school in order to become a doctor. Ascription limits access to status positions: A man cannot become a woman, a Boston Irishman cannot become a Lowell or Cabot, an Indian untouchable can never be a member of the Brahmin caste. Insofar as the number of persons who can fill a particular status is restricted—only a limited number of students are admitted to medical school, only one person at a time can be President, not everyone can rise to the top in industry—potential occupants must compete, demonstrating in some fashion their abilities to perform the relevant role.

One of the more significant aspects of a status is the value placed upon it, the respect or prestige it carries in the eyes of others. Each position—and its correlative role—is ranked by members of a society as superior or inferior. Doctors in the United States, to take an obvious example, have a higher social standing than pharmacists, and toolmakers rank higher than farm laborers. In many societies warriors have been more highly esteemed than merchants or artisans. Thus Herodotus, the ancient Greek historian, observed: "The Thracians, the Scyths, the Persians, the Lydians, and almost all other barbarians, hold the citizens who practice trades, and their children, in less repute than the rest, while they esteem as noble those who are aloof from handicrafts, and especially honour such as are given wholly to war." In classical China, on the other hand, warriors were ranked below scholars.

Status is used frequently to refer only to the ranking of a social position or role, or of the occupants of such roles, and one major aspect of any society is the hierarchy of roles and of persons, which constitutes one aspect of its organization or structure. This ranking is sociologically important because it contributes to the ordering of social interaction and the structure of social relationships and provides motivation for various kinds of so-

cial behavior; the by now familiar term "status-seeking" refers to behavior designed to enhance one's social standing or lead to the acquisition of a more prestigious social position.

Groups, Categories, and Statistical Aggregates

The complex array of roles and statuses that define the behavior of individuals and their relations with one another constitutes what sociologists call *social organization* or *social structure*. The term *social structure* is used occasionally to refer to any patterned regularity of behavior or interaction. This latter use emphasizes the element of pattern in the term "structure," but we shall stress the element of relationship among parts implicit in the word.

Social organization, however, also contains a variety of interconnected and often overlapping groups of collectivities, each with its own particular structure of roles and statuses. In everyday conversation, *group* is usually applied indiscriminately to many different collections of people. A handful of mountaineers operating an illicit still in the Kentucky hills, members of a ladies' club, a teen-age gang in Harlem or the Bronx, a Boy Scout troop, the 60,000 or so workers at the Ford River Rouge plant, the more than a million members of the United Automobile Workers, and the employees of U. S. Steel are all likely to be called "groups." So are the President's Cabinet, the some 100,000 people who each year attend the Army-Navy football game, and the mob of irate southerners who surrounded Little Rock High School when Negro students first tried to enter its doors in September, 1957. Each nation is frequently identified as a group, as are the innumerable families, clans, moieties, and tribes found among primitive peoples. Members of the Catholic Church, Jews, government employees, a movie audience, beatniks, the rich and the poor, those earning from $4,000 to $5,000 a year, members of the

Democratic or Republican Party, the Communist Party of the Soviet Union, professors, electricians, bankers, men, women, fans of some popular singer or movie actress, readers of comic books or of sociology texts—each of these is likely to be labeled in ordinary conversation as a group. Within some of these "groups" there may be still others: The Catholic Church is divided into parishes and dioceses, into a number of religious orders such as the Dominicans, Franciscans, and Jesuits; it contains such distinct entities as the college of Cardinals and the Curia Romana (the papal administration). Within the government bureaucracy are the innumerable offices, bureaus, agencies, departments, and interdepartmental committees, as well as informal cliques and sets of friends. Political parties have their national and state committees, precinct organizations, and factions; labor unions have locals, departments, and executive committees.

This legion of groups is obviously so diversified that it would be difficult, if not impossible, to characterize them in general terms. A family, with its relatively limited numbers, its recognized roles and statuses, and its sense of corporate identity clearly differs in important ways from the Catholic Church, with its elaborate hierarchical organization and its millions of members who share a set of beliefs and values and follow the same religious practices; from electricians or bankers who possess the same status but have little if any awareness of a collective identity; and from admirers of a popular singer who are grouped together simply because they share a single attribute. Sociologists therefore face the task of distinguishing types of human collectivities and establishing a precise language for their analysis.

As a first step in performing this task we may distinguish among social groups, social categories, and statistical aggregates.

A social group consists of a number of persons whose relationships are based upon a set of interrelated roles and statuses. They interact with one another in a more or less standardized fashion determined largely by the norms and values they accept. They are united or held together by a sense of common identity or a similarity of interests which enables them to differentiate members from nonmembers. The social group then is identified by three attributes: patterned interaction, shared or similar beliefs and values, and, to use Franklin H. Giddings' phrase, consciousness of kind.

In defining a social group in this way we have narrowed the meaning conventionally assigned to it, limiting its reference and making it somewhat more precise. A family, according to this definition, is a group, as is a labor union, a social club, a number of friends who see one another occasionally, and the students of a college or university. Men, women, owners of television sets, adolescents, hoboes, and readers of *True Story* magazine are not social groups.

These collections of people who do not possess the attributes of a group can be separated in turn into two distinct divisions. One, which we may call a *social category,* consists of persons who have a similar status and therefore in this respect perform the same social role—for instance, men, electricians, adolescents, bankers, or hoboes. The second, which we call a *statistical aggregate,* is made up of persons who possess a similar social attribute by virtue of which they can logically be thought of together—the readers of comic books and readers of *Harper's Magazine,* addicts of rock and roll and admirers of Brigitte Bardot, baseball fans, jazz devotees, and persons who commit suicide.

Although sociologists are chiefly concerned with social groups and categories, statistical aggregates are also, inevitably, important subjects for analysis. Often we wish to explain why people fall into particular aggregates, or to account for the differences between them. Why do some people read *Harper's Magazine* while others read *True Story?* Why do some Englishmen read the pontifical London *Times* while others read the tabloid *Daily Express?* Who are the readers of detective stories, the admirers of rock and roll, the people who commit suicide, and those who become drug addicts? In answering these questions, structural facts—that is, some information about the groups to which men belong and the statuses they occupy—will usually be necessary. Protestants commit suicide more often than Catholics, readers of *Harper's* are more likely to be professionals than readers of *True Story,* adolescents are more likely to prefer rock and roll than are adults. These facts provide the beginning of explanations which require some further knowledge of the nature of the groups people come from and of the roles they play.

Statistical aggregates are also important because they sometimes point to significant aspects of social structure or provide the basis for the emergence of social groups. A common interest in baseball, for example, or in modern jazz or antiques may be one of the ties that bind a group of friends together. Respect for physical prowess may be the basis upon which teen-age gangs select their leaders. An income of more than $10,000 per year may enable its recipients to achieve positions of high reputability in the community. In some cases, persons with similar attributes coalesce into groups: Fans of a popular singer become a mob trying to tear the shirt off his back or, more quietly, join fan clubs; rabid racists establish Citizens' Councils, or ride out in white sheets to terrorize Negroes; admirers of George Bernard Shaw establish Shavian societies.

Social categories share with statistical aggregates potentialities for the emergence of full-fledged groups. Because of this fact Morris Ginsberg has lumped together as *quasi-groups*

such entities as social classes, which, without being groups, are a recruiting field for groups, and whose members have certain characteristic modes of behavior in common; and other

incipient groups such as collections of individuals interested in the same pursuits or favouring the same policy, for example, employers of labour who have not yet formed any association in the defense of their interests, or individuals interested in particular sports, or in social reform, who yet possess no definite organization.[23]

By virtue of their common physical attributes, Negroes, for example, can be classified as a statistical aggregate. To the extent that they are assigned a particular status in society they become a social category. Because of the difficulties caused by their position they have tended to become "race conscious," to form voluntary organizations to improve their circumstances. They seek to eliminate discrimination and constraints imposed upon them because they are Negroes and to achieve the status their individual abilities warrant. Some wish racial attributes to be reduced merely to characteristics of a statistical aggregate, whereas others try to establish a distinctive culture and social identity as the basis for a cohesive social group.

One task of the sociologist is to specify the conditions under which the transformation from category or aggregate to group takes place. What forces, for example, lead a social class to become conscious of its existence and problems and to act as a more or less cohesive whole? When do workers form unions, employers an employers' association, or consumers a league for the protection of their interests? Why do movie fans join clubs and professional men join civic associations and professional societies?

The concepts of group, category, and statistical aggregate are sometimes difficult to apply to specific collections of people. Although many human aggregations are readily subsumed under one or another of these concepts, others are ambiguous in character and defy ready classification. From one point of view American physicians are merely a social category, from another they constitute a highly organized and powerful association. Many members of a social class have little sense of a collective identity, but others may be strongly "class-conscious" and seek to develop class-based organizations. Advocates of a proposed reform may be in process of establishing a new political group, and members of an emerging profession may be hesitantly feeling their way toward formation of a professional society.

These concepts, then, serve chiefly as heuristic devices, that is, they suggest questions and direct inquiry. Discussion in general terms of groups, social categories, and statistical aggregates takes us but a short step in the direction of systematic analysis. Merely determining that a particular collection of people is one or the other provides only a minimal beginning for systematic study; after this determination has been made one must proceed to account for the existence of a statistical aggregate, or explore the nature of a particular category and its significance for society, or analyze the structure and functions of a social group.

The definition of a social group is also essentially of heuristic value: It calls attention to significant variables which must be examined. Interaction, values, solidarity, the defining characteristics of social groups, are, after all, variable; they do not possess a fixed "value," if we may borrow mathematical terminology. There may be more or less interaction among persons who stand to one another in diverse kinds of relationships. Members of a group may subscribe to only one norm or belief or many, or may hold to their ideas with differing degrees of intensity. Members may be strongly or weakly identified with each other; the group, that is, may be more or less solidary. Each of these variables must then be examined and its relationship to others determined.

.   .   .

NOTES

1. Charles H. Cooley, *Human Nature and the Social Order,* New York: Scribner, 1902, p. 33 *n.*

2. Adam Ferguson, *Essay on the History of Civil Society* (7th ed.), Boston: Hastings, 1809, p. 4.

3. For a review of the literature on feral man see M. F. Ashley Montagu, *The Direction of Human Development,* New York: Harper, 1955, Ch. 11. For a detailed description and analysis of a case of a completely rejected child see Kingsley Davis, "Extreme Social Isolation of a Child," *American Journal of Sociology,* XLV (January, 1940), 554–565; and "Final Note on a Case of Extreme Isolation," *American Journal of Sociology,* LII (March, 1947), 432–447. A more recent report on a case of feral man is found in William F. Ogburn, "The Wolf Boy of Agra," *American Journal of Sociology,* LXIV (March, 1959), 449–454. A suggestive psychological interpretation of feral man is offered by Bruno Bettelheim, "Feral Children and Autistic Children," *American Journal of Sociology,* LXIV (March, 1959), 455–467.

4. For a detailed review of the meanings assigned to "culture," both past and present, see Alfred L. Kroeber and Clyde Kluckhohn, *Culture, a Critical Review of Concepts and Definitions,* New York: Random House Vintage Books, n.d. For an account of the various ways in which "culture" has been used since the end of the eighteenth century and of its applications in social criticism rather than social science, see the stimulating and suggestive study by Raymond Williams, *Culture and Society,* New York: Doubleday Anchor Books, 1959.

5. Gladys Bryson, *Man and Society,* Princeton: Princeton University Press, 1945.

6. Jay Rumney and Joseph Maier, *Sociology: The Science of Society,* New York: Schuman, 1953, p. 74.

7. Georg Simmel, *Sociology,* trans. by Kurt H. Wolff, New York: Free Press, 1950, p. 10.

8. Ralph Linton, *The Study of Man,* New York: Appleton, 1936, p. 91.

9. Ralph Linton, *The Cultural Background of Personality,* New York: Appleton, 1945, p. 125.

10. R. R. Marett, *Anthropology* (rev. ed.), London: Oxford, 1944, p. 183.

11. Talcott Parsons, *Essays in Sociological Theory,* New York: Free Press, 1949, p. 203.

12. William Graham Sumner, *Folkways,* Boston: Ginn, 1906, pp. 53–54.

13. See Kingsley Davis, *Human Society,* New York: Macmillan, 1949, p. 71.

14. Robert M. MacIver and Charles H. Page, *Society: An Introductory Analysis,* New York: Rinehart, 1949, p. 24.

15. John Kenneth Galbraith, *The Affluent Society,* Boston: Houghton Mifflin, 1958, p. 9.

16. Ernst Cassirer, *An Essay on Man,* New York: Doubleday Anchor Books, 1953, pp. 53–55.

17. A. L. Kroeber and Talcott Parsons, "The Concepts of Culture and of Social System," *American Sociological Review,* XXIII (October, 1958), 582–583.

18. See, for example, the selections by William Archer, Constant Coquelin, and Konstantin Stanislavsky in Toby Cole and Helen Krich Chinoy (eds.), *Actors on Acting,* New York: Crown, 1949.

19. Mirra Komarovsky, "Cultural Contradictions and Sex Roles," *American Journal of Sociology,* LII (November, 1946), 184–189.

20. Ely Chinoy, "Local Union Leadership," in Alvin W. Gouldner (ed.), *Studies in Leadership,* New York: Harper, 1950, p. 168.

21. Talcott Parsons, *The Social System,* New York: Free Press, 1951, pp. 439–447.

22. For an amusing characterization of the *tummler* see David Boroff, "The Catskills: Still Having Wonderful Time," *Harper's Magazine,* July, 1958, pp. 56–63.

23. Morris Ginsberg, *Sociology,* London: Butterworth, 1934, pp. 40–41.

7. A NORMATIVE THEORY OF CULTURE

GERTRUDE JAEGER *and* PHILIP SELZNICK

In this article, Gertrude Jaeger and Philip Selznick claim that the time has come for consideration of a rapprochement between the concept of culture as generally defined by social scientists on the one hand and the humanists on the other. They argue that a better theoretical foundation for the sociology of culture may be achieved by emphasis on: 1) the psychic source of culture in the quest for person-centered meanings and authentic experience, 2) symbolic elaboration as a major resource for, and product of, this quest for meaning, and 3) the esthetic potential in symbolization as well as in consummatory experience.

According to Jaeger and Selznick "to participate in culture is to be implicated in a system of symbolic meaning. The content of that system, and its quality, obviously make a difference for the way men think and behave."

Gertrude Jaeger is a sociologist at the University of California at Berkeley, coeditor of Major Social Problems (*1959*), *and coauthor of* The Apathetic Majority (*1966*) *and* The Tenacity of Prejudice (*1969*). *Her husband, Philip Selznick, is Professor of Sociology at the University of California at Berkeley. He is the author of* TVA and the Grass Roots (*1949*), The Organizational Weapon (*1952*), *and* Leadership in Administration (*1957*). *With Leonard Broom, he is coauthor of* Sociology (*1955*).

Few ideas in American social science have had so marked and pervasive an influence as the concept of culture. In its now familiar form, a somewhat crude and inelegant formulation has won the assent of most social scientists. It has also gained increasing currency among large sections of the educated public. Whatever our reservations, we cannot doubt that the idea of culture has met an intellectual and moral need, has advanced the growth of social studies, and has helped bring at least two generations of students to the brink of humility and self-knowledge.

Nevertheless, for many years we have felt a sense of disquiet with the social science meaning of culture, and we suspect that we are not entirely alone. This paper indicates some of the sources of that unease and offers a restatement of one intellectual position that, in our view, provides a more subtle and compelling theory of the nature of culture.

The most striking feature of conventional wisdom on this subject is the barrier erected between a purportedly scientific concept of culture and the way the word is used in our natural language and in the humanities. The "humanistic" concept is often explicitly counterposed to the "anthropological," [1] and, as things have gone, for "anthropological" we may read "sociological." Indeed, the discussion of culture among sociologists, especially among teachers of sociology, is heavily anthropological in both spirit and substance.

One result of this separation is to make of "high culture"—roughly all that is encompassed in the arts and intellectual life

Reprinted from the *American Sociological Review*, **29** (1964), 653–669, by permission of the authors and the American Sociological Association.

—a theoretical orphan. Indeed, the very term "high" is at best a grudging concession to what we are invited to take as non-scientific discourse. The scientific rhetoric, tight-lipped and non-normative, brooks no invidious distinctions. To the non-normative scientist high culture is just a part, and not a very special part, of some particular cultural order. It is a kind of sub-culture, perhaps judged to be high and better by those who share it, but not necessarily higher or better for those who have not learned to value it. In such an intellectual setting, it has been difficult to develop an adequate theory of high culture, and of its relation to the rest of culture.

For purposes of this discussion we have tried to find a formulation that would meet the following requirements:

1. retain the large merits of the now-conventional usage;
2. identify the distinctively cultural in human group life;
3. bridge the gap between social science and the humanities without subordinating either to the other;
4. overcome the theoretical split between research on "high culture" and more conventional studies of the cultural order;
5. suggest criteria for distinguishing the better from the worse.

In presenting this argument, we lean rather heavily on the philosophical perspective of John Dewey. In Dewey's pragmatism, and more particularly in his esthetic theory, may be found clues both to a normative theory of culture and to the basic continuity of culture and high culture.

Humanism and Anthropology

Let us begin by briefly reviewing a few salient differences between the humanistic and anthropological conceptions of culture. First, the humanist is selective. He separates out a segment of man's activities, interests, and products and designates them as cultural. Not every lasting product of group life is cultural, nor is culture something people automatically have because they live in society. By contrast, the anthropological view is non-selective. Culture is the entire social heritage. As Kroeber put it, culture is "that which the human species has and other social species lack . . . speech, knowledge, beliefs, customs, arts and technologies, ideals and rules . . . what we learn from other men, from our elders and the past, plus what we may add to it." [2] While this non-selective approach, following the lead of E. B. Tylor, is not always adhered to, it remains the dominant view.

The crudely omnibus character of the anthropological definition is partly justified by a special intellectual history. Until fairly recently, a chief theoretical concern for anthropology was to set off the cultural from the biological and in doing so to affirm the great impact of group experience on how men live, what they desire, and what becomes of them. In countering biological determinism, the anthropologist was undertaking a task of no particular interest to the humanist. The latter takes for granted that man owes everything to his history. For him the scientific issue is to understand the *quality* of culture and to account for variations in its forms and achievements. This difference in scholarly interest, in what is taken as problematic, accounts for much of the contrast in emphasis and conception.

Thus a second feature of the humanist's view of culture is that it is normative and evaluative. For him it makes sense to say that some people are more cultured than others and that some societies are more richly endowed with culture than others. The humanist is committed to the view— though he may hesitate to embrace it openly—that at least some universal values exist and that objective judgments of value may be warranted in inquiry. He denies that his assessments of culture, when based on responsible and scholarly investigation, are ethnocentric. Implicit in the humanist concept is the belief that ethnocentrism is a *variable,* not a gross brute fact of life—that groups and societies differ in the degree to which they produce ethnocentrism or, instead, encourage a broad appreciation for universal values. The anthropologist assumes a quite different posture. Fearful of the sin of ethnocentrism, he eschews evaluation. For him assertions that some people are more cultured than others or that some cultures may be assessed as better or richer than others are nonsensical. To be human is to have a culture. We are all equally human and we are all equally cultured. Since culture is the entire precipitate of group experience, it cannot be seen as embodying a distinctive good or a distinctive set of human potentialities.

For anthropologists judgments concerning the worth of cultures are necessarily ethnocentric. In logic, though perhaps not in practice, they believe that ethnocentrism is absolute and does not vary. If we judge another culture negatively, this is because our own culture has not taught us the values shared by the other culture; if we had the values of the other culture we would judge it positively. If we judge another culture positively, this is because at some point there is a convergence of cultural values. Thus even when values are transcultural, it is impossible to escape the closed circle of ethnocentrism. We are all culture-bound, and equally so.

These contrasting views reflect a similar moral impulse but a different educational strategy. It would be naive to suppose that the anthropological standpoint is single-mindedly scientific. On the contrary, much of anthropology has been a humanist revel, a lyrical celebration of man's common humanity, his uniqueness, his creativity, his universal capacity to fashion a moral identity. Without derogating the scientific component of anthropological investigation, surely its main motif

must be read as an affirmation of humane values.

Nowhere is the moral and educational aim of social science more clearly manifest than in the commitment to cultural relativism. In its dramatic demonstrations of cultural diversity, anthropology discovered a rich educational resource. This led to a characteristic strategy. Much would be gained for tolerance, for sympathetic understanding, for a deeper sense of human community, if the student were deeply impressed with the many different paths to group survival and to valued ways of life. At the same time, of course, he would be taught that, as a warrant of their common humanity, all men need and deserve respect despite their diverse habits and customs. Through this exquisite combination of an avowed relativism and an implicit universalism anthropology sought —and offered—a spiritual prophylactic, a way of escaping the sin of pride.

Signs of Convergence

Can there be a rapprochement between the humanist and the social science conceptions of culture? We think that this is both possible and desirable. It may even be likely. A number of trends in the recent history of social science contribute to that end.

1) Among these developments is a disposition within anthropology itself to formulate the meaning of culture in more selective, less omnibus terms. When Kluckhohn defined culture as "the distinctive way of life of a group of people, their complete design for living," [3] he was being selective, in at least two ways. First, such a formula is not really equivalent to the totality of socially learned behavior. Not everything socially transmitted is equally important to a society's distinctive way of life. The search here is for some organizing principle or set of principles, perhaps not exactly an ethos but something close to it. In this sense the aim of anthropolog-

ical study is not a complete ethnographic description but a theory of what gives the society at hand its special character.

We should also take seriously the conception of culture as a *"design* for living." A design for living is a set of implicit and explicit standards which, in any society, can be only approximately embodied in action. The society has its ideal father, son, workman, and friend, but the observed role, and even the learned role, may be a far cry from the cultural ideal. Whatever the theoretical ambiguities, and the bland, non-committal character of the textbook definitions, it is hard to escape the conclusion that, even for the anthropologist, culture has some special and intimate connection with what a society considers ideal. This concern for cultural *ideals* is at least an important step in the direction of the humanist view.

A more explicitly selective usage has been recommended by A. L. Kroeber and Talcott Parsons. In 1958 a joint communiqué announced their agreement on the desirability of distinguishing between culture and society.[4] (For "society" may be substituted such terms as "social system," "social organization," "social structure," or even "social relations.") Kroeber and Parsons recognized, of course, that the distinction they had in mind was already fairly commonplace, but their statement has the form of an authoritative utterance, a self-conscious effort to influence the course and content of social science theory.

Kroeber and Parsons recalled that in the anthropological tradition of Tylor and Boas culture designated all of human social behavior "that was independent of the genetic constitutions and biological characteristics of organisms."[5] The important nineteenth-century task, they asserted, was to distinguish social heredity from biological heredity, and in this task both sociologists and anthropologists cooperated. To designate what was "superorganic" the former used the omnibus term "society" and the latter the equally omnibus term

"culture." Both terms were roughly equivalent. This worked well enough, for a while. But now a distinction seems appropriate, based apparently on the more selective usage actually informing the more recent work of anthropologists and sociologists alike.

Here are the proffered definitions. "We suggest that it is useful to define the concept *culture* for most usages more narrowly than has been generally the case in the American anthropological tradition, restricting its reference to transmitted and created content and patterns of values, ideas, and other symbolic-meaningful systems as factors in the shaping of human behavior and the artifacts produced through behavior. On the other hand, we suggest that the term *society*—or more generally, *social system*—be used to designate the specifically relational system of interaction among individuals and collectivities."[6] The idea of social system is passed over lightly in this version, but it is obvious that the definition of culture was put together with more than a little sweat.

At this point we may note what Kroeber and Parsons take to be central to the idea of culture. The key terms are, of course, "values, ideas and other symbolic-meaningful systems." In this they come close to an older tradition in the study of culture. Sorokin distinguished the social and the cultural in much the same way, and the position of Alfred Weber on "civilization" and "culture," put forward in this country by R. M. MacIver, shows a similar emphasis.[7]

We find, in short, that a) a selective rather than an omnibus view of culture has support in recent commentary, and b) what is selected gives prominence to the ideal, the symbolic, and the meaningful.

2) Another trend of importance to the potential convergence of humanist and social science perspectives is the closer study of differential socialization. The discussion of socialization had for many years, and to some extent still has, a polemical im-

port. It has been another way of downgrading biological factors and emphasizing the dependence of man on social learning. Here again a moral impulse is affirmed. A recognition of the variety of human settings within which socialization takes place would encourage humane and civilized attitudes. But as these lessons have been taken for granted, and as social psychology has turned to more detailed and problem-oriented investigation, there has resulted a greater sensitivity to the unevenness of socialization, to the way this vital process varies in effectiveness under varying conditions. Some people are more socialized than others and this outcome depends in large measure on the character and quality of the agencies of cultural transmission. It is not only that people are socialized in different ways into a different content. It is rather that, within any given setting, some people are more committed to, more aware of, more sensitive to, more capable of participating in the ideals of the groups to which they belong and into which they are more or less effectively socialized. More drastically, some groups and social situations are simply inadequate to the task of socialization; at best they cannot transmit the ideals of the larger society; at worst they produce people radically incapable of genuine social participation.[8]

George H. Mead was primarily concerned with spelling out in detail the sense in which the self is always and ineluctably social. It is sometimes forgotten, however, that Mead included in his theory of self some propositions about growth and development. He understood at least some aspects of the difference between the enlargement of self and its restriction. He was not content to affirm that the self is a product of social experience. He went beyond this basic insight to ask questions about the quality of selfhood as that is related to the capacity of the group and the individual to transcend what is narrowing and stultifying and to embrace a perspective both liberating and liberal.[9]

Some students of society may continue to affirm that it is always content and never quality that is at stake in socialization. They will interpret delinquency, for example, as merely a different kind of behavior, aspiration, and belief resulting from differential association. On the other hand, there is an older and continuing tradition which distinguishes between "pathological" and other forms of deviance and interprets some kinds of socialization as not only different but faulty or incomplete.

Sociological interest in inadequate socialization is closely related to that portion of personality theory concerned with the quality of experience. Although even G. H. Mead sensed the reality of psychic impoverishment, it was Freud who really paid attention to it and provided a theoretical foundation for its study. Modern dynamic psychology has provided significant insights into the variety and complexity of human adaptation. In contrast to the pragmatist tradition, Freudian and neo-Freudian investigators have emphasized that adaptation is no necessary warrant of psychic growth or fulfillment. On the contrary, adaptation may be involuted and distorted, crippled and brutalized, spirtually withdrawn, socially incompetent. These findings, reaffirming common sense, have helped dim the optimistic visions of the recent past. They have reminded a sobered epoch that socialization, whatever else it may be, is a precarious venture and, to a large extent, a healing art.

Qualitatively considered, effective socialization produces high levels of personal and social competence. The well-tempered, well-socialized man is no small achievement. He is marked by sensibility, sophistication, and psychic adequacy. He understands the nuances of code and custom, the purposes that guide collective action, the spirit as well as the letter of the law. His is the "mature ego," capable of accepting frustration, governing irrational fears, making psychic commitments, sticking to the task at hand, and all the rest. Viewed in this light, the more cultured person is one for whom social participation is meaningful in the sense that he can appreciate, act out, and perhaps teach whatever richness there may be in the experience. This he cannot do without sensibility and sophistication; the integrity and worth of the experience are threatened if he lacks psychic adequacy.

The closer we come to the heart of culture, to the modes of thought and feeling that lend unity to diversity and define a way of life, the more important is sophistication and sensibility to the well-socialized man. In this there is more than a hint of convergence between the humanist ideal and the prescriptions of the clinical sociologist and psychologist.

3) Perhaps the most important line of study suggesting a convergence between the humanist and the social science views of culture is the work on mass society and mass culture. The attempt to understand mass society has inevitably directed attention to the quality of man's relatedness to other men and to symbols. Atomization, standardization, superficiality, alienation, apathy, compulsive conformity—this is the grim language of mass-society theory. Although "mass" suggests quantity, in fact most writing in this area reflects a concern for the quality of social and cultural participation. A persistent question is the effect of technology on the integrity of culture, that is, the capacity of values to retain their strength and subtlety in the face of widespread dehumanization of work and communication.

Humanist and anthropologist alike must see in mass society the principle of anticulture. Of the lessons of our age not least important is the truth that society can persist despite the attenuation of cultural meaning, the emptying-out of symbols, the transformation of institutions into organizations. It is possible to see much that is benign in mass society and to prefer the present, with all its shortcomings, over a past that had its own great limitations.

However we decide on that score, we must still confront the evidence that what anthropologists think of as a "valued way of life" has a hard time surviving in the world described by theorists of mass society.

The student of mass society offers small comfort to the doctrine of cultural relativism. Far from being trapped in ethnocentrism, the social scientist finds himself engaged in a critical interpretation of his own culture and, by extension, of any other that shows similar pathologies. At the same time, his diagnosis reaches to the core of humanist concern.

In the light of these trends, the time has come for a more thoroughgoing discussion of the theory of culture. The intellectual foundations for a more acceptable approach have long since been laid down. We propose to reopen the discussion and to restate the guidelines we think should be followed.

The Culture-Creating Act

To understand culture we must take a long step backward from its more obvious manifestations. We must look first to the *source* of culture and this we shall find in human nature and the human condition. A theory of the distinctively cultural must rest on an underlying model of persistent and universal human needs, aspirations, and mechanisms. This psychic bundle, in its encounter with characteristic environing conditions, produces the repetitive outcomes we call culture.

The primordial culture-creating act is the transformation of an impersonal setting into a personal one. We speak here of the beginning of culture, of its rudiments and roots, and not of its end. Although it is not often put this way, in fact a great deal of sociological study is devoted to this elementary striving. It might be said, indeed, that for the sociologist one of the most significant human experiences is man's encounter with impersonality. This anguished confrontation is not the whole of life, nor is it the foundation of everything social; but it does produce much of what is interesting to us in the reconstruction of the self and the social environment.

It cannot be said that man has a constant and uniform need to avoid impersonality. Obviously, impersonal relations are not only tolerated but actively desired and maintained. They have protective value for the individual and they are important to effective social organization. But there is a latent source of energy in most human groups that derives from the widespread disposition to break the bonds of impersonality, to spill over the boundaries of narrowly defined roles, to make the setting more satisfactory to the actor as a unified organic and psychic being. Perhaps the clearest warrant of this phenomenon is the work that must be put into the maintenance of impersonal relations in formal organizations. In this special sense, the formal system of organization is "unnatural." It requires self-conscious effort to maintain a disciplined and compartmented way of life, one that is alien to at least some of man's natural impulses.

This does not mean that every effort to relieve the pain and peril of impersonality has a cultural outcome. There are many ways of resisting the impersonal, including rage and destructiveness, the search for protective cover, the claim to personal favor or prerogative. These may have nothing to do with culture. The culture-creating act is more than an emotional response, surely more than flight, more also than a manipulative gambit. It is an effort to make the world rich with personal significance, to place the inner self upon the stage, to transform narrow instrumental roles into vehicles of psychic fulfillment. It implicates the self and strives to invest the environment with subjective relevance and meaning. In an older tradition we might have referred to this investment as "the objectification of spirit."

It has often been said: culture is the adjustment man makes to his environment; a culture is "the sum of men's adjustments to their life-conditions." [10] Culture is indeed a product of adaptation. But it would be better to say that culture is the adjustment of society to man *qua* man. Not every result of individual and social adaptation is culture. Not every human action implicates the self, nor is every human quest a quest for meaning. Man *qua* man is this actor and this seeker. He is, if you like, meaning-seeker and meaning-maker. He is existentialist man, for whom problems of commitment and authenticity, meaning and alienation, pose the unspoken issues of everyday life.

These ideas find some support in John Dewey's analysis of experience. We refer to his ideas, not as a complete theory, but as helpful starting points for the reopened discussion. Dewey's theory is inadequate because he never was able to make the leap from a biological model to a genuinely psychological one. Therefore his approach to self-involvement remains implicit and rudimentary. Nevertheless, his normative concept of experience is apt and helpful. And it offers a link, which Dewey himself made, to cultural participation and the cultural order.

Dewey's life-long emphasis on man as an adjustive being and on the need to bring scientific method to human choice did not imply that his only concern was with the efficacy of the means man uses to solve his problems. His additional and more distinctive concern for the interdependence of means and ends led him to the persistent query: what do men get out of the instruments they use, what payments do they receive in the coin of immediate satisfaction? Dewey was no great friend of the deferred gratification. To him, the quality of experience on the road to a remote end should have its own warrant in immediate satisfaction and fulfillment.

In his analysis of differences in the quality of experience, Dewey distinguished between experience-in-general and "having an experience." [11] We all single out events in which we have participated that we remember and speak of as *an* experience. Something aroused and held our interest, touched us deeply, engaged our emotions, focused our attention, stimulated some wholehearted response. *An* experience stands out as a unified segment of experience-in-general, distinguished from a background of the routine, the habitual, the stereotyped, the boring, from all the beginnings that go nowhere, from the aimless, the merely conventional, the indecisive, the unengaging.

In effect, Dewey was distinguishing between existing and living, between "going through the motions" and having a sense of heightened vitality. The distinction is a normative one, but it is not arbitrary or culture-bound. Having an experience in Dewey's sense is naturally and spontaneously valued. It is not the only human value, nor is it always given highest priority. But it is part of our common humanity that having an experience, with its qualities of vitality, response, interest, awareness, and meaningfulness, will be prized and sought. And to be denied the opportunity of experience is to suffer deprivation.

The capacity to have an experience—in contrast to merely existing and passively reacting to internal and external excitation—is not unique to man. Dewey argues that the hungry animal stalking its prey is in a different state of being from the animal that is merely reacting to chance stimuli of no great moment. [12] The urgency of biological need transforms the animal into something that is experiencing itself and its environment in some total way rather than merely reacting in segmental and superficial ways. Hunger implicates the animal in its entirety. It also transforms a hitherto neutral and emotionally indifferent environment into one that is alive with significance for the organism—into a setting of cues and hints, portents and omens, threats and promises. The environment becomes suffused with subjective meaning. It has both import and importance for the organism.

Dewey's fundamental interest is epistemological: in opposition to the dominant empiricist tradition, he asserts the ultimate interdependence of cognition and valuation. In the primeval act of biological adaptation, there is no distinction between recognition of things as objective signs and instrumentalities and recognition of things as subjective threats and promises. Indeed, if anything, cognitive discriminations wait on—they are existentially grounded in—discriminations of feeling and response.

For Dewey experience and meaning are emotional as well as cognitive. Meaning is not to be taken in a rationalist sense, as a product of merely cognitive awareness and interpretation. Meaning is meaning for the organism in its subjective wholeness, as a responsive unity. This is, of course, fundamental in Dewey's philosophy, which places great weight on subjectively experienced disequilibrium and on the ultimate unity of cognitive and emotional outcomes.

Although Dewey's approach is correct in the main, he characteristically does not pay enough attention to the discontinuities between man and the other organisms. Granted that many species have experiences and apprehend meanings, the human animal seems to have a distinctive disposition to seek out the meaningful and create vehicles to carry and sustain it. Man works upon his environment, both the physical and the social, to fashion a setting to which he can relate, and which can be related to him, as a person. This, as we have suggested, is the culture-creating act.

Culture and the Symbolic

The product of this activity is a world of symbols. Culture is created when, in the struggle against alienation, man transforms the instrumental and the impersonal, the physical and the organic, into a realm of evocative, expressive, person-centered meanings. No human resource is more impressive, none more subtle, than this remarkable capacity for symbolization.

It is not uncommon to speak of man as the symbol-making animal and to link the creation of symbols to the emergence of culture. But the theory of symbols, in philosophy as well as in sociology, remains inadequate to the task at hand. The main problem is a too ready reliance on an over-generalized notion of what symbols are and of the work they do.

Leslie White has stressed that man alone has culture because he is the only animal capable of creating symbols. White defines the symbol broadly as anything "the value or meaning of which is bestowed upon it by those who use it." [13] Thus he includes within his concept of symbol all "artificial" man-made signs. These encompass language (any word is a linguistic "symbol") as well as what we would call true cultural symbols, such as the Christian cross or the wearing of black to signify mourning. White's concept of the symbol is too broad, not only for our purposes but for his as well. As so often among anthropologists, he ties his discussion to a distinction between the sheerly biological order and the human order. But to raise man up it is sufficient to show that he can create language. Through language man transcends the limits of fixed biological and physical information systems. Significant as this capacity is, as a *foundation* of distinctively human achievement, it does not follow that language is necessarily part of a symbolic realm, in any significant theoretical meaning of symbol or symbolization. That man creates symbols is a capacity of another order, beyond the making of words and sentences. Language is essential to the emergence of mind and to transforming man from a reactive to a creative creature. But in itself language may be a bare-bones vehicle of communication, a technical artifact uninformed by —and making no contribution to—symbolically meaningful experience.

Perhaps our approach can be more sharply formulated if we distinguish three fundamental processes in the theory of signs: 1) *indication,* 2) *denotation,* and 3) *connotation.*

1) Because ours is a world of causality, any object or event, including an utterance, may function as a "natural sign," that is, as a probabilistic indicator of something else. Dark clouds are natural signs of rain. Birds at sea are a natural sign of nearby land. Death is a natural sign of disease. High personnel turnover is a natural sign of low morale. Obviously, such signs may be misleading and their efficacy depends upon objective empirical connections. Furthermore, that an event is taken as a sign is a human, and usually a social, decision. But for the most part language plays no special role in the realm of natural signs.

2) In denotation, as opposed to indication, there may be no connection in causality between the sign and its referent. Even if there is a connection, that is not the warrant of the sign. A denotative sign may be an object, as in the case of a tree that marks a boundary, but the characteristic denotative sign is a word. In the usual case the word "pencil" denotes a class of objects—or, as Susanne Langer insists, the idea of a pencil [14]—and in doing so exhausts its function.

3) The word "teacher" may *de*note one who occupies a position on a faculty, but the same word *con*notes a wide and not-fully-specified set of suggestions and overtones, such as authority, knowledge, wisdom, etc. That language has connotative as well as denotative meaning is familiar to common sense. What needs only to be added is that objects, too, can have connotative meaning. As a natural sign, the natural event, cloud, designates the presence of the natural event, rain. But clouds may be associated with a variety of ideas as well, and insofar as they are, they have connotative and not merely indicative meaning.

It is this capacity of objects and words to connote, rather than simply indicate and denote, that is the source of their capacity to symbolize. By itself, however, connotation does not add up to symbolization. An object or word may simply trigger a series of arbitrary associations, and these might be thought of as its connotations for a particular person at a particular time. A minimal condition of any sign, however, whether indicative, denotative, or connotative, is that there be some stability between the sign and its referent.

A sign becomes a symbol when the sign is responded to directly as a carrier of connotative meaning.[15] The symbolic world is inherently opaque. Insofar as the object functions as an indicative or denotative sign, it is "transparent." We do not respond to such a sign save by noting what it points to. It does not enter into our lives as a constitutive part of "an experience." If the sign arouses feeling, it does so only in its denotative capacity. It points to a possible experience—as clouds, after a drought, may point to welcomed rain—but it is not itself the center of "an experience." The emotional qualities that surround its referent do not pervade the sign, and we do not respond to the sign as we would to its referent. The sign points but does not embody. The non-symbolic sign has cognitive and instrumental worth, but it does not have human and consummatory significance.

The indicative or denotative sign may promise and prepare the way for a directly meaningful experience; the symbol is the vehicle of its fulfillment. This is so because the symbol itself takes on the human significance possessed by its referent. To the naturalist, the flock of birds may be a sign of land, and nothing more. To the sailor long at sea, the flock of birds may acquire symbolic status and he may respond to them much as he will later respond to his actual homecoming. Black may be merely a denotative sign of death, death merely a natural sign of disease. But when black is a true symbol of death, we respond to it much as we would humanly respond in the presence of death.

The word "symbol" is often used for both denotative and connotative signs. In that usage, of course, any word is a symbol. But we suggest that for a theory of culture it makes better sense to build the concept of symbol upon 1) the idea of connotation and 2) the idea that, when treated as embodiments of their connotations, signs are capable of evoking direct response and providing consummatory experience. On our view, therefore, symbols are usually objects, events, or images, not language *per se*. The word "black" as an English word and black as the cultural symbol for death are both indisputably man-made. But we are suggesting that it is the creation of black as the symbol for death, not the creation of "black" as the linguistic sign denoting a color, that marks the distinctively cultural order.

As human beings endowed with a certain neurological capacity, we are capable of creating language and understanding meanings, whether they are "literal" or symbolic. But cultural creativity is not the construction of language. It is the bestowal of symbolic meaning on things, acts, events, persons. The word "cross" may simply denote a physical object or a certain form, but it may also refer to the cross as a symbol. Some words, such as "God," attain an independent symbolic status. "God" is a denotative sign for an idea, but the very word itself has been treated as a genuine symbol or surrogate for the unknown and the sacred. On more ordinary levels, the name of a person is sometimes treated as a symbol of that person and not as a mere denotative sign: the name is treated with the same respect or lack of it that the person himself would be accorded. But that names may be symbols, or that language may refer to symbols or itself take on symbolic meaning, should not obscure the fundamental distinction between the denotative signs of language and true symbols.[16]

On the other hand, this distinction does

not derogate the contribution of language to symbolization. Symbols *are* man-made, and in part they are made by language. Much expressive language, including the primitive myth and folk tale, explores hidden meanings and creates a symbolic imagery. Ceremonial speeches recognize and even establish the symbolic significance of events and gatherings, for very often the common listening is the only experience that is meaningfully shared and that can provide the event with an interpretation. The style as well as the content of language contributes to symbolization. Through rhythm, alliteration, simile, metaphor, tone of voice—all the familiar devices of poetry, rhetoric, incantation—language induces a symbolic approach to the world.

Men create symbols in order to continue and sustain meaningful experience. The wearing of black respects and prolongs the experience of mourning, of confronted death. Festivities rich in symbolism can help consummate an experience that would otherwise be brief and incomplete. In the presence of the symbol, people respond in ways that nurture rather than attenuate the experience. Moreover, having had "an experience," men create a symbol of it in order that the experience may be re-evoked and relived. Durkheim said as much when he suggested that religious symbolism arose in part out of the desire to recreate the emotional uplift originally stemming from collective excitement.[17]

Symbols help to provide focus, direction, and shape to what otherwise might disintegrate into chaotic feeling or the absence of feeling. Mass political action gains coherence and discipline from symbolic leadership, ritual, and exhortation. Without symbolism, it is often difficult to transform an important occasion, such as a wedding, into a meaningful experience, as many unconventional and secularized couples have found to their dismay. By serving as vehicles of response, symbols can help transform a "mere" feeling, a vague somatic tension, into genuine emotion. Thus symbols do more than sustain emotion. They contribute to the emergence of emotion as a uniquely human attribute.

Sometimes an experience is so deep and moving that its emotional qualities spread out and pervade all that surrounds it and is related to it. In this way, some sensuous correlate of a significant event becomes a symbol of it and is capable of evoking response to itself. Perhaps the most important illustration of this is the capacity of a geographic *locale* to symbolize an event associated with it. The difficulty of making such associations in modern society has restricted man's opportunities for authentic symbolic experience.

A chief function of the culture symbol is to serve as a sensuous embodiment of what is abstract and ineffable. Because of language, men have the capacity to entertain abstract ideas and values and to be guided by them rather than by the vagaries of biological adjustment and transitory excitation. Without sensuous embodiment, however, ideas and values tend to lose their force, to be less easily retained in the mind, to be readily diverted. It might be added that when ideas and values change too rapidly, their symbolization is not apt to occur. As Susanne Langer says, with reference to art, "in a footloose society surfeited with influences, nothing is inviolate long enough to be governed by one clear feeling and to be really expressive of it." [18]

It is important to emphasize that any repetitive human act, any object, even the meanest product of man's contrivance, can become a symbol and thus take on cultural import. It does not follow, however, that everything is equally competent to do symbolic work, equally effective as a bearer of connotative meaning, equally capable of sustaining shared symbolic experience. Culture is built upon expressive symbolism, but not every symbol is a cultural symbol. Some symbols, e.g., personal or even family keepsakes, heirlooms, traditions, and rituals, may be too private and ungeneralized to be available to the community as vehicles of shared experience.[19] Other objects or activities may resist symbolic elaboration because they are too specialized and precise to sustain a penumbra of connotative meaning. Thus objects or activities vary in their capacity to be symbols, and symbols vary in the extent and nature of their contribution to culture.

With this background, we can essay a definition of culture. *Culture consists of everything that is produced by, and is capable of sustaining, shared symbolic experience.* Obviously, the key terms used here must be read in the light of the preceding discussion. Moreover, the definition is necessarily general and analytic. No concrete product or activity, not even religion or art, should be automatically classified as part of culture. Of course there is a high probability that these and related activities will stem from and contribute to shared symbolic experience. But the possibility remains that religion or art, though flourishing in other ways, may wither as contributors to culture.

The Strain Toward the Esthetic

We can now turn to the relation between culture, as we have just defined it, and high culture. The fundamental connection is not far to seek, and here again Dewey has offered some guidelines. His book *Art As Experience* is a critique of the separation of art and life, both in esthetic theory and in the social world. Dewey argued that the esthetic dimension of life has its roots in the nature of authentic experience. To think of art as mere embellishment, of the esthetic response as a psychic grace note, is a radical misreading of both man and society.

The task of philosophy of the fine arts, wrote Dewey, "is to restore continuity between the refined and intensified forms of experience that are works of art and the everyday events, doings, and sufferings that are universally recognized to constitute experience." [20] "When artistic objects are separated from both conditions of origin and operation in experience, a wall is built around them that renders almost opaque their general significance. . . . Art is remitted to a separate realm, where it is cut off from that association with the materials and aims of every other form of human effort. . . ." [21]

Dewey's argument about art and society rests on an elaboration of his theory of experience. Esthetic quality is "implicit in normal experience." When experience is meaningful and satisfying, when it is authentic, it takes on form and coherence, inner harmony and rhythm. "For only when an organism shares in the ordered relations of its environment does it secure the stability essential to living. And when the participation comes after a phase of disruption and conflict, it bears within itself the germs of a consummation akin to the esthetic." [22] The esthetic, in other words, is not a quality uniquely associated with works of art; on the contrary, the esthetic element is present in ordinary life when feeling is evoked whose very substance consists of what Dewey called "appreciated meanings."

Dewey's whole point is that there are other ways of having an esthetic experience than producing or viewing works of art. Even a practical activity will have esthetic quality, he says, "provided that it is integrated and moves by its own urge to fulfillment." [23] The satisfactions of authentic experience result from using the world not as a barely instrumental means but as an expressive medium. To strive for experience is to strive for expressiveness, for a state of affairs where the activity engaged in is so closely related to the emotions, attitudes, and content of the acting self as to be, like a work of art, their literal or material embodiment. The expressive act, he urges, tends quite naturally to assume the lineaments of esthetic or artistic form.

Taking our cue from Dewey, but reaching beyond his argument, we can now indicate what we have in mind by a "strain toward the esthetic" in culture. We mean by this that there is a tendency for the vehicles of symbolic meaning, the true artifacts of culture, to take on esthetic form. This hypothesis is based on an implicit theory of what constitutes an effective symbol, of what conditions must be met by the cultural artifact, in its own form and texture, if it is to carry the burden of symbolic meaning.

As has been said of the art object, the cultural artifact is "congealed meaning." While it is true that almost anything at all can carry cultural meaning, at least in a rudimentary way, it does not follow that everything is equally capable of doing so. *An effective symbol combines economy of statement with richness of expression.* Economy is needed for evocative clarity and force as well as to maintain an abstract and general import. Richness is needed to provide that shading of connotative meanings without which the symbol would degenerate, that is, trigger a reaction rather than evoke a response.[24] It appears that when this combination of symbolic economy and richness is achieved the result tends to be esthetic in form.

In accounting for the strain toward the esthetic it should be remembered that culture, though founded in individual need and fulfillment, is not a private phenomenon but a public one. Symbolic meanings are readily shared and form the basis of collective as well as of individual experience. This building up of public, shared symbolism itself generates esthetic outcomes, if only by intensifying the dual requirement of economy and enrichment just mentioned. It is interesting that the attenuation of culture, and with it of the esthetic quality of public artifacts, is associated with a standardization of symbols without concomitant enrichment.

If our argument has merit, it means that symbolic expression, including artistic expression, is central to the study of culture in the social sciences and not peripheral to it. It means that studies of high culture are not a thing apart, a peculiar and embarrassing intrusion on the world of anthropology and sociology. High culture has no monopoly on symbolic expression, but it is there that the vehicle of consummatory meaning—the representative object, the stylized form of action, the distinctive outlook on world and self—is given its most sophisticated and sensitive development. At the same time, cultural symbolism assimilated to the arts and intellectual life is inherently precarious, subject to attenuation, privatization, subordination to the narrower ends of esthetic creativity.

Thus we do not identify high culture with the entire cultural order. The cultural symbol is not necessarily an esthetic symbol nor is the esthetic symbol necessarily part of high culture. A village square, a pile of ruins, or a historic personage may become a cultural symbol without having much in the way of esthetic quality. We have argued that there is a *strain* toward the esthetic among cultural symbols, not that all cultural symbols are works of art. Our guess is that when a village square has symbolic meaning it will have, or there will be some effort to lend it, esthetic elaboration. But we recognize that there are other sources of symbolic "imprinting," e.g., the recurrent use of the square as a locale for ritual gatherings. While a venerable adobe wall or mud hut may be dubbed an historic monument, and have symbolic worth, it is more likely, we suppose, that what is preserved is not only symbolically meaningful but has some esthetic appeal. Culture heroes are not selected in beauty contests but the process of idealization "touches up" reality and makes the man's remembered image a more effective summoner of symbolic response.

The strain toward the esthetic is limited by the nature of the materials from which the cultural artifact is made, as well as by the use to which it is put. Many natural materials and objects do not lend themselves to extensive manipulation and elaboration. They are relatively limited in their plasticity and, by the same token, in their capacity to serve as connotative signs. Thanksgiving Turkey is a cultural symbol, but not a very good one. A well-roasted turkey is a heart-warming sight, but it is a fairly unvariable attainment. Though symbolic expression can be achieved, there is little variation allowed in the choice of materials to be used and not much leeway in what can be done with the turkey once he is prepared for roasting. On the other hand, more general symbols, such as a deity, or artifacts that allow wide variation in their making, such as buildings, can provide the basis for a richer symbolism. Given a choice of materials, and malleable ones, the craftsman can vary the symbolic object and thus evoke different nuances of emotion and response. Thus some of the conditions of a good work of art and of an effective cultural symbol are the same. Both should be capable of evoking non-conventionalized, non-sentimental, non-standard response. To be sure, even the best cultural symbols and the best works of art may decay in meaning and become conventionalized relics of a dead tradition.[25] But the esthetic potentialities of a medium of symbolization are importantly related to the depth and range of its cultural significance.

Another clue to the difference between the cultural and the esthetic symbol lies in the former's *historical* character. Because historical associations are imprinted upon it, the cultural symbol may be more arbitrary, more "free" than the esthetic symbol. The cultural symbol need not carry its meaning on its face. It need not be a "statement" of the qualities it symbolizes. The cultural symbol can evoke fear or reverence or joy without itself embodying the connoted meanings. This is most obvious for symbolic places and buildings, which depend for connotation not on the structures themselves but on historical as-

sociation. However, most symbolic objects are given some sort of elaboration, if only to signify what response is appropriate.

In esthetic elaboration the opportunity is presented to build meanings into the symbol itself by giving them a sensual rendering. To put it crudely, a cultural symbol may be made to "look like" its meanings; in some way, perhaps quite abstract, the art object "states" the meaning. This may be achieved by graphic or plastic means, or through the creation of stories or poetry in which metaphor becomes the master device for "collapsing" denotative and connotative meanings.

Any effort to transform an object so that its concrete, specific properties evoke a desired response will naturally draw upon art as a vital resource. Of course, the esthetic transformation may be better or worse, successful or unsuccessful. And if the "desired" response is superficial, conventional, standardized, merely sentimental, the esthetic quality of the elaboration suffers. If only for this reason, the quality of the art of a people may be a good *indicator* of the quality of symbolic experience in everyday life.

Even when the cultural symbol takes on esthetic qualities, it does not necessarily become part of high culture. In high culture symbolic expression is sophisticated and self-conscious. But esthetic elaboration goes on in many spheres of life and can make its contribution to the quality of culture without benefit of writer, artist, musician, or ballet-master. Folk art is not high art, but it is art nevertheless and reflects the universal striving for an effective symbolism and for authentic cultural experience.

Problems of a Normative Theory

The approach we have taken is explicitly normative. Like friendship, citizenship, law, education, science itself, culture is intimately associated with the realization of values.[26] An understanding of the nature of the values at stake, and the conditions of their realization, must form a part of the theory of culture. It is in this sense a normative theory, one that does not shrink from identifying some cultures as attenuated, some symbols as emptied out, some experiences as truncated or distorted.

As Sapir said, whatever culture is, it is a "good thing." [27] But this is not a matter of our own subjective preferences. Nor does it necessarily mean that culture is an unalloyed or unequivocal "good thing." A normative view of culture is a way of taking seriously the idea that culture is an adaptive product, a result of individual and social striving for symbolically meaningful experience. By the same token, if culture is a problem-solving achievement, it cannot be uniformly successful. The interdependence of culture, social organization, and technology guarantees that, quite apart from other limiting and distorting factors. Some model of cultural attainment is needed if the effect of these factors is to be weighed.

A normative theory of culture can keep philosophers and social scientists happily occupied for some time to come. Among the problems that need careful study is the relation between morality and cultural order. Suppose one society has a subtle and rich symbolic system but a barbaric moral order, manifested in brutality and worse; another society has a thin and underdeveloped symbolic system but decently dull human relations. Which has the "better" culture? We take the view that much is to be gained by avoiding the equation of the moral and the cultural. Rather, we think the relation between the two should be explored. There may well be an empirical tension, though probably not a fatal one, between enlightened moral orders and the development of culture.[28] To the extent that symbolization of persons and groups occurs, there is cultural enrichment. But symbolization can be demonic and go hand in hand with cruel and inhuman moral systems. Moral enlighten-

ment often depends upon the weakening of symbols, upon making profane what was formerly sacred, upon taking people for what they are and not for their symbolic status and value. When we look at culture with a fascinated eye, it is easy to forget that values realized through symbolic systems may inhibit the realization of other values that depend upon more instrumental, more rational, more disengaged behavior. On the other hand, a moral order may be weak and precarious if it does not produce cultural symbols, and is not sustained by them.

Is esthetic creativity and productivity a primary criterion in the evaluation of culture? The Aztecs had a highly developed esthetic sense. Should we therefore rank Aztec society as more cultured than other societies less creative esthetically? Not necessarily. It would be an error to make sheer production of esthetic objects the hallmark of culture. Such productivity, if it is the specialized activity of a high culture divorced from the life of society, may actually be a sign of cultural breakdown. The mark of culture, in a proper social science meaning, is not the development of the esthetic impulse in itself, nor is it the creation of a specialized artist class. It is rather that the ordinary objects and forms of group experience have symbolic value. Although we believe there is a strain toward the esthetic in culture, and that therein may be found the link between culture and high culture, it is the process of symbolization that is primary and basic. If cultural symbols naturally tend to take on esthetic form, quite apart from any desire to make them esthetic, then the absence of esthetic quality in everyday life is a sign of the attenuation of symbolic value in objects, acts, and relationships. The sheer presence of esthetic objects or activity is, however, no conclusive evidence that the quality of a culture, taken as a whole, is high.

A word might be said here about etiquette. In common sense, a cultured man is, among other things, a man of good manners. He behaves with a certain formality, restraint, and delicacy. Ordinarily, many would be inclined to say that this common sense notion has little to do with culture in the scholarly sense. Yet we venture to suggest that where there is genuine culture we also find good manners. People comport themselves in ways that sustain the symbolic meanings of social occasions. Gestures and actions themselves become symbolic, express the social meaning of an event, and thus contribute to authentic group experience. But manners also tend to have esthetic qualities, to be characterized by grace, form, and harmony. Manners can, of course, be merely formal, studied, emotionally empty prescriptions for maintaining the integrity of a social situation when personal feelings are absent or potentially disruptive. But if manners can degenerate into triviality, it is also true that symbolically meaningful social encounters tend to be expressed in the styles and rhythms of comportment. In a primitive and incipient way, the participant uses his own body as a medium of expression. His body becomes a symbolic object and tends to take on esthetic form. It is in this sense that the esthetic is a mark of culture, an indicator of symbolic value in ordinary life.

A normative concept of culture entails, of course, an appropriate theory of value. In contemporary social science, there is a strong tendency to adopt a "subjectivist" view of value. On this view, values come down to preferences, usually distinguished by their stability or scope from other, more transitory preferences. Ultimately, values are in people's hearts and heads, not in the world. It is people who give value to objects and institutions.

An alternative approach sees values as objective. This requires that the assertion, "friendship *is* a value" be recast to read: friendship *has* value. Friendship is then seen as an arrangement which (objectively and causally) can, under certain conditions, provide experiences that are felt as good and not merely said to be good. An objective value is not a disposition to act, however broad or fundamental. It is, or is the source of, a good experience of a certain kind.

An objective theory of value is sometimes confounded with, and stigmatized as, "absolutist." But if some social arrangement, such as monogamy, is objectively valuable, this does not mean that it is the exclusive source of value, even within its special sphere. Nor does it mean that monogamy always and everywhere makes the same contribution to human well-being, or has only positive attributes. That the same can be said of polygamy does not vitiate the objectivity of the values to be found in each.[29]

There is an important link between what is valued subjectively and what has value objectively. The value system of a group (what it "says" it values, or what may be inferred from group action and institutional history) helps to determine *which* objective values, and *how much* objective value, individuals in the group will actually have, experience, realize. Thus subjective value systems, together with social arrangements, vary in their capacity to promote the realization of objective values.

Conclusion

The import of our argument for theory and research in the sociology of culture can be briefly summarized. Mainly we have argued for the centrality of expressive symbolism in the theory of culture. We have tried to explicate and ground the notion that culture has something special to do with "symbolic-meaningful systems." This we have identified with expressive symbolism and treated it as the core of culture. The elements of culture are known by their contribution to the symbolic order, and this cannot be settled apart from empirical assessment. This holds for language, norms, values, knowledge, religion, and art as well as for any other social product.

We have reasoned that linguistic signs may be purely denotative and therefore without symbolic significance. Language that is narrowly technical lies outside the cultural sphere and may indeed be *destructive* of culture. Is this not the meaning of Orwell's vision of Newspeak in *1984?*

It was perceived that in thus abbreviating a name one narrowed and subtly altered its meaning, by cutting out most of the associations that would otherwise cling to it. The words *Communist International,* for instance, call up a composite picture of universal human brotherhood, red flags, barricades, Karl Marx, and the Paris Commune. The word *Comintern,* on the other hand, suggests merely a tightly knit organization and a well-defined body of doctrine. . . . In the same way, the associations called up by a word like *Minitrue* are fewer and more controllable than those called up by *Ministry of Truth.*[30]

As with language, so too with norms, values, and the rest. A great many norms, especially in modern society, are simply technical devices for maintaining practical social arrangements and getting work done. Some "technical" norms do carry symbolic meaning, especially those associated with traditional craftsmanship, but others do not. A norm becomes cultural, not by virtue of being a norm, but only insofar as it evokes symbolic response. It is understandable that a view of culture based on field work in largely tradition-directed communities should have implicitly taken all norms as symbolically meaningful and thus obscured an important distinction.

Much the same may be said for values, although in this case the probabilities are greater that anything prized for itself (if that is what we mean by value) will have symbolic import. Still, not everything prized by a social group has equal status as a cultural value. Some group values, such as efficiency, and some prescriptions, such as achievement, may reflect or be a prelude to the attenuation of culture. They may be relatively incapable of generating

and sustaining an effective context of symbolic meanings.

Again, knowledge is culture only insofar as it is a vehicle of expressive symbolism. A table of nutritive values of standard food portions is knowledge; so too is set theory and the technology of erosion control. Almost any part of the corpus of knowledge can take on symbolic significance at some time for some people, but this is always problematic. The sociology of knowledge, insofar as it is part of the sociology of culture, studies legal, scientific, theological, and other concepts, not for their technical meaning or for their function in social organization, but for their contribution to the symbolic order.

Thus a cultural interpretation of legal history looks to the imagery of the system and especially to those legal ideas, or to those ways of apprehending law, that have evocative and integrative force. Although contract was an important legal notion from an early period in Anglo-American law, it came into its own as a cultural symbol only after the heyday of 18th century contractualism in political theory. To 19th century courts contract symbolized an ideal way of ordering private arrangements, and this symbolism shed a benign light on decisions upholding dubiously free private bargains. Today contract has lost its hold upon the legal imagination, with important results both in and out of the law.

A sociologist attempting to investigate the cultural significance of industrial, political, military, or educational activity would get very little help from contemporary concepts of culture. But he would intuitively grasp the need for a selective approach and one that would appraise the symbolic significance of work, politics, war, or education. It is one thing to consider how different technologies affect worker morale. It is another to ask: What role has the assembly line played as a symbol of industrial organization? It is one thing to study the contribution of low levels of political participation to the stability of the political order. It is another to ask: How many voters see politics as a mode of self-expression, with concomitant demands that political programs conform to an appropriate symbolic imagery? Can we expect more of this in times of affluence, when people can "afford" the luxury of symbolic expression in politics? These questions suggest the selective emphasis of the sociology of culture.

Our emphasis on expressive symbolism in no way detracts from the chief pedagogical value of the older anthropological concept—the idea that culture is determining and that men are "culture-bound." To participate in culture is to be implicated in a system of symbolic meanings. The content of that system, and its qual-

ity, obviously make a difference for the way men think and behave. The symbolic meanings of culture become part of mind and self and this is the chief source of culture-boundedness. It may be argued, indeed, that the interpretation of culture as expressive symbolism only sharpens the insight and heightens the relevance of the traditional analyst of culture. At the same time, a better theoretical foundation is suggested for the study of change and variation in the *degree* of culture-boundedness and in the significance of cultural determinism for the integrity of the self. The study of cultural particularity is not an end in itself but an avenue to fundamental knowledge regarding man as a moral and psychic being.

NOTES

1. For example, by A. L. Kroeber and Clyde Kluckhohn, *Culture,* New York: Vintage Books, 1963, pp. 54–62. But note that Robert Redfield sought to accommodate the difference. See *Human Nature and the Study of Society,* Margaret Park Redfield (ed.), Chicago: University of Chicago Press, 1962, p. 55.

2. A. L. Kroeber, *Anthropology,* New York: Harcourt, Brace, 1948, p. 253.

3. Clyde Kluckhohn, "The Concept of Culture" in D. Lerner and H. D. Lasswell (eds.), *The Policy Sciences,* Stanford: Stanford University Press, 1951, p. 86.

4. A. L. Kroeber and Talcott Parsons, "The Concepts of Culture and of Social System," *American Sociological Review,* 23 (1958), 582–583.

5. *Ibid.,* p. 582.

6. *Ibid.,* p. 583.

7. Pitirim A. Sorokin, *Society, Culture and Personality,* New York: Harper, 1947, p. 313; Alfred Weber, *Fundamentals of Culture-Sociology: Social Process, Civilizational Process and Culture-Movement* (New York, 1939), mimeographed translation sponsored by the Works Progress Administration and the Department of Social Science, Columbia University, reprinted in part in Talcott Parsons, Edward Shils, Kaspar D. Naegele, Jesse R. Pitts (eds.), *Theories of Society,* New York: Free Press of Glencoe, 1961, Vol. II, pp. 1274–1283; R. M. MacIver and C. H Page, *Society. An Introductory Analysis,* New York: Rinehart, 1949, pp. 498 ff.; and R. M. MacIver, *Social Causation,* Boston: Ginn and Company, 1942, pp. 269–290.

8. "The youth most susceptible to violent-gang membership emerges from a social milieu that trains him inadequately for assuming constructive social roles . . . the defective socialization process to which he is subjected in the disorganized slum fosters a lack of social 'feelings.' " Lewis Yablonsky, *The Violent Gang,* New York: Macmillan, 1963, p. 196.

9. Not only the manner but "the degree to which the self is developed depends upon the community," specifically upon the capacity of the community to envision and embody values that deepen and enlarge experience, both social and "private." G. H. Mead, *Mind, Self and Society,* Chicago: University of Chicago Press, 1934, pp. 265–266.

10. W. G. Sumner and A. G. Keller, *The Science of Society,* 1, New Haven: Yale University Press, 1927, pp. 46–47, quoted in Kroeber and Kluckhohn, *op. cit.,* p. 105.

11. John Dewey, *Art as Experience,* New York: Capricorn Books, 1958, Chap. III, pp. 35–57.

12. John Dewey, *Logic: The Theory of Inquiry,* New York: Henry Holt, 1938, pp. 29–31.

13. Leslie White, *The Science of Culture,* New York: Farrar, Straus, 1949, p. 25.

14. Susanne K. Langer, *Philosophy in a New Key,* New York: Penguin Books, 1948, p. 49.

15. "The soldier who dies for his flag, dies for his country; but as a matter of fact, in his own consciousness, it is the flag that has the first place," Émile Durkheim, *The Elementary Forms of the Religious Life,* Glencoe, Ill.: Free Press, 1947, p. 220.

16. For another view, see Langer, *op. cit.* and the work of Ernst Cassirer, as developed in *The Philosophy of Symbolic Forms,* New Haven: Yale University Press, 1953, 3 vols., and more briefly stated in *Language and Myth,* New York: Harper, 1946.

17. Durkheim, *op. cit.,* pp. 214–216.

18. Susanne K. Langer, *Feeling and Form,* New York: Charles Scribner's Sons, 1953, p. 26.

19. In his study of early religion and the evolution of civic culture, Fustel de Coulanges took this as a problem and traced the transition from private to public symbolism. See *The Ancient City,* New York: Anchor, 1956.

20. Dewey, *Art as Experience,* p. 3.

21. *Loc. cit.*

22. *Ibid.,* p. 15.

23. *Ibid.,* p. 39.

24. On triggered, "unmediated" reactions and the degeneration of political symbols, see Philip Selznick, *The Organizational Weapon,* Glencoe, Ill.: Free Press, 1960, pp. 289–293.

25. The decay attendant on the proliferation and over-exposure of symbolic objects is discussed in S. Huizinga, *The Waning of the Middle Ages,* New York: Anchor, 1954, Chap. 12.

26. For fuller discussion of normative concepts in social science, see Philip Selznick, "Sociology and Natural Law," *Natural Law Forum,* 6 (1961), 84–108. See also Ernest Nagel, *The Structure of Science,* New York: Harcourt, Brace & World, 1961, pp. 490–495.

27. E. Sapir, "Culture, Genuine and Spurious," *American Journal of Sociology,* 29 (1924), p. 402. A genuine culture, he wrote, is "inherently harmonious, balanced, self-satisfactory . . . in which nothing is spiritually meaningless." To have such a culture, "the major activities of the individual must directly satisfy his own creative and emotional impulses, must always be something more than a means to an end."

28. This problem was considered by Redfield at a number of points. See, for example, *The Primitive World and Its Transformation,* Ithaca, N.Y.: Cornell University Press, 1953.

29. "With C. I. Lewis, we may speak of *intrinsic value* as 'experienced goodness,' the sense of satisfaction or fulfillment, the direct (that is, unmediated) experience of gratification. Judgments of value then say something, in effect, about the intrinsic values empirically associated with what is being judged." Abraham Kaplan, *The Conduct of Inquiry,* San Francisco: Chandler, 1964, p. 389.

30. George Orwell, *1984,* New York: Signet, 1961, pp. 252–253.

8. THE SILENT LANGUAGE

EDWARD T. HALL

In his book, The Silent Language, *Edward T. Hall states that "what people do is frequently more important than what they say." One needs to know more than the formal language of a given group in order to fully comprehend its way of life. In a very real sense, culture "talks." Culture provides the expressive symbols that guide behavior.*

In the following essay, Hall compares the people of the United States with those of certain Latin-American countries in terms of their differential concepts of space and time and social relationships. The bases for ethnocentric misunderstandings are made vividly apparent in Hall's brief description.

Edward T. Hall is now Professor of Anthropology at Northwestern University. Author of The Silent Language *(1959) and* The Hidden Dimension *(1965), he is the former President of Overseas Training and Research, Incorporated.*

There are deep and subtle differences between the people of the United States and their South American neighbors. Surface differences can be seen and dealt with. What defeats all of us are the hidden elements in man's psychological make-up whose presence are all too often not even suspected.

I will use the Spanish word *ocultos*—"not seen"—in a new sense to stand for these hidden psychological patterns that stand between peoples. Like germs that can't be seen, there are many *ocultos* that cause psychological difficulty. All one sees are the symptoms, the outward manifestation of the *oculto*.

I will particularize about three specific topics to demonstrate a principle. These are time, space, and friendship. *Ocultos* between the United States citizen and his neighbors differ in all three.

I first became aware of space as a patterned aspect of human behavior when I noted that people raised in other cultures handled it differently. In the Middle East I felt crowded and was often made to feel anxious.

"Natural" Distances

Fellow United States citizens, also, found it hard to adapt themselves to houses and offices arranged so differently, and often commented on how there was too little or too much space, and how much space was wasted. These spatial differences are not limited to offices and homes: towns, subway systems, and road networks usually follow patterns that appear curious to one not accustomed to the culture.

The "natural" way to describe space may be different in two cultures. For instance, I discovered in Japan that intersections of streets were named and the streets were not.

These differing ideas of space contain traps for the uninformed. A person raised in the United States is often likely to give an unintentional snub to a Latin Ameri-

Reprinted from *Américas,* **14** (February 1962), 5–8, monthly magazine published by the Pan American Union in English, Spanish, and Portuguese, by permission of the authors and the publisher.

can because of the way he handles space relationships, particularly the physical distance between individuals during conversations.

A conversation I once observed between a Latin and a North American began at one end of a 40-foot hall. I watched the two conversationalists until they had finally reached the other end of the hall.

This maneuver had been effected by a continual series of small backward steps on the part of the North American as he unconsciously retreated, searching for a comfortable talking distance. Each time, there was an accompanying closing of the gap, as his Latin friend attempted to reestablish his own accustomed conversation distance.

In formal business conversations in North America, the "proper" distance to stand when talking to another adult male who is simply a business acquaintance, is about two feet. This distance diminishes, of course, at social functions like the cocktail party, but anything under eight to ten inches is likely to irritate.

To the Latin, with his own *ocultos,* a distance of two feet seems remote and cold, sometimes even unfriendly. One of the things that gives the South or Central American the feeling that the North American is *simpatico* is when he is no longer made uncomfortable by closeness or being touched.

North Americans, working in offices in Latin America, may keep their local acquaintances at a distance—not the Latin American distance—by remaining behind a desk or typewriter. Even North Americans who have lived in Latin America for years have been known to use the "barricade approach" to communication, and to remain completely unaware of its cultural significance.

They are aware only that they "feel comfortable" when not crowded, without realizing that the distance and the desk often create an *oculto* that distorts or gives a cold tone to virtually everything

that takes place. The hold of the *oculto* is so strong, however, that the Latin is sometimes observed trying to "climb over" the intervening obstacles—leaning across the desk for instance—in order to achieve a distance at which he can communicate comfortably.

Latin Time Lag

As with space, there are many time *ocultos* that characterize each people. The North American has developed a language of time that involves much more than being prompt. He can usually tell you when his own *ocultos* have been violated, but not how they work. His blood pressure rises, and he loses his temper when he is kept waiting; this is because time and the ego have been linked.

As a rule, the longer a North American is kept waiting in his own setting, the greater the discrepancy between the status of the two parties. Because of their high status, important people can keep less important people waiting. Also, very important business takes precedence over less important business. The North American has developed a pattern for seeing one person at a time, but individual appointments aren't usually scheduled by the Latin American to the exclusion of other appointments. The Latin often enjoys seeing several people at once even if he has to talk on different matters at the same time.

In this setting, the North American may feel he is not being properly treated, that his dignity is under attack, even though this simply is not true. The Latin American clock on the wall may look the same, but it tells a different sort of time.

By the United States clock, a consistently tardy man is considered undependable. To judge a Latin American by the same time values is to risk a major error.

This cultural error may be compounded by a further miscalculation. Suppose the *Norteamericano* has waited 45 minutes or an hour and finally gets to see the Latin American with whom he has an appointment, only to be told, with many apologies, that "there is only five minutes—maybe a meeting can be arranged for tomorrow or next week?"

At this point, the North American's schedule has been "shot." If it is important, he will have to make the time. What he may not understand is an *oculto* common in Mexico, for example, and that is that one is very likely to take one's time before doing business, in order to provide time for "getting acquainted."

First meetings leave the North American with the feeling he isn't getting anywhere. If not forewarned he keeps trying to get down to business and stop "wasting time." This turns out to be a mistake.

In the United States, discussion is used as a means to an end: the deal. One tries to make his point with neatness and dispatch—quickly and efficiently. The North American begins by taking up major issues, leaving details for later, perhaps for technicians to work out.

Discussion, however, is to the Latin American an important part of life. It serves a different function and operates according to rules of form; it has to be done right. For the Latin American, the emphasis is on courtesy, not speed. Close friends who see each other frequently, shake hands when they meet and when they part.

For the Latin American it is the invisible social distance that is maintained, not the physical distance. Forming a new friendship or a business acquaintance must be done properly. The Latin first wants to know the human values of a new acquaintance—his cultural interests, his philosophy of life—not his efficiency. This is all accompanied by elaborate and graceful formal verbal expressions, which people in the United States have long felt too busy to take time for. They tend to assume familiarity very quickly, to invite new acquaintances to their homes after one or two meetings. But the Latin American entertains only friends of very long standing in his home—and never for business reasons.

Brief Northern Friendships

Of course, times are changing, because there are an increasing number of Latin businessmen who now demand punctuality even more strictly than in the North. However, there are still a great many times when the old patterns prevail and are not understood. The hidden differences seem to center around the fact that in the North, the ego of the man is more on the surface, whereas in the South preserving institutional forms is important.

It has been observed that in the United States, friendships may not be long lasting. People are apt to take up friends quickly and drop them just as quickly.

A feature influencing North American friendship patterns is that people move constantly (in the 12-year period from 1946–1958, according to United States census data, two thirds of those owning homes had moved, while virtually all those renting property had moved). The North American, as a rule, looks for and finds his friends next door and among those with whom he works.

There are for him few well-defined, hard-and-fast rules governing the obligations of friendship. At just what point our friendships give way to business opportunism or pressure from above is difficult to say. In this, the United States seems to differ from many other countries in the world.

Weight of Tradition

In Latin America, on the other hand, while friendships are not formed as quickly or as easily as in the United States, they often go much deeper and last longer. They almost always involve real obligations. It is important to stress that in Latin America your "friends" will not let you down. The fact that they, personally, are having difficulties is never an excuse for failing friends. You, in turn, are obligated to look out for their interests.

The weight of tradition presses the Latin American to do business within a circle of friends and relatives. If a product or service he needs is not available within his circle, he hesitates to go outside; if he does so, he looks for a new friend who can supply the want.

Apart from the cultural need to "feel right" about a new relationship, there is the logic of the business system. One of the realities of life is that it is dangerous to enter into business with someone over whom you have no "control." The difference between the two systems lies in the controls. One is formal, personal, and de-pends upon family and friends. The other is technical-legal, impersonal, and depends upon courts and contracts.

Europeans often comment on how candid the North American is. Being candid, he seeks this in others. What fools him is that the Latin American does not readily reciprocate. One has to be known and trusted—admitted into the circle of friendship—before this happens. Even then, what is not said may be just as important, and just as much noticed, as what is said.

Until we face up to the reality of the *ocultos,* and make them explicit, difficulties in communication are going to continue. *Ocultos* drain the great reservoir of good will that the people of the Americas feel in their hearts for each other.

9. THE ANALYSIS OF CULTURE

HARRY C. BREDEMEIER *and* RICHARD M. STEPHENSON

Culture, "the silent language," not only tells people what to perceive, it also provides certain response-channels. One learns what is (and was and will be), what is deemed pleasurable and what is painful, what is considered good and what is bad. Such cognitive, cathectic, and evaluative expectations differ markedly depending upon definitions of social situations. An additional form of variation is that concerned with the kind of "action problems" that face the individual in the course of everyday life.

Talcott Parsons has suggested that five such problems are inherent in every situation and that the structures of different situations vary with respect to how the problems are solved. The "problems" include qualities versus performance, universalism versus particularism, affectivity versus neutrality, diffuseness versus specificity, and self-orientation versus collectivity orientation. Harry C. Bredemeier and Richard M. Stephenson describe Parsons' "pattern variables" and then proceed to explain other ways of categorizing the forms and meanings of social action.

Harry C. Bredemeier and Richard M. Stephenson are both Professors of Sociology at Douglass College of Rutgers University. Together they wrote The Analysis of Social Systems (1962) *from which this selection is adapted.*

The first, and in a sense the most elementary, classification is one that distinguishes between cultural definitions telling people *what to perceive* and those that tell them *how to respond* to what they perceive. The first kind we call "cognitive" meanings. They tell people what *is* (or was, or will be, or might be). They include ideas of cause and effect relationships. For example, all the following are cognitive ideas:

The earth is flat.
The earth is round.
God created the world.
There is no God.
All men are mortal; Socrates is a man; therefore, Socrates is mortal.
If I go through a red light, the chances are 65 out of 100 that I'll get a ticket.

Notice that in these examples there is no necessary implication that cognitive ideas are "correct," or even that it is possible to ascertain whether or not they are correct. Obviously, the earth is not both round and flat, and obviously there is no scientific way of knowing whether there is or is not a God. All the ideas, nonetheless, are cognitive ideas because they tell people what *is* or "what the chances are" that something will happen. They might, to be sure, tell them incorrectly, but we are not at the moment concerned with correctness or incorrectness. Our point is that if people's cognitive ideas tell them that something is so, they will *act* as if it were so. This is only a special case of our basic proposition that human beings respond to their *definitions* of situations.

Not only do people depend upon symbols to tell them "what is" (that is, to channelize their perceptions); they also depend on symbols to channelize their *responses* to these perceptions. We can distinguish between two kinds of these response-channeling definitions. One we call "cathectic" ideas; the other we call "moral" or "evaluative" or "normative" ideas.[1]

Cathectic ideas consist of cultural definitions that define what is pleasurable and what is painful. At first glance, it may seem to be stretching things a bit to say that human beings need symbolic definitions to tell them what is pleasurable and what is painful. But, in fact, the human dependence on cultural meanings does extend even to this point. It is one thing, for example, to *cognize* caterpillars as possibly nutritious and a very different thing to define them as tasty. A moment's thought will tell you that we could find hundreds of illustrations of this point in the realm of food alone. It is enough merely to mention such expressions as cannibalism, dog steaks, fried cat liver, and rat soup to make the point.

We could also find hundreds of illustrations in the realm of sex, beauty, music, fashion, or housing. For example, the difference between even white teeth and filed pointed teeth, between the attractive feminine figure of the 1920's and that of Brigitte Bardot, between the music of Brahms and rock 'n roll—these will do to illustrate the point. So thoroughly do cathectic ideas intervene between men and the environment that they can determine such basic physiological responses as glandular secretions, sexual appetites, the pulse rate, the directions of peristalsis, and so on.

The second kind of definition helping to determine responses consists of "moral" or "normative" ideas. These are different from cognitive and cathectic ideas in that they add a dimension to human responses that, so far as we know, is completely absent from other animals. All animals, after all, perceive some aspects of reality and have tastes—although their perceptions and tastes are, to be sure, largely *biologically* dictated. But human beings also respond to the "goodness" or "badness" of things, the "virtuousness" or "wickedness," the "properness" or "impropriety" of things.

Evaluative ideas often take precedence over both cognitions and cathexes in determining action. Some things that are positively cathected may be morally tabooed, as in the case of many sexual pleasures; and some things that are *negatively* cathected may be *morally required*, as in the case of firemen entering burning buildings or men allowing women and children to leave a sinking ship first. Furthermore, actions that are *cognized* as being very efficient ways to achieve some gratification may be *morally prohibited*, such as cheating on an examination or poisoning one's rival in a love affair. All Americans cognize the horse and buggy as a means of transportation, but only Mennonites feel *morally* obliged to use it.

With these concepts in mind, it is possible to gain a better understanding of the way in which culture guides human behavior. The "barbarian invaders," as Ralph Linton has termed the infants of each generation, learn from their parents, teachers, and older children how to cognize, cathect, and evaluate the situations in which they are called upon to act. (The process by which they are taught their culture is aptly called by sociologists the "socialization" process. It is the process by which they are changed from nonsocial to social beings.)

The compelling nature of social "definitions of situations" has been dramatically demonstrated in laboratory experiments. Sherif has shown how group definitions affect individual perception in unstructured situations, while at the same time suggesting how such definitions become a property of the group.[2] In his experiment, he made use of the "autokinetic effect," in which a *stationary* point of light in a completely dark room *appears* to move. First, he had his subjects individually indicate over a period how far they thought the light moved. He found that each individual tended to establish a range of movement peculiar to himself. Next he put the individuals into two groups to see how the group would affect the individual's perception. One group was composed of individuals who had previously made judgments as individuals; the other, of individuals who had not previously participated in the experiment. In the group situation, he found that each of those who had previously established his own range of movement tended to converge judgment so that a group standard was established. Those who faced the experiment for the first time also developed a group judgment, but their convergence was closer than the initiated group. Furthermore, when an individual faced the experiment *alone,* after his group experience, he carried over in his individual perception the standard of his group.

Solomon Asch demonstrated that the effect of group definitions on individual judgment operates even in situations where objective differences could be readily perceived. His experiment involved judging the length of lines by matching a given line with one of three others, only one of which was of equal length to the line to be matched. Asch instructed a group of assistants (who pretended to be subjects along with one "naïve" subject) to insist that line A matched line B, when in fact line A did not. He found that the naïve subject in such a case nearly always changed his own objective judgments in favor of the group distortion.[3] Such experiments as these, repeated with variation by many researchers, have amply demonstrated that an individual's "definition of a situation" is affected by that held by the group. Projecting these findings into "real-life" situations, we can begin to understand how the cognitive, cathectic, and normative definitions held by groups of people are taken over by individuals, particularly when they are introduced in infancy and reinforced by the group for an extended period.

As the Sherif experiment suggests, the more vague and unstructured a stimulus, the greater the effect of factors not inherent in the stimulus itself. Where no objective standard exists, as in the autokinetic situation, the individual is particularly vulnerable to standards of judgment set by the group. In the case of *moral* judgments, which have no ultimate objective standards, it would appear that people are especially subject to group values, particularly in childhood, when such values are first established in the individual. Asch's research suggests that where objective standards do exist, the amount of concerted group consensus and pressure required to affect the judgment of individuals is greater, but that nonetheless such group pressure is extraordinarily difficult to withstand.

When fully socialized as members of a group, people have learned to single out certain aspects of situations as "the" significant aspects. They cognitively abstract from the total situation certain key characteristics, which have moral or cathectic *meanings* to them. Those aspects also have further cognitive meanings.

For example, when you enter a classroom or a lecture hall as a sociology student, there are literally thousands of aspects of the total situation which you do *not* cognize (if you have been socialized properly). The age of the chair you sit in, the kind of wood from which it is made, the architectural style of the building, the fact of your blood circulation, the chemistry of your digestion, the physics of the acoustics, and so on and on. You perceive only selected aspects—the professor glancing at his watch, for example, and that aspect has a meaning for you. You instantly deduce from it certain further cognitions ("He's going to start lecturing in a minute"); certain evaluative convictions ("He shouldn't start before everyone has a chance to get settled"); and perhaps certain cathexes ("I wish it were summer again!")

Variations in Cultural Definitions

The cognitive, cathectic, and evaluative expectations comprising the structure of situations may vary in several ways, in addition to the obvious variation in content. In the first place, they vary with respect to their precision. Some situations are precisely and minutely defined; the expectations are prescribed in minute detail and no deviation is permitted. Soldiers on parade, certain religious ceremonies and rituals, and formal Japanese tea ceremonies are examples. In most situations, however, the definition of the situation is less rigid. Students, for example, are supposed to be "attentive"; women are supposed to dress "attractively"; men are supposed to be "considerate" of their dates. But there is a wide range of behavior which would still be called "attentive," "attractive," or "considerate."

In the second and related place, different expectations fall at different points along a positive-negative continuum. Behavior might be required, preferred, permitted, tolerated, disapproved, or tabooed (prohibited). In the third place, expectations differ with respect to the person, situation, and time. Some apply to everyone in a group or a society (for example, the Ten Commandments); others are applicable only to subgroups within a culture (for example, women may and sometimes must wear hats in Catholic churches, men must not; haberdashers may advertise, physicians must not; in some parts of the South whites must be called "Miss" or "Mrs." but Negroes must not be). Some apply in nearly all situations, such as concepts of virtue or integrity; others apply only in specific situations, such as the exercise of competition in business relations

but not in friendship. Some are perceived as relatively transitory, such as fads and styles, whereas others are held to be valid for all times, such as religious and ethical beliefs.

Pattern Variables

A fourth kind of variation emphasized by some analysts is concerned with the kind of "action problem" that definitions help individuals to solve. Talcott Parsons has suggested that five such problems are inherent in every situation, and that the structures of different situations vary with respect to how they are solved. The five problems or "dilemmas" distinguished by Parsons are as follows:

1. Is Person A supposed to pay attention to what Person B *is* (a Negro, a woman, an American, a professor) or what he can *do* (cook, run, advise, teach)?
2. Is A supposed to be chiefly concerned with B's relationship to *himself* (*my* mother, *my* wife, *my* teammate), or with B's relationship to general principles (laws, standards of competence, rules of the game)?
3. Do evaluative standards take precedence over cathectic ones ("Die for your country!"), or is the reverse true ("Run for your life!")?
4. Is this a narrow, specific relationship (such as giving a waitress your dinner order), or a broad, diffuse one (such as asking your mother to fix your favorite food *and* iron your clothes *and* nurse you when you're sick *and* give you money, etc.)?
5. Is Individual A supposed to watch out only for his own interests ("What's in this for me?"), or is he supposed to give priority to B's interests ("What's best for him?")?

The different answers to these five questions give different definitions of situations.[4] We shall discuss each of these five problems in the order given above.

Qualities vs. performances

A distinction of far-reaching significance in social affairs is the distinction between two institutionalized ways of defining people: on the basis of their abilities or on the basis of certain of their qualities.

In one sense, this is a familiar distinction to Americans, who learn almost from kindergarten that "what a man *is* doesn't matter; it's what he can *do* that should determine his fate." These two opposing definitions are, of course, at the root of the national crisis over the treatment of Negroes. One tradition says that the *performances* of Negroes should determine their relationship to whites; another says that the sheer quality of "being Negro" should be the determining factor.

Since it is in the context of racial, ethnic, and religious conflict that most Americans think about the difference between emphasizing performances and emphasizing qualities, it is understandable that most people think of the "quality" orientation as "discrimination." This is misleading, however, for people *must* discriminate one object from another before they can act. What is critical is the question of the *basis* on which their cultural definitions lead them to discriminate.

All cultures, in some contexts, define certain qualities as "the" important things; in other contexts, certain performances are defined as important. In the American culture, when Individual A is a man looking for a wife he is *supposed* to discriminate on the basis of a quality: B's sex. Most people would be horrified and indignant if in such a situation he insisted on giving priority to what people can *do,* and chose to marry a homosexual male on the grounds that the latter could clean house and cook better than any of the available females. But there is nothing "automatic" about this; it is a matter of cultural definitions, as the following report by an anthropologist, Ralph Linton, indicates:

Men whose personalities were completely uncongenial to the warrior role assumed a special status, that of *berdache.* They wore women's costumes and carried on women's activities. . . . They continued to hunt and a little of the general pattern of male superiority still attached to them. Thus they were expected to be somewhat better than women even at women's tasks. The highest compliment which could be paid to a woman was to tell her that her beadwork was as fine or her lodge as well kept as that of a *berdache.* Some of the *berdache* were homosexual, but the majority apparently were not. In either case, the society's attitude toward them was entirely neutral. Even when they married other men there was only mild disapproval, and this fell upon the "husband," not the *berdache.* He was condemned for trying to get a partner who would not only keep his house but also hunt for him.[5]

In many other respects also, the American culture defines situations by assigning rights and obligations to people on the basis of their qualities. The difference between "women's work" and "men's work"; the different expectations of boys' and girls' behavior on dates, the privilege of voting simply by virtue of being twenty-one years old; the obligation of enlisted men in the armed forces to initiate the salute between commissioned officers and themselves—all these are examples of structured expectations based on qualities.

Universalism vs. particularism

A second way in which social structures differ is in terms of the kind of morality institutionalized—what we might call the "morality of principle," on the one hand, or the "morality of loyalty," on the other. The "morality of principle" consists of the expectation that one should treat everyone according to the same abstract, general, *universal* principles. The "morality of loyalty" is the expectation that one should treat people differently, depending on their *particular* relationship to one. Principle morality or universalism, for example, says that if you see your best friend cheating, you should report him to the professor. Loyalty, morality or particularism says that you should lie to the professor to protect your friend. Particularism says, "My country—may she ever be right; but right or wrong, my country!" Universalism says, "May she ever be right—if she wants my support."

When a professor gives grades to students "impartially," based only on the students' relation to *third* things, such as the exam questions, he is behaving universalistically. When he favors his son or daughter who happens to be in the class, thus emphasizing the student's relationship to *himself,* he is behaving particularistically.

These two contrasting expectations are often deeply rooted in people and invested with strong emotions. Such epithets as "traitor," "squealer," and "disloyal" attest to the indignation aroused by people who violate particularistic institutions. But the same people who indignantly cry "traitor" at someone who behaves universalistically in one situation will just as indignantly cry "corruption" at, let us say, a judge who *fails* to apply the law impersonally in another situation. This is a good illustration of our basic point that what arouses indignation is the violation of social definitions —which, however, vary from situation to situation. Thus, to illustrate the principle in another context, the woman who behaves particularistically as a jury member is dishonest, but if she does *not* behave particularistically as a wife, she is unfaithful. The situations in which loyalty is institutionalized are sharply different from those in which universalism is called for; and . . . the two kinds of definitions have very different consequences.

Affectivity [6] vs. neutrality

A third basic difference in the definition of different situations concerns the question of which has priority—cathectic definitions or evaluative ones? Every situation contains opportunities for people to get immediate gratifications—that is, it provides ways in which people can maximize their immediate pleasure. In some situa-

tions it is proper for them to do so, and in others, it is not. When it is proper, they are expected to be "affective"; when it is not, they are expected to be "neutral."

We briefly cited some examples of this above. Firemen, for example, could maximize their immediate gratifications by refusing to enter a burning building. Soldiers under fire could get great pleasure from deserting. There are opportunities for sexual pleasure in every situation involving males and females. Almost everyone could increase his immediate gratification by turning off the alarm in the morning and going back to sleep.

All such pleasures—avoiding pain or death, sex, sleep—are expected in some situations but not in others. When the definition of the situation calls for gratification and pleasure-oriented behavior, then people who insist upon giving priority to evaluative ideas are treated with indignation and scorn, or perhaps even as psychologically sick. The frigid woman or the impotent man, for example, who are too obsessed with the "immorality of sex" to be able to play adult sexual roles are familiar examples. The date who must leave the party at eleven o'clock in order to "get a good night's sleep" is a not unfamiliar bore.

It is significant, however, that the indignation felt toward people who are *neutral* when the situation calls for *affectivity* is considerably less than that felt toward people who are *affective* when the structure demands *neutrality.* The impotent man is more likely to be an object of ridicule than of hostility; but the reverse is true of the cowardly man. The reason for this, we may speculate, is that neutrality is rather harder to learn than affectivity, which "comes naturally," as it were. The infant is born with the ability to attempt to maximize pleasure and does not hesitate to complain about pain or discomfort. It takes a long time and considerable effort and frustration to acquire the ability to inhibit the desire for immediate gratification of every impulse and whim. It is on the side of neutrality, then, that the weight of a society's tradition tends to be thrown; and the greatest wrath is reserved for those who threaten to upset the hard-won victory over impulse.

Furthermore, the need for reliability and predictability of behavior is so great in the delicately balanced human division of labor that impulsive behavior is a serious threat. Compulsive behavior, on the other hand, which might prevent someone from being effective, is merely irritating. It has nowhere near the same possibilities of disruptive consequences. It is as if society prefers the risk of going too far in inhibiting some people to that of not going far enough in controlling the impulses of others.

For these reasons uncontrolled impulsiveness is likely to be more seriously punished in all societies than uncalled for restraint or inhibition. The American culture, moreover, has had a special dose of neutrality injected into it by Puritanism, which probably went as far toward devaluing affectivity as it is possible to go.

Diffuseness vs. specificity

A fourth way in which definitions of situations differ is with respect to the range of different activities the participants engage in with one another or the range of different experiences they share. In some situations, the expectations that A may legitimately (that is, according to the common definitions) have of B are sharply limited, involving only a fraction of A's and B's total personalities. The expectations are *specified* narrowly, as in a contract in which A promises to deliver ten tons of coal to B next Friday in exchange for $100, *and that's all.* Any other expectation these two might have of one another is illegitimate. For example, B must find someone else to mow his lawn, another person to teach him sociology, still another to cook his meals, and so on. Indeed, if B even so much as asks A to put the coal in the coalbin instead of dumping it on the sidewalk, it might be institutionally appropriate for A to retort, "That's not in our contract!" (or to communicate the same idea by inviting B to go where coal is highly redundant).

Specific relationships, in other words, are specialized ones. Situations that are defined *diffusely,* on the other hand, are situations in which the limits to the expectations one person might have of another are not specified. They perform not one but many functions for one another—or at least, it is legitimate for them to expect one another to do so if need should arise. Friends, for example, are traditionally supposed to "know no limits" to the sacrifices they will make for one another. In small rural communities or in preliterate, simple societies, neighbors and clan members may do virtually everything for one another—they hunt, fish, plant, harvest, nurse, worship, live, eat, and sleep together.

In modern, specialized, complex societies most situations are specific. Even the marriage relationship, as many sociologists have pointed out, no longer involves many of the functions that husbands and wives used to perform for one another. It is scarcely an exaggeration to say that there is virtually nothing the modern husband receives from his wife that he could not *legitimately* get elsewhere—and better, provided he could pay for it—save sex, love or companionship, and "blood children." Canning, cooking, washing, sewing, house cleaning, even child care are available from specialized experts; and many wives, in fact, simply act as liaison agents between the family and those specialists.

A simple test of whether a relationship is defined *specifically* or *diffusely* is to ask, "Who has the burden of proof—the person who wants to *in*clude something in the relationship, or the person who wants to *ex*clude something?" In a *specific* relationship, such as the coal seller–coal purchaser relationship, the person who wants to *in*clude something must prove that he has a right to do so—that it is legitimately a "part of the contract." In a *diffuse* relationship, such as a husband-wife relationship, the person who wants to *ex*clude something has the burden of proof. It is entirely possible, of course, that in a specific relationship the person who wants to include some new element in the relationship—or even many new elements—may be able to carry the burden of proof.

For example, a professor-student relationship is specific; it is supposed to be confined strictly to the interchange of knowledge about a certain subject. If a professor says to one of his students, "Where were you last Saturday night, whom were you with, what were you doing, and what time did you get home?" the student might very well reply, "That's none of your business." The student, properly, is denying the professor's right to include such subjects in their specific relationship. Still, the professor may be able to prove that he *does* have a right to include them *in terms of the specific relationship*. If he is a sociology or a psychology professor, for example, he may explain that he needs to know those things in order to be able to carry out his *specific task of explaining some point to the student*.

In the same way, the members of a *diffuse* relationship may be able to "prove" that a certain element which the other member wants to include in the relationship, in fact, should not be included. If a husband asks his wife to steal something, for example, the wife may legitimately refuse *if* the culture places her obligations to the larger society on a higher level than it places her obligation to her husband.

Self-orientation vs. collectivity orientation

The fifth and final way in which Talcott Parsons has suggested that social definitions might differ significantly is with respect to the kind of motivation institutionalized. On the one hand, individuals may be expected to attempt to further their own interests in the situation; on the other hand, they may be expected to subordinate their own interests to the interests of some larger collectivity. For example, when you buy a car you expect the salesman to give you a "sales talk," and you know that the sales talk will be designed not to meet *your* needs but the salesman's. By contrast, when you consult your physician about your health, you know fairly confidently that he will tell you what is best for *you,* even if he could use the extra money from an expensive operation.

It is easy to become confused about this distinction by arguing that the physician as well as the salesman is trying to further his own interests, only the physician is in a position in which he would get in trouble if it were discovered that he was prescribing operations on the basis of his own monetary needs rather than his patients' health needs. The difference in their "positions" is exactly the point we are making. The salesman is *expected* to ignore the customer's needs—they are up to the customer to protect in this situation. The "customer" as *patient,* however, is *not* supposed to protect or meet his own needs; the physician is.

This distinction has nothing whatever to do with the question of which is "more selfish" or "more altruistic"—the physician or the salesman. "Selfishness" and "altruism" are evaluative terms referring (not very informatively [7]) to individual character traits. We are dealing with only cognitive terms, in the first place; and in the second place, we are not talking about character traits. We are talking about *shared expectations*. Physicians, teachers, lawyers, engineers—all professional persons (at least)—are institutionally required to put their clients' interests ahead of their own, in the sense that all the clients have to do is to make their problems known in order to *obligate* the professional person to try to solve them to the best of his ability. In a sense, the client is the employer of the professional person (even though indirectly, as in the case of the student client); and he has an institutional right to expect his "employee" to give him his best effort and not to "rob the till," so to speak. The salesman, however, is not remotely the employee of the customer. They are independent bargainers.

The professional people may be extremely selfish, greedy, antisocial persons, so far as their personal characters are concerned; and the salesmen may be paragons of charity, sweetness, and altruism. None of that is relevant. The selfish physician must still pursue his ends by doing his best to meet his *patients'* problems; the kindly car salesman must meet his by making sales. (If he attempts to further his customer's interests, as one of the authors once did in a part-time job as a department store salesman, by telling the customer to go to another store where he could get a better bargain, the salesman simply won't be a salesman long!)

These five respects in which the structure of situations vary will appear again and again in our analysis of integration, adaptation, and decision making. The terminology is not the important thing, so the reader need not fret about such unfamiliar language as "specificity and diffuseness, affectivity and neutrality," and so on. When it is convenient to use the terms later on, they will be explained again. What is important is to understand what the terms are labels *for;* that is, to understand the difference between the structure of a situation calling for "affectivity," for example, and that of a situation calling for "neutrality."

Folkways and Mores

So far we have discussed four different ways in which sociologists find it convenient to distinguish among the cognitive, cathectic, and evaluative definitions that comprise "culture." We called attention to differences in the minuteness with which they regulate behavior; we noted that some are phrased positively, some permissively, and some negatively (thou shalt, thou may, thou shalt not); we observed that some apply to all the members of a group or a society whereas others apply only to special subgroups; and we described alternative ways in which five basic issues of social definition might be culturally resolved. Now, and finally, we must point out another way in which it is sometimes useful to analyze the prescriptions and prohibitions of culture into separate categories.

This is a classification that has become by now a part of everyday speech, in such familiar terms as "folkways," "mores," "customs," "enacted law," and "common law." These categories of social definition result from focusing attention on three characteristics of the *normative* or evaluative aspects of culture: their origin; the degree of importance attached to them by the members of a society or group; and the manner in which they are enforced.[8]

Two kinds of origin may be distinguished—tradition and organized enactment. That is, norms are simply divided into two categories—those whose origins are "lost in the mists of antiquity," such as the taboo on sexual relations between parents and children; and those that were enacted by a legislature of some kind, such as traffic laws or the national prohibition amendment. Second, norms are grouped into those about which people feel strongly and those about which they feel mildly. Third, they are divided into those which are enforced by some formal machinery, such as police and courts; and those which are enforced informally, through such means as spontaneous group ridicule or lynchings.

When these three distinctions are put together, the classification shown in Table 1 emerges.

Mores, as Table 1 indicates, are norms that are traditional, informally enforced, and invested with strong group feelings. Folkways are like mores in that they are informally enforced and traditional; but the members of the group do not attach so

Table 1. *Classification of Norms*

	Informal Enforcement		Formal Enforcement	
	Strong group feeling	*Mild group feeling*	*Strong group feeling*	*Mild group feeling*
Traditional	MORES	FOLKWAYS	COMMON LAW	
		(CUSTOMS)		
Enacted	XXX	XXXX	ENACTED LAW	

much importance to them. Both mores and folkways together are "customs."

The common law is traditional law, but unlike folkways and mores, the legal norms are formally enforced, simply by definition. No distinction is made between common-law norms about which the group feels strongly and those about which it feels mildly—that distinction would appear in the severity of the sanctions meted out by the enforcement agency. Enacted law, similarly, is formally enforced, with no distinction between "important" and "unimportant" statutes, except in terms of their sanctions.

As the two sets of X's in Table 1 indicate, there are no terms for norms that are enacted but for which no enforcement machinery exists. As Allen Barton suggests,[9] examples of these might be found in statutes prohibiting racial or religious discrimination, but with no "teeth" in them. They are not likely, then, to be very effective.

Structure and Institutionalization

When people know how to act in a situation—when they know what to expect of others and what is expected of them—we say that the situation is "structured" for them. This is to say that they have a common *definition* of the situation. When these expectations are not only cognized but are positively evaluated as well, the structure is said to be *institutionalized* in this group of people. That is, when expectations are institutionalized, people not only can predict how they and other members of the group will behave, but believe that they *should* behave that way. Moreover, they usually *want* to behave in the expected manner. If someone behaves contrary to an institutionalized expectation, other people are startled, indignant, scornful, or hostile. Punishment of one sort or another is visited on the violator, who himself ordinarily feels guilt or shame and embarrassment.

Situations, however, may be structured for individuals without the structure being institutionalized in the group. This is the case, for example, when two friends know they can count on one another to cheat but also know that cheating is "wrong"— at least in the eyes of most members of the group and probably in their own eyes as well. This distinction between structured and institutionalized interaction is made in order to emphasize the fact that people may interact in predictable, patterned ways that deviate from the normatively expected ways of the group.

The conditions under which people violate institutionalized definitions [are many]. Here we shall continue in another direction by noting that sometimes people encounter situations that are "unstructured" in either an institutional or a noninstitutional sense. Sometimes people may be brought together in situations where there are no institutionalized or structured expectations. Sometimes people may enter groups where there are highly institutionalized expectations, but they have not yet learned what these are. Sometimes, too, different persons may have incompatible expectations; they bring different definitions to the same situation. It is in such situations that the human dependence on shared cultural definitions is made vivid, for the feeling of not knowing what to expect—or even worse, what is expected —can be completely paralyzing; and the experience of discovering that one's expectations have been widely at variance with someone else's can be either infuriating or embarrassing, depending on the circumstances.

For example, when a boy sees himself as playing Romeo to a girl's Juliet, while all the time she sees him as playing Laertes to her Ophelia—both persons are in for a shock. At some point she is going to discover that the way he is holding her hand is not exactly brotherly; and at that point someone's definition of the situation is going to have to change. The situation will be restructured.

Such a situation illustrates the necessity not only of *clear* expectations but also of shared and complementary expectations. Individual A must know confidently what Individual B is like, how she will interpret his actions, what her responses will be, what response he is then supposed to make to her response, and so on, before he can act. But, in addition, she must know exactly the same things before they can *interact* in any stable way. Everyone, in other words, is dependent on symbolic definitions to tell him what things are and how to respond to them; but if the symbolic definitions are to be part of a *culture,* they must be widely shared by the members of a social system. Put another way, people can act on the basis of private, idiosyncratic, symbolic definitions; but if they are to *inter*act in a structured situation, there must be a *culture*—that is, *shared* definitions.

In the example we have chosen, of course—courtship, or the "dating game" —an element of uncertainty about the other person's response is itself institutionalized (in the American system) as part of the expectations. A slight amount of uncertainty, especially when institutionalized, adds a certain zest or thrill to the situation, as in any game. But the importance of even the uncertainty's being institutionalized becomes readily apparent if one considers introducing the same amount of uncertainty into the situation after a man and woman are married. Marriage, by definition, is an institution in which the expectations are supposed to be certain—which, for some people, is precisely what makes marriage dull and boring. But it is also precisely what makes it possible for the marriage partners to eat and sleep and to think about something besides the limpid pools of liquid twilight that are the beloved's eyes.

It should be emphasized, however, that not only is the "uncertainty" *institutionalized* in the dating game, as in a baseball game or a bridge game, but also the rules and signals governing the "players" behavior must be institutionalized before any interaction, except warfare, can take place. Just how far the boy is supposed to go, just what degree of resistance he is supposed to recognize as real rather than as part of the game, just which responses on the part of the girl mean encouragement—all these symbols, which might be very subtle, must be institutionalized if the situation is not to degenerate into open conflict. The tragicomedies of dating and courtship often result from boys and girls moving from a group in which one set of rules and signals were institutionalized into a different group with a different set.

The extreme of lack of structure occurs when the individual simply does not know what is expected. No doubt many readers can illustrate from their own experiences the anguish and near paralysis felt when they found themselves in a strange situation with no clear understanding of how to act. If the situation is one which in fact has a structure, although the individual in question does not know it, the remedy is the fairly simple one (however painful it might be) of learning it. In some cases, however, the situation is in fact unstructured; and then before interaction can go on, a structure must be found or created on the basis of past experience with similar situations. Something like this happens not infrequently perhaps in boy-girl relationships in the United States. One of the persons makes a very vague, general, essentially meaningless remark. (The ability even to take this first step, of course, requires a vast amount of past experience with symbols and their definitions.) In order to respond, the other person must pick out some range of meanings the remarks *might* have and give some response to that imputed meaning. If the response is in the direction desired by the first speaker, he or she responds to it in a manner corroborating the second speaker's guess, and the situation becomes gradually structured. The art of ambiguity in this kind of dialogue can be developed to a very fine point, indeed.

James D. Thompson and William J. McEwen have called this the "sounding out" process, and have described it as follows in the context of an effort to *shift* the structure of a situation from one kind to another.

The sounding out process can be illustrated by the problem of the boss with amorous designs on his secretary in an organization that taboos such relations. He must find some means of determining her willingness to alter the relationship, but he must do so without risking rebuff, for a showdown might come at the cost of his dignity or his office reputation, at the cost of losing her secretarial services, or in the extreme case at the cost of losing his own position. The "sophisticated" procedure is to create an ambiguous situation in which the secretary is forced to respond in one of two ways: 1) to ignore or tactfully counter, thereby clearly channeling the relationship back into an already existing pattern, or 2) to respond in a similarly ambiguous vein (if not in a positive one) indicating a receptiveness to further advances. It is important in the sounding out process that the situation be ambiguous for two reasons: 1) the secretary must not be able to "pin down" the boss with evidence if she rejects the idea, and 2) the situation must be far enough removed from normal to be noticeable to the secretary. The ambiguity of sounding out has the further

advantage to the participants that neither party alone is clearly responsible for initiating the change.[10]

With such very special exceptions as this, however, and this one in only a limited sense, human beings find most unstructured situations intolerable. Indeed, in a basic sense, they *are* intolerable, since human beings are as dependent on cultural definitions as insects are on "instincts." It has been reported, for example, that among certain primitive Australian tribes, where only a limited number of structures are recognized and those mostly kinship relations, the following action takes place whenever two strangers meet. They immediately begin to trace their lineage back through the generations, in the hope of finding at some point a common ancestor. If they succeed, they know the relation in which they stand to one another, and they then know how to act. If they fail, they have only one recourse—to attempt to kill each other.

Summary

Human responses to physical and biological stimuli depend upon the meaning assigned to those stimuli by cultural definitions. Cognitive ideas tell people what to "see" in the environment; cathectic definitions tell them what is pleasant and unpleasant about what they see; and evaluative ideas tell them what is morally good and bad about what they see.

Cultural definitions not only permit people to abstract different aspects of concrete reality; they also permit people to generalize about them. Both abilities—to abstract and to generalize—permit human beings to understand and respond to many aspects and relationships that are beyond the purview of nonhuman animals. Human beings also, however, may be as much the prisoners of their definitions as other animals are of their instincts.

In order for people to interact with one another, it is necessary for them to share common definitions. Five "dilemmas of actions" must be resolved by a common culture—the dilemmas indicated by these concepts: 1) qualities vs. performances; 2) universalism vs. particularism; 3) affectivity vs. neutrality; 4) diffuseness vs. specificity; 5) self-orientation vs. collectiv- ity orientation. The cultural solutions of these as well as other cognitive, cathectic, and evaluative definitions may vary with respect to their origin, the importance attached to them, their mode of enforcement, their minuteness, and their universality.

NOTES

1. Normative definitions are frequently referred to as "social norms." The term "norm" is also used in a statistical sense to indicate the average or most frequent attribute of a group. Neither usage is more "correct" than the other, but the distinction should be kept in mind. Throughout this [essay] we shall use "norm" to mean a shared moral evaluation.

2. M. Sherif, *The Psychology of Social Norms,* New York: Harper & Bros., 1936.

3. S. E. Asch, "Effects of Group Pressures upon Modification and Distortion of Judgments," in G. E. Swanson, T. M. Newcomb, and E. L. Hartley *et al.* (eds.), *Readings in Social Psychology* (2d ed.), New York: Holt, Rinehart and Winston, 1952.

4. They are *variable* ways of *patterning* relationships and probably for that reason the sociologist who originated this mode of analysis, Talcott Parsons, called it the "pattern variable" schema. See Talcott Parsons, *The Social System,* New York: Free Press of Glencoe, 1951, pp. 58–67.

5. Ralph Linton, *The Study of Man,* New York: Appleton-Century-Crofts, 1936, p. 480.

6. The term "affectivity" in this context comes from the word "affect," which, regrettably, has several different legitimate meanings and, to make matters worse, is widely used incorrectly as a synonym for "effect." Funk and Wagnalls' dictionary gives two meanings when the word is used as a verb: (1) To act upon or have an effect upon; (2) *to touch or move emotionally*. It is the second of these meanings that is the root of "affectivity" as used here. An attitude of "affectivity" is one that allows the person to be touched or moved emotionally.

7. Like all evaluative terms, they describe nothing about the person to whom they are applied, but simply report the attitudes of the person applying them. The evaluative sentence "He is selfish" is translatable into the cognitive sentence, "I think he ought to behave differently."

8. We are here following the analysis presented by Allen Barton, "The Concept of Property Space in Social Research," in Paul F. Lazarsfeld and Morris Rosenberg (eds.), *The Language of Social Research,* New York: Free Press of Glencoe, 1955, pp. 51–52.

9. *Ibid.,* p. 52.

10. James D. Thompson and William J. McEwen, "Organizational Goals and Environment," *American Sociological Review,* 23 (1958), p. 30.

10. THE OVERSOCIALIZED CONCEPTION OF MAN

DENNIS H. WRONG

What follows is, perhaps, the best known critique of the idea that man internalizes the norms of his society and develops his self-image by simple conformity to the expectations of others. Dennis H. Wrong suggests that sociologists need to develop a more complex, dialectical conception of human nature instead of the rigid view held by many theorists of "enculturation."

Dennis H. Wrong is Professor of Sociology at New York University. The author of Population and Society *(revised, 1967) and coeditor of* Readings in Introductory Sociology *(1967), he is a frequent contributor to* Dissent, Commentary, *and other journals of opinion.*

Gertrude Stein, bedridden with a fatal illness, is reported to have suddenly muttered, "What, then, is the answer?" Pausing, she raised her head, murmured, "But what is the question?" and died. Miss Stein presumably was pondering the ultimate meaning of human life, but her brief final soliloquy has a broader and humbler relevance. Its point is that answers are meaningless apart from questions. If we forget the questions, even while remembering the answers, our knowledge of them will subtly deteriorate, becoming rigid, formal, and catechistic as the sense of indeterminacy, of rival possibilities, implied by the very putting of a question is lost.

Social theory must be seen primarily as a set of answers to questions we ask of social reality. If the initiating questions are forgotten, we readily misconstrue the task of theory and the answers previous thinkers have given become narrowly confining conceptual prisons, degenerating into little more than a special, professional vocabulary applied to situations and events that can be described with equal or greater precision in ordinary language.

Forgetfulness of the questions that are the starting points of inquiry leads us to ignore the substantive assumptions "buried" in our concepts and commits us to a one-sided view of reality.

Perhaps this is simply an elaborate way of saying that sociological theory can never afford to lose what is usually called a "sense of significance;" or, as it is sometimes put, that sociological theory must be "problem-conscious." I choose instead to speak of theory as a set of answers to questions because reference to "problems" may seem to suggest too close a linkage with social criticism or reform. My primary reason for insisting on the necessity of holding constantly in mind the questions that our concepts and theories are designed to answer is to preclude defining the goal of sociological theory as the creation of a formal body of knowledge satisfying the logical criteria of scientific theory set up by philosophers and methodologists of natural science. Needless to say, this is the way theory is often defined by contemporary sociologists.

Yet to speak of theory as interrogatory may suggest too self-sufficiently intellec-

Reprinted from the *American Sociological Review,* **26,** 2 (April 1961), 183–193, by permission of the author and The American Sociological Association. This article was originally entitled "The Oversocialized Conception of Man in Modern Sociology."

tual an enterprise. Cannot questions be satisfactorily answered and then forgotten, the answers becoming the assumptions from which we start in framing new questions? It may convey my view of theory more adequately to say that sociological theory concerns itself with questions arising out of problems that are inherent in the very existence of human societies and that cannot therefore be finally "solved" in the way that particular social problems perhaps can be. The "problems" theory concerns itself with are problems *for* human societies which, because of their universality, become intellectually problematic for sociological theorists.

Essentially, the historicist conception of sociological knowledge that is central to the thought of Max Weber and has recently been ably restated by Barrington Moore, Jr. and C. Wright Mills [1] is a sound one. The most fruitful questions for sociology are always questions referring to the realities of a particular historical situation. Yet both of these writers, especially Mills, have a tendency to underemphasize the degree to which we genuinely wish and seek answers to trans-historical and universal questions about the nature of man and society. I do not, let it be clear, have in mind the formalistic quest for social "laws" or "universal propositions," nor the even more formalistic effort to construct all-encompassing "conceptual schemes." Moore and Mills are rightly critical of such efforts. I am thinking of such questions as, "How are men capable of uniting to form enduring societies in the first place?"; "Why and to what degree is change inherent in human societies and what are the sources of change?"; "How is man's animal nature domesticated by society?"

Such questions—and they are existential as well as intellectual questions—are the *raison d'être* of social theory. They were asked by men long before the rise of sociology. Sociology itself is an effort, under new and unprecedented historical conditions, to find novel answers to them.

They are not questions which lend themselves to successively more precise answers as a result of cumulative empirical research, for they remain eternally problematic. Social theory is necessarily an interminable dialogue. "True understanding," Hannah Arendt has written, "does not tire of interminable dialogue and 'vicious circles' because it trusts that imagination will eventually catch at least a glimpse of the always frightening light of truth." [2]

I wish briefly to review the answers modern sociological theory offers to one such question, or rather to one aspect of one question. The question may be variously phrased as, "What are the sources of social cohesion?"; or, "How is social order possible?"; or, stated in social-psychological terms, "How is it that man becomes tractable to social discipline?" I shall call this question in its social-psychological aspect the "Hobbesian question" and in its more strictly sociological aspect the "Marxist question." The Hobbesian question asks how men are capable of the guidance by social norms and goals that makes possible an enduring society, while the Marxist question asks how, assuming this capability, complex societies manage to regulate and restrain destructive conflicts between groups. Much of our current theory offers an oversocialized view of man in answering the Hobbesian question and an overintegrated view of society in answering the Marxist question.

A number of writers have recently challenged the overintegrated view of society in contemporary theory. In addition to Moore and Mills, the names of Bendix, Coser, Dahrendorf, and Lockwood come to mind. [3] My intention, therefore, is to concentrate on the answers to the Hobbesian question in an effort to disclose the oversocialized view of man which they seem to imply.

Since my view of theory is obviously very different from that of Talcott Parsons and has, in fact, been developed in opposition to his, let me pay tribute to his recognition of the importance of the Hobbesian question—the "problem of order," as he calls it—at the very beginning of his first book, *The Structure of Social Action*.[4] Parsons correctly credits Hobbes with being the first thinker to see the necessity of explaining why human society is not a "war of all against all"; why, if man is simply a gifted animal, men refrain from unlimited resort to fraud and violence in pursuit of their ends and maintain a stable society at all. There is even a sense in which, as Coser and Mills have both noted,[5] Parsons' entire work represents an effort to solve the Hobbesian problem of order. His solution, however, has tended to become precisely the kind of elaboration of a set of answers in abstraction from questions that is so characteristic of contemporary sociological theory.

We need not be greatly concerned with Hobbes' own solution to the problem of order he saw with such unsurpassed clarity. Whatever interest his famous theory of the origin of the state may still hold for political scientists, it is clearly inadequate as an explanation of the origin of society. Yet the pattern as opposed to the details of Hobbes' thought bears closer examination.

The polar terms in Hobbes' theory are the state of nature, where the war of all against all prevails, and the authority of Leviathan, created by social contract. But the war of all against all is not simply effaced with the creation of political authority: it remains an ever-present potentiality in human society, at times quiescent, at times erupting into open violence. Whether Hobbes believed that the state of nature and the social contract were ever historical realities—and there is evidence that he was not that simple-minded and unsociological, even in the seventeenth century—is unimportant; the whole tenor of his thought is to see the war of all against all and Leviathan dialectically, as coexisting and interacting opposites.[6] As

R. G. Collingwood has observed, "According to Hobbes . . . *a body politic is a dialectical thing,* a Heraclitean world in which at any given time there is a negative element."[7] The first secular social theorist in the history of Western thought, and one of the first clearly to discern and define the problem of order in human society long before Darwinism made awareness of it a commonplace, Hobbes was a dialectical thinker who refused to separate answers from questions, solutions to society's enduring problems from the conditions creating the problems.

What is the answer of contemporary sociological theory to the Hobbesian question? There are two main answers, each of which has come to be understood in a way that denies the reality and meaningfulness of the question. Together they constitute a model of human nature, sometimes clearly stated, more often implicit in accepted concepts, that pervades modern sociology. The first answer is summed up in the notion of the "internalization of social norms." The second, more commonly employed or assumed in empirical research, is the view that man is essentially motivated by the desire to achieve a positive image of self by winning acceptance or status in the eyes of others.

The following statement represents, briefly and broadly, what is probably the most influential contemporary sociological conception—and dismissal—of the Hobbesian problem: "To a modern sociologist imbued with the conception that action follows institutionalized patterns, opposition of individual and common interests has only a very limited relevance or is thoroughly unsound."[8] From this writer's perspective, the problem is an unreal one: human conduct is totally shaped by common norms or "institutionalized patterns." Sheer ignorance must have led people who were unfortunate enough not to be modern sociologists to ask, "How is order possible?" A thoughtful bee or ant would never inquire, "How is the social order of the hive or ant-hill possible?" for the opposite of that order is unimaginable when the instinctive endowment of the insects ensures its stability and built-in harmony between "individual and common interests." Human society, we are assured, is not essentially different, although conformity and stability are there maintained by non-instinctive processes. Modern sociologists believe that they have understood these processes and that they have not merely answered but disposed of the Hobbesian question, showing that, far from expressing a valid intimation of the tensions and possibilities of social life, it can only be asked out of ignorance.

It would be hard to find a better illustration of what Collingwood, following Plato, calls *eristical* as opposed to dialectical thinking: [9] The answer destroys the question, or rather destroys the awareness of rival possibilities suggested by the question which accounts for its having been asked in the first place. A reversal of perspective now takes place and we are moved to ask the opposite question: "How is it that violence, conflict, revolution, and the individual's sense of coercion by society manage to exist at all, if this view is correct?" [10] Whenever a one-sided answer to a question compels us to raise the opposite question, we are caught up in a dialectic of concepts which reflects a dialectic in things. But let us examine the particular processes sociologists appeal to in order to account for the elimination from human society of the war of all against all.

The Changing Meaning of Internalization

A well-known section of *The Structure of Social Action,* devoted to the interpretation of Durkheim's thought, is entitled "The Changing Meaning of Constraint." [11] Parsons argues that Durkheim originally conceived of society as controlling the individual from the outside by imposing constraints on him through sanctions, best illustrated by codes of law. But in Durkheim's later work he began to see that social rules do not "merely regulate 'externally' . . . they enter directly into the constitution of the actors' ends themselves." [12] Constraint, therefore, is more than an environmental obstacle which the actor must take into account in pursuit of his goals in the same way that he takes into account physical laws: it becomes internal, psychological, and self-imposed as well. Parsons developed this view that social norms are constitutive rather than merely regulative of human nature before he was influenced by psychoanalytic theory, but Freud's theory of the superego has become the source and model for the conception of the internalization of social norms that today plays so important a part in sociological thinking. The use some sociologists have made of Freud's idea, however, might well inspire an essay entitled, "The Changing Meaning of Internalization," although, in contrast to the shift in Durkheim's view of constraint, this change has been a change for the worse.

What has happened is that internalization has imperceptibly been equated with "learning," or even with "habit-formation" in the simplest sense. Thus when a norm is said to have been "internalized" by an individual, what is frequently meant is that he habitually both affirms it and conforms to it in his conduct. The whole stress on inner conflict, on the tension between powerful impulses and superego controls the behavioral outcome of which cannot be prejudged, drops out of the picture. And it is this that is central to Freud's view, for in psychoanalytic terms to say that a norm has been internalized, or introjected to become part of the superego, is to say no more than that a person will suffer guilt-feelings if he fails to live up to it, not that he will in fact live up to it in his behavior.

The relation between internalization and conformity assumed by most sociologists is suggested by the following passage from a recent, highly praised advanced textbook: "Conformity to institutionalized norms is, of course, 'normal.' The actor, having internalized the norms, feels something like a need to conform. His conscience would bother him if he did not." [13] What is overlooked here is that the person who conforms may be even more "bothered," that is, subject to guilt and neurosis, than the person who violates what are not only society's norms but his own as well. To Freud, it is precisely the man with the strictest superego, he who has most thoroughly internalized and conformed to the norms of his society, who is most wracked with guilt and anxiety.[14]

Paul Kecskemeti, to whose discussion I owe initial recognition of the erroneous view of internalization held by sociologists, argues that the relations between social norms, the individual's selection from them, his conduct, and his feelings about his conduct are far from self-evident. "It is by no means true," he writes, "to say that acting counter to one's own norms always or almost always leads to neurosis. One might assume that neurosis develops even more easily in persons who *never* violate the moral code they recognize as valid but repress and frustrate some strong instinctual motive. A person who 'succumbs to temptation,' feels guilt, and then 'purges himself' of his guilt in some reliable way (e.g., by confession) may achieve in this way a better balance, and be less neurotic, than a person who never violates his 'norms' and never feels conscious guilt." [15]

Recent discussions of "deviant behavior" have been compelled to recognize these distinctions between social demands, personal attitudes towards them, and actual conduct, although they have done so in a laboriously taxonomic fashion.[16] They represent, however, largely the rediscovery of what was always central to the Freudian concept of the superego. The main explanatory function of the concept is to show how people repress themselves, imposing checks on their own desires and thus turning the inner life into a battlefield of conflicting motives, no matter which side "wins," by successfully dictating overt action. So far as behavior is concerned, the psychoanalytic view of man is less deterministic than the sociological. For psychoanalysis is primarily concerned with the inner life, not with overt behavior, and its most fundamental insight is that the wish, the emotion, and the fantasy are as important as the act in man's experience.

Sociologists have appropriated the superego concept, but have separated it from any equivalent of the Freudian id. So long as most individuals are "socialized," that is, internalize the norms and conform to them in conduct, the Hobbesian problem is not even perceived as a latent reality. Deviant behavior is accounted for by special circumstances: ambiguous norms, anomie, role conflict, or greater cultural stress on valued goals than on the approved means for attaining them. Tendencies to deviant behavior are not seen as dialectically related to conformity. The presence in man of motivational forces bucking against the hold social discipline has over him is denied.

Nor does the assumption that internalization of norms and roles is the essence of socialization allow for a sufficient range of motives underlying conformity. It fails to allow for variable "tonicity of the superego," in Kardiner's phrase.[17] The degree to which conformity is frequently the result of coercion rather than conviction is minimized.[18] Either someone has internalized the norms, or he is "unsocialized," a feral or socially isolated child, or a psychopath. Yet Freud recognized that many people, conceivably a majority, fail to acquire superegos. "Such people," he wrote, "habitually permit themselves to do any bad deed that procures them something they want, if only they are sure that no authority will discover it or make them suffer for it; their anxiety relates only to the possibility of detection. Present-day society has to take into account the prevalence of this state of mind." [19] The last sentence suggests that Freud was aware of the decline of "inner-direction," of the Protestant conscience, about which we have heard so much lately. So let us turn to the other elements of human nature that sociologists appeal to in order to explain, or rather explain away, the Hobbesian problem.

Man the Acceptance-Seeker [20]

The superego concept is too inflexible, too bound to the past and to individual biography, to be of service in relating conduct to the pressures of the immediate situation in which it takes place. Sociologists rely more heavily therefore on an alternative notion, here stated—or, to be fair, overstated—in its baldest form: "People are so profoundly sensitive to the expectations of others that all action is inevitably guided by these expectations." [21]

Parsons' model of the "complementarity of expectations," the view that in social interaction men mutually seek approval from one another by conforming to shared norms, is a formalized version of what has tended to become a distinctive sociological perspective on human motivation. Ralph Linton states it in explicit psychological terms: "The need for eliciting favorable responses from others is an almost constant component of [personality]. Indeed, it is not too much to say that there is very little organized human behavior which is not directed toward its satisfaction in at least some degree." [22]

The insistence of sociologists on the importance of "social factors" easily leads them to stress the priority of such socialized or socializing motives in human behavior.[23] It is frequently the task of the sociologist to call attention to the intensity with which men desire and strive for the good opinion of their immediate associates in a variety of situations, particularly those where received theories or ideologies have unduly emphasized other motives such as financial gain, commitment to ideals, or the effects on energies and aspirations of arduous physical conditions. Thus sociologists have shown that factory workers are more sensitive to the attitudes of their fellow-workers than to purely economic incentives; that voters are more influenced by the preferences of their relatives and friends than by campaign debates on the "issues;" that soldiers, whatever their ideological commitment to their nation's cause, fight more bravely when their platoons are intact and they stand side by side with their "buddies."

It is certainly not my intention to criticize the findings of such studies. My objection is that their particular selective emphasis is generalized—explicitly or, more often, implicitly—to provide apparent empirical support for an extremely one-sided view of human nature. Although sociologists have criticized past efforts to single out one fundamental motive in human conduct, the desire to achieve a favorable self-image by winning approval from others frequently occupies such a position in their own thinking. The following "theorem" has been, in fact, openly put forward by Hans Zetterberg as "a strong contender for the position as the major Motivational Theorem in sociology": [24]

An actor's actions have a tendency to become dispositions that are related to the occurence [*sic*] of favored uniform evaluations of the actor and-or his actions in his action system.[25]

Now Zetterberg is not necessarily maintaining that this theorem is an accurate factual statement of the basic psychological roots of social behavior. He is, characteristically, far too self-conscious about the logic of theorizing and "concept formation" for that. He goes on to remark that "the maximization of favorable attitudes from others would thus be the counterpart in sociological theory to the maximization of profit in economic theory." [26] If by this it is meant that the theorem is to be understood as a heuristic rather than an empirical assumption, that sociology has a selective point of view which is just as abstract and partial as that of economics and the other social sciences, and if his view of theory as a set of logically connected formal propositions is granted provisional acceptance, I am in agreement. (Actually, the view of theory suggested at the beginning of this paper is a quite different one.)

But there is a further point to be made. Ralph Dahrendorf has observed that structural-functional theorists do not "claim that order *is based on* a general consensus of values, but that it *can be conceived of in terms of* such consensus and that, if it is conceived of in these terms, certain propositions follow which are subject to the test of specific observations." [27] The same may be said of the assumption that people seek to maximize favorable evaluations by others; indeed this assumption has already fathered such additional concepts as "reference group" and "circle of significant others." Yet the question must be raised as to whether we really wish to, in effect, define sociology by such partial perspectives. The assumption of the maximization of approval from others is the psychological complement to the sociological assumption of a general value consensus. And the former is as selective and one-sided a way of looking at motivation as Dahrendorf and others have argued the latter to be when it determines our way of looking at social structure. The oversocialized view of man of the one is a counterpart to the overintegrated view of society of the other.

Modern sociology, after all, originated as a protest against the partial views of man contained in such doctrines as utilitarianism, classical economics, social Darwinism, and vulgar Marxism. All of the great nineteenth and early twentieth century sociologists [28] saw it as one of their major tasks to expose the unreality of such abstractions as economic man, the gain-seeker of the classical economists; political man, the power-seeker of the Ma-

chiavellian tradition in political science; self-preserving man, the security-seeker of Hobbes and Darwin; sexual or libidinal man, the pleasure-seeker of doctrinaire Freudianism; and even religious man, the God-seeker of the theologians. It would be ironical if it should turn out that they have merely contributed to the creation of yet another reified abstraction in socialized man, the status-seeker of our contemporary sociologists.

Of course, such an image of man is, like all the others mentioned, valuable for limited purposes so long as it is not taken for the whole truth. What are some of its deficiencies? To begin with, it neglects the other half of the model of human nature presupposed by current theory: moral man, guided by his built-in superego and beckoning ego-ideal.[29] In recent years sociologists have been less interested than they once were in culture and national character as backgrounds to conduct, partly because stress on the concept of "role" as the crucial link between the individual and the social structure has directed their attention to the immediate situation in which social interaction takes place. Man is increasingly seen as a "role-playing" creature, responding eagerly or anxiously to the expectations of other role-players in the multiple group settings in which he finds himself. Such an approach, while valuable in helping us grasp the complexity of a highly differentiated social structure such as our own, is far too often generalized to serve as a kind of *ad hoc* social psychology, easily adaptable to particular sociological purposes.

But it is not enough to concede that men often pursue "internalized values" remaining indifferent to what others think of them, particularly when, as I have previously argued, the idea of internalization has been "hollowed out" to make it more useful as an explanation of conformity. What of desire for material and sensual satisfactions? Can we really dispense with the venerable notion of material "interests" and invariably replace it with the blander, more integrative "social values"? And what of striving for power, not necessarily for its own sake—that may be rare and pathological—but as a means by which men are able to *impose* a normative definition of reality on others? That material interests, sexual drives, and the quest for power have often been over-estimated as human motives is no reason to deny their reality. To do so is to suppress one term of the dialectic between conformity and rebellion, social norms and their violation, man and social order, as completely as the other term is suppressed by those who deny the reality of man's "normative orientation" or reduce it to the effect of coercion, rational calculation, or mechanical conditioning.

The view that man is invariably pushed by internalized norms or pulled by the lure of self-validation by others ignores—to speak archaically for a moment—both the highest and the lowest, both beast and angel, in his nature. Durkheim, from whom so much of the modern sociological point of view derives, recognized that the very existence of a social norm implies and even creates the possibility of its violation. This is the meaning of his famous dictum that crime is a "normal phenomenon." He maintained that "for the originality of the idealist whose dreams transcend his century to find expression, it is necessary that the originality of the criminal, who is below the level of his time, shall also be possible. One does not occur without the other." [30] Yet Durkheim lacked an adequate psychology and formulated his insight in terms of the actor's cognitive awareness rather than in motivational terms. We do not have Durkheim's excuse for falling back on what Homans has called a "social mold theory" of human nature. [31]

Social but Not Entirely Socialized

I have referred to forces in man that are resistant to socialization. It is not my purpose to explore the nature of these forces

or to suggest how we ought best conceive of them as sociologists—that would be a most ambitious undertaking. A few remarks will have to suffice. I think we must start with the recognition that *in the beginning there is the body*. As soon as the body is mentioned the specter of "biological determinism" raises its head and sociologists draw back in fright. And certainly their view of man is sufficiently disembodied and non-materialistic to satisfy Bishop Berkeley, as well as being de-sexualized enough to please Mrs. Grundy.

Am I, then, urging us to return to the older view of a human nature divided between a "social man" and a "natural man" who is either benevolent, Rousseau's Noble Savage, or sinister and destructive, as Hobbes regarded him? Freud is usually represented, or misrepresented, as the chief modern proponent of this dualistic conception which assigns to the social order the purely negative role of blocking and re-directing man's "imperious biological drives." [32] I say "misrepresented" because, although Freud often said things supporting such an interpretation, other and more fundamental strains in his thinking suggest a different conclusion. John Dollard, certainly not a writer who is oblivious to social and cultural "factors," saw this twenty-five years ago: "It is quite clear," he wrote, ". . . that he (Freud) does not regard the instincts as having a fixed social goal; rather, indeed, in the case of the sexual instinct he has stressed the vague but powerful and impulsive nature of the drive and has emphasized that its proper social object is not picked out in advance. His seems to be a drive concept which is not at variance with our knowledge from comparative cultural studies, since his theory does not demand that the 'instinct' work itself out with mechanical certainty alike in every varying culture." [33]

So much for Freud's "imperious biological drives!" When Freud defined psychoanalysis as the study of the "vicissitudes of the instincts," he was confirming, not denying, the "plasticity" of human nature insisted on by social scientists. The drives or "instincts" of psychoanalysis, far from being fixed dispositions to behave in a particular way, are utterly subject to social channelling and transformation and could not even reveal themselves in behavior without social molding any more than our vocal chords can produce articulate speech if we have not learned a language. To psychoanalysis man is indeed a social animal; his social nature is profoundly reflected in his bodily structure.[34]

But there is a difference between the Freudian view on the one hand and both sociological and neo-Freudian conceptions of man on the other. To Freud man is a *social* animal without being entirely a *socialized* animal. His very social nature is the source of conflicts and antagonisms that create resistance to socialization by the norms of any of the societies which have existed in the course of human history. "Socialization" may mean two quite distinct things; when they are confused an oversocialized view of man is the result. On the one hand socialization means the "transmission of the culture," the particular culture of the society an individual enters at birth; on the other hand the term is used to mean the "process of becoming human," of acquiring uniquely human attributes from interaction with others.[35] All men are socialized in the latter sense, but this does not mean that they have been completely molded by the particular norms and values of their culture. All

cultures, as Freud contended, do violence to man's socialized bodily drives, but this in no sense means that men could possibly exist without culture or independently of society.[36] From such a standpoint, man may properly be called as Norman Brown has called him, the "neurotic" or the "discontented" animal and repression may be seen as the main characteristic of human nature as we have known it in history.[37]

But isn't this psychology and haven't sociologists been taught to foreswear psychology, to look with suspicion on what are called "psychological variables" in contradistinction to the institutional and historical forces with which they are properly concerned? There is, indeed, as recent critics have complained, too much "psychologism" in contemporary sociology, largely, I think, because of the bias inherent in our favored research techniques. But I do not see how, at the level of theory, sociologists can fail to make assumptions about human nature.[38] If our assumptions are left implicit, we will inevitably presuppose of a view of man that is tailor-made to our special needs; when our sociological theory over-stresses the stability and integration of society we will end up imagining that man is the disembodied, conscience-driven, status-seeking phantom of current theory. We must do better if we really wish to win credit outside of our ranks for special understanding of man, that plausible creature [39] whose wagging tongue so often hides the despair and darkness in his heart.

NOTES

1. Barrington Moore, Jr., *Political Power and Social Theory,* Cambridge: Harvard University Press, 1958; C. Wright Mills, *The Sociological Imagination,* New York: Oxford University Press, 1959.

2. Hannah Arendt, "Understanding and Politics," *Partisan Review,* 20 (July-August, 1953), 392. For a view of social theory close to the one adumbrated in the present paper, see Theodore Abel, "The Present Status of Social Theory," *American Sociological Review,* 17 (April, 1952), 156–164.

3. Reinhard Bendix and Bennett Berger, "Images of Society and Problems of Concept Formation in Sociology," in Llewellyn Gross (ed.), *Symposium on Sociological Theory,* Evanston, Ill.: Row, Petersen & Co., 1959, pp. 92–118; Lewis A. Coser, *The Functions of Social Conflict,* Glencoe, Ill.: The Free Press, 1956; Ralf Dahrendorf, "Out of Utopia: Towards a Re-Orientation of Sociological Analysis," *American Journal of Sociology,* 64 (September,

1958), 115–127; and *Class and Class Conflict in Industrial Society*, Stanford, Calif.: Stanford University Press, 1959; David Lockwood, "Some Remarks on 'The Social System,'" *British Journal of Sociology*, 7 (June, 1956), 134–146.

4. Talcott Parsons, *The Structure of Social Action*, New York: McGraw-Hill Book Co., 1937, pp. 89–94.

5. Coser, *op. cit.*, p. 21; Mills, *op. cit.*, p. 44.

6. A recent critic of Parsons follows Hobbes in seeing the relation between the normative order in society and what he calls "the sub-stratum of social action" and other sociologists have called the "factual order" as similar to the relation between the war of all against all and the authority of the state. David Lockwood writes: "The existence of the normative order . . . is in one very important sense inextricably bound up with potential conflicts of interest over scarce resources . . . ; the very existence of a normative order mirrors the continual potentiality of conflict." Lockwood, *op. cit.*, p. 137.

7. R. G. Collingwood, *The New Leviathan*, Oxford: The Clarendon Press, 1942, p. 183.

8. Francis X. Sutton and others, *The American Business Creed*, Cambridge: Harvard University Press, 1956, p. 304. I have cited this study and, on several occasions, textbooks and fugitive articles rather than better-known and directly theoretical writings because I am just as concerned with what sociological concepts and theories are taken to mean when they are actually used in research, teaching, and introductory exposition as with their elaboration in more self-conscious and explicitly theoretical discourse. Since the model of human nature I am criticizing is partially implicit and "buried" in our concepts, cruder and less qualified illustrations are as relevant as the formulations of leading theorists. I am also aware that some older theorists, notably Cooley and MacIver, were shrewd and worldly-wise enough to reject the implication that man is ever fully socialized. Yet they failed to develop competing images of man which were concise and systematic enough to counter the appeal of the oversocialized models.

9. Collingwood, *op. cit.*, pp. 181–182.

10. *Cf.* Mills, *op. cit.*, pp. 32–33, 42. While Mills does not discuss the use of the concept of internalization by Parsonian theorists, I have argued elsewhere that his view of the relation between power and values is insufficiently dialectical. See Dennis H. Wrong, "The Failure of American Sociology," *Commentary*, 28 (November, 1959), 378.

11. Parsons, *op. cit.*, pp. 378–390.

12. *Ibid.*, p. 382.

13. Harry M. Johnson, *Sociology: A Systematic Introduction*, New York: Harcourt, Brace and Co., 1960, p. 22.

14. Sigmund Freud, *Civilization and Its Discontents*, New York: Doubleday Anchor Books, 1958, pp. 20–21.

15. Paul Kecskemeti, *Meaning, Communication, and Value*, Chicago: University of Chicago Press, 1952, pp. 244–245.

16. Robert Dubin, "Deviant Behavior and Social Structure: Continuities in Social Theory," *American Sociological Review*, 24 (April, 1959), 147–164; Robert K. Merton, "Social Conformity, Deviation, and Opportunity Structures: A Comment on the Contributions of Dubin and Cloward," *Ibid.*, pp. 178–189.

17. Abram Kardiner, *The Individual and His Society*, New York: Columbia University Press, 1939, pp. 65, 72–75.

18. Mills, *op. cit.*, pp. 39–41; Dahrendorf, *Class and Class Conflict in Industrial Society*, pp. 157–165.

19. Freud, *op. cit.*, pp. 78–79.

20. In many ways I should prefer to use the neater, more alliterative phrase "status-seeker." However, it has acquired a narrower meaning than I intend, particularly since Vance Packard appropriated it, suggesting primarily efforts, which are often consciously deceptive, to give the appearance of personal achievements or qualities worthy of deference. "Status-seeking" in this sense is, as Veblen perceived, necessarily confined to relatively impersonal and segmental social relationships. "Acceptance" or "approval" convey more adequately what all men are held to

seek in both intimate and impersonal relations according to the conception of the self and of motivation dominating contemporary sociology and social psychology. I have, nevertheless, been unable to resist the occasional temptation to use the term "status" in this broader sense.

21. Sutton and others, *op. cit.*, p. 264. Robert Cooley Angell, in *Free Society and Moral Crisis,* Ann Arbor: University of Michigan Press, 1958, p. 34, points out the ambiguity of the term "expectations." It is used, he notes, to mean both a factual prediction and a moral imperative, e.g. "England expects every man to do his duty." But this very ambiguity is instructive, for it suggests the process by which behavior that is non-normative and perhaps even "deviant" but nevertheless "expected" in the sense of being predictable, acquires over time a normative aura and becomes "expected" in the second sense of being socially approved or demanded. Thus Parsons' "interaction paradigm" provides leads to the understanding of social change and need not be confined, as in his use of it, to the explanation of conformity and stability. But this is the subject of another paper I hope to complete shortly.

22. Ralph Linton, *The Cultural Background of Personality,* New York: Appleton-Century Co., 1945, p. 91.

23. When values are "inferred" from this emphasis and then popularized, it becomes the basis of the ideology of "groupism" extolling the virtues of "togetherness" and "belongingness" that have been attacked and satirized so savagely in recent social criticism. David Riesman and W. H. Whyte, the pioneers of this current of criticism in its contemporary guise, are both aware, as their imitators and epigoni usually are not, of the extent to which the social phenomenon they have described is the result of the diffusion and popularization of sociology itself. See on this point Robert Gutman and Dennis H. Wrong, "Riesman's Typology of Character" (forthcoming in a symposium on Riesman's work to be edited by Leo Lowenthal and Seymour Martin Lipset), and William H. Whyte, *The Organization Man,* New York: Simon and Schuster, 1956, Chapters 3–5. As a matter of fact, Riesman's "inner-direction" and "other-direction" correspond rather closely to the notions of "internalization" and "acceptance-seeking" in contemporary sociology as I have described them. Riesman even refers to his concepts initially as characterizations of "modes of conformity," although he then makes the mistake, as Robert Gutman and I have argued, of calling them character types. But his view that all men are to some degree both inner-directed and other-directed, a qualification that has been somewhat neglected by critics who have understandably concentrated on his empirical and historical use of his typology, suggests the more generalized conception of forces making for conformity found in current theory. See David Riesman, Nathan Glazer, and Reuel Denny, *The Lonely Crowd,* New York: Doubleday Anchor Books, 1953, pp. 17 ff. However, as Robert Gutman and I have observed: "In some respects Riesman's conception of character is Freudian rather than neo-Freudian: character is defined by superego mechanisms and, like Freud in *Civilization and Its Discontents,* the socialized individual is defined by what is forbidden him rather than by what society stimulates him to do. Thus in spite of Riesman's generally sanguine attitude towards modern America, implicit in his typology is a view of society as the enemy both of individuality and of basic drive gratification, a view that contrasts with the at least potentially benign role assigned it by neo-Freudian thinkers like Fromm and Horney." Gutman and Wrong, "Riesman's Typology of Character," p. 4 (typescript).

24. Hans L. Zetterberg, "Compliant Actions," *Acta Sociologica,* 2 (1957), 189.

25. *Ibid.,* p. 188.

26. *Ibid.,* p. 189.

27. Dahrendorf, *Class and Class Conflict in Industrial Society,* p. 158.

28. Much of the work of Thorstein Veblen, now generally regarded as a sociologist (perhaps the greatest America has yet produced), was, of course, a polemic against the rational, calculating *homo economicus* of classical economics and a documentation of the importance in economic life of the quest for status measured by conformity to arbitrary and shifting conventional standards. Early in his first and most famous book Veblen made an observation on human nature resembling that which looms so large in contemporary sociological thinking: "The usual basis of self-respect," he wrote, "is the respect accorded by one's neighbors. Only individuals with an aberrant temperament can in the long run retain their self-esteem in the face of the disesteem of their fellows." *The Theory of the Leisure Class,* New York: Mentor Books, 1953, p. 38. Whatever the inadequacies of his psychological assumptions, Veblen did not, however, overlook other motivations to which he frequently gave equal or greater weight.

29. Robin M. Williams, Jr. writes: "At the present time, the literature of sociology and social psychology contains many references to 'Conformity'—conforming to norms, 'yielding to social pressure,' or 'adjusting to the requirements of the reference group.' . . . ; the implication is easily drawn that the actors in question are *motivated* solely in terms of conformity or non-conformity, rather than in terms of 'expressing' or 'affirming' internalized values . . ." (his italics). "Continuity and Change in Sociological Study," *American Sociological Review*, 23 (December, 1958), 630.

30. Emile Durkheim, *The Rules of Sociological Method*, Chicago: University of Chicago Press, 1938, p. 71.

31. George C. Homans, *The Human Group*, New York: Harcourt, Brace and Company, 1950, pp. 317–319.

32. Robert K. Merton, *Social Theory and Social Structure*, Revised and Enlarged Edition, Glencoe, Ill.: The Free Press, 1957, p. 131. Merton's view is representative of that of most contemporary sociologists. See also Hans Gerth and C. Wright Mills, *Character and Social Structure*, New York: Harcourt, Brace and Company, 1953, pp. 112–113. For a similar view by a "neo-Freudian," see Erich Fromm, *The Sane Society*, New York: Rinehart and Company, 1955, pp. 74–77.

33. John Dollard, *Criteria for the Life History*, New Haven: Yale University Press, 1935, p. 120. This valuable book has been neglected, presumably because it appears to be a purely methodological effort to set up standards for judging the adequacy of biographical and autobiographical data. Actually, the standards serve as well to evaluate the adequacy of general theories of personality or human nature and even to prescribe in part what a sound theory ought to include.

34. One of the few attempts by a social scientist to relate systematically man's anatomical structure and biological history to his social nature and his unique cultural creativity is Weston La Barre's *The Human Animal*, Chicago: University of Chicago Press, 1954. See especially Chapters 4–6, but the entire book is relevant. It is one of the few exceptions to Paul Goodman's observation that anthropologists nowadays "commence with a chapter on Physical Anthropology and then forget the whole topic and go on to Culture." See his "Growing up Absurd," *Dissent*, 7 (Spring, 1960), 121.

35. Paul Goodman has developed a similar distinction. *Op. cit.*, pp. 123–125.

36. Whether it might be possible to create a society that does not repress the bodily drives is a separate question. See Herbert Marcuse, *Eros and Civilization*, Boston: The Beacon Press, 1955; and Norman O. Brown, *Life Against Death*, New York: Random House, Modern Library Paperbacks, 1960. Neither Marcuse nor Brown are guilty in their brilliant, provocative, and visionary books of assuming a "natural man" who awaits liberation from social bonds. They differ from such sociological Utopians as Fromm, *op. cit.*, in their lack of sympathy for the de-sexualized man of the neo-Freudians. For the more traditional Freudian view, see Walter A. Weisskopf, "The 'Socialization' of Psychoanalysis in Contemporary America," in Benjamin Nelson (ed.), *Psychoanalysis and the Future*, New York: National Psychological Association for Psychoanalysis, 1957, pp. 51–56; Hans Meyerhoff, "Freud and the Ambiguity of Culture," *Partisan Review*, 24 (Winter, 1957), 117–130.

37. Brown, *op. cit.*, pp. 3–19.

38. "I would assert that very little sociological analysis is ever done without using at least an implicit psychological theory." Alex Inkeles, "Personality and Social Structure," in Robert K. Merton and others (eds.), *Sociology Today*, New York: Basic Books, 1959, p. 250.

39. Harry Stack Sullivan once remarked that the most outstanding characteristic of human beings was their "plausibility."

The Process and Impact of Socialization

11. SOCIALIZATION: FITTING MAN TO HIS SOCIETY

JOSEPH BENSMAN *and* BERNARD ROSENBERG

Ely Chinoy has said that culture is that which "defines appropriate or required modes of thinking, acting, and feeling." Gertrude Jaeger and Philip Selznick emphasized the importance of evaluating symbols and symbolic experience in understanding the nature of culture, a point partially illustrated by Edward T. Hall. Harry Bredemeier and Richard Stephenson discussed the ways in which human beings internalize the prescribed definitions of social situations presented to them in terms of standards for behavior, or norms.

In this article, Joseph Bensman and Bernard Rosenberg explain how cultural patterns—norms, values, ideas, and practices—are transmitted from generation to generation, from group to group, from one individual to another. This process of transmission is called socialization.

Socialization, as shall be shown, involves the learning of appropriate symbols that provide the means for communicating. It also involves the learning of particular roles which aid the person in developing his own self-image or identity.

Joseph Bensman is Professor of Sociology at City College of the City University of New York. With Arthur J. Vidich, he is coauthor of Small Town in Mass Society *(1958). Bernard Rosenberg is also Professor of Sociology at City College of the City University of New York. He is the author of* The Values of Veblen *(1956) and* Analyses of Con-

From *Mass, Class, and Bureaucracy: The Evolution of Contemporary Society*, by Joseph Bensman and Bernard Rosenberg, © 1963. Reprinted by permission of the authors and Prentice-Hall, Inc., Englewood Cliffs, New Jersey.

temporary Society (*1966*). *He is the editor of* Analyses of Contemporary Society (*1966*), *and coeditor of* Mass Culture (*1957*), Sociological Theory (*1957*), Mass Society in Crisis (*1964*), *and* Mass Culture: The Popular Arts in America. *Bensman and Rosenberg are coauthors of* Mass, Class, and Bureaucracy (*1963*), *from which this selection is adapted.*

Culture has continuity. Norms and patterns of behavior, like technology and level of economic development, may endure for many centuries. The cultural values inherent in Judaism, for example, have been passed on from generation to generation for several millennia; those embodied in Christianity, for nearly two thousand years. Even when culture changes very markedly through innovation and invention, new norms and patterns usually result from combinations or modifications of those that have long been in vogue. This continuity seems all the more remarkable to us when we reflect that any specific culture persists as a unique entity despite the complete turnover of its bearers in every generation. And in every generation the whole of a culture is transmitted to new generations. The process by which this occurs we call *socialization*.

Communication and Meaning in Socialization

The infant—a weak, dependent, completely helpless thing—is "aware" of only his inner tensions and biological needs, but not of what they are, much less how to allay or gratify them. Yet very shortly, to join others as a member of his society, he will have to master a complicated range of techniques, beliefs, and values. When this happens, we may say that he is socialized.

The baby, the human (or more accurately prehuman) infant, has unfocused biological needs, while in the lower orders of animal life, behavior is governed by biologically predetermined mechanisms. In these orders, learning is of minimal importance, although it does take place

(in some sense even among insects). But experience cannot accumulate, nor is behavior basically modified without previous biological changes. The environment which man builds for himself by transmitting his experience to others is qualitatively exclusive to his own species.

Infants, subject to internal pressures, hungers, tensions, and drives, are totally lacking in the means to ease or assuage them. They do not yet know what specific object or what kind of action will relieve their discomfort. Others know or know how to find out—and they alone can reduce the tension. When an infant cries, he may be hungry, wet, cold, stuck with a pin, or simply in need of being held. His mother, in tending to his needs, communicates to him the cause of his discomfort. Only then does he learn what was wrong. As Muzafer Sherif, a contemporary social psychologist, has said of the infant, "His earliest perceptions and discriminations, as well as actions, appear chiefly in relation to biologically significant objects and are then 'canalized' to objects and persons instrumental to such satisfactions." Sherif also observes:

The activity of a baby in the first weeks of his life is determined chiefly by the biogenic need with which he is born. From the standpoint of a socialized adult, his behavior may seem utterly chaotic and haphazard. But as Gesell put it so colorfully: "From the standpoint of 4-week-oldness his behavior is patterned, meaningful, significant." And the determiners of this 4-week-oldness are the physiological states of his organism. This general fact can be substantiated by anyone who carefully observes or cares for an infant. . . .

As the baby grows and develops, the opportunities for varied stimulation and contact with persons and objects in his environment increase. In many respects, the most important of these contacts arise in connection with feeding, sleep, elimination, and other physiological functions. It is not surprising, in view of what is known about the effects of the biogenic needs on the learning process, to find that the earliest discriminatory responses are preponderantly directed toward persons and objects related to the satisfaction of these needs. . . .[1]

In earliest infancy, by crying, the child establishes an elementary sort of social relationship, and by his mother's response he learns the meaning of his action. From this we see that even in its meagerest beginnings, socialization is based on the communication of meaning and value. Only as he is able to absorb the many meanings of social action and their value does the child begin to share in his culture.

As he repeats the process of "communication by crying"—and even it has infantile nuances—the child gradually masters a variety of other gestures that draw attention to his needs. Trial and error teach him which responses to expect. He communicates a limited range of emotion more effectively than before. He also observes that different persons respond to his gestures in different ways. For instance, his mother probably will tend to his every immediate need, his father may merely play with him, and strangers may not respond at all to any of his gestures. Realizing that there is a differential response to him, the child learns to choose his gestures and apply them appropriately. Thus, when he is distressed he signals his mother; with his father he is playful; and when in the presence of a stranger, he simply stares, wondering what to do next. Certain expectations become familiar. Others are unknown, unstructured, undefined—and yet to be learned.

Roles and Role-playing

A socially defined or collective expectation is called a *role*. It consists of the probable behavior that will be evoked in an individual by others under specified conditions, giving that behavior an indispensable measure of predictability. Without the roles assigned to us by our culture, group life, based on interpretative interaction among human beings, would be impossible.

For every function performed in society there is a role. The role of father defines that conduct which one can expect from a man in relation to his children. The manner in which he is expected to act as father—or for that matter, as son, husband, father-in-law, grandfather, brother, uncle, cousin, not to mention areas far removed from the family drama—we call *role expectancy,* and the actual response to this expectancy we may call *role performance* or *role fulfillment.* The father also expects specific behavior of his children, and a great part of their action takes the form of role fulfillment to the father's role expectancies. The process is interactive: it presupposes a certain mutuality in which role expectancies and role fulfillment produce role-playing.

At first the parent acts alone as a cultural agent. He defines the behavior of his child—and in doing so tells him what is expected of him. From parental reactions, the child comes to know which of his appeals for attention will be most effective. Ordinarily, he modifies his behavior to achieve desired responses.

Role-playing, however, does not take place merely on this interpersonal level. Whereas the infant recognizes only his physical discomforts and tensions, parents come to their relationship with children bearing a great many cultural expectations and definitions of behavior. They therefore judge the child by applying standards, values, conventions, and customs which have become "second nature" to them. It is in keeping with the parents' norms—those they have "internalized" from their culture—that demands are made on the child. Only in the earliest stages of infancy are the child's demands paramount. Thereafter, as the child matures, he discovers that some of his demands are met and others are not. His parents begin to say "No!" and to make it clear that only certain forms of behavior will evoke the response he seeks. Clyde Kluckhohn and Henry A. Murray, two gifted students of human personality, noting that the inculcation of social patterns is partly rewarding to a child who, without it, could do no more than grope toward a mastery of the many things he must learn, add:

> However, a child is also confronted by a multiplicity of Don'ts, each connected with some activity or place, or objects towards which he is naturally disposed, and a large number of Do's connected with actions toward which he is not disposed, at least at the time or in the manner indicated. If he is to avoid punishment and enjoy the rewards which adults have to offer, he must learn to inhibit or redirect certain insistent impulses, temporarily or permanently, as well as learn to force himself to perform certain other actions which at the time are repugnant to his feelings. After countless protestations and rebellions, the average child, with great reluctance, learns to do these things, to the extent of conforming to most of the patterns which are considered normal for his age.[2]

In all this there is a large ingredient of power—which is not the same as force, but connotes *latent* or *potential* force. Parents possess total power over their young child, granting to or withholding from him basic gratifications. This becomes more obvious as he matures beyond infancy. Their attitude is governed by the child's willingness or unwillingness to accept cultural standards. To the extent that he abides by these standards, he is accorded personal gratifications. But in addition to pleasing mother and father, his acceptable actions conform to an over-all culture of which he is unaware.

The above is highly oversimplified. We do not mean to suggest that socialization and the culture which it transmits rest only on power. Although it is necessarily an important factor, there are additional "mechanisms"—as they are known in psychoanalysis—which also facilitate the internalization of initially external norms.

In infancy, as we have said, the child makes demands by gestures, above all by crying, and does this without knowing what steps he might take to abate his discomfort or satisfy his needs. Although parent and child "communicate," it is the parent who responds to the child long before the child responds to the parent. In these earliest exchanges the child appears to be all-powerful: his little repertoire of noises quickly and effectively, not to say magically, produces the desired results. With greater maturity, however, it comes to him that he is not omnipotent, that, on the contrary, his parents have the power to do things (far beyond his capacity) not just for themselves, but for him as well. Gratification of the child's wants depends on his parents. Seeing this situation, the child wishes to be like his parents, to share the adults' apparently enormous powers, and to receive the benefits of affection and approval from these all-powerful figures. The illusion of omnipotence persists; only its locus is altered.

Identification as a Process in Socialization

In order to become like his parents, the child adopts their attitudes; he imitates and, in his own childish way, mirrors their speech, gesticulations, and general conduct. He begins simultaneously to enact the roles of both parent and child. He, for example, gives orders to himself and carries them out (with resultant confusion, slowly eliminated, in the use of personal pronouns). These attitudes and behavior patterns are no longer wholly external to the child; having at this stage become part of his personality, they are more than mere constraints to which he must bow. He has absorbed parental—and hence broadly cultural—values, in order to be more like those persons in his environment who are already socialized. This aspect of social learning is called *identification*.

Children almost always voluntarily accept attitudes and values internalized through identification at an early age. These attitudes and values come to be an integral part of the adult's personality, the backbone of his character formed from a cluster of norms somewhat less likely to change than those internalized later in life. Through identification, then, much of the parents' culture is selectively, not altogether predictably, but securely incorporated in the child, and he is well on his way to active, reciprocal membership in his society.

Role-playing is instrumental not only in socializing the child, but also in the emergence of his "self"; he develops a growing sense of identity and individuality. There is no self-consciousness without consciousness of others, and neither appears spontaneously.

When the child uses nonsymbolic gestures as his only means of communication, he cannot learn their meaning except by the response that others make to them. The interaction which ensues is initiated within himself—something he cannot know as a prisoner of his infantile "autism" (or egocentricity) and his own limited but "absolute" perceptions—and it is completed in the satisfaction he achieves from others. When the child learns to speak, or otherwise to symbolize, a decisive transformation takes place. He speaks —and hears himself just as if he were hearing someone else. He notices that others respond to him, and at the same time that he can respond to himself. He is able to "imagine" in advance the probable response his speech will elicit in others, and therefore to accept or reject the expectancy he arouses in them. The memory of repeated responses to his use of language enables him to think of—that is, anticipate—even in their absence, how others will react to his verbal cues. Moreover, he is able to censor his own thoughts and actions, and consequently, attune them to the responses he has evoked in those who are meaningful to him, his "significant others."

The impulse to act autonomously (in contrast to heteronomous conduct, determined by external control) was referred to as the "I" by George Herbert Mead, an enormously influential social philosopher. For Mead, the "I" suggested spontaneous biological drives and unconventionalized motives that might actuate an individual at any moment. The imagined effect of an action on others Mead called the "Me." Most of us are most of the time Me's, else we could not relate to each other as human beings. Yet all of us are sometimes (and always to some extent) I's, for otherwise we would be indistinguishable from one another. The Me is the individual seen as an object to the I. The I's and Me's taken together constitute the self, the individual sitting in judgment of his own impulse to act. As the self develops, a human being incorporates the norms 'round about him. These norms Mead more or less personified in his concept of "The Generalized Other." This terminology is dramatic—or better, dramaturgic —on purpose. It spotlights a fundamental fact about man in society, namely that he is a wearer of masks, a "person" in the original sense of the word. After a while, he acts imaginatively before an audience consisting solely of himself, selecting and screening what he will do in advance of his doing it.

Socialization as a Lifelong Process

Role-taking, identification, and internalization produce and form the self; they also bring about socialization of the child. Our earlier description dealt only with emerging roles in the infant's immediate family. Actually, role-taking is a generalized process of interpersonal relationships which occurs at all ages and in all situations.

As the child matures and extends the range of his personal relationships, he finds himself subject to new definitions to which he must make new responses and which involve the internalization of new aspects of culture. The fulfilling of the roles of playmate, friend, relative (in all its gradations), schoolmate, pupil, church attendant—all oblige him to incorporate new rules, norms, patterns of behavior, and skills. In each case rewards are offered. By responding appropriately, the individual gains some rewards, but only in the process of modifying his behavior so that he is a slightly different person as a result of each successive role fulfillment.

Since role-playing is present in all social relations, socialization is a continuous process which ends only with death. The role expectancies imposed on us change with age: the sub-teenager is given treatment different from the adolescent's, and each in turn is accorded treatment different from the young adult's or the oldster's. Moreover, every social position involves different sexual, occupational, membership, prestige, marital, and family roles, all changing within the lifetime of an individual and all involving the acquisition of new horizons, new perspectives, new skills, and new attitudes.

The mere repetition of social role-playing causes individuals to attach new meanings to values and experiences. At the beginning of any new relationship, a person attempts to learn the responses expected of him, those that he can expect of others, and the gratifications they involve. New role relationships may produce anxiety when he is not sure either of what is expected of him or how to go about doing it if he does know; they may involve new thrills or excitement in the effort to work out a novel relationship. In either case, new role relationships impart heightened self-consciousness, if only because the new roles are problematical. As a person learns a role situation, he soon knows what to expect and how to respond, and role-fulfillment loses the element of self-consciousness. It becomes habitual.

Thought, self-consciousness, and planning almost cease in the execution of habitual roles. However, self-consciousness

in role performance may be restored when either party changes the expectancies or gratifications involved, when the execution of one role involves the possibility of not fulfilling another role, or when fulfillment of an expectancy does not produce the anticipated effort.

A given pattern of role performance may disappear simply when parties to the relationship are not available, when other role fulfillment offers the same gratification, and when, through changes in a person's social position, old demands are no longer made upon him, or he no longer makes them upon others. So when a man is married, many bachelor roles which he played are no longer suitable to his new position. Instead, different and unfamiliar roles—those of husband, of in-law, of "stable member of the community"—fall upon his shoulders. Throughout his life, the individual, in fulfilling new roles, acquires new values.

Role-playing and the Transmission of Culture

Up to this point, we have considered role-playing from the standpoint of a particular individual who interacts with *others*. In this interaction the individual assimilates cultural elements (ways of thinking and acting) that are new for him. This absorption of culture is only one link in a chain that binds him to his fellows. The role definitions and cultural expectancies communicated to our hypothetical individual will eventually be communicated by him to still other people who are becoming habituated to new roles.

Society is a continuous chain of role expectancies and behavior resulting from role expectancies. To put it another way, society is a fairly stable network of social relationships based on relatively uniform and predictable behavior maintained between specific individuals in specified positions.

The continuous communication of role

expectancies standardizes them. There are standard definitions of what can be expected of—let us say—a doctor, a son, a husband, or even a brother-in-law. This does not mean that all doctors or all brothers act exactly the same way, but it does mean that when either fails to fulfill the "ideal" expectancy, others will frequently punish him for his deed. However, role expectancies are seldom so sharply defined that all individuals will respond to them in exactly the same way.

Whenever a human society exists, there is minimal agreement within it about what constitutes the core of a role and what behavior is considered adequate to its fulfillment.

Role Differentiation

Some roles are highly specialized, others are not. The actual or potential role of wife, for example, obviously applies at most to no more than half of a society. A specific occupational role—expectancies placed on an individual by virtue of his job or profession—are in each instance applicable to only a small proportion of the total society. No individual ever becomes socialized to the whole of his culture. Socialization is never complete, and no one person ever follows all the lines of socialization available to every member of his society.

Social Skills in Role-playing

Role-playing involves the development of certain social skills and techniques which facilitate the transmission of culture and the socialization of the individual. These skills also make it possible to receive those gratifications which are the end product of role-playing.

The basic skills are technical, psychological, and projective. Role-playing, above all, requires communication—for it means first the ability to recognize an expect-

ancy. The individual must be able to define a situation so that he can understand what kind of behavior is appropriate. At the same time, in order to achieve his ends, he must be able to communicate expectancies to others. The subtlety and complexity of this phenomenon has been lately best presented in several books and articles by Erving Goffman, a brilliant continuator of Mead's. We may sample a few specimens of Goffman's contribution:

> The expressiveness of the individual (and therefore his capacity to give impressions) appears to involve two radically different kinds of sign activity: the expression that he *gives* and the expression that he *gives off*. The first involves verbal symbols. This is communication in the traditional and narrow sense. The second involves a wide range of action that others can treat as symptomatic of the actor, the expectation being that the action was performed for reasons other than the information conveyed in this way.[3]

Goffman's interest has centered on "expressions given off," the "more theatrical and contextual kind, the nonverbal, presumably unintentional kind, whether this communication be purposely engineered or not." The author offers an illustration from his own observations in Shetland Isle:

> When a neighbor dropped in to have a cup of tea, he would ordinarily wear at least a hint of an expectant warm smile as he passed through the door into the cottage. Since lack of physical obstructions outside the cottage and lack of light within it usually made it possible to observe the visitor unobserved as he approached the house, islanders sometimes took pleasure in watching the visitor drop whatever expression he was manifesting and replace it with a sociable one just before reaching the door. However, some visitors, in appreciating that this examination was occurring, would blindly adopt a social face a long distance from the house, thus insuring the projection of a constant image.[4]

Perhaps because contemporary society affords so little leeway, Goffman leaves none at all for the "I." He endorses the position taken by an earlier sociologist,

Robert Ezra Park, that ". . . everyone is always and everywhere, more or less consciously playing a role. . . . It is in these roles that we know each other; it is in these roles that we know ourselves. . . . In a sense, and in so far as this mask represents the conception we have formed of ourselves—the role we are striving to live up to—this mask is our truer self, the self we would like to be. In the end, our conception of our role becomes second nature and an integral part of our personality. We come into the world as individuals, achieve character, and become persons." [5]

To strengthen his point by meeting a major criticism of it, Goffman distinguishes between behavior "onstage" or "frontstage" and behavior "backstage" thus:

Throughout Western society there seems to be one informal or backstage language of behavior, and another language of behavior for occasions when a performance is being presented. The backstage language consists of reciprocal first-naming, co-operative decision-making, profanity, open sexual remarks, elaborate griping, smoking, rough informal dress, "sloppy" sitting and standing posture, use of dialect or sub-standard speech, mumbling and shouting, playful aggressivity and "kidding," inconsiderateness for the other in minor but potentially symbolic acts, minor physical self-involvements, such as humming, whistling, chewing, nibbling, belching and flatulence. The frontstage of behavior language can be taken as the absence (and in some sense the opposite) of this. In general, then, backstage conduct is one which allows minor acts which might easily be taken as symbolic of intimacy and disrespect for others present and the region, while front region conduct is one which disallows such potentially offensive behavior. [6]

What goes on before the footlights and what goes on behind them, and not only in theaters, are indeed very different. Arnold Wesker, in his recent play, *The Kitchen,* has shown us with extraordinary vividness how great the disparity is between action in a restaurant "out front" where there are customers, and behind the scenes where food is being prepared.

We all feel that our behavior backstage is considerably more relaxed, natural, informal. But is it free (or even freer) of mask-wearing, of role-playing? Does the "true self" assert itself only when there are no outsiders to impress? Does it come out of hiding if "one's hair is down"? Or do we go on performing now for our teammates, colleagues, and friends as we did before for others? Our questions are rhetorical, our answer simple: the content changes, but the act remains. The swift adoption of a new role does not mean that role-playing has been transcended. Goffman explains the limitations of backstage informality:

First, when the audience is not present, each member of the team is likely to want to sustain the impression that he can be trusted with the secrets of the team and that he is not likely to play his part badly when the audience is present. While each team member will want the audience to think of him as a worthy character, he is likely to want his teammates to think of him as a loyal, well-disciplined performer. Secondly, there are often moments backstage when the performers will have to sustain one another's morale and maintain the impression that the show that is about to be presented will go over well or that has just been presented did not really go over so badly. Thirdly, if the team contains representatives of fundamental social divisions, such as different age-grades, different ethnic groups, etc., then some discretionary limits will prevail on freedom of backstage activity. Here, no doubt, the most important division is the sexual one, for there seems to be no society in which members of the two sexes, however closely related, do not sustain some appearances before each other. [7]
. . . One may feel obliged, when backstage, to act out of character in a familiar fashion and this can come to be more of a pose than the performance for which it was meant to provide a relaxation. [8]

It is clear that we shall have to look elsewhere than backstage for the I; perhaps it is both below and beyond the social sphere. But, mostly there is just the Me, and our world is the one pictured by Shakespeare, which is to say, a stage, "and all the men and women merely players." Further: "They have their exits and their entrances, And one man in his time plays many parts."

How well he plays them depends not only on his own organic equipment, which is indispensable, for without an adequate nervous system, he cannot hope to symbolize—which simply disables him as a human being. But there is also a social pathology of role-playing which cannot be ignored even though it does not cause total incapacitation. Derived partly from a biological condition (but embedded in and conditioned by man-made culture), this pathology has diverse social consequences of the first importance. It consists largely in the inability to interpret, project, or respond to the collective expectations of one's society.

NOTES

1. Muzafer Sherif, *An Outline of Social Psychology*, New York: Harper, 1948, pp. 51, 53.

2. Clyde Kluckhohn and Henry A. Murray, *Personality in Nature, Society and Culture*, New York: Knopf, 1948, p. 23.

3. Erving Goffman, *The Presentation of Self in Everyday Life*, Garden City, N.Y.: Anchor, 1958, p. 2.

4. *Ibid.*, p. 8.

5. Robert E. Park, *Race and Culture*, Glencoe, Ill.: Free Press, 1950, p. 249.

6. Goffman, *op. cit.*, p. 128.

7. *Ibid.*, pp. 129–130.

8. *Ibid.*, p. 134.

12. CONTINUITIES AND DISCONTINUITIES IN CULTURAL CONDITIONING

RUTH BENEDICT

This article is a classic and has been reprinted many times since it first appeared in 1938 in the journal, Psychiatry. *Here, with the deft skill that made her one of the world's most widely-read anthropologists, Ruth Benedict describes the difficult process of growing up, of learning to play the roles required of the adult after having internalized the ways of children.*

Her approach is comparative and she examines various methods of socialization, particularly with regard to the individual's roles as child and as father. Her analysis deals with three spheres of potential conflict: social responsibility, patterns of dominance and submissiveness, and sex role differentiation.

Ruth Benedict died in 1948. At the time of her death she was Professor of Anthropology at Columbia University. Author of many important studies in anthropology including Patterns of Culture *(1934),* Zūni Mythology *(1935),* Race: Science and Politics *(1940), and* The Chrysanthemum and the Sword *(1946), she also published several volumes of poetry under the pseudonym, Anne Singleton.*

All cultures must deal in one way or another with the cycle of growth from infancy to adulthood. Nature has posed the situation dramatically: on the one hand, the new born baby, physiologically vulnerable, unable to fend for itself, or to participate of its own initiative in the life of the group, and, on the other, the adult man or woman. Every man who rounds out his human potentialities must have been a son first and a father later and the two roles are physiologically in great contrast; he must first have been dependent upon others for his very existence and later he must provide such security for others. This discontinuity in the life cycle is a fact of nature and is inescapable. Facts of nature, however, in any discussion of human problems, are ordinarily read off not at their bare minimal but surrounded by all the local accretions of behavior to which the student of human affairs has become accustomed in his own culture. For that reason it is illuminating to examine comparative material from other societies in order to get a wider perspective on our own special accretions. The anthropologist's role is not to question the facts of nature, but to insist upon the interposition of a middle term between "nature" and "human behavior"; his role is to analyze that term, to document local man-made doctorings of nature and to insist that these doctorings should not be read off in any one culture as nature itself. Although it is a fact of nature that the child becomes a man, the way in which this transition is effected varies from one society to another, and no one of these particular cultural bridges should be regarded as the "natural" path to maturity.

From a comparative point of view our culture goes to great extremes in emphasizing contrasts between the child and the

Reprinted from *Psychiatry,* **1** (1938), 161–167, by special permission of the executors of the estate of Ruth Benedict and The William Alanson White Psychiatric Foundation, Inc. Copyright 1938 by The William Alanson White Psychiatric Foundation.

adult. The child is sexless, the adult estimates his virility by his sexual activities; the child must be protected from the ugly facts of life, the adult must meet them without psychic catastrophe; the child must obey, the adult must command this obedience. These are all dogmas of our culture, dogmas which in spite of the facts of nature, other cultures commonly do not share. In spite of the physiological contrasts between child and adult these are cultural accretions.

It will make the point clearer if we consider one habit in our own culture in regard to which there is not this discontinuity of conditioning. With the greatest clarity of purpose and economy of training, we achieve our goal of conditioning everyone to eat three meals a day. The baby's training in regular food periods begins at birth and no crying of the child and no inconvenience to the mother is allowed to interfere.* We gauge the child's physiological make-up and at first allow it food oftener than adults, but, because our goal is firmly set and our training consistent, before the child is two years old it has achieved the adult schedule. From the point of view of other cultures this is as startling as the fact of three-year old babies perfectly at home in deep water is to us. Modesty is another sphere in which our child training is consistent and economical; we waste no time in clothing the baby and in contrast to many societies where the child runs naked till it is ceremonially given its skirt or its pubic sheath at adolescence, the child's training fits it precisely for adult conventions.

In neither of these aspects of behavior is there need for an individual in our culture to embark before puberty, at puberty or at some later date upon a course of action which all his previous training has

tabued. He is spared the unsureness inevitable in such a transition.

The illustration I have chosen may appear trivial, but in larger and more important aspects of behavior, our methods are obviously different. Because of the great variety of child training in different families in our society, I might illustrate continuity of conditioning from individual life histories in our culture, but even these, from a comparative point of view, stop far short of consistency and I shall therefore confine myself to describing arrangements in other cultures in which training which with us is idiosyncratic, is accepted and traditional and does not therefore involve the same possibility of conflict. I shall choose childhood rather than infant and nursing situations not because the latter do not vary strikingly in different cultures but because they are nevertheless more circumscribed by the baby's physiological needs than is its later training. Childhood situations provide an excellent field in which to illustrate the range of cultural adjustments which are possible within a universally given, but not so drastic, set of physiological facts.

The major discontinuity in the life cycle is of course that the child who is at one point a son must later be a father. These roles in our society are strongly differentiated; a good son is tractable, and does not assume adult responsibilities; a good father provides for his children and should not allow his authority to be flouted. In addition the child must be sexless so far as his family is concerned, whereas the father's sexual role is primary in the family. The individual in one role must revise his behavior from almost all points of view when he assumes the second role.

I shall select for discussion three such contrasts that occur in our culture be-

---

* [*Editor's note:* Although the point is well taken, the specific example is no longer meaningful. In fact, in recent years, the pendulum has swung quite far in the direction of permissive feeding.]

tween the individual's role as child and as father: 1. responsible—nonresponsible status role. 2. dominance—submission. 3. contrasted sexual role. It is largely upon our cultural commitments to these three contrasts that the discontinuity in the life cycle of an individual in our culture depends.

1. Responsible—Non-Responsible Status Role

The techniques adopted by societies which achieve continuity during the life cycle in this sphere in no way differ from those we employ in our uniform conditioning to three meals a day. They are merely applied to other areas of life. We think of the child as wanting to play and the adult as having to work, but in many societies the mother takes the baby daily in her shawl or carrying net to the garden or to gather roots, and adult labor is seen even in infancy from the pleasant security of its position in close contact with its mother. When the child can run about it accompanies its parents still, doing tasks which are essential and yet suited to its powers, and its dichotomy between work and play is not different from that its parents recognize, namely the distinction between the busy day and the free evening. The tasks it is asked to perform are graded to its powers and its elders wait quietly by, not offering to do the task in the child's place. Everyone who is familiar with such societies has been struck by the contrast with our child training. Dr. Ruth Underhill tells me of sitting with a group of Papago elders in Arizona when the man of the house turned to his little three-year old granddaughter and asked her to close the door. The door was heavy and hard to shut. The child tried but it did not move. Several times the grandfather repeated, "Yes, close the door." No one jumped to the child's assistance. No one took the responsibility away from her. On the

other hand there was no impatience, for after all the child was small. They sat gravely waiting till the child succeeded and her grandfather gravely thanked her. It was assumed that the task would not be asked of her unless she could perform it, and having been asked the responsibility was hers alone just as if she were a grown woman.

The essential point of such child training is that the child is from infancy continuously conditioned to responsible social participation while at the same time the tasks that are expected of it are adapted to its capacity. The contrast with our society is very great. A child does not make any labor contribution to our industrial society except as it competes with an adult; its work is not measured against its own strength and skill but against high-geared industrial requirements. Even when we praise a child's achievement in the home we are outraged if such praise is interpreted as being of the same order as praise of adults. The child is praised because the parent feels well disposed, regardless of whether the task is well done by adult standards, and the child acquires no sensible standard by which to measure its achievement. The gravity of a Cheyenne Indian family ceremoniously making a feast out of the little boy's first snowbird is at the furthest remove from our behavior. At birth the little boy was presented with a toy bow, and from the time he could run about serviceable bows suited to his stature were specially made for him by the man of the family. Animals and birds were taught him in a graded series beginning with those most easily taken, and as he brought in his first of each species his family duly made a feast of it, accepting his contribution as gravely as the buffalo his father brought. When he finally killed a buffalo, it was only the final step of his childhood conditioning, not a new adult role with which his childhood experience had been at variance.

The Canadian Ojibwa show clearly

what results can be achieved. This tribe gains its livelihood by winter trapping and the small family of father, mother and children live during the long winter alone on their great frozen hunting grounds. The boy accompanies his father and brings in his catch to his sister as his father does to his mother; the girl prepares the meat and skins for him just as his mother does for her husband. By the time the boy is 12, he may have set his own line of traps on a hunting territory of his own and return to his parents' house only once in several months—still bringing the meat and skins to his sister. The young child is taught consistently that it has only itself to rely upon in life, and this is as true in the dealings it will have with the supernatural as in the business of getting a livelihood. This attitude he will accept as a successful adult just as he accepted it as a child.[1]

2. Dominance—Submission

Dominance—submission is the most striking of those categories of behavior where like does not respond to like but where one type of behavior stimulates the opposite response. It is one of the most prominent ways in which behavior is patterned in our culture. When it obtains between classes, it may be nourished by continuous experience; the difficulty in its use between children and adults lies in the fact that an individual conditioned to one set of behavior in childhood must adopt the opposite as an adult. Its opposite is a pattern of approximately identical reciprocal behavior, and societies which rely upon continuous conditioning characteristically invoke this pattern. In some primitive cultures the very terminology of address between father and son, and more commonly, between grandchild and grandson or uncle and nephew, reflects this attitude. In such kinship terminologies one reciprocal expresses each of these relationships so that son and father, for

instance, exchange the same term with one another, just as we exchange the same term with a cousin. The child later will exchange it with his son. "Father—son," therefore, is a continuous relationship he enjoys throughout life. The same continuity, backed up by verbal reciprocity, occurs far oftener in the grandchild—grandson relationship or that of mother's brother—sister's son. When these are "joking" relationships, as they often are, travelers report wonderingly upon the liberties and pretensions of tiny toddlers in their dealings with these family elders. In place of our dogma of respect to elders such societies employ in these cases a reciprocity as nearly identical as may be. The teasing and practical joking the grandfather visits upon his grandchild, the grandchild returns in like coin; he would be led to believe that he failed in propriety if he did not give like for like. If the sister's son has right of access without leave to his mother's brother's possessions, the mother's brother has such rights also to the child's possessions. They share reciprocal privileges and obligations which in our society can develop only between age mates.

From the point of view of our present discussion, such kinship conventions allow the child to put in practice from infancy the same forms of behavior which it will rely upon as an adult; behavior is not polarized into a general requirement of submission for the child and dominance for the adult.

It is clear from the techniques described above by which the child is conditioned to a responsible status role that these depend chiefly upon arousing in the child the desire to share responsibility in adult life. To achieve this little stress is laid upon obedience but much stress upon approval and praise. Punishment is very commonly regarded as quite outside the realm of possibility, and natives in many parts of the world have drawn the conclusion from our usual disciplinary methods that white parents do not love their children. If the child is not required to be submissive however, many occasions for punishment melt away; a variety of situations which call for it do not occur. Many American Indian tribes are especially explicit in rejecting the ideal of a child's submissive or obedient behavior. Prince Maximilian von Wied who visited the Crow Indians over a hundred years ago describes a father's boasting about his young son's intractability even when it was the father himself who was flouted; "He will be a man," his father said. He would have been baffled at the idea that his child should show behavior which would obviously make him appear a poor creature in the eyes of his fellows if he used it as an adult. Dr. George Devereaux tells me of a special case of such an attitude among the Mohave at the present time. The child's mother was white and protested to its father that he must take action when the child disobeyed and struck him. "But why?" the father said, "he is little. He cannot possibly injure me." He did not know of any dichotomy according to which an adult expects obedience and a child must accord it. If his child had been docile he would simply have judged that it would become a docile adult—an eventuality of which he would not have approved.

Child training which brings about the same result is common also in other areas of life than that of reciprocal kinship obligations between child and adult. There is a tendency in our culture to regard every situation as having in it the seeds of a dominance—submission relationship. Even where dominance—submission is patently irrelevant we read in the dichotomy, assuming that in every situation there must be one person dominating another. On the other hand some cultures, even when the situation calls for leadership, do not see it in terms of dominance—submission. To do justice to this attitude it would be necessary to describe their political and especially their economic arrangements, for such an attitude

to persist must certainly be supported by economic mechanisms that are congruent with it. But it must also be supported by—or what comes to the same thing, express itself in—child training and familial situations.

3. Contrasted Sexual Role

Continuity of conditioning in training the child to assume responsibility and to behave no more submissively than adults is quite possible in terms of the child's physiological endowment if his participation is suited to his strength. Because of the late development of the child's reproductive organs continuity of conditioning in sex experience presents a difficult problem. So far as their belief that the child is anything but a sexless being is concerned, they are probably more nearly right than we are with an opposite dogma. But the great break is presented by the universally sterile unions before puberty and the presumably fertile ones after maturation. This physiological fact no amount of cultural manipulation can minimize or alter, and societies therefore which stress continuous conditioning most strongly sometimes do not expect children to be interested in sex experience until they have matured physically. This is striking among American Indian tribes like the Dakota; adults observe great privacy in sex acts and in no way stimulate children's sexual activity. There need be no discontinuity, in the sense in which I have used the term, in such a program if the child is taught nothing it does not have to unlearn later. In such cultures adults view children's experimentation as in no way wicked or dangerous but merely as innocuous play which can have no serious consequences. In some societies such play is minimal and the children manifest little interest in it. But the same attitude may be taken by adults in societies where such play is encouraged and forms a major activity among small children. This is true among most of the Melanesian cultures of Southeast New Guinea; adults go as far as to laugh off sexual affairs within the prohibited class if the children are not mature, saying that since they cannot marry there can be no harm done.

It is this physiological fact of the difference between children's sterile unions and adults' presumably fertile sex relations which must be kept in mind in order to understand the different mores which almost always govern sex expression in children and in adults in the same culture. A great many cultures with pre-adolescent sexual license require marital fidelity and a great many which value pre-marital virginity in either male or female arrange their marital life with great license. Continuity in sex experience is complicated by factors which it was unnecessary to consider in the problems previously discussed. The essential problem is not whether or not the child's sexuality is consistently exploited—for even where such exploitation is favored in the majority of cases the child must seriously modify his behavior at puberty or at marriage. Continuity in sex expression means rather that the child is taught nothing it must unlearn later. If the cultural emphasis is upon sexual pleasure the child who is continuously conditioned will be encouraged to experiment freely and pleasurably, as among the Marquesans;[2] if emphasis is upon reproduction, as among the Zuni of New Mexico, childish sex proclivities will not be exploited, for the only important use which sex is thought to serve in his culture is not yet possible to him. The important contrast with our child training is that although a Zuni child is impressed with the wickedness of premature sex experimentation he does not run the risk as in our culture of associating this wickedness with sex itself rather than with sex at his age. The adult in our culture has often failed to unlearn the wickedness or the dangerousness of sex, a lesson which was impressed upon him strongly in his most formative years.

Discontinuity in Conditioning

Even from this very summary statement of continuous conditioning the economy of such mores is evident. In spite of the obvious advantages, however, there are difficulties in its way. Many primitive societies expect as different behavior from an individual as child and as adult as we do, and such discontinuity involves a presumption of strain.

Many societies of this type however minimize strain by the techniques they employ, and some techniques are more successful than others in ensuring the individual's functioning without conflict. It is from this point of view that age-grade societies reveal their fundamental significance. Age-graded cultures characteristically demand different behavior of the individual at different times of his life and persons of a like age-grade are grouped into a society whose activities are well oriented toward the behavior desired at that age. Individuals "graduate" publicly and with honor from one of these groups to another. Where age society members are enjoined to loyalty and mutual support, and are drawn not only from the local group but from the whole tribe as among the Arapaho, or even from other tribes as among the Wagawaga of Southeast New Guinea, such an institution has many advantages in eliminating conflicts among local groups and fostering intratribal peace. This seems to be also a factor in the tribal military solidarity of the similarly organized Masai of East Africa. The point that is of chief interest for our present discussion however is that by this means an individual who at any time takes on a new set of duties and virtues is supported not only by a solid phalanx of age mates but by the traditional prestige of the organized "secret" society into which he has now graduated. Fortified in this way, individuals in such cultures often swing between remarkable extremes of opposite behavior without apparent psychic threat. For example, the great majority exhibit prideful and non-conflicted behavior at each stage in the life cycle even when a prime of life devoted to passionate and aggressive head hunting must be followed by a later life dedicated to ritual and to mild and peaceable civic virtues.[3]

Our chief interest here, however, is in discontinuity which primarily affects the child. In many primitive societies such discontinuity has been fostered not because of economic or political necessity or because such discontinuity provides for a socially valuable division of labor, but because of some conceptual dogma. The most striking of these are the Australian and Papuan cultures where the ceremony of the "Making of Man" flourishes. In such societies it is believed that men and women have opposite and conflicting powers, and male children, who are of undefined status, must be initiated into the male role. In Central Australia the boy child is of the woman's side and women are tabu in the final adult stages of tribal ritual. The elaborate and protracted initiation ceremonies of the Arunta therefore snatch the boy from the mother, dramatize his gradual repudiation of her. In a final ceremony he is reborn as a man out of the men's ceremonial "baby pouch." The men's ceremonies are ritual statements of a masculine solidarity, carried out by fondling one another's *churingas,* the material symbol of each man's life, and by letting out over one another blood drawn from their veins. After this warm bond among men has been established through the ceremonies, the boy joins the men in the men's house and participates in tribal rites.[4] The enjoined discontinuity has been tribally bridged.

West of the Fly River in southern New Guinea there is a striking development of this Making of Men cult which involves a childhood period of passive homosexuality. Among the Keraki [5] it is thought that no boy can grow to full stature without playing the role for some years. Men slightly older take the active role and the older man is a jealous partner. The life cycle of the Keraki Indians includes, therefore, in succession, passive homosexuality, active homosexuality and heterosexuality. The Keraki believe that pregnancy will result from post-pubertal passive homosexuality and see evidences of such practices in any fat man whom even as an old man, they may kill or drive out of the tribe because of their fear. The ceremony that is of interest in connection with the present discussion takes place at the end of the period of passive homosexuality. This ceremony consists in burning out the possibility of pregnancy from the boy by pouring lye down his throat, after which he has no further protection if he gives way to the practice. There is no technique for ending active homosexuality, but this is not explicitly tabu for older men; heterosexuality and children however are highly valued. Unlike the neighboring Marindanim who share their homosexual practices, Keraki husband and wife share the same house and work together in the gardens.

I have chosen illustrations of discontinuous conditioning where it is not too much to say that the cultural institutions furnish adequate support to the individual as he progresses from role to role or interdicts the previous behavior in a summary fashion. The contrast with arrangements in our culture is very striking, and against this background of social arrangements in other cultures the adolescent period of *Sturm und Drang* with which we are so familiar becomes intelligible in terms of our discontinuous cultural institutions and dogmas rather than in terms of physiological necessity. It is even more pertinent to consider these comparative facts in relation to maladjusted persons in our culture who are said to be fixated at one or another pre-adult level. It is clear that if we were to look at our social arrangements as an outsider, we should infer directly from our family institutions and habits of child training that many individuals would not "put off childish things"; we should have to say that our adult activity demands traits that are interdicted in children, and that far from redoubling efforts to help children bridge this gap, adults in our culture put all the blame on the child when he fails to manifest spontaneously the new behavior or, overstepping the mark, manifests it with untoward belligerence. It is not surprising that in such a society many individuals fear to use behavior which has up to that time been under a ban and trust instead, though at great psychic cost, to attitudes that have been exercised with approval during their formative years. Insofar as we invoke a physiological scheme to account for these neurotic adjustments we are led to overlook the possibility of developing social institutions which would lessen the social cost we now pay; instead we elaborate a set of dogmas which prove inapplicable under other social conditions.

NOTES

1. Landes, Ruth, *The Ojibwa Woman,* Part 1, Youth—Columbia University Contributions to Anthropology, V. 31.

2. Ralph Linton, class notes on the Marquesans.

3. Henry Elkin, manuscript on the Arapaho.

4. Spencer, B., and Gillen, F. J., *The Arunta,* New York: Macmillan, 1927, 2 vols. Róheim, Géza, "Psycho-Analysis of Primitive Cultural Types," *Internat. Journal Psychoanal.* 13 (1932), 1–224—in particular, Chapter 3, on the Aranda, The Children of the Desert.

5. Williams, Francis E., *Papuans of the Trans-Fly,* Oxford, 1936.

13. CULTURAL COMPONENTS IN RESPONSES TO PAIN

MARK ZBOROWSKI

In this article, Mark Zborowski deals with the extent to which culture influences responses to the physiological manifestations of pain caused by disease or injury. He draws his evidence from a comparative examination of the attitudes and behavior of a selected number of Jewish, Italian, Irish, and "Old American" patients at a single veterans' hospital in New York City. By relating clinical observations to knowledge of differential child-rearing practices, varied perspectives on the relationships between children and their parents, as well as thoughts about pain and its alleviation, Zborowski, like Ruth Benedict, clearly demonstrates the impact of early socialization.

Mark Zborowski is an anthropologist and is currently on the research staff of Mount Zion Hospital in San Francisco. He is coauthor of Life Is with People (*1952*).

This paper reports on one aspect of a larger study: that concerned with discovering the role of cultural patterns in attitudes toward and reactions to pain which is caused by disease and injury—in other words, responses to spontaneous pain.

Some Basic Distinctions

In human societies biological processes vital for man's survival acquire social and cultural significance. Intake of food, sexual intercourse or elimination—physiological phenomena which are universal for the entire living world—become institutions regulated by cultural and social norms, thus fulfilling not only biological functions but social and cultural ones as well. Metabolic and endocrinal changes in the human organism may provoke hunger and sexual desire, but culture and society dictate to man the kind of food he may eat, the social setting for eating or the adequate partner for mating.

Moreover, the role of cultural and social patterns in human physiological activities is so great that they may in specific situations act against the direct biological needs of the individual, even to the point of endangering his survival. Only a human being may prefer starvation to the breaking of a religious dietary law or may abstain from sexual intercourse because of specific incest regulations. Voluntary fasting and celibacy exist only where food and sex fulfill more than strictly physiological functions.

Thus, the understanding of the significance and role of social and cultural patterns in human physiology is necessary to clarify those aspects of human experience which remain puzzling if studied only within the physiological frame of reference.

Pain is basically a physiological phenomenon and as such has been studied by physiologists and neurologists such as Harold Wolff, James Hardy, Helen Goodell, C. S. Lewis, W. K. Livingston and others. By using the most ingenious methods of investigation they have succeeded in clarifying complex problems of the physiology of pain. Many aspects of perception and reaction to pain were studied

Reprinted from the *Journal of Social Issues,* **8** (1953), 16–31, by permission of the author and the Society for the Psychological Study of Social Issues.

in experimental situations involving most careful preparation and complicated equipment. These investigators have come to the conclusion that "from the physiological point of view pain qualifies as a sensation of importance to the self-preservation of the individual." [1] The biological function of pain is to provoke special reactive patterns directed toward avoidance of the noxious stimulus which presents a threat to the individual. In this respect the function of pain is basically the same for man as for the rest of the animal world.

However, the physiology of pain and the understanding of the biological function of pain do not explain other aspects of what Wolff, Hardy and Goodell call the *pain experience,* which includes not only the pain sensation and certain automatic reactive responses but also certain "associated feeling states." [2] It would not explain, for example, the acceptance of intense pain in torture which is part of the initiation rites of many primitive societies, nor will it explain the strong emotional reactions of certain individuals to the slight sting of the hypodermic needle.

In human society pain, like so many other physiological phenomena, acquires specific social and cultural significance, and, accordingly, certain reactions to pain can be understood in the light of this significance. As Drs. Hardy, Wolff and Goodell state in their recent book, ". . . the culture in which a man finds himself becomes the conditioning influence in the formation of the individual reaction patterns to pain . . . A knowledge of group attitudes toward pain is extremely important to an understanding of the individual reaction." [3]

In analyzing pain it is useful to distinguish between self-inflicted, other-inflicted and spontaneous pain. Self-inflicted pain is defined as deliberately self-inflicted. It is experienced as a result of injuries performed voluntarily upon oneself, e.g., self-mutilation. Usually these injuries have a culturally defined purpose, such as achieving a special status in the society. It

can be observed not only in primitive cultures but also in contemporary societies on a higher level of civilization. In Germany, for instance, members of certain student or military organizations would cut their faces with a razor in order to acquire scars which would identify them as members of a distinctive social group. By other-inflicted pain is meant pain inflicted upon the individual in the process of culturally accepted and expected activities (regardless of whether approved or disapproved), such as sports, fights, war, etc. To this category belongs also pain inflicted by the physician in the process of medical treatment. Spontaneous pain usually denotes the pain sensation which results from disease or injury. This term also covers pains of psychogenic nature.

Members of different cultures may assume differing attitudes towards these various types of pain. Two of these attitudes may be described as pain expectancy and pain acceptance. Pain expectancy is anticipation of pain as being unavoidable in a given situation, for instance, in childbirth, in sports activities or in battle. Pain acceptance is characterized by a willingness to experience pain. This attitude is manifested mostly as an inevitable component of culturally accepted experiences, for instance, as part of initiation rites or part of medical treatment. The following example will help to clarify the differences between pain expectancy and pain acceptance: Labor pain is expected as part of childbirth, but while in one culture, such as in the United States, it is not accepted and therefore various means are used to alleviate it, in some other cultures, for instance in Poland, it is not only expected but also accepted, and consequently nothing or little is done to relieve it. Similarly, cultures which emphasize military achievements expect and accept battle wounds, while cultures which emphasize pacificistic values may expect them but will not accept them.

In the process of investigating cultural attitudes toward pain it is also important to distinguish between pain apprehension and pain anxiety. Pain apprehension reflects the tendency to avoid the pain sensation as such, regardless of whether the pain is spontaneous or inflicted, whether it is accepted or not. Pain anxiety, on the other hand, is a state of anxiety provoked by the pain experience, focused upon various aspects of the causes of pain, the meaning of pain or its significance for the welfare of the individual.

Moreover, members of various cultures may react differently in terms of their manifest behavior toward various pain experiences, and this behavior is often dictated by the culture which provides specific norms according to the age, sex and social position of the individual.

The fact that other elements as well as cultural factors are involved in the response to a spontaneous pain should be taken into consideration. These other factors are the pathological aspect of pain, the specific physiological characteristics of the pain experience, such as the intensity, the duration and the quality of the pain sensation, and, finally, the personality of the individual. Nevertheless, it was felt that in the process of a careful investigation it would be possible to detect the role of the cultural components in the pain experience.

The Research Setting

In setting up the research we were interested not only in the purely theoretical aspects of the findings in terms of possible contribution to the understanding of the pain experience in general; we also had in mind the practical goal of a contribution to the field of medicine. In the relationship between the doctor and his patient the respective attitudes toward pain may play a crucial role, especially when the doctor feels that the patient exaggerates his pain while the patient feels that the doctor minimizes his suffering. The same may be true, for instance, in a hospital where the members of the medical and nursing staff may have attitudes toward pain different from those held by the patient, or when they expect a certain pattern of behavior according to their cultural background while the patient may manifest a behavior pattern which is acceptable in his culture. These differences may play an important part in the evaluation of the individual pain experience, in dealing with pain at home and in the hospital, in administration of analgesics, etc. Moreover, we expected that this study of pain would offer opportunities to gain insight into related attitudes toward health, disease, medication, hospitalization, medicine in general, etc.

With these aims in mind the project was set up at the Kingsbridge Veterans Hospital, Bronx, New York,[4] where four ethnocultural groups were selected for an intensive study. These groups included patients of Jewish, Italian, Irish and "Old American" stock. Three groups—Jews, Italians and Irish—were selected because they were described by medical people as manifesting striking differences in their reaction to pain. Italians and Jews were described as tending to "exaggerate" their pain, while the Irish were often depicted as stoical individuals who are able to take a great deal of pain. The fourth group, the "Old Americans," were chosen because the values and attitudes of this group dominate in the country and are held by many members of the medical profession and by many descendants of the immigrants who, in the process of Americanization, tend to adopt American patterns of behavior. The members of this group can be defined as White, native-born individuals, usually Protestant, whose grandparents, at least, were born in the United States and who do not identify themselves with any foreign group, either nationally, socially or culturally.

The Kingsbridge Veterans Hospital was chosen because its population represents roughly the ethnic composition of New York City, thus offering access to a fair sample of the four selected groups, and also because various age groups were represented among the hospitalized veterans of World War I, World War II and the Korean War. In one major respect this hospital was not adequate, namely, in not offering the opportunity to investigate sex differences in attitude toward pain. This aspect of research will be carried out in a hospital with a large female population.

In setting up this project we were mainly interested in discovering certain regularities in reactions and attitudes toward pain characteristic of the four groups. Therefore, the study has a qualitative character, and the efforts of the researchers were not directed toward a collection of material suitable for quantitative analysis. The main techniques used in the collection of the material were interviews with patients of the selected groups, observation of their behavior when in pain and discussion of the individual cases with doctors, nurses and other people directly or indirectly involved in the pain experience of the individual. In addition to the interviews with patients, "healthy" members of the respective groups were interviewed on their attitudes toward pain, because in terms of the original hypothesis those attitudes and reactions which are displayed by the patients of the given cultural groups are held by all members of the group regardless of whether or not they are in pain although in pain these attitudes may come more sharply into focus. In certain cases the researchers have interviewed a member of the patient's immediate family in order to check the report of the patient on his pain experience and in order to find out what are the attitudes and reactions of the family toward the patient's experience.

These interviews, based on a series of open-ended questions, were focused upon the past and present pain experiences of the interviewee. However, many other areas were considered important for the understanding of this experience. For instance, it was felt that complaints of pain may play an important role in manipulating relationships in the family and the larger social environment. It was also felt that in order to understand the specific reactive patterns in controlling pain it is important to know certain aspects of child-rearing in the culture, relationships between parents and children, the role of infliction of pain in punishment, the attitudes of various members of the family toward specific expected, accepted pain experiences, and so on. The interviews were recorded on wire and transcribed verbatim for an ultimate detailed analysis. The interviews usually lasted for approximately two hours, the time being limited by the condition of the interviewee and by the amount and quality of his answers. When it was considered necessary an interview was repeated. In most of the cases the study of the interviewee was followed by informal conversations and by observation of his behavior in the hospital.

The information gathered from the interviews was discussed with members of the medical staff, especially in the areas related to the medical aspects of the problem, in order to get their evaluation of the pain experience of the patient. Information as to the personality of the patient was checked against results of psychological testing by members of the psychological staff of the hospital when these were available.

The discussion of the material presented in this paper is based on interviews with 103 respondents, including 87 hospital patients in pain and 16 healthy subjects. According to their ethno-cultural background the respondents are distributed as follows: "Old Americans," 26; Italians, 24; Jews, 31; Irish, 11; and others, 11.[5] In addition, there were the collateral interviews and conversations noted above with family members, doctors, nurses and other members of the hospital staff.

With regard to the pathological causes of pain the majority of the interviewees fall into the group of patients suffering from neurological diseases, mainly herniated discs and spinal lesions. The focusing upon a group of patients suffering from a similar pathology offered the opportunity to investigate reactions and attitudes toward spontaneous pain which is symptomatic of one group of diseases. Nevertheless, a number of patients suffering from other diseases were also interviewed.

This paper is based upon the material collected during the first stage of study. The generalizations are to a great extent tentative formulations on a descriptive level. There has been no attempt as yet to integrate the results with the value system and the cultural pattern of the group, though here and there there will be indications to the effect that they are part of the culture pattern. The discussions will be limited to main regularities within three groups, namely, the Italians, the Jews and the "Old Americans." Factors related to variations within each group will be discussed after the main prevailing patterns have been presented.

Pain Among Patients of Jewish and Italian Origin

As already mentioned, the Jews and Italians were selected mainly because interviews with medical experts suggested that they display similar reactions to pain. The investigation of this similarity provided the opportunity to check a rather popular assumption that similar reactions reflect similar attitudes. The differences between the Italian and Jewish culture are great enough to suggest that if the attitudes are related to cultural pattern they will also be different despite the apparent similarity in manifest behavior.

Members of both groups were described as being very emotional in their responses to pain. They were described as tending to exaggerate their pain experience and being very sensitive to pain. Some of the doctors stated that in their

opinion Jews and Italians have a lower threshold of pain than members of other ethnic groups, especially members of the so-called Nordic group. This statement seems to indicate a certain confusion as to the concept of the threshold of pain. According to people who have studied the problem of the threshold of pain, for instance Harold Wolff and his associates, the threshold of pain is more or less the same for all human beings regardless of nationality, sex or age.

In the course of the investigation the general impressions of doctors were confirmed to a great extent by the interview material and by the observation of the patients' behavior. However, even a superficial study of the interviews has revealed that though reactions to pain appear to be similar the underlying attitudes toward pain are different in the two groups. While the Italian patients seemed to be mainly concerned with the immediacy of the pain experience and were disturbed by the actual pain sensation which they experienced in a given situation, the concern of patients of Jewish origin was focused mainly upon the symptomatic meaning of pain and upon the significance of pain in relation to their health, welfare and, eventually, for the welfare of the families. The Italian patient expressed in his behavior and in his complaints the discomfort caused by pain as such, and he manifested his emotions with regard to the effects of this pain experience upon his immediate situation in terms of occupation, economic situation and so on; the Jewish patient expressed primarily his worries and anxieties as to the extent to which the pain indicated a threat to his health. In this connection it is worth mentioning that one of the Jewish words to describe strong pain is *yessurim,* a word which is also used to describe worries and anxieties.

Attitudes of Italian and Jewish patients toward pain-relieving drugs can serve as an indication of their attitude toward pain. When in pain the Italian calls for pain relief and is mainly concerned with the analgesic effects of the drugs which are administered to him. Once the pain is relieved the Italian patient easily forgets his sufferings and manifests a happy and joyful disposition. The Jewish patient, however, often is reluctant to accept the drug, and he explains this reluctance in terms of concern about the effects of the drug upon his health in general. He is apprehensive about the habit-forming aspects of the analgesic. Moreover, he feels that the drug relieves his pain only temporarily and does not cure him of the disease which may cause the pain. Nurses and doctors have reported cases in which patients would hide the pill which was given to them to relieve their pain and would prefer to suffer. These reports were confirmed in the interviews with the patients. It was also observed that many Jewish patients after being relieved from pain often continued to display the same depressed and worried behavior because they felt that though the pain was currently absent it may recur as long as the disease was not cured completely. From these observations it appears that when one deals with a Jewish and an Italian patient in pain, in the first case it is more important to relieve the anxieties with regard to the sources of pain, while in the second it is more important to relieve the actual pain.

Another indication as to the significance of pain for Jewish and Italian patients is their respective attitudes toward the doctor. The Italian patient seems to display a most confident attitude toward the doctor which is usually reinforced after the doctor has succeeded in relieving pain, whereas the Jewish patient manifests a skeptical attitude, feeling that the fact that the doctor has relieved his pain by some drug does not mean at all that he is skillful enough to take care of the basic illness. Consequently, even when the pain is relieved, he tends to check the diagnosis and the treatment of one doctor against the opinions of other specialists in the field. Summarizing the difference between

the Italian and Jewish attitudes, one can say that the Italian attitude is characterized by a present-oriented apprehension with regard to the actual sensation of pain, and the Jew tends to manifest a future-oriented anxiety as to the symptomatic and general meaning of the pain experience.

It has been stated that the Italians and Jews tend to manifest similar behavior in terms of their reactions to pain. As both cultures allow for free expression of feelings and emotions by words, sounds and gestures, both the Italians and Jews feel free to talk about their pain, complain about it and manifest their sufferings by groaning, moaning, crying, etc. They are not ashamed of this expression. They admit willingly that when they are in pain they do complain a great deal, call for help and expect sympathy and assistance from other members of their immediate social environment, especially from members of their family. When in pain they are reluctant to be alone and prefer the presence and attention of other people. This behavior, which is expected, accepted and approved by the Italian and Jewish cultures often conflicts with the patterns of behavior expected from a patient by American or Americanized medical people. Thus they tend to describe the behavior of the Italian and Jewish patient as exaggerated and over-emotional. The material suggests that they do tend to minimize the actual pain experiences of the Italian and Jewish patient regardless of whether they have the objective criteria for evaluating the actual amount of pain which the patient experiences. It seems that the uninhibited display of reaction to pain as manifested by the Jewish and Italian patient provokes distrust in American culture instead of provoking sympathy.

Despite the close similarity between the manifest reactions among Jews and Italians, there seem to be differences in emphasis especially with regard to what the patient achieves by these reactions and as to the specific manifestations of these reactions in the various social settings. For instance, they differ in their behavior at home and in the hospital. The Italian husband, who is aware of his role as an adult male, tends to avoid verbal complaining at home, leaving this type of behavior to the women. In the hospital, where he is less concerned with his role as a male, he tends to be more verbal and more emotional. The Jewish patient, on the contrary, seems to be more calm in the hospital than at home. Traditionally the Jewish male does not emphasize his masculinity through such traits as stoicism, and he does not equate verbal complaints with weakness. Moreover, the Jewish culture allows the patient to be demanding and complaining. Therefore, he tends more to use his pain in order to control interpersonal relationships within the family. Though similar use of pain to manipulate the relationships between members of the family may be present also in some other cultures it seems that in the Jewish culture this is not disapproved, while in others it is. In the hospital one can also distinguish variations in the reactive patterns among Jews and Italians. Upon his admission to the hospital and in the presence of the doctor the Jewish patient tends to complain, ask for help, be emotional even to the point of crying. However, as soon as he feels that adequate care is given to him he becomes more restrained. This suggests that the display of pain reaction serves less as an indication of the amount of pain experienced than as a means to create an atmosphere and setting in which the pathological causes of pain will be best taken care of. The Italian patient, on the other hand, seems to be less concerned with setting up a favorable situation for treatment. He takes for granted that adequate care will be given to him, and in the presence of the doctor he seems to be somewhat calmer than the Jewish patient. The mere presence of the doctor reassures the Italian patient, while the skepticism of the Jewish patient limits the reassuring role of the physician.

To summarize the description of the reactive patterns of the Jewish and Italian patients, the material suggests that on a semi-conscious level the Jewish patient tends to provoke worry and concern in his social environment as to the state of his health and the symptomatic character of his pain, while the Italian tends to provoke sympathy toward his suffering. In one case the function of the pain reaction will be the mobilization of the efforts of the family and the doctors toward a complete cure, while in the second case the function of the reaction will be focused upon the mobilization of effort toward relieving the pain sensation.

On the basis of the discussion of the Jewish and Italian material two generalizations can be made: 1) *Similar reactions to pain manifested by members of different ethno-cultural groups do not necessarily reflect similar attitudes to pain.* 2) *Reactive patterns similar in terms of their manifestations may have different functions and serve different purposes in various cultures.*

Pain Among Patients of "Old American" Origin

There is little emphasis on emotional complaining about pain among "Old American" patients. Their complaints about pain can best be described as reporting on pain. In describing his pain, the "Old American" patient tries to find the most appropriate ways of defining the quality of pain, its localization, duration, etc. When examined by the doctor he gives the impression of trying to assume the detached role of an unemotional observer who gives the most efficient description of his state for a correct diagnosis and treatment. The interviewees repeatedly state that there is no point in complaining and groaning and moaning, etc., because "it won't help anybody." However, they readily admit that when pain is unbearable they may react strongly, even to the point of crying, but they tend to do it when they are alone. Withdrawal from society seems to be a frequent reaction to strong pain.

There seem to be different patterns in reacting to pain depending on the situation. One pattern, manifested in the presence of members of the family, friends, etc., consists of attempts to minimize pain, to avoid complaining and provoking pity; when pain becomes too strong there is a tendency to withdraw and express freely such reactions as groaning, moaning, etc. A different pattern is manifested in the presence of people who, on account of their profession, should know the character of the pain experience because they are expected to make the appropriate diagnosis, advise the proper cure and give the adequate help. The tendency to avoid deviation from certain expected patterns of behavior plays an important role in the reaction to pain. This is also controlled by the desire to seek approval on the part of the social environment, especially in the hospital, where the "Old American" patient tries to avoid being a "nuisance" in the ward. He seems to be, more than any other patient, aware of an ideal pattern of behavior which is identified as "American," and he tends to conform to it. This was characteristically expressed by a patient who answered the question how he reacts to pain by saying, "I react like a good American."

An important element in controlling the pain reaction is the wish of the patient to cooperate with those who are expected to take care of him. The situation is often viewed as a team composed of the patient, the doctor, the nurse, the attendant, etc., and in this team everybody has a function and is supposed to do his share in order to achieve the most successful result. Emotionality is seen as a purposeless and hindering factor in a situation which calls for knowledge, skill, training and efficiency. It is important to note that this behavior is also expected by American or Americanized members of the medical or nursing staff, and the patients who do not fall into this pattern are viewed as deviants, hypochondriacs and neurotics.

As in the case of the Jewish patients, the American attitude toward pain can be best defined as a future-oriented anxiety. The "Old American" patient is also concerned with the symptomatic significance of pain which is correlated with a pronounced health-consciousness. It seems that the "Old American" is conscious of various threats to his health which are present in his environment and therefore feels vulnerable and is prone to interpret his pain sensation as a warning signal indicating that something is wrong with his health and therefore must be reported to the physician. With some exceptions, pain is considered bad and unnecessary and therefore must be immediately taken care of. In those situations where pain is expected and accepted, such as in the process of medical treatment or as a result of sports activities, there is less concern with the pain sensation. In general, however, there is a feeling that suffering pain is unnecessary when there are means of relieving it.

Though the attitudes of the Jewish and "Old American" patients can be defined as pain anxiety they differ greatly. The future-oriented anxiety of the Jewish interviewee is characterized by pessimism or, at best, by skepticism, while the "Old American" patient is rather optimistic in his future-orientation. This attitude is fostered by the mechanistic approach to the body and its functions and by the confidence in the skill of the expert which are so frequent in the American culture. The body is often viewed as a machine which has to be well taken care of, be periodically checked for disfunctioning and eventually, when out of order, be taken to an expert who will "fix" the defect. In the case of pain the expert is the medical man who has the "know-how" because of his training and experience and therefore is entitled to full confidence. An important element in the optimistic outlook is faith in the progress of science. Patients with intractable pain often stated that though at the present moment the doctors do not have the "drug" they will eventually discover it, and they will give the examples of sulfa, penicillin, etc.

The anxieties of a pain-experiencing "Old American" patient are greatly relieved when he feels that something is being done about it in terms of specific activities involved in the treatment. It seems that his security and confidence increases in direct proportion to the number of tests, X-rays, examinations, injections, etc. that are given to him. Accordingly, "Old American" patients seem to have a positive attitude toward hospitalization, because the hospital is the adequate institution which is equipped for the necessary treatment. While a Jewish and an Italian patient seem to be disturbed by the impersonal character of the hospital and by the necessity of being treated there instead of at home, the "Old American" patient, on the contrary, prefers the hospital treatment to the home treatment, and neither he nor his family seems to be disturbed by hospitalization.

To summarize the attitude of the "Old American" toward pain, he is disturbed by the symptomatic aspect of pain and is concerned with its incapacitating aspects, but he tends to view the future in rather optimistic colors, having confidence in the science and skill of the professional people who treat his condition.

Some Sources of Intra-Group Variation

In the description of the reactive patterns and attitudes toward pain among patients of Jewish and "Old American" origin certain regularities have been observed for each particular group regardless of individual differences and variations. This does not mean that each individual in each group manifests the same reactions and attitudes. Individual variations are often due to specific aspects of pain experience, to the character of the disease which causes the pain or to elements in the personality of the patient. However, there are also other factors that are instrumental in provoking these differences and which can still be traced back to the cultural backgrounds of the individual patients. Such variables as the degree of Americanization of the patient, his socioeconomic background, education and religiosity may play an important role in shaping individual variations in the reactive patterns. For instance, it was found that the patterns described are manifested most consistently among immigrants, while their descendants tend to differ in terms of adopting American forms of behavior and American attitudes toward the role of the medical expert, medical institutions and equipment in controlling pain. It is safe to say that the further is the individual from the immigrant generation the more American is his behavior. This is less true for the attitudes toward pain, which seem to persist to a great extent even among members of the third generation and even though the reactive patterns are radically changed. A Jewish or Italian patient born in this country of American-born parents tends to *behave* like an "Old American" but often expresses *attitudes* similar to those which are expressed by the Jewish or Italian people. They try to appear unemotional and efficient in situations where the immigrant would be excited and disturbed. However, in the process of the interview, if a patient is of Jewish origin he is likely to express attitudes of anxiety as to the meaning of his pain, and if he is Italian he is likely to be rather unconcerned about the significance of his pain for his future.

The occupational factor plays an important role when pain affects a specific area of the body. For instance, manual workers with herniated discs are more disturbed by their pain than are professional or business people with a similar disease because of the immediate significance of this particular pain for their respective abilities to earn a living. It was also observed that headaches cause more concern among intellectuals than among manual workers.

The educational background of the patient also plays an important role in his attitude with regard to the symptomatic meaning of a pain sensation. The more educated patients are more health-conscious and more aware of pain as a possible symptom of a dangerous disease. However, this factor plays a less important role than might be expected. The less educated "Old American" or Jewish patient is still more health-conscious than the more educated Italian. On the other hand, the less educated Jew is as much worried about the significance of pain as the more educated one. The education of the patient seems to be an important factor in fostering specific reactive patterns. The more educated patient, who may have more anxiety with regard to illness, may be more reserved in specific reactions to pain than an unsophisticated individual, who feels free to express his feelings and emotions.

The Transmission of Cultural Attitudes Toward Pain

In interpreting the differences which may be attributed to different socio-economic and education backgrounds there is enough evidence to conclude that these differences appear mainly on the manifest and behavioral level, whereas attitudinal patterns toward pain tend to be more uniform and to be common to most of the members of the group regardless of their specific backgrounds.

These attitudes toward pain and the expected reactive patterns are acquired by the individual members of the society from the earliest childhood along with

other cultural attitudes and values which are learned from the parents, parent-substitutes, siblings, peer groups, etc. Each culture offers to its members an ideal pattern of attitudes and reactions, which may differ for various sub-cultures in a given society, and each individual is expected to conform to this ideal pattern. Here, the role of the family seems to be of primary importance. Directly and indirectly the family environment affects the individuals' ultimate response to pain. In each culture the parents teach the child how to react to pain, and by approval or disapproval they promote specific forms of behavior. This conclusion is amply supported by the interviews. Thus, the Jewish and Italian respondents are unanimous in relating how their parents, especially mothers, manifested over-protective and over-concerned attitudes toward the child's health, participation in sports, games, fights, etc. In these families the child is constantly reminded of the advisability of avoiding colds, injuries, fights and other threatening situations. Crying in complaint is responded to by the parents with sympathy, concern and help. By their over-protective and worried attitude they foster complaining and tears. The child learns to pay attention to each painful experience and to look for help and sympathy which are readily given to him. In Jewish families, where not only a slight sensation of pain but also each deviation from the child's normal behavior is looked upon as a sign of illness, the child is prone to acquire anxieties with regard to the meaning and significance of these manifestations. The Italian parents do not seem to be concerned with the symptomatic meaning of the child's pains and aches, but instead there is a great deal of verbal expression of emotions and feelings of sympathy toward the "poor child" who happens to be in discomfort because of illness or because of an injury in play. In these families a child is praised when he avoids physical injuries and is scolded when he does not pay enough attention to bad weather, to drafts or when he takes part in rough games and fights. The injury and pain are often interpreted to the child as punishment for the wrong behavior, and physical punishment is the usual consequence of misbehavior.

In the "Old American" family the parental attitude is quite different. The child is told not to "run to mother with every little thing." He is told to take pain "like a man," not to be a "sissy," not to cry. The child's participation in physical sports and games is not only approved but is also strongly stimulated. Moreover, the child is taught to expect to be hurt in sports and games and is taught to fight back if he happens to be attacked by other boys. However, it seems that the American parents are conscious of the threats to the child's health, and they teach the child to take immediate care of any injury. When hurt the right thing to do is not to cry and get emotional but to avoid unnecessary pain and prevent unpleasant consequences by applying the proper first aid medicine and by calling a doctor.

Often attitudes and behavior fostered in a family conflict with those patterns which are accepted by the larger social environment. This is especially true in the case of children of immigrants. The Italian or Jewish immigrant parents promote patterns which they consider correct, while the peer groups in the street and in the school criticize this behavior and foster a different one. In consequence, the child may acquire the attitudes which are part of his home-life but may also adopt behavior patterns which conform to those of his friends.

The direct promotion of certain behavior described as part of the child-rearing explains only in part the influence of the general family environment and the specific role of the parents in shaping responses to pain. They are also formed indirectly by observing the behavior of other members of the family and by imitating their responses to pain. Moreover, attitudes toward pain are also influenced by various aspects of parent-child relationship in a culture. The material suggests that differences in attitudes toward pain in Jewish, Italian and "Old American" families are closely related to the role and image of the father in the respective cultures in terms of his authority and masculinity. Often the father and mother assume different roles in promoting specific patterns of behavior and specific attitudes. For example, it seems that in the "Old American" family it is chiefly the mother who stimulates the child's ability to resist pain, thus emphasizing his masculinity. In the Italian family it seems that the mother is the one who inspires the child's emotionality, while in the Jewish family both parents express attitudes of worry and concern which are transmitted to the children.

Specific deviations from expected reactive and attitudinal patterns can often be understood in terms of a particular structure of the family. This became especially clear from the interviews of two Italian patients and one Jewish patient. All three subjects revealed reactions and attitudes diametrically opposite to those which the investigator would expect on the basis of his experience. In the process of the interview, however, it appeared that one of the Italian patients was adopted into an Italian family, found out about his adoption at the age of fourteen, created a phantasy of being of Anglo-Saxon origin because of his physical appearance and accordingly began to eradicate everything "Italian" in his personality and behavior. For instance, he denied knowledge of the Italian language despite the fact that he always spoke Italian in the family and even learned to abstain from smiling, because he felt that being happy and joyful is an indication of Italian origin. The other Italian patient lost his family at a very early age because of family disorganization and was brought up in an Irish foster home.

The Jewish patient consciously adopted a "non-Jewish" pattern of behavior and attitude because of strong sibling rivalry. According to the respondent, his brother, a favored son in the immigrant Jewish family, always manifested "typical" Jewish reactions toward disease, and the patient, who strongly disliked the brother and was jealous of him, decided to be "completely different."

. . .

NOTES

1. James D. Hardy, Harold G. Wolff, and Helen Goodell, *Pain Sensations and Reactions,* Baltimore: Williams and Wilkins Company, 1952, p. 23.

2. *Ibid.,* p. 204.

3. *Ibid.,* p. 262.

4. I should like to take the opportunity to express my appreciation to Dr. Harold G. Wolff, Professor of Neurology, Cornell University Medical College, Dr. Hiland Flowers, Chief of Neuropsychiatric Service, Dr. Robert Morrow, Chief of Clinical Psychology Section, Dr. Louis Berlin, Chief of Neurology Section, and the Management of the hospital for their cooperation in the setting up of the research at the Kingsbridge Veterans Hospital.

5. Italian respondents are mainly of South Italian origin; the Jewish respondents, with one exception, are all of East European origin. Whenever the Jews are mentioned they are spoken of in terms of the culture they represent and not in terms of their religion.

14. THE FATE OF IDEALISM IN MEDICAL SCHOOL

HOWARD S. BECKER *and* BLANCHE GEER

Socialization is a lifelong process. It involves more than learning the rules of the general society or the norms and values of one's particular family, class, ethnic group, and social environment. In a highly complex society, the learning of occupational skills and professional roles often requires rather specialized and inclusive training in which the neophyte is initiated into the professional milieu by being divested of certain preconceived attitudes and expectations that are replaced by those that have relevance only to others who share the status he seeks to achieve. Entry into the military, the ministry, and the academy all involve particular indoctrination procedures. So, too, does medical training.

In this article, Howard S. Becker and Blanche Geer describe the socialization of medical students who, imbued with idealized images of the medical profession, undergo a transformation as they are exposed to the rigors of preclinical training, function as lowly men on the hospital staff hierarchy, and, eventually, emerge as fledgling physicians.

Howard S. Becker is Professor of Sociology at Northwestern University. Blanche Geer is Director of the Socialization Project at Northeastern University where she also teaches sociology. They are among the coauthors of Boys in White: Student Culture in Medical School *(1961). Becker is also the author of* Outsiders *(1963) and* The Other Side: Perspectives on Deviance *(1964), and the editor of* Social Problems *(1966).*

It makes some difference in a man's performance of his work whether he believes wholeheartedly in what he is doing or feels that in important respects it is a fraud, whether he feels convinced that it is a good thing or believes that it is not really of much use after all. The distinction we are making is the one people have in mind when they refer, for example, to their calling as a "noble profession" on the one hand or a "racket" on the other. In the one case they idealistically proclaim that their work is all that it claims on the surface to be; in the other they cynically concede that it is first and foremost a way of making a living and that its surface pretensions are just that and nothing more. Presumably, different modes of behavior are associated with these perspectives when wholeheartedy embraced. The cynic cuts corners with a feeling of inevitability while the idealist goes down fighting. *The Blackboard Jungle* and *Not as a Stranger* are only the most recent in a long tradition of fictional portrayals of the importance of this aspect of a man's adjustment to his work.

Professional schools often receive a major share of the blame for producing this kind of cynicism—and none more than the medical school. The idealistic young freshman changes into a tough, hardened, unfeeling doctor; or so the popular view has it. Teachers of medicine sometimes rephrase the distinction between the clinical and pre-clinical years into one between the "cynical" and "pre-cynical" years. Psychological research

Reprinted from the *American Sociological Review,* **23** (1958), 50–56, by permission of the authors and the American Sociological Association.

supports this view, presenting attitude surveys which show medical students year by year scoring lower on "idealism" and higher on "cynicism." [1] Typically, this cynicism is seen as developing in response to the shattering of ideals consequent on coming face-to-face with the realities of professional practice.

In this paper, we attempt to describe the kind of idealism that characterizes the medical freshmen and to trace both the development of cynicism and the vicissitudes of that idealism in the course of the four years of medical training. Our main themes are that though they develop cynical feelings in specific situations directly associated with their medical school experience, the medical students never lose their original idealism about the practice of medicine; that the growth of both cynicism and idealism are not simply developments, but are instead complex transformations; and that the very notions "idealism" and "cynicism" need further analysis, and must be seen as situational in their expressions rather than as stable traits possessed by individuals in greater or lesser degree. Finally, we see the greater portion of these feelings as being collective rather than individual phenomena.

Our discussion is based on a study we are now conducting at a state medical school,[2] in which we have carried on participant observation with students of all four years in all of the courses and clinical work to which they are exposed. We joined the students in their activities in school and after school and watched them at work in labs, on the hospital wards, and in the clinic. Often spending as much as a month with a small group of from five to fifteen students assigned to a particular activity, we came to know them well and were able to gather information in informal interviews and by overhearing the ordinary daily conversation of the group.[3] In the course of our observation and interviewing we have gathered much information on the subject of idealism. Of necessity, we shall have to present the very briefest statement of our findings with little or no supporting evidence.[4] The problem of idealism is, of course, manyfaceted and complex and we have dealt with it in a simplified way, describing only some of its grosser features.[5]

The Freshmen

The medical students enter school with what we may think of as the idealistic notion, implicit in lay culture, that the practice of medicine is a wonderful thing and that they are going to devote their lives to service to mankind. They believe that medicine is made up of a great body of well-established facts that they will be taught from the first day on and that these facts will be of immediate practical use to them as physicians. They enter school expecting to work industriously and expecting that if they work hard enough they will be able to master this body of fact and thus become good doctors.

In several ways the first year of medical school does not live up to their expectations. They are disillusioned when they find they will not be near patients at all, that the first year will be just like another year of college. In fact, some feel that it is not even as good as college because their work in certain areas is not as thorough as courses in the same fields in undergraduate school. They come to think that their courses (with the exception of anatomy) are not worth much because, in the first place, the faculty (being Ph.D.'s) know nothing about the practice of medicine, and, in the second place, the subject matter itself is irrelevant, or as the students say, "ancient history."

The freshmen are further disillusioned when the faculty tells them in a variety of ways that there is more to medicine than they can possibly learn. They realize it may be impossible for them to learn all they need to know in order to practice medicine properly. Their disillusionment becomes more profound when they discover that this statement of the faculty is literally true.[6] Experience in trying to master the details of the anatomy of the extremities convinces them that they cannot do so in the time they have. Their expectation of hard work is not disappointed; they put in an eight-hour day of classes and laboratories, and study four or five hours a night and most of the weekend as well.

Some of the students, the brightest, continue to attempt to learn it all, but succeed only in getting more and more worried about their work. The majority decide that, since they can't learn it all, they must select from among all the facts presented to them those they will attempt to learn. There are two ways of making this selection. On the one hand, the student may decide on the basis of his own uninformed notions about the nature of medical practice that many facts are not important, since they relate to things which seldom come up in the actual practice of medicine; therefore, he reasons, it is useless to learn them. On the other hand, the student can decide that the important thing is to pass his examinations and, therefore, that the important facts are those which are likely to be asked on an examination; he uses this as a basis for selecting both facts to memorize and courses for intensive study. For example, the work in physiology is dismissed on both of these grounds, being considered neither relevant to the facts of medical life nor important in terms of the amount of time the faculty devotes to it and the number of examinations in the subject.

A student may use either or both of these bases of selection at the beginning of the year, before many tests have been given. But after a few tests have been taken, the student makes "what the faculty wants" the chief basis of his selection of what to learn, for he now has a better idea of what this is and also has become aware that it is possible to fail examinations and that he therefore must learn the

expectations of the faculty if he wishes to stay in school. The fact that one group of students, that with the highest prestige in the class, took this view early and did well on examinations was decisive in swinging the whole class around to this position. The students were equally influenced to become "test-wise" by the fact that, although they had all been in the upper range in their colleges, the class average on the first examination was frighteningly low.

In becoming test-wise, the students begin to develop systems for discovering the faculty wishes and learning them. These systems are both methods for studying their texts and short-cuts that can be taken in laboratory work. For instance, they begin to select facts for memorization by looking over the files of old examinations maintained in each of the medical fraternity houses. They share tip-offs from the lectures and offhand remarks of the faculty as to what will be on the examinations. In anatomy, they agree not to bother to dissect out subcutaneous nerves, reasoning that it is both difficult and time-consuming and the information can be secured from books with less effort. The interaction involved in the development of such systems and short-cuts helps to create a social group of a class which had previously been only an aggregation of smaller and less organized groups.

In this medical school, the students learn in this way to distinguish between the activities of the first year and their original view that everything that happens to them in medical school will be important. Thus they become cynical about the value of their activities in the first year. They feel that the real thing—learning which will help them to help mankind—has been postponed, perhaps until the second year, or perhaps even farther, at which time they will be able again to act on idealistic premises. They believe that what they do in their later years in school under supervision will be about the same thing they will do, as physicians, on their own; the first year had disappointed this expectation.

There is one matter, however, about which the students are not disappointed during the first year: the so-called trauma of dealing with the cadaver. But this experience, rather than producing cynicism, reinforces the student's attachment to his idealistic view of medicine by making him feel that he is experiencing at least some of the necessary unpleasantness of the doctor. Such difficulties, however, do not loom as large for the student as those of solving the problem of just what the faculty wants.

On this and other points, a working consensus develops in the new consolidated group about the interpretation of their experience in medical school and its norms of conduct. This consensus, which we call *student culture*,[7] focuses their attention almost completely on their day-to-day activities in school and obscures or sidetracks their earlier idealistic preoccupations. Cynicism, griping, and minor cheating become endemic, but the cynicism is specific to the educational situation, to the first year, and to only parts of it. Thus the students keep their cynicism separate from their idealistic feelings and by postponement protect their belief that medicine is a wonderful thing, that their school is a fine one, and that they will become good doctors.

Later Years

The sophomore year does not differ greatly from the freshman year. Both the work load and anxiety over examinations probably increase. Though they begin some medical activities, as in their attendance at autopsies and particularly in their introductory course in physical diagnosis, most of what they do continues to repeat the pattern of the college science curriculum. Their attention still centers on the problem of getting through school by doing well in examinations.

During the third and fourth, or clinical years, teaching takes a new form. In place of lectures and laboratories, the students' work now consists of the study of actual patients admitted to the hospital or seen in the clinic. Each patient who enters the hospital is assigned to a student who interviews him about his illnesses, past and present, and performs a physical examination. He writes this up for the patient's chart, and appends the diagnosis and the treatment that he would use were he allowed actually to treat the patient. During conferences with faculty physicians, often held at the patient's bedside, the student is quizzed about items of his report and called upon to defend them or to explain their significance. Most of the teaching in the clinical years is of this order.

Contact with patients brings a new set of circumstances with which the student must deal. He no longer feels the great pressure created by tests, for he is told by the faculty, and this is confirmed by his daily experience, that examinations are now less important. His problems now become those of coping with a steady stream of patients in a way that will please the staff man under whom he is working, and of handling what is sometimes a tremendous load of clinical work so as to allow himself time for studying diseases and treatments that interest him and for play and family life.

The students earlier have expected that once they reach the clinical years they will be able to realize their idealistic ambitions to help people and to learn those things immediately useful in aiding people who are ill. But they find themselves working to understand cases as medical problems rather than working to help the sick and memorizing the relevant available facts so that these can be produced immediately for a questioning staff man. When they make ward rounds with a faculty member they are likely to be quizzed about any of the seemingly countless facts possibly related to the condition of the patient for whom they are "caring."

Observers speak of the cynicism that overtakes the student and the lack of concern for his patients as human beings. This change does take place, but it is not produced solely by "the anxiety brought about by the presence of death and suffering." [8] The student becomes preoccupied with the technical aspects of the cases with which he deals because the faculty requires him to do so. He is questioned about so many technical details that he must spend most of his time learning them.

The frustrations created by his position in the teaching hospital further divert the student from idealistic concerns. He finds himself low man in a hierarchy based on clinical experience, so that he is allowed very little of the medical responsibility he would like to assume. Because of his lack of experience, he cannot write orders, and he receives permission to perform medical and surgical procedures (if at all) at a rate he considers far too slow. He usually must content himself with "mere" vicarious participation in the drama of danger, life, and death that he sees as the core of medical practice. The student culture accents these difficulties so that events (and especially those involving patients) are interpreted and reacted to as they push him toward or hold him back from further participation in this drama. He does not think in terms the layman might use.

As a result of the increasingly technical emphasis of his thinking the student appears cynical to the non-medical outsider, though from his own point of view he is simply seeing what is "really important." Instead of reacting with the layman's horror and sympathy for the patient to the sight of a cancerous organ that has been surgically removed, the student is more likely to regret that he was not allowed to close the incision at the completion of the operation, and to rue the hours that he must spend searching in the fatty flesh for the lymph nodes that will reveal how far the disease has spread. As in other lines of work, he drops lay attitudes for those more relevant to the way the event affects someone in his position.

This is not to say that the students lose their original idealism. When issues of idealism are openly raised in a situation they define as appropriate, they respond as they might have when they were freshmen. But the influence of the student culture is such that questions which might bring forth this idealism are not brought up. Students are often assigned patients for examination and follow-up whose conditions might be expected to provoke idealistic crises. Students discuss such patients, however, with reference to the problems they create for the *student*. Patients with terminal diseases who are a long time dying, and patients with chronic diseases who show little change from week to week, are more likely to be viewed as creating extra work without extra compensation in knowledge or the opportunity to practice new skills than as examples of illness which raise questions about euthanasia. Such cases require the student to spend time every day checking on progress which he feels will probably not take place and to write long "progress" notes in the patient's chart although little progress has occurred.

This apparent cynicism is a collective matter. Group activities are built around this kind of workaday perspective, constraining the students in two ways. First, they do not openly express the lay idealistic notions they may hold, for their culture does not sanction such expression; second, they are less likely to have thoughts of this deviant kind when they are engaged in group activity. The collective nature of this "cynicism" is indicated by the fact that students become more openly idealistic whenever they are removed from the influence of student culture—when they are alone with a sociologist as they near the finish of school and sense the approaching end of student life, for example, or when they are isolated from their classmates and therefore are less influenced by this culture.[9]

They still feel, as advanced students, though much less so than before, that school is irrelevant to actual medical practice. Many of their tasks, like running laboratory tests on patients newly admitted to the hospital or examining surgical specimens in the pathology laboratory, seem to them to have nothing to do with their visions of their future activity as doctors. As in their freshman year, they believe that perhaps they must obtain the knowledge they will need in spite of the school. They still conceive of medicine as a huge body of proven facts, but no longer believe that they will ever be able to master it all. They now say that they are going to try to apply the solution of the practicing M.D. to their own dilemma: learn a few things that they are interested in very well and know enough about other things to pass examinations while in school and, later on in practice, to know to which specialist to send difficult patients.

Their original medical idealism reasserts itself as the end of school approaches. Seniors show more interest than students in earlier years in serious ethical dilemmas of the kind they expect to face in practice. They have become aware of ethical problems laymen often see as crucial for the physician—whether it is right to keep patients with fatal diseases alive as long as possible, or what should be done if an influential patient demands an abortion —and worry about them. As they near graduation and student culture begins to break down as the soon-to-be doctors are about to go their separate ways, these questions are more and more openly discussed.

While in school, they have added to their earlier idealism a new and peculiarly professional idealism. Even though they know that few doctors live up to the standards they have been taught, they intend always to examine their patients thoroughly and to give treatment based on firm diagnosis rather than merely to relieve symptoms. This expansion and trans-formation of idealism appear most explicitly in their consideration of alternative careers, concerning both specialization and the kind of arrangements to be made for setting up practice. Many of their hypothetical choices aim at making it possible for them to be the kind of doctors their original idealism pictured. Many seniors consider specialty training so that they will be able to work in a limited field in which it will be more nearly possible to know all there is to know, thus avoiding the necessity of dealing in a more ignorant way with the wider range of problems general practice would present. In the same manner, they think of schemes to establish partnerships or other arrangements making it easier to avoid a work load which would prevent them from giving each patient the thorough examination and care they now see as ideal.

In other words, as school comes to an end, the cynicism specific to the school situation also comes to an end and their original and more general idealism about medicine comes to the fore again, though within a framework of more realistic alternatives. Their idealism is now more informed although no less selfless.

Discussion

We have used the words "idealism" and "cynicism" loosely in our description of the changeable state of mind of the medical student, playing on ambiguities we can now attempt to clear up. Retaining a core of common meaning, the dictionary definition, in our reference to the person's belief in the worth of his activity and the claims made for it, we have seen that this is not a generalized trait of the students we studied but rather an attitude which varies greatly, depending on the particular activity the worth of which is questioned and the situation in which the attitude is expressed.

This variability of the idealistic attitude suggests that in using such an element of personal perspective in sociological analysis one should not treat it as homogeneous but should make a determined search for subtypes which may arise under different conditions and have differing consequences. Such subtypes presumably can be constructed along many dimensions. There might, for instance, be consistent variations in the medical students' idealism through the four years of school that are related to their social class backgrounds. We have stressed in this report the subtypes that can be constructed according to variations in the object of the idealistic attitude and variations in the audience the person has in mind when he adopts the attitude. The medical students can be viewed as both idealistic and cynical, depending on whether one has in mind their view of their school activities or the future they envision for themselves as doctors. Further, they might take one or another of these positions depending on whether their implied audience is made up of other students, their instructors, or the lay public.

A final complication arises because cynicism and idealism are not merely attributes of the actor, but are as dependent on the person doing the attributing as they are on the qualities of the individual to whom they are attributed.[10] Though the student may see his own disregard of the unique personal troubles of a particular patient as proper scientific objectivity, the layman may view this objectivity as heartless cynicism.[11]

Having made these analytic distinctions, we can now summarize the transformations of these characteristics as we have seen them occurring among medical students. Some of the students' determined idealism at the outset is reaction against the lay notion, of which they are uncomfortably aware, that doctors are money-hungry cynics; they counter this with an idealism of similar lay origin stressing the doctor's devotion to service. But this idealism soon meets a setback, as students find that it will not be relevant for awhile, since medical school has, it seems, little relation to the practice of medicine, as they see it. As it has not been refuted, but only shown to be temporarily beside the point, the students "agree" to set this idealism aside in favor of a realistic approach to the problem of getting through school. This approach, which we have labeled as the cynicism specific to the school experience, serves as protection for the earlier grandiose feelings about medicine by postponing their exposure to reality to a distant future. As that future approaches near the end of the four years and its possible mistreatment of their ideals moves closer, the students again worry about maintaining their integrity, this time in actual medical practice. They use some of the knowledge they have gained to plan careers which, it is hoped, can best bring their ideals to realization.

We can put this in propositional form by saying that when a man's ideals are challenged by outsiders and then further strained by reality, he may salvage them by postponing their application to a future time when conditions are expected to be more propitious.

NOTES

1. Leonard D. Eron, "Effect of Medical Education on Medical Students," *Journal of Medical Education*, 10 (1955), 559–566.

2. This study is sponsored by Community Studies, Inc., of Kansas City, Missouri, and is being carried on at the University of Kansas Medical School, to whose dean, staff, and students we are indebted for their wholehearted cooperation. Professor Everett C. Hughes of the University of Chicago is director of the project.

3. The technique of participant observation has not been fully systematized, but some approaches to this have been made. See, for example, Florence R. Kluckhohn, "The Participant Observer Technique in Small Communities," *American Journal of Sociology*, 45 (1940),

331–343; Arthur Vidich, "Participant Observation and the Collection and Interpretation of Data," *ibid.*, 60 (1955), 354–360; William Foote Whyte, "Observational Field-Work Methods," in Maria Jahoda, Morton Deutsch, and Stuart W. Cook (eds.), *Research Methods in the Social Sciences*, New York: Dryden Press, 1951, 2, pp. 393–514; and *Street Corner Society*, enlarged edition, Chicago: University of Chicago Press, 1955, pp. 279–358; Rosalie Hankey Wax, "Twelve Years Later: An Analysis of Field Experience," *American Journal of Sociology*, 63 (1957), 133–142; Morris S. Schwartz and Charlotte Green Schwartz, "Problems in Participant Observation," *American Journal of Sociology*, 60 (1955), 343–353; and Howard S. Becker and Blanche Geer, "Participant Observation and Interviewing: A Comparison," *Human Organization*, 16 (1957), 28–33. The last item represents the first of a projected series of papers attempting to make explicit the operations involved in this method. For a short description of some techniques used in this study, see Howard S. Becker, "Interviewing Medical Students," *American Journal of Sociology*, 62 (1956), 199–201.

4. A fuller analysis and presentation of evidence will be contained in a volume on this study now being prepared by the authors in collaboration with Everett C. Hughes and Anselm L. Strauss.

5. Renee Fox has shown how complex one aspect of this whole subject is in her analysis of the way medical students at Cornell become aware of and adjust to both their own failure to master all available knowledge and the gaps in current knowledge in many fields. See her "Training for Uncertainty," in Robert K. Merton, George G. Reader, and Patricia L. Kendall (eds.), *The Student Physician: Introductory Studies in the Sociology of Medical Education*, Cambridge: Harvard University Press, 1957, pp. 207–241.

6. Compare the description of student reaction in Fox, *op. cit.*, pp. 209–221 to this problem at Cornell.

7. The concept of student culture is analyzed in some detail in Howard S. Becker and Blanche Geer, "Student Culture in Medical School," *Harvard Educational Review*, 28 (1958), 70–80.

8. Dana L. Farnsworth, "Some Observations on the Attitudes and Motivations of the Harvard Medical Student," *Harvard Medical Alumni Bulletin*, January, 1956, 34.

9. See the discussion in Howard S. Becker, "Interviewing Medical Students," *op. cit.*

10. See Philip Selznick's related discussion of fanaticism in *TVA and the Grass Roots*, Berkeley: University of California Press, 1953, pp. 205–213.

11. George Orwell gives the layman's side in his essay, "How the Poor Die" in *Shooting an Elephant and Other Essays*, London: Secker and Warburg, 1950, pp. 18–32.

15. THE AMERICAN NUN

EDWARD WAKIN *and* FR. JOSEPH F. SCHEUER

Membership in a religious order involves far more than the ability to perform a set of ceremonial duties. One's novitiate is supposed to end with a total commitment to a way of life that is markedly different from that of the rest of the members of society. Yet, save for those who are entirely cloistered, even priests and nuns must learn to reconcile what is expected within the order and what one knows about (and sees in) the world beyond.

In this essay Edward Wakin and Father Joseph Scheuer describe the conflicts experienced by many American nuns.

Both authors are on the faculty of Fordham University. Wakin, a former newspaperman, is the author of Lonely Minority: The Modern Story of Egypts Copts *(1963) and* At the Edge of Harlem *(1964). Father Scheuer directs the LePlay Research, Inc. and teaches sociology. Together they wrote* The De-Romanization of the American Catholic Church *(1966).*

The American public has been introduced in recent months to a new image of the Catholic nun—a change from the genial ball-playing lady in formidable black and white to the graduate student pursuing a Ph.D. at Columbia or UCLA. A touch of style has been added to the nun's costume, and a number of nuns have been making news of a most untraditional kind. Sister Frances Catherine of Cincinnati, for instance, was admitted in May to practice before the U. S. Supreme Court; Sister Francetta Barberis, after retiring as a college president in Missouri, now actually wears secular clothes as consultant to the Job Corps.

The most dramatic departure, of course, has been provided by the nuns in civil-rights demonstrations. When they sang "We Shall Overcome" in Selma, the spirit belonged to Susan B. Anthony as well as Martin Luther King—for a struggle for emancipation has begun in the convent, spurred on by the Vatican Council. The American nun—with her vows to be poor, chaste, and obedient—is restive over the suffocating context of her religious life.

But the struggle must be put into its proper perspective. There are 180,000 women in no less than 480 orders—from A (for Adoratices, with 14 U.S. members) to Z (for Zelatrices, with 294 U.S. members). The few exceptions in graduate school, in important positions, or on picket lines do not make a revolution. They only symbolize a growing demand for change, and that demand is taking place in a tense and obstructive framework.

Within each separate community of nuns, efforts to modernize are accompanied by strong ideological differences. And within each convent, the gap between the older and younger generations is a pronounced one. This was confirmed firsthand when one of us discussed the main ideas in this article before gatherings of three orders of nuns; the differences between the generations are close to the surface. It is easy to provoke a heated debate in any convent on the problems facing the American nun.

Questions of reform focus on two charges—incompetence and irrelevance. In 1952, when leading sister-educators took stock in a nation-wide survey, only 13 of 255 orders responding said that they had programs which enabled their members to get bachelor's degrees. And 118 orders admitted they were cut off geographically from educational facilities they could use, either of their own or of accessible Catholic colleges.

In the past, undertrained and overworked sisters in parochial schools had taught hundreds of thousands of Catholic children; without them, parish schools could not have existed. But it became obvious in the postwar period that good intentions were scarcely enough. The Sister Formation Movement, which emerged in 1954, has addressed itself to the problem of competence, taking its name from the goal of complete formation along "human, Christian, intellectual, professional, religious, and apostolic" lines.

With nine-tenths of the Catholic women's religious communities in the country participating, the Sister Formation Conference directs a broad program aimed at upgrading professional qualifications. Its influence has been contagious, making it fashionable to seek both experience and education outside convent walls, even outside the Catholic ghetto. The goals of the movement include providing every young sister with a bachelor's degree, more education and training for older sisters, more advanced study for promising sisters, and sharing of educational facilities among the various orders.

The emancipation process thus follows a familiar pattern by beginning with educational opportunity. The more basic question of the relevance of the American nun remains. As Sister Charles Borromeo has written in the *National Catholic Reporter,* "I would like to accept the judgment that we are increasingly irrelevant in

modern America to the extent that we cling blindly to old forms and old psychological patterns." She adds a biting comment on the stereotyped nun: "Rigidity of gesture, the extremely soft voice, the posture of cringing before authority figures imply that vigor and vitality are somehow pagan or corrupting."

A Fortress Community

Strong criticism of the convent mentality and of isolation from the real world received international support when a leading liberal Cardinal, Leon Joseph Suenens of Belgium, wrote *The Nun in the World.* With its publication in 1962, the book became a manifesto for progressive-thinking nuns in America. Cardinal Suenens stated:

A community of nuns often gives the impression of being a fortress whose drawbridge is only furtively and fearfully lowered. . . . [P]hysical and psychological detachment from the world leads a religious to turn in on herself and her own community. Her world shrinks, and, if she is not careful, will end up no more than a few square yards in size. From this comes a distorted vision, seeing everything from one angle, measuring things against a diminished scale. From this comes also the contrived and artificial nature of certain customs in religious houses—a sort of "house etiquette," a stylized, stereotyped, and unnatural behavior. It has been said of certain congregations of nuns that they are the last stronghold of the very studied manners of the middle-class woman of the nineteenth century. . . .

An observer analyzing the part played by religious today cannot help being struck by their absence from the main spheres of influence at adult levels, spheres where they have a right to be and where their talents are called for and their presence is needed. . . . The religious of today appears to the faithful to be out of touch with the world as it is, an anachronism.

In reality, the more progressive nuns are struggling with a restrictive tradition in which change and custom, the modern and the old, mix uneasily. The American nun remains part of a traditional church society characterized by male dominance.

The Vatican Council itself has emphasized the secondary status of women by excluding them from its deliberations, thus ignoring thousands of nuns and millions of laywomen. Only belatedly, a handful of voteless woman auditors, both lay and religious, have been added. And the Sacred Congregation of Religious, which is responsible for the rules and regulations governing Catholic women's religious organizations, has no nuns involved directly in its work. In our society, the nun is not only a woman; she has joined a religious community structured along medieval lines. Women's orders were formed as subsidiaries of men's, and historical origins are not easily cast aside. Today, as in the past, the nun's work is primarily among the young, the sick, and the elderly—the woman's traditional role.

When St. Vincent de Paul and St. Louise de Marillac dismantled the cloisters in the seventeenth century, they made "their chapel the parish church, their cloister the streets of the city or wards of the hospitals." The result was the Daughters of Charity, the Church's first uncloistered community for women and now its largest group of religious women. Today in the United States, their work includes all the major activities of nuns: elementary, high-school, and college teaching; nursing and schools of nursing; homes for children, working girls, unmarried mothers; care of the aged; day nurseries; centers for child guidance, social work, and teaching of religion; retreats; home and foreign missions.

But the seventeenth-century problem of the cloister, which separated the nun physically from a needy world, has been replaced by the twentieth-century problem of "enclosure," which tends to cut her off psychologically from the real world. The modern nun can leave the cloister to teach, nurse, do welfare work, or even shop, but otherwise she is enclosed within the convent and bound by a restricted and tightly regulated round of activities. She is not only wrapped in a religious costume as contemporary as a suit of armor; she is entangled in myriad rules and restrictions of staggering pettiness. Like the child whose interfering parent wants to govern every part of her life, the nun must fight for her own personal maturity.

Time-Bound and Enclosed

Many nuns, however, defend these restrictions as safeguarding the spirit of their order's foundress. In a recent collection of essays about convent life, one nun went so far as to call the petty differences between communities "wholesome signs, indicating a noble ideal." She describes what would happen if Mrs. X took a group of sisters from different orders on an afternoon outing, a description which typifies both the entangling web of regulations and the acceptance of them by many of the victims.

Sister A may go for the ride, but she can't get out of the car or eat an ice-cream cone on the way. Sister B may go for the ride and get out of the car, but refreshments are taboo. Sister C may go for the ride and have her ice cream, but all within the sanctuary of the car. Sister D may go for the ride, get out of the car, and eat the ice-cream cone. She may even name her own flavor if Mrs. X isn't a dictator. Sister E? She may come out to the car and wave goodbye to the others.[1]

On the level of professional service, the negative results are predictable. Time-bound by an "horarium"—an all-embracing schedule of daily activities—sisters are prevented from carrying on the very life of service to which they commit themselves. Sister-teachers find it almost impossible to see the parents of their pupils, much less visit homes, since the hours when parents are freest are the very hours when sisters are confined to their convents. Some nursing sisters whose habits cover their ears find themselves hardly able to take blood-pressure readings or listen to the fetal heart.

Most sisters are restricted in opportunities to enlarge their horizons, to engage in learning experiences, to gain a firsthand appreciation of the things their lay contemporaries face. Sisters do get permission nowadays to attend meetings, lectures, or conventions, but under limitations and usually within the protective Catholic ghetto. While the situation is considerably more permissive for nuns on college faculties or for those pursuing graduate degrees, they are a small minority. For the bulk of American nuns, the demands of "enclosure" are stifling.

An outsider can only sense the impact of the system upon the individual nun. Here is what a sister who has been in a religious order for thirty years said—a sobering contrast to the lyrical accounts in the pietistic literature about convent life:

If only we'd go the whole way on *aggiornamento!* In the morning I drag myself out of bed too tired to think. I get down to the Chapel where we say Matins and Lauds, followed by a half-hour of mental prayer and twenty minutes of vocal prayers for the Church, the Community, and benefactors, and then Mass starts. By Communion time I'm lost in frustration because I can feel no fervor—only fatigue. Sometimes I kneel at the Communion railing wondering if I can possibly please God feeling as I do. Then we go to breakfast and are served in rank. Since I'm near the end of my particular table, I'm served near the last, and I practically choke with smoldering resentment—and yes, let me be honest—with scruples because I'm in such a bad humor every morning. Yet, I love to pray. What a joy and peace it would be if we just had meditation as a preparation for Mass. I could sing aloud with the best of them or join in hearty dialogue at Mass in all the glory of the new liturgy.[2]

The personality consequence of such a ritualized existence can be serious, and it is evident in the widespread concern about mental illness among Catholic women's religious orders. Sympathetic priests commonly encounter troubled sisters torn by tensions, conflicts of conscience, and self-doubts about the meaningfulness of their lives. Dr. John B. Wain, a Catholic physician with extensive experience treating nuns, has cited his "clinical impressions" in a penetrating article for the *Review for Religious*. He presents two generalizations based on his experience and conversations with Catholic doctors and religious nurses: "First, there is too much neurosis among religious. Second, much of it is avoidable or preventable." No realistic observer close to the situation would disagree.

Psychological Soundings

In a unique attempt to document the national aspects of the problem, Sister M. William Kelley collected data on hospitalization of sisters for mental illness. She found that nuns had a higher incidence of both psychotic disorders (particularly schizophrenia) and psychoneurotic disorders than American women in general. By comparing her 1956 findings with a similar study in 1936, Sister William found that the rate of hospitalization among sisters for mental illness had increased substantially—from 485 per 100,000 to 595. And while the rate for the small minority of cloistered nuns remained greater than for active nuns, that difference had also narrowed. In fact, the rate of hospitalization for mental illness had increased for active nuns while decreasing for cloistered nuns.

This led Sister William to make several likely hypotheses which underscore the tension between the traditional and the modern. She cites the sources of greater stress that may be contributing to greater numbers of mental breakdowns: overcrowded classrooms, understaffed hospitals, accreditation demands, and various other professional pressures facing religious today. In the past such strains were not nearly so severe. Today, the figures on increasing mental illness strongly suggest the system must be adjusted and that applicants for religious life must be better screened in the first place.

Both recommendations are made by psychologists familiar with religious life in America. As was indicated in the 1936 study particularly, many prepsychotic personalities are attracted to the religious life for what they think it will offer them. One of the leading practitioners in the expanding field of psychological testing for religious orders alerted the 1964 convention of the National Catholic Educational Association to the problem. Dr. Walter J. Coville of St. Vincent's Hospital in New York City warned that the traditional criteria for identifying promising applicants can be misleading, "for what often appears to be a virtue may actually be a neurosis." He cited those candidates "who conspicuously reveal themselves as docile, self-effacing; eager to comply, pious, and humble, but who actually are passive-dependent personality types." Insecure, filled with anxieties, eager to avoid responsibility, such types seek a neurotic escape to the religious life for shelter and support. Another type cited by Dr. Coville is the ambitious candidate who "needs to find status and recognition, and who may unwittingly exploit others" for her own benefit. His sobering caveat raises speculation on how many examples of both types have been admitted to the religious life in America. And how many have reached positions of power with neurotic traits that were interpreted as virtues?

The situation is complicated by recruiting patterns for the religious life. The decision to become a sister is usually made during the teen years, commonly under the influence and inspiration of teaching sisters. This magnifies the danger of unrealistic and immature decisions. In a study of 2,120 sisters entering the convent between 1885 and 1943, Bishop John Hagan found that the largest number (507) first thought of the convent at age ten, with the largest number (315) making the final decision at eighteen. The median age for entering the convent was nineteen.[3]

Once a young woman joins an order,

she becomes absorbed into the life of her religious community. Her training is designed to bring about total commitment to the religious order. First, as a "postulant" —for one to three years, depending on the order—then as a "novice" for one or more years, the young woman is under the strict control of a religious supervisor.

After the training period, the young woman takes her vows publicly before her religious community. At this point she formally makes her triple commitment to poverty, chastity, and obedience. These vows should ideally impose responsibilities both on the nuns and on the religious system itself, although the traditionalists stress only the nuns' responsibilities.

Yet the system should provide for healthy fulfillment of the vows in the collective life of the order or community (the terms are interchangeable in popular usage, though there are canonical differences). The small minority of cloistered nuns are limited to the convent and cut off from all outside contacts. The overwhelming majority of nuns in the United States are active sisters living in a convent.

Within the present-day convent, a sister's personal resources are often strained unnecessarily by the inbred community life, the suspicion of everything physical, restrictions on relationships with lay people, and the confined atmosphere. As one perceptive nun told us, "The cardinal sin of religious women is lack of charity of the tongue; it is more serious and more frequent than any other failing, causing more upsets in communities than any of the vows." Despite the admonition of psychologists, maladjustment and neurotic behavior are commonly attributed to a poor spiritual life, and a more intense spiritual life is regarded as a panacea.

When Chastity Goes Before Charity

Of the three vows, poverty is the least misused in America. In Europe, it is more common to confuse frugality with chill penury, with degrading and unhealthy living conditions. Nonetheless, the lingering presence of begging sisters and the continued risk of tuberculosis among young nuns in America suggest that there is still room for reform on the vow of poverty. Of the other two vows, chastity is widely distorted and obedience commonly misunderstood.

The difference between the generations of nuns is vividly illustrated in attitudes toward chastity. These samples of sex advice given by the older generation of nuns in Catholic high schools were collected from freshman coeds at an Eastern university: "Don't wear patent-leather shoes, else men see your underwear reflected in them." "Beware of men who lurk by stairways in order to stare up at you." "White reminds men of bed sheets." "Put talcum powder in your bath, so your body won't be reflected in the water."

Among older nuns, in particular, these attitudes are accompanied by a Bride of Christ mystique which romanticizes what is basically a medieval metaphor symbolized by the wedding band worn by nuns. In most religious communities, new members still wear bridal gowns at their reception, and it is even common for friends to hold bridal showers for girls about to enter a convent. The literature surrounding this symbolism is bizarre. A nun writing in *A Seal Upon My Heart,* published in 1956, said: "When I started out with my tremendous Lover, I had yet to learn that love is not so much receiving as giving, not so much possession as being possessed."

Other problems are hidden behind convent walls. Dr. Wain reported that gynecological complaints are often suffered for years before medical aid is sought; sometimes malignant tumors are not reported until they are inoperable. In the inhibited atmosphere of the convent, premenstrual tension among young nuns and menopause among older ones become extraheavy burdens. Left in relative ignorance in a society of women with limited worldly experience, the typical sister is likely to suffer more from the prevailing prudery than from her vow of chastity. She is easily shaken by temptations at what she may regard as the most inopportune times, though, as Dr. Wain notes, "it is probably not uncommon for religious and lay people to experience sexual feelings at the quiet times of recollection and Communion." It is not surprising that chastity, rather than charity, seems to emerge as the greatest single virtue in the convent culture of American sisters.

On the other hand, obedience represents the most significant problem for the American nun. As expected, the demands for renovation are strongest from the new kind of religious woman. She must balance her individual conscience with her acceptance of authority. She must accept curbs on her professional competence for nonprofessional reasons invoked by nonprofessional superiors. She must exist in a world of outmoded regulations and worn-out attitudes which drown her involvement in the contemporary world.

Bulwarks Against Emancipation

In discussing reform, it is important to stress the Church's dependence on the present system of religious orders; the orders, in turn, are committed to their own survival. A religious community is an economical and efficient source of women workers in the Church. By binding women into a community life, the Church has low-cost personnel for its schools, hospitals, and charitable institutions. Its extensive American operations would collapse without them.

While the total value of the contributed services of sisters is pure speculation, some indication can be found in their major area of activity, the schools. More than 100,000 sisters in education may account for as much as one-half of the total $2 billion estimated annual contributed value of the U.S. Catholic educational enterprise. Pope Pius XII is frequently quoted: "The apostolate of the Church is almost inconceivable without the help of religious women."

Nowadays, however, the traditional Catholic religious orders are no longer taken for granted as the only means to a life of religious commitment. "Many nuns and sisters," Cardinal Joseph Ritter of St. Louis has said, "precisely because of their own sense of fairness and humility, have come to doubt their usefulness in and to the Church. Young girls, possibly the religious of tomorrow, influenced by these criticisms, have mistrusted their own sense of vocation; many others have been advised that a more effective apostolate is open to them in the lay state."

The secular institute is a structural modernization of the traditional religious order. Its members remain in the world, earning a living, following their professions, without having to wear any religious uniform. Their vows or promises of poverty, chastity, and obedience are adjusted to the realities of the environment in which they perform apostolic work. They are still united in membership, and include several hundred Americans in such institutes as Caritas Christi, Oblate Missionaries of Mary Immaculate, and Rural Parish Workers of Christ the King. (The Grail, an international movement of both single and married women, has been a Catholic version of the Peace Corps for more than forty years, operating under a more flexible structure than the secular institute.)

But despite its potential, this alternative, which did not gain unequivocal papal recognition until 1947, has a limited future in the face of support by the Church establishment for the traditional religious orders, which constitute the vested interests of 480 religious superiors. For this reason, if for no other, the controversy over the life and role of the American nun is certain to continue within the present system along the familiar lines of emancipation for any minority: increasing education, expanding opportunities, greater freedom accompanied by pressure for even more freedom.

The restrictive status of nuns is being challenged within the Catholic Church, and the drive for more education and training for them is the main vehicle for reform. By establishing qualifications as professionals and as intellectual leaders, and by demonstrating an involvement in social issues, the sisters are trying to make their role more modern and more American.

They cannot manage reform on their own; they are still not free of the male-dominated establishment. Yet within their tight little islands, the religious orders must make extensive repairs and alterations in response to the demands of the progressive new nuns. They must do this to avoid decline, to reduce dropouts among their recruits, and to expand to meet the needs of a growing and more sophisticated Catholic population. For it is obvious that you cannot keep them behind convent walls once they have been on a picket line.

NOTES

1. *Convent Life,* Joan M. Lexau (ed.), Sister Mary Gilbert, S.N.J.M., New York: Dial Press, 1964.

2. Quoted by Sister Bertrande Meyers, D.C., in *Sisters for the 21st Century,* Sheed and Ward, 1965.

3. A nationwide picture of vocations and of the background of nuns still has not been drawn because of the Balkanized situation involving religious orders. Religious superiors have ruled

their own empires almost in isolation; only in 1956 was a beginning made toward grouping them cooperatively into a Conference of Major Superiors of Women Religious. Data on dropouts and on vocations are still treated as classified information—when available.

Some indication of social and family background is provided in a survey conducted at the Sister Formation college near St. Louis, Marillac College. A 1961 study of 150 Daughters of Charity at the college showed how deeply American their roots are. Slightly more than half had grandparents on both sides of the family who were born in America; only 15 per cent had three or four grandparents who were born abroad.

SUGGESTIONS FOR FURTHER READING
on *Society, Culture, and the Individual*

The Basic Concepts

BENEDICT, RUTH. *Patterns of Culture.* Originally published in 1934, now available in many editions. An examination of American culture in comparison to the lifeways of three primitive peoples.

CHILDE, V. GORDON, *Man Makes Himself.* New York: New American Library, 1951. A noted archaeologist looks at the evolution of culture.

HALL, EDWARD T. *The Silent Language.* Garden City, N.Y.: Doubleday, 1959. A theory for the examination of culture as a complex of message systems.

KLUCKHOHN, CLYDE. *Mirror for Man.* New York: McGraw-Hill, 1949. A popular introduction to cultural anthropology.

KROEBER, A. L., and CLYDE KLUCKHOHN. *Culture.* New York: Vintage, 1952. A critical review of concepts and definitions.

LIPSET, SEYMOUR MARTIN. *The First New Nation.* New York: Basic Books, 1963. A sociologist's view of the principal value systems of the American people in historical perspective.

MILLER, WARREN. *Russians as People.* New York: E. P. Dutton, 1961. A journalist's sensitive portrayal of the persisting patterns of Russian culture in Soviet society.

REDFIELD, ROBERT. *Peasant Society and Culture.* Chicago: University of Chicago Press, 1956. This book examines the nature of peasantry in various societies.

SERVICE, ELMAN R. *A Profile of Primitive Culture.* New York: Harper, 1958. Summaries of the culture patterns of twenty societies.

Process of Socialization

CLARK, KENNETH. *Dark Ghetto.* New York: Harper and Row, 1965. What it means to grow up "black" in a white man's world.

ELKIN, FREDERICK. *The Child and Society.* New York: Random House, 1960. An introduction to the study of the process of socialization.

GOFFMAN, ERVING. *The Presentation of Self in Everyday Life.* Garden City, N.Y.: Doubleday, 1959. A penetrating analysis of the ways in which people act in varied social settings.

GOODMAN, PAUL. *Growing Up Absurd.* New York: Random House, 1960. A critical examination of the result of socialization in the contemporary United States.

HOGGART, RICHARD. *The Uses of Literacy.* Boston: Beacon Press, 1957. The effects of mass media on values in the English working class.

LINTON, RALPH. *The Cultural Background of Personality.* New York: Appleton-Century-Crofts, 1945. A discussion of the effects of culture and social structure upon the individual.

MOORE, WILLIAM, JR. *The Vertical Ghetto.* New York: Random House, 1969. A study of everyday life in an urban housing project.

RIESMAN, DAVID, NATHAN GLAZER, and RUEL DENNY. *The Lonely Crowd.* Garden City, N.Y.: Doubleday, 1953. A study of the changing American character.

WHITING, JOHN, and IRVIN L. CHILD. *Child Training and Personality: A Cross-Cultural Study.* New Haven, Conn.: Yale University Press, 1958. A comparative study of child-rearing in several societies.

PART THREE
SOCIAL ORGANIZATION

Patterns of primary and
secondary relationships in a
variety of social settings

Edward A. Shils has written that "ideals and beliefs can only influence conduct alongside personal ties, primordial attachments, and responsibilities to corporate bodies. . . ." Thus, while the meaning of social life is defined by culture, actual behavior is manifest in various structured forms. Simply stated, culture refers to the conceptions men live by, and social organization to the ways men live together.

Sociology is the study of shared, patterned, human relationships. The concern of the sociologist is not with the individual *per se* but with the recurrent and predictable forms of social action in which human beings individually and collectively participate. Abstractly, these forms may be seen as ranging along a continuum, their "position" assessed by such variables as size, degree of formality, extensiveness of participation, and the nature or quality of involvement. At one pole is the ideal primary grouping: small in size, simple in rules which are more often implicit than explicit, intimate and coequal in membership, and marked by inclusive relationships that have their own intrinsic value. By contrast, a secondary grouping is large, the rules complex and highly formalized, the members joined by their ability to perform special tasks or by limited interests, relationships tend to be impersonal and highly stratified, and commitment is apt to be to the job, cause, or organization, not to fellow-members. Traditionally, sociologists and anthropologists have cited the close-knit, "folk" society as illustrative of one polar extreme and the heterogeneous, industrial, "associational" society—with its proliferation of special purpose organizations—of the other.

Of course, in reality these ideal constructs are only partial approximations. While primary and secondary relationships do exist, the former are not limited to the folk society, or the latter to the modern type. The study of the organization and content of complex societies reveals a wide array of social forms ranging from the most intimate of primary ties (as between the mother and her child) to the bonds of communal participation (as in the "project" or the neighborhood) to those which connect persons of similar background, race, or religion to the more tenuous links between those who are given similar status in the community or perform similar tasks (as, for example, professionals or civil servants). Even the groups properly called secondary (ranging from certain clubs to the corporation) often become the setting for unofficially sanctioned relationships that are highly personal in character. Not infrequently these are encouraged by the fact that the formal organization does not provide the adequate means for participants to overcome certain persistent problems leading to the unification of members against the system and, in some instances, to the establishment of new lines of communication and ultimately to the formation of "informal groups" within the bureaucratic situation.

This part of *The Study of Society* deals with two sorts of social organizations: those roughly set beneath the rubric "Small Groups and Large Organizations" and those grouped under the even looser label, "Communities." The division is heuristic for, as noted, communities (and societies) are also marked by varying sorts of patterned relationships.

The first set of papers begins with Edward A. Shils' rebuttal of the "myth of soulless modernity" (and the narration of his own studies of the primary group in many different circumstances). Shils' essay is followed by Charles Wright and Herbert Hyman's analysis of data which show the voluntary association membership of varying categories of Americans and Wilbert E. Moore's "The Organized Individual." The next three essays deal with bureaucracy: Philip Selznick's "Foundation of the Theory of Organization," S. E. Finer's description of the modern army, and Charles Page's view of "Bureaucracy's Other Face" based on his experiences as a naval officer in World War II.

In the section on communities, the reader will find Robert Redfield's famous statement on the nature of the ideal "folk society"; a description by Robert MacIver of "The Multi-Group Society"; a paper by Arthur Vidich and Joseph Bensman reporting on small-town living in a mass society; and Herbert Gans' penetrating critique of many of the shibboleths of sociologists who have accepted, at face value, the "disorganizing effect" of urban living. The last two essays also deal with urban life: Stanford M. Lyman and Marvin D. Scott's "Territoriality: A Neglected Sociological Dimension" and an illustration of the applicability of this concept by Gerald D. Suttles in his "Anatomy of a Chicago Slum."

Small Groups and Large Organizations

16. PRIMORDIAL, PERSONAL, SACRED AND CIVIL TIES

EDWARD A. SHILS

Modern society, as Edward Shils sees it, "is no Gesellschaft, *soulless, egotistical, loveless, faithless, utterly impersonal and lacking any integrative forces other than interest or coercion. It is held together by an infinity of personal attachments, moral obligations in concrete contexts, professional and creative pride, individual ambition, primordial affinities and a civil sense . . ." In this article, originally presented as a lecture on the relationship between sociological theory and research and then published in the* British Journal of Sociology, *Shils supports his contention by reviewing his own lifetime of experience studying and reporting—in Germany, the United States, and Great Britain—on personal ties, primary attachments, and the responsibilities of men to corporate bodies.*

This essay serves to illustrate the essential connection between patterns of culture and the nature of social organization. In addition, it provides the reader with a brief, but penetrating, resume of the theoretical premises of sociologists who, since the days of Comte, have attempted to understand and explain social cohesion and group solidarity.

Edward A Shils is Professor of Sociology and a member of the Committee on Social Thought at the University of Chicago. He is the author of The Present State of American Sociology *(1948),* The Torment of Secrecy *(1956),* The Intellectual Between Tradition and Modernity: The Indian Situation *(1961), and* Political Development in New States *(1962). He is coauthor of* Working Papers in the Theory of Action *(1953) and coeditor, with Talcott Parsons, of* Toward a General Theory of Action *(1951).*

Reprinted from the *British Journal of Sociology,* **8** (1957), 130–145, by permission of the author.

What sociologists and social anthropologists call the cultural value or belief system of a society can be lived up to only partially, fragmentarily, intermittently and only in an approximate way. The ideals of prophets and saints can take root only when they are attenuated, moderated and compromised with other contradictory ideals and with the demands of the situation and the needs of "the old Adam." Ideals and beliefs can only influence conduct alongside of personal ties, primordial attachments, and responsibilities in corporate bodies and they can come into play primarily in the form of vague notions regarding the Right and Good in concrete forms.

Sociologists and anthropologists might make it appear as if every man is implicitly a philosopher and a theologian with a coherent image of the cosmos and society and a hierarchy of standards of preference. This is, however, very far from the truth.

Man is much more concerned with what is near at hand, with what is present and concrete than with what is remote and abstract. He is more responsive on the whole to persons, to the status of those who surround him and the justice which he sees in his own situation than he is with the symbols of remote persons, with the total status system in the society and with the global system of justice. Immediately present authorities engage his mind more than remote ones. The ordinary man is however not a complete idiot in the Greek sense. In a dormant way, semi-conscious and peripheral, he too responds to the central authorities and symbols of the society. From time to time, as occasion requires, he comes more closely into contact with them; his consciousness is opened to them at election time, in times of national troubles, in great ceremonial occasions like the Coronation, in the same way in which an "Easter and Christmas" communicant enters into communion with divinity on these two great annual occasions, at his wedding, at the christening of his children, on the occasion of the death of a kinsman, a family member or a close friend. For the rest of the time, the ultimate values of the society, what is sacred to its members, are suspended amidst the distractions of concrete tasks, which makes the values ambiguous and thus gives freedom for individual innovation, creation, and adaptation.

Those who because of the needs of their personalities and the driving force of their reason come into contact with the symbols of the ultimate in the cosmos or in the sphere of justice and morality are impatient with existing tradition, regardless of whether they are "progressive" or seek to revive ancient virtues and "the good old times." They are impatient with anything less than whole-hearted commitment to the ideal as they see it. That is why the ideologist, be he prophet or revolutionary, is affronted by the ordinary man's attachment to his mates, to his pub, to his family, to his petty vanities in his job, to his vulgar gratifications, to his concern for the improvement of his conditions of life. That is also why the ideologist dislikes the politician, who aspires to do no more than to help to keep things running and to make piecemeal changes, and of course, the businessman, the manager, the technologist who works on a limited front.

Nonetheless the work of keeping society going at all times except moments of extreme crisis is the achievement of the workman at his task, the manager in his plant, the administrator bound by red tape, the father and mother in their family circle, a man among his friends, the expert at his narrow job; in brief, it is the achievement which follows from each person concerning himself with his task and his relationships as they exist around.

As I see it, modern society is no lonely crowd, no horde of refugees fleeing from freedom. It is no *Gesellschaft*, soulless, egotistical, loveless, faithless, utterly impersonal and lacking any integrative forces other than interest or coercion. It is held together by an infinity of personal attachments, moral obligations in concrete contexts, professional and creative pride, individual ambition, primordial affinities and a civil sense which is low in many, high in some, and moderate in most persons. It might be destroyed by modern warfare, or the exhaustion of its resources, the lack of initiative of its inventors and enterprisers might so hurt its competitive position in the economic world that it would be doomed to the pressure of a standard of living below what its members aspire to. Aside from these, it is in no danger of internal disintegration. Whatever danger it faces in this respect would be far less from those who are charged with faithlessness, and the inability to rise above their routine concerns, from the philistines, the dwellers in housing estates and new towns, than from those who think that society needs a new faith to invigorate it and give it a new impulse.

These remarks on some of the bonds which hold a large-scale society together have emerged from a long process of research and analysis, a process which began long before I was born and which will go on for a long time after the appearance of *Love, Belief and Civility* in which my own efforts to contribute to the process are contained. When I was asked to speak about the relationships of theory and research, I decided to make my analysis as concrete as possible, especially since the actually subsisting relationships are often obscured and falsified by an excessively schematic, excessively orderly picture. In order to be as concrete as possible I am reporting on my own experience of this relationship between research and theory; it is not because I think that my experience is more profound or more important than that of other workers in our disciplines that I have chosen this autobiographical form, but because I know it best. I think that I can best observe the often slovenly, often haphazard, and often unconscious elements in the relationship of theory and research by scrutinizing my own experience.

–1–

In 1887, in *Gemeinschaft und Gesellschaft,* Tönnies contrasted modern Western society, or *Gesellschaft,* which he saw as expediential, atomized, rationalistic and individualistic, with a state of very intense solidarity, in which individuality was kept in a rudimentary state and which he called *Gemeinschaft.* He saw instances of *Gemeinschaft* in extended families residing together, guilds, village communities, tribal societies, etc. These were all highly integrated, i.e., they had a high degree of conformity of action with expectations and the expectations covered a wide range of the actions of their members. After leaving Tönnies' hands, the notion of *Gemeinschaft* underwent a considerable extension which made explicit some of the implications of Tönnies' notion. A state of intense solidarity with highly affective overtones, even where the strong emotions did not always find direct expression, became one of the major variables in the analysis of social structure. Simmel, in his stress on the extremely individualistic, tradition-destroying forces of modern urban society, was in the same tradition. Durkheim, who was influenced by Comte's image of a society destroyed by rationalistic negativism and individualism, in seeking to establish a contrast with the disintegrate condition of modern Western society, focussed his attention on the same phenomenon as Tönnies, i.e., mechanical solidarity.

On the other side of the ocean, Charles Cooley, just after the turn of the century, and apparently without any connection with either Tönnies' or Durkheim's writings, fastened his attention on the same phenomenon—a state of intense and comprehensive solidarity in a relatively small group in which there is opportunity for direct interaction and a very pronounced feeling of "we-ness" in which "individualities have been fused." Neighbourhoods, families, the play groups of children were called "primary groups." Like Tönnies, Cooley intended to contrast the disagreeable, selfish, conflictful aspects of modern society with the ethos of the primary group. Like Tönnies, Cooley thought that the larger society could take its ethos from the rules of life of the small intensely bound group; he used the term "primary" because he believed that their "primary" nature lay in the fact that in such groups the higher ideals which could govern conduct in the larger society were formed.

The primary group became one of the major interests of American sociology in the period up to the beginning of the great depression and the accession to power of Adolf Hitler in Germany. W. I. Thomas and Robert Park, Ernest Burgess and other American writers referred to the family, the play group, the boys' gang, the tightly knit village community, the neighbourhood, as primary groups, all of which —with the exception of the boys' gang— they believed were being increasingly eroded by the individualism, the growth of rationality and large-scale organization, and the dissolution of moral consensus of American urban society. The late Professor Louis Wirth's essay on "Urbanism as a Way of Life" stated in extreme form the contrast between the moral solidarity of the primary group, and the anomic individualism, unrestrained by common moral standards, characteristic of modern urban society.

In 1935 Elton Mayo published *The Human Problems of an Industrial Civilization,* and not long after that T. N. Whitehead published *Leadership in a Free Society.* Both of these writers stressed the "impoverishment of social relations" in the modern factory by which they meant the absence of strong personal attachments of the workers and staff with each other. They derived all sorts of distressing consequences such as class conflict, industrial inefficiency and the like. (Neither

wrote with any indication of awareness of Cooley's, Simmel's, or Tönnies' writings on the same subject.)

In the early 1920's Professor Hermann Schmalenbach, in an essay on "Die soziologische Kategorie des Bundes" (in *Die Dioskuren,* vol. I), introduced a new note into the analysis of *Gemeinschaft.* Instead of using it to heighten the description of the individualism and moral dissensus of modern society, he analysed the concept itself and discovered that it covered a diversity of phenomena, which truth required to be separated from each other. He saw that it was possible for a state of intense and comprehensive solidarity to exist without those who shared it possessing either a common territory of origin and residence, a common place of work or ties of blood and sexual connection. When these primordial elements were isolated from the original concept of *Gemeinschaft,* the residue was the *Bund,* for which such terms as confraternity, brotherhood, league, band, gang are all poor translations but each of which brings to the fore the element of intense mutual attachment, independent of primordial ties. Schmalenbach's ideas were not taken up by other German sociologists and they remained utterly unknown in the English-speaking world. Nonetheless, I think that Schmalenbach's essay was the first stage in the turning away from the uncritical contrast, of *Gemeinschaft* and *Gesellschaft,* or primary group and the atomized large-scale society.

Before Schmalenbach, Max Weber had expounded an analysis, mostly by definition and classification, of the kindred phenomenon of the charismatic circle of prophet and apostles, and the corresponding conception of the sect as body membership which is a function of the state of mind of the members. The qualifying state of mind was a possession, by an intense relatively unmediated experience of contact with the sacred. Max Weber had gone further than Schmalenbach inasmuch as he saw that the *Bund*-like religious body, the charismatic sect, was disruptive of the civil order. He had also in his famous distinction between *Gesinnungsethik* and *Verantwortungsethik* which paralleled the distinction between "Sect" and "church," laid the foundations of the distinction between ideological and civil politics. But the foundations were not built upon by Max Weber in his theory of social structure, and they were not perceived by other workers in the same and neighbouring fields. I had read all these writers in the 1930's and failed to draw them into systematic relation with one another. I had been a fairly conscientious student of the Communist and Nazi movements but except for the abduction of the term "charisma" in an effort to describe the Nazi party in 1938 (before this became the fashion) and my awareness that the Nazis were enamoured of *Gemeinschaft*-like ideas, my theoretical "knowledge" lay unused.

In this period, I also read with great interest Lenin's *What is to be Done* and had noted his complaint that the working class, if left to itself, would not become revolutionary but would content itself with small improvements in its immediate situation; he had said that except for the active work of full-time professional revolutionaries, no revolution could take place. I utterly failed to see at this time the conceptual parallel of Lenin's distinction between economistic trade unionism and the professional revolutionary, Max Weber's more general distinction between *Alltag* (routine) and charisma, and his distinction between church and sect. It was some years before I perceived that Lenin and Weber were discussing with a frightful urgency the function of one type of primary group in the social system.

In 1941 I began some inquiries among groups of xenophobic nativists and Nazi sympathizers in Chicago. In my interviews with these zealots, and in my reading of their correspondence and publications, I was impressed by their passion for solidarity, their insistence on absolute loyalty of their members to the organization and their paranoid anxiety about the backsliding propensities of their fellow-members. They tended to refer every event in their personal affairs and in the larger world to the principles which they and their comrades sought to serve. In the incoherent farrago of the leaders of these groups, I discerned a set of themes: first, a dualistic conception of the world in which light fought against darkness, good against evil, Protestants against everyone else, Christians against everyone else, Americans (the same as Christians) against everyone else, everyone else against Jews and foreigners in an unceasing war for the destiny of the world; second, the need for unbreakable solidarity; third, a conviction of the permanently persistent efforts of the enemy to penetrate the organization of the children of light; fourth, closely connected therewith, a fear of the untrustworthiness of their comrades. To some extent they had assimilated the Nazi ideology from their German American associates, and they were also the heirs of the ideology of the *Dearborn Independent* and the Protocols of the Elders of Zion, which was in the air in the Middle West throughout the 1920's and 1930's. I got the impression, however, that if the culture of nativist extremism had not been there, my interviewees would have generated it themselves. Many of them were unsuccessful aspirants to charismatic leadership; they were ideologists by nature, however uneducated they were. They were "natural Manichaeans."

–3–

In the war years, I worked on German civilian and military morale. I had the good fortune for several years from early 1943 to be closely associated with Dr. Henry Dicks, who was at that time beginning to study the personality structure of the Nazi prisoners of war. Their attitudes as they emerged in the course of these investigations began to fall into a pattern which had been formed in my previous studies. The heavy stress on the value of comradeliness made me think back to Schmalenbach, and I began in a vague fumbling way to see the German army as an elaborate administrative and logistic framework for a network of primary groups. This insight did not come to me as a result of any clearly perceived prior hypothesis; it was, in fact, forced on me by the German zeal in the use of the word *Gemeinschaft* in all sorts of connections: e.g., *Frontgemeinschaft, Kampfgemeinschaft,* etc.

The integration of a large society through attachments which fell short of attachments to the central value system of the society now emerged in my mind as a possibility. It was the first time that the idea occurred to me. The ties which bound these primary groups to the larger structure remained obscure to me. I did not see that they were diverse and I did not see the pattern of their diversity.

There was a phenomenon which we called during the war the "hard core," that is, the convinced Nazis—obdurate, steadfast, unyielding as soldiers, stiffening and strengthening influences among their fellow soldiers. There was also the sergeant and the junior officer, more often than not non-Nazi, devoted to his men as a father or older brother would be, concerned to keep them alive while doing his job. At this time, I did not make a clear distinction in my mind between the apolitical officers and sergeants and those with a strong ideological bent, between the paternal, protective person and the "hard core." So I failed to perceive the distinction between the personal and the ideological, which later on seemed to me to be extremely significant. I treated both of them as leaders of the small groups, whose spirit permeated followers and strengthened them, each one separately and each one becoming the center of influence upon his comrades. There were other features of the outlook and conduct

of the German soldiers, the need to demonstrate masculinity, the tenderness taboo, the positive appreciation of discipline as a curb on the *"innere Schweinhund,"* of which I was made very acutely aware. At that time, however, they did not fit readily into my scheme of analysis of the nature of the military primary group and so they lay, noticed but unused. I saw how the soldier's attachment to his comrades and to the group which they formed held in check his own self-regarding impulses to protect the integrity of his own skin regardless of consequences and how this attachment caused him to accept obligations and expectations when otherwise he might be remiss. The discovery that the primary group—by the stiffening and fortification of weaklings and laggards through example, encouragement and protective affection—influenced military effectiveness was enough at that stage to set my mind at rest.

In 1944, I drafted an elaborate interview schedule which was then used by the interrogators of PWD/SHAEF, with modifications until the end of the war. (In this work I had the collaboration of Dr. Dicks and Professor Morris Janowitz, now of the University of Michigan.) When the war was over, I analysed the material which had been gathered by the interrogators. In the course of this analysis, I realized that Elton Mayo, Whitehead and Rothlisberger, in their studies of industrial morale, had been investigating exactly the same thing as I discovered in my studies of the German Army. They too discovered the influence of small, closely knit groups on the conduct of their members in the performance of tasks set them from the outside.

If I may place my own work at the end of a line of development which ran from Tönnies' *Gemeinschaft und Gesellschaft,* I would summarize it as follows: first: Tönnies described a single complex variable: *Gemeinschaft*—containing many heterogeneous elements—and described the ethos and structure of modern society in a way which excluded *Gemeinschaft* in principle; second: Cooley asserted that the ethos of the primary group could be and often were adopted as the ethos of the public life of the larger society; third: Max Weber, followed by Schmalenbach, distinguished the elements of intense and comprehensive attachment in *Gemeinschaft* from the primordial, ecological and biological bases with which they were merged in Tönnies' idea of *Gemeinschaft;* then Max Weber in his analysis of the tension between charismatic authority and the traditional and rational-legal types of authority disclosed another facet of the relationship between ethos of certain types of primary groups and the working of the larger society; and most important, Weber, by his intimation of the seed of charisma at the root of the rational-legal and traditional types of authority, provided the distinction between intense and moderate attachments to the ultimate values; fourth: Mayo perceived the dependence of the functioning of corporate bodies on the morale of primary groups; fifth: my own observations before and during the war singled out *a*) the affinity between political or ideological enthusiasm and a tendency to organize into primary groups; *b*) the dependence of corporate efficiency on primary group morale; *c*) the role of the mediating or linking person in binding the primary group to the corporate body (for this last point, I found support in Alexander Leighton's studies of the administration of the displaced Japanese camps).

Here were the elements from which I tried to develop my views on the role of primary groups in the reproduction and modification of the larger society.

–4–

In the Autumn of 1947, I presented a course of lectures at the London School of Economics, entitled the Primary Groups in the Social Structure, and repeated this course again in the Autumn of 1948. In this course, I dealt mainly with industrial and military primary groups, to some extent with religious primary groups, especially the store front Revivalist religious sect in the industrial centers in the United States, and the political primary groups such as conspiratorial and revolutionary cells. Although I dealt at some length with their internal structure, I did not attend particularly to the nature of the ties holding the members of the groups together. I devoted some time to the description of identification, in the usual psychoanalytic way, and without entering into elaborate detail, attributed the formation of primary groups and their effectiveness in influencing the conduct of their members to the "need for love," which I left without further analysis. I simply accepted it as a datum and attributed all primary groups to this—military, industrial, and religious. I did not attempt to refute Cooley's statement about the transmission of the ethos of primary groups into the public sphere but I was sceptical of it since I saw that things were really far more complicated than Cooley believed. I later concluded that the kind of primary group which endows a society with some of its values was one which Cooley had not really considered—the ideological primary group—and that its transmission could take place only if there were a real diminution of the intensity with which such values were experienced. At that time, however, I had not yet arrived at a clear distinction between ideological and personal primary groups. I knew they were different from each other and I felt a little uneasy about including religious and political sects as primary groups. They seemed to be different yet they also seemed to belong to the category of groups with a very intense solidarity, which demanded far-reaching individual renunciation on behalf of the group. They were characterized by an extreme "we-consciousness." There was much emotion involved in the mutual attachment which made them up. The fact that German Army primary groups contained both political and non-political elements made me think that the difference, although real, was not significant enough to place them into a totally different category, but the difference continued to make me uneasy for some time. I should add that I was also confused by Max Weber's usage of *charisma* in which he treated undifferentiatedly striking personal qualities and possession by the sacred. Attraction by the sacred quality of another individual and by his personality both appeared to be equally charismatic. It was difficult to break through the barrier created by Weber's own failure to distinguish these two possibilities.

In 1949, on the invitation of Professors Lazarsfeld and Merton, I was given the opportunity to reanalyse the material presented in *The American Soldier,* with respect to the role of primary group membership on fighting effectiveness. While I studied the primary group phenomenon in the American Army, I also went back to Georges Sorel, to write an introduction to a new edition of Sorel's *Reflection on Violence.* I now saw what had escaped me in my studies of Sorel two decades before: Sorel, the theorist of the "heroic" orientation in politics, believed that the right setting for the heroic life was the small conventicle of morally integral individuals who were possessed by the superior revolutionary morality. The correlation between an intense relationship to ultimate values, to sacred objects and symbols on the one side, and a closed conventicular life on the other was brought to the fore by my study of Sorel. The similarity of Sorel's notions of revolutionary heroism and Ernst Junger's appreciation of soldierly comradeship in the *Fronterlebnis,* and the difference between their kind of primary group and that of the largely apolitical American soldier who fought out of a general sense of obligation, comradely solidarity and the need to demonstrate manliness carried me beyond Schmalenbach into a greater awareness

that within what he called the *Bund* there were at least two separate types.

–5–

In the Autumn of 1949 and the Winter and early Spring of 1950, Professor Parsons and I wrote the "General Statement" and the "Values, Motives and Systems of Action" in *Towards a General Theory of Action.* Only two parts of this will concern us here, first the paradigm of interaction and the classification of the properties of objects. These highly abstract formulations are relevant here because they were thought by me at the time when we made them to clarify certain features of the primary group, and because further work on the primary group has shown wherein they must be revised and reformulated.

In the interaction paradigm, the two partners are treated as responding to each other's expectations and intentions, as perceived by the responding person. It is always, according to the paradigm, the prospective response, in attitude or action, of the other person which motivates our orientation towards him. No attention is paid in the paradigm to the qualitative properties of the individual apart from his approving or disapproving, loving or unloving response. The introduction of the normative element, derived from the culture, does not alter the fact that there is a gap between the interaction paradigm which, as formulated, takes into account only "personal" relations (dispositional states of mind or qualities) and "collaborative" relations (performances) and the classification of the properties of objects. The paradigm was not sufficiently differentiated. It did not take into account states of mind entailing beliefs, it did not take into account primordial qualities. Had we differentiated the paradigm a little more, while building in the base which we created, we could have closed the gap which existed between it and the classification of objects, at least with respect to primordial qualities. Had we done so, we would then have improved the classification of objects and made it more realistic.

As it was the classification has turned out to be largely correct but that was due more to inner theoretical necessity and the need for logical coherence than to an appreciation at the time of its connection with reality. It was indeed because we did not try it out on reality at once but we were satisfied with theoretical coherence that it was so cumbersome. Furthermore, although I was already troubled by the distinction between the person as an object and the belief-possessed person, the zealot or enthusiast, and had in my own field studies come directly into collision with the difference, it did not enter into the paradigm at all or into the classification in a realistic way. It was only when I read the work of the Swedish theologian, Anders Nygren, *Agape and Eros,* that I discovered the nature of my unclarity about religious and political revolutionary cells as primary groups. It was also in this connection that I saw what had to be done to repair our classification of objects.

This classification of objects was begun with the awareness, not sufficiently incorporated into the paradigm of interaction, that it was not only the other person's responses to us, that is, his approval or disapproval, or his action in conformity with or deviance from our expectations or desires that are significant, but also certain features or characteristics of the person which are not part of his action or of his personal attitude towards us. It had its points of departure into three phenomena: 1) the recognition that in responding to another person, one of the major criteria —and this is taken account of in the interaction-paradigm—is his personality, that is, his temperamental disposition, generally, and relation of that disposition to oneself as a person; 2) the distinction between performance and quality; 3) the distinction between classificatory and relational properties of objects which corresponds to the distinction between univer-

salistic and particularistic orientation (in the pattern variable scheme). It is clear to us from our common sense and general observation, as well as from the analysis of the conception of *Gemeinschaft,* that certain organic and physical properties, certain properties of the organism in relationship to the environment and unconnected with the social structure, had to be taken into account by us, because they were being taken into account in the actions of real, living human beings toward each other. After this came the distinction between "classificatory," e.g., sex, age, and physical properties and "relational" properties, e.g., biological relatedness and territorial location, both of which, it will be remembered, are grouped under the qualities of the organism.

So far so good. It may be noticed that we dealt in a very slip-shod way with beliefs as properties of objects. They were omitted entirely from the paradigm of interaction, and in the object classification, they are acknowledged to be the objects of orientations, but from our treatment of them in the text, it is clear that we did not perceive their significance in interaction and in the formation of social structures. Beliefs we treated as objects of orientation, but not as objects which are qualities of acting human beings. Although elsewhere in our work we repeatedly argued for the incorporation of cultural symbols in action, we only recognized them insofar as they were the objects of individual cognitive, appreciative or moral evaluation in themselves. The understanding of religious or ideological collectivities had been omitted from our analysis. This was another gap in our theoretical scheme which empirical research has helped to close.

–6–

In the late Spring of 1950, I went to Germany with Dr. Henry Dicks, who was then Nuffield Professor of Psychiatry at Leeds, to organize an inquiry, which I had designed, into the social structure of the

Soviet Army in the Second World War. The investigation was conducted through detailed interviews with deserters from the Soviet Army, or from Soviet prisoners of war who had been taken by the Germans and who had remained behind in Western Germany after the end of the war. The Soviet soldier's motivation in combat we found drew relatively little sustenance from any attachment to the central political and ideological symbols of the society in which they lived. Motivation came from three other sources instead: One, the morale of the small unit, i.e., the mutual support given by members of the group to each other and particularly the benevolent relationship of the junior officer and the non-commissioned officer to the men; secondly, the cult of manliness; third, diffuse patriotism, often contradictory to the ideological symbols of the ruling group; and fourth, fear and awe of authority. The resulting picture was very different from *Gemeinschaft* or *Gesellschaft* and insofar as the structure of the Army was a network of *Bund*-like bodies, it was certainly not of ideological *Bünde*. The Soviet Army was a very powerful organization which had a great deal of coherence, yet very little of that coherence seemed to come from attachment to ideological or political symbols, or even intense patriotism.

Here again, empirical analysis has forced a reformulation of theory. In our analysis of systems of value-orientation, we had, although pointing out that they could never be completely integrated, assumed that all parts, however mutually contradictory, were equally objects of orientation of the adult members of the society. The military studies revealed that participation in the central value system was very unequal in intensity and continuity, and that a large social organization could maintain a high degree of effectiveness (integration) with only a modicum of attachment to its value system.

It was possible therefore to correct this assumption without discarding the notion of a central value system. The difference in the degrees of intensity of attachment to a central system of value orientation was already contained in Max Weber's hint that the charismatic sensitivity can slumber within the rational-legal and traditional legitimations of authority. This had been touched on by Professor Parsons as early as *The Structure of Social Action* and I had made something of it in 1948 when I wrote an essay on Max Weber but in our analysis of systems of value orientation we did not distinguish between intense and attenuated attachments to those symbols. I cite this instance only to show to what an extent one's thought is always full of loose ends, and in what way the theoretical loose ends get tied together through research, and often that aspect of the research which is peripheral.

–7–

From the end of 1952, I had the good fortune to be drawn by Michael Young into a loose association with his research on family and kinship in the East End. The family had always been regarded as a primary group by Cooley, Park, Thomas, *et al.* The extended family had been treated as a prototype of the *Gemeinschaft*. Yet it was obviously different from the military, industrial and religious primary groups which I and others had previously studied. In our discussions of his early interviews, I observed what Schmalenbach had observed a long time before, namely, that the ecological or primordial base of the *Gemeinschaft* was different from the relationship itself. But there seemed to be something more important than this distinction. As one thought about the strengths and tensions in family attachments, it became apparent that the attachment was not merely to the other family member as a person, but as a possessor of certain especially "significant relational" qualities, which could only be described as primordial. The attachment to another member of one's kinship group is not just a function of interaction as Professor Homans would have it. It is because a certain ineffable significance is attributed to the tie of blood. Even where affection was not great, the tangibility of the attachment to the other person, by virtue of our perception of his membership in the kinship group, is clearly in evidence. The fact that both those factors operated in many of the more intensely knit families does not demonstrate that the two variables are one, but rather that two types of attachments each move in the same direction. The primordial or ecological basis of *Gemeinschaft* thus seemed to me to be not merely a precondition of the formation of *Gemeinschaft* but a very crucial property of the members which greatly influenced their conduct towards each other. At about this time, I was studying in connection with my work on primary groups Professor A. D. Nock's *Conversion* and Professor Martin P. Nilsson's various books on Greek religion, especially his *Greek Popular Religion*. In these books, the "coerciveness" of the primordial properties of object, the ties of blood and of common territory, was very strikingly portrayed. Nock's distinction between religions of belief and religions of primordial membership—the terms are my own—helped me very much here. Nock, Nilsson and Michael Young's material gave me a clearer idea of the truth of our classification of objects and of where we had been muddled. (I also saw by contrasting the East End families with the religious communities of the last century of the Roman Republic and the first century of the Empire, that the primordial property too could have had sacredness attributed to it. It too could be the object of attachments of different degrees of intensity.) But this would carry us too far afield for present purposes.

–8–

Cooley's proposition asserted a substantial harmony between the orientations in the primary group and the orientations in the Great Society. He asserted indeed that the values pursued and acknowledged in each of these spheres were identical. Mayo's research on small groups in industry and my own research on small groups in military organizations of diverse nationalities have cast considerable doubt on this. Indeed, my own examination of the extent to which the ordinary soldier understood and shared in the purposes of the war and in the symbols of the State on behalf of which the war was being fought, promulgated by the leaders who were directing the war, has shown that acceptance was usually vague, unintense, and although positive, as close to neutrality in concrete situations as it could be without being entirely absent.

I found that persons with an intense preoccupation, continuous and fervent, with the symbols associated with authority in the corporate organization, within which the primary groups were formed, seemed to be very different kinds of people from those who had a looser, more intermittent and less zealous attachment to the symbols. Conversely, those with strong personal attachments, that is attachments to the personal dispositions of their associates, seemed relatively unresponsive to the symbols of the larger society which were incorporated in the authorities of the society and its major organization.

The contemplation of "ideological primary groups" disclosed the phenomenon of "over-participation" in the system of ultimate values. The alternatives of "under-participation," moderate and attenuated participation, and "over-participation," were crystallized in my mind by an effort which I made in 1953 to describe, according to the theory of action, the structure of an alienated revolutionary party on the basis of autobiographies and personal records of former members, in an attempt to understand the nature of the tie and the resulting structure of persons who regard others in the light of their symbolic rather than personal significance. The central figures in these groups were just the opposite of the "under-participators." They were involved in the central value system with great intensity.

Shortly thereafter, in 1954, Mr. Berelson asked me to read and criticize the manuscript of the book which he and Professor Lazarsfeld were writing on the Presidential campaign of 1948 in Elmira, New York. The material gathered in this inquiry showed that the proportion of those with intense and continuous responses to symbols referring to the central value system were in a very small minority. The proportion of those with no response at all was likewise rather small and in between the large majority of the population maintained a very moderate interest which increased with the campaign. There seemed to be normal distribution of attachment to the central symbols of the society. This distribution, which is now displayed by the authors of *Voting* in their last chapter, is the prototype of the relationships which are maintained towards all the elements of the system of values prevailing in any society. Some are very much concerned with them, positively or negatively, some are not at all concerned with them—these are the "idiots" of whom Aristotle spoke—and most are in varying degrees of attenuation and dilution, intermittently concerned with them, acting in many situations from a mixture of considerations of personal attachment and a vague sense of duty in a role, and of a generalized, vague, occasional and sometimes only limiting sense of concern for the whole.

The civil attachment, the moderate pluralistic concern for the whole, among other things, is not the spirit of the primary group. Cooley's great hypothesis seems to fall to the ground when the ethos and tone necessary for the maintenance of civil society is seen to be inimical to the fervour and passion of the primary group. The ways in which the three different types of primary groups do, nonetheless, contribute to the integration of society, must however continue to be one of the major subjects of sociological inquiry.

–9–

I have dared to tell this rambling tale of my intellectual wanderings because I have thought that it might help sociologists to obtain a more just conception of the collaboration of research and theory. I think that the prevailing conceptions of this collaboration are usually erroneous. The earlier view of a steady progress from particular facts to general theories has now been replaced by the more sophisticated image of a hypothesis, derived from a general theory, being tested by a systematic scrutiny of particular facts: then the theory is either disconfirmed by the facts and is replaced by one more adequate to them or the hypothesis and corresponding theory are confirmed and the problem is settled. There are variations and complications of this latter schema but in all essentials this account of it is correct. It sees the relationship as an orderly process of truth. But in reality, nothing could be less truthful than this picture of scientific growth.

The growth of knowledge is a disorderly movement. It is full of instances of things known and overlooked, unexpected emergencies, and rediscoveries of long known facts and hypotheses which in the time of their original discovery had no fitting articulation and which found such articulation only after a considerable time. It was for the purpose of giving a relatively realistic picture of this disorderly process on a very narrow front that I have offered this record of my own experience.

It is an interesting question as to why sociologists hold this incorrect view of the relations between theory and research. Part of the difficulty arises from an erroneous conception of the nature of the growth of truth in physics, chemistry and the other well established and esteemed sciences. Part of the error arises, however, from the position of the sociologists in the scientific community.

Sociologists are at present, despite their increased numbers and prosperity, a depressed class. They feel themselves outside the pale of the more reputable sciences and they wish very much to be within it. They look for their elevation to "a theory" which will compel their general recognition. At the same time the theories which command attention in sociology are very abstract, very difficult to understand and even more difficult to use in the understanding of the world as we know it from our experience. They are especially difficult and probably impossible to use at present in the way in which sociologists think a scientific theory ought to be used.

These impediments do not in my opinion make them valueless in advancing our understanding. Far from it. In order, however, for these theories to improve our understanding they must be deprived of their salvationary and even of their awe-inspiring character. Sociologists must cease to look upon them as finished products, waiting to be applied, *in toto,* in an orderly and systematic way. They must be taken as general guides and not as specific directives. They must be brought into op-

eration only on the basis of a feeling of personal intimacy. They must be used only after an osmotic assimilation which involves discriminating acceptance and rejection, which rests on the sense of fitness and appropriateness rather than on any formal test. Although this counsel is full of pitfalls, I would say that sociologists will learn to use theory when they have also learned to trust their unconscious discriminatory powers. These might often be wrong, but without them there is little hope.

Theory will bear fruit in sociology only when it has been assimilated into the perception of concrete and particular events, and not as long as it is thought to be something which comes before and emerges from research. Sociological theory must be the explicit articulation of our thought about concrete events, and the explication of the presuppositions and implications of the thought so articulated. To put it differently it must be the comparison and not the court of judgment of our concrete observation. Only under those conditions will it enrich our research into particular situations and only then will it be enriched by that research.

17. VOLUNTARY ASSOCIATION MEMBERSHIPS OF AMERICAN ADULTS

CHARLES R. WRIGHT *and* HERBERT H. HYMAN

*It was Alexis de Tocqueville who described the United States as "a nation of joiners."
Ever since his book,* Democracy in America, *was published in 1835 this phrase has
become a part of the stereotyped view of social life in this country. In recent years,
sociologists have attempted to investigate the veracity of this assertion and their studies
suggest that membership in voluntary associations is neither universal nor uniform.*

*On the basis of their nationwide studies of the American people in general and of
certain specific racial and ethnic subgroups within the population, Charles Wright and
Herbert Hyman indicate that voluntary participation in such organizations as fraternal
and secret societies, unions, neighborhood, ethnic, special interest groups, veterans'
organizations, civic clubs, church fellowships, youth clubs, and professional and learned
societies varies considerably with such social correlates as socioeconomic status, occupation, urban or rural residence, and ethnicity.*

*Charles R. Wright is Associate Professor of Sociology at the University of California
at Los Angeles. He is the author of* Mass Communication *(1959). Herbert H. Hyman
is Professor of Sociology at Wesleyan University. His publications include* The Psychology of Status *(1942),* Interviewing in Social Research *(1954),* Survey Design and
Analysis: Principles, Cases, and Procedures *(1955),* Political Socialization *(1959), and*
Applications of Methods of Evaluation: Four Studies of the Encampment for Citizenship *(1962). He is coeditor with Eleanor Singer of* Readings in Reference Group Theory
and Research *(1968).*

Introduction

Several recent studies have demonstrated
the need for a thorough reappraisal of the
commonly held belief that Americans
are a nation of joiners. For example,
Komarovsky[1] and Axelrod[2] have provided evidence for urban dwellers, to
whom such behavior has been especially
attributed, that membership in a large
number of associations is not characteristic of many Americans and is far from
universally distributed throughout the various segments of the population.

Unfortunately, most investigators of the
problem have had to work within serious

limitations imposed by the nature of their
data. In some instances, the sampling procedures available to the investigator could
not provide adequate data.[3] In other instances, while the researcher was fortunate enough to have access to representative samples, the findings relate to such
circumscribed and limited universes as
small local communities, a single metropolis, or one social class within a particular
city.[4] What has been missing in the literature is evidence of the voluntary association memberships of Americans in general
and of important subgroups within the
nation, derived from adequate sampling of
the general population. The present paper

Reprinted from the *American Sociological Review,* **23** (1958), 284–294, by permission of the
authors and the American Sociological Association.

provides data that partially meet this need.

More specifically, the paper presents evidence bearing on the following problems: 1) the pattern of membership in voluntary associations of adult Americans in general, and of specific subgroups, such as racial and religious minorities; 2) some correlates of membership which might be considered determinants, for example, socio-economic status, urban or rural residence; and 3) some of the correlates of membership which might be considered consequences of significance to theories about such functions of voluntary association membership for society as interest in politics, voting, and charitable activity.

Method and Data

Solutions of these problems are provided by secondary analysis of recent survey data, where the universes studied often approximate the national adult population and where the samples have been drawn through probability designs. Through good fortune, a number of nationwide and local surveys conducted by the National Opinion Research Center [5] have contained one or more questions on voluntary association memberships. These items provide substantial information on the actual magnitude and pattern of voluntary association membership of the American people and of subgroups within the general population. Secondary analysis of these surveys can also provide evidence about numerous sociological determinants of membership, which have figured in past speculative discussions but have seldom been supported by much empirical data, for example, the effect of urbanization upon membership. In addition, the surveys often contain data on possible determinants of membership which have rarely been treated, either speculatively or empirically, in past writings. Thus data are available on various situational factors which might facilitate or impede membership and participation,

such as parenthood, residential mobility, travel time to work, and the like. For many of these latter analyses, it is necessary to consult sample surveys which were conducted on local rather than national populations, but here too all the inquiries have the merit of being based on large samples drawn by a probability design. Therefore, though limited to the cities or counties involved, they still constitute reliable evidence concerning hypotheses based on representative sampling. Finally, by secondary analysis tabulation of voluntary association membership is possible, not only by hypothesized determinants, but also by the customary questions asked in such surveys about attitudes, opinions, interests, conduct, and so on. In this manner, some empirical perspective can be obtained on the fundamental question of the functions of organizational membership for citizens in a democratic society.

Admittedly there are serious limitations to such secondary analysis. Foremost among these is the reliance put upon questions not primarily designed for the study of voluntary association memberships. Since data on such memberships were only incidental to the primary purposes of the surveys, the questioning in this area is not as thorough as would be desired. Furthermore, the wording of questions about membership varies from study to study, hence complicating the analysis. Nevertheless, we believe that these inherent limitations of secondary analysis are more than offset by the gains which have been outlined above.

The bulk of the analysis to be presented is based on two national probability samples of the adult, non-institutionalized population of the United States, over 21 years of age. The first sample contains 2,809 men and women, and the second 2,379. The studies were conducted in the years 1953 and 1955. In addition to the national data, findings on voluntary association membership were available for representative samples from NORC studies of the following localities: a large metropolitan area (New York metropolitan area represented by a probability sample of 1,053 cases drawn in 1951); a medium sized Western metropolis (Denver represented by a probability sample of 920 cases obtained in the spring of 1949); a small city and surrounding county (Findley and Hancock County, Ohio, represented by 535 cases drawn in May, 1952). The local findings on magnitude of membership and its social distribution are not presented in detail, although, where confirmation or contradiction occurs, some brief reference will be made. They will be used to examine hypotheses about particular variables, however, which are not demonstrable on a national scale.

Findings

Memberships of Americans

Data from the national surveys confirm the conclusions drawn by previous researchers based on local studies, which showed that a sizable group of Americans are not members of any voluntary associations and that only a minority belong to more than one such organization. Table 1 presents data from two surveys, one of which inquired about the voluntary association membership of *any* member of the family, the other survey pertained to activities of the respondent himself. Calculated either way, voluntary association membership is not a major characteristic of Americans. Nearly half of the families (47 per cent) and almost two-thirds of the respondents (64 per cent) belong to no voluntary associations. About a third of the families (31 per cent) and a fifth of the respondents belong to only one such organization. Only about a fifth of the families (21 per cent) and a sixth of the respondents (16 per cent) belong to two or more organizations. These findings hardly warrant the impression that Americans are a nation of joiners.[6]

Table 1. *Membership in Voluntary Associations for Two National Cross-Sections of American Adults, 1953 and 1955*

Number of Voluntary Associations	*Percentage of Families Whose Members Belong to Organizations as Indicated (1953)* *	*Percentage of Adults Who Were Themselves Members of the Organizations, as Indicated (1955)* †
None	47	64
One	31	20
Two	12	9
Three	5	4
Four or more	1	3
Unknown	4	0
	100%	100%
Total	(2,809)	(2,379)

* *"Does anyone in the family belong to any sort of club, lodge, fraternal order, or union with ten or more members in it?"* If yes, *"What organization? Any other?"* SOURCE: *NORC Survey 335.*

† *Union membership is not included in these data because the interviewing on organizational membership during this part of the survey concerned associations other than unions. The question was, "Do you happen to belong to any groups or organizations in the community here?"* If yes, *"Which ones? Any other?"* SOURCE: *NORC Survey 367.*

Data on the types of organizations to which Americans belong are also revealing. In the 1953 survey, which contained an account of organizations to which any family member belonged, only two (unions and fraternal or secret societies) have relatively large memberships, 23 per cent and 19 per cent respectively. Next in order are neighborhood-ethnic-special interest groups (8 per cent), veterans' organizations (7 per cent), civic organizations (5 per cent), church sponsored organizations (3 per cent), youth organizations (2 per cent), and professional and learned societies (2 per cent). These findings provide national perspective on the data recorded by former studies of local populations, such as the Detroit Area Study, in which unions and fraternal organizations also accounted for more of the citizens' voluntary memberships than any other type of association.[7]

Racial and religious subgroups

Table 2 presents figures on the membership patterns for two types of subgroups within American society: racial and religious. Comparison of Negro and white respondents shows that voluntary association membership is somewhat more characteristic of whites than Negroes. Less than half (46 per cent) of the white families and 63 per cent of the white respond-

Table 2. *Voluntary Association Memberships of Racial and Religious Subgroups Based on National Samples*

(A) Family Data (1953)	Per Cent of Families Whose Members Belong to:			
	No Organization	*One*	*Two or More*	*N (100%)*
Race *				
Negro	60	29	11	279
White	46	31	23	2,472
Religion †				
Jewish	31	37	32	99
Catholic	44	34	22	579
Protestant	49	30	21	1,992

SOURCE: *NORC Survey 335.*

(B) Respondent Data (1955)	Per Cent of Respondents Who Belong to:			
	No Organization	*One*	*Two or More*	*N (100%)*
Race ‡				
Negro	73	18	9	229
White	63	20	17	2,139
Religion §				
Jewish	45	25	30	71
Protestant	63	20	17	1,701
Catholic	69	17	14	519

* *Figures exclude 58 cases of other races or of unknown race.*
† *Figures exclude 139 cases who report some other religion or none at all.*
‡ *Figures exclude 11 cases of other races.*
§ *Figures exclude 88 cases who report some other religion or none at all.*
SOURCE: *NORC Survey 367.*

ents belong to no associations in contrast to 60 per cent of the Negro families and 73 per cent of the Negro adults. And nearly a quarter (23 per cent) of the white families belong to two or more organizations in contrast to only 11 per cent of the Negro families.

Differences in rates of membership also distinguish the major religious subgroups of the population. Whether measured on a family or individual basis, the highest rate of membership is found among the Jews. On a family basis, the next highest participants in voluntary associations are the Catholics (56 per cent), and the least active are the Protestants (51 per cent). Data on individual memberships, however, are different, with a higher percentage of Protestants than Catholics belonging to any organizations.

Interesting comparisons with national data on memberships of religious subgroups are available from the local studies of New York City and Denver. In both cities the ordering of memberships agrees with the national sample on individual memberships: the rate of membership is highest for Jews, next for Protestants and lowest for Catholics. In New York, 64 per cent of the Jewish respondents reported membership in at least one voluntary association, 54 per cent of the Protestants and 37 per cent of the Catholics. In Denver, the membership rates were 77 per cent for Jews, 65 per cent for Protestants and 55 per cent for Catholics. Thus the Catholic membership rates in these urban settings appear lower than those of the Jews and Protestants, as in the 1955 national survey.[8]

Social stratification and membership

On the local level, several studies have demonstrated a relationship between the social status of the respondent, as measured by a variety of indices, and membership in voluntary associations.[9] These studies generally agree that there is an increase in the percentage of memberships in formal associations the higher the status of the respondents. The magnitude of the difference in membership between classes varies considerably, however, from study to study. For example, Komarovsky found that 60 per cent of working class men in her sample of New Yorkers belonged to no voluntary association in contrast to only 53 per cent of white collar workers. Similarly Dotson's study of families in New Haven reported that 70 per cent of the working class adults in his sample belonged to no organizations. On the other hand, Bell and Force in a recent study of San Francisco report that even in low status neighborhoods about three-quarters of the men belong to at least one formal group.

Data from the national samples support the correlation between social status and membership. Table 3 presents data on the membership of the 1955 sample classified by five indices of social status: family income, education of respondent, interviewer's rating of family's level of living, occupation of head of household, and home ownership. Whichever index of status is used, an appreciably higher percentage of persons in higher status positions belong to voluntary associations than do persons of lower status. For example, fully 76 per cent of the respondents whose family income falls below 2,000 dollars do not belong to any organizations in contrast to only 48 per cent of those whose income is 7,500 dollars or more. Furthermore, there is an increase in the percentage of persons who belong to *several* organizations as social status increases. For example, only 7 per cent of the lowest income group belong to two or more associations in contrast to 30 per cent of the highest income group. Similar findings are obtained from inspection of the data on education, level of living, occupation, and home ownership, as examination of Table 3 reveals.[10]

One set of findings warrant special mention. The pattern of voluntary association membership among different occu-

Table 3. *Indices of Stratification and Voluntary Association Membership, 1955 ***

| | Per Cent Who Belong to: | | | |
	No Organization	One Organization	Two or More	No. of Cases (100%)
A. Income level				
Under $2,000	76	17	7	385
2,000–2,999	71	17	12	304
3,000–3,999	71	18	11	379
4,000–4,999	65	21	14	450
5,000–7,499	57	22	21	524
7,500 and over	48	22	30	328
B. Education				
0–6 years	83	12	5	348
7–8 years	73	17	10	522
9–11 years	67	20	13	495
12 years	57	23	20	610
1–3 years of college	46	24	30	232
4 years college or more	39	25	36	170
C. Level of living (Interviewer's rating)				
Very low	92	7	1	125
Below average	81	14	5	580
Average	61	22	17	1,318
Above average	43	25	32	288
Very high	18	18	64	44
D. Occupation				
Professional	47	24	29	259
Prop., mgrs., officials	47	24	29	294
Farm owners	58	28	14	265
Clerical and sales	59	21	20	240
Skilled labor	68	19	13	447
Semi-skilled labor	77	14	9	492
Service	73	18	9	142
Non-farm labor	79	16	5	155
Farm labor	87	13	0	54
Retired, unemployed	77	11	12	35
E. Home ownership				
Owns home	57	22	21	1,407
Rents	75	16	9	968

* *Data exclude union membership.*
SOURCE: *NORC Survey 367.*

pational levels indicates even less participation among blue collar workers than had been noted in previous local studies. For example, from 68 to 87 per cent of the blue collar workers belong to no organizations (not counting union membership), in contrast to 59 per cent of the white collar workers and 47 per cent of the businessmen and professionals. The higher rate of voluntary association membership among businessmen and professionals is clearly documented by the national data, which show that 29 per cent of the members of these two occupational categories belong to two or more organizations, in contrast with only 5 to 13 per cent of the blue collar workers. These data extend to the national level a relationship noted by Komarovsky in her New York study, namely that it is only in the business and professional classes that the majority is formally organized.

Urbanization and voluntary association membership

Voluntary associations customarily have been identified as characteristic of the urban way of life, and membership in such associations has been assumed to be more common for city residents than rural people. Recent observers, however, have noted that the spread of urbanization in America is reducing such differences between city and country. Williams,[11] for example, has noted that "Formally organized special-interest associations are most highly developed in urban areas, but have increasingly pervaded the open country as well." Nevertheless, we have lacked specific information on the differential rates of voluntary association membership of residents of various sized communities. A breakdown of national survey data provides considerable information on this question.

From the 1953 national survey it is possible to determine the number of associational affiliations of family members living in counties of varying degrees of urbanization, taking the size of the largest city in the county as a crude index of its degree of urbanism. Three types of counties can be examined: 1) highly urbanized counties, those with at least one city of 50,000 population or more; 2) moderately urbanized, with at least one city of 10,000 to 50,000 population; and 3) least urbanized, having no city of 10,000 or more.

Examination of the memberships of residents of these three types of counties reveals that only 57 per cent of the families who live in highly urbanized counties have members in at least one voluntary association, 53 per cent of those in moderately urbanized counties, and 41 per cent of those living in the least urbanized or predominantly rural counties. Thus some correlation appears between the degree of urbanization and voluntary association membership, although the difference between the most urban and least urban counties is not great.

But the type of county is only a crude index of the social atmosphere within which the citizen lives. Within each county, for example, there are areas of more *and* less urban nature. Therefore a finer breakdown is desirable in order to determine more precisely the relationship between urbanism and membership in voluntary associations. Table 4 presents data on membership according to urban, rural non-farm, and rural farm residences within each type of county.

Several interesting findings emerge. First, it appears that, with one exception (rural farm residents in moderately urbanized counties) the relationship between urbanization of county and membership in voluntary associations persists. That is, more of the residents of highly urbanized counties belong to organizations than do persons living in similar types of neighborhoods but in less urbanized counties. For example, only 42 per cent of the urbanites in highly urbanized counties belong to no organization, in contrast with 46 per cent of the urbanites in moderately urbanized counties, and 54 per cent in the least urbanized.

Secondly, within each type of county, rural farm residence is more closely associated with non-membership than is either rural non-farm or urban residence. For example, within highly urbanized counties 67 per cent of the rural farm residents belong to no voluntary association, in con-

Table 4.   *Urbanism and Voluntary Association Membership, 1953*

Per Cent of Families Whose Members Belong to:	Metropolitan Counties (with City of 50,000 or More)			Other Urbanized Counties (with City of 10–50,000)			Primarily Rural Counties (Have No Town of 10,000)		
	Urban Resi- dence	*Rural Non- farm*	*Rural Farm*	*Urban*	*RNF*	*RF*	*Urban*	*RNF*	*RF*
No organization	42	40	67	46	46	53	54	52	70
One organization	33	37	21	36	34	28	27	24	21
Two or more organizations	25	23	12	18	20	19	19	24	9
Total	100%	100%	100%	100%	100%	100%	100%	100%	100%
Cases	1,394	193	48	294	115	134	110	264	252

SOURCE: *NORC Survey 335.*

trast to only 40 per cent of the rural non-farm residents and 42 per cent of the urbanites.[12]

Third, there is *no* appreciable difference between the membership rates of urbanites and rural non-farm residents within any type of county. This finding, in connection with the second, suggests an interesting hypothesis about the spread of urbanism into American suburban and rural areas. If the countryside were becoming urbanized then one might expect that rural-urban differences would be minimal in counties which contained large cities and maximal in counties still rural. Such is not the case, at least with respect to voluntary association membership. True, the urban pattern of membership prevails in rural non-farm areas but it does not extend to rural farms. Furthermore, an anomaly (requiring further substantiation) appears in that rural farm persons living in *moderately* urbanized counties resemble their urban and rural non-farm neighbors more than do rural-ites in either highly urbanized or heavily rural counties. Perhaps this finding means that rural-urban differences in general are polarized—being greatest in both highly urban and highly rural counties and least in partially urbanized areas.

Some situational determinants of membership

In this section some data from the Denver survey are examined to clarify certain situational factors which might be presumed to affect urban participation in voluntary associations. Specifically, data are presented on the effect of length of residence in the community, length of residence at the same address, type of residence (for example, single family dwelling versus apartment), travel time to work, and family status (for example, single, married with children or without children). The presumed influence of such factors is illustrated by the hypothesis that long-time residents in the community or in the neighborhood are more likely to be involved in formal organizations. Or, persons living in apartments might be expected to participate less in voluntary associations than those living in single family dwellings. Persons who spend less time commuting to work, it may be argued, should have more time to devote to organizations and therefore should show a higher incidence of membership. Similarly, single men and women, who are unencumbered by children, might have more spare time and hence be more apt to

Table 5. *Some Situational Determinants of Voluntary Association Membership: Evidence from Denver Survey*

	Percentage of Each Type Who Belong to Voluntary Associations	No. of Cases in Base
A. Residential history		
Born in Denver or lived there		
at least 20 years	65	504
Lived in Denver less than 20 years	62	404
Lived in Denver at present address		
over 20 years	63	200
Lived at present address for		
5 to 20 years	67	346
Lived at present address less than 5 years	60	358
B. Residential mobility		
Moved to Denver from place of under		
2,500 population	61	272
Moved from place of 2,500 to		
25,000 population	60	205
Moved from place larger than 25,000	64	281
C. Type of residence		
Single family house, rented	57	81
Multiple family dwelling, rented	59	165
Apartment building, rented	60	117
Owned, all types of dwelling	67	512
D. Travel time to work		
45 minutes or more daily	60	81
35–44 minutes	70	185
30–34 minutes	64	256
25–29 minutes	66	192
Less than 25 minutes	57	205
E. Family status		
Men: Not married	66	79
Married, no children under 18 yrs. old	74	182
Married, with children under 18 yrs. old	82	162
Women: Not married	51	149
Married, no children under 18 yrs. old	53	174
Married, with children under 18 yrs. old	56	174

SOURCE: *Denver Community Survey, NORC-12B.*

belong to voluntary groups. Table 5 presents data which fail to support several of these arguments.

None of the residential factors shows a systematic relationship with the incidence of affiliation with voluntary associations. For example, persons born in Denver are hardly more likely to belong to voluntary associations than those who have arrived recently.[13] Apartment dwellers are slightly more likely to be voluntary association members than persons renting houses. Commuters who spent more than 45 minutes getting to work are about as likely to belong to organizations as are those people who have to travel only 25 minutes or less.

Only two of these situational factors—home ownership and family status—seem related to voluntary association membership. Home ownership as a determinant of membership, as brought out above, is related to social stratification. The data on family status show that married persons are more likely to be members of organizations than single persons; and that men and women with children are more likely to be members than childless couples. One might hypothesize that children—and perhaps the expectation of children—draw adults into participation in the voluntary associations in the urban community. This finding corroborates that of Janowitz in his study of Chicago residents in which he notes that neighborhood involvement often centers around activities connected with the rearing of children in a metropolis. As Janowitz remarks, on the neighborhood level, "children are not only the best neighbors in the community but they lead their parents to neighborhood community participation and orientation." [14]

Civic involvement of voluntary association membership

In this final section, data from the Denver Survey are presented which demonstrate psychological and behavioral differences between citizens who are members and those who are not members of formal organizations. Admittedly the data do not indicate that such differences can be attributed solely to the respondents' patterns of associational membership. Clearly several factors already established as correlates of membership (for example, high socio-economic status, occupation, place of residence) may also account for differences in political interest, voting and charitable acts of members and non-members. The authors feel, however, that comparison of members and non-members without controlling these associated factors is

proper insofar as the purpose is solely to *describe* the differences between persons who are or are not members of voluntary associations, regardless of the ultimate causes of such differences.[15] Hence Table 6 presents simple comparisons between the formally organized and unorganized, concerning their interest in political topics, voting records, and contributions to charity.

Several measures of interest in public affairs (including Presidential elections, unemployment, labor relations, minority problems, public schools, and city planning) indicate that persons belonging to voluntary associations are more concerned with such topics than are non-members. For example, fully 84 per cent of the Denverites who belonged to any voluntary association said they took a great deal of interest in Presidential elections, in contrast with only 73 per cent of the non-members. And members were more likely than non-members to be interested in city planning, 50 per cent to 31 per cent respectively.

Political interest is backed by participation in the political process, insofar as participation is measured by voting. Data on behavior in four elections—the 1944 Presidential, 1946 Congressional, 1947 City Charter, and 1948 Primary—indicate in every instance a greater percentage of voting among Denverites who were members of voluntary associations than among non-members.

Finally, in the non-political sphere of community life, charity, 72 per cent of the persons belonging to associations reported having made a contribution to the Community Chest in Denver, in contrast to 56 per cent of the non-members.

Thus three separate measures—interest in social issues, voting, and support of community charities—show that voluntary association participants are more involved civically than the non-members. Further research might fruitfully be addressed to such questions as the following: 1) to what extent does the citizen's inter-

Table 6.   *Political Interests and Behavior Associated with Voluntary Association Membership: Evidence from Denver Survey, 1949*

	Persons Who Were Members of:	
	No Organizations	*One or More Organizations*
A. Per cent who said they take "a great deal" of interest in:		
Presidential elections	73	84
Unemployment in the U.S.	53	57
The Denver public schools	33	50
City planning in Denver	31	50
Labor relations	31	45
The situation of Denver Negroes	23	35
B. Per cent who voted in each of the following elections:		
1944 Presidential	36	40
1946 Congressional	27	36
1947 City charter	15	24
1948 Primary	24	34
C. Per cent who report making a contribution to the Community Chest in Denver	56	72
Total cases	335	585

SOURCE: *Denver Community Survey, NORC-12B.*

est in public affairs lead him to join voluntary associations; 2) to what extent do the voluntary associations contribute to their members' interest in public affairs; 3) to what extent is membership in one or more voluntary associations functional for the citizen who has a great deal of interest in public affairs. Questions of this order, however, fall beyond the scope of this secondary analysis.[16]

Summary

A secondary analysis of two national and several local surveys provides evidence on the topics: the pattern of membership in voluntary associations of Americans in general and of such specific subgroups as class and religion; some possible determinants of membership, for example, socioeconomic status; and certain correlates of membership which relate to civic partici-

pation, for example, interest in public issues and voting.

The major findings are listed below in abbreviated form. In each case, the major source of data, that is, national or local survey, is indicated in parentheses. Subject to the qualifications noted above, the major findings are:

1. Voluntary association membership is not characteristic of the majority of Americans (National).
2. A relatively small percentage of Americans belong to two or more voluntary associations (National).
3. Membership is more characteristic of the white than Negro population (National).
4. Membership is more characteristic of Jewish than Protestant persons, and of Protestant than Catholics (National).
5. Membership is directly related to

socio-economic status, as measured by level of income, occupation, home ownership, interviewer's rating of level of living, and education (National).

6. Membership is more characteristic of urban and rural non-farm residents than of rural farm residents (National).

7. Membership does not appear to be related to a variety of situational factors, for example, length of residence in the community, length of residence at the same address, type of dwelling unit, commuting time to work (Denver).

8. Membership is related to family status, being higher for couples with children than without (Denver).

9. Membership is accompanied by a greater interest in such public affairs as unemployment problems, city planning, and public schools (Denver).

10. Membership is associated with voting in Presidential, Congressional and local elections (Denver).

11. Membership is associated with support for local charities (Denver).

NOTES

1. Mirra Komarovsky, "The Voluntary Associations of Urban Dwellers," *American Sociological Review,* 11 (1946), 686–698.

2. Morris Axelrod, "Urban Structure and Social Participation," *American Sociological Review,* 21 (1956), 13–18.

3. For example, Komarovsky's study, *op. cit.,* was based on responses of persons contacted at places of employment or other organizational meetings, hence not purporting to be a representative sample of New York adults.

4. For example, see the following studies: Scott Greer, "Urbanism Reconsidered: A Comparative Study of Local Areas in a Metropolis," *American Sociological Review,* 21 (1956), 19–25; Wendell Bell and Maryanne T. Force, "Urban Neighborhood Types and Participation in Formal Associations," *American Sociological Review,* 21 (1956), 25–34; Herbert Goldhamer, "Some Factors Affecting Participation in Voluntary Associations," unpublished Ph.D. dissertation (microfilmed), University of Chicago, 1942; Morris Axelrod, *op. cit.;* Floyd Dotson, "Patterns of Voluntary Association Among Urban Working-Class Families," *American Sociological Review,* 16 (1951), 687–693; Mirra Komarovsky, *op. cit.* Thus Greer's study used two census tracts within Los Angeles; Bell and Force employed four tracts within San Francisco; Goldhamer's study is confined to Chicago, Axelrod's to Detroit, Dotson's to New Haven, and Komarovsky's to New York City.

5. The authors wish to acknowledge their indebtedness to N.O.R.C. and to its director, Clyde Hart, who made the data available for secondary analysis, and to Jack Feldman, who provided many special tabulations.

6. To some extent, the open-ended form of the questions in the national studies might have reduced the proportion of memberships reported insofar as respondent recall might be faulty. There is some indication, however, that the impact of question format was not great in this instance. In the Denver study a card listing several types of organizations was handed to the respondent before he reported memberships. Under these conditions, 36 per cent of the Denverites reported that they belonged to no organizations, including unions. In the 1953 national survey, which used an open-ended question, 39 per cent of the urbanites living in large cities (1,000,000 or more) and 42 per cent of those living in any sizeable city (50,000 or more) reported no organizational memberships, including unions, for anyone in their family.

Obviously, primary research on voluntary association membership would require more and different questioning in this area, including check lists of organizations, investigation of the meaning of "belonging" to the respondent, etc. The data used in the current secondary analysis, however, were obtained from studies in which information on membership was only incidental to the primary purposes of the surveys, for which the open-ended questions sufficed. Confidence in the interpretation of the findings as indicative of low membership among Americans is increased through the use of data from *several* national and local surveys, which support one another, in general, despite variations in the wording of questions.

Of course, this is not to dispute the fact that, from a *comparative* point of view, Americans may be more prone to such membership than other national groups. Such a mode of analysis is illustrated, for example, by Arnold Rose, *Theory and Method in the Social Sciences,* Minneapolis: The University of Minnesota Press, 1954, pp. 72–115.

7. Axelrod, *op. cit.* Also see *A Social Profile of Detroit: 1952,* a report of the Detroit Area Study, Ann Arbor: The University of Michigan Press, 1952, pp. 13–19.

8. These findings are consistent with those reported by Bell and Force, *op. cit.,* from their study in San Francisco during 1953. They not only found that Protestants were more likely than Catholics to belong to formal associations but also that the relationship persisted even when economic level was controlled.

9. See, for example, Komarovsky, *op. cit.,* Dotson, *op. cit.,* and Bell and Force, *op. cit.*

10. Data from the 1953 sample on family participation in voluntary associations generally corroborated the findings presented above and hence are not reproduced here. In addition, several of the local studies contain data in support of the relationships described. For example, home ownership data were available in Denver and provided an opportunity to examine the influence of this factor within an urban setting. Here, as on the national level, home owners were more likely to be members than were renters, 67 per cent versus 59 per cent respectively. And in New York, families employing domestic help were more likely to be members than those without help, 73 per cent versus 45 per cent.

11. Robin Williams, *American Society: A Sociological Interpretation,* New York: Knopf, 1951, pp. 467–468.

12. The higher incidence of organizational membership among urban residents in contrast with their rural neighbors also was evident in the Hancock County, Ohio survey. In this survey a distinction was made between the residents of a small town (Findley, pop. approximately 24,000) and persons in the surrounding county. Fifty-six per cent of the Findley townspeople belonged to some voluntary association, in contrast to 49 per cent of the ruralites. For a recent summary of some surveys on rural memberships see Raymond Payne, "Some Comparisons of Participation in Rural Mississippi, Kentucky, Ohio, Illinois, and New York," *Rural Sociology,* 18 (1953), 171–172.

13. These data are consistent with those obtained in Hancock County, Ohio where 51 per cent of the persons who had resided in the county for 20 years or more were members of voluntary associations, 57 per cent of the 10–19 year residents were members, 58 per cent of the 5–8 year residents, and 57 per cent of the persons living there less than 5 years. The survey was conducted in May 1952. On the other hand, Zimmer, in a study of married men in a mid-western community of 20,000, found that membership in formal organizations increased directly with length of time in the community. Zimmer's relationship persisted within age, occupational and educational control categories. See Basil Zimmer, "Participation of Migrants in Urban Structures," *American Sociological Review,* 20 (1955), 218–224. And a recent study in Spokane, Washington indicates a relationship between mobility and voluntary association membership; see Howard Freeman, Edwin Novak and Leo Reeder, "Correlates of Membership in Voluntary Associations," *American Sociological Review,* 22 (1957), 528–533.

14. Morris Janowitz, *The Community Press in an Urban Setting,* Glencoe, Ill.: The Free Press, 1952, p. 124. Janowitz's remark is made in connection with family structure as a determinant of readership of the community press, but its import extends to other forms of involvement in community activities.

15. For a discussion of the differential demands of descriptive vs. explanatory analysis see Herbert Hyman, Survey Design and Analysis: Principles, Cases and Procedures, Glencoe, Ill.: The Free Press, 1955, especially pp. 121–124.

16. For examples of earlier theoretical and empirical work on the functions of voluntary association membership, see Rose, *op. cit.;* and Bernard Barber, "Participation and Mass Apathy in Associations," in Alvin Gouldner (ed.), *Studies in Leadership: Leadership and Democratic Action,* New York: Harper and Brothers, 1950, pp. 477–504.

18. THE ORGANIZED INDIVIDUAL

WILBERT E. MOORE

Where once stood the "minuteman," the "frontiersman," the "robber baron," and the "babbitt," now stands a new folk-type. To many people today, the "organization man" is the American par excellence. Over the past two decades numerous novelists, journalists and social scientists have attempted to portray the social structure of the large corporation, to describe its genesis and its future, and to dissect the life of the junior executive and those he seeks to emulate.

Here, in a selection taken from a chapter of Wilbert E. Moore's award-winning volume, The Conduct of the Corporation, *the inconsistencies which frequently exist between personal and corporate goals are examined. In "The Organized Individual," Professor Moore seeks to answer the question of why people work. The essay serves, once again, to illustrate the nature of adult socialization; it also provides the link between the study of informal social relationships and the nature of bureaucratic organizations.*

Wilbert E. Moore is currently Professor of Sociology at Denver University. In addition to The Conduct of the Corporation (*1962*), *Professor Moore is the author of* Industrial Relations and the Social Order (*1946, revised 1951*), Industrialization and Labor (*1951*), Economy and Society (*1955*), Man, Time and Society (*1963*), Social Change (*1963*), *and* The Impact of Industry (*1965*). *He is coeditor of* Twentieth Century Sociology (*1946*), Economic Growth: Brazil, India, Japan (*1955*), Labor Commitment and Social Change in Developing Areas (*1960*), *and* Industrialization and Society (*1963*).

The denizens of the large corporation have been widely portrayed as in a quite pathological state. They are, in fact, depicted as nearly comatose. Yet they appear to stir from their lethargy and display a fatal fascination with their own dissection. The picture, of course, is overdrawn to the point of caricature. The gray-flannel mind can indeed be found, and its owner's quest for conformity will keep the solitary crease in good order. They are a dull lot, the organization men, but not totally without interest or without their small hopes and fears, their tiny successes and failures. And it is easy enough to demonstrate that their organized apathy is quite unequal, and that they exist in an environment providing remarkable variety in the human fauna. The flora, too, are exotic, but those are mostly artificial status symbols and with those we are not, at the moment, concerned.

Bribed Cooperation

The relation between any individual and any group is at least a little uncertain. This is true even of the infant as he begins to develop a personality with "membership" in only one group, his family. Infants do not come with absolutely standard emotional and mental equipment, and in the complex interaction between infants and adults and older children, some friction, dissidence, and unpredictable outcomes must be expected. The situation is greatly complicated where the individual has multiple and often competing memberships and must exercise some effort if he is to preserve any integral identity, any cohesive life organization in the face of the pull-hauling of claims on his time, his energy, his basic loyalties.

The basic nexus between the member of a business concern and the corporate entity itself is the fact of employment. This relationship precedes all others, and all others are conditional on it for as long as the membership endures. Whatever else the member is doing there, he is basically earning a living or at least gaining an income. He normally achieves this desirable objective by performing tasks, by doing his duty. Whether he likes or dislikes his job may affect his performance, or it may not. Whether he likes or dislikes his associates, superiors, or the company as a whole is similarly of dubious relevance. Whether he cares about the organization, except that it survive and provide him with employment, may have no consequence at all.

If the organization were perfectly planned, perfectly secure in a benign environment, and perfectly staffed in terms of competent performers, the only link necessary between the individual and the organization would be whatever bribes the employer has to offer that are adequate to elicit the necessary performance. Cooperation would then be purely "structural," not motivational, a by-product of self-interest, not a shared and collective goal. For some workers at virtually all organizational levels this minimum affiliation is very nearly a true representation of the extent of their involvement. The proportions of persons whose cooperation is "bribed" is certainly higher than the proportions whose efforts are wholly selfless, dedicated to the common interest without thought of reward.

The bribes that corporations have to offer are numerous, but they invariably include money. The wage or salary is the way in which the specialized producer is permitted to become a generalized consumer. Workers generally constitute a small part of the consumers for goods they themselves produce; in capital goods production they have no use for the stuff at all. In an industrial society, there is no effective substitute for money as the link between production and consumption.

It is true that man does not live by bread alone; it is also true that money does not buy bread alone but a growing range of goods and services that "move through the market." The adult in our society who is not interested in money is probably certifiably insane.

Now it is equally true that employers offer and employees expect a great variety of "non-financial incentives." Some of these are simply deferred payments, like insurance and pension schemes, and others, such as security of employment, are simply assurance that the financial incentives will persist. Still others, such as safety measures or the comforts and amenities at the work place, have a price tag for the employer but not for the employee.

I do not mean to degrade the numerous studies that indicate that workers (including managers) are also interested in prestige and esteem, the approval of their peers and pleasant working relations with them, reasonable standards and fair treatment, a community fit to bring up their children in, and indeed a great variety of interests associated with the work place or the fact of employment. I do mean that these other interests and incentives are not substitutes for "adequate" financial reward. Within narrow limits, the employee may accept less money for a pleasanter job. He is either independently wealthy or plainly mad if he accepts no money for a pleasant job. If the non-financial characteristics of the job are viewed negatively by the employee or prospective worker, then financial rewards may overcome his distaste. This substitution too has its limits.

I think that it is this last point, the cost but limited effectiveness of purely financial incentives, that has led to the substantial distortion of the true situation in the thinking of many managers when the motives of hourly rated workers are up for consideration. The notion that workers can be bought off by kind words and attention to their irrationalities may be comforting to both the budget and the ego of managers, but the comfort is likely to be short-lived as experience demonstrates that the notion is false.

The true situation is complex but understandable. Below some "minimum" level, which of course varies by occupational level and tends to increase through time, the employee is likely to hold financial rewards as paramount and nearly exclusive. He cannot afford to be interested in, and indeed is likely to feel exploited by, "human relations" tricks. "Psychic income" buys no groceries at the supermarket. Beyond a minimum level of expectations, other, non-financial interests may loom larger in the worker's scheme of things. If forced to choose from among alternative job opportunities, he may even choose one paying a little less but offering other advantages. But the idea that this behavior represents a lack of interest in money is either stupid or willfully perverse. The worker would also clearly like to have more money.

Several years ago a leading commercial polling organization reported to its business clients on a study of production workers' attitudes. Of the various possible interests that workers valued in jobs, the pollsters reported, wages were seventh in importance. This "scientific" evidence, comforting to managerial wage negotiators dealing with unions, represented a deception that may have been deliberate. The question asked the sample of workers was, "What do you like best about your present job?" As a fair proportion of the workers were apparently dissatisfied with their wages, these did not do well in the popularity poll.

Managers who accept the notion that workers are not "primarily" interested in money are not notably self-sacrificing in appraising their own monetary value to the enterprise. Yet if one had to guess about the relative importance of financial incentives among workers and various categories of managers, one would guess that they are of greater importance to those who get less, the workers. And since the ordinary conditions of work also favor managers, non-managerial employees may show an especially sharp interest in the absolute size of the paycheck.

I am not here commenting on the equity of pay scales, but only on the nature of the individual employee's incentives for doing his job. All employees are bribed, at least with money, and some are also lured by additional homely pleasures. There is no reason to suppose that any category of workers, at least in industrial employment, is exceptionally irrational or benevolent in offering their services for pay. If several motives run in the same direction the individual avoids awkward choices among them, and the chance that the bribes are effective is greatly increased.

Commitment and Identification

My emphasis on bribes represents a deliberate attempt at bluntness about money matters and other motives. Yet bluntness may also distort and exaggerate, as when a spade is no longer a spade but a "bloody shovel." Most corporate employees exhibit more than a narrow self-interest in their jobs and their employer, an identification with persons and programs outside themselves, a sense of collective cooperation beyond their individual duties. The ways whereby contrived cooperation becomes conscientious reveal some further aspects of the relations between individuals and organizations.

Psychologists and sociologists interested in the way in which infants as untutored savages become more or less civilized adults refer to this transformation as the "socialization process." Socialization here has no reference to socialism or the confiscation of private property but rather to the formation of personality. The socialized individual learns a vast array of things from manual skills to expectations of others. He also "internalizes" values and codes of conduct and behaves in accordance with conscience and not solely in terms of external rewards and penalties. He knows and believes, perceives and feels, thinks and emotes. All of this happens in the context of interacting with others, complying with expectations of those who matter but finally including oneself as one who matters.

Most of the attention given to the socialization process has centered on infants and children, the progress from infancy to adulthood. Yet in the modern world the significance of adulthood is neither simple nor steady. The various adult roles cannot be entirely preconditioned in childhood. Some roles, such as rearing a family or earning a living, involve movement and progress. They do not remain stationary. If the individual is to behave properly in these roles, without continuous supervision and admonition, he must be socialized. The greater his mobility in roles or the greater the dynamic element in nominally "the same" position, the greater is the learning and character change required of him.

It is this process of adult socialization that figures largely in the work experience of the corporate employee or, for that matter, most breadwinners. He must learn the gross and subtle information and skills necessary to do his job and, to a degree, the attitudes appropriate to his function and position. The worker who passes both tests may be said to be *committed*. Bribed he may continue to be, but not exclusively so. He also will have performance standards and expectations, binding on himself and attributed to others in similar positions.

Expectations are important, however. When they are mutually shared by persons in comparable positions, the individual's own standards are externally reinforced. The workman's morale is likely to be eroded if the external reinforcement is only in the form of bribes and discipline but not the approval of significant others. Significant others may include superiors as well as peers, but only if our man "identifies" with them or seeks to emulate their success. Otherwise, all he will seek from superiors is fulfillment of his objective expectations, his terms and conditions of work, but not his subjective ones, the codes of behavior and standards of competence that can only be judged by those who share them.

The committed employee is also likely to be convinced of the importance of his own job for the accomplishment of the mission of his unit or of the whole concern. If this conviction gets no external confirmation at the work place—"no one appreciates me down there"—the individual's identification with the employer will certainly not persist. A feeling of futility pushes the participant back to a pure form of accepting bribes and wanting them to be high enough to offset his general dissatisfaction with his job. There is no guarantee of course that the individual's sense of his own importance is not neurotic, that is, out of touch with objective reality. One function of seeking out other jobs is, if successful, to restore the individual's self-confidence and incidentally to improve his bargaining position in extracting recognition from his employer if he remains.

There is very extensive evidence, from all sorts and circumstances of social life, that participation in decisions that affect the individual's life increases his involvement with the system as such. The man who helps make things happen rather than simply has them happen to him is better prepared to accept even some of the negative consequences. Some would argue that this is too little understood by those ultimately responsible for organizational policies, with the result that employees remain aloof and uninvolved. Others would argue that it is understood far too well, with the result that employees become captives of the employer, trapped by their participation in small matters and unable to question large issues.

For those concerned with large issues, on whom major responsibility rests for organizational success, the entrapment may be fairly complete even if self-imposed. If one can believe the testimony of biographers and the writers of magazine "profiles," the company becomes a sort of alter ego of the executive, with a corresponding reduction or distortion of other elements of normal human existence. Unable to divest himself of his official role, he "lives with" his job constantly. This is the ultimate in commitment and identification, the submersion of the individual in the organization sea. There is some doubt that this ultimate stage of organization is necessary. There is no doubt at all that it is abnormal in the statistical sense and probably in the psychological sense as well.

Conditional Love

Organizations and individuals initially face one another in a situation that reeks with uncertainty. Each may establish and maintain the relationship on a very tenuous basis, enduring it only so long as it meets the convenience of both parties. Or they may actually join in close, if chaste, embrace. Critics would even question the chastity of some relationships, for they feel that the individual loses his virtue without equivalent moral recompense.

Whyte's concern in *The Organization Man* is that the managerial employee is being smothered with kindness, to the destruction of both his individuality at work and his independence off the job. With income, amenities, and security, Whyte argues, the corporation encourages a kind of group conformity and a state of dependency.

I find it extremely doubtful that the quest for either security or conformity is any more prevalent now than in the past. It may, however, be more extensively realized in the large corporation. If the individual cannot gain either a sense of identity or a satisfactory sense of emotional security with individual components of the "faceless mass," he may lose himself in the mass itself and gain a sense of belonging by simply being common. There is no doubt that a number of pressures run in this direction, and particularly for the junior manager whose hopes and aspirations may be closely linked with the employer rather than with his colleagues or friends.

The man who "loves that company" or "loves that man" (his superior or someone above him) may find himself in the situation of the swain who goes a-courting and finds, despite his ardent pleas, that his love is unrequited. Security is likely to set in objectively only after several years of service and may never set in emotionally.

Uncertainty and anxiety are widely used as incentives. They may be generally effective in inducing a constrained conformity. In fact, for the immature they may induce a kind of pathetic dependence where the exceptional kind word or friendly gesture is given an exaggerated importance. ("He spoke to me today." "What did he say?" "He said, 'Get on with it Jones,' but his tone was friendly.") The evidence from psychology indicates that the child or man who has no emotional security and therefore slight basis for knowing where he stands on things is a poor risk in an uncertain situation or in one that provides moral dilemmas. He may be eager to please but end up doing the wrong thing or pleasing the wrong people.

Conditional love is generally what the corporation provides. Evidences of affection are tendered by the organization, not for the person as such, but for his obedient and compliant action. The source of excessive conformity, I am saying, is not a mutual relationship of stultifying affection, but a one-sided one. It is only in foolish novels that a marriage based on love by one party and convenience for the other ends up in deep mutual affection. The more probable outcome is a growing bitterness on the part of the "dependent" partner, and contempt on the part of the other. I do not doubt that "organization men" exist, but I do doubt that they can endure their futile search for affection, or *that the corporation can endure their unwanted, or rather, their welcome-but-excessive expressions of fealty.* Unstinting adulation palls and can only lead to increased coolness in the treatment of the craven captive, which may in turn increase his efforts to please. In the long term, the unacceptable admirer is a damned bore.

Endemic Pathologies

All administrative organizations are beset with various human frailties that cause chronic disorders in the ideal organizational structures. Some of these disorders are in fact common to most organizations, as they arise from the lack of an exact correspondence between collective and individual interests, the uncertain commitment of members to cooperative endeavors. Other pathological states are either peculiar to complex work organizations or flourish there to an unusually marked degree. This is why I have called them "endemic," like fungus infections in tropical areas.

FAVORITISM   "He's well meaning, and besides he's the boss's first cousin once removed." Nepotic practices in selection and promotion are probably less common in large corporations than in small ones, where the issue of competence may get intermixed with strong family financial control. But if kinship ties lose their strength in large organizations, perhaps because of explicit negative rules, other forms of social bonds do not. To reward one's friends and punish one's enemies is a common enough rule of conduct to persist even though it conflicts with the rule of competence. Naturally, favoritism flourishes most vigorously in filling positions that are fairly unexposed, that is, where neither personal qualifications nor the value of the performance can be specified easily. For example, "assistant managers" may be line officers and heirs apparent to higher office, but "assistants to the manager" have more ambiguous duties. Such positions indeed may represent part of the rather modest patronage that newcomers to the seats of power are accorded.

LETHARGY, SABOTAGE   "Don't sweat it." This crude advice from the vernacular is part of the arsenal of informal control devices used to discourage taking the demands of the job too seriously. Lethargic performance by the individual may arise from his own sense of futility and lack of recognition or from a properly sensitive response to the dampening pressure of his colleagues. Since every position is likely to entail a range of acceptable performance, "getting by" may be more common than pressing the upper limits. Sabotage, in its strict and original meaning of treading with wooden shoes or, in Veblen's language, the "conscientious withdrawal of efficiency," may actually take more effort than conscientious performance. Yet to the disgruntled employee anxious to fight the system, the trouble may be worthwhile. The tactics of delay and evasion may be as effectively disruptive as the flurry of apparently well-meaning errors. The handbook for organizational saboteurs has yet to be written, but one chapter would surely be devoted to the techniques of appearing to be very busy while actually doing nothing constructive at all.

CORRUPTION   "What's in it for me?" The substitution of individual for organizational interests is an omnipresent possibility in view of the "bribed" character of much organizational cooperation. Embezzlement is a crime available only to those entrusted with other people's money, but the requirements shade off into padded expense accounts, the conduct of personal business on company time, "liberating" office supplies or shop tools and materials, the use of company cars for week-end travel. Persons with the highest standards of personal honesty in their dealings with real people may have no hesitation in converting the property of that legal person, the corporation, to their own use. Notions of proprietorship through customary use may supersede the strictly legal rights of ownership. The man who would not dream of stealing a garden tool from a stranger may simply appropriate an office typewriter for his wife's personal correspondence. The attitude toward corporate property appears to have much in common with that toward public property. Belonging to "everyone," it may in effect be appropriated by those to whose custody it is assigned.

TECHNICISM "There's no reason; it's just policy." The principal fault that gives "bureaucracy" a bad name is the ritualistic compliance with rules and procedures without realistic reference to the goals to be accomplished or problems to be solved. "Red tape," once thought peculiar to governmental agencies, is in fact common to all very large organizations and many small ones. Rules are made to fit "type cases" but cases of the pure type may rarely arise. Safety for the officeholder lies with applying some rule not in rational disposal of the issues. Penalties, for the most part, are prescribed not for failure to achieve organizational ends or even for failing to believe in them but for violation of the procedural rules presumably designed to stipulate the means to be pursued. Those rules may have long since lost their original sense, or may be encumbered with so many modifications and exceptions as to encourage a petti-fogging legalism in interpretation. The "bureaucratic personality" takes comfort in his knowledge of the rules, and indeed this may be his only claim to excellence. If chaos ensues from the rules of law, that is not his problem. He didn't make the rules,

but he is intent on seeing that they are followed.

SAINTLINESS "Now if we all worked a little harder. . . ." Although not commonly understood, saints are more dangerous in organizations than sinners. Rules are made to control evil-doers, and penalties are prescribed for their misbehavior. But how can one punish exceptional virtue? Someone has expressed the view that the historic organizational strength of the Roman Catholic Church is best exemplified not by its adaptability to different times and places and not for its retention of the allegiance of half-hearted members but by its capacity for retaining and generally immunizing its devout extremists. The dedicated man is dangerous, partly because he sets standards that others cannot or will not follow. The saintly conservative who says, "I think we're tending to get a little sloppy," may attempt to achieve progress by going backward and restoring an ideal never officially abandoned but long since disregarded. The "saintly imperialist" who says, "I'll be glad to take on some additional responsibility," not only threatens the comfort of less avid performers but may threaten the security of those who thought they were already discharging the duties in question. The preacher of true virtue may of course only be attempting to get the official ideal modified to conform with practices, but unless that purpose is absolutely clear, his efforts are likely to be viewed with alarm and disruptive hostility.

SURVIVALISM "Don't break up a good team." Organizations do die, of course, and others are born. Yet keeping an organization going after its original mission has been accomplished or even after clear failure is a common kind of affliction in both public and private affairs. The National Foundation for Infantile Paralysis stayed in business after the discovery of the Salk vaccine, not only to help in rehabilitating polio victims but also to combat a considerable list of other human afflictions. Universities accept funds for setting up research organizations for particular projects. Part of the time and funds available will then be spent on developing proposals for other projects. Corporations set up temporary inter-divisional committees which then aspire to permanent divisional status in their own right. Occasionally survival may be assured by just being inconspicuous. Once a unit has a regular annual budget, it may be able to keep it almost in perpetuity as long as it is willing to curb its ambitions for larger resources. The agency may be dead, but no one may notice if it does not lie down.

Useful Troublemakers

Just as affliction may be good for character in some religious beliefs, so certain nuisances and discordant elements may be good for organizations, if one will just take a broad view of them. What is disadvantageous to individuals or other parts of the organizations may have positive benefits for the encompassing structure. Several such troublemakers are sufficiently standard to be characterized as types. I shall comment on certain of these.

MEMORY AND CONSCIENCE KEEPERS Despite my acerb comments at one or two earlier junctures about the preservers of rule and tradition, the problem is clearly one of balance. Standardization of many procedures is clearly more efficient than making them up anew on every occasion requiring action. But the standardized procedure must be known before it can be used. Although "universal" knowledge may be officially presumed, in fact some employees will be more expert than others. The neophyte in particular needs a source of advice, an expert in the law and lore. The degree of expertness is likely to have a high but not perfect correlation with length of service. Some men may, by this test, be old before their time, while others never grow up. The keepers of traditions and custodians of the corporate conscience

are likely to be regarded as dusty pedants, and indeed they often are. "Technicism" is their most common ailment, and if they reign unchallenged, "correct" behavior may lead to gradual decay. But continuity is also consequential, particularly in situations where substantial turnover prevails. The newcomer may eventually and in exasperation find ways of circumventing rules and precedents, but he is unlikely to be able to do so unless someone is around who knows what they are.

CONSCIENTIOUS OBJECTORS It is rather easier for a powerful executive to attract sycophantic subordinates than to discourage them. The "yes man" has become symbolic of the entourage of the mighty. Yet omniscience is accorded to few mortals, even among the successful men in corporate careers. The evidence and points of view appropriate for reasonably sound judgment are unlikely to appear unless doubt and disagreement are permitted and even moderately encouraged. The role of the objector is likely to be a dangerous one precisely because criticism may be asked for more earnestly than it is wanted or accepted when given. A recent magazine cartoon shows a man as a conspicuous minority of one in a raised-hand vote in the executive committee, and subsequently waiting his turn for interview in an employment agency. The "disagreeable fellow" may have a personality to fit the part, which can only add to the annoyance he may provoke. If some of his kind are not installed, no one may dare to say that the king, though majestic, is naked.

COURT JESTERS "Many a true word is spoken in jest," the adage goes, and this was precisely the function of the jester in the medieval royal courts. Humor, too, is a dangerous weapon, as the point may be as sharp as if it were hurled in anger by a "no man." Humor is commonly distasteful to serious-minded men, for it smacks of impiety. Yet I have seen some monstrously foolish corporate programs, which might have been scuttled soon after a little serious attention to objections, end in the disaster they deserved from the rolls of laughter that followed the first impious joke.

CREATORS The most effective counterbalance to the weighty hand of traditionalists is the innovator. The memory keepers are only troublesome because they impede progress by being virtuous. The creators are troublesome because they attempt to upset habit and custom, to defeat lethargic conformity. It has become increasingly popular for corporations to harbor "idea men," but that says nothing about their popularity in the organization. Intelligence, like humor, is not universally admired, and "bright" can be spoken as a curse as well as an accolade.

SINNERS Finally, I believe it is useful to note that evil has its place in the grand scheme of things and, paradoxically, may even do good. Laws are not made to be broken but to be kept. But without an occasional lawbreaker to evoke and renew the moral fervor of righteous men, the moral foundations of rules are likely to undergo steady decay. "Punishment," said the French sociologist Emile Durkheim, "is not meant for criminals but for honest men." By this he did not mean the deterrent effect of punishment that instills fear in the hearts of potential miscreants. Rather, he noted that wrongful acts provoke moral indignation on the part of those who obey and support the law. Without the occasion for righteous anger, the rules may lose their moral basis.

I do not mean to advocate mischief, because I do not think it necessary. All I am suggesting is that the occasional act of "disorganization" can have a salutary effect on the collective conscience. Like most other useful troublemakers, the wrong-doers are potentially beneficial only if they are kept in a strict minority. They represent the extreme rejection of the suffocating weight of conformity and as such may be accorded a nod of subdued respect.

19. FOUNDATIONS OF THE THEORY OF ORGANIZATION

PHILIP SELZNICK

To some writers, formal organization is the structural expression of rational action. But, as Philip Selznick points out in this article, such a definition ignores the true nature of corporate bodies. Organizations are a part of, not apart from, the general milieux in which they exist. Moreover, those who comprise these organizations are rarely capable of delimiting their attitudes and activities to the narrowly defined, formal roles demanded. They tend, rather, to resist depersonalization and react as "wholes."

The study of the organization involves assessment of two conceptually separable but empirically reciprocal frames of reference. There is, for example, the traditional emphasis upon the organizational system as an economy, a system of relationships that defines the availability of scarce resources and their allocation and that may be manipulated in terms of efficiency and effectiveness, that is, through delegation. There is also the view that organizational systems are adaptive social structures whose very existence is contingent upon the relationship between the control and the consent of participants. Deviation from the formal rules is not uncommon and frequently becomes institutionalized. Systematic evasions and informal associations are commonplace. The relevance of informal structures to organizational analysis, suggests Selznick, underlines the significance of conceiving of formal organizations as cooperative systems.

With these assertions as a baseline, Selznick develops a theory of organization utilizing the structural-functional model of analysis and stressing the process of "cooptation" as a means of maintaining the stability or the existence of the formal organization.

Philip Selznick is Professor of Sociology at the University of California at Berkeley. Titles of several of his published works appear on page 96 of this volume.

Trade unions, governments, business corporations, political parties, and the like are formal structures in the sense that they represent rationally ordered instruments for the achievement of stated goals. "Organization," we are told, "is the arrangement of personnel for facilitating the accomplishment of some agreed purpose through the allocation of functions and responsibilities." [1] Or, defined more generally, formal organization is "a system of consciously coordinated activities or forces of two or more persons." [2] Viewed in this light, formal organization is the structural expression of rational action. The mobilization of technical and managerial skills requires a pattern of coordination, a systematic ordering of positions and duties which defines a chain of command and makes possible the administrative integration of specialized functions. In this context *delegation* is the primordial organizational act, a precarious venture which requires the continuous elaboration of formal mechanisms of coordination and control. The security of all partici-

Reprinted from the *American Sociological Review*, **13** (1948), 25–35, by permission of the author and the American Sociological Association.

pants, and of the system as a whole, generates a persistent pressure for the institutionalization of relationships, which are thus removed from the uncertainties of individual fealty or sentiment. Moreover, it is necessary for the relations within the structure to be determined in such a way that individuals will be interchangeable and the organization will thus be free of dependence upon personal qualities.[3] In this way, the formal structure becomes subject to calculable manipulation, an instrument of rational action.

But as we inspect these formal structures we begin to see that they never succeed in conquering the non-rational dimensions of organizational behavior. The latter remain at once indispensable to the continued existence of the system of coordination and at the same time the source of friction, dilemma, doubt, and ruin. This fundamental paradox arises from the fact that rational action systems are inescapably imbedded in an institutional matrix, in two significant senses: 1) the action system—or the formal structure of delegation and control which is its organizational expression—is itself only an aspect of a concrete social structure made up of individuals who may interact as *wholes,* not simply in terms of their formal roles within the system; 2) the formal system, and the social structure within which it finds concrete existence, are alike subject to the pressure of an institutional environment to which some over-all adjustment must be made. The formal administrative design can never adequately or fully reflect the concrete organization to which it refers, for the obvious reason that no abstract plan or pattern can—or may, if it is to be useful—exhaustively describe an empirical totality. At the same time, that which is not included in the abstract design (as reflected, for example, in a staff-and-line organization chart) is vitally relevant to the maintenance and development of the formal system itself.

Organization may be viewed from two standpoints which are analytically distinct but which are empirically united in a context of reciprocal consequences. On the one hand, any concrete organizational system is an *economy;* at the same time, it is an *adaptive social structure.* Considered as an economy, organization is a system of relationships which define the availability of scarce resources and which may be manipulated in terms of efficiency and effectiveness. It is the economic aspect of organization which commands the attention of management technicians and, for the most part, students of public as well as private administration.[4] Such problems as the span of executive control, the role of staff or auxiliary agencies, the relation of headquarters to field offices, and the relative merits of single or multiple executive boards are typical concerns of the science of administration. The coordinative scalar, and functional principles, as elements of the theory of organization, are products of the attempt to explicate the most general features of organization as a "technical problem" or, in our terms, as an economy.

Organization as an economy is, however, necessarily conditioned by the organic states of the concrete structure, outside of the systematics of delegation and control. This becomes especially evident as the attention of leadership is directed toward such problems as the legitimacy of authority and the dynamics of persuasion. It is recognized implicitly in action and explicitly in the work of a number of students that the possibility of manipulating the system of coordination depends on the extent to which that system is operating within an environment of effective inducement to individual participants and of conditions in which the stability of authority is assured. This is in a sense the fundamental thesis of Barnard's remarkable study, *The Functions of the Executive.* It is also the underlying hypothesis which makes it possible for Urwick to suggest that "proper" or formal channels in fact function to "confirm and record" decisions arrived at by more personal means.[5] We meet it again in the concept of administration as a process of education, in which the winning of consent and support is conceived to be a basic function of leadership.[6] In short, it is recognized that control and consent cannot be divorced even within formally authoritarian structures.

The indivisibility of control and consent makes it necessary to view formal organizations as *cooperative* systems, widening the frame of reference of those concerned with the manipulation of organizational resources. At the point of action, of executive decision, the economic aspect of organization provides inadequate tools for control over the concrete structure. This idea may be readily grasped if attention is directed to the role of the individual within the organizational economy. From the standpoint of organization as a formal system, persons are viewed functionally, in respect to their *roles,* as participants in assigned segments of the cooperative system. But in fact individuals have a propensity to resist depersonalization, to spill over the boundaries of their segmentary roles, to participate as *wholes.* The formal systems (at an extreme, the disposition of "rifles" at a military perimeter) cannot take account of the deviations thus introduced, and consequently break down as instruments of control when relied upon alone. The whole individual raises new problems for the organization, partly because of the needs of his own personality, partly because he brings with him a set of established habits as well, perhaps, as commitments to special groups outside of the organization.

Unfortunately for the adequacy of formal systems of coordination, the needs of individuals do not permit a single-minded attention to the stated goals of the system within which they have been assigned. The hazard inherent in the act of delegation derives essentially from this fact. Delegation is an organizational act, having to do with formal assignments of functions and powers. Theoretically, these assignments are made to roles or official posi-

tions, not to individuals as such. In fact, however, delegation necessarily involves concrete individuals who have interests and goals which do not always coincide with the goals of the formal system. As a consequence, individual personalities may offer resistance to the demands made upon them by the official conditions of delegation. These resistances are not accounted for within the categories of coordination and delegation, so that when they occur they must be considered as unpredictable and accidental. Observations of this type of situation within formal structures are sufficiently commonplace. A familiar example is that of delegation to a subordinate who is also required to train his own replacement. The subordinate may resist this demand in order to maintain unique access to the "mysteries" of the job, and thus insure his indispensability to the organization.

In large organizations, deviations from the formal system tend to become institutionalized, so that "unwritten laws" and informal associations are established. Institutionalization removes such deviations from the realm of personality differences, transforming them into a persistent structural aspect of formal organizations.[7] These institutionalized rules and modes of informal cooperation are normally attempts by participants in the formal organization to control the group relations which form the environment of organizational decisions. The informal patterns (such as cliques) arise spontaneously, are based on personal relationships, and are usually directed to the control of some specific situation. They may be generated anywhere within a hierarchy, often with deleterious consequences for the formal goals of the organization, but they may also function to widen the available resources of executive control and thus contribute to rather than hinder the achievement of the stated objectives of the organization. The deviations tend to force a shift away from the purely formal system as the effective determinant of behavior to 1) a condition in which informal patterns buttress the formal, as through the manipulation of sentiment within the organization in favor of established authority; or 2) a condition wherein the informal controls effect a consistent modification of formal goals, as in the case of some bureaucratic patterns.[8] This trend will eventually result in the formalization of erstwhile informal activities, with the cycle of deviation and transformation beginning again on a new level.

The relevance of informal structures to organizational analysis underlines the significance of conceiving of formal organizations as cooperative systems. When the totality of interacting groups and individuals becomes the object of inquiry, the latter is not restricted by formal, legal, or procedural dimensions. The *state of the system* emerges as a significant point of analysis, as when an internal situation charged with conflict qualifies and informs actions ostensibly determined by formal relations and objectives. A proper understanding of the organizational process must make it possible to interpret changes in the formal system—new appointments or rules or reorganizations—in their relation to the informal and unavowed ties of friendship, class loyalty, power cliques, or external commitment. This is what it means "to know the score."

The fact that the involvement of individuals as whole personalities tends to limit the adequacy of formal systems of coordination does not mean that organizational characteristics are those of individuals. The organic, emergent character of the formal organization considered as a cooperative system must be recognized. This means that the *organization* reaches decisions, takes action, and makes adjustments. Such a view raises the question of the relation between organizations and persons. The significance of theoretical emphasis upon the cooperative *system* as such is derived from the insight that certain actions and consequences are enjoined independently of the personality of

the individuals involved. Thus, if reference is made to the "organization-paradox"—the tension created by the inhibitory consequences of certain types of informal structures within organizations—this does not mean that individuals themselves are in quandaries. It is the nature of the interacting consequences of divergent interests within the organization which creates the condition, a result which may obtain independently of the consciousness or the qualities of the individual participants. Similarly, it seems useful to insist that there are qualities and needs of leader*ship,* having to do with position and role, which are persistent despite variations in the character or personality of individual leaders themselves.

Rational action systems are characteristic of both individuals and organizations. The conscious attempt to mobilize available internal resources (e.g., self-discipline) for the achievement of a stated goal—referred to here as an economy or a formal system—is one aspect of individual psychology. But the personality considered as a dynamic system of interacting wishes, compulsions, and restraints defines a system which is at once essential and yet potentially deleterious to what may be thought of as the "economy of learning" or to individual rational action. At the same time, the individual personality is an adaptive structure, and this, too, requires a broader frame of reference for analysis than the categories of rationality. On a different level, although analogously, we have pointed to the need to consider organizations as cooperative systems and adaptive structures in order to explain the context of and deviations from the formal systems of delegation and coordination.

To recognize the sociological relevance of formal structures is not, however, to have constructed a theory of organization. It is important to set the framework of analysis and much is accomplished along this line when, for example, the nature of authority in formal organizations is reinterpreted to emphasize the factors of cohesion and persuasion as against legal or coercive sources.[9] This redefinition is logically the same as that which introduced the conception of the self as social. The latter helps make possible, but does not of itself fulfill, the requirements for a dynamic theory of personality. In the same way, the definition of authority as conditioned by sociological factors of sentiment and cohesion—or more generally the definition of formal organizations as cooperative systems—only sets the stage, as an initial requirement, for the formulation of a theory of organization.

Structural-Functional Analysis

Cooperative systems are constituted of individuals interacting as wholes in relation to a formal system of coordination. The concrete structure is therefore a resultant of the reciprocal influences of the formal and informal aspects of organization. Furthermore, this structure is itself a totality, an adaptive "organism" reacting to influences upon it from an external environment. These considerations help to define the objects of inquiry, but to progress to a system of predicates *about* these objects it is necessary to set forth an analytical method which seems to be fruitful and significant. The method must have a relevance to empirical materials, which is to say, it must be more specific in its reference than discussions of the logic or methodology of social science.

The organon which may be suggested as peculiarly helpful in the analysis of adaptive structures has been referred to as "structural-functional analysis."[10] This method may be characterized in a sentence: *Structural-functional analysis relates contemporary and variable behavior to a presumptively stable system of needs and mechanisms.* This means that a given empirical system is deemed to have basic needs, essentially related to self-maintenance; the system develops repetitive means of self-defense; and day-to-day

activity is interpreted in terms of the function served by that activity for the maintenance and defense of the system. Put thus generally, the approach is applicable on any level in which the determinate "states" of empirically isolable systems undergo self-impelled and repetitive transformations when impinged upon by external conditions. This self-impulsion suggests the relevance of the term "dynamic," which is often used in referring to physiological, psychological, or social systems to which this type of analysis has been applied.[11]

It is a postulate of the structural-functional approach that the basic need of all empirical systems is the maintenance of the integrity and continuity of the system itself. Of course, such a postulate is primarily useful in directing attention to a set of "derived imperatives" or needs which are sufficiently concrete to characterize the system at hand.[12] It is perhaps rash to attempt a catalogue of these imperatives for formal organizations, but some suggestive formulation is needed in the interests of setting forth the type of analysis under discussion. In formal organizations, the "maintenance of the system" as a generic need may be specified in terms of the following imperatives:

1) THE SECURITY OF THE ORGANIZATION AS A WHOLE IN RELATION TO SOCIAL FORCES IN ITS ENVIRONMENT This imperative requires continuous attention to the possibilities of encroachment and to the forestalling of threatened aggressions or deleterious (though perhaps unintended) consequences from the actions of others.

2) THE STABILITY OF THE LINES OF AUTHORITY AND COMMUNICATION One of the persistent reference-points of administrative decision is the weighing of consequences for the continued capacity of leadership to control and to have access to the personnel or ranks.

3) THE STABILITY OF INFORMAL RELATIONS WITHIN THE ORGANIZATION Ties of sentiment and self-interest are evolved

as unacknowledged but effective mechanisms of adjustment of individuals and sub-groups to the conditions of life within the organization. These ties represent a cementing of relationships which sustains the formal authority in day-to-day operations and widens opportunities for effective communication.[13] Consequently, attempts to "upset" the informal structure, either frontally or as an indirect consequence of formal reorganization, will normally be met with considerable resistance.

4) THE CONTINUITY OF POLICY AND OF THE SOURCES OF ITS DETERMINATION For each level within the organization, and for the organization as a whole, it is necessary that there be a sense that action taken in the light of a given policy will not be placed in continuous jeopardy. Arbitrary or unpredictable changes in policy undermine the significance of (and therefore the attention to) day-to-day action by injecting a note of capriciousness. At the same time, the organization will seek stable roots (or firm statutory authority or popular mandate) so that a sense of the permanency and legitimacy of its acts will be achieved.

5) A HOMOGENEITY OF OUTLOOK WITH RESPECT TO THE MEANING AND ROLE OF THE ORGANIZATION The minimization of disaffection requires a unity derived from a common understanding of what the character of the organization is meant to be. When this homogeneity breaks down, as in situations of internal conflict over basic issues, the continued existence of the organization is endangered. On the other hand, one of the signs of "healthy" organization is the ability to effectively orient new members and readily slough off those who cannot be adapted to the established outlook.

This catalogue of needs cannot be thought of as final, but it approximates the stable system generally characteristic of formal organizations. These imperatives are derived, in the sense that they represent the conditions for survival or self-maintenance of cooperative systems of organized action. An inspection of these needs suggests that organizational survival is intimately connected with the struggle for relative prestige, both for the organization and for elements and individuals within it. It may therefore be useful to refer to a *prestige-survival motif* in organizational behavior as a short-hand way of relating behavior to needs, especially when the exact nature of the needs remains in doubt. However, it must be emphasized that prestige-survival in organizations does not derive simply from like motives in individuals. Loyalty and self-sacrifice may be individual expressions of organizational or group egotism and self-consciousness.

The concept of organizational need directs analysis to the *internal relevance* of organizational behavior. This is especially pertinent with respect to discretionary action undertaken by agents manifestly in pursuit of formal goals. The question then becomes one of relating the specific act of discretion to some presumptively stable organizational need. In other words, it is not simply action plainly oriented internally (such as in-service training) but also action presumably oriented externally which must be inspected for its relevance to internal conditions. This is a prime importance for the understanding of bureaucratic behavior, for it is of the essence of the latter that action formally undertaken for substantive goals be weighed and transformed in terms of its consequences for the position of the officialdom.

Formal organizations as cooperative systems on the one hand, and individual personalities on the other, involve structural-functional homologies, a point which may help to clarify the nature of this type of analysis. If we say that the individual has a stable set of needs, most generally the need for maintaining and defending the integrity of his personality or ego; that there are recognizable certain repetitive mechanisms which are utilized by the ego in its defense (rationalization, projection, regression, etc.); and that overt and variable behavior may be interpreted in terms of its relation to these needs and mechanisms—on the basis of this logic we may discern the typical pattern of structural-functional analysis as set forth above. In this sense, it is possible to speak of a "Freudian model" for organizational analysis. This does not mean that the substantive insights of individual psychology may be applied to organizations, as in vulgar extrapolations from the individual ego to whole nations or (by a no less vulgar inversion) from strikes to frustrated workers. It is the *logic,* the *type* of analysis which is pertinent.

This homology is also instructive in relation to the applicability of generalizations to concrete cases. The dynamic theory of personality states a set of possible predicates about the ego and its mechanisms of defense which inform us concerning the propensies of individual personalities under certain general circumstances. But these predicates provide only tools for the analysis of particular individuals, and each concrete case must be examined to tell which operate and in what degree. They are not primarily organs of prediction. In the same way, the predicates within the theory of organization will provide tools for the analysis of particular cases. Each organization, like each personality, represents a resultant of complex forces, an empirical entity which no single relation or no simple formula can explain. The problem of analysis becomes that of selecting among the possible predicates set forth in the theory of organization those which illuminate our understanding of the materials at hand.

The setting of structural-functional analysis as applied to organizations requires some qualification, however. Let us entertain the suggestion that the interesting problem in social science is not so much why men act the way they do as why men in certain circumstances *must* act the way they do. This emphasis upon constraint, if accepted, releases us from an ubiquitous attention to behavior in general, and especially from any undue fixation upon statistics. On the other hand, it has what would seem to be the salutary consequence of focusing inquiry upon certain necessary relationships of the type "if . . . then," for example: If the cultural level of the rank and file members of a formally democratic organization is below that necessary for participation in the formulation of policy, then there will be pressure upon the leaders to use the tools of demagogy.

Is such a statement universal in its applicability? Surely not in the sense that one can predict without remainder the nature of all or even most political groups in a democracy. Concrete behavior is a resultant, a complex vector, shaped by the operation of a number of such general constraints. But there is a test of general applicability: it is that of noting whether the relation made explicit must be *taken into account* in action. This criterion represents an empirical test of the significance of social science generalizations. If a theory is significant it will state a relation which will either 1) be taken into account as an element of achieving control; or 2) be ignored only at the risk of losing control and will evidence itself in a ramification of objective or unintended consequences.[14] It is a corollary of this principle of significance that investigation must search out the underlying factors in organizational action, which requires a kind of intensive analysis of the same order as psychoanalytic probing.

A frame of reference which invites attention to the constraints upon behavior will tend to highlight tensions and dilemmas, the characteristic paradoxes generated in the course of action. The dilemma may be said to be the handmaiden of structural-functional analysis, for it introduces the concept of *commitment* or *involvement* as fundamental to organizational analysis. A dilemma in human behavior is represented by an inescapable commitment which cannot be reconciled with the needs of the organism or the social system. There are many spurious dilemmas which have to do with verbal contradictions, but inherent dilemmas to which we refer are of a more profound sort, for they reflect the basic nature of the empirical system in question. An economic order committed to profit as its sustaining incentive may, in Marxist terms, sow the seed of its own destruction. Again, the anguish of man, torn between finitude and pride, is not a matter of arbi-- trary and replaceable assumptions but is a reflection of the psychological needs of the human organism, and is concretized in his commitment to the institutions which command his life; he is in the world and of it, inescapably involved in its goals and demands; at the same time, the needs of the spirit are compelling, proposing modes of salvation which have continuously disquieting consequences for worldly involvements. In still another context, the need of the human organism for affection and response necessitates a commitment to elements of the culture which can provide them; but the rule of the super-ego is uncertain since it cannot be completely reconciled with the need for libidinal satisfactions.

Applying this principle to organizations we may note that there is a general source of tension observable in the split between "the motion and the act." Plans and programs reflect the freedom of technical or ideal choice, but organized action cannot escape involvement, a commitment to personnel or institutions or procedures which effectively qualifies the initial plan. *Der Mensch denkt, Gott lenkt.* In organized action, this ultimate wisdom finds a temporal meaning in the recalcitrance of the tools of action. We are inescapably committed to the mediation of human structures which are at once indispensable to our goals and at the same time stand between them and ourselves. The selection of agents generates immediately a bifurcation of interest, expressed in new centers of need and power, placing effective con-

straints upon the arena of action, and resulting in tensions which are never completely resolved. This is part of what it means to say that there is a "logic" of action which impels us forward from one undesired position to another. Commitment to dynamic, self-activating tools is of the nature of organized action; at the same time, the need for continuity of authority, policy, and character is pressing, and requires an unceasing effort to master the instruments generated in the course of action. This generic tension is specified within the terms of each cooperative system. But for all we find a persistent relationship between *need* and *commitment* in which the latter not only qualifies the former but unites with it to produce a continuous state of tension. In this way, the motion of constraint (as reflected in tension or paradox) at once widens and more closely specifies the frame of reference for organizational analysis.

For Malinowski, the core of functionalism was contained in the view that a cultural fact must be analyzed in its setting. Moreover, he apparently conceived of his method as pertinent to the analysis of all aspects of cultural systems. But there is a more specific problem, one involving a principle of selection which serves to guide inquiry along significant lines. Freud conceived of the human organism as an adaptive structure, but he was not concerned with all human needs, nor with all phases of adaptation. For his system, he selected those needs whose expression is blocked in some way, so that such terms as repression, inhibition, and frustration became crucial. All conduct may be thought of as derived from need, and all adjustment represents the reduction of need. But not all needs are relevant to the systematics of dynamic psychology; and it is not adjustment as such but reaction to frustration which generates the characteristic modes of defensive behavior.

Organizational analysis, too, must find its selective principle; otherwise the indiscriminate attempts to relate activity functionally to needs will produce little in the way of significant theory. Such a principle might read as follows: *Our frame of reference is to select out those needs which cannot be fulfilled within approved avenues of expression and thus must have recourse to such adaptive mechanisms as ideology and to the manipulation of formal processes and structures in terms of informal goals.* This formulation has many difficulties, and is not presented as conclusive, but it suggests the kind of principle which is likely to separate the quick and the dead, the meaningful and the trite in the study of cooperative systems in organized action.[15]

The frame of reference outlined here for the theory of organization may now be identified as involving the following major ideas: 1) the concept of organizations as cooperative systems, adaptive social structures, made up of interacting individuals, sub-groups and informal plus formal relationships; 2) structural-functional analysis, which relates variable aspects of organization (such as goals) to stable needs and self-defensive mechanisms; 3) the concept of recalcitrance as a quality of the tools of social action, involving a break in the continuum of adjustment and defining an environment of constraint, commitment, and tension. This frame of reference is suggested as providing a specifiable *area of relations* within which predicates in the theory of organization will be sought, and at the same time setting forth principles of selection and relevance in our approach to the data of organization.

It will be noted that we have set forth this frame of reference within the over-all context of social action. The significance of events may be defined by their place and operational role in a means-end scheme. If functional analysis searches out the elements important for the maintenance of a given structure, and that structure is one of the materials to be manipulated in action, then that which is functional in respect to the structure is also functional in respect to the action

system. This provides a ground for the significance of functionally derived theories. At the same time, relevance to control in action is the empirical test of their applicability or truth.

Cooptation as a Mechanism of Adjustment

The frame of reference stated above is in fact an amalgam of definition, resolution, and substantive theory. There is an element of *definition* in conceiving of formal organizations as cooperative systems, though of course the interaction of informal and formal patterns is a question of fact; in a sense, we are *resolving* to employ structural-functional analysis on the assumption that it will be fruitful to do so, though here, too, the specification of needs or derived imperatives is a matter for empirical inquiry; and our predication of recalcitrance as a quality of the tools of action is itself a *substantive theory,* perhaps fundamental to a general understanding of the nature of social action.

A theory of organization requires more than a general frame of reference, though the latter is indispensable to inform the approach of inquiry to any given set of materials. What is necessary is the construction of generalizations concerning transformations within and among cooperative systems. These generalizations represent, from the standpoint of particular cases, possible predicates which are relevant to the materials as we know them in general, but which are not necessarily controlling in all circumstances. A theory of transformations in organization would specify those states of the system which resulted typically in predictable, or at least understandable, changes in such aspects of organization as goals, leadership, doctrine, efficiency, effectiveness, and size. These empirical generalizations would be systematized as they were related to the stable needs of the cooperative system.

Changes in the characteristics of organizations may occur as a result of many different conditions, not always or necessarily related to the processes of organization as such. But the theory of organization must be selective, so that explanations of transformations will be sought within its own assumptions or frame of reference. Consider the question of size. Organizations may expand for many reasons —the availability of markets, legislative delegations, the swing of opinion—which may be accidental from the point of view of the organizational process. To explore changes in size (as of, say, a trades union) as related to changes in non-organizational conditions may be necessitated by the historical events to be described, but it will not of itself advance the frontiers of the theory of organization. However, if "the innate propensity of all organizations to expand" is asserted as a function of "the inherent instability of incentives" [16] then transformations have been stated within the terms of the theory of organization itself. It is likely that in many cases the generalization in question may represent only a minor aspect of the empirical changes, but these organizational relations must be made explicit if the theory is to receive development.

In a frame of reference which specifies needs and anticipates the formulation of a set of self-defensive responses or mechanisms, the latter appear to constitute one kind of empirical generalization or "possible predicate" within the general theory. The needs of organizations (whatever investigation may determine them to be) are posited as attributes of all organizations, but the responses to disequilibrium will be varied. The mechanisms used by the system in fulfillment of its needs will be repetitive and thus may be described as a specifiable set of assertions within the theory of organization, but any given organization may or may not have recourse to the characteristic modes of response. Certainly no given organization will employ all of the possible mechanisms which are theoretically available. When Barnard speaks of an "innate propensity of organi-zation to expand" he is in fact formulating one of the general mechanisms, namely, expansion, which is a characteristic mode of response available to an organization under pressure from within. These responses necessarily involve a transformation (in this case, size) of some structural aspect of the organization.

Other examples of the self-defensive mechanisms available to organizations may derive primarily from the response of these organizations to the institutional environments in which they live. The tendency to construct ideologies, reflecting the need to come to terms with major social forces, is one such mechanism. Less well understood as a mechanism of organizational adjustment is what we may term *cooptation*. Some statement of the meaning of this concept may aid in clarifying the foregoing analysis.

Cooptation is the process of absorbing new elements into the leadership or policy-determining structure of an organization as a means of averting threats to its stability or existence. This is a defensive mechanism, formulated as one of a number of possible predicates available for the interpretation of organizational behavior. Cooptation tells us something about the process by which an institutional environment impinges itself upon an organization and effects changes in its leadership and policy. Formal authority may resort to cooptation under the following general conditions:

1) When there exists a hiatus between consent and control, so that the legitimacy of the formal authority is called into question. The "indivisibility" of consent and control refers, of course, to an optimum situation. Where control lacks an adequate measure of consent, it may revert to coercive measures or attempt somehow to win the consent of the governed. One means of winning consent is to coopt elements into the leadership or organization, usually elements which in some way reflect the sentiment, or possess the confidence of the relevant public or mass. As a

result, it is expected that the new elements will lend respectability or legitimacy to the organs of control and thus reestablish the stability of formal authority. This process is widely used, and in many different contexts. It is met in colonial countries, when the organs of alien control reaffirm their legitimacy by coopting native leaders into the colonial administration. We find it in the phenomenon of "crisis-patriotism" wherein normally disfranchised groups are temporarily given representation in the councils of government in order to win their solidarity in a time of national stress. Cooptation is presently being considered by the United States Army in its study of proposals to give enlisted personnel representation in the court-martial machinery —a clearly adaptive response to stresses made explicit during the war, the lack of confidence in the administration of army justice. The "unity" parties of totalitarian states are another form of cooptation; company unions or some employee representation plans in industry are still another. In each of these cases, the response of formal authority (private or public, in a large organization or a small one) is an attempt to correct a state of imbalance by *formal* measures. It will be noted, moreover, that what is shared is the *responsibility* for power rather than power itself. These conditions define what we shall refer to as *formal cooptation*.

2) Cooptation may be a response to the pressure of specific centers of power. This is not necessarily a matter of legitimacy or of a general and diffuse lack of confidence. These may be well established; and yet organized forces which are able to threaten the formal authority may effectively shape its structure and policy. The organization in respect to its institutional environment—or the leadership in respect to its ranks—must take these forces into account. As a consequence, the outside elements may be brought into the leadership or policy-determining structure, may be given a place as a recognition of and concession to the resources they can inde-

pendently command. The representation of interests through administrative constituencies is a typical example of this process. Or, within an organization, individuals upon whom the group is dependent for funds or other resources may insist upon and receive a share in the determination of policy. This form of cooptation is typically expressed in informal terms, for the problem is not one of responding to a state of imbalance with respect to the "people as a whole" but rather one of meeting the pressure of specific individuals or interest-groups which are in a position to enforce demands. The latter are interested in the substance of power and not its forms. Moreover, an open acknowledgment of capitulation to specific interests may itself undermine the sense of legitimacy of the formal authority within the community. Consequently, there is a positive pressure to refrain from explicit recognition of the relationship established. This form of the cooptative mechanism, having to do with the sharing of power as a response to specific pressures, may be termed *informal cooptation*.

Cooptation reflects a state of tension between formal authority and social power. The former is embodied in a particular structure and leadership, but the latter has to do with subjective and objective factors which control the loyalties and potential manipulability of the community. Where the formal authority is an expression of social power, its stability is assured. On the other hand, when it becomes divorced from the sources of social power its continued existence is threatened. This threat may arise from the sheer alienation of sentiment or from the fact that other leaderships have control over the sources of social power. Where a formal authority has been accustomed to the assumption that its constituents respond to it as individuals, there may be a rude awakening when organization of those constituents on a non-governmental basis creates nuclei of power which are able effectively to demand a sharing of power.[17]

The significance of cooptation for organizational analysis is not simply that there is a change in or a broadening of leadership, and that this is an adaptive response, but also that *this change is consequential for the character and role of the organization.* Cooptation involves commitment, so that the groups to which adaptation has been made constrain the field of choice available to the organization or leadership in question. The character of the coopted elements will necessarily shape (inhibit or broaden) the modes of action available to the leadership which has won adaptation and security at the price of commitment. The concept of cooptation thus implicitly sets forth the major points of the frame of reference outlined above: it is an adaptive response of a cooperative system to a stable need, generating transformations which reflect constraints enforced by the recalcitrant tools of action.

NOTES

1. John M. Gaus, "A Theory of Organization in Public Administration," in *The Frontiers of Public Administration,* Chicago: University of Chicago Press, 1936, p. 66.

2. Chester I. Barnard, *The Functions of the Executive,* Cambridge: Harvard University Press, 1938, p. 73.

3. Cf. Talcott Parsons' generalization (after Max Weber) of the "law of the increasing rationality of action systems," in *The Structure of Social Action,* New York: McGraw-Hill, 1937, p. 752.

4. See Luther Gulick and Lydall Urwick (eds.), *Papers on the Science of Administration,* New York: Institute of Public Administration, Columbia University, 1937; Lydall Urwick, *The Elements of Administration,* New York: Harper, 1943; James D. Mooney and Alan C. Reiley, *The Principles of Organization,* New York: Harper, 1939; H. S. Dennison, *Organization Engineering,* New York: McGraw-Hill, 1931.

5. Urwick, *op. cit.,* p. 47.

6. See Gaus, *op. cit.* Studies of the problem of morale are instances of the same orientation, having received considerable impetus in recent years from the work of the Harvard Business School group.

7. The creation of informal structures within various types of organizations has received explicit recognition in recent years. See F. J. Roethlisberger and W. J. Dickson, *Management and the Worker,* Cambridge: Harvard University Press, 1941, p. 524; also Barnard, *op. cit.,* chap. ix; and Wilbert E. Moore, *Industrial Relations and the Social Order,* New York: Macmillan, 1946, chap. xv.

8. For an analysis of the latter in these terms, see Philip Selznick, "An Approach to a Theory of Bureaucracy," *American Sociological Review,* 8 (1943), 47–54.

9. Robert Michels, "Authority," *Encyclopedia of the Social Sciences,* New York: Macmillan, 1931, pp. 319 ff.; also Barnard, *op. cit.,* chap. xii.

10. For a presentation of this approach having a more general reference than the study of formal organizations, see Talcott Parsons, "The Present Position and Prospects of Systematic Theory in Sociology," in Georges Gurvitch and Wilbert E. Moore (eds.), *Twentieth Century Sociology,* New York: The Philosophical Library, 1945.

11. "Structure" refers to both the relationships within the system (formal plus informal patterns in organization) and the set of needs and modes of satisfaction which characterize the given type of empirical system. As the utilization of this type of analysis proceeds, the concept of "need" will require further clarification. In particular, the imputation of a "stable set of needs" to organizational systems must not function as a new instinct theory. At the same time, we cannot avoid using these inductions as to generic needs, for they help us to stake out our area of inquiry. The author is indebted to Robert K. Merton who has, in correspondence, raised some important objections to the use of the term "need" in this context.

12. For "derived imperative" see Bronislaw Malinowski, *The Dynamics of Culture Change,* New Haven: Yale University Press, 1945, pp. 44 ff. For the use of "need" in place of "motive"

see the same author's *A Scientific Theory of Culture,* Chapel Hill: University of North Carolina Press, 1944, pp. 89–90.

13. They may also *destroy* those relationships, as noted above, but the need remains, generating one of the persistent dilemmas of leadership.

14. See R. M. MacIver's discussion of the "dynamic assessment" which "brings the external world selectively into the subjective realm, conferring on it subjective significance for the ends of action." *Social Causation,* Boston: Ginn, 1942, chaps. 11, 12. The analysis of this assessment within the context of organized action yields the implicit knowledge which guides the choice among alternatives. See also Robert K. Merton, "The Unanticipated Consequences of Purposive Social Action," *American Sociological Review,* 1 (1936), 894–904.

15. This is not meant to deprecate the study of organizations as *economies* or formal systems. The latter represent an independent level, abstracted from organizational structures as cooperative or adaptive systems ("organisms").

16. Barnard, *op. cit.,* pp. 158–159.

17. It is perhaps useful to restrict the concept of cooptation to formal organizations, but in fact it probably reflects a process characteristic of all group leaderships. This has received some recognition in the analysis of class structure, wherein the ruling class is interpreted as protecting its own stability by absorbing new elements. Thus Michels made the point that "an aristocracy cannot maintain an enduring stability by sealing itself off hermetically." See Robert Michels, *Umschichtungen in den herrschenden Klassen nach dem Kriege,* Stuttgart: Kohlhammer, 1934, p. 39; also Gaetano Mosca, *The Ruling Class,* New York: McGraw-Hill, 1939, p. 413 ff. The alliance or amalgamation of classes in the face of a common threat may be reflected in formal and informal cooptative responses among formal organizations sensitive to class pressures. In *TVA and the Grass Roots,* Berkeley: University of California Press, 1949 [now available in a Harper Torchbook Edition, 1965], the author has made extensive use of the concept of cooptation in analyzing some aspects of the organizational behavior of a government agency.

20. THE MODERN ARMY AS A BUREAUCRACY

S. E. FINER

It has often been argued that "form follows function." The classic example used by those who hold this view is that of the growth and character of modern armies. The military has long been considered the prototype of bureaucratic organization, a system which delegates responsibility through fixed channels to maximize efficiency and effectiveness and in which specific prerogatives are allocated to those occupying particular positions in a hierarchy of authority. In addition, by developing an esprit de corps *among members, the professional military organization has a tendency to become the primary referent for its members' social existence.*

S. E. Finer's article presents the view that because of its organization and coherence, the military has great political advantages over civilian organizations.

Professor of Political Issues at The University of Keele in Great Britain, S. E. Finer is the author of A Primer of Public Administration (*1950*), Anonymous Empire: A Study of Lobby in Great Britain (*1958*), *and* The Man on Horseback: The Role of the Military in Politics (*1962*).

The armed forces have three massive political advantages over civilian organizations: a marked superiority in organization, a highly emotionalized symbolic status, and a monopoly of arms. They form a prestigious corporation or Order, enjoying overwhelming superiority in the means of applying force. The wonder, therefore, is not why this rebels against its civilian masters, but why it ever obeys them.

The Modern Army [1]

In practically every country of the world today, except possibly in one or two of the proto-dynastic survivals such as the Yemen, the army is marked by the superior quality of its organization. Even the most poorly organized or maintained of such armies is far more highly and tightly structured than any civilian group.

The fact that not all armies were highly organized in the past, or that they need not necessarily be so, is irrelevant here. Modern armies are *cohesive* and *hierarchical*. Some armies of the past have not been cohesive but have consisted of a mere multitude of men independent of one another and maintaining little contact between themselves. Others have not been hierarchical, but almost republican in their relations to their chiefs. The Spartan host and the Cossack settlements were cohesive enough, but republican as to command. The *voortrekkers* and the American frontiersmen were neither cohesive nor hierarchical formations. In the early stages of their development, some revolutionary armies (e.g. Fidel Castro's, or Pancho Villa's or Zapata's) resemble these primitive prototypes of the modern armies . . . but for the most part, and certainly for the time being, we are concerned only with the modern type of

Reprinted from *The Man on Horseback* (London: Pall Mall Press, Ltd., 1962; New York: Frederick A. Praeger, Inc., 1963), by permission of the author and the publishers. c. S. E. Finer 1962. This chapter was originally entitled "The Political Strengths of the Military."

army, characterized by its uniquely high level of organization.

Organization and coherence

"Non est potestas super terram quae comparetur" runs the quotation on the title page of Hobbes's *Leviathan*. May we not think likewise of the modern army?

The army is a *purposive* instrument. It is not a crescive institution like the church; it comes into being by fiat. It is rationally conceived to fulfil certain objects. One may be to assist the civil power, but the principal object is to fight and win wars. The highly peculiar features of its organization flow from this central purpose, not from the secondary one, and find in it their supreme justification. These features are 1) centralized command, 2) hierarchy, 3) discipline, 4) intercommunication, 5) *esprit de corps* and a corresponding isolation and self-sufficiency.

Military command is centralized. In practice, much is delegated to units in the field, but always within the supreme command's general directives and always subject to be resumed by it should occasion arise. A continuous chain of command links the very lowest echelons with the supreme H.Q. This centralization of authority derives from the basic object of the army—in military parlance it exists "to be fought" by its commanders and for this it must respond to their commands as a single unit.

The army is arranged in a pyramid of authority, a hierarchy, each echelon owing explicit and peremptory obedience to the orders of its superior. The army is therefore very highly stratified. Further to this, each echelon in the hierarchy is immediately and objectively identifiable by named rank and distinctive insignia. Authority is depersonalized; it is owed to the rank, not to the man, and it exactly corresponds to the rank, and the rank to the insignia. The importance of subordination and superordination is further enhanced by social practices prescribing a social distance be-

tween the superior and inferior ranks. The hierarchical structure, like centralization, derives from the army's basic imperative —to fight as a unit; it must have a supreme directing command—hence centralization; the command must transmit its orders from highest to lowest—hence hierarchy.

From high to low, each member is subject to discipline. The army is difficult to leave—desertion is punished heavily, and desertion on active service might even incur the death penalty. The chain of command is sacrosanct; everything is supposed to "go through the channels." In practice, this often is offset by the "Old Boy Net," whereby one can speed up the "usual channels." This is true of most large-scale organizations. It only thrives, however, where the organization has developed an *esprit de corps* (for which see below). Each echelon is subject to the orders of its superiors; failure to obey carries penalties, some exceedingly heavy. This obligation to unquestioning and prompt obedience is enhanced by the depersonalization of the soldier. The army is too big a machine to reck of individuals, and the soldier becomes a number. Extraneous considerations are thereby thrust aside, and obedience to superiors, recognized by their rank and insignia, becomes the dominant or sole criterion of action. This rule of obedience also springs from the army's primary purpose, i.e., successful combat. Unless it existed, the behavior of the units that are being "fought" would not be calculable. It must be calculable and predictable if the battle plan is to be executed.

Centralization of command, the hierarchical arrangement of authority and the rule of obedience—all are necessary to make the army respond as a unity to the word of command; but they in turn demand a nervous system, a network of communication. Armies have developed elaborate signal systems independent of the civil authorities. The most modern methods of telephone, wireless and teleprinter are supplemented by the older systems of physical communication—the despatch rider, and this in turn by the primitive methods of semaphore and the runner. For so important are communications that there must always be methods available, even the most clumsy. By these means the nervous articulation of every unit in the country and the combination of all arms and services is rendered *physically* possible. By the same token, the territorial dispersion of units, their geographical separation offers no impediment to their unity of decision and of action.

But any army which possessed only these characteristics and none other would hardly win a battle. Its unity would be entirely mechanical, wholly compulsive, singularly lifeless, and not very bellicose. An army must in addition be animated by consciousness of its martial purpose and inspired by a corporate spirit of unity and solidarity. What Durkheim called *organic* solidarity, namely a "system of different and special functions united by definite relationships," has to be supplemented by his (strangely named) *mechanical* solidarity, i.e. "a more or less organized *ensemble* of the beliefs and the sentiments common to all the members of the group." This can only be, as Durkheim says, "in proportion as the ideas and inclinations common to all the members . . . exceed in number and intensity those personal to each of them. . . ." [2]

This "more or less organized *ensemble* of the beliefs and sentiments common to all members of the group" is deliberately inculcated in armies and constitutes their vital spark—their *esprit de corps*. It is grounded on service to a cause—as with Cromwell's Ironsides or Trotsky's Red Army—but, much more commonly, on service to the nation. The inculcation of an extreme nationalism, often of the most rabid or it may be vulgar sort, is universal in the training of all but the very few ideological or religious armies. This is accompanied by the systematic disparagement of the foreigner, and the channeling

of all aggressive tendencies into hatred of the enemy.

Such indoctrination is supplemented by measures to inculcate a sense of solidarity. The newcomer is instructed in the history and traditions of his regiment. He is taught to respect its insignia and its colors. And all this is enhanced by some of the physical arrangements of the military life. The army differs in function from the society that surrounds it and this function requires that it be separate and segregated. It requires a common uniform, and this immediately distinguishes it from the civilian masses. It requires separate housing, in purely military quarters, the barracks. It demands a systematized nomadism moving from one garrison town to another. It demands a separate code of morals and manners from that of the civilian population, so that the normal freedoms of life—to take leave, to change one's employment, in some cases even to marry —are exercised only under surveillance and tutelage, and by permission. All this tends to enhance military solidarity by making the military life self-centered. It is easy, even, to inspire contempt for one's own nationals—the "civvies," *"les pékins," "les bourgeois"*—and so forth. The barracks becomes the world.[3]

Thus because of their centralization, hierarchy, discipline, intercommunication and *esprit de corps,* armies are much more highly organized than any civilian bodies. Few of these attain to the degree of organization obtained by even the most primitive of modern armies. The Roman Catholic Church certainly displays these five features; but it is a voluntary organization which the member may enter or leave as he thinks fit; for those of tepid faith the penalties for disobedience are feeble; its segregation from the laity is much less extreme than that of officer-corps from civilians. Firms and bureaucracies may possess these five characteristics too, but, once again, they are voluntary bodies, the sanctions for indiscipline are feeble and there is no segregation, no very special code of manners or rules that have to be obeyed, and no tutelage. Of political parties only the communist parties of the "popular democracies" resemble the armed forces. Not for nothing have they been described as "lay armies." Their high degree of organization and their formidably energetic *esprit de corps* are of the highest importance to the question of civilian control of the armed forces; [4] yet here again, they are neither as hierarchical, as severely disciplined, as physically interconnected, as armies, nor are they physically and psychologically separated from the rest of the population.

Modern armies, then, are usually far more highly organized than any other association within a state. This is not the only political advantage they possess. The military profession often—though not always—carries with it certain emotional associations. In so far as this is so, the army may enjoy a politically important moral prestige.

The military virtues

"Their sons," wrote Herodotus of the Persians, "are carefully instructed from their fifth to their twentieth year in three things alone—to ride, to draw the bow and to speak the truth." [5] Herein we see the prototype of the famed military virtues. These virtues—bravery, discipline, obedience, self-abnegation, poverty, patriotism, and the like—are associated, by long standing, with the soldier's choice of career. They are values which all esteem. Where they are identified with the military, these acquire a moral halo which is politically of profound importance.

Yet we must be cautious. The military are *not* universally well regarded. In Germany or Japan, up to 1945, their prestige was preternaturally high. In Egypt, during the same period and up to 1952, the profession of arms was despised; likewise, the Chinese soldier was despised until 1949. *Autres pays, autres moeurs.* Furthermore, in any one country, public opinion may be quite different at one period from what it is at another. This has been elegantly demonstrated, for the French army by Girardet.[6] After 1815 there was a reaction against all things military. The soldier was regarded as vulgar, uncouth, brutal. "These soldiers," writes Girardet (echoing the sentiments of that time), "who take up the middle of the pavement, noisy and arrogant; who often behave as in a conquered town, pursuing the women with their gross assiduities. . . ." Yet fifty years later general sentiment favored the soldier. The social prestige of the officer was very high and to marry a daughter to one became an object of middle-class ambition. Instead of stressing their stupidity or their unproductiveness, society sentimentalized over the "life of order, hierarchy, obedience and poverty." [7] Not very much later, after Sedan, the army became *"l'arche sainte,"* its hierarchical nature rendering it the darling of the Right, and its democratic mass basis the favorite of the Left.

Yet at most times and in most countries, traits like courage and discipline and self-sacrifice and patriotism, traits which seem almost characteristically to inhere in "the soldier," are esteemed and cherished. From this there arises, at the lowest, a sympathy for the armed forces; at its highest a veritable mystique.

. . . That it may become as it ought to be, the career of arms requires from those who seek or are called on to pursue it, certain specific qualities which we call the military virtues: valor, fidelity, patriotism. The exercise of these virtues to a very high degree is so essential to the career of arms that they constitute its characteristic feature, define its own peculiar spirit. They are the necessary conditions of the existence of the career, and if they disappeared it would disappear also. How can one conceive of a cowardly soldier, an unfaithful comrade, a warrior who betrays his country? No! To the extent that cowardice, disloyalty and treason arise, there is no force, there are no troops, there is no army. There is only a multitude in arms—and for that very reason more dangerous than any other. . . .

In internal structure, the army is not simply

a collection of men: it is an organism to which union, collaboration and solidarity are indispensable. Fidelity in the army is necessary to make sure that at all times all organs will carry out their duty. For this reason there must be no plots, no disunity, no mutual distrust; watchful of itself the army must expel from its midst, like dead bodies, those elements which do not belong to it in spirit, and whose hearts do not beat in unison with its own. . . .

For the soldier . . . there exists neither the hamlet, nor the region, nor the province, nor the colony: there is for him nothing but the national territory. He has no family, no relatives, no friends, no neighbours: only the people who live and work in the national territory. He has only—in a word—the fatherland; the fatherland in all its material expressions, in the totality of its sentiments and traditions, in all the beauty of its historical evolution and its future ideal. To it he must surrender all; safety, peace, family and life itself.[8]

Sentiments such as these would be re-echoed today in Cairo, Bagdad, Khartum; in Madrid or in Karachi; and wherever they are harbored they help lift the military to power. But even in London, or Washington, or Stockholm, an atmosphere of candor, self-sacrifice and vigor clings to the armed forces, and of all among the "powers that be" there is a tendency to esteem them as the most noble. Where and in so far as this happens, it constitutes a second political strength of the military.

The armed forces then are not only the most highly organized association in the state. They are a continuing corporation with an intense sentiment of solidarity, enjoying, in many cases, considerable favor. This formidable corporate body is more lethally and heavily armed than any other organization in the state, and indeed enjoys a near-monopoly of all effective weapons.

. . .

NOTES

1. What is said of the army here is to be taken also to apply, *mutatis mutandis,* to the air force and the navy.

2. Émile Durkheim, *La Division du Travail Social* (Paris, 1960), p. 99.

3. For proof, if it be needed, witness the plots and escapades that make up the tale of such television programs as *Sergeant Bilko.*

4. See p. 99 ff.

5. Herodotus, *History.* Everyman ed., Vol. 1, p. 72.

6. R. Girardet. *La Societé Militaire dans la France Contemporaine.*

7. *Ibid.,* Chapter 1.

8. Oliveira Salazar, *El Pensamiento de la Revolucion Nacional* (Buenos Aires, 1938), Chapter V, pp. 118–22, "Elogio de las Virtudes Militares."

21. BUREAUCRACY'S OTHER FACE

CHARLES H. PAGE

Possessed of fixed rules and traditional regulations, the American Navy represents the very kind of organization described by S. E. Finer. Yet, within the military organization (or any other bureaucracy), there exists an intricate set of informal norms which provide channels of circumvention of the formal methods of procedure. These unofficial patterns cannot be made public knowledge lest they alter the image of officially sanctioned behavior.

Using his own four-year experience as a naval officer (and participant-observer) as the basis for explaining the nature and function of "bureaucracy's other face," Charles H. Page illustrates the relationship between publicly-ratified and privately-sanctified dimensions of military life. He juxtaposes the conventional channels overtly symbolized by rank and rating with the informal structure marked by spontaneity and camaraderie and shows how an ostensibly "secondary interest group" has a tendency to take on, however temporarily, the characteristics of a "primary interest group." In addition, he presents important insights into "bureaucratic virtuosity" and, like Finer, discusses the difference between the professional military man and the civilian (in and out of uniform).

Charles H. Page is Professor of Sociology at the University of Massachusetts, Amherst. He is a Consulting Editor in Sociology at Random House, the author of Class and American Sociology: From Ward to Ross *(1940; revised 1970), and coauthor, with Robert M. MacIver, of* Society *(1949). With Morroe Berger and Theodore Abel, he is coeditor of* Freedom and Control in Modern Society *(1954). Page is also editor and coauthor of* Sociology and Contemporary Education *(1963).*

The Approach

The following remarks are being set down after having just completed almost four years of duty in the organization under discussion. At no time during that tour was there any attempt by the writer to analyze systematically the bureaucratic structure of which he was a part: from a research viewpoint he was at best a participant observer—with the emphasis upon participant. However, a sociologist let loose in an organization such as the United States Navy cannot avoid the temptation to "sociologize" his own experiences to some extent, illustrated in this instance by random notes and letters which form the basis of this paper and evidenced more generally by various articles recently published in the sociological journals.

For students of social structure, the sociology of professions and the study of bureaucracy, participation in a military organization is professionally instructive. To be sure, active membership carries with it participation much too intense for purposes of research. But the intensity of participation rarely precludes the mental application of conceptual schema, a rough

Reprinted from *Social Forces*, **25** (1946–1947), 88–94, by permission of the author and the University of North Carolina Press.

kind of observational testing of some hypotheses and, on occasion, when the participant "enjoys" an order-issuing position in the social structure, an opportunity to manipulate segments of it and thereby to submit certain hypotheses to a crude pragmatic checking. These form whatever "research" there has been made in support of the generalizations which follow.

The United States Navy as a segment of social organization is an example of rationally organized social structure wherein the officially designated roles are functionally geared to the fulfillment of its prescribed missions. In such structures, Merton has written,

> . . . there is integrated a series of offices, of hierarchized statuses, in which inhere a number of obligations and privileges closely defined by limited and specific rules. Each of these offices contains an area of imputed competence and responsibility. Authority, the power of control which derives from an acknowledged status, inheres in the office and not in the particular person who performs the official rôle. Official action ordinarily occurs within the framework of preexisting rules of the organization. The system of prescribed relations between the various offices involves a considerable degree of formality and clearly defined social distance between the occupants of these positions. Formality is manifested by means of a more or less complicated social ritual which symbolizes and supports the "pecking order" of the various offices. Such formality, which is integrated with the distribution of authority within the system, serves to minimize friction by largely restricting (official) contact to modes which are previously defined by the rules of the organization. Ready calculability of others' behavior and a stable set of mutual expectations is thus built up. Moreover, formality facilitates the interaction of the occupants of offices despite their (possibly hostile) private attitudes toward one another. In this way, the subordinate is protected from the arbitrary action of his superior, since the actions of both are constrained by a mutually recognized set of rules. Specific procedural devices foster objectivity and restrain the "quick passage of impulse into action." [1]

This long quotation ably describes many of the principal structural features of *bureaucracy,* and it is to this sociological category that the Navy (and other military organizations) must be assigned. Each sentence of Merton's statement depicts an aspect of bureaucratic structure of significance to the student of social organization and/or to the participant. Each of his sentences, too, could be used to point up an important feature of the Navy itself: the illustrations suggest themselves.

The approach, then, is one which stems from the functional analysis of social structures. There could be no attempt here, of course, to set down the Navy's total structural profile which such analysis requires. A gigantic contribution could be made to the social sciences, to the Navy and to the nation were this task undertaken. It would involve a thorough and objective study of the roles and established relationships within the Navy, of its goals and the institutionalized instrumentalities for their achievement, of the social pressures of all kinds operating within the structure, of the "occupational psychology" peculiar to it, and, most important, of the functional interrelations among all these. Those particular aspects of the Navy discussed below would form an integral part of the larger analysis. They are also characteristics that struck this student's sociological fancy and, it is maintained, are too frequently overlooked or "taken for granted" by many of the key members of the organization itself.

The Informal Structure

The Navy is a bureaucratic structure; more generally it is a large example of a secondary group. As a complex association it therefore is an instrumental organization designed to fulfill specified goals. The latter are established in the law of the land and receive extensive written expression in codes which govern the Navy's operations, down to the most detailed activities. Study of these codes and of the other documents which blueprint the formal institutional structure provides the Navy's neophyte with a knowledge of the rules, the groupings, and the officially sanctioned systems of procedure. He learns, for example, about missions, bureaus, divisions, sections, fleets, task forces, ranks, rates, courts martial, training programs, personnel selection. It is a complex picture and, especially in recent years, a rapidly changing one, but much of it can be gleaned from "the book."

All of this constitutes the *formal* structure of the Navy. A more systematic account of it than currently exists would be, I believe, of real value to both the professional Navy man, the "oldtimer," and to its new or temporary members. And a thorough documentation of the formal structure by a student of social organization would constitute an example of the kind of study of bureaucracy advocated by Max Weber.

However, such a study would fail to include a very significant part of the organization which is vital in any functional analysis. This aspect shall be termed the *informal structure*. Like the formal, it consists of rules, groupings, and sanctioned systems of procedure. They are informal because they are never recorded in the codes or official blueprints and because they are generated and maintained with a degree of spontaneity always lacking in the activities which make up the formal structure. These rules, groupings, and procedures do, nevertheless, form a structure, for, though not *officially* recognized, they are clearly and semi-permanently established, they are just as "real" and just as compelling on the membership as the elements of the official structure, and they maintain their existence and social significance throughout many changes of personnel.

The informal structure may be viewed as a part of the "culture" created within the organization. Military organization, like many other social structures of the secondary associational type, develops internal procedures, values, and sanctions peculiar to "institutions for the care of segregated persons," to use Willard Waller's expression. These are shaped, to some extent, as a method of circumventing the formal structure; they form the core of the "inmate culture." The Navy, no less than other organizations of semi-isolation such as colleges, penitentiaries, and political parties, has its own *internal* traditions, its own caucuses, cliques, and pressure-groups, its own status-systems and compelling values, its own routines and "grape-vine" procedures, which are the inmate's very own and which are hidden to the outsider and the fresh newcomer.

The latter, whether an enlisted "boot" or the newly commissioned officer about to experience his sixty-day indoctrination, from the viewpoint of this analysis, has two large segments of Navy organization to learn. The high-pressure instruction of the indoctrination school or boot camp, the Navy teacher and his own study of the documents can reveal the intricacies of the Navy's formal structure. This teaching and learning task can be and usually is accomplished quickly and efficiently. But knowledge of the informal structure, which is at least as necessary for successful participation, must be gained through experience in the group itself. The Navy has its own definition of maturity: its measure is the extent to which the individual becomes hep to the inner culture. The speed with which the individual "learns the ropes" is determined by many factors, including his preconceptions of Navy life, the particular niche which he occupies in the service, the sensitivity he displays to the existence and operational significance of the informal structure and, of special importance, his role in the organization as defined by the attitudes and reactions of the other inmates.

The existence and importance of the informal structure of the Navy would hardly be denied by any experienced participant. To be sure, the newly graduated officer of an indoctrination school, having just completed two months' training in the most rarefied, formal Navy atmosphere, sometimes comes smack against the informal structure with a shock of disillusionment. (I have seen this experienced, indeed, by a sociologist-turned-Naval officer, by one whose relative sophistication concerning the nature of social organization would presumably have led him to suspect what he was to encounter.) Nevertheless, the informal structure is shrouded in a group-imposed cloak of semi-mystery: one of its chief features is the sanctity which protects it from exposure to the uninitiated eye. Anyone who ventured to explore and to spell out the intricacies of and the operations within the informal structure of the Navy would very likely be tagged with the kind of "muckraking" label which was attached to Lincoln Steffens' early studies of urban political parties or, on a different level, Freud's explorations of the workings of the human psyche. It is characteristic of the informal structure of bureaucracies, including the Navy's, to resist exposure.

This characteristic is not entirely attributable, by any means, to the fear of the members that unsavory elements will be brought to light. While this fear always plays some role in keeping off the record the "inside picture" of any bureaucracy, it is to one of the features of the informal structure itself that more importance must be assigned. For the informal structure serves the very significant role of providing a *channel of circumvention* of the formally prescribed rules and methods of procedure. No organization feels that it can afford to publicize those methods (by which certain problems are solved, it is important to note) which are antithetical to the officially sanctioned and, in this case, strongly sanctified methods dear to the traditions of the group.

Many pressing problems develop within the Navy, *efficient* solutions for which are not possible within the framework of the official institutional structure. Some of these are solved through openly recognized "extra-legal" methods; in so far as such methods prove useful and are not in extreme opposition to the traditional procedures they tend to become codified and thus to become part of the formal structure. A large illustration of this process would be the array of new personnel practices developed during World War II. However, many other problems continue to be solved through the operation of the informal structure. The persistence of these methods (which are "illegal" rather than "extra-legal") derives from the fact that the problems solved thereby demand circumventional treatment and are, in truth, partly caused by the formality and the officially defined requisites of the bureaucratic structure.

Such a problem is the constant and, to the initiated, conspicuous one of official communication between officers. Official communications in most cases must, according to the regulations, be routed through the "chain of command" for whatever endorsements the officers in the chain judge appropriate. This regulation is clearly an essential requirement from the viewpoint of the efficiency demands of military organization. Its absence would render meaningless the role of commanding officer, and it is thus certain that no attempt would be made to eliminate it. Yet very frequently the circumvention of this regulation appears as precisely the solution of a pressing problem. When such a development occurs the individuals involved, if they are sophisticated in the ways of their organization, will operate on the level of the informal structure wherein a solution is usually possible, and will thereby avoid that bureaucratic frustration so frequently felt by those who are strict followers of "the book." Of course, many problems which are solved by circumventing the chain of command on the informal level are of a self-interest nature and the solutions benefit only the initiating individuals, but there are many others the solutions for which utilize the "grape-vine" machinery which are of significance to the entire unit or units involved.

Whichever the case, resort to the informal methods is usually denied and almost always condemned, sometimes most hotly by those most adept and experienced in their use. This is not to suggest hypocrisy in any conscious sense, but rather to stress that quality of the bureaucratic structure which requires *public* sanctification of the formal procedures and *private* sanctification of the informal. For no experienced member of the organization, in the realization of his dependence upon both, would seriously advocate the elimination of either.

The informal structure of the Navy extends from bottom to top of the official hierarchy and, horizontally, across all branches of the service. Throughout it is marked by and encourages *spontaneity*. Almost the opposite is the case with the formal. Thus the informal structure circumvents, once more, in that it provides an area of behavior for the membership where the rigid demands of protocol and regulation go by the boards.

This characteristic is broadly illustrated by the status and role configurations which develop in all units on the informal level. Whereas the official status hierarchy is overtly symbolized by rank and rate, the informal pattern is revealed only by examination of the distinctly unofficial and frequently semi-concealed inter-personal attitudes of the membership. Application of the techniques of sociography to a Naval unit would turn up the attraction and repulsion patterns, the "natural leaders" and the "rejected types" which typify the informal structure. Rarely, if ever, would this configuration parallel the formal. The latter, to be sure, influences the shaping of the informal status pattern, evidenced, for example, in the fact that the demarcation between enlisted personnel and officers usually (though not always: witness its breakdown in flight crews) is present on both the formal and informal

levels; or in the fact that the officially established social isolation of the commanding officer is frequently matched informally. This is only to say, however, that the informal and formal structures affect each other, as do all elements within the organization. An essential function of the informal structure is the provision of a spontaneity area wherein abuse of officialdom is a chief mark.

The need for such a spontaneity area is more keenly felt and its development more extensive and apparent in those locations more separated from the "outer world" than in Naval activities in the United States. This is evidenced in the various land-based units in the Pacific known to the writer. One extreme example, an island air-base whose position and absence of native population guaranteed almost no contact with extra-Navy persons, had experienced a major structural change from the time that it had been based in the United States. In this case the informal structure had almost altogether lost its private sanctification and stood, in large measure, as the officially recognized pattern of this group of temporary island residents. One visiting officer described this as a "breakdown" of the organization. This was clearly not the case, as shown by the high morale and the effective accomplishment of missions. What had "broken down" was a large part of the formal structure, or rather it had been submerged as the informal structure rose into overt recognition and use. Fortunately the "skipper" as well as several other officers and petty officers were "natural leaders": their status and role definitions were somewhat parallel in the two structures. However, unmistakable indications of the superordination of the informal included the replacement of the social isolation of the commanding officer by his very keen participation in all activities of the unit, the submergence of the rejected types whatever their rank or rate to the informally defined roles, the emergence of the natural leaders to what amounted to official recognition, the abandonment of most of the officially governing protocol (except in the treatment of visitors), and accomplishment of the day-to-day and long-run tasks with efficiency, zeal, and spontaneous initiative not characteristic of official bureaucratic machinery.

This extreme case of the emergence of the "hidden" informal structure illustrates a process which is always present to some degree when a Naval unit moves from an area which provides a surrounding community, say a west-coast city, to one where it must act as its own community, say a small Pacific atoll. An important implication for the member of such an organization who assumes command responsibility or assists in its administration is that he should learn as much as possible about the informal structure of which he is a part as early in the game as possible. Good skippers do.

For the good skipper realizes, whatever the language he might use to describe it, that important changes are due whenever the segment of bureaucratic structure which he directs shifts scene so as to be forced to turn in upon itself in seeking a *community* of living. The Naval unit, ordinarily and essentially an association promoting officially defined secondary interests, to use R. M. MacIver's distinction, becomes as well a temporary primary interest group. The commanding officer adds to his directorship of the means organization the role of participant, and perhaps leader, in an ends group.

This distinction permits a further characterization on the informal structure: it contains the elements which typify the primary group. Within it can be observed the development of friendships and cliques, the interplay of love and hate, award and punishment at intimate face-to-face level and spontaneity of expression. The intense impersonality of the official bureaucracy is frequently matched in degree by the highly personal quality found unofficially within it. The primary nature of the informal structure, which is partially compensatory and is manifested in varying extents when the Naval unit is "stateside," becomes very markedly compensatory and shows itself much more clearly when the organization is semi- or wholly isolated. As the unit becomes (by necessity) its own community, then, the otherwise hidden face of the informal structure appears. Sometimes its emergence is quite upsetting to the green officer, just recently carefully trained in the details of the official structure but untutored in the off-the-record ways of the Navy folk. Incidentally, this educational neglect could be remedied.

The green officer, however, usually learns his organizational ropes rapidly on his island base. And he may learn them, in a sense, too well. For when the unit moves on to a thickly populated area of friendly people, say Manila or Shanghai, or back to the "States," it moves through a reverse organizational process. As it again gains an adjacent outer world its own community tends to disappear, the informal structure regains its inner sanctity, and formal protocol and regulation take on their original roles. This readjustment and realignment of the elements of the total structure leave some individuals lagging —both officers and enlisted. They are often the executive or personnel officer's toughest problems.

There are a number of other personnel peculiarities of the Navy which are intimately related to the structural features of the organization. The following section points to some of them.

Bureaucratic Structure and Personality

Merton, in the article quoted earlier, describes the confusion of ends and means which so frequently occurs in bureaucratic structures. The governing rules of such organizations which prescribe the methods of procedure and officially define the relationships among the parts of the structure, designed as means, often become for the membership, or part of it, ends in themselves. Certainly all established bureaucracies are marked, with varying degrees of emphasis, by the phenomenon of "instrumental values becoming terminal values."

This is outstandingly the case in military organizations, including the Navy. Military organizations must, if they are to fulfill their basic purposes, so carefully define the rules and so engender devotion to them that "reliability of response" is guaranteed. It is clear that the demands of battle, to use the extreme and necessarily the governing example, require nothing less. Much of the official experience of Naval personnel is "drill" which teaches a devotion to procedures without which a Naval commander would be, for practical purposes, without command. The need for such routinization of response stands behind the traditional use, in both Navy and Army, of close order drill which forms such an imposing and wearying part of the early training of both enlisted and officer personnel. The willing acceptance of close order drill by the newcomers is frequently negated by the drillmaster's identification of this *method* of disciplining response with end values.

Close order drill is the most conspicuous example of the routinization of procedure which typifies military life. The detail and precision of definition of, say, the manual of arms are extended to every segment of the Navy's formal structure. Thus there are the officially correct ways of writing letters, greeting fellow personnel, executing air maneuvers, loading weapons, burying the dead, reporting infractions of the rules, fixing the seating for dinners, hailing a ship from a boat, packing one's clothing for travel, *ad infinitum*. The absorption of these various techniques and methods represents the formal side of learning the Navy procedure. It represents also a process which all too frequently sanctifies for the learners the methods themselves, induces a non-logical "pride of craft," and enhances the role and sometimes the prestige of the "bureaucratic virtuosos." The latter are found throughout the official hierarchy. The master of red tape is as likely to be the long-experienced petty officer whose knowledge of the niceties of "the book" frequently awes the recruit as the veteran admiral who discourages his new flag secretary by constant correctness re rule and protocol. Part of the measure of the effectiveness of a member of the organization is, indeed, precisely his mastery of the details of the elaborate mechanisms of correct procedure.

Such mastery, however, when combined with allegiance to the methods reaching the point of sanctification lessens effectiveness. Colonel Blimps are by no means confined to the British Army, and as in the case of that fictitious but realistic arch-type, they are most subject to "exposure" and to "shelving" during times of rapid change in the organizational structure. For sanctification of the methods always induces a defense of those which have been long established, and creates on the level of personality not only resistance to necessary change but an inflexibility which handicaps the organization. In such instances response has become, as it were, too reliable. This situation encourages the sudden elevation to positions of importance of many individuals whose records during the comparative static days of peace were marked by careless observance of traditional methods and by an unseemly desire to institute change. Witness, for example, the rapid rise of the "flying admirals" and the somewhat reluctant recognition of the achievements of Colonel Carlson and his Marine "Raiders." In similar manner, the wartime requirement of increasing flexibility gives scope to the abilities and initiative of many reserve officers whose personalities are not weighted with a near life-time of tribute to traditional procedures. However great the contribution of the reserve officers to the war effort has been in this respect, it must also be noted that many of them responded so intensely to their indoctrination in the formal ways of the Navy that their keen allegiance to the latter seriously lessened whatever flexibility and initiative traits they otherwise possessed.

This confusion of ends and means, common to all bureaucratic structures, assumes an especially interesting and significant form in the Navy's concept of *tradition*. Usually tradition is taken to mean the set of morale-evoking values associated with the deeds of heroes, the accomplishment of large victories in the past, and the esteemed virtues which should be sought by Naval personnel. These may be termed the *spiritual tradition* of the Navy and form, of course, a segment of that more extensive complex, the spiritual tradition of the nation. Both nation and Navy make effective and necessary use of these traditional values in the stimulation of loyalty, morale, and pride. The Navy as a professional organization could not operate successfully in the absence of this tradition which provides the ultimate judgment of current achievements and therefore performs an essential function. Frequently, however, the values of the spiritual tradition become attached to considerations which are essentially matters of technological or organizational efficiency. The latter problems, such as the question of building more aircraft carriers and fewer battleships or the elimination of the bureau structure in the Navy Department or the methods of selecting officer personnel, demand "cold-blooded" analysis and solution. It is no doubt a sensible as well as a necessary procedure to evoke the glories of the past to enhance loyalty and pride in present membership. But it is confusing and sometimes harmful to argue the merits of proposed organizational or technological changes on the basis of appeal to traditional practice. Sacred indeed are the grand exploits of John Paul Jones, but there should be no sacred significance attached to the fact that his ships were wooden.

The identification of traditional values with matters of sheer efficacy is an inevitable process in a bureaucratic structure of long standing. This is not to say that all members are unable to see this distinction and to reason quite clearly about even such tradition-loaded problems as the present proposal to combine the two services; but it is to say that bureaucratic structure is constantly exerting a pressure on its membership to mentally attach the symbols of sacred tradition to the secular concerns of current moment. This pressure is felt throughout the membership: by temporary as well as permanent personnel, by sailor and officer both. The degree to which it shapes the thinking, and therefore affects decision-making, however, varies greatly from group to group within the structure.

Least susceptible to non-logical identification of traditional values with instrumental concerns are probably the "one-hitch" sailors of peace-time and the "duration" enlisted personnel of war. The latter are in several senses the "people's Navy": their values reflect to a much greater extent than others their civilian training and experiences. This is somewhat less true of reserve officers who are also "civilians in uniform," but who have usually experienced an especially intense indoctrination which always includes an emphasis upon Navy tradition. The majority of reserve officers "mature" fairly rapidly after indoctrination, but a few, at least, retain almost a reverential awe of all to which the symbols of the traditions of their temporary profession have been attached. This attachment is felt even more keenly by the professional sailor, i.e., the enlisted man who repeatedly "ships over" and makes his career the Navy. It is most apparent among the Annapolis trained U.S.N. officers, the true professionals of Naval science and practice. Generalizations concerning personality tendencies of any of these groups are dangerous because of the wide range of temperament and intellectual attainment which exists in each of them.

It may be hypothesized, however, that in the last group, the "regular" officers of the Navy, exist certain attitude and behavior patterns peculiar to the occupation and perpetuated by the character of the bureaucratic structure. Of these, strong in-group loyalty is the most often remarked and most easily discerned. While it is true that the graduates of the United States Naval Academy develop internal cliques and antagonisms, these are generally overshadowed by a strong feeling of common ties with each other and an attitude of dissociation toward all outgroups. This feeling and this attitude are the result, of course, of the common Annapolis training at the start and the subsequent experiences largely confined within an occupational structure of bureaucratic design and marked by compelling values of professional tradition. It is not surprising, however annoying it may be on occasion, that Naval officers feel more "at home" with, say, their British equivalents (in whom may be perceived very similar occupational traits) than with American representatives of other professions such as law or medicine. Nor is it surprising that reserve officers, sometimes finding themselves, so to say, "on the outside," tend to develop counter-attitudes which enhance their own self-view at the expense of the "trade school boys," to use a symptomatic epithet. From the viewpoint of the Annapolis man, the reserve officer is an outsider lacking proper initiation into and maturation within the "culture" of his own world. The demands of war often cause the closest kind of collaboration and of sympathy and understanding between regular and reserve, but as these demands lessen and the Navy approaches the more static stage of the war-peace cycle, the in-group-out-group manifestations reappear.

Identification with the in-group and dissociative attitudes toward the outsider are interestingly illustrated by the professional Navy man's reaction to the Navy's "client-public." The officeholders of many bureaucratic structures, as they become expert in the skills of their organizations and as they take on the "bureaucratic viewpoint," tend to develop antipathy toward the clients the organizations serve. This is no less, and perhaps more, the case with the Navy than with civilian administrative bureaus of the Federal Government. The client-public of the Navy is the nation itself; it is understandable that this relationship receives strong emphasis in the training of officers and major rank in their professional ethic. All officers would insist that they are indeed the servants of the people. However, there is within the governmental agencies perhaps no professional body which, on the level of attitude, so dissociates itself from its citizen clients and their political representatives. To be sure, this is in part the result of the Naval officer's officially correct insistence to stay "free of politics," but it is also a manifestation of the bureaucratic expert's inevitable antagonism toward the inexpert persons he serves. Occasionally this antagonism reaches the point of revulsion, and almost always it leads to in-group criticism of the member who sometimes strays from the Navy fold into the area of political citizenship. In the best of the tradition going back to Jones himself I am the people's servant, so the Navy mind runs, but keep me free of the plain clothes citizen and the politician who cannot tell a tactic from a strategy, a binnacle from a pelican hook. Repeatedly the civilian in or out of uniform resents such an attitude which may appear to him as an unjustifiable ambivalence. The "justification," it has been argued, is to be found in the character of the structure of which the Naval officer is a part.

NOTE

1. R. K. Merton, "Bureaucratic Structure and Personality," *Social Forces,* 18 (1940), 561–568.

Societies and Communities

22. THE FOLK SOCIETY·

ROBERT REDFIELD

Although many scholars have discussed the "folk-urban continuum," few have had greater impact than anthropologist Robert Redfield. Here his classic article, "The Folk Society," is reprinted to illustrate both the utility of ideal types as methodological and conceptual tools and to indicate the specific form and content of the simplest form of communal social organization.

Redfield begins by suggesting that one way to understand oneself is to examine something quite different. Thus, an ideal type of folk society is contrasted with modern urbanized society. The folk society is characterized as small, isolated, nonliterate, and homogeneous; it has a strong sense of group solidarity. The ways of living are conventionalized into a coherent system that was earlier defined as "culture." Behavior in the folk society is traditional, spontaneous, and personal; there is no legislation or habit of experiment and reflection for intellectual ends. Kinship, its relationships and institutions are the type categories of experience and the familial group is the unit of action. The sacred prevails over the secular; the economy is one of status rather than of market. These related characteristics are restated in terms of "folk mentality."

Robert Redfield died in 1958. At the time of his death he was Robert M. Hutchins Distinguished Service Professor at the University of Chicago. Redfield's long list of publications include four monographs: Tepotztlan *(1930),* Chan Kom *(1934),* The Folk

Reprinted from the *American Journal of Sociology,* **52** (1947), 293–308, by permission of the University of Chicago Press.

Culture of Yucatan (*1941*), *and* The Village That Chose Progress: Chan Kom Revisited (*1950*). *He also wrote* The Primitive World and Its Transformations (*1953*), The Little Community (*1955*), *and* Peasant Society and Culture (*1956*).

–1–

Understanding of society in general and of our own modern urbanized society in particular can be gained through consideration of the societies least like our own: the primitive, or folk, societies.[1] All societies are alike in some respects, and each differs from others in other respects; the further assumption made here is that folk societies have certain features in common which enable us to think of them as a type —a type which contrasts with the society of the modern city.[2]

This type is ideal, a mental construction. No known society precisely corresponds with it, but the societies which have been the chief interest of the anthropologist most closely approximate it. The construction of the type depends, indeed, upon special knowledge of tribal and peasant groups. The ideal folk society could be defined through assembling, in the imagination, the characters which are logically opposite those which are to be found in the modern city, only if we had first some knowledge of nonurban peoples to permit us to determine what, indeed, are the characteristic features of modern city living. The complete procedure requires us to gain acquaintance with many folk societies in many parts of the world and to set down in words general enough to describe most of them those characteristics which they have in common with each other and which the modern city does not have.

In short, we move from folk society to folk society, asking ourselves what it is about them that makes them like each other and different from the modern city. So we assemble the elements of the ideal type. The more elements we add, the less will any one real society correspond to it.

As the type is constructed, real societies may be arranged in an order of degree of resemblance to it. The conception develops that any one real society is more or less "folk." But the more elements we add, the less possible it becomes to arrange real societies in a single order of degree of resemblance to the type, because one of two societies will be found to resemble the ideal type strongly in one character and weakly in another, while in the next society strong resemblance will lie in the latter character and not in the former. This situation, however, is an advantage, for it enables us to ask and perhaps answer questions, first, as to whether certain characters tend to be found together in most societies, and then, if certain of them do, why.

Anyone attempting to describe the ideal folk society must take account of and in large degree include certain characterizations which have been made of many students, each of whom has been attentive to some but not to all aspects of the contrast between folk and modern urban society. Certain students have derived the characterization from examination of a number of folk societies and have generalized upon them in the light of contrast provided by modern urban society; the procedure defined above and followed by the writer. This is illustrated by Goldenweiser's characterization of five primitive societies. He says that they are small, isolated, nonliterate; that they exhibit local cultures; that they are relatively homogeneous with regard to the distribution of knowledge, attitudes, and functions among the population; that the individual does not figure as a conspicuous unit; and that knowledge is not explicitly systematized.[3]

In other cases the students have compared the state of certain societies at an early time with the same, or historical descendant of the same, society at a later time. In this way Maine arrived at his influential contrasts between society based on kinship and society based on territory, and between a society of status and one of contract.[4] In the case of this procedure, as in the case of the next, broad and illuminating conceptions are offered us to apply to folk societies as we contrast them with modern urban society. We are to find out if one of the contrasting terms is properly applicable to folk society and the other term to modern urban society.

In the work of still other students there is apparent no detailed comparison of folk with urbanized societies or of early society with later; rather, by inspection of our own society or of society in general, contrasting aspects of all society are recognized and named. This procedure is perhaps never followed in the unqualified manner just described, for in the instances about to be mentioned there is evidence that folk or ancient society has been compared with modern urbanized society. Nevertheless, the emphasis placed by men of this group is upon characteristics which, contrasting logically, in real fact coexist in every society and help to make it up. Here belongs Tönnies' contrast between *Gemeinschaft* and *Gesellschaft,* or that aspect of society which appears in the relations that develop without the deliberate intention of anyone out of the mere fact that men live together, as contrasted with that aspect of society which appears in the relations entered into deliberately by independent individuals through agreement to achieve certain recognized ends.[5] Comparable is Durkheim's distinction between that social solidarity which results from the sharing of common attitudes and sentiments and that which results from the complementary functional usefulnesses of the members of the group. In the "social segment"—the form of society existing in terms of "mechanical solidarity"—the law is "repressive"; in the "social organ"—the

form of society existing in terms of "organic solidarity"—the law is "restitutive." [6]

It may be asked how closely the constructed type arrived at by any one investigator who follows the procedure sketched above will resemble that reached by another doing the same. It may be supposed that to the extent to which the real societies examined by the one investigator constitute a sample of the range and variety of societies similar to the sample constituted by the societies examined by the other, and to the extent that the general conceptions tentatively held by the one are similar to those held by the other, the results will be (except as modified by other factors) the same. For the purposes of understanding which are served by the method of the constructed type, however, it is not necessary to consider the question. The type is an imagined entity, created only because through it we may hope to understand reality. Its function is to suggest aspects of real societies which deserve study, and especially to suggest hypotheses as to what, under certain defined conditions, may be generally true about society. Any ideal type will do; although it is safe to assert that the ideal construction has most heuristic value which depends on close and considered knowledge of real folk societies and which is guided by an effective scientific imagination—whatever that may be.

–2–

"The conception of a 'primitive society' which we ought to form," wrote Sumner, "is that of small groups scattered over a territory." [7] The folk society is a small society. There are no more people in it than can come to know each other well, and they remain in long association with each other. Among the Western Shoshone the individual parental family was the group which went about, apart from other families, collecting food; a group of families would assemble and so remain for a few weeks, from time to time, to hunt together; during the winter months such a group of families would form a single camp.[8] Such a temporary village included perhaps a hundred people. The hunting or food-collecting bands considered by Steward, representing many parts of the world, contained, in most cases, only a few score people.[9] A Southwestern Pueblo contained no more than a few thousand persons.

The folk society is an isolated society. Probably there is no real society whose members are in complete ignorance of the existence of people other than themselves; the Andamanese, although their islands were avoided by navigators for centuries, knew of outsiders and occasionally came in contact with Malay or Chinese visitors.[10] Nevertheless, the folk societies we know are made up of people who have little communication with outsiders, and we may conceive of the ideal folk society as composed of persons having communication with no outsider.

This isolation is one half of a whole of which the other half is intimate communication among the members of the society. A group of recent castaways is a small and isolated society, but it is not a folk society; and if the castaways have come from different ships and different societies, there will have been no previous intimate communication among them, and the society will not be composed of people who are much alike.

May the isolation of the folk society be identified with the physical immobility of its members? In building this ideal type, we may conceive of the members of the society as remaining always within the small territory they occupy. There are some primitive peoples who have dwelt from time immemorial in the same small valley, and who rarely leave it.[11] Certain of the Pueblos of the American Southwest have been occupied by the same people or their descendants for many generations. On the other hand, some of the food-collecting peoples, such as the Shoshone

Indians and certain aborigines of Australia, move about within a territory of very considerable extent; and there are Asiatic folk groups that make regular seasonal migrations hundreds of miles in extent.

It is possible to conceive of the members of such a society as moving about physically without communicating with members of other groups than their own. Each of the Indian villages of the midwest highlands of Guatemala is a folk society distinguishable by its customs and even by the physical type of its members from neighboring villages, yet the people are great travelers, and in the case of one of the most distinct communities, Chichicastenango, most of the men travel far and spend much of their time away from home.[12] This does not result, however, in much intimate communication between those traveling villagers and other peoples. The gipsies have moved about among the various peoples of the earth for generations, and yet they retain many of the characteristics of a folk society.

Through books the civilized people communicate with the minds of other people and other times, and an aspect of the isolation of the folk society is the absence of books. The folk communicate only by word of mouth; therefore the communication upon which understanding is built is only that which takes place among neighbors, within the little society itself. The folk has no access to the thought and experience of the past, whether of other peoples or of their own ancestors, such as books provide. Therefore, oral tradition has no check or competitor. Knowledge of what has gone before reaches no farther back than memory and speech between old and young can make it go; behind "the time of our grandfathers" all is legendary and vague. With no form of belief established by written record, there can be no historical sense, such as civilized people have, no theology, and no basis for science in recorded experiment. The only form of accumulation of experience, except the tools and other enduring articles of manufacture, is the increase of wisdom which comes as the individual lives longer; therefore the old, knowing more than the young can know until they too have lived that long, have prestige and authority.

The people who make up a folk society are much alike. Having lived in long intimacy with one another, and with no others, they have come to form a single biological type. The somatic homogeneity of local, inbred populations has been noted and studied. Since the people communicate with one another and with no others, one man's learned ways of doing and thinking are the same as another's. Another way of putting this is to say that in the ideal folk society, what one man knows and believes is the same as what all men know and believe. Habits are the same as customs. In real fact, of course, the differences among individuals in a primitive group and the different chances of experience prevent this ideal state of things from coming about. Nevertheless, it is near enough to the truth for the student of a real folk society to report it fairly well by learning what goes on in the minds of a few of its members, and a primitive group has been presented, although sketchily, as learned about from a single member. The similarity among the members is found also as one generation is compared with its successor. Old people find young people doing, as they grow up, what the old people did at the same age, and what they have come to think right and proper. This is another way of saying that in such a society there is little change.

The members of the folk society have a strong sense of belonging together. The group which an outsider might recognize as composed of similar persons different from members of other groups is also the group of people who see their own resemblances and feel correspondingly united. Communicating intimately with each other, each has a strong claim on the sympathies of the others. Moreover, against such knowledge as they have of societies other than their own, they emphasize their own mutual likeness and value themselves as compared with others. They say of themselves "we" as against all others, who are "they." [13]

Thus we may characterize the folk society as small, isolated, nonliterate, and homogeneous, with a strong sense of group solidarity. Are we not soon to acknowledge the simplicity of the technology of the ideal folk society? Something should certainly be said about the tools and tool-making of this generalized primitive group, but it is not easy to assign a meaning to "simple," in connection with technology which will do justice to the facts as known from the real folk societies. The preciseness with which each tool, in a large number of such tools, meets its needs in the case of the Eskimo, for example, makes one hesitate to use the word "simple." Some negative statements appear to be safe: secondary and tertiary tools—tools to make tools—are relatively few as compared with primary tools; there is no making of artifacts by multiple, rapid, machine manufacture; there is little or no use of natural power.

There is not much division of labor in the folk society: what one person does is what another does. In the ideal folk society all the tools and ways of production are shared by everybody. The "everybody" must mean "every adult man" or "every adult woman," for the obvious exception to the homogeneity of the folk society lies in the differences between what men do and know and what women do and know. These differences are clear and unexceptional (as compared with our modern urban society where they are less so). "Within the local group there is no such thing as a division of labor save as between the sexes," writes Radcliffe-Brown about the Andaman Islanders. ". . . Every man is expected to be able to hunt pig, to harpoon turtle and to catch fish, and also to cut a canoe, to make bows and arrows and all the other objects that are made by men." [14] So all men share the same interests and have, in general, the same experience of life.

We may conceive, also, of the ideal folk society as a group economically independent of all others: the people produce what they consume and consume what they produce. Few, if any, real societies are completely in this situation; some Eskimo groups perhaps most closely approach it. Although each little Andamanese band could get along without getting anything from any other, exchange of goods occurred between bands by a sort of periodic gift-giving.

The foregoing characterizations amount, roughly, to saying that the folk society is a little world off by itself, a world in which the recurrent problems of life are met by all its members in much the same way. This statement, while correct enough, fails to emphasize an important, perhaps the important, aspect of the folk society. The ways in which the members of the society meet the recurrent problems of life are conventionalized ways; they are the results of long intercommunication within the group in the face of these problems; and these conventionalized ways have become interrelated within one another so that they constitute a coherent and self-consistent system. Such a system is what we mean in saying that the folk society is characterized by "a culture." A culture is an organization or integration of conventional understandings. It is, as well, the acts and the objects, in so far as they represent the type characteristic of that society, which express and maintain these understandings. In the folk society this integrated whole, this system, provides for all the recurrent needs of the individual from birth to death and of the society through the seasons and the years. The society is to be described, and distinguished from others, largely by presenting this system.

This is not the same as saying, as was said early in this paper, that in the folk society what one man does is the same as what another man does. What one man does in a mob is the same as what another man does, but a mob is not a folk society. It is, so far as culture is concerned, its very antithesis.[15] The members of a mob (which is a kind of "mass") each do the same thing, it is true, but it is a very immediate and particular thing, and it is done without much reference to tradition. It does not depend upon and express a great many conventional understandings related to one another. A mob has no culture. The folk society exhibits culture to the greatest conceivable degree. A mob is an aggregation of people doing the same simple thing simultaneously. A folk society is an organization of people doing many different things successively as well as simultaneously. The members of a mob act with reference to the same object of attention. The members of a folk society are guided in acting by previously established comprehensive and interdependent conventional understandings; at any one time they do many different things, which are complexly related to one another to express collective sentiments and conceptions. When the turn comes for the boy to do what a man does, he does what a man does; thus, though in the end the experiences of all individuals of the same sex are alike, the activities of the society, seen at a moment of time, are diverse, while interdependent and consistent.

The Papago Indians, a few hundred of them, constituted a folk society in southern Arizona. Among these Indians a war party was not so simple a thing as a number of men going out together to kill the enemy. It was a complex activity involving everybody in the society both before, during, and after the expedition and dramatizing the religious and moral ideas fundamental to Papago life.[16] Preparation for the expedition involved many practical or ritual acts on the part of the immediate participants, their wives and children, previously successful warriors, and many others. While the party was away, the various relatives of the warriors had many things to do or not to do—prayer, fasting, preparation of ritual paraphernalia, etc. These were specialized activities, each appropriate to just that kind of relative or other category of person. So the war was waged by everybody. These activities, different and special as they were, interlocked, so to speak, with each other to make a large whole, the society-during-a-war-expedition. And all these specialized activities obeyed fundamental principles, understood by all and expressed and reaffirmed in the very forms of the acts—the gestures of the rituals, the words of songs, the implied or expressed explanations and admonitions of the elders to the younger people. All understood that the end in view was the acquisition by the group of the supernatural power of the slain enemy. This power, potentially of great positive value, was dangerous, and the practices and rituals had as their purposes first the success of the war party and then the draining-off of the supernatural power acquired by the slaying into a safe and "usable" form.

We may say, then, that in the folk society conventional behavior is strongly patterned: it tends to conform to a type or a norm. These patterns are interrelated in thought and in action with one another, so that one tends to evoke others and to be consistent with the others. Every customary act among the Papago when the successful warriors return is consistent with and is a special form of the general conceptions held as to supernatural power. We may still further say that the patterns of what people think should be done are closely consistent with what they believe is done, and that there is one way, or a very few conventional ways, in which everybody has some understanding and some share, of meeting each need that arises.[17] The culture of a folk society is, therefore, one of those wholes which is greater than its parts. Gaining a livelihood takes support from religion, and the relations of men to men are justified in the conceptions held of the supernatural world or in some other aspect of the culture. Life, for the member of the folk society, is not one activity and then another and different one; it is one large activity out of which one part may not be separated without affecting the rest.

A related characteristic of the folk society was implied when it was declared that the specialized activities incident to the Papago war party obeyed fundamental principles understood by all. These "principles" had to do with the ends of living, as conceived by the Papago. A near-ultimate good for the Papago was the acquisition of supernatural power. This end was not questioned; it was a sort of axiom in terms of which many lesser activities were understood. This suggests that we may say of the folk society that its ends are taken as given. The activities incident to the war party may be regarded as merely complementarily useful acts, aspects of the division of labor. They may also, and more significantly, be seen as expressions of unquestioned common ends. The folk society exists not so much in the exchange of useful functions as in common understandings as to the ends given. The ends are not stated as matters of doctrine, but are implied by the many acts which make up the living that goes on in the society. Therefore, the morale of a folk society—its power to act consistently over periods of time and to meet crises effectively is not dependent upon discipline exerted by force or upon devotion to some single principle of action but to the concurrence and consistency of many or all of the actions and conceptions which make up the whole round of life. In the trite phrase, the folk society is a "design for living."

What is done in the ideal folk society is done not because somebody or some people decided, at once, that it should be done, but because it seems "necessarily" to flow from the very nature of things. There is, moreover, no disposition to reflect upon traditional acts and consider them objectively and critically. In short, behavior in the folk society is traditional, spontaneous, and uncritical. In any real folk society, of course, many things are done as a result of decision as to that particular action, but as to that class of actions tradition is the sufficient authority. The Indians decide now to go on a hunt; but it is not a matter of debate whether or not one should, from time to time, hunt.

The folkways are the ways that grow up out of long and intimate association of men with each other; in the society of our conception all the ways are folkways. Men act with reference to each other by understandings which are tacit and traditional. There are no formal contracts or other agreements. The rights and obligations of the individual come about not by special arrangement; they are, chiefly, aspects of the position of the individual as a person of one sex or the other, one age-group or another, one occupational group or another, and as one occupying just that position in a system of relationships which are traditional in the society. The individual's status is thus in large part fixed at birth; it changes as he lives, but it changes in ways which were "foreordained" by the nature of his particular society. The institutions of the folk society are of the sort which has been called "crescive"; they are not of the sort that is created deliberately for special purposes, as was the juvenile court. So, too, law is made up of the traditional conceptions of rights and obligations and the customary procedures whereby these rights and obligations are assured; legislation has no part in it.

If legislation has no part in the law of the ideal folk society, neither has codification, still less jurisprudence. Radin has collected material suggesting the limited extent to which real primitive people do question custom and do systematize their knowledge.[18] In the known folk societies they do these things only to a limited extent. In the ideal folk society there is no objectivity and no systematization of knowledge as guided by what seems to be its "internal" order. The member of this mentally constructed society does not stand off from his customary conduct and subject it to scrutiny apart from its meaning for him as that meaning is defined in culture. Nor is there any habitual exercise of classification, experiment, and abstraction for its own sake, least of all for the sake of intellectual ends. There is common practical knowledge, but there is no science.

Behavior in the folk society is highly conventional, custom fixes the rights and duties of individuals, and knowledge is not critically examined or objectively and systematically formulated; but it must not be supposed that primitive man is a sort of automaton in which custom is the mainspring. It would be as mistaken to think of primitive man as strongly aware that he is constrained by custom. Within the limits set by custom there is invitation to excel in performance. There is lively competition, a sense of opportunity, and a feeling that what the culture moves one to do is well worth doing. "There is no drabness in such a life. It has about it all the allurements of personal experience, very much one's own, of competitive skill, of things well done."[19] The interrelations and high degree of consistency among the elements of custom which are presented to the individual declare to him the importance of making his endeavors in the directions indicated by tradition. The culture sets goals which stimulate action by giving meaning to it.[20]

It has been said that the folk society is small and that its members have lived in long and intimate association with one another. It has also been said that in such societies there is little critical or abstract thinking. These characteristics are related to yet another characteristic of the folk society: behavior is personal, not impersonal. A "person" may be defined as that social object which I feel to respond to situations as I do, with all the sentiments and interests which I feel to be my own; a person is myself in another form, his qualities and values are inherent within him, and his significance for me is not merely one of utility. A "thing," on the other hand, is a social object which has no claim upon my sympathies, which responds to me, as I conceive it, mechanically; its value for me exists in so far as it serves my end. In the folk society all human beings admitted to the society are treated as persons; one does not deal impersonally ("thing-fashion") with any other participant in the little world of that society. Moreover, in the folk society much besides human beings is treated personally. The pattern of behavior which is first suggested by the inner experience of the individual—his wishes, fears, sensitivenesses, and interests of all sorts—is projected into all objects with which he comes into contact. Thus nature, too, is treated personally: the elements, the features of the landscape, the animals, and especially anything in the environment which by its appearance or behavior suggests that it has the attributes of mankind—to all these are attributed qualities of the human person.[21]

In short, the personal and intimate life of the child in the family is extended, in the folk society, into the social world of the adult and even into inanimate objects. It is not merely that relations in such a society are personal; it is also that they are familial. The first contacts made as the infant becomes a person are with other persons; moreover, each of these first persons, he comes to learn, has a particular kind of relation to him which is associated with that one's genealogical position. The individual finds himself fixed within a constellation of familial relationships. The kinship connections provide a pattern in terms of which, in the ideal folk society, all personal relations are conventionalized and categorized. All relations are personal. But relations are not, in content of specific behavior, the same for everyone. As a mother is different from a father, and a grandson from a nephew, so are these classes of personal relationship, originating in genealogical connection, extended outward into all relationships

whatever. In this sense, the folk society is a familial society. Lowie[22] as demonstrated the qualification that is to be introduced into the statement of Maine[23] that the primitive society is organized in terms of kinship rather than territory. It is true that the fact that men are neighbors contributes to their sense of belonging together. But the point to be emphasized in understanding the folk society is that whether mere contiguity or relationship as brother or as son is the circumstance uniting men into the society, the result is a group of people among whom prevail the personal and categorized relationships that characterize families as we know them, and in which the patterns of kinship tend to be extended outward from the group of genealogically connected individuals into the whole society. The kin are the type persons for all experience.

This general conception may be resolved into component or related conceptions. In the folk society family relationships are clearly distinguished from one another. Very special sorts of behavior may be expected by a mother's brother of his sister's son, and this behavior will be different from that expected by a father's brother of his brother's son. Among certain Australian tribes animals killed by a hunter must be divided so that nine or ten certain parts must be given to nine or ten corresponding relatives of the successful hunter—the right ribs to the father's brother, a piece of the flank to the mother's brother, and so on.[24] The tendency to extend kinship outward takes many special forms. In many primitive societies kinship terms and kinship behavior (in reduced degree) are extended to persons not known to be genealogically related at all, but who are nevertheless regarded as kin. Among the central Australians, terms of relationship are extended "so as to embrace all persons who come into social contact with one another. . . . In this way the whole society forms a body of relatives."[25] In the folk society groupings which do not arise out of genealogical connection are few, and those that do exist tend to take on the attributes of kinship. Ritual kinship is common in primitive and peasant societies in the forms of blood brotherhood, godparental relationships, and other ceremonial sponsorships.[26] These multiply kinship connections; in these cases the particular individuals to be united depend upon choice. Furthermore, there is frequently a recognizedly fictitious or metaphorical use of kinship terms to designate more casual relationships, as between host and guest or between worshiper and deity.[27]

The real primitive and peasant societies differ very greatly as to the forms assumed by kinship. Nevertheless, it is possible to recognize two main types. In one of these the connection between husband and wife is emphasized, while neither one of the lineages, matrilineal or patrilineal, is singled out as contrasted with the other. In such a folk society the individual parental family is the social unit, and connections with relatives outside this family are of secondary importance. Such family organization is common where the population is small, the means of livelihood are by precarious collection of wild food, and larger units cannot permanently remain together because the natural resources will not allow it. But where a somewhat larger population remains together, either in a village or in a migratory band, there often, although by no means always, is found an emphasis upon one line of consanguine connection rather than the other with subordination of the conjugal connection.[28] There results a segmentation of the society into equivalent kinship units. These may take the form of extended domestic groups or joint families (as in China) or may include many households of persons related in part through recognized genealogical connection and in part through the sharing of the same name or other symbolic designation; in the latter case we speak of the groups as clans. Even in societies where the individual parental family is an independent economic unit, as in the case of the eastern Eskimo, husband and wife never become a new social and economic unit with the completeness that is characteristic of our own society. When a marriage in primitive society comes to an end, the kinsmen of the dead spouse assert upon his property a claim they have never given up.[29] On the whole, we may think of the family among folk peoples as made up of persons consanguinely connected. Marriage is, in comparison with what we in our society directly experience, an incident in the life of the individual who is born, brought up, and dies with his blood kinsmen. In such a society romantic love can hardly be elevated to a major principle.

In so far as the consanguine lines are well defined (and in some cases both lines may be of importance to the individual) [30] the folk society may be thought of as composed of families rather than of individuals. It is the familial groups that act and are acted upon. There is strong solidarity within the kinship group, and the individual is responsible to all his kin as they are responsible to him. "The clan is a natural mutual aid society. . . . A member belongs to the clan, he is not his own; if he is wrong, they will right him; if he does wrong, the responsibility is shared by them." [31] Thus, in folk societies wherein the tendency to maintain consanguine connection has resulted in joint families or clans, it is usual to find that injuries done by an individual are regarded as injuries against his kinship group, and the group takes the steps to right the wrong. The step may be revenge regulated by custom or a property settlement. A considerable part of primitive law exists in the regulation of claims by one body of kin against another. The fact that the folk society is an organization of families rather than an aggregation of individuals is further expressed in many of those forms of marriage in which a certain kind of relative is the approved spouse. The customs by which in many primitive societies a man is expected to marry his deceased brother's widow or a woman to marry her deceased sister's husband express the view of marriage as an undertaking between kinship groups. One of the spouses having failed by death, the undertaking is to be carried on by some other representative of the family group. Indeed, in the arrangements for marriage—the selection of spouses by their relatives, in bride-price, dowry, and in many forms of familial negotiations leading to a marriage—the nature of marriage as a connubial form of social relations between kindreds finds expression.

It has been said in foregoing paragraphs that behavior in the folk society is traditional, spontaneous, and uncritical, that what one man does is much the same as what another man does, and that the patterns of conduct are clear and remain constant throughout the generations. It has also been suggested that the congruence of all parts of conventional behavior and social institutions with each other contributes to the sense of rightness which the member of the folk society feels to inhere in his traditional ways of action. In the well-known language of Sumner, the ways of life are folkways; furthermore, the folkways tend to be also mores—ways of doing or thinking to which attach notions of moral worth. The value of every traditional act or object or institution is, thus, something which the members of the society are not disposed to call into question; and should the value be called into question, the doing so is resented. This characteristic of the folk society may be briefly referred to by saying that it is a sacred society. In the folk society one may not, without calling into effect negative social sanctions, challenge as valueless what has come to be traditional in that society.

Presumably, the sacredness of social objects has its source, in part, at least, in the mere fact of habituation; probably the individual organism becomes early adjusted to certain habits, motor and mental, and to certain associations between one activity and another or between certain sense experiences and certain activities, and it is almost physiologically uncomfortable to change or even to entertain he idea of change. There arises "a feeling of impropriety of certain forms, of a particular social or religious value, or a superstitious fear of change." [32] Probably the sacredness of social objects in the folk society is related also to the fact that in such well-organized cultures acts and objects suggest the traditions, beliefs, and conceptions which all share. There is reason to suppose that when what is traditionally done becomes less meaningful because people no longer know what the acts stand for, life becomes more secular. [33] In the repetitious character of conventional action (aside from technical action) we have ritual; in its expressive character we have ceremony; in the folk society ritual tends also to be ceremonious, and ritual-ceremony tends to be sacred, not secular.

The sacredness of social objects is apparent in the ways in which, in the folk society, such an object is hedged around with restraints and protections that keep it away from the commonplace and the matter-of-fact. [34] In the sacred there is alternatively, or in combination, holiness and dangerousness. When the Papago Indian returned from a successful war expedition, bringing the scalp of a slain Apache, the head-hairs of the enemy were treated as loaded with a tremendous "charge" of supernatural power; only old men, already successful warriors and purified through religious ritual, could touch the object and make it safe for incorporation into the home of the slayer. Made into the doll-like form of an Apache Indian, it was, at last, after much ceremonial preparation, held for an instant by the members of the slayer's family, addressed in respect and awe by kinship terms, and placed in the house, there to give off protective power. [35] The Indians of San Pedro de la Laguna, Guatemala, recognize an officer, serving for life, whose function it is to keep custody of ten or a dozen Latin breviaries printed in the eighteenth century and to read prayers from one or another of these books on certain occasions. No one but this custodian may handle the books, save his assistants on ceremonial occasions, with his permission. Should anyone else touch a book he would go mad or be stricken with blindness. Incense and candles are burnt before the chest containing the books, yet the books are not gods—they are objects of sacredness.[36]

In the folk society this disposition to regard objects as sacred extends, characteristically, even into the subsistence activities and into the foodstuffs of the people. Often the foodstuffs are personified as well as sacred. "My granduncle used to say to me," explained a Navajo Indian, " 'if you are walking along a trail and see a kernel of corn, pick it up. It is like a child lost and starving.' According to the legends corn is just the same as a human being, only it is holier. . . . When a man goes into a cornfield he feels that he is in a holy place, that he is walking among Holy People. . . . Agriculture is a holy occupation. Even before you plant you sing songs. You continue this during the whole time your crops are growing. You cannot help but feel that you are in a holy place when you go through your fields and they are doing well." [37] In the folk society, ideally conceived, nothing is solely a means to an immediate practical end. All activities, even the means of production, are ends in themselves, activities expressive of the ultimate values of the society.

–3–

This characterization of the ideal folk society could be greatly extended. Various of the elements that make up the conception could be differently combined with one another, and this point or that could be developed or further emphasized and its relations shown to other aspects of the conception. For example, it might be pointed out that where there is little or no systematic and reflective thinking the customary solutions to problems of practical action only imperfectly take the form of really effective and understood control of the means appropriate to accomplish the desired end, and that, instead, they tend to express the states of mind of the individuals who want the end brought about and fear that it may not be. We say this briefly in declaring that the folk society is characterized by much magic, for we may understand "magic" to refer to action with regard to an end—to instrumental action—but only to such instrumental action as does not effectively bring about that end, or is not really understood in so far as it does, and which is expressive of the way the doer thinks and feels rather than adapted to accomplishing the end. "Magic is based on specific experience of emotional states . . . in which the truth is revealed not by reason but by the play of emotions upon the human organism . . . magic is founded on the belief that hope cannot fail nor desire deceive." [38] In the folk society effective technical action is much mixed with magical activity. What is done tends to take the form of a little drama; it is a picture of what is desired.

The nature of the folk society could, indeed, be restated in the form of a description of the folk mind. This description would be largely a repetition of what has been written in foregoing pages, except that now the emphasis would be upon the characteristic mental activity of members of the folk society, rather than upon customs and institutions. The man of the folk society tends to make mental associations which are personal and emotional, rather than abstractly categoric or defined in terms of cause and effect. ". . . Primitive man views every action not only as adapted to its main object, every thought related to its main end, as we should perceive them, but . . . he associates them with other ideas, often of a religious or at least a symbolic nature. Thus he gives to them a higher significance than they seem to us to deserve." [39] A very similar statement of this kind of thinking has been expressed in connection with the thinking of medieval man; the description would apply as well to man in the folk society:

From the causal point of view, symbolism appears as a sort of short-cut of thought. Instead of looking for the relation between two things by following the hidden detours of their causal connections, thought makes a leap and discovers their relation, not in a connection of cause or effects, but in a connection of signifiation or finality. Such a connection will at once appear convincing, provided only that the two things have an essential quality in common which can be referred to a general value. . . . Symbolic assimilation founded on common properties presupposes the idea that these properties are essential to things. The vision of white and red roses blooming among thorns at once calls up a symbolic association in the medieval mind: for example, that of virgins and martyrs, shining with glory, in the midst of their persecutors. The assimilation is produced because the attributes are the same: the beauty, the tenderness, the purity, the colours of the roses are also those of the virgins, their red color that of the blood of the martyrs. But this similarity will only have a mystic meaning if the middle-term connecting the two terms of the symbolic concept expresses an essentiality common to both; in other words, if redness and whiteness are something more than names for physical differences based on quantity, if they are conceived of as essences, as realities. The mind of the savage, of the child, and of the poet never sees them otherwise.[40]

The tendency to treat nature personally has recognition in the literature as the "animistic" or "anthropomorphic" quality of primitive thinking, and the contrast between the means-ends pattern of thought more characteristic of modern urban man and the personal thought of primitive man has been specially investigated.[41]

In the foregoing account no mention has been made of the absence of economic behavior characteristic of the market in the folk society. Within the ideal folk society members are bound by religious and kinship ties, and there is no place for the motive of commercial gain.

There is no money and nothing is measured by any such common denominator of value. The distribution of goods and services tends to be an aspect of the conventional and personal relationships of status which make up the structure of the society: goods are exchanged as expressions of good will and, in large part, as incidents of ceremonial and ritual activities. "On the whole, then, the compulsion to work, to save, and to expend is given not so much by a rational appreciation of the [material] benefits to be received as by the desire for social recognition, through such behavior." [42]

The conception sketched here takes on meaning if the folk society is seen in contrast to the modern city. The vast, complicated, and rapidly changing world in which the urbanite and even the urbanized country-dweller live today is enormously different from the small, inward-facing folk society, with its well-integrated and little-changing moral and religious conceptions. At one time all men lived in these little folk societies. For many thousands of years men must have lived so; urbanized life began only very recently, as the long history of man on earth is considered, and the extreme development of a secularized and swift-changing world of society is only a few generations old.

The tribal groups that still remain around the edges of expanding civilization are the small remainders of this primary state of living. Considering them one by one, and in comparison with the literate or semiliterate societies, the industrialized and the semi-industrialized societies, we may discover how each has developed forms of social life in accordance with its own special circumstances. Among the polar Eskimos, where each small family had to shift for itself in the rigors of the arctic environment, although the ties of kinship were of great importance, no clans or other large unilateral kinship groups came into existence. The sedentary Haida of the Queen Charlotte Islands were divided into two exogamous kinship groups, each composed of clans, with intense pride of decent and healthy rivalry between them. Among the warring and nomadic Comanche initiative and resourcefulness of the individual were looked on more favorably than among the sedentary and closely interdependent Zuni. In West Africa great native states arose, with chiefs and courts and markets, yet the kinship organization remained strong; and in China we have an example of slow growth of a great society, with a literate élite, inclosing within it a multitude of village communities of the folk type. Where cities have arisen, the country people dependent on those cities have developed economic and political relationships, as well as relationships of status, with the city people, and so have become that special kind of rural folk we call peasantry.[43] And even in the newer parts of the world, as in the United States, many a village or small town has, perhaps, as many points of resemblance with the folk society as with urban life.

Thus the societies of the world do not range themselves in the same order with regard to the degree to which they realize all of the characteristics of the ideal folk society. On the other hand, there is so marked a tendency for some of these characteristics to occur together with others that the interrelations among them must be in no small part that of interdependent variables. Indeed, some of the interrelations are so obvious that we feel no sense of problem. The smallness of the folk society and the long association together of the same individuals certainly is related to the prevailingly personal character of relationships. The fewness of secondary and tertiary tools and the absence of machine manufacture are circumstances obviously unfavorable to a very complex division of labor. Many problems present themselves, however, as to the conditions in which certain of these characteristics do not occur in association, and as to the circumstances under which certain of them may be expected to change in the direction of their opposites, with or without influencing others to change also.

A study of the local differences in the festival of the patron village saint in certain communities of Yucatan indicates that some interrelationship exists in that case.[44] In all four communities, differing as to their degrees of isolation from urban centers of modifying influence, the festival expresses a relationship between the village and its patron saint (or cross) which is annually renewed. In it a ritual and worship are combined with a considerable amount of play. The chief activities of the festival are a novena, a folk dance, and a rustic bullfight. In all four communities there is an organization of men and women who for that year undertake the leadership of the festival, handing over the responsibility to a corresponding group of successors at its culmination. So far the institution is the same in all the communities studied. The differences appear when the details of the ritual and play and of the festal organization are compared, and when the essential meanings of these acts and organizations are inquired into. Then it appears that from being an intensely sacred act, made by the village as a collectivity composed of familially defined component groups, with close relationship to the system of religious and moral understandings of the people, the festival becomes, in the more urbanized communities, chiefly an opportunity for recreation for some and of financial profit for others, with little reference to moral and religious conceptions.

In the most isolated and otherwise most folklike of the communities studied the organization of the festival is closely integrated with the whole social structure of the community. The hierarchy of leaders of the community, whose duties are both civil and religious, carry on the festival: It is the chiefs, the men who decide disputes and lead in warfare, who also take principal places in the religious processions and in the conduct of the ceremonies. The community, including several neighboring settlements, is divided into five groups, membership in which descends in the male line. The responsibility for leading the prayers and preparing the festal foods rests in turn on four men chosen from each of the five groups. The festival is held at the head village, at the shrine housing the cross patron of the entire community. The festival consists chiefly of solemnly religious acts: masses, rosaries, procession of images, kneeling of worshipers. The ritual offerings are presented by a special officer, in all solemnity, to the patron cross; certain symbols of divinity are brought from the temple and exposed to the kneeling people as the offerings are made. The transfer of the responsibility to lead the festival is attended by ceremony in an atmosphere of sanctity: certain ritual paraphernalia are first placed on the altar and then, after recitation of prayers and performance of a religious dance, are handed over, in view of all, from the custodians of the sacred charge for that year to their successors.

In the villages that are less isolated the festival is similar in form, but it is less well integrated with the social organization of the community, is less sacred, and allows for more individual enterprise and responsibility. These changes continue in the other communities studied, as one gets nearer to the city of Merida. In certain seacoast villages the festival of the patron saint is a money-getting enterprise of a few secular-minded townspeople. The novena is in the hands of a few women who receive no help from the municipal authorities; the bullfight is a commercial entertainment, professional bullfighters being hired for the occasion and admission charged; the folk dance is little attended. The festival is enjoyed by young people who come to dance modern dances and to witness the bullfight, and it is an opportunity to the merchants to make a profit. What was an institution of folk culture has become a business enterprise in which individuals, as such, take part in secular ends.

The principal conclusion is that the less isolated and more heterogeneous communities of the peninsula of Yucatan are the more secular and individualistic and the more characterized by disorganization of culture. It further appeared probable that there was, in the changes taking place in Yucatan, a relation of interdependence among these changing characteristics, especially between the disorganization of culture and secularization. "People cease to believe because they cease to understand, and they cease to understand because they cease to do the things that express the understandings." [45] New jobs and other changes in the division of labor bring it about that people cannot participate in the old rituals; and, ceasing to participate, they cease to share the values for which the rituals stood. This is, admittedly, however, only a part of the explanation.

The conception of the folk society has stimulated one small group of field workers to consider the interdependence or independence of these characteristics of society. In Yucatan isolation, homogeneity, a personal and "symbolic" view of nature, importance of familial relationships, a high degree of organization of culture, and sacredness of sanctions and institutions were all found in regular association with each other. It was then reported that in certain Indian communities on or near Lake Atitlan in Guatemala this association of characteristics is not repeated. [46] As it appeared that these Guatemalan communities were not in rapid change, but were persisting in their essential nature, the conclusion was reached that "a stable society can be small, unsophisticated, homogeneous in beliefs and practices," have a local, well-organized culture, and still be one "with relationships impersonal, with formal institutions dictating the acts of individuals, and with family organization weak, with life secularized, and with individuals acting more from economic or other personal advantage than from any deep conviction or thought of the social good." It was further pointed out that in these Guatemalan societies a "primitive world view," that is, a disposition to treat nature personally, to regard attributes as entities, and to make "symbolic" rather than causal connections, coexists with a tendency for relations between man and man to be impersonal, commercial, and secular, as they tend to be in the urban society.[47]

These observations lead, in turn, to reconsideration of the circumstances tending to bring about one kind of society or one aspect of society rather than another. The breakdown of familial institutions in recent times in Western society is often ascribed to the development of the city and of modern industry. If, as has been reported, familial institutions are also weak in these Guatemalan villages, there must be alternative causes for the breakdown of the family to the rise of industry and the growth of the city, for these Guatemalan Indians live on or near their farms, practice a domestic handicraft manufacture, and have little or nothing to do with cities. It has been suggested that in the case of the Guatemalan societies the development, partly before the Conquest and partly afterward, of a pecuniary economy with a peddler's commerce, based on great regional division of labor, together with a system of regulations imposed by an élite with the use of force, may be the circumstances that have brought about reduction in the importance of familial institutions and individual independence, especially in matters of livelihood.[48]

The secular character of life in these highland villages of the Lake Atitlan region is not so well established as in the individuated character of life, but if life is indeed secular there, it is a secularity that has developed without the influence of high personal mobility, of the machine, and of science. In a well-known essay Max Weber showed how capitalistic commercialism could and did get along with piety in the case of the Puritans.[49] So it may appear that under certain conditions a literate and, indeed, at least partly urbanized society may be both highly commercial and sacred—as witness, also, the Jews—while under certain other conditions an otherwise folklike people may become individualistic, commercial, and perhaps secular. It is, of course, the determination of the limiting conditions that is important.

NOTES

1. Neither the term "primitive" nor any other is denotative, and none has sufficient generally accepted precise meaning to allow us to know in just what characters of a society to discover the degree to which it is or is not "primitive," "simple," or whatever. The words "nonliterate" or "preliterate" do call attention to a particular character, literacy, but understanding is still required as to when a society is "literate" and as to what form or degree of literacy has significance. There are head-hunting tribes, in other respects as primitive as were the Pawnee Indians in the seventeenth century, that have knowledge of writing. In certain Mexican villages most children and many adults have formal knowledge of the arts of reading and writing, but in most other respects these village societies are much more like tribal societies than they are like our western cities.

The word "folk," which will be used in this paper, is no more precise than any other. It is used here because, better than others, it suggests the inclusion in our comparisons of peasant and rustic people who are not wholly independent of cities and because in its compounds, "folklore" and "folk song," it points, in a rough way, to the presence of folklore and folk songs, as recognized by the collector of such materials, as a sign of a society to be examined in making up the characterization of the ideal type with which we are here concerned. But the question of the word to be used is of small importance.

2. The reader may compare the conception developed in this paper with the ideal "sacred society" characterized by Howard Becker in "Ionia and Athens," Ph.D. dissertation, University of Chicago, 1930, pp. 1–16; with similar conceptions developed in chapter i of *Social Thought from Lore to Science* by Harry Elmer Barnes and Howard Becker, Boston, New York: D.C.

Heath & Co., 1938; and with the application of the conception in *The Sociology of the Renaissance* by Alfred von Martin, London: Kegan Paul, Trench, Truburn & Co., Ltd., 1945.

3. A. A. Goldenweiser, *Early Civilization,* New York: Knopf, 1922, pp. 117–118.

4. Henry Maine, *Ancient Law,* London: J. Murray, 1861.

5. Ferdinand Tönnies, *Gemeinschaft und Gesellschaft* (1st ed., 1887), trans. and ed. by Charles P. Loomis as *Fundamental Concepts of Sociology,* New York: American Book Co., 1940.

6. *Émile Durkheim on the Division of Labor in Society,* a translation by George Simpson of *De la division du travail social,* New York: Macmillan Co., 1933; Howard Becker, "Constructive Typology in the Social Sciences," *American Sociological Review,* 5 (1940), 40–55; reprinted in Harry Elmer Barnes, Howard Becker, and Frances Bennett Becker (eds.), *Contemporary Social Theory,* New York: D. Appleton-Century Co., 1940, Part I.

7. W. G. Sumner, *Folkways,* Boston: Ginn & Co., 1907, p. 12.

8. Julian Steward, *Basin-Plateau Aboriginal Sociopolitical Groups,* Smithsonian Institution, Bureau of American Ethnology, Bull. 120, Washington, D.C.: Government Printing Office, 1938, pp. 230–234.

9. Julian Steward, "Economic and Social Basis of Primitive Bands," *Essays in Anthropology Presented to A. L. Kroeber,* Berkeley: University of California Press, 1936, pp. 341–342.

10. A. R. Radcliffe-Brown, *The Andaman Islanders,* Cambridge: University Press, 1933, pp. 6–9.

11. A. L. Kroeber, *Handbook of Indians of California,* Smithsonian Institution, Bureau of American Ethnology, Bull. 78, Washington, D.C.: Government Printing Office, 1925, p. 13.

12. Robert Redfield, "Primitive Merchants of Guatemala," *Quarterly Journal of Inter-American Relations,* I, No. 4, 42–56.

13. Sumner, *op. cit.,* pp. 13–15.

14. Radcliffe-Brown, *op. cit.,* p. 43.

15. Herbert Blumer, "Mass Behavior and the Motion Picture," *Publications of the American Sociological Society,* 29 (1935), 115–127.

16. Ruth Underhill, "The Autobiography of a Papago Woman," *American Anthropological Association Memoirs,* No. 46 (1936).

17. Ralph Linton, *The Study of Man,* New York: D. Appleton-Century Co., 1936, chap. xvi, esp. p. 283.

18. Paul Radin, *Primitive Man as Philosopher,* New York: D. Appleton-Century Co., 1927.

19. A. A. Goldenweiser, "Individual, Pattern and Involution," *Essays in Anthropology Presented to A. L. Kroeber,* Berkeley: University of California Press, 1936, p. 102.

20. Ruth Benedict, *Patterns of Culture,* Boston and New York: Houghton Mifflin Co., 1934.

21. Ruth Benedict, "Animism," *Encyclopaedia of the Social Sciences.*

22. Robert H. Lowie, *The Origin of the State,* New York: Harcourt, Brace & Co., 1927, pp. 51–73.

23. Maine, *op. cit.*

24. A. W. Howitt, *The Native Tribes of Southeastern Australia,* New York: Macmillan Co., 1904, p. 759.

25. A. R. Radcliffe-Brown, "Three Tribes of Western Australia," *Journal of the Royal Anthropological Institute,* 43, 150–151.

26. Benjamin Paul, "Ritual Kinship: With Special Reference to Godparenthood in Middle America" (Ph.D. thesis, University of Chicago, 1942).

27. E. C. Parsons, "Notes on Zuni," Part II, *American Anthropological Association Memoirs,* Vol. 4, No. 4 (1917).

28. Ralph Linton, *The Study of Society,* New York: Century Co., p. 159.

29. Ruth Benedict, "Marital Property Rights in Bilateral Societies," *American Anthropologist,* 38 (1936), 368–373.

30. Peter Murdock, "Double Descent," *American Anthropologist,* 42, Part I (1940), 555–561.

31. Edwin W. Smith and Andrew Murray Dale, *The Ila-Speaking Peoples of Northern Rhodesia,* London: Macmillan & Co., Ltd., 1920, I, 296.

32. Franz Boas, *Primitive Art,* Oslo, 1927, p. 150.

33. Robert Redfield, *The Folk Culture of Yucatan,* Chicago: University of Chicago Press, 1941, p. 364.

34. Émile Durkheim, *The Elementary Forms of the Religious Life,* London: Allen & Unwin, 1926.

35. Underhill, *op. cit.,* p. 18.

36. Benjamin Paul, unpublished MS.

37. W. W. Hill, "The Agricultural and Hunting Methods of the Navaho Indians," *Yale University Publications in Anthropology,* No. 18, New Haven: Yale University Press (1938), p. 53.

38. Bronislaw Malinowski, "Magic, Science and Religion," in *Science, Religion and Reality,* ed. Joseph Needham, New York: Macmillan Co., 1925, p. 80.

39. Franz Boas, *The Mind of Primitive Man,* New York: Macmillan Co., 1938, p. 226.

40. J. Huizinga, *The Waning of the Middle Ages,* London: Arnold & Co., 1924, pp. 184–185. This "symbolic" kind of thinking is related to what Lévy-Bruhl called "participation" (see L. Lévy-Bruhl, *How Natives Think* [New York: Knopf, 1925], esp. chap. ii).

41. Hans Kelsen, "Causality and Retribution," *Philosophy of Science,* 8 (1941), 533–556; and Kelsen, *Society and Nature,* Chicago: University of Chicago Press, 1944.

42. Raymond Firth, *Primitive Economics of the New Zealand Maori,* New York: E. P. Dutton & Co., 1929, p. 484. See also, Firth, *Primitive Polynesian Economy,* London: George Routledge & Sons, 1939, esp. chap. x, "Characteristics of a Primitive Economy."

43. Robert Redfield, "Introduction," in Horace Miner, *St. Denis: A French-Canadian Parish,* Chicago: University of Chicago Press, 1940.

44. Redfield, *The Folk Culture of Yucatan.*

45. *Ibid.,* p. 364.

46. Sol Tax, "Culture and Civilization in Guatemalan Societies," *Scientific Monthly,* 48 (1939), 467.

47. Sol Tax, "World View and Social Relations in Guatemala," *American Anthropologist,* 43 (1941), 27–42.

48. Redfield, *The Folk Culture of Yucatan,* pp. 365–367.

49. Max Weber, "Protestant Ethics and the Spirit of Capitalism," cited in Kemper Fullerton, "Calvinism and Capitalism," *Harvard Theological Review,* 21, 163–195.

23. THE MULTI-GROUP SOCIETY

ROBERT M. MACIVER

In contrast to the ideal folk society where age and sex are the principal criteria for dividing the population into meaningful categories, industrial society is, by its very nature, multigroup. It is comprised of a plethora of bodies differentiated not only by age and sex, but by class and occupation and religion and race and ethnicity and personal interests. The problem of the complex society is to come to terms with these variegated interest groups, to find some means of reconciling their existence with the exigencies of modern life. The specific differences are not the same in all advanced societies; yet, the underlying problem remains the topic of discussion throughout the world. It is the so-called "search for a community."

In this short selection, Robert M. MacIver discusses the nature of the multigroup society and comments on both the character of group differences and the necessity to adapt to them.

Robert M. MacIver is Columbia Lieber Professor Emeritus of Political Philosophy and Sociology, Columbia University. One of the world's most distinguished sociologists, he has published over twenty books in six productive decades. A partial sampling is illustrative of his range of interest and scholarly productivity: Community: A Sociological Study *(1917),* The Elements of Social Science *(1921),* Society *(1931),* Leviathan and People *(1939),* Social Causation *(1942),* The Ramparts We Guard *(1950),* Great Moral Dilemmas in Literature *(1955),* The Challenge of the Passing Years; My Encounters with Time *(1962),* Assault on Poverty *(1965),* The Prevention and Control of Delinquency *(1966), and* Politics and Society *(1968).* The Web of Government, *from which this selection is adapted, was published in 1947.*

Our main argument to this point is that the relation of man to the many groups and forms of organization to which he is more nearly or more distantly, more deeply or more superficially, attached is not solved by making one of these, whether the state or any other, the sole or inclusive object of his devotion, the one social focus of his being. There are other forms of order than the simple uni-centered order. There is the order of the balance and inter-adjustment of many elements. The conception of the all-inclusive all-regulating state is as it were a pre-Copernican conception of the social system. It appeals to the primitive sense of symmetry. As we explore more deeply the social universe we must discard it and frame a conception more adequate to social reality. In this exploration we learn, among other things, to understand better the nature of the multi-group society of modern man.

With this theme we shall deal here very briefly. We start from the fact that men have many different kinds of interest, that some of these are universal, in the sense that they are pursued by all men everywhere—all seek alike the satisfaction of certain elementary needs—while some are particular, making appeal to some men and not to others. Now since organization conveys power men learn to join with others so as to pursue their interests more effectively, each for each as well as each for all. Some of these interests are purely distributive, as are most economic interests. These we may speak of as like interests. The benefits of organization then accrue to each separately, so that the proceeds become private dividends, privately enjoyed by each. Other interests are *common,* in such wise that what each receives does not divide the product of the collectivity or lessen the benefits available to all the rest. To this class belong our cultural interests, the advance of knowledge, the exploration of art, of thought, of literature, of religion, and so forth. While the individual explorer or creator may receive particular awards, honors, or emoluments, the things that he explores or creates are potentially for all men. The wells of knowledge and of inspiration are not less full for the number who drink of them. When a man makes shoes it is for private use. When he makes a work of art or literature it is generally available, in one way or another, for the enjoyment of those who care for it.

Thus we can distinguish two types of organization, according to the nature of their product, leaving aside those that are intermediate or that in some manner combine both functions. Let us consider particularly the character of the second type. The cultural interests of men are exceedingly diverse and they exist on every level from the highest to the lowest. Many men have many minds. Children subjected to the same conditions and to the same influences react in very different ways. The attitudes of every group differ from the attitudes of every other. There is much incompatibility of outlook, of opinion and belief, of interpretation, of enjoyment, of the whole realization of life. Different men find very different sustenance within the fields of culture. In the seeking of this sustenance they are most themselves, most

alive, most creative. Whether the sustenance be refined or vulgar, ample or meager, it is always that through which man seeks fulfillment. Everything else on earth is for the spirit that is in man nothing but apparatus or mechanism.

To satisfy this need men weave manifold relationships with their fellows. These extend from the give-and-take of love or comradeship through informal neighborly groupings for recreation, gossip, and so forth, up to the world-wide religious brotherhoods. There are two conclusive reasons why the numerous organizations thus engendered cannot be co-ordinated, over any range of territory great or small, under the aegis of the state. One is that the various organizations of the same cultural species are not only dissimilar in viewpoint, in method, in system of values, but actually antipathetic, alien, or hostile to one another in these respects. The differences are not reconcilable, nor are they so unimportant that they could be omitted from some universal charter or creed that would seek to embrace the different faiths within a single organizational fold. There are schools and styles in every form of art, in every field of cultural expression. The followers of any one abjure the other schools and styles. They take delight in their own, in the difference itself. Religions may alike proclaim the brotherhood of man or the fatherhood of God, but each has its own conception of the fatherhood. To co-ordinate them all into one would be to destroy their characteristic qualities, to drain them of their vitality. Coordination could be imposed only by sheer compulsion, and there is essential truth, even if the statement be too strongly worded, in the comment of the absolutist Hobbes, "Belief and unbelief never follow men's commands." Here we reach the second reason why neither the state nor any other form of organization can be all-embracing. Every way of life and every way of thought is nourished from within. It is the conviction that counts, the habit of mind, the devotion to a cause, the impulse to artistic expression, the congeniality of the group. It cannot be controlled from without, it cannot be directed by an indifferent or alien power. The creative force of all culture lies in its own spontaneity. It is killed by compulsion, reduced to a lifeless mechanism. Only the arrogance of the tyrant or of the dogmatist denies this truth. The dogmatist, secure in his own faith, would refuse other men the right to theirs, blindly seeking to destroy in them the same spirit of devotion from which he nourishes his own being.

This truth was appreciated by T. H. Green, Hegelian though he was. In his *Lectures on the Principles of Political Obligation* he put forward the thesis that the state should not command the doing of things the value of which depends on the spirit in which they are performed and not on the mere externals of performance. This thesis is relevant to the whole area of cultural pursuits, though of course there arise marginal issues. We may put forward as a corollary of this thesis the further point that wherever actions are of such a kind that the performance of them by one group in one manner or style does not impede the performance of them by other groups in a diverse or contradictory manner or style such actions should not be on intrinsic grounds subject to coordination by the state or any other collectivity. When we say "on intrinsic grounds" we mean that, for example, no one should be forbidden to worship in his own way because the ruling powers entertain a religious objection to that form of worship. If however the worship involved, say, headhunting or any other interference with the liberties of other men or any infringement of a criminal law that itself was not motivated by religious considerations but only by regard for public safety, then the performance would be subject to ban or control on extrinsic grounds. Our formula applies to the whole business of the expression of opinion, to the great realms of art and of thought in every form. One man is not precluded from advancing his opinion because another man has a contrary opinion. One man is not prevented from worshiping his own God because another man worships a different kind of God. Thus the objective conditions of public order do not demand uniformity in the cultural realm.

There is some contrast here between the cultural realm and the realm presided over by the organizations that fall predominantly within our second type. Economic activities, for example, cannot be left to the free arbitrament of individuals and groups without serious interference with public order. Thus an employer cannot lower the wages of his employees below the prevailing rate without seriously affecting the business of other employers who may have more concern for the welfare of their workers. He cannot extend the hours of labor without doing harm to his fellow employers as well as to his employees. He cannot "run his own business in his own way" as though it were a private imperium islanded from the rest of the world. No more can a man rightly claim to use his property in any way that seems good to him. His property not only is the fruit of the co-operative labor of many men but also it is the potential if not the actual source of the livelihood of others. If he neglects it, lets it run to waste or ruin, or actually destroys it he is injuring his fellows. He does the same thing if, say, he buys a patent from an inventor so as to prevent its exploitation, for the sake of his own greater profit. But there is no end of such examples. The economic order is a vast network of interdependence.

It might be claimed that a like statement could be made concerning the cultural order. A man cannot ventilate his opinions, cannot write a popular novel, cannot even worship his God without having some influence somehow on others. But there is a crucial difference. One man influences another in this manner because the other is freely responsive to that influence. We may adjudge the influence good or bad. We may condemn and oppose it. That also is our right. Opinions and creeds are for ever in conflict. Every man must find and respond to his own. There is no other way save compulsion, and we have already shown how alien and perilous that is. Moreover, with respect to economic relations the effect of one man's action on that of another is external and even automatic. The effect is measurable. We have a common standard, an objective index. Economic advantage, economic prosperity, has the same meaning for all men, even though some are more devoted to it than others. Thus the main objections that apply to the control of opinion are not relevant here. There is in fact only one relevant limit to specific economic controls, and that is precisely the consideration how far such controls conduce to the general economic welfare, how far they are efficient, how far they may go without restraining the spirit of initiative and enterprise, the spring of energy, vision, and responsibility, without which organization degenerates into the wasteful routine of bureaucracy.

Let us return, however, to our first conclusion, that the many cultural organizations of society have not and cannot have any one focus, cannot without losing their identity and their function be amalgamated and absorbed as mere departments of the state. Now we face the question of the inter-adjustment of all these organizations, and of the groups who maintain them, within the ordered yet free life of the community. Here is the essential problem of our multi-group society.

In every range and at every stage of social life this problem exists. In the simplest societies it is embryonic, and it reaches its full proportions only in the ambit of the modern nation. In the world of Western civilization it first became acute when various religious groups broke away from the universalism of the mediaeval church. The assumption that every community, every state, must have a single religion had a tremendous hold over the minds of most men. Only the sheer impossibility of maintaining this assumption at length persuaded them that they could live decently together, as members of one community, with those who professed a different faith. Centuries of persecution, war, and civil strife were needed to achieve this result. Manifestations of the old intolerance persist in the more liberal states while new forms of it, not associated with a religious principle, have appeared in some other states and shown a virulence not surpassed by the most extreme instances of earlier times. The full requirement of cultural liberty has rarely, if ever, been realized. In democratic countries it is now *politically* established. These countries have advanced far since the days when the king of one of them announced that he would "make the extirpation of the heretics his principal business." Gradually they passed from persecution to toleration and from toleration to the position that a man's religion is no concern of the state. The Edict of Nantes in 1598 was the first acknowledgment of a Roman Catholic government that "heretics" should be accorded civil rights, but even as late as 1776 the greatest of French radicals could assert that it was "impossible for men to live at peace with those they believe to be damned." In Protestant countries Roman Catholics were at length "tolerated," but it was only in 1819 that even England admitted them to citizenship. As for Jews, they have suffered longer and more grievously from persecution and the denial of civil rights than those who professed any other religion.

The principle set out in the First Amendment of the United States Constitution, that no law shall be enacted respecting an establishment of religion, has in effect been accepted by most democratic countries as well as by some others that cannot be placed in that category. But the problem of the multi-group society is not solved merely by the formal recognition of equality before the law. Such equality can exist while nevertheless minority groups or groups in an inferior economic or social position may be subject to such discrimination that they are practically excluded from participation in the life of the community. An outstanding example is the situation of the Negroes in the United States, particularly in the South. Other groups suffer discrimination to different degrees. The Jewish people are exposed to it but so in a measure are various ethnic groups, especially those of Eastern European countries, while yet stronger disabilities are applied against the Chinese, the Japanese, and the people of India. If we add to these groups the American Indians, the Filipinos, the Mexicans and other Latin-Americans we get the picture of à country constitutionally dedicated to the equality of men that nevertheless exhibits a complex pattern of rifts and fissures ramifying across the life of the community.

In different countries the problem takes different shapes. While in the United States minority groups are dispersed throughout the population, in some other countries they have a territorial locus, as in the Balkan area. Sometimes ethnic differences are associated with differences of religion. Often the disadvantaged groups occupy an inferior economic status. Not infrequently there is political as well as social and economic discrimination. This situation is found in its extreme form in colonial possessions, where the usual relation of majority and minority is reversed in favor of a dominant alien group.

Under all conditions the discrimination of group against group is detrimental to the well-being of the community. Those who are discriminated against are balked in their social impulses, are prevented from developing their capacities, become warped or frustrated, secretly or openly nurse a spirit of animosity against the dominant group. Energies that otherwise might have been devoted to constructive service are diverted and consumed in the friction of fruitless conflict. The dominant group, fearing the loss of its privileges, takes its stand on a traditional conservatism and loses the power of adapting itself to the changing times. The dominated, unless they are sunk in the worse apathy of sullen impotence, respond to subversive doctrines that do not look beyond the overthrow of the authority they resent. Each side conceives a false image of the other, denying their common humanity, and the community is torn asunder.

There is no way out of this impasse, apart from revolution, except the gradual readjustment of group relations in the direction of equality of opportunity—not merely of legal equality. Since this readjustment requires the abandonment of habits and traditions, the breaking of taboos, the reconstruction of the distorted images cherished by each group of the other, and the recognition that the narrower interests and fears and prides that stimulate discrimination and prejudice are adverse to the common good and often empty cr vain, its achievement can be effected only through the arduous and generally slow processes of social education. The sense of community, dissipated by the pervading specialization of interests, needs to be reinforced. The common values of the embracing culture need to be reasserted and again made vital. The provision of equality of opportunity will not of itself bring about any such result. It will serve chiefly by removing a source of division that stands obdurately in the way of social cohesion. Only when this obstacle is removed can the positive values of the multi-group society be cultivated—if we have the wisdom to seek and to find them.

The sense of the need of community, if not the sense of community, is still alive and seeks embodiment. It is witnessed to by men's devotion to the nation and by their attachment to some local community they feel—or once felt—to be their home. But these bonds do not satisfy the need, do not sufficiently provide the experience of effective solidarity. The nation is too wide and too diverse. The local community is too heterogeneous, if it is large, or too limited, if it is small. Often the attachment to it is nostalgic or merely sentimental. So the unit gropes for a more satisfying unity, seeking to recover the spirit of co-operative living that animated the uni-group society. Sometimes men seek to recover it by methods that would reimpose the old order on the new. They would restore the myth of the uni-group society; they would make the all-inclusive state the sufficient focus of our moral and spiritual being; they would even, as totalitarians, ruthlessly co-ordinate out of existence our cultural heterogeneity. But there is no road back. The course of civilization is as irreversible as time itself. We have left behind the one-room social habitation of our ancestors. We have built ourselves a house of many mansions. Somehow we must learn to make it ours.

24. SMALL TOWN IN MASS SOCIETY: SPRINGDALE'S IMAGE OF ITSELF

ARTHUR J. VIDICH *and* JOSEPH BENSMAN

What is life like in a small town located in the middle of a mass society? How do the people who live in such a place see themselves?

In this descriptive selection, Arthur J. Vidich and Joseph Bensman indicate the color and quality of social participation in Springdale, a hamlet in upstate New York. Here is a community of "plain folk" rapidly becoming a relic of a passing era, clinging to its identity as a rural village. Here is a town whose citizens reckon that the only virtues are the homely ones and that they must maintain their style of life against the growing encroachment of urban ways. Clearly, they will face a dilemma in a society of accelerating urbanization, but for the "present" Springdale remains a small town in word and deed.

Arthur J. Vidich is Professor and Chairman of the Department of Sociology and Anthropology at the New School for Social Research. He has written Small Town and Mass Society *(1968), and, with Maurice Stein, has edited* Identity and Anxiety *(1960) and* Sociology on Trial *(1963). Joseph Bensman is Professor of Sociology at City College of the City University of New York. He is the coauthor of* Mass, Class, and Bureaucracy *(1963).*

Vidich and Bensman are coauthors of Small Town in Mass Society: Class, Power and Religion in a Rural Community *(1958).*

"Just Plain Folks"

When one becomes more intimately acquainted with the people of Springdale, and especially with the more verbal and more prominent inhabitants, one finds that they like to think of themselves as "just plain folks." The editor of the paper, in urging people to attend public meetings or in reporting a social event, says, "all folks with an interest" should attend or "the folks who came certainly had a good time." Almost any chairman of a public gathering addresses his audience as folks —"all right, folks, the meeting will get underway"—and the interviewer in his work frequently encounters the same expression—"the folks in this community," "the townfolk," "the country folk," "good folks," and "bad folks." Depending on context, the term carries with it a number of quite different connotations.

First and foremost, the term serves to distinguish Springdalers from urban dwellers, who are called "city people," an expression which by the tone in which it is used implies the less fortunate, those who are denied the wholesome virtues of rural life. City people are separated from nature and soil, from field and stream, and are caught up in the inexorable web of impersonality and loneliness, of which the public statement in Springdale is: "How can people stand to live in cities?" In an understandable and ultimate extension of this valuation one may occasionally hear references to the rural or country folk, in contrast to the villagers, the former being regarded by Springdalers as the "true folk."

The self-designation as "folk" includes everyone in the community; by its generality of reference it excludes neither the rich nor the poor, for everyone can share equally in the genuine qualities ascribed by the term. This is not to say that the community does not recognize scoundrels and wastrels in its own environment; quite the contrary, the scoundrel and allied types become all the more noticeable in the light of the dominant genuineness of rural life. It is rather to say that the standard of judgment by which character is assessed in Springdale includes no false or artificial values. To be one of the folks requires neither money, status, family background, learning, nor refined manners. It is, in short, a way of referring to the equalitarianism of rural life.

The term also includes a whole set of moral values: honesty, fair play, trustworthiness, good-neighborliness, helpfulness, sobriety, and clean-living. To the Springdaler it suggests a wholesome family life, a man whose spoken word is as good as a written contract, a community of religious-minded people, and a place where "everybody knows everybody" and "where you can say hello to anybody." The background image of urban society and city people gives force and meaning to the preferred rural way of life.

Rural Virtues and City Life

The sense of community-mindedness and identification has its roots in a belief in the inherent difference between Springdale and all other places, particularly the nearby towns and big cities. For the Springdaler surrounding towns all carry stigmata which are not found in Springdale: the county seat is the locus of vice and corruption, the Finnish settlement is "red," University Town is snobbish and aloof, and Industrial Town is inhuman, slummy and foreign. In the big city the individual is anonymously lost in a hostile and dog-eat-dog environment. Being in the community gives one a distinct feeling of living in a protected and better place, so that in spite of occasional internal quarrels and the presence of some unwholesome characters, one frequently hears it said that "there's no place I'd rather live . . . there isn't a better place to raise a family . . . this is the best little town in the whole country." In the face of the outer world, Springdalers "stick up for their town."

The best example of community identification occurs when newspapers of neighboring towns choose to publicize negative aspects of Springdale life: making banner headlines over the dismissal of a school principal, publishing the names of youthful criminal offenders who come from good families. In such instances, irrespective of issue or factional position, anyone with an interest in the community comes to its defense: "We may have our troubles, but it's nothing we can't handle by ourselves—and quicker and better if they'd leave us alone." A challenge to the image of Springdale as a preferred place cuts deep and helps to re-create the sense of community when it is temporarily lost.

It is interesting that the belief in the superiority of local ways of living actually conditions the way of life. Springdalers *make an effort* to be friendly" and "*go out of their way* to help newcomers." The newspaper always emphasizes the positive side of life; it never reports local arrests, shotgun weddings, mortgage foreclosures, lawsuits, bitter exchanges in public meetings, suicides or any other unpleasant happening. By this constant focus on warm and human qualities in all public situations, the public character of the community takes on those qualities and, hence, it has a tone which is distinctly different from city life.

Relationships with nearby towns, in spite of the occasional voicing of hostility, also have a sympathetic and friendly competitive aspect. No one in Springdale would gloat over another town's misfortunes, such as a serious fire or the loss of an industry. Athletic rivalries have long histories and although there is a vocabulary of names and yells for "enemies," these simply stimulate competitiveness and arouse emotions for the night of the contest. No one takes victory or defeat seriously for more than a day or two and only in a very rare instance is there a public incident when outsiders visit the town. "Nobody really wants trouble with other towns."

When one goes beyond neighboring communities, the Springdaler leaps from concrete images of people and places to a more generalized image of metropolitan life. His everyday experiences give him a feeling of remoteness from the major centers of industry, commerce and politics. His images are apt to be as stereotyped as those that city people hold concerning the country. Any composite of these images would certainly include the following:

1. Cities breed corruption and have grown so big and impersonal that they are not able to solve the problems they create.
2. Cities are an unwholesome environment for children and families, and have had an unhealthy effect on family morals.
3. Urban politicians and labor leaders are corrupt and represent anti-democratic forces in American life.
4. Washington is a place overridden with bureaucrats and the sharp deal, fast-buck operator, both of whom live like parasites off hard-working country folk.
5. Industrial workers are highly paid for doing little work. Their leaders foment trouble and work against the good of the country.
6. Cities are hotbeds of un-American sen-timent, harbor the reds and are incapable of educating their youth to Christian values.
7. Big universities and city churches are centers of atheism and secularism and in spite of occasional exceptions have lost touch with the spiritual lesson taught by rural life.
8. Most of the problems of country life have their origin in the effects which urban life has on rural ways.

What is central, however, is the feeling of the Springdaler that these things do not basically affect him. While he realizes that machinery and factory products are essential to his standard of life and that taxation and agricultural policy are important, he feels that he is independent of other features of industrial and urban life, or, better, that he can choose and select only the best parts. The simple physical separation from the city and the open rural atmosphere makes it possible to avoid the problems inherent in city life. Personal relations are face-to-face and social gatherings are intimate, churchgoing retains the quality of a family affair, the merchant is known as a person, and you can experience the "thrill of watching nature and the growth of your garden." Springdalers firmly believe in the virtues of rural living, strive to maintain them and defend them against anyone who would criticize them.

"Neighbors Are Friends"

Almost all of rural life receives its justification on the basis of the direct and personal and human feelings that guide people's relations with each other. No one, not even a stranger, is a stranger to the circumambience of the community. It is as if the people in a deeply felt communion bring themselves together for the purposes of mutual self-help and protection. To this end the community is organized for friendliness and neighborliness, so much so that the terms "friends" and "neighbors" almost stand as synonyms for "folk."

In its most typical form neighborliness occurs in time of personal and family crisis—birth, death, illness, fire, catastrophe. On such occasions friends and neighbors mobilize to support those in distress: collections of money are taken, meals are prepared by others, cards of condolence are sent. A man whose house or barn has burned may unexpectedly find an organized "bee" aiding in reconstruction. Practically all organizations have "sunshine" committees whose sole purpose is to send greeting cards. These practices are so widespread and ultimately may include so many people that an individual, unable to acknowledge all this friendliness personally, will utilize the newspaper's "card of thanks" column to express his public appreciation.

Borrowing and "lending back and forth" is perhaps the most widespread act of neighborliness. Farmers say they like to feel that "in a pinch" there is always someone whom they can count upon for help—to borrow tools, get advice, ask for labor. In spite of the advent of mechanized and self-sufficient farming and consequently the reduction of the need for mutual aid, the high public value placed on mutual help is not diminished. Though a farmer may want to be independent and wish to avoid getting involved in other people's problems and, in fact, may privately resent lending his machinery, it is quite difficult for him to refuse to assist his neighbor if asked. Even where technological advance has made inroads on the need for the practice, to support the public creed remains a necessity.

For housewives in a community where "stores don't carry everything" domestic trading and borrowing is still a reality; they exchange children's clothing and *do* borrow salt and sugar. In Springdale they say "you never have to be without . . . if you need something bad enough you can always get it: of course, sometimes people

overdo it and that makes it bad for everybody, but after a while you find out who they are." The process of selectively eliminating the bad practitioners makes it possible to keep the operation of the practice on a high plane.

Neighborliness has its institutional supports and so is given a firm foundation. Ministers and church groups make it a practice to visit the sick in hospitals and homes and to remember them with cards and letters, and all other organizations— the Legion, Masons, Community Club, book clubs—designate special committees to insure that remembrance is extended to the bereaved and ill. The Legion and Community Club "help our own" with baskets of food and clothing at Christmas time and organize fund drives to assist those who are "burned out." The ideology of neighborliness is reflected in and reinforced by the organized life of the community.

To a great extent these arrangements between friends and neighbors have a reciprocal character: a man who helps others may himself expect to be helped later on. In a way the whole system takes on the character of insurance. Of course some people are more conscious of their premium payments than others and keep a kind of mental bookkeeping on "what they owe and who owes them what," which is a perfectly permissible practice so long as one does not openly confront others with unbalanced accounts. In fact, the man who knows "exactly where he stands" with his friends and neighbors is better advised than the one who "forgets and can't keep track." The person who is unconsciously oblivious of what others do for him and distributes his own kindness and favor without thinking is apt to alienate both those whom he owes and doesn't owe. The etiquette for getting and giving in Springdale is an art that requires sensitive adjustments to the moods, needs and expectations of others. This ability to respond appropriately in given situations is the sign of the good neighbor. That this sensitivity is possessed by large numbers of people is attested to by the fact that friendliness and neighborliness contribute substantially to the community's dominant tone of personalness and warmth.

Of course, everyone does not participate equally or at the same level in being a good friend and neighbor. Deviations and exceptions are numerous. Neighborliness is often confined to geographical areas and to socially compatible groups. The wife of the lawyer is on neighborly terms with others like herself rather than with the wife of a carpenter. Farmers necessarily have less to do with people in the village and teachers are more apt to carry on friendly relations with each other. Those who are not willing to both give and take find themselves courteously eliminated from this aspect of local life. "People who are better off" simply by possessing sufficient resources do not find it necessary to call on friends and neighbors for help, though "everyone knows that if you went and asked them for something, they'd give it to you right away." Others have a more "independent turn of mind" and "will get by with what they have, no matter what, just to be free of mind"; the ideology of neighborliness is broad enough to include them "so long as they don't do anyone harm." The foreign elements, particularly the Poles, limit their everyday neighboring to their own group, but still by community definitions they are good neighbors because "you can always trust a Pole to deal square . . . if they owe you anything, they will always pay you back on time." Some folks are known as "just good people" who by choice "keep to themselves." By isolating themselves within the community they neither add nor detract from the neighborly quality of community life and so do not have an effect on the public character of the town.

The only group which does not fall within the purview of the conception of friend and neighbor is the 10 percent of the population that live "in shacks in the hills." The people who live in shacks "can't be trusted"; "they steal you blind"; "if you're friendly to them, they'll take advantage of you"; "if you lend them something you'll never see it again"; "they're bad . . . no good people . . . live like animals." Hence by appropriately extending the social definition to give it a broader base than mutual aid, all groups in the community, except the shack people, fulfill the image of good friend and neighbor. The self-conception then reinforces itself, serves as a model for achievement and adds to the essential appearance of community warmth.

Good Folks and Bad Folks

"Of course, there are some people who just naturally have a dirty mouth. You'll find them anywhere you go and I'd be lying if I said we didn't have a few here." The "dirty mouth" is a person who not only fabricates malicious gossip about his enemies but also wantonly and carelessly spreads his fabrications. He commits the double *faux pas* of being deliberately malicious and of not observing the etiquette of interpersonal relations, and he is perhaps the most despised person in the community.

There are a whole range of personal qualities which are almost unanimously disapproved in Springdale. These are identified in the person

"who holds a grudge . . . who won't ever forget a wrong done to him."

"who can't get along with other people . . . who won't ever try to be friendly and sociable."

"who gives the town a bad name . . . always raising up a ruckus . . . always trying to stir up trouble."

"who trys to be something he isn't . . . the show-off . . . the braggart."

"who thinks he's better than everybody else . . . who thinks he's too good for the town

. . . who thinks he's a cut above ordinary folks."

"who is bossy . . . thinks his ideas are always the best . . . tries to run everything . . . wants to be the center of attention all the time without working for it."

"who makes money by cheating people . . . who hasn't made his money honestly . . . you can't figure out where he got all that money."

"whom you can't trust . . . whose word is no good . . . who doesn't do what he says he was going to do . . . who doesn't carry through on anything."

In almost the exact reverse, the qualities of a good member of the community are found in the person who

"forgives and forgets . . . lets bygones be bygones . . . never dredges up the past . . . lets you know that he isn't going to hold it against you."

"is always doing something for the good of the town . . . gives willingly of his time and money . . . supports community projects . . . never shirks when there's work to be done."

"gets along with everybody . . . always has a good word . . . goes out of his way to do a good turn . . . never tries to hurt anybody . . . always has a smile for everybody."

"is just a natural person . . . even if you know he's better than you, he never lets you know it . . . never tries to impress anybody just because he has a little more money . . . acts like an ordinary person."

"always waits his turn . . . is modest . . . will work along with everybody else . . . isn't out for his own glory . . . takes a job and does it well without making a lot of noise."

"worked hard for what he's got . . . deserves every penny he has . . . doesn't come around to collect the first day of the month . . . you know he could be a lot richer."

"stands on his word . . . never has to have it in writing . . . does what he says . . . if he can't do it he says so and if he can he does it . . . always does it on time."

Springdalers affirm that on the whole most people have these qualities. They are the qualities of "average folk" and "we like to think of ourselves as just a little above the average." "Average people can get things done because nobody has any high-blown ideas and they can all work together to make the community a better place to live."

What is interesting about the usual definitions of good and bad people are the types that are excluded entirely. At this level those who go unrecognized, even in the negative statements, are the intellectuals, the bookish and the introverts. In a community that places a high premium on being demonstrably average, friendly and open, the person who appears in public and "doesn't say much" is a difficult character to understand: "he's a good fellow, but you never know what he's thinking." "Book reading and studying all the time," while they have a place, "shouldn't be carried too far . . . you have to keep your feet on the ground, be practical." The intellectual is respected for his education, is admired for his verbal facility and sometimes can provide the right idea, but nevertheless he is suspect and "shouldn't be allowed to get into positions of responsibility." It is apparent that where stereotyped public definitions do not easily fit, nonconformity is still tolerated so long as it does not seriously interfere with the workings of the town.

In the community setting the test case of the toleration and sympathy for nonconformity lies in attitudes toward cranks, psychotics and "odd" personalities: the ex-minister who writes poetry, the hermit who lives in the woods, the woman obsessed with the legal correctness of her husband's will, the spinster who screams at callers, the town moron and the clinical catatonic. Needless to say these represent only a small percentage of the population. The point is that Springdale is able to absorb, protect and care for them; when in the infrequent instance they intrude on the public scene, they are treated with the same sympathy and kindness accorded a child. So long as non-conformity does not interfere with the normal functioning of the town, no price is exacted from the non-conformist. At the worst, the nonconforming types are surrounded by humor. They become local "characters" who add color and interest to the everyday life of the community; because they are odd and different, they are always available as a standard conversational piece. In this way the community demonstrates its kindness and "lives and lets live."

"We're All Equal"

With the exception of a few "old cranks" and "no goods," it is unthinkable for anyone to pass a person on the street without exchanging greetings. Customarily one stops for a moment of conversation to discuss the weather and make inquiries about health; even the newcomer finds others stopping to greet him. The pattern of everyone talking to everyone is especially characteristic when people congregate in groups. Meetings and social gatherings do not begin until greetings have been exchanged all around. The person who feels he is above associating with everyone, as is the case with some newcomers from the city, runs the risk of being regarded a snob, for the taint of snobbishness is most easily acquired by failing to be friendly to everyone.

It is the policy of the Community Club to be open to "everyone, whether dues are paid or not" and hardly a meeting passes without a repetition of this statement. Those who are the leaders of the community take pride in this organization specifically because it excludes no one, and this fact is emphasized time and again in public situations. Wherever they can, community leaders encourage broad participation in all spheres of public life: everyone is urged and invited to attend public meetings and everyone is urged to "vote not as a duty, but as a privilege." The equality at the ballot box of all men, each according to his own conscience, in a community where you know all the candidates personally, where votes can't be bought and where you know the poll-keepers, is the hallmark of equality that underpins all other equality. "Here no man counts more than any other"; this is stated in every affirmation of rural political equality—"if you don't like the rascals, use your vote to kick them out."

In the private sphere—at what is commonly regarded as the level of gossip, either malicious or harmless—Springdalers tend to emphasize the negative and competitive qualities of life. One learns about domestic discords, sexual aberrations, family skeletons, ill-gained wealth, feuds, spite fences, black sheep, criminal records and alcoholism. The major preoccupation, however, is reserved for "what he's worth" in the strictly monetary and material meaning of the expression. The image of the sharp trading farmer, the penny-wise homemaker and the thrifty country folk is reflected in reverse in this concern with the state of other people's finances and possessions. All men, from the bartender to the clergyman, are capable of such concern typically expressed as follows:

"I'd say he's worth at least $30,000. Why the cows and buildings are worth that alone."

"You'd think a man with his money would give more than $50 to the church."

"The reason he's got so much is because he never spends any, hasn't taken a vacation for thirty years, never contributes a cent to anything."

"There's a man who's got a fortune and you'd never guess it."

"What I couldn't do with his dough."

"The way they spend money, you'd think it was like picking leaves off a tree."

"There's a guy making $2,800 and he's got a new Pontiac."

"Up to his neck in debt and he walks around like he had a million."

"Lend him a cent and you'll never see it again."

"He cleaned up during the war."

"There isn't anything he can't turn into a dollar."

"Figure it out. He's working, his wife's working, they haven't got any kids and they're collecting rent on two houses besides."

"He could be doing well if he stopped drinking."

"He may be taking in more than me, but then he's killing himself doing it."

"If he'd loosen up and be human, this town would be a better place for everybody."

"But, then, I haven't done so bad myself. There's the car, only four years left on the house and two kids through school."

These and similar statements, however, serve the function of enabling a person to calculate his relative financial standing. They are encountered almost everywhere in private gossip, but remain unspoken and hidden in ordinary public situations.

The social force of the idea finds its most positive expression in a negative way. The ladies of the book clubs, the most exclusive and limited membership groups in Springdale, find themselves in the ambiguous position of having to be apologetic for their exclusiveness. Because they are select in a community which devalues standoffishness, they are the only groups that are defensive in meeting the rest of the public. To the observer, they explain, "It's not that we want to be exclusive. It's just that sixteen is all you can manage in a book club. If anybody wants to be in a book club, she can start her own, like the Wednesday Group." By the same token they receive a large share of resentment; any number of vulgar expressions refer to this feminine section of the community.

The public ideology of equality has its economic correlates. One must not suppose that inequalities in income and wealth go unnoticed; rather, they are quite closely watched and known in Springdale. However, such differences, as in the image of the frontier community, are not publicly weighed and evaluated as the measure of the man.

In everyday social intercourse it is a social *faux pas* to act as if economic ine-

qualities make a difference. The wealthiest people in town, though they have big homes, live quite simply without servants. The serviceman, the delivery boy and the door-to-door canvasser knock at the front door and, though they may feel somewhat awkward on carpeted floors, are asked to enter even before stating their business. A man who flaunts his wealth, or demands deference because of it, is out of tune with a community whose "upper class" devalues conspicuous consumption and works at honest pursuits. "What makes the difference is not the wealth but the character behind it."

It is not a distortion to say that the good man is the working man and in the public estimation the fact of working transcends, indeed explains, economic differentials; work has its own social day of judgment and the judgment conferred is self-respect and respectability. Work, in the first instance, is the great social equalizer, and the purest form of work which serves as a yardstick for all other work is farm work. By this mechanism the "hard-working poor man" is superior to the "lazy rich man." The quotation marks are advised and indicate the hypotheticalness of the case because in common usage the two, work and wealth, go together. Where they don't it is because of misfortune, catastrophe, bad luck or simply because the man is young and work has not yet had a chance to pay its dividends. But even wealth is the wrong word. Work is rather juxtaposed beside such terms as rich, solvent, well-off; wealth implies more economic differentiation than Springdalers like to think exists in their community. Thus, the measure of a man, for all public social purposes, is the diligence and perseverance with which he pursues his economic ends; the "steady worker," the "good worker," the "hard worker" in contrast to the "fly-by-night schemer," the "band-wagon jumper," and the "johnny-come-lately." For the Springdaler the test case is the vulgar social climber, the person who tries to "get in with the better people" by aping them in dress and possessions which only money can buy. In spite of the social and economic differences visible to the outside observer, the pervading appearance of the community is that of a social equality based on the humanness of rural life.

The Etiquette of Gossip

Like other small rural communities Springdale must face the classic problem of preserving individual privacy in the face of a public ideology which places a high valuation on positive expressions of equalitarianism and neighborliness. The impression of community warmheartedness which is given by the free exchange of public greetings and the easy way "everybody gets along with everybody else" has its counterpart in the absence of privacy implied by the factor of gossip. The observer who has been in the community for a length of time realizes that "everybody isn't really neighborly . . . that some people haven't talked to each other for years . . . that people whom you might think are friends hate each other . . . that there are some people who are just naturally troublemakers . . . that he'd skin his own grandmother for a buck." However, such statements are never made in public situations. The intimate, the negative and the private are spoken in interpersonal situations involving only two or three people. Gossip exists as a separate and hidden layer of community life.

That is why it is at first difficult for the observer to believe the often-repeated statement that "everybody knows everything about everybody else in Springdale," or, as stated otherwise, "in a small town you live in a glass house." It develops that the statements are true only to a degree: while one learns intimate and verifiable details of people's private lives, these never become the subject of open, public discussion.

What is interesting about gossip is that in Springdale it seldom hurts anyone. Because it occurs in small temporarily closed circles and concerns those who are not present, the subject of the gossip need never be aware of it. Moreover, the *mores* demand, or better still one should say that it is an iron law of community life, that one not confront the subject of gossip with what is said about him. For this reason, though everyone engages in the practice, no one *has* to learn what things are being said about him. In the rare instance where one hears about gossip about oneself, it comes as a distinct shock "to think that so-and-so could have said that about me."

In a way, then, it is true that everyone knows everything about everyone else but, because of the way the information is learned, it does not ordinarily affect the everyday interpersonal relations of people; in public view even enemies speak to each other. When the victim meets the gossiper, he does not see him as a gossip and the gossiper does not let the privately gained information affect his public gestures; both greet each other in a friendly and neighborly manner and, perhaps, talk about someone else. Because the people of the community have this consideration for other people's feelings ("we like to think of ourselves as considerate and kind, not out to hurt anybody . . . that's one of the main reasons you live in a small town") relationships between people always give the impression of personalness and warmth.

The etiquette of gossip which makes possible the public suppression of the negative and competitive aspects of life has its counterpart in the etiquette of public conversation which always emphasizes the positive. There are thus two channels of communication that serve quite different purposes. In public conversation one hears comments only on the good things about people—"a man who has always done good things for the town"; "a swell guy"; "she's always doing good things for people"; "a person who never asks anything in return." More than this, the level of public conversation always focuses on the collective success of the community and the individual successes of its members. People comment on the success of a charitable drive, on the way a money-raising project "went over the top," on "what a good program it was," on the excellence of the actors' performance. These same themes become the subject of self-congratulatory newspaper articles. When failures occur, when the play "was a flop," as of course must happen from time to time, one senses what is almost a communal conspiracy against any further public mention of it. So too with the successes of individuals—the man who after many years of diligence finally gets a good job,

the person who completes a correspondence course, the local girl who gets a college degree, the local boy who makes good in the city, the man who finally succeeds in establishing himself in business, the winner of a contest, the high scorer, the person who has his name in a city newspaper—all such successes are given recognition in conventional conversation and in the press. At the public level all types of success are given public recognition while failure is treated with silence. It is because of the double and separate set of communication channels that negative gossip seldom colors the friendly ethos and the successful mood of the public life of the community.

25. URBANISM AND SUBURBANISM AS WAYS OF LIFE: A RE-EVALUATION OF DEFINITIONS

HERBERT J. GANS

In 1938 Louis Wirth published an essay entitled "Urbanism as a Way of Life." It has long been used as a companion to the piece by Robert Redfield (on folk society) because in it Wirth outlined what he saw to be the characteristics of the city dweller— the urban-type—in contrast to the member of the simple, preindustrial folk community. Persisting in the view that the city was the antithesis of the folk society, Wirth emphasized its depersonalizing, transitory and segmental qualities, suggesting that primary ties and other aspects of an integrated and settled existence would be replaced by secondary relationships. For many years his thesis has been the baseline for urban studies, his definitions the generally accepted views of city living.

In "Urbanism and Suburbanism as Ways of Life," Herbert Gans cogently presents Wirth's principal points and then seeks to reevaluate them in the light of recent empirical research. Gans contends that Wirth actually based his generalizations upon limited study of the inner city (and one city at that) and did not take into account the varied quality of life within the city and the larger metropolitan area. His critique includes a set of propositions on the characteristics—the social organization and ecology— of the inner city, the outer city, and the suburbs.

Herbert J. Gans is Professor of Sociology and Education at Teachers College and Research Associate, Institute of Urban Studies, Columbia University. An urban sociologist, he is the author of The Urban Villagers: Group and Class in the Life of Italian-Americans *(1962),* The Levittowners *(1967), and* People and Plans *(1968), and numerous articles in both professional and general journals of opinion.*

The contemporary sociological conception of cities and of urban life is based largely on the work of the Chicago School, and its summary statement in Louis Wirth's essay, "Urbanism as a Way of Life." [1] In that paper, Wirth developed a "minimum sociological definition of the city" as "a relatively large, dense and permanent settlement of socially heterogeneous individuals." [2] From these prerequisites, he then deduced the major outlines of the urban way of life. As he saw it, number, density, and heterogeneity created a social structure in which primary-group relationships were inevitably replaced by secondary contacts that were impersonal, segmental, superficial, transitory, and often predatory in nature. As a result, the city dweller became anonymous, isolated, secular, relativistic, rational, and sophisticated. In order to function in the urban society, he was forced to combine with others to organize corporations, voluntary associations, representative forms of government, and the impersonal mass media of communications. [3] These replaced the primary groups and the integrated way of life found in rural and other pre-industrial settlements.

Wirth's paper has become a classic in urban sociology, and most texts have followed his definition and description faithfully.[4] In recent years, however, a considerable number of studies and essays have questioned his formulations.[5] In addition, a number of changes have taken place in cities since the article was published in 1938, notably the exodus of white residents to low- and medium-priced houses in the suburbs, and the decentralization of industry. The evidence from these studies and the changes in American cities suggest that Wirth's statement must be revised.

There is yet another, and more important reason for such a revision. Despite its title and intent, Wirth's paper deals with urban-industrial society, rather than with the city. This is evident from his approach. Like other urban sociologists, Wirth based his analysis on a comparison of settlement types, but unlike his colleagues, who pursued urban-rural comparisons, Wirth contrasted the city to the folk society. Thus, he compared settlement types of pre-industrial and industrial society. This allowed him to include in his theory of urbanism the entire range of modern insitutions which are not found in the folk society, even though many such groups (e.g., voluntary associations) are by no means exclusively urban. Moreover, Wirth's conception of the city dweller as depersonalized, atomized, and susceptible to mass movements suggests that his paper is based on, and contributes to, the theory of the mass society.

Many of Wirth's conclusions may be relevant to the understanding of ways of life in modern society. However, since the theory argues that all of society is now urban, *his analysis does not distinguish ways of life in the city from those in other settlements within modern society.* In Wirth's time, the comparison of urban and pre-urban settlement types was still fruitful, but today, the primary task for

urban (or community) sociology seems to me to be the analysis of the similarities and differences between contemporary settlement types.

This paper is an attempt at such an analysis; it limits itself to distinguishing ways of life in the modern city and the modern suburb. A re-analysis of Wirth's conclusions from this perspective suggests that his characterization of the urban way of life applies only—and not too accurately—to the residents of the inner city. The remaining city dwellers, as well as most suburbanites, pursue a different way of life, which I shall call "quasi-primary." This proposition raises some doubt about the mutual exclusiveness of the concepts of city and suburb and leads to a yet broader question: whether settlement concepts and other ecological concepts are useful for explaining ways of life.

The Inner City

Wirth argued that number, density, and heterogeneity had two social consequences which explain the major features of urban life. On the one hand, the crowding of diverse types of people into a small area led to the segregation of homogeneous types of people into separate neighborhoods.[6] On the other hand, the lack of physical distance between city dwellers resulted in social contact between them, which broke down existing social and cultural patterns and encouraged assimilation as well as acculturation—the melting pot effect.[7] Wirth implied that the melting pot effect was far more powerful than the tendency toward segregation and concluded that, sooner or later, the pressures engendered by the dominant social, economic, and political institutions of the city would destroy the remaining pockets of primary-group relationships.[8] Eventually, the social system of the city would resemble Tönnies' *Gesellschaft*—a way of life which Wirth considered undesirable.

Because Wirth had come to see the city

as the prototype of mass society, and because he examined the city from the distant vantage point of the folk society—from the wrong end of the telescope, so to speak—his view of urban life is not surprising. In addition, Wirth found support for his theory in the empirical work of his Chicago colleagues. As Greer and Kube [9] and Wilensky [10] have pointed out, the Chicago sociologists conducted their most intensive studies in the inner city.[11] At that time, these were slums recently invaded by new waves of European immigrants and rooming house and skid row districts, as well as the habitat of Bohemians and well-to-do Gold Coast apartment dwellers. Wirth himself studied the Maxwell Street Ghetto [of Chicago], an inner-city Jewish neighborhood then being dispersed by the acculturation and mobility of its inhabitants.[12] Some of the characteristics of urbanism which Wirth stressed in his essay abounded in these areas.

Wirth's diagnosis of the city as *Gesellschaft* must be questioned on three counts. First, the conclusions derived from a study of the inner city cannot be generalized to the entire urban area. Second, there is as yet not enough evidence to prove—nor, admittedly, to deny—that number, density, and heterogeneity result in the social consequences which Wirth proposed. Finally, even if the causal relationship could be verified, it can be shown that a significant proportion of the city's inhabitants were, and are, isolated from these consequences by social structures and cultural patterns which they either brought to the city, or developed by living in it. Wirth conceived the urban population as consisting of heterogeneous individuals, torn from past social systems, unable to develop new ones, and therefore prey to social anarchy in the city. While it is true that a not insignificant proportion of the inner city population was, and still is, made up of unattached individuals,[13] Wirth's formulation ignores the fact that this population consists mainly of relatively homogeneous groups, with social

and cultural moorings that shield it fairly effectively from the suggested consequences of number, density, and heterogeneity. This applies even more to the residents of the outer city, who constitute a majority of the total city population.

The social and cultural moorings of the inner city population are best described by a brief analysis of the five types of inner city residents. These are:

1. the "cosmopolites";
2. the unmarried or childless;
3. the "ethnic villagers";
4. the "deprived"; and
5. the "trapped" and downward mobile.

The "cosmopolites" include students, artists, writers, musicians, and entertainers, as well as other intellectuals and professionals. They live in the city in order to be near the special "cultural" facilities that can only be located near the center of the city. Many cosmopolites are unmarried or childless. Others rear children in the city, especially if they have the income to afford the aid of servants and governesses. The less affluent ones may move to the suburbs to raise their children, continuing to live as cosmopolites under considerable handicaps, especially in the lower-middle-class suburbs. Many of the very rich and powerful are also cosmopolites, although they are likely to have at least two residences, one of which is suburban or exurban.

The unmarried or childless must be divided into two subtypes, depending on the permanence or transience of their status. The temporarily unmarried or childless live in the inner city for only a limited time. Young adults may team up to rent an apartment away from their parents and close to a job or entertainment opportunities. When they marry, they may move first to an apartment in a transient neighborhood, but if they can afford to do so, they leave for the outer city or the suburbs with the arrival of the first or second child. The permanently unmarried may stay in the inner city for the remainder of their lives, their housing depending on their income.

The "ethnic villagers" are ethnic groups which are found in such inner city neighborhoods as New York's Lower East Side, living in some ways as they did when they were peasants in European or Puerto Rican villages.[14] Although they reside in the city, they isolate themselves from significant contact with most city facilities, aside from workplaces. Their way of life differs sharply from Wirth's urbanism in its emphasis on kinship and the primary group, the lack of anonymity and secondary-group contacts, the weakness of formal organizations, and the suspicion of anything and anyone outside their neighborhood.

The first two types live in the inner city by choice; the third is there partly because of necessity, partly because of tradition. The final two types are in the inner city because they have no other choice. One is the "deprived" population: the very poor; the emotionally disturbed or otherwise handicapped; broken families; and, most important, the non-white population. These urban dwellers must take the dilapidated housing and blighted neighborhoods to which the housing market relegates them, although among them are some for whom the slum is a hiding place, or a temporary stop-over to save money for a house in the outer city or the suburbs.[15]

The "trapped" are the people who stay behind when a neighborhood is invaded by non-residential land uses or lower-status immigrants, because they cannot afford to move, or are otherwise bound to their present location.[16] The "downward mobiles" are a related type; they may have started life in a higher class position, but have been forced down in the socio-economic hierarchy and in the quality of their accommodations. Many of them are old people, living out their existence on small pensions.

These five types all live in dense and heterogeneous surroundings, yet they have such diverse ways of life that it is hard to see how density and heterogeneity could exert a common influence. Moreover, all but the last two types are isolated or detached from their neighborhood and thus from the social consequences which Wirth described.

When people who live together have social ties based on criteria other than mere common occupancy, they can set up social barriers regardless of the physical closeness of the heterogeneity of their neighbors. The ethnic villagers are the best illustration. While a number of ethnic groups are usually found living together in the same neighborhood, they are able to *isolate* themselves from each other through a variety of social devices. Wirth himself recognized this when he wrote that "two groups can occupy a given area without losing their separate identity because each side is permitted to live its own inner life and each somehow fears or idealizes the other."[17] Although it is true that the children in these areas were often oblivious to the social barriers set up by their parents, at least until adolescence, it is doubtful whether their acculturation can be traced to the melting pot effect as much as to the pervasive influence of the American culture that flowed into these areas from the outside.[18]

The cosmopolites, the unmarried, and the childless are *detached* from neighborhood life. The cosmopolites possess a distinct subculture which causes them to be disinterested in all but the most superficial contacts with their neighbors, somewhat like the ethnic villagers. The unmarried and childless are detached from their neighborhood because of their life-cycle stage, which frees them from the routine family responsibilities that entail some relationship to the local area. In their choice of residence, the two types are therefore not concerned about their neighbors, or the availability and quality of local community facilities. Even the well-to-do can choose expensive apartments in or near poor neighborhoods, because if they have children, these are sent to special schools and summer camps which effectively isolate them from neighbors. In addition, both types, but especially the childless and unmarried, are transient. Therefore, they tend to live in areas marked by high population turnover, where their own mobility and that of their neighbors creates a universal detachment from the neighborhood.[19]

The deprived and the trapped do seem to be affected by some of the consequences of number, density, and heterogeneity. The deprived population suffers considerably from overcrowding, but this is a consequence of low income, racial discrimination, and other handicaps, and cannot be considered an inevitable result of the ecological make-up of the city.[20] Because the deprived have no residential choice, they are also forced to live amid neighbors not of their own choosing, with ways of life different and even contradictory to their own. If familial defenses against the neighborhood climate are weak, as is the case among broken families and downward mobile people, parents may lose their children to the culture of "the street." The trapped are the unhappy people who remain behind when their more advantaged neighbors move on; they must endure the heterogeneity which results from neighborhood change.

Wirth's description of the urban way of life fits best the transient areas of the inner city. Such areas are typically heterogeneous in population, partly because they are inhabited by transient types who do not require homogeneous neighbors or by deprived people who have no choice, or may themselves be quite mobile. Under conditions of transience and heterogeneity, people interact only in terms of the segmental roles necessary for obtaining local services. Their social relationships thus display anonymity, impersonality, and superficiality.[21]

The social features of Wirth's concept of urbanism seem therefore to be a result of residential instability, rather than of number, density, or heterogeneity. In fact, heterogeneity is itself an effect of residential instability, resulting when the influx of transients causes landlords and realtors to stop acting as gatekeepers—that is, wardens of neighborhood homogeneity.[22] Residential instability is found in all types of settlements, and, presumably, its social consequences are everywhere similar. These consequences cannot therefore be identified with the ways of life of the city.

The Outer City and the Suburbs

The second effect which Wirth ascribed to number, density, and heterogeneity was the segregation of homogeneous people into distinct neighborhoods,[23] on the basis of "place and nature of work, income, racial and ethnic characteristics, social status, custom, habit, taste, preference and prejudice." [24] This description fits the residential districts of the *outer city*.[25] Although these districts contain the majority of the city's inhabitants, Wirth went into little detail about them. He made it clear, however, that the socio-psychological aspects of urbanism were prevalent there as well.[26]

Because existing neighborhood studies deal primarily with the exotic sections of the inner city, very little is known about the more typical residential neighborhoods of the outer city. However, it is evident that the way of life in these areas bears little resemblance to Wirth's urbanism. Both the studies which question Wirth's formulation and my own observations suggest that the common element in the ways of life of these neighborhoods is best described as *quasi-primary*. I use this term to characterize relationships between neighbors. Whatever the intensity or frequency of these relationships, the interaction is more intimate than a secondary contact, but more guarded than a primary one.[27]

There are actually few secondary relationships, because of the isolation of residential neighborhoods from economic institutions and workplaces. Even shopkeepers, store managers, and other local functionaries who live in the area are treated as acquaintances or friends, unless they are of a vastly different social status or are forced by their corporate employers to treat their customers as economic units.[28] Voluntary associations attract only a minority of the population. Moreover, much of the organizational activity is of a sociable nature, and it is often difficult to accomplish the association's "business" because of the members' preference for sociability. Thus, it would appear that interactions in organizations, or between neighbors generally, do not fit the secondary-relationship model of urban life. As anyone who has lived in these neighborhoods knows, there is little anonymity, impersonality or privacy.[29] In fact, American cities have sometimes been described as collections of small towns.[30] There is some truth to this description, especially if the city is compared to the actual small town, rather than to the romantic construct of anti-urban cities.[31]

Postwar suburbia represents the most contemporary version of the quasi-primary way of life. Owing to increases in real income and the encouragement of home ownership provided by the FHA, families in the lower-middle class and upper working class can now live in modern single-family homes in low-density subdivisions, an opportunity previously available only to the upper and upper-middle classes.[32]

The popular literature describes the new suburbs as communities in which conformity, homogeneity, and other-direction are unusually rampant.[33] The implication is that the move from city to suburb initiates a new way of life which causes considerable behavior and personality change in previous urbanites. A preliminary analysis of data which I am now collecting in Levittown, New Jersey, suggests, however, that the move from the city to this predominantly lower-middle-class suburb does not result in any major behavioral changes for most pople. Moreover, the changes which do occur reflect the move from the social isolation of a transient city or suburban apartment building to the quasi-primary life of a neighborhood of single-family homes. Also, many of the people whose life has changed reported that the changes were intended. They existed as aspirations before the move, or as reasons for it. In other words, the suburb itself creates few changes in ways of life. Similar conclusions have been reported by Berger in his excellent study of a working-class population newly moved to a suburban subdivision.[34]

A Comparison of City and Suburb

If urban and suburban areas are similar in that the way of life in both is quasi-primary, and if urban residents who move out to the suburbs do not undergo any significant changes in behavior, it would be fair to argue that the differences in ways of life between the two types of settlements have been overestimated. Yet the fact remains that a variety of physical and demographic differences exist between the city and the suburb. However, upon closer examination, many of these differences turn out to be either spurious or of little significance for the way of life of the inhabitants.[35]

The differences between the residential areas of cities and suburbs which have been cited most frequently are:

1. Suburbs are more likely to be dormitories.
2. They are further away from the work and play facilities of the central business districts.
3. They are newer and more modern than city residential areas and are designed for the automobile rather than for pedestrian and mass-transit forms of movement.

4. They are built up with single-family rather than multi-family structures and are therefore less dense.
5. Their populations are more homogeneous.
6. Their populations differ demographically: they are younger; more of them are married; they have higher incomes; and they hold proportionately more white collar jobs.[36]

Most urban neighborhoods are as much dormitories as the suburbs. Only in a few older inner city areas are factories and offices still located in the middle of residential blocks, and even here many of the employees do not live in the neighborhood.

The fact that the suburbs are farther from the central business district is often true only in terms of distance, not travel time. Moreover, most people make relatively little use of downtown facilities, other than workplaces.[37] The downtown stores seem to hold their greatest attraction for the upper-middle class;[38] the same is probably true of typically urban entertainment facilities. Teen-agers and young adults may take their dates to first-run movie theaters, but the museums, concert halls, and lecture rooms attract mainly upper-middle-class ticket-buyers, many of them suburban.[39]

The suburban reliance on the train and the automobile has given rise to an imaginative folklore about the consequences of commuting on alcohol consumption, sex life, and parental duties. Many of these conclusions are, however, drawn from selected high-income suburbs and exurbs, and reflect job tensions in such hectic occupations as advertising and show business more than the effects of residence.[40] It is true that the upper-middle-class housewife must become a chauffeur in order to expose her children to the proper educational facilities, but such differences as walking to the corner drug store and driving to its suburban equivalent seem to me of little emotional, social, or cultural import.[41] In addition, the continuing shrinkage in the number of mass-transit users suggests that even in the city many younger people are now living a wholly auto-based way of life.

The fact that suburbs are smaller is primarily a function of political boundaries drawn long before the communities were suburban. This affects the kinds of political issues which develop and provides somewhat greater opportunity for citizen participation. Even so, in the suburbs as in the city, the minority who participate are the professional politicians, the economically concerned businessmen, lawyers and salesmen, and the ideologically motivated middle- and upper-middle-class people with better than average education.

The social consequences of differences in density and house type also seem overrated. Single-family houses on quiet streets facilitate the supervision of children; this is one reason why middle-class women who want to keep an eye on their children move to the suburbs. House type also has some effects on relationships between neighbors, insofar as there are more opportunities for visual contact between adjacent homeowners than between people on different floors of an apartment house. However, if occupants' characteristics are also held constant, the differences in actual social contact are less marked. Homogeneity of residents turns out to be more important as a determinant of sociability than proximity. If the population is heterogeneous, there is little social contact between neighbors, either on apartment-house floors or in single-family-house blocks; if people are homogeneous, there is likely to be considerable social contact in both house types. One need only contrast the apartment house located in a transient, heterogeneous neighborhood and exactly the same structure in a neighborhood occupied by a single ethnic group. The former is a lonely, anonymous building; the latter, a bustling micro-society. I have observed similar patterns in suburban areas: on blocks where people are homogeneous, they socialize; where they are heterogeneous, they do little more than exchange polite greetings.[42]

Suburbs are usually described as being more homogeneous in house type than the city, but if they are compared to the outer city, the differences are small. Most inhabitants of the outer city, other than well-to-do homeowners, live on blocks of uniform structures as well—for example, the endless streets of rowhouses in Philadelphia and Baltimore or of two-story duplexes and six-flat apartment houses in Chicago. They differ from the new suburbs only in that they were erected through more primitive methods of mass production. Suburbs are of course more predominantly areas of owner-occupied single homes, though in the outer districts of most American cities homeownership is also extremely high.

Demographically, suburbs as a whole are clearly more homogeneous than cities as a whole, though probably not more so than outer cities. However, people do not live in cities or suburbs as a whole, but in specific neighborhoods. An analysis of ways of life would require a determination of the degree of population homogeneity within the boundaries of areas defined as neighborhoods by residents' social contacts. Such an analysis would no doubt indicate that many neighborhoods in the city as well as the suburbs are homogeneous. Neighborhood homogeneity is actually a result of factors having little or nothing to do with the house type, density, or location of the area relative to the city limits. Brand new neighborhoods are more homeogeneous than older ones, because they have not yet experienced resident turnover, which frequently results in population heterogeneity. Neighborhoods of low- and medium-priced housing are usually less homogeneous than those with expensive dwellings because they attract families who have reached the peak of occupational and residential mobility, as well as young families who are just starting their climb and will eventually move to neighborhoods of higher status. The latter, being accessible only to high-income people, are therefore more homogeneous with respect to other resident characteristics as well. Moreover, such areas have the economic and political power to slow down or prevent invasion. Finally, neighborhoods located in the path of ethnic or religious group movement are likely to be extremely homogeneous.

The demographic differences between cities and suburbs cannot be questioned, especially since the suburbs have attracted a large number of middle-class child-rearing families. The differences are, however, much reduced if suburbs are compared only to the outer city. In addition, a detailed comparison of suburban and outer city residential areas would show that neighborhoods with the same kinds of people can be found in the city as well as the suburbs. Once again, the age of the area and the cost of housing are more important determinants of demographic characteristics than the location of the area with respect to the city limits.

Characteristics, Social Organization, and Ecology

The preceding sections of the paper may be summarized in three propositions:

1. As concerns ways of life, the inner city must be distinguished from the outer city and the suburbs; and the latter two exhibit a way of life bearing little resemblance to Wirth's urbanism.
2. Even in the inner city, ways of life resemble Wirth's description only to a limited extent. Moreover, economic condition, cultural characteristics, life-cycle stage, and residential instability explain ways of life more satisfactorily than number, density, or heterogeneity.
3. Physical and other differences between city and suburb are often spurious or

without much meaning for ways of life.

These propositions suggest that the concepts urban and suburban are neither mutually exclusive, nor especially relevant for understanding ways of life. They—and number, density, and heterogeneity as well —are ecological concepts which describe human adaptation to the environment. However, they are not sufficient to explain social phenomena, because these phenomena cannot be understood solely as the consequences of ecological processes. Therefore, other explanations must be considered.

Ecological explanations of social life are most applicable if the subjects under study lack the ability to *make choices,* be they plants, animals, or human beings. Thus, if there is a housing shortage, people will live almost anywhere, and under extreme conditions of no choice, as in a disaster, married and single, old and young, middle and working class, stable and transient will be found side by side in whatever accommodations are available. At that time, their ways of life represent an almost direct adaptation to the environment. If the supply of housing and of neighborhoods is such that alternatives are available, however, people will make choices, and if the housing market is responsive, they can even make and satisfy explicit *demands.*

Choices and demands do not develop independently or at random; they are functions of the roles people play in the social system. These can best be understood in terms of the *characteristics* of the people involved; that is, characteristics can be used as indices to choices and demands made in the roles that constitute ways of life. Although many characteristics affect the choices and demands people make with respect to housing and neighborhoods, the most important ones seem to be *class*—in all its economic, social and cultural ramifications—and *life-cycle stage.*[43] If people have an opportunity to choose, these two characteristics will go far in explaining the kinds of housing and neighborhoods they will occupy and the ways of life they will try to establish within them.

Many of the previous assertions about ways of life in cities and suburbs can be analyzed in terms of class and life-cycle characteristics. Thus in the inner city, the unmarried and childless live as they do, detached from neighborhood, because of their life-cycle stage; the cosmopolites, because of a combination of life-cycle stage and a distinctive but class-based subculture. The way of life of the deprived and trapped can be explained by low socioeconomic level and related handicaps. The quasi-primary way of life is associated with the family stage of the life-cycle, and the norms of child-rearing and parental role found in the upper working class, the lower-middle class, and the non-cosmopolite portions of the upper-middle and upper classes.

The attributes of the so-called suburban way of life can also be understood largely in terms of these characteristics. The new suburbia is nothing more than a highly visible showcase for the ways of life of young, upper-working-class and lower-middle-class people. Ktsanes and Reissman have aptly described it as "new homes for old values." [44] Much of the descriptive and critical writing about suburbia assumes that as long as the new suburbanites lived in the city, they behaved like upper-middle-class cosmopolites and that suburban living has mysteriously transformed them.[45] The critics fail to see that the behavior and personality patterns ascribed to suburbia are in reality those of class and age.[46] These patterns could have been found among the new suburbanites when they still lived in the city and could now be observed among their peers who still reside there—if the latter were as visible to critics and researchers as are the suburbanites.

Needless to say, the concept of "characteristics" cannot explain all aspects of ways of life, either among urban or suburban residents. Some aspects must be explained by concepts of social organization that are independent of characteristics. For example, some features of the quasi-primary way of life are independent of class and age, because they evolve from the roles and situations created by joint and adjacent occupancy of land and dwellings. Likewise, residential instability is a universal process which has a number of invariate consequences. In each case, however, the way in which people react varies with their characteristics. So it is with ecological processes. Thus, there are undoubtedly differences between ways of life in urban and suburban settlements which remain after behavior patterns based on residents' characteristics have been analyzed, and which must therefore be attributed to features of the settlement.[47]

Characteristics do not explain the causes of behavior; rather, they are clues to socially created and culturally defined roles, choices, and demands. A causal analysis must trace them back to the larger social, economic, and political systems which determine the situations in which roles are played and the cultural content of choices and demands, as well as the opportunities for their achievement.[48] These systems determine income distributions, educational and occupational opportunities, and in turn, fertility patterns, child-rearing methods, as well as the entire range of consumer behavior. Thus, a complete analysis of the way of life of the deprived residents of the inner city cannot stop by indicating the influence of low income, lack of education, or family instability. These must be related to such conditions as the urban economy's "need" for low-wage workers, and the housing market practices which restrict residential choice. The urban economy is in turn shaped by national economic and social systems, as well as by local and regional ecological processes. Some phenomena can be explained exclusively by reference to these ecological processes.

However, it must also be recognized that as man gains greater control over the natural environment, he has been able to free himself from many of the determining and limiting effects of that environment. Thus, changes in local transportation technology, the ability of industries to be footloose, and the relative affluence of American society have given ever larger numbers of people increasing amounts of residential choice. The greater the amount of choice available, the more important does the concept of characteristics become in understanding behavior.

Consequently, the study of ways of life in communities must begin with an analysis of characteristics. If characteristics are dealt with first and held constant, we may be able to discover which behavior patterns can be attributed to features of the settlement and its natural environment.[49] Only then will it be possible to discover to what extent city and suburb are independent—rather than dependent or intervening—variables in the explanation of ways of life.

This kind of analysis might help to reconcile the ecological point of view with the behavioral and cultural one, and possibly put an end to the conflict between conceptual positions which insist on one explanation or the other.[50] Both explanations have some relevance, and future research and theory must clarify the role of each in the analysis of ways of life in various types of settlement.[51] Another important rationale for this approach is its usefulness for applied sociology—for example, city planning. The planner can recommend changes in the spatial and physical arrangements of the city. Frequently, he seeks to achieve social goals or to change social conditions through physical solutions. He has been attracted to ecological explanations because these relate behavior to phenomena which he can affect. For example, most planners tend to agree with Wirth's formulations, because they stress number and density, over which the planner has some control. If the undesirable social conditions of the inner city could be traced to these two factors, the planner could propose large-scale clearance projects which would reduce the size of the urban population, and lower residential densities. Experience with public housing projects has, however, made it apparent that low densities, new buildings, or modern site plans do not eliminate anti-social or self-destructive behavior. The analysis of characteristics will call attention to the fact that this behavior is lodged in the deprivations of low socioeconomic status and racial discrimination, and that it can be changed only through the removal of these deprivations. Conversely, if such an analysis suggests residues of behavior that can be attributed to ecological processes or physical aspects of housing and neighborhoods, the planner can recommend physical changes that can really affect behavior.

A Re-evaluation of Definitions

The argument presented here has implications for the sociological definition of the city. Such a definition relates ways of life to environmental features of the city *qua* settlement type. But if ways of life do not coincide with settlement types, and if these ways are functions of class and life-cycle stage rather than of the ecological attributes of the settlement, a sociological definition of the city cannot be formulated.[52] Concepts such as city and suburb allow us to distinguish settlement types from each other physically and demographically, but the ecological processes and conditions which they synthesize have no direct or invariate consequences for ways of life. The sociologist cannot, therefore, speak of an urban or suburban way of life.

Conclusion

Many of the descriptive statements made here are as time-bound as Wirth's.[53]

Twenty years ago, Wirth concluded that some form of urbanism would eventually predominate in all settlement types. He was, however, writing during a time of immigrant acculturation and at the end of a serious depression, an era of minimal choice. Today, it is apparent that high-density, heterogeneous surroundings are for most people a temporary place of residence; other than for the Park Avenue or Greenwich Village cosmopolites, they are a result of necessity rather than choice. As soon as they can afford to do so, most Americans head for the single-family house and the quasi-primary way of life of the low-density neighborhood, in the outer city or the suburbs.[54]

Changes in the national economy and in government housing policy can affect many of the variables that make up housing supply and demand. For example, urban sprawl may eventually outdistance the ability of present and proposed transportation systems to move workers into the city; further industrial decentralization can forestall it and alter the entire relationship between work and residence. The expansion of present urban renewal activities can perhaps lure a significant number of cosmopolites back from the suburbs, while a drastic change in renewal policy might begin to ameliorate the housing conditions of the deprived population. A serious depression could once again make America a nation of doubled-up tenants.

These events will affect housing supply and residential choice; they will frustrate but not suppress demands for the quasi-primary way of life. However, changes in the national economy, society, and culture can affect people's characteristics—family size, educational level, and various other concomitants of life-cycle stage and class. These in turn will stimulate changes in demands and choices. The rising number of college graduates, for example, is likely to increase the cosmopolite ranks. This might in turn create a new set of city dwellers, although it will probably do no more than encourage the development of cosmopolite facilities in some suburban areas.

The current revival of interest in urban sociology and in community studies, as well as the sociologist's increasing curiosity about city planning, suggest that data may soon be available to formulate a more adequate theory of the relationship between settlements and the ways of life within them. The speculations presented in this paper are intended to raise questions; they can only be answered by more systematic data collection and theorizing.

NOTES

1. Louis Wirth. "Urbanism as a Way of Life," *American Journal of Sociology,* 44 (1938), 1–24. Reprinted in Paul Hatt and Albert J. Reiss, Jr. (eds.), *Cities and Society.* Glencoe, Ill.: The Free Press, 1957, pp. 46–64.

2. *Ibid.,* p. 50.

3. *Ibid.,* pp. 54–60.

4. Richard Dewey. "The Rural-Urban Continuum: Real but Relatively Unimportant," *American Journal of Sociology,* 66 (1960), 60–66.

5. Morris Axelrod. "Urban Structure and Social Participation," *American Sociological Review,* 21 (1956), 13–18; Dewey, *op. cit.;* William H. Form, *et al.,* "The Compatibility of Alternative Approaches to the Delimitation of Urban Sub-areas," *American Sociological Review,* 19 (1954), 434–440; Herbert J. Gans, *The Urban Villagers: A Study of the Second Generation Italians in the West End of Boston.* Boston: Center for Community Studies, December 1959 (mimeographed); Scott Greer, "Urbanism Reconsidered: A Comparative Study of Local Areas in a Metropolis," *American Sociological Review,* 21 (1956), 19–25; Scott Greer, and Ella Kube, "Urbanism and Social Structure: A Los Angeles Study," in Marvin B. Sussman (ed.), *Community Structure and Analysis.* New York: Thomas Y. Crowell Company, 1959, pp. 93–112; Morris Janowitz, *The Community Press in an Urban Setting.* Glencoe, Ill.: The Free Press, 1952; Albert J. Reiss, Jr., "An Analysis of Urban Phenomena," in Robert M. Fisher (ed.), *The Metropolis in Modern Life.* Garden City, N.Y.: Doubleday & Company, Inc., 1955, pp. 41–49; Albert J. Reiss, Jr., "Rural-Urban and Status Differences in Interpersonal Contacts," *American Journal of Sociology,* 65 (1959), 182–195; John R. Seeley, "The Slum: Its Nature, Use and Users," *Journal of the American Institute of Planners,* 25 (1959), 7–14; Joel Smith, William Form, and Gregory Stone. "Local Intimacy in a Middle-Sized City," *American Journal of Sociology,* 60 (1954), 276–284; Gregory P. Stone, "City Shoppers and Urban Identification: Observations on the Social Psychology of City Life," *American Journal of Sociology,* 60 (1954), 36–45; William F. Whyte, Jr., *Street Corner Society.* Chicago: The University of Chicago Press, 1955; Harold L. Wilensky, and Charles Lebeaux, *Industrial Society and Social Welfare.* New York: Russell Sage Foundation, 1958; Michael Young, and Peter Willmott. *Family and Kinship in East London.* London: Routledge & Kegan Paul, Ltd., 1957.

I shall not attempt to summarize these studies, for this task has already been performed by Dewey, Reiss, Wilensky, and others.

6. Wirth, *op cit.,* p. 56.

7. *Ibid.,* p. 52.

8. *Ibid.,* pp. 60–62.

9. Greer and Kube, *op. cit.,* p. 112.

10. Wilensky, *op. cit.,* p. 121.

11. By the *inner city,* I mean the transient residential areas, the Gold Coasts and the slums that generally surround the central business district, although in some communities they may continue for miles beyond that district. The *outer city* includes the stable residential areas that house the working- and middle-class tenant and owner. The *suburbs* I conceive as the latest and most modern ring of the outer city, distinguished from it only by yet lower densities, and by the often irrelevant fact of the ring's location outside the city limits.

12. Louis Wirth. *The Ghetto,* Chicago: The University of Chicago Press, 1928.

13. Arnold M. Rose. "Living Arrangements of Unattached Persons," *American Sociological Review,* 12 (1947), 429–435.

14. Gans, *op. cit.*

15. Seeley, *op. cit.*

16. *Idem;* The trapped are not very visible, but I suspect that they are a significant element in what Raymond Vernon has described as the "gray areas" of the city. See Raymond Vernon, *The Changing Economic Function of the Central City,* New York: Committee on Economic Development, Supplementary Paper No. 1, January 1959.

17. Greer, *op. cit.,* p. 283.

18. If the melting pot has resulted from propinquity and high density, one would have expected second-generation Italians, Irish, Jews, Greeks, Slavs, etc. to have developed a single "pan-ethnic culture," consisting of a synthesis of the cultural patterns of the propinquitous national groups.

19. The corporation transients (see William F. Whyte, Jr., *The Organization Man,* New York: Simon & Schuster, 1956; Wilensky and Lebeaux, *op. cit.*), who provide a new source of residential instability to the suburb, differ from city transients. Since they are raising families, they want to integrate themselves into neighborhood life, and are usually able to do so, mainly because they tend to move into similar types of communities wherever they go.

20. The negative social consequences of overcrowding are a result of high room and floor density, not of the land coverage of population density which Wirth discussed. Park Avenue residents live under conditions of high land density, but do not seem to suffer visibly from overcrowding.

21. Whether or not these social phenomena have the psychological consequences Wirth suggested depends on the people who live in the area. Those who are detached from the neighborhood by choice are probably immune, but those who depend on the neighborhood for their social relationships—the unattached individuals, for example—may suffer greatly from loneliness.

22. Needless to say, residential instability must ultimately be traced back to the fact that, as Wirth pointed out, the city and its economy attract transient—and, depending on the sources of outmigration, heterogeneous—people. However, this is a characteristic of urban-industrial society, not of the city specifically.

23. By neighborhoods or residential districts I mean areas demarcated from others by distinctive physical boundaries or by social characteristics, some of which may be perceived only by the residents. However, these areas are not necessarily socially self-sufficient or culturally distinctive.

24. Wirth, *op. cit.,* p. 56.

25. For the definition of *outer city,* see Footnote 11.

26. Wirth, *loc. cit.*

27. Because neighborly relations are not quite primary, and not quite secondary, they can also become *pseudo-primary;* that is, secondary ones disguised with false affect to make them appear primary. Critics have often described suburban life in this fashion, although the actual prevalence of pseudo-primary relationships has not been studied systematically in cities or suburbs.

28. Stone, *op. cit.*

29. These neighborhoods cannot, however, be considered as urban folk societies. People go out of the area for many of their friendships, and their allegiance to the neighborhood is neither intense nor all-encompassing. Janowitz has aptly described the relationship between resident and neighborhood as one of "limited liability." See Janowitz, *op. cit.,* chap. 7.

30. Were I not arguing that ecological concepts cannot double as sociological ones, this way of life might best be described as small-townish.

31. Arthur J. Vidich, and Joseph Bensman. *Small Town in Mass Society: Class, Power and Religion in a Rural Community.* Princeton, N.J.: Princeton University Press, 1958.

32. Harold Wattell. "Levittown: A Suburban Community," in William M. Dobriner (ed.), *The Suburban Community.* New York: G. P. Putnam's Sons, 1958, pp. 287–313.

33. Bennett Berger. *Working Class Suburb: A Study of Auto Workers in Suburbia.* Berkeley, Calif.: University of California Press, 1960; Vernon, *op. cit.*

34. Berger, *op. cit.*

35. They may, of course, be significant for the welfare of the total metropolitan area. Cf. Wattell, *op. cit.*

36. Otis Dudley Duncan, and Albert J. Reiss, Jr. *Social Characteristics of Rural and Urban Communities, 1950,* New York: John Wiley & Sons, 1956, p. 131.

37. Donald L. Foley. "The Use of Local Facilities in a Metropolis," in Paul Hatt and Albert J. Reiss, Jr. (eds.), *Cities and Society.* Glencoe, Ill.: The Free Press, 1957, pp. 237–247; and Christen T. Jonassen, *The Shopping Center versus Downtown,* Columbus, Ohio: Bureau of Business Research, Ohio State University, 1955.

38. Jonassen, *op. cit.,* pp. 91–92.

39. A 1958 study of New York theater goers showed a median income of close to $10,000 and 35 per cent were reported as living in the suburbs. See John Enders, *Profile of the Theater Market.* New York: Playbill, undated and unpaged.

40. A. C. Spectorsky. *The Exurbanites,* Philadelphia: J. B. Lippincott, 1955.

41. I am thinking here of adults; teen-agers do suffer from the lack of informal meeting places within walking or bicycling distance.

42. Herbert J. Gans. "Planning and Social Life: An Evaluation of Friendship and Neighbor Relations in Suburban Communities," *Journal of the American Institute of Planners,* 27 (1961), 134–140.

43. These must be defined in dynamic terms. Thus, class includes also the process of social mobility, stage in the life-cycle, and the processes of socialization and aging.

44. Thomas Ktsanes, and Leonard Reissman. "Suburbia: New Homes for Old Values," *Social Problems,* 7 (1959–60), 187–194.

45. Leonard J. Duhl. "Mental Health and Community Planning," in *Planning 1955,* Chicago: American Society of Planning Officials, 1956, pp. 31–39; Erich Fromm, *The Sane Society,* New York: Rinehart & Co., Inc., 1955, pp. 154–162; David Riesman, "The Suburban Sadness," in William M. Dobriner (ed.), *The Suburban Community,* New York: G. P. Putnam's Sons, 1958, pp. 375–408; William F. Whyte, Jr., *The Organization Man, op. cit.*

46. William M. Dobriner. "Introduction: Theory and Research in the Sociology of the Suburbs," in William M. Dobriner (ed.), *The Suburban Community, op. cit.,* pp. xiii–xxviii.

47. Sylvia Fleis Fava. "Contrasts in Neighboring: New York City and a Suburban Community," in William M. Dobriner (ed.), *The Suburban Community, op. cit.,* pp. 122–131.

48. This formulation may answer some of Duncan and Schnore's objections to socio-psychological and cultural explanations of community ways of life. See Otis Dudley Duncan, and Leo F. Schnore, "Cultural, Behavioral and Ecological Perspectives in the Study of Social Organization," *American Journal of Sociology,* 65 (1959), 132–155.

49. The ecologically oriented researchers who developed the Shevsky-Bell social area analysis scale have worked on the assumption that "social differences between the populations of urban neighborhoods can conveniently be summarized into differences of economic level, family characteristics and ethnicity." See Wendell Bell, and Maryanne T. Force. "Urban Neighborhood Types and Participation in Formal Associations," *American Sociological Review,* 21 (1956), 26. However, they have equated "urbanization" with a concept of life-cycle stage by using family characteristics to define the index of urbanization. See Bell and Force, *op. cit.;* Scott Greer, "The Social Structure and Political Process of Suburbia," *American Sociological Review,* 25 (1960), 514–526; Greer and Kube, *op. cit.* In fact, Bell has identified suburbanism with familism. See Wendell Bell, "Social Choice, Life Styles and Suburban Residence," in William M. Dobriner (ed.), *The Suburban Community, op. cit.,* pp. 225–247.

50. Duncan and Schnore, *op. cit.*

51. Dobriner, *op. cit.,* p. xxii.

52. Because of the distinctiveness of the ways of life found in the inner city, some writers propose definitions that refer only to these ways, ignoring those found in the outer city. For

example, popular writers sometimes identify "urban" with "urbanity," i.e., "cosmopolitanism." However, such a definition ignores the other ways of life found in the inner city. Moreover, I have tried to show that these ways have few common elements, and that the ecological features of the inner city have little or no influence in shaping them.

53. Even more than Wirth's they are based on data and impressions gathered in the large Eastern and Midwestern cities of the United States.

54. Personal discussions with European planners and sociologists suggest that many European apartment dwellers have similar preferences, although economic conditions, high building costs, and the scarcity of land make it impossible for them to achieve their desires.

26. TERRITORIALITY: A NEGLECTED SOCIOLOGICAL DIMENSION

STANFORD M. LYMAN *and* MARVIN D. SCOTT

Recently students of human communities have offered some new views of the old concept of "territoriality," the attempt to control space, once again linking homo sapien to his animal brother. Here two sociologists outline what they define as "a neglected sociological dimension."

Stanford M. Lyman and Marvin D. Scott begin by distinguishing four types of territory (public- home-, interactional-, and body-territories), three types of territorial encroachment (violation, invasion, and contamination) and several reaction patterns (turf defense, insulation, and linguistic collusion). Then, explaining that certain groups, spatially deprived of free territory, develop means of modifying their inner space (that is, their bodies), they offer some significant observations about lower-class urban Negro youth.

Stanford M. Lyman is Associate Professor of Sociology at the University of Nevada. Author of many articles on social deviance, Lyman has also published Accounts in Deviance and Respectability *(1968). Marvin D. Scott received his Ph.D. from the University of California at Berkeley and teaches sociology at Sonoma State College.*

All living organisms observe some sense of territoriality,[1] that is, some sense— whether learned or instinctive to their species—in which control over space is deemed central for survival.[2] Although man's domination over space is potentially unlimited, in contemporary society it appears that men acknowledge increasingly fewer *free* territories for themselves.[3]

Free territory is carved out of space and affords opportunities for idiosyncrasy and identity. Central to the manifestation of these opportunities are boundary creation and enclosure. This is so because activities that run counter to expected norms need seclusion or invisibility to permit unsanctioned performance, and because peculiar identities are sometimes impossible to realize in the absence of an appropriate setting.[4] Thus the opportunities for freedom of action—with respect to normatively discrepant behavior and maintenance of specific identities—are intimately connected with the ability to attach boundaries to space and command access to or exclusion from territories.

In American society where territorial encroachment affects nearly all members of society, certain segments of the population are particularly deprived, namely, Negroes, women, youth, and inmates of various kinds. With these categories in mind, this paper re-introduces a neglected dimension of social analysis important to understanding deprived groups.

Our strategy is twofold: first, to bring together under a new set of organizing concepts the notions of types of territory, types of territorial encroachment, and types of responses to encroachment; and second, to specify the reactions of spatially deprived groups.

Reprinted from *Social Problems*, **12**, 4 (1967), 236–249, by permission of the authors and The Society for the Study of Social Problems.

The Types of Territories

We can distinguish four kinds of territories, namely, *public territories, home territories, interactional territories* and *body territories*.

Public territories

Public territories are those areas where the individual has freedom of access, but not necessarily of action, by virtue of his claim to citizenship.[5] These territories are officially open to all, but certain images and expectations of appropriate behavior and of the categories of individuals who are normally perceived as using these territories modify freedom. First, it is commonly expected that illegal activities and impermissible behavior will not occur in public places. Since public territories are vulnerable to violation in both respects, however, policemen are charged with the task of removing lawbreakers from the scene of their activities and restricting behavior in public places.[6]

Second, certain categories of persons are accorded only limited access to and restricted activity in public places. It is expected, for instance, that children will not be playing in public playgrounds after midnight; that lower-class citizens will not live—although they might work—in areas of middle-class residence; and that Negroes will not be found leisurely strolling on the sidewalks of white neighborhoods, though they might be found laying the sewer pipe under the streets.

Since the rights of such discrepant groups to use these territories as citizens sometimes contradicts the privileges accorded them as persons, such territories are not infrequently the testing grounds of challenges to authority. The wave of sit-ins, wade-ins, and demonstrations in racially segregated restaurants, public beaches, and schools constitute an outstanding recent example. Informal restrictions on access to public territories often violate unenforced or as yet untested

rights of citizens. Since the informal delineation of some of these territories implies the absence of certain persons, their presence stands out. Policemen frequently become allies of locals in restricting citizenship rights when they remove unseemly persons from territories which they do not regularly habituate, or when they restrict certain categories of persons to specific areas.[7]

Public territories are thus ambiguous with respect to accorded freedoms. First, the official rights of access may be regularly violated by local custom. Second, status discrepancy may modify activity and entrance rights. For example, the ambiguity in the distinction between minors and adults is a source of confusion and concern in the regulation of temporal and access rights to those whose status is unclear. Finally, activities once forbidden in public may be declared permissible, thus enlarging the freedom of the territory; or activities once licit may be proscribed, thus restricting it. Hence display of female breasts is now permitted in San Francisco nightclubs, but not on the streets or before children. Nude swimming enjoys police protection at certain designated beaches, but watching nude swimmers at these same beaches is forbidden to those who are attired.

Home territories

Home territories are areas where the regular participants have a relative freedom of behavior and a sense of intimacy and control over the area. Examples include makeshift club houses of children, hobo jungles, and homosexual bars. Home and public territories may be easily confused. In fact "the areas of public places and the areas of home territories are not always clearly differentiated in the social world and what may be defined and used as a public place by some may be defined and used as a home territory by others."[8] Thus, a home territory that also may be used as a public one is defined by its regular use by specific persons or categories of persons and by the particular "territorial stakes" or "identity pegs" that are found in such places. The style of dress and language among the patrons at a bar may immediately communicate to a homosexual that he has arrived in home territory, while a heterosexual passerby who pauses for a drink may be astonished or outraged when he is accosted for sexual favors from the stranger seated next to him. Large-scale clandestine brotherhoods indoctrinate their members in secret codes of dress and demeanor so that regardless of their later travels they can unobtrusively communicate their fraternal identity and ask for assistance from one another in otherwise public places. Home territories sometimes enjoy a proactive status, beyond the presence of their inhabitants, in the form of reserved chairs, drinking mugs, signs or memorabilia that serve to indicate special and reserved distinctions.

Home territories may be established by "sponsorship" or "colonization." An example of the former is found in the merchant emigrants from China who established caravansaries in certain quarters of Occidental cities which served as public trading establishments but also as living quarters, employment agencies, meeting places, and courts for their *Landsmänner*.[9] Colonization occurs when a person or group lays claim to a formally free territory by virtue of discovery, regular usage, or peculiar relationship. Thus certain restaurants become home territories to those who are impressed with their first meal there; to those who eat there on specific occasions, such as luncheons, birthdays, or after sporting events; and to those who are intimate with the waitress.

Loss of home status may be occasioned by the death or resignation of a sponsor, by violation of the previously established usages, by rejection, or by conquest. Erstwhile "regulars" at a bar may discover they are no longer warmly greeted nor eligible for a free drink when the proprietor dies or when their patronage becomes irregular. Homosexuals may desert a "queer bar" when it becomes a place which heterosexuals frequent to observe deviant behavior.

It is precisely because of their officially open condition that public areas are vulnerable to conversion into home territories. The rules of openness are sufficiently broad and ambiguous so that restrictions on time, place, and manner are difficult to promulgate and nearly impossible to enforce. Armed with a piece of chalk children can change the public sidewalk into a gameboard blocking pedestrian traffic. Despite building codes and parental admonitions youngsters convert abandoned buildings or newly begun sites into forts, clubs, and hideaways.[10]

But children are not the only colonizers on the public lands. Beggars and hawkers will stake out a "territory" on the sidewalks or among the blocks and occupy it sometimes to the exclusion of all others similarly employed. The idle and unemployed will loiter on certain street corners, monopolizing the space, and frightening off certain respectable types with their loud, boisterous, or obscene language, cruel jests, and suggestive leers. Members of racial and ethnic groups colonize a portion of the city and adorn it with their peculiar institutions, language, and rules of conduct.[11] Ethnic enclaves, like certain notorious homosexual bars and prisons on open-house day, are often "on display" to non-ethnics who thus grant legitimacy to the colony's claim for territorial identity.

Among the most interesting examples of colonizing on the public lands are those attempts by youths to stake out streets as home territories open only to members of their own clique and defended against invasion by rival groups. Subject always to official harassment by police and interference by other adults who claim the streets as public territories, youths resolve the dilemma by redefining adults as non-persons whose seemingly violative presence on the youth's "turf" does not challenge the latter's proprietorship. Streets are most vulnerable to colonizing in this manner and indeed, as the early studies of the Chicago sociologists illustrated so well, streets and knots of juxtaposed streets become unofficial home areas to all those groups who require relatively secluded yet open space in which to pursue their interests or maintain their identities.[12]

Interactional territories

Interactional territories refer to any area where a social gathering may occur. Surrounding any interaction is an invisible boundary, a kind of social membrane.[13] A party is an interactional territory, as are the several knots of people who form clusters at parties. Every interactional territory implicitly makes a claim of boundary maintenance for the duration of the interaction. Thus access and egress are governed by rules understood, though not officially promulgated, by the members.

Interactional territories are characteristically mobile and fragile. Participants in a conversation may remain in one place, stroll along, or move periodically or erratically. They may interrupt only to resume it at a later time without permanently breaking the boundary or disintegrating the group. Even where "settings" are required for the interaction, mobility need not be dysfunctional if the items appropriate to the setting are movable. Thus chemists may not be able to complete a discussion without the assistance of a laboratory, but chess players may assemble or disassemble the game quite readily and in the most cramped quarters. Similarly, so long as Negroes were chattel slaves slaveholders might move them anywhere where their services or appearance were needed.

The fragility of interactional territories is constantly being tested by parvenus and newcomers. The latter, even when they possess credentials entitling them to entrance into the interactional circle, break down ongoing interaction and threaten it by requiring all to start over again, end it

instead, and begin a new subject of common interest, or disintegrate.[14] Parvenus are a greater threat since their presence breaks the boundaries of the interaction and challenges the exclusiveness of the group. They may be repulsed, or accepted fully, though the latter is less likely than the granting of a "temporary visa," i.e., rights to interact for the instant occasion with no promise of equal rights in the future.

Body territories

Finally, there are body territories, which include the space encompassed by the human body and the anatomical space of the body. The latter is, at least theoretically, the most private and inviolate of territories belonging to an individual. The rights to view and touch the body are of a sacred nature, subject to great restriction. For instance, a person's rights to his own body space are restricted where norms govern masturbation, or the appearance and decoration of skin. Moreover, rights of others to touch one's body are everywhere regulated, though perhaps modern societies impose greater restrictions than others.[15]

Body territory is also convertible into home territory. The most common method is marriage in a monogamous society in which sexual access to the female is deemed the exclusive right of the husband so long as he exercises propriety with respect to his status. Ownership, however, is not necessarily or always coterminous with possession, so that sexual rivalry might continue illegitimately after a marital choice has been made and erupt in trespass on the husband's sexual property.[16] Under situations where women are scarce, such as nineteenth-century overseas Chinese communities in the United States, sexual property was institutionalized through organized prostitution, and the few Chinese wives among the homeless men were carefully secluded.[17]

Body space is, however, subject to creative innovation, idiosyncrasy, and destruction. First, the body may be marked or marred by scars, cuts, burns, and tattoos. In addition, certain of its parts may be inhibited or removed without its complete loss of function. These markings have a meaning beyond the purely anatomical. They are among the indicators of status or stigma. They can be signs of bravado as was the dueling scar among German students, or of criminality as is a similar scar on Italians and Negroes in America. Loss of an eye may prevent one's entrance into dental school, but at least one clothing manufacturer regards one-eyed men as status symbols for starched shirts. Tattoos may memorialize one's mother or sweetheart as well as indicate one's seafaring occupation.

The human organism exercises extraterritorial rights over both internal and external space. In the latter instance the space immediately surrounding a person is also inviolate.[18] Thus conversations among friends are ecologically distinguishable from those between acquaintances or strangers. A person who persists in violating the extraterritorial space of another of the same sex may be accused of tactlessness and suspected of homosexuality, while uninvited intersex invasion may indicate unwarranted familiarity.[19] Moreover, eye contact and visual persistence can be a measure of external space. Thus two strangers may look one another over at the proper distance, but as they near one another, propriety requires that they treat one another as non-persons unless a direct contact is going to be made.[20]

Control over "inner space" is the quintessence of individuality and freedom. Violations of "inner space" are carried out by domination, ranging in intensity from perception of more than is voluntarily revealed to persuasion and ultimately hypnosis.[21] Demonstration of idiosyncrasy with respect to "inner space" is exemplified by the modifications possible in the presentation of self through the uses of the several stimulants and depressants.

Territorial Encroachment

We can distinguish three forms of territorial encroachment: violation, invasion, and contamination.

VIOLATION of a territory is unwarranted use of it. Violators are those who have repulsed or circumvented those who would deny them access. Violators are also, by virtue of their acts, claimants in some sense to the territory they have violated. Their claim, however, may vary in scope, intensity, and objective. Children may violate the graves of the dead by digging "for treasure" in the cemetery, but unlike ghouls, they are not seeking to remove the bodies for illicit purposes. Some territories may be violated, however, merely by unwarranted entrance into them. Among these are all those territories commonly restricted to categorical groups such as toilets, harems, nunneries, and public baths—areas commonly restricted according to sex. Other territories may not be necessarily violated by presence but only by innovative or prohibited use. Thus some parents regard family-wide nudity as permissible, but hold that sexual interest or intercourse among any but the married pair is forbidden. Interactional territories are violated when one or more of the legitimate interactants behaves out of character.[22]

INVASION of a territory occurs when those not entitled to entrance or use nevertheless cross the boundaries and interrupt, halt, take over, or change the social meaning of the territory. Such invasions, then, may be temporary or enduring.

CONTAMINATION of a territory requires that it be rendered impure with respect to its definition and usage. Cholera may require that a portion of the city be quarantined. In a racial caste society the sidewalks may be contaminated by low caste persons walking upon them. Home territories may be contaminated by pollution or destruction of the "home" symbols. Orthodox Jews may destroy their dinnerware when an unwary maid has accidentally mixed the milk and meat dishes. Heterosexuals who regularly congregate at a bar sometimes discontinue their patronage when known homosexuals begin frequenting the bar. (This example illustrates a continuum in the process of territorial encroachment from invasion to contamination.) Interactional territories may be contaminated by sudden odors, especially if they emanate from one of the interactants, or by indiscreet language, e.g., obscenity, among those for whom identification with such language constitutes a loss of face or a reduction in status.[23]

Contamination of bodily territories occurs whenever the immediate space of or around the body is polluted. The removal by bathing of material involuntarily attached to the skin constitutes a ritualized purification rite of considerable importance in industrial societies.[24] However, body space may be contaminated in many ways, by smell, look, touch, and by proximity to contaminated persons or things. The sensitivity with respect to touch illustrates the complex nature of this contamination and also its peculiarly social character. The rules regarding touch are highly developed in American society and are clear indicators of social distance between individuals and groups.[25] Typically, older people can touch younger ones, but suspicions of sexual immorality modify such contacts. Women who are friends or relatives may greet one another with a light kiss (commonly called a "peck") on the cheek, but not on the lips. Men who are long absent may be greeted by male friends and relatives with a hearty embrace and a touching of the cheeks, but the embrace must not be overlong or tender. Indeed, "rough-housing," mockfighting, and pseudo-hostility are commonly employed in masculine affective relationships. Touch which would otherwise be contaminating is exempt from such designation when it takes place in situations of intense social action, e.g., on a dance floor, or in situations when the actors are not privileged to interact, e.g., on

crowded buses. At other times bodies contaminated by impermissible contacts are restored to their pure state by apologies.

Body space may be contaminated by a kind of negative charismatic contact whereby objects which, though neutral in themselves, carry contaminating effect when transferred directly to the body. Thus a comb or toothbrush may not be lent or borrowed in certain circles since to use someone else's tools of personal hygiene is to contaminate oneself. Typically, when clothing, especially clothing that will directly touch the skin, is lent, it is proper for the lender to assure the borrower that the apparel is clean, and that it has not been worn by anyone since its last cleaning.[26] A more striking example involves the rule of some shops forbidding Negroes from trying on clothes—their skin being regarded as a source of pollution. Similarly, drinking from the same glass as another is discouraged as a matter of hygiene among the middle class and as a source of pollution if it occurs among persons of different races or castes.

Reaction to Encroachment

We have already suggested that something of a reciprocal relation exists between the territorial types. For example, a public swimming pool—while officially open to all persons—might be conceived by certain regular users as an exclusive area. Strangers seeking access by virtue of their diffuse civic rights might be challenged by those whose sense of peculiar propriety is thus violated. Such a confrontation (sometimes called "when push meets shove") could result in retreat on the part of the party seeking admittance, flight on the part of those favoring denial, or strategy and tactics on the part of the contending parties to expand the area of legitimate access on the one hand, and withhold entirely or restrict the meaning of entry on the other.

Of course, the occupants of a territory

may extend its use to others whose presence is not regarded as a threat. The most common situation is that in which common usage will not destroy or alter the value of the territory.[27] When public territories have been colonized by users who do not fully monopolize the space, who embroider it by their presence, or whose occupancy still allows for other public and colonizing usages, the colonists will not be seriously opposed. Delinquent gangs who often define the streets of a neighborhood as a home territory do not usually regard the presence of local adults and children as an encroachment on their own occupancy. Unwarranted intrusion on interactional territories may be countenanced if the unwelcome guest indicates his willingness to be present on this occasion alone with no future rights of reentry, or to listen only and not to interrupt the proceedings. Bodies usually invulnerable to feel and probe by strangers may be violated if circumstances render the act physically safe, socially irrelevant, or emotionally neutral. Thus female nurses may massage their male patients with mutual impunity, and striptease dancers may perform unclothed upon a raised stage out of reach of the audience.[28] However, all such contacts will tend to be defined as territorial encroachment when the claimants threaten obliteration, monopoly, or fundamental alteration of a territory. Under these conditions, the holders of territory are likely to react to unwelcome claimants in terms of *turf defense, insulation,* or *linguistic collusion.*

Turf defense

Turf defense is a response necessitated when the intruder cannot be tolerated. The animal world provides a multitude of examples which are instructive with respect to the human situation.[29] Here we may be content, however, to confine ourselves to the human scene. When Chinese merchants sought "colonizing" rights among the urban merchants of San Francisco, they were welcomed and honored. A few years later, however, the appearance of Chinese miners in the white Americans' cherished gold fields called forth violent altercations and forced removals.[30] In contemporary American cities delinquent gangs arm themselves with rocks, knives, tire irons, and zip guns to repel invaders from other streets.[31] Among the "primitive" Kagoro the choice of weapons is escalated in accordance with the social distance of the combatants; poison spears and stratagems are employed exclusively against hostile strangers and invaders.[32]

Turf defense is an ultimate response, however. Other more subtle repulsions or restrictions are available to proprietors wishing to maintain territorial control.

Insulation

Insulation is the placement of some sort of barrier between the occupants of a territory and potential invaders. The narrow streets, steep staircases, and regularized use of Cantonese dialects in Chinatowns serve notice on tourists that they may look over the external trappings of Chinese life in the Occidental city but not easily penetrate its inner workings. Distinct uniforms distinguishing status, rights, and prerogatives serve to protect military officers from the importunities of enlisted men, professors from students, and doctors from patients.[33] Bodily insulation characteristically takes the form of civil inattention and may be occasioned by a subordinate's inability to repel invasion directly. Another common form of insulation involves use of body and facial idiom to indicate impenetrability. It may be effected by the use of sunglasses,[34] or attained accidentally, by dint of culturally distinct perceptions of facial gestures, as, for example, often happens to orientals in Western settings.[35] It can also be attained by conscious efforts in the management and control of the mouth, nostrils, and especially the eyes.[36]

Linguistic collusion

Linguistic collusion involves a complex set of processes by which the territorial integrity of the group is reaffirmed and the intruder is labelled as an outsider. For example, the defending interactants may engage one another in conversation and gestures designed to so confuse the invader that he responds in a manner automatically labelling him eligible for either exclusion from the group or shameful status diminution. In one typical strategy the defending interactants will speak to one another in a language unfamiliar to the invader. Ethnic enclaves provide numerous examples. Jewish and Chinese storekeepers will speak Yiddish and Cantonese respectively to their clerks when discussing prices, bargaining rights, and product quality in the presence of alien customers. Negroes may engage one another in a game of "the dozens" in the presence of intruding whites, causing the latter considerable consternation and mystification.[37] And teenagers develop a peer group argot (frequently borrowed from Negro and jazz musician usages) which sets them apart from both children and adults, and which, incidentally, is most frequently cited as proof for the claim that a distinctive youth culture does exist in the United States.

In another recognizable strategy, the participants continue to engage in the same behavior but in a more exaggerated and "staged" manner. Mood and tone of the voice are sometimes regulated to achieve this effect. Thus persons engaged in conversation may intensify their tone and include more intra-group gestures when an outsider enters the area. Professors may escalate the use of jargon and "academese" in conversations in the presence of uninvited students or other "inferiors." Homosexuals engaged in flirtations in a "gay" bar may exaggerate their femininity when heterosexuals enter the establishment. Such staged displays call attention to the exclusive culture of the interactants and suggest to the outsider that he is bereft of the cards of identity necessary to participate.

Reaction to the Absence of Free Space

There are some segments of society that are systematically denied free territories. One outstanding example is that of lower-class urban Negro youth. Their homes are small, cramped, and cluttered and also serve as specialized areas of action for adults; their meeting places are constantly under surveillance by the agents of law enforcement and social workers; and, when in clusters on the street, they are often stopped for questioning and booked "on suspicion" by the seemingly ever-present police.[38]

What is the condition of Negro youth in particular appears to be an exaggerated instance of the trend with respect to denial of freedom among youth in general. Thus it has been suggested that youth are adrift somewhere between humanism and fatalism, i.e., between situations in which they feel they have control over their destinies and those in which such control is in the hands of forces outside youth's individual direction and influence.[39] In such a situation one response is to seek to maximize the area of freedom, the situations in which one can exercise liberty and license, the times one can be cause rather than effect. Among lower-class youth the carving of home territories out of the space provided as public ones is common and has already been noted. Note also, however, the frequency with which youth-created home territories are subject to invasion, violation, and contamination and the relative vulnerability of youth home territories to such encroachments.

Exercising freedom over body territory provides a more fruitful approach to those for whom public territories are denied and home territories difficult or impossible to maintain. The body and its attendant inner and external space have an aura of ownership and control about them that is impressed upon the incumbent. The hypothesis we wish to suggest here is that as other forms of free territory are perceived to be foreclosed by certain segments of the society, these segments, or at least those elements of the segments not constrained by other compelling forces, will utilize more frequently and intensively the area of body space as a free territory. Three forms of such utilization are prominent: *manipulation, adornment,* and *penetration.*

MANIPULATION rests upon the fact that the body is adjustable in a greater number of ways than are positively sanctioned and that by modifying the appearance of the self one can establish identity, and flaunt convention with both ease and relative impunity. Thus children, separated from one another for being naughty and enjoined from conversation, may sit and "make faces" at one another, conforming to the letter of their punishment but violating its principle. Teenagers, denied approval for the very sexual activity for which they are biologically prepared, and also enclosed more and more from private usage of public territories for such purposes, have developed dance forms which involve little or no body contact but are nevertheless suggestive of the most intimate and forbidden forms of erotic interaction. Further, male youth—enjoined from verbal scatological forms by customs and by rules of propriety—have developed a gesture language by which they can communicate the desired obscenity without uttering it.

ADORNMENT of the body is another response.[40] By covering, uncovering, marking, and disfiguring the body individuals can at least partly overcome whatever loss of freedom they suffer from other encroachments. Both the French "bohemians" of the nineteenth century and the disaffected American Negro youths of the twentieth have exhibited themselves as "dandies," [41] while the ascetic Doukho-bors of British Columbia disrobe entirely and in public when challenged by authority.[42] Body space may also be attended by filling in the apertures in nose, mouth and ears by rings, bones, and other emblematic artifacts; by marking upon the skin with inks and tattoos; and by disfigurements, scars, and severance of non-vital members. An alternative mode of adornment, that appears to be directed definitely against elements of the core culture, is the refusal to use instruments of personal hygiene. We have already noted how these instruments acquire a peculiar aspect of the personal charisma of the user so that people do not customarily borrow the comb, toothbrush, and razor of another unless the contamination that occurs thereby is neutralized. Here, however, adornment occurs by simply *not* washing, combing, shaving, cutting the hair, etc. Like public nudity this form of assertiveness and reaction to oppression has the advantage of inhibiting a like response among those who are offended by the appearance created thereby, but, unlike stripping in public, has the added advantage of being legal.

PENETRATION refers to the exploitation and modification of inner space in the search for free territory. One might hypothesize that the greater the sense of unfreedom, the greater the exercise of body liberty so that penetration is an escalated aspect of manipulation and adornment. There is, as it were, a series of increasing gradations of body space. The ultimate effort is to gain freedom by changing one's internal environment. The simplest form of this is cultivating a vicarious sense of being away, of transporting the self out of its existential environment by musing, daydreaming, or relapsing into a reverie.[43] However, voluntary reorganization of the inner environment can be assisted by alcohol and drugs. Contemporary college youth sometimes partake of hallucinogenic and psychedelic drugs in order to make an inner migration (or "take a trip" as the popular idiom has it).

Conclusions

The concept of territoriality offers a fruitful approach for the analysis of freedom and situated action. Although the early school of ecology in American sociology provided a possible avenue for this kind of exploration, its practitioners appear to have eschewed the interactionist and phenomenological aspects of the subject in favor of the economic and the biotic. Nevertheless, much of their work needs to be examined afresh for the clues it provides for understanding the nature and function of space and the organization of territories. Similarly the work done by the students of non-human animal association provides clues to concept formation and suggestions for research. Here we may mention several potentially fruitful areas. The first involves cross-cultural studies of territoriality. Such studies would attempt to describe in greater specificity the constituent features of types of territoriality, the ways in which they vary, and their interrelationships. Using a cross-cultural perspective would also serve to specify generic forms of reactions to territorial encroachment and to establish how certain contexts predispose one type of response rather than another. A second area of research would focus on a variety of deviant behaviors (e.g., crime, juvenile delinquency, drug addiction) with the purpose of understanding the part the territorial variable plays in the etiology of such behaviors. Finally, we may suggest that micro-sociological studies of territoriality—which are perhaps more amenable to rigorous research design—may be extrapolated to an analysis of macro-sociological inquiries, especially in the realm of international affairs.

NOTES

1. The concept of territoriality was introduced into sociological analysis in the twenties under the label of "the ecological school." For an early statement see Robert E. Park, Ernest W. Burgess, and R. D. McKenzie, *The City,* Chicago: University of Chicago Press, 1925. For a summary and bibliography of the school see Milla Aissa Alihan, *Social Ecology,* N.Y.: Columbia University Press, 1938. An updated version of this school is found in James A. Quinn, *Human Ecology,* Englewood Cliffs, N.J.: Prentice-Hall, 1950, and Amos H. Hawley, *Human Ecology, A Theory of Community Structures,* N.Y.: The Ronald Press, 1950.

   Originating in animal studies, "territoriality" still looms large as an organizing concept in ethology. For a summary statement see C. R. Carpenter, "Territoriality: A Review of Concepts and Problems," in A. Roe and G. Simpson, editors, *Behavior and Evolution,* New Haven: Yale University Press, 1958, pp. 224–250.

   For a challenging argument that sociological investigation can fruitfully employ the techniques of comparative ethology—especially to such subjects as territoriality—see Lionel Tiger and Robin Fox, "The Zoological Perspective in Social Science," *Man,* I., 1 (March, 1966), esp. p. 80.

   Only very recently have sociologists revived ecological thinking to include a truly *interactional* dimension. The outstanding contributor is, of course, Edward T. Hall. See his *The Silent Language,* Garden City, N.Y.: Doubleday and Co., 1959, and *The Hidden Dimension,* Garden City, N.Y.: Doubleday and Co., 1966. For a masterful application of the concept of territoriality in interactional terms see Erving Goffman, *Asylums,* Garden City, N.Y.: Doubleday and Co., Anchor Books, 1961, pp. 227–248. In a slightly different vein see the interesting efforts of Robert Sommer, "Studies in Personal Space," *Sociometry,* 22 (September, 1959), 247–260, and the writings of Roger Barker, especially his "Roles, Ecological Niches, and the Psychology of the Absent Organism," paper presented to the conference on the Propositional Structure of Role Theory, University of Missouri, 1962.

2. For the argument that human territoriality is a natural rather than a cultural phenomenon see Robert Ardrey, *The Territorial Imperative,* New York: Atheneum, 1966, pp. 3–41.

3. The idea of "free territory" is derived from Goffman, *loc. cit.*

4. See Erving Goffman, *The Presentation of Self in Everyday Life,* Garden City, N.Y.: Doubleday Anchor Books, 1959, p. 22.

5. The term "citizenship" is used in a sense similar to that employed by T. H. Marshall in *Class, Citizenship and Social Development,* Garden City, N.Y.: Doubleday Anchor Books, 1965, esp. pp. 71–134.

6. See Harvey Sacks, "Methods in Use for the Production of a Social Order: A Method for Warrantably Informing Moral Character," Center for the Study of Law and Society, University of California, Berkeley, 1962; and Aaron Cicourel, *The Social Organization of Juvenile Justice,* unpublished manuscript.

7. See Jerome Skolnick, *Justice Without Trial,* New York: John Wiley, 1966, pp. 96–111 *et passim;* and Sacks, *op. cit.*

8. Sherri Cavan, "Interaction in Home Territories," *Berkeley Journal of Sociology,* 5 (1963), 18.

9. See Stanford M. Lyman, *The Structure of Chinese Society in Nineteenth Century America,* unpublished Ph.D. dissertation, Berkeley: University of California, 1961.

10. Indeed, children are among the most regular and innovative creators of home territories from the space and material available to the public in general. Speaking of their peculiar tendency to violate the rules governing trespass, William Prosser has aptly observed, "Children, as is well known to anyone who has been a child, are by nature unreliable and irresponsible people, who are quite likely to do almost anything. In particular, they have a deplorable tendency to stray upon land which does not belong to them, and to meddle with what they find there." "Trespassing Children," *California Law Review* (August, 1959), p. 427.

11. Ethnic groups in the process of assimilation sometimes discover to their astonishment that the isolated slum wherein they have traditionally and unwillingly dwelt is in fact a home territory possessed of cherished values and irreplaceable sentiments. A militant Negro thus writes: "For as my son, Chuck, wrote me after exposure to the Negro community of Washington: 'I suddenly realized that the Negro ghetto is not a ghetto. It is home.' " John Oliver Killens, *Black Man's Burden,* New York: Trident Press, 1965, p. 94.

12. Harvey W. Zorbaugh, *The Gold Coast and the Slums,* Chicago: University of Chicago Press, 1929. See also Jane Jacobs, *The Death and Life of Great American Cities,* N.Y.: Vintage Books, 1961, pp. 29–142.

13. See Erving Goffman, *Behavior in Public Places,* N.Y.: The Free Press of Glencoe, 1963, pp. 151–165 *et passim.*

14. An excellent illustration of the several facets of this process and attendant issues in social gatherings is found in David Riesman, *et al.,* "The Vanishing Host," *Human Organization* (Spring, 1960), pp. 17–27.

15. Talcott Parsons notes that "the very fact that affectionate bodily contact is almost completely taboo among men in American society is probably indicative of [the limited nature of intra-sex friendship] since it strongly limits affective attachment." *The Social System,* Glencoe, Ill.: Free Press, 1951, p. 189. For an empirical study and analysis of touching relations see Erving Goffman, "The Nature of Deference and Demeanor," *American Anthropologist,* 58 (June, 1956), pp. 473–502.

16. See Kingsley Davis, *Human Society,* New York: Macmillan, 1948, pp. 19–193.

17. Lyman, *op. cit.,* pp. 97–111.

18. The perceptions of Simmel on this subject surpass all others and we are indebted to his work. Thus Simmel has noted: "In regard to the 'significant' [i.e., "great"] man, there is an inner compulsion which tells one to keep at a distance and which does not disappear even in intimate relations with him. The only type for whom such distance does not exist is the individual who has no organ for perceiving distance. . . . The individual who fails to keep his distance from a great person does not esteem him highly, much less too highly (as might superficially appear to be the case); but, on the contrary, his importune behavior reveals lack of proper respect. . . . The same sort of circle which surrounds a man—although it is value-accentuated in a very different sense—is filled out by his affairs and by his characteristics. To penetrate this circle by taking notice, constitutes a violation of personality. Just as material property is, so to speak, an extension of the ego, there is also an intellectual private property, whose violation effects a lesion of the ego in its very center." Georg Simmel, "Secrecy and Group Communication," reprinted in T. Parsons, *et al., Theories of Society,* New York: The

Free Press of Glencoe, 1961, p. 320. For an updated statement of Simmel's point see Goffman, *Behavior in Public Places, op. cit.*

19. An interesting dilemma in this respect arises for the deaf and myopic. In attempting to appear as "normals" they may overstep another's territorial space and thus call attention to the very stigma they wish to conceal. On the problems of those who are stigmatized see Goffman, *Stigma,* Englewood Cliffs, N.J.: Prentice-Hall, 1963.

20. Goffman refers to this as "civil inattention." See *Behavior in Public Places, op. cit.*

21. Compare the remarks by Simmel, *op. cit.,* p. 321. "In the interest of interaction and social cohesion, the individual *must* know certain things about the other person. Nor does the other have the right to oppose this knowledge from a moral standpoint, by demanding the discretion of the first: he cannot claim the entirely undisturbed possession of his own being and consciousness, since this discretion might harm the interests of his society. . . . But even in subtler and less unambiguous forms, in fragmentary beginnings and unexpressed notions, all of human intercourse rests on the fact that everybody knows somewhat more about the other than the other voluntarily reveals to him; and those things he knows are frequently matters whose knowledge the other person (were he aware of it) would find undesirable." See also Goffman, *The Presentation of Self in Everyday Life, op. cit.,* pp. 1–16.

22. The structural properties and parameters of interactional territories in unserious gatherings have been admirably presented by Georg Simmel. See his "The Sociology of Sociability," *American Journal of Sociology,* (November, 1949), 254–261. Reprinted in Parsons, *et al., Theories of Society, op. cit.,* pp. 157–163.

23. Here perhaps it is worth noting that language has a "tactile" dimension, in the sense that to be "touched" audially by certain terms is to be elevated or reduced in status. For Southern Negroes to be publicly addressed as "Mr.," "Miss," and "Mrs.," and by last names is considered so relevant for removal of caste barriers that legal action to require these usages has been undertaken. We may also note that genteel persons are polluted by audial contact with slang, obscenity, and, on occasion, idiomatic expression.

24. See Horace Miner, "Body Ritual Among the Nacirema," *American Anthropologist,* 55, No. 3, 1956.

25. Note such phrases as "I wouldn't touch him with a ten-foot pole"; "she's under my skin"; "he's a pain in the neck," and "Look, but don't touch." For the rules regarding touch see Erving Goffman, "The Nature of Deference and Demeanor," *op. cit.*

26. Robin Williams has shown that one test of social distance among the races in America is their unwillingness to try on clothing at an apparel shop when they have witnessed that clothing tried on and rejected by members of another—and supposedly inferior—race. Robin Williams, *Strangers Next Door,* Englewood Cliffs, N.J.: Prentice-Hall, 1964, pp. 125–130.

27. Our usage is similar to that employed in describing the relationships in plant-communities. "The majority of individuals of a plant-community are linked by bonds other than those mentioned—bonds that are best described as *commensal.* The term commensalism is due to Van Beneden, who wrote 'Le commensal est simplement un compagnon de table'; but we employ it in a somewhat different sense to denote the relationship subsisting between species which share with one another the supply of food-material contained in soil and air, and thus feed at the same table." Robert E. Park and Ernest W. Burgess, *Introduction to the Science of Sociology,* Chicago: University of Chicago Press, 1921, p. 175. (Adapted from Eugenius Warming, *Oecology of Plants,* London: Oxford University Press, 1909, pp. 12–13, 91–95.)

28. Ann Terry D'Andre, "An Occupational Study of the Strip-Dancer Career," paper delivered at the annual meetings of the Pacific Sociological Association, Salt Lake City, Utah, 1965.

29. See Ardrey, *op. cit.,* p. 210, who writes: "Biology as a whole asks but one question of a territory: is it defended? Defense defines it. Variability becomes the final description." See also Konrad Lorenz, *On Aggression,* New York: Harcourt, Brace and World, 1966, pp. 33–38 *et passim.*

30. See Mary Coolidge, *Chinese Immigration,* New York: Henry Holt, 1909, pp. 15–26, 255–256.

31. See Lewis Yablonsky, *The Violent Gang,* New York: Macmillan, 1962, pp. 29–100 for a good ethnography of urban gangs. For an analytical treatment see Frederic M. Thrasher, *The Gang;* Chicago: University of Chicago Press, 1927, pp. 97–100, 116–129.

32. See M. G. Smith, "Kagoro Political Development," *Human Organization* (Fall, 1960), pp. 137–149.

33. It is now a commonplace of sociological irony that persons thus insulated are vulnerable once the insulating material is removed or ubiquitously available. Thus non-coms will insult officers in clubs when both are out of uniform, psychiatrists will be mistaken for patients at dances held in the recreation room of an insane asylum, and students will adopt an inappropriate familiarity with professors not wearing a coat and tie.

34. See Goffman, *Behavior in Public Places, op. cit.,* p. 85 for a succinct account of the elements of this process as a form of civil inattention.

35. Kathleen Tamagawa, *Holy Prayers in a Horse's Ear,* New York: Long, Smith, Inc., 1932, pp. 144–151 *et passim.* Andre M. Tao-Kim-Hai, "Orientals are Stoic," in F. C. Macgregor, *Social Science in Nursing,* New York: Russell Sage, 1960, pp. 313–326.

36. See Georg Simmel, "The Aesthetic Significance of the Face," in Kurt H. Wolff (ed.), *Georg Simmel 1858–1918,* Columbus: Ohio State University Press, 1959, pp. 280–281.

37. The usual situation is quite the reverse, however. The "dozens" and other verbal contest forms are most frequently used by Negroes within the ethnic enclave out of earshot and view of whites. See Roger D. Abrahams, *Deep Down in the Jungle,* Hatboro, Penn.: Folklore Associates, esp. pp. 41–64.

38. See Carl Werthman, *Delinquency and Authority,* M.A. Thesis, University of California, Berkeley, 1964.

39. David Matza, *Delinquency and Drift,* New York: John Wiley, 1964.

40. Many suggestive essays on this subject can be found in *Dress, Adornment, and the Social Order,* in M. E. Roach and J. B. Eicher (eds.), N.Y.: John Wiley, 1965.

41. See Cesar Grana, *Bohemian vs. Bourgeois,* New York: Basic Books, 1964, and Harold Finestone, "Cats, Kicks, and Color," *Social Problems,* 5, 1 (1957), 3–13.

42. See Harry B. Hawthorn (ed.), *The Doukhobors of British Columbia,* Vancouver, B.C.: The University of British Columbia and Dent & Sons, 1955.

43. Goffman, *Behavior in Public Places, op. cit.,* pp. 69–75.

27. ANATOMY OF A CHICAGO SLUM

GERALD D. SUTTLES

Theory into practice. In the following essay Gerald D. Suttles gives ample evidence for the importance of using "the neglected concept" territoriality. His report is based upon excerpts from a larger study of the social structure of the Near West Side of Chicago, a multiethnic community with a social order all its own. (The area Suttles describes is the locale of many sociological studies dating back to the 1920s.)

Gerald D. Suttles teaches sociology at the University of Chicago. He has recently published The Social Order of the Slum *(1968), a book which received the C. Wright Mills Award from the Society for the Study of Social Problems in 1969.*

In its heyday, the Near West Side of Chicago was the stronghold of such men as Al (Scarface) Capone and Frank (The Enforcer) Nitti, and served as the kindergarten for several figures still active in the underworld. For convenience, I will call this part of Chicago the Addams area—after Jane Addams, who founded Hull House there. The name is artificial, since it is never used by the local residents.

The Addams area is one of the oldest slums in Chicago, and researchers have invaded it almost as often as new minority groups have. Like most slums, it remains something of a mystery. In some ways it is easiest to describe the neighborhood by describing how its residents deviate from the public standards of the wider community. The area has, for example, a high delinquency rate, numerous unwed mothers, and several adolescent "gangs." It is tempting to think that the residents are simply people suffering from cultural deprivation, unemployment, and a number of other urban ills. And if the residents insist upon the irrelevance of the standards of the wider community and the primacy of their own, this can be dismissed as sour grapes or an attempt to make of necessity a virtue.

Seen from the inside, however, Addams area residents require discipline and self-restraint in the same way as the wider community does. Conventional norms are not rejected but emphasized differently, or suspended for established reasons. The vast majority of the residents are quite conventional people. At the same time, those who remain in good standing are often exceptionally tolerant of and even encouraging to those who are "deviant."

Certainly the social practices of the residents are not just an inversion of those of the wider society, and the inhabitants would be outraged to hear as much. Nor is the neighborhood a cultural island with its own distinct and imported traditions. The area's internal structure features such commonplace distinctions as age, sex, territoriality, ethnicity, and personal identity. Taken out of context, many of the social arrangements of the Addams area may seem an illusory denial of the beliefs and values of the wider society. But actually the residents are bent on ordering local relations because the beliefs and evaluations of the wider society do not provide adequate guidelines for conduct.

In anthropology, territorial grouping has been a subject of continued interest. Most anthropological studies begin by focusing upon social groupings that can be

Reprinted in condensed form from *The Social Order of the Slum: Ethnicity and Territoriality in the Inner City,* by permission of the author and the University of Chicago Press.

defined by their areal distribution. In turn, many of the social units singled out for particular attention—the domestic unit, the homestead, the tribe, and so forth—frequently have locality as one of their principles of organization. And where locality and structural forms do not coincide, anthropologists have regarded this discrepancy as a distinct problem that raises a number of theoretical and methodological issues.

The most obvious reason for focusing on locality groups is that their members cannot simply ignore one another. People who routinely occupy the same place must either develop a moral order that includes all those present or fall into conflict. And because almost all societies create a public morality that exceeds the capabilities of some of its members, territorial groups are always faced with the prospect of people whose public character does not warrant trust. In the United States a very large percentage of our population fails to meet the public standards we set for measuring someone's merit, trustworthiness, and respectability.

Many groups have avoided compromising these ideals of public morality by territorial segregation. More exactly, they have simply retreated and left valuable portions of the inner city to those they distrust. Obviously, this practice has its limits—it tends to aggregate those who are poor, unsuccessful, and disreputable in the same slum neighborhoods. These people must compromise the ideals of public morality or remain permanently estranged from one another.

In slum neighborhoods, territorial aggregation usually comes before any common social framework for assuring orderly relations. After all, ethnic invasion, the encroachment of industry, and economic conditions constantly reshuffle slum residents and relocate them around new neighbors. Since the residents lack obvious grounds for assuming mutual trust, a combination of alternatives seems to offer the most promising course:

Social relations can be restricted to only the safest ones. Families can withdraw to their households, where they see only close relatives. Segregation by age, sex, and ethnicity are maneuvers that will prevent at least the most unfair and most likely forms of conflict and exploitation. Remaining close to the household cuts down on the range of anonymity and reduces the number of social relations. The general pattern, then, should be a fan-shaped spatial arrangement, with women and children remaining close by the house while males move progressively outwards, depending on their age.

Slum residents can assuage at least some of their apprehensions by a close inquiry into one another's personal character and past history. Communication, then, should be of an intimate character and aimed toward producing personal rather than formal relations. In turn, social relations will represent a sort of private compact in which particular loyalties replace impersonal standards of worth.

Neither of these patterns will immediately produce a comprehensive framework within which a large number of slum residents can safely negotiate with one another. The segregation by age, sex, and territorial groups, however, does provide a starting point from which face-to-face relations can grow and reach beyond each small territorial aggregation. The development of personal relations furnishes both a moral formula and a structural bridge between groups. Within each small, localized peer group, continuing face-to-face relations can eventually provide a personalistic order. Once these groups are established, a single personal relation between them can extend the range of such an order. Thus, with the acceptance of age-grading and territorial segregation, it becomes possible for slum neighborhoods to work out a moral order that includes most of their residents.

The Addams area actually consists of four different sections, each occupied predominantly by Negroes, Italians, Puerto

Ricans, and Mexicans. And each of these sections falls into a somewhat different stage in its development of a provincial order.

Despite this difference and others, all four ethnic sections share many characteristics and seem headed along the same social progression. The overall pattern is one in which age, sex, ethnic, and territorial units are fitted together like building blocks to create a larger structure. I have termed this pattern "ordered segmentation" to indicate two related features: (1) the orderly relationship between groups; and (2) the order in which groups combine in instances of conflict and opposition. This ordered segmentation is not equally developed in all ethnic sections but, in skeletal outline, it is the common framework within which groups are being formed and social relations are being cultivated.

My own experiences within the Addams area and the presentation of this volume are heavily influenced by the ordered segmentation of the neighborhood. I took up residence in the area in the summer of 1963 and left a little fewer than three years later.

As I acquired friends and close informants, my own ethnicity became a serious problem. A few people worked over my genealogy trying to find some trace that would allot me to a known ethnic group. After close inquiry, one old Italian lady announced with peals of laughter, "Geraldo, you're just an American." She did not mean it as a compliment, and I remember being depressed. In the Addams area, being without ethnicity means there is no one you can appeal to or claim as your own.

Only after a year or more in the Addams area was I able to penetrate the private world of its families, street-corner groups, and insular establishments. These are the groupings within which Addams area residents are least cautious and most likely to expose themselves. In large part my experience with these groups is limited

to many adolescent male street-corner groups and my own adult friends, who formed a group of this type.

By far the most striking contrast is between the Negro and the Italian sections. For instance, almost all the Negroes live in public housing; the Italians usually control both their households and commercial establishments. The Negroes have very similar incomes and almost no political power; among the Italians, there *is* some internal differentiation of income and political power. Such differences draw the Italians and Negroes apart and generate radically different styles of life.

In most ways, the Puerto Rican section is the least complex of those in the Addams area. There are no more than 1100 Puerto Ricans in the section and, within broad age ranges, most of them know one another. Until 1965, no named groups had emerged among the Puerto Ricans.

The Mexicans are more numerous, and several named groups have developed among the teenagers. Unlike the Italians, however, the Mexican groups have not survived into adulthood. The Mexicans seem to have much in common with the Italians, and frequently their relationships are congenial. What gives the Mexicans pause is the occasional necessity to divide their loyalties between the Italians and the Negroes.

Although one must not overemphasize the extent of differences between all these ethnic sections, such differences as do occur loom large in the Addams area. The residents are actively looking for differences among themselves. The ethnic sections in the area constitute basic guidelines from which the residents of each section can expect certain forms of reciprocity, and anticipate the dangers that may be in store elsewhere.

The portion of the Addams area now controlled by the Italians is only a residue from the encroachments of the three other ethnic groups. But in total land space, it is the largest of any controlled by a single ethnic group. In population, it is not exceptionally big, though, and throughout the section an unusually high percentage of Mexicans have been accepted by the Italians as neighbors.

What the Italians lack in numbers, they often make up for by their reputation for using sheer force and for easy access to "influence" or "connections." It is said, for example, that many of the Italians are "Outfit people," and that many more could rely on mobsters if they needed help. Also, it is the general view that the Italians control both the vice and patronage of the First Ward, a political unit that includes the spoils of the Loop—downtown Chicago.

There are some very famous Italians in the Addams area, and they frequently get a spread in the city newspapers. There are many others not nearly so prominent but whose personal histories are still known in the neighborhood. At least five Italian policemen live in the area, and a few more who grew up there are assigned to the local district. The other ethnic groups have not a single resident or ex-resident policeman among them. Most of the precinct captains are also Italian; and, outside the projects, the Italians dominate those jobs provided by public funds. There are a number of Italian businessmen, each of whom controls a few jobs. It is also widely believed that they can "sponsor" a person into many of the industries of the city— the newsstands in the Loop, the city parks, the beauty-culture industry, a large printing company, and a number of clothing firms.

While there is some substance to this belief in Italian power and influence, it is actually quite exaggerated. Many of the Italian political figures seem to have little more than the privilege of announcing decisions that have been made by others. In most of the recent political actions that have affected the area, they have remained mute and docile. When the Medical Center was built and then extended, they said nothing. The Congress and the Dan Ryan Expressways were constructed with the local politicians hardly taking notice. Finally, when the University of Illinois was located at Congress Circle, the politicians, mobsters, and—indeed—all the male residents accepted it without even a show of resistance. In fact, only a group of Italian and Mexican housewives took up arms and sought to save some remnant of the neighborhood.

The Italians' notoriety for being in the rackets and having recourse to strong-arm methods is also a considerable exaggeration, or at least a misinterpretation. The majority of the local Italians are perfectly respectable people and gain nothing from organized crime. Yet, many of the common family names of the area have been sullied by some flagrant past episode by a relative. And in the area, family histories remain a basis for judging individual members and are extended to include all persons who share the same name. In another neighborhood, this information might be lost or ignored as improper; in the Addams area, it is almost impossible to keep family secrets, and they are kept alive in the constant round of rumor and gossip.

The local Italians themselves contribute to their reputation—because on many occasions they find it advantageous to intimate that they have connections with the Outfit. For example, outsiders are often flattered to think that they are in the confidence of someone who knows the underworld. Also, it is far more prestigious to have other people believe that one's background is buried in crime and violence than in public welfare. In America, organized crime has always received a certain respect, even when this respect had to be coerced. A recipient of public welfare is simply dismissed as unimportant. And during the Depression many of the Italians went on welfare.

"Right People" Can Protect Them

In addition, some of the Italians feel that a reputation of being in with the "right people" can in some circumstances ensure them against victimization. They often hint about their connections with the Outfit when facing the members of another ethnic group under uncertain odds, or when in an argument among themselves. Yet with friends and relatives, the Italians often complain bitterly of how they are maligned by the press and by their neighbors.

Ironically, the Italians are cautious in their dealings with one another; more than any other group, they are intimidated by the half-myth that is partly of their own creation. And indirectly this myth gives them considerable cohesion, and a certain freedom from the judgments and actions of the wider society. It is almost impossible to persuade one of them to make a complaint to the police, for instance, because of their fear of the Outfit; indeed, they shun all public sources of social control. They handle grievances, contracts, and exchanges in a very informal manner, usually limited to the immediate parties. If in need, they exact aid in the form of favors and generally ignore sources available to the general public. As a result, the Italians have been able to sustain among themselves the image of an independent, powerful, and self-confident people.

Behind the Scenes Bargaining

Yet the cohesion and solidarity of the Italians are very limited. They are based primarily on the suspicion that social arrangements are best made by private settlements. This suspicion, in turn, is based on the assumption that recourse to public means can do little more than excite retaliation and vengeance. These same suspicions and doubts undermine the possibilities of a unified and explicit stance by the Italians toward the wider community and political organization. First, very few of them believe that the others will cooperate in joint efforts unless it is to their personal advantage or they are under some dire

threat. Second, the Italians simply fear that a united public stand will elicit a similar posture on the part of their adversaries and eliminate the opportunity for private negotiations. Accordingly, the Italians either shun public confrontations or slowly draw away, once so engaged. In retrospect, the spirit of *omerta* seems ineffectual when it confronts the explicit efforts of the wider community. (Literally, *omerta* means a conspiracy between thieves. The Italians use it to mean any private agreement that cannot be safely broached before the general public.)

The inability of the Italians to accept or engage in public appeals leaves them somewhat bewildered by the Negroes' civil-rights movement. By the Italians' standards, the Negroes are "making a federal case" out of something that should be handled by private agreement. Indeed, even those who accept the justice of the Negroes' cause remain perplexed by the Negroes' failure to approach *them* in some informal manner. Throughout the summer of 1964, when demonstrators were most active, the Italians always seemed aggrieved and surprised that the Negroes would "pull such a trick" without warning. The Negroes took this view as a "sham" and felt that the Italians had ample reason to anticipate their demands. To the Italians this was not the point. Of course, they knew that the Negroes had many long-standing demands and desires. What struck the Italians as unfair about the Negroes' demonstrations was their tactics: sudden public confrontations, without any chance for either side to retreat or compromise with grace.

Ultimately, both the Italians and Negroes did take their differences behind closed doors, and each settled for something less than their public demands. The main bone of contention was a local swimming pool dominated by the Italians and their Mexican guests.

In the background, of course, was the oppressive belief that the benefits of social life make up a fixed quantity and are already being used to the maximum. Thus, even the most liberal Italians assume that any gain to the Negroes must be their loss. On their own part, the Negroes make the same assumption and see no reason why the Italians should give way without a fight. Thus, whatever good intentions exist on either side are overruled by the seeming impracticality or lack of realism.

The Italians' career in the Addams area has been shaped by a traditional world view that relies heavily on a belief in "natural man." For example, it is felt to be "natural" for men to be sexual predators; for mothers to love their children, regardless of what their children do; for girls to connive at marriage; for boys to hate school; for a businessman to cheat strangers; and for anyone to choose pleasure in preference to discipline and duty. Implicit in the concept of natural man is the conviction that moral restraints have little real power in a situation in which they contradict man's natural impulses. Civilization is a mere gloss to hide man's true nature.

Often, although not always, man's natural impulses are at odds with his moral standards. Indeed, otherwise there would be no need for the church, the police, the government, and all other bodies of social control. But it is not always possible for these external bodies of social control to keep track of what people are doing. Inevitably, then, there will be occasions when people are free to choose between acting naturally and acting morally. For their own part, the Italians may have considerable conviction of their personal preferences for morality. In their dealings with other people, however they have little faith in this thin thread of individual morality. Correspondingly, to them their own personal morality becomes utterly impractical and must be replaced by whatever amoral expedient seems necessary for self-defense.

The general outcome seems to be an overwhelming distrust of impersonal or "voluntary" relationships. The other side

of the coin is an equally strong tendency to fall back on those relationships and identities where one's own welfare is guaranteed by "natural inclinations." For the most part these are kin relations, close friendship, common regional origins (*paesani*), joint residential unity, and sacred pledges like marriage, God, parenthood, etc. Thus, the Italians in the Addams area have tended to turn in upon themselves and become a provincial moral world.

Actually, many of the Italians are quite "Americanized." Frequently, though, these people lead something of a double life. During the daytime they leave the neighborhood and do their work without much thought of their ethnicity. When they come home in the evening, they are obliged to reassume their old world identity. This need not be so much a matter of taste as necessity. Other people are likely to already know their ethnicity, and evasions are likely to be interpreted as acts of snobbery or attempts at deception. Moreover, members of the other three ethnic groups refuse to accept such a person's Americanization, no matter how much it is stressed. To others, an attempt to minimize one's ethnicity is only a sly maneuver to escape responsibility for past wrongs or to gain admission into their confidence. Finally, there are still many old-timers in the neighborhood, and it would be very ill-mannered to parade one's Americanism before them. Thus, within the bounds of the local neighborhood, an Italian who plays at being an "American" runs the risk of being taken as a snob, phony, opportunist, coward, or fink.

Among the Italians themselves, notions of ethnicity are particularly well-elaborated. For the most part, these internal subdivisions are based on regional origins in Italy. By contrast, the other ethnic groups have very little internal differentiation. The Negroes make only a vague distinction between those raised in the South and those raised in the North. Among the former, Mississippians are sometimes singled out for special contempt. However, none of these divisions lead to cohesive social unities. But among the Italians their *paesani* (regional origins) take on great importance, and it remains the first perimeter beyond the family within which they look for aid or feel themselves in safe hands. Most *paesani* continue to hold their annual summer picnics and winter dance. Some have grown into full-scale organizations with elected officers, insurance plans, burial funds, and regular poker sessions.

Of all the ethnic groups in the Addams area, the Italians still have the richest ceremonial life. Aside from the annual *paesani* dances and picnics, there are parades, *feste,* and several other occasions. In the summer, their church holds a carnival that duplicates much of the Italian *feste.* On Columbus Day there is a great parade in the Loop, exceeded in grandeur only by the one held by the Irish on St. Patrick's Day. During Lent there are several special religious events and afterwards a round of dances, parties, and feasts. Throughout the summer a local brass band periodically marches through the streets playing arias from Puccini and Verdi. Sidewalk vendors sell Italian lemonade, sausages, and beef sandwiches. Horsedrawn carts go about selling grapes during the fall winemaking season, tomatoes when they are ready to be turned to paste, and fruit and vegetables at almost any time of the year.

Communal Ceremonies and Festivities

Even weddings, communions, funerals, and wakes maintain some of their communal nature. Weddings are usually known of beforehand and often attract a number of onlookers as well as those invited. Afterwards the couple and their friends drive around the neighborhood in decorated cars, honking their horns at one another and whomever they recognize on the streets. Parochial-school children usually receive first communion as a

group and attract a good deal of attention. tion of the neighborhood. On this sort of and funeral processions often tour a por- Wakes are also open to almost anyone, occasion, the Mexicans follow much the same practice, although they lack full control of a local church where they can carry out these affairs to the same extent as the Italians. Among the Negroes and Puerto Ricans, weddings, funerals, and religious events tend to be quite private affairs, open through invitation alone.

The Italians are also favored by the relatively long period over which many of them have been able to know one another and to decide upon whom they can or cannot trust. Over time, a considerable amount of information has been accumulated on many people, and this circulates in such a way as to be available to even a fairly recent resident. Moreover, the intertwining of social relations has become so extensive that contact with one person often opens passage to many others. In this sense, "getting acquainted" is almost unavoidable for a new resident.

The forms of social organization in the Italian section are far more extensive and complicated than those of the other ethnic groups. At the top are two groups, the "West Side Bloc" and the "Outfit," which share membership and whose participants are not all from the Addams area. The West Side Bloc is a group of Italian politicians whose constituency is much larger than the Addams area but which includes a definite wing in the area. Generally its members are assumed to belong to or to have connections with the Outfit. A good deal of power is attributed to them within the local neighborhood, city, state, and nation. The Outfit, more widely known as the Syndicate, includes many more people, but it is also assumed to reach beyond the Addams area. Locally, it is usually taken to include almost anyone who runs a tavern or a liquor store, or who relies on state licensing or city employment. A few other businessmen and local toughs are accredited with membership because of their notorious immunity to law enforcement or their reputed control of "favors."

Indirectly, the Outfit extends to a number of adult social-athletic clubs (s.a.c.'s). These clubs invariably have a store-front where the members spend their time in casual conversation or drink, or play cards. A few of their members belong to the Outfit, and a couple of these clubs are said to have a "regular game" for big stakes. Each group is fairly homogeneous in age, but collectively the groups range between the late 20's up to the late 60's.

Below these adult s.a.c.'s are a number of other s.a.c.'s that also have a clubhouse, but whose members are much younger. As a rule, they are somewhat beyond school age, but only a few are married, and practically none have children. To some degree, they are still involved in the extra-familial life that occupies teenagers. Occasionally they have dances, socials, and impromptu parties. On weekends they still roam around together, attending "socials" sponsored by other groups, looking for girls or for some kind of "action." Within each young man's s.a.c., the members' ages cover a narrow range. Together, all the groups range between about 19 and the late 20's. They form a distinct and well-recognized age grade in the neighborhood because of their continuing involvement in those cross-sexual and recreational activities open to unmarried males.

Nevertheless, these young men's s.a.c.'s are somewhat outside the full round of activities that throw teenagers together. A good portion of their time is spent inside their clubhouse out of sight of their rivals or most bodies of social control. Most members are in their 20's and are able to openly enjoy routine forms of entertainment or excitement that the wider community provides and accepts. When they have a dance or party, it is usually restricted to those whom they invite. Being out of school, they are not forced each day to confront persons from beyond their neighborhood. Since many of them have

cars, they need not trespass too much on someone else's domain.

The s.a.c.'s are not assumed to have any active role in the Outfit. At most, it is expected that they might be able to gain a few exemptions from law enforcement and an occasional "favor," e.g., a job, a chance to run an illegal errand, a small loan, someone to sign for their clubhouse charter (required by law), and the purchase of stolen goods or of anything else the boys happen to have on hand. It is assumed that they could solicit help from the Outfit if they got into trouble with another group, but very rarely are they drawn into this type of conflict. Almost invariably the opponent is a much younger "street group" that has encroached on what the s.a.c. considers its "rights"—e.g., tried to "crash" one of their parties, insulted them on the streets, made noise nearby, or marked up their clubhouse. Even at these times, their actions seem designed to do little more than rid themselves of a temporary nuisance. Once rid of their tormentors, they usually do not pursue the issue further, and for good reason. To charter such a club requires three cosigners, and these people may withdraw their support if the group becomes too rowdy. Also, they have a landlord to contend with, and he can throw them out for the same reason. Finally, they cannot afford to make too many enemies; they have a piece of property, and it would be only too easy for their adversaries to get back at them. Unlike all the groups described in the other three sections, they have a stake in maintaining something like law and order.

All the remaining Italian groups include members who are of high-school age. While they too call themselves s.a.c.'s, none of them have a storefront. All of them do have an established "hangout," and they correspond to the usual image of a street-corner group.

While the street groups in this section of the area often express admiration for the adult s.a.c.'s, they seldom develop in an unbroken sequence into a full-fledged adult s.a.c. Usually when they grow old enough to rent a store-front they change their name, acquire new members from groups that have been their rivals, and lose a few of their long-term members. Some groups disband entirely, and their members are redistributed among the newly formed s.a.c.'s. Of the 12 young men's and adult s.a.c.'s, only one is said to have maintained the same name from the time it was a street-corner group. Even in this case some members have been added and others lost. Together, then, the Italian street-corner groups make up the population from which future young men's s.a.c.'s are drawn, but only a few street-corner groups form the nucleus of a s.a.c.

Conceptually, the Italian street groups and the older s.a.c.'s form a single unity. In the eyes of the boys, they are somewhat like the steps between grammar school and college. While there may be dropouts, breaks, and amalgamations, they still make up a series of steps through which one can advance with increasing age. Thus, each street group tends to see the adult s.a.c.'s as essentially an older and more perfect version of itself. What may be just as important is their equally strong sense of history. Locally, many of the members in the street groups can trace their group's genealogy back through the Taylor Dukes, the 40 game, the Genna Brothers, and the Capone mob. Actually, there is no clear idea of the exact order of this descent line; some people include groups that others leave out. Moreover, there is no widespread agreement on which specific group is the current successor to this lineage. Nonetheless, there is agreement that the groups on Taylor Street have illustrious progenitors. On some occasions this heritage may be something of a burden, and on others a source of pride. In any case, it is unavoidable, and usually the Italian street group prefaces its own name with the term "Taylor." Among the younger groups this is omitted only when their name is an amalgam made up from a specific street corner or block. Only the adult s.a.c.'s regularly fail to acknowledge in their name the immediate territory within which they are situated.

Direct Line of Succession from the Outfit

Since they see themselves in a direct line of succession to groups reputed to be associated with the Outfit, these street-corner groups might be expected to have a strong criminal orientation. In the Addams area, however, the Italian groups are best known for their fighting prowess, and their official police records show no concentration on the more utilitarian forms of crime. The fact is that, like the other adolescent groups in the area, the Italian boys are not really free to choose their own goals and identities. Territorial arrangements juxtapose them against similar groups manned by Negro and Mexican boys. If the Italian street-corner groups fail to define themselves as fighting groups, their peers in the other ethnic groups are certainly going to assume as much.

There is also considerable rivalry between Italian street-corner groups of roughly the same age. Commonly they suspect each other of using force to establish their precedence. In turn, each group seems to think it must at least put on a tough exterior to avoid being "pushed around." Privately there is a great deal of talk among them about the Outfit and about criminal activities, but it is academic in the sense that there is no strong evidence that their behavior follows suit.

It is interesting that the adult s.a.c.'s that actually have members in the rackets avoid any conspicuous claims about their criminal activities or fighting abilities. Their names, for example, are quite tame, while those of the street groups tend to be rather menacing. And their dances, leisure-time activities, and interrelationships are quite private and unpretentious. Unlike the street groups, they never wear clothing that identifies their group membership. The older men in the s.a.c.'s make no apparent attempt to establish a publicly-known hierarchy among themselves. Other people occasionally attribute more respect to one than another of them, but there seems to be little consensus on this. On their own part, the older groups seem to pay little attention to their relative standing and to be on fairly good terms. During my three years in the area, I never heard of them fighting among themselves.

Unlike the Negro and Mexican ethnic sections, there are no female counterparts to the named Italian street-corner groups. A very few Italian girls belong to two Mexican girls' groups that "hung" in the Mexican section. This, in itself, was exceptional; almost always the minority members in a street group are from a lower-ranking ethnic group. The Italian girls, however, are under certain constraints that may be lacking for those in the other ethnic groups. Naturally, their parents disapprove of such a blatant display of feminine unity. The Italian parents may gain stature by their power and precedence in comparison to the Negro and Mexican adults. Yet what seems far more significant is the general form that boy-girl relationships take among the Italians. On either side, the slightest hint of interest in the other sex is likely to be taken in the most serious way; as either a rank insult or a final commitment. Thus, any explicit alliance between a boys' and girls' group can be interpreted in only one of two ways: (1) all the girls are "laying" for the boys, or (2) they are seriously attached to each other. Neither side seems quite willing to betray so much and, thus, they avoid such explicit alliances.

This dilemma was quite evident on many occasions while I was observing the Italian boys and girls. The girls seemed extraordinarily coy when they were in a "safe" position—with their parents, in church, etc. When alone and on their own they became equally cautious and non-committal. On public occasions, the boys seemed almost to ignore the girls and even to snub them. On Taylor Street, for instance, an Italian boys' group and an Italian girls' group used to hang about 10 feet from each other. Almost invariably they would stand with their backs to each other, although there were many furtive glances back and forth. During almost two years of observation, I never saw them talk. Later, I was surprised to learn that everyone in each group was quite well-known to the other. For either of them to have acknowledged the other's presence openly, however, would have been too forward. The boys are quite aware of this dilemma and complain that the girls are not free enough to be convenient companions. This, they say, is one reason why they have to go elsewhere to date someone. At the same time, they perpetuate the old system by automatically assuming that the slightest sign of interest by a girl makes her fair game. Out of self-defense, the girls are compelled to keep their distance. On private occasions, of course, there are many Italian boys and girls who sneak off to enjoy what others might consider an entirely conventional boy-girl relationship (petting, necking). In public, though, they studiously ignore each other. Throughout my time in the area I never saw a young Italian couple hold hands or walk together on the sidewalk.

The Barracudas were the first Mexican street-corner group to emerge in the Italian section. They first became a named group in the spring of 1964, and all members were Mexican.

Once established, the Barracudas installed themselves in the northwest corner of Sheridan Park. Virtually every Italian street group in the area makes use of this park, and several have their hangout there. Other people in turn refer to the Italian groups collectively as "the guys from the Park." The park itself is partitioned into a finely graduated series of more or less private enclosures, with the most private hangout going to the reigning group and the least private to the weakest group. The northwest corner of the park is the most exposed of any portion, and this is where the Barracudas installed themselves. Even in this lowly spot, they were much resented by the other groups. To the Italians the Park was almost a sacred charge, and the Mexicans' intrusion was a ritual pollution. The Barracudas were harassed, ridiculed, and insulted. On their own part, they became belligerent and vaunted all sorts of outrageous claims about themselves. Soon the situation deteriorated and the Italian groups became extremely harsh with the Barracudas. Since the Barracudas were no match for even some of the younger Italian groups, they removed themselves to one member's house.

Their new hangout placed them in an anomalous position. Ethnically they were identified as a Mexican group. Yet they were located in a part of the area that had been conceded to the Puerto Ricans. And individually most of them continued to reside in the Italian section. The general result seems to have been that the Barracudas were isolated from any of the other group hierarchies and placed in opposition to every group in the area. Within a year every white group was their enemy, and the Negroes were not their friends. The Barracudas responded in kind and became even more truculent and boastful. More than any group in the area, they openly embraced the stance of a fighting group. They wrote their name all over the neighborhood and even on some of the other groups' hangouts. In the meantime, they made a clubhouse out of a lean-to adjacent to a building on Harrison Street. Inside they installed a shield on which they wrote "hate," "kill," and other violent words. Carrying a weapon became almost routine with them, and eventually they collected a small arsenal. In time they had several small-scale fights with both the Italians from the Park and the Mexicans around Polk and Laflin. In due course,

they acquired so many enemies that they could hardly risk leaving the immediate area of their hangout. At the same time, some of them began to go to Eighteenth Street, where they had "connections"— relatives. This only brought them into conflict with other groups in this neighborhood. By the summer of 1965, the Barracudas were as isolated and resentful as ever.

"Incognitos" and the "Pica People"

There are two other groups in the Italian section, the Pica People and the Incognitos. The groups' names are themselves an expression of their isolation. The Incognitos self-consciously avoided comparison with the other groups: They did not hang in the Park, hold socials, or become involved in any of the local sidewalk confrontations. About the same age as the Contenders, the Incognitos were notably different in their exclusion from the local round of praise and recriminations.

"Pica People" is a derisive name meant as an insult for five young men about 19 to 25 years of age. Although these five individuals associate regularly, they claim no group identity and become angry when called the Pica People. Unlike the Incognitos, the Pica People are well known and often accused of some predatory display. They do not fight for group honor, but there is friction between them and all the other street-corner groups in the Addams area.

It was impossible to determine how these two groups came into existence. (I talked only twice with the Incognitos, who simply said they "grew up together." Local people started calling the Pica People by that name after a movie in which the "Pica People" were sub-humans. I knew some of the members of this group, but they became so angry at any mention of the name that I could not discuss it with them.) What is known of their composition may throw some light on why they were excluded from the structure of the other groups. All informants described the Incognitos as "good guys," still in school and no trouble to anyone. They were not considered college boys but, if asked, most informants said they thought some of them might go to college. Local youth agencies made no attempt to work with them, and the entire neighborhood seemed to feel they were not dangerous. Other street-corner groups in the Italian section did not look down on them, but they did exempt them from the ambitions that brought other groups into opposition.

The Pica People were just the opposite. All members were boastful of their alleged Outfit connections and their ability to intimidate other people. But the Pica People possessed so many personal flaws that they were rather useless to the Outfit. One member was slightly claustrophobic. Another was so weak that even much younger boys pushed him around. A third had an exceedingly unfortunate appearance. Under the circumstances, their pretensions became laughable.

Extremes of Street Corner Groups

The Incognitos and the Pica People seem to represent the extremes of a range in which the street-corner group is considered the normal adolescent gathering. Modest and well-behaved youngsters are excluded as exceptions, as are criminally inclined but unsuccessful young men. Both of these groups fell outside the range considered normal by the local residents and were thereby dissociated from the total group hierarchy.

The social context of the Italian street groups is somewhat different from that of the street groups in the other three ethnic sections. Among the Italians, the major share of coercive power still remains in adult hands. The wider community may not be very pleased with the form *their* power takes, but it is the only case where the corporate power of the adolescents is

tempered by that of the adults. Also, since many of the same adults have an active role in distributing some of the benefits that are held in store by the wider community, their power is augmented. Perhaps the most obvious result of the adults' ascendency is that the adolescents do not simply dismiss them or adulthood as unimportant. A more immediate consequence is to give many of the adults the prerogative of exacting considerable obedience from the local adolescents. It is not at all uncommon to see an Italian adult upbraid and humble one of the local youths. Not all adults have this privilege; but many do, and their example provides a distinct contrast to the other ethnic groups where similar efforts would be futile.

In the long run, the effectiveness of these coercive controls among the Italians may do little more than confirm their convictions that, outside of natural tendencies, there is no guarantee to moral conduct except economic and numerical strength. Within their own little world, however, such coercive measures constitute a fairly effective system of social control. Personal privacy and anonymity are almost impossible. In turn, each person's known or assumed connections dampen most chances at exploitation because of the fear of unknown consequences. Thus, the opportunities for immorality presented by transient relations and "fair game" are fairly rare. Within these limits, such an authoritarian system of social control will work. Outside their own section, of course, these conditions do not hold; and the Italian boys find themselves free to seize whatever advantages or opportunities present themselves. Among themselves, they are usually only a rowdy and boisterous crowd. With strangers or in other parts of the Addams area, they become particularly arrogant and unscrupulous.

With these qualifications, it appears that well-established adolescent street-corner groups are quite compatible with strong adult authority and influence. In fact, judging from the Italian section, these adolescent street-corner groups seem to be the building blocks out of which the older and more powerful groups have originated. The younger groups continue to replenish the older ones and help maintain the structure within which adults are shown deference.

Moreover, the total age-graded structure of groups in the Italian section relates youngsters to the wider society both instrumentally and conceptually. The Italian street groups see themselves as replacements in an age structure that becomes progressively less provincial. At the upper age level, groups even stop prefacing their name with the term "Taylor"; and a few of their members have a place in the wider society through the Outfit and West Side Bloc. The relationship between these age grades also provides a ladder down which favors and opportunities are distributed. The wider community may hesitate at accepting the legitimacy of these trans-actions, but they are mostly of a conventional form. The "Outfit" and the "West Side Bloc" have a strong interest in maintaining a degree of social order, and the sorts of wanton violence associated with gangs do not at all fit their taste.

In Conclusion

The Addams area is probably a more orderly slum than many others, and it departs sharply from the common image of an atomized and unruly urban rabble. For all its historical uniqueness, the neighborhood does establish the possibility of a moral order within its population. The recurrence of the circumstances that led to its organization is as uncertain as the future of the Addams area itself. In spite of all these uncertainties, the Addams area shows that slum residents are intent upon finding a moral order and are sometimes successful in doing so.

on *Social Organization*

Small Groups and Large Organizations

BLAU, PETER M. *Bureaucracy in Modern Society*. New York: Random House, 1956. An introduction to the study of bureaucracy.

BLAU, PETER M., and W. RICHARD SCOTT. *Formal Organizations*. San Francisco: Chandler, 1962. A comparative examination of the types and dynamics of formal organizations.

CROZIER, MICHAEL. *The Bureaucratic Phenomenon*. Chicago: University of Chicago Press, 1964. A study of bureaucracy in France in comparison with other societies.

ETZIONI, AMATAI. *Complex Organizations*. New York: Free Press, 1961. A theoretical paradigm for the analysis of large organizations in terms of the role of compliance.

GRANICK, DAVID. *The Red Executive*. Garden City, N.Y.: Doubleday, 1961. A study of the high level bureaucrat in Russian industry.

HARE, PAUL, EDGAR F. BORGETTA, and ROBERT F. BALES, eds. *Small Groups*. Revised edition. New York: Alfred A. Knopf, 1965. A collection of studies on social interaction.

HOMANS, GEORGE C. *The Human Group*. New York: Harcourt, Brace, 1950. A theory for the study of social relationships is developed with illustrations drawn from several major sociological and anthropological studies.

MERTON, ROBERT K., *et al.*, eds. *Reader in Bureaucracy*. Glencoe, Ill.: Free Press, 1962. A collection of articles.

MOORE, WILBERT E. *The Conduct of the Corporation*. New York: Random House, 1962. An award-winning description of the organization of the large business firm in America.

OLMSTED, MICHAEL S. *The Small Group*. New York: Random House, 1959. An introduction to the study of small groups with case illustrations.

WHYTE, WILLIAM FOOTE. *Street Corner Society*. Enlarged edition. Chicago: University of Chicago Press, 1955. A study of social relationships in an Italian-American neighborhood.

WHYTE, WILLIAM H. *The Organization Man*. New York: Simon and Schuster, 1956. A provocative study of the junior executive at home and at work.

Communities

BALTZELL, E. DIGBY, ed. *Search for Community in Modern Society*. New York: Harper and Row, 1969. A collection of essays by historians and social scientists.

CAHNMAN, WERNER, and JEAN COMHAIRE. *How Cities Grew*. Madison, N.J.: Florham Park Press, 1959. The historical sociology of cities.

GANS, HERBERT. *The Levittowners*. New York: Pantheon, 1967. A study of life in a newly built suburban town.

GANS, HERBERT. *The Urban Villagers*. New York: Free Press, 1962. Groups and classes in the neighborhood life of Italian-Americans in a large city.

HATT, PAUL K., and ALBERT J. REISS, eds. *Cities and Society*. Glencoe, Ill.: Free Press, 1957. An excellent reader in urban sociology.

JACOBS, JANE. *The Death and Life of Great American Cities*. New York: Random House, 1961. A polemic against the current trend of city planning.

LYFORD, JOSEPH. *The Airtight Cage*. New York: Harper and Row, 1966. A journalistic report on New York's West Side.

LYND, ROBERT, and HELEN LYND. *Middletown*. New York: Harcourt, Brace and World, 1956. A reprint of a famous sociological study of a small Midwestern town. Originally published in 1929.

OSOFSKY, GILBERT. *Harlem: The Making of a Ghetto*. New York: Harper and Row, 1966. The history of Harlem from 1890–1930.

POLL, SOLOMON. *The Hasidic Community of Williamsburg*. New York: Free Press, 1962. A study of a small community of Hasidic Jews living in Brooklyn.

REDFIELD, ROBERT. *The Little Community*. Chicago: University of Chicago Press, 1955. Some notes on the study of communities as wholes.

WARREN, ROLAND L. *The Community in America*. Chicago: Rand McNally, 1963. A reassessment of a number of community studies, and a paradigm for the analysis of the community as a social entity.

PART FOUR
STRATIFICATION AND
DIFFERENTIATION

Systems of inequality
and distinction based upon
social, economic, and
ethnic differences

In all societies individuals are differentiated by biological and social criteria. People are ranked in hierarchical fashion, as superior or inferior, according to those attributes that are deemed important. Even in the most primitive societies, where subsistence is the primary concern, distinctions are made in terms of age groupings, sex, and kinship. More advanced societies are divided into distinct social strata, with those persons higher on the scale having access to greater opportunities for wealth, prestige, and social control.

Opportunities for mobility are dependent upon the socially defined system of stratification. Where a rigid caste system exists, there is little hope for individual advancement. Status is fixed by birth and marriage is endogamous. In some societies, with a feudal social structure, the estate system provides limited channels for mobility and individuals are sometimes able to change their estates by royal decree, by marriage to someone of higher position, by military service, or by entering the clergy. In agricultural societies, where status is directly related to the ownership and use of land, the estate system is most prevalent.

In industrial societies, where land tenure is relatively unimportant, skill and income tend to become the relevant measures of social position. In such societies class systems emerge. Ideally, every individual has the opportunity to gain recognition through personal ability and performance, regardless of birth or previous conditions of inequality. While greater opportunities do exist in a class system for movement up and down the mobility ladder, there is no society where individual merit, in and of itself, is the sole criterion for determining status.

In the United States, for example, "fluid ascription" is the term frequently used to describe the current nature of social stratification. This means that, although birth plays a large part in ascribing socioeconomic status, it is—and has been—possible for many to realize the ambitions of the "American Dream" and move upward in the stratification hierarchy. No longer pyramid shaped, the graphic representation of the American class system is now more accurately portrayed as a diamond. Yet, there are still many who have not been able to achieve that modicum of affluence that would admit them to the ranks of the middle (or even the working) class. They comprise what Michael Harrington has aptly called "the other America."

Foreign-born persons, members of certain religious groups, those who live in isolated areas or whose skills are not needed, and especially, those with darker skins are often categorically denied the right to fulfill their own potentialities in the "pursuit of happiness." As Kurt Mayer has said, "If the absence of estatelike characteristics makes the American class system unique, it is likewise true that the intrusion of racial castelike features is almost without parallel in modern Western experience." A critical aspect of placement in the status hierarchy of American society is that of ethnic and racial group membership.

In Part Four, two themes are examined: social class, and racial and ethnic patterns of differentiation. In the first instance discussion is opened with a translation of Max Weber's famous essay, "Class, Status, and Party." This is followed by two more well-known articles: Kingsley Davis and Wilbert E. Moore's discussion of the universality and functional necessity of social stratification, and a critique of Davis-Moore by Melvin M. Tumin.

The next paper offers a portrait of the American class system as seen by William Lloyd Warner (director of the well known Yankee City Series) and his associates. Then, zeroing in on those people situated at the bottom of most ranking schemes (including Warner's), S. M. Miller offers further refinement. His essay on "The American Lower Class: A Typological Approach" is followed by Norbert Wiley's "The Ethnic Mobility Trap." Wiley's paper offers a bridge between the section on Social Class and the one on Race and Ethnicity.

The second set of papers continues focusing on the United States. It starts with Milton M. Gordon's consideration of the meaning of structural pluralism for American life and a description of the nature of residential segregation and its effect upon the assimilation process by Stanley Lieberson. Also included is Peter I. Rose's study "Strangers in Their Midst," a report on small-town Jews and their neighbors.

"Discrimination and the American Creed," Robert Merton's famous essay about the relationship between prejudice and discrimination, is followed by Gerald D. Berreman's "Caste in India and the United States" and Kenneth B. Clark's documentation of the impact of segregation on those who live in Harlem. The last paper is an analysis of research on "Ethnicity as an Influence on Behavior," by Andrew Greeley.

Social Class

28. CLASS, STATUS, PARTY

MAX WEBER

*Few men have influenced the study of social stratification (and sociology in general)
more than the German sociologist, Max Weber. His discussion of "class, status, and
party" and of "ethnic segregation" and "caste" are basic reading for all concerned with
the distribution of wealth, prestige, and power. Indeed, Weber's ideas have generated
much of the research and theorizing discussed in this section. It is for these various
reasons that precedent is broken and an essay, written long before World War II, is
presented here.*

*Max Weber was born in Germany in 1864 and died there in 1920. Early in his career,
he served as Professor of Economics at Freiburg University and at Heidelberg. Later,
he became Professor of Sociology at the University of Munich. His most famous work,*
The Protestant Ethic and the Spirit of Capitalism, *was published in 1904. He also
wrote* The Theory of Social and Economic Organization, The Sociology of Religion,
Religion of China, Religion of India, Ancient Judaism, Sociology of Law, Economy and
Society, *and* Methodology of the Social Sciences.

From *Max Weber: Essays in Sociology,* edited and translated by H. H. Gerth and C. Wright
Mills. Copyright 1946 by Oxford University Press, Inc. Reprinted by permission. The first
sentence in paragraph one and the several definitions in this selection which are in brackets do
not appear in the original text. They have been taken from other contexts of *Wirtschaft und
Gesellschaft.*

1: Economically Determined Power and the Social Order

Law exists when there is a probability that an order will be upheld by a specific staff of men who will use physical or psychical compulsion with the intention of obtaining conformity with the order, or of inflicting sanctions for infringement of it. The structure of every legal order directly influences the distribution of power, economic or otherwise, within its respective community. This is true of all legal orders and not only that of the state. In general, we understand by "power" the chance of a man or of a number of men to realize their own will in a communal action even against the resistance of others who are participating in the action.

"Economically conditioned" power is not, of course, identical with "power" as such. On the contrary, the emergence of economic power may be the consequence of power existing on other grounds. Man does not strive for power only in order to enrich himself economically. Power, including economic power, may be valued "for its own sake." Very frequently the striving for power is also conditioned by the social "honor" it entails. Not all power, however, entails social honor: The typical American Boss, as well as the typical big speculator, deliberately relinquishes social honor. Quite generally, "mere economic" power, and especially "naked" money power, is by no means a recognized basis of social honor. Nor is power the only basis of social honor. Indeed, social honor, or prestige, may even be the basis of political or economic power, and very frequently has been. Power, as well as honor, may be guaranteed by the legal order, but, at least normally, it is not their primary source. The legal order is rather an additional factor that enhances the chance to hold power or honor; but it cannot always secure them.

The way in which social honor is distributed in a community between typical groups participating in this distribution we may call the "social order." The social order and the economic order are, of course, similarly related to the "legal order." However, the social and the economic order are not identical. The economic order is for us merely the way in which economic goods and services are distributed and used. The social order is of course conditioned by the economic order to a high degree, and in its turn reacts upon it.

Now: "classes," "status groups," and "parties" are phenomena of the distribution of power within a community.

2: Determination of Class Situation by Market Situation

In our terminology, "classes" are not communities; they merely represent possible, and frequent, bases for communal action. We may speak of a "class" when (1) a number of people have in common a specific causal component of their life chances, in so far as (2) this component is represented exclusively by economic interests in the possession of goods and opportunities for income, and (3) is represented under the conditions of the commodity or labor markets. [These points refer to "class situation," which we may express more briefly as the typical chance for a supply of goods, external living conditions, and personal life experiences, in so far as this chance is determined by the amount and kind of power, or lack of such, to dispose of goods or skills for the sake of income in a given economic order. The term "class" refers to any group of people that is found in the same class situation.]

It is the most elemental economic fact that the way in which the disposition over material property is distributed among a plurality of people, meeting competitively in the market for the purpose of exchange, in itself creates specific life chances. According to the law of marginal utility this mode of distribution excludes the nonowners from competing for highly valued goods; it favors the owners and, in fact, gives to them a monopoly to acquire such goods. Other things being equal, this mode of distribution monopolizes the opportunities for profitable deals for all those who, provided with goods, do not necessarily have to exchange them. It increases, at least generally, their power in price wars with those who, being propertyless, have nothing to offer but their services in native form or goods in a form constituted through their own labor, and who above all are compelled to get rid of these products in order barely to subsist. This mode of distribution gives to the propertied a monopoly on the possibility of transferring property from the sphere of use as a "fortune," to the sphere of "capital goods"; that is, it gives them the entrepreneurial function and all chances to share directly or indirectly in returns on capital. All this holds true within the area in which pure market conditions prevail. "Property" and "lack of property" are, therefore, the basic categories of all class situations. It does not matter whether these two categories become effective in price wars or in competitive struggles.

Within these categories, however, class situations are further differentiated: on the one hand, according to the kind of property that is usable for returns; and, on the other hand, according to the kind of services that can be offered in the market. Ownership of domestic buildings; productive establishments; warehouses; stores; agriculturally usable land, large and small holdings—quantitative differences with possibly qualitative consequences—; ownership of mines; cattle; men (slaves); disposition over mobile instruments of production, or capital goods of all sorts, especially money or objects that can be exchanged for money easily and at any time; disposition over products of one's own labor or of others' labor differing according to their various distances from consumability; disposition over transferable monopolies of any kind—all these distinctions differentiate the class situations of the propertied just as does the "meaning" which they can and do give to the utilization of property, especially to property which has money equivalence. Accordingly, the propertied, for instance, may belong to the class of rentiers or to the class of entrepreneurs.

Those who have no property but who offer services are differentiated just as much according to their kinds of services as according to the way in which they make use of these services, in a continuous or discontinuous relation to a recipient. But always this is the generic connotation of the concept of class: that the kind of chance in the *market* is the decisive moment which presents a common condition for the individual's fate. "Class situation" is, in this sense, ultimately "market situation." The effect of naked possession *per se,* which among cattle breeders gives the nonowning slave or serf into the power of the cattle owner, is only a forerunner of real "class" formation. However, in the cattle loan and in the naked severity of the law of debts in such communities, for the first time mere "possession" as such emerges as decisive for the fate of the individual. This is very much in contrast to the agricultural communities based on labor. The creditor-debtor relation becomes the basis of "class situations" only in those cities where a "credit market," however primitive, with rates of interest increasing according to the extent of dearth and a factual monopolization of credits, is developed by a plutocracy. Therewith "class struggles" begin.

Those men whose fate is not determined by the chance of using goods or services for themselves on the market, e.g. slaves, are not, however, a "class" in the technical sense of the term. They are, rather, a "status group."

3: Communal Action Flowing from Class Interest

According to our terminology, the factor that creates "class" is unambiguously economic interest, and indeed, only those interests involved in the existence of the "market." Nevertheless, the concept of "class-interest" is an ambiguous one: even as an empirical concept it is ambiguous as soon as one understands by it something other than the factual direction of interests following with a certain probability from the class situation for a certain "average" of those people subjected to the class situation. The class situation and other circumstances remaining the same, the direction in which the individual worker, for instance, is likely to pursue his interests may vary widely, according to whether he is constitutionally qualified for the task at hand to a high, to an average, or to a low degree. In the same way, the direction of interests may vary according to whether or not a *communal* action of a larger or smaller portion of those commonly affected by the "class situation," or even an association among them, e.g. a "trade union," has grown out of the class situation from which the individual may or may not expect promising results. [Communal action refers to that action which is oriented to the feeling of the actors that they belong together. Societal action, on the other hand, is oriented to a rationally motivated adjustment of interests.] The rise of societal or even of communal action from a common class situation is by no means a universal phenomenon.

The class situation may be restricted in its effects to the generation of essentially *similar* reactions, that is to say, within our terminology, of "mass actions." However, it may not have even this result. Furthermore, often merely an amorphous communal action emerges. For example, the "murmuring" of the workers known in ancient oriental ethics: the moral disap- proval of the workmaster's conduct, which in its practical significance was probably equivalent to an increasingly typical phenomenon of precisely the latest industrial development, namely, the "slow down" (the deliberate limiting of work effort) of laborers by virtue of tacit agreement. The degree in which "communal action" and possibly "societal action," emerges from the "mass actions" of the members of a class is linked to general cultural conditions, especially to those of an intellectual sort. It is also linked to the extent of the contrasts that have already evolved, and is especially linked to the *transparency* of the connections between the causes and the consequences of the "class situation." For however different life chances may be, this fact in itself, according to all experience, by no means gives birth to "class action" (communal action by the members of a class). The fact of being conditioned and the results of the class situation must be distinctly recognizable. For only then the contrast of life chances can be felt not as an abso- lutely given fact to be accepted, but as a resultant from either (1) the given distri- bution of property, or (2) the structure of the concrete economic order. It is only then that people may react against the class structure not only through acts of an intermittent and irrational protest, but in the form of rational association. There have been "class situations" of the first category (1), of a specifically naked and transparent sort, in the urban centers of antiquity and during the Middle Ages; es- pecially then, when great fortunes were accumulated by factually monopolized trading in industrial products of these lo- calities or in foodstuffs. Furthermore, under certain circumstances, in the rural economy of the most diverse periods, when agriculture was increasingly ex- ploited in a profit-making manner. The most important historical example of the second category (2) is the class situation of the modern "proletariat."

4: Types of "Class Struggle"

Thus every class may be the carrier of any one of the possibly innumerable forms of "class action," but this is not necessarily so. In any case, a class does not in itself constitute a community. To treat "class" conceptually as having the same value as "community" leads to distortion. That men in the same class situation regularly react in mass actions to such tangible situations as economic ones in the direction of those interests that are most adequate to their average number is an important and after all simple fact for the understanding of historical events. Above all, this fact must not lead to that kind of pseudoscientific operation with the concepts of "class" and "class interests" so frequently found these days, and which has found its most classic expression in the statement of a talented author, that the individual may be in error concerning his interests but that the "class" is "infallible" about its interests. Yet, if classes as such are not communities, nevertheless class situations emerge only on the basis of communalization. The communal action that brings forth class situations, however, is not basically action between members of the identical class; it is an action between members of different classes. Communal actions that directly determine the class situation of the worker and the entrepreneur are: the labor market, the commodities market, and the capitalistic enterprise. But, in its turn, the existence of a capitalistic enterprise presupposes that a very specific communal action exists and that it is specifically structured to protect the possession of goods *per se,* and especially the power of individuals to dispose, in principle freely, over the means of production. The existence of a capitalistic enterprise is preconditioned by a specific kind of "legal order." Each kind of class situation, and above all when it rests upon the power of property *per se,* will become most clearly efficacious when all other determinants of

reciprocal relations are, as far as possible, eliminated in their significance. It is in this way that the utilization of the power of property in the market obtains its most sovereign importance.

Now "status groups" hinder the strict carrying through of the sheer market principle. In the present context they are of interest to us only from this one point of view. Before we briefly consider them, note that not much of a general nature can be said about the more specific kinds of antagonism between "classes" (in our meaning of the term). The great shift, which has been going on continuously in the past, and up to our times, may be summarized, although at the cost of some precision: the struggle in which class situations are effective has progressively shifted from consumption credit toward, first, competitive struggles in the commodity market and, then, toward price wars on the labor market. The "class struggles" of antiquity—to the extent that they were genuine class struggles and not struggles between status groups—were initially carried on by indebted peasants, and perhaps also by artisans threatened by debt bondage and struggling against urban creditors. For debt bondage is the normal result of the differentiation of wealth in commercial cities, especially in seaport cities. A similar situation has existed among cattle breeders. Debt relationships as such produced class action up to the time of Cataline. Along with this, and with an increase in provision of grain for the city by transporting it from the outside, the struggle over the means of sustenance emerged. It centered in the first place around the provision of bread and the determination of the price of bread. It lasted throughout antiquity and the entire Middle Ages. The propertyless as such flocked together against those who actually and supposedly were interested in the dearth of bread. This fight spread until it involved all those commodities essential to the way of life and to handicraft production. There were only incipient discussions of wage disputes in antiquity and in the Middle Ages. But they have been slowly increasing up into modern times. In the earlier periods they were completely secondary to slave rebellions as well as to fights in the commodity market.

The propertyless of antiquity and of the Middle Ages protested against monopolies, pre-emption, forestalling, and the withholding of goods from the market in order to raise prices. Today the central issue is the determination of the price of labor.

This transition is represented by the fight for access to the market and for the determination of the price of products. Such fights went on between merchants and workers in the putting-out system of domestic handicraft during the transition to modern times. Since it is quite a general phenomenon we must mention here that the class antagonisms that are conditioned through the market situation are usually most bitter between those who actually and directly participate as opponents in price wars. It is not the rentier, the share-holder, and the banker who suffer the ill will of the worker, but almost exclusively the manufacturer and the business executives who are the direct opponents of workers in price wars. This is so in spite of the fact that it is precisely the cash boxes of the rentier, the share-holder, and the banker into which the more or less "unearned" gains flow, rather than into the pockets of the manufacturers or of the business executives. This simple state of affairs has very frequently been decisive for the role the class situation has played in the formation of political parties. For example, it has made possible the varieties of patriarchal socialism and the frequent attempts—formerly, at least—of threatened status groups to form alliances with the proletariat against the "bourgeoisie."

5: Status Honor

In contrast to classes, *status groups* are normally communities. They are, however, often of an amorphous kind. In contrast to the purely economically determined "class situation" we wish to designate as "status situation" every typical component of the life fate of men that is determined by a specific, positive or negative, social estimation of *honor*. This honor may be connected with any quality shared by a plurality, and, of course, it can be knit to a class situation: class distinctions are linked in the most varied ways with status distinctions. Property as such is not always recognized as a status qualification, but in the long run it is, and with extraordinary regularity. In the subsistence economy of the organized neighborhood, very often the richest man is simply the chieftain. However, this often means only an honorific preference. For example, in the so-called pure modern "democracy," that is, one devoid of any expressly ordered status privileges for individuals, it may be that only the families coming under approximately the same tax class dance with one another. This example is reported of certain smaller Swiss cities. But status honor need not necessarily be linked with a "class situation." On the contrary, it normally stands in sharp opposition to the pretensions of sheer property.

Both propertied and propertyless people can belong to the same status group, and frequently they do with very tangible consequences. This "equality" of social esteem may, however, in the long run become quite precarious. The "equality" of status among the American "gentlemen," for instance, is expressed by the fact that outside the subordination determined by the different functions of "business," it would be considered strictly repugnant—wherever the old tradition still prevails—if even the richest "chief," while playing billiards or cards in his club in the evening, would not treat his "clerk" as in every sense fully his equal in birthright. It would be repugnant if the American "chief" would bestow upon his "clerk" the condescending "benevolence" marking a distinction of "position," which the German chief can never dissever from his attitude. This is one of the most important reasons why in America the German "clubbyness" has never been able to attain the attraction that the American clubs have.

6: Guarantees of Status Stratification

In content, status honor is normally expressed by the fact that above all else a specific *style of life* can be expected from all those who wish to belong to the circle. Linked with this expectation are restrictions on "social" intercourse (that is, intercourse which is not subservient to economic or any other of business's "functional" purposes). These restrictions may confine normal marriages to within the status circle and may lead to a complete endogamous closure. As soon as there is not a mere individual and socially irrelevant imitation of another style of life, but an agreed-upon communal action of this closing character, the "status" development is under way.

In its characteristic form, stratification by "status groups" on the basis of conventional styles of life evolves at the present time in the United States out of the traditional democracy. For example, only the resident of a certain street ("the street") is considered as belonging to "society," is qualified for social intercourse, and is visited and invited. Above all, this differentiation evolves in such a way as to make for strict submission to the fashion that is dominant at a given time in society. This submission to fashion also exists among men in America to a degree unknown in Germany. Such submission is considered to be an indication of the fact that a given man *pretends* to qualify as a gentleman. This submission decides, at least *prima facie,* that he will be treated as such. And this recognition becomes just as important for his employment chances in "swank" establishments, and above all, for social intercourse and marriage with "esteemed"

families, as the qualification for dueling among Germans in the Kaiser's day. As for the rest: certain families resident for a long time, and, of course, correspondingly wealthy, e.g. "F. F. V.," i.e. "First Families of Virginia," or the actual or alleged descendants of the "Indian Princess" Pocahontas, of the Pilgrim fathers, or of the Knickerbockers, the members of almost inaccessible sects and all sorts of circles setting themselves apart by means of any other characteristics and badges . . . all these elements usurp "status" honor. The development of status is essentially a question of stratification resting upon usurpation. Such usurpation is the normal origin of almost all status honor. But the road from this purely conventional situation to legal privilege, positive or negative, is easily traveled as soon as a certain stratification of the social order has in fact been "lived in" and has achieved stability by virtue of a stable distribution of economic power.

7: "Ethnic" Segregation and "Caste"

Where the consequences have been realized to their full extent, the status group evolves into a closed "caste." Status distinctions are then guaranteed not merely by conventions and laws, but also by *rituals.* This occurs in such a way that every physical contact with a member of any caste that is considered to be "lower" by the members of a "higher" caste is considered as making for a ritualistic impurity and to be a stigma which must be expiated by a religious act. Individual castes develop quite distinct cults and gods.

In general, however, the status structure reaches such extreme consequences only where there are underlying differences which are held to be "ethnic." The "caste" is, indeed, the normal form in which ethnic communities usually live side by side in a "societalized" manner. These ethnic communities believe in blood relationship and exclude exogamous marriage and social intercourse. Such a caste situation is part of the phenomenon of "pariah" peoples and is found all over the world. These people form communities, acquire specific occupational traditions of handicrafts or of other arts, and cultivate a belief in their ethnic community. They live in a "diaspora" strictly segregated from all personal intercourse, except that of an unavoidable sort, and their situation is legally precarious. Yet, by virtue of their economic indispensability, they are tolerated, indeed, frequently privileged, and they live in interspersed political communities. The Jews are the most impressive historical example.

A "status" segregation grown into a "caste" differs in its structure from a mere "ethnic" segregation: the caste structure transforms the horizontal and unconnected coexistences of ethnically segregated groups into a vertical social system of super- and subordination. Correctly formulated: a comprehensive societalization integrates the ethnically divided communities into specific political and communal action. In their consequences they differ precisely in this way: ethnic coexistences condition a mutual repulsion and disdain but allow each ethnic community to consider its own honor as the highest one; the caste structure brings about a social subordination and an acknowledgment of "more honor" in favor of the privileged caste and status groups. This is due to the fact that in the caste structure ethnic distinctions as such have become "functional" distinctions within the political societalization (warriors, priests, artisans that are politically important for war and for building, and so on). But even pariah people who are most despised are usually apt to continue cultivating in some manner that which is equally peculiar to ethnic and to status communities: the belief in their own specific "honor." This is the case with the Jews.

Only with the negatively privileged status groups does the "sense of dignity" take a specific deviation. A sense of dignity is the precipitation in individuals of social honor and of conventional demands which a positively privileged status group raises for the deportment of its members. The sense of dignity that characterizes positively privileged status groups is naturally related to their "being" which does not transcend itself, that is, it is to their "beauty and excellence" ($\chi\alpha\lambda o$-$\chi\dot\alpha\gamma\alpha\vartheta\iota\alpha$). Their kingdom is "of this world." They live for the present and by exploiting their great past. The sense of dignity of the negatively privileged strata naturally refers to a future lying beyond the present, whether it is of this life or of another. In other words, it must be nurtured by the belief in a providential "mission" and by a belief in a specific honor before God. The "chosen people's" dignity is nurtured by a belief either that in the beyond "the last will be the first," or that in this life a Messiah will appear to bring forth into the light of the world which has cast them out the hidden honor of the pariah people. This simple state of affairs, and not the "resentment" which is so strongly emphasized in Nietzsche's much admired construction in the *Genealogy of Morals,* is the source of the religiosity cultivated by pariah status groups. In passing, we may note that resentment may be accurately applied only to a limited extent; for one of Nietzsche's main examples, Buddhism, it is not at all applicable.

Incidentally, the development of status groups from ethnic segregations is by no means the normal phenomenon. On the contrary, since objective "racial differences" are by no means basic to every subjective sentiment of an ethnic community, the ultimately racial foundation of status structure is rightly and absolutely a question of the concrete individual case. Very frequently a status group is instrumental in the production of a thoroughbred anthropological type. Certainly a status group is to a high degree effective in producing extreme types, for they select personally qualified individuals (e.g., the Knighthood selects those who are fit for warfare, physically and psychically). But selection is far from being the only, or the predominant, way in which status groups are formed: Political membership or class situation has at all times been at least as frequently decisive. And today the class situation is by far the predominant factor, for of course the possibility of a style of life expected for members of a status group is usually conditioned economically.

8: Status Privileges

For all practical purposes, stratification by status goes hand in hand with a monopolization of ideal and material goods or opportunities, in a manner we have come to know as typical. Besides the specific status honor, which always rests upon distance and exclusiveness, we find all sorts of material monopolies. Such honorific preferences may consist of the privilege of wearing special costumes, of eating special dishes taboo to others, of carrying arms —which is most obvious in its consequences—the right to pursue certain non-professional dilettante artistic practices, e.g. to play certain musical instruments. Of course, material monopolies provide the most effective motives for the exclusiveness of a status group; although, in themselves, they are rarely sufficient, almost always they come into play to some extent. Within a status circle there is the question of intermarriage: the interest of the families in the monopolization of potential bridegrooms is at least of equal importance and is parallel to the interest in the monopolization of daughters. The daughters of the circle must be provided for. With an increased inclosure of the status group, the conventional preferential opportunities for special employment grow into a legal monopoly of special offices for the members. Certain goods become objects for monopolization by status groups. In the typical fashion these include "entailed estates" and frequently also the possessions of serfs or bondsmen and, finally, special trades. This monopolization occurs positively when the status group is exclusively entitled to own and to manage them; and negatively when, in order to maintain its specific way of life, the status group must *not* own and manage them.

The decisive role of a "style of life" in status "honor" means that status groups are the specific bearers of all "conventions." In whatever way it may be manifest, all "stylization" of life either originates in status groups or is at least conserved by them. Even if the principles of status conventions differ greatly, they reveal certain typical traits, especially among those strata which are most privileged. Quite generally, among privileged status groups there is a status disqualification that operates against the performance of common physical labor. This disqualification is now "setting in" in America against the old tradition of esteem for labor. Very frequently every rational economic pursuit, and especially "entrepreneurial activity," is looked upon as a disqualification of status. Artistic and literary activity is also considered as degrading work as soon as it is exploited for income, or at least when it is connected with hard physical exertion. An example is the sculptor working like a mason in his dusty smock as over against the painter in his salon-like "studio" and those forms of musical practice that are acceptable to the status group.

9: Economic Conditions and Effects of Status Stratification

The frequent disqualification of the gainfully employed as such is a direct result of the principle of status stratification peculiar to the social order, and of course, of this principle's opposition to a distribution of power which is regulated exclusively through the market. These two factors operate along with various individual ones, which will be touched upon below.

We have seen above that the market and its processes "knows no personal distinctions": "functional" interests dominate it. It knows nothing of "honor." The status order means precisely the reverse, viz.: stratification in terms of "honor" and of styles of life peculiar to status groups as such. If mere economic acquisition and naked economic power still bearing the stigma of its extra-status origin could bestow upon anyone who has won it the same honor as those who are interested in status by virtue of style of life claim for themselves, the status order would be threatened at its very root. This is the more so as, given equality of status honor, property *per se* represents an addition even if it is not overtly acknowledged to be such. Yet if such economic acquisition and power gave the agent any honor at all, his wealth would result in his attaining more honor than those who successfully claim honor by virtue of style of life. Therefore all groups having interests in the status order react with special sharpness precisely against the pretensions of purely economic acquisition. In most cases they react the more vigorously the more they feel themselves threatened. Calderon's respectful treatment of the peasant, for instance, as opposed to Shakespeare's simultaneous and ostensible disdain of the *canaille* illustrates the different way in which a firmly structured status order reacts as compared with a status order that has become economically precarious. This is an example of a state of affairs that recurs everywhere. Precisely because of the rigorous reactions against the claims of property *per se*, the "parvenu" is never accepted, personally and without reservation, by the privileged status groups, no matter how completely his style of life has been adjusted to theirs. They will only accept his descendants who have been educated in the conventions of their status group and who have never besmirched its honor by their own economic labor.

As to the general *effect* of the status order, only one consequence can be stated, but it is a very important one: the hindrance of the free development of the market occurs first for those goods which status groups directly withheld from free exchange by monopolization. This monopolization may be effected either legally or conventionally. For example, in many Hellenic cities during the epoch of status groups, and also originally in Rome, the inherited estate (as is shown by the old formula for indiction against spendthrifts) was monopolized just as were the estates of knights, peasants, priests, and especially the clientele of the craft and merchant guilds. The market is restricted, and the power of naked property *per se,* which gives its stamp to "class formation," is pushed into the background. The results of this process can be most varied. Of course, they do not necessarily weaken the contrasts in the economic situation. Frequently they strengthen these contrasts, and in any case, where stratification by status permeates a community as strongly as was the case in all political communities of antiquity and of the Middle Ages, one can never speak of a genuinely free market competition as we understand it today. There are wider effects than this direct exclusion of special goods from the market. From the contrariety between the status order and the purely economic order mentioned above, it follows that in most instances the notion of honor peculiar to status absolutely abhors that which is essential to the market: higgling. Honor abhors higgling among peers and occasionally it taboos higgling for the members of a status group in general. Therefore, everywhere some status groups, and usually the most influential, consider almost any kind of overt participation in economic acquisition as absolutely stigmatizing.

With some over-simplification, one might thus say that "classes" are stratified according to their relations to the production and acquisition of goods; whereas "status groups" are stratified according to the principles of their *consumption* of goods as represented by special "styles of life."

An "occupational group" is also a status group. For normally, it successfully claims social honor only by virtue of the special style of life which may be determined by it. The differences between classes and status groups frequently overlap. It is precisely those status communities most strictly segregated in terms of honor (viz. the Indian castes) who today show, although within very rigid limits, a relatively high degree of indifference to pecuniary income. However, the Brahmins seek such income in many different ways.

As to the general economic conditions making for the predominance of stratification by "status," only very little can be said. When the bases of the acquisition and distribution of goods are relatively stable, stratification by status is favored. Every technological repercussion and economic transformation threatens stratification by status and pushes the class situation into the foreground. Epochs and countries in which the naked class situation is of predominant significance are regularly the periods of technical and economic transformations. And every slowing down of the shifting of economic stratifications leads, in due course, to the growth of status structures and makes for a resuscitation of the important role of social honor.

10: Parties

Whereas the genuine place of "classes" is within the economic order, the place of "status groups" is within the social order, that is, within the sphere of the distribution of "honor." From within these spheres, classes and status groups influence one another and they influence the legal order and are in turn influenced by it. But "parties" live in a house of "power."

Their action is oriented toward the ac-

quisition of social "power," that is to say, toward influencing a communal action no matter what its content may be. In principle, parties may exist in a social "club" as well as in a "state." As over against the actions of classes and status groups, for which this is not necessarily the case, the communal actions of "parties" always mean a societalization. For party actions are always directed toward a goal which is striven for in planned manner. This goal may be a "cause" (the party may aim at realizing a program for ideal or material purposes), or the goal may be "personal" (sinecures, power, and from these, honor for the leader and the followers of the party). Usually the party action aims at all these simultaneously. Parties are, therefore, only possible within communities that are societalized, that is, which have some rational order and a staff of persons available who are ready to enforce it. For parties aim precisely at influencing this staff, and if possible, to recruit it from party followers.

In any individual case, parties may represent interests determined through "class situation" or "status situation," and they may recruit their following respectively from one or the other. But they need be neither purely "class" nor purely "status" parties. In most cases they are partly class parties and partly status parties, but sometimes they are neither. They may represent ephemeral or enduring structures. Their means of attaining power may be quite varied, ranging from naked violence of any sort to canvassing for votes with coarse or subtle means: money, social influence, the force of speech, suggestion, clumsy hoax, and so on to the rougher and more artful tactics of obstruction in parliamentary bodies.

The sociological structure of parties differs in a basic way according to the kind of communal action which they struggle to influence. Parties also differ according to whether or not the community is stratified by status or by classes. Above all else, they vary according to the structure of domination within the community. For their leaders normally deal with the conquest of a community. They are, in the general concept which is maintained here, not only products of specially modern forms of domination. We shall also designate as parties the ancient and medieval "parties," despite the fact that their structure differs basically from the structure of modern parties. By virtue of these structural differences of domination it is impossible to say anything about the structure of parties without discussing the structural forms of social domination *per se*. Parties, which are always structures struggling for domination, are very frequently organized in a very strict "authoritarian" fashion . . .

Concerning "classes," "status groups," and "parties," it must be said in general that they necessarily presuppose a comprehensive societalization, and especially a political framework of communal action, within which they operate. This does not

mean that parties would be confined by the frontiers of any individual political community. On the contrary, at all times it has been the order of the day that the societalization (even when it aims at the use of military force in common) reaches beyond the frontiers of politics. This has been the case in the solidarity of interests among the Oligarchs and among the democrats in Hellas, among the Guelfs and among Ghibellines in the Middle Ages, and within the Calvinist party during the period of religious struggles. It has been the case up to the solidarity of the landlords (international congress of agrarian landlords), and has continued among princes (holy alliance, Karlsbad decrees), socialist workers, conservatives (the longing of Prussian conservatives for Russian intervention in 1850). But their aim is not necessarily the establishment of new international political, i.e., *territorial,* dominion. In the main they aim to influence the existing dominion.*

---

* The posthumously published text breaks off here. We omit an incomplete sketch of types of "warrior estates." [Note by editors Hans Gerth and C. Wright Mills.]

29. SOME PRINCIPLES OF STRATIFICATION

KINGSLEY DAVIS *and* WILBERT E. MOORE

Sociologists have long contended that social stratification, or hierarchical inequality, is present—and has been present—in all types of human societies. To Kingsley Davis and Wilbert E. Moore, stratification is a functional necessity.

In this article, Davis and Moore discuss what they see as the universal features of social stratification and suggest the variant forms of stratification found in different societies, patterns that are dependent upon such factors as the functional importance of specific positions and the scarcity of personnel to play certain necessary social roles. The authors examine the relationship between social stratification and such aspects of the social order as religion, government, economics, and technical knowledge. Their article ends with the presentation of a typology of stratification systems.

Since it first appeared in 1945, this essay has been used frequently as a basic point of departure for students of sociology.

Kingsley Davis is Professor of Sociology at the University of California, Berkeley. He is the author of The Modern Urban Revolution (*1967*) *and many studies in demography, as well as one of the most useful introductory textbooks in sociology,* Human Society (*1948*). *He is also coauthor, with Harry C. Bredemeier and Marion J. Levy, of* Modern American Society (*1950*).

Wilbert E. Moore is Professor of Sociology at Denver University. A partial listing of his published works appears on page 220 of this volume.

In a previous paper some concepts for handling the phenomena of social inequality were presented.[1] In the present paper a further step in stratification theory is undertaken—an attempt to show the relationship between stratification and the rest of the social order.[2] Starting from the proposition that no society is "classless," or unstratified, an effort is made to explain, in functional terms, the universal necessity which calls forth stratification in any social system. Next, an attempt is made to explain the roughly uniform distribution of prestige as between the major types of positions in every society. Since, however, there occur between one society and another great differences in the degree and kind of stratification, some attention is also given to the varieties of social inequality and the variable factors that give rise to them.

Clearly, the present task requires two different lines of analysis—one to understand the universal, the other to understand the variable features of stratification. Naturally each line of inquiry aids the other and is indispensable, and in the treatment that follows the two will be interwoven, although, because of space limitations, the emphasis will be on the universals.

Throughout, it will be necessary to keep in mind one thing—namely, that the discussion relates to the system of positions,

Reprinted from the *American Sociological Review*, **10** (1945), 242–249, by permission of the authors and the American Sociological Association.

not to the individuals occupying those positions. It is one thing to ask why different positions carry different degrees of prestige, and quite another to ask how certain individuals get into those positions. Although, as the argument will try to show, both questions are related, it is essential to keep them separate in our thinking. Most of the literature on stratification has tried to answer the second question (particularly with regard to the ease or difficulty of mobility between strata) without tackling the first. The first question, however, is logically prior and, in the case of any particular individual or group, factually prior.

The Functional Necessity of Stratification

Curiously, however, the main functional necessity explaining the universal presence of stratification is precisely the requirement faced by any society of placing and motivating individuals in the social structure. As a functioning mechanism a society must somehow distribute its members in social positions and induce them to perform the duties of these positions. It must thus concern itself with motivation at two different levels: to instill in the proper individuals the desire to fill certain positions, and, once in these positions, the desire to perform the duties attached to them. Even though the social order may be relatively static in form, there is a continuous process of metabolism as new individuals are born into it, shift with age, and die off. Their absorption into the positional system must somehow be arranged and motivated. This is true whether the system is competitive or non-competitive. A competitive system gives greater importance to the motivation to achieve positions, whereas a non-competitive system gives perhaps greater importance to the motivation to perform the duties of the positions; but in any system both types of motivation are required.

If the duties associated with the various positions were all equally pleasant to the human organism, all equally important to societal survival, and all equally in need of the same ability or talent, it would make no difference who got into which positions, and the problem of social placement would be greatly reduced. But actually it does make a great deal of difference who gets into which positions, not only because some positions are inherently more agreeable than others, but also because some require special talents or training and some are functionally more important than others. Also, it is essential that the duties of the positions be performed with the diligence that their importance requires. Inevitably, then, a society must have, first, some kind of rewards that it can use as inducements, and, second, some way of distributing these rewards differentially according to positions. The rewards and their distribution become a part of the social order, and thus give rise to stratification.

One may ask what kind of rewards a society has at its disposal in distributing its personnel and securing essential services. It has, first of all, the things that contribute to sustenance and comfort. It has, second, the things that contribute to humor and diversion. And it has, finally, the things that contribute to self-respect and ego expansion. The last, because of the peculiarly social character of the self, is largely a function of the opinion of others, but it nonetheless ranks in importance with the first two. In any social system all three kinds of rewards must be dispensed differentially according to positions.

In a sense the rewards are "built into" the position. They consist in the "rights" associated with the position, plus what may be called its accompaniments or perquisites. Often the rights, and sometimes the accompaniments, are functionally related to the duties of the position. (Rights as viewed by the incumbent are usually duties as viewed by other members of the community.) However, there may be a host of subsidiary rights and perquisites that are not essential to the function of the position and have only an indirect and symbolic connection with its duties, but which still may be of considerable importance in inducing people to seek the positions and fulfil the essential duties.

If the rights and perquisites of different positions in a society must be unequal, then the society must be stratified, because that is precisely what stratification means. Social inequality is thus an unconsciously evolved device by which societies insure that the most important positions are conscientiously filled by the most qualified persons. Hence every society, no matter how simple or complex, must differentiate persons in terms of both prestige and esteem, and must therefore possess a certain amount of institutionalized inequality.

It does not follow that the amount or type of inequality need be the same in all societies. This is largely a function of factors that will be discussed presently.

The Two Determinants of Positional Rank

Granting the general function that inequality subserves, one can specify the two factors that determine the relative rank of different positions. In general those positions convey the best reward, and hence have the highest rank, which a) have the greatest importance for the society and b) require the greatest training or talent. The first factor concerns function and is a matter of relative significance; the second concerns means and is a matter of scarcity.

DIFFERENTIAL FUNCTIONAL IMPORTANCE Actually a society does not need to reward positions in proportion to their functional importance. It merely needs to give sufficient reward to them to insure that they will be filled competently. In other words, it must see that less essential positions do not compete successfully with more essential ones. If a position is easily filled, it need not be heavily rewarded, even though

important. On the other hand, if it is important but hard to fill, the reward must be high enough to get it filled anyway. Functional importance is therefore a necessary but not a sufficient cause of high rank being assigned to a position.[3]

DIFFERENTIAL SCARCITY OF PERSONNEL Practically all positions, no matter how acquired, require some form of skill or capacity for performance. This is implicit in the very notion of position, which implies that the incumbent must, by virtue of his incumbency, accomplish certain things.

There are, ultimately, only two ways in which a person's qualifications come about: through inherent capacity or through training. Obviously, in concrete activities both are always necessary, but from a practical standpoint the scarcity may lie primarily in one or the other, as well as in both. Some positions require innate talents of such high degree that the persons who fill them are bound to be rare. In many cases, however, talent is fairly abundant in the population but the training process is so long, costly, and elaborate that relatively few can qualify. Modern medicine, for example, is within the mental capacity of most individuals, but a medical education is so burdensome and expensive that virtually none would undertake it if the position of the M.D. did not carry a reward commensurate with the sacrifice.

If the talents required for a position are abundant and the training easy, the method of acquiring the position may have little to do with its duties. There may be, in fact, a virtually accidental relationship. But if the skills required are scarce by reason of the rarity of talent or the costliness of training, the position, if functionally important, must have an attractive power that will draw the necessary skills in competition with other positions. This means, in effect, that the position must be high in the social scale—must command great prestige, high salary, ample leisure, and the like.

HOW VARIATIONS ARE TO BE UNDER-STOOD Insofar as there is a difference between one system of stratification and another, it is attributable to whatever factors affect the two determinants of differential reward—namely, functional importance and scarcity of personnel. Positions important in one society may not be important in another, because the conditions faced by the societies, or their degree of internal development, may be different. The same conditions, in turn, may affect the question of scarcity; for in some societies the stage of development, or the external situation, may wholly obviate the necessity of certain kinds of skill or talent. Any particular system of stratification, then, can be understood as a product of the special conditions affecting the two aforementioned grounds of differential reward.

Major Societal Functions and Stratification

RELIGION The reason why religion is necessary is apparently to be found in the fact that human society achieves its unity primarily through the possession by its members of certain ultimate values and ends in common. Although these values and ends are subjective, they influence behavior, and their integration enables the society to operate as a system. Derived neither from inherited nor from external nature, they have evolved as part of culture by communication and moral pressure. They must, however, appear to the members of the society to have some reality, and it is the role of religious belief and ritual to supply and reinforce this appearance of reality. Through belief and ritual the common ends and values are connected with an imaginary world symbolized by concrete sacred objects, which world in turn is related in a meaningful way to the facts and trials of the individual's life. Through the worship of the sacred objects and the beings they symbolize, and the acceptance of supernatural prescriptions that are at the same time codes of behavior, a powerful control over human conduct is exercised, guiding it along lines sustaining the institutional structure and conforming to the ultimate ends and values.

If this conception of the role of religion is true, one can understand why in every known society the religious activities tend to be under the charge of particular persons, who tend thereby to enjoy greater rewards than the ordinary societal member. Certain of the rewards and special privileges may attach to only the highest religious functionaries, but others usually apply, if such exists, to the entire sacerdotal class.

Moreover, there is a peculiar relation between the duties of the religious official and the special privileges he enjoys. If the supernatural world governs the destinies of men more ultimately than does the real world, its earthly representative, the person through whom one may communicate with the supernatural, must be a powerful individual. He is a keeper of sacred tradition, a skilled performer of the ritual, and an interpreter of lore and myth. He is in such close contact with the gods that he is viewed as possessing some of their characteristics. He is, in short, a bit sacred, and hence free from some of the more vulgar necessities and controls.

It is no accident, therefore, that religious functionaries have been associated with the very highest positions of power, as in theocratic regimes. Indeed, looking at it from this point of view, one may wonder why it is that they do not get *entire* control over their societies. The factors that prevent this are worthy of note.

In the first place, the amount of technical competence necessary for the performance of religious duties is small. Scientific or artistic capacity is not required. Anyone can set himself up as enjoying an intimate relation with deities, and nobody can successfully dispute him. Therefore, the factor of scarcity of personnel does not operate in the technical sense.

One may assert, on the other hand, that religious ritual is often elaborate and religious lore abstruse, and that priestly ministrations require tact, if not intelligence. This is true, but the technical requirements of the profession are for the most part adventitious, not related to the end in the same way that science is related to air travel. The priest can never be free from competition, since the criteria of whether or not one has genuine contact with the supernatural are never strictly clear. It is this competition that debases the priestly position below what might be expected at first glance. That is why priestly prestige is highest in those societies where membership in the profession is rigidly controlled by the priestly guild itself. That is why, in part at least, elaborate devices are utilized to stress the identification of the person with his office—spectacular costume, abnormal conduct, special diet, segregated residence, celibacy, conspicuous leisure, and the like. In fact the priest is always in danger of becoming somewhat discredited—as happens in a secularized society—because in a world of stubborn fact, ritual and sacred knowledge alone will not grow crops or build houses. Furthermore, unless he is protected by a professional guild, the priest's identification with the supernatural tends to preclude his acquisition of abundant worldly goods.

As between one society and another it seems that the highest general position awarded the priest occurs in the medieval type of social order. Here there is enough economic production to afford a surplus, which can be used to support a numerous and highly organized priesthood; and yet the populace is unlettered and therefore credulous to a high degree. Perhaps the most extreme example is to be found in the Buddhism of Tibet, but others are encountered in the Catholicism of feudal Europe, the Inca regime of Peru, the Brahminism of India, and the Mayan priesthood of Yucatan. On the other hand, if the society is so crude as to have no surplus and little differentiation, so that every priest must be also a cultivator or hunter, the separation of the priestly status from the others has hardly gone far enough for priestly prestige to mean much. When the priest actually has high prestige under these circumstances, it is because he also performs other important functions (usually political and medical).

In an extremely advanced society built on scientific technology, the priesthood tends to lose status, because sacred tradition and supernaturalism drop into the background. The ultimate values and common ends of the society tend to be expressed in less anthropomorphic ways, by officials who occupy fundamentally political, economic, or educational rather than religious positions. Nevertheless, it is easily possible for intellectuals to exaggerate the degree to which the priesthood in a presumably secular milieu has lost prestige. When the matter is closely examined the urban proletariat, as well as the rural citizenry, proves to be surprisingly godfearing and priest-ridden. No society has become so completely secularized as to liquidate entirely the belief in transcendental ends and supernatural entities. Even in a secularized society some system must exist for the integration of ultimate values, for their ritualistic expression, and for the emotional adjustments required by disappointment, death, and disaster.

GOVERNMENT Like religion, government plays a unique and indispensable part in society. But in contrast to religion, which provides integration in terms of sentiments, beliefs, and rituals, it organizes the society in terms of law and authority. Furthermore, it orients the society to the actual rather than the unseen world.

The main functions of government are, internally, the ultimate enforcement of norms, the final arbitration of conflicting interests, and the overall planning and direction of society; and externally, the handling of war and diplomacy. To carry out these functions it acts as the agent of the entire people, enjoys a monopoly of force, and controls all individuals within its territory.

Political action, by definition, implies authority. An official can command because he has authority, and the citizen must obey because he is subject to that authority. For this reason stratification is inherent in the nature of political relationships.

So clear is the power embodied in political position that political inequality is sometimes thought to comprise all inequality. But it can be shown that there are other bases of stratification, that the following controls operate in practice to keep political power from becoming complete: a) The fact that the actual holders of political office, and especially those determining top policy must necessarily be few in number compared to the total population. b) The fact that the rulers represent the interest of the group rather than of themselves, and are therefore restricted in their behavior by rules and mores designed to enforce this limitation of interest. c) The fact that the holder of political office has his authority by virtue of his office and nothing else, and therefore any special knowledge, talent, or capacity he may claim is purely incidental, so that he often has to depend upon others for technical assistance.

In view of these limiting factors, it is not strange that the rulers often have less power and prestige than a literal enumeration of their formal rights would lead one to expect.

WEALTH, PROPERTY, AND LABOR   Every position that secures for its incumbent a livelihood is, by definition, economically rewarded. For this reason there is an economic aspect to those positions (e.g. political and religious) the main function of which is not economic. It therefore becomes convenient for the society to use unequal economic returns as a principal means of controlling the entrance of persons into positions and stimulating the performance of their duties. The amount of the economic return therefore becomes one of the main indices of social status.

It should be stressed, however, that a position does not bring power and prestige *because* it draws a high income. Rather, it draws a high income because it is functionally important and the available personnel is for one reason or another scarce. It is therefore superficial and erroneous to regard high income as the cause of a man's power and prestige, just as it is erroneous to think that a man's fever is the cause of his disease.[4]

The economic source of power and prestige is not income primarily, but the ownership of capital goods (including patents, good will, and professional reputation). Such ownership should be distinguished from the possession of consumers' goods, which is an index rather than a cause of social standing. In other words, the ownership of producers' goods is properly speaking, a source of income like other positions, the income itself remaining an index. Even in situations where social values are widely commercialized and earnings are the readiest method of judging social position, income does not confer prestige on a position so much as it induces people to compete for the position. It is true that a man who has a high income as a result of one position may find this money helpful in climbing into another position as well, but this again reflects the effect of his initial, economically advantageous status, which exercises its influence through the medium of money.

In a system of private property in productive enterprise, an income above what an individual spends can give rise to possession of capital wealth. Presumably such possession is a reward for the proper management of one's finances originally and of the productive enterprise later. But as social differentiation becomes highly advanced and yet the institution of inheritance persists, the phenomenon of pure ownership, and reward for pure ownership, emerges. In such a case it is difficult to prove that the position is functionally important or that the scarcity involved is anything other than extrinsic and accidental. It is for this reason, doubtless, that the institution of private property in productive goods becomes more subject to criticism as social development proceeds toward industrialization. It is only this pure, that is, strictly legal and functionless ownership, however, that is open to attack; for some form of active ownership, whether private or public, is indispensable.

One kind of ownership of production goods consists in rights over the labor of others. The most extremely concentrated and exclusive of such rights are found in slavery, but the essential principle remains in serfdom, peonage, encomienda, and indenture. Naturally this kind of ownership has the greatest significance for stratification, because it necessarily entails an unequal relationship.

But property in capital goods inevitably introduces a compulsive element even into the nominally free contractual relationship. Indeed, in some respects the authority of the contractual employer is greater than that of the feudal landlord, inasmuch as the latter is more limited by traditional reciprocities. Even the classical economics recognized that competitors would fare unequally, but it did not pursue this fact to its necessary conclusion that, however it might be acquired, unequal control of goods and services must give unequal advantage to the parties to a contract.

TECHNICAL KNOWLEDGE The function of finding means to single goals, without any concern with the choice between goals, is the exclusively technical sphere. The explanation of why positions requiring great technical skill receive fairly high rewards is easy to see, for it is the simplest case of the rewards being so distributed as to draw talent and motivate training. Why they seldom if ever receive the highest rewards is also clear: the importance of

technical knowledge from a societal point of view is never so great as the integration of goals, which takes place on the religious, political, and economic levels. Since the technological level is concerned solely with means, a purely technical position must ultimately be subordinate to other positions that are religious, political, or economic in character.

Nevertheless, the distinction between expert and layman in any social order is fundamental, and cannot be entirely reduced to other terms. Methods of recruitment, as well as of reward, sometimes lead to the erroneous interpretation that technical positions are economically determined. Actually, however, the acquisition of knowledge and skill cannot be accomplished by purchase, although the opportunity to learn may be. The control of the avenues of training may inhere as a sort of property right in certain families or classes, giving them power and prestige in consequence. Such a situation adds an artificial scarcity to the natural scarcity of skills and talents. On the other hand, it is possible for an opposite situation to arise. The rewards of technical position may be so great that a condition of excess supply is created, leading to at least temporary devaluation of the rewards. Thus "unemployment in the learned professions" may result in a debasement of the prestige of those positions. Such adjustments and readjustments are constantly occurring in changing societies; and it is always well to bear in mind that the efficiency of a stratified structure may be affected by the modes of recruitment for positions. The social order itself, however, sets limits to the inflation or deflation of the prestige of experts: an over-supply tends to debase the rewards and discourage recruitment or produce revolution, whereas an undersupply tends to increase the rewards or weaken the society in competition with other societies.

Particular systems of stratification show a wide range with respect to the exact position of technically competent persons.

This range is perhaps most evident in the degree of specialization. Extreme division of labor tends to create many specialists without high prestige since the training is short and the required native capacity relatively small. On the other hand it also tends to accentuate the high position of the true experts—scientists, engineers, and administrators—by increasing their authority relative to other functionally important positions. But the idea of a technocratic social order or a government or priesthood of engineers or social scientists neglects the limitations of knowledge and skills as a basic for performing social functions. To the extent that the social structure is truly specialized the prestige of the technical person must also be circumscribed.

Variation in Stratified Systems

The generalized principles of stratification here suggested form a necessary preliminary to a consideration of types of stratified systems, because it is in terms of these principles that the types must be described. This can be seen by trying to delineate types according to certain modes of variation. For instance, some of the most important modes (together with the polar types in terms of them) seem to be as follows:

a) THE DEGREE OF SPECIALIZATION The degree of specialization affects the fineness and multiplicy of the gradations in power and prestige. It also influences the extent to which particular functions may be emphasized in the invidious system, since a given function cannot receive much emphasis in the hierarchy until it has achieved structural separation from the other functions. Finally, the amount of specialization influences the bases of selection. Polar types: *Specialized, Unspecialized.*

b) THE NATURE OF THE FUNCTIONAL EMPHASIS In general when emphasis is put on sacred matters, a rigidity is introduced that tends to limit specialization and hence the development of technology. In addition, a brake is placed on social mobility, and on the development of bureaucracy. When the preoccupation with the sacred is withdrawn, leaving greater scope for purely secular preoccupations, a great development, and rise in status, of economic and technological positions seemingly takes place. Curiously, a concomitant rise in political position is not likely, because it has usually been allied with the religious and stands to gain little by the decline of the latter. It is also possible for a society to emphasize family functions—as in relatively undifferentiated societies where high mortality requires high fertility and kinship forms the main basis of social organization. Main types: *Familistic, Authoritarian (Theocratic* or sacred, and *Totalitarian* or secular), *Capitalistic.*

c) THE MAGNITUDE OF INVIDIOUS DIFFERENCES What may be called the amount of social distance between positions, taking into account the entire scale, is something that should lend itself to quantitative measurement. Considerable differences apparently exist between different societies in this regard, and also between parts of the same society. Polar types: *Equalitarian, Inequalitarian.*

d) THE DEGREE OF OPPORTUNITY The familiar question of the amount of mobility is different from the question of the comparative equality or inequality of rewards posed above, because the two criteria may vary independently up to a point. For instance, the tremendous divergences in monetary income in the United States are far greater than those found in primitive societies, yet the equality of opportunity to move from one rung to the other in the social scale may also be greater in the United States than in a hereditary tribal kingdom. Polar types: *Mobile* (open), *Immobile* (closed).

e) THE DEGREE OF STRATUM SOLIDARITY Again the degree of "class solidarity" (or the presence of specific organizations to promote class interests) may vary to some extent independently of the other criteria, and hence is an important principle in classifying systems of stratification. Polar types: *Class organized, Class unorganized.*

External Conditions

What state any particular system of stratification is in with reference to each of these modes of variation depends on two things: 1) its state with reference to the other ranges of variation, and 2) the conditions outside the system of stratification which nevertheless influence that system. Among the latter are the following:

a) THE STAGE OF CULTURAL DEVELOPMENT As the cultural heritage grows, increased specialization becomes necessary, which in turn contributes to the enhancement of mobility, a decline of stratum solidarity, and a change of functional emphasis.

b) SITUATION WITH RESPECT TO OTHER SOCIETIES The presence or absence of open conflict with other societies, of free trade relations or cultural diffusion, all influence the class structure to some extent. A chronic state of warfare tends to place emphasis upon the military functions, especially when the opponents are more or less equal. Free trade, on the other hand, strengthens the hand of the trader at the expense of the warrior and priest. Free movement of ideas generally has an equalitarian effect. Migration and conquest create special circumstances.

c) SIZE OF THE SOCIETY A small society limits the degree to which functional specialization can go, the degree of segregation of different strata, and the magnitude of inequality.

Composite Types

Much of the literature on stratification has attempted to classify concrete systems into a certain number of types. This task is deceptively simple, however, and should come at the end of an analysis of elements and principles, rather than at the beginning. If the preceding discussion has any validity, it indicates that there are a number of modes of variation between different systems, and that any one system is a composite of the society's status with reference to all these modes of variation. The danger of trying to classify whole societies under such rubrics as *caste, feudal,* or *open class* is that one or two criteria are selected and others ignored, the result being an unsatisfactory solution to the problem posed. The present discussion has been offered as a possible approach to the more systematic classification of composite types.

NOTES

1. Kingsley Davis, "A Conceptual Analysis of Stratification," *American Sociological Review,* 7 (1942), 309–321.

2. The writers regret (and beg indulgence) that the present essay, a condensation of a longer study, covers so much in such short space that adequate evidence and qualification cannot be given and that as a result what is actually very tentative is presented in an unfortunately dogmatic manner.

3. Unfortunately, functional importance is difficult to establish. To use the position's prestige to establish it, as is often unconsciously done, constitutes circular reasoning from our point of view. There are, however, two independent clues: a) the degree to which a position is functionally unique, there being no other positions that can perform the same function satisfactorily; b) the degree to which other positions are dependent on the one in question. Both clues are best exemplified in organized systems of positions built around one major function. Thus, in most complex societies the religious, political, economic, and educational functions are handled by distinct structures not easily interchangeable. In addition, each structure possesses many different positions, some clearly dependent on, if not subordinate to, others. In sum, when an institutional nucleus becomes differentiated around one main function,

and at the same time organizes a large portion of the population into its relationships, the *key* positions in it are of the highest functional importance. The absence of such specialization does not prove functional unimportance, for the whole society may be relatively unspecialized; but it is safe to assume that the more important functions receive the first and clearest structural differentiation.

4. The symbolic rather than intrinsic role of income in social stratification has been succinctly summarized by Talcott Parsons, "An Analytical Approach to the Theory of Social Stratification," *American Journal of Sociology,* 45 (1940), 841–862.

30. STRATIFICATION: A CRITICAL ANALYSIS

MELVIN M. TUMIN

In the previous article Kingsley Davis and Wilbert E. Moore argued that systems of social stratification (or structured social inequality) are both inevitable and functional. In this essay Melvin Tumin raises some penetrating questions about certain assumptions of Davis and Moore. The debate, which has continued, is one of the best known in modern sociology.

Melvin M. Tumin is Professor of Sociology and Anthropology at Princeton University. A list of his many publications is presented on page 62 of this volume.

The fact of social inequality in human society is marked by its ubiquity and its antiquity. Every known society, past and present, distributes its scarce and demanded goods and services unequally. And there are attached to the positions which command unequal amounts of such goods and services certain highly morally-toned evaluations of their importance for the society.

The ubiquity and the antiquity of such inequality has given rise to the assumption that there must be something both inevitable and positively functional about such social arrangements.

Clearly, the truth or falsity of such an assumption is a strategic question for any general theory of social organization. It is therefore most curious that the basic premises and implications of the assumption have only been most casually explored by American sociologists.

The most systematic treatment is to be found in the well-known article by Kingsley Davis and Wilbert Moore, entitled "Some Principles of Stratification." [1] More than twelve years have passed since its publication, and though it is one of the very few treatments of stratification on a high level of generalization, it is difficult to locate a single systematic analysis of its reasoning. It will be the principal concern of this paper to present the beginnings of such an analysis.

The central argument advanced by Davis and Moore can be stated in a number of sequential propositions, as follows:

1. Certain positions in any society are functionally more important than others, and require special skills for their performance.
2. Only a limited number of individuals in any society have the talents which can be trained into the skills appropriate to these positions.
3. The conversion of talents into skills involves a training period during which sacrifices of one kind or another are made by those undergoing the training.
4. In order to induce the talented persons to undergo these sacrifices and acquire the training, their future positions must carry an inducement value in the form of differential, i.e., privileged and disproportionate access to the scarce and desired rewards which the society has to offer. [2]
5. These scarce and desired goods consist of the rights and perquisites attached

Reprinted from the *American Sociological Review,* **18** (1953), 387–394, by permission of the author and the American Sociological Association. This article was originally entitled "Some Principles of Stratification: A Critical Analysis."

to, or built into, the positions, and can be classified into those things which contribute to (a) sustenance and comfort, (b) humor and diversion, (c) self-respect and ego expansion.

6. This differential access to the basic rewards of the society has as a consequence the differentiation of the prestige and esteem which various strata acquire. This may be said, along with the rights and perquisites, to constitute institutionalized social inequality, i.e., stratification.

7. Therefore, social inequality among different strata in the amounts of scarce and desired goods, and the amounts of prestige and esteem which they receive, is both positively functional and inevitable in any society.

Let us take these propositions and examine them *seriatim*.[3]

(*1*) *Certain positions in any society are more functionally important than others and require special skills for their performance.*

The key term here is "functionally important." The functionalist theory of social organization is by no means clear and explicit about this term. The minimum common referent is to something known as the "survival value" of a social structure.[4] This concept immediately involves a number of perplexing questions. Among these are: (a) the issue of minimum vs. maximum survival, and the possible empirical referents which can be given to those terms; (b) whether such a proposition is a useless tautology since any *status quo* at any given moment is nothing more and nothing less than everything present in the *status quo*. In these terms, all acts and structures must be judged positively functional in that they constitute essential portions of the *status quo*; (c) what kind of calculus of functionality exists which will enable us, at this point in our development, to add and subtract long and short range consequences, with their mixed qualities, and arrive at some summative judgment regarding the rating an act or structure should receive on a scale of greater or lesser functionality? At best, we tend to make primarily intuitive judgments. Often enough, these judgments involve the use of value-laden criteria, or, at least, criteria which are chosen in preference to others not for any sociologically systematic reasons but by reason of certain implicit value preferences.

Thus, to judge that the engineers in a factory are functionally more important to the factory than the unskilled workmen involves a notion regarding the dispensability of the unskilled workmen, or their replaceability, relative to that of the engineers. But this is not a process of choice with infinite time dimensions. For at some point along the line one must face the problem of adequate motivation for *all* workers at all levels of skill in the factory. In the long run, *some* labor force of unskilled workmen is as important and as indispensable to the factory as *some* labor force of engineers. Often enough, the labor force situation is such that this fact is brought home sharply to the entrepreneur in the short run rather than in the long run.

Moreover, the judgment as to the relative indispensability and replaceability of a particular segment of skills in the population involves a prior judgment about the bargaining-power of that segment. But this power is itself a culturally shaped *consequence* of the existing system of rating, rather than something inevitable in the nature of social organization. At least the contrary of this has never been demonstrated, but only assumed.

A generalized theory of social stratification must recognize that the prevailing system of inducements and rewards is only one of many variants in the whole range of possible systems of motivation which, at least theoretically, are capable of working in human society. It is quite conceivable, of course, that a system of norms could be institutionalized in which the idea of threatened withdrawal of services, except under the most extreme circumstances, would be considered as absolute moral anathema. In such a case, the whole notion of relative functionality, as advanced by Davis and Moore, would have to be radically revised.

(2) *Only a limited number of individuals in any society have the talents which can be trained into the skills appropriate to these positions (i.e., the more functionally important positions).*

The truth of this proposition depends at least in part on the truth of proposition 1 above. It is, therefore, subject to all the limitations indicated above. But for the moment, let us assume the validity of the first proposition and concentrate on the question of the rarity of appropriate talent.

If all that is meant is that in every society there is a *range* of talent, and that some members of any society are by nature more talented than others, no sensible contradiction can be offered, but a question must be raised here regarding the amount of sound knowledge present in any society concerning the presence of talent in the population.

For, in every society there is some demonstrable ignorance regarding the amount of talent present in the population. *And the more rigidly stratified a society is, the less chance does that society have of discovering any new facts about the talents of its members.* Smoothly working and stable systems of stratification, wherever found, tend to build-in obstacles to the further exploration of the range of available talent. This is especially true in those societies where the opportunity to discover talent in any one generation varies with the differential resources of the parent generation. Where, for instance, access to education depends upon the wealth of one's parents, and where wealth is differentially distributed, large segments of the population are likely to be deprived of the chance even to *discover* what are their talents.

Whether or not differential rewards and opportunities are functional in any one generation, it is clear that if those differentials are allowed to be socially inherited by the next generation, then, the stratification system is specifically dysfunctional for the discovery of talents in the next generation. In this fashion, systems of social stratification tend to limit the chances available to maximize the efficiency of discovery, recruitment and training of "functionally important talent." [5]

Additionally, the unequal distribution of rewards in one generation tends to result in the unequal distribution of motivation in the succeeding generation. Since motivation to succeed is clearly an important element in the entire process of education, the unequal distribution of motivation tends to set limits on the possible extensions of the educational system, and hence, upon the efficient recruitment and training of the widest body of skills available in the population.[6]

Lastly, in this context, it may be asserted that there is some noticeable tendency for elites to restrict further access to their privileged positions, once they have sufficient power to enforce such restrictions. This is especially true in a culture where it is possible for an elite to contrive a high demand and a proportionately higher reward for its working by restricting the numbers of the elite available to do the work. The recruitment and training of doctors in modern United States is at least partly a case in point.

Here, then, are three ways, among others which could be cited, in which stratification systems, once operative, tend to reduce the survival value of a society by limiting the search, recruitment and training of functionally important personnel far more sharply than the facts of available talent would appear to justify. It is only when there is genuinely equal access to recruitment and training for all potentially talented persons that differential rewards can conceivably be justified as functional. And stratification systems are apparently *inherently antagonistic* to the development of such full equality of opportunity.

(*3*) *The conversion of talents into skills involves a training period during which sacrifices of one kind or another are made by those undergoing the training.*

Davis and Moore introduce here a concept, "sacrifice" which comes closer than any of the rest of their vocabulary of analysis to being a direct reflection of the rationalizations, offered by the more fortunate members of a society, of the rightness of their occupancy of privileged positions. It is the least critically thought-out concept in the repertoire, and can also be shown to be least supported by the actual facts.

In our present society, for example, what are the sacrifices which talented persons undergo in the training period? The possibly serious losses involve the surrender of earning power and the cost of the training. The latter is generally borne by the parents of the talented youth undergoing training, and not by the trainees themselves. But this cost tends to be paid out of income which the parents were able to earn generally by virtue of *their* privileged positions in the hierarchy of stratification. That is to say, the parents' ability to pay for the training of their children is part of the differential *reward* they, the parents, received for their privileged positions in the society. And to charge this sum up against sacrifices made by the youth is falsely to perpetuate a bill or a debt already paid by the society to the parents.

So far as the sacrifice of earning power by the trainees themselves is concerned, the loss may be measured relative to what they might have earned had they gone into the labor market instead of into advanced training for the "important" skills. There are several ways to judge this. One way is to take all the average earnings of age peers who did go into the labor market for a period equal to the average length of the training period. The total income, so calculated, roughly equals an amount which the elite can, on the average, earn back in the first decade of professional work, over and above the earnings of his age peers who are not trained. Ten years is probably the maximum amount needed to equalize the differential.[7] There remains, on the average, twenty years of work during each of which the skilled person then goes on to earn far more than his unskilled age peers. And, what is often forgotten, there is then still another ten or fifteen year period during which the skilled person continues to work and earn when his unskilled age peer is either totally or partially out of the labor market by virtue of the attrition of his strength and capabilities.

One might say that the first ten years of differential pay is perhaps justified, in order to regain for the trained person what he lost during his training period. But it is difficult to imagine what would justify continuing such differential rewards beyond that period.

Another and probably sounder way to measure how much is lost during the training period is to compare the per capita income available to the trainee with the per capita income of the age peer on the untrained labor market during the so-called sacrificial period. If one takes into account the earlier marriage of untrained persons, and the earlier acquisition of family dependents, it is highly dubious that the per capita income of the wage worker is significantly larger than that of the trainee. Even assuming, for the moment, that there is a difference, the amount is by no means sufficient to justify a lifetime of continuing differentials.

What tends to be completely overlooked, in addition, are the psychic and spiritual rewards which are available to the elite trainees by comparison with their age peers in the labor force. There is, first, the much higher prestige enjoyed by the college student and the professional-school student as compared with persons in shops and offices. There is, second, the extremely highly valued privilege of having greater opportunity for self-development. There is, third, all the psychic gain involved in being allowed to delay the assumption of adult responsibilities such as earning a living and supporting a family. There is, fourth, the access to leisure and freedom of a kind not likely to be experienced by the persons already at work.

If these are never taken into account as rewards of the training period it is not because they are not concretely present, but because the emphasis in American concepts of reward is almost exclusively placed on the material returns of positions. The emphases on enjoyment, entertainment, ego enhancement, prestige and esteem are introduced only when the differentials in these which accrue to the skilled positions need to be justified. If these other rewards were taken into account, it would be much more difficult to demonstrate that the training period, as presently operative, is really sacrificial. Indeed, it might turn out to be the case that even at this point in their careers, the elite trainees were being differentially rewarded relative to their age peers in the labor force.

All of the foregoing concerns the quality of the training period under our present system of motivation and rewards. Whatever may turn out to be the factual case about the present system—and the factual case is moot—the more important theoretical question concerns the assumption that the training period under *any* system must be sacrificial.

There seem to be no good theoretical grounds for insisting on this assumption. For, while under any system certain costs will be involved in training persons for skilled positions, these costs could easily be assumed by the society-at-large. Under these circumstances, there would be no need to compensate anyone in terms of differential rewards once the skilled positions were staffed. In short, there would be no need or justification for stratifying social positions on *these* grounds.

(4) *In order to induce the talented persons to undergo these sacrifices and acquire the training, their future positions must carry an inducement value in the form of differential, i.e., privileged and disproportionate access to the scarce and desired rewards which the society has to offer.*

Let us assume, for the purposes of the discussion, that the training period is sacrificial and the talent is rare in every conceivable human society. There is still the basic problem as to whether the allocation of differential rewards in scarce and desired goods and services is the only or the most efficient way of recruiting the appropriate talent to these positions.

For there are a number of alternative motivational schemes whose efficiency and adequacy ought at least to be considered in this context. What can be said, for instance, on behalf of the motivation which De Man called "joy in work," Veblen termed "instinct for workmanship" and which we latterly have come to identify as "intrinsic work satisfaction"? Or, to what extent could the motivation of "social duty" be institutionalized in such a fashion that self interest and social interest come closely to coincide? Or, how much prospective confidence can be placed in the possibilities of institutionalizing "social service" as a widespread motivation for seeking one's appropriate position and fulfilling it conscientiously?

Are not these types of motivations, we may ask, likely to prove most appropriate for precisely the "most functionally important positions?" Especially in a mass industrial society, where the vast majority of positions become standardized and routinized, it is the skilled jobs which are likely to retain most of the quality of "intrinsic job satisfaction" and be most readily identifiable as socially serviceable. Is it indeed impossible then to build these motivations into the socialization pattern to which we expose our talented youth?

To deny that such motivations could be institutionalized would be to overclaim our present knowledge. In part, also, such a claim would seem to derive from an assumption that what has not been institutionalized yet in human affairs is incapable of institutionalization. Admittedly, historical experience affords us evidence we cannot afford to ignore. But such evidence cannot legitimately be used to deny absolutely the possibility of heretofore untried alternatives. Social innovation is as important a feature of human societies as social stability.

On the basis of these observations, it seems that Davis and Moore have stated the case much too strongly when they insist that a "functionally important position" which requires skills that are scarce, "must command great prestige, high salary, ample leisure, and the like," if the appropriate talents are to be attracted to the position. Here, clearly, the authors are postulating the unavoidability of very specific types of rewards and, by implication, denying the possibility of others.

(5) *These scarce and desired goods consist of rights and perquisites attached to, or built into, the positions and can be classified into those things which contribute to (a) sustenance and comfort; (b) humor and diversion; (c) self-respect and ego expansion.*

(6) *This differential access to the basic rewards of the society has as a consequence the differentiation of the prestige and esteem which various strata acquire. This may be said, along with the rights and perquisites, to constitute institutionalized social inequality, i.e., stratification.*

With the classification of the rewards offered by Davis and Moore there need be little argument. Some question must be raised, however, as to whether any reward system, built into a general stratification system, must allocate equal amounts of all three types of reward in order to function effectively, or whether one type of reward may be emphasized to the virtual neglect of others. This raises the further question regarding which type of emphasis is likely to prove most effective as a differential

inducer. Nothing in the known facts about human motivation impels us to favor one type of reward over the other, or to insist that all three types of reward must be built into the positions in comparable amounts if the position is to have an inducement value.

It is well known, of course, that societies differ considerably in the kinds of rewards they emphasize in their efforts to maintain a reasonable balance between responsibility and reward. There are, for instance, numerous societies in which the conspicuous display of differential economic advantage is considered extremely bad taste. In short, our present knowledge commends to us the possibility of considerable plasticity in the way in which different types of rewards can be structured into a functioning society. This is to say, it cannot yet be demonstrated that it is *unavoidable* that differential prestige and esteem shall accrue to positions which command differential rewards in power and property.

What does seem to be unavoidable is that differential prestige shall be given to those in any society who conform to the normative order as against those who deviate from that order in a way judged immoral and detrimental. On the assumption that the continuity of a society depends on the continuity and stability of its normative order, some such distinction between conformists and deviants seems inescapable.

It also seems to be unavoidable that in any society, no matter how literate its tradition, the older, wiser and more experienced individuals who are charged with the enculturation and socialization of the young must have more power than the young, on the assumption that the task of effective socialization demands such differential power.

But this differentiation in prestige between the conformist and the deviant is by no means the same distinction as that between strata of individuals each of which operates *within* the normative order, and is composed of adults. The *latter* distinction, in the form of differentiated rewards and prestige between social strata is what Davis and Moore, and most sociologists, consider the structure of a stratification system. The *former* distinctions have nothing necessarily to do with the workings of such a system nor with the efficiency of motivation and recruitment of functionally important personnel.

Nor does the differentiation of power between young and old necessarily create differentially valued strata. For no society rates its young as less morally worthy than its older persons, no matter how much differential power the older ones may temporarily enjoy.

(7) *Therefore, social inequality among different strata in the amounts of scarce and desired goods, and the amounts of prestige and esteem which they receive, is both positively functional and inevitable in any society.*

If the objections which have heretofore been raised are taken as reasonable, then it may be stated that the only items which any society *must* distribute unequally are the power and property necessary for the performance of different tasks. If such differential power and property are viewed by all as commensurate with the differential responsibilities, and if they are culturally defined as *resources* and not as rewards, then, no differentials in prestige and esteem need follow.

Historically, the evidence seems to be that every time power and property are distributed unequally, no matter what the cultural definition, prestige and esteem differentiations have tended to result as well. Historically, however, no systematic effort has ever been made, under propitious circumstances, to develop the tradition that each man is as socially worthy as all other men so long as he performs his appropriate tasks conscientiously. While such a tradition seems utterly utopian, no known facts in psychological or social science have yet demonstrated its impossibility or its dysfunctionality for the continuity of a society. The achievement of a full institutionalization of such a tradition seems far too remote to contemplate. Some successive approximations at such a tradition, however, are not out of the range of prospective social innovation.

What, then, of the "positive functionality" of social stratification? Are there other, negative, functions of institutionalized social inequality which can be identified, if only tentatively? Some such dysfunctions of stratification have already been suggested in the body of this paper. Along with others they may now be stated, in the form of provisional assertions, as follows:

1. Social stratification systems function to limit the possibility of discovery of the full range of talent available in a society. This results from the fact of unequal access to appropriate motivation, channels of recruitment and centers of training.

2. In foreshortening the range of available talent, social stratification systems function to set limits upon the possibility of expanding the productive resources of the society, at least relative to what might be the case under conditions of greater equality of opportunity.

3. Social stratification systems function to provide the elite with the political power necessary to procure acceptance and dominance of an ideology which rationalizes the *status quo*, whatever it may be, as "logical," "natural" and "morally right." In this manner, social stratification systems function as essentially conservative influences in the societies in which they are found.

4. Social stratification systems function to distribute favorable self-images unequally throughout a population. To the extent that such favorable self-images are requisite to the development of the creative potential inherent in men, to

that extent stratification systems function to limit the development of this creative potential.

5. To the extent that inequalities in social rewards cannot be made fully acceptable to the less privileged in a society, social stratification systems function to encourage hostility, suspicion and distrust among the various segments of a society and thus to limit the possibilities of extensive social integration.

6. To the extent that the sense of significant membership in a society depends on one's place on the prestige ladder of the society, social stratification systems function to distribute unequally the sense of significant membership in the population.

7. To the extent that loyalty to a society depends on a sense of significant membership in the society, social stratification systems function to distribute loyalty unequally in the population.

8. To the extent that participation and apathy depend upon the sense of significant membership in the society, social stratification systems function to distribute the motivation to participate unequally in a population.

Each of the eight foregoing propositions contains implicit hypotheses regarding the consequences of unequal distribution of rewards in a society in accordance with some notion of the functional importance of various positions. These are empirical hypotheses, subject to test. They are offered here only as exemplary of the kinds of consequences of social stratification which are not often taken into account in dealing with the problem. They should also serve to reinforce the doubt that social inequality is a device which is uniformly functional for the role of guaranteeing that the most important tasks in a society will be performed conscientiously by the most competent persons.

The obviously mixed character of the functions of social inequality should come as no surprise to anyone. If sociology is sophisticated in any sense, it is certainly with regard to its awareness of the mixed nature of any social arrangement, when the observer takes into account long as well as short range consequences and latent as well as manifest dimensions.

Summary

In this paper, an effort has been made to raise questions regarding the inevitability and positive functionality of stratification, or institutionalized social inequality in rewards, allocated in accordance with some notion of the greater and lesser functional importance of various positions. The possible alternative meanings of the concept "functional importance" has been shown to be one difficulty. The question of the scarcity or abundance of available talent has been indicated as a principal source of possible variation. The extent to which the period of training for skilled positions may reasonably be viewed as sacrificial has been called into question. The possibility has been suggested that very different types of motivational schemes might conceivably be made to function. The separability of differentials in power and property considered as resources appropriate to a task from such differentials considered as rewards for the performance of a task has also been suggested. It has also been maintained that differentials in prestige and esteem do not necessarily follow upon differentials in power and property when the latter are considered as appropriate resources rather than rewards. Finally, some negative functions, or dysfunctions, of institutionalized social inequality have been tentatively identified, revealing the mixed character of the outcome of social stratification, and casting doubt on the contention that

Social inequality is thus an unconsciously evolved device by which societies insure that the most important positions are conscientiously filled by the most qualified persons.[8]

NOTES

1. *American Sociological Review,* 10 (April, 1945), 242–249. An earlier article by Kingsley Davis, entitled, "A Conceptual Analysis of Stratification," *American Sociological Review,* 7 (June, 1942), 309–321, is devoted primarily to setting forth a vocabulary for stratification analysis. A still earlier article by Talcott Parsons, "An Analytical Approach to the Theory of Social Stratification," *American Journal of Sociology,* 45 (November, 1940), 849–862, approaches the problem in terms of why "differential ranking is considered a really fundamental phenomenon of social systems and what are the respects in which such ranking is important." The principal line of integration asserted by Parsons is with the fact of the normative orientation of any society. Certain crucial lines of connection are left unexplained, however, in this article, and in the Davis and Moore article of 1945 only some of these lines are made explicit.

2. The "scarcity and demand" qualities of goods and services are never explicitly mentioned by Davis and Moore. But it seems to the writer that the argument makes no sense unless the goods and services are so characterized. For if rewards are to function as differential inducements they must not only be differentially distributed but they must be both scarce and demanded as well. Neither the scarcity of an item by itself nor the fact of its being in demand is sufficient to allow it to function as a differential inducement in a system of unequal rewards. Leprosy is scarce and oxygen is highly demanded.

3. The arguments to be advanced here are condensed versions of a much longer analysis entitled, *An Essay on Social Stratification.* Perforce, all the reasoning necessary to support some of the contentions cannot be offered within the space limits of this article.

4. Davis and Moore are explicitly aware of the difficulties involved here and suggest two "independent clues" other than survival value. See preceding article.

5. Davis and Moore state this point briefly in the preceding article but do not elaborate it.

6. In the United States, for instance, we are only now becoming aware of the amount of productivity we, as a society, lose by allocating inferior opportunities and rewards, and hence, inferior motivation, to our Negro population. The actual amount of loss is difficult to specify precisely. Some rough estimate can be made, however, on the assumption that there is present in the Negro population about the same range of talent that is found in the White population.

7. These are only very rough estimates, of course, and it is certain that there is considerable income variation within the so-called elite group, so that the proposition holds only relatively more or less.

8. See preceding Davis and Moore article.

31. SOCIAL CLASS IN AMERICA

WILLIAM LLOYD WARNER, MARCIA MEEKER, *and*
KENNETH ELLS

The senior author of the famous "Yankee City Series" and several collaborators offer a brief overview of the meaning and nature of social class in American society. While dated in one sense, what William Lloyd Warner, Marcia Meeker, and Kenneth Ells said in the late 1940s has considerable relevance today. The reader should take special notice of the explanations given for why there is a social class system in this country, especially in view of the preceding debate over the functions and dysfunctions of social stratification.

William Lloyd Warner is Professor of Social Research at Michigan State University. He is the author of many books including Democracy in Jonesville (*1949*), Social Class in America (*1949*), The Living and the Dead (*1959*), Family of God: A Symbolic Study of Christian Life in America (*1961*), American Life: Dream and Reality (*1962*), *and* Yankee City (*1963*). *Professor Warner is coauthor and editor of many others. Marcia Meeker is currently a Research Associate with the New Mexico State Department of Education. She is working on a statistical study of the status of New Mexican schools. Kenneth Ells is a psychologist at the California Institute of Technology.*

The American Dream and Social Class

In the bright glow and warm presence of the American Dream all men are born free and equal. Everyone in the American Dream has the right, and often the duty, to try to succeed and to do his best to reach the top. Its two fundamental themes and propositions, that all of us are equal and that each of us has the right to the chance of reaching the top, are mutually contradictory, for if all men are equal there can be no top level to aim for, no bottom one to get away from; there can be no superior or inferior positions, but only one common level into which all Americans are born and in which all of them will spend their lives. We all know such perfect equality of position and opportunity does not exist. All Americans are not born into families of equal posi-tion: some are born into a rich man's aristocracy on the Gold Coast; some into the solid comfort of Suburbia's middle classes; and others into a mean existence among the slum families living on the wrong side of the tracks. It is common knowledge that the sons and daughters of the Gold Coasts, the Main Lines, and Park Avenues of America are more likely to receive recognition for their efforts than the children of the slums. The distance these fortunate young people travel to achieve success is shorter, and the route up easier, than the long hard pull necessary for the ambitious children of the less fortunate middle class. Though everyone has the common right to suc-ceed, it is not an equal "right"; though there is equality of rank for some of us, there is not equality of rank for all of us.

When some men learn that *all* the

Reprinted from *Social Class in America* by William Lloyd Warner, Marcia Meeker, and Kenneth Ells, N.Y.: Science Research Association, 1949, by permission of the authors and publisher.

American Dream does not fit *all* that is true about the realities of our life, they denounce the Dream and deny the truth of *any* of it. Fortunately, most of us are wiser and better adjusted to social reality; we recognize that, though it is called a Dream and though some of it is false, by virtue of our firm belief in it we have made some of it true. Despite the presence of social hierarchies which place people at higher and lower levels in American communities, the principles of democracy do operate; the Christian dogma that all men are equal in the sight of God because He is our Father and we are His spiritual children, buttressed by the democratic faith in the equality of men and the insistence on their equal rights as citizens, is a powerful influence in the daily life of America.

From grade school on, we have learned to cite chapter and verse proving from the lives of many of the great men of American history that we can start at the bottom and climb to the highest peaks of achievement when we have a few brains and a will to do. Our mass magazines and newspapers print and reprint the legendary story of rags to riches and tell over and over again the Ellis-Island-to-Park-Avenue saga in the actual lives of contemporary successful immigrant men and women. From mere repetition, it might be thought the public would tire of the theme; the names are all that vary and the stories, like those of children, remain the same. But we never do tire of this theme, for it says what we need to know and what we want to hear.

Among people around us, we sometimes recognize men who have got ahead, who have been successfully upward-mobile, and who have reached levels of achievement beyond even the dreams of most men. Many Americans by their own success have learned that, for them, enough of the Dream is true to make all of it real. The examples from history, from the world around us, and from our own experience provide convincing evi-

dence that, although full equality is absent, opportunity for advancement is present sufficiently to permit the rise of a few from the bottom and a still larger number from the middle to the higher economic and social levels. Although we know the statement that everyone is equal but that some men are higher than others is contradictory, and although some of us smile or become angry when we hear that "all of us are equal but some are more equal than others," we still accept both parts of this proposition either by understressing one part of the proposition or by letting all of it go as a paradox we feel to be true.

Our society does an excellent job in giving us an explicit knowledge of, and good argument for, the equalitarian aspects of our life. We have much scholarly knowledge about the workings of democracy, but we have little scientific knowledge about the powerful presence of social status and how it works for good and evil in the lives of all of us. Yet to live successfully and adaptively in America, every one of us must adjust his life to each of these contradictions, not just one of them, and we must make the most of each. Our knowledge of the democratic aspects of America is learned directly as part of our social heritage, but our understanding of the principle of social status tends to be implicit and to be learned obliquely and through hard and sometimes bitter experience. The lives of many are destroyed because they do not understand the workings of social class.[1]

It is the hope of the authors that this book will provide a corrective instrument which will permit men and women better to evaluate their social situations and thereby better adapt themselves to social reality and fit their dreams and aspirations to what is possible.

Our great state papers, the orations of great men, and the principles and pronouncements of politicians and statesmen tell us of the equality of all men. Each school boy learns and relearns it; but most of us are dependent upon experience and indirect statement to learn about "the wrong side of the tracks," "the Gold Coast and the slums," and "the top and bottom of the social heap." We are proud of those facts of American life that fit the pattern we are taught, but somehow we are often ashamed of those equally important social facts which demonstrate the presence of social class. Consequently, we tend to deny them or, worse, denounce them and by so doing deny their existence and magically make them disappear from consciousness. We use such expressions as "the Century of the Common Man" to insist on our democratic faith; but we know that, ordinarily, for Common Men to exist as a class, un-Common superior and inferior men must also exist. We know that every town or city in the country has its "Country Club set" and that this group usually lives on its Gold Coast, its Main Line, North Shore, or Nob Hill, and is the top of the community's social heap. Most of us know from novels such as those of Sinclair Lewis of the Main Streets that run through all our towns and cities, populated by Babbitts or, more explicitly stated, by "the substantial upper-middle class"; and by now, thanks to another group of novelists such as Erskine Caldwell, we know there is a low road, a Tobacco Road, that runs not only by the ramshackle houses of the poor whites of the South, but by the tarpaper shanties of the slums and river bottoms or Goat Hills of every town and city in the United States.

The "superior people" of Marquand's New England, "the North Shore crowd," divided into a top level of "old families" with a set of values and a way of life rated above those of the "new families," are matched by Philadelphia's "Main Line" families in Christopher Morley's *Kitty Foyle* and by similar groups in many other novels which report on the dominance of "the upper classes" in all regions of the United States. Reading them, together with similar novels reporting on Suburbia and Main Street for the middle

classes and those on the Tobacco Roads and the city slums for the lower levels, gives one the understanding that throughout the towns and cities of America the inhabitants are divided into status levels which are ways of life with definite characteristics and values. Talking to and observing the people of these communities demonstrate that they, too, know how real these status levels are, and they prove it by agreeing among themselves about the levels and who belongs to them in their particular city.

Although well aware of social class, social scientists have been more concerned with their theories and with quarreling among themselves about what social class is than with studying its realities in the daily lives of the people.[2] Until recently, they have lagged behind the novelists in investigating what our classes are, how they operate in our social life, and what effect they have on our individual lives.

But recent scientific studies of social class in the several regions of the United States demonstrate that it is a major determinant of individual decisions and social actions; that every major area of American life is directly and indirectly influenced by our class order; and that the major decisions of most individuals are partly controlled by it. To act intelligently and know consciously how this basic factor in American life affects us and our society, it is essential and necessary that we have an explicit understanding of what our class order is, how it works, and what it does to the lives and personalities who live in it. Our most democratic institutions, including our schools, churches, business organizations, government, and even our family life, are molded by its all-pervading and exceedingly subtle but powerful influence.

The researches on social class in the several regions of the United States[3] make it possible to fill in much of the missing knowledge necessary to give Americans such explicit understanding of social class and to answer some of the important questions we raise about it when adjusting to the realities of our existence. Reduced to their simplicities these questions are: What is social class? How are social classes organized? And how do they function in the individual and the community? How do we use such knowledge to adjust ourselves more satisfactorily to the world around us? What is the effect of class on buying and selling and other problems of business enterprise, on the problems of personnel, on school and education, on the church and religion, on the acceptance and rejection of the communications of mass media such as the radio, magazine, newspaper, and motion picture? And, above all, are there effective and simple techniques of studying and applying the social-class concept so that those who are not specialized class analysts can apply such knowledge to the practical problems of their business or profession or to the research problems of the scientist?

.   .   .

The Structural Imperative—Why We Have a Class System

The recognition of social class and other status hierarchies in this country comes as no surprise to students of society. Research on the social life of the tribes and civilizations of the world clearly demonstrates that some form of rank is always present and a necessity for our kind of society.

Just as students of comparative biology have demonstrated that the physical structure of the higher animals must have certain organs to survive, so students of social anthropology have shown that the social structures of the "higher," the more complex, societies must have rank orders to perform certain functions necessary for group survival.

When societies are complex and service large populations, they always possess some kind of status system which, by its own values, places people in higher or lower positions. Only the very simple hunting and gathering tribes, with very small populations and very simple social problems, are without systems of rank; but when a society is complex, when there are large numbers of individuals in it pursuing diverse and complex activities and functioning in a multiplicity of ways, individual positions and behaviors are evaluated and ranked.[4] This happens primarily because, to maintain itself, the society must co-ordinate the efforts of all its members into common enterprises necessary for the preservation of the group, and it must solidify and integrate all these enterprises into a working whole. In other words, as the division of labor increases and the social units become more numerous and diverse, the need for co-ordination and integration also increases and, when satisfied, enables the larger group to survive and develop.

Those who occupy co-ordinating positions acquire power and prestige. They do so because their actions partly control the behavior of the individuals who look to them for direction. Within this simple control there is simple power. Those who exercise such power either acquire prestige directly from it or have gained prestige from other sources sufficiently to be raised to a co-ordinating position. For example, among many primitive peoples a simple fishing expedition may be organized so that the men who fish and handle each boat are under the direction of one leader. The efforts of each boat are directed by the leader and, in turn, each boat is integrated into the total enterprise by its leader's taking orders from his superior. The same situation prevails in a modern factory. Small plants with a small working force and simple problems possess a limited hierarchy, perhaps no more than an owner who bosses all the workers. But a large industrial enterprise, with complex activities and problems, like General Motors, needs an elaborate hierarchy of supervision. The position in a great industrial empire which integrates and co-ordinates all the positions beneath it throughout all the supervising levels down to the workers has great power and prestige. The same holds true for political, religious, educational, and other social institutions; the more complex the group and the more diverse the functions and activities, the more elaborate its status system is likely to be.

The studies of other societies have demonstrated one other basic point: the more complex the technological and economic structure, the more complex the social structure; so that some argue (the Marxians and many classical economists) that technological advancement is the cause of social complexity and all class and status systems. It cannot be denied that economic and technological factors are important in the determination of class and status orders. We must not lose sight of the fact, however, that the social system, with its beliefs, values, and rules, which governs human behavior may well determine what kind of technology and what kind of economic institutions will survive or thrive in any given tribe or nation. In any case, social complexity is necessary for economic advancement. Furthermore, social complexity is a basic factor determining the presence or absence of class.

The Marxians have argued that the economic changes our society is undergoing always result in a class war in which "the proletariat" will be triumphant and out of which a "classless society" will result. The authors do not agree with them for several reasons. The principal reasons are: (1) the presence of a class order does not necessarily mean class conflict—the relations of the classes can be and often are amiable and peaceful; (2) classless societies (without differential status systems) are impossible where there is complexity for the reasons previously given. Russia's communistic system, supposedly designed to produce a pure equalitarian society, necessarily has citizens who are ranked above and below each other. Generals,

there, outrank privates; commissars, the rank and file; and members of the Politburo, the ordinary comrade. Occupants of these higher ranks in Russia tend to associate together; those of the lower ranks form their own groups. Their children are trained according to the rank of their parents. This means that the younger generation learns these status differences, thereby strengthening status differences between levels and fostering the further development of social class in Communistic Russia.

All this has occurred despite the fact the Russians have removed the means of production from private hands and placed them under the control of the State ("the people"). The economic factor which by Marxian doctrine produced social classes is largely absent; yet social hierarchies and social classes are present for the reason that Russia is a complex society and needs them to survive.

These status trends in Russia will undoubtedly continue, for her population is vast, her peoples diverse, her problems immensely complex; and elaborate systems of co-ordination and control are necessary for such a nation to maintain itself. The Communist ideals of economic and political equality cannot produce perfect equality within the complexities of Russian life.

But let us return to the United States. We, too, have a complex, highly diverse society. We, too, possess an elaborate division of labor and a ramified technology. And we, too, possess a variety of rank orders built on the need of maintaining unity and cohesion in making our common enterprises successful. Men occupying high and low positions possess families. Their families and their activities are identified with their social position. Families of the same position tend to associate together. They do this informally or through cliques, associations, or other institutions. This social matrix provides the structure of our class system. Children are always born to their families' position.

Through life they may increase or decrease their status. The family thereby strengthens and helps maintain our class order. Social status in America is somewhat like man's alimentary canal; he may not like the way it works and he may want to forget that certain parts of it are part of him, but he knows it is necessary for his very existence. So a status system, often an object of our disapproval, is present and necessary in our complex social world.

If we cannot eliminate the system of status, we can and must work to keep it as democratic and equalitarian as possible. To be successful we must see to it that each American is given his chance to move in the social scale. This ideal of equality of opportunity is essential for our democracy. To do this intelligently, we must know what our class order is and what can be done to make it conform most closely to the needs of the American people.

The remainder of this chapter will briefly summarize what we now know about our social classes and how they are organized and function in the towns and cities of the several regions of the United States. We will start with the New England Yankees and then go on to the Middle and Far West and end up with the South before we take up the question of the common features of American class and what it is as a status system.

Class Among the New England Yankees

Studies of communities in New England clearly demonstrate the presence of a well-defined social-class system.[5] At the top is an aristocracy of birth and wealth. This is the so-called "old family" class. The people of Yankee City say the families who belong to it have been in the community for a long time—for at least three generations and preferably many generations more than three. "Old family" means not only old to the community but old to the class. Present members of the

class were born into it; the families into which they were born can trace their lineage through many generations participating in a way of life characteristic of the upper class back to a generation marking the lowly beginnings out of which their family came. Although the men of this level are occupied gainfully, usually as large merchants, financiers, or in the higher professions, the wealth of the family, inherited from the husband's or the wife's side, and often from both, has been in the family for a long time. Ideally, it should stem from the sea trade when Yankee City's merchants and sea captains made large fortunes, built great Georgian houses on elm-lined Hill Street, and filled their houses and gardens with the proper symbols of their high position. They became the 400, the Brahmins, the Hill Streeters to whom others looked up; and they, well-mannered or not, looked down on the rest. They counted themselves, and were so counted, equals of similar levels in Salem, Boston, Providence, and other New England cities. Their sons and daughters married into the old families from these towns and at times, when family fortune was low or love was great, they married wealthy sons and daughters from the newly rich who occupied the class level below them. This was a happy event for the fathers and mothers of such fortunate young people in the lower half of the upper class, an event well publicized and sometimes not too discreetly bragged about by the parents of the lower-upper-class children, an occasion to be explained by the mothers from the old families in terms of the spiritual demands of romantic love and by their friends as "a good deal and a fair exchange all the way around for everyone concerned."

The new families, the lower level of the upper class, came up through the new industries—shoes, textiles, silverware—and finance. Their fathers were some of the men who established New England's trading and financial dominance throughout America. When New York's Wall

Street rose to power, many of them transferred their activities to this new center of dominance. Except that they aspire to old-family status, if not for themselves then for their children, these men and their families have a design for living similar to the old-family group. But they are consciously aware that their money is too new and too recently earned to have the sacrosanct quality of wealth inherited from a long line of ancestors. They know, as do those about them, that, while a certain amount of wealth is necessary, birth and old family are what really matter. Each of them can cite critical cases to prove that particular individuals have no money at all, yet belong to the top class because they have the right lineage and right name. While they recognize the worth and importance of birth, they feel that somehow their family's achievements should be better rewarded than by a mere second place in relation to those who need do little more than be born and stay alive.

The presence of an old-family class in a community forces the newly rich to wait their turn if they aspire to "higher things." Meanwhile, they must learn how to act, fill their lives with good deeds, spend their money on approved philanthropy, and reduce their arrogance to manageable proportions.

The families of the upper and lower strata of the upper classes are organized into social cliques and exclusive clubs. The men gather fortnightly in dining clubs where they discuss matters that concern them. The women belong to small clubs or to the Garden Club and give their interest to subjects which symbolize their high status and evoke these sentiments necessary in each individual if the class is to maintain itself. Both sexes join philanthropic organizations whose good deeds are an asset to the community and an expression of the dominance and importance of the top class to those socially beneath them. They are the members of the Episcopalian and Unitarian and, occasionally, the Congregational and Presbyterian churches.

Below them are the members of the solid, highly respectable upper-middle class, the people who get things done and provide the active front in civic affairs for the classes above them. They aspire to the classes above and hope their good deeds, civic activities, and high moral principles will somehow be recognized far beyond the usual pat on the back and that they will be invited by those above them into the intimacies of upper-class cliques and exclusive clubs. Such recognition might increase their status and would be likely to make them members of the lower-upper group. The fact that this rarely happens seldom stops members of this level, once activated, from continuing to try. The men tend to be owners of stores and belong to the large proprietor and professional levels. Their incomes average less than those of the lower-upper class, this latter group having a larger income than any other group, including the old-family level.

These three strata, the two upper classes and the upper-middle, constitute the levels above the Common Man. There is a considerable distance socially between them and the mass of the people immediately below them. They comprise three of the six classes present in the community. Although in number of levels they constitute half the community, in population they have no more than a sixth, and sometimes less, of the Common Man's population. The three levels combined include approximately 13 per cent of the total population.

The lower-middle class, the top of the Common Man level, is composed of clerks and other white-collar workers, small tradesmen, and a fraction of skilled workers. Their small houses fill "the side streets" down from Hill Street, where the upper classes and some of the upper-middle live, and are noticeably absent from the better suburbs where the upper-middle concentrate. "Side Streeter" is a term often used by those above them to imply an inferior way of life and an inconsequential status. They have accumulated little property but are frequently home owners. Some of the more successful members of ethnic groups, such as the Italians, Irish, French-Canadians, have reached this level. Only a few members of these cultural minorities have gone beyond it; none of them has reached the old-family level.

The old-family class (upper-upper) is smaller in size than the new-family class (lower-upper) below them. It has 1.4 per cent, while the lower-upper class has 1.6 per cent, of the total population. Ten per cent of the population belongs to the upper-middle class, and 28 per cent to the lower-middle level. The upper-lower is the most populous class, with 34 per cent, and the lower-lower has 25 per cent of all the people in the town.

The prospects of the upper-middle-class children for higher education are not as good as those of the classes above. One hundred per cent of the children of the two upper classes take courses in the local high school that prepare them for college, and 88 per cent of the upper-middle do; but only 44 per cent of the lower-middle take these courses, 28 per cent of the upper-lower, and 26 per cent of the lower-lower. These percentages provide a good index of the position of the lower-middle class, ranking it well below the three upper classes, but placing it well above the upper-lower and the lower-lower.[6]

The upper-lower class, least differentiated from the adjacent levels and hardest to distinguish in the hierarchy, but clearly present, is composed of the "poor but honest workers" who more often than not are only semi-skilled or unskilled. Their relative place in the hierarchy of class is well portrayed by comparing them with the classes superior to them and with the lower-lower class beneath them in the category of how they spend their money.

A glance at the ranking of the proportion of the incomes of each class spent on ten items (including such things as rent and shelter, food, clothing, and education,

among others) shows, for example, that this class ranks second for the percentage of the money spent on food, the lower-lower class being first and the rank order of the other classes following lower-middle according to their place in the social hierarchy. The money spent on rent and shelter by upper-lower class is also second to the lower-lower's first, the other classes' rank order and position in the hierarchy being in exact correspondence. To give a bird's-eye view of the way this class spends its money, the rank of the upper-lower, for the percentage of its budget spent on a number of common and important items, has been placed in parentheses after every item in the list which follows: food (2), rent (2), clothing (4), automobiles (5), taxes (5), medical aid (5), education (4), and amusements (4–5). For the major items of expenditure the amount of money spent by this class out of its budget corresponds fairly closely with its place in the class hierarchy, second to the first of the lower-lower class for the major necessities of food and shelter, and ordinarily, but not always, fourth or fifth to the classes above for the items that give an opportunity for cutting down the amounts spent on them. Their feelings about doing the right thing, of being respectable and rearing their children to do better than they have, coupled with the limitations of their income, are well reflected in how they select and reject what can be purchased on the American market.[7]

The lower-lower class, referred to as "Riverbrookers" or the "low-down Yankees who live in the clam flats," have a "bad reputation" among those who are socially above them. This evaluation includes beliefs that they are lazy, shiftless, and won't work, all opposites of the good middle-class virtues belonging to the essence of the Protestant ethic. They are thought to be improvident and unwilling or unable to save their money for a rainy day and, therefore, often dependent on the philanthropy of the private or public agency and on poor relief. They are sometimes said to "live like animals" because it is believed that their sexual mores are not too exacting and that pre-marital intercourse, post-marital infidelity, and high rates of illegitimacy, sometimes too publicly mixed with incest, characterize their personal and family lives. It is certain that they deserve only part of this reputation. Research shows many of them guilty of no more than being poor and lacking in the desire to get ahead, this latter trait being common among those above them. For these reasons and others, this class is ranked in Yankee City below the level of the Common Man (lower-middle and upper-lower). For most of the indexes of status it ranks sixth and last.

Class in the Democratic Middle West and Far West

Cities large and small in the states west of the Alleghenies sometimes have class systems which do not possess an old-family (upper-upper) class. The period of settlement has not always been sufficient for an old-family level, based on the security of birth and inherited wealth, to entrench itself. Ordinarily, it takes several generations for an old-family class to gain and hold the prestige and power necessary to impress the rest of the community sufficiently with the marks of its "breeding" to be able to confer top status on those born into it. The family, its name, and its lineage must have had time to become identified in the public mind as being above ordinary mortals.

While such identification is necessary for the emergence of an old-family (upper-upper) class and for its establishment, it is also necessary for the community to be large enough for the principles of exclusion to operate. For example, those in the old-family group must be sufficiently numerous for all the varieties of social participation to be possible without the use of new-family members; the family

names must be old enough to be easily identified; and above all there should always be present young people of marriageable age to become mates of others of their own class and a sufficient number of children to allow mothers to select playmates and companions of their own class for their children.

When a community in the more recently settled regions of the United States is sufficiently large, when it has grown slowly and at an average rate, the chances are higher that it has an old-family class. If it lacks any one of these factors, including size, social and economic complexity, and steady and normal growth, the old-family class is not likely to develop.

One of the best tests of the presence of an old-family level is to determine whether members of the new-family category admit, perhaps grudgingly and enviously and with hostile derogatory remarks, that the old-family level looks down on them and that it is considered a mark of advancement and prestige by those in the new-family group to move into it and be invited to the homes and social affairs of the old families. When a member of the new-family class says, "We've only been here two generations, but we still aren't old-family," and when he or she goes on to say that "they (old family) consider themselves better than people like us and the poor dopes around here let them get away with it," such evidence indicates that an old-family group is present and able to enforce recognition of its superior position upon its most aggressive and hostile competitors, the members of the lower-upper, or new-family, class.

When the old-family group is present and its position is not recognized as superordinate to the new families, the two tend to be co-ordinate and view each other as equals. The old-family people adroitly let it be known that their riches are not material possessions alone but are old-family lineage; the new families display their wealth, accent their power, and prepare their children for the development of a future lineage by giving them the proper training at home and later sending them to the "right" schools and marrying them into the "right" families.

Such communities usually have a five-class pyramid, including an upper class, two middle, and two lower classes.[8]

Jonesville, located in the Middle West, approximately a hundred years old, is an example of a typical five-class community. The farmers around Jonesville use it as their market, and it is the seat of government for Abraham County. Its population of over 6,000 people is supported by servicing the needs of the farmers and by one large and a few small factories.

At the top of the status structure is an upper class commonly referred to as "the 400." It is composed of old-family and new-family segments. Neither can successfully claim superiority to the other. Below this level is an upper-middle class which functions like the same level in Yankee City and is composed of the same kind of people, the only difference being the recognition that the distance to the top is shorter for them and the time necessary to get there much less. The Common Man level, composed of lower-middle- and upper-lower-class people, and the lower-lower level are replicas of the same classes in Yankee City. The only difference is that the Jonesville ethnics in these classes are Norwegian Lutherans and Catholic Poles, the Catholic Irish and Germans having been absorbed for the most part in the larger population; whereas in Yankee City the ethnic population is far more heterogeneous, and the Catholic Irish are less assimilated largely because of more opposition to them, and because the church has more control over their private lives.

. . .

The communities of the mountain states and Pacific Coast are new, and many of them have changed their economic form from mining to other enterprises; consequently, their class orders are similar to those found in the Middle West. The older

and larger far western communities which have had a continuing, solid growth of population which has not destroyed the original group are likely to have the old-family level at the top with the other classes present; the newer and smaller communities and those disturbed by the destruction of their original status structure by large population gains are less likely to have an old-family class reigning above all others. San Francisco is a clear example of the old-family type; Los Angeles, of the more amorphous, less well-organized class structure.

. . .

The Generalities of American Class

It is now time to ask what are the basic characteristics of social status common to the communities of all regions in the United States and, once we have answered this question, to inquire what the variations are among the several systems. Economic factors are significant and important in determining the class position of any family or person, influencing the kind of behavior we find in any class, and contributing their share to the present form of our status system. But, while significant and necessary, the economic factors are not sufficient to predict where a particular family or individual will be or to explain completely the phenomena of social class. Something more than a large income is necessary for high social position. Money must be translated into socially approved behavior and possessions, and they in turn must be translated into intimate participation with, and acceptance by, members of a superior class.

This is well illustrated by what is supposed to be a true story of what happened to a Mr. John Smith, a newly rich man in a far western community. He wanted to get into a particular social club of some distinction and significance in the city. By indirection he let it be known, and was told by his friends in the club they had submitted his name to the membership committee.

Mr. Abner Grey, one of the leading members of the club and active on its membership committee, was a warm supporter of an important philanthropy in this city. It was brought to his attention that Mr. Smith, rather than contributing the large donation that had been expected of him, had given only a nominal sum to the charity.

When Mr. Smith heard nothing more about his application, he again approached one of the board members. After much evasion, he was told that Mr. Grey was the most influential man on the board and he would be wise to see that gentleman. After trying several times to make an appointment with Mr. Grey, he finally burst into Grey's offices unannounced.

"Why the hell, Abner, am I being kept out of the X club?"

Mr. Grey politely evaded the question. He asked Mr. Smith to be seated. He inquired after Mr. Smith's health, about the health of his wife, and inquired about other matters of simple convention.

Finally, Mr. Smith said, "Ab, why the hell am I being kept out of your club?"

"But, John, you're not. Everyone in the X club thinks you're a fine fellow."

"Well, what's wrong?"

"Well, John, we don't think you've got the *kind* of money necessary for being a good member of the X club. We don't think you'd be happy in the X club."

"Like hell I haven't. I could buy and sell a half dozen of some of your board members."

"I know that, John, but that isn't what I said. I did not say the amount of money. I said the kind of money."

"What do you mean?"

"Well, John, my co-workers on the charity drive tell me you only gave a few dollars to our campaign, and we had you down for a few thousand."

For a moment Mr. Smith was silent. Then he grinned. So did Mr. Grey. Smith took out his fountain pen and checkbook. "How much?"

At the next meeting of the X club Mr. Smith was unanimously elected to its membership.

Mr. Smith translated his money into philanthropy acceptable to the dominant group, he received their sponsorship, and finally became a participant in the club. The "right" kind of house, the "right" neighborhood, the "right" furniture, the proper behavior—all are symbols that can ultimately be translated into social acceptance by those who have sufficient money to aspire to higher levels than they presently enjoy.

To belong to a particular level in the social-class system of America means that a family or individual has gained acceptance as an equal by those who belong in the class. The behavior in this class and the participation of those in it must be rated by the rest of the community as being at a particular place in the social scale.

Although our democratic heritage makes us disapprove, our class order helps control a number of important functions. It unequally divides the highly and lowly valued things of our society among the several classes according to their rank. Our marriage rules conform to the rules of class, for the majority of marriages are between people of the same class. No class system, however, is so rigid that it completely prohibits marriages above and below one's own class. Furthermore, an open class system such as ours permits a person during his lifetime to move up or down from the level into which he was born. Vertical social mobility for individuals or families is characteristic of all class systems. The principal forms of mobility in this country are through the use of money, education, occupation, talent, skill, philanthropy, sex, and marriage. Although economic mobility is still important, it seems likely now that more people move to higher positions by education than by any other route. We have indicated before this that the mere possession of money is insufficient for gaining and keeping a higher social position. This is equally true of all other forms of mobility. In every case there must be social acceptance.

Class varies from community to community. The new city is less likely than an old one to have a well-organized class order; this is also true for cities whose growth has been rapid as compared with those which have not been disturbed by huge increases in population from other regions or countries or by the rapid displacement of old industries by new ones. The mill town's status hierarchy is more likely to follow the occupational hierarchy of the mill than the levels of evaluated participation found in market towns or those with diversified industries. Suburbs of large metropolises tend to respond to selective factors which reduce the number of classes to one or a very few. They do not represent or express all the cultural factors which make up the social pattern of an ordinary city.

Yet systematic studies from coast to coast, in cities large and small and of many economic types, indicate that, despite the variations and diversity, class levels do exist and that they conform to a particular pattern of organization.

How Class Operates in Our Daily Lives

Because social class permeates all parts of our existence, it is impossible to do more than indicate how it enters consciously or unconsciously into the success and failure of business, professional, and other occupations or to show how knowledge of its effects is necessary for increasing the predictive qualities of much of the research done by psychologists and social scientists. Class is vitally significant in marriage and training children as well as in most social activities of a community. Status plays a decisive role in the formation of personality at the various stages of development,

for if young people are to learn to live adaptively as mature people in our society they must be trained by the informal controls of our society to fit into their places.

Education is now competing with economic mobility as the principal route to success. Today fewer men rise from the bottom to the top places in industry and business than did a generation ago. More and more, the sons of executives are replacing their fathers in such positions, leaving fewer positions into which the sons of those farther down can climb from the ranks. Captains of industry educate their sons to take their places or to occupy similar places in other industries. Also, more and more top jobs in industry are being filled by men coming from the technical and engineering schools or from the universities. The route up for them is no longer through a hierarchy of increasing skill to management and ownership as it was two generations ago. The prudent mobile man today must prepare himself by education if he wishes to fill an important job and provide his family with the money and prestige necessary to get "the better things of life."

Social-class research demonstrates that our educational system performs the dual task of aiding social mobility and, at the same time, working effectively to hinder it. This ceases to be a paradox when all the facts are examined. In the lower grades, our public schools are filled by children from all walks of life. Since education is free in the public schools, since everyone has a right to it and our laws try to keep children in school, and since it is common knowledge that "if you want to get ahead you must get an education," it would be assumed that children at, and below, the Common Man level would stay in school and equip themselves for mobility. Such is not the case. The social and educational systems work to eliminate the majority of them and permit only a few to get through. It has been estimated that, whereas 80 per cent of the upper- and upper-middle-class children actually go to college, only 20 per cent of the lower-middle and five per cent of the lower-class children get there.[9] The evidence indicates that most, if not all, of the children of the top classes complete their preparation and go on to college, whereas those from the lower classes start dropping out in the grade schools and continue to do so in increasing numbers in high school. Only a very few of them go on to college. The educational conveyor belt drops lower-class children at the beginning and bottom of the educational route and carries those from the higher classes a longer distance, nearly all the upper-class children going to the end of the line.

If the teachers and school administrators in grade and high schools know the class positions of the children who enter their schools they can predict who will and who will not get to college. Furthermore, with such knowledge the educator can act to change a negative prediction to a positive one for the bright, ambitious lower- and lower-middle-class children, whose chances for higher education are now very slight.

The reason for the high mortality rate among the lower-class children becomes apparent when one examines the relation of the teachers and the other children to them. We now know that the intelligence of lower-class children is not responsible for their failures in school for often their I.Q.'s are equal to those of children higher up. Although inferior intelligence has been the most frequent and plausible explanation,[10] I.Q. tests equated to social class demonstrate that differential intelligence is not the answer.

Teachers, it must be said, although one of the most democratically minded groups in America, tend to favor the children of the classes above the Common Man and to show less interest in those below that level. Studies in the Deep South, New England, and the Middle West indicate that they rate the school work of children from the higher classes in accordance with their family's social position and conversely give low ratings to the work of the lower-class children.

To illustrate how the system of rating the child's abilities and attainments is relative to his position in the social-class order, we will quote from *Who Shall Be Educated?*[11] on what happens in Old City in the Deep South.

"In some elementary schools where there is more than one classroom per grade there is a section system by which students are rated and put together into A section, B section, C section, and more if necessary. In Old City, we find such a system. Each grade is divided into three sections: A, B, and C. This division into sections pervades the whole school system but of necessity it has less formal characteristics in the later years of high school. The junior high-school principal says of these sections:

When a child enters school he is put into one of three sections according to what the teacher thinks his ability is. When you have dealt with children much you soon find that you can pretty well separate them into three groups according to ability. Then if a child shows more ability he may be shifted into a higher group or if he fails he may be moved into a lower group.

"Sometime later when this same principal was asked whether there seemed to be any class distinctions between the sections, he answered:

There is to some extent. You generally find that children from the best families do the best work. That is not always true but usually it is so. The children from the lower class seem to be not as capable as the others. I think it is to some extent inheritance. The others come from people who are capable and educated, and also the environment probably has a great effect. They come to school with a lot of knowledge already that the others lack.

"Whatever one may think of this principal's theory in explanation of the correlation between social position and school section, this correlation holds true. There is a strong relationship between social status and rank in school. An analysis of the classes of three years in which the social position of 103 girls was known, shows that:

1. of the ten upper-class girls, eight were in section A, one in B, and one in C
2. of the seven upper-middle class girls, six were in section A and one in B
3. of the thirty-three girls from lower middle and indeterminate middle class, twenty-one were in section A, ten in section B, and two in section C
4. of the fifty-three lower-class girls, only six were in section A, twenty-eight in section B, and nineteen in section C.

"A teacher in junior high school was willing and able to talk more explicitly about these sections than was the principal quoted above. This teacher was asked if there was 'much class feeling in the school' and she said:

Oh, yes, there is a lot of that. We try not to have it as much as we can but of course we can't help it. Now, for instance, even in the sections we have, it is evident. Sections are supposed to be made up just on the basis of records in school but it isn't and everybody knows it isn't. I know right in my own A section I have children who ought to be in B section, but they are little socialites and so they stay in A. I don't say there are children in B who should be in A but in the A section there are some who shouldn't be there. We have discussed it in faculty meetings but nothing is ever done.

"Later on, she said:

Of course, we do some shifting around. There are some border-liners who were shifted up to make the sections more nearly even. But the socialites who aren't keeping up their standard in the A section were never taken into B or C section and they never will. They don't belong there socially. Of course, there are some girls in A section who don't belong there socially, but almost everyone of the socialites is in A.

"In Old City the ranking of students in their classrooms is clearly influenced by

status considerations." The democratically minded educator asks how this can be. The answer is that most of it is done through ignorance of social class and how it operates in our lives. To be more specific, part of the general answer lies within the teacher as a product of our class system. The teacher conscientiously applies his own best values to his rating of the child. The middle-class teacher, and over three-fourths of teachers are middle-class, applies middle-class values. For him, upper- and upper-middle-class children possess traits that rank high and are positive; lower-class children have characteristics that are negative and are ranked low.

Perhaps the most powerful influence of social class on the educational careers of our children, and certainly one of the most decisive and crucial situations in settling the ultimate class position of children from the Common Man and lower-class levels, is the influence of other children on the child's desire to stay in school. If the world of the child is pleasant, rewarding, and increases his self-esteem, he is likely to want to stay and do well. If it is punishing and decreases his self-respect, he is likely to do poorly and want to quit.

In a study of children's ratings of other children in a middle western community, Neugarten found that the children of the upper and upper-middle classes were rated high by all other children for such traits as good looks, liking for school, leadership, friendship, and many other favorable personal traits; lower-class children were ranked low or, more often than not, were given a negative rating and were said to be bad looking, dirty, and "people you would not want for friends." [12] When it is remembered that these children were only in the fifth and sixth grades and that each child in these grades was supposedly rated by all other children with no reference to status, we can see how quickly class values influence behavior and have their decisive effect in molding the personalities and influencing the life careers of Americans from their earliest years. School for the children of the populous lower classes is not the satisfactory place it is for the middle and upper classes. Given children of equal intellect, ability, and interest, it can be predicted by the use of class analysis that a large percentage of those from the lower classes will be out of school before the sophomore year in high school and that none of the upper-class children, except those physically or mentally handicapped, will quit school.

If our society is to use more effectively the brains and native talent of this great army of young people, it must learn how to train them. To do this, it must keep them in school long enough to equip them with the skills and disciplines necessary for them to function satisfactorily in our economic and social world. Children, as well as teachers and school administrators, must have a conscious and explicit understanding of social class and a simple and easy way to use such knowledge in solving problems. Personality and I.Q. tests are important instruments to guide the teacher, but unless they are supplemented with instruments to measure and count the effects of social class they are insufficient. We believe the instructions in this book for the measurement of social class provide much of the necessary information.

Studies of the relations of workers and managers in business and industry demonstrate how class continues to operate selectively when the young people leave school. Management is bringing college-trained men into the lower ranks of supervisors and promoting fewer from the ranks because it finds that the workers, while good men technically, do not have the necessary knowledge about handling men and relating themselves effectively to the higher reaches of management. Their education is often insufficient to make them good prospects for continuing advancement. The hiring of formally educated men effectively puts a ceiling over the legitimate aspirations of workers expecting to rise in the ranks. The blocking

of the worker's mobility and the encouragement of college-trained men is the ultimate payoff of what began in the grade schools. Mobility for workers is becoming more difficult; this means for the United States generally that the American Dream is becoming less real.[13]

Studies of the personalities of workers and managers now being made demonstrate that the effects of social-class and mobility drives are clearly discernible and demonstrably a part of the personality of individuals.[14]

In another area, studies of magazine subscriptions show that the class factor is of real importance in the selection of magazines. Readers from different class levels prefer various magazines on the basis of the different symbolic appeal of the stories and pictures. The Yankee City research showed that class entered not only into the purchase of magazines but into newspaper reading.[15] Later research indicates it has a decided effect on radio listening.

A casual examination of the advertising displayed in various magazines demonstrates that advertising agencies and their clients often waste their money because they are ignorant of the operation of class values in their business. This is not surprising since so many status factors have to be considered. The class distribution of readers of the periodicals published in America varies enormously. The readers of certain magazines are confined to the narrow limits of the classes above the Common Man, others to the lower classes, still others to the Common Man level, but there are some who are not confined to any one segment, being well distributed throughout all class levels. The editors of the magazines last designated, intuitively, by trial and error, or some better means, have chosen reading matter which appeals to all levels. The others, not knowing how to extend their readership or appealing deliberately to a narrow range, have a status-limited range of readers.

The readers to whom the advertiser is appealing may or may not be the potential purchasers of his product. The product may be of such a nature that it appeals to only a narrow segment of the total society; to advertise in those media which have readers largely from other strata or to pay for advertising in journals which appeal to every level is a waste of money.

Although advertising agencies often spend their money foolishly when judged by class criteria, the fault is not always theirs, for frequently the manufacturer or retailer does not know how his product appeals to the different classes. Sometimes the product will appeal to but one level, but often a product might appeal to, and be used by, all class levels, were the producer aware of how his product is valued at different social levels. It is certain that the use and meaning of most objects sold on the American market shift from class to class.

The soap opera is a product of contemporary radio. The average upper-middle-class radio listener has little interest in soap operas; in fact, most of this group are actively hostile to these curious little dramas that fill the daytime air waves. Yet, millions and millions of American women listen daily to their favorite soap operas, and advertisers of certain commodities have found them invaluable in selling their products.

Research has shown that the soap opera appeals particularly to the level of the Common Man. The problems raised in these folk dramas, their characters, plot, and values have a strong positive appeal to women of this class level, whereas they have little appeal to women above the Common Man level.[16]

Other researchers demonstrate that furniture, including drapes, floor coverings, chairs and other seating facilities, is class-typed.

Another phenomenon of class, social mobility, is enormously important in the daily lives of Americans and, to a very great degree, determines how they will act on the job or at home. Recent studies of executives in large business enterprises clearly demonstrate that the success or failure of all of them is partly determined by the presence or absence of a "mobility drive." Our research shows that when a family loses its desire to achieve and advance itself, this very often is reflected in the executive's "slowing down" or being unwilling to make the effort necessary for success as a manager. On the other hand, some men are too aggressively mobile and stir up trouble by their overly ambitious desires and their ruthless competition.

Tests combining knowledge of social class and personality demonstrate the necessity of knowing not only what the man's status level is, what it has been, and what he wants it to be, but how the class values and beliefs of his early training have become integral parts of his personality, and ever-present guides for what he thinks, what he feels, and how he acts. Those concerned with selecting executives need a personality inventory and a man's I.Q. to predict how a man will function in a given job; but they also need to find out what his experiences in our status order have done to his individuality and character structure.

Every aspect of American thought and action is powerfully influenced by social class; to think realistically and act effectively, we must know and understand our status system.

. . .

NOTES

1. Jurgen Ruesch, Martin B. Loeb, *et al., Chronic Disease and Psychological Invalidism; a Psychosomatic Study,* New York: American Society for Research in Psychosomatic Problems, 1946. A research at the University of California Hospital by Ruesch and others which demonstrates that this can be literally true; their results show how certain serious physical and mental ailments are directly attributable to social class and mobility strivings and anxieties.

2. See Chapter 15 of Warner *et al., Social Class in America,* New York: Science Research Associates, 1949, for a list of some of their publications and comments about each publication.

3. For a commentary on some of these see Chapter 15 of Warner, *op. cit.*

4. See the reference to Hobhouse, Wheeler, and Ginsberg, *The Material Culture and Social Institutions of the Simpler Peoples,* in Chapter 15 of Warner, *op. cit.*

5. See Chapter 15 of Warner, *op. cit.,* for a description of the several volumes of "Yankee City Series." New and poorly organized towns sometimes have class systems which have no old-family (upper-upper) class.

6. See W. Lloyd Warner and Paul S. Lunt, *The Social Life of a Modern Community,* Vol. I, "Yankee City Series," New Haven: Yale University Press, 1941, pp. 58–72.

7. The evidence for the statements in this paragraph can be found in *The Social Life of a Modern Community, op. cit.,* pp. 287–300.

8. It is conceivable that in smaller communities there may be only three, or even two, classes present.

9. Robert J. Havighurst and Hilda Taba, *Adolescent Character and Personality,* New York: John Wiley & Sons, 1948.

10. The unpublished studies of Allison Davis, Robert J. Havighurst, and their collaborators on the class bias *within* the I.Q. tests themselves provide strong evidence to show that the tests are not "culture free" but reflect the middle- and upper-class cultural bias of those who fabricate them. For example, the tests, being largely products of upper-middle-class people, reflect their biases and only middle- and higher-class children are properly prepared to take them.

11. W. Lloyd Warner, Robert J. Havighurst, and Martin B. Loeb, *Who Shall Be Educated?* New York: Harper & Bros., 1944, pp. 73–74.

12. Bernice L. Neugarten, "Social Class and Friendship among School Children," *American Journal of Sociology,* 51, No. 4 (January, 1946), 305–13.

13. See W. Lloyd Warner and J. O. Low, *The Social System of the Modern Factory,* Vol. IV, "Yankee City Series," New Haven: Yale University Press, 1947, for a discussion of how many of the strikes and conflicts with management are determined by the factor of worker's blocked opportunity.

14. The ordinary tests of personnel offices fail completely to account for social mobility and class factors, yet the predictive value of these factors for the success of managers in different kinds of jobs is very high.

15. See Warner and Lunt, *The Social Life of a Modern Community,* Chapter XIX; and W. Loyd Warner and William E. Henry, "Radio Daytime Serial: A Symbolic Analysis," *Genetic Psychology Monographs,* 37 (1948), 3–71.

32. THE AMERICAN LOWER CLASS: A TYPOLOGICAL APPROACH

S. M. MILLER

In this essay S. M. Miller indicates the two traditional methods of defining "lower class" (one in terms of "class" characteristics such as income and role, the other according to life styles, for example, "the culture of poverty"). The author suggests that the two approaches be combined. A fourfold (or "2 x 2") table is presented indicating the following types of lower-class people: the stable poor, the strainers, the copers, and the unstables.

S. M. Miller is Professor of Education and Sociology at New York University. He has been Program Advisor in Social Development for the Ford Foundation. He is coauthor of The Dynamics of the American Economy *(1956) and of* Social Class and Social Policy *(1968) and is coeditor of* Applied Sociology: Opportunities and Problems *(1965).*

In recent years increasing attention has been directed to the "lower class"—those existing at the economic and social margins of society. The current concern with the limited economic prospects of school drop-outs,[1] the discussions of "hard-core," and "multi-problem" families,[2] the casualties of the welfare state,[3] the analysis of the number of Americans living below the "poverty line," [4] and of the "submerged fifth" in Britain [5]—all reflect the growing awareness of the underprivileged in presumably affluent welfare societies of a high level of industrialization.

Much confusion exists in these discussions. Those concerned with psychological and social dislocations ("disorganization" is the commonly used word) tend to underestimate the importance of economic pressures, and those interested in economic deprivation frequently discount the role of social and psychological problems in preventing people from coping with their difficulties. Who is or is not "lower class" is a moot point, as different axes of demarcation are utilized. As I have explained elsewhere, I prefer to use terms like the "new working class" rather than that of the "lower class." Since most of the literature is couched in terms of the "lower class," I have used this term here despite my objections to it.

A way of classifying a population is a way of thinking about them. A frequent practice is to classify that large number of people who are members of households where the breadwinner is not involved in some kind of white-collar (*i.e.*, middle-class) occupation as "lower class." [6] This category is then considered to have high homogeneity and is treated as though it constituted a group with great centrality of attitudinal and behavioral patterns. This orientation has probably led to much of the confusion and conflict in discussions of the characteristics of those at the lower end of the social structure. For example, the inconsistent results concerning methods of child-rearing may be due to the variations from study to study among those who are sampled as members of the "lower class."

It is becoming a more common, though not a consistent practice, to mark off dis-

Reprinted from *Social Research*, **31**, 1 (1964), by permission of the author and publisher.

tinctions within the manual category. Frank Riessman and I [7] have argued that a working class of skilled and semi-skilled regular workers should be distinguished from unskilled, irregular workers who might be called "lower class." Preferably, the latter group might be called by less invidious terms like the "unskilled," "marginal workers," or "underprivileged workers," restricting this latter term, used by Allison Davis, to a narrow scope.[8] But even where a distinction is made between the "working class" and the "lower class," the criteria of classification are frequently obscure or conflicting.

Two approaches, not always clearly noted, are employed in defining the "lower class." One approach emphasizes the definition of groups in terms of "class" characteristics, especially economic role or income. The other employs "cultural" or "status" criteria such as style of life. The Hollingshead index, based on occupation, education and place of residence, is in the tradition of the first approach.[9] Walter Miller's discussion [10] of the "lower-class subculture" is along the lines of the second. Social workers' discussions of the "lower-class client" and the "multi-problem family" almost always employ style-of-life indicators.

The two approaches intertwine but seem to make independent contributions to elucidating the characteristics of the "lower class" or the poor. Consequently, I have brought them together in an effort to move away from a broadly and vaguely defined "lower class" into a specification of types of lower-class individuals. The effort is to utilize class and status variables in categorizing a population. The combination of the two produces problems, but these may be outweighed by the difficulties and obscurities produced by the current shifting between the two sets of dimensions in discussing groupings and issues: Walter Miller's "lower class" [11] is not Lee Rainwater's.[12]

Obviously other dimensions like education or region should also be employed.

Class and status dimensions should be more carefully marked off than in the following discussion. Unfortunately the material to do an adequate job is lacking. The purpose here is to show one way of approaching the problem of differentiation among the poor in order to direct more attention to the recognition of variations among the poor.

The Class Criterion

The advantage of using an economic indicator in defining the lower class is that it specifies a political-economic category to which legislation and other remedial programs could be devoted. Emphasis on style-of-life indicators can be confusing because the meaning of attitudes or behavior or what they lead to can be quite different for the rich, for the middling well-off, for those "getting by," and for the poor. The same behavior may have different roots and consequences in varying milieus.

On the other hand, the class or occupational criterion is not as clearcut as it appears. Some unskilled workers have stable, fairly well-paid jobs and are thus not a pressing social or economic problem. (This is particularly true where the unskilled worker is employed in a unionized, mass-production factory.) Many semi-skilled and fewer skilled workers suffer some degree of irregularity of employment, especially due to seasonal factors. Another problem is that a considerable number of poor families (35 to 50 per cent) have no member in the labor force.[13]

Consequently, I would suggest that an income criterion is more useful today than an occupational criterion in the definition of the lower class. The recent analyses of poverty in the United States can be employed for this purpose.[14] They show remarkable agreement, despite their different procedures, in estimating that one-quarter to one-fifth of the United States population lives below the poverty line. The level of income defining poverty varies depending on family size, composition, age, region, and type of community. For our purposes we can ignore these complexities and put the poverty line at a $4,000 family income, following Keyserling. It is the population falling below this line which, if we want to use the term, could be called "lower class," or "low income," or "the poor."

The advantage of utilizing the economic criterion, and particularly the income definition, is that it specifies a socio-economic category towards which policy can be directed. For example, Morgan reports,[15] following Lampman's earlier lead, that 10 billion dollars would bring all spending units now below the poverty line to an income level above poverty. Questions of the distribution of income and of social services can be pinpointed then in terms of how they affect this particular population.

Obviously, income levels and sources of income vary considerably among the low-income population. Keyserling distinguishes between the very poor, the poor and a higher income group who suffer what he terms "deprivation" but not outright poverty. What income level is used affects deeply the characteristics of the poor. Lampman uses lower income limits than Keyserling or Morgan. Consequently, he describes a poor population with 50 per cent of the heads of households out of the labor market, while the others, using a higher income level to define poverty, report only 35 per cent of the heads as out of the labor market. We do not have data but it is reasonable to deduce that a higher percentage of Lampman's poor are on welfare than is true of Morgan's or Keyserling's.

Clearly, different income cut-off points shape the characteristics of the low-income group. The lower the income level used, the more economically and socially different are the poor.

Definitions of poverty and the poor are not technical problems but social and ideological issues. The recipients of low income are not basically a "welfare poor." Only one-fifth of Morgan's poor receive welfare assistance. The social scientists and social service specialists who write of the "welfare poor" are discussing only a slice of the poor; those concerned with "hard-core" and "multi-problem families" are, in turn, analyzing only a very thin wedge of this small slice.

The income criterion has several components: the level of income, the stability or regularity of income, and the source of income (employment or welfare). A number of observers believe that it makes a difference, holding income constant, whether a family is supported by welfare or not. The knowledge for making a refined classification of these components is lacking. I have resorted therefore to combining them into one indicator of economic security (roughly combining income and stability), and then dichotomizing this indicator into the two simple dimensions of high (security) and low (insecurity). Lumping together these components and dichotomizing them is inadequate.[16] But we cannot at present describe each of the cells of what should be an 8-cell or 16-cell table. I think, however, that the cells of a 4-cell table can be usefully discussed. This capsulated table should rapidly be expanded as we acquire more knowledge and understanding.

The Style-of-Life Criterion

The style-of-life variable also offers difficulties. It refers at least to attitudes and behavior in the areas of family relationships and consumption patterns. A major difficulty is that the content of the "lower-class style-of-life" is debatable. Further, evaluative judgments (as implied in the concepts of "family disorganization," "social disorganization," or "family instability") are invariably involved. As yet, it is not possible to formulate a clean-cut classification which avoids cultural biases

Table 1   *Types of Economic Security and Familial Stability*

		Familial Stability +	Instability −
Security	+	++(1)	+−(2)
Economic			
Insecurity	−	−+(3)	−−(4)

and still is of use in formulating a judgment about the impact of life-style on individuals. For example, does the absence of a permanent male figure mean that the family is inevitably "unstable," and that children are necessarily psychologically deformed by living in such a family? Assessments such as these are difficult to make because much of our knowledge and theorizing about fatherless families is based on middle-class situations.

I employ the notion of "familial stability/instability," a dichotomization of style of life, to summarize a variety of elements. Familial stability patterns are characterized by families coping with their problems—the children are being fed, though not necessarily on a schedule; the family meets its obligations so that it is not forced to keep on the move; children are not getting into much more trouble than other children of the neighborhood. These are not satisfactory indicators; they are, at best, suggestive of the kind of behavior which is characteristic of stability among the low income population. The aim is to be able to describe the degrees of effectiveness of different styles of life in handling the same environment, granted that our vocabulary is inadequate for this task.

Class and Status

The two approaches can be welded together by cross-classifying the two dimensions of the two variables of economic security and familial stability in the 2 x 2 table above.

Cell 1 is referred to as the stable poor;

cell 2, the strained; cell 3, the copers; and cell 4, the unstable.

To some extent, life-cycle stages may be involved here, as some young people escape from cell 4 via cell 2 or cell 3 to cell 1, representing a more stable pattern, and beyond. Or families may drop with age from cell 1 to cell 3, where they have lowered economic security but maintain family stability.

Each of the cells contains many variants. While I believe the four types are an improvement over analysis in terms of *the* lower class, it is important to recognize that each type has many variations. One kind of variation is determined by whether the family is stationary in its particular pattern or moving to greater or less security-stability. *My general orientation is to emphasize flux, rather than assuming a permanent position in a pattern.*

The Stable Poor

Cell 1 (the stable poor) is characterized by stability, economically and familially. This cell points to the regularly employed, low-skill, stable poor families.

The rural population, both farm and non-farm, undoubtedly make up the bulk of the stable poor, since this is the majority of the American poor: a re-calculation of Morgan's data suggests that only 30 per cent of the poor live in metropolitan areas. The majority of all the poor and of the stable poor are white rural Southern populations. In addition, the non-urban poor are probably represented in this cell to a greater extent than they are among all the poor. Aged persons are also over-represented and constitute a large part of the poor who suffer from downward mobility, since most of them were better off at earlier points in their lives. Left-over third-generation immigrant populations in large cities are probably under-represented.[17]

A number of Negro families are of the stable poor. They have higher social status in the Negro community than their economic counterparts have in the white community because of the general scaling down of incomes and occupational levels of Negroes in the United States. For reasons discussed below, Negroes and other groups affected by discrimination are probably becoming more important politically as well as in relative size among the urban stable poor.

The children of cell 1 families are of all the children of the poor those most likely to be educationally and occupationally mobile. Cell 1 might be considered the "take-off" cell, representing the phase necessary before many can really make a big advance. But this is a dangerous metaphor, for obviously many youth from families in more difficult circumstances are able to make considerable gains.

The stable poor, then, are a varied group; one component, the aged, has a poor economic future, except to the extent that social security and old-age payments improve, and a declining future as an intact family unit.

The Strained

Cell 2 (the strained) portrays a secure economic pattern, but an unstable family pattern. This might involve a life-cycle problem, *i.e.,* at certain points the families of low-wage, unskilled workers are likely to exhibit unstable patterns. Examples might be "wild" younger workers or alcoholic older workers who disturb family functioning. Or, the pattern could manifest the beginning of a move into cell 4, as a low-income family finds increasing difficulty in maintaining its economic security because of family and personal problems or the economic situation. Obviously, the two possibilities may be closely connected.

Movement may be viewed inter-generationally as well as in terms of life-cycle patterns. Many of the offspring of strained families "may fail to match the economic security of their parents" and experience inter-generational skidding.[18]

Strained familial relations may not, however, result in skidding. In earlier periods, immigrant groups faced considerable internal strain arising from the conflict between the younger and older generations in the course of acculturation. Nonetheless, the second generation generally improved its economic circumstances. The instability of today's strained families is regarded as more "pathological" than that of the immigrant populations, although some social work accounts of families at the turn of the century differ little from current reports of "poor family functioning." The current stress is on parents' fighting and drinking, illicit sexual relations of parents, and neglect or brutality towards the children. Whether the economically secure and familially unstable are characterized by these patterns is not clear. If they are not, the offspring of the strained family may not be a prey to skidding. Further, not all children of deeply conflicting or hostile families are inevitably unable to maintain or improve their economic position.

I have looked at cell 2 as a transitional condition. This view may be misleading: many families persist with a low but steady income and a great deal of internal strain.

The Copers

The copers of cell 3 manifest economic insecurity and familial stability—families and individuals having a rough time economically but managing to keep themselves relatively intact. This group probably increases considerably during periods of extensive unemployment. Probably a considerable number of Negroes are in this group and their children are more likely to be mobile than those living in cell 2-type situations.

This cell probably contains a disproportionate number of families affected by downward mobility. Both Morgan [19] and I [20] have shown the sizable number of sons of non-manual workers who end up in manual (and sometimes low-income) positions. In Great Britain 40 per cent of those born in non-manual families move into manual occupations. Many of these downwardly mobile persons are probably more likely to retain a stable family style than others in the same economic predicament. As in other situations, however, a minority of the downwardly mobile may manifest extreme familial instability, which would place them in cell 4. Limited data suggest that children of downwardly mobile families have a better chance of rising occupationally than children of families which have been at this low level for some generations. [21]

The Unstable

In cell 4, the unstable have neither economic nor personal stability. It is this group which is probably most generally called the "lower class," and Jerome Cohen has suggested to me that the term "lower class" might be usefully restricted to this group. Since this recommendation is unlikely to be consistently utilized by social workers, economists, sociologists, political scientists and others interested in low-income populations, I have not adopted it, preferring to focus attention on the varied segments of the low-income population. Within the unstable group there are degrees of stability and strain— *not every family is a "hard-core case" or has a "multi-agency problem."* Nor do we have sufficient data over time to assert that once in cell 4, always in cell 4. It may be that families and individuals occasionally manifest both economic and personal

instability, then overcome these problems for a while. Later they may again suffer from illness, unemployment, emotional upset or familial instability.

As important in some ways as distinguishing cell 4 from the other three cells which make up the lower class, is it to note that cell 4 contains an extremely varied grouping. In it are partially urbanized Negroes new to the North and to cities, remaining slum residents of ethnic groups which have largely moved out of the slums, and long-term (inter-generational) poor white families, the *déclassés* of Marx. Also included are the physically handicapped and the aged who have dropped through the class structure. *The low-income class generally and the unstable in particular comprise a category of unskilled, irregular workers, broken and large families, and a residual bin of the aged, physically handicapped and mentally disturbed.*

In some cases, social characteristics handicap the low-income groups: for example, recent rurality (resulting in unfamiliarity with urban problems and lack of appropriate skills) and discrimination. These groups—Negroes, former mountaineer whites—have the worst problems. They also have perhaps the greatest potential because removing their social limitations would lead to major change. Their handicaps are less self-inflicted and self-sustaining. This may not be as true for mountaineer whites as for Negroes. Aside from people dropping into the poverty class along the life-and-physical-cycle, the whites in the lower class who have no good, *i.e.,* social, reason for being there, are most likely to be intractable to change.

Hylan Lewis [22] has suggested the categories of clinical, pre-clinical and sub-clinical to delineate patterns among the poor. I would substitute the word "chronic" for "clinical." The chronic poor refers to the long-term dependents, part of whom are the "hard-core"; the pre-chronic poor are a high-risk group who are moving toward a chronic situation but have not yet become chronically dependent. The sub-chronic poor are those who have many characteristics of dependence but have a greater ability to cope with their problems.[23]

A number of forces can lead individuals into chronic dependence. *Lower-class life is crisis-life, constantly trying to "make do" with string where rope is needed.* Anything can break the string. Illness is most important—"Got a job but I got sick and lost it"; "We managed until the baby got sick." The great incidence of physical afflictions among the poor—frequently unknown to the victim—are obvious to any casual observer. Particularly striking are the poor teeth of many. The tendency of lower-class people to somaticize their emotional difficulties may be influenced by the omnipresence of illness.

Familial and personal instability may be the sources as well as the consequences of difficulties. While some frequent concomitants of low-income life such as matrifocality do not inevitably produce grave difficulties in family life, they frequently do. Alcoholism, an inability to handle aggression, hostility or dependence—one's own or others' toward one—can deeply disturb family functioning. A variety of direct personal aid may be necessary.

Sophistication along these lines of analysis has frequently tended to denigrate the importance of structural factors in producing "personal inadequacies," "social disabilities," and "familial instability." The work of Raymond Smith[24] and Edith Clarke[25] strongly suggests that illegitimacy is related to economic conditions—the better the economic conditions among the "lower-class" Negroes of the Caribbean, the lower the rate of illegitimacy. Kunstadter[26] similarly argues that matrifocality as a "lower-class" trait is related to a particular set of economic characteristics.

Prolonged unemployment, irregular employment, and low income are important forces leading to a chronic pattern. Low-paid and irregularly employed individuals do not develop an image of the world as predictable and as something with which they are able to cope. The control or direction of events appears to be (and frequently is) an unattainable achievement. When these individuals suffer long-term unemployment, they are less likely than other unemployed, who have had the experience of fairly regular employment, to maintain personal stability. (Maslow[27] has argued that those who have had a stable past are more able to manage in disastrous circumstances than those who have had considerable prior deprivation.) A high-employment economy has relatively fewer hard-core cases than a low-employment economy. The American community studies suggest that the lower class is smaller in numbers in times of prosperity than in periods of depression. Peter Townsend in an informal lecture recently declared that during the 1930's in England it was believed that 500,000 to 1,000,000 of those not working were unemployable. In 1940, with the pressures of the war, it was discovered that only 100,000 were really unemployable. Thus, structural change would be of great importance in reducing chronic dependence.

Strategies

Three basic policies are possible: (1) direct economic change, such as providing steadier employment, or raising incomes through the provision of a national minimum level of income; (2) direct services, such as case work activities to strengthen the ego-functioning of the individual, or family assistance through homemaker help; (3) indirect change affecting the climate—social, psychological, political—of the neighborhoods in which the poor live.

What would lead one type of low-income population in a given direction would not work at all for another type. A panacea does not exist because there is no one thing which will have a pervasive impact in all cases. What is crucial for one type of problem may be insignificant for others.

I find the concept of elasticity useful here.[28] It points to the extent of change resulting from input of additional services or income. Some types of the poor have high income elasticity—a little change in income produces a big change in behavior; other types may have low income elasticity but have high education elasticity or high case work elasticity. Still other types will respond rapidly and deeply to new housing, to a steady job, to counseling, or to a package of such ingredients rather than to, say, case work alone. The concept of elasticity brings into focus the issue of different remedies for various types of problems. The issues of costs, and of substitution or choice of different services or resources are made vivid by confrontation with the concepts of elasticity and productivity (the return per unit of expenditure).

The stable, those in cell 1, would be immediately helped if their incomes were raised so that they came closer to the American standard of life. Unionization of industries in which they work (especially in service trades and occupations), shifts from low productivity land and industries to highly productive industries, and occupational retraining would be important. In some situations, individuals have to be prepared for retraining (where, for example, the level of literacy is low) or aided in moving to new localities where opportunities are greater. They may need help in adjusting to new urban conditions, but this adjustment would probably not be very difficult where jobs and housing are adequate. The stable poor, in short, would have a high income elasticity, rapidly improving and adjusting to increases in their income.

The inadequacy of social services and payments in the United States forces many into cell 1. Improving and extending social security, which at present maintains many only at the level of penury while a substantial number are not covered by it,

would move large numbers of persons from cells 2, 3, and 4 into cell 1 and lead many of the stable poor into the society. Harrington[29] and Titmuss[30] have pointed out that social services in the United States and Britain do not seem to be benefiting the poor as much as those in the middle income range. Obviously, changes in social policy are necessary here.

Some of the strained of cell 2 might require some case work help in improving family conditions and operations, but other approaches might also be effective. If these persons live in a locality that manifests high rates of disturbances, they might be helped by moving to new areas. For some, an improvement in economic conditions may be necessary in order to get deeper family changes. Undoubtedly, a number are not sensitive to income changes or to neighborhood climate change, and sustained case work help would be necessary.

Familial instability may be a carry-over from an earlier period when the family suffered from economic insecurity; the family has not caught up with its economic improvements. But, as Seymour S. Bellin and Jerome Cohen have pointed out, in some families where economic conditions have improved after a long period of economic deprivation and family difficulties, withdrawing the stress of economic insecurity may be insufficient. The toll of the stress frequently must be overcome. Special help may be necessary to bring about familial changes of great importance. Social agencies should be adapted so that they are able to meet the requirements of these families at the time of need and to provide aid in ways which fit the outlook of these families.

The copers of cell 3, who maintain family stability in the face of grave economic difficulties, obviously need economic aid. Many of them would be helped by improvement in welfare payments and practices; others, where there is a working head of household, would be advanced by regularization of work and/or shifting to more remunerative fields. The needs of the stable and of the copers would seem to be similar. Improvement of the economic dimension would push more of the copers into the mobility possibilities of the stable poor of cell 1 and beyond.

Cell 4, containing the unstable, is the most discussed grouping of the poor today. Many, if not most of those in this category are on welfare allotments; women head many of the family units. A general improvement in economic conditions would not have much economic impact on the unstable because they are largely out of the labor force and out of the economy. It is widely believed that unstable families do not have a high income elasticity but the evidence is not strong. Specific programs aimed at this group would be important. Present-day welfare services are insufficient since they are largely budgetary and policing activities. Concentration on improving the educational achievement of the youth of these families would perhaps be more important than a diffuse effort to achieve better family functioning.[31] A number of interesting and aggressive case work services have been offered, but their degree of long-term success is unclear. A variety of direct services may be effective with some of these families, including continuous homemaking and baby-sitting services, provisions for nurseries and all-day schools, and consumer buying protection.

It may be that a less direct approach would be effective. It would involve trying to mobilize politically the communities in which the unstable live with the more stable poor so as to provide greater feelings of strength and control. Improvement of family conditions may be anticipated. But far more important, a general change in a low-income community, precipitated perhaps by the mobile, the strained and the copers, may spread to affect the unstable of the community as well. The social actionists, of whom Saul Alinsky is the best-known, have this implicit strategy.

In all of the strategies it is necessary to

be clear about what exactly is the target population. This is frequently determined on the basis of the numbers involved, though there is always the delicate choice of helping a lot of people a little or a few people a lot. The second step is to discover what works with whom. There is probably nothing that will help all lower-class people in one move although, as suggested above, a steady, meaningful, well-paid job as a general base of action should not be underestimated. A decent level of living as the minimal responsibility of an affluent society may be a crucial goal. But there are certain things that alone will help some groups. We have to find the right things for the right groups at the right time.

Political Action

The poor are not rapidly declining; inequality in income and wealth appear to have been increasing in recent years; the incomes of Negroes are no longer advancing relative to those of whites; pension and assistance schemes are maintaining many in poverty rather than providing a "welfare state" standard. The decline in the number of poor between 1947 and 1957 has been due, Lampman contends, to general economic advance rather than to a redistribution of income and wealth in favor of the poor. Improvements in social services and a decrease in inequality would require a shift in the allocation of national product towards improving the relative position of the bottom 20 per cent of the population.

These issues are political ones. They will be affected by the possibility that the present American poor may prove to be more politically active than is usually true of the poor. If this happens, it will be because a large slice of the urban poor is made up of Negroes who have ethnic as well as economic forces moving them. Samuel Lubell [32] has argued that Negroes in large cities will furnish a new base for Democratic ward machines. They are becoming more and more politically active and demanding. This self-organization is not only important in getting changes from the government, but it is also serving to change lower-class Negro communities from within. Local leaders are developing, and the orientation of many community agencies to provide leadership and direction to lower-class communities will become increasingly ineffective. The conservative orientation of gaining change and social advance through an harmonious arrangement with local power forces is being superseded by disadvantaged groups themselves actively pressuring for the kinds of changes—in housing, in schools and the like—that they believe to be important.

As these pressures build up it is likely that the *desegregation issue will emerge as a social class issue* affecting all lower-class persons, and not only as a racial issue affecting Negroes alone. Mexican-Americans and Puerto Ricans, who, with Negroes, increasingly make the poor of the large metropolis a "colored poor," are moving into the stable and coping patterns and beginning to develop political effectiveness. Poverty may not be treated as a racial issue affecting only Negroes. *Even where Negroes operate alone, the impact of their demands will affect all the poor as they achieve better schools, better housing, better jobs, better social services.*

Cause and Consequence

A good deal of the tone of discussions of the lower class, even by sociologists, has a negative quality. On the other hand, a few seem to have a romantic feeling about the lower class, particularly its juvenile delinquents, whom they see as rebels against the horrors of middle-class, conformist America. The former view suffers from the assumption that the lower class has little potential for change; the latter, that there is nothing better in present-day America to which it can change.

Among other things, the glorification theme ignores, as Frank Riessman has pointed out, the impact on the lower class of its limited education.[33] The negative view frequently confuses, as Keyserling has noted, cause and consequence. The personal instability of many lower-class persons may be a consequence of economic instability as well as a cause of it. The chain of cause-and-effect over time frequently becomes blurred. An effective way of cutting into the chain so that change will occur becomes the key issue. My feeling is that structural forces have been underplayed recently as a mode of change, while the "culture of poverty" has been overstressed.[34]

The negative view has the danger of not seeing positive elements in lower-class life. By ignoring these elements, social policies can frequently worsen them. For example, in an exciting study of a Puerto Rican slum, Helen Icken Safa has analyzed the community and familial solidarity of the residents of a slum barrio. When families were moved into public housing, community ties were weakened. Perhaps this was because the project social workers centered their efforts on the wife, while the husband's role and responsibility in the family and community diminished.[35]

It is perhaps a "heuristic" fallacy, as Riessman has said, to believe that lower-class people are willing and capable of positive change. This is not always true, but if professionals and social reformers lack confidence in the poor, little can be accomplished either in the social services or in political action. An optimistic outlook may not insure success, but without optimism, it is doubtful if anything can be moved. Frequently, disenchantment and cynicism capture accurately a slice of life, but they are also immobilizing, for they ignore the constructive and energizing role of hope.[36]

Conclusion

A clearly defined "lower class" does not exist. As Peter Townsend has noted, the population embraced by this term is a varied, changing group:

"A misconception is that in a relatively prosperous society most individuals have the capacity to meet any contingency in life. Only a poor and handicapped minority need special protection or help. This ignores the infinite diversities and changing conditions to be found in any population. Men gain or fall in status and living standards; at one stage of their life their dependencies are minimal, at others unduly numerous; sometimes they need exceptional help to achieve qualifications and skills held to be desirable by society; and at all times they are susceptible to the vicissitudes of prolonged ill health, disability, redundancy of unemployment, and bereavement, which they are usually powerless to control or even reasonably anticipate. Unanticipated adversity is not the peculiar experience of one fixed section of the working class."[37]

In England, Dahrendorf contends,[38] the unskilled category represents a temporary condition; individuals at various stages of the life cycle may drop into it, but for only a comparatively few is it a permanent position. In the United States this is not as true, and if caste pressures grow, it will be even less true.

The changing economy of America is producing new property relations; at the same time it is producing new working classes and lower-income classes.[39] The analysis of data and the development of our concepts have not kept up with the increasing differentiation within these populations. Many pressures and counterpressures exist in any stratum. Despite a modal pattern, considerable variety in values and behavior occurs. Since cross-pressures affect the lower class to a considerable extent,[40] we should look for *types* of behavior patterns even among people apparently very similar in objective characteristics. Those at the social bottom see only a vague and ill-defined "them" above them, and those above believe that those below are all rather similar. But those at the top know how much differentiation within the top actually takes place; those at the bottom are aware of much more differentiation than are the outsiders looking in. In particular, what has been taken as typical of the most unstable bottom group has been generalized to apply to all who are poor or who are manual workers.

The label "the lower class" increasingly distorts complicated reality. We must begin to demarcate types of poor people more sharply if we are to be able to understand and interpret behavior and circumstance and to develop appropriate social policies. Evaluations of commentators are frequently masked as description. The interpretation of behavior frequently assumes that all outcomes are necessarily desired and normatively prescribed. Antisocial behavior is viewed as heavily sanctioned rather than as the interaction of weak sanctions and difficult reality conditions.

The resurgence of interest in the poor augurs well for a rethinking of the new kind of poverty in the "welfare state," which is unlike the mass unemployment of the 1930's or the grinding poverty of the employed workers of the nineteenth century. Our "received wisdom" should be superseded by new categories and concepts. New wine is being poured into old conceptual bottles and the special quality of the new is being lost.

NOTES

1. *Cf.* Patricia Cayo Sexton, *Education and Income: Inequalities in our Public Schools,* New York: Viking Press, 1961, pp. 10 ff., and S. M. Miller, Carolyn Comings and Betty Saleem, *The School Dropout Problem—Syracuse,* Albany: New York State Division for Youth and the Syracuse University Youth Development Center, 1963. Herman P. Miller points out that the disadvantage of not having a college diploma grew from 1939 to 1958. See his "Money Value of an Education," *Occupational Outlook Quarterly* (September, 1961), 4.

2. Janet E. Weinandy, *Families Under Stress,* Syracuse: Syracuse University Youth Development Center, 1962.

3. Audrey Harvey, *Casualties of the Welfare State,* Fabian Tract 321, London: Fabian Society, 1959.

4. Michael Harrington, *The Other America: Poverty in the United States,* New York: The Macmillan Co., 1962; Conference on Economic Progress, *Poverty and Deprivation in the United States,* Washington, D.C.: Conference on Economic Progress, 1961; the main author of this analysis is Leon Keyserling and it is known as the "Keyserling Report"; Gabriel Kolko, *Wealth and Power in the United States,* New York: Frederick Praeger, 1962; Robert J. Lampman, "The Low Income Population and Economic Growth," *Study Paper No. 12,* Joint Economic Committee, Congress of the United States, December 16, 1959, Washington, D.C.: Government Printing Office, 1959; James N. Morgan *et al., Income and Welfare in the United States,* New York: McGraw-Hill and Company, 1962.

5. Brian Abel-Smith, "Whose Welfare State?" in Norman MacKenzie (ed.), *Conviction,* London: MacGibbon and Kee, 1958.

6. "The terms 'lower class' and 'middle class' are used here to refer to systems of behavior and concerns rather than groups defined in conventional economic terms." William C. Kvaraceus and Walter B. Miller, *Delinquent Behavior: Culture and the Individual,* Washington, D.C.: National Education Association, 1959, p. 62.

7. S. M. Miller and Frank Riessman, "The Working-Class Subculture: A New View," *Social Problems,* IX (Summer, 1961), 86–97.

8. Allison Davis, "The Motivation of the Underprivileged Worker," in William Foote Whyte (ed.), *Industry and Society,* New York: McGraw-Hill and Company, 1946, pp. 84–106.

9. August B. Hollingshead and Frederick C. Redlich, *Social Class and Mental Illness: A Community Study,* New York: John Wiley & Sons, 1958, pp. 387–97.

10. Walter B. Miller, "Lower-Class Culture as a Generating Milieu of Gang Delinquency," *Journal of Social Issues,* XIV, 3 (1958), 6, footnote 3. In his penetrating analysis, Miller notes the existence of "subtypes of lower-class culture" but does not pursue this point. While his emphasis is on cultural characteristics such as "female-based" household and "serial monogamy" mating patterns, he elsewhere employs educational, occupational and income variables to define the lower class. See his "Implications of Urban Lower-Class Culture for Social Work," *Social Service Review* (September, 1959), 229 ff. His major stress is on cultural or status characteristics as defining the lower-class culture.

11. *Ibid.*

12. Lee Rainwater assisted by Karol Kane Weinstein, *And the Poor Get Children,* Chicago: Quadrangle Books, 1960. See also the distinctions made within the lower-lower class by Martin Loeb, "Social Class and the American Social System," *Social Work,* 6 (April, 1961), 16.

13. Keyserling, *op. cit.,* Lampman, *op. cit.*

14. See footnote 4.

15. Morgan, *op. cit.,* p. 3.

16. Not all families receiving welfare assistance should automatically be classified in the economically insecure category. For the aged, perhaps, welfare assistance does not constitute a lack of security. In general, however, the fact of welfare assistance would put a family in the economically insecure category.

17. Richard Cloward and Lloyd Ohlin, *Delinquency and Opportunity,* Glencoe, Ill.: The Free Press, 1960.

18. Dennis Wrong, in a personal communication, has influenced this and the following paragraph. "Skidding" is discussed in Harold Wilensky and Hugh Edwards, "The Skidder: Ideological Adjustments of Downward Mobile Workers," *American Sociological Review,* 24 (April, 1959), 215–231.

19. Morgan, *op. cit.*

20. S. M. Miller, "Comparative Social Mobility," *Current Sociology,* IX, 1 (1960), 1–89,

21. *Ibid.,* pp. 32–33.

22. Hylan Lewis, "Child Rearing Among Low Income Families," Washington Center for Metropolitan Studies, June 8, 1961. This paper and others by Lewis are among the most stimulating on the problems of low-income patterns. Also see Hyman Rodman, "The Lower-Class Value Stretch," *Social Forces,* 42 (December, 1963).

23. I have used the terms "dependent" and "dependence" here for want of a sharper term; I find the concept of dependence murky and frequently used to cover a variety of conditions which a writer does not like.

24. Raymond T. Smith, *The Negro Family in British Guiana,* London: Routledge & Kegan Paul, Ltd., 1956.

25. Edith Clarke, *My Mother Who Fathered Me,* New York: Humanities Press, 1957.

26. Peter Kunstadter, "A Survey of the Consanguine and Matrifocal Family," *American Anthropologist,* 65 (February, 1963), 56–66.

27. A. H. Maslow, *Motivation and Personality,* New York: Harper & Bros., 1953, pp. 80–106.

28. Carlsson has reintroduced the concept of elasticity into sociological thinking. Gosta Carlsson, "Okonomische Ungleichheit und Lebenschanchen," *Kolner Zeitschrift für Soziologie,* 5 (1961), 189–199.

29. Harrington, *op. cit.*

30. Richard Titmuss, *Essays on 'The Welfare State,'* London: George Allen & Unwin, 1958, Chapter 2, "The Social Division of Welfare," and *Income Distribution and Social Change,* Toronto: University of Toronto Press, 1962. Although Titmuss is a seminal thinker in analyzing changes in the social structure of the modern society, he has been almost completely ignored by American sociologists.

31. *Cf.* S. M. Miller, "Poverty and Inequality in America: Implications for the Social Services," *Child Welfare* (November, 1963), 424–5. Republished in the Syracuse University Youth Development Center Reprint Series.

32. In his syndicated column which appeared in the *Syracuse Herald-Journal* (Nov. 14, 1961).

33. Frank Riessman, *The Culturally Deprived Child,* New York: Harper & Brothers, 1962.

34. Harrington seems frequently to write and speak as though all low-income persons are bound in an immutable chain of apathy and ineffectiveness, characteristics of "the culture of poverty." He has obviously extended this term beyond the intent of Oscar Lewis who introduced it in his *Five Families,* New York: Basic Books, 1959, and in *The Children of Sanchez,* New York: Random House, 1961. Warren Hagstrom has countered this view in his "The Power of the Poor," Syracuse University Youth Development Center, 1963.

35. Helen Icken Safa, "From Shanty Town to Public Housing," Syracuse University Youth Development Center, 1962. The peculiar stresses of public housing life may be functional equivalents of the economic conditions of matrifocality discussed by Kunstadter.

36. *Cf.* S. M. Miller and Frank Riessman, "Working Class Authoritarianism: A Critique of Lipset," *British Journal of Sociology* (September, 1961).

37. Peter Townsend, "Freedom and Equality," *New Statesman,* LXI, No. 1570 (April 14, 1961), 574.

38. Ralf Dahrendorf, *Unskilled Labour in British Industry,* unpublished Ph.D. thesis, London School of Economics, 1956, pp. 429–430.

39. S. M. Miller, "Poverty, Race and Politics," in Irving Louis Horowitz (ed.), *The New Sociology: Essays on Social Values and Social Theory in Honor of C. Wright Mills,* New York: Oxford University Press, 1964.

40. See Miller and Riessman, *op. cit.,* and Hylan Lewis, *op. cit.*

33. THE ETHNIC MOBILITY TRAP AND STRATIFICATION THEORY

NORBERT F. WILEY

According to Norbert F. Wiley, "a mobility trap is a structural condition in which the means for moving up within a stratum are contrary to those for moving to the next higher stratum." Using the metaphor of climbing a tree rather than a ladder, Wiley shows the significance of the internal structure of ethnic groups for members who want to move up—and for those who want to move out.

Wiley's paper is an important contribution to the growing literature on class and ethnicity and, like Milton M. Gordon's notion of the ethclass, it already has influenced many sociologists interested in the stratification of American society.

Norbert F. Wiley teaches sociology at the University of Illinois. A specialist in political sociology and social stratification, he has published in several contemporary sociological journals.

The sociology of American ethnic groups has centered on ethnic acculturation and assimilation, both as pure processes and as social problems. From the viewpoint of stratification, though, these processes are cases of large-scale social mobility, and the history of American mobility is largely the history of ethnic assimilation. In examining ethnicity and mobility together, much can be learned about both. This paper will consider ethnic mobility, not as such, but as a source of new ideas for stratification theory. Ethnic mobility has been characterized by a special form of mobility which, although found elsewhere, is most easily identified in the ethnic case. Once we have named and defined this mechanism, we will consider its explanatory value.

The mobility chances of ethnic group members are often subject to special complications, not only because of discrimination, but because of features within the ethnic structure itself; for the group is usually internally stratified to some degree and offers in-group opportunities alongside of those in the larger society. This duality of intra- versus extra-group mobility is further complicated if the group is moving upward as a bloc. The individual ethnic may have to make special decisions concerning his career plans. Not only must he choose, for example, whether to aim for a job in the professions, a bureaucracy, or small business. He also faces the question of ethnicity, whether to move with it or against it, to capitalize on it or disregard it. If he makes the wrong decision, he may find himself in a mobility trap, and these exist in abundance in all fluid stratification systems.

Briefly, a mobility trap is an opportunity for mobility which offers a good deal less than it seems to, and, once pursued, permits release only at the cost of some downward mobility. The first section of this paper will be an elaboration of this definition, especially in relation to ethnic

Reprinted from *Social Problems,* **15,** 2 (Fall 1967), 147–159, by permission of the author and The Society for the Study of Social Problems.

groups, and it should be regarded as an attempt to form a usable concept. This will be followed by a "discussion" section in which the concept will be related more systematically to the theory of stratification.

Metaphors and Concept Formation

To give a clearer definition of the mobility trap it will be necessary to sketch the picture of the opportunity structure which it assumes. Such pictures are usually related to some simple metaphor, and much of the theorizing in this area is influenced, perhaps unconsciously, by half-hidden metaphors.[1] Before giving our own, mention will be made of two others in relation to which ours can be more clearly seen.

Perhaps the most common metaphor is that of the "social ladder," the "ladder of success" and kindred notions. For our purposes this metaphor has two important features. Social strata are visualized in a continuous hierarchical line; that is, the ladder is a straight one and no rungs are missing. Secondly, it can be climbed, and the means of climbing are the same at all levels. It is implicit that ability and hard work determine one's place on the ladder. This optimistic picture is favored by people who are themselves in the upper strata and feel a bit guilty about being there.

A second cluster of metaphors centers around the notion of physical restraint. People speak of "beating your head against a wall," "running down a blind alley," "being on a treadmill," and so on. This picture has implications exactly opposite to those of the previous one. Social strata are not continuous; they are clearly separated. Also, climbing into a higher stratum is impossible. This picture is favored by dissatisfied people in the lower levels of the system.

The notion of the mobility trap assumes a picture that is a compromise between the two already given.[2] The opportunity system is to be visualized as a tree and mobility as tree climbing. This image is invoked when people speak of being "out on a limb," and it is the limbs that are its distinctive part. The limbs are like strata, leading gently upward but primarily outward and away from all chance of serious ascent. Normally the climber who wants to hit the top will avoid the limbs as much as possible and concentrate on the trunk.

This metaphor has implications that parallel those of the previous ones. One is that the limbs, or strata, are both continuous and discrete. On the dimension of height the limbs overlap leaving no gaps in the structure. In physical contact, however, they are discrete, with good-sized gaps in between.[3] Secondly, mobility is, in a sense, both possible and impossible. If a person is at the top of an isolated limb, direct ascent may be impossible; but if he retreats to the trunk or can reach an overhead limb, mobility is possible, for the sole connection between limbs is often at the base, by way of the trunk. To the people who are blithely climbing the limb in pursuit of a dead-end form of mobility, the truly mobile person may be pitied or scorned, for he will appear to be moving downward. Actually he is preparing to leave the stratum at its only exit, at the bottom. *The essence of the mobility trap is this: the means for moving up within a stratum are contrary to those for moving to the next higher stratum.* In other words there is a conflict between intra- and inter-stratum mobility norms. For those on a limb this paradox is obscured, for their limited vantage point persuades them to move in the wrong direction.[4]

A few examples will make this clearer. To a boy in the slums, social advancement within a delinquent gang by accumulating tattoos, knife skills and a police record is a limb. Spending his free time in a settlement house with the social workers is the trunk. To a slum girl, sexual promiscuity with its instant popularity is a limb. Sexual restraint and a marriage to a mobile young man may be the trunk. To a bright young factory worker, the blue collar hierarchy is a limb, and becoming a foreman may be its outermost point.[5] Going back to school in pursuit of a college degree is the trunk. To a young business executive, long and faithful service to one employer may be a limb, and job-hopping the trunk.

To the mobile person the trap is the limb, especially if it is long, low and lateral. Mobility comes not only from persistent and dedicated climbing. More important is knowing how to distinguish the limbs from the trunk, and even in knowing when to climb out on a strong safe limb to avoid falling from a slippery trunk. Ultimately the trap is a state of mind, and for those without further aspirations it can be as cozy as a nest. Nevertheless it is based solidly on the structure of the system, and its reality will become clear if an attempt is made to leave it.

Up to now we have done two things. We have presented a picture which gives metaphorical, and admittedly pre-scientific, support to certain stratification variables that are presently without such support. These variables are (a) degrees of continuity or discontinuity between adjacent strata, (b) degrees of hierarchy or subordination-superordination between adjacent strata, (c) degrees of mobility opportunity, depending on location in the structure, and (d) multi-dimensionality in the forms of equality, e.g. as they appear in Max Weber's class-status-party formulation. The second thing we have done is to draw out one concept from this metaphorical base and give it an initial definition.

I should add that the picture of the tree is deliberately overdrawn to fix it securely as a reference point. In the discussion section, I will consider which points are overdrawn and what theoretical contributions a picture of this kind could reasonably lead to.

Types of Mobility Traps

Without attempting to be systematic or exhaustive, we can see at least four fairly common types of mobility traps. This listing is not meant to be a formal classification but a further attempt to sharpen a definition, by means of a rough enumeration.

(1) The "age-grade trap" consists in the tendency of age groups to adopt prestige standards which conflict with those of older age groups. Too much advancement within such a stratum makes it difficult, upon leaving the group, to adjust to the standards of the next. The most marked instance occurs during adolescence, in a different version for each sex and social class.[6] In later life the woman who has responded too well to motherhood faces the "empty nest," and the man who has over-adjusted to his occupation faces a vacuous retirement.

(2) The "overspecialization trap" is found in highly specialized administrative jobs, usually at the lower levels, which are dead-end positions in themselves, and whose skills do not help much for the performance of higher activities. The occupant who takes his duties too seriously, treating them as an effective mobility investment, may find himself at once narrowed and indispensable, thus becoming unpromotable.[7] A special variant of this trap falls to those who are given that fake promotion called being "kicked upstairs," for they are shorn of power and come to specialize solely in ritual.

(3) The "localite trap" exists in those professions which, while once pursued with one employer in one locale, are beginning to require a series of job changes within a national market loosely controlled by the major employers and top professionals. Such professions as social worker, planner, school superintendent, university professor and clergyman are in various stages of this transition. These occupations have two distinct power and prestige arenas: the local, which is diminishing in importance, and the national, which is growing. Broadly speaking, the trap consists in pursuing local prestige at the expense of national.

(4) The final type is the "minority group trap," including not only ethnic and racial groups, but, under some conditions, religious, female, radical political and other relatively powerless groups which offer advancement within their ghettos. This case is a trap in the most nearly literal sense because it is often a mechanism of deliberate suppression by majority group people. The ethnic sub-type has special qualities which will be given further analysis.

Ethnic Mobility Patterns

The mobility trap is often a great pitfall for the ambitious member of an ethnic group. As long as his group exists as a visible and integrated body of people, it is a limb on which there is limited opportunity for mobility. The limb will often have immediate attraction, since in-group opportunities will be the more visible as well as being continuous with existing social bonds. The mobile ethnic can choose the relatively safe and comfortable course of pursuing whatever opportunities exist within the group; or, to the extent that the majority group permits, he can take the more adventuresome and lonely course of leaving the group to climb the trunk. The latter option is not equally open to all groups. For Negroes it is almost impossible to get off the limb, except in a limited sense. For a relatively assimilated group like the Irish, it is extremely easy. But in all groups, depending on their state of assimilation, the choice is there to be made.[8]

Once made, the choice may have social and psychological effects which make it irreversible. One who chooses the ethnic career in such fields as journalism, politics or the professions will become imbedded in a firm network of ethnic relations—in his family, religion, occupation and club memberships—from which he can almost never extricate himself. On the other hand, one who leaves his group—a Negro who passes into white society, a Jew who

becomes a Christian, an Italian who changes his name or a Catholic who leaves the Church—may never be able to fully re-enter his group.

In either case something will be lost as well as gained: higher opportunities will be lost if the choice is made in the ethnic direction, and the warmth of the ethnic community if the choice is made in the "outside" direction. Also, in either case the person will gradually deepen his "commitment," in the sense that choices in other areas of life will develop as offshoots of the original choice, thereby making it too costly to change.[9] But movement out on a limb entails something more than a commitment; for, not only will it be difficult to retreat or change, it will also be difficult to advance beyond a certain point. The "ethnic" choice thus limits options and maneuverability considerably more than does the "outside" choice.

It is the in-group career that is the classic ethnic trap, for while it is attractive and emotionally rewarding, it usually has a low ceiling, and there is no easy way out into the world at large.[10] This form of mobility, which is tied to a minority subculture and can go only so far, has been an important part of American social experience, and I will argue that it has contributed to several of the characteristic marks of the American stratification system.

A more complete analysis of ethnic mobility as such should take account of other forms of entrapment that can occur if there are fast changes in the balance between internal and external opportunity. Internal opportunity sometimes increases unexpectedly, from a new wave of immigration, a political breakthrough, or some other change that augments the mobility value of ethnic membership. In those cases the members who have moved outside the group (trunk-climbers) might find these new internal opportunities unavailable to them. On the other hand, assimilation sometimes increases faster than expected, and ethnic careerists find themselves stranded in a declining market. These barriers, which arise from fluctuations in the dynamics of acculturation, should be added to the major barrier we have already described; and, to return to the metaphor, one might think of the limbs as growing or dying, in a none too predictable manner. But these processes only elaborate the basic proposition that ethnic mobility has often moved somewhat off the main line of ascent, into trap-like situations, and this has given both mild advantages and more serious disadvantages to ethnic members.

Discussion

Origins of mobility traps

The metaphor of the tree, just as that of the social ladder or brick wall, is, of course, an overstatement; for frequently the normal mobility within a stratum leads directly, without any branching effect, into the next stratum. A dead-end is reached only when there is a structural discontinuity between strata. This exists when two contiguous strata have incompatible norms, such that mobility within the lower stratum requires the adoption of attitudes and skills which are a liability for entering the next stratum.

Discontinuities can come about through social change, as when educational programs, occupations and other mobility investments become obsolescent; or, as we have emphasized in this paper, they may arise from systematic group conflict along such lines as ethnicity, religion or class.[11] In either case discontinuity is a matter of degree, and its measurement would require a comparison of the mobility norms of adjacent strata and an examination of mobility careers, both upward and downward. Also, the degree of discontinuity can change over time, and individuals can, for example, become trapped with skills and reputations that are tied to an obsolete conflict or cooperative relation.

The significance of normative discontinuity between ethnic groups depends also on how severely the subordinate group is being held down. If the subordination is quite severe, requiring a large amount of coercion, the normative discontinuity is largely just an instrument of power—a means of subordinating the minority group—and not a basic cause of blocked mobility. When suppression is a minor factor, however—when it is relatively easy to get off the limb—the conflict of mobility norms is not just the reflection of a basically coercive relationship; it has an originating influence of its own. The notion of the mobility trap has its more central meaning in the latter case.

Apart from these important questions of degree and empirical measurement, a structural discontinuity can be recognized qualitatively by two attributes that were touched on lightly in the preceding section. These are (1) the prevalence of a by-passing or "leap-frog" type of mobility from the bottom of the lower stratum (up the trunk) directly to the bottom of the next higher stratum, and (2) the inability of upper stratum people to judge correctly the internal norms and ranks of lower stratum people.

Mobility from the bottom

There have been a number of observations in the sociological literature of that form of social mobility which by-passes the person's own stratum and jumps immediately into the higher stratum. Robert Merton, for example, examined the case of the World War II army recruit who, unlike the typical recruit, strongly accepted the official rules and regulations of the army.[12] In adopting these attitudes the recruits at once conformed closely to the expectations of the official army and deviated from the expectations of informal recruit life. Thus, they ranked low in informal recruit society; for in following the norms of a higher stratum they had to violate the informal norms. Yet it was these same recruits who, four months later, had the larger proportion of promotions to Private First Class. From the point of view of the informal recruit ranking system, mobility came more frequently from the bottom.

In commenting on this case Merton emphasized the psychological factor of reference group orientation and the special preparation for mobility which he called "anticipatory socialization." It should also be pointed out, though, that these responses are especially characteristic of mobility between discontinuous strata and that failure to make these responses may lead into a mobility trap. For all socialization is, at least in part, anticipatory, but when strata are discontinuous there are two distinct lines of anticipatory socialization, internal and external, and the degree of difference and stress between them depends on the degree of discontinuity between strata.

Perhaps the classic picture of the two lines of socialization is that of the "corner boys" and the "college boys" in Whyte's *Street Corner Society*.[13] The corner boys were being socialized toward an opportunity ceiling in ethnic politics or rackets, while the college boys were being groomed for professional or managerial positions. Both types of socialization had a future reference, but that of the college boys was more consciously and visibly anticipatory because it went against the grain, socially speaking, and had little social support. The notion of anticipatory socialization, then, has a special explanatory power only when it is in preparation for a by-passing form of mobility.

Merton's example of mobility from the bottom is only one of many that are frequently met. Others are the high school bookworm, the well-behaved convict, the "company man" in the factory, and other institutional types who, while ranking low in their own strata, nevertheless have the best chance of mobility (getting into college, becoming paroled, getting promoted to foreman or management, as the case may be).[14]

In general, mobility from the bottom seems most likely when intergroup conflict exists to some extent and the preparation for mobility requires a nonconformity if not a disloyalty to one's own stratum. If the conflict is too mild, the discontinuity in mobility norms will not develop very far; if it is too severe, mobility between strata might stop altogether. A medium degree of conflict therefore seems to be the optimum condition for producing mobility from the bottom. Accordingly, anticipatory socialization, in Merton's technical sense, is most useful when the avenue of opportunity is only partly open. When this avenue is completely closed, anticipatory socialization is useless, and when it is completely open it is not needed.

This does not mean that everyone at the bottom of a limb or stratum has a better chance of mobility than those above them. Mobility chances are greater only for those who are deviating from their own group's norms to conform to those of the higher group. There will be others at the bottom who rank low from both points of view, that of their own stratum and that of the higher one. These people are spiritually at home in their own stratum, and they might be called "centrals" as distinguished from the "marginals" who are preparing for mobility. One would expect that the centrals and marginals would typically withdraw from and dislike each other, bringing about a basic disunity at the bottom.

In the situation we are describing, downward mobility too should be leapfrog, although in this case the movement is from the bottom of one stratum all the way down to the bottom of the next lower stratum. For even though the person is now in a lower stratum, he will still have the habits and attitudes of the superior stratum. These habits, being incompatible with the norms of his new stratum, will make him rank low as soon as he enters it. In other words, a downwardly mobile person, formerly a "central" at the bottom of the superior stratum, will fall to the bottom of his new stratum, and this will place him in the role of a "marginal," for his moral attachment will still be to the norms of the higher stratum. The relation between marginals who have fallen and those getting ready to rise should be harmonious and mutually supportive, although this would have to be investigated.

The disunity of the lower stratum, between the two types of marginals and the centrals, has consequences for intergroup relations. It weakens the potential of the lower group for collective action along the lines of political or economic conflict. This can be interpreted as a self-regulating or equilibrating mechanism for the entire society in the following way. An initial conflict produces a normative discontinuity between strata; discontinuity produces the by-passing form of mobility; this, in turn, results in a disunity between centrals and marginals; and the final effect is a restriction on the potential for conflict. So conflict, through its effect on mobility, places limits on its own escalation. On the other hand, if the original condition is one of injustice for the lower stratum, the self-regulating process tends to perpetuate the injustice by weakening the power of the lower group to defend itself.

Cross-class misperception

Another sign of discontinuity between strata is the tendency of upper stratum people to err in perceiving the norms of the lower stratum, either by seeing no norms at all ("moral anarchy") or by extrapolating upper stratum norms onto the lower stratum. In American ethnic history the superior groups have often regarded the inferiors as child-like, depraved, "disorganized," and generally without moral controls. Contemporary white attitudes toward Negroes often exhibit this misperception, just as do attitudes which management holds toward labor in some industries.

When upper stratum norms are ex-tended to the lower stratum, an inaccurate picture of the internal ranking in the lower stratum results. This error makes it difficult to achieve cooperative action between groups, because statuses are unrecognized and norms unwittingly broken. The classic case is that of the middle-class social worker who assumes that the mobility-oriented lower-class male, who ranks high on middle-class criteria, must thereby also rank high in lower-class society. The attempt to "reach" lower-class youths through such "leaders" is the perennial error of the group social worker. The same mistake is often made when teachers try to influence the informal life of their students, managers try to reach their workers, and higher ethnic groups try to reach lower ethnic communities. Closer to home is the case of the sociologist who, in studying a discontinuous community status arrangement, leans too heavily on the opinions of upper status people to judge the internal order of people in lower strata.

Pathological results of mobility

Another condition that may be an attribute of a structural discontinuity is an unusually great amount of stress for the mobile person. A great deal has been written about the stress and personal breakdown that presumably results from mobility, especially downward mobility. Taking their cue from Durkheim, who related suicide rates to mobility, many scholars have argued that mobility loosens moral and social bonds, creates stress, and produces various forms of self-destructive and anti-social behavior.[15] Other studies have challenged or denied this hypothesis.[16] Perhaps the relation between mobility and stress depends on other factors, such as the degree of discontinuity between strata. Earlier it was pointed out that the social, and presumably also the psychological, loss of downward mobility is greater when strata are discontinuous. Similarly the upwardly mobile person, under discontinuous conditions, has the stress of living with two opposed normative systems, and this might scar him even after the mobility has succeeded.

More concretely, this might mean that mobility between manual and nonmanual work, in either direction, would produce the greatest stress within industries with the bitterest labor-management cleavage, perhaps Kerr and Siegel's strike-prone industries.[17] It might mean that mobility from an ethnic group that is subject to intense prejudice will produce more stress than mobility from less disfavored ethnic groups. It might also be that movement up and out of a relatively fundamentalistic religion will produce more stress than other mobility-linked changes of religion.

On the other hand, mobility stress should be least when the two strata present a continuous gradation of norms and little hostility or conflict. In fact upward mobility, far from being pathological, might have a healthy effect on the personality. It may be, then, that the relation between mobility and pathology could fruitfully be re-examined from the preceding viewpoint.[18]

Status consistency and mobility traps

In the recent sociological literature two varieties of status inconsistency have been investigated: positional and reputational. Positional inconsistency exists when a person or group has a high position on one status dimension, such as income, and a low position on another, such as education.[19] Reputational inconsistency exists when a person or group receives different degrees of status or honor from different segments of the community.[20] For example, a parvenu family of great visible wealth might be ranked at the pinnacle of local society by the working class but ranked considerably lower in the eyes of the local "upper uppers." Similarly a professional gambler might rank considerably higher by lower-class standards than by those of the middle class.

Most of the inconsistency research has been on the social and psychological effects of positional inconsistency and very little has been on reputational inconsistency, but the concept of the mobility trap is closely related to both.[21] If a status arrangement is characterized by mobility traps and structural discontinuities it will also have reputational inconsistencies, for, just as with the inconsistent person, the trapped person has a claim to high rank within his own stratum but finds this claim disapproved by members of other strata. The structural base for this form of status inconsistency can be traced to a tree-like opportunity system.

Positional inconsistency bears a more complex relation to the mobility trap. This type of inconsistency can exist only to the extent that there is independence or autonomy among status dimensions, such that a change in rank along one dimension does not necessarily cause or require changes along another. Status dimensions differ in their degrees of autonomy, or, to look at it from above rather than below, they differ in their "lifting power" to eventually raise a person along dimensions other than the one on which the original penetration was made. Max Weber, for example, pointed out that in the long run economic mobility would usually bring about "status" mobility, but that status mobility was less likely to bring about economic mobility.[22] If we consider the five dimensions of income, occupation, education, interaction level, and consumption style, one could argue that the lifting power, especially inter-generationally, is greatest with income and occupation, less with education, and least with interaction level and consumption style. Consumption style in particular seems to be the weakest mobility investment, and for many it is a sop which barely hides their resignation to the impossibility of more basic mobility.[23]

If the lifting power of a dimension, or of a specific line of activity within a dimension, is weak, then a commitment to this dimension or line is a mobility trap.

An investment in interaction contacts, such as joining an expensive club, or in consumption style, such as buying an overly expensive house—especially when these actions deepen the person's commitment to the culture of his stratum—will probably have weak returns on other dimensions. Similarly education can sometimes lead a person into an inconsistent situation, particularly when the training program or institution has low prestige or a declining market value. Of course even occupational and income achievements can sometimes be traps in the long run, but this is less common.

This discussion implies that the dynamics of positional inconsistency are crucial. If the inconsistency leads, over a period of time, to a new consistency at a higher level, there may be little stress for the person, for he may be experiencing the gradual consolidation of his overall status. If the passage of time does not bring a gradual consolidation of position, the person will sense that he is in a trap and may experience greater stress. Such attributes as the type of inconsistency, the length of time it has persisted, the person's age, and the presence of children should, accordingly, be related to the various "effects" of inconsistency. In any event positional inconsistency, just as reputational inconsistency, fits into a structural model such as we have proposed.

Mobility traps and politics

One of the special qualities of the United States is that, although there does not seem to be a great deal more occupational mobility than in other industrial countries, there is an unusually free amount of movement along the pure prestige dimensions of interaction and consumption. This may be one of the reasons why Americans believe that occupational mobility too is *far greater* than in other countries. This may also be the basis for the widespread sense of underlying social equality, even in the face of economic inequality, that Americans seem to feel.[24] Most working-class Americans can easily identify themselves as middle class if they choose to emphasize the dimensions of interaction and consumption.

The pure prestige dimensions though, having little "lifting power," are mobility traps, and, in the long run, give little more than an illusory form of mobility. Yet they may have the effect of draining off a great deal of discontent that might otherwise express itself in political radicalism. Once again we see that mobility traps can have moderating political effects.

Looking at the same question historically, the ethnic heterogeneity of the United States is often cited as a reason for the absence of a strong socialist party in American history, the assumption being that heterogeneity prevented communication and solidarity among the working class. But this diversity had another important effect. It permitted a great deal of internal mobility into ethnically protected positions in small business and the professions. In other words the working class was not only divided into discrete branches of the social structure; the branches were slanted upwards and mobile ethnics could advance to some extent without threatening those on higher limbs.[25]

I have been arguing that mobility traps and inconsistencies have moderating political effects, but some sociologists have found that inconsistent people, in the positional sense, are more politically extreme, either to the right or to the left, than consistent people are.[26] This seems to lead to the conclusion that inconsistency has the overall effect of political radicalization. Yet if we look at the whole system, as distinct from the individuals within it, the effect may still be conservative. To the people at the bottom of the system, who are all too consistent, the possibility of social ascent—even though it be only on one dimension, into an inconsistent posture—may give them a certain amount of hope which prevents them from becoming more radical. Those who do make these limited forms of ascent into mobility traps of some kind probably have a much more optimistic picture of the opportunity structure than they would have if they had remained at the bottom. Status inconsistency and mobility traps, then, may contribute to keeping the whole political system in the Democratic-Republican center, at the cost of pushing some inconsistents a bit to the right or left of the main line.

Conclusion

This paper has been a systematic attempt at concept formation and elaboration. We began by arguing that metaphors influence creativity by screening new ideas. Then we presented a new metaphor in the area of stratification and explored it as a source of ideas, first in the area of ethnic mobility and then in a variety of other problem areas. This led to the reformulation of several stratification concepts and the discovery of a few new hypotheses.

This kind of qualitative speculation seems especially called for in the area of stratification, for the existing networks of concepts tend to be centered around the conflict or consensus poles, and many of the most important realities lie in the middle.

NOTES

1. The importance of metaphor as a creative instrument in science has been discussed in Max Black, "Metaphor" and "Models and Archetypes" in his *Models and Metaphors,* Ithaca, N.Y.: Cornell University Press, 1962, pp. 25–47 and 219–243. The role of metaphor in sociology is evaluated in Maurice R. Stein, "The Poetic Metaphors of Sociology," in Maurice Stein and Arthur Vidich (eds.), *Sociology on Trial,* Englewood Cliffs, N.J.: Prentice-Hall, 1963, pp. 173–182.

2. We are ignoring a third metaphor which is of the greatest historical importance, but is now generally obsolete in industrialized countries. This is the notion of a social "organism" in which each person has his indispensable part to play and does not attempt to move to another part. A current metaphor which fills a somewhat similar purpose is the notion that people are laterally distributed in "all walks of life." This is invoked on national holidays and at other times when it is useful to deny the very existence of inequality.

3. The old question of whether social strata are continuous or discrete is an oversimplification resulting partly from the use of misleading metaphors.

4. Several of my colleagues who read this paper criticized the assertion that mobility usually requires a temporary retreat or loss of prestige. They urged instead that movement directly from one limb to another is the more common reality. I have not accepted this suggestion because I think it would limit the utility of the metaphor and blur the theoretical implications I will draw from it. My concern is more with finding usable concepts than with representational accuracy.

5. A disadvantage of linear mobility conceptions is that they cannot account for the overlap between blue and white collar occupations. The top of the blue collar limb is actually higher, at least in income, than the bottom of the white collar limb.

6. See James S. Coleman, *The Adolescent Society,* New York: The Free Press of Glencoe, 1961.

7. For a related point see Merton's discussion of the over-conforming bureaucrat in Robert K. Merton, *Social Theory and Social Structure,* revised and enlarged edition, Glencoe, Ill.: The Free Press, 1957, pp. 197–202.

8. In speaking of mobility as involving a choice I do not mean that anyone can achieve mobility merely by choosing to do so. The choice, rather, is in whether or not and in what way to *attempt* mobility. The chance of success is a resultant of the kind of choice and the location in the opportunity structure. Some locations are, of course, just about hopeless, regardless of choice and effort.

9. Howard S. Becker, "Notes on the Concept of Commitment," *American Journal of Sociology,* 66 (July, 1960), 32–40.

10. Jews have been somewhat of an exception in the United States, for they have been able to stay within their group while experiencing considerable mobility. Although the qualities of the Jewish limb have been favorable (high, nearly vertical, etc.), it has been, and in some ways still is, a limb. Kurt Lewin was referring especially to Jews trapped on the top of the limb in his discussion of "Self-Hatred among Jews," *Contemporary Jewish Record,* 4 (June, 1941), 219–232.

11. In feudal societies discontinuities between strata are normal and accepted, often with very little conflict. My discussion is limited to the United States and, perhaps, to similar industrial societies.

12. Merton, *op. cit.,* pp. 262–271.

13. In Part I of William Foote Whyte, *Street Corner Society,* Chicago: University of Chicago Press, 1964.

14. In European history a somewhat similar process of mobility from the bottom seems to have occurred in the development of capitalism and the middle class. Pirenne traces the origins of the middle class to the poorest and most rootless medieval people. To some extent this process continues, he argues, as successive changes in the forms of capitalism draw new waves of enterprising people from below. See Henri Pirenne, "Stages in the Social History of Capitalism," in Reinhard Bendix and Seymour Martin Lipset (eds.), *Class, Status and Power,* Glencoe, Ill.: The Free Press, 1953, pp. 501–517.

15. Much of this literature is reviewed in Bruno Bettelheim and Morris Janowitz, *Social Change and Prejudice,* New York: The Free Press of Glencoe, 1964; and in Harold L. Wilensky and Hugh Edwards, "The Skidder: Ideological Adjustments of Downward Mobile Workers," *American Sociological Review,* 24 (April, 1959), 215–231.

16. Robert J. Kleiner and Seymour Parker, "Goal-Striving, Social Status, and Mental Disorder: A Research Review," *American Sociological Review,* 28 (April, 1963), 189–203; Warren Breed, "Occupational Mobility and Suicide among White Males," *American Sociological Review,* 28 (April, 1963), 179–188; H. Warren Dunham, Patricia Phillips, and Barbara Srinivasan, "A Research Note on Diagnosed Mental Illness and Social Class," *American Sociological Review,* 31 (April, 1966), 223–27; Robert W. Hodge and Donald J. Treiman, "Occupational Mobility and Attitude Toward Negroes," *American Sociological Review,* 31 (February, 1966), 93–102.

17. Clark Kerr and Abraham J. Siegel, "The Interindustry Propensity to Strike—An International Comparison," in Clark Kerr, *Labor and Management in Industrial Society,* Garden City, N.Y.: Anchor Books, 1964, pp. 105–147.

18. It might be useful to classify industries, or "situses," according to how much mobility there is across the manual-nonmanual line. According to my line of reasoning, the more the internal mobility the less the structural discontinuity and the less the mobility stress. Another implication of the present perspective is that in countries with strong feudal remnants, such as France and West Germany, there should be more mobility stress than in countries without these remnants, such as the United States or Canada.

19. Much of the research on positional inconsistency is cited and briefly summarized in Gerhard Lenski, *Power and Privilege,* New York: McGraw-Hill, 1966, pp. 86–88 and 408–410.

20. Reputational inconsistency is not usually thought of as a form of status inconsistency, nor has it gone under the present name before, so it is somewhat arbitrary to decide what studies do or do not belong under this heading. One study that analyzes several forms of reputational inconsistency, though, is Gregory P. Stone and William H. Form, "Instabilities in Status: The Problem of Hierarchy in the Community Study of Status Arrangements," *American Sociological Review,* 18 (April, 1953), 149–162. A comparative study which treats "status consensus" (which amounts to reputational consistency) in three communities is David L. Westby, "Status Arrangements in Three Michigan Communities," unpublished Ph.D. thesis, Michigan State University, 1962.

21. I suppose that positional inconsistency has been favored by researchers because it avoids the tedious local evaluations and judgments that are necessary for reputational research. Yet positional research is not pursued without logical cost, for in all of this research, from Lenski's on, there is a serious theoretical weakness. This is the assumption that prestige standards are rigid hierarchies that submit to high-powered quantitative analysis. Specifically it is assumed

that widespread community or national agreement exists on (a) which prestige dimensions are most important, (b) whether they are equal in importance, (c) whether the values or scores on each dimension can be ranked, and (d) whether these ranks fall into interval scales. It may be that the margin of error in these assumptions is greater than the variation that is usually found in status consistency.

Also, the consensus assumption conflicts with the assumption that individuals can vary to any extent in their status profiles, from complete consistency to complete inconsistency. It would seem more plausible that as the number of inconsistent people increases, the consensus on prestige standards will decrease. A large number of inconsistent people will jar and loosen up the standards, with the result that their own inconsistency will decrease as standards lose their precision.

22. Max Weber, "Class, Status, Party," in Bendix and Lipset (eds.), *op. cit.,* pp. 63–75.

23. Ely Chinoy, *Automobile Workers and the American Dream,* Boston: Beacon Press, 1965, p. 126.

24. Comparative mobility rates are discussed in Lenski, *op. cit.,* pp. 410–417. "Ideological equalitarianism" in the United States is discussed in Seymour Martin Lipset and Reinhard Bendix, *Social Mobility in Industrial Society,* Berkeley and Los Angeles: University of California Press, 1960, pp. 76–81. Lipset and Bendix's notion of "equalitarianism of manners" is equivalent to my notion of interaction and consumption freedom, but I believe they make a more optimistic interpretation of it than I do.

25. The same protected market existed for Negro professionals and small businessmen in the South, although desegregation in the consumption sphere seems to be undercutting this protection. See James A. Geschwender, "Desegregation, the Educated Negro, and the Future of Social Protest in the South," *Sociological Inquiry,* 35 (Winter, 1965), 58–68.

26. This literature is reviewed and challenged on empirical grounds, however, in K. Dennis Kelly and William J. Chambliss, "Status Consistency and Political Attitudes," *American Sociological Review,* 31 (June, 1966), 375–382.

Race and Ethnicity

34. ASSIMILATION IN AMERICA: THEORY AND REALITY

MILTON M. GORDON

Norbert F. Wiley's article, the last to appear in the preceding section, provides an appropriate bridge between the American sociologist's concern with social stratification and differentiation on the basis of race and creed and color. As Wiley suggests, ethnicity is—and has long been—an important variable in status ascription.

In "Assimilation in America: Theory and Reality," Milton M. Gordon delves more deeply into the problem of ethnicity. Gordon presents three ideologies promulgated by the Founding Fathers and their descendants and by the immigrants and their spokesmen related to the nature of adapting varied ethnic groups to American life. The three theses are called "Anglo-conformity," "the melting pot," and "cultural pluralism." After tracing the historical background of these three points of view, Gordon offers his own analysis in which he suggests that while acculturation has taken place in large measure, the country has remained structurally pluralistic.

Milton M. Gordon is Professor of Sociology at the University of Massachusetts. He is the author of Social Class in American Sociology (*1958*) *and* Assimilation in American Life (*1964*).

Reprinted from *Daedalus,* **90** (1961), *Ethnic Groups in American Life,* 263–285, by permission of the author and the American Academy of Arts and Sciences, Brookline, Massachusetts.

Three ideologies or conceptual models have competed for attention on the American scene as explanations of the way in which a nation, in the beginning largely white, Anglo-Saxon, and Protestant, has absorbed over 41 million immigrants and their descendants from variegated sources and welded them into the contemporary American people. These ideologies are Anglo-conformity, the melting pot, and cultural pluralism. They have served at various times, and often simultaneously, as explanations of what has happened—descriptive models—and of what should happen—goal models. Not infrequently they have been used in such a fashion that it is difficult to tell which of these two usages the writer has had in mind. In fact, one of the more remarkable omissions in the history of American intellectual thought is the relative lack of close analytical attention given to the theory of immigrant adjustment in the United States by its social scientists.

The result has been that this field of discussion—an overridingly important one since it has significant implications for the more familiar problems of prejudice, discrimination, and majority-minority group relations generally—has been largely preempted by laymen, representatives of belles lettres, philosophers, and apologists of various persuasions. Even from these sources the amount of attention devoted to ideologies of assimilation is hardly extensive. Consequently, the work of improving intergroup relations in America is carried out by dedicated professional agencies and individuals who deal as best they can with day-to-day problems of discriminatory behavior, but who for the most part are unable to relate their efforts to an adequate conceptual apparatus. Such an apparatus would, at one and the same time, accurately describe the present structure of American society with respect to its ethnic groups (I shall use the term "ethnic group" to refer to any racial, religious, or national-origins collectivity), and allow for a considered formulation of

its assimilation or integration goals for the foreseeable future. One is reminded of Alice's distraught question in her travels in Wonderland: "Would you tell me, please, which way I ought to go from here?" "That depends a good deal," replied the Cat with irrefutable logic, "on where you want to get to."

The story of America's immigration can be quickly told for our present purposes. The white American population at the time of the Revolution was largely English and Protestant in origin, but had already absorbed substantial groups of Germans and Scotch-Irish and smaller contingents of Frenchmen, Dutchmen, Swedes, Swiss, South Irish, Poles, and a handful of migrants from other European nations. Catholics were represented in modest numbers, particularly in the middle colonies, and a small number of Jews were residents of the incipient nation. With the exception of the Quakers and a few missionaries, the colonists had generally treated the Indians and their cultures with contempt and hostility, driving them from the coastal plains and making the western frontier a bloody battleground where eternal vigilance was the price of survival.

Although the Negro at that time made up nearly one-fifth of the total population, his predominantly slave status, together with racial and cultural prejudice, barred him from serious consideration as an assimilable element of the society. And while many groups of European origin started out as determined ethnic enclaves, eventually, most historians believe, considerable ethnic intermixture within the white population took place. "People of different blood" [sic]—write two American historians about the colonial period, "English, Irish, German, Huguenot, Dutch, Swedish —mingled and intermarried with little thought of any difference." [1] In such a society, its people predominantly English, its white immigrants of other ethnic origins either English-speaking or derived largely from countries of northern and western Europe whose cultural divergences from the English were not great, and its dominant white population excluding by fiat the claims and considerations of welfare of the non-Caucasian minorities, the problem of assimilation understandably did not loom unduly large or complex.

The unfolding events of the next century and a half with increasing momentum dispelled the complacency which rested upon the relative simplicity of colonial and immediate post-Revolutionary conditions. The large-scale immigration to America of the famine-fleeing Irish, the Germans, and later the Scandinavians (along with additional Englishmen and other peoples of northern and western Europe) in the middle of the nineteenth century (the so-called "old immigration"), the emancipation of the Negro slaves and the problems created by post-Civil War reconstruction, the placing of the conquered Indian with his broken culture on government reservations, the arrival of the Oriental, first attracted by the discovery of gold and other opportunities in the West, and finally, beginning in the last quarter of the nineteenth century and continuing to the early 1920's, the swelling to proportions hitherto unimagined of the tide of immigration from the peasantries and "pales" of southern and eastern Europe —the Italians, Jews, and Slavs of the so-called "new immigration," fleeing the persecutions and industrial dislocations of the day—all these events constitute the background against which we may consider the rise of the theories of assimilation mentioned above. After a necessarily foreshortened description of each of these theories and their historical emergence, we shall suggest analytical distinctions designed to aid in clarifying the nature of the assimilation process, and then conclude by focusing on the American scene.

Anglo-Conformity

"Anglo-conformity" [2] is a broad term used to cover a variety of viewpoints about assimilation and immigration; they all assume the desirability of maintaining English institutions (as modified by the American Revolution), the English language, and English-oriented cultural patterns as dominant and standard in American life. However, bound up with this assumption are related attitudes. These may range from discredited notions about race and "Nordic" and "Aryan" racial superiority, together with the nativist political programs and exclusionist immigration policies which such notions entail, through an intermediate position of favoring immigration from northern and western Europe on amorphous, unreflective grounds ("They are more like us"), to a lack of opposition to any source of immigration, as long as these immigrants and their descendants duly adopt the standard Anglo-Saxon cultural patterns. There is by no means any necessary equation between Anglo-conformity and racist attitudes.

It is quite likely that Anglo-conformity in its more moderate aspects, however explicit its formulation, has been the most prevalent ideology of assimilation goals in America throughout the nation's history. As far back as colonial times, Benjamin Franklin recorded concern about the clannishness of the Germans in Pennsylvania, their slowness in learning English, and the establishment of their own native-language press.[3] Others of the founding fathers had similar reservations about large-scale immigration from Europe. In the context of their times they were unable to foresee the role such immigration was to play in creating the later greatness of the nation. They were not at all men of unthinking prejudices. The disestablishment of religion and the separation of church and state (so that no religious group—whether New England Congregationalists, Virginian Anglicans, or even all Protestants combined—could call upon the federal government for special favors or support, and so that man's religious conscience should be free) were cardinal points of the new national policy they fostered. "The Government of the United States," George Washington had written to the Jewish congregation of Newport during his first term as president, "gives to bigotry no sanction, to persecution no assistance."

Political differences with ancestral England had just been written in blood; but there is no reason to suppose that these men looked upon their fledgling country as an impartial melting pot for the merging of the various cultures of Europe, or as a new "nation of nations," or as anything but a society in which, with important political modifications, Anglo-Saxon speech and institutional forms would be standard. Indeed, their newly won victory for democracy and republicanism made them especially anxious that these still precarious fruits of revolution should not be threatened by a large influx of European peoples whose life experiences had accustomed them to the bonds of despotic monarchy. Thus, although they explicitly conceived of the new United States of America as a haven for those unfortunates of Europe who were persecuted and oppressed, they had characteristic reservations about the effects of too free a policy. "My opinion, with respect to immigration," Washington wrote to John Adams in 1794, "is that except of useful mechanics and some particular descriptions of men or professions, there is no need of encouragement, while the policy or advantage of its taking place in a body (I mean the settling of them in a body) may be much questioned; for, by so doing, they retain the language, habits and principles (good or bad) which they bring with them." [4] Thomas Jefferson, whose views on race and attitudes toward slavery were notably liberal and advanced for his time, had similar doubts concerning the effects of mass immigration on American institutions, while conceding that immigrants, "if they come of themselves . . . are entitled to all the rights of citizenship." [5]

The attitudes of Americans toward foreign immigration in the first three-quarters of the nineteenth century may correctly be described as ambiguous. On the one hand, immigrants were much desired, so as to swell the population and importance of states and territories, to man the farms of expanding prairie settlement, to work the mines, build the railroads and canals, and take their place in expanding industry. This was a period in which no federal legislation of any consequence prevented the entry of aliens, and such state legislation as existed attempted to bar on an individual basis only those who were likely to become a burden on the community, such as convicts and paupers. On the other hand, the arrival in an overwhelmingly Protestant society of large numbers of poverty-stricken Irish Catholics, who settled in groups in the slums of Eastern cities, roused dormant fears of "Popery" and Rome. Another source of anxiety was the substantial influx of Germans, who made their way to the cities and farms of the mid-West and whose different language, separate communal life, and freer ideas on temperance and sabbath observance brought them into conflict with the Anglo-Saxon bearers of the Puritan and Evangelical traditions. Fear of foreign "radicals" and suspicion of the economic demands of the occasionally aroused workingmen added fuel to the nativist fires. In their extreme form these fears resulted in the Native-American movement of the 1830's and 1840's and the "American" or "Know-Nothing" party of the 1850's, with their anti-Catholic campaigns and their demands for restrictive laws on naturalization procedures and for keeping the foreign-born out of political office. While these movements scored local political successes and their turbulences so rent the national social fabric that the patches are not yet entirely invisible, they failed to influence national legislative policy on immigration and immigrants; and their fulminations inevitably provoked the expected reactions from thoughtful observers.

The flood of newcomers to the westward expanding nation grew larger, reaching over one and two-thirds million between 1841 and 1850 and over two and one-half million in the decade before the Civil War. Throughout the entire period, quite apart from the excesses of the Know-Nothings, the predominant (though not exclusive) conception of what the ideal immigrant adjustment should be was probably summed up in a letter written in 1818 by John Quincy Adams, then Secretary of State, in answer to the inquiries of the Baron von Fürstenwaerther. If not the earliest, it is certainly the most elegant version of the sentiment, "If they don't like it here, they can go back where they came from." Adams declared: [6]

They [immigrants to America] come to a life of independence, but to a life of labor—and, if they cannot accommodate themselves to the character, moral, political and physical, of this country with all its compensating balances of good and evil, the Atlantic is always open to them to return to the land of their nativity and their fathers. To one thing they must make up their minds, or they will be disappointed in every expectation of happiness as Americans. They must cast off the European skin, never to resume it. They must look forward to their posterity rather than backward to their ancestors; they must be sure that whatever their own feelings may be, those of their children will cling to the prejudices of this country.

The events that followed the Civil War created their own ambiguities in attitude toward the immigrant. A nation undergoing wholesale industrial expansion and not yet finished with the march of westward settlement could make good use of the never faltering waves of newcomers. But sporadic bursts of labor unrest, attributed to foreign radicals, the growth of Catholic institutions and the rise of Catholics to municipal political power, and the continuing association of immigrant settlement with urban slums revived familiar fears. The first federal selective law restricting immigration was passed in 1882, and Chinese immigration was cut off in the same year. The most significant development of all, barely recognized at first, was the change in the source of European migrants. Beginning in the 1880's, the countries of southern and eastern Europe began to be represented in substantial numbers for the first time, and in the next decade immigrants from these sources became numerically dominant. Now the notes of a new, or at least hitherto unemphasized, chord from the nativist lyre began to sound—the ugly chord, or discord, of racism. Previously vague and romantic notions of Anglo-Saxon peoplehood, combined with general ethnocentrism, rudimentary wisps of genetics, selected tidbits of evolutionary theory, and naive assumptions from an early and crude imported anthropology produced the doctrine that the English, Germans, and others of the "old immigration" constituted a superior race of tall, blonde, blue-eyed "Nordics" or "Aryans," whereas the peoples of eastern and southern Europe made up the darker Alpines or Mediterraneans—both "inferior" breeds whose presence in America threatened, either by intermixture or supplementation, the traditional American stock and culture. The obvious corollary to this doctrine was to exclude the allegedly inferior breeds; but if the new type of immigrant could not be excluded, then everything must be done to instill Anglo-Saxon virtues in these benighted creatures. Thus, one educator writing in 1909 could state: [7]

These southern and eastern Europeans are of a very different type from the north Europeans who preceded them. Illiterate, docile, lacking in self-reliance and initiative, and not possessing the Anglo-Teutonic conceptions of law, order, and government, their coming has served to dilute tremendously our national stock, and to corrupt our civic life. . . . Everywhere these people tend to settle in groups or settlements, and to set up here their national manners, customs, and observances. Our task is to break up these groups or settlements, to assimilate and amalgamate these people as a part of our American race, and to implant in their children, so far as can be done, the Anglo-Saxon conception of righteousness, law and order, and popular government, and to awaken in them a reverence for our democratic institutions and for those things in our national life which we as a people hold to be of abiding worth.

Anglo-conformity received its fullest expression in the so-called Americanization movement which gripped the nation during World War I. While "Americanization" in its various stages had more than one emphasis, it was essentially a consciously articulated movement to strip the immigrant of his native culture and attachments and make him over into an American along Anglo-Saxon lines—all this to be accomplished with great rapidity. To use an image of a later day, it was an attempt at "pressure-cooking assimilation." It had prewar antecedents, but it was during the height of the world conflict that federal agencies, state governments, municipalities, and a host of private organizations joined in the effort to persuade the immigrant to learn English, take out naturalization papers, buy war bonds, forget his former origins and culture, and give himself over to patriotic hysteria.

After the war and the "Red scare" which followed, the excesses of the Americanization movement subsided. In its place, however, came the restriction of immigration through federal law. Foiled at first by presidential vetoes, and later by the failure of the 1917 literacy test to halt the immigrant tide, the proponents of restriction finally put through in the early 1920's a series of acts culminating in the well-known national-origins formula for immigrant quotas which went into effect in 1929. Whatever the merits of a quantitative limit on the number of immigrants to be admitted to the United States, the provisions of the formula, which discriminated sharply against the countries of southern and eastern Europe, in effect institutionalized the assumptions of the rightful dominance of Anglo-Saxon patterns in the land. Reaffirmed with only slight modifications in the McCarran-Walter Act of 1952, these laws, then, stand as a legal monument to the creed of Anglo-

conformity and a telling reminder that this ideological system still has numerous and powerful adherents on the American scene.

The Melting Pot

While Anglo-conformity in various guises has probably been the most prevalent ideology of assimilation in the American historical experience, a competing viewpoint with more generous and idealistic overtones has had adherents and exponents from the eighteenth century onward. Conditions in the virgin continent, it was clear, were modifying the institutions which the English colonists brought with them from the mother country. Arrivals from non-English homelands such as Germany, Sweden, and France were similarly exposed to this fresh environment. Was it not possible, then, to think of the evolving American society not as a slightly modified England but rather as a totally new blend, culturally and biologically, in which the stocks and folkways of Europe, figuratively speaking, were indiscriminately mixed in the political pot of the emerging nation and fused by the fires of American influence and interaction into a distinctly new type?

Such, at any rate, was the conception of the new society which motivated that eighteenth-century French-born writer and agriculturalist, J. Hector St. John Crèvecoeur, who, after many years of American residence, published his reflections and observations in *Letters from an American Farmer.*[8] Who, he asks, is the American?

He is either an European, or the descendant of an European, hence that strange mixture of blood, which you will find in no other country. I could point out to you a family whose grandfather was an Englishman, whose wife was Dutch, whose son married a French woman, and whose present four sons have now four wives of different nations. *He* is an American, who leaving behind him all his ancient prejudices and manners, receives new ones from the new mode of life he has embraced, the new government he obeys, and the new rank he holds. He becomes an American by being received in the broad lap of our great *Alma Mater*. Here individuals of all nations are melted into a new race of men, whose labours and posterity will one day cause great changes in the world.

Some observers have interpreted the open-door policy on immigration of the first three-quarters of the nineteenth century as reflecting an underlying faith in the effectiveness of the American melting pot, in the belief "that all could be absorbed and that all could contribute to an emerging national character." [9] No doubt many who observed with dismay the nativist agitation of the times felt as did Ralph Waldo Emerson that such conformity-demanding and immigrant-hating forces represented a perversion of the best American ideals. In 1845, Emerson wrote in his Journal: [10]

I hate the narrowness of the Native American Party. It is the dog in the manger. It is precisely opposite to all the dictates of love and magnanimity; and therefore, of course, opposite to true wisdom. . . . Man is the most composite of all creatures. . . . Well, as in the old burning of the Temple at Corinth, by the melting and intermixture of silver and gold and other metals a new compound more precious than any, called Corinthian brass, was formed; so in this continent,—asylum of all nations,—the energy of Irish, Germans, Swedes, Poles, and Cossacks, and all the European tribes,—of the Africans, and of the Polynesians,—will construct a new race, a new religion, a new state, a new literature, which will be as vigorous as the new Europe which came out of the smelting-pot of the Dark Ages, or that which earlier emerged from the Pelasgic and Etruscan barbarism. *Le Nature aime les croisements.*

Eventually, the melting-pot hypothesis found its way into historical scholarship and interpretation. While many American historians of the late nineteenth century, some fresh from graduate study at German universities, tended to adopt the view that American institutions derived in essence from Anglo-Saxon (and ultimately Teutonic) sources, others were not so sure.[11] One of these was Frederick Jackson Turner, a young historian from Wisconsin, not long emerged from his graduate training at Johns Hopkins. Turner presented a paper to the American Historical Association, meeting in Chicago in 1893. Called "The Significance of the Frontier in American History," this paper proved to be one of the most influential essays in the history of American scholarship, and its point of view, supported by Turner's subsequent writings and his teaching, pervaded the field of American historical interpretation for at least a generation. Turner's thesis was that the dominant influence in the shaping of American institutions and American democracy was not this nation's European heritage in any of its forms, nor the forces emanating from the eastern seaboard cities, but rather the experiences created by a moving and variegated western frontier. Among the many effects attributed to the frontier environment and the challenges it presented was that it acted as a solvent for the national heritages and the separatist tendencies of the many nationality groups which had joined the trek westward, including the Germans and Scotch-Irish of the eighteenth century and the Scandinavians and Germans of the nineteenth. "The frontier," asserted Turner, "promoted the formation of a composite nationality for the American people. . . . In the crucible of the frontier the immigrants were Americanized, liberated, and fused into a mixed race, English in neither nationality nor characteristics. The process has gone on from the early days to our own." And later, in an essay on the role of the Mississippi Valley, he refers to "the tide of foreign immigration which has risen so steadily that it has made a composite American people whose amalgamation is destined to produce a new national stock." [12]

Thus far, the proponents of the melting-pot idea had dealt largely with the diversity produced by the sizeable immigration from the countries of northern and western Europe alone—the "old immigration," consisting of peoples with cultures and physical appearance not greatly different from those of the Anglo-Saxon stock. Emerson, it is true, had impartially included Africans, Polynesians, and Cossacks in his conception of the mixture; but it was only in the last two decades of the nineteenth century that a large-scale influx of peoples from the countries of southern and eastern Europe imperatively posed the question of whether these uprooted newcomers who were crowding into the large cities of the nation and the industrial sector of the economy could also be successfully "melted." Would the "urban melting pot" work as well as the "frontier melting pot" of an essentially rural society was alleged to have done?

It remained for an English-Jewish writer with strong social convictions, moved by his observation of the role of the United States as a haven for the poor and oppressed of Europe, to give utterance to the broader view of the American melting pot in a way which attracted public attention. In 1908, Israel Zangwill's drama, *The Melting Pot,* was produced in this country and became a popular success. It is a play dominated by the dream of its protagonist, a young Russian-Jewish immigrant to America, a composer, whose goal is the completion of a vast "American" symphony which will express his deeply felt conception of his adopted country as a divinely appointed crucible in which all the ethnic divisions of mankind will divest themselves of their ancient animosities and differences and become fused into one group, signifying the brotherhood of man. In the process he falls in love with a beautiful and cultured Gentile girl. The play ends with the performance of the symphony and, after numerous vicissitudes and traditional family opposition from both sides, with the approaching marriage of David Quixano and his beloved. During the course of these developments, David, in the rhetoric of the time, delivers himself of such sentiments as these: [13]

America is God's crucible, the great Melting Pot where all the races of Europe are melting and re-forming! Here you stand, good folk, think I, when I see them at Ellis Island, here you stand in your fifty groups, with your fifty languages and histories, and your fifty blood hatreds and rivalries. But you won't be long like that, brothers, for these are the fires of God you've come to—these are the fires of God. A fig for your feuds and vendettas! Germans and Frenchmen, Irishmen and Englishmen, Jews and Russians—into the Crucible with you all! God is making the American.

Here we have a conception of a melting pot which admits of no exceptions or qualifications with regard to the ethnic stocks which will fuse in the great crucible. Englishmen, Germans, Frenchmen, Slavs, Greeks, Syrians, Jews, Gentiles, even the black and yellow races, were specifically mentioned in Zangwill's rhapsodic enumeration. And this pot patently was to boil in the great cities of America.

Thus around the turn of the century the melting-pot idea became embedded in the ideals of the age as one response to the immigrant receiving experience of the nation. Soon to be challenged by a new philosophy of group adjustment (to be discussed below) and always competing with the more pervasive adherence to Anglo-conformity, the melting-pot image, however, continued to draw a portion of the attention consciously directed toward this aspect of the American scene in the first half of the twentieth century. In the mid-1940's, a sociologist who had carried out an investigation of intermarriage trends in New Haven, Connecticut, described a revised conception of the melting process in that city and suggested a basic modification of the theory of that process. In New Haven, Ruby Jo Reeves Kennedy [14] reported from a study of intermarriages from 1870 to 1940 that there was a distinct tendency for the British-Americans, Germans, and Scandinavians to marry among themselves—that is, within a Protestant "pool"; for the Irish, Italians, and Poles to marry among themselves—a Catholic "pool"; and for the Jews to marry other Jews. In other words, intermarriage was taking place across lines of nationality background, but there was a strong tendency for it to stay confined within one or the other of the three major religious groups, Protestants, Catholics, and Jews. Thus, declared Mrs. Kennedy, the picture in New Haven resembled a "triple melting pot" based on religious divisions, rather than a "single melting pot." Her study indicated, she stated, that "while strict endogamy is loosening, religious endogamy is persisting and the future cleavages will be along religious lines rather than along nationality lines as in the past. If this is the case, then the traditional 'single-melting-pot' idea must be abandoned, and a new conception, which we term the 'triple-melting-pot' theory of American assimilation, will take its place as the true expression of what is happening to the various nationality groups in the United States." [15] The triple-melting-pot thesis was later taken up by the theologian, Will Herberg, and formed an important sociological frame of reference for his analysis of religious trends in American society, *Protestant-Catholic-Jew*.[16] But the triple-melting-pot hypothesis patently takes us into the realm of a society pluralistically conceived. We turn now to the rise of an ideology which attempts to justify such a conception.

Cultural Pluralism

Probably all the non-English immigrants who came to American shores in any significant numbers from colonial times onward—settling either in the forbidding wilderness, the lonely prairie, or in some accessible urban slum—created ethnic enclaves and looked forward to the preservation of at least some of their native cultural patterns. Such a development, natural as breathing, was supported by the later accretion of friends, relatives, and countrymen seeking out oases of familiarity in a strange land, by the desire of the settlers to rebuild (necessarily in miniature) a society in which they could communicate in the familiar tongue and maintain familiar institutions, and, finally, by the necessity to band together for mutual aid and mutual protection against the uncertainties of a strange and frequently hostile environment. This was as true of the "old" immigrants as of the "new." In fact, some of the liberal intellectuals who fled to America from an inhospitable political climate in Germany in the 1830's, 1840's, and 1850's looked forward to the creation of an all-German state within the union, or, even more hopefully, to the eventual formation of a separate German nation, as soon as the expected dissolution of the union under the impact of the slavery controversy should have taken place.[17] Oscar Handlin, writing of the sons of Erin in mid-nineteenth-century Boston, recent refugees from famine and economic degradation in their homeland, points out: "Unable to participate in the normal associational affairs of the community, the Irish felt obliged to erect a society within a society, to act together in their own way. In every contact therefore the group, acting apart from other sections of the community, became intensely aware of its peculiar and exclusive identity.[18] Thus cultural pluralism was a fact in American society before it became a theory—a theory with explicit relevance for the nation as a whole, and articulated and discussed in the English-speaking circles of American intellectual life.

Eventually, the cultural enclaves of the Germans (and the later arriving Scandinavians) were to decline in scope and significance as succeeding generations of their native-born attended public schools, left the farms and villages to strike out as individuals for the Americanizing city, and generally became subject to the influences of a standardizing industrial civilization. The German-American community, too, was struck a powerful blow by the accumulated passions generated by World

War I—a blow from which it never fully recovered. The Irish were to be the dominant and pervasive element in the gradual emergence of a pan-Catholic group in America, but these developments would reveal themselves only in the twentieth century. In the meantime, in the last two decades of the nineteenth, the influx of immigrants from southern and eastern Europe had begun. These groups were all the more sociologically visible because the closing of the frontier, the occupational demands of an expanding industrial economy, and their own poverty made it inevitable that they would remain in the urban areas of the nation. In the swirling fires of controversy and the steadier flame of experience created by these new events, the ideology of cultural pluralism as a philosophy for the nation was forged.

The first manifestations of an ideological counterattack against draconic Americanization came not from the beleaguered newcomers (who were, after all, more concerned with survival than with theories of adjustment), but from those idealistic members of the middle class who, in the decade or so before the turn of the century, had followed the example of their English predecessors and "settled" in the slums to "learn to sup sorrow with the poor." [19] Immediately, these workers in the "settlement houses" were forced to come to grips with the realities of immigrant life and adjustment. Not all reacted in the same way, but on the whole the settlements developed an approach to the immigrant which was sympathetic to his native cultural heritage and to his newly created ethnic institutions.[20] For one thing, their workers, necessarily in intimate contact with the lives of these often pathetic and bewildered newcomers and their daily problems, could see how unfortunate were the effects of those forces which impelled rapid Americanization in their impact on the immigrants' children, who not infrequently became alienated from their parents and the restraining influence of family authority. Were not their

parents ignorant and uneducated "Hunkies," "Sheenies," or "Dagoes," as that limited portion of the American environment in which they moved defined the matter? Ethnic "self-hatred" with its debilitating psychological consequences, family disorganization, and juvenile delinquency, were not unusual results of this state of affairs. Furthermore, the immigrants themselves were adversely affected by the incessant attacks on their culture, their language, their institutions, their very conception of themselves. How were they to maintain their self-respect when all that they knew, felt, and dreamed, beyond their sheer capacity for manual labor—in other words, all that they *were*—was despised or scoffed at in America? And—unkindest cut of all—their own children had begun to adopt the contemptuous attitude of the "Americans." Jane Addams relates in a moving chapter of her *Twenty Years at Hull House* how, after coming to have some conception of the extent and depth of these problems, she created at the settlement a "Labor Museum," in which the immigrant women of the various nationalities crowded together in the slums of Chicago could illustrate their native methods of spinning and weaving, and in which the relation of these earlier techniques to contemporary factory methods could be graphically shown. For the first time these peasant women were made to feel by some part of their American environment that they possessed valuable and interesting skills—that they too had something to offer—and for the first time, the daughters of these women who, after a long day's work at their dank "needletrade" sweatshops, came to Hull House to observe, began to appreciate the fact that their mothers, too, had a "culture," that this culture possessed its own merit, and that it was related to their own contemporary lives. How aptly Jane Addams concludes her chapter with the hope that "our American citizenship might be built without disturbing these foundations which were laid of old time." [21]

This appreciative view of the immigrant's cultural heritage and of its distinctive usefulness both to himself and his adopted country received additional sustenance from another source: those intellectual currents of the day which, however overborne by their currently more powerful opposites, emphasized liberalism, internationalism, and tolerance. From time to time, an occasional educator or publicist protested the demands of the "Americanizers," arguing that the immigrant, too, had an ancient and honorable culture, and that this culture had much to offer an America whose character and destiny were still in the process of formation, an America which must serve as an example of the harmonious cooperation of various heritages to a world inflamed by nationalism and war. In 1916 John Dewey, Norman Hapgood, and the young literary critic, Randolph Bourne, published articles or addresses elaborating various aspects of this theme.

The classic statement of the cultural pluralist position, however, had been made over a year before. Early in 1915 there appeared in the pages of *The Nation* two articles under the title "Democracy *versus* the Melting-Pot." Their author was Horace Kallen, a Harvard-educated philosopher with a concern for the application of philosophy to societal affairs, and, as an American Jew, himself derivative of an ethnic background which was subject to the contemporary pressures for dissolution implicit in the "Americanization," or Anglo-conformity, and the melting-pot theories. In these articles Kallen vigorously rejected the usefulness of these theories as models of what was actually transpiring in American life or as ideals for the future. Rather he was impressed by the way in which the various ethnic groups in America were coincident with particular areas and regions, and with the tendency for each group to preserve its own language, religion, communal institutions, and ancestral culture. All the while, he pointed out, the immigrant has been

learning to speak English as the language of general communication, and has participated in the over-all economic and political life of the nation. These developments in which "the United States are in the process of becoming a federal state not merely as a union of geographical and administrative unities, but also as a cooperation of cultural diversities, as a federation or commonwealth of national cultures," [22] the author argued, far from constituting a violation of historic American political principles, as the "Americanizers" claimed, actually represented the inevitable consequences of democratic ideals, since individuals are implicated in groups, and since democracy for the individual must by extension also mean democracy for his group.

The processes just described, however, as Kallen develops his argument, are far from having been thoroughly realized. They are menaced by "Americanization" programs, assumptions of Anglo-Saxon superiority, and misguided attempts to promote "racial" amalgamation. Thus America stands at a kind of cultural crossroads. It can attempt to impose by force an artificial, Anglo-Saxon oriented uniformity on its peoples, or it can consciously allow and encourage its ethnic groups to develop democratically, each emphasizing its particular cultural heritage. If the latter course is followed, as Kallen puts it at the close of his essay, then,[23]

The outlines of a possible great and truly democratic commonwealth become discernible. Its form would be that of the federal republic; its substance a democracy of nationalities, cooperating voluntarily and autonomously through common institutions in the enterprise of self-realization through the perfection of men according to their kind. The common language of the commonwealth, the language of its great tradition, would be English, but each nationality would have for its emotional and involuntary life its own peculiar dialect or speech, its own individual and inevitable esthetic and intellectual forms. The political and economic life of the commonwealth is a single unit and serves as the foundation and background for the realization of the distinctive individuality of each *natio* that composes it and of the pooling of these in a harmony above them all. Thus "American civilization" may come to mean the perfection of the cooperative harmonies of "European civilization"—the waste, the squalor and the distress of Europe being eliminated—a multiplicity in a unity, an orchestration of mankind.

Within the next decade Kallen published more essays dealing with the theme of American multiple-group life, later collected in a volume.[24] In the introductory note to this book he used for the first time the term "cultural pluralism" to refer to his position. These essays reflect both his increasingly sharp rejection of the onslaughts on the immigrant and his culture which the coming of World War I and its attendant fears, the "Red scare," the projection of themes of racial superiority, the continued exploitation of the newcomers, and the rise of the Ku Klux Klan all served to increase in intensity, and also his emphasis on cultural pluralism as the democratic antidote to these ills. He has since published other essays elaborating or annotating the theme of cultural pluralism. Thus, for at least forty-five years, most of them spent teaching at The New School for Social Research, Kallen has been acknowledged as the originator and leading philosophical exponent of the idea of cultural pluralism.

In the late 1930s and early 1940s the late Louis Adamic, the Yugoslav immigrant who had become an American writer, took up the theme of America's multicultural heritage and the role of these groups in forging the country's national character. Borrowing Walt Whitman's phrase, he described America as "a nation of nations," and while his ultimate goal was closer to the melting-pot idea than to cultural pluralism, he saw the immediate task as that of making America conscious of what it owed to all its ethnic groups, not just to the Anglo-Saxons. The children and grandchildren of immigrants of non-English origins, he was convinced,

must be taught to be proud of the cultural heritage of their ancestral ethnic group and of its role in building the American nation; otherwise, they would not lose their sense of ethnic inferiority and the feeling of rootlessness he claimed to find in them.

Thus, in the twentieth century, particularly since World War II, "cultural pluralism" has become a concept which has worked its way into the vocabulary and imagery of specialists in intergroup relations and leaders of ethnic communal groups. In view of this new pluralistic emphasis, some writers now prefer to speak of the "integration" of immigrants rather than of their "assimilation."[25] However, with a few exceptions,[26] no close analytical attention has been given either by social scientists or practitioners of intergroup relations to the meaning of cultural pluralism, its nature and relevance for a modern industrialized society, and its implications for problems of prejudice and discrimination—a point to which we referred at the outset of this discussion.

Conclusions

In the remaining pages I can make only a few analytical comments which I shall apply in context to the American scene, historical and current. My view of the American situation will not be documented here, but may be considered as a series of hypotheses in which I shall attempt to outline the American assimilation process.

First of all, it must be realized that "assimilation" is a blanket term which in reality covers a multitude of subprocesses. The most crucial distinction is one often ignored—the distinction between what I have elsewhere called "behavioral assimilation" and "structural assimilation."[27] The first refers to the absorption of the cultural behavior patterns of the "host" society. (At the same time, there is frequently some modification of the cultural patterns of the immigrant-receiving country, as well.) There is a special term for this process of cultural modification or "behavioral assimilation"—namely, "acculturation." "Structural assimilation," on the other hand, refers to the entrance of the immigrants and their descendants into the social cliques, organizations, institutional activities, and general civic life of the receiving society. If this process takes place on a large enough scale, then a high frequency of intermarriage must result. A further distinction must be made between, on the one hand, those activities of the general civic life which involve earning a living, carrying out political responsibilities, and engaging in the instrumental affairs of the larger community, and, on the other hand, activities which create personal friendship patterns, frequent home intervisiting, communal worship, and communal recreation. The first type usually develops so-called "secondary relationships," which tend to be relatively impersonal and segmental; the latter type leads to "primary relationships," which are warm, intimate, and personal.

With these various distinctions in mind, we may then proceed.

Built on the base of the original immigrant "colony" but frequently extending into the life of successive generations, the characteristic ethnic group experience is this: within the ethnic group there develops a network of organizations and informal social relationships which permits and encourages the members of the ethnic group to remain within the confines of the group for all of their primary relationships and some of their secondary relationships throughout all the stages of the life cycle. From the cradle in the sectarian hospital to the child's play group, the social clique in high school, the fraternity and religious center in college, the dating group within which he searches for a spouse, the marriage partner, the neighborhood of his residence, the church affiliation and the church clubs, the men's and the women's social and service organizations, the adult clique of "marrieds," the vacation resort, and then, as the age cycle nears completion, the rest home for the elderly and, finally, the sectarian cemetery —in all these activities and relationships which are close to the core of personality and selfhood—the member of the ethnic group may if he wishes follow a path which never takes him across the boundaries of his ethnic structural network.

The picture is made more complex by the existence of social class divisions which cut across ethnic group lines just as they do those of the white Protestant population in America. As each ethnic group which has been here for the requisite time has developed second, third, or in some cases, succeeding generations, it has produced a college-educated group which composes an upper middle class (and sometimes upper class, as well) segment of the larger groups. Such class divisions tend to restrict primary group relations even further, for although the ethnic-group member feels a general sense of identification with all the bearers of his ethnic heritage, he feels comfortable in intimate social relations only with those who also share his own class background or attainment.

In short, my point is that, while *behavioral assimilation* or acculturation has taken place in America to a considerable degree, *structural assimilation,* with some important exceptions has not been extensive.[28] The exceptions are of two types. The first brings us back to the "triple-melting-pot" thesis of Ruby Jo Reeves Kennedy and Will Herberg. The "nationality" ethnic groups have tended to merge within each of the three major religious groups. This has been particularly true of the Protestant and Jewish communities. Those descendants of the "old" immigration of the nineteenth century, who were Protestant (many of the Germans and all the Scandinavians), have in considerable part gradually merged into the white Protestant "subsociety." Jews of Sephardic,

German, and Eastern-European origins have similarly tended to come together in their communal life. The process of absorbing the various Catholic nationalities, such as the Italians, Poles, and French Canadians, into an American Catholic community hitherto dominated by the Irish has begun, although I do not believe that it is by any means close to completion. Racial and quasi-racial groups such as the Negroes, Indians, Mexican-Americans, and Puerto Ricans still retain their separate sociological structures. The outcome of all this in contemporary American life is thus pluralism—but it is more than "triple" and it is more accurately described as *structural pluralism* than as cultural pluralism, although some of the latter also remains.

My second exception refers to the social structures which implicate intellectuals. There is no space to develop the issue here, but I would argue that there is a social world or subsociety of the intellectuals in America in which true structural intermixture among persons of various ethnic backgrounds, including the religious, has markedly taken place.

My final point deals with the reasons for these developments. If structural assimilation has been retarded in America by religious and racial lines, we must ask why. The answer lies in the attitudes of both the majority and the minority groups and in the way these attitudes have interacted. A saying of the current day is, "It takes two to tango." To apply the analogy, there is no good reason to believe that white Protestant America has ever extended a firm and cordial invitation to its minorities to dance. Furthermore, the attitudes of the minority-group members themselves on the matter have been divided and ambiguous. Particularly for the minority religious groups, there is a certain logic in ethnic communality, since there is a commitment to the perpetuation of the religious ideology and since structural intermixture leads to intermarriage and the possible loss to the group of the

intermarried family. Let us, then, examine the situation serially for various types of minorities.

With regard to the immigrant, in his characteristic numbers and socioeconomic background, structural assimilation was out of the question. He did not want it, and he had a positive need for the comfort of his own communal institutions. The native American, moreover, whatever the implications of his public pronouncements, had no intention of opening up his primary group life to entrance by these hordes of alien newcomers. The situation was a functionally complementary standoff.

The second generation found a much more complex situation. Many believed they heard the siren call of welcome to the social cliques, clubs, and institutions of white Protestant America. After all, it was simply a matter of learning American ways, was it not? Had they not grown up as Americans, and were they not culturally different from their parents, the "greenhorns"? Or perhaps an especially eager one reasoned (like the Jewish protagonist of Myron Kaufmann's novel, *Remember Me To God,* aspiring to membership in the prestigious club system of Harvard undergraduate social life), "If only I can go the last few steps in Ivy League manners and behavior, they will surely recognize that I am one of them and take me in." But, alas, Brooks Brothers suit notwithstanding, the doors of the fraternity house, the city men's club, and the country club were slammed in the face of the immigrant's offspring. That invitation was not really there in the first place; or, to the extent it was, in Joshua Fishman's phrase, it was a " 'look me over but don't touch me' invitation to the American minority group child." [29] And so the rebuffed one returned to the homelier but dependable comfort of the communal institutions of his ancestral group. There he found his fellows of the same generation who had never stirred from the home fires. Some of these had been too timid to

35. RESIDENTIAL SEGREGATION AND ETHNIC ASSIMILATION

STANLEY LIEBERSON

Milton M. Gordon's article specified and summarized three paths to assimilation in America frequently cited by historians of immigration. In reappraising immigration history with the eye of the sociologist, Gordon concluded that "Anglo-conformity" was never an unqualified success (despite the fact that many new Americans adapted themselves to the general ways of the dominant society), that the concept of the "melting pot" was more a myth than a reality, and that "cultural pluralism" was a fact of social life long before it ever became a theory of adjustment.

In the selection presented below, Stanley Lieberson examines the patterns of residential segregation of a number of specific immigrant groups in each of ten cities in an effort to ascertain the impact of ecological factors upon other aspects of ethnic assimilation. His sources of data are the United States census reports of 1930 and 1950.

Lieberson's analysis reveals that spatial isolation is an important variable in determining the extensiveness of assimilation as measured by such crude indices as the ability to speak English, the proclivity to become citizens, the tendency to move upward in the occupation hierarchy, and the extensiveness of intermarriage. In Gordon's terms, Lieberson's first three indices would be measures of "cultural assimilation," the fourth, a measure of "structural assimilation."

Stanley Lieberson is Professor of Sociology at the University of Wisconsin. He is the author of Ethnic Patterns in American Cities *(1963) and coauthor of* Metropolis and Region in Transition *(1969).*

The importance human ecologists attribute to the spatial distributions of human populations and social institutions is not only widely known but, if anything, misunderstood by many of their fellow social scientists. The ecologist's interest in space is often taken as evidence either of a preoccupation with the "subsocial" or of an esthetic satisfaction derived from locating social events in terms of gradients, "natural areas," multicolored maps, and the like. That this monolithic pursuit is to be found in the works of human ecologists—both present and past—ignores the

far less constricted rationale which may be offered for this concern.

For example, during the heyday of European immigration to the United States, the propensity of immigrants to first locate in ghettoes and their later movements out of these areas of first settlement were frequently utilized as a measure or index of an ethnic group's assimilation. Studies of such diverse urban centers as Chicago,[1] Durban,[2] Montreal,[3] Paris,[4] and the major cities of Australia[5] attest to the widespread existence of residential segregation and its usefulness as an indicator of ethnic

stray; others were ethnic ideologists committed to the group's survival; still others had never really believed in the authenticity of the siren call or were simply too passive to do more than go along the familiar way. All could now join in the task that was well within the realm of the sociologically possible—the build-up of social institutions and organizations within the ethnic enclave, manned increasingly by members of the second generation and suitably separated by social class.

Those who had for a time ventured out gingerly or confidently, as the case might be, had been lured by the vision of an "American" social structure that was somehow larger than all subgroups and was ethnically neutral. Were they, too, not Americans? But they found to their dismay that at the primary group level a neutral American social structure was a mirage. What at a distance seemed to be a quasi-public edifice flying only the all-inclusive flag of American nationality turned out on closer inspection to be the clubhouse of a particular ethnic group— the white Anglo-Saxon Protestants, its operation shot through with the premises and expectations of its parental ethnicity. In these terms, the desirability of whatever invitation was grudgingly extended to those of other ethnic backgrounds could only become a considerably attenuated one.

With the racial minorities, there was not even the pretense of an invitation. Negroes, to take the most salient example, have for the most part been determinedly barred from the cliques, social clubs, and churches of white America. Consequently, with due allowance for internal class differences, they have constructed their own network of organizations and institutions, their own "social world." There are now many vested interests served by the pres-

ervation of this separate communal life, and doubtless many Negroes are psychologically comfortable in it, even though at the same time they keenly desire that discrimination in such areas as employment, education, housing, and public accommodations be eliminated. However, the ideological attachment of Negroes to their communal separation is not conspicuous. Their sense of identification with ancestral African national cultures is virtually nonexistent, although Pan-Africanism engages the interest of some intellectuals and although "black nationalist" and "black racist" fringe groups have recently made an appearance at the other end of the communal spectrum. As for their religion, they are either Protestant or Catholic (overwhelmingly the former). Thus, there are no "logical" ideological reasons for their separate communality; dual social structures are created solely by the dynamics of prejudice and discrimination, rather than being reinforced by the ideological commitments of the minority itself.

Structural assimilation, then, has turned out to be the rock on which the ships of Anglo-conformity and the melting pot have foundered. To understand that behavioral assimilation (or acculturation) without massive structural intermingling in primary relationships has been the dominant motif in the American experience of creating and developing a nation out of diverse peoples is to comprehend the most essential sociological fact of that experience. It is against the background of "structural pluralism" that strategies of strengthening intergroup harmony, reducing ethnic discrimination and prejudice, and maintaining the rights of both those who stay within and those who venture beyond their ethnic boundaries must be thoughtfully devised.

Reprinted from *Social Forces,* **40** (1961), 52–57, by permission of the author and the University of North Carolina Press.

NOTES

1. Allan Nevins and Henry Steele Commager, *America: The Story of a Free People,* Boston: Little, Brown, 1942, p. 58.

2. The phrase is the Coles's. See Stewart G. Cole and Mildred Wiese Cole, *Minorities and the American Promise,* New York: Harper, 1954, chap. 6.

3. Maurice R. Davie, *World Immigration,* New York: Macmillan, 1936, p. 36, and (cited therein) "Letter of Benjamin Franklin to Peter Collinson, 9th May, 1753, on the condition and character of the Germans in Pennsylvania," in *The Works of Benjamin Franklin, with notes and a life of the author,* by Jared Sparks (Boston, 1828), vol. 7, pp. 71–73.

4. *The Writings of George Washington,* collected and edited by W. C. Ford, New York: G. P. Putnam's Sons, 1889, vol. 12, p. 489.

5. Thomas Jefferson, "Notes on Virginia, Query 8;" in *The Writings of Thomas Jefferson,* ed. A. E. Bergh, Washington: The Thomas Jefferson Memorial Association, 1907, vol. 2, p. 121.

6. *Niles' Weekly Register,* vol. 18, 29 April 1820, pp. 157–158; also, Marcus L. Hansen, *The Atlantic Migration, 1607–1860,* pp. 96–97.

7. Ellwood P. Cubberly, *Changing Conceptions of Education,* Boston: Houghton Mifflin, 1909, pp. 15–16.

8. J. Hector St. John Crèvecoeur, *Letters from an American Farmer,* New York: Albert and Charles Boni, 1925; reprinted from the 1st edn., London, 1782, pp. 54–55.

9. Oscar Handlin (ed.), *Immigration as a Factor in American History,* Englewood Cliffs, N.J.: Prentice-Hall, 1959, p. 146.

10. Quoted by Stuart P. Sherman in his Introduction to *Essays and Poems of Emerson,* New York: Harcourt, Brace, 1921, p. xxxiv.

11. See Edward N. Saveth, *American Historians and European Immigrants, 1875–1925,* New York: Columbia University Press, 1948.

12. Frederick Jackson Turner, *The Frontier in American History,* New York: Henry Holt, 1920, pp. 22–23, 190.

13. Israel Zangwill, *The Melting Pot,* New York: Macmillan, 1909, p. 37.

14. Ruby Jo Reeves Kennedy, "Single or Triple Melting-Pot? Intermarriage Trends in New Haven, 1870–1940," *American Journal of Sociology,* 49 (1944), 331–339. See also her "Single or Triple Melting-Pot? Intermarriage in New Haven, 1870–1950," *ibid.,* 58 (1952), 56–59.

15. —— "Single or Triple Melting-Pot? . . . 1870–1940," p. 332 (author's italics omitted).

16. Will Herberg, *Protestant-Catholic-Jew,* Garden City: Doubleday, 1955.

17. Nathan Glazer, "Ethnic Groups in America: From National Culture to Ideology," in Morroe Berger, Theodore Abel, and Charles H. Page (eds.), *Freedom and Control in Modern Society,* New York: D. Van Nostrand, 1954, p. 161; Marcus Lee Hansen, *The Immigrant in American History,* Cambridge: Harvard University Press, 1940, pp. 129–140; John A. Hawgood, *The Tragedy of German-America,* New York: Putnam's, 1940, *passim.*

18. Oscar Handlin, *Boston's Immigrants,* revised edition, Cambridge: Harvard University Press, 1959, p. 176.

19. From a letter (1883) by Samuel A. Barnett; quoted in Arthur C. Holden, *The Settlement Idea,* New York: Macmillan, 1922, p. 12.

20. Jane Addams, *Twenty Years at Hull House,* New York: Macmillan, 1914, pp. 231–258; Arthur C. Holden, *op. cit.,* pp. 109–131, 182–189; John Higham, *Strangers in the Land,* New Brunswick: Rutgers University Press, 1955, p. 236.

21. Jane Addams, *op. cit.,* p. 258.

22. Horace M. Kallen, "Democracy *versus* the Melting-Pot," *The Nation,* 18 and 25 February 1915; reprinted in his *Culture and Democracy in the United States,* New York: Boni and Liveright, 1924; the quotation is on p. 116.

23. Kallen, *Culture and Democracy . . .,* p. 124.

24. Kallen, *op. cit.*

25. See W. D. Borrie *et al., The Cultural Integration of Immigrants* (a survey based on the papers and proceedings of the UNESCO Conference in Havana, April 1956), Paris, UNESCO, 1959; and William S. Bernard, "The Integration of Immigrants in the United States" (mimeographed), one of the papers for this conference.

26. See particularly Milton M. Gordon, "Social Structure and Goals in Group Relations"; and Nathan Glazer, "Ethnic Groups in America; From National Culture to Ideology," both articles in Berger, Abel, and Page, *op. cit.;* S. N. Eisenstadt, *The Absorption of Immigrants,* London: Routledge and Kegan Paul, 1954; and W. D. Borrie *et al., op. cit.*

27. Milton M. Gordon, "Social Structure and Goals in Group Relations," p. 151.

28. See Erich Rosenthal, "Acculturation without Assimilation?" *American Journal of Sociology,* 66 (1960), 275–288.

29. Joshua A. Fishman, "Childhood Indoctrination for Minority-Group Membership and the Quest for Minority-Group Biculturism in America," in Oscar Handlin, ed., *Group Life in America,* Cambridge: Harvard University Press.

assimilation. Indeed, during the twenties and thirties, ethnic residential patterns were a major research interest of sociologists and others.

However, another dimension to the residential segregation of ethnic and racial groups is frequently overlooked. That is, not only can the residential patterns of ethnic groups be viewed as a significant element in the study of their assimilation and as an indicator of other elements of assimilation but, further, residential segregation has an effect on other aspects of ethnic assimilation. Hawley has hypothesized that physical isolation is a necessary condition for the maintenance of subordinate ethnic group status and, further, that "Redistribution of a minority group in the same territorial pattern as that of the majority group results in a dissipation of subordinate status and an assimilation of the subjugated group into the social structure." [6] Hawley's reasoning is based on the dual effect of residential segregation, that is, both as a factor accenting the differences between groups by heightening their visibility and, secondly, as a factor enabling the population to keep its peculiar traits and group structure. Evidence exists to support both of Hawley's contentions. For example, after finding that the greater the number of Negroes arrested in a district in Philadelphia, the greater the overestimation by policemen of the Negro rate in the district, Kephart has concluded that visibility increases at a more rapid rate than sheer number.[7] And Lieberson has shown close associations exist between the spatial distributions of ethnic populations in Chicago and the location of ethnic physicians' offices.[8]

This paper examines the impact of ethnic residential patterns on other aspects of their assimilation. Roughly 10 ethnic groups in each of 10 United States cities in 1930 were studied in terms of the relationships between their spatial distribution and citizenship, intermarriage, and ability to speak English. In addition, for a more limited number of groups and cities, the impact of residential segregation on occupational composition of ethnic groups was considered for 1950.

Data and Methods

With one exception, published and unpublished United States census reports for 1930 and 1950 were the sources for all analyses made below. Because census tract data were available for only a limited number of cities in 1930, the 10 cities under investigation were not selected randomly.[9] Since the 1930 census gives an unusually extensive array of data on various aspects of immigrant and second generation behavior, it was all the more necessary to include cities for which segregation indexes could be computed. The larger immigrant and second generation groups were studied in each city.

Residential segregation was computed by using indexes of dissimilarity in a manner similar to that utilized in several recent studies.[10] With the exception of Chicago where Community Areas were used, segregation of immigrant groups from the native white population of each city was determined on the basis of their degree of similarity in their intracity census tract distributions. Indexes of dissimilarity were also used to compare the degree of similarity in occupational composition between groups. These indexes range from 0 (complete similarity) to 100 (complete dissimilarity).

Kendall's rank order correlation, *tau,* is the only measure of association used in this study. This type of nonparametric correlation is of particular value in this study since it permits the use of partial correlations.

Findings

Citizenship status

Naturalization is by no means a perfect indicator of an individual's assimilation. Thus some naturalized immigrants later

Table 1.   *Rank Order Correlations (tau) Between Naturalization Status, Year of Arrival, and Segregation of Selected Immigrant Groups from Native Whites, 1930*

City	Percent of Foreign Born Who Are Aliens and:		Segregation Foreign Born from Native Whites and:	
	Segregation Foreign Born from Native Whites (1)	*Median Year of Arrival* (2)	*Median Year of Arrival* (3)	*Percent of Foreign Born Who Are Aliens (Holding Median Year of Arrival Constant)* (4)
Boston	.47	.62	.18	.46
Buffalo	.29	.64	.29	.14
Chicago	.42	.73	.24	.37
Cincinnati	.44	.76	.42	.17
Cleveland	.64	.78	.69	.22
Columbus	.24	.71	.31	.03
Philadelphia	.42	.58	.47	.20
Pittsburgh	.56	.44	.47	.45
St. Louis	.56	.49	.56	.40
Syracuse	.50	.86	.50	.16

Note: Citizenship data for foreign born groups in Columbus, Cincinnati, and Syracuse based on all immigrants 21 years of age and older in 1930. Citizenship data for other cities based on immigrants of all ages except those not reporting their status.

return to their country of origin whereas not all immigrants remaining in the United States for 20 or more years adopt American citizenship. Nevertheless, it seems reasonable to use citizenship status "as an indication that the assimilative process has proceeded to a moderate extent at least. The fact of naturalization is indicative of an attitude towards the country very different from that of the immigrant who shows no desire to take out naturalization papers." [11]

In 1930, there was a persistent association in all 10 cities between the variations between immigrant groups in their segregation from native whites and their propensity to remain aliens, that is, groups highly segregated from native whites also have proportionately large numbers of adult males who are aliens (Table 1, column 1). These high rank order correlations between segregation and percent alien indicate nothing more than that the spatial distributions of immigrant groups

may be used as an indicator of at least one additional dimension of assimilation. In order to infer that the residential segregation of immigrant groups affects the propensities of immigrants to change their citizenship, it is necessary to consider whether this association would exist independently of other major factors influencing the acquisition of American citizenship such as length of residence in the United States and ability to read and write in the English language.

Since literacy in English was not a prerequisite to obtaining first papers,[12] we have at least partially eliminated this factor by considering only the proportions of immigrants who have remained aliens, that is, who had obtained neither first nor second papers. However, if we view acquisition of American citizenship as largely a unilateral and irreversible process, then it is reasonable to assume that length of residence in the United States would be a major influence, that is, immigrants living in the country for a longer period would be less likely to be aliens than more recent migrants. Consequently, the positive associations between immigrant group differences in length of residence and their proportions alien (Table 1, column 2) are not surprising. Since length of residence is also associated with the degree of immigrant segregation (column 3), the fact that the partial *tau* between segregation and citizenship status remains positive (although lower) in all 10 cities (column 4) indicates that immigrant residential segregation decreases the proportion of a group taking at least minimal steps towards obtaining United States citizenship. Thus the magnitude of an immigrant group's isolation from the native white population appears to play a role in influencing the extent to which members of the group are prone to give up ties with their country of birth.

Intermarriage

In terms of theories with probability types of analysis, the examination of simply the number of exogamous and endogamous marriages for members of different ethnic groups is an inadequate indicator of group differentials in the propensity to intermarry. That is, the larger a group is in a given city, the greater the proportion of intragroup marriages we would expect for the group even if members of all groups chose their mates randomly.[13] Due to the limited data available, a rather crude indicator of intermarriage must be used; namely, the percent of the second generation whose parents are of mixed nativity, that is, one parent foreign born and one parent native. The second generation of a given nationality was categorized by the Census Bureau into those who had both parents born in a foreign country and those who had one foreign parent and one native parent. As was noted in an earlier study using similar data, "It should not be overlooked that in many cases the native parent is a second-generation member of the same stock as the foreign parent, but the census data do not permit us to distinguish such cases from those involving intermarriage in a stricter sense."[14] It should also be added that we have no information about the number of cases in which there was intermarriage between persons who were born in different foreign countries and that all of the intermarriage material is based on the nativity classifications of offspring, that is, the second generation. Differential fertility and migration, to name but two factors, tend to reduce the usefulness of such data.

Nevertheless, the relationship between segregation from native whites and inter-

Table 2. *Rank Order Correlations (tau) Between Residential Segregation and Intermarriage, 1930*

City	Foreign Born Segregation from Native Whites and Percent of Second Generation with Both Parents Foreign Born
Boston	.60
Buffalo	.69
Chicago	.73
Cincinnati	.53
Cleveland	.78
Columbus	.71
Philadelphia	.67
Pittsburgh	.78
St. Louis	.64
Syracuse	.83

marriage (as measured by the crude indicator discussed above) is a very strong one. In each city, the proportion of the second generation having "mixed" parents is inversely related to the magnitude of the foreign born group's segregation from the native white population (Table 2). And, regardless of methodological shortcomings, these results are consistent with the assumption that residential propinquity is a factor in choice of mate.[15] Thus the more segregated a foreign born group, the more likely marriages are to occur between members of the same group.

Ability to speak English

Turning to the problem of language spoken by immigrants, one would expect to find an interaction between ability to speak English and segregation from native whites. Assuming that all native whites are able to speak English but no other language, then the larger the proportion of a given immigrant group able to speak English, the smaller the proportion of the immigrant group who would be hampered or handicapped by language differences in their location near native whites. Such would also be the case for native whites if we continue our somewhat arbitrary assumption that they all speak English but no other additional language. From this point of view, ability to speak English can be used as an independent variable in considering the fluctuations between immigrant groups in their segregation from native whites in a city. On the other hand, one could easily enough reverse the line of reasoning and assume that isolated foreign born groups would have less reason and opportunity to learn English than a group widely dispersed among the native white population. Thus, in the latter case, ability to speak English would be the dependent variable and immigrant segregation from native whites the independent variable. At any rate, not only would we expect an interaction between the magnitude of an immigrant group's segregation from native whites and their ability to speak English but, further, it would be necessary to take into account the effect of length of residence in the United States on the ability

Table 3. *Rank Order Correlations (tau) Between Ability to Speak English, Year of Arrival, and Segregation of Selected Immigrant Groups from Native Whites, 1930*

City	Percent of Foreign Born Able to Speak English and:		Segregation Foreign Born from Native Whites and:	
	Segregation Foreign Born from Native Whites (1)	*Median Year of Arrival* (2)	*Median Year of Arrival* (3)	*Ability to Speak English (Holding Median Year of Arrival Constant)* (4)
Boston	.71	.42	.18	.71
Buffalo	.53	.00	.29	.55
Chicago	.44	.44	.24	.38
Cincinnati	.29	.47	.42	.11
Cleveland	.40	.49	.69	.10
Columbus	.40	.40	.31	.32
Philadelphia	.84	.49	.47	.79
Pittsburgh	.49	.44	.47	.35
St. Louis	.51	.47	.56	.34
Syracuse	.64	.75	.50	.47

of immigrants to speak English. That is, length of residence would presumably affect the ability of immigrants to speak English.

The *tau* correlations presented in Table 3 indicate that ability to speak English and segregation are correlated in the direction expected, that is, the more highly segregated an immigrant group is from native whites, the larger the proportion unable to speak English (column 1). Similarly, median length of residence for the immigrant groups in each city is positively related to their ability to speak English (column 2). There is but one exception, Buffalo, where the correlation is nil. Column 3 indicates the correlations considered earlier which show some relationship between length of residence and degree of segregation. Taking into account the findings that both segregation and ability to speak English are in part functions of length of residence in the United States, the partial *tau* correlations between segregation and ability to speak English are computed (column 4). Although these partial correlations are generally lower than the correlations found without taking into account length of residence (compare columns 1 and 4), they are nevertheless all positive and indicate an association between ability to speak English and segregation from native whites even after length of residence is taken into account.

Occupational composition

Although the use of ethnic occupational composition as an indicator of assimilation is a moot procedure, there is little doubt that the nature of an ethnic group's participation in the economy of a city is an extremely significant dimension of its adaptation to the new society. Hawley has suggested that residential segregation—regardless of its causes—"is a restriction of opportunity; it hampers the flow of knowledge and experience and thus impedes diversification of interests and occupations." [16] One would therefore expect the occupational composition of highly segregated ethnic groups to be more sharply differentiated from native whites than the occupational composition of those groups less spatially isolated from the native white population. This association is found in four of the five cities for which both occupational and residential data were computed. That is, with the exception of Boston, immigrant occupational segregation from native whites varies with the magnitude of their residential segregation from the native whites in their city (Table 4, column 2).

Table 4. *Rank Order Correlations (tau) Between Residential Segregation of Selected Foreign Born Groups from Native Whites and Foreign Born Occupational Segregation from Native Whites; Deviation of Second Generation Males, Ages 25–44, from "Expected" Occupational Composition, 1950*

City *	Number of Groups (1)	Occupational and Residential Segregation (2)	Deviation from Expected Occupational Composition and Residential Segregation (3)
Boston	7	−.05	.14
Chicago	9	.50	.50
Cleveland	8	.29	.36
Philadelphia	7	.52	.24
Pittsburgh	8	.64	.29

* *Occupational data based on Standard Metropolitan Areas; residential data based on central cities.*

Not withstanding the importance of these descriptive associations, the critical problem involves determining whether the magnitude of residential segregation influences the occupational composition of ethnic groups. Clearly, there are a number of general social forces operating to influence an individual's choice of occupation, for example, sex, educational attainment, father's occupation, age, and the like. If ethnic groups differ in these attributes, then we would expect the groups to vary in their degree of occupational similarity to that of the native white population. The influence of segregation on one such general societal pattern is considered below.

Intergenerational occupational mobility

It is fairly evident that father's occupation influences the occupations his sons select. For example, one would hardly expect the sons of laborers to have the same occupational distribution as the sons of professionals in a community. Using unpublished data gathered by Gladys L. Palmer for 1950,[17] male intergenerational occupational mobility rates were determined on the basis of data for four combined cities; Chicago, Los Angeles, Philadelphia, and San Francisco. This intergenerational mo-

bility table yielded rates that were largely in the direction one would expect. For example, 29 percent of the sons of professional workers were professionals themselves, whereas only 4 percent of the sons of laborers were professionals. By contrast, 3 percent of the sons of professionals were laborers, whereas 10 percent of the sons of laborers were themselves laborers.[18]

By applying these rates to the occupational composition of each group of older foreign born males in a city, the "expected" occupational distribution of each second generation group of younger males was obtained. Assuming that second generation males between the ages of 25 and 44 in 1950 were the sons of immigrant males of the same nationality who were at least 45 years old in 1950 in a given city and, further, barring questions of differential fertility, mortality, and migration, it is possible to compare the actual occupational composition of second generation males with the composition expected on the basis of the society's intergenerational occupational mobility rates.

Despite the admittedly arbitrary nature of the assumptions, the results in Table 5 indicate that for a number of groups a fairly good prediction of the occupational

Table 5. *Indexes of Dissimilarity Between the Actual Occupational Distribution of Selected Groups of Second Generation Males (25 to 44 Years of Age) and the Occupational Distribution Expected on the Basis of Intergenerational Mobility Patterns in Several Large United States Cities, 1950*

Groups	Boston	Chicago *	Cleveland	Philadelphia *	Pittsburgh
England and Wales	5.04	5.78	11.76	11.68	12.68
Ireland	13.64	12.26	8.28	8.98	11.63
Norway	—	10.01	—	—	—
Sweden	15.42	13.72	—	—	—
Germany	9.70	8.66	10.34	12.54	14.45
Poland	8.82	13.71	15.54	16.14	20.35
Czechoslovakia	—	9.30	13.42	—	20.51
Austria	—	8.51	11.98	7.28	19.69
Russia	25.22	23.79	19.04	22.61	14.66
Italy	7.68	8.99	5.75	9.07	10.43

* Indexes of dissimilarity adjusted for the group's estimated proportion of the total male population in the four cities for which generational mobility patterns were obtained. These adjustments led to minor changes and did not affect the groups' rank order in either Chicago or Philadelphia.

composition of second generation males could have been made simply on the basis of the general social pattern of intergenerational mobility. That is, knowledge of the occupations of the fathers of second generation males combined with the general intergenerational occupational mobility patterns yields predictions of the occupational composition of second generation members that is fairly close to their actual occupational distributions. But, further, the magnitudes of the deviations in Table 5 are related to the degree of residential segregation of the foreign born groups from native whites in 1950. The correlations shown in column 3 of Table 4 indicate a persistent pattern in which the more segregated an immigrant group, the greater its deviation from the general intergenerational occupational mobility patterns that exist in our society.

Summary and Conclusion

The magnitude of an immigrant group's residential isolation from the native white population in a city influences other dimensions of the group's assimilation. Highly segregated groups are less apt to become citizens or speak English; and these associations hold after differences between groups in their length of residence are taken into account. In addition, the degree of intermarriage is influenced by an immigrant group's residential segregation. That is, keeping in mind that an admittedly crude indicator was used, groups highly segregated residentially tend to have low rates of intermarriage. Finally, applying intergenerational mobility tables to the occupational patterns of second generation groups in five metropolises for which such data were available, it was found that highly segregated first generation groups were more apt to have second generation members deviate from the general pattern of intergenerational occupational choice.

These results may be viewed in two closely related contexts. First, the differential residential segregation of ethnic groups in American cities is an important factor in the assimilation of ethnic groups. Segregation is not only a significant dimension to assimilation but, further, the magnitude of a group's segregation appears to influence other aspects of the group's assimilation. In this respect, support is offered for Hawley's hypothesis that residential dispersion is a basic prerequisite for ethnic assimilation.

Secondly, the results of this inquiry may be used in calling to the reader's attention the fact that examination of the spatial distributions of human populations or social institutions is not merely a convenient tool or indicator for research purposes—as important as this may be—but is, additionally, a potentially significant factor in interpreting and predicting differences in social behavior.

NOTES

1. Otis Dudley Duncan and Stanley Lieberson, "Ethnic Segregation and Assimilation," *American Journal of Sociology,* 64 (1959), 364–374.

2. Leo Kuper, Hilstan Watts, and Ronald Davies, *Durban: A Study in Racial Ecology,* London: Jonathan Cape, 1958.

3. Eva R. Younge, "Population Movements and the Assimilation of Alien Groups in Canada," *Canadian Journal of Economics and Political Science,* 10 (1944), 372–380.

4. Robert Gessain and Madeleine Doré, "Facteurs Comparés d'assimilation chez des Russes et des Arméniens," *Population,* I (1946), 99–116.

5. Jerzy Zubrzycki, "Ethnic Segregation in Australian Cities," paper read at International Population Conference, Vienna, 1959.

6. Amos H. Hawley, "Dispersion Versus Segregation: Apropos of a Solution of Race Problems," *Papers of the Michigan Academy of Science, Arts, and Letters,* 30 (1944), 674.

See, also, Royal Institute of International Affairs, *Nationalism,* London: Oxford University Press, 1939, pp. 281–283.

7. William M. Kephart, "Negro Visibility," *American Sociological Review,* 19 (1954), 462–467.

8. Stanley Lieberson, "Ethnic Groups and the Practice of Medicine," *American Sociological Review,* 23 (1958), 542–549.

9. For a list of cities for which such data were gathered in 1930, see Howard Whipple Green and Leon E. Truesdell, *Census Tracts in American Cities (Census Tract Manual),* revised edition, Washington: United States Department of Commerce, Bureau of the Census, 1937.

10. Otis Dudley Duncan and Beverly Duncan, "Residential Distribution and Occupational Stratification," *American Journal of Sociology,* 60 (1955), 493–503; Duncan and Lieberson, *op. cit.;* Kuper, Watts, and Davies, *op. cit.*

11. W. Burton Hurd, "Racial Origins and Nativity of the Canadian People," in Dominion Bureau of Statistics, *Seventh Census of Canada, 1931,* Vol. 13, *Monographs,* Ottawa: Edmond Cloutier, 1942, p. 662.

12. Bureau of the Census, *Fifteenth Census of the United States: 1930, Population,* Vol. 2, Washington, D.C.: Government Printing Office, 1933, p. 401.

13. Franco Savorgnan, "Matrimonial Selection and the Amalgamation of Heterogeneous Groups," *Population Studies,* supplement (March, 1950), pp. 59–67.

14. Duncan and Lieberson, *op. cit.,* p. 370.

15. See, for example, Marvin R. Koller, "Residential and Occupational Propinquity," in Robert F. Winch and Robert McGinnis (eds.), *Marriage and the Family,* New York: Henry Holt, 1953, pp. 429–434.

16. Hawley, *op. cit.,* p. 672.

17. For a description of the study, see Gladys L. Palmer, *Labor Mobility in Six Cities,* New York: Social Science Research Council, 1954.

18. For the complete table, see Stanley Lieberson, "Comparative Ethnic Segregation and Assimilation," Ph. D. dissertation, University of Chicago, 1960, p. 255.

36. STRANGERS IN THEIR MIDST: SMALL-TOWN JEWS AND THEIR NEIGHBORS

PETER I. ROSE

In Beyond the Melting Pot, *Nathan Glazer and Daniel Patrick Moynihan flatly state that "the point about the melting pot is that it did not happen—at least not in New York, and* mutatis mutandis, *in those parts of America which resemble New York." Stanley Lieberson's article gives empirical evidence to indicate the fact that members of ethnic minorities do, indeed, tend to congregate into their own enclaves in our large cities. But what is the situation when a member of a minority group ventures into the hinterlands and settles in a small town? How does the "stranger" in the midst of alien territory adapt to community life? Where does he fit in the social structure? And how is he received?*

The study discussed below is one of the few attempts to investigate the relationship between a selected group of outsiders who chose to settle in small, rural communities, and their "hosts." The attitudes and behavior of both small-town Jews and their Christian neighbors are examined.

Peter I. Rose is Professor and Chairman of the Department of Sociology and Anthropology at Smith College and a Visiting Professor at Yale. He is author of They and We *(1964),* The Subject is Race *(1968), contributing editor of* The Ghetto and Beyond: Essays on Jewish Life in America *(1969), and editor of the two volume anthology,* Americans from Africa *(1970).*

For many years social scientists and historians have been trying to piece together a composite portrait of American Judaism. Owing to their predominant pattern of city residence, research has been focused on the urban dwelling Jews, and the Jews of the United States have been characterized as a metropolitan people. There is, however, a scattered minority of American Jews living in little hamlets and rural villages who do not fully fit this urban image. Such people do not reside in old style ghettoes, in ethnic neighborhoods, or in modern homogeneous suburbs. Unlike their urban coreligionists, they are not members of on-going Jewish communities. They are strangers in alien territory.

Critical examination of Jewish life in the small community would seem to be a logical extension of research in the study of American Judaism and the nature of Jewish-Gentile relations. Yet, while the literature offers a wealth of information about the urban Jew in America, there is a dearth of published material about his "country cousin." And what there is is limited to sketchy life histories, journalistic descriptions, and anecdotal recollections of the experiences of individuals who have lived in, visited, or passed through little villages, appearing in such publications as *Midstream, Commentary,* and *Congress Weekly.*[1]

In an attempt to add to the general

Reprinted from *The Jewish Journal of Sociology* (England), **3** (1961), 174–191, by permission of the author and the World Jewish Congress.

literature on Jewish life on the American scene, to assess Jewish-Gentile relations in this neglected setting, and to re-examine the ubiquitous concept of "marginal man," an extensive study of the small-town Jews of New York State was conducted in 1958.[2] Because the small-town Jew is so often cast in the role of being an ambassador of "his people" to the Gentiles, a parallel study was simultaneously carried out with non-Jewish small-towners also living in upstate New York.

Data were gathered to seek answers to several questions. To what extent do group traditions persist in cases of relative isolation? Does indentification wane when unsupported by fellow members of one's own group? How intensive are relationships between the stranger and the world in which he has chosen to live? What kinds of adjustments does he have to make? And, finally, to what extent does interpersonal contact with an isolated minority member influence the stereotypic conceptions and misconceptions held by the majority group members about him?

The Research Design

Investigation was confined to one particular area of the country: "rural" New York State. Operationally, "rural communities" and "small-town Jews" were defined as follows:

> Rural communities are those communities with fewer than 10,000 permanent residents, in non-metropolitan counties of New York State, excluding all towns in the Catskill mountain region, in Westchester county, and on Long Island.

> Small-town Jews are persons identifying themselves as being Jewish living in "rural communities" having 10 or fewer Jewish families.

The first of the two studies was an attempt to document and analyze the background, beliefs, and behavior of small-town Jews and to study and record their attitudes relating to the communities where they reside. We were particularly anxious to explore the areas of religiosity,

community satisfaction, associations, and patterns of socialization.

Respondents were located through initial contact with twenty individuals who were known to the writer; each lived in a small town in one of twenty different counties. These persons provided the names of all the Jews they knew who fit the criteria established for designating "small-town Jews." These persons, in turn, supplied additional names. This technique, called "pyramiding," provided 180 names in two weeks.

Of the 180 names twenty were randomly selected; and these individuals and their families, together with the original key informants, were personally interviewed in the Spring of 1958. The 160 in the remaining group were mailed detailed questionnaires which asked a number of questions about origins, family life, satisfaction with small-town living, religious beliefs and practices, organizational affiliations, and attitudes about their relative isolation.

In *every* instance—whether in the interview setting or in responding to the survey—respondents were told that research was being conducted on Jews living in small towns and that *their* help was needed to tell *their* story accurately. In no cases did those to be personally interviewed refuse to cooperate; and in the case of the mail survey, 80 per cent responded.[3]

The second study was designed to gather information on the impressions and attitudes of small-town community leaders about themselves and their images and attitudes about minority groups. Data were collected on the relationship between generalized prejudices and attitudes toward Jews, Negroes, and "foreigners"; the extent to which isolated Jewish persons might influence stereotypes; and the nature of interpersonal contact and socialization between Gentiles and Jews in rural communities.

The names of community leaders were obtained by writing to the mayor or clerk of each village selected and asking that a form designating 25 statuses of leadership —in business, the professions, in government and politics, in education and social service, and in agriculture—be filled out with the appropriate names and returned.

Twenty towns were included in this second survey. All had fewer than 5,000 residents. Ten towns had from one to three Jewish families; the remaining group had none.

In all, 315 questionnaires which complemented those sent to Jewish participants were mailed. With two follow-up appeals a total of 60 per cent were returned.[4]

Jewish Life in the Rural Community

DEALERS AND DOCTORS   Almost to a man the Jews of New York's rural areas are outsiders and not native sons. Most are urban-emigrants who settled in small towns after having spent the early part of their lives in American or European cities. Only 4 per cent were born in the communities where they now live. Of the remaining majority half were born in one of the large American metropolitan centers and 12 per cent in middle-sized cities in the United States. Thirty per cent were born in Europe, many of them refugees from Nazi-dominated Germany and Austria.

How did these urban Jews happen to settle in such hamlets? Two-thirds came for business reasons. These are, in the main, second generation East European immigrants. Many began their careers as traveling salesmen and peddlers who settled down and started a little general store in one of the towns along the circuit. Here they remained and here they prospered.

In addition to these "dealers," the other major group are refugee physicians who fled to America only to find it difficult to establish practices in urban areas. A large number of such doctors were placed in small towns by refugee agencies or professional groups.

Besides these two major groups, there are several lawyers, teachers, insurance brokers, cattle dealers, and farmers to be found within the sample group.

When asked to place themselves into the upper, upper middle, lower middle, or working class, 74 per cent marked "upper middle." Only three respondents felt they were "working class": two teachers and one tenant farmer. It was from the ranks of the professional people that the greatest percentage of "upper class" self-ratings came. The high self-evaluation of socio-economic status is reflected in the relatively high incomes of the small-town Jews. In response to the question "Roughly, what was the total income for your family last year?" 30 per cent said their income exceeded $20,000, 37 per cent gave $10,-000–$20,000, 30 per cent $5,000–$10,000, and only 3 per cent indicated that they made less than $5,000 per annum.

Owing to the large proportion of professional Jews in the sample (36 per cent), it is not surprising to find a high level of education. Seventy per cent of those questioned hold at least a Bachelor of Arts degree or its European equivalent. The small-town Jews indicated, however, that only 11 per cent of their parents had college diplomas and 56 per cent said that their parents had gone to the eighth grade or less. As for their own children, nine out of ten parents in the sample indicated that one or more of their children would (or did) obtain at least a college degree.

When asked about their political affiliations 27 per cent said they consider themselves Republicans "in most political matters"; 29 per cent are Democrats and the rest marked "independent." However, it is interesting to note that a number of "Republicans" wrote in the margin of the questionnaire saying that they were "registered Republicans whose loyalty lies in the Democratic camp."

Finally, respondents were asked the following question: "Basically, do you consider yourself more a rural person or more an urban person?" Two-thirds of the group said "urban."

ONCE A JEW. . . . Eighty-six per cent of the small-town Jews placed themselves in some "Jewish" category: Orthodox, Conservative or Reform. *All* expressed some feeling of religious and/or cultural identity with Judaism. Those who said they did not fit into any of the three categories are not apostates as their response to this particular query might appear to suggest. Rather they tended to qualify their answers with statements like: "I'm a liberal Jew," "My family are ethical Jews," or "We're Jews, that's all."

Three-fourths said they belonged to some religious congregation. At the same time almost all persons said they "rarely" or "never" attend religious services since the synagogue to which they belong is too far away. (Estimates ranged from 15 to 100 miles.)

While they are too isolated to establish some form of Jewish communal existence, many keep traditional observances at home. For example, over half celebrate the Passover holidays, 25 per cent never serve bacon or ham, and 15 per cent maintain strictly kosher homes importing meat from distant cities. The attempt to maintain the traditions of the faith is found in both the "immigrant" and "refugee" groups. The latter, however, is less likely to display Jewish and Israeli artifacts in the home.

The deep-seated sense of Jewish-identification is evident in the following random excerpts from several interviews:

I came to this community from New York. There I was raised in a real ghetto. All my friends and associates were Jews. I went to *heder,* to *shul,* etc., like everybody else. This was our way of life. Although I wanted to get out of the city and away from the ghetto, I never wanted to forget I was a Jew. This is my fate and I try to live up to it in every way.

Another respondent phrased it this way:

Most people like us are city-folk living in rural areas. While our homes are here, our roots are somewhere else. . . . We bring the past with us when we go into upstate communities like this. Part of this past is our religion. We see ourselves as Jews and so does the community. . . .

All told, most small-town Jews maintain some affective connection with their religion even when they leave the geographic boundaries of the urban Jewish community.

A housewife summed up the expressions of many when she said:

We're not what one might call observant Jews. Yet there are certain traditions we like to keep. We have a *mezuzah* in the doorway and a *menorah* on the mantle. We celebrate some of the holidays like the High Holy Days and Passover. We light the *Shabbas* candles and things like that. And, I must say I like a good piece of *gefilte* fish when I can get it. Yet we eat pork, work on Saturday . . . why sometimes I even go to Midnight Mass with my friends.

"Irrespective of whether you follow religious practices or attend synagogue, do you consider yourself a religious person?" Each person answered this question by placing himself somewhere along a continuum of "very religious" to "not religious at all." Five per cent considered themselves "very religious," while 62 per cent felt that they were "moderately" so. Thirty-six per cent said "somewhat religious" and 7 per cent said they were "not religious at all."

A strikingly high correlation appeared when one compares the degree to which a person considers himself religious with the extent to which he practices religious observances, and with the nature of affiliation, that is, whether Orthodox, Conservative, or Reform. Taking these three items together we constructed the Religiosity Scale which allowed us to simplify analysis by using this single measure of "traditional" religiousness. Respondents were broken into three groups: high, medium, and low on religiosity.

In communities having several Jewish families the presence of co-religionists tends to reinforce religious identity and to

Table 1.   *Religiosity and the Number of Jews*

Religiosity	Number of Jewish Families in Town			
	1	*2*	*3–5*	*6–10*
	%	%	%	%
Low	66	62	59	42
Medium	27	32	26	26
High	7	6	15	32
	100	100	100	100
	(31)	(21)	(44)	(24)

support religious practices. Table 1 graphically illustrates the fact that in towns with more Jews, religiosity is higher among Jewish respondents.

In addition to this demographic factor it was found that religiosity is correlated with several background factors. Those highest in socio-economic status (by self-rating and income) are lowest in religiosity. In relation to occupation, those in the medical arts (mainly of the refugee group) are most apt to be low in this expression of religiousness, while those in agriculture tend to be the highest. This was borne out in the interviews. We spoke to the daughter of an immigrant from Russia, a man who became a cattle-dealer in a small upstate community where he raised his family. She related:

Our religion was very important to us. We sang Hebrew songs and spoke Yiddish in the house. I couldn't speak English until I first went to school. . . . To my father the family was the core of Jewish life and so we learned about Jews and our religion through discussions at home, through books, through stories. We were always very Jewish.

And a Jewish farmer had this to say:

It's funny, but though we're really out of touch with Jews we're the ones who try to keep up the traditions. . . . We think of ourselves as more Orthodox than anything. You know, the Gentile farmers around us are pretty religious too. If you can't go to church, then you have to bring religion into the home.

Furthermore, we found that small-town Jews who are low in religiosity are more apt to see themselves as more "urban" than "rural" even though these very people live, most often, in the tiniest hamlets. And those low in religiosity tend to feel Gentile members of the community consider them "different from" rather than "typical of" most Jews while those highly religious stress the reverse; they feel non-Jews think they are typical of Jewish people.

Although respondents were asked the difficult question of telling how they felt others saw them, it seems that they answered mainly in terms of their own self-images. Among those who said they felt they were viewed as "different" the following kinds of reasons were given: "don't conform to stereotypes," "better assimilated," "differ in physical features," "gentler and less crude," "quieter." Most of the adjectives were related to personal demeanor. Moreover, this group felt that Gentiles considered them as "unique" Jews and suggested that they were more likely to be seen as exceptions to commonly held beliefs.

Those who felt they were seen as "typical" tended to give quite opposite reasons; reasons which were related to positive stereotypic images. "I'm wealthy and well-educated," "I still maintain the traditions and practices of Judaism," "have a Jewish name." In other words, these people felt they were viewed as recognizably Jewish, and most expressed the belief that their behavior was, for Gentiles, typical of Jews.

AMBASSADORS TO THE GENTILES Being strangers in a Gentile world, many respondents appear to be more conscious of being Jewish than do their urban cousins who live in the centers of ethnic communities. In one form or other *every* respondent indicated that there are times when he is called upon to represent *the Jews.* Here, as several stated, they are "ambassadors to the *goyim.*" Most often this occurs when interfaith functions are held in the community. There the local priest and minister are accompanied by the Jewish merchant to "give balance to the program."

Frequently the Jew serves as a "representative of his people" in less formal settings. He is called upon to give "the Jewish point of view" or to explain why Jews do one thing and not another. When the townsfolk turn to the Jews for information, the respondents related that they often feel a deep sense of responsibility and of inadequacy.

For example, one man told me:

You know, we're curiosities around town. The people always heard about Jews but never met one. Then we appeared. Real live Jews. After some hesitancy they began to ask us all kinds of questions. . . . Often I wished I could answer all of them. . . .

A housewife allowed:

My children have been asked to explain about *Chanukah,* to tell the story of Moses, to explain what the *Mogen David* is. They wanted to know and my kids were the likely ones to ask.

And a merchant had this to say:

"I can't understand it. As kids we learned that the Jews killed Christ. Tell me, [respondent's name]," he says to me, "is it true?" As a Jew, and the only one this guy ever knew personally, I'm supposed to have all the answers.

FRIENDS AMONG NEIGHBORS   In small towns Jews find that there are few limitations on formal and informal social participation and interaction. All but 17 per cent indicated that they were members of some mixed organization. Over 45 per cent said they belonged to professional, business, and social groups. In addition, one-third are members of fraternal orders like the Masons or Elks.

When asked which organization (national or local) gave them the most satisfaction, almost every respondent listed some local (thereby non-Jewish) group. A druggist had this to say:

I think I've been a member of every damn organization in this town. From member of the volunteer firemen to president of the school board. Discrimination? Not in any organizations, that's for sure.

And the owner of a small chain of department stores said:

This is my community. These are my people in many more ways than Jews are. After all, our neighbors are friendly, all the organizations accept us, so we make friends here. This is home. When I join an organization they know they're taking in a Jew but it doesn't make any difference. . . . I've been President of Rotary, on the Chamber of Commerce, a member of the Masonic Lodge, and Secretary of the Rod and Gun Club.

This reflects the attitudes of most people interviewed.

We asked questions about discrimination against Jews. Eighty-seven per cent said they could not think of any community organizations they would not wish to join because of antisemitic feeling. In addition, 81 per cent said they knew of no discrimination of any kind being practiced in their communities.

However, it is important to note that while most say they personally have not experienced antisemitism, many are of the opinion that they are being exempted from commonly held stereotypes about Jews. Many respondents feel that latent antisemitism exists among some community members, but that Gentiles view *them* as being "different from other Jews." Fortunately we are able to compare these expressions with those of non-Jews. In the second study we found that what the Jews feel as the true pulse of community sentiment is not always the reality of the attitudes of Gentiles.

In predicting what we would find along the lines of socializing between Jews and non-Jews we hypothesized that close proximity to Gentile neighbors and the lack of opportunity to have day-to-day contact with members of a Jewish community would lead to a degree of intimate interfaith socializing unparalleled in larger communities. The majority of persons who were interviewed substantiated this prediction. For example:

Everyone has close friends. In the city Jewish people tend to cling together. But in the rural village, when you are a minority of one, you associate completely with Gentiles. While it's rare in the city for Jews and Gentiles to be invited to one another's home for informal visiting, this is an everyday occurrence in the little community.

In the small town Jews are more than participants in formal community functions. In most instances they are an integral part of the social life of their towns. For the adults this includes such activities as parties, trips, dances, bridge clubs, and just plain "dropping in." For the children this often means playing together, going to parties, and frequent instances of dating.

In over 50 per cent of all cases small-town Jews designated a Gentile person as their closest friend. Yet, 30 per cent said they feel "more comfortable" with Jews than with non-Jews, especially in social situations. Those highest on religiosity, identifying most strongly with traditional Judaism, are most apt to feel this way.

AND THE NEXT GENERATION That the strength of identification with Judaism plays a major role in determining patterns of and feelings about informal socializing with Gentiles becomes even clearer when we examine the attitudes of Jewish parents toward their children. Since 90 per cent of the respondents are parents, we were able to get reactions to a number of questions; reactions which indicate a firm conviction that Jewish identity should not only be maintained but intensified. Thus, while a

high degree of informal interaction is practiced, the small-town Jews, like their urban co-religionists, are anxious for their children to keep the faith and to marry Jews. As a result they send them to Jewish summer camps and, when they are through with high school, encourage them to attend large, metropolitan universities. And, although they themselves are satisfied with rural living, few expect their children to return to the small town after graduation.

Here is the opinion of a retired business man:

We've lived here ever since the children—I have three—were born. They grew up among Gentile people. I don't think they ever met another Jew until they were fifteen or sixteen. In no case were they ever discriminated against. My son was captain of the basketball team and played ball for the local Altar Boys Baseball Club. My daughters always went around with local kids and dated boys from school. I can't say I was happy about this, but I didn't try to stop them. Yet, despite a number of crushes on certain fellows, they never got real serious about any of them. . . . When they graduated from high school they all went to college in the city. There they met Jewish people. . . . I'm really happy that my children all married Jews. It's easier that way.

It seems safe to say that the small-town Jew is similar to the city-dwelling Jew to the extent that he wants his children to remain Jews. He is firmly opposed to interfaith marriage. To him this represents either the confrontation of too many social problems or alienation from Judaism: both are considered highly undesirable. Complete assimilation into the Christian community is not the goal of the American Jew. This means giving up a part of himself, a part that sometimes even he cannot explain. Rather, the Jew in New York and "East Podunk" wants to remain a hyphenated American, sharing the "best of both." No better example of this is to be found than in the rural hamlet.

THE BEST OF BOTH Stonequist, Park and others have characterized the Jew as a disturbed marginal man,[5] an eternal stranger [6] unable to reconcile the traditions of his people with the counter-forces of the majority world; "one whom fate has condemned to live in two societies and in two, not merely different, but antagonistic cultures." [7] One might expect to find ample support for such a definition among the small-town Jews who live away from the mainstream of Jewish life. Yet, rather than being on the periphery of two cultures, the ex-urban Jew seems to have internalized the best of each. He is more a part of his community than he is apart from it. He is far more assimilated to the Gentile milieu than his urban cousin. But, as indicated above, he remains a Jew.

While he strongly identifies with fellow Jews—a reference group he can "feel" rather than "touch"—and in many ways expresses a feeling of kinship with his people, he has adapted himself to the folkways of the small town in a variety of ways. He enjoys the advantages of sharing two "cups of life" and, in a word, is bi-cultural. This duality (rather than marginality) causes the majority of respondents to come to agreement with one who stated:

> You see, we feel we have the best of both . . . Judaism with all its tradition, its stress on culture, on learning, on freedom. . . . And the fact that we live in a small town with nice people and good, clean air. . . . We wouldn't trade either for the world.

All told, those who can reconcile the past with the present find that they can share a little of each of their different cultures. Those who find satisfaction in the small community generally seem to agree with one woman who said:

> It's funny. I never thought a city girl like me would like small-town living. But I've changed. I honestly enjoy the lack of sophistication at Home Bureau meetings, the knock-down-drag-out fights at school meetings, the gossip that never escapes anyone. I love the scenery, the simplicity, and the lack of formality here. Sometimes I miss the city. A good play, a concert, a corned beef sand-

wich! But we get away each year and spend a few days in New York. After about three days I've had enough. I'm ready for home. I want to go back to. . . .

and with a lawyer originally from New York City:

> I guess having been raised in the city makes you appreciate a community such as this even more than if you were born here. It's just nice not to have to be on the go all the time. . . . There was a time when I would have laughed if somebody suggested that I might wind up in the sticks. But here I am and loving every minute of it. People accept you for what you are, not who you are. . . .

Naturally those who gave such enthusiastic testimonials for small-town living were among the most satisfied with their lives in the rural community. Yet only 14 per cent of all respondents expressed true dissatisfaction. Two main reasons were most frequently given for disliking the small town. First, there was general dissatisfaction with rural living. "This town is too provincial for me." "Progress is nil. I just wish we could get out." "I'd take the impersonality of the city any day over the gossipy closeness of this burg." The second kind of dissatisfaction related to isolation from other Jews. "Frankly I would be much happier if we could be with Jews more often." "My wife is not happy here. She'd much rather be some place where she can pick up the phone and talk to the girls. We miss Jewish contacts." "If I had it to do over again, I surely wouldn't move out to the sticks. I'd rather be where there are more Jewish people."

Why do they not move out? The answer is provided by a merchant:

> We always plan to leave here for a larger community. My business keeps me here, as it furnishes me with a good income. If I could leave, I would. The small town is too backward for me.

It must be remembered that the dissatisfied residents are deviant cases. The majority of respondents express some degree of satisfaction with their communities. They were either "very satisfied" (50 per cent) or "somewhat satisfied" (36 per cent).

Satisfaction seems to depend upon whether or not town people are cordial and accepting of strangers. In most cases isolated Jews are, as several interviewees put it, "curiosities and strangers." Generally the burden is on the Jew himself; at least he thinks so. If he accepts the ways of the rural village in which he resides, that is, if he joins the local lodge, contributes to the funds, buys his food and some clothing in town, takes an interest in community affairs, he is "in." According to a storekeeper:

> The secret of a Jew living in a small town —happily—is to assimilate as soon as possible—but, always to remember he's a Jew.

And a doctor said:

> In small rural towns one is accepted for what he is. Religion plays a minor fact in your being accepted. If one is honest and equitable in his dealings with others, you are placed in the forefront of things. . . .

MINORITY ADJUSTMENT   The brief description of the findings of our study of Jewish life in the small town are but excerpts from the original report. Yet it is hoped they shed some illumination on the life of the isolated member of one minority group and indicate the role of the ethnic ambassador. From this first study several generalizations are suggested. 1) Those who leave the confines of the ghetto or ethnic community are frequently anxious to seek economic and social betterment, to find acceptance in the new setting without loss of ethnic identity. 2) Once the minority member enters the new "alien" situation, he finds himself in the position of representing his "people" to the community at large. As a stranger his ethnic identity becomes particularly salient to the community and to himself. More often than not, consciousness of minority membership increases when one be-

comes an isolate. 3) The minority member who lives in the milieu of the majority has infinitely greater opportunity to adapt himself to the folkways of the dominant group than does one who lives in the middle of the ethnic community.

Opinions of Community Leaders

For that part of the research which was designed to tap the attitudes of the majority group we chose to get reactions of community leaders. Such individuals were selected because it was felt that they would have the greatest opportunity to have contact with the widest number of persons in their towns. In addition, being in positions of formal leadership in such small villages (average population 2,500) meant that these same persons would most likely play informal leadership roles as well; they would be the pace-setters for community opinion. It also seemed logical to assume that a higher percentage of community leaders would have closer contact with Jews than rank and file citizens.

Many of the same kind of questions used in the first section of the study were asked of respondents in the second. In addition, a number of items referred directly or indirectly to attitudes about Jews and other minority group members.

Piecing together the varied comments of several different Gentile opinion leaders, all of whom live in one village in central New York State, we have a rough image of "native" small-towners, their attitudes toward the community, general prejudice, and the effects of contact with minority representatives.

> I have lived in this town all my life. . . . I feel that in the small, rural community people are friendly to one another. A common greeting is "Hello Joe" . . . truly a warm feeling, one of belonging. . . . I love it here.

> Well, I'm an American, since before the War of 1812. I guess I feel this makes me a little better. I'm not prejudiced. I just prefer to be with my own kind and I'm sure they'd [Jews, Negroes, and foreigners] prefer to mix together too. . . .

There are only two Jewish families here and they are highly regarded—one man is a business man. The other is a very fine attorney. No comparison with New York City Jews. They're different. . . .

I run a store and come into contact with salesmen of different races. I have three Jewish salesmen, all three are good men. There is none of this pushing and trying to sell stuff you don't need like in the city. . . .

THE NATIVES While the small-town Jews are generally outsiders who migrated to the rural community, most of the Gentile respondents were born and raised in their towns or in similar small villages. Only one-fifth of the total group were born in cities and a mere 2 per cent were born abroad. Like the Jews, some who came from the outside came for business reasons. But unlike the Jews, most "newcomers" settled down in small towns because of marriage to a community member, because of cheaper housing, or for health reasons.

These people are mainly of old "Yankee" stock with 38 per cent claiming that their families—that is, their father's father's family—came to America before 1800. Members of this group tend to call themselves "American," "Scotch-Irish," or "Holland-Dutch" in their self-descriptions. Those whose families immigrated during the nineteenth century are more apt to be of German or Irish descent. The most recent group are most often of Italian origins.

The occupations of those respondents are widely varied, ranging from farmers to bankers, from ministers to mill-hands. Like the Jewish small-towners, most place themselves in the upper middle class. Their average annual family income is, however, half of that of the Jewish respondents, i.e. $7,500. Half of the Gentile participants are self-employed as compared with 80 per cent of the Jewish group.

Thirty-nine per cent of the Gentiles said they had a college education or had gone beyond college; 64 per cent had at least a high school education. Like the Jews they too have high aspirations for their children. Seventy-six per cent of these persons are Protestant (the remainder Catholic); two-thirds are Republicans; and two out of every three see themselves as more "rural" than "urban."

When asked about satisfaction with their communities the most typical response was "This is home." By and large the respondents were highly satisfied with their communities (68 per cent) and an additional one-fourth expressed moderate satisfaction. For this group community satisfaction is dependent upon such variables as length of residence, the ties one has to one's home town, and the progressiveness of the community.

When asked for comments a highly satisfied respondent wrote:

This is a small, rural, closely knit community where newcomers have to make every effort to become an insider. The effort, however, I feel is well worth it. We are not too far from a large city (but far enough to be away from the clatter), our school is excellent and religious relations in this community are excellent. While this town is pretty conservative, I find a great deal of satisfaction in the slow, easy-going pace. I've lived here since I was a boy and wouldn't leave for anything.

For contrast here is the comment of a dissatisfied resident of the *same* community.

Passivity, complacency and a sheer lack of or neglect of economic intellect in this community has been responsible for the apparent degeneration of atmosphere and attitude in all things related to even a reasonable degree of progress. This, of course, offers nothing of value to the high school generation. It offers nothing to newcomers. All in all, a community which was once great is slowly but most certainly annihilating itself.

ETHNOCENTRISM AND "THE GOOD OLD DAYS" In some instances dissatisfaction with one's town is unrelated to whether the community is a good place to live and work or not; rather it seems to depend upon the image of what the town itself should be (or what it might have been) and what it has become.

Although the lack of change or progress appeared the most significant factor for dissatisfaction with community life, there are some residents who have *become* dissatisfied precisely because changes have occurred. Not the least of these changes is the influx of outsiders to a number of small towns. In almost every village included in our sample there were two or three respondents who longed for the old days, who resented the intrusion of newcomers, who could not accept change as progress.

Several examples serve to illustrate their attitudes:

I am sure foreign people make a mistake in keeping customs of their own land alive and featured in this country. If this country meets their expectations, they should forget the folklore of Europe, St. Patrick's Day Parades, German Days, and get behind American things. If they can't do this they should be returned to the land they love. This country is supposed to be the world's melting pot. If they won't melt, they should not belong.

We have a lot of foreigners here. . . . They're all right, keep in their own place, go to their own church. But I must say it isn't really the same any more. This town has a great heritage, it was settled before the Revolution. . . . I don't mean to imply that I am prejudiced or that I dislike foreigners. We all have our place in this great country of ours. I just think it a shame that outsiders like those who live here, have to keep their old ways. It makes it harder for them to be accepted.

These persons were among a small group of respondents (21 per cent) who agreed with the following statement: "This country would be better off if there were not so many foreigners here." They were also in agreement with "Religions which preach unwholesome ideas should be suppressed," as were 56 per cent of the sample group; and with the statement "Americans must be on guard against the power of the Catholic church," with which one-quarter of all respondents also agreed.

Such attitudes indicate ethnocentric thinking. A Scale of Ethnocentrism based upon responses to the first two questions cited above and one which stated "Some people say that most people can be trusted. Others say you can't be too careful in your dealings with people. How do you feel about it?" was used to assess general prejudice.

A high degree of ethnocentrism is, in most cases, highly correlated with poor paying jobs, low educational attainment, small-town origins, occupations involving working with "things" rather than "people," and "old family" status. If one is ethnocentric, one tends to be more "success-oriented" and less apt to want to be "independent." The highly ethnocentric individual is more likely to indicate a need to belong and express a strong desire to be accepted by others. Those who see themselves as being *upper class* and those who feel they belong to the *working class* are higher in their distaste for outsiders than "middle-class" individuals. Little difference is found between Catholics and Protestants or along political lines.

Does the opportunity to interact with minority members affect the general prejudice expressed by the small-town Gentile? Without a panel study over time it is virtually impossible to answer this query. However, the data do indicate that contact is related to the amount of generalized ethnocentrism one feels, but *only* when this contact is close enough to permit social interaction to occur. As will be noted in Table 2, those who have close association with Jews and Negroes have a much lower degree of ethnocentrism than those who rarely communicate with members of these two groups or have no contact in the community at all.

ATTITUDES TOWARDS JEWS AND THE "EXEMPTION MECHANISM" Prejudice against Jews is more prevalent in the attitudes of the Gentiles (at least among community leaders) than the Jews themselves imagine. Many of the community leaders subscribe to traditional stereotypes about

Jews. For instance, 83 per cent agree with the statement "Jews tend to be more money-minded than most people"; 80 per cent agree that "Jews tend to be shrewder business men than most people"; and 77 per cent agree that "Jews tend to be more aggressive than most people."

Thus most of the respondents feel that Jews in general possess these "characteristic traits." Whether or not a Jew lives in town is not crucial for changes in stereotyping. Merely buying in a "Jewish store" or visiting a Jewish physician may only perpetuate generalized images of Jews. Many of the small-town Jews in New York State do, in fact, fulfill several of the classic stereotypes; especially for those who never get to know them individually. As a group, they are frequently in business. They are more liberal politically. They do tend to possess an urbane demeanor and are thus natural recipients of the traditional suspicions of "city slickers." And their children, being strongly motivated, do tend to do especially well in school. Here there is ample support for the "kernel of truth" hypothesis.

Yet expressions of attitudes and actual behavior are sometimes contradictory. Close examination of the data disclosed the fact that when interaction takes place

at an *equal status* level, community leaders, even those with negative images of Jews as a group, tend to accept individual Jews as exceptions to the rule. They see them as being "different."

In general, respondents who have personal and intimate contact with local Jews view their close acquaintances as less clannish, quieter, less flashy, and less radical than they imagine Jews to be. Here are three excerpts of statements appearing on the last page of the mailed questionnaire.

My experience as to Jewish residents of this community is probably not typical. A high-class, wealthy, cultured, refugee Jewish family came here in 1940 and we have been very close friends ever since then, both professionally and socially. They seem, to me, very different from most Jews.

Frankly, I'm not too fond of Jews. I've heard too much about how they stick together, how they can chisel you, how they try to get ahead. Yet, here in —— there is a Jewish family who are not at all like this. They are fine, intelligent, honest citizens and very close friends of ours.

When the —— came to this community everyone was suspicious. We knew what Jews were like and we didn't like what we knew. After a while we found that they were pretty nice folks. We looked at them as a different kind of Jew. They didn't seem the Brooklyn

Table 2. *Ethnocentrism and the Nature of Contact with Jews and Negroes Living in the Community*

Degree of Ethnocentrism	Jews			Negroes		
	No Contact *	*Impersonal Contact* †	*Personal Contact* ‡	*No Contact* *	*Impersonal Contact* †	*Personal Contact* ‡
	%	%	%	%	%	%
High	32	33	10	30	50	13
Medium	34	32	36	36	14	31
Low	34	35	54	34	36	56
	100	100	100	100	100	100
	(88)	(46)	(39)	(124)	(14)	(39)

* "No Contact" means that respondents say there are no members of this group living in their community and also includes those who "don't know" whether or not the group is represented in their town.

† "Impersonal Contact" refers to respondents who say they know members of this group but only "to speak to" or someone they "see around."

‡ "Personal Contact" refers to respondents who say they know members of this group who call them by their first names, to whom they can say what they really think, or close friends with whom they can discuss confidential matters.

type. Thinking about it now I have the feeling that our children build their image of what a Jew is supposed to be from the contact they have with the children of this Jewish family. Sometimes we have warped ideas about what we think is true. . . .

Repeated *personal* and *informal* contact in the home and around town can serve as a significant factor leading towards the ultimate reduction of prejudice against Jews. Exemption is perhaps an important intermediate step in breaking down predispositions towards minority groups.

One further statement serves to illustrate this proposition:

When a Jewish family first moved in we wanted them to prove themselves to us. It must have been hard on them but they came through like troopers. They became an important part of the community. They showed us a different kind of Jew. No Shylock. Knowing them for twenty years now when I think of Jews I think of them. I used to think about some mean, hook-nosed character.

MAJORITY REACTION The following generalizations are tentatively offered based upon the study of the community leaders of twenty small towns in New York State: 1) In the small community the minority group member is constantly in direct contact with the majority group. As he gets to know their ways, they cannot help but get to know him. He stands upon the threshold of influencing deep-seated images. He can reinforce such images or aid in the recasting of these by those with whom he interacts. 2) The isolated minority member rarely constitutes a threat to the established order and community members are often willing to accept the individual outsider despite ar-

ticulated expressions of prejudice. 3) Repeated and intensive contact and personal association often tend to change the mental picture of the isolate from being "different from" to be "typical of" the group he represents. Exemption is viewed as an instrumental step in the ultimate reduction of prejudice.

A Final Note

On the basis of the two studies reported here, it is logical to predict that increasing interaction with Jewish "representatives," especially those who have spent their early years in the small town, would have a decided effect on changing the overall attitudes of Gentiles toward Jews. A study of the children of small-towners would provide the information needed to test this hypothesis. But any research of this kind would necessarily have to be conducted in the very near future.

As is stated in the summary of the original report:

Another prediction is, unfortunately perhaps, in order. With the tremendous rate of post-teen out-migration on the part of the offspring of Jews living in rural communities we wonder whether the small-town Jew is, in reality, a disappearing type in the spectrum of American Jewry. Most Jews who settled in small villages did so prior to World War II. Since that time few have chosen to live in such communities. Now the children are grown and rapidly leaving the nest to live in larger centers. Although some children will return to run the business, our studies suggest that small as it now is, the population of American Jews living in small communities will increasingly diminish in the years to come. . . .[8]

NOTES

1. See, for example, Toby Shafter, "The Fleshpots of Maine," *Commentary,* 7 (January–June 1949) 60–67; Earl Raab, "Report from the Farm," *Commentary,* 8 (July–December 1949) 475–479; Harry Golden, "The Jews of the South," *Congress Weekly,* 31 December 1951; Lee J. Levinger, "The Disappearing Small-Town Jew," *Commentary,* 14 (July–December 1952) 157–163; Louise Laser, "The Only Jewish Family in Town," *Commentary* (December 1959) 489–496; and a letter to the Editor from Gerald M. Phillips, "Jews in Rural America," *Commentary* (February 1960), 163.

2. This research was sponsored by The Anti-Defamation League of B'nai B'rith, 315 Lexington Avenue, New York City. The original manuscript is entitled *Strangers in Their Midst, A Sociological Study of the Small-Town Jew and His Neighbors,* Cornell University, 1959. The project title was that of the "Cornell Community Studies."

3. Approximately 25 per cent of those who did not respond were randomly selected and attempts were made to interview each. Of this group two persons claimed they were no longer Jews and refused. Both were German refugees and had married non-Jews *prior* to their immigration to America. Two persons were deceased. The remaining group all identified themselves as Jews. Four permitted themselves to be interviewed and the information gathered was consistent with that of the less reluctant respondents. One individual refused to be interviewed and expressed the general feeling that such a study could do little to enhance Jewish-Gentile relations.

4. That slightly less than two-thirds responded suggests the possibility of a selective bias in the second part of the study. Time and budget did not permit the personal follow-up of non-respondents similar to that in the first study.

5. Everett V. Stonequist, *The Marginal Man: A Study in Personality and Culture Conflict,* New York, 1937; and Robert E. Park, "Human Migration and the Marginal Man," *American Journal of Sociology,* 33 (1928), 881–893.

6. Georg Simmel, "The Stranger," *The Sociology of Georg Simmel,* Kurt H. Wolff, trans., Glencoe, Ill., 1950, 402–408; and Robert E. Park and Ernest W. Burgess, *Introduction to the Science of Sociology,* Chicago, 1921, 286.

7. Park, "Human Migration . . . ," *op. cit.,* 891.

8. Rose, *op. cit.,* 279–280.

37. DISCRIMINATION AND THE AMERICAN CREED

ROBERT K. MERTON

Few articles on so volatile a subject as intergroup relations have the "staying power"
of the one that follows. It is more than two decades since Robert K. Merton pub-
lished "Discrimination and the American Creed," yet it remains a classic commentary
on the conditions conducive to conformity to and deviation from the American creed
of equal access to justice, freedom, and opportunity for all as expressed in both
attitudinal and behavioral responses to national, regional, and communal norms.

Suggesting that allegiance to the creed is highly variable and depends upon relevant
factors in one's social milieu, Merton goes on to state, ". . . the problems of racial
and ethnic inequities are not expressible as a discrepancy between high cultural
principles and low social conduct [as Gunnar Myrdal would put it]. It is a relation not
between two variables, official creed and private practice, but between three: first, the
cultural creed honored in cultural tradition and partly enacted in law; second, the
beliefs and attitudes of individuals regarding the principles of the creed; and third, the
actual practices of individuals with reference to it." Merton graphically expresses
his position in a typology which takes into account variant attitudes and patterns of
behavior. His four types— the "unprejudiced non-discriminator," the "unpreju-
diced discriminator," the "prejudiced non-discriminator," and the "prejudiced dis-
criminator"—are presented and described in detail. The essay ends with a set of
assumptions underlying suggested social policy for the reduction of racial and ethnic
discrimination relevant to the variant categories presented in the paradigm.

While some of the examples used by Merton now seem dated, the ideas put forth
both for the analysis and the solution of intergroup conflict continue to remain germane.

Robert K. Merton is Professor of Sociology at Columbia University. A partial list
of his numerous publications is presented on page 31 of this volume.

The primary function of the sociologist is to search out the determinants and consequences of diverse forms of social behavior. To the extent that he succeeds in fulfilling this role, he clarifies the alternatives of organized social action in a given situation and of the probable outcome of each. To this extent, there is no sharp distinction between pure research and applied research. Rather, the difference is one between research with direct implications for particular problems of social action and research which is remote from these problems. Not infrequently, basic research which has succeeded only in clearing up previously confused concepts may have an immediate bearing upon the problems of men in society to a degree not approximated by applied research oriented exclusively to these problems. At least, this is the assumption underlying the present paper: clarification of apparently unclear and confused concepts in the sphere of race and ethnic relations is a step necessarily prior to the devising of effective programs for reducing intergroup conflict and for promoting equitable access to economic and social opportunities.

In an effort toward such clarification, I shall consider first the place of the creed of equitable access to opportunity in American culture; second, the relations of this creed to the beliefs and practices of Americans; third, the diverse types of orientation toward discrimination *and* prejudice; fourth, the implications for organized action of the recognition of these diverse types; and fifth, the expectable consequences of alternative lines of action in diverse social contexts.

The American Creed: As Cultural Ideal, Personal Belief and Practice

The American creed as set forth in the Declaration of Independence, the preamble of the Constitution and the Bill of Rights has often been misstated. This part of the cultural heritage does *not* include the patently false assertion that all men are created equal in capacity or endowment. It does *not* imply that an Einstein and a moron are equal in intellectual capacity or that Joe Louis and a small, frail Columbia professor (or a Mississippian Congressman) are equally endowed with brawny arms harboring muscles as strong as iron bands. It does *not* proclaim universal equality of innate intellectual or physical endowment.

Instead, the creed asserts the indefeasible principle of the human right to full equity—the right of equitable access to justice, freedom and opportunity, irrespective of race or religion or ethnic origin. It proclaims further the universalist doctrine of the dignity of the individual, irrespective of the groups of which he is a part. It is a creed announcing full moral equities for all, not an absurd myth affirming the equality of intellectual and physical capacity of all men everywhere. And it goes on to say that though men

differ in innate endowment, they do so as individuals, not by virtue of their group memberships.

Viewed sociologically, the creed is a set of values and precepts embedded in American culture, to which Americans are expected to conform. It is a complex of affirmations, rooted in the historical past and ceremonially celebrated in the present, partly enacted in the laws of the land and partly not. Like all creeds, it is a profession of faith, a part of cultural tradition sanctified by the larger traditions of which it is a part.

It would be a mistaken sociological assertion, however, to suggest that the creed is a fixed and static cultural constant, unmodified in the course of time, just as it would be an error to imply that as an integral part of the culture, it evenly blankets all subcultures of the national society. It is indeed dynamic, subject to change and in turn promoting change in other spheres of culture and society. It is, moreover, unevenly distributed throughout the society, being institutionalized as an integral part of local culture in some regions of the society and rejected in others.

Nor does the creed exert the same measure of control over behavior in diverse times and places. In so far as it is a "sacred" part of American culture, hallowed by tradition, it is largely immune to direct attack. But it may be honored simply in the breach. It is often evaded, and the evasions themselves become institutionalized, giving rise to what I may call the "institutionalized evasion of institutional norms." Where the creed is at odds with local beliefs and practices, it may persist as an empty cultural form partly because it is so flexible. It need not prove overly obstructive to the social, psychological and economic gains of individuals, because there are still so many avenues for conscientiously ignoring the creed in practice. When necessary for peace of mind and psychological equilibrium, individuals indoctrinated with the creed who find themselves deviating from its precepts may readily explain how their behavior accords with the spirit of the creed rather than with its sterile letter. Or the creed itself is re-interpreted. Only those of equal endowment should have equal access to opportunity, it is said, and a given race or ethnic group manifestly does not have the requisite capacity to be deserving of opportunity. To provide such opportunities for the inferior of mind would be only wasteful of national resources. The rationalizations are too numerous and too familiar to bear repetition. The essential point is that the creed, though invulnerable to direct attack in some regions of the society, is not binding on practice. Many individuals and groups in many areas of the society systematically deny through daily conduct what they affirm on periodic ceremonial or public occasions.

This gap between creed and conduct has received wide notice. Learned men and men in high public positions have repeatedly observed and deplored the disparity between ethos and behavior in the sphere of race and ethnic relations. In his magisterial volumes on the American Negro, for example, Gunnar Myrdal called this gulf between creed and conduct "an American dilemma," and centered his attention on the prospect of narrowing or closing the gap. The President's Committee on Civil Rights, in their report to the nation, and . . . President [Truman] himself, in a recent message to Congress, have called public attention to this "serious gap between our ideals and some of our practices."

But valid as these observations may be, they tend so to simplify the relations between creed and conduct as to be seriously misleading both for social policy and for social science. All these high authorities notwithstanding, the problems of racial and ethnic inequities are not expressible as a discrepancy between high cultural principles and low social conduct. It is a relation not between two variables, official creed and private practice, but between three: first, the cultural creed honored in

cultural tradition and partly enacted into law; second, the beliefs and attitudes of individuals regarding the principles of the creed; and third, the actual practices of individuals with reference to it.

Once we substitute these three variables of cultural idea, belief and actual practice for the customary distinction between the two variables of cultural ideals and actual practices, the entire formulation of the problem becomes changed. We escape from the virtuous but ineffectual impasse of deploring the alleged hypocrisy of many Americans into the more difficult but potentially effectual realm of analyzing the problem in hand.

To describe the problem and to proceed to its analysis, it is necessary to consider the official creed, individuals' beliefs and attitudes concerning the creed, and their actual behavior. Once stated, the distinctions are readily applicable. Individuals may *recognize* the creed as part of a cultural tradition, *without having any private conviction of its moral validity or its binding quality*. Thus, so far as the beliefs of individuals are concerned, we can identify two types: those who genuinely believe in the creed and those who do not (although some of these may, on public or ceremonial occasions, profess adherence to its principles). Similarly, with respect to actual practices: conduct may or may not conform to the creed. But, and this is the salient consideration: *conduct may or may not conform with individuals' own beliefs concerning the moral claims of all men to equal opportunity.*

Stated in formal sociological terms, this asserts that attitudes and overt behavior vary independently. *Prejudicial attitudes need not coincide with discriminatory behavior.* The implications of this statement can be drawn out in terms of a logical syntax whereby the variables are diversely combined, as can be seen in the following typology.

By exploring the interrelations between prejudice and discrimination, we can identify four major types in terms of their

A Typology of Ethnic Prejudice and Discrimination

	Attitude Dimension: * Prejudice and Non-prejudice	Behavior Dimension: * Discrimination and Non-discrimination
Type I: Unprejudiced non-discriminator	+	+
Type II: Unprejudiced discriminator	+	−
Type III: Prejudiced non-discriminator	−	+
Type IV: Prejudiced discriminator	−	−

* Where (+) = *conformity to the creed and* (−) = *deviation from the creed. For a brief note on the uses of paradigms such as this, see the appendix to this paper.*

attitudes toward the creed and their behavior with respect to it. Each type is found in every region and social class, though in varying numbers. By examining each type, we shall be better prepared to understand their interdependence and the appropriate types of action for curbing ethnic discrimination. The folk-labels for each type are intended to aid in their prompt recognition.

Type I: the unprejudiced non-discriminator or all-weather liberal

These are the racial and ethnic liberals who adhere to the creed in both belief and practice. They are neither prejudiced nor given to discrimination. Their orientation toward the creed is fixed and stable. Whatever the environing situation, they are likely to abide by their beliefs: hence, the *all-weather* liberal.

This is, of course, the strategic group which *can* act as the spearhead for the progressive extension of the creed into effective practice. They represent the solid foundation both for the measure of ethnic equities which now exist and for the future enlargement of these equities. Integrated with the creed in both belief and practice, they would seem most motivated to influence others toward the same democratic outlook. They represent a reservoir of culturally legitimatized goodwill which can be channeled into an active program for extending belief in the creed and conformity with it in practice.

Most important, as we shall see pres-

ently, the all-weather liberals comprise the group which can so reward others for conforming with the creed, as to transform deviants into conformists. They alone can provide the positive social environment for the other types who will no longer find it expedient or rewarding to retain their prejudices or discriminatory practices.

But though the ethnic liberal is a *potential* force for the successive extension of the American creed, he does not fully realize this potentiality in actual fact, for a variety of reasons. Among the limitations of effective action are several fallacies to which the ethnic liberal seems peculiarly subject. First among these is the *fallacy of group soliloquies*. Ethnic liberals are busily engaged in talking to themselves. Repeatedly, the same groups of like-minded liberals seek each other out, hold periodic meetings in which they engage in mutual exhortation and thus lend social and psychological support to one another. But however much these unwittingly self-selected audiences may reinforce the creed among themselves, they do not thus appreciably diffuse the creed in belief or practice to groups which depart from it in one respect or the other.

More, these group soliloquies in which there is typically wholehearted agreement among fellow-liberals tend to promote another fallacy limiting effective action. This is the *fallacy of unanimity*. Continued association with like-minded individuals tends to produce the illusion that a large measure of consensus has been achieved in the community at large. The unanimity regarding essential cultural axioms which obtains in these small groups provokes an overestimation of the strength of the movement and of its effective inroads upon the larger population which does not necessarily share these creedal axioms. Many also mistake participation in the groups of like-minded individuals for effective action. Discussion accordingly takes the place of action. The reinforcement of the creed for oneself is mistaken for the extension of the creed among those outside the limited circle of ethnic liberals.

Arising from adherence to the creed is a third limitation upon effective action, the *fallacy of privatized solutions* to the problem. The ethnic liberal, precisely because he is at one with the American creed, may rest content with his own individual behavior and thus see no need to do anything about the problem at large. Since his own spiritual house is in order, he is not motivated by guilt or shame to work on a collective problem. The very freedom of the liberal from guilt thus prompts him to secede from any *collective* effort to set the national house in order. He essays a *private* solution to a *social* problem. He assumes that numerous individual adjustments will serve in place of a collective adjustment. His outlook, compounded of good moral philosophy but poor sociology, holds that each individual must put his own house in order and fails to recognize that privatized solutions cannot be effected for problems which are essentially social in nature. For clearly, if each person *were* motivated to abide by the American creed, the problem would not be likely to exist in the first place. It is only when a social environment is established by conformists to the creed that deviants can in due course be brought to modify their behavior in the direction of conformity. But this "environment" can be constituted only through collective effort and not through private adherence to a public creed. Thus we have the paradox

that the clear conscience of many ethnic liberals may promote the very social situation which permits deviations from the creed to continue unchecked. Privatized liberalism invites social inaction. Accordingly, there appears the phenomenon of the inactive or passive liberal, himself at spiritual ease, neither prejudiced nor discriminatory, but in a measure tending to contribute to the persistence of prejudice and discrimination through his very inaction.

The fallacies of group soliloquy, unanimity and privatized solutions thus operate to make the potential strength of the ethnic liberals unrealized in practice.

It is only by first recognizing these limitations that the liberal can hope to overcome them. With some hesitancy, one may suggest initial policies for curbing the scope of the three fallacies. The fallacy of group soliloquies can be removed only by having ethnic liberals enter into organized groups not comprised merely by fellow-liberals. This exacts a heavy price of the liberal. It means that he faces initial opposition and resistance rather than prompt consensus. It entails giving up the gratifications of consistent group support.

The fallacy of unanimity can in turn be reduced by coming to see that American society often provides large rewards for those who express their ethnic prejudice in discrimination. Only if the balance of rewards, material and psychological, is modified will behavior be modified. Sheer exhortation and propaganda are not enough. Exhortation verges on a belief in magic if it is not supported by appropriate changes in the social environment to make conformity with the exhortation rewarding.

Finally, the fallacy of privatized solutions requires the militant liberal to motivate the passive liberal to collective effort, possibly by inducing in him a sense of guilt for his unwitting contribution to the problems of ethnic inequities through his own systematic inaction.

One may suggest a unifying theme for

the ethnic liberal: goodwill is not enough to modify social reality. It is only when this goodwill is harnessed to social-psychological realism that it can be used to reach cultural objectives.

Type II: the unprejudiced discriminator or fair-weather liberal

The fair-weather liberal is the man of expediency who, despite his own freedom from prejudice, supports discriminatory practices when it is the easier or more profitable course. His expediency may take the form of holding his silence and thus implicitly acquiescing in expressions of ethnic prejudice by others or in the practice of discrimination by others. This is the expediency of the timid: the liberal who hesitates to speak up against discrimination for fear he might lose status or be otherwise penalized by his prejudiced associates. Or his expediency may take the form of grasping at advantages in social and economic competition deriving solely from the ethnic status of competitors. This is the expediency of the self-assertive: the employer, himself not an anti-Semite or Negrophobe, who refuses to hire Jewish or Negro workers because "it might hurt business"; the trade union leader who expediently advocates racial discrimination in order not to lose the support of powerful Negrophobes in his union.

In varying degrees, the fair-weather liberal suffers from guilt and shame for departing from his own effective beliefs in the American creed. Each deviation through which he derives a limited reward from passively acquiescing in or actively supporting discrimination contributes cumulatively to this fund of guilt. He is, therefore, peculiarly vulnerable to the efforts of the all-weather liberal who would help him bring his conduct into accord with his beliefs, thus removing this source of guilt. He is the most amenable to cure, because basically he wants to be cured. His is a split conscience which motivates him to cooperate actively with those who

will help remove the source of internal conflict. He thus represents the strategic group promising the largest returns for the least effort. Persistent re-affirmation of the creed will only intensify his conflict; but a long regimen in a favorable social climate can be expected to transform the fair-weather liberal into an all-weather liberal.

Type III: the prejudiced non-discriminator or fair-weather illiberal

The fair-weather illiberal is the reluctant conformist to the creed, the man of prejudice who does not believe in the creed but conforms to it in practice through fear of sanctions which might otherwise be visited upon him. You know him well: the prejudiced employer who discriminates against racial or ethnic groups until a Fair Employment Practice Commission, able and willing to enforce the law, puts the fear of punishment into him; the trade union leader, himself deeply prejudiced, who does away with Jim Crow in his union because the rank-and-file demands that it be done away with; the businessman who foregoes his own prejudices when he finds a profitable market among the very people he hates, fears or despises; the timid bigot who will not express his prejudices when he is in the presence of powerful men who vigorously and effectively affirm their belief in the American creed.

It should be clear that the fair-weather illiberal is the precise counterpart of the fair-weather liberal. Both are men of expediency, to be sure, but expediency dictates different courses of behavior in the two cases. The timid bigot conforms to the creed only when there is danger or loss in deviations, just as the timid liberal deviates from the creed only when there is danger or loss in conforming. *Superficial similarity in behavior of the two in the same situation should not be permitted to cloak a basic difference in the meaning of this outwardly similar behavior,* a difference which is as important for social policy as it is for social science. Whereas the timid bigot is under strain when he conforms to the creed, the timid liberal is under strain when he deviates. For ethnic prejudice has deep roots in the character structure of the fair-weather bigot, and this will find overt expression unless there are powerful countervailing forces, institutional, legal and interpersonal. He does not accept the moral legitimacy of the creed; he conforms because he must, and will cease to conform when the pressure is removed. The fair-weather liberal, on the other hand, is effectively committed to the creed and does not require strong institutional pressure to conform; continuing interpersonal relations with all-weather liberals may be sufficient.

This is the one critical point at which the traditional formulation of the problem of ethnic discrimination as a departure from the creed can lead to serious errors of theory and practice. Overt behavioral deviation (or conformity) may signify importantly different situations, depending upon the underlying motivations. Knowing simply that ethnic discrimination is rife in a community does not, therefore, point to appropriate lines of social policy. It is necessary to know also the distribution of ethnic prejudices and basic motivations for these prejudices as well. Communities with the same amount of overt discrimination may represent vastly different types of problems, dependent on whether the population is comprised by a large nucleus of fair-weather liberals ready to abandon their discriminatory practices under slight interpersonal pressure or a large nucleus of fair-weather illiberals who will abandon discrimination only if major changes in the local institutional setting can be effected. Any statement of the problem as a gulf between creedal ideals and prevailing practice is thus seen to be overly-simplified in the precise sense of masking this decisive difference between the type of discrimination exhibited by the fair-weather liberal and by the fair-weather illiberal. That the gulf-between-ideal-and-practice does not

adequately describe the nature of the ethnic problem will become more apparent as we turn to the fourth type in our inventory of prejudice and discrimination.

Type IV: the prejudiced discriminator or the all-weather illiberal

This type, too, is not unknown to you. He is the confirmed illiberal, the bigot pure and unashamed, the man of prejudice consistent in his departures from the American creed. In some measure, he is found everywhere in the land, though in varying numbers. He derives large social and psychological gains from his conviction that "any white man (including the village idiot) is 'better' than any nigger (including George Washington Carver)." He considers differential treatment of Negro and white not as "discrimination," in the sense of unfair treatment, but as "discriminating," in the sense of showing acute discernment. For him, it is as clear that one "ought" to accord a Negro and a white different treatment in a wide diversity of situations, as it is clear to the population at large that one "ought" to accord a child and an adult different treatment in many situations.

This illustrates anew my reason for questioning the applicability of the usual formula of the American dilemma as a gap between lofty creed and low conduct. For the confirmed illiberal, ethnic discrimination does *not* represent a discrepancy between *his* ideals and *his* behavior. His ideals proclaim the right, even the duty, of discrimination. Accordingly, his behavior does not entail a sense of social deviation, with the resultant strains which this would involve. The ethnic illiberal is as much a conformist as the ethnic liberal. He is merely conforming to a different cultural and institutional pattern which is centered, not about the creed, but about a doctrine of essential inequality of status ascribed to those of diverse ethnic and racial origins. To overlook this is to overlook the well-known *fact* that our national culture is divided into a number of local subcultures which are not consistent among themselves in all respects. And again, to fail to take this fact of different subcultures into account is to open the door for all manner of errors of social policy in attempting to control the problems of racial and ethnic discrimination.

This view of the all-weather illiberal has one immediate implication with wide bearing upon social policies and sociological theory oriented toward the problem of discrimination. The extreme importance of the social surroundings of the confirmed illiberal at once becomes apparent. For as these surroundings vary, so, in some measure, does the problem of the consistent illiberal. The illiberal, living in those cultural regions where the American creed is widely repudiated and is no effective part of the subculture, has his private ethnic attitudes and practices supported by the local mores, the local institutions and the local power-structure. The illiberal in cultural areas dominated by a large measure of adherence to the American creed is in a social environment where he is isolated and receives small social support for his beliefs and practices. In both instances, the *individual* is an illiberal, to be sure, but he represents two significantly different *sociological types*. In the first instance, he is a *social conformist*, with strong moral and institutional reinforcement, whereas in the second, he is a *social deviant*, lacking strong social corroboration. In the one case, his discrimination involves him in further integration with his network of social relations; in the other, it threatens to cut him off from sustaining interpersonal ties. In the first cultural context, personal change in his ethnic behavior involves alienating himself from people significant to him; in the second context, this change of personal outlook may mean fuller incorporation in groups meaningful to him. In the first situation, modification of his ethnic views requires him to take the path of greatest resistance whereas in the second,

it may mean the path of least resistance. From all this, we may surmise that any social policy aimed at changing the behavior and perhaps the attitudes of the all-weather illiberal will have to take into account the cultural and social structure of the area in which he lives.

Some Assumptions Underlying Social Policies for the Reduction of Racial and Ethnic Discrimination

To diagnose the problem, it appears essential to recognize these several types of men, and not to obscure their differences by general allusions to the "gulf-between-ideals and practice." Some of these men discriminate precisely because their local cultural ideals proclaim the duty of discrimination. Others discriminate only when they find it expedient to do so, just as still others fail to translate their prejudices into active discrimination when *this* proves expedient. It is the existence of these three types of men, in a society traditionally given over to the American creed, who constitute "the racial problem" or "the ethnic problem." Those who practice discrimination are *not* men of one kind. *And because they are not all of a piece, there must be diverse social therapies, each directed at a given type in a given social situation.*

Were it not for widespread social policies to the contrary, it would be unnecessary to emphasize that there is no single social policy which will be adequate for all these types in all social situations. So far as I know, sociological science has not yet evolved knowledge for application to this problem sufficient to merit great confidence in the results. But it has reached the point where it can suggest, with some assurance, that different social types in different social contexts require different social therapies if their behavior is to be changed. To diagnose these several types, therefore, may not be an "academic" exercise, in the too-frequent and dolorous sense of the word "academic." However scanty our knowledge, if action is to be taken, such diagnoses represent the first step toward pragmatic social therapy. The unprejudiced discriminator will respond differently from the prejudiced non-discriminator and he, in turn, differently from the prejudiced discriminator or all-weather illiberal. And each of these will respond according to the social composition of the groups and community in which he is involved.

In setting forth my opinions on the strategy of dealing with ethnic and racial discrimination, I hope it is plain that I move far beyond the adequately accredited knowledge provided by sociology to this point. In 1948, neither the rigorous theory nor many needed data are at hand to "apply" sociological science to this massive problem of American society. But moving from the slight accumulation of sociological knowledge at my disposal, it may be possible to suggest some considerations which it presently seems wise to take into account. For at scattered points, our knowledge may be sufficient to detect probably erroneous assumptions, though it is not always adequate to set out probably sound assumptions.

It is sometimes assumed that discrimination and its frequent though not invariable adjunct, prejudice, are entirely the product of ignorance. To be sure, ignorance *may* support discrimination. The employer unfamiliar with the findings of current anthropology and psychology, for example, may discriminate against Negroes on the ground of the honest and ignorant conviction that they are inherently less intelligent than whites. But, in general, there is no indication that ignorance is the major source of discrimination. The evidence at hand does not show that ethnic and racial discrimination is consistently less common among those boasting a college education than among the less well educated.

To question the close connection between ignorance and discrimination is to raise large implications for social policy. For if one assumes that ignorance and error are alone involved, obviously all that need be done by way of curbing prevalent discriminatory practices is to introduce a program of education concerning racial and ethnic matters, on a scale yet unimagined. Mass education and mass propaganda would at once become the sole indicated tools for action. But there are few who will accept the implications of this assumption that simple ignorance is a major or exclusive source of discrimination and urge that formal education alone can turn the trick. If some seem to be saying this, it is, I suspect, because they are begging the question; they are using the phrase "education on racial and ethnic matters" in an equivocal sense to mean "eradication of racial and ethnic prejudices." But, of course, that is precisely the question at issue: what *are* the procedures most likely to eradicate prejudice and discrimination?

If the assumption of ignorance as the root-source of discrimination is put to one side, then we must be prepared to find that discrimination is in part sustained by a socialized reward-system. When a population is divided into sub-groups, some of which are set apart as inferior, even the lowliest member of the ostensibly superior group derives psychic gains from this institutionalized superiority of status. This system of discrimination also supplies preferential access to opportunity for the more favored groups. The taboos erect high tariff walls restricting the importation of talent from the ethnic outgroups. But we need not assume that such psychic, social and economic gains are *sufficient* to account for the persistence of ethnic discrimination in a society which has an ideal pattern proclaiming free and equal access to opportunity. To be sure, these rewards supply motivation for discrimination. But men favor practices which give them differential advantages only so long as there is a moral code which defines these advantages as "fair." In the absence of this code, special advantage is not typically exploited. Were this not the case, the doctrine of Hobbes would stand unimpaired: everyone would cheat—in personal, economic and other institutional relations. Yet even the most cynical observer would not suggest that chicanery and cheating are the typical order of the day in all spheres, even where fear of discovery is at a minimum. This suggests that discrimination is sustained not only by the direct gains to those who discriminate, but also by cultural norms which *legitimize* discrimination.

To the extent that the foregoing assumptions are valid, efforts to minimize discrimination must take into account at least three sets of factors sustaining discriminatory practices. And each of these points toward distinct, though interrelated, lines of attack on the forces promoting discrimination. First, mass education and propaganda would be directed toward the reduction of sheer ignorance concerning the objective attributes of ethnic groups and of the processes of intergroup relations and attitudes. Second, institutional and interpersonal programs would seek to reduce the social, psychic and economic gains presently accruing to those who discriminate. And third, long-range efforts would be required to reinforce the legitimacy of the American creed as a set of cultural norms applicable to all groups in the society.

One gains the impression that certain secular trends in the society are slowly affecting each of these three fronts. On the educational front, we find an increasing proportion of the American population receiving higher schooling. And in the course of schooling, many are exposed for the first time to salient *facts* regarding ethnic and racial groups. Preconceptions notwithstanding, higher educational institutions even in the Deep South do not

teach discredited myths of race superiority; if race is treated at all, it is in substantially factual terms countering the cognitive errors now sustaining race discrimination. Without assuming that such education plays a basic role, I suggest that in so far as it is at all effective, it undermines erroneous conceptions of racial and ethnic qualities.

On the economic front, secular change moves with geological speed but consistently in the same positive direction. This secular trend is represented in slow shifts in the occupational composition of Negroes and other ethnic groups toward a perceptibly higher average level. Again, the importance of these slight shifts should not be exaggerated. As everyone knows, prejudice and its frequent corollary in action, discrimination, are resistant, if not entirely immune, to the coercion of sheer facts. Yet the white agricultural laborer does recognize, at some level of his self, the improbability of his "superiority" to the Negro physician or university president. The discrepancy between achieved occupational status and ascribed caste status introduces severe strains upon the persistence of rationalized patterns of social superiority. As occupational and educational opportunity expand for Negroes, the number of Negroes with class status higher than that of many whites will grow and with it the grounds for *genuinely believing,* no matter what one's protestations, that "any white man is better than any nigger" will be progressively eroded. This secular change is, of course, a two-edged sword: every economic advance of the Negro invites increased hostility and resentment. But no major change in social structure occurs without the danger of temporarily increased conflict (though it is a characteristic of the liberal to want the rose without the thorn, to seek major change without conflict). In any event, it seems plausible that the secular trend of occupational change presently militates against the unimpeded persistence of discrimination.

On the third front of the reinforcement of the American creed, the impressionistic picture is not so clear. But even here, there is one massive fact of contemporary history which points to a firmer foundation for this cultural doctrine. In a world riven with international fears, the pressure for national consensus grows stronger. Ethnic and racial fissures in the national polity cannot so lightly be endured. (Consider the concessions commonly given these groups in times of war.) This tendency is enhanced as men become sensitized to the balance of world population and recognize that firm alliances must be built with non-white peoples, ultimately, it is hoped, in a world alliance. From these pressures external to the nation, there develops an increasing movement toward translating the American creed from a less than fully effective ideology into a working code governing the behavior of men. Slight, yet not unimpressive, signs of this change are evident. In the realm of institutional organizations, there is growing pressure upon government, universities, trade unions and churches to govern themselves by the words they profess. In the realm of interpersonal relations, one has a marked impression of increasing relations between members of diverse racial and ethnic groups. (This change in the pattern of private relations must remain conjectural, until social research searches out the needed *facts*. Periodic researches into the frequency of interracial and interethnic friendships would provide a barometer of interpersonal relations [necessarily invisible to the individual observer] which could be used to supplement current information on institutional changes and public decisions.)

These assumptions of the strategic significance of the three major fronts of social policy on race and ethnic relations and these impressions of secular trends now in progress on each front provide the basis for a consideration of social strategies for the reduction of discrimination.

Implications of the Typology for Social Policy

This necessary detour into the assumptions underlying social policy leads us back to the main path laid down in the account of the four main types appearing in our typology of prejudice and discrimination. And again, however disconcerting the admission may be, it is essential to note that we must be wholly tentative in drawing out the implications of this typology for social policy, for the needed sociological theory and data are plainly inadequate to the practical demands of the situation. Yet if we cannot confidently establish the procedures which should be followed, we can perhaps exclude the procedures which are likely to be unproductive. The successive elimination of alternative procedures is some small gain.

In approaching problems of policy, two things are plain. First, these should be considered from the standpoint of the militant ethnic liberal, for he alone is sufficiently motivated to engage in positive action for the reduction of ethnic discrimination. And second, the fair-weather liberal, the fair-weather illiberal and the all-weather illiberal represent types differing sufficiently to require diverse kinds of treatment.

Treatment of the fair-weather liberal

The fair-weather liberal, it will be remembered, discriminates only when it appears expedient to do so, and experiences some measure of guilt for deviating from his own belief in the American creed. He suffers from this conflict between conscience and conduct. Accordingly, he is a relatively easy target for the all-weather liberal. He represents the strategic group promising the largest immediate returns for the least effort. Recognition of this type defines the first task for the militant liberal who would enter into a collective effort to make the creed a viable and effective set of social norms rather than a ceremonial myth. And though the tactics which this definition of the problem suggests are numerous, I can here only allude to one of these, while emphasizing anew that much of the research data required for fuller confidence in this suggestion are not yet at hand. But passing by the discomforts of our ignorance for the moment, the following would seem to be roughly the case.

Since the fair-weather liberal discriminates only when it seems rewarding to do so, the crucial need is so to change social situations that there are few occasions in which discrimination proves rewarding and many in which it does not. This would suggest that ethnic liberals self-consciously and deliberately seek to draw into the social groups where they constitute a comfortable majority a number of the "expedient discriminators." This would serve to counteract the dangers of self-selection through which liberals come to associate primarily with like-minded individuals. It would, further, provide an interpersonal and social environment for the fair-weather liberal in which he would find substantial social and psychological gains from abiding by his own beliefs, gains which would more than offset the rewards attendant upon occasional discrimination. It appears that men do not long persist in behavior which lacks social corroboration.

We have much to learn about the role of numbers and proportions in determining the behavior of members of a group. But it seems that individuals generally act differently when they are numbered among a minority rather than the majority. This is not to say that minorities abdicate their practices in the face of a contrary-acting majority, but only that the same people are subjected to different strains and pressures according to whether they are included in the majority or the minority. And the fair-weather liberal who finds himself associated with militant ethnic liberals may be expected to forego his occasional deviations into discrimination; he may move from category II into category I; this at least is suggested by the Columbia-Lavanburg researches on ethnic relations in the planned community.

This suggestion calls attention to the possible significance for policy of the composition of a local population with respect to the four types found in our typology, a consideration to which I shall presently return in some detail. But first it is necessary to consider briefly the problems attending policies for dealing with the illiberal.

Treatment of the fair-weather illiberal

Because his *beliefs* correspond to those of the full-fledged liberal, the fair-weather liberal can rather readily be drawn into an interpersonal environment constituted by those of a comparable turn of mind. This would be more difficult for the fair-weather illiberal, whose beliefs are so fully at odds with those of ethnic liberals that he may, at first, only be alienated by association with them. If the initial tactic for the fair-weather liberal, therefore, is a change in interpersonal environment, the seemingly most appropriate tactic for the fair-weather illiberal is a change in the institutional and legal environment. It is, indeed, probably this type which liberals implicitly have in mind when they expect significant changes in behavior to result from the introduction of controls on ethnic discrimination into the legal machinery of our society.

For this type—and it is a major limitation for planning policies of control that we do not know his numbers or his distribution in the country—it would seem that the most effective tactic is the institution of legal controls administered with strict efficiency. This would presumably reduce the amount of *discrimination* practiced by the fair-weather illiberal, though it might *initially* enhance rather than reduce his *prejudices*.

Despite large libraries on the subject, we have little by way of rigorous knowledge indicating how this group of prejudiced but coercible conformists can be brought to abandon their prejudices. But something is known on a research basis of two methods which are *not* effective, information important for social policy since groups of ethnic liberals do commonly utilize these two apparently ineffectual methods. I refer, first, to mass propaganda for "tolerance" and second, the formation of interracial groups seeking to promote tolerance among their members.

Available evidence suggests rather uniformly that propaganda for ethnic equity disseminated through the channels of mass communication does not appreciably modify prejudice. Where prejudice is deep-seated, it serves too many psychological functions for the illiberal to be relinquished in response to propaganda, emanating from howsoever prestigeful a source. The propaganda is either evaded through misinterpretation or selectively assimilated into his prejudice-system in such a fashion as to produce a "boomerang" effect of intensified prejudice.[1] Seemingly, propaganda for ethnic tolerance has a more important effect upon the propagand*ist,* who comes to feel that he "is doing something" about diffusing the American creed, than upon the prejudiced people who are the ostensible objects of the propaganda. It is at least plausible that *the great dependence of ethnic liberals upon propaganda for tolerance persists because of the morale function the propaganda serves for the liberals who feel that something positive is being accomplished.*

A second prevalent tactic for modifying the prejudice of the fair-weather illiberal is that of seeking to draw him into interethnic groups explicitly formed for the promotion of tolerance. This, too, seems largely ineffectual, since the deeply prejudiced individual will not enter into such groups of his own volition. As a consequence of this process of self-selection, these tolerance groups soon come to be comprised by the very ethnic liberals who initiated the enterprise.

This barrier of self-selection can be partially hurdled only if the ethnic illiberals are brought into continued association with militant liberals in groups devoted to significant common values, quite remote from objectives of ethnic equity as such. Thus, as our Columbia-Lavanburg researches have found, many fair-weather illiberals *will* live in interracial housing projects in order to enjoy the rewards of superior housing at a given rental. And some of the illiberals thus brought into personal contact with various ethnic groups under the auspices of prestigeful militant liberals come to modify their prejudices. It is, apparently, only through interethnic collaboration, initially enforced by pressures of the situation, for immediate and significant objectives (other than tolerance) that the self-insulation of the fair-weather illiberal from rewarding interethnic contacts can be removed.

But however difficult it may presently be to affect the *prejudicial sentiments* of the fair-weather illiberal, his *discriminatory practices* can be lessened by the uniform, prompt and prestigeful use of legal and institutional sanctions. The critical problem is to ascertain the proportions of fair-weather and all-weather illiberals in a given local population in order to have some clue to the probable effectiveness or ineffectiveness of anti-discrimination legislation.

Treatment of the all-weather illiberal

It is, of course, the hitherto confirmed illiberal, persistently translating his prejudices into active discrimination, who represents the most difficult problem. But though he requires longer and more careful treatment, it is possible that he is not beyond change. In every instance, his social surroundings must be assiduously taken into account. It makes a peculiarly large difference whether he is in a cultural region of bigotry or in a predominantly "liberal" area, given over to verbal adherence to the American creed, at the very least. As this cultural climate varies, so must the prescription for his cure and the prognosis for a relatively quick or long delayed recovery.

In an unfavorable cultural climate—and this does not necessarily exclude the benign regions of the Far South—the immediate resort will probably have to be that of working through legal and administrative federal controls over extreme discrimination, with full recognition that, in all probability, these regulations will be systematically evaded for some time to come. In such cultural regions, we may expect nullification of the law as the common practice, perhaps as common as was the case in the nation at large with respect to the Eighteenth Amendment, often with the connivance of local officers of the law. The large gap between the new law and local mores will not *at once* produce significant change of prevailing practices; token punishments of violations will probably be more common than effective control. At best, one may assume that significant change will be fitful, and excruciatingly slow. But secular changes in the economy may in due course lend support to the new legal framework of control over discrimination. As the economic shoe pinches because the illiberals do not fully mobilize the resources of industrial manpower nor extend their local markets through equitable wage-payments, they may slowly abandon some discriminatory practices as they come to find that these do not always pay—even the discriminator. So far as discrimination is concerned, organized counteraction is possible and some small results may be expected. But it would seem that wishes father thoughts, when one expects basic changes in the immediate future in these regions of institutionalized discrimination.

The situation is somewhat different with regard to the scattered, rather than aggregated, ethnic illiberals found here and there throughout the country. Here the mores and a social organization oriented toward the American creed still have some measure of prestige and the resources of a majority of liberals can be mobilized to isolate the illiberal. In these surroundings, it is possible to move the all-weather illiberal toward Type III—he can be brought to conform with institutional regulations, even though he does not surrender his prejudices. And once he has entered upon this role of the dissident but conforming individual, the remedial program designed for the fair-weather illiberal would be in order.

Ecological Bases of Social Policy

Where authenticated data are few and scattered and one must make *some* decision, whether it be the decision to act in a given fashion or not to take action at all, then one must resort to reasonable conjecture as the basis for policy. That is what I have done in assuming throughout that policies designed to curb ethnic discrimination must be oriented toward differences in the composition of a population with respect to the four types here under discussion. It is safe to assume that communities and larger areas vary in the proportion of these several types. Some communities may have an overwhelming majority of militant liberals, in positions of authority and among the rank-and-file. Others may be short on ethnic liberals but long on fair-weather illiberals who respond promptly though reluctantly to the pressure of institutional controls. It would seem reasonable to suppose that different social policies of control over discrimination would be required as these ecological distributions of prejudice-discrimination types vary.

This assumption is concretized in the conjectural distributions of these types set

Hypothetical Class and Regional Profiles and Cultural Clichés Identifying Each Type in the Prejudice-Discrimination Typology

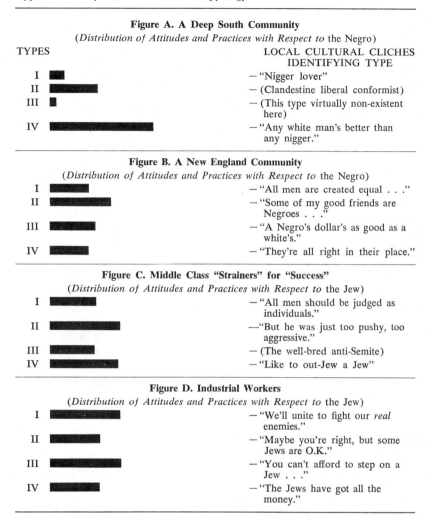

Figure A. A Deep South Community
(*Distribution of Attitudes and Practices with Respect to* the Negro)

TYPES   LOCAL CULTURAL CLICHES IDENTIFYING TYPE

I — "Nigger lover"

II — (Clandestine liberal conformist)

III — (This type virtually non-existent here)

IV — "Any white man's better than any nigger."

Figure B. A New England Community
(*Distribution of Attitudes and Practices with Respect to* the Negro)

I — "All men are created equal . . ."

II — "Some of my good friends are Negroes . . ."

III — "A Negro's dollar's as good as a white's."

IV — "They're all right in their place."

Figure C. Middle Class "Strainers" for "Success"
(*Distribution of Attitudes and Practices with Respect to* the Jew)

I — "All men should be judged as individuals."

II — "But he was just too pushy, too aggressive."

III — (The well-bred anti-Semite)

IV — "Like to out-Jew a Jew"

Figure D. Industrial Workers
(*Distribution of Attitudes and Practices with Respect to* the Jew)

I — "We'll unite to fight our *real* enemies."

II — "Maybe you're right, but some Jews are O.K."

III — "You can't afford to step on a Jew . . ."

IV — "The Jews have got all the money."

forth in the following charts. Consider the same legislation aimed at curbing job discrimination against the Negro as this might operate in a community in the Far South and in New England. Since it runs counter to the strongly entrenched attitudes of the large majority in the one community and not in the other, we may suppose that the same law will produce different results in the two cases. This must be put in a reasonable time perspective. Conceivably, the short-term and the long-term effects may differ widely. But with respect to both the long and the short term, it matters greatly whether there is a sufficient local nucleus of ethnic liberals in positions of prestige and authority. The ecological and social distribution of the prejudice-discrimination types is of central importance in assessing the probable outcome. Whether a law providing for equitable access to jobs will in fact produce this result depends not only on the law itself as on the rest of the social structure.

The law is a small, though important, part of the whole. Unless a strong economic and social base for its support exists in a community, the law will be nullified in practice.

Figures C and D set forth, again conjecturally, the distribution of the prejudice-discrimination types with respect to the Jew among middle-class "strainers" and industrial workers. Should research find that the industrial worker stratum indeed has a larger proportion of militant ethnic liberals than the middle classes, then initial support of an active anti-discrimination policy might most effectively be sought there. But whatever the actual facts might show, the policy-maker attuned to the realities as well as the objectives of the problem would do well to take these into account in the design of his program.

If makers of policy are to escape utopianism on the one hand and pessimistic inaction on the other, they must utilize diverse procedures for modifying attitudes and behavior according to the distribution of these prejudice-discrimination types.

Finally, though action cannot, perhaps, wait upon continued research, it is suggested that the following kinds of information are needed as a basis for effective anti-discrimination policy:

1. An inventory to determine the relative proportions in various areas of these four prejudice-discrimination types;
2. Within each area, an inventory of these proportions among the several social classes, major associations, and nationality groups;
3. Periodic audits of these proportions, thus providing a barometric map of ethnic attitudes and practices repeatedly brought up to date and marking the short-run and secular trends in diverse areas and groups;
4. Continuing studies of the consequences of various programs designed to promote ethnic equities, thus reducing the wastage presently entailed by well-intentioned, expensive and ineffectual programs.

This is a large research order. But the American creed, as set down in the basic moral documents of this nation, seems deserving of the systematic exercise of our social intelligence fully as much as it is deserving of our moral resolution.

NOTE

1. There is a large literature bearing on this point. For recent discussions, see P. F. Lazarsfeld, "Some Remarks on the Role of Mass Media in So-called Tolerance Propaganda," *Journal of Social Issues, Summer,* 1947; P. F. Lazarsfeld and R. K. Merton, "Media of Mass Communication, Popular Taste, and Organized Social Action," in Lyman Bryson (ed.), *Communication of Ideas,* New York, Institute for Religious and Social Studies, 1948; M. Jahoda and E. Cooper, "Evasion of Propaganda: How Prejudiced People Respond to Anti-prejudice Propaganda," *Journal of Psychology,* 23 (1947), 15–25. For an appraisal of the inadequate research to date on this problem, see R. M. Williams, Jr., *The Reduction of Intergroup Tensions,* New York, Social Science Research Council, 1947, 32 ff. The absence of adequate evidence attesting the *pragmatic* (not statistical) significance of tolerance propaganda suggests that propaganda programs now represent an act of faith on the part of propagandists.

38. CASTE IN INDIA AND THE UNITED STATES

GERALD D. BERREMAN

*For many years there has been controversy over whether or not the concept "caste"
is appropriate to describe the barriers which exist between white and black Americans.
Some contend that the term is appropriate only to India; others argue that it has
far wider usage and that it is not only appropriate but is useful as a concept to define
particular kinds of intergroup situations cross-culturally. Gerald D. Berreman supports
the latter view.*

*Having compared patterns of race relations in southern United States with
relations between the untouchables and other castes of India, Berreman suggests
that the two systems are structurally similar though they differ in content and origin.
He defines a caste system as "a hierarchy of endogamous divisions in which membership
is hereditary and permanent." The hierarchy pertains not merely to inequities in
status but also to inequities in access to goods and services and more general
opportunities.*

*Gerald D. Berreman is Professor of Anthropology at the University of California,
Berkeley. He has spent many years studying kinship and caste arrangements in
India and is the author of* Hindus of the Himalaya *(1963). He has also published an
important monograph on anthropological fieldwork,* Behind Many Masks *(1962).*

Many writers who have contributed to the
vast literature on the caste system in India
have emphasized its unique aspects and
ignored or denied the qualities it shares
with rigid systems of social stratification
found in other societies. Others have
claimed to find caste systems or caste
groups in such widely scattered areas as
Arabia, Polynesia, Africa, Guatemala,
and Japan.[1] Some observers refer to
Negro-white relations in the United States,
and particularly in the South, as being
those of caste,[2] a usage which others, including C. S. Johnson, Oliver C. Cox, and,
more recently, G. E. Simpson and J. M.
Yinger, have criticized. This paper will
compare the relationship between "touchable," especially twice-born, and "untouchable" castes in India with that between Negroes and whites in the southern
United States.

Caste can be defined so that it is applicable only to India, just as it is possible to
define narrowly almost any sociocultural
phenomenon. Indianists have traditionally
held to specific, usually enumerative, definitions. Indeed, the caste system in India
has several unique features, among which
are its religious aspects, its complexity,
and the degree to which the caste is a
cohesive group that regulates the behavior
of its members. Within India there is con-

Reprinted from the *American Journal of Sociology,* **64** (1960), 120–127, by permission of the
author and The University of Chicago Press. Copyright © 1960 by The University of Chicago
Press.

siderable variation in the characteristics of, and the relations among, the groups to which the term "caste" is applied.

However, caste can be accurately defined in broader terms. For many purposes similar social facts may be usefully categorized together, despite differences which, while not denied, are not crucial to the purposes at hand. For purposes of cross-cultural comparison this is necessary: for the study of social process, and with the aim of deriving generalizations, caste is a concept which might well be applied cross-culturally. For these purposes a caste system may be defined as a *hierarchy of endogamous divisions in which membership is hereditary and permanent.* Here hierarchy includes inequality both in status and in access to goods and services. Interdependence of the subdivisions, restricted contacts among them, occupational specialization, and/or a degree of cultural distinctiveness might be added as criteria, although they appear to be correlates rather than defining characteristics.

This definition is perhaps best viewed as describing an ideal type at one end of a continuum along which systems of social stratification might be ranged. There can be little doubt that the systems in India and the southern United States would fall far toward the caste extreme of the continuum.[3] It now becomes necessary to look at the differences cited as crucial by those who object to use of the term "caste" in both societies. The objections raised by those interested in structure, relationships, and interaction will be discussed here; the objections of those interested in specific content will be ignored—not because the latter objections are less cogent, but because they are less relevant to the comparison of social systems.[4]

Johnson sees many similarities in the two systems but objects to identifying both as caste, since "a caste system is not only a separated system, it is a stable system in which changes are socially impossible; the

fact that change cannot occur is accepted by all, or practically all, participants. . . . No expenditure of psychological or physical energy is necessary to maintain a caste system." [5] Simpson and Yinger agree with Johnson and further object that, in the United States, "we lack a set of religious principles justifying a rigid system of social stratification and causing it to be willingly accepted by those at all levels." [6] Cox lists a number of features of a caste system (i.e., caste in India) which distinguish it from an interracial situation (i.e., Negro-white relations in America), important among which are its "nonconflictive," "nonpathological," and "static" nature, coupled with absence of "aspiration and progressiveness." [7]

Central to these distinctions is that caste in India is passively accepted and endorsed by all on the basis of religio-philosophical explanations which are universally subscribed to, while Negro-white relations in America are characterized by dissent, resentment, guilt, and conflict. But this contrast is invalid, resulting, as it does, from an idealized and unrealistic view of Indian caste, contrasted with a more realistic, pragmatic view of American race relations. Indian caste is viewed as it is supposed to work rather than as it does work; American race relations are seen as they do work rather than as they are supposed, by the privileged, to work. The traditional white southerner, asked to describe relations between the races, will describe the Negro as happy in his place, which he may quote science and Scripture to justify. This is similar to the explanations offered for the Indian system by the advantaged.

The point here is that ideal intercaste behavior and attitudes in India are much like those in America, while the actual interaction and attitudes are also similar. Commonly, ideal behavior and attitudes in India have been contrasted with real behavior and attitudes in America—a fact which has led to a false impression of difference. Similarly, comparisons of race relations in the rapidly changing urban or industrial South with caste relations in slowly changing rural or agrarian India lead to erroneous conclusions. Valid comparison can be made at either level, but must be with comparable data. The impact on intergroup relations of the social and economic changes which accompany urban life seems to be similar in both societies. Recent literature on village India and on the changing caste functions and caste relations in cities and industrial areas presents a realistic picture which goes far toward counteracting traditional stereotypes of Indian caste.[8]

In a study of caste functioning in Sirkanda, a hill village of northern Uttar Pradesh, India, I was struck by the similarity of relations between the twice-born and untouchable castes to race relations in the southern United States.[9] In both situations there is a genuine caste division, according to the definition above. In the two systems there are rigid rules of avoidance between castes, and certain types of contacts are defined as contaminating, while others are non-contaminating. The ideological justification for the rules differs in the two cultures, as do the definitions of the acts themselves; but these are cultural details. The tabooed contacts are symbolically rather than literally injurious as evidenced by the many inconsistencies in application of the rules.[10] Enforced deference, for example, is a prominent feature of both systems. Lack of deference from low castes is not contaminating, but it is promptly punished, for it implies equality. The essential similarity lies in the fact that the function of the rules in both cases is to maintain the caste system with institutionalized inequality as its fundamental feature. In the United States, color is a conspicuous mark of caste, while in India there are complex religious features which do not appear in America, but in both cases dwelling area, occupation, place of worship, and cultural behavior, and so on, are important symbols associated with caste status. The crucial fact is

that caste status is determined, and therefore the systems are perpetuated, by birth: membership in them is ascribed and unalterable. Individuals in low castes are considered inherently inferior and are relegated to a disadvantaged position, regardless of their behavior. From the point of view of the social psychology of intergroup relations, this is probably the most important common and distinct feature of caste systems.

In both the United States and India, high castes maintain their superior position by exercising powerful sanctions, and they rationalize their status with elaborate philosophical, religious, psychological, or genetic explanations. The latter are not sufficient in themselves to maintain the systems, largely because they are incompletely accepted among those whose depressed positions they are thought to justify. In both places castes are economically interdependent. In both there are great differences in power and privilege among, as well as class differences within, castes and elaborate barriers to free social intercourse among them.

Similarities in the two caste systems extend throughout the range of behavior and attitudes expressed in relations among groups. An important and conspicuous area of similarity is associated with competition for certain benefits or "gains" which are personally gratifying and/or socially valued and which by their nature or under the circumstances cannot be enjoyed by all equally. Competitive striving is, of course, not unique to caste organization; it is probably found to some extent in all societies. It is subject to a variety of social controls resulting in a variety of forms of social stratification, one of which is a caste system as defined here. However, the genesis of caste systems is not here at issue.[11]

The caste system in India and in the United States has secured gains for the groups established at the top of the hierarchy. Their desire to retain their position for themselves and their children accounts for their efforts to perpetuate the system. John Dollard, in his discussion of "Southerntown," identifies their gains as economic, sexual, and in prestige.

In the economic field, low-caste dependence is maintained in India as in America by economic and physical sanctions. This assures not only greater high-caste income but a ready supply of free service and cheap labor from the low castes. It also guarantees the continuing availability of the other gains. In India it is the most explicitly recognized high-caste advantage.

The sexual gain for the southern white caste is defined by Dollard, quoting whom I will substitute "high caste" and "low caste" for "white" and "Negro," respectively. In this form his definition fits the Indian caste system equally well.

In simplest terms, we mean by a "sexual gain" the fact that [high-caste] men, by virtue of their caste position, have access to two classes of women, those of the [high] and [low] castes. The same condition is somewhat true of the [low-caste] women, except that they are rather the objects of the gain than the choosers, though it is a fact that they have some degree of access to [high-caste] men as well as men of their own caste. [Low-caste] men and [high-caste] women, on the other hand, are limited to their own castes in sexual choices.[12]

This arrangement is maintained in the Indian caste system, as it is in America, by severe sanctions imposed upon any low-caste man who might venture to defy the code, by the toleration accorded high-caste men who have relations with low-caste women, and by the precautions which high-caste men take to protect their women from the low castes.

High-caste people gain, by virtue of their caste status alone, deference from others, constant reinforcement of a feeling of superiority, and a permanent scapegoat in the lower castes. Dollard has stated the implications of this gain in prestige, and, again substituting a caste designation for a racial one, his statement describes the Indian system perfectly:

The gain here . . . consists in the fact that a member of the [high] caste has an automatic right to demand forms of behavior from [low-caste people] which serve to increase his own self-esteem.

It must always be remembered that in the end this deference is demanded and not merely independently given.[13]

Ideally the high-caste person is paternalistic and authoritarian, while the low-caste person responds with deferential, submissive, subservient behavior. Gallagher might have been describing India rather than America when he noted: "By the attitudes of mingled fear, hostility, deprecation, discrimination, amused patronage, friendly domination, and rigid authoritarianism, the white caste generates opposite and complementary attitudes in the Negro caste." [14]

An additional high-caste gain in India is the religious tradition which gives people of high caste promise of greater rewards in the next life than those of low caste. People can increase their rewards in the next life by fulfilling their traditional caste duty. For high castes, this generally results in increasing the economic advantages and prestige acquired in this life, while it requires that the low castes subordinate their own economic gains and prestige in this life to the service and honor of high castes. Thus, for high-caste people, behavior leading to immediate rewards is consistent with ultimate rewards, while, for low-caste people, behavior required for the two rewards is contradictory.

These advantages are significant and recognized reasons for maintenance of the system by the privileged groups.[15] They are expressed in folklore, proverbs, and jokes; for instance, a story tells that, as the funeral procession of an old landlord passed two untouchable women going for water, one hand of the corpse fell from under the shroud and flopped about. One of the women turned to the other and remarked, "You see, Takur Singh is dead, but he still beckons to us." Other stories recount the avariciousness of Brahmins in their priestly role, the hardheartedness of landlords and the like.

The compensatory gains for low-caste people are cited more often by high-caste advocates of the system than by those alleged to enjoy them. They are gains common to authoritarian systems everywhere and are usually subject to the will of the dominant groups.

As noted above, India is frequently cited as an example of a society in which people of deprived and subject status are content with their lot, primarily justifying it by religion and philosophy. This is the characteristic of caste in India most often cited to distinguish it from hereditary systems elsewhere, notably in the southern United States. On the basis of my research and the literature, I maintain that this is not accurate and therefore not a valid distinction. Its prevalence is attributable in part, at least, to the vested interests of the advantaged and more articulate castes in the perpetuation of the caste system and the maintenance of a favorable view of it to outsiders. The same arguments and the same biases are frequently presented by apologists for the caste system of the southern United States.

In both systems there is a tendency to look to the past as a period of halcyon amity and to view conflict and resentment as resulting from outside disturbances of the earlier normal equilibrium. Alien ideas, or large-scale economic disturbances, or both, are often blamed for reform movements and rebellion. Such explanations may account for the national and regional reform movements which find their advocates and followers primarily among the educated and social elites; they do not account for the recurrent grass-roots attempts, long endemic in India, to raise caste status; for the state of mind which has often led to low-caste defections from Hinduism when the op-

portunity to do so without fear of major reprisals has presented itself; nor for the chronic resentment and tension which characterizes intercaste relations in even so remote a village as Sirkanda, the one in which I worked.

Among the low or untouchable castes in Sirkanda, there was a great deal of readily expressed resentment regarding their caste position. Specific complaints revolved around economic, prestige, and sexual impositions by the high castes. Although resentment was suppressed in the presence of people of the dominant high castes, it was readily expressed where their was no fear of detection or reprisal.[16] Low-caste people felt compelled to express village loyalties in public, but in private acts and attitudes caste loyalties were consistently and intensely dominant when the two conflicted.

Caste, as such, was not often seriously questioned in the village. Objections were characteristically directed not at "caste" but at "my position in the caste hierarchy."

In the multicaste system of India, abolition of the system evidently seems impossible from the point of view of any particular caste, and a change in its rank within the system is viewed by its members as the only plausible means of improving the situation. Moreover, abolition would destroy the caste as a group which is superior to at least some other groups, and, while it would give caste members an opportunity to mingle as equals with their superiors, it would also force them to mingle as equals with their inferiors. Abolition, even if it could be accomplished, would thus create an ambivalent situation for any particular caste in contrast to the clear-cut advantages of an improvement in rank.

In the dual system of the southern United States where the high caste is clearly dominant, abolition of the caste division may be seen by the subordinate group as the only plausible remedy for their deprived position. Furthermore, they have nothing to lose but their inferior status, since there are no lower castes. There are, of course, Negroes and organized groups of Negroes, such as the black supremacist "Muslims" recently in the news in the United States, who want to invert the caste hierarchy; conversely, there are low-caste people in India who want to abolish the entire system. But these seem to be atypical viewpoints. The anticaste religions and reform movements which have from time to time appealed with some success to the lower castes in India, for example, Buddhism, Islam, Christianity, Sikhism, have been unable, in practice, to remain casteless. This seems to be a point of real difference between Indian and American low-caste attitudes, for in America objection is more characteristically directed toward the system as such.[17]

In Sirkanda those low-caste people who spoke most piously against high-caste abuses were likely to be equally abusive to their caste inferiors. However, no low caste was encountered whose members did not seriously question its place in the hierarchy. A sizable literature is accumulating concerning castes which have sought to alter their status.[18] Such attempts were made in Sirkanda. A more common reaction to deprived status on the part of low-caste people was what Dollard calls "passive accommodation" coupled with occasional ingroup aggression.[19]

In both America and India there is a tendency for the person of low caste to "laugh it off" or to become resigned. In Sirkanda low-caste people could not avoid frequent contacts with their superiors, because of their proximity and relative numbers. Contacts were frequently informal, but status differences and the dangers of ritual pollution were not forgotten. An untouchable in this village who covered up his bitter resentment by playing the buffoon received favors denied to his more sullen caste fellows. The irresponsible, simple-minded untouchable is a widespread stereotype and one which he, like

the Negro, has found useful. Similarly, sullen resignation, with the attendant stereotype of lazy shiftlessness, is a common response, typified in the southern Negro axiom, "Do what the man says." This, too, helps him avoid trouble, although it does little for the individual's self-respect. Aggression against the economically and numerically dominant high castes in Sirkanda was too dangerous to be a reasonable alternative. It was discussed by low-caste people in private but was rarely carried out. Even legitimate complaints to outside authority were avoided in view of the general belief that the high-caste's wealth would insure an outcome unfavorable to the low castes—a belief well grounded in experience.

Since they harbored indignation and resentment, a number of rationalizations of their status were employed by low-caste people, apparently as mechanisms to lessen the sting of reality. Thus, they often attributed their caste status to relative wealth and numbers: "If we were wealthy and in the majority, we would make the high castes untouchable."

Three more explanations of their caste status were consistently offered by low-caste people. These had the effect of denying the legitimacy of their low-caste position:

1) Members of the entire caste (or subcaste) group would deny that they deserved the low status to which they had been assigned. One example:

Englishmen and Muslims are untouchables because they have an alien religion and they eat beef. This is as it should be. We are Hindus and we do not eat beef, yet we, too, are treated as untouchables. This is not proper. We should be accorded higher status.

No group would admit to being lowest in the caste hierarchy.

2) People might grant that the caste of their clan, lineage, or family was of low status but deny that their particular group really belong to it. I have not encountered a low-caste group which did not claim

high-caste ancestry or origin. Thus a typical comment is:

> Yes, we are drummers by occupation, but our ancestor was a Brahmin who married a drummer woman. By rights, therefore, we should be Brahmins, but in such cases the high castes here go against the usual custom and assign the child the caste of his low-caste parent rather than of his father, from whom a person inherits everything else.

3) A person might grant that his own caste and even his lineage or family were of low status, but his explanation would excuse him from responsibility for it. Such explanations were supplied by Brahmins who, as the most privileged caste and the recipients of religiously motivated charity from all castes, have a vested interest in maintenance of the system and its acceptance by those at all levels. An individual's horoscope would describe him as having been of high caste and exemplary behavior in a previous life and therefore destined for even greater things in the present life. However, in performing some religiously meritorious act in his previous existence, he inadvertently sinned (e.g., he was a raja, tricked by dishonest servants who did not give to the Brahmin the charity he intended for them). As a result he had to be punished in this life with a low rebirth.

Thus, no one said, in effect, "I am of low status and so are my family members and my caste-fellows, and justly so, because of our misdeeds in previous lives." To do so would lead to a psychologically untenable position, though one advocated by high-caste people and by orthodox Hinduism. Rationalizations or beliefs such as these form a consistent pattern—they are not isolated instances. Neither are they unique to the village or culture reported here: the literature reveals similar beliefs elsewhere in North India.[20] They evidently indicate something less than enthusiastic acceptance of caste position and, meanwhile, they perhaps alleviate or divert resentment.

That people remain in an inferior position, therefore, does not mean that they do so willingly, or that they believe it is justified, or that they would do anything in their power to change it, given the opportunity. Rationalizations of caste status which are consistent and convincing to those who are unaffected or who benefit from them seem much less so to those whose deprivation they are expected to justify or explain. Adherence to a religious principle may not significantly affect the attitudes and behavior to which logic would seem, or to which dogma attempts, to tie it. A comparison of the realities of caste attitudes and interaction in India and the United States suggests that no group of people is content to be low in a caste hierarchy—to live a life of inherited deprivation and subjection—regardless of the rationalizations offered them by their superiors or constructed by themselves. This is one of many points on which further cross-cultural comparison, and only cross-cultural comparison of caste behavior might be conclusive.

It should be evident that the range of similarities between caste in India and race relations in America, when viewed as relations among people, is wide and that the details are remarkably similar in view of the differences in cultural context. Without denying or belittling the differences, I would hold that the term "caste system" is applicable at the present time in the southern United States, if it is applicable anywhere outside of Hindu India, and that it can be usefully applied to societies with systems of hierarchical, endogamous subdivisions whose membership is hereditary and permanent, wherever they occur. By comparing caste situations, so defined, it should be possible to derive further insight, not only into caste in India, but into a widespread type of relations between groups—insight which is obscured if we insist upon treating Indian caste as entirely unique.

NOTES

1. E. D. Chapple and C. S. Coon, *Principles of Anthropology,* New York: Henry Holt & Co., 1942, p. 437; S. F. Nadel, "Caste and Government in Primitive Society," *Journal of the Anthropological Society of Bombay,* New Series VIII (1954), 9–22; M. M. Tumin, *Caste in a Peasant Society,* Princeton, N.J.: Princeton University Press, 1952; J. D. Donoghue, "An Eta Community in Japan: The Social Persistence of Outcaste Groups," *American Anthropologist,* 59 (1957), 1000–1017.

2. E.g., Allison Davis, Kingsley Davis, John Dollard, Buell Gallagher, Gunnar Myrdal, Kenneth Stampp, Lloyd Warner.

3. The Tira of Africa, for example, would not fall so far toward this extreme (cf. Nadel, *op. cit.,* pp. 18 ff.).

4. As a matter of fact, ignorance of the details of content in the patterns of relations between whites and Negroes in the United States has prevented many Indianists from seeing very striking similarities. Two contrasting views of the cross-cultural applicability of the concept of caste have appeared since this paper was written: F. C. Bailey, "For a Sociology of India?" *Contributions to Indian Sociology,* No. 3 (July, 1959), 88–101, esp. 97–98; and E. R. Leach, "Introduction: What Should We Mean by Caste?" in *Aspects of Caste in South India, Ceylon and North-west Pakistan* ("Cambridge Papers in Social Anthropology," No. 2 [Cambridge: Cambridge University Press, 1959]), pp. 1–10.

5. C. S. Johnson, *Growing Up in the Black Belt,* Washington, D.C.: American Council on Education, 1941, p. 326.

6. G. E. Simpson and J. M. Yinger, *Racial and Cultural Minorities,* New York: Harper, 1953, p. 328.

7. O. C. Cox, "Race and Caste: A Distinction," *American Journal of Sociology,* 50 (1945) 360 (see also his *Caste, Class and Race,* Garden City, N.Y.: Doubleday, 1948).

8. See, for example, the following community studies: F. G. Bailey, *Caste and the Economic Frontier,* Manchester: University of Manchester Press, 1957; Berreman, *op. cit.;* S. C. Dube, *Indian Village,* Ithaca, N.Y.: Cornell University Press, 1955; Oscar Lewis, *Village Life in Northern India,* Urbana: University of Illinois Press, 1958; McKim Marriott (ed.), *Village India* (American Anthropological Association Memoir No. 83 [Chicago: University of Chicago Press, 1955]); M. E. Opler and R. D. Singh, "The Division of Labor in an Indian Village," in *A Reader in General Anthropology,* ed. C. S. Coon, New York: Henry Holt, 1948, pp. 464–96; M. N. Srinivas *et al., India's Villages* (Development Department, West Bengal: West Bengal Government Press, 1955). See also, for example, the following studies of caste in the contemporary setting: Bailey, *op. cit.;* N. K. Bose, "Some Aspects of Caste in Bengal," *American Journal of Folklore,* 71 (1958), 397–412; Leach, *op. cit.;* Arthur Niehoff, *Factory Workers in India* ("Milwaukee Public Museum Publications in Anthropology," No. 5 [1959]); M. N. Srinivas, "Caste in Modern India," *Journal of Asian Studies,* 16 (1957), 529–548; and the several articles comprising the symposium on "Caste in India" contained in *Man in India,* 39 (1959), 92–162.

9. The following discussion is based not exclusively on the Sirkanda materials but on observations and literature in non-hill areas as well. The hill area presents some distinct regional variations in caste structure, important among which is the absence of intermediate castes—all are either twice-born or untouchable. This leads to a dichotomous situation, as in the United States, but one which differs in that there are important caste divisions on either side of the "pollution barrier" (cf. Bailey, *op. cit.,* p. 8; Berreman, *op. cit.,* pp. 389 ff.). Relations across this barrier do not differ greatly from similar relations among plains castes, although somewhat more informal contact is allowed—pollution comes about less easily—in the hills.

10. The symbolic acts—the "etiquette" of caste relations—in India and in America are often remarkably similar. The symbolism in America is, of course, not primarily religious as much as it is in India, although the sacred aspects in India are often far from the minds of those engaging in the acts and are not infrequently unknown to them.

11. Cf. Nadel, *op. cit.*

12. John Dollard, *Caste and Class in a Southern Town,* Garden City, N.Y.: Doubleday, 1957, p. 135 (cf. Berreman, *op. cit.,* pp. 470 ff.).

13. Dollard, *op. cit.,* p. 174. Nadel, speaking of caste in general, has noted that "the lower caste are despised, not only unhappily under-privileged; they bear a stigma apart from being unfortunate. Conversely, the higher castes are not merely entitled to the possession of coveted privileges, but are also in some way exalted and endowed with a higher dignity" (Nadel, *op. cit.,* p. 16).

14. B. G. Gallagher, *American Caste and the Negro College,* New York: Columbia University Press, 1938, p. 109.

15. Cf. Pauline M. Mahar, "Changing Caste Ideology in a North Indian Village," *Journal of Social Issues,* 14 (1958), 51–65, esp. pp. 55–56; Kailash K. Singh, "Intercaste Tensions in Two Villages in North India" (unpublished Ph.D. dissertation, Cornell University, 1957), pp. 184–185; and M. N. Srinivas, "The Dominant Caste in Rampura," *American Anthropologist,* 61 (1959), 1–16, esp. p. 4.

16. Elaborate precautions were often taken by informants to insure against any possibility that their expressions of feeling might become known to their caste superiors, which is very similar to behavior I have observed among Negroes of Montgomery, Alabama.

17. Whether this difference in attitude is widely correlated with multiple, as compared to dual, caste systems, or is attributable to other differences in the Indian and American situations, can be established only by further comparative work.

18. E.g., Opler and Singh, *op. cit.,* p. 476; B. S. Cohn, "The Changing Status of a Depressed Caste," in Marriott (ed.), *op. cit.,* pp. 53–77; and Bailey, *op. cit.,* pp. 220–226.

19. Dollard, *op. cit.,* p. 253.

20. Cf. E. T. Atkinson, *The Himalayan Districts of the North-Western Provinces of India* (Allahabad: North-Western Provinces and Oudh Press, 1886), 3, 446; B. S. Cohn, "The Camars of Senapur: A Study of the Changing Status of a Depressed Caste" (unpublished Ph.D. dissertation, Cornell University, 1954), pp. 112 ff.; and D. N. Majumdar, *The Fortunes of Primitive Tribes,* Lucknow: Universal Publishers Ltd., 1944, p. 193.

39. THE PSYCHOLOGY OF THE GHETTO

KENNETH B. CLARK

*For nonwhites in the United States, segregation is more than an ecological
phenomenon. It creeps into every nook and cranny of daily life. Its effect is not
difficult to observe. One need not be a sociologist to see that the "gray areas" of our
great cities, those sandwiched between the better residential neighborhoods and the
commercial centers, and the "brown areas" of the rural districts are blighted by
deprivation and despair. And one need not be a psychologist to see that those who live
in these urban and rural slums are marked by oppression. But many people have not
bothered to look, and as Ralph Ellison so poignantly reminds his readers, the denizens of
America's Harlems have been aptly called "invisible men."*

*In recent years the invisible man and his problems have come into the open. In
this selection, the psychologist Kenneth B. Clark presents a portrait of life in the black
ghetto. He describes the difficulty of growing up black in a white man's world. He
analyzes the family life in the black ghetto and its deleterious effect upon the male's
self-image. And he describes the rationalizations of whites for their persistent discrimination against black people.*

*The complexity of black-white relations in the United States cannot be adequately
summarized in a single essay. Yet, Clark's commentary raises a number of fundamental
questions relevant both to the sociology of race relations and to those who seek
an end to those inequities still extant in a society which claims the American creed
as a touchstone of the democratic way of life.*

*Kenneth B. Clark is Professor of Psychology and Director, Social Dynamics Re-
search Institute at City College of the City University of New York and the author of*
Prejudice and Your Child *(1955),* The Negro Protest *(1963), and* Dark Ghetto
(1965). He is also coeditor, with Talcott Parsons, of The Negro American *(1966).
Dr. Clark is one of the founders of Harlem Youth Opportunities Unlimited and is
an elected member of the New York State Board of Regents. His testimony on
the psychological effects of segregation was regarded by many as an influential factor
in the 1954 Supreme Court decision overturning the "separate but equal" doctrine.*

It is now generally understood that chronic and remediable social injustices corrode and damage the human personality, thereby robbing it of its effectiveness, of its creativity, if not its actual humanity. No matter how desperately one seeks to deny it, this simple fact persists and in- trudes itself. It is the fuel of protests and revolts. Racial segregation, like all other forms of cruelty and tyranny, debases all human beings—those who are its victims, those who victimize, and in quite subtle ways those who are merely accessories.

This human debasement can only be

comprehended as a consequence of the society which spawns it. The victims of segregation do not initially desire to be segregated, they do not "prefer to be with their own people," in spite of the fact that this belief is commonly stated by those who are not themselves segregated. A most cruel and psychologically oppressive aspect and consequence of enforced segregation is that its victims can be made to accommodate to their victimized status and under certain circumstances to state that it *is* their desire to be set apart, or to agree that subjugation is not really detrimental but beneficial. The fact remains that exclusion, rejection, and a stigmatized status are not desired and are not voluntary states. Segregation is neither sought nor imposed by healthy or potentially healthy human beings.

Human beings who are forced to live under ghetto conditions and whose daily experience tells them that almost nowhere in society are they respected and granted the ordinary dignity and courtesy accorded to others will, as a matter of course, begin to doubt their own worth. Since every human being depends upon his cumulative experiences with others for clues as to how he should view and value himself, children who are consistently rejected understandably begin to question and doubt whether they, their family, and their group really deserve no more respect from the larger society than they receive. These doubts become the seeds of a pernicious self- and group-hatred, the Negro's complex and debilitating prejudice against himself.

The preoccupation of many Negroes with hair straighteners, skin bleachers, and the like illustrates this tragic aspect of American racial prejudice—Negroes have come to believe in their own inferiority. In recent years Negro men and women have rebelled against the constant struggle to become white and have given special emphasis to their "Negroid" features and hair textures in a self-conscious acceptance of "negritude"—a whole-hearted embracing of the African heritage. But whether a Negro woman uses hair straightener or whether she highlights her natural hair texture by flaunting *au naturel* styles, whether a Negro man hides behind a neat Ivy League suit or wears blue jeans defiantly in the manner of the Student Nonviolent Coordinating Committee (SNCC), each is still reacting primarily to the pervasive factor of race and still not free to take himself for granted or to judge himself by the usual standards of personal success and character. It is still the white man's society that governs the Negro's image of himself.

Fantasy Protections

Many Negroes live sporadically in a world of fantasy, and fantasy takes different forms at different ages. In childhood the delusion is a simple one—the child may pretend that he is really white. When Negro children as young as three years old are shown white- and Negro-appearing dolls or asked to color pictures of children to look like themselves, many of them tend to reject the dark-skinned dolls as "dirty" and "bad" or to color the picture of themselves a light color or a bizarre shade like purple. But the fantasy is not complete, for when asked to identify which doll is like themselves, some Negro children, particularly in the North, will refuse, burst into tears, and run away. By the age of seven most Negro children have accepted the reality that they are, after all, dark skinned. But the stigma remains; they have been forced to recognize themselves as inferior. Few if any Negroes ever fully lose that sense of shame and self-hatred.

To the Negro child the most serious injury seems to be in the concept of self-worth related directly to skin color itself. Because school is a central activity at this age, his sense of inferiority is revealed most acutely in his lack of confidence in himself as a student, lack of motivation to learn, and in problems of behavior—a gradual withdrawal or a growing rebellion. The effects of this early damage are difficult to overcome, for the child who never learns to read cannot become a success at a job or in a society where education and culture are necessary. In addition, there is the possibility that poor teaching, generally characteristic of the ghetto schools, tends to reinforce this sense of inferiority and to give it substance in the experience of inferior achievement. The cycle that leads to menial jobs and to broken homes has then begun; only the most drastic efforts at rehabilitation can break that cycle.

The obsession with whiteness continues past childhood and into adulthood. It stays with the Negro all his life. Haryou [Harlem Youth Opportunities Unlimited] recorded a conversation between teen-age boys about their hair styles that reflected this obsession.

You know, if he go in there with his hair slick up like white, they might go for him better, you know.

They might use him for a broom or a mop.

Well, why do you wear "brushes?"

Why do I wear "brushes?" It's a blind, a front. Are you saying that I'm ignorant?

He's a playboy. He like to do his hair like that. He's ashamed of his own hair, you know. He feels bad that he's black and now he wants to be half and half. He wants to be a half-breed.

When your great granmammy was taken advantage of in the fields, what was happening then? Have you ever seen a light-skinned African? Have you ever seen an African your color?

No.

All right then; two bird dogs don't make nothing but a bird dog.

You don't have to go all the way, getting your hair slicked.

I don't have to go all the way black either, do I?

What are you going to do? You can't go all the way white.

Teen-age Negroes often cope with the ghetto's frustrations by retreating into fantasies related chiefly to their role in society. There is, for example, a fantasy employed by many marginal and antisocial teen-agers, to pretend to knowledge about illicit activities and to a sexual urbanity that they do not, really, have. They use as their models the petty criminals of the ghetto, whose colorful, swaggering style of cool bravado poses a peculiar fascination. Some pretend falsely to be pimps, some to have contacts with numbers runners. Their apparent admiration of these models is not total but reflects a curious combination of respect, of contempt, and, fundamentally, of despair. Social scientists who rely on questionnaires and superficial interviews must find a way to unravel this tangled web of pretense if their conclusions are to be relevant.

Among the young men observed at Haryou, fantasy played a major role. Many of these marginal, upward-striving teen-agers allowed others to believe that they were college students. One young man told his friends that he was a major in psychology. He had enrolled in the classes of a Negro professor with whom he identified, and he described those lectures in detail to his friends. The fact is that he was a dropout from high school. Others dressed like college students and went to college campuses where they walked among the students, attempting to feel a part of a life they longed for and could not attain. Some carried attaché cases wherever they went—often literally empty. One carried ordinary books camouflaged by college bookcovers and pretended to "study" in the presence of friends. Most of these young men were academically at the fifth- or sixth-grade reading level; none was in college. Another youngster who said he was in college planned to become a nuclear physicist. He spoke most convincingly about his physics and math courses and discussed the importance of Negroes' going into the field. Within a year, however, he had been dropped for nonattendance from the evening session of the municipal college at which he was enrolled. He had not taken even a first course in physics and had not been able to pass the elementary course in mathematics. He explained this failure in a complicated story and reported that he now intended to get a job. Later he described his new job in the executive training program of a high-status department store downtown. He was saving for college where he would continue with nuclear physics. He carried an attaché case to work each day. But the truth was that he was not in an executive training program at all; he had a job as a stock clerk. Yet the fantasy was one of performance; there was truth in his dreams, for if he had been caught in time he might have become a scientist. He did have the intellectual potential. But as a Negro, he had been damaged so early in the educational process that not even the surge of motivation and his basic intelligence could now make his dreams effective. His motivation was sporadic and largely verbal; his plans were in the realm of delusion. To some, this form of social schizophrenia might seem comic, but a more appropriate response is tears, not laughter.

Sex and Status

In Negro adults the sense of inadequate self-worth shows up in lack of motivation to rise in their jobs or fear of competition with whites; in a sense of impotence in civic affairs demonstrated in lethargy toward voting, or community participation, or responsibility for others; in family insta-

bility and the irresponsibility rooted in hopelessness.

But, because, in American life, sex is, like business advancement, a prime criterion of success and hence of personal worth, it is in sexual behavior that the damage to Negro adults shows up in especially poignant and tragic clarity. The inconsistency between the white society's view of the Negro as inferior and its sexual exploitation of Negroes has seemed to its victims a degrading hypocrisy. Negroes observe that ever since slavery white men have regarded Negroes as inferior and have condemned interracial marriage while considering illicit sexual relationships with Negro women appropriate to their own higher status. The white man in America has, historically, arranged to have both white and Negro women available to him; he has claimed sexual priority with both and, in the process, he has sought to emasculate Negro men. Negro males could not hold their women, nor could they defend them. The white male tried to justify this restriction of meaningful competition with the paradoxical claim that Negro males were animal-like and brutish in their appetites and hence to be feared and shunned by white women. The ironic fact has been that, given the inferiority of their racial status, Negro males have had to struggle simply to believe themselves men. It has long been an "inside" bit of bitter humor among Negroes to say that Negro men should bribe their wives to silence.

Certain Negro women of status who have married white men report that their choice was related to their discovery that the Negro men they knew were inferior in status, interests, and sophistication and hence unsuitable as partners. Many problems of race and sex seem to follow this principle of the self-fulfilling prophecy. The Negro woman of status may see the Negro male as undesirable as a sexual partner precisely because of his low status in the eyes of whites. Unlike a white female who may reassure herself that the lower the status of the male, the more satisfying he is as a sexual partner, the upper-class Negro female tends to tie sexual desirability to status and exclude many Negro males as undesirable just because their status is inferior. It is a real question whether this "discovery" is based on fact or whether these women are not accepting the white society's assumption of the low status of Negro men and therefore expecting them to be weak. On the other hand, frustrated, thrill-seeking white males or females who have been told all their lives that Negroes are primitive and uninhibited may seek and find sexual fulfillment among the same Negroes who are cool, distant, or hostile in their relationship to other Negroes. In sexual matters it appears that those who expect weakness or gratification often find what they expect.

As Negro male self-esteem rises in the wake of the civil rights movement, one interesting incidental fact is that any Negro woman who is known to be the mistress of a white public official—and particularly any mistress of a segregationist—has been put under a growing pressure to break that relationship. In the past, Negroes tended to suppress their bitterness about such illicit relationships, accepting the white male's evaluation of himself and of them, and in a sense forgiving the Negro woman for submitting to the temptation of protection and economic gain. In the last decade, however, Negro mistresses of white officials are more openly rejected and are regarded as one of the "enemy."

White men were accustomed to possessing Negro women without marriage, but today the fact that a number of white men are married to Negro women of status, particularly those who are well known in the theatrical world, indicates that Negro women are placing higher value upon their own dignity than many other Negro women were permitted to in the past—and so are the white men who marry them. But, though a Negro woman may gain status by marrying into the white community, Negro men, even in the North, remain vulnerable if they seek to cross racial lines and to break this most fearsome of social taboos. When they have done so they have paid a tremendous price—lynching, murder, or a prison sentence in the South, social condemnation in the North—but, above all, the price of their own self-doubt and anxiety. The full complexity of social disapproval and personal doubt is difficult to resist psychologically even when the law allows and protects such nonconformist behavior.

The emerging, more affirmative sexual pride among Negro males may have as one of its consequences an increasing trend toward more open competition between white and Negro males for both white and Negro females. One of the further consequences would probably be an intensification of hostility of white males toward interracial couples and toward the white female participants, reflecting the desire on the part of the white male to preserve his own competitive advantage. One would expect him then to employ his economic and political power—without suspecting the fundamental basis of his antagonism—to maintain the inferior status of the Negro male for as long as possible. An important level of racial progress will have been reached when Negro and white men and women may marry anyone they choose, without punishment, ostracism, ridicule, or guilt.

The Negro Matriarchy and the Distorted Masculine Image

Sexual hierarchy has played a crucial role in the structure and pathology of the Negro family. Because of the system of slavery in which the Negro male was systematically used as a stud and the Negro female used primarily for purposes of breeding or for the gratification of the white male, the only source of family continuity was through the female, the dependence of the child on his mother.

This pattern, together with the continued post-slavery relegation of the Negro male to menial and subservient status, has made the female the dominant person in the Negro family. Psychologically, the Negro male could not support his normal desire for dominance. For the most part he was not allowed to be a consistent wage earner; he could not present himself to his wife and children as a person who had the opportunity or the ability to compete successfully in politics, business, and industry. His doubts concerning his personal adequacy were therefore reinforced. He was compelled to base his self-esteem instead on a kind of behavior that tended to support a stereotyped picture of the Negro male—sexual impulsiveness, irresponsibility, verbal bombast, posturing, and compensatory achievement in entertainment and athletics, particularly in sports like boxing in which athletic prowess could be exploited for the gain of others. The Negro male was, therefore, driven to seek status in ways which seemed either antisocial, escapist, or socially irresponsible. The pressure to find relief from his intolerable psychological position seems directly related to the continued high incidence of desertions and broken homes in Negro ghettos.

The Negro woman has, in turn, been required to hold the family together; to set the goals, to stimulate, encourage, and to protect both boys and girls. Her compensatory strength tended to perpetuate the weaker role of the Negro male. Negro boys had the additional problem of finding no strong male father figure upon which to model their own behavior, perhaps one of the reasons for the prevalent idea among marginal Negroes that it is not masculine to sustain a stable father or husband relationship with a woman. Many young men establish temporary liaisons with a number of different women with no responsibility toward any. Among Negro teen-agers the cult of going steady has never had the vogue it seems to have among white teen-agers; security for Ne-groes is found not in a relationship modeled after a stable family—for they have seen little of this in their own lives—but upon the relationship they observed in their own home: unstable and temporary liaisons. The marginal young Negro male tends to identify his masculinity with the number of girls he can attract. The high incidence of illegitimacy among Negro young people reflects this pervasive fact. In this compensatory distortion of the male image, masculinity is, therefore, equated with alleged sexual prowess.

The middle-class white and Negro male often separates women into two categories, good women with whom he will go steady and marry, and others with whom he has and will continue to have sexual relations alone. The lower-class Negro is, in a way, more sophisticated than either in his refusal to make undemocratic distinctions between "good girls" and "others." The consistently higher illegitimacy rate among Negroes is not a reflection of less virtue or greater promiscuity, but rather of the fact that the middle-class teen-agers are taught the use of contraceptives and learn how to protect themselves from the hazards of premarital and illicit sexual contacts. The middle-class girl is able to resort to abortions, or she gives birth secretly, surrendering the child for adoption. In the case of marginal young people, or the upwardly mobile Negro, what contraceptive ideas he has are unreliable; and rarely does the girl participate in protection, in part because it is taken as a sign of masculinity for the male to supervise such matters. Illegitimacy among these groups, therefore, is a consequence, in large part, of poverty and ignorance.

Among Negro middle-class families the attitude toward sex is vastly different from that among marginal and lower-class Negro groups. The middle-class Negro fears he will be identified with the Negro masses from whom he has escaped or tried to escape, and sex is a focal point of anxiety. The middle-class girl is often so rigidly protected that normal sexual behavior is inhibited, or she learns to be sophisticated about the use of contraceptives. For her, as for white middle-class girls, sex is tied to status and aspirations. She wants to make a good marriage—marriage to a white man might even be available—and the motivation to avoid illevitimate pregnancy is great.

The marginal young people in the ghetto, through their tentative and sporadic relationships, are seeking love, affection, and acceptance perhaps more desperately than young people elsewhere Person-to-person relationships are, for many, a compensation for society's rejection. They are, in a sense, forced to be quite elemental in their demands, and sex becomes more important for them than even they realize. They act in a cavalier fashion about their affairs, trying to seem casual and cool, but it is clear nonetheless that they are dominated by the complexity of their needs.

The girl, like the boy, has no illusions. Unlike the middle-class girl who believes —or demands—that each relationship should be forever, and who tries to hold on to the boy, the marginal Negro lower-class girl is realistic about the facts of the situation. Nor does she expect to hold the boy. Sex is important to her, but it is not, as in middle-class society, a symbol of status, to be used to rise into a better family or a higher income bracket. The marginal Negro female uses her sex, instead, to gain personal affirmation. She is desired, and that is almost enough. The relationship, whatever its social and psychological limitations, is pure in the same sense as innocence—that is, it is not contaminated by other goals. For her and for the boy, sex is time-contained, with its own intrinsic worth and value, not animal in its expression, but related to the urgent human need for acceptance; it is sophisticated, not primitive.

This innocent sophistication includes the total acceptance of the child if a child comes. In the ghetto, the meaning of the illegitimate child is not ultimate disgrace.

There is not the demand for abortion or for surrender of the child that one finds in more privileged communities. In the middle class, the disgrace of illegitimacy is tied to personal and family aspirations. In lower-class families, on the other hand, the girl loses only some of her already limited options by having an illegitimate child; she is not going to make a "better marriage" or improve her economic and social status either way. On the contrary, a child is a symbol of the fact that she is a woman, and she may gain from having something of her own. Nor is the boy who fathers an illegitimate child going to lose, for where is he going? The path to any higher status seems closed to him in any case.

Illegitimacy in the ghetto cannot be understood or dealt with in terms of punitive hostility, as in the suggestion that unwed mothers be denied welfare if illegitimacy is repeated. Such approaches obscure, with empty and at times hypocritical moralizing, the desperate yearning of the young for acceptance and identity, the need to be meaningful to someone else even for a moment without implication of a pledge of undying fealty and foreverness. If, when the girl becomes pregnant, the boy deserts or refuses to marry her, it is often because neither can sustain an intimate relationship; both seem incapable of the tenderness that continues beyond immediate gratification. Both may have a realistic, if unconscious, acceptance of the fact that nothing else is possible; to expect —to ask—for more would be to open oneself to the inevitable rejections, hurts, and frustrations. The persistent experience of rejection spills over into the anticipation and acceptance of rejection in a love relationship. This lack of illusion stems from the fact that there can be no illusion in any other area of life. To expose oneself further to the chances of failure in a sustained and faithful relationship is too large to risk. The intrinsic value of the relationship is the only value because there can be no other.

Among most lower-class Negroes, competition in sex is predominantly heterosexual and free. In the Negro middle class sexual freedom and expression are often identified with lower-class status, and many men and women are therefore governed chiefly by their inhibitions and cannot act freely in matters of sex. The men may be impotent, the women frigid, and both afflicted with guilt. Some compensate for the restraints on sexual adequacy and fulfillment through fantasies and boasting about a false prowess. Other middle-class Negro men retreat into noncommittal peripheral relationships with women, avoiding all alternatives—homosexuality, heterosexuality, or verbal bombasts—as risks requiring more ego strength than their resources permit. Instead, a blank and apathetic sexlessness dominates their lives. They withdraw from all commitment to another person seeking refuge from the dangers of personal vulnerability.

Considering the depth and the complexity of the need, aggressive sexual behavior may, for many of the racially damaged, make the difference between personal stability and instability. Until the lower-class Negro is free to compete for and to win the socially acceptable rewards of middle-class society, the ghetto's pattern of venereal disease, illegitimacy, and family instability will remain unbroken. But when that time comes, no one can expect destructive sexual activity to cease abruptly. What is more likely is a shift to another, some would say "higher," level of behavior; then the Negro's sexual "misbehavior" will be indistinguishable in all respects from that of the respectables—with full participation in divorce, abortions, adultery, and the various forms of jaded and fashionable middle- and upper-class sexual explorations. There might even be the possibility of sexual fulfillment and health.

White Rationalizations

It is now rare even for the most ardent apologist for the *status quo* seriously to assert that the American pattern of segregation has beneficial consequences. Some do, however, continue to argue that the Negro's inferiority and inherent character defects demand that he be segregated. Others suggest that the chances of his developing those traits and characteristics which would make him more acceptable to the white community would be greater if he would function within his own community until he demonstrates that he is worthy of associating with others. Among the questions which remain unanswered by this type of argument are : Under what circumstances is the Negro ever adjudged worthy or deserving of association with others, and how can he be expected to develop these traits of "worthiness" under conditions which tend to perpetuate characteristics of unworthiness as described by the proponents of this position themselves? In the belief no doubt that this was a statement of compassion, one white opponent of New York's school integration plan said: "If I were God, what would I do to improve the lot of the Negro? If I were God, I'd make everybody white." [1] To sensitive Negroes, this betrays the ultimate condescension—the belief that to *be* Negro means irrevocable rejection.

Even this point of view is not logically consistent, since the same individuals who reject Negroes as offensive have no difficulty, as we have noted above, in accepting Negroes in close and at times intimate association and relationship, for example, as servants or menials or mistresses, as long as the inferior position of the Negro and the dominant position of the white is clearly perceived and accepted by both.

The answers to these questions cannot be found in any single devil—but must be sought in the compliant or accessory role of many in society. However, more privileged individuals understandably may need to shield themselves from the inevitable conflict and pain which would result from their acceptance of the fact that they *are* accessories to profound injustice. The tendency to discuss disturbing social issues such as racial discrimination, segregation, and economic exploitation in detached, legal, political, socio-economic, or psychological terms as if these persistent problems did not involve the suffering of actual human beings is so contrary to empirical evidence that it must be interpreted as a protective device. After World War II, the bulk of the German people *could not know* what was going on in the death camps. The people of Mississippi *had to believe* in 1964 that the disappearance and death of the three civil rights workers in that state was a diversionary strategy plotted by civil rights groups. Negroes generally expected that a grand jury in New York City *would have found* that it was justifiable homicide performed in the line of duty for a white policeman to kill a fifteen-year-old Negro boy who was "attacking him with a penknife." Insensitivity is a protective device. Among its more primitive examples are: The prevalent beliefs that the predicament of the masses of Negroes reflects their inherent racial inferiority; that the poor are to blame for the squalor and despair of the slums; that the victims of social injustice are somehow subhuman persons who cause and perpetuate their own difficulties; that the more responsible and superior people of the society not only have no obligation for the "irresponsibles" but must be vigilant to see that all of the power of government is used to protect them and their children from them; and that any contrary or compassionate interpretation of the plight of the poor or the rejected is merely the sentimental and naive expression of impractical do-gooders or "bleeding hearts."

More subtle and obscure forms of protection against facing the consequences of social injustice are to be found among those social scientists who cultivate that degree of academic detachment which blocks meaningful or insightful study of human affairs. The preoccupation with trivia—as if this were the ultimate scientific virtue and goal—leads to the irrele-

vance of much social science research. It is interesting to speculate on the significance of the fact that during the ten years after the U. S. Supreme Court school desegregation decision, an increasing number of social scientists have raised questions concerning the "scientific validity" of the psychological and sociological data cited by the Court as evidence of the damage which segregation inflicts upon personality. Not one of these critics had questioned these data and their interpretations prior to the Court's decision, although the studies on which they were based had been published and available for critical reactions for many years prior to their use in the historic decision.

Certain students of jurisprudence have also criticized the Court's decision on the grounds that the Brown decision, which ruled that state laws requiring or permitting racial segregation in public schools violated the equal protection clause of the Fourteenth Amendment, was based upon flimsy sociological and psychological data rather than upon more stable and heretofore determining legal grounds. This, too, is a purist approach rooted in the belief that detachment or enforced distance from the human consequences of persistent injustice is objectively desirable. It may rather be of service primarily as a subconscious protection against personal pain and direct involvement in moral controversies.

The language and the emphasis of the Court's decision made any such evasion of the human costs of racial segregation quite difficult. The Court insisted upon a simple and direct statement of the reality:[2]

To separate them from others of similar age and qualifications solely because of their race generates a feeling of inferiority as to their status in the community that may affect their hearts and minds in a way unlikely ever to be undone. The effect of this separation on their educational opportunities was well stated by a finding in the Kansas case by a court which nevertheless felt compelled to rule against the Negro plaintiffs: Segregation of white and colored children in public schools has a detrimental effect upon the colored children. The impact is greater when it has the sanction of the law: for the policy of separating the races is usually interpreted as denoting the inferiority of the Negro group. A sense of inferiority affects the motivation of a child to learn. Segregation with the sanction of the law, therefore, has a tendency to retard the educational and mental development of Negro children and to deprive them of some of the benefits they would receive in a racially integrated school system.

The obscuring function of legal technicalities and the equivocations of social science jargon were rejected and in their place was offered an understandable statement of the inevitable anguish of rejected and stigmatized human beings.

The pervasive need to turn one's back on any clear evidence of man's inhumanity to man exemplified in the cool objective approach is probably most clearly seen, though in a more subtle form, in the detached "professionalism" of many social workers and in the selective isolation of many psychiatrists and clinical psychologists. Some members of these "helping fields," too, have often defended as objectivity what, to the client, feels more like insensitivity. Furthermore, in their preoccupation with the problem of the individual and their insistence upon reducing him to a manageable system of assumptions, the disturbing and dehumanizing social realities behind his personal agony may be avoided. With the professional perspective which constricts social vision to the impulses, strengths, and weaknesses of the individual "client" as if these can be isolated from the injustices and pathologies of his life, these professionals need not confront the difficult problems of nature and origin of the social injustices nor run the risks of conflict with the many vested interests which tend to perpetuate the problems of the poor and the rejected. This posture is built into the nature of their training and

reinforced by their complex role as agents of the more privileged classes and the admitted and irrevocable fact of their identification with the middle classes. The professionals themselves would point out, also, that the routinizing pressure of bureaucratic procedures, and a heavy case load of human suffering dull the edge of concern and that the most sensitive among them feel, within the structure, uncertain and helpless as to how to address themselves to the problem of social change. It is not surprising, altogether, that compassion is usually sooner or later subordinated to accommodation; yet it is hard for many to understand why they are irrelevant to the root problems of the poor.

Some theorists and practitioners maintain that it is not within their power or training to attempt to help working-class and low-status people because the problems of these people are psychosocial and, since they cannot be "reached," are not amenable to the psychotherapeutic and casework techniques thought to be helpful in working with middle-class individuals. Some professionals tend to limit their role to that of models or interpreters of the middle-class norms of speech, behavior, dress, values, and ways of handling problems and feelings. In view of their status and psychological distance, the social worker's concern to "relate to" the "client" seems pathetic in its failure of elemental empathy. The stated or unstated goal of this type of "therapeutic" relationship must then become that of helping the client "adjust" to his life realities, i.e., to keep him from "acting out" his rebellion in antisocial or self-destructive ways and thereby to function more effectively *within* the continuing pathology of his society. These goals are consistent with the *status quo* convenience of the middle class. They are consistent with the benign artificiality of response from these professionals which repels the members of the working class, for whom the immediate and pressing realities of their daily lives alone seem relevant. That middle-class individuals are not equally repelled may be an indication of the extent to which pretenses and protective detachment have become norms of middle-class adjustment —particularly in a society of accepted injustice. This is not to say that individual therapy is not needed and cannot be effective. It is to say that such procedures are not effective where social pathology is at the root of the individual's maladjustment. It is a real question whether adjustment or indifference to the reality of injustice is not the real neurosis, and rebellion the evidence of health.

Moral Objectivity

Objectivity, without question essential to the scientific perspective when it warns of the dangers of bias and prejudgment in interfering with the search for truth and in contaminating the understanding of truth, too often becomes a kind of a fetish which serves to block the view of truth itself, particularly when painful and difficult moral insights are involved. The question of the nature of objectivity in law, in science, in human relationships, is complex and cannot be resolved by attempts to make it synonymous with the exclusion of feeling and value. Objectivity that implies detachment or escape from psychological reality decreases understanding and can be used merely to avoid the problem. In the social sciences, the cult of objectivity seems often to be associated with "not taking sides." When carried to its extreme, this type of objectivity could be equated with ignorance. When the social psychology department of an outstanding Eastern university received a substantial grant to endow a chair in the field of race relations, the responsible officials of that department decided that, in order to obtain the most objective person, they should consider no one who had worked extensively in the field of race relations. Indeed, they decided to appoint someone who had

had no experience in this field at all, and chose a man whose major contribution to psychology was rather in the field of the experimental psychology of visual discrimination. Perhaps the guiding assumption was that the problem of American race relations was to be understood in the most fundamental terms of the capacity of the rods and cones of the human retina to differentiate color! Imagine, however, if a chair in nuclear science were to be filled in any university, how transparently absurd it would seem to choose a man with no experience in the field, on the grounds that he thereby would be more objective! The fact that this did not seem absurd to scholars in the case of race relations is a revealing commentary. It may be that where essential human psychological and moral issues are at stake, noninvolvement and noncommitment and the exclusion of feeling are neither sophisticated nor objective, but naive and violative of the scientific spirit at its best. Where human feelings are part of the evidence, they cannot be ignored. Where anger is the appropriate response, to exclude the recognition and acceptance of anger, and even to avoid the feeling itself as if it were an inevitable contamination, is to set boundaries upon truth itself. If a scholar who studied Nazi concentration camps did not feel revolted by the evidence no one would say he was unobjective, but rather fear for his sanity and moral sensitivity. Feeling may twist judgment, but the lack of feeling may twist it even more. And to insist on quantitative measurement and analysis of certain phenomena, of, for example, love or friendship, is to distort the nature of the phenomenon itself. It is not to enlarge truth, but to constrict it.

Even to pose an hypothesis is to move away from literal objectivity, *if* objectivity is to be defined as total openmindedness. Objectivity should play a role not in the refusal to make hypotheses, but in the rigorous assessment of the evidence accumulated for that hypothesis, so as to guard, as far as possible, against any distortion of these facts. When one cares deeply what the answer to a question is, one must exercise even greater care to examine the evidence than if the answer is of no personal consequence. To refuse science the right to deal with such phenomena is to set intolerable limits, for moral decisions, like all others, should be based on fact. Responsible objectivity includes the totality of reality, not a part alone.

NOTES

1. *The New York Times Magazine,* September 20, 1964, p. 122.
2. *Brown v. Board of Education,* 347 U.S. 483 (1954).

40. ETHNICITY AS AN INFLUENCE ON BEHAVIOR

FR. ANDREW GREELEY

At a time when research on the plight of black Americans (and other "colored" minorities) is plentiful, very little work is being conducted on the traditional "white ethnics." Many people so labeled are in a quandary about the changes they see around them. Angry and afraid rather than guilty, they resent the encroachment of others on their turf. And it is not only in the realm of race relations that various ethnic groups have their own opinions. As Father Andrew Greeley shows here, ethnicity influences behavior in a variety of spheres of American life.

Father Andrew M. Greeley is Lecturer in Sociology at the University of Chicago. A specialist on the sociology of religion, he is the author of Religion and Careers *(1963),* The Education of Catholic Americans *(1966), and* The Changing Catholic College *(1967).*

One suspects that when the social historians of, let us say, the twenty-third or twenty-fourth century, look back on the era that we now presume to describe as the modern world, they will find two or three social phenomena of extraordinary interest. One is certainly the demographic revolution—the astonishing increase in the population level of the world that has occurred in the past century and a half. The second will be the westernization and industrialization of the non-Western world; and the third, unless I miss my guess, will be the formation of a new nation on the North American continent made up of wildly different nationality groups. The historians of the future will find it hard to believe that it could have happened that English, Scotch, and Welsh, Irish, Germans, Italians, and Poles, Africans, Indians—both Eastern and Western—Frenchmen, Spaniards, Finns, Swedes, Lebanese, Danes, Armenians, Croatians, Slovenians, Greeks, and Luxemburgers, Chinese, Japanese, Filipinos, and Puerto Ricans would come together to form a nation that not only would survive, but, all things considered,

survive reasonably well. I further suspect that the historians of the future will be astonished that American sociologists, the product of this gathering in of the nations, could stand in the midst of such an astonishing social phenomenon and take it so much for granted that they would not bother to study it.

They will find it especially astonishing in light of the fact that ethnic differences, even in the second half of the twentieth century, proved far more important to men than did the differences in philosophy or economic system. Men who would not die for a premise or a dogma or a division of labor, would more or less cheerfully die for a difference rooted in ethnic origins. Chinese and Malay fight each other in South East Asia; Ibo and Hausa in Nigeria; Greek and Turk on Cyprus; Czech and Slovak in Czechoslovakia; Arab and Jew in the Middle East; black (at least so-called) fights white (at least relatively) in the United States; [1] and the French and the English, running out of colonial peoples with which to contend, now renew the feud that the Hundred Years' War never did settle. Finally, along the lines of

Reprinted by permission of the author.

the Shamrock curtain another feud simmers, and Frank O'Connor's immortal words, spoken from the secure position of his own agnosticism, are as true as ever: "The north of Ireland contains the best Protestants in the world and the south of Ireland, the best Catholics, and there is nary a single Christian in the whole lot."

In this paper I wish to cover four topics: (1) Some remarks about the nature of ethnic groups; (2) comments on the present lack of information about the social correlates of ethnicity; (3) a summary of some tables on ethnic differences; and (4) certain recommendations for what might be very loosely called "policy."

Ethnicity in American Society

Ethnic groups, in the sense we are using the term, are to be defined as human collectivities based on an assumption of common origin, real or imaginary. As E. K. Francis points out, in commenting on this essentially Weberian definition, the ethnic collectivity represents an attempt on the part of men to keep alive during their pilgrimage from *Gemeinschaft* to *Gesellschaft,* from peasant commune to industrial metropolis, some of the diffuse, ascriptive, particularistic modes of behavior that were common to their past. One is not an ethnic in one's native village, but only when one has left that village for the city or left one's country for the New World. In Ireland we were Mayo men or Cork men; in Italy, Baresi or Neopolitans or Sicilians; in Germany, Swabians or Bavarians or Saxons; we became Irish, Italian, German, only when the host society chose to define us as such and we found that the primordial ties of soil and blood could best be described in such terms in the new setting in which we found ourselves. Our ethnic group provided for us a pool of preferred role opposites in various areas of our lives. It was perhaps necessary in the large corporate structures to interact with whomever the random possi-

bilities of the economic system put at the workbench or the desk next to us. But when it came to choosing our wife, our poker or bridge partner, our precinct captain, our doctor, our lawyer, our real estate broker, our construction contractor, our clergyman, and even our psychiatrists, we felt much more at ease if we could choose those of whom we could say, "After all, they're our kind of people." Furthermore, it was even a big help if, when we approached the personnel office of a large corporation, we could say at least to someone in that office, "My mother knows your mother." [2]

It is assumed, I think, by people for whom ethnicity is a relevant variable, that members of ethnic groups share certain common values about the behavior of opposites in intimate role relationships. I would hypothesize, at least until further research proves me wrong, that the principal variations among ethnic groups will be found to be in the expectations one has of a parent or sibling or child or spouse or cousin or a niece or an aunt or a friend, and I would suggest that it is precisely this common core of assumptions about how one behaves in intimate relationships that is most difficult for an acculturation process to erase and that is most likely to survive for generations, if not permanently, among the descendants of ethnic immigrants.

The sociological profession has assumed for the last three decades that ethnicity is not a relevant variable in American society, and that intermarriage is rapidly eliminating the ethnic groups. Curiously enough, little or no evidence has been provided to back up this assumption, and the evidence that does exist (much of it collected by my student, Harold Abramson) would indicate that while ethnic intermarriage does occur, it is generally a highly selective form of intermarriage, and that it has by no means eliminated the ethnic collectivities.

But if ethnic groups seem to the behavioral scientist to be unimportant, there are many other citizens of our republic who think differently—politicians, church administrators, real estate men, and the more sophisticated public educators, to name but a few such groups. The balanced ticket, the ethnic parish, the nationality suburb, are all too obvious on the American scene, even if the inhabitants of Cambridge, Hyde Park, Madison, Ann Arbor, and Berkeley haven't noticed lately.

The exact composition of ethnic groups, who belongs to a group, to what extent formal organizations are necessary, or what role formal institutions play, the relationship between ethnic groups and the mother country, are all subjects for research—research which, alas, one must report simply has not been done. The questions at issue are fascinating, however. It is clear to anyone who has observed them closely that the American Irish are not the Irish Irish, nor are they the English Irish, and that all three groups have something in common with one another. Being Irish in the United States, for example, no longer involves as it once did deep concern about the political fortunes of the Irish Republic. Not so long ago I was visiting a Catholic girls' college in the heartland of America and I noticed a sign on the bulletin board announcing that shortly the Irish Club of the college would hold its monthly meeting. I asked the young lady who was showing me through the college if she belonged to the Irish Club and she admitted that she not only belonged to it, but was its president. "Peggy," I said to her, "do you know what the six counties are?" She admitted that she did not, and I said, "Have you ever heard of the Sein fein?" and she admitted that she did not know what it was. "And," I said, "have you ever heard of the Easter rising of the I.R.A.?" and she admitted her ignorance. Finally, I said, "Peggy, do you know who Eamon de Valera is?" She brightened at that question. "Isn't he the Jewish man that is the Lord Mayor of Dublin?" she asked.

Information about Ethnic Groups

The basic response to the question about which this paper is concerned is that there isn't any demographic, socioeconomic, or sociopsychological information about the latter stages of the acculturation processes of the American ethnic group; it simply does not exist and is not likely to exist in the foreseeable future. In all likelihood, no attempt will be made to collect such information until it is too late. The Census Bureau now provides only data on the foreign-born and tells us nothing about the second, third, or the fourth generation of the ethnic immigrant groups. If one looks under the title "Ethnicity" in the indices of the behavioral science journals, one can find articles about Eskimos and Navahos, about tribes in Africa and New Guinea, and even occasionally about black-white relationships, but precious little else. Ethnic questions are not routinely included in survey research questionnaires, and for all the wild assertions about ethnic voting patterns (based usually on the foreign-born percentages of the Census tract data), national samples of political behavior rarely break up the American religious groups into their ethnic components.

Even though graduate students are interested in writing dissertations on the subject (a strange application of Hansen's law), faculty members who feel qualified to moderate such dissertations are almost nonexistent. The sprightly Glazer and Moynihan book (*Beyond the Melting Pot*) offers interesting data and speculations about New York City, but New York City is not, as startling as it may seem in the present set of circumstances, the whole republic. Herbert Gans' book about the Italians of Boston (*The Urban Villagers*) is extremely suggestive, but one looks in vain for imitators of Gans. Fishman's book on language loyalty (*Language Loyalty in the U.S.*) is extremely valuable but quite narrow in its focus; it tells us nothing, for example, about ethnic groups like the Irish who speak only English, and that sometimes not too well. Gordon's book (*Assimilation in American Life*) is, as far as I know, the only serious attempt to state some general propositions about ethnicity in American society. When one attempts to persuade on the exigencies of ethnic research as important, one is told first that the question is quite irrelevant because of the workings of the assimilation process, and second that it is a highly sensitive issue which might offend people if pushed too vigorously. How something can be irrelevant and sensitive, no longer an issue and still offensive, is one of those great paradoxes that we gentlemen adventurer sociologists must learn to live with. One can submit articles on ethnicity to even such respectable journals as *The Public Interest* and not even expect the courtesy of having the articles rejected; and proposals, even technically sound ones, to governmental agencies are likely to be rejected without even the formality of a visit from the site committee. Ethnic study is out and one wonders if there is any likelihood that it is not going to stay out.

I shall not speculate at great length as to the reason for this nonexistence of interest in research on ethnic groups, but one is truly hard put to know why the last serious sociological study of American Poles was done by Thomas and Znaniecki in 1958. It could be that ethnic material is not particularly suited for multiple regression analysis, or it could be, if one wants to take a very sinister interpretation, advanced to me and one middle-aged Ph.D. from Columbia (not Peter Rossi), that those who have trained the present generation of younger American sociologists repressed the possibility of ethnic research from their consciousness because of their own profound ambivalence about their personal ethnic backgrounds.

Be that as it may, we do not have the information, and because we lack information it is hard to come to grips with the question of ethnic groups in either a meaningfully theoretical or practically opera-

tional way. Is everyone an ethnic? Do we all belong to some larger collectivity that stands between the family and society and is somehow based on common origins? Are Protestants an ethnic group? Are Texans? Are intellectuals? What is the relationship between ethnicity and religion? My own inclination is to say that most all of us need some collectivity with which to identify ourselves, and that many, if not most of us, are still inclined to fall back on the primordial bonds of blood and land. In some sections of the country, to be a white Anglo-Saxon Protestant is definitely to be an ethnic, and I suspect that to be an intellectual and a Texan may well be to be ethnic. However, it seems to me that the really relevant piece of research information that is not available to us is under what set of circumstances which kind of people find which ethnic values and behavior appropriate? We need to know, therefore, both the basic demographic information about the ethnic groups—who they are, where they are, what they are doing —and also what value and behavioral correlates of ethnicity have survived in modern society. Finally, it would help to know how these ethnic collectivities relate to more organized groups of society, either those that could be called formal ethnic institutions or those that are intimately connected with nationality origins such as political parties and churches.

Some Available Data

In this section of the paper I propose to comment on some tables gathered in secondary analysis of NORC research data. These tables are cited to show that ethnic differences still do persist in American society, and also to fulfill at least in part what is basically an impossible task—to report on the social and demographic correlates of ethnicity.[3]

In Table 1 we learn that the Irish are the most successful of the Catholic immigrant groups in terms of their occupation,

Table 1.   (*Percent*)

Item	Irish	German	Italian	French	Polish
Duncan 8–10	32	31	13	22	17
High school graduate	77	62	51	42	46
More than $14,000	24	19	17	7	18
High on general knowledge scale	18	9	7	5	3
Democratic	70	65	67	70	77
"Very happy"	41	36	35	40	27
High on "sacramental" index	32	31	13	22	30
High on "religious extremism" index	19	20	24	28	34
High on "racism" index	44	46	54	51	61
High on "anti-Semitism" index	29	47	43	54	52
High on "open-mindedness" index	52	48	42	40	43
Low on anomie scale	64	51	47	49	43
	(328)	(361)	(370)	(177)	(184)

their education, and their income, while the Italians and the Polish are the least successful. The Germans seem to have less education and less income than the Irish, though the distribution on the Duncan occupational scale is not appreciably different from that of the Irish and they do not score nearly as high as the Irish on the general knowledge index that was available in the data.

The Poles are the most loyal to the Democratic party, while the Germans and the Italians are the least loyal, though even here two-thirds of the respondents were Democratic, and the spread of twelve percentage points between the Germans and Poles is, one supposes, not terribly great. There is little difference in religious behavior between the Irish, the Germans, and the Poles, though the French and the Italians seem to be substantially less devout than the other three groups. The Irish and the French score highest on the happiness measure, and the Poles, with true slavic sobriety, score the lowest. Similarly, the French and the Poles have the highest scores on an index of religious extremism, and the Irish and the Germans, the lowest scores. The racism scores are highest among the Poles and lowest among the Irish and the Germans. The Irish are lowest on the anti-Semitism index; the French and the Poles are the highest. The Irish are

also most likely to score high on open-mindedness and low on anomie, with the Germans just behind them, and the other three groups trailing.

In summary, as one might suspect, the earlier immigrant groups are both the most socially successful and the most tolerant, but there are enough differences, say, between the Irish and the Germans and between the Italians and the Poles to suggest that other factors are at work besides the time at which one's parents washed up on the American shores.

In Table 2 we devote some passing attention to regional differences among ethnic groups. The Eastern Irish are more likely to be Democratic than the Middle Western Irish, while exactly the reverse seems to be true of the Germans. All four ethnic groups seem to be more religious in the Middle West than in the East. The middle western Irish seem somewhat more liberal politically, as do the Germans from that region. The middle western Poles, on the other hand, seem to be more ethnocentric than their counterparts on the East Coast.

In Table 3 we attempt to see if education explains the differences we have observed among the five ethnic groups, and discover that even among high school graduates the Poles and the Italians and the French score higher on measures of

Table 2.   (*Percent*)

Item	Eastern [a]				Middle Western [b]			
	Irish	*German*	*Italian*	*Polish*	*Irish*	*German*	*Italian*	*Polish*
High on general knowledge scale	15	8	5	1	14	8	8	2
Democratic	76	56	67	70	64	67	69	80
"Very happy"	45	36	33	32	34	35	37	29
High on "sacramental" index	28	16	10	13	44	37	22	21
High on "religious extremism" index	23	20	26	35	15	22	19	39
High on "racism" index	44	51	50	54	41	48	48	64
High on "anti-Semitism" index	31	44	44	55	30	53	45	53
High on "open-mindedness" index	53	42	43	47	49	47	35	39
Low on anomie scale	66	52	41	49	61	54	59	40

[a] *New England and Middle Atlantic*
[b] *East North Central and West North Central*
Other regions are excluded.

Table 3.   (*Percent*)

Item	Did Not Graduate from High School					High School Graduate				
	Irish	*German*	*Italian*	*French*	*Polish*	*Irish*	*German*	*Italian*	*French*	*Polish*
Duncan 8–10	5	4	2	1	5	30	25	18	22	21
Professional or manager	5	5	0	4	5	46	37	32	18	24
More than $14,000	12	12	10	14	13	28	24	26	16	23
High on general knowledge scale	4	1	1	1	0	22	14	12	11	6
Democratic	79	69	79	75	83	67	63	59	63	70
"Very happy"	28	29	30	39	22	44	40	40	40	32
High on "sacramental" index	5	4	2	1	5	36	33	15	35	15
High on "religious extremism" index	27	31	29	36	44	15	14	20	17	25
High on "racism" index	55	54	58	56	64	43	36	48	28	60
High on "anti-Semitism" index	36	61	51	60	60	28	40	37	46	44
High on "open-mindedness" index	52	42	38	37	39	52	50	45	45	47
Low on anomie scale	45	41	41	39	38	69	57	53	61	50
	(72)	(131)	(175)	(101)	(96)	(256)	(230)	(195)	(76)	(87)

racism, anti-Semitism, and religious extremism than do the Irish, and in most instances, the Germans. Interestingly enough, high school graduation seems to make less difference on the racial question for Polish respondents than it does for the members of the other four ethnic groups.

In Table 4 we try to determine to what extent the differences we have uncovered can be explained away by the different

Table 4.   (*Percent*)

Item	First and Second Generation					Third or Later Generation				
	Irish	Ger-man	French	Ital-ian	Pol-ish	Irish	Ger-man	French	Ital-ian	Pol-ish
Duncan 8–10	21	14	10	5	12	25	20	16	12	16
Professional or manager	21	17	26	10	18	24	29	27	17	9
More than $14,000	24	15	20	7	20	24	21	13	8	17
High on general knowledge scale	19	10	5	3	2	18	10	16	7	5
Democratic	69	64	70	74	77	71	66	51	72	76
"Very happy"	30	36	34	49	27	45	37	43	37	24
High on "sacramental" index	32	23	13	26	19	32	33	11	23	16
High on "religious extremism" index	16	20	26	26	38	17	20	12	27	20
High on "racism" index	53	55	53	45	51	43	41	54	35	67
High on "anti-Semi-tism" index	35	55	46	53	53	28	44	35	52	53
High on "open-minded-ness" index	55	42	40	34	47	51	50	45	44	37
Low on anomie scale	52	48	47	49	48	70	54	50	60	43
	(76)	(109)	(294)	(70)	(111)	(225)	(216)	(62)	(79)	(58)

generational composition of the ethnic groups, and see that, even holding generation as constant as we can with our relatively small sample, the Irish and the Germans tend to be more socially successful and less ethnocentric than do the Italians and the Poles, although later generation Italians have the lowest score on the racism scale. It is further worth noting that third generation Poles score higher on the racism measure than do earlier generation Poles, perhaps because the Polish population is at the present time in the first phase of the home-owning stage in American society, and hence the one most to be threatened by the migration of Negro population in the urban centers of the nation.

In Table 5 we try to combine controls for generation and education, though the case bases here in this table are so small that one can generalize from the table only with great risk. Even among the high school graduates who are at least the grandchildren of immigrants, the Irish,

Germans, and Poles seem to be more successful in occupational prestige and income than the Italians or French. The Irish are the best informed, with the Germans and Italians taking second place on this measure; and the Italians are the most likely to have migrated out of the Democratic party. The Irish and the French are the happiest, hopefully putting to rest forever the notion that the Celts are a morose and melancholy lot, and I shall leave to others such as Dr. Rossi to explain why the descendants of sunny Italy seem so gloomy, though with only twenty-nine of them in the table, one could easily argue that the whole sample was made up of somber Milanese.

The Poles consistently score highest on the measures of ethnocentrism, the Irish being the lowest on anti-Semitism (the American Jewish Committee please note), and the Germans and French the lowest on racism. The Irish—or at least the Irish in our sample—are the least anomic and

Table 5.   (*Percent*)

Item	Third Generation or Later, High School Graduates				
	Irish	*Ger-man*	*Ital-ian*	*French*	*Pol-ish*
Duncan 8–10	31	34	12	21	32
Professional or manager	45	47	37	31	22
More than $14,000	26	22	3	11	21
High on general knowledge scale	26	17	20	9	11
Democratic	67	61	51	76	62
"Very happy"	47	38	26	48	32
High on "sacramental" index	32	32	10	39	20
High on "religious extremism" index	14	15	20	26	31
High on "racism" index	39	30	54	29	61
High on "anti-Semitism" index	25	38	32	43	59
High on "open-mindedness" index	51	56	51	40	34
Low on anomie scale	74	60	44	60	61
	(131)	(102)	(29)	(31)	(24)
N s for other tables:					
Third generation, did not graduate	(22)	(37)	(11)	(31)	(16)
First or second generation, did not graduate	(9)	(33)	(153)	(47)	(69)
First or second generation, did graduate	(29)	(26)	(123)	(18)	(27)

the Italians the most, and the Germans the most open-minded and the Poles the least open-minded.

Table 6 is presented not because one has a great deal of confidence in it, but simply because it gives some comparative information for non-Catholic ethnic groups. It should be remembered that the case bases here are very small and that the WASP group includes many southern whites. Table 6 A does show, however, in comparison with the percentages for the Irish, Polish, and Italians in Table 1, a fairly close similarity in percentages claiming to be "very happy." It is reassuring to know that the laws of probability still do work.

Similarly, the differences between the Irish and the Polish on racial issues (at least in 1962 when the data were collected) are similar to those reported in Table 1. Furthermore, it would appear that the Irish were the least likely of the three Catholic groups to vote for their

fellow Irish Catholic, John Kennedy, for the presidency. One must note of Table 6 C that the Jewish percentage is obviously quite inaccurate.

Table 6 D would suggest that on certain matters of sexual morality the Irish and the WASP constitute a moderate group with the Jews being the more "liberal," the Italians more conservative, and the Poles ambivalent, approving of petting more than anyone else, and of having intercourse much less than the Irish and the WASPs.

Finally, in Table 6 E, we note that Jews and Protestants are more abstemious in their dealings with John Barleycorn than are the Catholics, and by and large, the Irish are successful in confirming their reputation for being quite apt when it comes to "downing a few."

There is some other research material available which can be summarized in one paragraph. Ethnicity predicts, as we might

Table 6.   *A. HAPPINESS*

"Taken all together, how would you say things are these days—would you say that you
are very happy, pretty happy, or not too happy?"

Item	WASP	Irish	Polish	Italian	Jewish
Very	37	47	28	31	14
Pretty	47	38	59	52	55
Not too	16	18	13	17	31
N	(227)	(64)	(39)	(59)	(43)

B. ATTITUDES ON RACE (Percent)

Item	WASP	Irish	Polish	Italian	Jewish
Negro children should go to separate schools	64	20	38	17	30
Negroes should be on separate sections of streetcars and buses	22	5	21	14	8
Unfavorable to Negroes living in same block	41	25	46	36	30

C. VOTING IN 1960 ELECTION (Percent)

Item	WASP	Irish	Polish	Italian	Jewish
Voting for Kennedy	43	76	82	88	57

D. ATTITUDES ON COURTSHIP PRACTICES

(Percentage rating practice as "acceptable for male when he is engaged")

Item	WASP	Irish	Polish	Italian	Jewish
Kissing	96	95	97	94	92
Petting	63	55	70	42	63
Intercourse	18	22	13	5	49

(Percentage rating practice as "acceptable for female when she is engaged")

Kissing	95	93	95	95	92
Petting	57	53	63	41	63
Intercourse	14	14	8	5	45

E. ATTITUDES TOWARD DRINKING (Percent)

Item	WASP	Irish	Polish	Italian	Jewish
Abstainers	33	11	10	10	23
Twice a week	28	41	32	15	44
Neglect meals	14	17	17	6	25
Don't remember next day	14	12	11	4	17
Toss down fast	26	28	19	7	35
Make socializing more enjoyable	36	64	74	45	38
Make less self-conscious	19	27	18	11	14

expect, occupational choice. Germans, regardless of religion, are more likely to choose careers in science and engineering than any other group. Jews overchoose medicine and law. The Irish overchoose law, political science, history, and the diplomatic service. (In the June, 1961 sample, one-half of those who said they were going to take the foreign service exams were Catholic and one-quarter of them were Irish Catholic, suggesting that the Mick migrate from the precinct to the Embassy. Whether this be social progress or not is, one supposes, a matter of values.) Polish and other slavic groups are less likely to approve of bond issues. Irish react to sickness with fierce bravery that represses symptoms, while Italians react with an emotional intensity that, if anything, exaggerates the symptoms. And this, ladies and gentlemen, is about all there is to say.

One could, I suppose, attempt to evolve explanations for the phenomena reported in the tables accompanying this article. But given the weak state of our theory on ethnic groups, the scarcity of data, and the general unreliability of the case bases on which the critical comparisons are based, one would probably be wasting one's time. These tables establish what they were intended to establish—ethnicity is still a predictor variable of some relevance in American society.

"Policy" Recommendations

I would suggest that there are two reasons which would justify research in American ethnic groups, even though the subject is not one which seems to me to be inherently interesting.

First of all, there are immediate social problems which our society faces that cannot be solved unless we understand more about the operation of the ethnic factor. One need not look at the statistics in my tables about Polish attitudes on race questions to know that there is an acute problem here, not, at least, if one lives in

Chicago. But beyond mythological explanations it is extremely difficult to attribute a cause for this phenomenon. It would be extremely helpful, not to say imperative, if we understood more about the antipathy of certain ethnic groups to other ethnic groups.

Secondly, since it seems likely that many of the problems existing in the United States and in the whole world today are based on, or at least focus about the presumed differences in origin, one would want to know as much as possible about the ethnicity, the root of these differences, in order to understand how people of diverse origin and values can live with each other in peace—at least in relative peace. This may, in the final analysis, be the ultimate contribution that our multiple melting-pot society is able to make to the rest of the world.

In my judgment, the first thing we must do is collect the basic demographic and socioeconomic information which simply does not exist now. We must know who and where and what the major ethnic groups are and not merely the large groups of which we have spoken in this paper, but also the smaller groups which may be even more instructive for understanding a multiple melting-pot model of society. The Greeks, the Armenians, the Luxemburgers, the Lebanese are still very much with us and there might be a lot to be learned from them. Once we have the basic demographic information, then we could go on to attitude and value studies and the more complicated questions of the impact of ethnicity on social structure. I say we could, because in all honesty, I don't really believe that we will. In fact, I don't even believe that we are going to start putting ethnicity on survey research questionnaires as a standard item.

Let me conclude with a story whose point I think I need not emphasize. I was standing in front of a church in the west of Ireland, camera in hand, attempting to record the church which I thought just possibly was the place of my grandfather's baptism. The parish priest who was out cutting his hedge despite the rain, approached me, noted that I was a new man around here, and introduced himself. I must say I was a bit surprised when, on hearing my name, he remarked, "Ah, yes, you'd be the sociologist fellow from Chicago," and then added, "Would you be wantin' your grandfather's baptismal record, now?"

I admitted that the idea hadn't occurred to me, and he shook his head in discouragement. "Ah," he said, "fine sociologist you are." "Do a lot of people come seek-

ing such records?" I asked. He shook his head gravely. "Indeed they do," he said, "indeed they do. Those poor people, you know, they've been in the states now for three generations and they come seeking roots; they want to know who they are; they want to know all about their past and their ancestors. The poor people, I feel so sorry for them. Well," he continued, "the least we can do is be of some help to them. That's why I had all their baptismal records put on microfilm. It makes it a lot easier for people to find their roots."

NOTES

1. Though I am sure that a visitor from Nigeria would be hard put many times to tell who was black and who was white in the United States.

2. In the recent mayoral campaign in Chicago a Polish Republican was opposing the incumbent Irish Democratic mayor. In a television interview the Republican candidate went down the list of Democratic administrators of the city and indicated one by one why he would replace them. Only one name was omitted and that was the Director of the Commission on Human Relations, who was, curiously enough, of Polish origin. The interviewer asked what would be done with this administrator. The Republican candidate shrugged his shoulders and said that after all, he and the administrator had grown up in the same neighborhood and that, as far as he could see, the administrator was doing a reasonably good job. That their mothers knew each other can be left to the future historians to determine.

3. It should be noted that all the respondents represented in Tables 1 through 5 were Roman Catholic, and that the "French" were largely French Canadian.

SUGGESTIONS FOR FURTHER READING
on *Stratification and Differentiation*

Social Class

BALTZELL, E. DIGBY. *Philadelphia Gentleman*. Glencoe, Ill.: Free Press, 1958. The social bases of traditional upper class status in one part of the United States.

BENDIX, REINHARD, and SEYMOUR MARTIN LIPSET, eds. *Class, Status and Power*. Revised edition. Glencoe, Ill.: Free Press, 1966. A reader in social stratification.

BOTTOMORE, T. B. *Elites and Society*. New York: Basic Books, 1964. A critique of theories about rulers and the ruled.

BRODERSEN, ARVID. *The Soviet Worker*. New York: Random House, 1966. A study in labor and government in soviet society.

LOCKWOOD, DAVID. *The Black-Coated Worker*. London: Allen and Unwin, 1958. A study of class consciousness in Britain.

MAYER, KURT. *Class and Society*. New York: Random House, 1955. An introduction to the study of social stratification.

MILLS, C. WRIGHT. *White Collar*. New York: Oxford University Press, 1951. An assessment of America's new middle classes.

PACKARD, VANCE. *The Status Seekers*. New York: McKay, 1959. A journalist's summary of studies of stratification in the United States much criticized by academic sociologists.

SHOSTAK, ARTHUR, and WILLIAM GOMBERG, eds. *Blue Collar World*. Englewood Cliffs, N.J.: Prentice-Hall, 1964. An anthology of studies of the American worker.

THOMPSON, E. P. *The Making of the English Working Class*. New York: Vintage, 1966. An economic history.

TUMIN, MELVIN M. *Social Stratification*. Englewood Cliffs, N.J.: Prentice-Hall, 1964. A small text on the forms and functions of inequality.

Racial and Ethnic Patterns

BROWN, CLAUDE. *Manchild in the Promised Land*. New York: Macmillan, 1965. An autobiographical account of a childhood in Harlem.

GLAZER, NATHAN, and DANIEL PATRICK MOYNIHAN. *Beyond the Melting Pot*. Cambridge: Harvard-M.I.T. Press, 1963. A study of the Negroes, Puerto Ricans, Jews, Italians, and Irish of New York City.

GORDON, MILTON M. *Assimilation in American Life*. New York: Oxford University Press, 1964. The role of race, religion, and national origins in the "integration process."

MALCOLM X. *The Autobiography of*. New York: Grove Press, 1964. The life experience of this famous black American.

PARSONS, TALCOTT, and KENNETH B. CLARK, eds. *The Negro American*. Boston: Houghton Mifflin Company, 1966. An excellent collection of essays on the social, economic, and political life of black Americans and their relations with white.

ROSE, ARNOLD M., ed. *Minority Problems*. New York: Harper and Row, 1965. A collection of fifty-four recent articles on intergroup relations.

ROSE, PETER I. *They and We*. New York: Random House, 1964. An introduction to the study of racial and ethnic relations in the United States.

ROSE, PETER I. (ed.). *Americans from Africa.* New York: Atherton, 1970. Papers on eight controversies on the black experience. Volume I: *Slavery and Its Aftermath;* Volume II: *Old Memories, New Moods.*

SHIBUTANI, TAMOTSU, and KIAN W. KWAN. *Ethnic Stratification.* New York: Macmillan, 1965. A textbook on the comparative study of racial and ethnic relations.

WAGLEY, CHARLES, and MARVIN HARRIS. *Minorities in the New World.* New York: Columbia University Press, 1958. Six case studies: Indians in Brazil and Mexico, Negroes in Martinique and the United States, French Canadians, and Jews in the United States.

WILLIAMS, ROBIN M., JR., et al. *Strangers Next Door.* Englewood Cliffs, N.J.: Prentice-Hall, 1964. A nationwide study of ethnic relations in American communities.

PART FIVE
SELECTED SOCIAL
INSTITUTIONS

Normative systems which
regulate conduct and define
social relationships
in various spheres of life

Herbert Spencer, one of sociology's founding fathers, described society as a composite of interdependent parts, organs, or institutions. To Spencer, institutions were viewed as aspects of the social order, conceptually separable according to the functions they serve: sustaining functions (as, for example, the family), distributing functions (the economic system), and regulating functions (political organizations, ecclesiastical bodies, systems of social control, or, what he called "restraints").

To this day, the concept of institution remains a focal point for sociological analysis. Contemporary sociologists define the concept in various ways and some still hold to Spencer's basic organic analogy specifying both the anatomical (organizational) and physiological (functional) characteristics of the principal segments of the social *corpus*. Yet, recognition of the fact that what have been called institutions are, at bottom, not simply segments of society but networks of ideas related to specific aspects of social life has led many modern sociologists to define institutions as normative systems, collections of folkways, mores and laws (or "modes of action") that regulate overt behavior and serve to organize and define social relationships in various spheres.

In Part Five theoretical essays and empirical reports which treat several selected institutional systems are presented. The first section is concerned with familial norms and relationships.

It is more than cliché to say that the family gets the individual first and has the greatest influence upon the development of personality and social character. The family is both the locus of the most intimate of human relationships and the primary agency of socialization. In all societies, the family ascribes initial status to the individual, teaches him the basic skills, instills aspirations and sets limits upon them, and provides him with models of performance. In addition, the family is the transmission belt linking the past to the future, relaying the ever-cumulating and ever-changing cultural traditions of ancestors to the neophyte members of society who, in turn, pass them on in modified form to their offspring.

Though authority structures, lineage systems, residential patterns, attitudes toward sexual mores and marriages, marital arrangements, and techniques of child rearing are highly varied, the family is a basic unit in the dynamic structure of every society. While always affected by the wider culture of the society of which it is a part, the family system is instrumental in influencing behavior and social relationships of individuals not only "round the hearth," but in wider areas of social life.

Essays on the family by William J. Goode, John Sirjamaki, and Marvin B. Sussman and Lee Burchinal indicate the changing role of this particular institution in the social and economic revolution that is sweeping the world, describe the cultural configurations of American family life, and examine the nature of the "Kin Family Network." Taken together these articles raise some serious questions about the future of the family in modern, industrial countries.

The second set of papers deals with the economic institution, that aspect of the social order concerned with the organization of production, the patterning of consumption, and the distribution and exchange of such resources as land, capital, and manpower. Like the family, economic systems vary markedly from one society to another.

"Primitive" societies are often primitive technologically. Their members are limited to primary tools and live at a level of meager subsistence and beyond the mainstream of modern life. At the other end of the continuum are the "advanced" societies such as the United States, Canada, Japan, the Soviet Union, and the nations of Europe, which are possessed of elaborate technologies, intricate bureaucracies, highly differentiated and mobile labor forces, and high levels of productivity.

The papers in this section are concerned with such advanced societies and our primary focus is on the United States, a nation in which, some have argued, the economic system is the linchpin of society, determining the nature of social stratification, the values of the people, and making its presence felt in every sector—family, school, church, and government.

In the first three essays on the economic system, Daniel Bell discusses changes in the economic and social structure of capitalistic America, Peter F. Drucker describes what he calls the "employee society," and Melvin M. Tumin describes "Business as a Social System." The last article is comparative. Here, Alex Inkeles and Peter H. Rossi compare occupational prestige in six industrial countries suggesting, that in spite of widespread cultural variability, modernity has a pervasive quality.

All societies have institutioned means of dealing with the regulation of the rules of conduct, the establishment of legitimate authority, and the exercise of social control. The expression of these political and legal arrangements is a fascinating subject for comparative analysis; so, too, is the study of the covert meanir gs which underlie political forms. Political sociologists are concerned with understanding the nature and extent of participation in the political process, with leadership and power relationships, and with the connection between political and other institutions.

Three essays—by Robert Bierstedt, Robert Dahl, and William Kornhauser—are grouped under the rubric "The Polity." Together, they illustrate the problem of defining what is meant by "authority," the relationship between the citizen and the state, the question of whether the "power elite" or "veto groups" dominate in the American political order, and responses to authority by various segments of the body politic.

In an earlier section on "Culture and the Individual," the process of socialization was defined, discussed, and illustrated. It was suggested that through socialization cultural perspectives (ideas, values, beliefs) are inculcated and roles (or behavioral expectations) are specified and internalized. The family is the primary agency of initial socialization. In some societies it is responsible for training throughout life. In advanced and advancing societies, however, formal indoctrination to both the ideological and technical requirements for operational effectiveness is increasingly served by "education." The school system often serves the functions of technical *and* political indoctrination. Education is frequently used as the principal avenue of social mobility or, conversely, as a means of perpetuating social differences.

Talcott Parsons, in the first essay in the section on education, sees the school class as a social system. His concern is with how the school affects the students. James Coleman looks at the other side of the coin and discusses the viewpoints of the students themselves. A. H. Halsey deals with changing functions of higher education, while Leila Sussmann relates what happens when the American system of higher education is transplanted into another society (in this case, Puerto Rico).

The last normative system considered here is religion. Religion is an institution "in the round." It encompasses sacred beliefs, prescribed rites and rituals, communities of believers, and, in many cases, special forms of social organization. To many it is the very core of the integrative life offering a reason for existence, emotional out-lets, and a basis for social cohesion.

These functions are discussed in detail in J. Milton Yinger's theoretical statement on the sociology of religion. Religious organization is the subject of Bryan R. Wilson's paper, the second selection in this section. The third paper deals with the nature of the "ethnic church" in America; it is taken from Marshall Sklare's book, *Conservative Judaism*. The last paper, by Father Joseph H. Fichter, describes the special problem of racial integration in American churches.

The Family

41. THE FAMILY AS AN ELEMENT IN THE WORLD REVOLUTION

WILLIAM J. GOODE

Our examination of several selected examples of literature dealing with the family in various cultures begins with an essay by William J. Goode. After dispelling a few of the many common misconceptions about the nature of the family, including the "classical family of Western nostalgia" and the corresponding myths that exist in other parts of the world, Goode turns from fancy to fact. He compares Japanese and Chinese family systems and describes the role each has played (and continues to play) in adapting to the revolution of modern industrialization now sweeping the globe. Using these cases as points of departure, Goode discusses the dynamism of familial systems in relation to the general issue of social and economic development.

William J. Goode is Professor of Sociology at Columbia University and the author of World Revolution and Family Patterns, *which won the MacIver Award for the best book in sociology in 1965. He is also the author of* Religion Among the Primitives *(1951),* After Divorce *(1956), and* The Family *(1964), and is coauthor of* Methods in Social Research *(1952). He is editor of a volume of* Readings on The Family and Society *(1964) and of* The Dynamics of Modern Society *(1966).*

This essay is a reprint of the pamphlet *The Family as an Element in the World Revolution* published by the Institute of Life Insurance, by permission of the author and the publisher.

It was a cynic of uncommon disillusionment who claimed that Adam and Eve, when they ate the apple in the Garden of Eden, became aware not of their shame and nakedness, but of their more fundamental and far-reaching predicament: they were living in a family and from that point on would therefore know no peace.

The cynic's observation of the enormous consequences of the family and its effect on people's lives is matched by the wisdom of the gret philosopher Plato, who, over two millennia ago decided to eliminate the family system from his Utopia, because the family, as the keystone of the class system, was an impediment to the achievement of equal opportunity for all.

This recognition that the family is not a passive conduit through which the social tradition is passed from one generation to another, and is not merely the repository of ancient virtue and morality, but rather takes an active role in the social structure, has a special force today. For, as with bewildering rapidity societies and nations are being transformed around us, we need greater understanding than ever before to guide, resist, or facilitate the massive forces of social change.

If we want to achieve more systematic knowledge of how family patterns affect the larger social structure, we must go beyond the casual intermittent insights of either cynicism or sagacity and carry out a difficult, disciplined program of research. We must substitute fact for fancy and hard study for literary creation.

In examining the important role played by the family in social change two warnings are especially necessary.

First, we must be prepared to analyze, not moralize, in an area where our emotions are easily aroused. When we *distinguish* analysis and description from moralizing and evaluation it is not necessary to place a greater value on one or the other. Evaluation is a central fact of being human—of social action itself. But it is most appropriate after the facts are in. Evaluation without facts is blind prejudice.

Preaching often disguises impoverished data.

Second, if we wish to understand how family systems play a role in world change we need a base point from which to measure change. To study alteration we must know what the family itself is changing *from*. This brings out our second warning: we must be prepared to yield some of our most cherished clichés and myths and see them coolly destroyed. The history of every family system in the world is partly myth. It is usually an idealized, stylized literary fabrication, at best describing a minority of upper class families, and often having little relevance to the lives of most people. This is true for recent history as well as for our own time with which we are more familiar. But because we are familiar with our own time does not mean we have knowledge of it. Familiarity only provides surface images and must not be confused with the knowledge which comes from a systematic study of facts.

For example, one of the literary myths that was killed by fact just a decade ago was that the lower class family was a vast network of extended kinfolk, warm and sympathetic, and that if hot-tempered in domestic life, it did not usually consider divorce to be a solution to its conflicts, if only because of the cost.

Although we would understand our society better if we possessed adequate data, oddly enough no one has yet mapped the very basic pattern of class differences in the American family system. The few hard facts we *do* have show that for decades the divorce rate has actually been higher in the lower social strata, and the kin network has also been smaller there.

Another cliché recent research has demolished concerns the large household that was thought to be the average family of the past. Not only did most Americans in the past *not* live out their lives in large households made up of many generations, but (again contrary to myth) this was also true of Chinese and Indians too.

To turn to a more specific case in which

social research contradicts bluntly a key matrimonial myth: studies correlating dates of marriage with dates of first birth show that as many as one-fourth of U.S. marriages are attended by a small but influential guest—the growing fetus in the bride. This may shock you, but I doubt that this is a new phenomenon, or, that it is evidence of family decay in our corrupt, urbanized era. I suspect that this pattern was common in U.S. rural areas in the past. I *know* that in the Western countries from which most of our ancestors came, this pattern can be traced back for hundreds of years.

Perhaps I should not offer more examples. It might strain your credulity if I went further and expressed my doubt that family life in our grandfather's generation was much happier or more virtuous than at present. In any event, what I suggest— referring to such recent studies—is that we must be prepared to give up some of our clichés if we seriously mean to investigate how the family operates. We must be prepared to cast aside not only what I have called the "classical family of Western nostalgia" but also the corresponding family myths of other countries. We may argue that the Chinese communists distort the Chinese family of the past when they call it "feudal," but honest classical Chinese scholars also distorted the past, and called their family system "Mandarin," drawing a picture of enlightened scholarship, wise humanitarianism, an all-powerful male as the clan patriarch ruling over a great household, all living in serenity, with never a divorce to mar its calm content.

Let us turn from myths to reality. Japan provides a good illustration of what has been learned in recent research about the importance of the family in an early stage of the great societal transformation that so many countries are now undergoing. We see a dramatic contrast between the success of the Japanese leaders who, in answer to the threat from the industrial West, carried out the Meiji Restoration in 1868 and then reshaped the social institu-

tions of their country, and the failure of the Chinese to move ahead with any effectiveness during the same period. As one analyst has summarized it: The Japanese "started close to bankruptcy, used almost no foreign capital, established uneconomic heavy industries, organized and maintained a modern military and navy establishment, changed their governmental system radically, altered their system of production and consumption of goods and services to one in which modern industry was strategic, erected and conducted many highly profitable modern enterprises, made literacy virtually universal . . ." and taught their people a new pattern of social relations that was characteristic of the Western market system.[1] Moreover, this task, perhaps the only genuine instance of an underdeveloped country lifting itself entirely by its own bootstraps, was carried out by World War I, that is, within a period of about five decades. China, on the other hand, faced with a similar situation, found no such solution for its problems. The case is the more convincing, because the Meiji leaders were determined to confine the spread of personal freedom, especially in family matters, to what was absolutely necessary for the goals desired. In contrast to the modern era, in which the family system may contribute to social change through its new emphasis on freedom, the Meiji leaders sought to yield to the family no more than was necessary, and instead to *use* the family group as a positive element in industrialization. The case is complex, and only a brief listing of the important elements can be given here. Specifically, we can see that differences in the Chinese and Japanese family systems had a marked effect on the relative economic success of the two countries, despite their similar situations at that time.

Under the Chinese family system, all sons inherited equally, which meant that family capital could not ordinarily be held intact. By contrast, in Japan, one son— usually the eldest—inherited all, which meant that wealth could accumulate in one family line, and a decision to invest could more easily be made.

Second, and perhaps most important, Chinese familism asserted that a man owed his first duty to his family elders, and that if duty to Emperor conflicted with duty to his father, the latter would be upheld. The greatest of Chinese sins was to be unfilial. By contrast, though a Japanese owed a duty to his father, there was no comparable boundary setting off the family from nonfamily, father from Emperor. An unbroken chain of fealty stretched from each individual through his father and his father's lord or leader, and through successively higher levels in the feudal system to the great princes and the Emperor. Since each family was so linked, orders and requests from above were more likely to be obeyed, including those requiring renunciation or sacrifice. The radical changes needed for industrialization included putting warriors to work or using them for policemen, taking land from great lords to be used as capital for new enterprises, and even asking those whose tasks had largely been symbolic or ornamental, actually to get to work. Nevertheless, these links of family with State held firm.

Third, Chinese familism considered nepotism a duty, not a crime. Any man who rose by his own energy and talent was expected to carry upward with him a goodly number of family members. Such a burden was less likely in Japan, where the class barriers were more difficult to cross, but where *adoption* was a major route of social ascent. A Japanese might disinherit an untalented son in favor of an able adopted son, an almost unthinkable act in China. The adopted son in turn was *not* compelled to carry his former family with him. This meant that Chinese efficiency was handicapped by nepotism, while a Japanese man of station was free to look for an able successor, and the son he adopted was free of the duty to give favors to his family of birth. Consequently, the Japanese could more easily rise to the

new achievements required by industrialism.

Fourth, precisely because upward class mobility was possible in China, if a man was successful in business there was little accumulation of a family lore or tradition in those areas that were of greatest importance in the new era of capitalism. How did this happen? The Chinese merchant had a *lowly* social rank, even when he had some power because of his money, and as a consequence his prime aim was to acquire enough wealth to cease being a merchant, to educate his sons to become scholars, or at least to live like gentlemen. The gentry could own land, and live in a traditional style but the scholarship that was the foundation of the Chinese civil service had little relevance to the needs of the new economic system. Thus, the emphasis on family mobility through the accumulation of learning prevented the accumulation of the merchant's economic skills and knowledge. In short, the successful Chinese, the man who by talent and energy moved upward, moved away from the very knowledge that would have facilitated industrialization. By contrast, the Japanese merchant had little or no opportunity of moving his family upward, and little reason to urge his sons to become gentlemen. Confined to a narrower kind of mobility, Japanese merchant family lines were ready to provide appropriate financial and economic skills when the Meiji Restoration opened the doors to the new economic enterprises.

Here then, we have a dramatic example of how, when Western influences began to penetrate two societies of similar situations but differing family structures, these differences helped to shape their widely divergent histories of success or failure as a modern industrial society.

We do not, however, assert that the family system is the prime mover, the root force of any society; for when all things are in flux, it is difficult to say that any particular element is basically responsible. But the family system does play an important role. It has a force and power of its own, to shape, resist, or facilitate the main trends and currents of social change.

I believe that we are now in a new phase of world history. We may well wonder whether the family is any more than simply a passive agent in *this* great movement. Let us consider what it is, and what part is played by the family within it.

We are now in the midst of a world revolution. Every society is being profoundly altered. This is a unique event: For the first time in world history, a common set of forces is changing radically the quality of living among the three billion people who inhabit this planet. These deep transmutations will continue throughout our lifetimes. From one perspective, this movement may be called progress. But, as is true of all progress, it means the destruction of the old, including the parts with which we may have been living comfortably.

This revolution is not the spectacular spread of Communism immediately after World War II, or the less publicized but striking failure of Communism to continue that extension in the last few years. Both of these are only transitory and surface events compared with this world revolution. Moreover, both drew their strength from this greater revolution, not vice versa.

The driving force of the radical transformation is this: for the first time the peoples of the world have become afflicted with a disturbing *wish* to change and to improve their economic position; to become industrialized. It is tempting to see this as a banality, an obvious process: of course, people want the goods produced by Western countries: are they not obviously superior? But like so many seemingly obvious "facts," this one misses the point where it is not plainly wrong. For it is not true that other peoples have always wanted most of our goods. Though they did see the advantages of possessing our guns, and a small number of our tools, most people did not, at first contact, want more of *all*

our goods; they simply wanted more of their own.

The more fundamental point is that the lust for goods is merely one facet of an underlying aspiration. More than the goods themselves, people want the machines to make them with, the magic and the power that these machines both symbolize and make real. The *still* deeper wish, the root and wellspring from which the transmuting force comes, is a vision, expectation, and demand that freedom of choice be no longer denied. This is the *real* revolution. It expresses a radical ideology, even when its implementation takes a form that we consider politically retrograde. It denies the right of powerful countries to rule the less powerful, even if the conquest is hundreds of years in the past. It proclaims instead that people have the right to rule—or even misrule—themselves. It undermines the legitimacy of feudal regimes in which lord and serf exchange protection for labor. Rather, people prefer to work for wages, since money permits them to make their own purchase choices. The ideology denies the authority of elders, or a caste system, to determine a man's occupation, and asserts instead that a man may follow his own bent, suiting his talents to the changing rewards of the open market. Nor does it adjust easily to the tradition of an ancient class system, which in its rigidity sought to keep each man in the social position where he was born. Instead, this revolutionary doctrine claims that a man may rise if he wishes. This new belief opens geographical choice as well, not only through new forms of transportation, but through the physical protection given to those who wander, and through the economic opportunities that make that movement profitable. One consequence of this massive hunger for self-determination has been the rapid overthrow of both colonial empires and old native despotisms, and the swift overthrow of new governments whose people were impatient for progress. Another has been the frequent temporary—and sometimes longer lasting

—success of native or imported Communist leaders in many countries, *because* Communist promises have coincided with these aspirations: new jobs, land, the vote, the overthrow of privileged groups.

Indeed, as a sociologist I would point out that the tragic irony of the underdeveloped nations has been that their leaders believe our secret lies in our machines and money, whereas in fact it is in our social institutions. It is easy to see the machines; the institutions are more subtle, and are difficult to observe or to copy. They believe that if they can have the machines, they can achieve the freedom they seek without additional guidance or knowledge. Unfortunately, very likely the facts are exactly opposite. It was the ideas and the social system of the West, and more particularly of the Puritans, that made possible our great wealth.

But the apparent short-sightedness of such leaders may not be self-defeating in the long run. For it is not only the factory that is being introduced. In some form or another, the new ideology may well enter before the factory, and begin to change people's attitudes and aspirations, paving the way for new modes of behavior. The new, revolutionary philosophy presses for freedom in many areas of life, and thus changes in ideas and the social system may not merely follow the factory; they may lay the groundwork for it.

It seems clear that at our most cautious we must concede the crucial importance of these social ideas and institutions, since they begin to affect public decisions, laws and constitutions even before any substantial industrialization has occurred. Therefore, I repeat, we must begin to examine closely the family, a social institution that is usually omitted from contemporary analyses of social change. We must understand it if we are to understand the great swirl of alteration in which the world now lives, for the family itself is in a state of flux everywhere.

What has been the reason for neglecting this vital institution? It has been assumed too readily that one can easily predict the kind of family system that will be found in a society if one knows its technological or economic system. But, oddly enough, despite this supposition no one has yet succeeded in even *stating* such determinate relations, let alone proving them. Moreover, an increasing body of evidence, some of which I have already reported here, suggests the family system may be an *independent* set of variables, having its own effect on the total societal dynamics.

The relations of family changes to other social and economic changes can more easily be studied now than fifteen years ago. The more highly developed nations have come to see that their destinies are now intertwined with those of the newer nations. Bidding for their political backing, the industrialized nations must offer economic leadership, but to do so rationally requires research. Experts in the newer nations have also begun to carry out research, often in order to demonstrate to richer nations their needs. Thereby, hundreds of studies of social change are furnishing a massive, if sometimes chaotic and ill-planned, mountain of data for us to think about, to organize, and to understand. From such hopeful visions of the future, then, the facts emerge, with which we can better comprehend the interaction of family and the larger social structure.

Revolutionaries seek the significance of the family clearly and use this knowledge; they seek the support of the young, the educated, the women, the disadvantaged. In every new fundamental law or constitution—whether in Algeria or China, Tunisia or Viet-Nam, Japan or India, the family has been juridically changed—it has been changed far ahead of public opinion, and in the direction of greater freedom for the individual. Obviously, those who have sought to bring about these changes believe what they offer will attract followers, and will yield the new energies for development which freedom seems to release.

The main outlines of the shifts are clear enough. Family systems of the world are gradually moving toward a form of the family known as the conjugal family, in which the unit is comprised of parents and children and only very limited extended kinship relationships. Thereby, the power of a lineage to control a young couple diminishes. Under the new form, young people begin to have the right to choose their own spouses, and love becomes a major basis of mate-choice. They are no longer dependent on the elders to furnish a dowry or brideprice before they can marry, and elders do not determine the permissible marriage age. The young couple chooses where they are to live, usually setting up their own household. After marriage, they make their own decision as to how many children they will have. Parents have less authority over children, and husbands have less control over their wives. If husband and wife do not find this union congenial, both have the freedom to dissolve it, and to form a new alliance. Thus, the divorce rate is high (though not necessarily higher than in traditional family systems), and so is the remarriage rate.

Such a system offers more freedom to the individual, even if we may deplore some of its other consequences. By permitting personal choice of one's spouse, as against the fiat of family elders, it offers a much wider network from which to select a mate and thus helps to erode ancient class barriers. By denying the traditional authority of the male it offers the woman some scope for personal development.

Not only are many subject peoples in revolt; in much of the world women and children are rebelling too.

At the same time, this is a system that fits the needs of industrialization remarkably well. Industrialization requires that positions be filled on the basis of achievement, not family position; it requires movement and fluidity of labor, rather than geographical fixity based on family location. It requires decisions to be made rationally, rather than by a set of family elders. It needs the additional talents of women, which are wasted in most systems.

These fundamental family changes are part of the broader alterations in the social and economic structures of the world's societies, and also contribute to them. In so brief a compass, we cannot look closely at more than two of these family changes.

Let us first consider the flow of talent into the posts where it can best be used, without which the peoples of the world have no hope of realizing their new aspiration for growth and freedom. The emotional cohesion by which the family makes its most important contribution to the individual's development is at the same time a deterrent to such an easy flow. No family system—East or West—supports the occupational placement of men and women solely on the basis of merit. In all systems, the parents at any given class level strive with more or less success to exclude from their ranks those at a lower position—by controlling "dates" and friendships among their children, by controlling marriage, the granting of jobs, or by political and financial agreements.

However, the shift toward a conjugal family system, in which the young have greater freedom to date and choose their own mates, or to dissolve their union, or to seek a new job distant from any kin, at least reduces the effect of traditional systems which have stifled the easy utilization of talent. Obviously, if a new nation is to maximize growth, it must limit the number of jobs and opportunities that are under the control of family elders who will allot them to their kin rather than to the ablest candidates. The importance of such a restriction, so characteristic of this conjugal pattern toward which the world's family systems are moving, may be seen in an interesting paradox—one which shows how significant the family is in hindering or facilitating a nation's growth.

Theoretical formulations, which I summarized a moment ago, in pointing out how this system yields freedom and the flow of talent, suggest that an extreme form of conjugal system, whatever its emotional costs, meets the labor needs of industrialism better than does any other system. But herein lies a paradox: the families that are most *successful* in an industrial system, i.e., the middle and upper classes, have in fact more frequent and extended communication and exchanges with extended kin, control more effectively the dating and premarital behavior of their children, grant less freedom in choice of mate, and have a lower divorce rate—i.e., the families that are most successful actually adjust the least to industrial needs. Phrased crudely, lower class families adjust to the need of industrialism; middle and upper class families adjust industrialism to *their* needs, and resist the pressures toward a conjugal system. Or, phrased still differently, the key positions held by the elite make more profitable the maintenance of their kinship links.

This relationship between class and family structure—again, I remind you, the mapping of such relationships is only in its infancy—seems to have been typical in Western society for centuries. The key class difference is that when the economic or political system expanded, the upper strata could control the new jobs because it was they who initiated the expansion. The Church offered many new opportunities in the eleventh and twelfth centuries, with the creation of nunneries, monasteries, and churches, and the elite could offer them in exchange for family obedience.

The commercial and political opportunities in colonial expansion also permitted elite elders to maintain control over the young, since it was the elite who organized that expansion. By contrast, elders in lower strata families must permit their young to leave, having no better alternative to offer them; and cannot demand subservience, if the young can do even better without their blessing.

In some countries this problem has been partly solved by the overthrow of the elite and their government, but we know from other revolutions that after the turmoil has calmed down and the new order has settled in, the sons of the elite will still enjoy a statistically higher chance of getting privileged posts than will sons of peasants—if only because they are better educated. Moreover, whatever our democratic prejudices, there is no reason to suppose that the sons of the elite are *less* able; and since new countries typically suffer from a shortage of trained people, to forbid them good positions would actually hamper the country's development.

If the crucial factor that will differentiate the countries which will grow quickly from those which do not, is their effective utilization of manpower, the flow of talent, the importance of the family processes is once more suggested. What is significant is not the class *origin* of the new generation of leaders, but whether their family and kin groups can still control their placement, and their decisions after placement. If nepotism is to be avoided, then those countries that most fully accept the ideology and behavioral patterns of the conjugal system will be most successful at it. The ideology urges the young to rebel against traditional authority, but it also undermines the confidence of their elders in the rightness of that control. Where the new family system succeeds in offering its kind of freedom, the rest of the social system is also likely to create its new forms of personal development and opportunity, the essence of the revolution we are discussing today. At the least, the *degree* of control and nepotism will be diminished.

There is a second, but related, element in this shift in family patterns. We will treat it briefly, although it is an emotion-laden topic, the utilization of womanpower. Countries in which women are not freed to take jobs are not likely to enjoy the fruits of the revolution we now have under our lens. I hasten to point out that women work in *all* societies. But industrialism is the first kind of social structure in world history that has permitted women to obtain jobs and to advance on their own merits, independent of the decisions of husbands or fathers. Imperial Rome, for example, gave many personal liberties to women. It did not, however, allow them scope for autonomous growth, without which political equality is meaningless, and participation in family decisions empty.

Freeing half of the country's talent for its development and enrichment may seem rational, but the accompanying alteration of family patterns which inevitably results is especially difficult. Women are largely untrained, and their men resent the personal rights which women demand when they begin to obtain jobs on their own. Even in the highly industrialized Western countries, it is striking that women of the lower strata are more likely to work because their men are less able to prevent them from doing so, and less likely to work toward the upper strata, where their men have more authority. In no country have men been willing to take over the jobs traditionally held by women. Indeed, I suggest that the Chinese commune system enjoyed one advantage by assuring men a continuation of the traditional home services such as food preparation, laundry, and child care, but in the communes assigning these tasks to women. Consequently, although the Chinese male still resists equalitarianism strongly, even in the face of official pressures, he can at least avoid "women's work." But in spite of some reversion to the traditional sex division of labor, Chinese women were given far greater scope for their abilities than ever before, and their progress has been enormous.

I have emphasized here the importance of the family system in the world revolution we are witnessing, in which hundreds of millions of people are acquiring new aspirations for goods and education, for the freedom to choose and move and work as they wish. And I have noted the importance of the family form toward which the world's societies are moving. This form, buttressed and heralded by an ideology of freedom, is the conjugal family, in which the major emphasis is on the parents and children as a unit with fewer social ties with the extended kin network. It releases people from older family rigidities, and contributes to the development of the society and economy which in turn yield more opportunities for its members.

But I have hinted more than once that precisely because a family system is important, the new form can hinder as well as facilitate. Its impact on the larger social processes is sometimes great, and deserves serious research, but clearly not all its consequences are to be admired.

We cannot leave this exploration of only partially charted regions without a final comment, from an entirely different stance. Let us remember, even while holding firmly to the analytic and cosmic view presented here, that if societies are changing, then so are *people,* and that in such personal terms this means tragedy as well as liberation. New rights for the wife may mean lessened privilege for the husband. Freedom, after all, has its other face. Whether, on balance we welcome the change or deplore it, depends on our personal values, and no one else can judge for us.

A Japanese son will still take care of his widowed mother in his household, but if she grew up in a rural household where her own mother was paid increasing respect with age and ruled as matriarch behind the public authority of her husband, she may feel a nagging sense of disappointment as a modern widow, when she is denied that experience. Doubtless most of you are pleased that the Arab husband learns that divorce is an increasingly awkward, tedious, and costly action, far more than it was for his father, but many Arab men are annoyed that they cannot so lightly dismiss their wives as their fathers and grandfathers could. I dare say that most of you also learn with approval that young Chinese brides no longer bring tea to their mothers-in-law in the morning, rub their feet, or bow in submission before the elder woman's authority, but many elderly Chinese feel that they have been dismissed, cast out, or neglected by an unfeeling younger generation.

The spread of the conjugal family pattern with its greater personal freedom arouses dismay among many people, who see in it freedom's other face, which is irresponsibility, disorganization, and the personal burden of failure. Under a system of arranged marriages, they point out, perhaps most people did not find love, but the slow or quick dissolution of love in the new system brings pain and trauma. In the older systems, the women and young people carried great burdens, but in time they too acquired wisdom, and were given respect, living out a full cycle in which each part was part of an unbroken and meaningful unity. Now, no one knows what his family obligations are, and no one is paid respect for wisdom, while the young and the women have lost the protection which was once theirs in exchange for their submission. I do not urge the gloomy philosophy that for every gain there is an equal loss; simply that we must also be aware not only of the concomitant losses, but also of the essential fact that it is our personal values which determine whether they *are* to be counted as losses.

In my own values, the greater effectiveness of the new family patterns in a developing industrialism is not a sufficient justification. The new system, like the industrial system that comes with it, creates great personal difficulties and forces upon us a nearly continuous challenge. Perhaps its primary justification—and this massive revolution will not be stopped, whether or not we find a justification for it —is that it presents to more individuals at least the *potentiality* of greater fulfillment, even if most people do not achieve it or even seek it. In any event, I confidently predict that after the establishment of a conjugal system, people in every country will, as we do here, look backward wistfully to the idealized past, and agree with one another in their thoughtful moments on how much better the past family system used to be, in the good old days that never were.

NOTE

1. Marion J. Levy, "Contrasting Factors in the Modernization of China and Japan," in Simon S. Kuznets, Wilbert E. Moore, and Joseph J. Spengler (eds.), *Economic Growth: Brazil, India, Japan,* Durham, N.C.: Duke University Press, 1955, pp. 528–529.

42. CULTURE CONFIGURATIONS IN THE AMERICAN FAMILY

JOHN SIRJAMAKI

Viewing a cultural analysis of the dominant configurations of the family as an alternative to more traditional approaches to family study, John Sirjamaki's article dovetails rather neatly with the point of view expressed by William J. Goode. Sirjamaki defines culture configurations as the approved rules or sentiments, existing at a covert level, that motivate the overt behavior of individuals and integrate it into meaningful patterns. Such configurations, when applied to the family, express its value system.

An analysis of the middle-class American family suggests that at least eight such value themes are identifiable. Taken together they represent an idealized model of family life in the United States to which most Americans refer (but not all are capable of realizing).

John Sirjamaki is Professor of Sociology at the State University of New York at Buffalo. He is the author of The American Family in the Twentieth Century *(1953) and* The Sociology of Cities *(1964). He has recently revised Earl H. Bell's textbook,* Social Foundations of Human Behavior *(1966).*

Most sociological studies of the family deal with it either as a social system or as a social institution. An important supplement to these approaches is the cultural analysis of the family in terms of its dominant configurations. When these can be specified for the family, it is possible to interpret the basic moral ideas which give the family its distinctive and identifying characteristics.

Culture configurations are the moral principles which comprise the social philosophy of a society. They are patterns of covert behavior; as such, they are the culturally approved rules or sentiments which motivate overt behavior and which integrate it into consistent patterns; and they can be deduced only from behavior. Such configurations exist on the level of the culture and arise in the context of everyday living. Members of a society compre-

hend the meaning of such precepts in the process of socialization, even when they are expressed tenuously or obscurely; and, indeed, configurations are difficult to state abstractly inasmuch as they generally operate below the level of awareness. Taken together, the configurations delineate the ethos of a culture.[1]

Configurations are thus the basic units of the value system of a society. They differ from the absolute ethics of religious or philosophical systems in that they are mundane, practical, this-worldly; having developed within the culture, they express the dominant values which are thought to be necessary for the continued functioning of the society. Ordinarily configurational values are stigmatized by philosophers as base and inferior; Fromm has called them "socially immanent ethics" as contrasted to universal ethics.[2] For the social scientist,

Reprinted from the *American Journal of Sociology,* **53** (1948), 464–470, by permission of the author and The University of Chicago Press.

however, it is necessary to understand the configurations of a culture, since they motivate behavior much more continuously than do absolute ethical systems. The configurations will tend to support the total culture and to achieve an interrelatedness among themselves. As Sumner indicated, there is a strain for consistency in the mores.[3]

The concept of the configurations of the culture, and a knowledge of the manner in which these are expressed within an institution, illuminates the study of the family. Configurations reach into the most intimate areas of individual and family behavior; they furnish the meanings and determine right and wrong behavior in courting, in husband-wife and parent-child relationships, in heterosexual social activity, and in ideas about sex. Thus they supply the moral sentiments by which family members are influenced and make explicable the vagaries of their behavior.

At least four qualifications may be raised concerning the validity of applying culture configurations to the study of the American family. First, since such configurations are inferred by the investigator from the overt behavior of people, he must have available a considerable amount of observational data which, however, is currently lacking. Second, the use of such configurations should await an analysis of the total culture, and this has been attempted thus far in the most tentative manner.[4] The analysis of parts of the culture, however, will assist in the determination of the total culture ethos. Third, generalizations about American culture must be stated in the most broad terms and can attempt only to strike an average, since regional and ethnic subcultures obviously differ from the main pattern. To whom, it may be asked, do configurations apply? The answer is that configurations are generally valid, or will tend to become so, for the entire American society, in the sense that they represent the moral standards by which all behavior is evaluated, and which exert a social pressure to secure some de-

gree of conformance. Families of ethnic minorities thus quite apparently have patterns dissimilar to those of native-born families, but in time the American culture configurations come to influence the actions of at least the immigrant children and to bring their behavior into conformity with the general requirements of society. Finally, configurations are not easily amenable to quantification; they may seem to be accurately stated, but they are difficult to measure. There is no real answer to this objection other than to predicate the statement of configurations upon as careful objective analysis as is possible. A value system patently exists in every culture, and its appraisal should be sought by the social scientist.

The following configurations, among others, appear in the American family:

1) MARRIAGE IS A DOMINATING LIFE-GOAL, FOR MEN AS WELL AS FOR WOMEN It is felt that married life is the normal, desired condition for all adults, that it brings the greatest personal happiness and fulfilment, and that it permits the proper exercise of sex for the procreation of children and for individual satisfaction. The single adult life by contrast, according to this attitude, is empty and barren. That there is a considerable societal concern that women marry is generally recognized, but the greater courting and sexual initiative assumed by men has obscured the comparable pressure on them to marry, and adult men who postpone marriage into their thirties become objects of distress and conspiracy among friends and relatives. Most Americans marry in their twenties, and, for a considerable share of them, marriage at that age means a happy union of individual volition and social pressure.

Long ago Professor E. A. Ross pointed out that Americans are the most marrying nation in Western Christendom. United States census figures have shown that since 1890 they have married in steadily increasing proportions and at earlier ages.[5] About 92 per cent of adults will have been married at some time in their lives by the age of sixty-five, and this is a sufficiently high number to suggest that nearly all persons marry who are physically and mentally capable of contracting marriage.

2) THE GIVING AND TAKING IN MARRIAGE SHOULD BE BASED ON PERSONAL AFFECTION AND CHOICE Marriage is thought to be preeminently the linking of the lives of two young people drawn to each other by personal attraction. Arranged marriages, or those based on fraud or calculation, receive considerable disapprobation.

Dating is thought by many sociologists to precede serious courting and to be an educational process leading to it. Waller first analyzed it in terms of its distinctive cultural patterns.[7] In dating, the young woman undoubtedly receives the greatest cultural estimation of her personal qualities: merely to be a young, nubile female of attractive phenotype means that she is the object of considerable masculine attention and chivalry.[8] But despite this high evaluation of young women, most men grow up in American society with the assumption, culturally derived, that the decision to marry rests with them; they expect in the fulness of time to lead some dear girl to the altar. Women, on the other hand, regardless of their personal qualities, can never be completely sure that they will receive a marriage proposal which they can consider seriously, or, more to the point, be asked to marry by the man upon whom they have fastened their desire.[9] The culture does not permit them to undertake active courting by themselves; to be a man-chaser is to suffer an ostracism which is enforced by the women themselves. Women are obviously not completely helpless in these sentimental matters, but they must use guile and finesse to bring the male to their side.

Since the biological fact of bisexuality predisposes women for the having and rearing of children, and therefore for the maintenance of a home, they are compelled to drive as good a bargain in the marriage market as they can. This they can manage only by a careful exploitation of the rules which specify correct maidenly deportment. Men, on the other hand, have greater volition in their marriage choices and are much more disposed as a result to manage their marital ventures in the bathos of culturally approved romance.

3) THE CRITERION OF SUCCESSFUL MARRIAGE IS THE PERSONAL HAPPINESS OF HUSBAND AND WIFE Mutual compatibility is made the basis of marriage, and marital bliss becomes dependent upon the emotional sentiments, fluctuating and volatile as they may be, with which a couple regard their relationship. Ultimately their fullest felicity is believed to be achieved by having children, whose arrival and subsequent nurture are viewed as bringing satisfaction to basic biological and social needs. Childless couples are sometimes regarded as possessed of a selfishness which blights their union. Happiness in marriage is thus predicated upon a personal equation, the individual satisfaction and the opportunity for development of the couple.

The cultural accent upon happiness in marriage is of relatively recent origin. Marriages are ordinarily contracted and their success gauged by their contribution in the struggles of life. These may be the partnership cooperation of man and wife, the production of children, the social recognition of adult status, or the stability of marital status. Many such marriages may be buttressed by institutional supports, the most important of which is generally the exchange of property. The spouses may be selected for each other by the parents or other adults, after a careful scrutiny of their relative merits and upon some property agreement, in the belief that normal young people, once married, can fashion for themselves a successful marital life.[10]

A corollary of the American patterns of courtship and marriage which is not always recognized is the logical necessity of a relatively easy system of divorce. From a cultural viewpoint, if marriages are made on the basis of personal and inevitably shifting emotions, without the added support of other institutional devices, then they should be equally easy to dissolve. Persons marry to find happiness and, finding it not, turn to divorce as a way out. The present high divorce rate, therefore, is in this sense made explicable and partially condoned by the cultural rules of marriage.

4) THE BEST YEARS OF LIFE ARE THOSE OF YOUTH, AND ITS QUALITIES ARE THE MOST DESIRABLE A high evaluation is placed upon youth and early middle age in American society, while the old are sometimes treated with indifference and even callousness. Youth is regarded as a period of innocence, energy, and enthusiasm; it is inventive and pragmatic when faced with new experiences and is glad of change— qualities fondly believed to be typical of Americans in general.

Among the young, the unmarried girl, aged perhaps twenty, attractive of face and limb, is the center of attraction in thought and deed. In other societies young men, or old men, or mothers are variously regarded as ideal symbols; [11] in the United States it is the young, pretty girl. She therefore receives at this age the greatest gratification of her ego drives which will probably ever come to her. With men the ideal age is somewhere in the thirties; they need time in which to win occupational and social placement and need not depend so much upon chronological age for their acceptance.

From this high esteem on youth there derive important social consequences. Wherever the young are involved, whether it be in the conduct of schools, or juvenile delinquency, or maltreatment of children, or provision for their play opportunities, there is likely to be at least a quick emotional response to their needs.

Such sentiments as these do not, of course, arise in a social vacuum. They exist, rather, and become understandable in terms of American social history. Youth has received a high evaluation, precisely because its resourcefulness and resilience

were valued qualities in the exploitation and development of the American continent. There have been, in addition, as compared to the age groups in European societies, relatively high proportions in the younger age categories in the American population; Americans have in this sense been a young people and correspondingly eager to admire the virtues of youth. The aged, on the other hand, have emerged as a significant social group only recently, and they are not yet favorably regarded.

Related to this cultural theme of youth is the existence of a considerable rift, not to say antagonism, between the generations. The conflict between the old and the young is common enough in human groups; what is significant is its intensity in American society. This is due, in large part, to the rapidity of social change in the United States and to the differing rates with which the generations have adjusted to those changes. Keller speaks somewhat nostalgically of the aged in primitive society as revered "repositories of wisdom,"[12] in American society they are unlikely to be regarded as possessors of a truth that has any relationship to their age.[13]

5) CHILDREN SHOULD BE REARED IN A CHILD'S WORLD AND SHIELDED FROM TOO EARLY PARTICIPATION IN ADULT WOES AND TRIBULATIONS This configuration is obviously closely related to the high cultural esteem of youth. It is modified by social class: the sentiment is held most strongly by the upper levels of society, much less so by the lower, but even among the poor the social conditions of the American community prevent a too considerable precocity among the children.[14]

The cultural ideal is that children shall mature slowly in terms of their nature and age-sex grades in a prolonged child's world, which is characterized by a segregated class of children's activities.[15] In this juvenile social world they are allowed to grow, develop their abilities, indulge in play, and occasionally to perform such small and often artificial tasks as may be assigned them. Generally they are protected from the responsibilities of adults, and laws and custom prevent their too early gainful employment. In many American homes, particularly in the cities, there is actually not much useful work that children can perform even if they wish. Especially in middle-class families is the configuration most completely observed. The child is accepted as an individual, and his relationships with parents are often warm and affectionate.

Folsom has contrasted this pattern with that which prevails in certain western European families, in which the child is incorporated into the family of adults and in which he lives in their world rather than in a segregated youth society.[16] Moreover, unlike the American middle-class child who may become somewhat exhibitionist in his behavior because of the attention shown him, the European youth is often hastened along in the process of maturation and trained to deference and respect toward parents and elders in general.

Such training as the American child receives may start him off with a psychologically secure character structure,[17] but in other respects it prepares him inadequately for later life. Sometimes he has not broken the emotional ties with his parents or developed definite heterosexual interests; hence his fondness for "Mom."[18] During World War II the British thought the American soldier adolescent.[19] James Graham Leyburn has pointed out that the American family is itself often at fault because of its inadequate integration with the larger community.[20] It may be unable, as a result, to prepare and to place its members into job, school, clique and class, association, and other social relationships in the society. Thus it delays the processes of maturation.

6) THE EXERCISE OF SEX SHOULD BE CONTAINED WITHIN WEDLOCK Prior to marriage premarital intercourse is strongly condemned, and sex knowledge is kept hidden from children lest it be damaging to their moral character. After marriage,

adultery is similarly proscribed. Sex may thus be legitimately expressed only within marriage, and the speaking of marriage vows makes highly moral sexual behavior which before then had been grossly immoral. The couple, previously prohibited from intercourse, may now embark upon an active, and socially approved, sex life. Sex, to speak figuratively, explodes upon marriage.

About sex there is considerable tension, preoccupation, frustration, shame, and deceit in American society. Judeo-Christian influences, and more immediately Puritanism, have given a sinful cast to sex and have condoned its expression in marriage only because of the grossly physical method of human reproduction. The tradition has particularly valued virginity, more especially in women, before marriage. But the strong interdictions upon sex have tended to heighten rather than to lessen the fascination with sex which exists among Americans. The furtiveness with which it is often approached and the numerous colloquialisms which refer to it indicate the uneasiness with which it is treated. Kinsey's exploration of the sex histories of American males has documented their actual performances.[21] These data indicate that the sex configuration is held with varying intensity at the several levels of society, apparently least so in the lower class. Even here, however, the materials reemphasize the manner in which restrictive cultural attitudes condition and limit sexual outlets.

7) FAMILY ROLES OF HUSBAND AND WIFE SHOULD BE BASED ON A SEXUAL DIVISION OF LABOR, BUT WITH THE MALE STATUS BEING SUPERIOR According to this configuration, the husband is head of his family, its main economic support, and its representative in the larger community. Women, consigned to domesticity, are mothers and homemakers. These roles, biologically and culturally conditioned, provide for the structuring of all types of heterosexual relationships, in which the presumption of dominance generally rests

with the males. Men are trained to develop the qualities necessary to fulfil their roles in economic, social, sexual, and other activities and to view themselves with self-respect when they have secured a competence in their performances. Women, too, are trained to their respective feminine roles, and these generally involve some degree of catering to men, somewhat as a complement to the expectation of greater male initiative. Terman's analysis of the desired pattern of sex typing in husband and in wife indicated how the cultural conception of the manly man and the womanly woman falls into the cultural mold.[22]

Women's behavior is governed by a double standard of morality which expects greater masculine enterprise not only in the sexual spheres but in many other areas of life. Women live, in male estimation, under a blanket of oppressive mores which restrains their ordinary, everyday movements. Where men have a relative freedom of action, women must cater to a public opinion of what is womanly behavior. In social life women are under greater disapproval than men when they smoke or indulge in narcotics. On the job they may encounter much male prejudice which affects their pay and possibilities of promotion. They are more protected by social legislation which governs their hours and conditions of employment.[23]

These cultural attitudes persist despite the social and economic events of modern times which have released women from the control of husbands and fathers. Before the law women have achieved a near-equality with men; they may seek gainful employment and retain their earnings; they have equal rights with men to education; they have all the freedoms necessary to live their own lives as they wish. Democratic sentiments further foster the desire that women develop as persons to enjoy the manifold blessings of American life and to have many of the privileges given men.

Women are thus caught in a process of social change, in which the cultural configuration restrains them to traditional roles, while new ones are proffered by economic and social forces. There is much confusion among them as a result. The young college girl, for example, may have difficulty in knowing to which force to respond: should she be content with the domestic role and look to the main chance of marriage, or should she seek outlets which include both marriage and other roles?[24] Apparently some urban upper-level women find the puzzle extremely hard to resolve and respond to it neurotically.[25]

Men, too, it must be pointed out, suffer in the realignment of roles, since they as much as women are conditioned to the status quo and may find it hard to accommodate themselves to change.

8) INDIVIDUAL, NOT FAMILIAL, VALUES ARE TO BE SOUGHT IN FAMILY LIVING The family is obviously affected by the considerable cultural affirmation of individualism, and the lack of a tradition of familism in American culture has further aided in the development of a configuration in which the family exists for the benefit of its members. The emphasis has been upon the individualization of all members of the family, the children as well as the parents, the wife as much as the husband. Obviously, the husband's prerogatives, nurtured in the bosom of the patriarchal family have had to be parceled out to the other members.

There are many important social consequences from the stress on individualism in the family. On the one hand, its promise is for the richer, fuller development of personality. On the other hand, it weakens the unity of the family. The stresses of American life, including industrialization, urbanization, internal migration, and social class, press hard against the frail shell of the family, attenuated as it is by the thinning of larger kin groups and often limited to its own resources in times of crisis. Further, since the family is not primarily important in placing its members into positions in the larger community, its members feel the strain of loyalties divided between the family and the outside affiliations.

If some of the configurations of the American family have been correctly stated, they indicate a social philosophy in which the values of individualism are paramount, or, more specifically, those which support the development of individual personality in the context of family and community relationships. A primary stress is placed on the family as a social group rather than on the functions which it performs for society. The family exists for its members rather than the members for the family. In this respect the family is in relatively close adjustment to the total culture, in which the democratic realization of the potentialities of all its members is an ideal.

But the family is preeminently an association based on antagonistic cooperation, and in times of hardship the antagonisms may predominate. The straining of family members for individualistic goals may blunt their sense of obligation to each other and to the larger society. When achievement of the desired values for which they grope seems far off and difficult, individualism may decay into gross egotism and selfishness. The family based on the chimera of personal values seems then faced with a dolorous future.

The American family, however, is not without resources. Contributing to its strength is the immense popularity of marriage, and through marriage the possibility of parenthood, both of them regarded as major life-goals. Staying power is also given the family by the affection and compatibility which draws two people into marriage, the warmth of relationships between parents and children, and the individualization of all members of the family. The structure of the family is such as to permit the desired nurturing of stable and democratic personalities.

In view of the ethos of the culture the direction of evolutionary change in the family, and of desirable efforts at rational adjustments, is in the continued emphasis upon the social relationships within the family and upon the family as a social system through which fundamental life-purposes can be achieved.

NOTES

1. I have adhered to Clyde Kluckhohn's definition of configuration in his chapter, "Patterning as Exemplified in Navaho Culture," in Leslie Spier, A. Irving Hallowell, and Stanley S. Newman (eds.), *Language, Culture, and Personality*, Menasha, Wis.: Sapir Memorial Publication Fund, 1941, pp. 109–130, and exemplified in part in Clyde Kluckhohn and Dorothea Leighton, *The Navaho*, Cambridge: Harvard University Press, 1946, pp. 216–238. My indebtedness is considerable to Ruth Benedict, "Configurations of Culture in North America," *American Anthropologist*, 34 (1932), 1–27, and *Patterns of Culture*, Boston: Houghton Mifflin, 1934. For the study of value systems configuration has appeared to be a more useful concept than most, in that it refers to positive rules which organize behavior into patterns, while the mores are generally stated as unitary negative injunctions (see William Graham Sumner, *Folkways*, Boston: Ginn & Co., 1906, p. 30; and William Graham Sumner and Albert Galloway Keller, *The Science of Society*, New Haven: Yale University Press, 1927, I, 33–35). Bronislaw Malinowski has used the concept of "charter" in his definition of a social institution as a means of studying values, *A Scientific Theory of Culture and Other Essays*, Chapel Hill: University of North Carolina Press, 1944, pp. 52–53. Alfred McClung Lee has analyzed social values from an interesting and useful approach in "Levels of Culture as Levels of Social Generalization," *American Sociological Review*, 10 (1945), 485–495, and in "Social Determinants of Public Opinions," *International Journal of Opinion and Attitude Research*, 1 (1947), 12–29.

2. Erich Fromm, *Man for Himself*, New York: Rinehart, 1947, p. 241.

3. *Op. cit.*, pp. 5–6.

4. John Sirjamaki, "A Footnote to the Anthropological Approach to the Study of American Culture," *Social Forces*, 25 (1947), 253–263; Clyde Kluckhohn, "The American Culture:

Definition and Prophecy. Part II. The Way of Life," *Kenyon Review*, 3 (1941), 160–179; Clyde Kluckhohn and Florence R. Kluckhohn, "American Culture: Generalized Orientations and Class Patterns," in Lyman Bryson, Louis Finkelstein, and R. M. MacIver (eds.), *Conflicts of Power in Modern Culture*, New York: Harper & Bros., 1947, pp. 106–128; Andrew G. Truxal and Francis E. Merrill, *The Family in American Culture*, New York: Prentice-Hall, 1947, pp. 29–199; Robert S. Lynd, *Knowledge for What?* Princeton: Princeton University Press, 1939, pp. 63–99; Robert S. Lynd and Helen Merrell Lynd, *Middletown: A Study in American Culture*, New York: Harcourt, Brace, 1929, and *Middletown in Transition*, New York: Harcourt, Brace, 1937; and Oscar Waldemar Junek, "What Is the Total Pattern of Our Western Civilization? Some Preliminary Observations," *American Anthropologist*, 48 (1946), 397–406.

5. *Sixteenth Census of the United States, 1940, Population*, IV, Part I, 16.

6. *Fifteenth Census of the United States, 1930, Population*, Vol. II, chapter on marital condition.

7. Willard Waller, "The Rating and Dating Complex," *American Sociological Review*, 2 (1937), 727–734.

8. Weston LaBarre, "Social Cynosure and Social Structure," *Journal of Personality*, 14 (1946), 171.

9. Ernest R. Grover, *Marriage*, New York: Henry Holt, Inc., 1933, pp. 89–90.

10. Ralph Linton, *The Study of Man*, New York: D. Appleton-Century, 1936, p. 175.

11. LaBarre, *op. cit.*, p. 179.

12. Sumner and Keller, *op. cit.*, p. 464.

13. Margaret Park Redfield, "The American Family: Consensus and Freedom," *American Journal of Sociology*, 52 (1946), 177.

14. W. Lloyd Warner and Paul S. Lunt, *The Social Life of a Modern Community*, New Haven: Yale University Press, 1941, pp. 92–111; and Allison Davis, Burleigh B. Gardner, and Mary R. Gardner, *Deep South*, Chicago: University of Chicago Press, 1941, pp. 84–136.

15. Joseph K. Folsom, *The Family and Democratic Society*, New York: John Wiley & Sons, Inc., 1943, p. 184.

16. *Ibid.*, p. 105.

17. Abram Kardiner, *The Psychological Frontiers of Society*, New York: Columbia University Press, 1945, p. 361.

18. Edward A. Strecker, *Their Mothers' Sons*, Philadelphia: J. B. Lippincott Co., 1946, and Philip Wylie, *Generation of Vipers*, New York: Farrar & Rinehart, Inc., 1942.

19. Mass-Observation, London, "Portrait of an American?" *International Journal of Opinion and Attitude Research*, 1 (1947), p. 96.

20. In lecture at Yale University, May 2, 1947.

21. Alfred C. Kinsey, Wardell B. Pomeroy, and Clyde E. Martin, *Sexual Behavior in the Human Male*, Philadelphia: W. B. Saunders Co., 1948.

22. Lewis M. Terman, *Psychological Factors in Marital Happiness*, New York: McGraw-Hill Book Co., Inc., 1938, pp. 145–166.

23. Constantine Panunzio, *Major Social Institutions*, New York: Macmillan Co., 1939, p. 430.

24. Mirra Komarovsky, "Cultural Contradictions and Sex Roles," *American Journal of Sociology*, 52 (1946), 184–189.

25. Ferdinand Lundberg and M. F. Farnham, *Modern Woman: The Lost Sex*, New York: Harper and Bros., 1947.

43. KIN FAMILY NETWORK

MARVIN B. SUSSMAN *and* LEE BURCHINAL

In the preceding essay John Sirjamaki offers an overview of the model American middle-class family. Even such a portrait, Marvin B. Sussman and Lee Burchinal would argue, is somewhat distorted. They suggest that in family sociology there is an "academic cultural lag" between rather outdated family theory and empirical reality. Focusing on the role of the extended kin family system, Sussman and Burchinal seek to dispel certain persistent myths.

Marvin B. Sussman is Chairman of the Department of Sociology at Case Western Reserve University. He is coauthor of Walking Patient: A Study in Outpatient Care *(1967), editor of* Society and Rehabilitation *(1966), and coeditor of* Sourcebook in Marriage and the Family *(revised, 1968). Lee Burchinal is Director of the Division of Research Training in the Bureau of Research, United States Office of Education. His publications include* Career Choice of Rural Youth in a Changing Society: A Summary of Research.

Introduction

Most Americans reject the notion that receiving aid from their kin is a good thing. The proper ideological stance is that the individual and his family should fend for themselves. The family in this instance is nuclear in structure and consists of husband and wife and children. Further investigation would probably reveal that most of these rejectors are receiving or have received financial and other types of aid from their kin long after the time they were supposed to be on their own. After marriage many are involved within a network of mutual assistance with kin, especially with parents. Moreover, one would find that independence of the nuclear family of procreation is being maintained. Where independence is threatened, it is probably due to other causes. The rejection of the idea of receiving aid from kin and actually being helped by them is another case of discrepancy between belief and practice.

Discrepancies between belief and practice of "ideal" and "real" behavior are common in our society. In family sociology the reason is "academic cultural lag"; the lag between apparently antiquated family theory and empirical reality. The theory stresses the social isolation and social mobility of the nuclear family while findings from empirical studies reveal an existing and functioning extended kin family system closely integrated within a network of relationships and mutual assistance along bilateral kinship lines and encompassing several generations.[1]

The major purpose of this paper is to reduce the lag between family theory and research in so far as it concerns the functioning of the American kin family network and its matrix of help and service among kin members. The procedure is to review relevant theory and conclusions de-

Reprinted from the *Journal of Marriage and the Family,* **24,** 3 (August 1962), 231–240 by permission of the authors and the National Council on Family Relations. This article was originally entitled: "Kin Family Network: Unheralded Structure in Current Conceptualizations of Family Functioning."

rived from research on kin family networks completed by sociologists and anthropologists. Appropriate modifications of existing theory which posits the notion of the isolated nuclear family are then suggested.[2]

Nuclear Family Theory

Durkheim, Simmel, Toënnies and Mannheim have stressed that the family in urban society is a relatively isolated unit. Social differentiation in complex societies requires of its members a readiness to move, to move to where there are needs for workers and where there are opportunities for better jobs.

American social theorists such as Linton,[3] Wirth[4] and Parsons,[5] support this position. Parsons suggests that the isolated nuclear family system consisting of husband and wife and offspring living independent from their families of orientation is ideally suited to the demands of occupational and geographical mobility which are inherent in modern industrial society. Major obligations, interactions and nurturance behavior occur within the nuclear family. While bonds exist between the nuclear family and other consanguineous relatives and affinals of the kin group, these lack significance for the maintenance of the individual conjugal family.

Family sociologists generally accept the isolated nuclear theory as promulgated above. They report the changes in the structure and functions of the American family system which have occurred as the system has adapted to the demands of a developing industrial society. There is general agreement that the basic functions reserved for the family are procreation, status placement, biological and emotional maintenance and socialization.[6] However, these functions are generally analyzed in the context of the "isolated" nuclear family. The functions of intergenerational and bilateral kin family networks regarding the processes of biological and emotional

maintenance or socialization are given little attention by theorists or analysts. The conclusion reached is that demands associated with occupational and geographical mobility have brought about a family pattern in urban areas consisting of relatively isolated nuclear family units which operate without much support from the kinship system.

The textbooks are written by family sociologists. Few among them, either texts on the sociology of the family or those written for marriage and family preparation courses, give theoretical or empirical treatment to the maintenance of the family system by the mutual assistance activities of the kin group. Among the texts examined, only one considers in any detail financial arrangements among kin members.[7] One result of the review of basic family and preparation for marriage texts regarding current knowledge of the functioning of the kin network and its matrix of help and service is that the theory of the isolated nuclear family prevails.

Discussion of the Theoretical Argument

The lack of research until the 1950's and the almost complete omission of the topic, kin family network and its matrix of help and services, in family texts are closely related. If the generalized description of the American family system as atomistic and nuclear were valid, there would be very little exchange of financial help or services within the kin family network. Parental support of married children or exchange of services and other forms of help among kin members would be comparatively rare and hence, unimportant.[8] Research would be unnecessary and discussion of the subject, except in crisis situations, could be safely omitted from textbook discussions. However, accepting this theory as essentially valid without considerable empirical substantiation has contributed to errors in descriptions of kin family

Functional Analysis of Parental Aid to Married Children

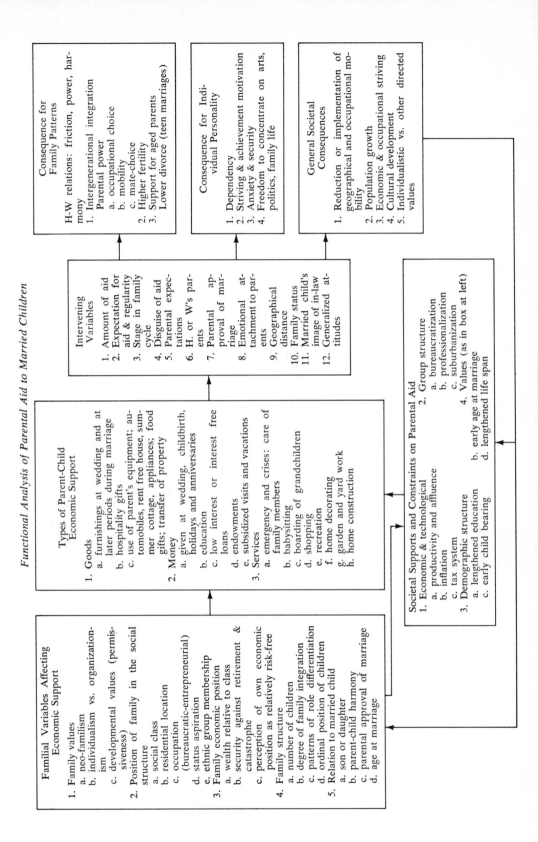

Consequence for Family Patterns

H-W relations: friction, power, harmony
1. Intergenerational integration
   Parental power
   a. occupational choice
   b. mobility
   c. mate-choice
2. Higher fertility
3. Support for aged parents
   Lower divorce (teen marriages)

Consequence for Individual Personality
1. Dependency
2. Striving & achievement motivation
3. Anxiety & security
4. Freedom to concentrate on arts, politics, family life

General Societal Consequences
1. Reduction or implementation of geographical and occupational mobility
2. Population growth
3. Economic & occupational striving
4. Cultural development
5. Individualistic vs. other directed values

Intervening Variables
1. Amount of aid
2. Expectation for aid & regularity
3. Stage in family cycle
4. Disguise of aid
5. Parental expectations
6. H. or W's parents
7. Parental approval of marriage
8. Emotional attachment to parents
9. Geographical distance
10. Family status
11. Married child's image of in-law
12. Generalized attitudes

Types of Parent-Child Economic Support
1. Goods
   a. furnishings at wedding and at later periods during marriage
   b. hospitality gifts
   c. use of parent's equipment; automobiles, rent free house, summer cottage, appliances; food gifts; transfer of property
2. Money
   a. given at wedding, childbirth, holidays and anniversaries
   b. education
   c. low interest or interest free loans
   d. endowments
   e. subsidized visits and vacations
3. Services
   a. emergency and crises: care of family members
   b. babysitting
   c. boarding of grandchildren
   d. shopping
   e. recreation
   f. home decorating
   g. garden and yard work
   h. home construction

Societal Supports and Constraints on Parental Aid
1. Economic & technological
   a. productivity and affluence
   b. inflation
   c. tax system
2. Group structure
   a. bureaucratization
   b. professionalization
   c. suburbanization
3. Demographic structure
   a. lengthened education
   b. early age at marriage
   c. early child bearing
4. Values (as in box at left)
   b. early age at marriage
   d. lengthened life span

Familial Variables Affecting Economic Support
1. Family values
   a. neo-familism
   b. individualism vs. organization-ism
   c. developmental values (permissiveness)
2. Position of family in the social structure
   a. social class
   b. residential location
   c. occupation (bureaucratic-entrepreneurial)
   d. status aspiration
   e. ethnic group membership
3. Family economic position
   a. wealth relative to class
   b. security against retirement & catastrophe
   c. perception of own economic position as relatively risk-free
4. Family structure
   a. number of children
   b. degree of family integration
   c. patterns of role differentiation
   d. ordinal position of children
5. Relation to married child
   a. son or daughter
   b. parent-child harmony
   c. parental approval of marriage
   d. age at marriage

networks and aid patterns among families. A new empiricism emerging in the late 1940's questioned the persistence of the isolated nuclear family notion and presented evidence to support the viability of kin family network in industrial society.

The ideal description of the isolated nuclear character of the American family system cannot be applied equally to all segments of American society. Regional, racial, ethnic, and rural and urban, as well as socio-economic status differences in modified extended relations and family continuity patterns are known to exist. Family continuity and inheritance patterns of families in several social strata have been described.[9] Among upper-class families direct, substantial and continuous financial support flows from the parents, uncles, aunts, and grandparents to the children both before and after marriage. Only by receiving substantial kin support can the young high-status groom and his bride begin and sustain their family life at the financial and social level which is shared by their parents, other relatives and their friends. This support frequently includes obtaining a position for the husband in his or his in-law family's economic enterprise.

Members of lower-class kin groups generally have few financial resources with which to assist married children. Among certain European ethnic groups some effort is made to assist the young couple at marriage; the notion of a dowry still persists. Generally, however, there is little knowledge, tradition or tangible forms of assistance transmitted to children which directly aids children in establishing or enhancing their socio-economic status.[10] Kin support in this class most frequently takes the form of providing services and sharing what financial resources are available at the time of crises or of exchanging nonmonetary forms of aid. Marginal financial resources and the impact of unemployment hits all kin members alike.[11]

The description of the isolated, nuclear American family system, if valid, is most suited to the white, urban, middle-class segment of American society.[12] Presumably, the leisure time of the members of these families is absorbed in the activities of secondary, special interest social groups. Since urban, lower-class family members participate less than middle-class family members in voluntary organizations, it is believed that social activities of adult lower-class family members are restricted to informal visiting patterns. Visiting with relatives would be a significant proportion of all of their social relations. However, prevailing sociological theory suggests that the disparities between an extended kin family system and the requirements of a mobile labor force and intergenerational family discontinuities generated by social mobility should be reflected in the lack of continuity among lower-class families as well as among middle-class families.

The degree to which urban lower- or middle-class families function as relatively isolated from their extended kin family systems is critical for all subsequent discussions of the question of kinship network and its matrix of help and service. Unless there is a reasonable frequent occurrence of primary group interaction among kin members, very likely there will be an insignificant help pattern.

The emphasis on the atomistic character of urban families has contributed to incorrect assumptions concerning interaction within the kinship matrix. It has led family sociologists to incorrectly assume that assistance among kin members was comparatively rarely sought or offered. A reconsideration of these assumptions is necessary. The bases of reconsideration are logical constructs and empirical realities set forth in the following data.

Family Networks and Mutual Aid: Conceptualization and Research

A theory is here considered to be composed of logically interrelated propositions which explain phenomena. Concepts are elements of a theory, defining what is to be observed. Concepts by themselves cannot be construed as a theory. They require integration into a logical scheme to become a theory.

The existence of a modified extended family with its intricate network of mutual aid in lieu of the isolated nuclear family notion is probably more of a conceptualization than a theory. However, it approaches the state of being a theory since it is not an isolated concept but is integrated with other propositions concerned with the maintenance over time of the family and other social systems of the society.

Family networks and their patterns of mutual aid are organized into a structure identified as a "modified extended family" adopted to contemporary urban and industrial society.[13] This structure is composed of nuclear families bound together by affectional ties and by choice. Geographical propinquity, involvement of the family in the occupational placement and advancement of its members, direct intervention into the process of achieving social status by members of nuclear family units, and a rigid hierarchical authority structure are unrequired and largely absent. The modified extended family functions indirectly rather than directly to facilitate the achievement and mobility drives of component families and individual members. Its tasks complement those of other social systems. By achieving integration with other social systems, concerned with the general goals of maintenance and accomplishment of these systems, the extended family network cannot be considered as an isolated or idiosyncratic concept. Its elements require organization as logically interrelated propositions and whereupon it should emerge as a theory replacing the prevalent one of the isolated nuclear family.

Our concepts die hard and one way to speed their demise is to examine the evidence supporting the new ones. Evidence and measurement are difficult terms to define. When do you have evidence and when have you achieved a measurement? The reader will have to judge. The approach here is to examine the writings and research emerging from several disciplines. In some cases the work is focused on testing hypotheses or describing relationships relevant to the new conceptualization. In others, the discussions and findings emerge incidentally to the major purpose of the study. There are cases of serendipity. They occur more frequently than one would expect and add to the uncertainty of the notion of the isolated nuclear family.

One assumption of the isolated nuclear family conceptualization is that the small nuclear family came into existence in Western Europe and the United States as a consequence of the urban-industrial revolution. Furthermore its small size is ideally suited for meeting requirements of an industrial society for a mobile workforce. The effect of the urban-industrial revolution is to produce a small sized family unit to replace the large rural one. This assumption can be challenged. A study of different societies reveals that industrialization and urbanization can occur with or without the small nuclear family.[14]

If household size reflects in any way the structure and characteristics of the joint extended family in India, then little changes have occurred in this system during the period of industrialization in India from 1911 to 1951.[15]

The uprooting of the rural family, the weakening of family ties, and the reshaping of the rural family form into a nuclear type as a consequence of the industrial revolution are disclaimed for one Swiss town in a recent investigation. On the contrary many fringe rural families were stabilized and further strengthened in their kin ties from earning supplementary income in nearby factories. Able-bodied members obtained work nearby and no longer had to leave the family unit in search of work. Families which moved closer to their place of employment were accommodated in row houses; these units facilitated the living together of large family groups.[16] These findings question the impact of industrialization upon the structure and functioning of the pre-industrial family.

It is difficult to determine if the conditions of living during the transition from a rural to an industrial society ended the dominance of the classical extended family and replaced it with a modified kin form, or if it was replaced by the nuclear one. The question is whether the modified extended family has existed since industrialization occurred; is it a recent phenomenon or an emergent urban familism departure from the traditional nuclear form; or is it non-existent? The evidence to support either of these positions is inconclusive. It remains however that the family network described variously as "an emergent urban familism" or "modified extended family" exists and functions in the modern community.

The family network and its functions of mutual aid have implications for the functioning of other social systems. With the growth of large metropolitan areas and concomitant occupational specialization, there is less need for the individual to leave the village, town, city or suburb of the urban complex in order to find work according to his training. Large urban areas supply all kinds of specialized educational and occupational training. The individual can remain in the midst of his kin group, work at his speciality and be the recipient of the advantages or disadvantages preferred by the kin family network. If individuals are intricately involved within a kin family network, will they be influenced by kin leaders and be less amenable to influence by outsiders; will they seek basic gratifications in kin relationships in lieu of the work place or the neighborhood; will they modify drastically current patterns of spending leisure time thus affecting current leisure forms and social systems?[17]

Empirical evidence from studies by investigations in a variety of disciplines substantiate the notion that the extended kin family carries on multitudinous activities that have implications for the functioning of other social systems of the society. The major activities linking the network are mutual aid and social activities among kin related families. Significant data have been accumulated on the mutual aid network between parents and their married child's family in a number of separate and independent investigations.[18,19,20] The conclusions are:

1. Help patterns take many forms, including the exchange of services, gifts, advice and financial assistance. Financial aid patterns may be direct as in the case of the young married couples Burchinal interviewed; or indirect and subtle, such as the wide range of help patterns observed by Sussman, Sharp and Axelrod.

2. Such help patterns are probably more widespread in the middle- and working-class families and are more integral a feature of family relationships than has been appreciated by students of family behavior. Very few families included in available studies reported neither giving nor receiving aid from relatives. However, these relationships until recently have not been the subject of extensive research.

3. The exchange of aid among families flows in several directions, from parents to children and vice versa, among siblings, and less frequently, from more distant relatives. However, financial assistance generally appears to flow from parents to children.

4. While there may be a difference in the absolute amount of financial aid received by families of middle- and working-class status, there are insignificant differences in the proportion of families in these two strata who report receiving, giving or exchanging economic assistance in some form.

5. Financial aid is received most commonly during the early years of married life. Parents are probably more likely to support financially "approved" than "dis-

Table 1.   *Direction of Service Network of Respondent's Family and Related Kin by Major Forms of Help*

Major Forms of Help and Service	Direction of Service Network				
	*Between Respondent's Family and Related Kin Per Cent**	*From Respondents to Parents Per Cent**	*From Respondents to Siblings Per Cent**	*From Parents to Respondents Per Cent**	*From Siblings to Respondents Per Cent**
Any Form of Help	93.3	56.3	47.6	79.6	44.8
Help During Illness	76.0	47.0	42.0	46.4	39.0
Financial Aid	53.0	14.6	10.3	46.8	6.4
Care of Children	46.8	4.0	29.5	20.5	10.8
Advice (Personal and Business)	31.0	2.0	3.0	26.5	4.5
Valuable Gifts	22.0	3.4	2.3	17.6	3.4

* *Totals do not add up to 100 per cent because many families received more than one form of help of service.*
* *Marvin B. Sussman, "The Isolated Nuclear Family: Fact or Fiction," Social Problems 6 (Spring, 1959), 338.*

approved" ones, such as elopements, interfaith and interracial marriages. Support can be disguised in the form of substantial sums of money or valuable gifts given at the time of marriage, at the time of the birth of children, and continuing gifts at Christmas, anniversaries or birthdays. High rates of parental support are probably associated with marriages of children while they are still in a dependency status; those among high school or college students are examples.

6. Research data are inadequate for assessing the effects of parental aid on family continuity and the marital relations of the couple receiving aid. Few studies report associations between the form and amount of aid given with the parents' motivations for providing aid. Additional studies on these points are necessary before the implications of aid to married children can be better known.[21]

Social activities are principal functions of the kin family network. The major forms are interfamily visitation, participation together in recreational activities, and ceremonial behavior significant to family unity. Major research findings are:

1. Disintegration of the extended family in urban areas because of lack of contact is unsupported and often the contrary situation is found. The difficulty in developing satisfactory primary relationships outside of the family in urban areas makes the extended family *more important* to the individual.[22]

2. Extended family get-togethers and joint recreational activities with kin dominate the leisure time pursuits of urban working-class members.[23]

3. Kinship visiting is a primary activity of urban dwelling and outranks visitation patterns found for friends, neighbors, or co-workers.[24,25,26,27,28]

4. Among urban middle classes there is an almost universal desire to have interaction with extended kin, but distance among independent nuclear related units is a limiting factor.[29]

5. The family network extends between generational ties of conjugal units. Some structures are identified as sibling bonds,[30] "occasional kin groups," [31] family circles and cousin clubs.[32] These structures perform important recreational, ceremonial, mutual aid, and often economic functions.

Services performed regularly throughout the year or on occasions are additional functions of the family network. The findings from empirical studies are:

1. Shopping, escorting, care of children, advice giving and counselling, cooperating with social agencies on counselling and welfare problems of family members are types of day-to-day activities performed by members of the kin network.[33,34]

2. Services to old persons such as physical care, providing shelter, escorting, shopping, performing household tasks, sharing of leisure time, etc. are expected and practiced roles of children and other kin members. These acts of filial and kin responsibility are performed voluntarily without law or compulsion.[35,36,37,38,39,40,41,42]

3. Families or individual members on the move are serviced by units of the family network. Services range from supplying motel-type accommodations for vacationing kin passing through town, to scouting for homes and jobs for kin, and in providing supportive functions during the period of in-migration and transition from rural to the urban pattern of living.[43,44,45,46,47]

4. Services on occasions would include those performed at weddings or during periods of crisis, death, accident, disaster, and personal trouble of family members. A sense of moral obligation to give service or acknowledgement of one's kin appropriate to the occasion is found among kin members. The turning to kin when in trouble before using other agencies established for such purposes is the mode rather than the exception.[48,49,50,51]

5. General supportive behavior from members of the kin family network facilitates achievement and maintenance of family and community status.[52] Supportive behavior of kin appears to be instrumental in affecting fertility rates among component family members.[53]

A convergence of many of these findings occurs in the work of Eugene Litwak. In an extensive study of a middle-class population Litwak tests several hypotheses on the functional properties of the isolated nuclear family for an industrial society: (a) occupational mobility is antithetical to

extended family relations; (b) extended family relations are impossible because of geographical mobility. His findings summarized briefly are: 1) The extended kin family as a structure exists in modern urban society at least among middle-class families; 2) Extended family relations are possible in urban industrial society; 3) Geographical propinquity is an unnecessary condition for these relationships; 4) Occupational mobility is unhindered by the activities of the extended family, such activities as advice, financial assistance, temporary housing, and the like provide aid during such movement; and 5) The classical extended family of rural society or its ethnic counterpart are unsuited for modern society, the isolated nuclear family is not the most functional type, the most functional being a modified extended kin family.[54]

Conclusions

There exists an American kin family system with complicated matrices of aid and service activities which link together the component units into a functioning network. The network identified by Litwak as extended family relations is composed of nuclear units related by blood and affinal ties. Relations extend along generational lines and bilaterally where structures take the form of sibling bonds and ambilineages, i.e., the family circle or cousin club.

As a consequence of limited historical work and particularistic developments in theory and research in sociology there is uncertainty concerning the impact of industrialization upon the structure and function of the pre-industrial family. Was the extended classical type found in rural society replaced by a nuclear one, or did it evolve into the modified kin form described in this paper? It is suggested that the notion of the isolated nuclear family stems from theories and research on immigrant groups coming into the city to work during the period of urbanization in Western society.[55] Anomie in family behavior resulted from individual and institutional failure to make appropriate adjustments required by this migration. The coldness and indifference of the workplace and the city as a steel and concrete bastion contributed to a feeling of aloneness and isolation. The basic concern of the inmigrant was survival in an unknown manmade jungle. Survival was related to dependence upon small family units. These could make quicker and more complete adjustments to the new ways of urban life. The ethos of a competitive and expanding industrial society supported the flexibility of movement now possible by an atomistic unit. Every man is for himself, every man should be unencumbered by ties that will hinder his economic or social progress, and every man should seize opportunities to better himself. One assumption of this position is that early urban man had little time for concern or activity with kinsmen. A more logical assumption is that isolation, a depressive workplace, and uncertainty produced greater reliance upon kin. Once new immigrants became established in the city they served as informants, innkeepers, and providers for later kin arrivals.[56] Once these followers arrived the kin family network then functioned most effectively to protect and acculturate their members into urban ways.

Major activities of this network are that members give to each other financial aid and goods of value, and a wide range of services at specific times and under certain conditions. The aid and service provided within the network supplement rather than displace the basic activities of nuclear family units. Kinship behavior assists more than negates the achievement of status and occupational advance of component families and their members.

The main flow of financial aid is along generational lines, from parents to young married children and from middle-aged parents to aged parents. Such aid is not restricted to emergencies, but may be given at various occasions such as support for education, to start a family, at time of marriage, to begin a career, and the like.

The network is used among middle-class families as a principal source of aid and service when member families or individuals are in personal difficulty, in times of disaster and crisis, and on ceremonial occasions. There are some indications that established working-class families are following the same pattern. Some situations cannot be handled by the nuclear unit alone, e.g., destruction of the family home by a tornado; while other situations involve more than one nuclear family or individual member, e.g., the death of an aging parent. In such situations there are mutual expectations of going to the aid of kin. Aid is sought from the most immediate kin chiefly along sibling or generational lines. Then it is followed by help from more distant kin.

In many instances everyday or weekly activities link together the members of the kin family network. Joint participation in leisure time activities is possible because of reduction of the work week. Visiting among kin is facilitated by high speed highways and other conveyances of a modern transportation system. Constant communication among kin members is possible by the widespread adoption on all class levels of the telephone as a household necessity.[57,58]

The feasibility of the kin network in modern society is due to the existence of modern communication and transportation systems which facilitate interaction among members; a bureaucratic industrial structure suited to modern society which removes the responsibility for job placement from the network will still permit the network of concentrate on activities intended to aid the social and economic achievement of network members; [59,60] and expansion of metropolitan areas in which individuals can obtain educational, occupational and status objectives without leaving their kin area. Kin members can live some distance from each other within the metropolitan area and still have relationships within the network. Nuclear units function autonomously. Decisions on what and when to act are responsibilities of the nuclear family. Influence may be exerted by the kin group upon the nuclear units so that the latter may make the "right" decision. However the kin group seldom directs the decision or action of the nuclear family in a given situation. Immunity from such control is guaranteed by legal and cultural norms which reaffirm the right and accountability of the nuclear family in such situations. The role of the family kin network is supportive rather than coercive in its relationship with the nuclear family.

Understanding of the family as a functioning social system interrelated with other social systems in society is possible *only by rejection of the isolated nuclear family concept.* Accepting the isolated nuclear family as the most functional type today has led to erroneous conclusions concerning the goals and functions of these other social systems. In social service fields, for instance, institutions establish goals and programs concerned with caring for individuals and families who are unable to fend for themselves. Institutions assume that the family unit is a small and isolated unit easily injured and upset by the many problems it faces in contemporary society. The therapeutic approach is to treat the individual or at best the members of the nuclear family. The kin network is overlooked. Often nuclear families respond hesitantly to the overtures of these institutions; the nuclear unit prefers to find solutions to its problems within the family kin network. When such solutions are impossible then the specialized service institution may be used. How the operations of the kin family network affect the functioning of other social systems is yet to be established. Their positive or negative effects are unknown. Some beginning research on this problem is now underway.[61]

NOTES

1. The authors adopt Eugene Litwak's interpretation of the modified extended family. It is one that "does not require geographical propinquity, occupational nepotism, or integration, and there are no strict authority relations, but equalitarian ones." See "Geographical Mobility and Extended Family Cohesion," *American Sociological Review,* 25 (June, 1960), 385. The components of the system are neolocal nuclear families in a bilateral or generational relationship. This system is referred to as the "Kin Family Network."

2. The implications of parental support to the married child's family for the functioning of the American family system is discussed in another paper. The major question is whether parental aid affects the independence of the married child's family. "Parental Aid to Married Children: Implications for Family Functioning" in *Marriage and Family Living* (November, 1962).

3. Ralph Linton, "The Natural History of the Family," in Ruth N. Anshen, *The Family: Its Function and Destiny,* New York: Harpers, 1959, pp. 45–46.

4. Louis Wirth, "Urbanism As a Way of Life," *American Journal of Sociology,* 44 (July, 1938), 1–24.

5. All by the same author, see Talcott Parsons, "The Kinship System of the Contemporary United States," *American Anthropologist,* 45 (January–March, 1943), 22–38; "Revised Analytical Approach to the Theory of Social Stratification," in R. Bendix and S. M. Lipset (eds.), *Class, Status and Power,* Glencoe, Ill.: Free Press, 1953, p. 166 ff.; "The Social Structures of the Family," in Ruth Anshen, *op. cit.,* p. 263 ff.; Parsons and Robert F. Bales, *Family, Socialization and Process,* Glencoe, Ill.: Free Press, 1955, pp. 3–33.

6. Compare Robert F. Winch, *The Modern Family,* New York: Holt, 1952, and William J. Goode, "The Sociology of the Family," in Robert K. Merton, Leonard Broom and Leonard S. Cottrell, Jr. (eds.), *Sociology Today,* New York: Basic Books, 1959, pp. 178–196.

7. Evelyn M. Duvall, *Family Development,* Chicago: Lippincott, 1957, pp. 129–133, 206–210.

8. See Reuben Hill, *Families Under Stress,* New York: Harpers, 1949.

9. W. Lloyd Warner and Paul S. Lunt, *The Social Life of a Modern Community,* New Haven, Connecticut: Yale University Press, 1941. See also Cavan, *The American Family,* New York: T. Y. Crowell, pp. 119–187, for a review of other studies of social status differentials in family behavior.

10. R. E. L. Faris, "Interactions of Generations and Family Stability," *American Sociological Review,* 12 (April, 1947), 159–164.

11. Ruth S. Cavan, "Unemployment-Crisis of the Common Man," *Marriage and Family Living,* 21 (May, 1959), 139–146.

12. Someone has facetiously suggested the samples of white, urban, middle-class Protestant respondents be labeled as WUMP samples. If family sociologists continue to draw samples principally from this segment of our social structure or wish to limit generalizations to this segment, there would be more than a facetious basis for arguing for the merit of the convenient shorthand expression represented by WUMP.

13. Eugene Litwak, *op. cit.,* p. 355. See also by the same author, "Occupational Mobility and Extended Family Cohension," *American Sociological Review,* 25 (February, 1960), 10.

14. Sidney M. Greenfield, "Industrialization and the Family in Sociological Theory," *American Journal of Sociology,* 67 (November, 1961), 312–322.

15. Henry Orenstein, "The Recent History of the Extended Family in India," *Social Problems,* 8 (Spring, 1961), 341–350.

16. Rudolph Braun, *Industrialisierung Volksleben,* Erbenback-Zierrich: Reutsch, 1960.

17. A. O. Haller raises interesting questions on the significance of an emerging urban familism. See "The Urban Family," *American Journal of Sociology,* 66 (May, 1961), 621–622.

18. Marvin B. Sussman, "The Help Pattern in the Middle-Class Family," *American Sociological Review,* 18 (February, 1953), 22–28. For related analyses by the same author, see "Parental Participation in Mate Selection and Its Effect Upon Family Continuity," *Social Forces,* 32 (October, 1953), 76–81; "Family Continuity: Selective Factors Which Affect Relationships Between Families at Generational Levels," *Marriage and Family Living,* 16 (May, 1954), 112–120; "Activity Patterns of Post Parental Couples and Their Relationship to Family Continuity," *Marriage and Family Living,* 27 (November, 1955), 338–341; "The Isolated Nuclear Family: Fact or Fiction," *Social Problems,* 6 (Spring, 1959), 333–340; "Intergenerational Family Relationships and Social Role Changes in Middle Age," *Journal of Gerontology,* 15 (January, 1960), 71–75.

19. Harry Sharp and Morris Axelrod, "Mutual Aid Among Relatives in an Urban Population," in Ronald Freedman and associates (eds.), *Principles of Sociology,* New York: Holt, 1956, pp. 433–439.

20. Lee G. Burchinal, "Comparisons of Factors Related to Adjustment in Pregnancy-Provoked and Non-Pregnancy-Provoked Youthful Marriages," *Midwest Sociologist,* 21 (July, 1959), 92–96; also by the same author, "How Successful Are School-Age Marriages?" *Iowa Farm Science,* 13 (March, 1959), 7–10.

21. Further analyses on the implications of parental aid to married children are found in a paper, "Parental Aid to Married Children: Implications for Family Functioning," in *Marriage and Family Living,* November, 1962.

22. William H. Key, "Rural-Urban Differences and the Family," *Sociological Quarterly,* 2 (January, 1961), 49–56.

23. F. Dotson, "Patterns of Voluntary Association Among Urban Working Class Families," *American Sociological Review,* 16 (October, 1951), 689–693.

24. Morris Axelrod, "Urban Structure and Social Participation," *American Sociological Review,* 21 (February, 1956), 13–18.

25. Scott Greer, "Urbanism Reconsidered," *American Sociological Review,* 21 (February, 1956), 22–25.

26. Wendell Bell and M. D. Boat, "Urban Neighborhoods and Informal Social Relations," *American Journal of Sociology,* 43 (January, 1957), 381–398.

27. Marvin B. Sussman and R. Clyde White, *Hough: A Study of Social Life and Change,* Cleveland: Western Reserve University Press, 1959.

28. Paul J. Reiss, "The Extended Kinship System of the Urban Middle Class," unpublished Ph.D. dissertation, Harvard University, 1959.

29. E. Franklin Frazier, "The Impact of Urban Civilization Upon Negro Family Life," in P. K. Hatt and H. S. Reiss, Jr. (eds.), *Cities and Society,* Glencoe, Ill.: Free Press, 1957, rev. ed., pp. 495–496.

30. Elaine Cumming and David M. Schneider, "Sibling Solidarity: A Property of American Kinship," *American Anthropologist,* 63 (June, 1961), 498–507.

31. Millicent Ayoub, "American Child and his Relatives: Kindred in Southwest Ohio," project supported by the Public Health Service, 1961, Dr. Ayoub in continuing her studies under the subtitle, "The Nature of Sibling Bond." She examines the solidarity or lack of it between siblings in four focal subsystems and at different stages of the life cycle.

32. William E. Mitchell, "Descent Groups Among New York City Jews," *The Jewish Journal of Sociology,* 3 (1961), 121–128; "Lineality and Laterability in Urban Jewish Ambilineages," read at the 60th Annual Meeting of the American Anthropological Association in Philadelphia, Pa., November 16, 1961; and William E. Mitchell and Hope J. Leichter, "Urban Ambilineages and Social Mobility," unpublished paper based on research from the project, "Studies in Family Interaction," sponsored jointly by the Jewish Family Service of New York City and the Russell Sage Foundation.

33. Sussman, *op. cit.,* "The Help Pattern in the Middle Class Family."

34. Hope J. Leichter, "Kinship and Casework," paper read at the meetings of the Groves Conference, Chapel Hill, North Carolina, 1959; "Life Cycle Changes and Temporal Sequence in a Bilateral Kinship System," read at the annual meetings of the American Anthropological Association, 1958; Washington, D.C. "Normative Intervention in an Urban Bilateral Kinship System," paper read at the meetings of the American Anthropological Association, 1959.

35. John Kosa, Leo D. Rachiele, and Cyril O. Schommer, S. J., "Sharing the Home with Relatives," *Marriage and Family Living,* 22 (May, 1960), 129–131.

36. Alvin L. Schorr, *Filial Responsibility in a Modern American Family,* Washington, D.C.; Social Security Administration, U. S. Department of Health, Education and Welfare, 1960, pp. 11–18.

37. Peter Townsend, *The Family Life of Older People: An Inquiry in East London,* London: Routledge and Kegan Paul, 1957.

38. Michael Young and Peter Willmott, *Kinship and Family in East London,* Glencoe, Ill.: Free Press, 1957.

39. Elizabeth Bott, *Family and Social Network,* London: Tavistock Publications, Ltd., 1957.

40. See *Adjustment in Retirement,* by Gordon F. Streib and Wayne E. Thompson, *Journal of Social Issues,* 14 (1958). Streib and Thompson have done the most creative thinking and analysis of data on these points.

41. Ethel Shanas, "Older People and Their Families," paper given at the meetings of the American Sociological Association, September, 1961. A more complete report is in *Family Relationships of Older People,* Health Information Foundation, 1961.

42. The best treatment of uses of leisure during the later years of life is found in Robert W. Kleemeier (ed.), *Aging and Leisure,* New York: Oxford University Press, 1961. See particularly the chapters by Wilensky, Streib and Thompson.

43. M. B. Sussman and R. C. White, *op. cit., Hough: A Study of Social Life and Change.*

44. C. Wright Mills, Clarence Senior, and Rose K. Goldsen, *Puerto Rican Journey,* New York: Harper Bros., 1950, pp. 51–55.

45. James S. Brown, Harry K. Schwarzweller, and Joseph J. Mangalam, "Kentucky Mountain Migration and the Stem Family: An American Variation on a Theme by LePlay," paper given at the meetings of the American Sociological Association, September 1, 1961.

46. Peter H. Rossi, *Why Families Move,* Glencoe, Ill.: Free Press, 1955, pp. 37–38.

47. Earl L. Koos, *Families in Trouble,* New York: Columbia University Press, 1946.

48. Sussman, *op. cit.*, "Family Continuity: Selective Factors Which Affect Relationships Between Families at Generational Levels."

49. Seymour S. Bellin, *Family and Kinship in Later Years*, N.Y. State Dept. of Mental Hygiene, Mental Health Research Unit Publication, 1960.

50. Sharp and Axelrod, *op. cit.*, "Mutual Aid Among Relatives."

51. Enrico L. Wuarantelli, "A Note on the Protective Function of the Family in Disasters," *Marriage and Family Living*, 22 (August, 1960), 263–264.

52. Bernard Barber, "Family Status, Local-Community Status, and Social Stratification: Three Types of Social Ranking," *Pacific Sociological Review*, 4, 1 (Spring, 1961), 3–10. In this paper Barber challenges the current conceptualization of social class for designating an individual's position and power within a community. He differentiates social class position, family status and local-community statuses into three types of social ranking. Each one has its own structure and functions; each allocates position, power and prestige; and each has its own range of variation. The family kin network and support received from it determines family status. President Kennedy's family and its extended family relations illustrates the point of this thesis.

53. David Goldberg, "Some Recent Developments in Fertility Research," Reprint No. 7, *Demographic and Economic Change in Developed Countries*, Princeton University Press, 1960. Recent fertility research has focused upon the relationship of family organization to differential fertility since variations in family planning and family size cannot be explained by differences in socio-economic status. One variable of family organization is the family kin network. Goldberg observes, "—and incidentally one which may ultimately prove fruitful in cross-cultural studies, is a consideration of the relative benevolence of the environment in defraying the economic and social costs of having children. Here it is hypothesized that the greater the amount of help available from one's community or kinship system the weaker the desire to prevent or postpone pregnancy." *Ibid.*, p. 9.

54. Eugene Litwak, "The Use of Extended Family Groups in the Achievement of Social Goals: Some Policy Implications," *Social Problems*, 7 (Winter, 1959–60), 177–187; *op. cit.*, "Occupational Mobility and Extended Family Cohesion"; *op. cit.*, "Geographical Mobility and Family Cohesion."

55. Key, *op. cit.*, "Rural-Urban Differences and the Family," p. 56; Sussman, *op. cit.*, "The Isolated Nuclear Family: Fact or Fiction," p. 340.

56. Key discusses this point in his paper "Rural-Urban Differences and the Family," *op. cit.* From studies on immigration to the United States and geographical movement of families within the country one concludes that family members perform invasion of scout roles and then attract other kin into their communities and neighborhoods.

57. Several empirical studies are currently in progress on the extensity of kin family network functions in metropolitan areas. Robert W. Habenstein and Alan D. Coult are conducting one in Kansas City on "The Functions of Extended Kinship in an Urban Milieu." "The purpose of this research is to discover, describe, and analyse the social correlates and functions of extended kinship in representative samples of blue collar and white collar socio-economic classes in Kansas City," p. 1, Research Proposal, July 1, 1961.

58. A second study is being undertaken by Marvin B. Sussman and Sherwood B. Slater in Cleveland, Ohio. "The objectives of the Cleveland Study are to investigate the working and middle-class families; to compare the kinship networks of 'illness' and 'non-illness' families; to estimate the normative form of kinship networks for social class and family life cycle stages to variations in normative patterns," p. 1, Research Plan, September 27, 1961.

59. One investigation being conducted by John Bennett is concerned with the variations in business operations due to kinship behavior. Business organization practice according to current theory operates with bureaucratic, universalistic, and impartial norms. Bennett is investigating the compatibility and conflict between these bureaucratic norms and those which characterize the kinship network, particularistic behavior for idiosyncratic situations. "Kinship in American Business Organization," meetings of the Central States Anthropological Society, May, 1961.

60. William Mitchell, "Lineality and Laterality in Urban Jewish Ambilineages," *op. cit.*, finds some integration of kinship and business activity. There is a tendency to "Throw business to kin members."

61. Hope J. Leichter, *op. cit.*, see footnote 34.

The Economic System

44. THE BREAKUP OF FAMILY CAPITALISM

DANIEL BELL

Dating back to Roman times, the fusion in European societies of the institutions of property and of family was instrumental in circumscribing a class system in which the varied levels were marked by distinctive styles of life and by recognition of one's relative place in the social and political hierarchy. Those who ranked high often gained their prominent and powerful positions through "family capitalism" and maintained them by means of "dynastic" marriages and through inheritance laws designed to preserve the inalienable title to property.

In the United States, despite the lack of a traditional landed gentry and the fact that land was a far more marketable commodity than it was in Europe, and despite the high value placed upon individual mobility and achievement, certain similarities were in evidence from the early days of settlement until the turn of this century. Family enterprises did exist and flourish here as in Europe and great fortunes made by merchants in the seventeenth and eighteenth centuries and by enterprising businessmen in the nineteenth, depended, in large measure, upon family solidarity. Moreover, although it never established clear hegemony over large segments of society, there was a traditional symbiosis between business acumen, social prestige, and political power for many of America's "leading" families.

Reprinted from *The End of Ideology* (New York: The Free Press, 1960), pp. 160–178, by permission of the author.

American-style family capitalism began to break up during the turbulent years between 1890 and 1910 to be replaced by "finance capitalism" and corporate owner-ship. The background and changes in the American economic system are presented and analyzed in Daniel Bell's article.

Daniel Bell is Professor of Social Relations at Harvard University. He is the author of Work and Its Discontents (*1956*), The End of Ideology (*1960*), The Reforming of General Education: The Columbia College Experience in its National Setting (*1966*), *and* Toward the Year 2000: Work in Progress (*1968*), *and is the editor of* The Radical Right (*1963*).

The story of the rise and fall of social classes in Western society, as Pirenne and Schumpeter have pointed out, is that of the rise and fall of families. Without un-derstanding that fact, as many American sociologists, accustomed to viewing class position in individualistic terms, have failed to do, one cannot understand the peculiar cohesiveness of dominant eco-nomic classes in the past, or the sources of the breakup of power in contemporary society today.

Capitalism is not only, as Marx saw it, an economic system with employer-worker relations and classes formed on strictly economic lines, but a social system wherein power has been transmitted through the family, and where the satis-factions of ownership lay, in part, in the family name, by which the business enter-prise was known. (In Marcel Pagnol's *Fanny* the ecstatic hope of Panisse is to add the words "and Son" over the door of his shop, a practice long maintained by commercial enterprises.)

The social organization of the family rested on two institutions: property and the "dynastic" marriage. Property, sanc-tioned by law and reinforced by the coer-cive power of the state, meant power; the "dynastic" marriage was a means of con-serving and, through inheritance laws, of transmitting property, and so preserving, as the case might be, the continuity of the family enterprise. (A classic instance of this process, perhaps, was the assumption of Gustav von Bohlen of the family name of Krupp, when the line of the famous

German steel company lacked male heirs.)

The relationship of property to family structure is one of the oldest institutions in Western society, reaching far back to the Roman law of land. Land, historically, was the oldest and most basic form of property and power. In Roman law, prop-erty did not inhere in a particular person, in the head of the family; property in-hered in the heir. And when the heir be-came head of the family, the property no longer belonged to him, but to his heirs. This "fiction," as Sir Henry Maine called it, regarding the ownership of property, was necessary to preserve its "inaliena-bility," i.e., the fact that it could not be freely disposed of at will. The effort to freely dispose of land—to make it aliena-ble—to rid it of all entails, strict settle-ments, primogenitures, and the like, was part of the effort to make property a free commodity. In English law, it was not until 1925, in fact, that all impediments to the alienability of property were com-pletely removed.

In philosophical terms, the *linked* insti-tutions of property and family were al-ways seen as a necessary precondition to established society. When Godwin and Condorcet, at the turn of the nineteenth century, insisted that progress and free-dom lay only in striking the bonds of marriage and sharing all property, they were answered for all bourgeois society by Parson Malthus, who insisted that without the restraints of family and property the "natural" instincts to lust and licentiousness would assert themselves so freely that population would break all bounds, outstrip the growth of resources, and result in privation and misery for the multitude rather than happiness. The Essay on Population, in fact, was not an exercise in demography, but a sermon in morals.

But more than economic or moral considerations were involved in the linkage of the family and property systems. Through the fusion of the two institutions, a class system was maintained: people met at the same social levels, were educated in common schools appropriate to their wealth, shared the same manners and morals, read the same books and held similar prejudices, mingled in the same milieus—in short, created and shared a distinctive style of life.

The singular fact is that in the last seventy-five years the old relation between the two institutions of property and family, which, Malthus maintained, represented the "fundamental laws" of society, has broken down. The specific reasons for this breakdown are too complex for a short sketch, but the process is clear. In bourgeois society, marriage was a means of keeping sex relations within bounds; in bourgeois marriage, as Denis de Rougement wittily observed, every woman had a husband and desired a lover; the great Continental novels of the nineteenth century, Tolstoy's *Anna Karenina,* Flaubert's *Madame Bovary,* with their geometry of adultery, pointed up this paradox. The growth of romanticism, the high premium on individual attachment and free choice, the translation of passion into secular and carnal terms—all worked against the system of "dynastic" marriage. The emancipation of women meant, in one sense, the disappearance of one of the stable aspects of bourgeois society. If women could marry freely, crossing class lines if they so desired, then the economic enterprise with which the "dynastic" marriage was intertwined would lose some of its staying power.

But there are also reasons more indigenous to the nature of the economic system why the mode of family capitalism has given way. Some are general: the decline of the extended family or clan narrowed the choice of heirs competent to manage the enterprise; the increasing importance of professional techniques placed a high premium on skill rather than blood relationships. These reasons apply largely to the United States, and principally to those corporate areas where managerial and technical skill refuse simply to be agencies of family domination and want to lead in their own right. Yet in Europe, as studies by David Landes, for example, have shown, the continuity of family enterprise has been remarkable. And the continuing existence of such family enterprises, with its caution, conservatism, and fear of allowing outside capital to enter into its affairs, argues Landes, is one of the chief reasons, until now, for the slow rate of economic growth on the Continent.

The situation in America, from the start, has been somewhat different. One important reason is that title to almost all land in the United States has been held in fee simple, rather than entail as in Europe, and family founders have been comparatively unable to impose their wishes regarding the conservation of property upon successive generations. Another is that there has been in the United States, for a variety of complex reasons, a tradition—or at least a myth—whereby the son does not succeed the father but strikes out for himself. These two factors, historical and socio-psychological, have been distinctive elements which hindered the development of a full system of family capitalism in the United States.

Yet efforts to create such a system were constantly being made. As Bernard Bailyn has pointed out in his study of American merchants in the seventeenth century, the rise of business enterprise in the United States was due not to individual initiative but to family solidarity. The family was the source of initial capital, and from the extended family one could draw a variety of skills for the growth of the enterprise. Family enterprises were quite common along the eastern seaboard—particularly in the major cities of Boston, Philadelphia, and New York—in the post-colonial period, and "society" was made up of these leading family clans. The constant movement westward, the vast speculations, the wild economic swings, all acted as disruptive factors.

With the rapid industrialization after the Civil War, the new enterprises often began as family groups. In a capitalist society, control of money and credit, the sources of capital formation, is the fulcrum of power. Few of the companies that began were public corporations. They drew capital from family holdings and expanded by "self-financing." Most of the large "middle-sized" industries in the country have been typical family enterprises. This has been most true of textiles and brewing, but equally of others. International banking, characteristically, has been a "family" affair because of the "secret" nature of much of the business and the need for people one could trust to be placed in different parts of the world. The same reasons apply to shipping. Packing, for historical reasons, has been a closely-held family set of enterprises, as have chemicals, soap, and newspapers. The big "names" in American industry began as "family" names: du Pont, Swift, Armour, Grace, Ford, Olin chemical, Dow, etc. Even today, most major newspapers are family-owned, rather than being public corporations on the market.

The family system had a social counterpart as well: the domination, by the leading family, of the towns in which the family enterprise resided; and, since most industrial enterprise, at least in the late nineteenth and early twentieth century were located in river-valley areas, the stratification had a topographical correlate as well: the workers lived in the valley because the factory was located there, and the family owners lived "on the hill" because it had the commanding view.

However much family capitalism has entrenched itself in many middle-sized enterprises and left its mark on so many cities, it never succeeded in establishing its hegemony in the area of large-scale capital industries. For this, one has to look to the peculiar set of economic events which mark the crucial period of American capitalism, the period from 1890–1910.

The breakup of family capitalism began, roughly, around the turn of the century, when American industry, having overextended itself, underwent a succession of crises. At this point, the bankers, with their control of the money and credit market, stepped in and reorganized and took control of many of the country's leading enterprises. The great mergers at the turn of the century, typified by the formation of United States Steel, marked the emergence of "finance capitalism" in this country.

By their intervention, the investment bankers, in effect, tore up the social roots of the capitalist order. By installing professional managers—with no proprietary stakes themselves in the enterprise, unable therefore to pass along their power automatically to their sons, and accountable to outside controllers—the bankers effected a radical separation of property and family.

The men who made the "modern" corporation were not family enterprisers. Nor were they just bureaucratic managers administering a finished set of routines. The "corporate organizers" were a special breed, often engineers, whose self-conscious task was to build a new economic form, and whose rewards were not primarily money—few accumulated the large fortunes made by a Carnegie, a Rockefeller, a Harriman, or a Ford—but status achievements and, ultimately, some independent power of their own. Thus, T. N. Vail, who created American Telephone & Telegraph, Elbert Gary, who became the public relations face of U.S. Steel ("he never saw a blast furnace until he died," said Ben Stolberg once, bitterly), Alfred P. Sloan, who fashioned the decentralized structure of General Motors, Gerard Swope, who held together General Electric, Walter Teagle, who rationalized Standard Oil, left no personal dynasties, nor do the corporations bear their names; but their imprint on American society is indelible. Following them, the "young men from the provinces," passing through the classrooms of the Harvard Business School, now had an avenue by which to ascend to high social as well as economic positions. Thus family capitalism gave way to social mobility.

In time, however, the power of the bankers, too, declined as the managers became able, especially in the last twenty years, to detach themselves from financial controls and win independent power in their enterprises. In some cases they were able to do this because they, the corporate engineers, were strong individuals; even more important was the enforced separation, by the New Deal measures, of investment and banking functions, which limited the investment bankers' control of the money market; but, most important of all, perhaps, was the fact that the tremendous growth of American corporations enabled them to finance their expansion from their own profits rather than by borrowing on the money market.

The breakup of family capitalism may explain, in part, the "dynamic" nature of modern American capitalism, for the establishment of independent managerial controls has produced a new impetus and new incentives. Unable to withdraw enormous sums of wealth from their corporations, as, say, Andrew Carnegie did from his steel company, the chief status drives of the managers have been performance and growth. Such aims, combined with the changed tax laws, have stimulated a high and constant degree of reinvestment of profits. Whereas only 30 per cent of corporate profits in 1929 were reinvested, about 70 per cent of corporate profits in the postwar years were plowed back for expansion.

The fact that the new managers have lacked a class position buttressed by tradition has given rise to a need on their part for an ideology to justify their power and prestige. In no other capitalist order, as in the American, has this drive for an ideology been pressed so compulsively. In other orders it was less needed. Private property was always linked, philosophically, to a system of natural rights; thus, property itself provided a moral justification. But private productive property, especially in the United States, is largely a fiction, and rarely does one hear it invoked any longer as the moral source of the corporate executive's power. As we have had in the corporation the classic shift from ownership to managerial control, so, on the symbolic level, we have the shift from "private property" to "enterprise" as the justification of power. And, as with any ideology, the symbol itself sometimes becomes a propelling force, and "performance" for its own sake has become a driving motive of the American corporate head.

Sociologically, the breakup of family capitalism is linked to a series of shifts in power in Western society as a whole. No longer are there America's "Sixty Families" (or even France's "Two Hundred"). Family capitalism meant social and political as well as economic dominance. It does so no longer. Many middle-sized enterprises are still family-owned, with son succeeding father (e.g., breweries), and many towns, like St. Louis and Cincinnati, still reveal the marks of the old dominance by families, but by and large the system of family control is finished—so much so, that a classic study of American life like R. S. Lynd's *Middletown in Transition,* with its picture of the "X" family dominating the town, has in less than twenty years become a picture of the past rather than of contemporary society.

Two "silent" revolutions in the relations between power and class position in modern society seem to be in process. One is a change in the *mode of access* to power insofar as inheritance alone is no longer all-determining; the other is a change in the *nature of power-holding itself* insofar as technical skill rather than property, and political position rather than wealth, have become the basis on which power is wielded.

The two "revolutions" proceed simultaneously.[1] The chief consequence, politically, is the breakup of the "ruling class." A ruling class may be defined as a power-holding group which has both an established *community* of interest and a *continuity* of interest. Today, there is an "upper class" and a "ruling group." Being a member of the "upper class" (i.e., having differential privileges and being able to pass those privileges along to one's designees) no longer means that one is a member of the ruling group, for rule is now based on other than the traditional criteria of property; the modern ruling groups are essentially coalitions, and the means of passing on the power they possess, or the institutionalization of any specific modes of access to power (the political route, or military advancement), is not yet fully demarked and established.

NOTE

1. One of the great problems for the social analysis of power is the "foreshortening" of time as regards the stable organization of power. The ownership of private property as a basic *mode* of power held constant, in Western law, for nearly two thousand years; and within that time, property as land, was long a dominant form. Within that mode of power, specific family groups might retain power over a span of as many as ten generations. Even where new means of access to power were introduced, such as the *condottieri* of Italy, who simply seized booty, the legitimation of power involved property. In the last hundred and fifty years we have witnessed a rapid breakdown both of the *mode* of power itself and the stability of family and social groups whose power is based on that mode. Hence the difficulty in locating viable time periods for the measurement of power.

45. THE EMPLOYEE SOCIETY

PETER F. DRUCKER

Since the breakup of family capitalism, large-scale business organizations have dominated the structure of the American economy. Many small businesses have been replaced by corporations and the personal bonds between owners and workers have been replaced by more tenuous social arrangements. To many writers, including Peter F. Drucker, America has become an employee society, a hierarchical system in which relationships are defined in terms of statuses, not personalities, and rules are set forth as a result of negotiation between such new social organs as management and union.

Drucker describes this "employee society" and discusses the problems that have been—and are being—created for the individual and the society in this age of organization. The following article was originally published three years before the label "organization man" became a part of the American vernacular.

Peter F. Drucker is a management consultant and writer and has taught at both New York University and Bennington College. A frequent contributor to magazines, he is the author of Germany: The Last Four Years *(1937),* The End of Economic Man *(1939),* The Future of Industrial Man *(1942),* Concept of the Corporation *(1946),* The Anatomy of the Industrial Order *(1950),* The Practice of Management *(1954),* Landmarks of Tomorrow *(1959),* The Effective Executive *(1967), and* Recent Future: Guidelines to our Changing Society *(1968). He is also coauthor of* Power and Democracy in America *(1961).*

American society during the last fifty years has become an employee society. It is not only that the great majority of our people these days expect to spend most, if not all, of their working lives as employees. "Employeeship," to coin a term, colors the social values, the social mores, and the folklore of our society. It increasingly determines and sets the ethos of American society.

If we look at this phenomenon as students of society, the most important thing that stands out is that our society has changed from an employer society to an employee society. And perhaps the most significant change is not the emergence of the "employee" but the disappearance of the "employer."

Fifty years ago the people who were employed—even then a very large and significant part of our population, if not close to an actual satistical majority—worked predominantly for an employer. Of course a great many people still have an employer today. But in the large organization—and in a good many smaller ones—that is, in the qualitatively, socially, and morally decisive realm, people, while they work for a "boss," do not work for an "employer." The boss is himself an employee who in turn works for a boss—and so does the next boss and the next and the next. In the entire organization there is nobody who is not himself an employee working for a boss.

This is a change of tremendous social importance. It means, in the first place, that this employee society is a hierarchical

Reprinted from the *American Journal of Sociology,* **58** (1953), 358–363, by permission of the author and The University of Chicago Press.

system—a system in which everybody is related to people through his relationship to a strictly impersonal, strictly objective, strictly abstract thing, the "organization," the "corporation," the "government agency," etc. It means, second, that this is a society which is based on, and ruled by, status.[1]

A little over a hundred years ago that brilliant Irishman, Sir Henry Sumner Maine, coined the famous epigram that the course of Western history over the preceding century had been "from status to contract." We can today say that the course of American history—if not of Western history altogether—during the last fifty years has been "from contract to status." In the place of the personal relationship between employer and employee based on a contract which obligated the employee to contribute to the employer's goal—a goal defined in terms of property interest primarily—we now have a social system in which the relationship of people to one another is defined by their relative status in respect to a goal and purpose which lies entirely outside all of them, though they are all subordinated to it and cooperate toward its fulfilment. To be sure, the relationship of each individual member to that abstract being, the organization, the corporation, the government agency, is still based on contract, that is, on a voluntary agreement between two parties considered, at least for purposes of law, as equal, independent, and mobile. But the relationships within the organization are all based on status. And it is status therefore that rules and governs the employee society.

1) A new ruling group has emerged in our society—management. It is a ruling group which derives its authority and its responsibilities squarely from function, that is, from its status relationship to the organization, and not from anything it possesses such as property, birth, inherited magical power, or military force. Nor does it derive its position from the authority of superior knowledge or through so-

cially accepted objective tests of achievement or accomplishment; in other words, it is not based on the standing of a profession. Its position, its power, and its responsibilities rest solely on indispensable function. This is equally true incidentally in a free-enterprise society such as ours as in a society of democratic socialism or in a totalitarian state.

This raises basic problems for the student of society. In the first place, "management" itself is a remarkable social phenomenon. Of course it is not unprecedented; one can find, in the long history of mankind, ruling groups which, similarly, were based on function rather than on a sanction either in ideas or in power. But, in Western society at least, such a ruling group is so rare as to be practically unprecedented. And the study of management as a new social phenomenon, its functioning, its internal structure, its relationship to the other groups within society, both inside and without the organization, etc., is thus a major area of research and study for anybody interested in society. Also there are major problems of social policy to solve: the responsibilities of management within and without the organization; the internal organization of management, especially in the very large organization; above all, the question of the succession to management and of making certain of an adequate supply of competent and tested management people for tomorrow's management.

But there are also basic problems of the social order. Is it possible in any society to have a ruling group which bases its claim to power and responsibility exclusively on function, as the adherents of Mr. Burnham and of his "Managerial Revolution" claim? Or must a ruling group have a basis in the beliefs of society—or in its purposes? How do we make management accountable? Is this a problem of making management "professional," as many people in management itself seem to think? Or is this a problem of introducing formal methods of responsibility and accountability, and, if so, to whom and how should management be held responsible?

But the emergence of management has also brought with it another new and basic institution—the labor union. Again, it is not totally unprecedented. The tribunate in republican Rome is a very close analogy, as I have pointed out elsewhere.[2] But again here is an institution so rare in our history as to be still without theory or analysis. And it presents therefore extraordinary problems of social theory and social analysis, especially as both of the theories regarding the nature, structure, and function of trade-unionism held by an earlier generation have been proved totally inadequate: the revolutionary class-war theory of nineteenth-century Marxism and the concept of the trade-union as primarily if not exclusively an economic institution out to get "more"—the concept that still dominates American trade-union thinking by and large.[3]

2) The second major question posed by the fact that the employee society is a status society is: Can the values and beliefs of our American society be realized in the employee society and how? The very fact that the citizen spends the best part of his waking hours as an employee and at work; that in being an employee lies not only his livelihood but increasingly the realization of all his hopes, ambitions, and dreams; and that being an employee carries with it the threat of unemployment, increasingly a threat of social, if not of political, disenfranchisement, means that our basic social values and beliefs either must be realized in and through the employee society or become increasingly abortive.

The employee society offers opportunities, practically unlimited, to realize the basic values and beliefs of our free society. These values and beliefs, however, will not realize themselves but need social action of courage, wisdom, and imagination to become fulfilled in the new society. Whether one agrees with this analysis or not, the fact remains that in the employee

society we have a new and in essential respects a radically different society from the one in which our values and beliefs were first developed.

3) Finally, out of the realization that the employee society is a status society comes the question of the position and function of the individual in it, and especially of his rights in the society—and against it. Here is a status society. Yet we believe, and rightly, in equal opportunities for the individual, both as a matter of elementary justice on which the promise of our society is based and because the employee society, perhaps more than any other, demands the maximum utilization of all the human resources at its command. Hence we have the problem of a society of fixed status for the position but of extreme mobility for the individual to move from fixed position to fixed position —not again an unprecedented but certainly a novel situation.

Above all, we have the problems of squaring the necessary and indeed essential individual rights against society with the needs of society and of its members.

A perfect example of this is the development of the "right to the job," that is, the increasing tendency to give the individual within the organization exclusive and preemptive claims to a certain position. Very few realize how far we have already gone—through legislation, through union contracts, through custom —in establishing such a right to the job.[4] Indeed, it has been called a property right; to a very substantial extent the individual in the employee society, especially the individual in the lower ranks of the hierarchy, enjoys two of the essentials of property in respect to his job. He has the right to the exclusive enjoyment of the fruits of the job; and his exclusive and preemptive possession is guaranteed by such safeguards as seniority rules, union-shop or closed-shop provisions, pension rights, severance pay, jurisdictional rules, and the like. Only the third element of a true property right—the right to dispose of the property—has not been established, though there are some beginnings.

But while this may very well be not only a necessary but a desirable development, and one that gives the individual the independence and autonomy which he has to enjoy in any society to be an individual, a person, and a citizen, the problems and dangers are also obvious. At what point do one individual's rights oppress and deny those of others? At what point do his rights, instead of strengthening society, undermine its values, beliefs, promises, if not its ability to function and to survive? Few would today advocate that the individual employee be given the right to dispose of his job through sale, pledge, or testament; but there are certainly many who believe that it is both legitimate and desirable to expand the right in the job to the point where the present incumbents control access to the trade, craft, or industry in such a way as to derive the maximum return from their jobs, regardless of the injury done to other citizens through denying them a livelihood or to society through restricting the number of trained people. Many also believe that the right to be promoted should be part of the right to the job; but the claim that promotion follow strict seniority is nothing but a demand that opportunities be feudalized, that is, be considered extensions of the job rather than rights of the person. This is only one area in which the attempt to give the individual rights as an individual within the employee society raises problems of social justice, values, order, and cohesion.

For two hundred years or longer economists have assumed that all "advanced" economic organization must be based on exchange and organized in and through the market. But that is not true of the employee society. Within the enterprise, that is, as an employee, the individual is not in a market system. Nor is he in an exchange economy. He is in what the anthropologists call a "redistributive" economy. He contributes his work to the whole, receiving in return a share of the work of the whole, that is, of the proceeds of the total product. The market model of the theoretical economist sheds no light at all on this structure; it may be understood by reference to such economic systems as the medieval manor, or the great many "primitive" civilizations, in which all the producers bring their products to a central storage place and then receive their share from the central governing organ. Similarly in the modern business enterprise all "producers" contribute their work and then receive from the central governing organ their share.

Now this share is not determined by the exchange equivalences of the market. In the first place, it would be absolutely impossible to determine the exact economic contribution to the total product of any one employee or any one group of employees. A whole discipline has grown up around the attempt to find economically rational criteria for wage and salary determination; we have an entire economic mythology trying to find a market rationale for executive salaries, where obviously the rationale is nothing more or less than status within the hierarchy. But these attempts have not been very impressive, nor can they be. For what determines the share is not the economic contribution but the standing of the individual within the social group, determined by status in the organization, level of authority and responsibility, tradition, and prestige; that is, by typically social rather than economic criteria. And, even more important perhaps, the individual does not operate on the basis of a contract or a multitude of contracts either with the other producers (though it is with them that he "exchanges his labor," especially in the mass-production system) or with the ultimate consumer of the product, who, however, economically is really his "exchange partner." He receives his share from a central governing organ, management, which decides how to distribute the total product, what share each group is to receive, who has a bigger claim, and so on. It is typical of such a redistributive system not only that the size of share is largely based on power considerations but also that we talk of management's determining the amount of compensation or rewards received by each group as its share, even though, economically speaking, management is nothing but a reduction gear between the ultimate consumer and the producer, a broker who, economically speaking, has no power of determination whatsoever. For the decision how to redistribute in a redistributive society always presupposes an organ of political power. And it is the political decision that is important; the economic decision—that is, how much there is to distribute—is typically determined by outside considerations, namely, by how much the market pays for the total product. It is therefore not relevant to the relationships within the system, nor is it usually a problem or a cause for dispute.

From this redistributive function of management, incidentally, any real theory of the labor union will have to start. For the function of the union is primarily to be an opposition to, and a limitation of, the management power to determine the distribution of the total product and the share of individuals and groups in it. To want "more" and to fight for status and recognition for the workingman are certainly important aims for organized labor. But before and beyond them comes the opposition to management as the governing power of a redistributive system which can use political power to mete out economic punishments and rewards and economic control to demand political allegiance and submission.[5] And the central question of union policy and of public policy toward unionism is clearly whether this opposition of the labor union to management's redistributive power should be based on an acceptance of management as the necessary, if not the legitimate, ruling organ, with unionism as a limiting and balancing factor, or on rejection of and

opposition to management, with the union as an alternative.

As a redistributive system the modern enterprise is an extremely difficult and complex one, so peculiar as to be unique. On the one hand, practically all redistributive systems of which we have any knowledge redistribute physically the same products the members produced. But the modern enterprise sells the product, and sells it on a market, so that a market determines how much there is to distribute. Second, redistribution was practically everywhere made in kind, whereas in the modern enterprise it is made in money, that is, in purchasing power for other goods. Unique, too, is the situation at the other end of the system. Every redistributive system we know, other than the modern enterprise, is a closed system. Its members belong to it as tribesmen, subjects, serfs, or slaves. But this new redistributive system, modern enterprise, operates in a labor market. Its members can come and go. And the enterprise is forever in competition for them with other enterprises. Inside, in other words, the enterprise is a redistributive system. But it is totally submerged on the outside in market systems; that is, in systems which in structure, relationship, and values are radically different if not incompatible. This creates tremendous problems of economic theory and economic analysis.

The fact that the modern enterprise is a redistributive system raises the problem of the meaning of financial rewards and incentives. It seems that differentials between pay rates are of more importance in the social structure of the enterprise than the pay rates themselves. Hints come from the abundant material on the effectiveness or ineffectiveness of various kinds of incentive pay and from the discovery, in all our surveys, that the wives, who are not part of the employee society, look upon wage primarily as an economic reward and as something to buy things with; that is, they look upon it economically—so much so that at times they resemble remarkably the economic man of early nineteenth-century economics. The men, on the other hand—or rather the people in employment, since this is not primarily a difference between the sexes but a difference between those who are part of the employee society and those who are only connected with it—look upon wage and salary largely as social status symbols, pertaining to their relationship with the other members of the group and denoting their relative status.

The basic work of research still has to be done. It is primarily a job not of gathering data but of thinking through the problem and of formulating the basic theoretical concepts for analyzing it. Perhaps our best starting point would be Aristotle's conception of the determinants of economic rewards—his concept of justice and his emphasis on the role of economic rewards as strengthening the fraternal bonds of the community.[6]

Other basic areas of investigation are, for instance, the whole problem of the relationship between men, the group, and the actual job they are doing. It has been fashionable of late, particularly in the human relations school, to assume that the actual job, its technology, and its mechanical and physical requirements are relatively unimportant compared to the social and psychological situation of men at work. But this assumption is totally at variance with the observable facts.[7] A real study of the relationship between technol-ogy, using the word in its broadest sense, and social organization has yet to be started.

There is furthermore the whole problem of the position of the family in an employee society where work is carried on away from the home and where the family is connected with the work of the world only through father's paycheck. There is, too, a tremendous problem of education: What education is needed in an employee society? What are the role and function of education? And what education is needed within the employee society, within the work situation, within the organization?

The emergence of the employee society offers the student of society a tremendous challenge and opportunity. But to live up to this challenge he will need better tools than are available to him, especially an adequate methodology. All three methodologies in vogue today—the quantitative, the psychological, and the anthropological—have proved inadequate to develop basic concepts. Yet the most urgent and most important job today is precisely to develop adequate conceptual tools. There is no lack of case studies or of statistical material; indeed, the last fifteen years have brought a veritable avalanche of surveys, case studies, and factual descriptions—much of it, alas, without focus or direction. But basic concepts still have to be developed. No earlier generation of students, I believe, has ever had a greater opportunity or faced a greater challenge.

NOTES

1. The word "status" is used here in its precise scientific, not in the vague, propagandistic, meaning given to it during the early nineteenth century and still occasionally found in the literature. It does not imply a static society—in fact, some of the most mobile societies were status societies of pronounced character, such as, for instance, the monastic orders of the early and high Middle Ages. Nor does it imply a highly stratified society; middle-class England in early Victorian days—in which status had become all but completely submerged—was, for instance, extremely highly stratified. That a society is based on status means only that its basic social relationships are determined objectively by social function or position rather than either personally or through a man's position in the kinship system.

2. *The New Society,* New York: Harper & Bros., 1950.

3. On this whole problem see *ibid.,* and also Frank Tannenbaum, *A Philosophy of Labor,* New York: Alfred A. Knopf, Inc., 1951.

4. Joseph M. Juran, of the Graduate Engineering School of New York University, has brought together, so far unpublished, a mass of material, surprising even to those most familiar with unionism and industry, in respect both to the extent to which the right to the job has been developed in our society and to the speed at which it is developing.

5. This function of the labor union is certainly the reason why American management, by and large, prefers the AF of L to the CIO, even though the former is generally fully as militant, imposes more burdensome restrictions (on output, on productivity, on management's freedom of action, and on its right to hire and fire) and has a poorer record of observing a contract than the typical CIO union. But the egalitarianism of the major CIO unions with their steady pressure toward elimination of pay differentials and toward one basic wage rate is a direct attack on management's power to redistribute, which is the very root of management's power altogether. On the other hand, the AF of L, in emphasizing differentials, accepts management's function; it only demands a share in it. It would be interesting and important to raise the question whether the meteoric rise of the AF of L during the last few years—to where it now outnumbers the CIO 2 to 1—has anything to do with this basic attitude and is, for instance, related to the tremendous recovery of management's prestige and prominence in American society during the last ten or twelve years. [*Editor's note:* Since this article was originally published the AF of L and CIO have merged.]

6. In this discussion I am greatly indebted to Karl Polanyi and his pioneering studies in the nature and structure of economic institutions. See Karl Polanyi, *The Great Transformation,* Boston: Beacon, 1957.

7. See especially Charles Walker, *The Man at the Assembly Line,* Cambridge: Harvard University Press, 1952.

46. BUSINESS AS A SOCIAL SYSTEM

MELVIN M. TUMIN

In the author's own words, this "paper is an attempt to sketch out some of the actual assumptions on which people operate, as opposed to those that we have assumed to be characteristic of their basic premise systems." Melvin M. Tumin's paper is at once a critique of misplaced emphasis by many behavioral scientists and an example of how systematic assessment of social realities might best be conducted. His subject is the business world.

Melvin M. Tumin is Professor of Sociology and Anthropology at Princeton University. His many books are listed on page 62 of this volume.

Implicit in the title of this paper is an assumption which needs to be looked at closely, namely, that there is a uniformity and homogeneity in the world of business which permits one to generalize about business, businessmen, business activities, and business organizations. In an important way, of course, this assumption is false. For at certain levels of abstraction there is no uniform entity called business, no single activity called business enterprise, no homogeneous institutional arrangement called the corporation, nor any group of identical actors called businessmen.

Businessmen are as diverse as doctors in what they think, say, do, and want. Business ideology is as heterogeneous as religious ideology, if not more so. Business activities are as variegated as all the activities that go under the name of education or recreation. And the totality of actors, ideals, relationships, actions, and consequences that are characterized loosely as all belonging in some way to the world of business (as distinct, let us say, from religion or politics) comprises a pretty heterogeneous bundle, about which we generalize and to which we impute uniformities only at some considerable risk, and with obvious loss of specificity and correspondence with any actual person, corporation, or activity.

It is immediately evident, however, that the behavioral sciences have seen fit to assume that generalizations in these other equally diverse fields—religion, recreation, education, politics and the like—are possible, and we have proceeded well and wisely, on that assumption, toward the discovery of some very significant general findings. All this, let it be noted, in spite of the great diversities of activity, personnel and organization that claim to belong to the worlds of religion or politics or education or family life. In short, there seems to be no good reason to give up the scientific game as far as these other human activities are concerned. Quite the contrary, there seems to be every good reason to play at the game even more determinedly and resolutely. And by extension, there would seem to be identically good reasons to follow this behavioral science approach in the study of the work of business men, ideas, activities, and organizations.

But we do not have to defend this approach in terms of analogy from other fields alone. We need go back no further

Reprinted from *Behavioral Science*, **9**, 2 (April 1964), 120–130, by permission of the author and the publisher.

than the Hawthorne study to see how indispensable such an approach proved in getting at some basic problems of motivation, moral productivity, and organizational cohesion. Only by assuming that the actors were normal humans motivated in much the same way as others, subject to numerous economically irrational impulses, guided in their actions by sensitivity to their peers and the norms of their peer groups, concerned with status and rank and recognition, involved in networks of relationships outside the workshop that impinged importantly on the roles inside the workshop: only when these facts were recognized was it possible to begin to clear up the otherwise mysterious fluctuations in productivity, morale, and identification. And one wonders how long these apparent mysteries might have remained just that if the insights of the behavioral sciences, just then emerging, had been ignored and, instead, some market model of supply and demand of labor and the nature of work motives had been insisted upon.

The Behavioral Science Approach

One sees, then, in the Hawthorne study two general assumptions that underlie the approach through behavioral science. First, there are underlying patterns of behavior and incentives and motives of behavior that can be discovered by patient and imaginative scientific inquiry. Second, human activities, interests, and motives that take place in the workshop are part and parcel of *general* human motives, interests, and activities, sufficiently part and parcel so that any particularities they may exhibit because they take place within the world of business and work are best seen as special versions of more general human themes, rather than as matters so unique and different from all other systems of motives and interests as to defy broad scientific analysis.

Both these assumptions have been carried forward since the Hawthorne days in the works and labors of distinguished students of business activity, whose various contributions need only be mentioned to remind us of how valuable it has been to come at the world of production and distribution as though it were a social institution, subject to the same kinds of approaches and analyses as other social institutions. Think, for instance, of the insights and understandings that have been developed as a result of viewing business as though it were a bureaucratic organization; or, more generally, as a sample of a formal organization; or as a cultural unit and complex in interaction with others; or as an aspect of the culture that has absorbed many of the same basic general cultural themes (e.g., the Calvinist ethic) as other forms of current human action. Consider also what we have learned by assuming that the business executive is a sample of all executives rather than something *sui generis;* or that businessmen are probably as good a sample of irrationality in human conduct as preachers, teachers, and draymen; or that the wives and children of businessmen are subject to the same strains and pressures of dual and triple loyalties as the wives and children of men connected with other worlds—politics, or education, or whatever.

We are reminded by these observations, and by such names as Berle, Means, Drucker, Moore, Barnard, Dubin, Argyris, Simon, Gouldner, W. H. Whyte, David Riesman, C. Wright Mills, Georges Friedmann, and others, that we have come a long way in our understanding of the internal and external structures and functionings of business since the days of Frederic Taylor, and that however tempting it may be to invoke the shades of Taylor once again (especially when the going is rough, from the businessman's point of view), there is probably little to be gained and a great deal to be lost if one tries to ignore what the behavioral scientists have produced in the last thirty years or more.

The Businessman and the Social Sciences

It would seem pointless and gratuitous to take so long to insist that it is important for the business world to keep itself sensitive to and informed about developments in the behavioral sciences, if it were not for the fact that businessmen seem so largely to have ignored the social sciences and hence have profited so apparently little from those sciences, by comparison with how much social scientists have added to their general knowledge by studying and understanding business systems. It is, of course, hard to know exactly just how well informed businessmen keep themselves about anything, unless one is among them, and among many of them, and among a good sample of them. And one might well point to a conference such as this to indicate how concerned the world of business actually is with the behaviorial sciences: this conference, and the various new developments regarding business schools and their curriculums about which one hears so many encouraging things. But I venture to say that business schools are one thing and business enterprises are quite another. From simple role theory—by now part and parcel of any sociological journeyman's bag of tools —one would deduce that the schools of business, located as they are within the framework of universities, would be much more sensitized to the need to keep *au courant* of the work being done by colleagues in other colleges of their universities and would feel the general university pressures toward basic research. By contrast, business enterprises, having no such leg inside of university life, would tend to feel much less pressure to keep informed about theoretical problems and research findings, except as, either by accident or by the pressure of some urgent practical problem, they deliberately seek some social science advice and counsel. But few, if any, of the people I know (including myself) who have served as part-time con-

sultants to various kinds of business firms have very much enthusiasm for the degree of interest shown by these firms in social science research methods or findings, where these are not directly and immediately relevant to pressing problems. And if my experiences in consulting are in any way representative, I would note a further deplorable tendency on the part of firms to try to involve a social science consultant in practical customer problems—at which level the social scientist is usually no good at all—instead of discovering ways in which to utilize the social scientist's grasp of general problems and his hoped-for knowledge of the best among the current research materials. This is not to mention the instances in which business firms, having risked hiring a social science team for research into their own organizational problems, have seen fit to discharge the teams and reject their findings when these appeared to involve reversing certain of the more egregious extensions of Parkinson's laws of unnecessary growth. Such incidents suggest that all social science research within firms should be cleared by and responsible to the absolutely top executive, and only by and to him, if the research is to last any decent length of time. Otherwise, the pinched egos and feet stepped on willy-nilly at lower reaches of the organizational labyrinths create hosts of embittered lower-level officials, not excluding vice-presidents, who come to view the social science research teams as threats to their existence, not to mention the threats to any possible growth and expansion of their respective subkingdoms.

In all these matters one sees that corporations, corporation executives, and so-called rational hard-headed businessmen are susceptible to sudden fits of soft-headedness and irrationality just like the rest of mankind—if by irrationality we mean watching out for one's own personal interests first, whenever these appear to be in any way threatened by the interests of the organization—whatever those may be.

Principles of Conduct

But here I am anticipating. For what I should like to do in the rest of this paper is to examine in some detail a few of the major principles of organizational and individual conduct exemplified in business activities and organizations, but also more generally in all human activities and organizations. I do not propose simply to summarize what I think to be the best and most reliable of the findings of previous investigators. Any careful reading of the outstanding works in the field, with which you are all undoubtedly familiar, will provide that kind of information. Rather, I should like to try to indicate the extent to which business is a social system and may be viewed as such, by indicating the extent to which certain overarching themes of conduct govern and guide its organizations and personnel in perhaps the same way and to the same degree as is true of other social systems.

In all of this I am not unmindful of the *special* ways in which business organizations and activities need to be viewed because they are primarily business in their orientations; nor am I unmindful of the extent to which there is considerable variation within the business world itself. Yet, again, I would assert that it is important to ask and discover whether there are not certain generally pervasive themes and norms which more or less reflect the central and dominant tendencies of the world of business.

I think here of two categories of generalizations, one which refers to what I would call organizing myths, and the other referring to certain principles of conduct which it seems to me are operative even though they do not receive overt recognition.

In talking of myths and covert principles of conduct I am here specifying something characteristic of all social institutions. For in such institutions, there are always implicit certain general themes that are detectable and formulatable by the scientific observer, however much the actors themselves may fail to recognize and/or admit the existence of these themes. So, too, in every culture complex there are always implicit rules of conduct in accordance with which the members seem to behave, even though they may wish to deny and/or conceal that these rules are operative. So here we are dealing with the subsurface, yet operating, myths of the organization and principles of conduct of its members.

First, then, to the organizing myths.

Organizing Myths

The myth of infallibility

One can epitomize this in the statement that the true church is never in error; only its fallible human members are capable of error. The distinction, as you will recognize, is that between the true and institutional church. In business institutions, one finds statements of principles, intentions, and ideals, plus membership systems and work loads organized beautifully by structural and flow charts, designating with great cleanliness and clarity the lines of responsibility and power. That version of the organization can never go wrong. If something does go wrong, as almost always it does and will, the blame is placed on some deficient individual, or on some misunderstanding, or on some misconception by others of what the organization intended. But the formal organization, with its ideals and goals and means and flow charts, is immune to error. In this regard, it is noteworthy that while I have written scores of letters to various business firms to complain of some unwarranted insult or egregious inefficiency or obvious dereliction of duty by some employee or another, and while I have almost always received some kind of reply, since I always address these letters to the personal attention of the president or the chairman of the board, I have never once received anything by way of response but self-justification and self-exculpation. I have never received an admission of error in the sense that the official who responds concedes that something structurally inadequate in the organization itself produced the complained-of behavior.

This myth operates not only *within* each organization but for the whole world of business, so that if some business firm is caught red-handed at some illegal (or only some immoral) act, one is amazed at the speed with which spokesmen for what is amusingly called the Industry, or for All of Business, rush into print to assure everyone either that the wrongdoer is not really a member of the tribe; or that his motives have been misunderstood and his actions misinterpreted; or that, in fact, the charge of immorality or illegality is simply a malicious charge brought by persons who hate business. By such action the unity of the tribe is ritually affirmed, however much the various clans may go for each other's jugular veins in between such incidents.

The myth of social indispensability, or Apres nous, le deluge

A second organizing theme that is indispensable to executive morale and that almost always evokes laughter when it is announced seriously—as it almost always is—by executives through their highly-paid spokesmen, is the claim that the welfare of the entire community or nation, or even of the world, is contingent upon the welfare of the given organization and its profitable sales record. It is implied, if not made explicit, that if the given organization does not do well, or (horrors!) should fail, the entire society would experience a matching disaster. Charles Wilson was the first to have the splendid nerve to make public this belief of the intimate relationship between the welfare of General Motors and of the United States. But obviously, this is something widely believed in, or at least claimed, by many organizations, and there seems to be an informal cultural pressure to adopt this attitude, however ludicrous it latently is for *everyone* in *every* organization to hold to this notion. Lest one think this incredible delusion is characteristic of businesses alone, it should be noted that such non-profit organizations as colleges and universities, all 1,400 of the degree-granting variety, operate with this myth and find it perhaps even more indispensable to their continued functioning than do businesses. It would be impossible to nerve oneself to approach possible donors of capital gifts if one could not come to them with all the assurance of social indispensability. Moreover, this is highly functional for gift solicitation, since it permits otherwise functionless and insignificant people to delude themselves into believing that by giving to Podunk or Squeegee they are thereby making a significant contribution to the total educational enterprise and, of course, directly to total national welfare.

The myth of individual indispensability

A corollary of this organizational myth is a belief in oneself that grows in depth of conviction, scope of coverage, and explicitness of claim in direct proportion to one's power in an organization. This myth seems to be the particular favorite of chief executives, who frequently sacrifice themselves, as they see it, because while they don't want immodestly to insist that they are indispensable, it is difficult for them to imagine how anyone else could possibly do the job as well, if at all. I have never yet met a chief executive of anything who didn't believe this and believe it firmly (it is safe, after all, only for a chief executive to believe it and say it). This explains why it is incredibly rare for a chief executive to put his job on the line in defense of principles if there is really a showdown involving his job. At such points one suspects that motives other than those of belief in indispensability and concern for institutional welfare are dominant. But in the nature of the case, these are difficult to prove.

The myth of the necessary bias

This most interesting idea functions beautifully to exclude outsiders with objective perspectives and with nonorganizational criteria from examining the workings of institutions or from assuming any power in or over them. This is the myth summarized in the question "Have you ever met a payroll?" The implication here is obvious, and obviously wrong. It is about as sensible as insisting that one should be a horse in order to judge a horse show. Experience can be as bad a teacher as good. Whether we learn from experience and what we learn depends on what kind of experience we have and what attitudes we bring to the experience. Most experiences only serve to harden early-established biases and distorted perceptions by the process of selective ignoring of contrary evidence.

More dangerous still is the implication that somehow only those whose vested interests lie deeply with organizational success have the right and the ability to criticize effectively and relevantly. Such a principle would render democratic government and science inoperative. It is probably even worse for businesses, which claim to be rational and adaptive, to insist on such a principle.

The myth of the sacredness of the status quo nunc et ante

This myth has two dimensions. The first asserts that what was good enough for grandfather is good enough for us, a rule by which previous practices are endowed with the halo of time without regard for their suitability, past or present. Putting it very moderately, one may say that there is

no necessary relationship between the age of a custom or practice and its suitability at any given time. If anything, the older a custom is the more likely is it to be unsuitable for today's times and goals. It is curious how some really ancient principles of social organization and antique theories of motivation persist in business institutions and ideologies in spite of abundant evidence that they were dead and useless long ago.

The second aspect of this type of thinking forms the core of a Panglossian view of the world. It affirms, as did Candide's noble mentor, that anything that is, *must* be, and must be good, for if it didn't have to *be,* and if it weren't the best of all possible things, it wouldn't *be.* Naturally, organizations use this myth only to defend what they like, feeling free to invoke quite contrary principles to discredit ideas or practices they consider inimical to their interests.

The myth of universal applicability

This myth insists that the same principles along which business enterprises are theoretically run, and the same criteria of success and failure, are principles and criteria that ought to be used to operate and to judge the success and failure of other human activities, such as family life, schools, and the like. If time permitted, it would be perfectly easy to show how the extrapolation of business criteria into family life destroys families and how the insistence that schools operate according to canons of efficiency, measured in terms of dollars and cents, is guaranteed to ruin any school, no matter how good the school may have been before these business criteria were imposed. Businessmen tend to be blinded by the holy light emanating from the word "efficiency," as though somehow the invocation of this word dispelled any foolish notions about the importance of other criteria. One rarely hears anyone asking "Efficient for what?"—and whether the "what" that is stated has anything to do with the values sought in family life or schooling or religion.

Several important purposes are served, I think, by calling attention to these operative myths. In the first instance, we are reminded by them that business is a social institution comparable in certain salient and central ways to other social institutions, and hence subject to the same kind of objective study and as capable of profiting from that study as any other organized human enterprise that cares to take inventory of what it is doing and where it is going.

In the second instance, the recitation of these myths may serve to convey some sense of the degree of cynicism, disbelief, and discount with which the self-proclaimed motives, interests, and operations of business are greeted by many of the general public. To the extent that the world of business cares about being taken seriously, perhaps even loved (as apparently many businessmen feel they ought to be), further self-scrutiny in order to adjust its operations and public claims to the level of the acceptable and the believable may be urgently required.

Finally, these myths unquestionably serve some important positive functions for organizations as they are presently structured, and as some managers believe they should continue to be structured. But one cannot overlook the fact that several of these myths also render an organization considerably less susceptible to that kind of continuing self-evaluation and critical self-analysis which guarantees the effective adaptation of an organization to changing conditions. For these myths serve to minimize rationality in the strict sense of that term; they devalue the relevance of outside criticism and negatively sanction inside criticism; and they set any organization that operates on their terms in opposition and hostility to other non-business institutions in the society, as well as to other members of the business community.

Covert Principles of Conduct

Having said this much, we can now turn to look at some major principles of conduct that seem to me to be operative in the business world and to be unwittingly promoted by business itself. I have in mind the fact that our levels of expectation, hence our norms, hence our surprises and confirmations, hence our assurances, our anxieties, and our moral indignations, derive from certain basic premises we hold axiomatically about the nature of man and the fundamental characteristics of his social behavior. Thus, if we assume that all men are by nature good, we are surprised when they are evil, we get indignant about it, we are made anxious by it, we feel threatened by it, and we feel compelled to eliminate it. Our surprises and reactions would, of course, be very different (or they would be if we were consistent) if we held as axiomatic instead that men are evil by nature or that men are nothing by nature. We would have very different senses of what is possible in human affairs and very different tolerance levels and sets of prescriptions as to what ought to be done.

"Normal" and "deviant" behaviors

The behavioral sciences themselves have for some time operated on a series of axiomatic premises that gregariousness, kindness, gratitude, honesty, reciprocity, consideration of others, and many other such virtues, central to the liberal credo of life, are in fact the basic tendencies in human behavior and that contrary behavior-forms are to be viewed as unexpected, deviant, problematic, and demanding explanation.

In fact, of course, both the so-called normal and deviant behaviors equally require explanation. The process by which conformist behavior is produced is as complex as the process by which deviation is induced. And we may not, therefore, properly assume that the statistically most frequent and the morally most widely accepted forms of behavior may be left unanalyzed, on the assumption that "that's human nature."

But I wish to make a stronger point, to the effect that much of what passes for acceptable behavior and what in fact appears to be satistically most frequent may actually be much more difficult for society to produce than what is considered deviant and problematic and characteristic only of a minority; for in the very nature of becoming a human being, which can take place only in an interactional context, the refractory organism is forced to make certain vital surrenders of self and to observe certain restraints which continue to be viewed by him throughout life as relatively costly for the gains achieved.

The evidence in support of this contention is to be found in three kinds of individuals:

1. Those who have been inadequately socialized, by virtue of age or neglect or both. "Socialization" here may be a social science euphemism for a much stronger process more closely resembling terrorization.

2. Those who have rejected the dominant modes of psychic bookkeeping practiced by their neighbors because they have found the so-called profits of normative behavior to be too small indeed for the prices paid—e.g., criminals, delinquents, drug addicts, alcoholics, prostitutes. While these "types" deviate fairly frequently, almost all of us, if not all of us, deviate in like manner at one time or another.

3. Persons in extreme circumstances such as prisons, prison camps, concentration camps, severe settings, or in conditions of extreme deprivation under nominal freedom.

All three types of persons reveal in their behavior some tendencies to react to the world and others around them in ways which seem to represent what all men would think, say, feel, be, and do if they were not otherwise restrained, impelled, motivated, rewarded, threatened, or in some way contained.

That most people do not appear to operate in ways similar to persons in extreme situations is due, in the first instance, to the obvious fact that most people are not ordinarily in extreme situations; but just as important is the fact that systems built during the socialization process tend to work well at any given moment, when the pressures to the contrary are not very severe. What is startling, however, is how badly these control systems work when the pressure does get severe. The behavior of persons in extreme circumstances, so well documented in recent years, reveals how thin is the veneer of civilization, how shallow, tentative, and flimsy the control systems. So little by way of deprivation or even the threat of it is required, so little by way of imbalance in one's psychic books is needed, to strip the controls and restraints of their effectiveness. And none of us dare say with any certainty how much of what deprivation we would endure before we surrendered the supposed benefits of civilized behavior for other forms of behavior akin to those exhibited by persons in extreme circumstances: betrayal, bestiality, even murder.

On general principles by now well established, we must consider the behavior exhibited under pressure as an expression—albeit more unrestrained—of what we are always ready to do unless otherwise controlled, rather than as a magically-appearing new dimension otherwise totally alien to the organism.

When the extreme behavior forms are seen in this light, we are warned that there is always danger that some version of these extravagant actions will be evoked unless very great pains are taken to repress them and to elicit the more acceptable forms. No permanent guarantees are ever possible. Constant vigilance, motivation, control, inducement, and persuasion are necessary. Neither the "benign" nor the "malignant" form is more "natural" to the human being. Both are best seen, in view of what little we know today, as equi potential forms of behavior. What determines how much of each will be expressed in human relations depends very much on what themes the culture insists upon, what forms it rewards, what types of actions it solicits and praises.

With this much by way of introduction, we can now briefly examine some principles of individual and group conduct which stand in quite stark opposition to those principles ordinarily assumed to be the "normal" and the "natural" in human relationships. They are offered here, we repeat, as suggestions of what men will be like with each other, in small and large aggregates, unless they are otherwise restrained, impelled, or motivated.

The principle of least significant morality and most immoral member

In any social group, the moral behavior of the group as an average will tend to sink to that of the least moral participant, and the least moral participant will, in that sense, control the group unless he is otherwise restrained and/or expelled. Such is the case in business agreements, especially on pricing, for instance. Moore has put it: "Competitive tactics, as long as limiting rules are absent, vague or unenforced, provide rich ground for this principle to flourish. A new strategy, however immoral, must be matched by other players if they are going to stay in the game." [1]

Put in psychological terms, this principle affirms that the most neurotic member of a group will control the group unless he is otherwise restrained or expelled. The reason is simple. The most neurotic member is likely to be the most irresponsible member, caring least for the group norms and "group welfare" because he is least able to care for them.

The special relevance of this principle for the world of business relations derives from the fact that the central theme of "successful" business conduct is almost completely harmonious with it. For business conduct is held to be successful when, through intense competition, one contestant secures maximum personal gain in scarce resources, to the detriment and loss of other contestants. While business ideology is not devoid of rules of "decent" conduct in this intense competitive process, such rules are not likely to be very effective if, as must always be expected, one of the contestants, seeking to maximize his chances for winning, departs from the rules. At that point, the other competitors must restrain or expel him from the game, or in self-defense, must be willing to employ the deviant tactics themselves. The temptation to follow the leader in this resort to deviant tactics is apparently very strong.

This suggests that the principle of least morality flourishes in an environment where competition for scarce and valued goods is the dominant modality.

Of course, the business world may insist that the competitive theme has produced "results," and yet decry the extrapolation of this business theme to other areas of social life. But it is quite clear that business also strenuously insists that such "greatness" as American society may be able to claim is tied intimately to its capacity to produce material goods and services, and that such capacity to produce is itself intimately dependent upon the operations of the process of intense competition aimed at maximum personal gain. In short, by its own words and deeds the business world promotes the spread of the theme of competition and the measurement of success in terms of acquisition of material rewards to the rest of the culture. In the process, wittingly or unwittingly, a general atmosphere is created that is highly nurturant of the principle of least morality.

Bad money may not always drive out good money, though it almost always does. But "bad" conduct surely drives out "good" conduct with predictable vigor and speed.

The principle of least effort and least participation

Quite friendly to and consonant with the principle of least morality is the principle of least effort and least participation. It says in effect that in any social organization the contribution of any and all members will tend to sink to the minimum possible unless otherwise exhorted or impelled. This is not to overlook the power of various exhortations, motivations, and impulsions to the contrary. But it notes that in any collective enterprise, where there are unequal amounts of personal benefit to be gained from effective participation in those enterprises, effort will be exerted proportionate to the amount of possible gain—social, psychological, or material—that the individual perceives is in store for him. Such concepts as community spirit, *esprit de corps,* good citizenship, and the like therefore represent ideological and quasiutopian exhortations.

We are warned by this principle to suspect the amount of altruism present in the high-level community involvements of spirited and leading citizens. Altruism is perhaps the most difficult of all human sentiments to muster. In social organization, then, our question should be not why do some people lag, but why do any people participate at all.

The principle of least unity

Perhaps underlying all these principles is one mother principle I choose to call the principle of least unity. It urges, in effect, that all men tend to fly apart and stay apart from each other unless otherwise impelled. Social aggregation is thus an extraordinary achievement. It is apparently secured at considerable cost or deception to all the individuals involved. It is always tentative, as are the rules of safe conduct that are required to maintain aggregation.

Our problem, therefore, is not so much to understand why some men are refractory and do not make good group members as to understand why and how anyone comes to be bound to any social aggregate. The implications here are that deviation is the underlying tendency and that conformity is an extraordinary phenomenon, especially in the extent to which it is achieved against basic impulses to the contrary.

The principle of least rationality

A fourth principle has to do with the role of rationality in organizational conduct. We ordinarily mark the turn of civilization by the influx of rationality as a general principle. But we have a research fortune to make, I think, by investigating the large-scale irrationality that permeates even the so-called most rational organizations such as business. The principle of least rationality asserts that unless otherwise restrained, organizational functionaries will follow those alternatives which are most in accordance with their private sentiments and least in accord with some supposed rationally-calculated organizational requirements. This is not the same as the principle of least significant morality. Here we comment on the contrast between sentiment and dispassionate mind as ingredients in behavior, whereas the principle of morality contrasts norms with antinorms. Only in some contexts does the moral requirement coincide with the rational requirement. In most other cases we find that the norms of the community tend to embody quite strong ingredients of sentiment and fantasy and fear. But even these represent a compromise with what people would do if they could get away with it. There is, I believe, no organization in the world, no matter how rationalistic its ideology, that is not effectively colored by, if not primarily attuned to, certain stated or unstated sentimental preferences rather than to dispassionate rational calculations.

The principle of least consistency

A derivative from the principle of least rationality is the principle of least consistency. This principle affirms that any sequence of actions viewed collectively will exhibit maximum inconsistency unless otherwise governed. The reason here is simply that where consistency is judged by some principles of rational conduct, and when these are the logics of those who at the moment are the masters, the tendency will be widespread among other participants to try to get each new decision to conform to their own desires and hence to exhibit maximum dissonance with previous organizational decisions, except by coincidence. Another way of stating this principle would be to put it in terms of dissonance and consonance theory and to urge in those terms that a major principle of human psychic life is that of the compatibility of dissonance. We learn quickly how to organize our various *illogics* into an over-all scheme, one that is logical for us in view of our sentiments and private wishes, however dissonant by some external principle of logic our behaviors may be.

The principle of maximum ego inflation

A psychological principle of considerable importance, and decidedly consonant with the foregoing principles, is one which I call the principle of maximum ego inflation. Unless otherwise impelled, I suggest, men will follow that course of behavior designed to enhance their own favorable conceptions of themselves to the maximum available, being restricted in this only by the extent to which other of their own sentiments and antisocial impulses may overwhelm their desire for ego gratification. Impulses directed at body and psychic gratifications often compete with ego impulses, where these are confined to gratification in the form of favorable responses from others.

The importance of the drive for maximum ego gratification resonates through many areas of social life. It warns us of the limits of acceptable ideas where these may touch the limits of ego image. It warns us that if ego defeat is incurred, one is more likely than ever to see the principles of least moral behavior being put into motion. Morality is maintained to the extent that ego is enhanced by moral behavior and the reception given it. Take away such reception and approval, and much of the normally available restraint on irrationality and impulse gratification is withdrawn as well. This is why community organization, as ordinarily conceived, is so difficult to maintain. For the chance to distribute adequate ego gratification, and hence to bind large numbers of people to an organization, is very limited where recognition is considered a scarce resource and where membership is valued in proportion to skill or level of contribution. The average business enterprise is so characterized.

I will mention briefly three other principles. They are (1) the principle of maximum cruelty; (2) the principle of least reciprocity; and (3) the principle of the most proximate pecker.

The first, that of maximum cruelty, asserts that under conditions of unrestrained power and no socialization to the contrary, individuals will exhibit the maximum possible cruelty to each other. Kindness and consideration are hard-won exceptions.

The second principle, that of least reciprocity, urges that in any status hierarchy, favors extended to persons lower in the hierarchy will be reciprocated by maximum rejection and most deliberate punishment, where possible, of the individual who provided the assistance. Here gratitude is the hard-won and costly alternative. Without socialization to this sentiment and without very severe sanctioning, individuals will reciprocate favors extended to them when they are down with the most effective blow or kick they can contrive when they are up.

Finally, the principle of the most proximate pecker describes behavior in hierarchies where conflict is possible and where scapegoats are available. One will tend to peck, this principle urges, at those most proximate in the pecking order: at those just below, by reason of absence of power of retaliation, and at those just above, by reason of most availability, most social proximity, and most threat of one's own further degradation.

Consequences

The special relevance of these principles for those who govern business organizations but who, at the same time, are concerned with the quality of life and social relationships in the nonbusiness sectors of society, is that business principles and themes have proven to be very contagious, invading other institutional spheres and dominating them to the extent that business principles and themes come to be substituted for themes indigenous to these other institutions. In passing, one may cite one of the most evident examples, namely, the extent to which a man's adequacy as a husband and father has come increasingly to be judged in terms of the standard of living he provides for his family. When this criterion dominates, and when there are discernible different standards of living for various segments of the society, there is an implied and very consequential judgment that those who earn less are by that token and to that degree relatively inadequate as husbands and parents. One suspects that a good deal of family pathology arises directly out of such a context.

So, too, other themes central to business life and conduct stand in sharp antithesis and thematic hostility to principles of human relationships and group behavior that are ordinarily considered to be eminently desirable. Among such business themes are the belief in the value of sharply graded hierarchies of status and rank; nondemocratic processes of decision-making; inequalities in distribution of rewards and psychic gratifications; and the over-all insistence that the only viable theory of motives is that which holds that maximal self-interest must somehow be appealed to and evoked.

The dissonance between such themes and those promulgated for family life, religion, education, recreation, and democratic community and government organization is all too clear. As a result, one may fairly say that what business stands for, ideologically insists upon, and tries to get adopted as general principles of conduct, run directly against and reduce the chances of evoking affection and love as principles of relationship, identification with an enterprise as a source of voluntary and conscientious labor, and a sense of significant membership in an organization arising out of effective participation in decision-making.

Identification, affection, a sense of significant membership: these are among the most powerful restraints and controls that can be internalized and that can reduce the otherwise dominant tendencies to seek one's maximal gain at commensurate cost and loss to others. In promoting themes quite inimical to identification, affection, and significant membership, business thereby and to that extent tends to bring out, standardize, and reward the most unsocialized impulses of man. However much we may value what else business produces in this way, we cannot afford to ignore these general cultural consequences. Nor ought we to forget that there is resonance here, so that the very themes which business promotes, having secured reinforcement through adoption in other institutional contexts, then are played out more intensely still in the business world once again.

Finally, one may at least question whether the avowed goal of business—namely, profitable productivity—is best served by those views of man's nature and his motives that seem currently to dominate business thinking. Could it be that business might serve its own avowed interests much more effectively if it restructured its operations and recast its themes in order to attempt to evoke the kind of identification with an enterprise, concern for its outcome, and sense of significant membership in it that have proven, in other institutions like the family and the church, to be able to evoke extraordinary amounts of conscientious giving of one's best, without thought or concern for differentiated rewards?

NOTE

1. Moore, W. E. *The Conduct of the Corporation,* New York: Random House, 1962, p. 267.

47. NATIONAL COMPARISONS OF OCCUPATIONAL PRESTIGE

ALEX INKELES *and* PETER H. ROSSI

Despite the cultural variability of six industrial countries—the United States, Great Britain, New Zealand, Japan, Germany, and the Union of Soviet Socialist Republics, studies of occupational prestige as measured by surveys of popular opinion indicate a relatively standard hierarchy. Alex Inkeles and Peter H. Rossi, who made statistical comparisons of poll data, suggest that the high international correlations are due to certain universal features of the industrial occupational system.

Physicians uniformly ranked highest in all societies studied, with important government officials, professors, scientists, lawyers, accountants, and engineers all receiving high ratings by those whose attitudes were polled. Where there is some variation it is found particularly with regard to agricultural and service occupations.

Alex Inkeles is Professor of Sociology at Harvard University. He is the author of Public Opinion in Soviet Russia: A Study in Mass Persuasion (*1950*), What is Sociology? (*1964*), *the first volume in a series of studies in sociology of which he is the general editor, and* Social Change in Soviet Russia (*1968*). *He is also editor of* Readings in Modern Sociology (*1966*) *and coeditor of* The Soviet Citizen (*1959*), Soviet Society (*1961*), *and* Soviet Citizen: Daily Life in a Totalitarian Society (*1968*).

Peter H. Rossi is Professor of Sociology at the University of Chicago and Director of the National Opinion Research Center. His publications include Why Families Move (*1955*) *and* The Politics of Urban Renewal (*1961*), *which he edited with R. A. Dentler and others. He is also coeditor of* The Education of Catholic Americans (*1966*) *and* New Media and Education (*1966*).

During the latter part of the nineteenth and the first half of the twentieth centuries the factory system of production was introduced, at least on a small scale, to most areas of the world. The factory has generally been accompanied by a relatively standard set of occupations, including the factory manager (sometimes also owner) and his administrative and clerical staff, engineering and lesser technical personnel, foremen, skilled, semiskilled, and unskilled workers. In the factory, authority and responsibility are allocated largely according to the degree of technical or administrative competence required for the job. In addition, the allocation of material and social rewards, the latter generally in the form of deference, is closely adjusted to levels of competence and degrees of authority and responsibility. The pattern of differentiation of authority is undoubtedly functionally necessary to the productive activity of the factory, and it may be that the associated pattern of reward differentiation is also functionally necessary.

There is, however, no clear-cut imperative arising from the structure of the factory as such which dictates how the in-

Reprinted from the *American Journal of Sociology,* **61** (1956), 329–339, by permission of the authors and The University of Chicago Press. Copyright 1955 by The University of Chicago Press.

cumbents of its typical statuses should be *evaluated* by the population at large. One possibility is that in popular esteem the typical occupations will stand relative to one another in a rank order strictly comparable to their standing in the formal hierarchy of competence, authority, and reward in the factory. It is also possible, however, that the popular evaluation of these occupations will be quite different. Indeed, where the factory system has been introduced into societies like those of Spain or Japan, with well-established values based on tradition and expressive of the culture, one might expect significant differences between an occupation's standing in the formal hierarchy of the industrial system and its position in the popular ranking scheme.

Thus the interaction of the two systems —the standardized modern occupational system and the individual national value pattern for rating occupations—presents an interesting and important problem in comparative sociology.

We may posit two extreme positions in this interaction, while granting that it might be difficult to find live exponents of either. The extreme "structuralist" would presumably insist that the modern industrial occupational system is a highly coherent system, relatively impervious to influence by traditional culture patterns. Indeed, he might go so far as to insist that the traditional ranking system would in time have to be subsumed under, or integrated into, the industrial system. Consequently, his argument would run, even such occupations as priest, judge, provincial governor, not part of the modern occupational system and often given unusual deference, would come in time to have roughly the same standing relative to one another and to other occupations, no matter what their national cultural setting.

By contrast, an extreme "culturalist" might insist that within each country or culture the distinctive local value system would result in substantial—and, indeed, sometimes extreme—differences in the

evaluation of particular jobs in the standardized modern occupational system. For example, he might assume that in the United States the company director would be rated unusually high because of our awe of the independent businessman and large corporations or that in the Soviet Union the standing of industrial workers would be much higher relative to managerial personnel than in Germany, with its emphasis on sharply differentiated status hierarchies. Furthermore, he might argue that the more traditional occupational roles assigned special importance in particular cultures would continue to maintain their distinctive positions in the different national hierarchies. Indeed, he might hold that the characteristic roles of the modern industrial system would come to be subsumed within the traditional rating system, each factory occupation being equated with some traditional occupation and then assigned a comparable rank.

A systematic test of these contrasting positions is not beyond the capacity of contemporary social research. A standard list of occupations—say thirty or forty in number—might be presented for evaluation to comparable samples from countries presenting a range of culture types and degrees of industrialization. The list should contain both standard industrial occupations and the common, but differentially valued, traditional roles (e.g., priest, legislator, etc.).

Data are available which, though far from completely adequate, will carry us a long way beyond mere speculation on these matters. In the postwar years studies of occupational ratings have been conducted in and reported on five relatively industrialized countries: the United States, Great Britain, New Zealand, Japan, and Germany.[1] In addition, the authors have available previously unpublished data for a sixth country, the Soviet Union.

Since these six studies[2] were, on the whole, undertaken quite independently, our ideal research design is clearly far from being fulfilled. Nevertheless, the data do permit tentative and exploratory cross-national comparisons.

The Comparability of Research Designs

The elements of similarity and difference in the six studies may be quickly assessed from the following summary of their essential features:

A. Population studied

United States: National sample of adults fourteen years and over; 2,920 respondents

Japan: Sample of males twenty to sixty-eight years of age in the six large cities of Japan; 899 respondents

Great Britain: Written questionnaires distributed through adult-education centers and other organizations; 1,056 returns (percentage return unspecified)

U.S.S.R.: Sample of displaced persons, mostly in DP camps near Munich, Germany, and some former DP's now residing on eastern seaboard of U.S.; 2,100 written questionnaires

New Zealand: Sample collected mainly by interviews with inhabitants of town of 2,000 partly by mailed questionnaires (12 per cent returns) sent out to town of 4,000; 1,033 questionnaires and interviews used

Germany: 1,500 Schleswig-Holsteiners: vocational-school students, university students, and male adults (not otherwise specified); adult sample only used here

B. Overlap among occupations studied

Each study involved a different number of occupations, ranging from 88 in the case of the National Opinion Research Center American study to 13 in the Soviet research. Only the New Zealand and the British groups studied exactly the same occupations. Each of the remaining four studies used a dif-

ferent, but partially overlapping, set of occupations.

In order to make comparisons between pairs of countries, each occupation studied in each research was matched, when possible, with an occupation in the data gathered in the other country. In many cases it was necessary to disregard the information about an occupation in one of the paired countries because no comparable occupation was studied in the other. In other instances, in order to increase the number of occupations which could be compared for any given pair of countries, occupations were matched which were only very roughly comparable, e.g., Buddhist priest and minister, or collective farm chairman and farm owner and operator. In most cases, however, a direct correspondence characterizes the pairs of occupations which are being equated. The reader is invited to turn to Table 5 (p. 568), where the lists of occupations used from each of the researchers are printed. The occupations listed on any row or line were matched. The number of pairs of similar or identical occupations for each cross-national comparison is shown in Table 1.

C. Nature of rating task

United States: Respondents were asked: ". . . Please pick out the statement that best gives your own *personal opinion* of the *general standing* that such a job has. Excellent standing, good standing, average standing, somewhat below average, poor standing."

Japan: Respondents were given a set of thirty cards and asked: ". . . Think of the general reputations they have with people, and sort them into five or more groups, from those which people think highly of to those which are not thought so well of."

Great Britain: Respondents were told:

Table 1.   *Number of Identical or Similar Occupations Rated Between Six Countries*

	U.S.	Great Britain	U.S.S.R.	Japan	New Zealand	Germany
United States	—	24	10	25	24	20
Great Britain	—	—	7	14	30	12
U.S.S.R.	—	—	—	7	7	8
Japan	—	—	—	—	14	19
New Zealand	—	—	—	—	—	12
Total occupations studied	88	30	13	30	30	38

"We should like to know in what order, *as to their social standing,* you would grade the occupations in the list given to you. [Rate them] . . . in terms of five main social classes . . . ABCDE."

U.S.S.R.: Respondents were asked: "Taking everything into consideration, how desirable was it to have the job of (———) in the Soviet Union? Very desirable? Desirable? So-so? Undesirable? Very undesirable?"

New Zealand: Same as in Great Britain.

Germany: The source is unfortunately not very specific about the rating task assigned. The respondents were apparently asked to rank-order a list of 38 occupations presented as one slate.

D. Computing prestige position

   With the exception of the German study, each research presents a "prestige score" for each of the occupations studied. These scores, computed variously, represent in each case the "average" rating given to each of the occupations by the entire sample of raters used. The German study presented only the rank-order positions of the occupations.

One is not sure whether differences between nations are generated by the differences in the questionnaires or the differences in the nations themselves. However, similarities in the prestige hierarchies, particularly when they are striking, are somewhat strengthened by the same lack of comparability in research designs and in the occupations matched to one another. Similarities may be interpreted as showing the extent to which design and other differences are overcome by the comparability among the prestige hierarchies themselves.

Comparability of Occupational Prestige Hierarchies

Since each study included some occupations used in another study, it is possible to compare the prestige hierarchies of occupations in pairs of countries by computing correlation coefficients for the scores (or ranks) of occupations. The fifteen correlation coefficients which result are presented in Table 2.[3] It will be seen immediately that the levels of correlation are considerably higher than the magnitude to be expected if there were only rough agreement on placement in the top and bottom halves of the prestige hierarchy. Indeed, twelve of the fifteen coefficients are above .9, and only one is below .8. The three coefficients below .9 all concern the Soviet ratings, which, it will be recalled, involve only a very small number of occupations, maximizing the chances for lower correlations arising from merely one or two "mismatches."

Table 2.* *Correlations Between Prestige Scores (or Ranks) Given to Comparable Occupations in Six National Studies*

	U.S.S.R.	Japan	Great Britain	New Zealand	U.S.	Germany †
U.S.S.R.	—	.74	.83	.83	.90	.90
Japan	—	—	.92	.91	.93	.93
Great Britain	—	—	—	.97	.94	.97
New Zealand	—	—	—	—	.97	.96
United States	—	—	—	—	—	.96
Av. correlation	.84	.89	.93	.93	.94	.94

* *See Table 1 for numbers of occupations involved in each comparison.*
† *All coefficients are product-moment correlations, with the exception of those involving Germany, which are rank-order coefficients.*

For most of the comparisons, furthermore, the findings go beyond establishing mere comparability of rank orders. With the exception of the correlations involving Germany each coefficient represents the relationships between prestige *scores* given to the same occupations in two different nations. Hence there is a high relationship between the relative "distance" between occupations, as expressed in score differences, as well. In other words, if, of two occupations, one is given a much lower score than the other by the raters in one country, this difference in prestige scores and not merely crude rank order also obtains in another country.

It should also be noted that these high correlations were obtained by using samples of occupations which were not strictly identical from country to country, including such very crude comparisons already mentioned as that of collective farm chairman and farm owner and operator. One may anticipate that if the occupations studied were more uniform, the similarities of prestige hierarchies from country to country would be even higher.

In other words, *despite the heterogeneity in research design, there exists among the six nations a marked degree of agreement on the relative prestige of matched occupations.* To this extent, therefore, it appears that the "structuralist" expectation is more nearly met than is the expectation based on the culturalist position.

Each of the six nations differs in the extent to which its prestige hierarchy resembles those of other nations. The average of the correlations for each nation, contained in the bottom row of Table 2, expresses these differences among nations quantitatively. Thus we may see that the American and German occupational prestige hierarchies are most similar to those of other nations, while the Soviet and Japanese hierarchies are most dissimilar. When we consider that the Soviet Union and Japan are, of the six, the more recently industrialized cultures, we may see there some small degree of evidence for the culturalist position.

Furthermore, if we examine the correlations among the three nations which have the closest cultural ties and which share a common historical background and language—Great Britain, the United States, and New Zealand—we find these coefficients to be among the highest in Table 2. Again, the evidence to some extent supports the interpretation of a small "cultural" effect. However, the coefficients in question are not sufficiently distinguished in size from those involving Germany [4] and the three Anglo-Saxon nations to allow much weight to be given to the influence of the common Anglo-Saxon culture. In other words, whatever the national differences between the six, they do not greatly affect the general pattern of the prestige hierarchy.

National Patterns of Occupational Prestige

Although the relationships among the six occupational hierarchies are very high, they do not indicate one-to-one correspondences among the national ranks of occupations. Each nation shows some variation from every other, and the international discrepancies may perhaps throw further light on the relationships between social structure, culture, and occupational prestige.

One possibility is that unique aspects of the culture or social structure of a particular country determine distinctive appraisals of a certain type or types of occupation. National differences are thus to be interpreted in a unique fashion for each country.

A second possible explanation is that it is the type of occupation which engenders disagreement, some occupations being similarly rated everywhere and others yielding no consistent rating. To some extent these contrasting explanations are similar, respectively, to the culturalist and structuralist positions discussed earlier.

Here again the available data place marked limits on the possibility of a definitive answer, but it is nevertheless feasible for us to go some distance in exploring the problem. In order to obtain some means by which to assess the presence or absence of disagreement among nations, regression equations were computed to predict the prestige positions of the occupations in one country as against the prestige positions of the comparable occupations in each other country. Ten such equations were computed, interrelating the prestige hierarchies in the United States, Japan, Great Britain, New Zealand, and the Soviet Union but excluding Germany, since the published data on that country indi-

cated only the rank order of occupations. Those occupations which lay more than one standard deviation of the estimate off the regression lines were arbitrarily characterized as occupations over which there was a disagreement between the two nations involved.

Applying this criterion, we have, in Table 3, (p. 566) presented the discrepancies in ratings between all the relevant pairs of nations. The columns show the occupations rated higher by a given country in relation to each of the other countries represented in the rows. Reading the table by rows, we find the occupations rated lower by one country than by other nations, not forgetting that each comparison of a pair of countries involves a somewhat different set of occupations from the comparison of ratings for any other two countries. Only a few occupations, such as farmer, teacher, doctor, factory manager, and some form of industrial worker, were rated in all five countries and therefore appear in all the pairs of comparisons. Some occupations, such as judge, were rated in only two countries and therefore appear in only one paired comparison.[5]

Table 3 serves to highlight the special positions held by certain occupations in particular countries. For example, the Japanese Buddhist priest rates lower than a minister in each of the three available comparisons, and this undoubtedly reflects the cultural differences in structure and role between the Buddhist religion in Japan and the Judeo-Christian religion in the three Anglo-Saxon countries. Equally notable is the consistently lower position of farm manager as rated by displaced persons from the Soviet Union. While the occupation collective farm chairman is not strictly comparable to those with which it is matched, there can be no doubt that the displaced persons regard that occupation with a special ambivalence arising out of the position of agriculture in the Soviet economy during the last three decades.

Table 3. Discrepancies * in the Rating of Matched Occupations by Pairs of Nations

	Rated Higher in Japan	Rated Higher in U.S.	Rated Higher in Great Britain	Rated Higher in New Zealand	Rated Higher in U.S.S.R.
Rated lower in Japan		Minister, farmer, insurance agent, carpenter	Minister, farmer, insurance agent	Minister, farmer, insurance agent	Accountant
Rated lower in U.S.	Company director, labor leader, reporter (news), street sweeper, shoe shiner		Accountant, chef, street sweeper	Accountant, farmer, truck driver, street sweeper	Engineer, worker
Rated lower in Great Britain	Reporter (news), street sweeper	Civil servant, truck driver, minister, building contractor, electrician		Truck driver	Worker
Rated lower in New Zealand	Reporter (news), street sweeper	Civil servant, building contractor, bookkeeper, electrician, dock worker	Chef, bartender		Worker
Rated lower in U.S.S.R.	Factory manager, farmer	Scientist, farmer	Farmer	Farmer	

* We consistently designate any cited occupation by the title closest and most familiar to Americans. For example, we used minister in preference to Buddhist priest, electrician rather than fitter (electrical). For the exact titles see Table 5.

Despite the clarity with which a particular occupation may stand out, it is difficult to find any definite *pattern* characterizing the disagreements expressed by any one country. Of course, such a pattern, if it does exist, may be obscured in our data by the modest number of occupations rated by each country. There are seldom more than one or two occupations of a given type in each of the comparisons, and it is hazardous to assume from the fact, for example, that since the Japanese rate the occupation newspaper reporter higher than Americans, Britishers, or New Zealanders, they would rate occupations *of this type* higher than the other two countries. Nevertheless, it will be noticed that in the country with the largest number of comparisons, the instances of disagreement involve a wide variety of quite disparate occupations. Those rated higher in the United States, for example, range from building contractor to farmer and from scientist to dock worker and appear to have little in common. The same range and absence of a common denominator are shown by the occupations rated lower in the United States. Futhermore, the discrepancies do not consistently appear in all the relevant comparisons: farm owner is out of line in only two out of four comparisons; as to truck driver, the two recorded disagreements go in opposite directions, that occupation being rated higher in comparison with Britain and lower in comparison with New Zealand.

International Comparability of Types of Occupation

If there is no clear-cut pattern of deviance by country, is there perhaps a tendency for certain types of occupation to be foci of disagreement? Perhaps if we classify occupations according to the features of social structure or culture to which they are most closely related, we may gain further insight into the interaction between culture, social structure, and occupational prestige hierarchies. To explore this question, we grouped all the occupations into seven basic types: industrial, clerical and commercial, professional, political, traditional crafts, agricultural, and service occupations.[6] In Table 4 we have indicated the number of international comparisons between pairs among the five countries, again excluding Germany, which could be made involving the occupations in each class of occupations. We have also indicated the proportions of those comparisons which yielded disagreements. Disagreements were recorded on the same

Table 4.   *Discrepancies in Prestige Position According to Type of Occupation*

Occupation Types *	Proportion of Discrepancies (per cent)	No. of Comparisons
Professional	16	31
Industrial	24	29
Political	25	16
Traditional crafts	27	11
Clerical and commercial	32	37
Agricultural	50	16
Service	63	20

* Examples of occupations included in each type are as follows: Professional: *doctor, minister, teacher, etc.;* industrial: *industrial worker, company director, factory manager, engineer;* political: *judge, civil servant, etc.;* traditional crafts: *bricklayer, carpenter, fisherman;* clerical and commercial: *accountant, bookkeeper, salesman, small entrepreneur, etc.;* agricultural: *farm owner and operator, farm hand;* service: *shoe shiner, barber, porter, streetcar conductor, etc.*

Table 5

	United States		Germany		Great Britain		New Zealand		Japan		U.S.S.R.
Occupation	Score	Occupation	Rank	Occupation	Score	Occupation	Score	Occupation	Score	Occupation	Score
Physician	93	Doctor	2	Medical officer	1.3	Medical officer	1.4	Doctor	7.0	Doctor	75
State governor	93							Prefectural gov.	3.8		
College professor	89	Univ. professor	1					Univ. professor	4.6		
Scientist	89									Scientific worker	73
County judge	87			Civil servant	6.0	Civil servant	7.0	Local court judge	4.7		
Head of dept. in state government	87	High civil servant (Regierungsrat—höherer Beamter)	4					Section head of a government office	7.2		
Minister	87	Minister (Pfarrer)	6	Non-conformist minister	6.4	Non-conformist minister	5.9	Priest of a Buddhist temple	12.5		
Architect	86	(Elec. engineer)[a]	10	Country solicitor	2.6	Country solicitor	3.8	(Architect)	9.5		
Lawyer	86										
Member of board of directors of large corporation	86	Factory director (Fabrikdirektor)	5	Company director	1.6	Company director	3.6	Officer of large company	5.5	Factory manager	65
Civil engineer	84	Elec. engineer	10					(Architect)[b]	9.5	Engineer	73
Owner of factory that employs about 100 people	82							Owner of a small or medium-sized factory	10.2		
Accountant for a large business	81			Chartered accountant	3.2	Chartered accountant	5.7	(Company office clerk)[c]	16.1	Bookkeeper	62

Occupation		Occupation		Occupation		Occupation		Occupation		Occupation	
Captain in regular army	80	Major (in armed forces)	8							Officer in the armed services	58
Building contractor	79			Jobbing master builder	11.4	Jobbing master builder	10.7				
Instructor in public schools (teacher)	78	Elem.-school teacher (Volksschullehrer)	11	Elem.-school teacher	10.8	Elem.-school teacher	10.3	Elem.-school teacher	11.7	Teacher	55
Farm owner and operator	76	Farmer (Bauer—mittelgrosser Betrieb)	13	Farmer	7.3	Farmer	8.1	Small independent farmer	16.4	Chairman of collective farm	38
Official of international labor union	75							Chairman of national labor federation	10.8		
Electrician	73			Fitter (elec.)	17.6	Fitter (elec.)	15.8				
Trained machinist	73	Skilled industrial worker (Industrie-facharbeiter)	24								
Reporter on daily newspaper	71			News reporter	11.8	News reporter	13.8	Newspaper reporter	11.2		
Bookkeeper	68	Bank teller (bookkeeper in bank)	19	Routine clerk	16.1	Routine clerk	16.4	Company office clerk	16.1	(Bookkeeper) [d]	62

[a] Used here only for comparison with Japan. For comparison with other countries, see line beginning "United States civil engineer."

[b] Architect is the only occupation of a technical nature in Japan and was used here as a comparison only with the Soviet Union.

[c] Used here only for comparison with the Soviet Union. For comparison with other countries, see line beginning "United States bookkeeper."

[d] Used here only for comparison with Japan. For comparison with other countries, see line beginning "United States accountant for a large business."

Table 5—Continued

Occupation	Score	Occupation	Rank	Occupation	Score	Occupation	Score	Occupation	Score	Occupation	Score
United States:		*Germany:*		*Great Britain:*		*New Zealand:*		*Japan:*		*U.S.S.R.*	
Insurance agent	68	Insurance agent	20	Insurance agent	14.6	Insurance agent	16.1	Insurance agent	20.2		
Traveling salesman for wholesale concern	68			Commercial traveler	12.0	Commercial traveler	14.1				
Policeman	67	Postman	23	Policeman	16.1	Policeman	15.5	Policeman	16.4		
Mail carrier	66										
Carpenter	65	Carpenter	18	Carpenter	18.6	Carpenter	17.0	Carpenter	20.2		
Corporal in regular army	60	Non-commissioned officer	31								
Machine operator in factory	60	Machine operator (Maschinennenschlosser-Geselle)	26	(Composite of fitter, carpenter, bricklayer, tractor driver, coal hewer) [e]	20.5	(Composite of fitter, carpenter, bricklayer, tractor driver, coal hewer) [e]	20.9	Latheman	21.1	Rank-and-file worker	48
Barber	59	Barber	16					Barber	20.5		
Clerk in a store	58	Store clerk (Verkäufer im Lebensmittel geschäft)	28	Shop assistant	20.2	Shop assistant	20.2	Department-store clerk	19.8		
Fisherman who owns own boat	58							Fisherman	22.0		
Streetcar motorman	58	Conductor	33					Bus driver	20.9		
Restaurant cook	54			Chef	13.8	Chef	21.8				

				Rank-and-file collective farmer
Truck driver 54		Carter 25.8	Carrier [f] 20.2	18
Farm hand 50	Farm laborer (worker) 36	Agricultural laborer 25.5	Agricultural laborer 24.4	
Coal miner 49		Coal hewer 23.2	Coal hewer 24.7	Coal miner 23.7
Restaurant waiter 48	Waiter (Kellner) 30			
Dock worker 47		Dock laborer 27.0	Dock laborer 28.3	
Bartender 44		Barman 26.4	Barman 28.3	
Street sweeper 34	(Unskilled laborer) [g] 38	Road sweeper 28.9	Road sweeper 28.9	Road worker 24.8
Shoe shiner 33				Shoe shiner 26.9
	Bricklayer 27	Bricklayer 20.2	Bricklayer 19.3	
	Clothing-store owner 12			Owner of a retail store 15.3
	Tailor 14			Tailor 17.7
	Street peddler 35			Street-stall keeper 24.9
		Business manager 6.0	Business manager 5.3	
		Works manager 6.4	Works manager 7.9	
		News agent and tobacconist 15.0	News agent and tobacconist 15.4	
		Tractor driver 23.0	Tractor driver 22.8	
		Railway porter 25.3	Railway porter 25.3	

e Used here only for comparison with the Soviet Union. For comparison with other countries, see individual occupations as they appear later in the table.
f As there was no comparable occupation in New Zealand, the occupation substituted was carrier.
g Used here only for comparison with Japan.

basis as in the preceding table, that is, on the basis of predictions from regression equations.

Because our findings so far have so strongly supported the structuralist expectation concerning the influence of industrialization in producing uniformity, our initial expectation may well be that occupations closely allied to the industrial system will enjoy highly comparable standings from country to country, while occupations more remotely connected would be the focus of international discrepancies. Table 4 indicates that industrial occupations do enjoy comparable standing in all five countries. Nevertheless, the *lowest* proportion of disagreements is shown by the professions. In addition, other occupational types, such as the political occupations and the traditional crafts, which are not necessarily closely allied to the industrial system, manifested levels of disagreement as low as that enjoyed by the industrial occupations. Only the agricultural and service occupations yield a degree of disagreement which sets them apart from the other occupational groups.

Accounting for these discrepancies appears to require a combination of arguments. In the first place, some types of nonindustrial occupations are easily assimilated to the industrial system. The traditional crafts serve as the prime example here, since the skills involved in such occupations as bricklayer, carpenter, and plumber have a close resemblance to the skills of industrial workers. Indeed, some crafts have been partly incorporated into the industrial system, and, it may be argued, such occupations are easily placed within the hierarchy of industrial occupations and may tend to assume roughly the same position *vis-à-vis* industrial occupations. Likewise, some professions, such as engineering and applied scientific research, have a most immediate connection with the industrial system, and others, such as architecture, are easily equated with it.

However, closeness or assimilability to the industrial system will not suffice to explain the relatively stable position of other professions, such as doctor. Nor will it serve to explain the low proportion of disagreement concerning the political occupations. We must recognize that the nations being compared have certain structural and cultural features in common, in addition to the presence of industry. For example, they share certain needs, as for socialization, and values, such as health and systematic knowledge, which insure relatively comparable standing to doctors, teachers, and scientists. Furthermore, all the countries compared have in common the national state, with which is associated a relatively standardized occupational structure ranging from ministers of state to local bureaucrats. In addition, both the professions and the political occupations are highly "visible," and agreement as to their standing is probably facilitated by the relatively objective and easily perceived indexes of power, knowledge, and skill manifested by their incumbents.

The types of occupation which generate the greatest amount of disagreement are highly variant and unstandardized or difficult to assimilate to the industrial structure. Agriculture may be conducted, as in Japan, on relatively small holdings, on collective farms as in the U.S.S.R., or, as in the western plains of the United States, in "agricultural factories." Being a farmer means very different things in each of the five countries, quite unlike the standardized image of the machinist or the factory manager. It can be anticipated, however, that as agriculture tends to be similarly organized in different countries, agricultural occupations will achieve more uniform standing.

The "service" occupations—barber, shoe shiner, chef, street sweeper—show the greatest amount of variation. Many of them antedate the industrial system and are in agrarian as well as industrial societies. They have no fixed position relative to the industrial order, nor are they similar to typical industrial occupations, as are many of the traditional crafts. They therefore appear to be most easily evaluated according to the traditional culture. Personal service in countries like Japan and Great Britain, in which a servant class was historically well developed and benefited from intimate association with an aristocratic upper class, may still be regarded as not so degrading as in the more democratic societies, such as the United States and New Zealand. In fact, the greatest discrepancy to be found among all the comparisons involves the differences in prestige position accorded to chef in Great Britain as compared with either the United States or New Zealand, although in the case of the former the match was poor, since the comparable occupation was "restaurant cook." As these services come to be organized and mechanized— as in modern laundries or restaurants— they will become more thoroughly integrated into the larger economic order and may in time achieve more strictly comparable status from country to country.

All told, it would appear from this examination of international discrepancies that a great deal of weight must be given to the cross-national similarities in social structure which arise from the industrial system and from other common structural features, such as the national state. The greatest incidence of discrepancies occurs for occupations which are hardest to fit into either the one or the other structure. To this extent the structuralist position which we outlined earlier seems to be more heavily borne out in these data.

Summary and Conclusion

To sum up, our examination of occupational ratings in six modern industrialized countries reveals an extremely high level of agreement, going far beyond chance expectancy, as to the relative prestige of a wide range of specific occupations, despite the variety of sociocultural settings in which they are found. This strongly suggests that there is a relatively invariable hierarchy of prestige associated with the industrial system, even when it is placed in the context of larger social systems which are otherwise differentiated in important respects. In addition, the fact that the countries compared also have in common the national state and certain needs or values, such as interest in health, apparently also contributes to the observed regularity of the ratings, since both professional and political occupations are foci of agreement. Perhaps the most striking finding is the extent to which the different classes of occupation have been woven together into a single relatively unified occupational structure, more or less common to the six countries. At the same time, there is strong evidence that this relatively standardized occupational hierarchy does not apply without major exception to all occupations in all large-scale industrialized societies. In some instances, important disagreement may arise from the distinctive role of a single occupation in a particular country. In the majority of cases, however, the disagreement appears to involve certain classes of occupation, notably agricultural and service, about which there is only modest agreement. Disagreement probably reflects differences in the length and "maturity" of industrialization in various countries but also clearly results from differentiations in sociocultural systems which may well be relatively enduring.

NOTES

1. Additional studies of occupational prestige are available for the United States and for Australia. The authors decided to restrict the United States data to the most comprehensive study available. The Australian case (Ronald Taft, "The Social Grading of Occupations in Australia," *British Journal of Sociology,* 4 [1953]) was not included in this report because it was felt that little was to be gained by the inclusion of another Anglo-Saxon country.

2. (1) A. A. Congalton, "The Social Grading of Occupations in New Zealand," *British Journal of Sociology,* 4 (1953) (New Zealand data); (2) John Hall and D. Caradog Jones, "The Social

Grading of Occupations," *British Journal of Sociology,* 1 (1950) (Great Britain); (3) National Opinion Research Center, "Jobs and Occupations: A Popular Evaluation," in Reinhard Bendix and S. Martin Lipset, *Class, Status, and Power* (Glencoe, Ill.: Free Press, 1953) (United States data); (4) the Schleswig-Holstein data are taken from an article published in *Der Spiegel,* June 30, 1954, reporting a study by Professor Karl-Martin Bolte, of Christian-Albrecht University, in Kiel, Germany, to be published early in 1955; (5) Research Committee, Japan Sociological Society, "Report of a Sample Survey of Social Stratification and Mobility in the Six Large Cities of Japan" (mimeographed; December 1952) (the authors are grateful to Professor Kunio Odaka, of the University of Tokyo, for bringing this valuable study to their attention); and (6) the Soviet materials were collected by the Project on the Soviet Social System of the Russian Research Center at Harvard University.

3. Note that the correlation coefficients are all product-moment correlations, with the exception of the five coefficients involving the German study, which are rank-order correlations. With the exception noted, these coefficients represent the degree of similarity between the prestige *scores* given to the occupations.

4. Since the correlations involving Germany are rank-order correlations, it is difficult to make comparisons of such coefficients with others in Table 1. However, the relationship between rank-order correlations and product-moment correlations is rather high in the upper ranges, and it can be taken for granted that if prestige scores were available for the German ratings, the analysis shown in Table 2 would not be materially altered.

5. Table 5 will be found a useful aid in this connection, since by reading across the rows of that table one can tell quickly how many times a particular occupation was evaluated and by which national samples.

6. See note to Table 4 for examples of occupations included in each type.

The Polity

48. THE PROBLEM OF AUTHORITY

ROBERT BIERSTEDT

There is order in social life, order maintained by various expressions of institutionalized authority. In this essay, Robert Bierstedt examines the problem of defining authority, which, he contends, is at the very bottom of any adequate theory of social structure.

Bierstedt begins by saying what authority is not. It is no "competence" ("he is an authority on Bach . . ."), nor is authority the same as "leadership," for, although a leader may request that his orders be followed, an authority can demand compliance. In short, leadership, like competence, falls under the heading of influence, and authority pertains to the exercise of social control through clearly defined status arrangements between those in superordinate positions and those in positions below. Authority is expressed in a variety of ways in different societies and in different segments of the same society.

These ideas are more fully developed in terms of broader sociological considerations in the pages that follow.

Robert Bierstedt is Professor of Sociology at New York University. His published works include The Social Order: An Introduction to Sociology *(1957; revised 1963),* The Making of Society *(1959), and* Émile Durkheim *(1966).*

Reprinted from *Freedom and Control in Modern Society*, edited by Morroe Berger, Theodore Abel, and Charles H. Page (New York: Van Nostrand, 1954), pp. 67–81, by permission of the author and the publisher.

In the vast complexity which is a human society the exercise of authority is a constant and pervasive phenomenon. Society indeed is impossible without order—in a larger sense society is synonymous with order [1]—and it is authority which serves as the foundation of much of the order which society exhibits. Every day thousands of persons interact with thousands of others in relationships which involve superordination and subordination, the issuance of commands and obedience to them, the announcements of decisions by some and the acceptance of these decisions by others. Here we have a phenomenon of considerable significance and one which requires serious sociological analysis. What is it, in short, that confers upon some men the right to command, upon others the obligation to obey? Why should anyone exercise this right, anyone owe this duty? How does authority contribute to the order which all of the members of a society desire, those who obey as well as those who exact obedience?

If we seek examples of the exercise of authority we shall find them in every sector of society. It is authority which enables the jailor to hand to Socrates the cup of hemlock with the rueful but reasonable expectation that he will drink it; authority which enables the elders of the synagogue to execrate, curse, and cast out Spinoza with all the maledictions written in the book of the law; authority which confers upon an American president the right to remove an imperious general from his commands. On less exalted levels it is authority which enables a vice-president to dictate to his secretary, a sales-manager to assign territories to his salesmen, a personnel manager to employ and discharge workers, an umpire to banish a player from a baseball game, a policeman to arrest a citizen, and so on through innumerable situations. All these can serve to illustrate the ubiquitous character of the phenomenon we are about to analyze.

In inaugurating an inquiry into the nature of authority, however, it is advisable to exercise several cautions. In the first place the sociological literature on this subject, astonishingly enough, is somewhat scanty. Indeed, Florian Znaniecki remarked as late as 1935 that he was unacquainted with any sociological monograph on authority, although he conceded that the historical and political literature was "very rich." [2] In the second place, Roberto Michels, in an article specifically devoted to this problem, an article rich in insights, says nevertheless that "It is futile to discuss the *raison d'être* of authority." [3] Observations like these suggest at least some of the difficulties which an analysis will encounter.

A second caution concerns the fact that the problem of authority is susceptible to treatment on several different levels. One of these levels might be called the philosophic. Here the problem is the apparent opposition between liberty and authority. The literature here, of course, is voluminous, and it embraces in an important sense the entire history of political philosophy from Plato to MacIver. It is an issue, in fact, which is of continuing concern to philosopher and citizen alike. It is not, however, the problem we wish to pursue in this place. Another level might be called the political, that is, the level on which the competence of the political scientist is most relevant. Here we should meet, for example, problems of political obligation, of the particular kind of authority represented by the law, of the delegation of powers, of political power in general, and of public administration. On problems of this kind too there is a large literature and one which it would not be possible to examine in the space at our disposal. There is, however, a third level on which a discussion might proceed, and this level we shall call the sociological. It is less abstract than the first of the levels mentioned and less restricted in scope than the second. On this level we shall be interested in authority wherever we meet it and not only in the political organization of society.

One should not have to contend that the problem of authority in this last sense belongs to sociology. It is indeed obvious that the problem of authority rests at the very bottom of an adequate theory of the social structure. When MacIver, for example, seeks "the authority beyond the authority of government" he knows that even government, in a sense, is not merely a political phenomenon but primarily and fundamentally a social phenomenon, and that the matrix from which government springs itself possesses an order and a structure. If anarchy is the contrary of government so anomie is the contrary of society. Authority, in other words, is by no means a purely political phenomenon in the narrow sense of the word. For it is not only in the political organization of society, but in all of its organization, that authority appears. Each association in society, no matter how small or how temporary it might be, has its own structure of authority.[4]

Before discussing the nature of authority proper it will be convenient if we first distinguish it from two other phenomena with which it is sometimes confused. The first of these is competence. Thus, we commonly speak of a given person as "an authority" on a given subject. Branch Rickey, for example, is an authority on baseball, Lou Little on football, Emily Post on etiquette, Arturo Toscanini on music, Charles H. Goren on bridge, and every professor on the subject he teaches. In this sense authority is related to influence but not to power, and in this sense it has nothing to do with legitimacy and nothing with obligation. It is recognition of competence which encourages us to accept the opinions of those who have achieved prominence and prestige in their special fields of endeavor. There is nothing compulsory about this acceptance, and if we accede at all to opinions of this kind it is as a tribute to eminence rather than as an obeisance to authority. We voluntarily respect the competence of others, but authority requires our submission. When

the situation involves competence, furthermore, one may choose one "authority" rather than another, Casey Stengel rather than Branch Rickey, for example, or Herman Hickman rather than Lou Little, and so on. Competence, in other words, exerts influence; authority exacts obedience.[5]

It is interesting to note in this connection that our language tricks us into error. When we speak of an order or a command having been issued by "competent authority," we do not, curiously enough, mean competence at all. We mean not that the authority is competent, but that it is legitimate. In an inferior position, for example, we may obey the command of a superior whose authority we recognize even when it seems unreasonable, and disobey a command which seems reasonable if we question the authority of the alleged superior to issue it. Superior knowledge, superior skill, and superior competence need not be involved in the exercise of "competent" authority. As Talcott Parsons points out, the treasurer of a corporation may have the authority to sign checks disbursing the corporation's funds, but this does not imply that the treasurer is a better "check-signer" than any one of hundreds of others.[6] The authority to sign checks, in short, has little relation to the capacities of individuals and much less to the caliber of their calligraphy. Robert MacIver, similarly, has said that "The man who commands may be no wiser, no abler, may be in no sense better than the average of his fellows; sometimes, by any intrinsic standard, he is inferior to them."[7]

In view of considerations like these it is difficult to determine why Roberto Michels should begin his discussion with the statement that "Authority is the capacity, innate or acquired, for exercising ascendancy over a group."[8] We shall contend, on the contrary, that there is no clear sense in which authority is a capacity, that it is certainly not innate, and that it is never acquired except in the process of social organization. We shall further contend that it always has an institutional and never, except indirectly, a personal origin.[9]

The second phenomenon with which authority is sometimes confused is the phenomenon of leadership. Here again, for reasons which have considerable cogency, it seems desirable to maintain a distinction. It cannot be said that Max Weber, who otherwise contributed so many penetrating observations on this problem, maintained complete clarity on this point. It is the introduction of charismatic authority into his treatment which prompts this reservation. Weber, as is well known, distinguished charismatic authority from traditional authority on the one hand and from rational-legal authority on the other. Charisma, of course, is a gift of grace which, imputed to a leader by his followers, gives a divine sanction, encouragement, and even justification to his actions. A charismatic leader is believed to be different from other men; he rises above them because he is touched with divinity; there is something of the celestial afflatus about him. It is interesting to notice that persons whose achievements are so impressive that they distinguish them from the multitude are frequently suspected of charisma,[10] and indeed it is of significance for the sociologist of religion that the attribution of charisma seems to be the initial stage in apotheosis.

But leadership is not authority. As in the case of competence, no one is required to follow a leader and no one involuntarily satisfies a leader's desire or grants a leader's wish. The fiat of the leader lacks legitimacy. One may follow or not and no sanction except possibly the informal sanction of being regarded as odd by other followers is applied to those who abstain. The situation is different with respect to authority. A leader can only request, an authority can require. The person subjected to an order by "competent authority" has no alternative but to obey.[11] The examination must be taken at the appointed time, taxes must be paid, the draft induction notice must be observed.[12] Obedience to an authoritative command is not a matter of a subordinate's arbitrary decision. Leadership depends upon the personal qualities of the leader in the situations in which he leads. In the case of authority, however, the relationship ceases to be personal and, if the legitimacy of the authority is recognized, the subordinate must obey the command even when he is unacquainted with the person who issues it. In a leadership relation the person is basic; in an authority relation the person is merely a symbol.

We may summarize these observations by noting that an authority relationship is one of superordination and subordination; the leadership relationship, on the contrary, is one of dominance and submission. These are independent variables. Superordinates may or may not be dominant individuals in a psychological sense; subordinates may or may not be submissive.[13] The exercise of authority does not necessarily involve a personal relationship of any kind. As suggested immediately above, those who exercise authority, especially in the large-scale associations of complex societies, are frequently unaware of the individual identities of the persons over whom the authority is exercised and, conversely, the latter may be unaware of the personal identity of the former. In a military establishment, for example, thousands of men are sent to the far corners of the earth by an official whom they have never seen and whose name they may even fail to recognize. This official, in turn, is unacquainted with the men thus subjected to his command and he may not see or even sign the paper which dispatches them to their destinations. It would be inappropriate to contend that there is any leadership in this situation or that this kind of authority, as Michels has suggested, marks some kind of capacity, "innate or acquired," for ascendancy. Leadership, in short, like competence, is a species of influence; authority is a function of power.

Once we have distinguished authority from competence and from leadership we are prepared to indulge in some statements of a more positive character. Our first observation is perhaps the obvious one that authority is always a property of social organization. Where there is no organization there is no authority. Authority appears only in the organized groups—the associations—of society, never in unorganized groups or in the unorganized community. An absence of organization implies an absence of authority. There is authority only within an association, never in the interstices between associations. The exercise of authority, furthermore, never extends beyond the limits of the association in which it is institutionalized and which gives it support and sanction. The dean of women, for example, may require all women students to be in their domiciles at a certain hour in the evening, but such an order can have no effect upon the young women of the community who are not students at the university. The collector of internal revenue may not examine a candidate for the degree of doctor of philosophy, a policeman may not decide a close play at second base, and so on through all the situations of society.[14] This observation, of course, contributes nothing to the analysis of the phenomenon; it merely gives it a locus. But the locus is significant. If we ask where in society authority obtains, we shall reply in associations, and never anywhere else.

If authority is created in the organization of an association it is necessary, accordingly, to examine the process in which an unorganized group is transformed into an organized one. In this process several things happen. In the first place, informal procedures and patterns of interaction come to be standardized as norms. In the second place, roles come to be standardized as statuses. It is the institutionalization of procedures into norms and roles into statuses which results in the formal organization of the association. Norms and statuses then constitute the structure of the association; they are its organization. More particularly, the role of leader, which one or several members of the group have been playing, comes to be institutionalized in one or several statuses to which authority is now attached in accordance with the norms. These roles become statuses in order that the stability of the association may be assured and its continuity guaranteed.

It is apparent that no association of any size or degree of complexity can maintain a constant membership. The inexorable process of life itself determines that the personnel of the association will change over the course of time. Some associations, of course, cannot survive the individual departures of the people who comprise them because they have no method of recruitment.[15] Any association whose members wish it to survive and to gain an independence of particular personnel must institutionalize its roles into statuses and must create authority where initially there was only leadership. The leader who has been instrumental in organizing the association may subsequently be indisposed or withdraw from the circle of his followers. Unless his role has been institutionalized such a contingency would jeopardize the association's existence. After it has been institutionalized the leader may even be deposed from whatever position of authority he may occupy without damage to the group. A structure is thus necessary if associations are to survive flow of individuals in and out of membership. The supreme test of the organization of an association, in fact, is satisfied when it can sustain a total turnover in personnel.

The formal organization of an association, in short, is constituted of norms and statuses. The norms are attached to the statuses and not to the persons who occupy them. The norms involve rights, duties, privileges, obligations, prerogatives, and responsibilities as they are attached to particular statuses in the structure of the association. The right to exercise authority, that is, the right to make decisions and to enforce them, is now attached to certain statuses, and this right receives the support of all those who belong to the association and who conform to its norms. But the exercise of authority is not only a right; it is also a duty. The occupation of certain statuses implies the obligation to make decisions in the name of the association and the obligation to enforce them.

It is important to recognize that authority is never exercised except in a status relationship. As a right and as a duty it is always attached to a status and is never a matter of purely personal privilege. When an individual issues a command in his own name rather than in the name of the status or position which he occupies, we have a sure indication that it is leadership, not authority, which is being exercised. Sometimes, of course, there is a penumbra of uncertainty with respect to the authority vested in a status, and the right to make a decision, as in jurisdictional disputes, may be more hotly contested than the policy which the decision involves. Similarly, the authority of one status is always exercised over another status and never over an individual as such. It is not the case that Mr. Jones, the vice-president, issues orders to Mr. Jackson, the cashier of a bank. It is the vice-president who issues orders to the cashier in independence of the identity of the individuals who occupy these statuses. Authority is thus a function of the formal organization of an association, and it is exercised in accordance with specific and usually statutory norms and statuses. It makes no appearance in the informal organization. The superordination and subordination of associational statuses is characteristic of all formal social organization and it is this hierarchical arrangement, this stratification of statuses, which permits and indeed makes possible the exercise of authority.

That authority involves a status and not a personal relationship can be illustrated in addition by some interesting cases of status reversal which alter the superordination and subordination of two individuals. One factory-worker may be subordinate to another in the status hierarchy of the factory. In the union local to which they both belong, on the other hand, the latter may be subordinate to the former. In the Navy a commander of the line exercises military authority over all lieutenant commanders, both line and staff, but when he occupies the status of patient he is subject to the orders of a lieutenant commander of the medical corps who occupies the status of doctor. On a civic committee an employer may occupy a status subordinate to that of one of his own employees. For that matter, the President of the United States, superior in several hierarchies, takes orders from the officers of the Secret Service who are charged with the protection of his person. It is obvious that examples of this kind could be multiplied.

In spite of this important distinction it would be improvident to ignore the fact that personal factors do enter into status relationships and that the latter are seldom "pure" except in cases where the two individuals involved are wholly unaware of each other's identity. It is a fact that persons evaluate each other "intrinsically" in terms of their personalities and not only "extrinsically" in terms of their conformity to the norms which their statuses impose upon them. It is an additional fact that the informal organization of an association sometimes takes precedence over its formal organization. Subordinates in these situations frequently exhibit capacities as leaders and begin to play leadership roles; superordinates, on the other hand, frequently withdraw informally from the responsibilities of their statuses and exercise only a nominal authority.[16] Nor can we ignore the familiar phenomenon by which the possession of a status involving authority exerts an influence upon personality. Otherwise submissive individuals, "dress'd in a little brief authority," sometimes assume an authoritarian air, and otherwise dominant individuals, stripped of the perquisites of status, sometimes exhibit a new humility. Recognition of the intrusion of psychological factors does not alter the fact, however, that authority is exercised in a status relationship and not in a personal relationship, and that the relationship becomes increasingly impersonal with increase in associational size.

What, now, sustains the authority exercised by some people over others? Why should a subordinate obey a superordinate when he disapproves of the command? Why, in fact, does subordination not imply agreement, insubordination dissent? Why does an inferior obey a superior whom he may obviously dislike, whom he may never have met, or to whom in other relations he may be totally indifferent? A preliminary answer to these questions has already been suggested: both the superior and the inferior recognize that they are operating in a status relationship and not a personal relationship and that personal sentiments are irrelevant to the exercise of authority in the situation. Indeed, a person is expected and even required to exercise the same kind of authority over friends and intimates that he does over enemies and strangers. In the ideal case the exercise of authority is wholly objective, impartial, impersonal, and disinterested. The judge who has violated a traffic regulation is expected to fine himself.[17]

This observation, however, does not answer the more general question. The reasons people submit to authority, in the larger focus, are the reasons which encourage them to obey the law, to practice the customs of their society, and to conform to the norms of the particular associations to which they belong. This question has received a comprehensive discussion in the literature of political philosophy and sociology and the treatment which Robert M. MacIver has given to it in several of his works is unexcelled.[18] This treatment requires no recital or repetition here. But the reason why men in general conform to the norms does not always explain why particular men accept particular authority especially in situations where the person who exercises authority introduces new norms, when he exercises, in effect, a legislative function. What supports the authority in these instances?

The only possible answer to this question is that authority in these, as in all other cases, is supported, sanctioned, and sustained by the association itself. The person who exercises it is recognized as an agent of the group. He represents the group. He acts not in his own but in the group's name. Insubordination now is a threat not to a personal relationship but to the continued existence of the group. It is an assault upon the group, a denial of the validity of its norms, and, even more significantly, an attack by an individual upon a majority. Since authority is attached to a status, in a system of statuses supported by the majority of the members, and since this system of statuses is synonymous with the organization of an association, it is apparent that any disinclination to accept the status arrangement and the exercise of authority involved in it implies a disinclination to accept the group itself. It is the majority of the members of an association who support its structure and who sustain the authority exercised in particular statuses in accordance with particular norms. If we seek the rationale of authority, therefore, we find it in the very factors which induce men to form associations in the first place, to band together in organized groups, and to perpetuate these associations. It is the desire for stability and continuity which guarantees that the exercise of legitimate authority will be maintained in the statuses of the association, not as an underwriting of particular decisions, but as a bulwark behind the organization of the association itself. An individual who rejects this authority is jeopardizing the continued existence of the association.[19] The ultimate answer therefore to the question of what sustains the authority exercised in an association of any kind is that this authority is sustained by a majority of the association's own members.[20]

We have finally to inquire whether authority is a phenomenon exercised by coercion or by consent. Does the person who accepts a command from superior authority do so, in short, because he has to or because he wants to? Both Barnard and MacIver seem to accept the latter alternative. Barnard, for example, speaking primarily of the nonpolitical associations of society (but including the army), says, "The existence of net inducement is the only reason for accepting *any* order as having authority," and, even more strongly, "The decision as to whether an order has authority or not lies with the persons to whom it is addressed, and does not reside in 'persons of authority' or those who issue these orders." [21] His discussion emphasizes the view that the direction of authority proceeds from the bottom up rather than from the top down in any associational hierarchy. MacIver, similarly, speaking of political authority and the governmental associations of society, says that the identification of authority with power is "inept" and further that "The accent is primarily on right, not power. Power alone has no legitimacy, no mandate, no office." [22] Kingsley Davis, on the other hand, refers to authority as "a system of normatively sanctioned power;" [23] Horace Kallen calls authority "the sanctioned exercise of indirect coercion;" [24] for Lasswell and Kaplan authority is synonymous with "formal power;" [25] and the present writer has defined it as "institutionalized power." [26] Finally, Michels, meeting the dilemma head-on as it were, insists that "Even when authority rests on mere physical coercion it is accepted by those ruled, although the acceptance may be due to a fear of force." [27]

A possible solution to this apparent contrariety of opinions rests in a distinction between two kinds of associations, voluntary and involuntary. In a voluntary association membership is a matter of consent, and people voluntarily give their allegiance to it. They conform to the norms of the association for the same reason, let us say, that they conform to the rules of the games which they play; that is, they conform because the desire to play exceeds the desire to win. Similarly, they accept the authority of others in voluntary associations because the desire to belong exceeds the desire to make independent decisions on matters of associational concern. This is doubtless what Barnard means above by "net inducement." The candidate for the degree of doctor of philosophy, for example, accepts the authority of his examiners to ask him questions, a student accepts the authority of the instructor to evaluate his academic work, and an employee accepts the authority of his employer to assign his duties. In voluntary associations, in short, authority rests upon consent, and it might be appropriate in these circumstances to define authority as institutionalized leadership.

In involuntary associations, however, the situation is somewhat different. A soldier may not defy the order of a superior officer, a citizen may not ignore the demands of the tax-collector, and a prisoner certainly may not refuse to accept the authority of his guards. In certain associations, in other words, voluntary withdrawal is impossible, and these are what we should be inclined to call involuntary associations. In associations like these it would be somewhat unrealistic to deny that coercion is present in the exercise of authority. It is in these situations that authority becomes a power phenomenon, and it is in these that we can define authority as institutionalized power. In voluntary associations, then, we could say that authority is institutionalized leadership; in involuntary associations that it is institutionalized power. In the former authority rests upon consent; in the latter, upon coercion.

This solution, however, is not quite satisfactory. In the first place it is not always easy to distinguish between voluntary and involuntary associations. The distinction is one of degree. There are many associations, in addition, which one may voluntarily join but from which one may not voluntarily withdraw. In the second place, and possibly more important, authority which may or may not be accepted hardly qualifies as authority in accordance with the ordinary connotation of the term. There is something mandatory, not merely arbitrary, about the acceptance of authority and no analysis can quite rationalize this mandatory element away and retain the full significance of the phenomenon. Furthermore, even in what we have called voluntary associations a member who refuses to submit to constituted authority is ordinarily required, in an exercise of authority, to resign. If he refuses to resign there must be still another exercise of authority to compel his withdrawal from the association and to repel the threat to the group as a whole which his insubordination entails. In view of these considerations it would seem as if our problem requires yet another answer.

In order to find this answer we have to dare an apparent disagreement with MacIver. In order to retain the central connotation of the concept we are examining it seems desirable to assert that authority is always a power phenomenon. It is power which confers authority upon a command. But it is sanctioned power, institutionalized power. The power resides in the majority of the members. It is the majority which supports and sustains the association and its norms. This observation enables us to say that authority is always delegated. Its ultimate source is the power of the majority. The formation of an association, its stability and its continuity, involves the formal delegation of the power which resides in the majority to one or several of the group's members as agents of the whole. It is true, of course, that an individual's membership in an association may be a matter of consent and he may

similarly be free to withdraw. But so long as he remains a member, the authority exercised by his superordinates, supported by the majority of the members, is mandatory and not a matter of voluntary determination. The consent in these cases applies to membership in the association and not to the acceptance of the particular commands of constituted authority. Membership may be voluntary, but acceptance of authority is mandatory. It is one of the conditions of membership. Stated alternatively, an individual may be free to belong or not to belong to a particular association, but as a member he is not free to question or to reject the authority exercised by other individuals in accordance with the norms of the association. Considerations like these encourage us to conclude that when consent is involved, as it is in voluntary associations, it applies to the fact of membership and not to the acceptance of authority.

The disagreement with MacIver, however, is only apparent and stems from a slightly different conception of power. We can agree that "power alone has no legitimacy, no mandate, no office," and that authority is not simple power in this sense. But when we say that authority is institutionalized power we attribute a legitimacy, a mandate, and an office to its exercise, and with this proposition there is every indication that MacIver would agree.[28] We have attempted in this chapter to discover how this institutionalization occurs and how it characterizes every association, every organized group, in society. We have suggested in addition that the institutionalization of power is a process which occurs in the formal organization of groups and that it is institutionalized in them as authority. Without the support of the power which resides in the majority of the members of associations there would be no such phenomenon as authority. MacIver's definition of authority as "the established *right*, within any social order, to determine policies, to pronounce judgments on relevant issues, and to settle controversies," [29] is therefore quite in accord with the argument of this chapter. We have merely attempted to show how this right becomes established and how it is sustained. We should maintain, in conclusion, that it is difficult to explain these processes without recourse to the concept of power.

NOTES

1. On the problem of order in general, see Florian Znaniecki, *Cultural Sciences: Their Origin and Development,* Urbana: University of Illinois Press, 1952, Introduction and Chapters 1, 2, and 6.

2. *Social Actions,* New York: Farrar and Rinehart, 1936, p. 673.

3. "Authority," *Encyclopedia of the Social Sciences,* 2, pp. 319–321.

4. The word "association," throughout this paper, is exactly synonymous with "organized group."

5. This distinction has more recondite consequences of a political character than can be considered in this place. Ernest Barker has suggested, for example, that the authority of science can be used to perfect the science of authority. *Reflections on Government,* London: Oxford University Press, 1942, p. 232. See his discussion of this issue, pp. 231–234, and especially the note to p. 232.

6. Note 4 to p. 58 in Max Weber, *The Theory of Social and Economic Organization,* edited by Talcott Parsons, New York: Oxford University Press, 1947.

7. *The Web of Government,* New York: The Macmillan Co., 1947, p. 13.

8. *Loc. cit.*

9. In one sphere, however, it is especially difficult to dissociate the authority of competence from the authority of legitimacy. This is the sphere of religious authority. It is clear that the authority of a philosopher, for example, is the authority of competence and that the authority of the praetor, on the contrary, is the authority of power. But what shall we say about the authority of the pontiff? What supports the decretal issued by a religious hierarch? Is it his competence, the unique capacity imputed to him of direct communication with the deity? Or is it his authority which stems from his superior administrative position in the hierarchy? This situation introduces difficulties of a special and interesting kind and requires, unfortunately, a more elaborate analysis than we can give it here.

10. The biographer of John Maynard Keynes, for example, permits himself to speculate as follows: "In making a final appraisement of Keynes' influence, some may seek to attribute it to a gift or special power that lies outside the range of normal human qualities; they may seek for some mysterious aptitude, some nameless gift, bestowed on him from the unseen world." From R. F. Harrod, *The Life of John Maynard Keynes,* New York: Harcourt, Brace & Co., 1951, p. 646. This suggestion is immediately rejected, but if sophisticated scholars can allude, however lightly, to such a possibility, it is easy to see how the multitude, in any society, might concede charisma to those whose extraordinary achievements win them extraordinary devotion.

11. Unless, as we shall subsequently observe, the situation is rearranged in such a manner that the subordinate is able to withdraw from it.

12. An amusing story comes from England concerning the Londoner who, upon receiving his draft induction notice, replied, "See Luke 14:20." ("I have married a wife and therefore I cannot come.") To which the War Office answered, "Your attention is drawn to Luke 7:8." ("For I also am a man set under authority, having under me soldiers, and I say unto one, Go, and he goeth; and to another, Come, and he cometh.")

13. Leadership qualities, of course, are frequently involved in a man's rising to a position of authority, but this is another process. Frequency is not necessity, as can be seen in countless illustrations, from the monarch to the sheriff, where no test of leadership—or of competence —is imposed.

14. An instance of error in this respect concerns the late General Patton. On a tour of inspection at an army post he became annoyed at a telephone lineman who paid no attention to

his passing and who continued to work at the top of the pole. The lineman refused in addition to obey the general's peremptory command to come down from the pole and stand at attention. At this point the general, near apoplexy as the story goes, demanded to know the man's name and company. The name is unimportant; the company was the Bell Telephone Company.

15. This is Simmel's "broken-plate" pattern.

16. On the intrinsic and extrinsic evaluation of persons see E. T. Hiller, *Social Relations and Structures,* New York: Harper & Brothers, 1947, Chapters 13, 14, and 38. For an illuminating article on formal and informal organization see Charles H. Page, "Bureaucracy's Other Face," *Social Forces,* 25 (1946), 88–94.

17. The writer is indebted to Talcott Parsons for the suggestion that in the ideal case authority is as impersonal as a traffic light.

18. See particularly the section entitled "How and Why Men Obey," *The Web of Government,* pp. 73–81 *et passim;* and *Society: An Introductory Analysis* (with Charles H. Page), New York: Rinehart & Co., Inc., 1949, pp. 142–146 and the whole of Chapter 9, pp. 189–209. For an interesting discussion, one which depends to some extent upon MacIver's, see F. Lyman Windolph, *Leviathan and Natural Law,* Princeton: Princeton University Press, 1951, Chapter 2. This problem ultimately becomes a problem in moral philosophy, the problem of the proper relationship between the individual and his society.

19. Chester I. Barnard has noted in this connection that: "If objective authority is flouted for arbitrary or merely temperamental reasons, if, in other words, there is deliberate attempt to twist an organization requirement to personal advantage . . . then there is a deliberate attack on the organization itself." *The Functions of the Executive,* Cambridge: Harvard University Press, 1938, p. 171.

20. For an elaboration of the role of majorities in organized groups see Robert Bierstedt, "The Sociology of Majorities," *American Sociological Review,* 13 (1948), 700–710.

21. *The Functions of the Executive,* pp. 163, 166.

22. *The Web of Government,* pp. 83, 85.

23. *Human Society,* New York: The Macmillan Co., 1949, p. 48.

24. "Coercion," *Encyclopedia of the Social Sciences, op. cit.,* 3, p. 618.

25. Harold D. Lasswell and Abraham Kaplan, *Power and Society,* New Haven: Yale University Press, 1950, p. 133.

26. "An Analysis of Social Power," *American Sociological Review,* 15 (1950), 733 ff.

27. "Authority," *Encyclopedia of the Social Sciences, op. cit.,* Vol. II, p. 319.

28. Although it involves an additional issue, and one which we have no space to discuss, authority is distinguishable from force in that it always makes some appeal to rationality. An act of authority is not susceptible to argument but it does, in contrast to an act of force, attempt to satisfy the criterion of reason.

29. *The Web of Government,* p. 83. See also *Society,* pp. 146–147.

49. POLITICAL MAN

ROBERT DAHL

Robert Dahl suggests that, while man is a social animal, he is not necessarily a political one. At least not all men are equally "political" (in the sense that all are social). There are marked differences between apolitical individuals and those who are involved as voters, power seekers, and leaders. Moreover, as Dahl points out, the involvement itself varies in terms of degrees of interest, amount of concern over particular issues, the extent of information available, the willingness to participate, and, of course, the idiosyncratic proclivities of citizens.

Robert Dahl is Sterling Professor of Political Science at Yale University. His books include Who Governs? *(1961),* Modern Political Analysis *(1963), and* Political Oppositions in Western Democracy *(1966).*

An elementary starting point for all political theory is the existential fact that members of the human species live together. With few exceptions human beings do not carry on their lives in complete isolation. Whatever may be the elements of instinct, habit, necessity, or choice that induce people to form societies, man has amply demonstrated for thousands of years that he is a social animal. Yet though man is a social animal, neither by instincts nor by learning is he necessarily a political animal—at least not in quite the same sense. Even though they live in a society, men need not concern themselves with the politics of that society, nor participate actively in political life, nor cherish the political institutions and values of their society. Some people do, to be sure; but many . . . do not.

Nonetheless, simply because human beings are social they also develop political systems. Evidently they cannot dwell together without entering into relationships of influence; whenever these relationships become stable and repetitive, political systems exist.

In this looser sense, then, one might say (with Aristotle) that man *is* a political animal. Whatever his own values and concerns as a social being man is inevitably enmeshed in political systems—whether or not he likes or even notices the fact.

However, the individuals who find themselves within the boundaries of a political system are by no means equally concerned with political life. Some people are indifferent to politics, others are more deeply involved. Even among those who are heavily involved in politics, only some actively seek power. And among the power-seekers, some gain more power than the rest.

These four groups—the apolitical strata, the political strata, the power-seekers, and the powerful—can be illustrated in this way:

From Robert A. Dahl, *Modern Political Analysis*, © 1963. Reprinted by permission of the author and Prentice-Hall, Inc., Englewood Cliffs, New Jersey.

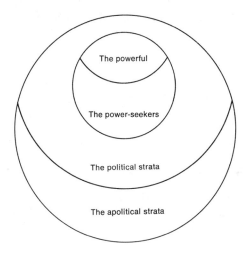

The powerful

The power-seekers

The political strata

The apolitical strata

The Political Strata

The political strata consist of individuals who are psychologically "involved" in governmental decisions. There are various ways in which individuals may be psychologically "involved" in decisions; these different forms of involvement usually run together, but they need not. Four dimensions of involvement in a decision are:

1. Interest—how curious one is to know what is happening.
2. Concern—how important one feels the decision is.

3. Information—how much knowledge one has about the decision.
4. Activity—how much one overtly participates in the decision.

In the United States, and probably in most societies, these four dimensions are correlated. For example, a person who has little interest in a presidential campaign and little concern about the outcome of the election is less likely to acquire information about the campaign and the issues involved, and is also less likely to vote in the election itself, than a citizen who has a great deal of interest and concern.[1] Tables 1 and 2 show how interest, concern, and voting turnout were related in the 1956 presidential campaign.

Table 3 illustrates the relationship between activity and information in the 1956 election. It is hardly surprising, of course, that those who participated most in the 1956 campaign were more familiar with the issues than those who participated less.

Voting, of course, is only one kind of activity. A study of registered voters in New Haven, Connecticut, included a wide variety of activities in addition to voting —nine having to do with campaigns and elections and four having to do with activities outside campaigns. When both interest and concern were combined into a

Table 1.   *RELATION OF DEGREE of Interest in Campaign to Voting Turnout, 1956*

	Degree of Interest in Campaign [a]		
	Not Much Interested	*Somewhat Interested*	*Very Much Interested*
Voted	58%	72%	87%
Did not vote	42	28	13
	100%	100%	100%
Number of cases	540	695	520

Source: *A. Campbell,* et al., The American Voter *(New York: Wiley, 1960), p. 103.*
[a] *Respondents were classified according to their responses to the following question: "Some people don't pay much attention to the political campaigns. How about you? Would you say that you have been very much interested, somewhat interested, or not much interested in following the political campaigns so far this year?"*

Table 2.   *RELATION OF DEGREE of Concern about Election Outcome to Voting Turn-out, 1956*

	Degree of Concern over Election Outcome [a]			
	Don't Care at All	*Don't Care Very Much*	*Care Somewhat*	*Care Very Much*
Voted	52%	69%	76%	84%
Did not vote	48	31	24	16
	100%	100%	100%	100%
Number of cases	230	367	627	459

Source: Ibid., *p. 104.*
[a] *Respondents were classified according to their responses to the following question: "Generally speaking, would you say that you personally care a good deal which party wins the presidential election this fall, or that you don't care very much which party wins?"*

Table 3.   *RELATION OF POLITICAL PARTICIPATION to Level of Issue Familiarity, 1956*

Issue Familiarity		Level of Participation		
		Low	*Medium*	*High*
High	4	16%	30%	45%
	3	17	27	27
	2	18	19	16
Low	1	49	24	12
		100%	100%	100%
	N	394	770	515

Source: *V. O. Key, Jr.,* Public Opinion and American Democracy *(New York: Knopf, 1961), Table 8.1, p. 185.*

Table 4.   *RELATION BETWEEN ACTIVITY in Local Affairs, Interest, Concern, and Information (New Haven, Conn., 1959)*

	Extent of Activity				
	Least	*Low*	*Medium*	*High*	*Highest*
Highly interested and concerned	16%	27%	47%	64%	72%
Highly informed	20%	17%	21%	39%	62%
Number of cases (total)	188	148	89	68	29

single measure, the relationship with activity was very strong. As might be expected, citizens who were the most active in local affairs were also likely to be better informed.

The Apolitical Strata

Because there are several dimensions of involvement, and because each dimension is more or less continuous, the political stratum shades off gradually into the apolitical strata; an exact boundary between the political strata and the apolitical strata must, therefore, be arbitrary. Nonetheless, it is probably true that in most political systems those who display great political interest, concern, information, and activity are not a large proportion of the adults; generally, no doubt, they are a minority. Even in a democratic society the political strata do not include all citizens, for even in democracies a sizeable number of citizens are apathetic about politics and relatively inactive. There are, to be sure, variations from one democracy to another and from time to time; but the existence of political apathy and indifference among many citizens in a democracy seems to be nearly universal. Even the Greek city-states, which are sometimes held up as models of democratic participation (aside from the slaves), were not immune. In Athens, for example, the *demos* was often indifferent. Aristotle wrote of fourth century Athens:

Payment for attendance at the assembly was, at first, a step which they (i.e., the restored democrats, once more in control after the perturbations at the end of the Peloponnesian War) refused to take. The citizens, however, failed to attend; and the presidents of the assembly were driven to one device after another in order to induce the populace to present themselves for the purpose of ratifying measures. In these circumstances Agyrrhius began by providing an obol a day for attendance: Heraclides . . . increased it to two obols; and Agyrrhius afterward advanced it to three.

By Aristotle's time, citizens received 6 obols a day for attending the Assembly, the town meeting of Athens.[2]

Sometimes, too, New England town meetings are regarded as a model. But just as in Athens, in New England towns many citizens were unconcerned about exercising their rights or fulfilling their political obligations. In New Haven, for example, the problem seems to have been a persistent one. In 1642 the General Court of the Colony "voted that any freeman who after due warning, should fail to appear in the General Courts before the Secretary finished the roll-call, should be fined 1s. 6d; and that any of the rest of the planters who should be absent after their names were read, should be fined one shilling. The novelty of the first few years had worn away, and attendance at the General Courts seemed, to many, burdensome." A century later the problem was still unsolved in New Haven. In 1784 the old colonial town officially became a city, and the first city elections were held. Of some 600 males living in the city, about 250 were excluded as voters either because they could not meet the property requirements or because they had been loyal to Great Britain. Of the 343 eligible males, about one-fourth failed to take the oath and hence could not vote in the first election. Although most of those who were qualified to vote did actually vote for the mayoralty candidates, two days later only about a hundred citizens (out of 261 eligible) showed up to vote for the councilmen.[3]

The problem is still acute today. Only a minority of adult American citizens vote regularly and participate in other ways. In 1950 two well-known pollsters reported the results of a survey of political activities among a cross-section sample of 8,000 adult Americans. The results are shown in Table 6. Except for voting once or more in the preceding four years, only a minority—usually a small minority—of the respondents had engaged in the forms of political activity listed.

Obviously man is not instinctively a political animal. It is true that few people ever live outside a political system; it is also true that by the standards of most of us the benefits of living in political systems far outweigh the disadvantages. Nonetheless, though human beings must and do live in political systems and share the benefits of political life, they do not necessarily participate in political life; they are not necessarily interested in poli-

Table 5. *POLITICAL ACTIVITIES OF AMERICAN CITIZENS*

Voting	
Once or more in last four years	75%
Three times or more	47
Five times or more	21
Discussing public issues with others	
Discusses frequently and takes an equal share in the conversation	21
Discusses frequently and usually tries to convince others he is right	6
Belonging to organizations that take stands on public issues	
Belongs to one or more such organizations	31
Belongs to two or more	7
Written or talked to congressman or other public official to give own opinion on a public issue	
One or more times in past year	13
Two or more times in past year	7
Worked for election of a political candidate in last four years	11
Contributed money to a party or candidate in last four years	7

Source: *Julian L. Woodward and Elmo Roper, "Political Activity of American Citizens,"* The American Political Science Review, *Vol. 44 (December, 1950), pp. 872–885.*

tics, nor do they always care what happens in politics, know much about political events, or share in making decisions. In most political systems, in fact, the political stratum is a minority of the adult population. Moreover, those who are *highly* interested, concerned, informed, and active are an even smaller minority within the political stratum.

Why is it that even in modern societies with widespread education, universal suffrage, and democratic political systems the apolitical stratum is so large? To answer this question would require much more space than can be given here, but a short if somewhat formal answer can be indicated. Essentially there seem to be three reasons why an individual does not become involved in politics.

1. *An individual is unlikely to get involved in politics if he places a low valuation on the rewards to be gained from political involvement relative to the rewards expected from other kinds of human activity.* For many people political activity is a good deal less gratifying than other outlets—family, friends, recreation, and the like. For many, political involvement yields far less affection, income, se-

curity, respect, excitement, and other values than working at one's job, watching television, reading, fishing, playing with the children, attending a football game, or assembling a new hi-fi set. For many, the rewards of political involvement are distant and vague, whereas the rewards of other activities are more immediate and concrete. In short, for many people the opportunity costs of political involvement are simply too high to make it worthwhile. These people are unwilling to forego immediate, certain, and concrete benefits or gratifications derived from non-political activities in order to obtain the more remote, uncertain, and abstract benefits that might ensue from political participation.

Just why political involvement is not more rewarding for more people is a question for which no short or easy answer is possible. The explanation, no doubt, turns on the fact that man is not by instinct a reasonable, reasoning civic-minded being. Many of his most imperious desires and the source of many of his most powerful gratifications can be traced to ancient and persistent biological and physiological drives, needs, and wants. Organized political life arrived late in man's evolution;

Table 6. *RELATION OF SENSE of Political Efficacy to Voting Turnout in the 1956 Presidential Election*

	Sense of Political Efficacy				
	Low				*High*
Voted	52%	60%	75%	84%	91%
Did not Vote	48	40	25	16	9
	100%	100%	100%	100%	100%
Number of cases	263	343	461	501	196

Source: *Campbell,* et al., op. cit., *Table 5–6, p. 105.*

today man learns how to behave as a political man with the aid and often with the hindrance of instinctive equipment that is the product of a long prior development. To avoid pain, discomfort, and hunger; to satisfy drives for sexual gratification, love, security and respect—these needs are insistent and primordial. The means of satisfying them quickly and concretely generally lie outside political life.

2. *An individual is unlikely to get involved in politics if he thinks that the probability of his influencing the outcome of events, of changing the balance of rewards by means of his political involvement, is low.* Individuals do not engage in activity merely because the *possible* rewards are high, if the *probability* of gaining the rewards is very low. Even though the pay-off to Irish Sweepstakes winners is very high, not everyone buys a ticket, for many people feel that the chance of winning is so slight that they are simply throwing their money away. In the same way, citizens who are pessimistic about their capacity to influence political events may eschew politics on the ground that what they do won't matter anyway. Voters sometimes neglect to vote because they feel that one vote won't change the outcome; citizens often fail to press their views on public officials because they believe that public officials won't pay attention to people like themselves.

Surveys show a strong relationship between a person's sense of political efficacy (the confidence that what one does really matters) and the extent of his political involvement. The weaker one's sense of political efficacy, the less likely one is to become involved. Table 6 is a typical illustration of this relationship. The table shows a strong relation between a sense of political efficacy and voting turnout in the 1956 presidential election. Of those with the highest confidence, 91 per cent voted, compared with only 52 per cent among those with the lowest degree of confidence.

Figure 2 shows another example. This table shows the relationship among a sample of voters in New Haven between the sense of political efficacy and a general index of local action. The index of local action combines a large variety of campaign, electoral, and non-campaign activities and thus is a more comprehensive measure of political involvement than mere voting.

The confidence one has in one's capacity to be effective in political life depends on many factors. In the United States the sense of efficacy rises with income, social standing, political experience, and, most of all, education. Of course, a person's sense of confidence may also simply reflect a realistic appraisal of his influence. Thus it is hardly surprising that among sub-leaders in various political organizations in New Haven, more than 8 out of 10 possess a relatively high sense of efficacy (Fig. 3). Probably one's "personality" has some bearing on one's sense of efficacy. Optimism or pessimism about

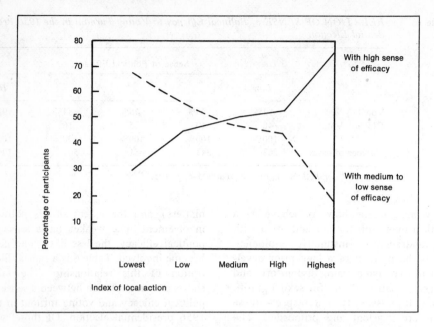

Figure 2. The more a person participates in local affairs, the more likely he is to have a high sense of political efficacy. (Source: Robert A. Dahl, "Who Governs? Democracy and Power in an American City" (New Haven: Yale University Press, 1961), p. 288.)

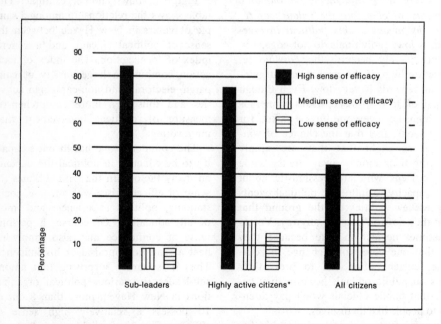

Figure 3. Sub-leaders have a very high sense of political efficacy. (Source: Dahl, op. cit., p. 289.)

one's chances of influencing policy is probably related to deeper personality factors, such as an underlying sense of confidence or lack of confidence that pervades a person's entire outlook.

3. *An individual is unlikely to get involved in politics if he believes that the outcome will be relatively satisfactory to him without his involvement.* A citizen who believes that some political decision is important might nevertheless not become involved if he feels quite confident that the decision will turn out well anyway. Just as low confidence in one's political efficacy discourages participation, so high confidence in the all-round justice, legitimacy, stability, and fairness of decisions in one's political system may make one's own participation seem unnecessary. One might expect political involvement to decrease during periods of prosperity and rise during depressions. A comparison of the turnout in United States presidential elections and major periods of depression and prosperity does indeed show some relation; though so many factors influence voting turnout that the results must be interpreted cautiously. However, the percentage of eligible voters who voted in presidential elections climbed to a sharp peak in 1876 during the depression that lasted from 1873–1878. The Greenback Movement and Populism were undoubtedly stimulated by the depressions of 1873–1878 and 1893–1897. The percentage of eligible voters who went to the polls rose during the Great Depression of 1929–1939.

Power-Seekers and Leaders

Within the political strata, some persons seek power much more actively than others. And some persons gain much more power than others. Within the political strata, then, there is a sub-stratum of *power-seekers* and a sub-stratum of powerful *leaders.*

You will notice that what we have just said is a restatement of two propositions set forth as empirical characteristics of political systems:

1. Some members of the political system seek to gain influence over the policies, rules, and decisions enforced by the government.

2. Political influence is distributed unevenly among adult members of a political system.

Now to seek power and to gain power are by no means the same thing. Although the two phenomena—seeking power and gaining power—are sometimes confused, clearly they are distinguishable. Not only are some power-seekers unsuccessful in their efforts to gain power; some people who gain power may not actually seek it. This might occur, for example, among those who, like a monarch or a feudal lord, acquire their power by inheritance. In Table 7 the two different dimensions are combined to yield four categories.

Table 7.   *SEEKING POWER AND GAINING POWER*

		Extent of Seeking Power	
		Little or No Active Search	*Highly Active Search*
Extent of power gained	Much	Powerful leaders who do not seek power	Successful power-seekers
	Little or none	Non-leaders who do not seek power	Unsuccessful power-seekers

We have, then, two important questions: Why do some people seek more power than others? And why do some people gain more power than others?

The Power-Seekers

Every human being has access to resources of some kind. His resources may be pitifully meager—a tiny barren patch of land that barely yields enough food to sustain his life, the labor-time he sells to a landlord for a pittance, a primitive wooden hoe. Or his resources may be enormous and varied—the wealth of a pasha, a famous family name, control over means of communication, a high public position, widespread popularity, a disciplined and loyal band of associates and followers, a far-flung bureaucracy for acquiring intelligence and analyzing information.

These resources could, in principle, nearly always be applied to more than a single purpose. The poor half-starved peasant in his wintry hour of need could burn his wooden hoe in a last desperate struggle to survive; he could use it to club an intruder or drive off an animal; or he and his fellows could use their labor-time and their hoes to overpower the landlord and rob his grain bin.

Nearly always, too, these resources could, in principle, be applied to change the expected behavior of someone else, in a word: to influence others. Frequently, in fact, these resources could be used to create a threat of severe penalties and thus offer the chance of gaining power over others.

Generally, then, human beings have access to some political resources, however paltry these may be. But human beings have many goals. Often, too, they can employ different means to achieve a given goal. Not all men apply their resources to gaining power. Yet some, the power-seekers, do. Why?

The answers to this question can be grouped into three categories.

1. Men seek power, it is said, in order to achieve the collective good. They wish to protect the interests of all citizens, achieve justice for all, benefit the state, or provide for life, liberty, and the pursuit of happiness. This is the argument attributed to Socrates in Plato's *Republic:*

> So far as arts are concerned, then, no art ever studies or enjoins the interests of the superior or stronger party, but always that of the weaker over which it has authority.
>
> Thrasymachus assented to this at last, though he tried to put up a fight. I then went on:
>
> So the physician, as such, studies only the patient's interest, not his own . . . ; and the ship's captain . . . will study and enjoin the interests of his subordinates, not his own.
>
> He agreed reluctantly.
>
> And so with government of any kind: no ruler, insofar as he is acting as ruler, will study or enjoin what is for his own interest. All that he says and does will be said and done with a view to what is good and proper for the subject for whom he practises his art.[4]

Now the difficulty with this debate between Socrates (or Plato) and Thrasymachus is that the two men are talking right past one another. This often happens in political controversy; each opponent vigorously flails an argument the other did not make, and thereby fails to meet head-on the precise point the other did make. In this case Socrates was making a *normative* argument, Thrasymachus an *empirical* one. Socrates met Thrasymachus' attempt to describe how rulers generally *do* act by indicating how good rulers *ought* to act.

Socrates and Plato knew perfectly well that rulers of states do not in fact always rule in the interests of their subjects. Indeed, to both Socrates and Plato the very meaning of a bad or perverted state was that the rulers did not seek the good of those over whom they ruled. Later on in the *Republic* Plato undertakes a description of the tyrant:

> . . . In every one of us, even those who seem most respectable, there exist desires, terrible in their untamed lawlessness, which reveal themselves in dreams. . . . Thus,

when nature or habit or both have combined the traits of drunkenness, lust, and lunacy, then you have the perfect specimen of the despotic man. . . . When the number of such criminals and their hangers-on increases and they become aware of their strength, then it is they who, helped by the folly of the common people, create the despot out of that one among their number whose soul is itself under the most tyrannical despotism.[5]

In sum, many political philosophers have argued that leaders *should* seek power in order to exercise authority for the good of all. But probably no student of politics has ever really argued that this is the only reason, or even the principal reason, why men *do* in fact seek power.

2. Men seek power, it has been argued, in conscious pursuit of their self-interest. This was the argument of Thrasymachus that Socrates purported to attack. Thrasymachus had said (according to Plato).

What I say is that "just" or "right" means nothing but what is to the interest of the stronger party. . . . In every case the laws are made by the ruling party in its own interest; a democracy makes democratic laws, a despot autocratic ones, and so on. By making these laws they define as "right" for their subjects whatever is for their own interest, and they call anyone who breaks them a "wrongdoer" and punish him accordingly. This is what I mean: in all states alike "right" has the same meaning, namely what is for the interest of the party established in power, and that is the strongest.[6]

Thrasymachus may well have represented an early Greek attempt to find naturalistic explanations for political behavior. Since nearly all we know of him comes from his enemy Plato, his argument in the *Republic* is probably somewhat distorted. Evidently Thrasymachus was trying to explain how it is that although rulers always proclaim that they are seeking justice, different rulers impose different ideas of justice on their states. To Thrasymachus the obvious explanation of the paradox was that each ruler was simply pursuing his own self-interest; "justice" as it was actually defined in the laws of each state was a mere ideological rationalization for the self-interest of the rulers. It is quite possible that Thrasymachus used his analysis to uphold traditional Athenian democratic institutions against subversion by supporters of oligarchy who insisted that they and they alone were concerned for the good of the state. Undoubtedly he also employed his analysis to undermine the appeal of Plato's elaborate defense of aristocracy, which Thrasymachus probably believed was no more than a brilliant rationalization for the antidemocratic ambitions of the oligarchical faction in Athens.[7]

Thrasymachus' hypothesis that men deliberately seek power for reasons of self-interest has been restated many times. Hobbes, for example, held that men were impelled by their passions and guided by their reason. Passion is the wind that fills the sails, reason the hand on the rudder. Man, to use another metaphor, is a chariot pulled by the wild horses of passion and steered by reason. Men's desires are insatiable, but reason dictates prudence. With the aid of his reason, man can discover the general rules or precepts that will enable him to improve his chances of gaining the ends his passions dictate. All men, then, seek power in order to satisfy their passions. But reason tells them *how* to seek power so as to reduce frustration, defeat, and the chances of violent death.

One difficulty with this hypothesis, as Plato rightly saw, is that the notion of "self-interest," which seems transparently obvious, is actually very complex. What one views as his "self" depends on one's identifications, and evidently these vary a good deal. How one perceives the "self" is not wholly instinctive, it seems, but also a matter of social learning. Likewise, what one considers to be in the "interest" of the self is shaped by learning, experience, tradition and culture. Consequently, to attribute an act to self-interest does not explain very much. As a distinguished modern psychologist has said:

. . . the self comprises all the precious things and persons who are relevant to an individual's life, so that the term selfish loses its original connotation, and the proposition that man is selfish resolves itself into the circular statement that people are concerned with the things they are concerned with.[8]

Jones' self-interest can mean Jones' pursuit of advantages for himself alone. Or it can mean his attempt to obtain advantages of all kinds for himself and his family. The Jones family now becomes the "self" and its "interests" run from acquisitiveness to zoology. Or Jones' self-interest can mean his attempt to obtain advantages for larger strata with which he identifies—his neighborhood, region, class, religion, ethnic group, race, nation. Thus both the "self" with which Jones identifies and the range of ends he regards as in the "interests" of the self may be extremely narrow or very wide, depending on learning, experience, tradition and culture. Anthropological studies testify to the fact that notions of "self," "interest," and "self-interest" vary widely among human beings.

A second objection to rational self-interest as an explanation is posed by post-Freudian psychology. Thrasymachus, Hobbes, Jeremy Bentham, and Marx all interpreted the search for power as "rational" and conscious pursuit of self-interest. But Freud showed that the "desires, terrible in their untamed lawlessness," of which Socrates spoke did more than drive human beings into conflict with one another (as Hobbes argued); they also drive human beings into conflict with themselves. These inner conflicts, according to Freud, are fierce gales that often blow out the flickering light of reason. Reason, as Freud saw it, cannot always guide the chariot drawn by passion, for these violent steeds turn on one another and in their battle the reins of reason become entangled.

Freud discovered, analyzed, and stated what those keen students of human psychology, the great playwrights and novelists, had always known. But since Freud's day, several social scientists have attempted to develop systematic theories dealing with the search for power.

3. Men seek power, some recent students of politics argue, from unconscious motives. One of the most influential contemporary explanations of power-seeking is Lasswell's. His theory can be summarized as follows. The power-seeker pursues power as a means of compensating for psychological deprivations suffered during childhood. Typical deprivations that engender power-seeking are a lack of respect and affection at an early age. The self, then, suffers damage; the individual acquires a low estimate on the self. (The self usually includes more than the "primary ego," the "I" or "me"; it includes parents, wife, children, friends, countrymen, co-religionists and others.) In childhood, adolescence, or perhaps later, the power-seeker learns to compensate for this low estimate of the worth of his "self" by pursuing power. He comes to believe that by acquiring power he can either make the self better, and hence more loved and respected, or he can change the attitudes of others about his "self." With power he will become important, loved, respected, admired. He hopes, then, to acquire through power relationships the affection and respect he failed to acquire in his family relationships. None of this behavior, of course, need be impelled by conscious, "rational" thought. On the contrary, a great deal of the motivation is likely to be unconscious. The power-seeker does not necessarily have much insight into why he seeks power; he rationalizes his power-seeking in terms acceptable to his conscious values and perhaps the prevailing ideology among those with whom he identifies. In comparison with other people, then, the power-seeker is a person who:

a. Places a high value on gaining power.
b. Demands power (and other values) for the self (the primary ego plus incorporated symbols of other egos).

c. Has relatively high confidence that he can gain power.

d. Acquires at least a minimum proficiency in the skills of power.[9]

Lasswell himself has questioned whether his power-seeker is likely to be very effective in *achieving* power, since he is likely to stimulate too much dislike and distrust to acquire much support. Robert Lane also argues that a number of recent findings suggest that a strong desire to gain power over other people is not correlated with political activity, at least in democratic systems. Lane furnishes several explanations for this paradox:

a. "To be successful in politics a person must have sufficient interpersonal skills to relate himself effectively to other men and must not be so consumed with power drives that he loses touch with reality. A person with a raging desire for power . . . will constantly alienate his supporters, thereby making the achievement of power impossible for him."

b. "One of the most common sources of the need for power over others is the deeper need for reassurance about the self. . . . This need for reassurance is, of course, related to lack of self-confidence, feelings of unworthiness, or low esteem. (But) . . . a feeling of personal effectiveness is highly related to participation."

c. "The power-seeker may find his needs sublimated in other ways than political activity, at least as this term is ordinarily defined." [10]

Conclusion

Of the three explanations for seeking power that we have explored, none seems entirely satisfactory. However, our discussion does suggest several conclusions:

First, whatever the reasons may be, some people do seek power more intently than others.

Second, scientific knowledge about the personalities and motives of power-seekers is still scanty. Everyone agrees that some people seek power more ardently than others, but authorities disagree over why they do.

Third, it seems evident that men seek power not only for its own sake but because of its instrumental value. Power can be used to gain a great variety of ends. Depending on culture, society, economy, and political system, power (as Lasswell and many others have pointed out) can be used to acquire fame, reverence, security, respect, affection, wealth and many other values. It is not surprising, then, that men should seek power; nor should we necessarily assume that power-seeking is abnormal or pathological. In its instrumental character, power is like money. Some men invest more effort in gaining money than others do; they do not necessarily do so because they value money, as such, more highly than others but because they see money as an instrument to other goals.

Fourth, power-seeking, like other behavior, is no doubt usually a compound of conscious and unconscious motives. Men who seek power may know some of the reasons why they do so; we can hardly expect them to know all the reasons.

Fifth, it seems unlikely that all power-seekers have substantially similar personalities. There are too many different reasons, conscious and unconscious, why one might want power, and too many variations in the costs and benefits of power from one political system to another and from one time to another. Undoubtedly both Caligula and Abraham Lincoln sought power. Yet it is highly implausible to suppose that Caligula and Lincoln had even approximately the same kind of personality.

The Powerful

Not all power-seekers, we have said, gain power. Indeed, though it is probably uncommon, some men who do not seek to gain and wield power may nevertheless exercise it. Why do some people gain more power than others?

In principle, if one gains more power than another (over X, with respect to Y) [11] then we may look to two possible sources of explanation to account for differences in the amount of power—to differences in the amount of resources used, and to differences in the skill or efficiency with which the resources are applied. Some people use more resources to gain power than others do. Some people use what resources they have more efficiently, more skillfully.

Why do some people use more resources than others do to gain power? Presumably because they expect to "gain more" by doing so. I may "gain more" than you from a given action either because the action is "less costly" to me or because the outcome of the action is "more valuable" to me. If A has more resources than B—if, say, A is wealthier than B—then a given outlay is less costly for A than for B (all other things being equal) because A has to forgo fewer alternatives than B. Or, in the language of the economist, A's opportunity costs are lower.

A man of wealth and a good deal of leisure can devote 60 hours a week to non-paying political activities at considerably lower opportunity cost than the man who has to work long hours to make a living. In short, if A has more resources than B, the opportunity costs of allocating a given amount of those resources to gaining power are less for A than for B. A can make the same outlays as B at less opportunity cost or more outlays at the same opportunity cost. In general, then, some people use more resources to gain power than others do because they have access to more resources. And, all other things being equal, it is reasonable to expect that people with more resources would gain more power. To this extent, then, differences in power and power-seeking are related to differences in objective circumstances.

However, "all other things" are not usually equal. Even if their resources were objectively identical, A might allocate a greater share of his resources in order to gain power if he places a higher value on the results. Why might A place a higher value than B on the results of an outlay of resources to gain power?

Because A might expect different results from B.

Because, though both expect the same results, A and B use different values or different scales to appraise the results.

Because, though they expect the same results, A feels more confident about the outcome than B does.

However, A's application of more resources may not result in more power (measured in any of the ways described in the last chapter) if B has more skill than A. A deft politician may accomplish more with little than a clumsy politician can accomplish with a great deal. Why then do some people have more skill in politics than others?

This is a difficult question to answer. To try to do so would carry on beyond the limits of this book. In brief, however, there are three possible explanations for a difference in skill between two persons, whatever the skill may be, whether walking a tightrope over the Niagara, playing the part of Mimi in "La Boheme," or serving as majority leader in the United States Senate. These are:

1. Genetic differences.
2. Differences in opportunities to learn.
3. Differences in incentives to learn.

The first two are differences in situations, the third is a difference in motivations.

The question we started out to answer a moment ago, you may remember, was, Why do some people gain more power than others? Let us now summarize our explanation.

Once again, the argument points to the conclusion that men who gain power need to be similar to one another only in cer-

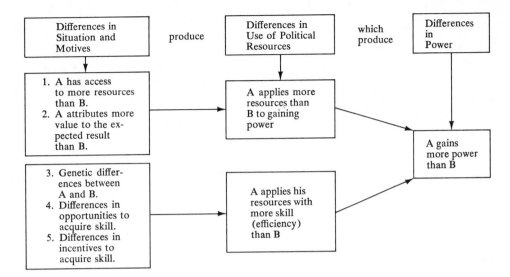

tain formal respects. In fact, the concrete characteristics of leaders seem to vary a good deal in different political systems, different times, and different situations. Leaders have different social origins, different resources, different skills, different personalities. Among those who have sought and gained power, the range of human types runs from Napoleon Bonaparte, the Corsican upstart, to Winston Churchill, descendant of seven Dukes of Marlborough; from Caesar, the military genius, to Woodrow Wilson, historian, political scientist, and college president; from the detached and reflective Hadrian to Savonarola, the fanatic; from the regal Elizabeth the First to Madame de Pompadour, the witty mistress of Louis XV; from the serene stoicism of the philosopher Marcus Aurelius to the neurosis of Hitler and the paranoia of Stalin; from Caligula to Lincoln.

NOTES

1. Robert Lane, *Political Life,* New York: Free Press, 1959, pp. 143 ff., and Angus Campbell, *et al., The American Voter,* New York: Wiley, 1960, pp. 101 ff.

2. Aristotle, *On the Constitution of Athens,* Appendix IV, in Barker (ed.), pp. 379, 383.

3. Charles H. Levermore, *The Republic of New Haven,* Baltimore: Johns Hopkins University Press, 1886, pp. 44, 231.

4. *The Republic of Plato,* translated with introduction and notes by F. M. Cornford, New York: Oxford University Press, 1945, pp. 23–24. The English translations of Plato's *Republic* often vary somewhat, but in the passages quoted here the differences are not significant. The student may wish to compare *The Dialogues of Plato,* translated by B. Jowett, New York: Random House, 1937, I, 607–608; and *Plato, The Republic,* translated by P. Shorey, New York: Putnam, The Loeb Classical Library, 1930, p. 63.

5. *The Republic of Plato,* in Cornford, trans., *op. cit.,* pp. 297, 298 and 300.

6. *Ibid.,* p. 18.

7. On this point see Eric A. Havelock, *The Liberal Temper in Greek Politics,* New Haven: Yale University Press, 1957, p. 231 and *passim.*

8. Gardner Murphy, "Social Motivation," in G. Lindzey (ed.), *Handbook of Social Psychology,* Cambridge, Mass.: Addison-Wesley, 1954, 2 Vols., 2, 625. On the influence of social learning on the self, see also E. H. Erikson, *Childhood and Society,* New York: Norton, 1950.

9. Harold Lasswell, *Power and Personality,* New York: Norton, 1948, Ch. 3, "The Political Personality," *passim.*

10. Lane, *op. cit.,* pp. 126–128.

11. For convenience, the clause in parenthesis will be dropped from time to time, though it would be formally necessary to give more precise meaning to the sentence.

50. "POWER ELITE" OR "VETO GROUPS"?

WILLIAM KORNHAUSER

William Kornhauser is concerned with the origin, change, distribution, sustenance, and consequences of power in the United States. He begins by presenting two well-known theses: C. Wright Mills' contention that America is ruled by a central "power elite" and David Riesman's argument that diversified interests are served by a plurality of "veto groups" which maintain a balance of authority.

After comparing the somewhat polemical assertions of Mills and Riesman on a number of critical points, Kornhauser specifies certain fundamental issues in the analysis of power relationships that, he feels, must be explored before the disagreements may be fruitfully resolved.

William Kornhauser is Professor of Sociology at the University of California in Berkeley. He is the author of Politics of Mass Society (*1959*) and of Scientists in Industry: Conflict and Accommodation (*1962*).

In the 50's two books appeared purporting to describe the structure of power in present-day America. They reached opposite conclusions: where C. Wright Mills found a "power elite," David Riesman found "veto groups." Both books have enjoyed a wide response, which has tended to divide along ideological lines. It would appear that *The Power Elite* has been most favorably received by radical intellectuals, and *The Lonely Crowd* has found its main response among liberals. Mills and Riesman have not been oblivious to their differences. Mills is quite explicit on the matter: Riesman is a "romantic pluralist" who refuses to see the forest of American power inequalities for the trees of short-run and discrete balances of power among diverse groups. [244] [1] Riesman has been less explicitly polemical, but he might have had Mills in mind when he spoke of those intellectuals "who feel themselves very much out of power and who are frightened of those who they think have the power," and who "prefer to be scared by the power structures they conjure up

than to face the possibility that the power structure they believe exists has largely evaporated." [257–258] [2]

I wish to intervene in this controversy just long enough to do two things: 1) locate as precisely as possible the items upon which Riesman and Mills disagree; and 2) formulate certain underlying issues in the analysis of power that have to be met before such specific disagreements as those between Riesman and Mills can profitably be resolved.

We may compare Mills and Riesman on power in America along five dimensions:

1) structure of power: how power is distributed among the major segments of present-day American society;
2) changes in the structure of power: how the distribution of power has changed in the course of American history;
3) operation of the structure of power: the means whereby power is exercised in American society;
4) bases of the structure of power: how

social and psychological factors shape and sustain the existing distribution of power;

5) consequences of the structure of power: how the existing distribution of power affects American society.

Structure of Power

It is symptomatic of their underlying differences that Mills entitles his major consideration of power simply "the power elite," whereas Riesman has entitled one of his discussions "who has the power?" Mills is quite certain about the location of power, and so indicates by the assertive form of his title. Riesman perceives a much more amorphous and indeterminate power situation, and conveys this view in the interrogative form of his title. These contrasting images of American power may be diagrammed as two different pyramids of power. Mills' pyramid of power contains three levels:

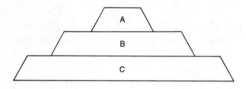

The apex of the pyramid (A) is the "power elite": a unified power group composed of the top government executives, military officials, and corporation directors. The second level (B) comprises the "middle levels of power": a diversified and balanced plurality of interest groups, perhaps most visibly at work in the halls of Congress. The third level (C) is the "mass society": the powerless mass of unorganized and atomized people who are controlled from above.

Riesman's pyramid of power contains only two major levels:

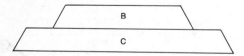

The two levels roughly correspond to Mills' second and third levels, and have been labeled accordingly. The obvious difference between the two pyramids is the presence of a peak in the one case and its absence in the other. Riesman sees no "power elite," in the sense of a single unified power group at the top of the structure, and this in the simplest terms contrasts his image of power in America with that of Mills. The upper level of Riesman's pyramid (B) consists of "veto groups": a diversified and balanced plurality of interest groups, each of which is primarily concerned with protecting its jurisdiction by blocking efforts of other groups that seem to threaten that jurisdiction. There is no decisive ruling group here, but rather an amorphous structure of power centering in the interplay among these interest groups. The lower level of the pyramid (C) comprises the more or less unorganized public, which is sought as an ally (rather than dominated) by the interest groups in their maneuvers against actual or threatened encroachments on the jurisdiction each claims for itself.

Changes in the Structure of Power

Riesman and Mills agree that the American power structure has gone through four major epochs. They disagree on the present and prospective future in the following historical terms: Mills judges the present to represent a fifth epoch, whereas Riesman judges it to be a continuation of the fourth.

The first period, according to Mills and Riesman, extended roughly from the founding of the republic to the Jacksonian era. During this period, Riesman believes America possessed a clearly demarcated ruling group, composed of a "landed-gentry and mercantalist-money leadership." [239] According to Mills, "the important fact about these early days is that social life, economic institutions, military establishment, and political order coincided, and men who were high politicians also played key roles in the economy and, with their families, were among those of the reputable who made up local society." [270]

The second period extended roughly from the decline of Federalist leadership to the Civil War. During this period power became more widely dispersed, and it was no longer possible to identify a sharply defined ruling group. "In this society," Mills writes, "the 'elite' became a plurality of top groups, each in turn quite loosely made up." [270] Riesman notes that farmer and artisan groups became influential, and "occasionally, as with Jackson, moved into a more positive command." [240]

The third period began after the Civil War and extended through McKinley's administration in Riesman's view [240] and until the New Deal according to Mills. [271] They agree that the era of McKinley marked the high point of the unilateral supremacy of corporate economic power. During this period, power once more became concentrated, but unlike the Federalist period and also unlike subsequent periods, the higher circles of economic institutions were dominant.

The fourth period took definite shape in the 1930's. In Riesman's view this period marked the ascendancy of the "veto groups," and rule by coalitions rather than by a unified power group. Mills judges it to have been so only in the early and middle Roosevelt administrations: "In these years, the New Deal as a system of power was essentially a balance of pressure groups and interest blocs." [273]

Up to World War II, then, Mills and Riesman view the historical development of power relations in America along strikingly similar lines. Their sharply contrasting portrayal of present-day American power relations begins with their diverging assessments of the period beginning about 1940. Mills envisions World War II and its aftermath as marking a new era in American power relations. With war as the major problem, there arises a new power group composed of corporate, governmental, and military directors.

The formation of the power elite, as we may now know it, occurred during World War II and its aftermath. In the course of the organization of the nation for that war, and the consequent stabilization of the war-like posture, certain types of man have been selected and formed, and in the course of these institutional and psychological developments, new opportunities and intentions have arisen among them.[3]

Where Mills sees the ascendancy of a power elite, Riesman sees the opposite tendency toward the dispersal of power among a plurality of organized interests:

There has been in the last fifty years a change in the configuration of power in America, in which a single hierarchy with a ruling class at its head has been replaced by a number of "veto groups" among which power is dispersed [239].

The shifting nature of the lobby provides us with an important clue as to the difference between the present American political scene and that of the age of McKinley. The ruling class of businessmen could relatively easily (though perhaps mistakenly) decide where their interests lay and what editors, lawyers, and legislators might be paid to advance them. The lobby ministered to the clear leadership, privilege, and imperative of the business ruling class. Today we have substituted for that leadership a series of groups, each of which has struggled for and finally attained a power to stop things conceivably inimical to its interests and, within far narrower limits, to start things. [246–247]

In short, both Mills and Riesman view the current scene from an historical perspective; but where one finds a hitherto unknown *concentration* of power, the other finds an emerging *indeterminacy* of power.

Operation of the Structure of Power

Mills believes the power elite sets all important public policies, especially foreign policy. Riesman, on the other hand, does not believe that the same group or coalition of groups sets all major policies, but rather that the question of who exercises power varies with the issue at stake: most groups are inoperative on most issues, and all groups are operative primarily on those issues that vitally impinge on their central interests. This is to say that there are as many power structures as there are distinctive spheres of policy. [256]

As to the modes of operation, both Mills and Riesman point to increasing *manipulation,* rather than command or persuasion, as the favored form of power play. Mills emphasizes the secrecy behind which important policy-determination occurs. Riesman stresses not so much manipulation under the guise of secrecy as manipulation under the guise of mutual tolerance for one another's interests and beliefs. Manipulation occurs, according to Riesman, because each group is trying to hide its concern with power in order not to antagonize other groups. Power relations tend to take the form of "monopolistic competition": "rules of fairness and fellowship [rather than the impersonal forces of competition] dictate how far one can go." [247] Thus both believe the play of power takes place to a considerable extent backstage; but Mills judges this power play to be under the direction of one group, while Riesman sees it as controlled by a mood and structure of accommodation among many groups.

Mills maintains that the mass media of communication are important instruments of manipulation: the media lull people to sleep, so to speak, by suppressing political topics and by emphasizing "entertainment." Riesman alleges that the mass media give more attention to politics and problems of public policy than their audiences actually want, and thereby convey the false impression that there is more interest in public affairs than really exists in America at the present time. Where Mills judges the mass media of communication to be powerful political instruments in American society [315–316], Riesman argues that they have relatively little significance in this respect. [228–231]

Bases of the Structure of Power

Power tends to be patterned according to the structure of interests in a society. Power is shared among those whose interests coincide, and divides along lines where interests diverge. To Mills, the power elite is a reflection and solidification of a *coincidence of interests* among the ascendant institutional orders. The power elite rests on the "many interconnections and points of coinciding interests" of the corporations, political institutions, and military services. [19] For Riesman, on the other hand, there is an amorphous power structure, which reflects a *diversity of interests* among the major organized groups. The power structure of veto groups rests on the divergent interests of political parties, business groups, labor organizations, farm blocs, and a myriad of other organized groups. [247]

But power is not a simple reflex of interests alone. It also rests on the capabilities and opportunities for cooperation among those who have similar interests, and for confrontation among those with opposing interests. Mills argues in some detail that the power elite rests not merely on the coincidence of interests among major institutions but also on the "psychological similarity and social intermingling" of their higher circles. [19] By virtue of similar social origins (old family, upper-class background), religious affiliations (Episcopalian and Presbyterian), education (Ivy League college or military academy), and the like, those who head up the major institutions share codes and values as well as material interests. This makes for easy communication, especially when many of these people already know one another, or at least know many people in common. They share a common way of life, and therefore possess both the will and the opportunity to integrate their lines of action as representatives of key institutions. At times this integration involves "explicit co-ordination," as during war. [19–20] So much for the bases of power at the apex of the structure.

At the middle and lower levels of power, Mills emphasizes the lack of independence and concerted purpose among those who occupy similar social positions.

In his book on the middle classes,[4] Mills purports to show the weakness of white-collar people that results from their lack of economic independence and political direction. The white-collar worker simply follows the more powerful group of the moment. In his book on labor leaders,[5] Mills located the alleged political impotence of organized labor in its dependence on government. Finally, the public is conceived as composed of atomized and submissive individuals who are incapable of engaging in effective communication and political action. [302 ff.]

Riesman believes that power "is founded, in large measure, on interpersonal expectations and attitudes." [253] He asserts that in addition to the diversity of interest underlying the pattern of power in America there is the psycho-cultural fact of widespread feelings of weakness and dependence at the top as well as at the bottom of the power structure: "If businessmen feel weak and dependent they do in actuality become weaker and more dependent, no matter what material resources may be ascribed to them." [253] In other words, the amorphousness of power in America rests in part on widespread feelings of weakness and dependence. These feelings are found among those whose position in the social structure provides resources that they could exploit, as well as among those whose position provides less access to the means of power. In fact, Riesman is concerned to show that people at all levels of the social structure tend to feel weaker than their objective position warrants.

The theory of types of conformity that provides the foundation of so much of Riesman's writings enters into his analysis of power at this point. The "other-directed" orientation in culture and character helps to sustain the amorphousness of power. The other-directed person in politics is the "inside-dopester," the person who possesses political competence but avoids political commitment. This is the dominant type in the veto groups, since other-direction is prevalent in the strata

from which their leaders are drawn. "Both within the [veto] groups and in the situation created by their presence, the political mood tends to become one of other-directed tolerance." [248] However, Riesman does not make the basis of power solely psychological:

This does not mean, however, that the veto groups are formed along the lines of character structure. As in a business corporation there is room for extreme inner-directed and other-directed types, and all mixtures between, so in a veto group there can exist complex "symbiotic" relationships among people of different political styles. . . . Despite these complications I think it fair to say that the veto groups, even when they are set up to protect a clearcut moralizing interest, are generally forced to adopt the political manners of the other-directed. [249]

Riesman and Mills agree that there is a widespread apathy in American society, but they disagree on the social distribution of political apathy. Mills locates the apathetic primarily among the lower social strata, whereas Riesman finds extensive apathy in higher as well as lower strata. Part of the difference may rest on what criteria of apathy are used. Mills conceives of apathy as the lack of political meaning in one's life, the failure to think of personal interests in political terms, so that what happens in politics does not appear to be related to personal troubles.[6] Riesman extends the notion of apathy to include the politically uninformed as well as the politically uncommitted.[7] Thus political indignation undisciplined by political understanding is not a genuine political orientation. Riesman judges political apathy to be an important *basis* for amorphous power relations. Mills, on the other hand, treats political apathy primarily as a *result* of the concentration of power.

Consequences of the Structure of Power

Four parallel sets of consequences of the structure of power for American society may be inferred from the writings of Mills and Riesman. The first concerns the impact of the power structure on the interests of certain groups or classes in American society. Mills asserts that the existing power arrangements enhance the interests of the major institutions whose directors constitute the power elite. [276 ff.] Riesman asserts the contrary: no one group or class is decisively favored over others by the culminated decisions on public issues. [257]

The second set of consequences concerns the impact of the structure of power on the quality of politics in American society. Here Mills and Riesman are in closer agreement. Mills maintains that the concentration of power in a small circle, and the use of manipulation as the favored manner of exercising power, lead to the decline of politics as public debate. People are decreasingly capable of grasping political issues, and of relating them to personal interests.[8] Riesman also believes that politics has declined in meaning for large numbers of people. This is not due simply to the ascendancy of "veto groups," although they do foster "the tolerant mood of other-direction and hasten the retreat of the inner-directed indignants." [251] More important, the increasing complexity and remoteness of politics make political self-interest obscure and aggravate feelings of impotence even when self-interest is clear.[9]

The third set of consequences of the American power structure concerns its impact on the quality of power relations themselves. Mills contends that the concentration of power has taken place without a corresponding shift in the bases of legitimacy of power: power is still supposed to reside in the public and its elected representatives, whereas in reality it resides in the hands of those who direct the key bureaucracies. As a consequence, men of power are neither responsible nor accountable for their power. [316–317] Riesman also implies that there is a growing discrepancy between the facts of power and the images of power, but for the opposite reason from Mills: power is more widely dispersed than is generally believed. [257–258]

Finally, a fourth set of consequences concerns the impact of the power structure on democratic leadership. If power tends to be lodged in a small group that is not accountable for its power, and if politics no longer involves genuine public debate, then there will be a *severe weakening of democratic institutions,* if not of leadership (the power elite exercises leadership in one sense of the term, in that it makes decisions on basic policy for the nation). Mills claims that power in America has become so concentrated that it increasingly resembles the Soviet system of power:

> Official commentators like to contrast the ascendancy in totalitarian countries of a tightly organized clique with the American system of power. Such comments, however, are easier to sustain if one compares mid-twentieth-century Russia with mid-nineteenth-century America, which is what is often done by Tocqueville-quoting Americans making the contrast. But that was an America of a century ago, and in the century that has passed, the American elite have not remained as patrioteer essayists have described them to us. The "loose cliques" now head institutions of a scale and power not then existing and, especially since World War I, the loose cliques have tightened up. [271]

If, on the other hand, power tends to be dispersed among groups that are primarily concerned to protect and defend their interests rather than to advance general policies and their own leadership, and if at the same time politics has declined as a sphere of duty and self-interest, then there will be a *severe weakening of leadership.* Thus Riesman believes that "power in America seems to [be] situational and mercurial; it resists attempt to locate it." [257] This "indeterminacy and amorphousness" of power inhibits the development of leadership: "Where the issue involves the country as a whole, no individual or group leadership is likely to be very effective, because the entrenched veto

TWO PORTRAITS OF THE AMERICAN POWER STRUCTURE

	Mills	*Riesman*
Levels	a. Unified power elite b. Diversified and balanced plurality of interest groups c. Mass of unorganized people who have practically no power over elite	a. No dominant power elite b. Diversified and balanced plurality of interest groups c. Mass of unorganized people who have some power over interest groups
Changes	a. Increasing concentration of power	a. Increasing dispersion of power
Operation	a. One group determines all major policies b. Manipulation of people at the bottom by group at the top	a. Who determines policy shifts with the issue b. Monopolistic competition among organized groups
Bases	a. Coincidence of interests among major institutions (economic, military, governmental)	a. Diversity of interests among major organized groups b. Sense of weakness and dependence among those in higher as well as lower status
Consequences	a. Enhancement of interests of corporations, armed forces, and executive branch of government b. Decline of politics as public debate c. Decline of responsible and accountable power—loss of democracy	a. No one group or class is favored significantly over others b. Decline of politics as duty and self-interest c. Decline of capacity for effective leadership

groups cannot be budged." [257] "Veto groups exist as defense groups, not as leadership groups." [248] Yet Riesman does not claim that the decline of leadership directly threatens American democracy, at least in the short run: the dispersion of power among a diversity of balancing "veto groups" operates to support democratic institutions even as it inhibits effective leadership. The long run prospects of a leaderless democracy are of course less promising.

In the second part of this paper, I wish to raise certain critical questions about Riesman's and Mills' images of power. One set of questions seeks to probe more deeply the basic area of disagreement in their views. A second set of questions concerns their major areas of agreement.

Power usually is analyzed according to its distribution among the several units of a system. Most power analysts construe the structure of power as a *hierarchy*—a rank-order of units according to their

amount of power. The assumption often is made that there is only one such structure, and that all units may be ranked vis-à-vis one another. Units higher in the hierarchy have power over units lower in the structure, so there is a one-way flow of power. Mills tends to adopt this image of the structure of power.

Riesman rejects this conception of the power structure as mere hierarchy:

The determination of who [has more power] has to be made all over again for our time: we cannot be satisfied with the answers given by Marx, Mosca, Michels, Pareto, Weber, Veblen, or Burnham. [255]

The image of power in contemporary America presented [in *The Lonely Crowd*] departs from current discussions of power which are usually based on a search for a ruling class. [260]

Riesman is not just denying the existence of a power elite in contemporary American society; he is also affirming the need to consider other aspects of power than only its unequal distribution. He is especially concerned to analyze common responses to power:

If the leaders have lost the power, why have the led not gained it? What is there about the other-directed man and his life situation which prevents the transfer? In terms of situation, it seems that the pattern of monopolistic competition of the veto groups resists individual attempts at power aggrandizement. In terms of character, the other-directed man simply does not seek power; perhaps, rather, he avoids and evades it. [275]

Whereas Mills emphasizes the *differences* between units according to their power, Riesman emphasizes their *similarities* in this respect. In the first view, some units are seen as dominated by other units, while in the second view, all units are seen as subject to constraints that shape and limit their use of power *in similar directions.*

The problem of power is not simply the differential capacity to make decisions, so that those who have power bind those who do not. Constraints also operate on those who are in decision-making positions, for if these are the places where acts of great consequence occur, so are they the targets for social pressures. These pressures become translated into restrictions on the alternatives among which decision-makers can choose. Power may be meaningfully measured by ascertaining the range of alternatives that decision-makers can realistically consider. To identify those who make decisions is not to say how many lines of action are open to them, or how much freedom of choice they enjoy.

A major advance in the study of power is made by going beyond a formal conception of power, in which those who have the authority to make decisions are assumed to possess the effective means of power and the will to use it. Nor can it be assumed that those not in authority lack the power to determine public policy. The identification of effective sources of power requires analysis of how *decision-makers are themselves subject to various kinds of*

constraint. Major sources of constraint include 1) opposing elites and active publics; and 2) cultural values and associated psychological receptives and resistances to power. A comparison of Mills and Riesman with respect to these categories of constraint reveals the major area of disagreement between them.

Mills implies that both sources of constraint are by and large inoperative on the highest levels of power. 1) There is little opposition among the top power-holders. Since they are not in opposition to one another, they do not constrain one another. Instead, they are unified and mutually supportive. Furthermore, there are few publics to constrain the elite. Groups capable of effective participation in broad policy determination have been replaced by atomized masses that are powerless to affect policy, since they lack the social bases for association and communication. Instead, people in large numbers are manipulated through organizations and media controlled by the elite. 2) Older values and codes no longer grip elites, nor have they been replaced by new values and codes that could regulate the exercise of power. Top men of power are not constrained either by an inner moral sense or by feelings of dependence on others. The widespread permissiveness toward the use of expedient means to achieve success produces "the higher immorality," that is to say, elites that are irresponsible in the use of power.

In sharp contrast to Mills, Riesman attaches great importance to both kinds of constraints on decision-makers. 1) There is a plethora of organized groups, "each of which has struggled for and finally attained a power to stop things conceivably inimical to its interests." [247] Furthermore, there is extensive opportunity for large numbers of people to influence decision-makers, because the latter are constrained by their competitive relations with one another to bid for support in the electoral arena and more diffusely in the realm of public relations. 2) The cultural emphasis on "mutual tolerance" and social conformity places a premium on "getting along" with others at the expense of taking strong stands. People are psychologically disposed to avoid long-term commitments as a result of their strong feelings of dependence on their immediate peers. "Other-directed" persons seek approval rather than power.

In general, the decisive consideration in respect to the restraint of power is the presence of multiple centers of power. Where there are many power groups, not only are they mutually constrained; they also are dependent on popular support, and therefore responsive to public demands. Now, there are many readily observable cases of institutionalized opposition among power groups in American society. In the economic sphere, collective bargaining between management and labor is conflict of this kind; and to the extent that "countervailing power" among a few large firms has been replacing competition among many small firms in the market place, there is a *de facto* situation of opposition among economic elites. In the political sphere, there is a strong two-party system and more or less stable factionalism within both parties, opposition among interest blocs in state and national legislatures, rivalry among executive agencies of government and the military services, and so forth.

Mills relegates these conflicting groups to the middle levels of power. Political parties and interest groups, both inside and outside of government, are not important units in the structure of power, according to Mills. It would seem that he takes this position primarily with an eye to the sphere of foreign policy, where only a few people finally make the big decisions. But he fails to put his argument to a decisive or meaningful test: he does not examine the pattern of decisions to show that foreign policy not only is made *by* a few people (this, after all, is a constitutional fact), but that it is made *for their particular interests.* Mills' major premise

seems to be that all decisions are taken by and for special interests; there is no action oriented toward the general interests of the whole community. Furthermore, Mills seems to argue that because only a very few people occupy key decision-making *positions,* they are free to decide on whatever best suits their particular interests. But the degree of *autonomy* of decision-makers cannot be inferred from the *number* of decision-makers, nor from the *scope* of their decisions. It is determined by the character of decision-making, especially the dependence of decision-makers on certain kinds of *procedure* and *support.*

Just as Mills is presenting a distorted image of power in America when he fails to consider the pressures on those in high positions, so Riesman presents a biased picture by not giving sufficient attention to *power differentials* among the various groups in society. When Riesman implies that if power is dispersed, then it must be relatively equal among groups and interests, with no points of concentration, he is making an unwarranted inference. The following statement conjures up an image of power in America that is as misleading on its side as anything Mills has written in defense of his idea of a power elite.

> One might ask whether one would not find, over a long period of time, that decisions in America favored one group or class . . . over others. Does not wealth exert its pull in the long run? In the past this has been so; for the future I doubt it. The future seems to be in the hands of the small business and professional men who control Congress, such as realtors, lawyers, car salesmen, undertakers, and so on; of the military men who control defense and, in part, foreign policy; of the big business managers and their lawyers, finance-committee men, and other counselors who decide on plant investment and influence the rate of technological change; of the labor leaders who control worker productivity and worker votes; of the black belt whites who have the greatest stake in southern politics; of the Poles, Italians, Jews, and Irishmen who have stakes in foreign policy, city jobs, and ethnic, religious and cultural organizations; of the editorializers and storytellers

who help socialize the young, tease and train the adult, and amuse and annoy the aged; of the farmers—themselves a warring congeries of cattlemen, corn men, dairymen, cotton men, and so on—who control key departments and committees and who, as the living representatives of our inner-directed past, control many of our memories; of the Russians and, to a lesser degree, other foreign powers who control much of our agenda of attention; and so on. [257]

It appears that Riesman is asking us to believe that power differentials do not exist, but only differences in the spheres within which groups exercise control.

If Riesman greatly exaggerates the extent to which organized interests possess equal power, nevertheless he poses an important problem that Mills brushes aside. For Riesman goes beyond merely noting the existence of opposition among "veto groups" to suggest that they operate to smother one another's initiative and leadership. It is one thing for interest groups to constrain one another; it is something else again when they produce stalemate. Riesman has pointed to a critical problem for pluralist society: the danger that power may become fragmented among so many competing groups that effective general leadership cannot emerge.

On Mills' side, it is indisputable that American political institutions have undergone extensive centralization and bureaucratization. This is above all an *institutional* change wrought by the greatly expanded scale of events and decisions in the contemporary world. But centralization cannot be equated with a power elite. There can be highly centralized institutions and at the same time a fragmentation of power among a multiplicity of relatively independent public and private agencies. Thus Riesman would appear to be correct that the substance of power lies in the hands of many large organizations, and these organizations are not unified or coordinated in any firm fashion. If they were, surely Mills would have been able to identify the major mechanisms that could produce this result. That he has failed to

do so is the most convincing evidence for their nonexistence.

To complete this analysis, we need only remind ourselves of the fundamental area of agreement between our two critics of American power relations. Both stress *the absence of effective political action* at all levels of the political order, in particular among the citizenry. For all of their differences, Mills and Riesman agree that there has been a decline in effective political participation, or at least a failure of political participation to measure up to the requirements of contemporary events and decisions. This failure has not been compensated by an increase in effective political action at the center: certainly Riesman's "veto groups" are not capable of defining and realizing the community's general aspirations; nor is Mills' "power elite" such a political agency. Both are asserting the inadequacy of political associations, including public opinion, party leadership, Congress, and the Presidency, even as they see the slippage of power in different directions. In consequence, neither is sanguine about the capacity of the American political system to provide responsible leadership, especially in international affairs.

If there is truth in this indictment, it also may have its sources in the very images of power that pervade Mills' and Riesman's thought. They are both inclined toward a negative response to power; and neither shows a willingness to confront the idea of a political system and the ends of power in it. Riesman reflects the liberal suspicion of power, as when he writes "we have come to realize that men who compete primarily for wealth are relatively harmless as compared with men who compete primarily for power." That such assertions as this may very well be true is beside the point. For certainly negative consequences of power can subsist alongside of positive ones. At times Riesman seems to recognize the need for people to seek and use power if they as individuals and the society as a whole are to develop to the fullest of their capacities. But his dominant orientation toward power remains highly individualistic and negative.

Mills is more extreme than Riesman on this matter, since he never asks what is socially required in the way of resources of power and uses of power, but instead is preoccupied with the magnitude of those resources and the (allegedly) destructive expropriation of them by and for the higher circles of major institutions. It is a very limited notion of power that construes it only in terms of coercion and conflict among particular interests. Societies require arrangements whereby resources of power can be effectively used and supplemented for public goals. This is a requirement for government, but the use of this term should not obscure that fact that government either commands power or lacks effectiveness. Mills does not concern himself with the *ends* of power, nor with the conditions for their attainment. He has no conception of the bases of political order, and no theory of the functions of government and politics. He suggests nothing that could prevent his "power elite" from developing into a full-blown totalitarianism. The logic of Mills' position finally reduces to a contest between anarchy and tyranny.

The problem of power seems to bring out the clinician in each of us. We quickly fasten on the pathology of power, whether we label the symptoms as "inside-dopesterism" (Riesman) or as "the higher immorality" (Mills). As a result, we often lose sight of the ends of power in the political system under review. It is important to understand that pivotal decisions increasingly are made at the national level, and that this poses genuine difficulties for the maintenance of democratic control. It is also important to understand that a multiplicity of public and private agencies increasingly pressure decision-makers, and that this poses genuine difficulties for the maintenance of effective political leadership. But the fact remains that there have been periods of centralized decision-making *and* democratic control, multiple constraints on power *and* effective leadership. There is no simple relationship between the extent to which power is equally distributed and the stability of democratic order. For a democratic order requires strong government as well as public consent by an informed citizenry. Unless current tendencies are measured against both sets of needs, there will be little progress in understanding how either one is frustrated or fulfilled. Finally, in the absence of more disciplined historical and comparative analysis, we shall continue to lack a firm basis for evaluating such widely divergent diagnoses of political malaise as those given us by Mills and Riesman.

NOTES

1. Page references in the text for remarks by C. Wright Mills refer to *The Power Elite*, New York: Oxford University Press, 1956.

2. Page references in the text for remarks by David Riesman refer to *The Lonely Crowd*, New York: Doubleday Anchor, 1953.

3. C. Wright Mills, "The Power Elite," in A. Kornhauser (ed.), *Problems of Power in American Society*, Detroit: Wayne University Press, 1957, p. 161.

4. *White Collar*, New York: Oxford University Press, 1951.

5. *The New Men of Power*, New York: Harcourt, Brace and Company, 1948.

6. *White Collar*, p. 327.

7. David Riesman and Nathan Glazer, "Criteria for Political Apathy," in Alvin W. Gouldner (ed.), *Studies in Leadership*, New York: Harper & Brothers, 1950.

8. *White Collar*, pp. 342–350.

9. "Criteria for Political Apathy," p. 520.

Education

51. THE SCHOOL CLASS AS A SOCIAL SYSTEM

TALCOTT PARSONS

When formalized into a separate sphere, education takes on characteristic structural forms. There is a school system in which a double hierarchy inevitably develops: one pertaining to the relationship between administrators, teachers, and students; the other regarding graduated levels of educational progress. Moreover, the school itself and each of its grades or classes may be seen as social systems in miniature. Being a product and part of the wider social milieu (and often subject to control of outsiders), it is not surprising that schools and school classes frequently reflect the social patterns of society at large.

In this essay, Talcott Parsons examines the structure of the American school system, comments on its methods of assessing "cognitive" and "moral" achievement, and, using the school class as a unit of analysis, discusses the external bases for differentiation at both the elementary and secondary level. Parsons sees the school as a channel of social selection as well as an agency of socialization.

Talcott Parsons is Professor of Sociology in the Department of Social Relations at Harvard University. A partial listing of his many books is presented on page 44 of this volume.

This essay will attempt to outline, if only sketchily, an analysis of the elementary and secondary school class as a social system, and the relation of its structure to its primary functions in the society as an agency of socialization and allocation.

Reprinted from the *Harvard Educational Review,* **29** (1959), 297–318, by permission of the author and the publisher.

While it is important that the school class is normally part of the larger organization of a school, the class rather than the whole school will be the unit of analysis here, for it is recognized both by the school system and by the individual pupil as the place where the "business" of formal education actually takes place. In elementary schools, pupils of one grade are typically placed in a single "class" under one main teacher, but in the secondary school, and sometimes in the upper elementary grades, the pupil works on different subjects under different teachers; here the complex of classes participated in by the same pupil is the significant unit for our purposes.

The Problem: Socialization and Selection

Our main interest, then, is in a dual problem: first of how the school class functions to internalize in its pupils both the commitments and capacities for successful performance of their future adult roles, and second of how it functions to allocate these human resources within the role-structure of the adult society. The primary ways in which these two problems are interrelated will provide our main points of reference.

First, from the functional point of view the school class can be treated as an agency of socialization. That is to say, it is an agency through which individual personalities are trained to be motivationally and technically adequate to the performance of adult roles. It is not the sole such agency; the family, informal "peer groups," churches, and sundry voluntary organizations all play a part, as does actual on-the-job training. But, in the period extending from entry into first grade until entry into the labor force or marriage, the school class may be regarded as the focal socializing agency.

The socialization function may be summed up as the development in individuals of the commitments and capacities which are essential prerequisites of their future role-performance. Commitments may be broken down in turn into two components: commitment to the implementation of the broad *values* of society, and commitment to the performance of a specific type of role within the *structure* of society. Thus a person in a relatively humble occupation may be a "solid citizen" in the sense of commitment to honest work in that occupation, without an intensive and sophisticated concern with the implementation of society's higher-level values. Or conversely, someone else might object to the anchorage of the feminine role in marriage and the family on the grounds that such anchorage keeps society's total talent resources from being distributed equitably to business, government, and so on. Capacities can also be broken down into two components, the first being competence or the skill to perform the tasks involved in the individual's roles, and the second being "role-responsibility" or the capacity to live up to other people's expectations of the interpersonal behavior appropriate to these roles. Thus a mechanic as well as a doctor needs to have not only the basic "skills of his trade," but also the ability to behave responsibly toward those people with whom he is brought into contact in his work.

While on the one hand, the school class may be regarded as a primary agency by which these different components of commitments and capacities are generated, on the other hand, it is, from the point of view of the society, an agency of "manpower" allocation. It is well known that in American society there is a very high, and probably increasing, correlation between one's status level in the society and one's level of educational attainment. Both social status and educational level are obviously related to the occupational status which is attained. Now, as a result of the general process of both educational and occupational upgrading, completion of high school is increasingly coming to be the norm for minimum satisfactory educational attainment, and the most significant line for future occupational status has come to be drawn between members of an age-cohort who do and do not go to college.

We are interested, then, in what it is about the school class in our society that determines the distinction between the contingents of the age-cohort which do and do not go to college. Because of a tradition of localism and a rather pragmatic pluralism, there is apparently considerable variety among school systems of various cities and states. Although the situation in metropolitan Boston probably represents a more highly structured pattern than in many other parts of the country, it is probably not so extreme as to be misleading in its main features. There, though of course actual entry into college does not come until after graduation from high school, the main dividing line is between those who are and are not enrolled in the college preparatory course in high school; there is only a small amount of shifting either way after about the ninth grade when the decision is normally made. Furthermore, the evidence seems to be that by far the most important criterion of selection is the record of school performance in elementary school. These records are evaluated by teachers and principals, and there are few cases of entering the college preparatory course against their advice. It is therefore not stretching the evidence too far to say broadly that the primary selective process occurs through differential school performance in elementary school, and that the "seal" is put on it in junior high school.[1]

The evidence also is that the selective process is genuinely assortative. As in virtually all comparable processes, ascriptive as well as achieved factors influence the outcome. In this case, the ascriptive factor is the socio-economic status of the child's family, and the factor underlying his op-

portunity for achievement is his individual ability. In the study of 3,348 Boston high school boys on which these generalizations are based, each of these factors was quite highly correlated with planning college. For example, the percentages planning college, by father's occupation, were: 12 per cent for semi-skilled and unskilled, 19 per cent for skilled, 26 per cent for minor white collar, 52 per cent for middle white collar, and 80 per cent for major white collar. Likewise, intentions varied by ability (as measured by IQ), namely, 11 per cent for the lowest quintile, 17 per cent for the next, 24 per cent for the middle, 30 per cent for the next to the top, and 52 per cent for the highest. It should be noted also that within any ability quintile, the relationship of plans to father's occupation is seen. For example, within the very important top quintile in ability as measured, the range in college intentions was from 29 per cent for sons of laborers to 89 per cent for sons of major white collar persons.[2]

The essential points here seem to be that there is a realtively uniform criterion of selection operating to differentiate between the college and the non-college contingents, and that for a very important part of the cohort the operation of this criterion is not a "put-up job"—it is not simply a way of affirming a previously determined ascriptive status. To be sure, the high-status, high-ability boy is very likely indeed to go to college, and the low-status, low-ability boy is very unlikely to go. But the "cross-pressured" group for whom these two factors do not coincide [3] is of considerable importance.

Considerations like these lead me to conclude that the main process of differentiation (which from another point of view is selection) that occurs during elementary school takes place on a single main axis of *achievement*. Broadly, moreover, the differentiation leads up through high school to a bifurcation into college-goers and non-college-goers.

To assess the significance of this pattern, let us look at its place in the socialization of the individual. Entering the system of formal education is the child's first major step out of primary involvement in his family of orientation. Within the family certain foundations of his motivational system have been laid down. But the only characteristic fundamental to later roles which has been clearly been "determined" and psychologically stamped in by that time is sex role. The postoedipal child enters the system of formal education clearly categorized as boy or girl, but beyond that his *role* is not yet differentiated. The process of selection, by which persons will select and be selected for categories of roles, is yet to take place.

On grounds which cannot be gone into here, it may be said that the most important single predispositional factor with which the child enters the school is his level of *independence*. By this is meant his level of self-sufficiency relative to guidance by adults, his capacity to take responsibility and to make his own decisions in coping with new and varying situations. This, like his sex role, he has as a function of his experience in the family.

The family is a collectivity within which the basic status-structure is ascribed in terms of biological position, that is, by generation, sex, and age. There are inevitably differences of performance relative to these, and they are rewarded and punished in ways that contribute to differential character formation. But these differences are not given the sanction of institutionalized social status. The school is the first socializing agency in the child's experience which institutionalizes a differentiation of status on nonbiological bases. Moreover, this is not an ascribed but an achieved status; it is the status "earned" by differential performance of the tasks set by the teacher, who is acting as an agent of the community's school system. Let us look at the structure of this situation.

The Structure of the Elementary School Class

In accord with the generally wide variability of American institutions, and of course the basically local control of school systems, there is considerable variability of school situations, but broadly they have a single relatively well-marked framework.[4] Particularly in the primary part of the elementary grades, i.e., the first three grades, the basic pattern includes one main teacher for the class, who teaches all subjects and who is in charge of the class generally. Sometimes this early, and frequently in later grades, other teachers are brought in for a few special subjects, particularly gym, music, and art, but this does not alter the central position of the main teacher. This teacher is usually a woman.[5] The class is with this one teacher for the school year, but usually no longer.

The class, then, is composed of about 25 age-peers of both sexes drawn from a relatively small geographical area—the neighborhood. Except for sex, in certain respects, there is initially no formal basis for differentiation of status within the school class. The main structural differentiation develops gradually, on the single main axis indicated above as achievement. That the differentiation should occur on a single main axis is insured by four primary features of the situation. The first is the initial equalization of the "contestants" status by age and by "family background," the neighborhood being typically much more homogeneous than is the whole society. The second circumstance is the imposition of a common set of tasks which is, compared to most other task-areas, strikingly undifferentiated. The school situation is far more like a race in this respect than most role-performance situations. Third, there is the sharp polarization between the pupils in their initial equality and the *single* teacher who is an adult and "represents" the adult world. And fourth, there is a relatively systematic process of evaluation of the pupils' performances. From the point of view of a pupil, this evaluation, particularly (though not exclusively) in the form of report card marks, constitutes reward and/or punishment for past performance; from the viewpoint of the school system acting as an allocating agency, it is a basis of *selection* for future status in society.

Two important sets of qualifications need to be kept in mind in interpreting this structural pattern, but I think these do not destroy the significance of its main outline. The first qualification is for variations in the formal organization and procedures of the school class itself. Here the most important kind of variation is that between relatively "traditional" schools and relatively "progressive" schools. The more traditional schools put more emphasis on discrete units of subject-matter, whereas the progressive type allows more "indirect" teaching through "projects" and broader topical interests where more than one bird can be killed with a stone. In progressive schools there is more emphasis on groups of pupils working together, compared to the traditional direct relation of the individual pupil to the teacher. This is related to the progressive emphasis on co-operation among the pupils rather than direct competition, to greater permissiveness as opposed to strictness of discipline, and to a de-emphasis on formal marking.[6] In some schools one of these components will be more prominent, and in others, another. That it is, however, an important range of variation is clear. It has to do, I think, very largely with the independence-dependence training which is so important to early socialization in the family. My broad interpretation is that those people who emphasize independence training will tend to be those who favor relatively progressive education. The relation of support for progressive education to relatively high socio-economic status and to "intellectual" interests and the like is well known. There is no contradiction between these emphases both on independence and

on co-operation and group solidarity among pupils. In the first instance this is because the main focus of the independence problem at these ages is vis-à-vis adults. However, it can also be said that the peer group, which here is built into the school class, is an indirect field of expression of dependency needs, displaced from adults.

The second set of qualifications concerns the "informal" aspects of the school class, which are always somewhat at variance with the formal expectations. For instance, the formal pattern of nondifferentiation between the sexes may be modified informally, for the very salience of the one-sex peer group at this age period means that there is bound to be considerable implicit recognition of it—for example, in the form of teachers' encouraging group competition between boys and girls. Still, the fact of coeducation and the attempt to treat both sexes alike in all the crucial formal respects remain the most important. Another problem raised by informal organization is the question of how far teachers can and do treat pupils particularistically in violation of the universalistic expectations of the school. When compared with other types of formal organizations, however, I think the extent of this discrepancy in elementary schools is seen to be not unusual. The school class is structured so that opportunity for particularistic treatment is severely limited. Because there are so many more children in a school class than in a family and they are concentrated in a much narrower age range, the teacher has much less chance than does a parent to grant particularistic favors.

Bearing in mind these two sets of qualifications, it is still fair, I think, to conclude that the major characteristics of the elementary school class in this country are such as have been outlined. It should be especially emphasized that more or less progressive schools, even with their relative lack of emphasis on formal marking, do not constitute a separate pattern, but rather a variant tendency within the same pattern. A progressive teacher, like any other, will form opinions about the different merits of her pupils relative to the values and goals of the class and will communicate these evaluations to them, informally if not formally. It is my impression that the extremer cases of playing down relative evaluation are confined to those upper-status schools where going to a "good" college is so fully taken for granted that for practical purposes it is an ascribed status. In other words, in interpreting these facts the selective function of the school class should be kept continually in the forefront of attention. Quite clearly its importance has not been decreasing; rather the contrary.

The Nature of School Achievement

What, now, of the content of the "achievement" expected of elementary school children? Perhaps the best broad characterization which can be given is that it involves the types of performance which are, on the one hand, appropriate to the school situation and, on the other hand, are felt by adults to be important in themselves. This vague and somewhat circular characterization may, as we mentioned earlier, be broken down into two main components. One of these is the more purely "cognitive" learning of information, skills, and frames of reference associated with empirical knowledge and technological mastery. The *written* language and the early phases of mathematical thinking are clearly vital; they involve cognitive skills at altogether new levels of generality and abstraction compared to those commanded by the pre-school child. With these basic skills goes assimilation of much factual information about the world.

The second main component is what may broadly be called a "moral" one. In earlier generations of schooling this was known as "deportment." Somewhat more generally it might be called responsible citizenship in the school community. Such things as respect for the teacher, consideration and co-operativeness in relation to fellow-pupils, and good "work-habits" are the fundamentals, leading on to capacity for "leadership" and "initiative."

The striking fact about this achievement content is that in the elementary grades these two primary components are not clearly differentiated from each other. Rather, the pupil is evaluated in diffusely general terms; a *good* pupil is defined in terms of a fusion of the cognitive and the moral components, in which varying weight is given to one or the other. Broadly speaking, then, we may say that the "high achievers" of the elementary school are both the "bright" pupils, who catch on easily to their more strictly intellectual tasks, and the more "responsible" pupils, who "behave well" and on whom the teacher can "count" in her difficult problems of managing the class. One indication that this is the case is the fact that in elementary school the purely intellectual tasks are relatively easy for the pupil of high intellectual ability. In many such cases, it can be presumed that the primary challenge to the pupil is not to his intellectual, but to his "moral," capacities. On the whole, the progressive movement seems to have leaned in the direction of giving enhanced emphasis to this component, suggesting that of the two, it has tended to become the more problematical.[7]

The essential point, then, seems to be that the elementary school, regarded in the light of its socialization function, is an agency which differentiates the school class broadly along a single continuum of achievement, the content of which is relative excellence in living up to the expectations imposed by the teacher as an agent of the adult society. The criteria of this achievement are, generally speaking, undifferentiated into the cognitive or technical component and the moral or "social" component. But with respect to its bearing on societal values, it is broadly a differentiation of *levels* of capacity to act in accord with these values. Though the relation is far from neatly uniform, this differentiation underlies the processes of selection for levels of status and role in the adult society.

Next, a few words should be said about the out-of-school context in which this process goes on. Besides the school class, there are clearly two primary social structures in which the child participates: the family and the child's informal "peer group."

Family and Peer Group in Relation to the School Class

The school age child, of course, continues to live in the parental household and to be highly dependent, emotionally as well as instrumentally, on his parents. But he is now spending several hours a day away from home, subject to a discipline and a reward system which are essentially independent of that administered by the parents. Moreover, the range of this independence gradually increases. As he grows older, he is permitted to range further territorially with neither parental nor school supervision, and to do an increasing range of things. He often gets an allowance for personal spending and begins to earn some money of his own. Generally, however, the emotional problem of dependence-independence continues to be a very salient one through this period, frequently with manifestations by the child of compulsive independence.

Concomitantly with this, the area for association with age-peers without detailed adult supervision expands. These associations are tied to the family, on the one hand, in that the home and yards of children who are neighbors and the adjacent streets serve as locations for their activities; and to the school, on the other hand, in that play periods and going to and from school provide occasions for informal association, even though organized extracurricular activities are introduced only later. Ways of bringing some of this activity under another sort of adult supervision are found in such organizations as the boy and girl scouts.

Two sociological characteristics of peer groups at this age are particularly striking. One is the fluidity of their boundaries, with individual children drifting into and out of associations. This element of "voluntary association" contrasts strikingly with the child's ascribed membership in the family and the school class, over which he has no control. The second characteristic is the peer group's sharp segregation by sex. To a striking degree this is enforced by the children themselves rather than by adults.

The psychological functions of peer association are suggested by these two characteristics. On the one hand, the peer group may be regarded as a field for the exercise of independence from adult control; hence it is not surprising that it is often a focus of behavior which goes beyond independence from adults to the range of adult-*disapproved* behavior; when this happens, it is the seed bed from which the extremists go over into delinquency. But another very important function is to provide the child a source of non-adult approval and acceptance. These depend on "technical" and "moral" criteria as diffuse as those required in the school situation. On the one hand, the peer group is a field for acquiring and displaying various types of "prowess"; for boys this is especially the physical prowess which may later ripen into athletic achievement. On the other hand, it is a matter of gaining acceptance from desirable peers as "belonging" in the group, which later ripens into the conception of the popular teen-ager, the "right guy." Thus the adult parents are augmented by age-peers as a source of rewards for performance and of security in acceptance.

The importance of the peer group for socialization in our type of society should be clear. The motivational foundations of character are inevitably first laid down through identification with parents, who are generation-superiors, and the generation difference is a type example of a hierarchical status difference. But an immense part of the individual's adult role performance will have to be in association with status-equals or near-equals. In this situation it is important to have a reorganization of the motivational structure so that the original dominance of the hierarchical axis is modified to strengthen the egalitarian components. The peer group plays a prominent part in this process.

Sex segregation of latency period peer groups may be regarded as a process of reinforcement of sex-role identification. Through intensive association with sex-peers and involvement in sex-typed activities, they strongly reinforce belongingness with other members of the same sex and contrast with the opposite sex. This is the more important because in the coeducational school a set of forces operates which specifically plays down sex-role differentiation.

It is notable that the latency period sex-role pattern, instead of institutionalizing relations to members of the opposite sex, is characterized by an avoidance of such relations, which only in adolescence gives way to dating. This avoidance is clearly associated with the process of reorganization of the erotic components of motivational structure. The pre-oedipal objects of erotic attachment were both intra-familial and generation-superior. In both respects there must be a fundamental shift by the time the child reaches adulthood. I would suggest that one of the main functions of the avoidance pattern is to help cope with the psychological difficulty of overcoming the earlier incestuous attachments, and hence to prepare the child for assuming an attachment to an age-mate of opposite sex later.

Seen in this perspective, the socialization function of the school class assumes a particular significance. The socialization

functions of the family by this time are relatively residual, though their importance should not be underestimated. But the school remains adult-controlled and, moreover, induces basically the same kind of identification as was induced by the family in the child's pre-oedipal stage. This is to say that the learning of achievement-motivation is, psychologically speaking, a process of identification with the teacher, of doing well in school in order to please the teacher (often backed by the parents) in the same sense in which a pre-oedipal child learns new skills in order to please his mother.

In this connection I maintain that what is internalized through the process of identification is a reciprocal pattern of role-relationships.[8] Unless there is a drastic failure of internalization altogether, not just one, but both sides of the interaction will be internalized. There will, however, be an emphasis on one or the other, so that some children will more nearly identify with the socializing agent, and others will more nearly identify with the opposite role. Thus, in the pre-oedipal stage, the "independent" child has identified more with the parent, and the "dependent" one with the child-role vis-à-vis the parent.

In school the teacher is institutionally defined as superior to any pupil in knowledge of curriculum subject-matter and in responsibility as a good citizen of the school. In so far as the school class tends to be bifurcated (and of course the dichotomization is far from absolute), it will broadly be on the basis, on the one hand, of identification with the teacher, or acceptance of her role as a model; and, on the other hand, of identification with the pupil peer group. This bifurcation of the class on the basis of identification with teacher or with peer group so strikingly corresponds with the bifurcation into college-goers and non-college-goers that it would be hard to avoid the hypothesis that this structural dichotomization in the school system is the primary source of the selective dichotomization. Of course in detail the relationship is blurred, but certainly not more so than in a great many other fields of comparable analytical complexity.

These considerations suggest an interpretation of some features of the elementary teacher role in American society. The first major step in socialization, beyond that in the family, takes place in the elementary school, so it seems reasonable to expect that the teacher-figure should be characterized by a combination of similarities to and differences from parental figures. The teacher, then, is an adult, characterized by the generalized superiority, which a parent also has, of adult status relative to children. She is not, however, ascriptively related to her pupils, but is performing an occupational role—a role, however, in which the recipients of her services are tightly bound in solidarity to her and to each other. Furthermore, compared to a parent's, her responsibility to them is much more universalistic, this being reinforced, as we saw, by the size of the class; it is also much more oriented to performance rather than to solicitude for the emotional "needs" of the children. She is not entitled to suppress the distinction between high and low achievers, just because not being able to be included among the high group would be too hard on little Johnny—however much tendencies in this direction appear as deviant patterns. A mother, on the other hand, must give *first* priority to the needs of her child, regardless of his capacities to achieve.

It is also significant for the parallel of the elementary school class with the family that the teacher is normally a woman. As background it should be noted that in most European systems until recently, and often today in our private parochial and non-sectarian schools, the sexes have been segregated and each sex group has been taught by teachers of their own sex. Given coeducation, however, the woman teacher represents continuity with the role of the mother. Precisely the lack of differentiation

in the elementary school "curriculum" between the components of subject-matter competence and social responsibility fits in with the greater diffuseness of the feminine role.

But at the same time, it is essential that the teacher is not a mother to her pupils, but must insist on universalistic norms and the differential reward of achievement. Above all she must be the agent of bringing about and legitimizing a differentiation of the school class on an achievement axis. This aspect of her role is furthered by the fact that in American society the feminine role is less confined to the familial context than in most other societies, but joins the masculine in occupational and associational concerns, though still with a greater relative emphasis on the family. Through identification with their teacher, children of both sexes learn that the category "woman" is not co-extensive with "mother" (and future wife), but that the feminine role-personality is more complex than that.

In this connection it may well be that there is a relation to the once-controversial issue of the marriage of women teachers. If the differentiation between what may be called the maternal and the occupational components of the feminine role is incomplete and insecure, confusion between them may be avoided by insuring that both are not performed by the same persons. The "old maid" teacher of American tradition may thus be thought of as having renounced the maternal role in favor of the occupational.[9] Recently, however, the highly affective concern over the issue of married women's teaching has conspicuously abated, and their actual participation has greatly increased. It may be suggested that this change is associated with a change in the feminine role, the most conspicuous feature of which is the general social sanctioning of participation of women in the labor force, not only prior to marriage, but also after marriage. This I should interpret as a process of structural differentiation in that the same category of persons is permitted and even expected to engage in a more complex set of role-functions than before.

The process of identification with the teacher which has been postulated here is furthered by the fact that in the elementary grades the child typically has one teacher, just as in the pre-oedipal period he had one parent, the mother, who was the focus of his object-relations. The continuity between the two phases is also favored by the fact that the teacher, like the mother, is a woman. But, if she acted only like a mother, there would be no genuine reorganization of the pupil's personality system. This reorganization is furthered by the features of the teacher role which differentiate it from the maternal. One further point is that while a child has one main teacher in each grade, he will usually have a new teacher when he progresses to the next higher grade. He is thus accustomed to the fact that teachers are, unlike mothers, "interchangeable" in a certain sense. The school year is long enough to form an important relationship to a particular teacher, but not long enough for a highly particularistic attachment to crystallize. More than in the parent-child relationship, in school the child must internalize his relation to the teacher's *role* rather than her particular personality; this is a major step in the internalization of universalistic pattern.

Socialization and Selection in the Elementary School

To conclude this discussion of the elementary school class, something should be said about the fundamental conditions underlying the process which is, as we have seen, simultaneously 1) an emancipation of the child from primary emotional attachment to his family, 2) an internalization of a level of societal values and norms that is a step higher than those he can learn in his family alone, 3) a differentiation of the school class in terms both of actual achievement and of differential

valuation of achievement, and 4) from society's point of view, a selection and allocation of its human resources relative to the adult role system.[10]

Probably the most fundamental condition underlying this process is the sharing of common values by the two adult agencies involved—the family and the school. In this case the core is the shared valuation of *achievement*. It includes, above all, recognition that it is fair to give differential rewards for different levels of achievement, so long as there has been fair access to opportunity, and fair that these rewards lead on to higher-order opportunities for the successful. There is thus a basic sense in which the elementary school class is an embodiment of the fundamental American value of equality of opportunity, in that it places value *both* on initial equality and on differential achievement.

As a second condition, however, the rigor of this valuational pattern must be tempered by allowance for the difficulties and needs of the young child. Here the quasi-motherliness of the woman teacher plays an important part. Through her the school system, assisted by other agencies, attempts to minimize the insecurity resulting from the pressures to learn, by providing a certain amount of emotional support defined in terms of what is due to a child of a given age level. In this respect, however, the role of the school is relatively small. The underlying foundation of support is given in the home, and as we have seen, an important supplement to it can be provided by the informal peer associations of the child. It may be suggested that the development of extreme patterns of alienation from the school is often related to inadequate support in these respects.

Third, there must be a process of selective rewarding of valued performance. Here the teacher is clearly the primary agent, though the more progressive modes of education attempt to enlist classmates more systematically than in the traditional pattern. This is the process that is the direct source of intra-class differentiation along the achievement axis.

The final condition is that this initial differentiation tends to bring about a status system in the class, in which not only the immediate results of school work, but a whole series of influences, converge to consolidate different expectations which may be thought of as the children's "levels of aspiration." Generally some differentiation of friendship groups along this line occurs, though it is important that it is by no means complete, and that children are sensitive to the attitudes not only of their own friends, but of others.

Within this general discussion of processes and conditions, it is important to distinguish, as I have attempted to do all along, the socialization of the individual from the selective allocation of contingents to future roles. For the individual, the old familial identification is broken up (the family of orientation becomes, in Freudian terms, a "lost object") and a new identification is gradually built up, providing the first-order structure of the child's identity apart from his originally ascribed identity as son or daughter of the "Joneses." He both transcends his familial identification in favor of a more independent one and comes to occupy a differentiated status within the new system. His personal status is inevitably a direct function of the position he achieves, primarily in the formal school class and secondarily in the informal peer group structure. In spite of the sense in which achievement-ranking takes place along a continuum, I have put forward reasons to suggest that, with respect to this status, there is an important differentiation into two broad, relatively distinct levels, and that his position on one or the other enters into the individual's definition of his own identity. To an important degree this process of differentiation is independent of the socio-economic status of his family in the community, which to the child is a prior ascribed status.

When we look at the same system as a selective mechanism from the societal point of view, some further considerations become important. First, it may be noted that the valuation of achievement and its sharing by family and school not only provides the appropriate values for internalization by individuals, but also performs a crucial integrative function for the system. Differentiation of the class along the achievement axis is inevitably a source of strain, because it confers higher rewards and privileges on one contingent than on another within the same system. This common valuation helps make possible the acceptance of the crucial differentiation, especially by the losers in the competition. Here it is an essential point that this *common* value of achievement is shared by units with different statuses in the system. It cuts across the differentiation of families by socio-economic status. It is necessary that there be realistic opportunity and that the teacher can be relied on to implement it by being "fair" and rewarding achievement to whoever shows capacity for it. The fact is crucial that the distribution of abilities, though correlated with family status, clearly does not coincide with it. There can then be a genuine selective process within a set of "rules of the game."

This commitment to common values is not, however, the sole integrative mechanism counteracting the strain imposed by differentiation. Not only does the individual pupil enjoy familial support, but teachers also like and indeed "respect" pupils on bases independent of achievement-status, and peer-group friendship lines, though correlated with position on the achievement scale, again by no means coincide with it, but cross-cut it. Thus there are cross-cutting lines of solidarity which mitigate the strains generated by rewarding achievement differentially.[11]

It is only *within* this framework of institutionalized solidarity that the crucial selective process goes on through selective rewarding and the consolidation of its results into a status-differentiation within the school class. We have called special attention to the impact of the selective process on the children of relatively high ability but low family status. Precisely in this group, but pervading school classes generally, is another parallel to what was found in the studies of voting behavior.[12] In the voting studies it was found that the "shifters"—those voters who were transferring their allegiance from one major party to the other—tended, on the one hand, to be the "cross-pressured" people, who had multiple status characteristics and group allegiances which predisposed them simultaneously to vote in opposite directions. The analogy in the school class is clearly to the children for whom ability and family status do not coincide. On the other hand, it was precisely in this group of cross-pressured voters that political "indifference" was most conspicuous. Nonvoting was particularly prevalent in this group, as was a generally cool emotional tone toward a campaign. The suggestion is that some of the pupil "indifference" to school performance may have a similar origin. This is clearly a complex phenomenon and cannot be further analyzed here. But rather than suggesting, as is usual on common sense grounds, that indifference to school work represents an "alienation" from cultural and intellectual values, I would suggest exactly the opposite: that an important component of such indifference, including in extreme cases overt revolt against school discipline, is connected with the fact that the stakes, as in politics, are very high indeed. Those pupils who are exposed to contradictory pressures are likely to be ambivalent; at the same time, the personal stakes for them are higher than for the others, because what happens in school may make much more of a difference for their futures than for the others, in whom ability and family status point to the same expectations for the future. In particular for the upwardly mobile pupils, too much emphasis on school success would pointedly suggest "burning their bridges" of association with their

families and status peers. This phenomenon seems to operate even in elementary school, although it grows somewhat more conspicuous later. In general I think that an important part of the anti-intellectualism in American youth culture stems from the *importance* of the selective process through the educational system rather than the opposite.

One further major point should be made in this analysis. As we have noted, the general trend of American society has been toward a rapid upgrading in the educational status of the population. This means that, relative to past expectations, with each generation there is increased pressure to educational achievement, often associated with parents' occupational ambitions for their children.[13] To a sociologist this is a more or less classical situation of anomic strain, and the youth-culture ideology which plays down intellectual interests and school performance seems to fit in this context. The orientation of the youth culture is, in the nature of the case, ambivalent, but for the reasons suggested, the anti-intellectual side of the ambivalence tends to be overtly stressed. One of the reasons for the dominance of the anti-school side of the ideology is that it provides a means of protest against adults, who are at the opposite pole in the socialization situation. In certain respects one would expect that the trend toward greater emphasis on independence, which we have associated with progressive education, would accentuate the strain in this area and hence the tendency to decry adult expectations. The whole problem should be subjected to a thorough analysis in the light of what we know about ideologies more generally.

The same general considerations are relevant to the much-discussed problem of juvenile delinquency. Both the general upgrading process and the pressure to enhanced independence should be expected to increase strain on the lower, most marginal groups. The analysis of this paper has been concerned with the line between college and non-college contingents; there is, however, another line between those who achieve solid non-college educational status and those for whom adaptation to educational expectations at *any* level is difficult. As the acceptable minimum of educational qualification rises, persons near and below the margin will tend to be pushed into an attitude of repudiation of these expectations. Truancy and delinquency are ways of expressing this repudiation. Thus the very *improvement* of educational standards in the society at large may well be a major factor in the failure of the educational process for a growing number at the lower end of the status and ability distribution. It should therefore not be too easily assumed that delinquency is a symptom of a *general* failure of the educational process.

Differentiation and Selection in the Secondary School

It will not be possible to discuss the secondary school phase of education in nearly as much detail as has been done for the elementary school phase, but it is worthwhile to sketch its main outline in order to place the above analysis in a wider context. Very broadly we may say that the elementary school phase is concerned with the internalization in children of motivation to achievement, and the selection of persons on the basis of differential capacity for achievement. The focus is on the *level* of capacity. In the secondary school phase, on the other hand, the focus is on the differentiation of *qualitative types* of achievement. As in the elementary school, this differentiation crosscuts sex role. I should also maintain that it cross-cuts the levels of achievement which have been differentiated out in the elementary phase.

In approaching the question of the types of capacity differentiated, it should be kept in mind that secondary school is the principal springboard from which

lower-status persons will enter the labor force, whereas those achieving higher status will continue their formal education in college, and some of them beyond. Hence for the lower-status pupils the important line of differentiation should be the one which will lead into broadly different categories of jobs; for the higher-status pupils the differentiation will lead to broadly different roles in college.

My suggestion is that this differentiation separates those two components of achievement which we labelled "cognitive" and "moral" in discussing the elementary phase. Those relatively high in "cognitive" achievement will fit better in specific-function, more or less technical roles; those relatively high in "moral" achievement will tend toward diffuser, more "socially" or "humanly" oriented roles. In jobs not requiring college training, the one category may be thought of as comprising the more impersonal and technical occupations, such as "operatives," mechanics, or clerical workers; the other, as occupations where "human relations" are prominent, such as salesmen and agents of various sorts. At the college level, the differentiation certainly relates to concern, on the one hand, with the specifically intellectual curricular work of college and, on the other hand, with various types of diffuser responsibility in human relations, such as leadership roles in student government and extracurricular activities. Again, candidates for post-graduate professional training will probably be drawn mainly from the first of these two groups.

In the structure of the school, there appears to be a gradual transition from the earliest grades through high school, with the changes timed differently in different school systems. The structure emphasized in the first part of this discussion is most clearly marked in the first three "primary" grades. With progression to the higher grades, there is greater frequency of plural teachers, though very generally still a single main teacher. In the sixth grade and sometimes in the fifth, a man as main teacher, though uncommon, is by no means unheard of. With junior high school, however, the shift of pattern becomes more marked, and still more in senior high.

By that time the pupil has several different teachers of both sexes [14] teaching him different subjects, which are more or less formally organized into different courses—college preparatory and others. Furthermore, with the choice of "elective" subjects, the members of the class in one subject no longer need be exactly the same as in another, so the pupil is much more systematically exposed to association with different people, both adults and age-peers, in different contexts. Moreover, the school he attends is likely to be substantially larger than was his elementary school, and to draw from a wider geographical area. Hence the child is exposed to a wider range of statuses than before, being thrown in with more age-peers whom he does not encounter in his neighborhood; it is less likely that his parents will know the parents of any given child with whom he associates. It is thus my impression that the transitions to junior high and senior high school are apt to mean a considerable reshuffling of friendships. Another conspicuous difference between the elementary and secondary levels is the great increase in high school of organized extracurricular activities. Now, for the first time, organized athletics become important, as do a variety of clubs and associations which are school-sponsored and supervised to varying degrees.

Two particularly important shifts in the patterning of youth culture occur in this period. One, of course, is the emergence of more positive cross-sex relationships outside the classroom, through dances, dating, and the like. The other is the much sharper prestige-stratification of informal peer groupings, with indeed an element of snobbery which often exceeds that of the adult community in which the school exists.[15] Here it is important that though

there is a broad correspondence between the prestige of friendship groups and the family status of their members, this, like the achievement order of the elementary school, is by no means a simple "mirroring" of the community stratification scale, for a considerable number of lower-status children get accepted into groups including members with higher family status than themselves. This stratified youth system operates as a genuine assortative mechanism; it does not simply reinforce ascribed status.

The prominence of this youth culture in the American secondary school is, in comparison with other societies, one of the hallmarks of the American educational system; it is much less prominent in most European systems. It may be said to constitute a kind of structural fusion between the school class and the peer-group structure of the elementary period. It seems clear that what I have called the "human relations" oriented contingent of the secondary school pupils are more active and prominent in extracurricular activities, and that this is one of the main foci of their differentiation from the more impersonally- and technically-oriented contingent. The personal qualities figuring most prominently in the human relations contingent can perhaps be summed up as the qualities that make for "popularity." I suggest that, from the point of view of the secondary school's selective function, the youth culture helps to differentiate between types of personalities which will, by and large, play different kinds of roles as adults.

The stratification of youth groups has, as noted, a selective function; it is a bridge between the achievement order and the adult stratification system of the community. But it also has another function. It is a focus of prestige which exists along side of, and is to a degree independent of, the achievement order focusing on school work as such. The attainment of prestige in the informal youth group is itself a form of valued achievement. Hence, among those individuals destined for higher status in society, one can discern two broad types: those whose school work is more or less outstanding and whose informal prestige is relatively satisfactory; and vice versa, those whose informal prestige is outstanding, and school performance satisfactory. Falling below certain minima in either respect would jeopardize the child's claim to belong in the upper group.[16] It is an important point here that those clearly headed for college belong to peer groups which, while often depreciative of intensive concern with studies, also take for granted and reinforce a level of scholastic attainment which is necessary for admission to a good college. Pressure will be put on the individual who tends to fall below such a standard.

In discussing the elementary school level it will be remembered that we emphasized that the peer group served as an object of emotional dependence displaced from the family. In relation to the pressure for school achievement, therefore, it served at least partially as an expression of the lower-order motivational system *out* of which the child was in process of being socialized. On its own level, similar things can be said of the adolescent youth culture; it is in part an expression of regressive motivations. This is true of the emphasis on athletics despite its lack of relevance to adult roles, of the "homosexual" undertones of much intensive same-sex friendship, and of a certain "irresponsibility" in attitudes toward the opposite sex—e.g., the exploitative element in the attitudes of boys toward girls. This, however, is by no means the whole story. The youth culture is also a field for practicing the assumption of higher-order responsibilities, for conducting delicate human relations without immediate supervision and learning to accept the consequences. In this connection it is clearly of particular importance to the contingent we have spoken of as specializing in "human relations."

We can, perhaps, distinguish three different levels of crystallization of these youth-culture patterns. The middle one is that which may be considered age-appropriate without clear status-differentiation. The two key-notes here seem to be "being a good fellow" in the sense of general friendliness and being ready to take responsibility in informal social situations where something needs to be done. Above this, we may speak of the higher level of "outstanding" popularity and qualities of "leadership" of the person who is turned to where unusual responsibilities are required. And below the middle level are the youth patterns bordering on delinquency, withdrawal, and generally unacceptable behavior. Only this last level is clearly "regressive" relative to expectations of appropriate behavior for the age-grade. In judging these three levels, however, allowance should be made for a good many nuances. Most adolescents do a certain amount of experimenting with the borderline of the unacceptable patterns; that they should do so is to be expected in view of the pressure toward independence from adults, and of the "collusion" which can be expected in the reciprocal stimulation of age-peers. The question is whether this regressive behavior comes to be confirmed into a major pattern for the personality as a whole. Seen in this perspective, it seems legitimate to maintain that the middle and the higher patterns indicated are the major ones, and that only a minority of adolescents comes to be confirmed in a truly unacceptable pattern of living. This minority may well be a relatively constant proportion of the age cohort, but apart from situations of special social disorganization, the available evidence does not suggest that it has been a progressively growing one in recent years.

The patterning of cross-sex relations in the youth culture clearly foreshadows future marriage and family formation. That it figures so prominently in school is related to the fact that in our society the element of ascription, including direct parental influence, in the choice of a marriage partner is strongly minimized. For the girl, it has the very important significance of reminding her that her adult status is going to be very much concerned with marriage and a family. This basic expectation for the girl stands in a certain tension to the school's curricular coeducation with its relative lack of differentiation by sex. But the extent to which the feminine role in American society continues to be anchored in marriage and the family should not be allowed to obscure the importance of coeducation. In the first place, the contribution of women in various extra-familial occupations and in community affairs has been rapidly increasing, and certainly higher levels of education have served as a prerequisite to this contribution. At the same time, it is highly important that the woman's familial role should not be regarded as drastically segregated from the cultural concerns of the society as a whole. The educated woman has important functions *as wife and mother,* particularly as an influence on her children in backing the schools and impressing on them the importance of education. It is, I think, broadly true that the immediate responsibility of women for family management has been increasing, though I am very skeptical of the alleged "abdication" of the American male. But precisely in the context of women's increased family responsibility, the influence of the mother both as agent of socialization and as role model is a crucial one. This influence should be evaluated in the light of the general upgrading process. It is very doubtful whether, apart from any other considerations, the motivational prerequisites of the general process could be sustained without sufficiently high education of the women who, as mothers, influence their children.

Conclusion

With the general cultural upgrading process in American society which has been going on for more than a century, the educational system has come to play an increasingly vital role. That this should be the case is, in my opinion, a consequence of the general trend to structural differentiation in the society. Relatively speaking, the school is a specialized agency. That it should increasingly have become the principal channel of selection as well as agency of socialization is in line with what one would expect in an increasingly differentiated and progressively more upgraded society. The legend of the "self-made man" has an element of nostalgic romanticism and is destined to become increasingly mythical, if by it is meant not just mobility from humble origins to high status, which does indeed continue to occur, but that the high status was attained through the "school of hard knocks" without the aid of formal education.

The structure of the public school system and the analysis of the ways in which it contributes both to the socialization of individuals and to their allocation to roles in society is, I feel, of vital concern to all students of American society. Notwithstanding the variegated elements in the situation, I think it has been possible to sketch out a few major structural patterns of the public school system and at least to suggest some ways in which they serve these important functions. What could be presented in this paper is the merest outline of such an analysis. It is, however, hoped that it has been carried far enough to suggest a field of vital mutual interest for social scientists on the one hand and those concerned with the actual operation of the schools on the other.

NOTES

1. The principal source for these statements is a study of social mobility among boys in ten public high schools in the Boston metropolitan area, conducted by Samuel A. Stouffer, Florence R. Kluckhohn, and the present author. Unfortunately the material is not available in published form.

2. See table from this study in J. A. Kahl, *The American Class Structure,* New York: Rinehart & Co., 1953, p. 283. Data from a nationwide sample of high school students, published by the Educational Testing Service, show similar patterns of relationships. For example, the ETS study shows variation, by father's occupation, in proportion of high school seniors planning college, of from 35 per cent to 80 per cent for boys and 27 per cent to 79 per cent for girls. From *Background Factors Related to College Plans and College Enrollment among High School Students,* Princeton: Educational Testing Service, 1957.

3. There seem to be two main reasons why the high-status, low-ability group is not so important as its obverse. The first is that in a society of expanding educational and occupational opportunity the general trend is one of upgrading, and the social pressures to downward mobility are not as great as they would otherwise be. The second is that there are cushioning mechanisms which tend to protect the high status boy who has difficulty "making the grade." He may be sent to a college with low academic standards, he may go to schools where the line between ability levels is not rigorously drawn, etc.

4. This discussion refers to public schools. Only about 13 per cent of all elementary and secondary school pupils attend non-public schools, with this proportion ranging from about 22 per cent in the Northeast to about 6 per cent in the South. U. S. Office of Education, *Biennial Survey of Education in the United States, 1954–56,* Washington, D.C.: U. S. Government Printing Office, 1959, chap. 2, "Statistics of State School Systems, 1955–56," Table 44, p. 114.

5. In 1955–56, 13 per cent of the public elementary school instructional staff in the United States were men. *Ibid.,* p. 7.

6. This summary of some contrasts between traditional and progressive patterns is derived from general reading in the literature rather than any single authoritative account.

7. This account of the two components of elementary school achievement and their relation summarizes impressions gained from the literature, rather than being based on the opinions of particular authorities. I have the impression that achievement in this sense corresponds closely to what is meant by the term as used by McClelland and his associates. Cf. D. C. McClelland *et al., The Achievement Motive,* New York: Appleton-Century-Crofts, Inc., 1953.

8. On the identification process in the family see my paper, "Social Structure and the Development of Personality," *Psychiatry,* 21 (1958), 321–340.

9. It is worth noting that the Catholic parochial school system is in line with the more general older American tradition, in that the typical teacher is a nun. The only difference in this respect is the sharp religious symbolization of the difference between mother and teacher.

10. The following summary is adapted from T. Parsons, R. F. Bales, *et al., Family, Socialization and Interaction Process,* Glencoe, Ill.: The Free Press, 1955, esp. chap. 4.

11. In this, as in several other respects, there is a parallel to other important allocative processes in the society. A striking example is the voting process by which political support is allocated between party candidates. Here, the strain arises from the fact that one candidate and his party will come to enjoy all the perquisites—above all the power—of office, while the other will be excluded for the time being from these. This strain is mitigated, on the one hand, by the common commitment to constitutional procedure, and, on the other hand, by the fact that the nonpolitical bases of social solidarity, which figure so prominently as determinants of voting behavior, still cut across party lines. The average person is, in various of his roles, associated with people whose political preference is different from his own; he therefore could not regard the opposite party as composed of unmitigated scoundrels without introducing a rift within the groups to which he is attached. This feature of the electorate's structure is brought out strongly in B. R. Berelson, P. F. Lazarsfeld, and W. N. McPhee, *Voting,* Chicago: University of Chicago Press, 1954. The conceptual analysis of it is developed in my own paper, " 'Voting' and the Equilibrium of the American Political System" in E. Burdick and A. J. Brodbeck (eds.), *American Voting Behavior,* Glencoe, Ill.: The Free Press, 1959.

12. *Ibid.*

13. J. A. Kahl, "Educational and Occupational Aspirations of 'Common Man' Boys," *Harvard Educational Review,* 23 (1953), 186–203.

14. Men make up about half (49 per cent) of the public secondary school instructional staff. *Biennial Survey of Education in the United States, 1954–56, op. cit.,* chap. 2, p. 7.

15. See, for instance, C. W. Gordon, *The Social System of the High School: A Study in the Sociology of Adolescence,* Glencoe, Ill.: The Free Press, 1957.

16. J. Riley, M. Riley, and M. Moore, "Adolescent Values and the Riesman Typology" in S. M. Lipset and L. Lowenthal (eds.), *The Sociology of Culture and the Analysis of Social Character,* Glencoe, Ill.: The Free Press, 1960.

52. THE ADOLESCENT SUBCULTURE AND ACADEMIC ACHIEVEMENT

JAMES S. COLEMAN

Talcott Parsons, in his analysis of the school class as a social system, treats the perspectives and activities of adolescents in relation to their assessment by the adult society. He views the school itself as a filter through which students are sifted and graded according to culturally defined norms of achievement.

Academic achievement and the status accorded to students who excel in terms of conventional standards used by educators may also be examined from the point of view of peers. Here, as James S. Coleman has found, the students' *values, those of the adolescent subculture rather than of the adult world, are exceedingly important. Coleman studied the prestige accorded to various types of students—the star athlete, the most popular, the most brilliant—by those attending ten different kinds of high schools in midwestern United States. He found that, in all schools, academic achievement was not given as much weight as other activities in prestige allocation. Coleman's findings suggest that adolescent subcultures may actually be deterrents to academic achievement.*

That "two cultures" may be in conflict over the criteria for assessing a "good" member of the community raises important questions for sociological theory and educational policy.

James S. Coleman is Professor and Chairman of the Department of Social Relations at The Johns Hopkins University. He is the author of Community Conflict (1957), The Adolescent Society (1961), and Introduction to Mathematical Sociology (1964). He is coauthor of Union Democracy (1956).

Industrial society has spawned a peculiar phenomenon, most evident in America but emerging also in other Western societies: adolescent subcultures, with values and activities quite distinct from those of the adult society—subcultures whose members have most of their important associations within and few with adult society. Industrialization, and the rapidity of change itself, has taken out of the hands of the parent the task of training his child, made the parent's skills obsolescent, and

put him out of touch with the times—unable to understand, much less inculcate, the standards of a social order which has changed since he was young.

By extending the period of training necessary for a child and by encompassing nearly the whole population, industrial society has made of high school a social system of adolescents. It includes, in the United States, almost all adolescents and more and more of the activities of the adolescent himself. A typical example is

Reprinted from the *American Journal of Sociology*, **65** (1960), 337–347, by permission of the author and The University of Chicago Press. Copyright © 1960 by The University of Chicago Press.

provided by an excerpt from a high-school newspaper in an upper-middle-class suburban school:

SOPHOMORE DANCING FEATURES CHA CHA
Sophomores, this is your chance to learn how to dance! The first day of sophomore dancing is Nov. 14 and it will begin at 8:30 A.M. in the Boys' Gym. . . .
No one is required to take dancing but it is highly recommended for both boys and girls. . . .
If you don't attend at this time except in case of absence from school, you may not attend at any other time. Absence excuses should be shown to Miss —— or Mr. ——.

In effect, then, what our society has done is to set apart, in an institution of their own, adolescents for whom home is little more than a dormitory and whose world is made up of activities peculiar to their fellows. They have been given as well many of the instruments which can make them a functioning community: cars, freedom in dating, continual contact with the opposite sex, money, and entertainment, like popular music and movies, designed especially for them. The international spread of "rock-and-roll" and of so-called American patterns of adolescent behavior is a consequence, I would suggest, of these economic changes which have set adolescents off in a world of their own.

Yet the fact that such a subsystem has sprung up in society has not been systematically recognized in the organization of secondary education. The theory and practice of education remains focused on *individuals;* teachers exhort individuals to concentrate their energies in scholarly directions, while the community of adolescents diverts these energies into other channels. The premise of the present research is that, if educational goals are to be realized in modern society, a fundamentally different approach to secondary education is necessary. Adults are in control of the institutions they have established for secondary education; tradition-

ally, these institutions have been used to mold children as individuals toward ends which adults dictate. The fundamental change which must occur is to shift the focus: to mold social communities as communities, so that the norms of the communities themselves reinforce educational goals rather than inhibit them, as is at present the case.

The research being reported is an attempt to examine the status systems of the adolescent communities in ten high schools and to see the effects of these status systems upon the individuals within them. The ten high schools are all in the Midwest. They include five schools in small towns (labeled *0–4* in the figures which follow), one in a working-class suburb (*6*), one in a well-to-do suburb (*9*), and three schools in cities of varying sizes (*5, 7,* and *8*). All but No. *5,* a Catholic boys' school, are coeducational, and all but it are public schools.

The intention was to study schools which had quite different status systems, but the similarities were far more striking than the differences. In a questionnaire all boys were asked: "How would you most like to be remembered in school: as an athletic star, a brilliant student, or most popular?" The results of the responses for each school are shown in Figure I,[1] where the left corner of the triangle represents 100 per cent saying "star athlete"; the top corner represents 100 per cent saying "brilliant student"; and the right corner represents 100 per cent saying "most popular." Each school is representedly a point whose location relative to the three corners shows the proportion giving each response.

The schools are remarkably grouped somewhat off-center, showing a greater tendency to say "star athlete" than either of the other choices. From each school's point is a broken arrow connecting the school as a whole with its members who were named by their fellows as being "members of the leading crowd." In al-

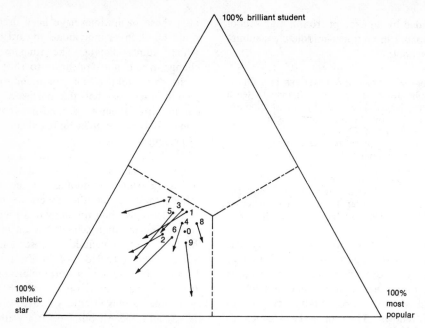

Figure 1. Positions of Schools and Leading Crowds in Boys' Relative Choice of Brilliant Student, Athletic Star, and Most Popular

most every case, the leading crowd tends in the direction of the athlete—in all cases *away* from the ideal of the brilliant student. Again, for the leading crowds as well as for the students as a whole, the uniformity is remarkably great; not so great in the absolute positions of the leading crowds but in the direction they deviate from the student bodies.

This trend toward the ideal of the athletic star on the part of the leading crowds is due in part to the fact that the leading crowds include a great number of athletes. Boys were asked in a questionnaire to name the best athlete in their grade, the best student, and the boy most popular with girls. In every school, without exception, the boys named as best athletes were named more often—on the average over twice as often—as members of the leading crowd than were those named as best students. Similarly, the boy most popular with girls was named as belonging to the leading crowd more often than the best student, though in all schools but the well-to-do suburb and the smallest rural

town (schools *9* and *0* on Fig. I) less often than the best athlete.

These and other data indicate the importance of athletic achievement as an avenue for gaining status in the schools. Indeed, in the predominantly middle-class schools, it is by far the most effective achievement for gaining a working-class boy entrée into the leading crowd.

Similarly, each girl was asked how she would like to be remembered: as a brilliant student, a leader in extracurricular activities, or most popular. The various schools are located on Figure II, together with arrows connecting them to this leading crowd. The girls tend slightly less, on the average, than the boys to want to be remembered as brilliant students. Although the alternatives are different, and thus cannot be directly compared, a great deal of other evidence indicates that the girls—although better students in every school—do not want to be considered "brilliant students." They have good reason not to, for the girl in each grade in each of the schools who was most often

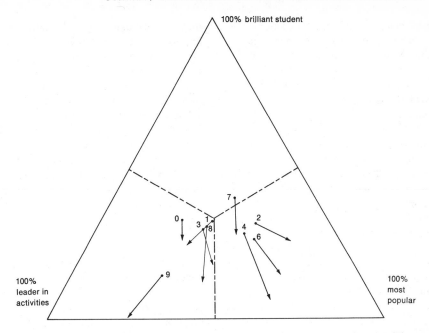

Figure 2. Positions of Schools and Leading Crowds in Girls' Relative Choice of Brilliant Student, Activities Leader, and Most Popular

named as best student has fewer friends and is less often in the leading crowd than is the boy most often named as best student.

There is, however, diversity among the schools in the attractiveness of the images of "activities leader" and "popular girl" (Fig. II). In five (*9, 0, 3, 8,* and *1*), the leader in activities is more often chosen as an ideal than is the popular girl; in four (*7, 6, 2,* and *4*) the most popular girl is the more attractive of the two. These differences correspond somewhat to class background differences among the schools: *2, 4, 6,* and *7,* where the activities leader is least attractive, have the highest proportion of students with working-class backgrounds. School *9* is by far the most upper-middle-class one and by far the most activities-oriented.

The differences among the schools correspond as well to differences among the leading crowds: in schools *2, 4,* and *6,* where the girls as a whole are most oriented to being popular, the leading crowds are even more so; in the school where the girls are most oriented to the ideal of the activities leader, No. *9,* the leading crowd goes even further in that direction.[2] In other words, it is as if a pull is exerted by the leading crowd, bringing the rest of the students toward one or the other of the polar extremes. In all cases, the leading crowd pulls away from the brilliant-student ideal.

Although these schools vary far less than one might wish when examining the effects of status systems, there are differences. All students were asked in a questionnaire: "What does it take to get into the leading crowd?" On the basis of the answers, the relative importance of various activities can be determined. Consider only a single activity, academic achievement. Its importance for status among the adolescents in each school can be measured simply by the proportion of responses which specify "good grades," or "brains" as adolescents often put it, as a means of entrée into the leading crowd. In all the schools, academic achievement was of less importance than other matters, such as being an athletic star among the boys, being a cheerleader or being good-looking among the girls, or other attributes. Other measures which were obtained of the importance of academic achievement in the adolescent status system correlate highly with this one.[3]

If, then, it is true that the status system of adolescents *does* affect educational goals, those schools which differ in the importance of academic achievement in the adolescent status system should differ in numerous other ways which are directly related to educational goals. Only one of those, which illustrates well the differing pressures upon students in the various schools, will be reported here.

In every social context certain activities are highly rewarded, while others are not. Those activities which are rewarded are the activities for which there is strong competition—activities in which everyone with some ability will compete. In such activities the persons who achieve most should be those with most potential ability. In contrast, in unrewarded activities, those who have most ability may not be motivated to compete; consequently, the persons who achieve most will be persons of lesser ability. Thus in a high school where basketball is important, nearly every boy who might be a good basketball player will go out for the sport, and, as a result, basketball stars are likely to be the boys with the most ability. If in the same school volleyball does not bring the same status, few boys will go out for it, and those who end up as members of the team will not be the boys with most potential ability.

Similarly, with academic achievement: in a school where such achievement brings few social rewards, those who "go out" for scholarly achievement will be few. The high performers, those who receive good grades, will not be the boys whose ability is greatest but a more mediocre few. Thus the "intellectuals" of such a society, those defined by themselves and others as the best students, will not in fact be those with most intellectual ability. The latter, knowing where the social rewards lie, will be off cultivating other fields which bring social rewards.

To examine the effect of varying social pressures in the schools, academic achievement, as measured by grades in school, was related to I.Q. Since the I.Q. tests differ from school to school, and since each school had its own mean I.Q. and its own variation around it, the ability of high performers (boys who made A or A— average) [4] was measured by the number of standard deviations of their average I.Q.'s above the mean. In this way, it is possible to see where the high performers' ability lay, relative to the distribution of abilities in their school.[5]

The variations were great: in a small-town school, No. *1,* the boys who made an A or A— average had I.Q.'s 1.53 standard deviations above the school average; in another small-town school, No. *0,* their I.Q.'s were only about a third this distance above the mean, .59. Given this variation, the question can be asked: Do these variations in ability of the high performers correspond to variations in the social rewards for, or constraints against, being a good student?

Figure III shows the relation for the boys between the social rewards for academic excellence (i.e., the frequency with which "good grades" was mentioned as a means for getting into the leading crowd) and the ability of the high performers, measured by the number of standard deviations their average I.Q.'s exceed that of the rest of the boys in the school. The relation is extremely strong. Only one school, a parochial boys' school in the city's slums, deviates. This is a school in which many boys had their most important associations outside the school rather than in it, so that its student body constituted far less of a social system, less able to dispense social rewards and punishments, than was true of the other schools.

Similarly, Figure IV shows for the girls the I.Q.'s of the high performers.[6] Unfor-

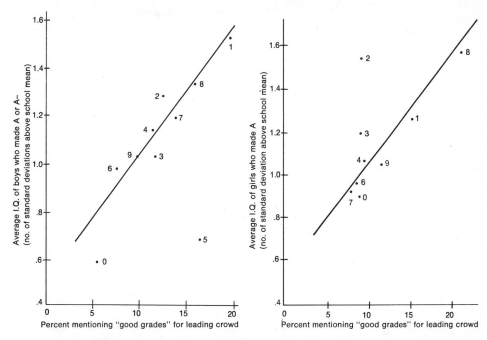

Figure 3. I.Q.'s of High Achieving Boys by Importance of Good Grades Among Other Boys

Figure 4. I.Q.'s of High Achieving Girls by Importance of Good Grades Among Other Girls

tunately, most of the schools are closely bunched in the degree to which good grades are important among the girls, so that there is too little variation among them to examine this effect as fully as would be desirable. School *2* is the one school whose girls deviate from the general relationship.

The effect of these values systems on the freedom for academic ability to express itself in high achievement is evident among the girls as it is among the boys. This is not merely due to the school facilities, social composition of the school, or other variables: the two schools highest in the importance of scholastic achievement for both boys and girls are *1* and *8*, the first a small-town school of 350 students and the second a city school of 2,000 students. In both there are fewer students with white-collar backgrounds than in schools *9* or *3*, which are somewhere in the middle as to value placed on academic achievement, but are more white-collar

than in schools *7* or *4*, which are also somewhere in the middle. The highest expenditure per student was $695 per year in school *9*, and the lowest was little more than half that, in school *4*. These schools are close together on the graphs of Figures III and IV.

It should be mentioned in passing that an extensive unpublished study throughout Connecticut, using standard tests of achievement and ability, yielded consistent results. The study found no correlation between per pupil expenditure in a school and the achievement of its students relative to their ability. The effects shown in Figures III and IV suggest why: that students with ability are led to achieve only when there are social rewards, primarily from their peers, for doing so—and these social rewards seem little correlated with per pupil expenditure.

So much for the effects as shown by the variation among schools. As mentioned earlier, the variation among schools was

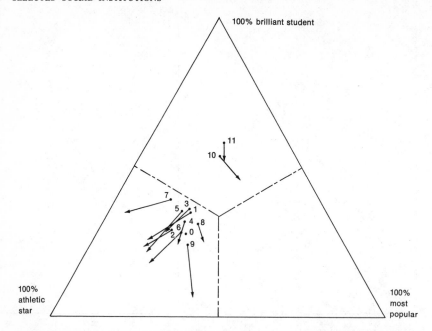

Figure 5. Positions of Schools and Leading Crowds in Boys' Relative Choice of Brilliant Student, Athletic Star, and Most Popular (Two Private Schools [10, 11] included)

not nearly so striking in this research as the fact that, in all of them, academic achievement did not count for as much as other activities. In every school the boy named as best athlete and the boy named as most popular with girls was far more often mentioned as a member of the leading crowd, and as someone to "be like," than was the boy named as the best student. And the girl named as best dressed, and the one named as most popular with boys, was in every school far more often mentioned as being in the leading crowd, and as someone to "be like," than was the girl named as the best student.

The relative unimportance of academic achievement, together with the effect shown earlier, suggests that these adolescent subcultures are generally deterrents to academic achievement. In other words, in these societies of adolescents those who come to be seen as the "intellectuals" and who come to think so of themselves are not really those of highest intelligence but are only the ones who are willing to work hard at a relatively unrewarded activity.

The implications for American society as a whole are clear. Because high schools allow the adolescent subcultures to divert energies into athletics, social activities, and the like, they recruit into adult intellectual activities people with a rather mediocre level of ability. In fact, the high school seems to do more than allow these subcultures to discourage academic achievement; it aids them in doing so. To indicate how it does and to indicate how it might do differently is another story, to be examined below.

Figures I and II, which show the way boys and girls would like to be remembered in their high school, demonstrate a curious difference between the boys and the girls. Despite great variation in social background, in size of school (from 180 to 2,000), in size of town (from less than a thousand to over a million), and in style of life of their parents, the proportion of boys choosing each of the three images by which he wants to be remembered is very nearly the same in all schools. And in every school the leading crowd "pulls" in

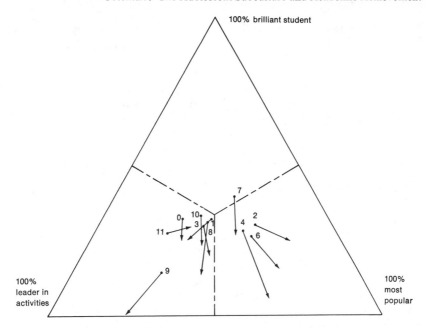

Figure 6. Positions of Schools and Leading Crowds in Girls' Relative Choice of Brilliant Student, Activities Leader, and Most Popular (Two Private Schools [10, 11] included)

similar directions: at least partly toward the ideal of the star athlete. Yet the ideals of the girls in these schools are far more dispersed, and the leading crowds "pull" in varying directions, far less uniformly than among the boys. Why such a diversity in the same schools?

The question can best be answered by indirection. In two schools apart from those in the research, the questionnaire was administered primarily to answer a puzzling question: Why was academic achievement of so little importance among the adolescents in school *9?* Their parents were professionals and business executives, about 80 per cent were going to college (over twice as high a proportion as in any of the other schools), and yet academic excellence counted for little among them. In the two additional schools parental background was largely held constant, for they were private, coeducational day schools whose students had upper-middle-class backgrounds quite similar to those of school *9.* One (No. *10*) was in the city; the other (No. *11*), in a subur-

ban setting almost identical to that of No. *9.* Although the two schools were added to the study to answer the question about school *9,* they will be used to help answer the puzzle set earlier: that of the clustering of schools for the boys and their greater spread for the girls. When we look at the responses of adolescents in these two schools to the question as to how they would like to be remembered, the picture becomes even more puzzling (Figs. V and VI). For the boys, they are extremely far from the cluster of the other schools; for the girls, they are intermingled with the other schools. Thus, though it was for the boys that the other schools clustered so closely, these two deviate sharply from the cluster; and for the girls, where the schools already varied, these two are not distinguishable. Furthermore, the leading crowds of boys in these schools do not pull the ideal toward the star-athlete ideal as do those in almost all the other schools. To be sure, they pull away from the ideal of the brilliant student, but the pull is primarily toward a social image, the most popular. Among the girls, the leading crowds pull in different directions and are nearly indistinguishable from the other schools.

The answer to both puzzles, that is, first, the great cluster of the boys and now, in these two additional schools, the greater deviation, seems to lie in one fact: the boys' interscholastic athletics. The nine public schools are all engaged in interscholastic leagues which themselves are knit together in state tournaments. The other school of the first ten, the Catholic school, is in a parochial league, where games are just as hotly contested as in the public leagues and is also knit together with them in tournaments.

Schools *10* and *11* are athletically in a world apart from this. Although boys in both schools may go in for sports, and both schools have interscholastic games, the opponents are scattered private schools, constituting a league in name only. They take no part in state or city tournaments and have almost no publicity.

There is nothing for the girls comparable to the boys' interscholastic athletics. There are school activities of one sort or another, in which most girls take part, but no interscholastic games involving them. Their absence and the lack of leagues which knit all schools together in systematic competition means that the status system can "wander" freely, depending on local conditions in the school. In athletics, however, a school and the community surrounding it, cannot hold its head up if it continues to lose games. It *must* devote roughly the same attention to athletics as do the schools surrounding it, for athletic games are the only games in which it engages other schools and, by representation, other communities.

These games are almost the only means a school has of generating internal cohesion and identification, for they constitute the only activity in which the school participates *as* a school. (This is well indicated by the fact that a number of students in school *10,* the private school which engages in no interscholastic games, has been concerned by a "lack of school spirit.") It is as a consequence of this that the athlete gains so much status: he is doing something for the school and the community, not only for himself, in leading his team to victory, for it is a school victory.

The outstanding student, in contrast, has little or no way to bring glory to his school. His victories are always purely personal, often at the expense of his classmates, who are forced to work harder to keep up with him. It is no wonder that his accomplishments gain little reward and are often met by ridiculing remarks, such as "curve-raiser" or "grind," terms of disapprobation which have no analogues in athletics.

These results are particularly intriguing, for they suggest ways in which rather straightforward social theory could be used in organizing the activities of high schools in such a way that their adolescent subcultures would encourage, rather than discourage, the channeling of energies into directions of learning. One might speculate on the possible effects of city-wide or state-wide "scholastic fairs" composed of academic games and tournaments between schools and school exhibits to be judged. It could be that the mere institution of such games would, just as do the state basketball tournaments in the midwestern United States, have a profound effect upon the educational climate in the participating schools. In fact, by an extension of this analysis, one would predict that an international fair of this sort, a "Scholastic Olympics," would generate interscholastic games and tournaments within the participating countries.

NOTES

1. I am grateful to James A. Davis and Jacob Feldman, of the University of Chicago, for suggesting such graphs for presenting responses to trichotomous items in a population.

2. This result could logically be a statistical artifact because the leaders were included among students as a whole and thus would boost the result in the direction they tend. However, it is not a statistical artifact, for the leading crowds are a small part of the total student body. When they are taken out for computing the position of the rest of the girls in each school, schools *2*, *4, 6,* and *7* are still the most popularity-oriented, and school *9* the most activities-oriented.

3. Parenthetically, it might be noted that these measures correlate imperfectly with the proportion of boys or girls who want to be remembered as brilliant students. These responses depend on the relative attractiveness of other ideals, which varies from school to school, and upon other factors unrelated to the status system.

4. In each school but *3* and *8,* those making *A and A* — constituted from 6 to 8 per cent of the student body. In order to provide a correct test of the hypothesis, it is necessary to have the same fraction of the student body in each case (since I.Q.'s of this group are being measured in terms of number of standard deviations above the student body). To adjust these groups, enough *6*'s were added (each being assigned the average I.Q. of the total group of *6*'s) to bring the proportion up to 6 per cent (from 3 per cent in school *3,* from 4 per cent in school *8*).

5. The I.Q. tests used in the different schools were: *0*) California Mental Maturity (taken seventh, eighth, or ninth grade); *1*) California Mental Maturity (taken eighth grade); *2*) SRA Primary Mental Abilities (taken tenth grade); *3*) California Mental Maturity (taken ninth grade; seniors took SRA PMA, which was tabulated as a percentile, and they have been omitted from analysis reported above); *4*) Otis (ninth and tenth grades; taken eighth grade); Kuhlman Finch (eleventh and twelfth grades, taken eighth grade); *5*) Otis (taken ninth grade); *6*) California Mental Maturity (taken eighth grade); *7*) California Mental Maturity (taken eighth grade); *8*) Otis (taken ninth or tenth grade); and *9*) Otis (taken eighth grade).

6. For the girls, only girls with a straight-*A* average were included. Since girls get better grades than boys, this device is necessary in order to make the sizes of the "high-performer" group roughly comparable for boys and for girls. Schools differed somewhat in the proportion of *A*'s, constituting about 6 per cent of the students in the small schools, only about 3 per cent in schools *6* and *7,* 1 per cent in *8,* and 2 per cent in *9.* In *8* and *9,* enough girls were added and assigned the average grade of the *7* (*A*—) group to bring the proportion to 3 per cent, comparable with the other large schools. The difference, however, between the large and small schools was left.

53. THE CHANGING FUNCTIONS OF UNIVERSITIES

A. H. HALSEY

The structural and functional aspects of educational systems are of particular interest to sociologists concerned with the process of modernization. Specialized education is both a response to certain social and technical needs and an instrumentality of social change.

In the essay below, A. H. Halsey discusses the background and nature of higher education in those societies whose cultures are now based on advanced technological achievements. He shows how colleges and universities began to eschew traditional parochialism by expanding their research activities and professional training facilities to meet the requirements of the industrial society. In doing so they became (and continue to be) more closely integrated with society in general and increased their potential influence as sources of economic and social change.

A. H. Halsey is a Fellow of Nuffield College at Oxford University. With Jean Floud he is coauthor of a trend report and bibliography on the sociology of education in Current Sociology, 7 (*1958*) *published by UNESCO. He is also coauthor of* Social Class and Educational Opportunity (*1958*), *and coeditor of* Education, Economy, and Society: A Reader in the Sociology of Education (*1961*).

Introduction

The main thesis of this essay concerns the relation of higher education to social structure and involves the notion of a type of society—the technological society [1]— toward which Western industrial countries are more or less rapidly moving. The mark of the educational institutions of a technological society is that they are in a special sense crucial to its maintenance and, through the institutionalization of technological research, to its further development.

In the medieval and industrial periods the history of the universities in relation to the economy is one of imperfect and usually belated adaptation to the occupational demands of a culture gradually increasing in its complexity. In the technological society the system of higher education no longer plays a passive role: it becomes a determinant of economic development and hence of stratification and other aspects of social structure. However, the stage reached and the speed of advance toward the technological society is conditioned by the strength of the earlier traditions of higher learning in any given industrial country.

Universities and Social Structures

The basic function of education is the preservation and transmission of culture. In this broad sense all societies are educative. Sociologists of education, however, confine their studies largely to those societies in which there is a sufficiently complex culture to require its preservation and transmission by specialized agencies.

Reprinted from *The Harvard Educational Review,* **30** (1960), 118–127, by permission of the author and the publisher. This article was originally entitled "The Changing Functions of Universities in Advanced Industrial Societies."

Higher education is such a specialized agency charged with the conservation of the most highly prized beliefs and intellectual skills in the cultural heritage.

Accordingly organizations of higher education must be seen as partially independent of, but functioning in relation to, such other aspects of social structure as government, the economy and religious and military organizations. The existence of the higher learning presupposes certain social conditions, notably a level of economic and political development that affords the possibility of "idleness" for a scholarly class.[2] Indeed universities always play a role in stratification because, controlling access to highly valued cultural elements, they are intrinsically inegalitarian. As Durkheim pointed out, "to find an absolutely homogeneous and egalitarian education, it would be necessary to go back to prehistoric societies in the structure of which there is no differentiation."[3]

An adequate analysis of contemporary university developments therefore requires a theory of change involving multiple causes, conditions, and consequences. But the crucial connection, in this context, is with the economy. This is basically because development of knowledge is always likely to issue from its conservation and, in fact, has done so intermittently throughout the history of higher learning. More particularly it is so because, in response to the demands set up by modern industrialism and scientific warfare, research has become institutionalized in universities. The universities have therefore become an established source of instability to the technology and hence to the economy. And at the same time they are the training institutions for the skilled manpower required by a complex technology.

Universities and the Emergence of Industrialism

The present linkage of the university to the economy in industrial society is direct and obvious through the market for professional manpower and through research activities in the applied sciences. It was not always so. Richard Hofstadter has contrasted the present situation with the period before the American Civil War: "In the middle of the 20th century, the American student of the history of higher education will find it hard to understand why college teaching responded so slowly to social change unless he realizes that the old-time colleges were not organically knit into the fabric of economic life."[4] The European universities were, in their medieval origins, an organic part of religious rather than economic life and this was true even of the much later American foundations where, until the early years of the 18th century, the majority of graduates became clergymen.[5] The subsequent development of new economic functions for the universities with the rise of industrialism is only one aspect, though an important one, of the broader process of secularization of learning which spread with the Renaissance and which, through the teaching of Wyclif, Ockham and Duns Scotus, had already disturbed Oxford in the 14th century.[6] A negligible proportion of the alumni of modern western universities enters the ministry.[7]

However, the typical transition of universities from their earlier functional emphasis was not a simple story of extension in provision for secular professional training as a response to the demands of developing industrialism. On the contrary there was an overlapping and, in England at least, still observable phase in which the universities were dominated by their function as preserves of the aristocratic and gentry classes. Indeed the history of European and American universities in the age of coal and steam industrialism is one of successful resistance, by ideological and other elements in the "superstructure," to the pressures set up by economic change.[8] Max Weber's view of education as a differentiating agency, socializing individuals into the total style of life of the strata for which they are destined, has to be used as if in application to an aristocratic "structure of domination" up to the Second World War. In this sense higher education has been essentially a phenomenon of status rather than class; a process directed "against the market." [9]

Traditionally the university has rightly been seen as primarily devoted to the education, moral and physical as well as intellectual, of the "cultivated man" [10] with its emphasis on "character," "service," poised and rounded personality, and an easy amateur command of the nonspecialist skill appropriate to a ruling class in a world of steam navigation, gunpowder, and manuscript.[11] For the lower strata the educational equivalent in Europe has been a simple literacy heavily imbued with ideas of docility, piety and nationalism.

Vocationalism was resisted in the European universities long after the religious domination of curricula had been overcome and long after secular universities had been founded on the basis of state and industrial patronage. Thus the creation of the University of Berlin in the early years of the 19th century, which set the tone for much of the subsequent modernization of universities in Europe and America, "was intended primarily to develop knowledge, secondarily and perhaps as a concession, to train the professional and the official classes." [12] In America the land grant colleges created after the Morrill Act of 1862 failed, despite the lead given by Wisconsin [13] to create a comprehensive link between higher education and agriculture, through either research or teaching, until after the First World War. In England the great champion of the modern universities, T. H. Huxley, asserted before the Cowper Commission of 1892 that "the primary business of the universities is with pure knowledge and pure art—independent of all application to practice; with progress in culture not with increase in wealth." [14]

The emergence of the modern British universities as undergraduate professional schools, though it begins with the foundation of the University of London, is largely a 20th-century phenomenon and even then is explicable primarily in terms of the continued command held by Oxford and Cambridge over the avenues of entry into the national elites. Even in America, where the absence of an indigenous aristocracy made professional and technological training more acceptable, it was absorbed into the universities more by their extension into graduate schools than by revision of undergraduate curricula.[15]

The aristocratic domination of universities which was typical of Europe in the 18th century, with its American equivalent in the education of ministers and lawyers as community leaders, continued despite the shifting class basis of power in the 19th and early 20th century. However, this did not preclude the more limited function of higher education as an agent of social mobility, of assimilation into elite groups, of "resocialization" for a selected minority of able boys from the lower strata. The 19th-century American colleges and the German universities both recruited from the middle and lower classes. And in England with the beginning of expansion of professional and administrative employment in the second half of the century, "the old and the new middle classes needed avenues of employment which would provide both prestige and relatively high income for their sons." [16] But the working classes were scarcely touched by these developments.[17]

In any case, as Hofstadter says of the American college, "Education was for gentlemen, it was designed to create among them a core of central knowledge that would make of them a community of the educated." [18] And even Veblen's bitter classic, though directed against "the conduct of universities by businessmen" and the perversion of scholarly values by the predatory ethics of business, describes an example of the ideal university man as one striving for "lifelike imitation of a country gentleman." [19]

Universities and Technological Society

A new relationship is now discernible. In general, whereas both Weber and Veblen saw the university as a corporate structure in process of adaptation (Veblen thought betrayal) to industrial society,[20] W. H. Whyte,[21] writing forty years later, had to see it as an integral part of the organization of a technological society. Development in this direction has its origins in the 19th century application of science to industrial processes, the "invention of invention," and the slow subsequent development of technological professions in agriculture, chemistry, metallurgy, mechanical and electrical engineering, etc. However it begins to become clear as a direct relationship of economic organization to the higher learning only with escape from the economic depressions of the 1930's and the search for high productivity of the war and postwar years. Both as research organizations and as training establishments, the institutions of higher education in this period have been drawn more closely into the economy either directly or through the state. The exchange of ideas, people, and contracts between university departments and research institutes and their counterparts in private industry and government agencies is such as to merge these organizations and to assimilate the life styles of their staff.

Basically, the new functions reflect a new stage in the development of the means of production in which, as Drucker puts it, "the highly educated man has become the central resource of today's society, the supply of such men the true measure of its economic, military, and even its political potential." [22] The class formation appropriate to the new means of production is one in which educational institutions play a crucial role. The search for talent to man the economy implies democratization of access to education and the development of selective processes. Schools, colleges and universities become the agencies through which

"achievement" in the occupational role is largely determined and in which the forces of "ascription" and "achievement" contend to determine the life chances of individuals.

The educational characteristics of a technological society are clearest where they are most advanced—in America. The explosive expansion which has taken place there in the demand for high scientific manpower has not only created conditions of chronic shortage of supply; it has also transformed the universities. In 1900 the percentage of American 18–21-year-olds enrolled in institutions of higher education was 4.0. It doubled in the next twenty years and again in the following twenty years to 15.6 in 1940. Since then expansion has been even more rapid until, in 1956, the figure was about one third.[23] Under these circumstances the function of universities as nurseries for elite groups is overlaid by their new function as a mass higher education service in an emergent technological society. The "community of the educated" similarly tends to disappear.[24] Meanwhile it should be noticed that the structure of higher education has adapted itself to the new conditions by forming itself into a status hierarchy or "academic procession" [25] with graded access to "achievement" and power in the stratification system.[26]

Russia is the same kind of society in the sense that higher education is geared closely to the economy which, in this case, is controlled centrally in the interests of maximizing economic growth. At first glance the USSR appears to be educationally underdeveloped. It has proportionately only half as many secondary-school graduates as the U.S.A. and only 16 per 1000 of its people have had higher education compared with the American figure of 44.[27] But the essential feature of the Russian case is that the sharp break with earlier social traditions which was made possible by the Revolution resulted in the development of a system of higher education adjusted directly to the demand for technological manpower. Thus in the supply of professional and scientific workers to agriculture, medicine, engineering, etc., the Russian system is as far advanced as the American. For example, in engineering and science the number of graduates per 1000 of the population is 9 in the USSR and 10 in the U.S.A.

The different points reached by these two countries in their advance towards the technological society is indicated by the fact that in Russia the percentage of science and engineering graduates to all graduates is 55 whereas in America it is 21. This certainly does not mean that in America the higher learning either already is or is becoming less closely geared to the economy. On the contrary there is a strong tendency for business to increase its influence over the content of American higher education as is indicated by the decline of the fundamental disciplines and the rise of applied subjects, especially those connected with business administration and commerce.[28] The "extra" output of American graduates in the humanities and social sciences mainly reflects the professionalization of the tertiary sectors of American industry and may be viewed as an adornment of the affluent society, which Russia has yet to become.

The British case is instructive as one in which the medieval and aristocratic traditions of the universities have hitherto acted as a powerful brake against movement towards the technological society. British university life has been dominated by Oxford and Cambridge since the defeat of the migration to Stamford in 1334.[29] In the 14th century Oxford and Cambridge, backed by royal power, established themselves as national institutions with a monopoly over the higher learning. The monopoly was challenged frequently but unsuccessfully until the rise of the universities in the great industrial cities of the 19th century, and even then monopoly only gave way to pre-eminence.[30] The challenge of industrialism and nonconformity was met partly by reform and expansion of the ancient foundations, partly by assimilation of the sons of successful business men through the colleges and the "public schools" which supply them, and partly by sending staff to the newly created universities.

As a result a two tier structure emerged in the early 20th century. Oxford and Cambridge were national universities connected with the national elites of politics, administration, business and the liberal professions. The rest were provincial, all of them, including London, taking most of their students from their own region [31] and training them in undergraduate professional schools for the newer technological and professional occupations created by industrialism such as chemistry, electrical engineering, state grammar school teaching and the scientific civil service.

Since the war, as may be seen from Table 1, a new wave of expansion, with some emphasis on science and the technologies, has been taking place. But the

Table 1. *Percentage Distribution of Full-time University Students by Faculties in the United Kingdom in 1938–39 and 1956–57*

Faculty	1938–39 (N = 50,002)	1956–57 (N = 89,866)
Arts	44.7	43.1
Pure science	15.3	22.2
Medicine, dentistry	26.8	17.4
Technology, agriculture	13.2	17.3
Total	100.0	100.0

SOURCE: *University Development 1952–1957, H.M.S.O. Cmd. 534.*

Table 2. *Geographical Origins of University Students * in English Universities, 1908–56*

| University | Per Cent Students Drawn from within 30 Miles | | |
	1908–09	1948–49	1955–56
Birmingham	—	56	38
Bristol	87	39	26
Leeds	78	60	40
Liverpool	75	62	55
Manchester	73	59	48
University College, London	66	53	43

* For the United Kingdom as a whole, including Oxford and Cambridge, the proportion of university students living at home fell from 41.7 per cent in 1938–39 to 34.6 per cent in 1951–52 and further to 26.6 per cent in 1956–57. (University Development 1952–57, H.M.S.O. Cmd. 534, Table VII.)

pace of expansion is much slower than in the U.S.A. or the USSR. The elite conception of the university continues to dominate development plans. Oxford and Cambridge are again expanding to assimilate the rising technological elite through the Cavendish Laboratories and Churchill College. A scrimmage for precedence on the second tier is taking place among the modern universities and the newly emancipated university colleges; and, in the process, the provincial universities are being nationalized. An indication of this trend may be had from the proportion of students drawn from within 30 miles of the university. In Table 2 some examples have been calculated from the Returns from Universities and University Colleges to the University Grants Committee.

Meanwhile a third tier in the structure of higher education is being formed by Colleges of Advanced Technology and Teacher Training Colleges offering courses of three years duration. The creation of this new level in the hierarchy is to the emerging technological economy what the provincial universities were to large-scale industrialism.

Conclusion

Throughout the period of emerging industrialism in Europe and America the principal social function of the universities has been that of status differentiation of elites with some assimilation of students from the lower strata. But the progressive secularization of higher learning since medieval times has increased the potential of the universities as sources of technological and therefore of social change until now they are beginning to occupy a place as part of the economic foundation of a new type of society. In this new technological society educational institutions are expanded not only to exercise research functions but also to play a central role in the economy and the system of stratification as agencies for selection, training, and occupational placement of individuals.

Movement toward this state of affairs is uneven among the Western industrial countries. A comparison of America, Russia and Britain shows that it is furthest advanced in America where professionalization has entered the tertiary sectors of industry and has resulted in far-reaching modifications of the content of university studies. It is fastest in Russia where the supply of graduates is closely attuned to the needs of a fast developing economy. It is slowest in Britain where the legacy of the traditional status-differentiating function of Oxford and Cambridge persists and where the response to technological change is most strongly contained within an educational hierarchy corresponding to the power and prestige pyramid of the wider society.

NOTES

1. *Cf.* J. E. Floud and A. H. Halsey, "The Sociology of Education—A Trend Report and Bibliography," *Current Sociology* 7 (1958).

2. More strictly, in the incipient phase of the development of higher learning, a "vicarious leisure class." *cf.* T. Veblen, *The Theory of the Leisure Class,* London: Allen and Unwin, Ltd., 1924, p. 367.

3. E. Durkheim, *Education and Sociology,* trans. S. D. Fox, Glencoe, Ill.: The Free Press, 1956, p. 69.

4. R. Hofstadter and C. P. Hardy, *The Development and Scope of Higher Education in the United States,* New York: Columbia University Press, 1952, p. 21.

5. 70% of the first few years of Harvard graduates (in the 1640's) became clergymen and nearly 73% of Yale graduates between 1701–1719. *cf.* Hofstadter, *op. cit.,* pp. 6–9.

6. Cf. A. R. Myers, *England in the Late Middle Ages (1307–1536),* London: Penguin Books, 1952, pp. 72–77.

7. At Yale it was reduced to 6% by 1900. In 1955 2% of those admitted to Oxford and Cambridge went to read theology, the figure for the modern British universities being 0.4%. R. K. Kelsall, *Applications for Admission to Universities,* London: Association of Universities of British Commonwealth, 1957, Table 1.

8. An excellent brief analysis of the impact of technology and science on the higher learning in Britain is given in Sir Eric Ashby, *Technology and the Academics,* London: The Macmillan Company, 1958.

9. Though access to it, in accordance with Weber's general definition of status, is in the long run determined by access to market opportunities.

10. Weber points out that, " 'the cultivated man,' rather than the 'specialist' has been the end sought by education and has formed the basis of social esteem in such various systems as the feudal, theocratic, and patrimonial structures of domination: in the English notable administration, in the old Chinese patrimonial bureaucracy as well as under the rule of demagogues in the so-called Hellenic democracy." H. Gerth & C. Mills, *From Max Weber,* London: Kegan Paul, 1948, p. 242.

11. "In the 18th century while the gentry ruled, the country [England] had practically no officials; the Church and the Law were allied powers. . . . The Universities accordingly developed on lines convenient to the ruling caste, as seats in which the youth of the country could acquire a modicum of classical learning; they gave an intellectual sanction to the domination of the gentry and brought up the young men to be gentlemen, accepting and exemplifying the ideals of a class. And such, despite the far-reaching reforms of the 19th century, Oxford and Cambridge remain to this day to a very large extent." W. Dibelius, *England,* trans. M. A. Hamilton, London: Jonathan Cape Ltd. 1929, p. 409.

12. A. Flexner, *Universities: American, English, German,* New York: Oxford University Press, 1930, p. 312.

13. *Cf.* C. McCarthy, *The Wisconsin Idea,* New York: The Macmillan Company, 1912.

14. Quoted in C. Bibby, "T. H. Huxley's Idea of a University," *Universities Quarterly,* 10 (1956).

15. It is noteworthy that only very recently have investigations of socialization into specialized professional groups such as the medical profession become a significant part of the sociological study of university life, e.g., R. K. Merton *et al., The Student Physician: Introductory Studies in the Sociology of Medical Education,* Cambridge, Mass.: Harvard University Press, 1957. H. Becker and B. Greer, "Student Culture in Medical School," *Harvard Educational Review,* 28 (1958), 70–80.

16. D. V. Glass, "Education," in M. Ginsberg (ed.), *Law and Opinion in the Twentieth Century,* London: Stevens, 1959, p. 326.

17. *Cf.* D. V. Glass, *ibid.* Of the generation of working-class boys born between 1910 and 1929 only 1.4% went to a university. For the best available statistical description see J. E. Floud, "The Educational Experience of the Adult Population of England and Wales as at July, 1949,"

in D. V. Glass (ed.), *Social Mobility in Britain,* London: Free Press, 1954. Writing of the German universities in 1929, Flexner (*op. cit.,* p. 337) states, "It has been estimated that at this moment not exceeding three per cent of the university students come from the working classes, and the number was formerly even smaller." In the American system of higher education initial access has traditionally been more open but selection *within* the system ("drop-out") has been more severe and along class lines. This basic contrast between American and English education is discussed in an interesting fashion by Ralph Turner in his "Sponsored and Contest Mobility and the School System," *American Sociological Review* 25 (1960), 855–867.

18. Hofstadter, *op. cit.,* p. 11.

19. T. Veblen, *The Higher Learning in America,* New York: B. W. Huebsch, 1918, p. 164. He goes on, "The incumbent had no distinguishing marks either as a teacher or a scholar, and neither science nor letters will be found in his debt."

20. *Cf.* J. E. Floud and A. H. Halsey, *loc. cit.*

21. W. H. Whyte, *The Organization Man,* New York: Simon and Schuster, 1956.

22. P. F. Drucker, *The Landmarks of Tomorrow,* London: Heinemann, 1959, p. 87.

23. *Cf.* N. DeWitt, "Basic Comparative Data on Soviet and American Education," *Comparative Education Review,* 2 (1958), 9.

24. It was once maintained in part by the role of two or three major universities as training institutions for all university faculty. But with expansion this integrating factor operates less and less. The minor universities are forced to become self-recruiting. Thus the status exclusiveness of the high-prestige universities is preserved though the distribution of academic talent may be widening. *Cf.* T. Caplow and R. J. McGee, *The Academic Market-Place,* New York: Basic Books, 1958, p. 211 *et seq.*

25. D. Riesman, *Constraint and Variety in American Education,* New York: Doubleday Anchor Books, 1958, Ch. 1.

26. E. Haveman and P. S. West, in their *They Went to College: The College Graduate in America Today,* New York: Harcourt, Brace, 1952, show that marked differences in earning increment are to be gained from attendance at the high-prestige universities like Princeton as compared with the ordinary run of state universities.

27. For this and the following figures, *cf.* DeWitt, *loc. cit.,* also his *Soviet Professional Manpower,* Washington: National Science Foundation, 1955, especially pp. 254–258, where a comparison is made of the supply of professional manpower in the USSR and U.S.A.

28. *Cf.* W. H. Whyte, *op. cit.,* pp. 80–82.

29. H. Rashdall, *The Universities of Europe in the Middle Ages,* Oxford: The Clarenden Press, 1936, III, 89–90.

30. *Cf.* E. A. Shils, "The Intellectuals. Great Britain," *Encounter,* 6 (1955), and A. Halsey, "British Universities and Intellectual Life," *Universities Quarterly,* 12 (1958), 141–152.

31. See Table 2.

54. EDUCATION IN PUERTO RICO: THE U. S. MODEL TRANSPLANTED

LEILA SUSSMANN

What happens when American public education principles and practices are transplanted in another cultural setting? Leila Sussmann sought an answer to this question through an extensive study of postwar changes in the Puerto Rican system of secondary and higher education.

Among many other important findings, the researcher discovered that while "democratization of access" was widespread it was accompanied by increasing segregation of the socially advantaged and disadvantaged in the private and public sector respectively and by a growing divergence of academic achievement between the two sectors. Such self-segregation was found to have no necessary connection with race. It was, rather, a class phenomenon.

Leila Sussmann is Professor of Sociology at Tufts University. Her publications include Dear F. D. R.: A Study in Political Letterwriting *(1963),* High School to University in Puerto Rico *(1965), and* Social Objectives in Educational Planning *(1967).*

The genius of American schooling is its "commitment to popular education." [1] This commitment is the essence of the U.S. model in Puerto Rico. The goal is to provide schooling for as many youths to as high a level as the economy will permit. If selection is necessary due to scarce resources, the criterion should be ability, but ability tempered by consideration for the socially caused disadvantages of lower class homes and schools. So runs the egalitarian ethos of Puerto Rican education.

Along with the populist bent of her ideology, Puerto Rico's educational system has been shaped by rapid economic growth since World War II. The Island gained semi-autonomy in 1940. With the impetus provided by the war, the new government launched a successful campaign of industrialization. The rising Gross Commonwealth Product made greater resources available for education,

and the growing literacy of the labor force was a lure for investors. It is well known that the success of the famed *Operation Bootstrap* owed much to Puerto Rico's unique political and economic ties to the United States. As U.S. citizens, Puerto Ricans have the right to migrate to the continent free of quota restrictions. Large numbers of young adults exercised this right in the forties and fifties, thereby helping to keep population growth within manageable bounds. [2] Since the Island is part of the U.S. defense system, none of her budget need be spent for defense. Her integration into the U.S. tariff and monetary systems is attractive to continental investors. Because Puerto Rico has no representative in Congress, she pays no federal taxes. At the same time she received direct and indirect federal aid during the postwar period estimated by one scholar at more than $175 million a year. [3]

Reprinted from *Sociology of Education*, **41** (Fall 1968), 321–341, by permission of the author and The American Sociological Association. This article was originally entitled "Democratization and Class Segregation in Puerto Rican Schooling: The U. S. Model Transplanted."

These economic advantages have few parallels in other developing countries and for that reason Puerto Rico's educational development is an atypical case. Nevertheless, rapid achievement of mass schooling is becoming a more influential pattern throughout the world, and its outcomes, even under special conditions, are worth study. Three of the important outcomes in Puerto Rico will be mentioned briefly here and discussed more fully below.

First, Puerto Rico has emulated the U.S. both in striving after numbers and leaving quality to take care of itself. For a country of her wealth, she has a school system characterized by high enrollment ratios and low quality. Her enrollment ratios rival those of the most industrialized nations of Europe; but indexes of school quality resemble those of less developed countries.

Second, "equal educational opportunity," in one meaning of that phrase, is well-realized in Puerto Rico. In 1960 there was an unusually close approach to equal rates of attendance at senior high school and university for youths of diverse social origins; this, despite the fact that only a third of the eligible age group was in senior high school and fewer than eight percent in B.A. programs at the university. The upper and upper middle classes had nothing like the disproportionate share of selective education that their counterparts long maintained in the older industrial nations.

Third, accompanying the postwar enrollment expansion and the democratization of access to higher schooling, there appeared a sharp social class segregation of secondary schools. The private sector of secondary education was increasingly preferred by middle class families. By 1960, public and private high schools were different worlds, socially and academically. The private schools recruited mainly from the top ability quintile and the higher social classes, while the public high schools had a heterogeneous social and academic composition. Social class and ability segregation were creeping into university education as well.

As I have shown in detail elsewhere, Puerto Rico constitutes an exception to the rule that the demand of the working classes for selective education does not begin to be met until the middle class demand has been filled.[4] (This is the rule for the countries for which there are data, at any rate.) In Puerto Rico equality of access to senior high school for children of different social classes was closely approached while the enrollment of the upper and upper middle classes was still under 50 percent. My main point here is that this radical democratization of access was accompanied by social class segregation of the high schools, in this case a cleavage between the public and private sectors. This is a new form of educational inequality since the private schools, attended exclusively by high status youths from educationally strong families are, by virtue of that fact if no other, qualitatively superior to the heterogeneous public high schools. The academic achievement of the private school graduates is strikingly superior to that of the graduates of the public high schools.

Democratization of access has had similar consequences in the United States. Not only our "neighborhood" elementary schools, but also our high schools and colleges are social class-segregated and correlatively ability-segregated in no small degree.

The phenomenon is old, but I suspect that segregation has sharpened as mass access to higher education has progressed. Inequality of access may be waning, only to be replaced by differential chances to get a high quality education, which in its way is just as significant. While the educational level of the whole population has risen, the educational gap between the social classes, especially if measured by amount learned rather than years of schooling, may be as wide as ever. To prove such an assertion for the U.S. is a huge undertaking, although important fragments of documentation are in hand.[5] In the small Commonwealth of Puerto Rico, some parts of the process—democratization of access accompanied by social class segregation of the high schools—stand out clearly.

Numbers and Quality in Puerto Rican Schooling

The economic and educational history of Puerto Rico from the American occupation to 1960 falls into three periods: 1899–1927; 1928–1940; and 1940–1960. During the first period, American investment flowed into corporate sugar plantations. Gross product and "social overhead" capital increased, but population grew even faster. Most of the sugar profits returned to the continent and the Puerto Rican people remained very poor.

At the time of the U.S. occupation, the population was 77 percent illiterate. Ninety-two percent of the children aged 5–17 were not in school. In accord with its declared intention that the people of its territories should gain full citizenship, the U.S. government began establishing a system of compulsory schooling. The goal of universal education enjoyed wide support in the Island, and the growth of schooling in Puerto Rico during the first 25 years of U.S. rule was substantial. It is difficult to find a yardstick to measure just how substantial. U.S. and Puerto Rican authorities habitually made the comparison with the continental United States, and of course found Puerto Rico's school system lagging. Comparison with countries at the same level of economic development in 1925 would be more appropriate except for the fact that Puerto Rico, as a colony, was exempt from many expenses independent nations must bear. She spent 45 percent of Insular and municipal receipts on education in 1925 as compared with an average for the continental states of 28 percent of state and local receipts. Thus, although she had a larger proportion of

her population in the school-going ages than North Carolina, the state which came nearest in this respect, and she was also poorer, Puerto Rico spent as much per pupil on education in 1925 as did North Carolina.[6]

Another possible but imperfect comparison could be made with nations which had reached Puerto Rico's 1925 economic development level around 1958. This comparison is convenient because the data are readily available. It puts Puerto Rico at an advantage in the sense mentioned above. She is being compared with independent nations which could afford to spend less on education; but it puts her at a disadvantage in the sense that the emphasis on education as the route to development was worldwide in 1958 as it had not been in 1925. For example, few European nations had more than 10 percent of the age group enrolled in secondary education in 1925; the U.S. had 25 percent and Puerto Rico had 8 percent.

If the comparison with nations equally developed in 1958 is made, using Harbison and Myers' tabulations of UNESCO data, Puerto Rico in 1925 falls into the range of the "partially developed" or "Level II" countries. As compared with those countries, her elementary school enrollment was above the mean and her secondary enrollments were just at the mean.[7] Enrollments in higher education cannot be compared because there are no data on how many Puerto Ricans were receiving higher education abroad. Harbison and Myers include those students in their reports on Level II countries. Puerto Rico was a little below the Level II mean in teacher/pupil ratios. This stood not so much for very large classes as for double sessions: A three-hour school day which allowed one teacher and classroom to serve two groups of pupils, morning and afternoon. Half-time schooling at the elementary level has been Puerto Rico's characteristic means for raising school enrollments within the limits of her resources. In 1925 the short school day was partly compensated for by a long school year: 180 days as compared with North Carolina's 139 days and an average for the continent of 164 days.[8] Puerto Rico's per pupil expenditure in elementary education in 1925 was more than three times that of the Latin American "partially developed countries" in 1958.[9] As a result the teachers were, on this comparison, well-paid, well-trained, and of high calibre. An investigation by a team of educators from Teachers College found that students going into elementary teaching were above the academic average of high school graduates and equal in academic quality to freshmen entering the liberal arts courses at the University of Puerto Rico at the time.[10] The holding power of the Puerto Rican schools was well above the Level II average: fourth grade pupils in the Island were 45 percent as many as first grade pupils while the Level II mean was 18 percent as many.

The most striking indication that the quality of Puerto Rico's schools in 1925 was high for a country with so little wealth comes from the results of Stanford Achievement Tests administered by the investigators from Teachers College. The tests, translated as literally as possible from the English, were given to over 10,000 children in grades 2 through 12, chosen to represent all geographical areas of the Island. There were examinations in Spanish, English and arithmetic, and also in science, history and literature. Since the latter three subjects were not taught at all in the Puerto Rican elementary schools— the time was devoted instead to teaching English—the children did very poorly in them. However, in the language and arithmetic tests they were close to, and sometimes above, the U.S. continental norms. In arithmetic computation and reasoning the children in the first four grades surpassed the continental children even on some tests administered in English. They also did better in the early grades on the Pinter non-language mental ability tests. U. S. children overtook and slightly sur-

passed the Puerto Rican pupils at grades 7, 8 and 9.[11]

Rough though these comparisons are, they support the view that mass expansion of schooling at whatever cost to quality was *not* the educational policy of Puerto Rico in 1925. There was great pressure from the urban areas for faster growth of secondary education, but the Teachers College consultants recommended giving first priority to universal elementary education of high quality.

Any debate which might have arisen concerning priorities was stilled by the world depression which reached Puerto Rico in 1928. The Island went into an economic decline lasting until 1940 which brought the growth of elementary school enrollment ratios to a halt. The same was true of changes in holding-power and double sessions. Pupil/teacher ratios became even less favorable than they had been. The urban-rural gap in school facilities, always large, grew larger. According to Education Commissioner José Gallardo in 1943, ". . . the existing differences in available facilities in the urban and rural zones of each municipality . . . are almost incredible." Only the senior high schools gained ground; their enrollment ratio went from eight percent of the age group in 1925 to 23 percent in 1947 while their pupil/teacher ratio remained unchanged at 30. Thus the urban demand for higher secondary schooling remained strong and effective, despite U.S. expert opinion.

The next distinct phase of educational growth dates from World War II to 1960. Wartime investment stimulated a spurt of economic development. Puerto Rico drew immense vitality from her newly-won autonomy and from the brilliance of her first elected Governor, Luis Muñoz Marín. He and his lieutenants initiated Operation Bootstrap which raised the Puerto Rican Commonwealth's gross product from $391,105,000 in 1940 to $1,878,000,000 in 1962 and per capita income from $213 to $680.

With increased financial resources at their disposal and the growth rate of the school-age population declining, the Puerto Rican government in 1950 set new school enrollment goals to be reached by 1960. The goals were reached before the target date. A few statistics will convey just how great an expansion of school attendance was compressed into a decade. In 1950, 72.5 percent of the 6–12 year olds were enrolled in elementary school, and in 1960, 82.6 percent.[12] In 1950, 32.4 percent of the 13–15 year olds were enrolled in junior high school, and in 1960, 52.9 percent. In 1950, 17.6 percent of the 16–18 year olds were enrolled in senior high school and in 1960, 32.1 percent. The proportion of high school seniors going on to a bachelor of arts college program did not rise during the decade. On the contrary, it fell slightly, but the proportion of the college-*age* group entering a four-year college course did increase. Eighteen years was the modal age of University of Puerto Rico freshman. Enrollment in the freshman year of a B.A. program as a proportion of 18 year olds was 2.7 percent in 1945, 5.6 percent in 1952, and 8.6 percent in 1960. If the college age group is defined as 18–21 year olds inclusive (as Puerto Rican official statistics define it), the number attending college or university in 1960, including two-year curricula, was 16 percent of the age group. Using 20–24 year olds as the college age group, the proportion, including two-year curricula, was about 12 percent.

Contemplating these school enrollments in 1960, Puerto Rican officials found them too low, but the United Nations Yearbook called them unusually high for a country of Puerto Rico's income. A comparison with Harbison and Myers' cross-national data for the same period bears out the UN interpretation. By 1960 Puerto Rico belonged economically either at the top of their Level III range, the "semi-advanced countries," or at the bottom of their Level IV range, the "advanced" countries. Her GNP per capita was midway between the Level III and Level IV means. Her percent of population engaged in agriculture was at the mean of Level IV. But her proportion of population in the school-going age cohorts was still as high as that of *any* "semi-advanced" country. Puerto Rico had not attained the low birth rate of the most industrialized nations. Nevertheless, her school enrollment ratios equalled the mean of Level IV, the "advanced countries."

Data collected by the OECD from its member nations (all of them Level IV by Harbison and Myers' yardsticks) calculate school enrollment ratios in a different way from UNESCO, which favors Puerto Rico even more.[13] By this method of calculation her school enrollment ratios were equal to those of the most advanced industrial countries in the world excepting only Canada and the U.S.

On indexes of quality, however, Puerto Rico did not match the Level IV countries. Both her recurrent per-pupil expenditures and her pupil/teacher ratios were inferior to theirs, despite the fact that she was still spending a higher proportion of GNP on education—five percent—than any of the advanced countries. These resources were spread wide and thin. For five of the years between 1947 and 1957 the proportion of all elementary pupils on double session rose to an unprecedented 75 percent. The pupil/teacher ratio went up to 60. There were no substitute teachers in the elementary schools. That fact, plus the high rate of teacher absences (due to low morale) left classes uncovered to an extent of five percent loss in the children's instructional time. Holidays were frequent. According to a report of the Superior Council of Education, the school year, subtracting teacher absences and holidays, lasted seven months. This is more than a month shorter than the school year of 1925.

The low morale among teaching staff contributed to an acute teacher shortage. A government planning report said that from 1955 to 1958 teachers had been leaving their jobs twice as fast as they were being trained.[14] It was difficult for the school system to compete with the private sector for educated personnel. In contrast to 1925 the teaching profession was not recruiting outstanding people. Students at the College of Education of the University of Puerto Rico had the lowest entrance examination scores of any freshmen in the University.[15]

In order to staff classrooms the standards for *normalista* training are distressingly low. For example one professor found that his *normalista* class had a third-grade-level reading proficiency in Spanish and a second-grade-level reading proficiency in English. Math and science teachers in the public schools frequently have never taken these subjects in college, and many English teachers cannot speak English.[16]

The high schools, too, underwent great changes between 1950 and 1960. In the twenties the public high schools of Puerto Rico had been college-preparatory institutions. Their curriculum was academic, offering English, Spanish, History, Mathematics, French, Latin, Science, and some Home Economics and Manual Training. They were located in the large cities and had room for only eight percent of the age group. They recruited meritocratically, on the basis of elementary school grades. After a probationary first year, "adjustments" were made. The competitive places in these public high schools were highly prized. They were the training ground for those who would go abroad to universities and return to the best positions in government, the professions, and commerce. The private high schools were patronized by students who had failed to gain acceptance in the public.

By the 1950's the public high schools were enrolling nearly a third of the age group. Commercial and vocational schools had been built to meet a growing demand. Graduates of these non-academic curricula increased by 78 percent in the 1940's as compared with a 121 percent increase in graduates of the college preparatory course. In the 1950's, the tables were turned; commercial and vocational graduates increased by 196 percent as compared with an 85 percent growth in college preparatory graduates.[17] At this point Puerto Rico implemented a long-standing U.S. recommendation for comprehensive high schools. The college preparatory course was dropped, leaving the "general" curriculum as the sole academic course of study. A few metropolitan high schools offered all three curricula: general, commercial, and vocational, and many offered the general and commercial courses. Rural high schools offered *only* the general curriculum. The academic requirements of the general curriculum were actually a bit lower than those of the commercial and vocational; however, the general course left room for many electives, while the other two curricula were filled up with special, non-academic requirements. In effect the college-preparatory curriculum became informal. Able, college-oriented students in the general curriculum were encouraged to take many academic electives while the others were encouraged to elect easier courses. My 1960 sample survey of Purto Rican high school seniors showed that the general curriculum attracted the most and least able students while the other two curricula drew from the middle of the ability range.[18]

This transformation of the Puerto Rican public high school differed in several ways from the shift to the mass terminal high school which had occurred in the U.S. a generation before. Although most Puerto Rican high school graduates of the 50's did not go to college, a majority were *oriented* to going there. Fifty-eight percent of all high school seniors in my 1960 survey said they planned to go to college. This was slightly higher than the proportion of high school seniors who had said they had college plans in the U.S. ETS survey of 1955. However, the proportion of Puerto Rican students actually entering college the following autumn was lower than in the U.S.[19] Furthermore, in Puerto Rico the difference in college plans among students in the different curricula was very slight. Commercial and vocational students had college plans almost as frequently as general curriculum students, but the rates of actual college *entry* differed sharply among planners from the different curricula. In short, the high school became a mass institution which was *de facto* terminal for most of its graduates, but it continued to be defined by its clientele as a college-preparatory institution. There was constant public pressure to make reality match this definition. Recalling Martin Trow's description of the two transformations of the U.S. high school, first from a select, college-preparatory academy to a mass terminal institution; and then to a mass college-preparatory institution,[20] it looks as though Puerto Rico telescoped these two transformations into one.

In all the public high schools in 1957–1958 there were only five qualified physics teachers. Five hundred mathematics teachers were needed but only 39 were qualified. The social studies, best supplied of the academic subjects, had 384 qualified teachers for 564 positions.[21] It is not surprising that under these conditions, student achievement declined:

A large company that hires only high school graduates reported that it rejects 70 percent of job applicants due to failure to pass a simple test in mathematics and mechanics designed for ninth graders. The Vocational Rehabilitation and Education Division's new technical school, selecting high school graduates with at least a B average, requires three years for a two year training course in order to overcome deficiencies in mathematics, Spanish, and English.[22]

The University of Puerto Rico was also in trouble qualitatively. One of its most sympathetic consultants, Rexford Guy Tugwell, called it "little more than a junior college." Not much upper college work was offered since, due to the stu-dents' poor preparation, it took the better part of four years to cover the work of freshman and sophomore level. In a report on the University of Puerto Rico written in 1959, Frank Bowles estimated that many freshmen arrived at the U.P.R. with a deficiency of a whole grade level in terms of preparation.[23] One could never discover this fact from looking at admissions records. My analysis of these showed that freshmen entering the U.P.R. in 1960 had many *more academic credits* in their high school records than entrants of 1952 or 1944;[24] yet their professors found these groups of freshmen successively less prepared.

Except that it deluged the students with a plethora of introductory courses, the University made no institutional effort to overcome their academic deficiencies.[25] Many students handled the problem by registering for an overload of courses and then withdrawing just before final examinations from those they thought they would fail. The U.P.R. permitted such overloads and withdrawals without penalty. The courses dropped could then be repeated and passed another year, or the student could keep taking new courses until he had, by trial and error, passed a sufficient number to graduate. This was often a long, discouraging process. A majority of entrants never obtained a degree. My data, compiled from individual records of all students who entered as freshmen at the Rio Piedras campus in 1952, show that 33 percent obtained a B.A. within four years; 13 percent obtained one within eight years; and 54 percent had not obtained a degree by 1960.[26]

Toward the end of the 50's, talk of a "crisis of quality" in the schools led to a round of evaluations by Puerto Rican educators and outside consultants. The Superior Council on Education administered tests in arithmetic, Spanish and English to 32,942 pupils in grades 4, 6, 9 and 12. Unfortunately, the published results contained no bench-mark comparisons with any outside group or previous period, so that the overall scores are very difficult to interpret. Important internal comparisons were made, however. Urban students did consistently better than rural, and students on single session did consistently better than those on double session in every subject. The report furnished a few illustrations of what it described as the "very unsatisfactory situation." In the fourth grade 57 percent of the pupils answered the problem of "16 minus 7" incorrectly; 59 percent could not multiply 9 by 8. Nineteen percent in the 6th grade and 13 percent in the ninth grade could not subtract 31 from 60; 81 percent in the 6th grade and 77 percent in the ninth grade could not divide ¾ by $\frac{6}{12}$.[27] A team of European consultants reported that in many fourth grades they visited 20 percent to 50 percent of the pupils could not read.[28]

Nearly all observers agreed that achievement levels were down since 1940. The increase in double sessions, the lowered quality of teaching personnel, the cuts in instructional time all contributed to the decline. However, part of it was due to the fact that the expanded school system had finally reached the most disadvantaged sector of the child population, those "first generations" to attend school who need a *higher* investment of instructional resources to attain the achievement levels of children whose parents have been schooled. But Puerto Rico's investment per elementary school pupil was virtually unchanged in 1960 from what it had been in 1925: $56 per year as compared with the earlier $50.[29]

The huge effort of the 1950's attained its goals. Nearly every Puerto Rican child had his "chance at school." The high schools were transformed from élite to popular institutions, and the same was true of the University. The price was a decline in quality throughout the system. Half-time schooling plagued the elementary schools. The high school students who were university-bound took more academic courses than their predecessors

and apparently learned less. The University had a huge dropout problem and lacked a true upper college. Many Puerto Rican educators said that the 1950's having been the decade of expansion, the 1960's must become the decade of quality improvement. But popular pressure for still further expansion of high school and university places was very strong. Slowing down the growth in favor of raising the academic standards could prove politically difficult for a popularly elected government.

Egalitarian Policy

Behind the expansion of the Puerto Rican school system in the fifties was a passionate concern for equal educational opportunity. Frank Bowles' 1959 report on higher education claimed ". . . Puerto Rico has accepted and tried to meet the need for expansion without recognizing that standards have been lowered in the process. Thereby the lowered standards have become embedded in and have affected all tax supported education in the Island."

If the educators gave too little thought to quality, it was because of their overriding devotion to equity. They wanted as nearly as possible to "equalize" educational chances. The spirit in which they made policy is well expressed in the following quotation:

At the present time there are 7 towns with first grades organized in single sessions (a six-hour school day) and 10 with second grades organized (in single sessions). The total number of children in these grades on single sessions reached 8209 last year. There were also 12,106 in these three grades on interlocking sessions (a five-hour school day) which makes a total of 20,315. That is to say that by organizing all the first, second, and third grades on double sessions (a three-hour day) it would be possible to make room for 20,315 new pupils next year. In this way, the opportunities of those now in the first three grades would be equalized and at the same time opportunity would be increased for

20,000 of those who are not in school. Why should 664 first grade students have a double opportunity, that is to say a complete day of classes when all the rest who are 74,499 have to make do with a half day? Why should one-fourth of those in third grade receive a full day while three-quarters receive only a half day? [30]

One can point to many educational policies of the 50's which sacrificed quality to equity, at times with awareness of the price. An instance was the continued practice of giving preference to children past the normal school-entry age over those who had just reached it, in admissions to first grade. The Teachers' College report criticized this practice in 1925, pointing out that overage children had a high dropout rate, whereas younger children tended to remain in school longer, and thus to be a better "investment" risk. The Puerto Rican educators knew the facts; but they felt it unjust to children who were originally excluded from school for lack of space to deprive them altogether of their chance to get an education. Hopefully, with further expansion, the younger children could be accommodated a year or two later. However, expansion never quite caught up with the need. Overage entrants continued to receive preference, and as a consequence the Puerto Rican school system has unusually large numbers of students who are older than the proper age for their grade level.

The rejection of any form of ability grouping in the elementary schools also had an egalitarian rationale. In particular, separating more able pupils from the others so that they could have an enriched curriculum or go through the regular one faster was considered a kind of an unacceptable "élitism."

The college-preparatory curriculum was dropped in the 50's and the general, commercial, and vocational curricula incorporated into comprehensive high schools in order to guarantee what the British call "parity of esteem" for all three courses of study. To the same end, the Superior Council on Education dropped *all specific subject requirements* for entry to the University of Puerto Rico. In theory, this opened the way to the university for graduates of any of the three high school curricula. They were all made eligible, that is, to take the University entrance examination. No doubt this formal equality of chances to enter the University supported the heavy college-orientation which I described above. But, as I pointed out, the facts were at variance with the doctrine. Competition for university entry was becoming more intense because the proportion of high school graduates who applied for admission grew, while the proportion of graduates admitted remained the same. As a result, the number of high school academic credits on the records of entering freshmen at the U.P.R. rose steadily, *after* the formal requirements for academic courses were dropped. Graduates of the commercial and vocational curricula lost out on the entrance examination for lack of this academic preparation. My data show that in 1960 their entrance examination performance was poorer than that of graduates of the general curriculum even with ability test scores held constant.[31]

In the 1950's too, an Island-wide competitive entrance examination became for the first time part of the University of Puerto Rico admissions procedure. Prior to that, entrance had been based on high school grades. However a study by the Superior Council on Education in 1948 demonstrated that a graduation index of "B" from a small (usually rural or small town) public high school was predictive of about the same university performance as a grade of "C" from a large (usually metropolitan) high school. The entrance examination was intended to correct for these differences in high school standards. However the policy adopted was actually a compromise. The high school graduation index and the entrance examination score were given equal weight and averaged to form the "admissions index."

Using the entrance examination alone would have been more purely meritocratic; but it would have penalized the rural as compared with the urban applicants, and the public school as compared with the private school applicants. For instance, the entrants to the College of Education in 1960 had scored second in their entering class on the basis of high school graduation indexes, but last on the basis of their entrance examination scores. They consisted disproportionately of girls from rural and small town high schools. Had admission to the university been based on the entrance examination alone, some of them would not have been admitted. Thus the meritocratic principle was tempered with the populist one, keeping the road to the University open for a good many youths whose homes and earlier schooling had left them academically disadvantaged.[32]

Equality of Access

The extent to which youths of different social origins gain access to senior high school and university education is only partly a matter of social policy. Aspirations to higher education have diffused far more rapidly to every social stratum in U.S. and Puerto Rican society[33] than in European. In the U.S., high enrollment ratios have been cause and consequence of the diffusion. However, the relationship between the enrollment ratio in secondary or higher education and parity of attendance rates as between the social strata is not a simple one. Expansion of the enrollment ratio is not necessarily associated with increased parity. Within limits total enrollment and parity of access for the different social strata can vary independently. For instance, a doubling of places in British grammar schools from 12 percent to 23 percent of the age group resulted in only a small reduction of social class differentials in rates of attendance. Of course when enrollment approaches

100 percent, as in the U.S. high school, it is self-evident that social class differentials decline. In fact when the enrollment from the upper social strata approaches saturation, further expansion can only come from below and *must* result in some equalization of social class attendance rates.

The evidence is that the expansion of selective education in Europe has not so far been associated with a decline of social class differentials in access. The upper and upper middle classes have continued to receive a disproportionate share of the new places. In the U.S., access to high school education for children of the manual strata seems to have levelled up only after the attendance rate of the non-manual strata was close to its ceiling. Something similar appears to be true in higher education. Expansion since 1947 has been associated with some equalization of attendance rates between the manual and non-manual classes. However, the equalization set in at a point when 78 percent of non-manual sons and 66 percent of non-manual daughters who graduated from high school were attending college; for the professional and technical classes the percentages were 83 and 78. Thus the U.S. is no exception to what has been the rule: substantial room in selective schools is made only after the demand of the non-manual strata has been filled.

It is striking, therefore, that Puerto Rico *is* an exception to the rule. In the Island only 32 percent of the age group was attending high school in 1960, as compared with 87 percent in the U.S. Yet, if the parity ratio of the two sets of high school seniors are put side by side, it is clear that parity of access was as far advanced in Puerto Rico as in the U.S. with the exception of children of farm laborers. It was much farther advanced than in Bridgeport, Connecticut, or Seattle, Washington at the time (1930) when only 30 percent of *their* youth were in high school. And this parity of access was achieved despite the fact that the non-manual classes in Puerto Rico still had an attendance rate in the 12th grade of less than 50 percent. Recruitment to the prestigeful status of high school senior in Puerto Rico was radically democratic.[34]

Recruitment to the status of college freshman was less so. Still, a comparison of parity ratios for freshmen at the University of Puerto Rico in 1960, when 8.6 percent of the age cohort were entering B.A. programs, with freshman in the U.S. which had 20 percent of the age cohort entering them, suggests that Puerto Rico will also achieve parity of access to higher education at an earlier stage of growth of universities than the United States. Recruitment to higher education there is already more democratic than it is in European countries with similar enrollment ratios.[35] Puerto Rico's mass education system clearly follows the U.S. pattern and, in some ways, is outrunning its model. In particular, the Commonwealth has admitted large numbers of urban working class youths to the privilege of higher schooling at a time when more than half the offspring of the middle classes are still denied it.

Social Class Segregation

Equal access is not the whole of equal educational opportunity. If high schools and colleges were alike in quality and prestige, it would be. But that situation is most nearly approached in countries where access is severely exclusive. In the U.S. the secondary schools and the colleges and universities are extremely diverse in curricula, in the social and ability composition of their clientele, and in the prestige of their diplomas. Mass extension of higher schooling has been accompanied by internal differentiation. A non-selected mass student population with a wide range of preparation, capacity, and occupational aspirations can only be served by a diversity of educational offerings. The diversity is not random, however. In high schools

and colleges, as well as elementary schools, the social and academic composition of the student body varies sharply from institution to institution and quality is positively correlated with the presence of a high proportion of high SES students. Thus "Educational inequalities linked to social class differences are not wiped out by the growth of mass higher education, but find their expression in the internal differentiation of the system." [36] Unequal access to high school and university is replaced by unequal access to schooling of high quality.

In the U.S. social class segregation in education is masked by the size and heterogeneity of our school systems. Though it exists in considerable degree, it has not been the socially visible irritant that racial segregation has become. The more socially visible fact has been the overall expansion. In Puerto Rico, the expansion and democratization of high school education and the withdrawal of the middle classes to private high schools were pretty much compressed into a space of 15 years. Between 1944 and 1960 the public and private sectors expanded with equal speed but their relative prestige was abruptly reversed. The private high schools, largely Catholic, became the prestige institutions where formerly they had been receivers for the public high school rejects. Whereas in 1944, U.P.R. freshmen were 84 percent public school graduates and 16 percent private school graduates, in 1960 they were 69 percent from the public and 31 percent from the private high schools.[37] The two groups of high school students were becoming mutually hostile and the existence of private schools was a potential political issue.[38]

In 1960 the private and public high schools catered to very distinct clienteles. The social composition of public and private high school seniors in my 1960 sample is shown in Table 1. The socio-educational index used to classify students in the table is a combination of father's occupation and education.[39] More than half of the private high school seniors and less than a fifth of the public came from the top two SES strata. Data which indicate the trend toward increasing difference in the social composition of public and private high schools between 1944 and 1960 are shown in Table 2 which gives the social composition of University of Puerto Rico entrants from the public and private sectors.

High school seniors in my 1960 sample were given a group ability test. The results for the public and private sectors are shown in Table 3. Fifty-nine percent of the private high school seniors scored in the top quintile. Private high school students scored higher in every subject than the public school seniors in the achievement tests administered by the Superior Council on Education in 1959. The graduates of private high schools showed increasing superiority between 1944 and 1960 on the University of Puerto Rico entrance examination and in grade indexes at the end of the freshman year. In 1960, private school entrants to the U.P.R. scored higher on the entrance examination than the public school entrants, even with ability held constant, a fact which suggests that they were not only a more able group but had received superior high school training.

The pattern of academic and social segregation of high school students which obtained in 1960 had the effect of cancelling out the correlation between social class and ability *within* the private schools on the one hand, and *within* the general curriculum of the public high schools on the other, although there was such a correlation for high school seniors as a whole. However, the correlation between student's SES and ability reappeared at the University where public and private school graduates were merged into one student body. As late as 1944, there was no correlation between father's occupation and entrance examination scores among freshmen entering the U.P.R. However, by 1952, a correlation had appeared and in 1960, it had become stronger. (Table 4) The same was true of grades at the end of the freshman year. (Table 5)

Using these data to hypothesize about the past, I would surmise that, prior to the 50's, the correlation between social class and measured ability was screened out at the public senior high school level by a selective and meritocratic admissions policy. The expansion of secondary education allowed the correlation to appear in the high school population as a whole; but the segregation of public and private sectors eliminated it within each sector. However, the state university, which kept itself accessible to the graduates of all high schools, was then faced with the problem of handling the gap between its socially

Table 1. *Socio-Educational Status of Public and Private High School Seniors in Puerto Rico—1960*

SES Stratum	Public	Private	Total
	Percent		
I (High)	8%	28%	11%
II	10	25	12
III	16	23	17
IV	29	12	26
V	25	12	23
VI (Low)	12	. .	11
N (100%) [a]	(1279)	(251)	(1530)

[a] *A few cases where socio-educational status could not be determined are omitted from the table.*

Table 2. Occupations of Fathers of Public and Private High School Graduates Admitted to U.P.R. at Rio Piedras

Occupation of Student's Father:	Public			Private Catholic			Other Private		
	1944 %	1952 %	1960 %	1944 %	1952 %	1960 %	1944 %	1952 %	1960 %
Professionals, semi-professionals and higher-white-collar	30	20	18	33	34	50	37	48	69
Lower-white-collar	6	11	15	6	10	13	7	13	10
Retail proprietors	22	20	16	31	30	17	30	19	10
Manual workers	23	23	32	18	9	10	11	2	5
Farm owners and managers	12	11	8	10	7	5	9	2	1
Farm laborers and farm foremen	1	1	2	..	..	..	..	..	1
Other	6	14	9	2	10	5	6	16	4
Total	100%	100%	100%	100%	100%	100%	100%	100%	100%
	(N = 542) [a]	(N = 907)	(N = 1148)	(N = 51)	(N = 143)	(N = 390)	(N = 54)	(N = 95)	(N = 138)

[a] This table is not based on a sample, but includes all entrants at Rio Piedras, U.P.R.

Table 3.   *Ability Distribution of Public and Private High School Seniors, in Puerto Rico, 1960*

	Percent	
Ability Quintile	*Public*	*Private*
Top	19	59
2nd	21	13
3rd	20	13
4th	19	7
Bottom	21	8
(N = 100%)	(1312)	(253)

and academically superior and inferior students. Already in 1960 there were distinct patterns of recruitment to the several colleges on the main campus of the U.P.R. at Rio Piedras. The Colleges of Natural Science and Humanities recruited, respectively, the boys and the girls of highest social status and academic ability. The College of Education recruited the lowest-status, least able girls. The Colleges of Business, Pharmacy and Social Sciences recruited the least able boys and also the middling ability groups of both sexes. Despite these differences, these colleges remained united as one huge urban campus. However, the movement for community colleges, already strong in 1960, will relieve the Rio Piedras campus of some of its financially and academically poorest

students. It will also add a new stratum of still poorer students (academically and financially) to the bottom of the pyramid. It is predictable that a further expansion of higher education will bring with it more internal differentiation still, although whether there will be much growth of private higher education is not clear. In 1960, the private denominational universities of Puerto Rico were somewhat easier to enter than the state University of Puerto Rico. Their academic standards differed little from the U.P.R.'s. A private university of high quality did not seem a likely possibility. However, there were pressures for decentralization of the U.P.R., which had three campuses and over 20,000 students. The most probable development is a further differentiation of

Table 4.   *Occupational Status of Students' Fathers and Mean Examination Score by Year, University of Puerto Rico at Rio Piedras*

	Mean Entrance Examination Scores		
	1944–1945	*1952–1953*	*1960–1961*
Occupational Status of Students' Fathers:			
Professional, proprietary and executive	238	137	170
Semi-professional and higher white collar	236	129	161
Lower white collar	248	128	157
Small business	228	122	151
Skilled labor	239	121	146
Semi- and unskilled labor	230	117	143
Farmer	213	111	145
Farmer laborer	... *	... *	138

* *Fewer than 10 cases.*

Table 5. *Occupational Status of Students' Fathers and Mean Freshman Index by Year, University of Puerto Rico at Rio Piedras*

	Mean Freshman Index		
	1944–1945	*1952–1953*	*1960–1961*
Occupational Status of Students' Fathers:			
Professional, proprietary and executive	2.13	2.46	2.49
Semi-professional and higher white collar	2.35	2.34	2.34
Lower white collar	2.46	2.33	2.14
Small business	2.15	2.24	2.06
Skilled labor	2.13	2.20	2.10
Semi- and unskilled labor	2.30	2.33	2.04
Farmer	2.00	2.20	2.06
Farm laborer	....*	....*	1.89

* *Fewer than 10 cases.*

social recruitment and quality within the state system of higher education.

Conclusion

The case of Puerto Rico demonstrates that access to selective schooling for the children of different social strata can be roughly equalized at a point where the enrollment ratio of the upper strata is not near saturation. Since this did not occur in either Europe or the U.S., the Puerto Rican exception is important. It suggests that the same might occur in other industrializing countries although the factors conducive to such a development are not clear. Speed of educational expansion together with a strong egalitarian ethos seem to be two favorable conditions. A third, perhaps, is the absence of a strongly developed pre-industrial class structure.[40]

However, the Puerto Rican case also suggests that rapid democratization of access is accompanied by segregation of the social classes into separate schools of disparate quality. By the time education reaches the stage of mass expansion (which democratization implies), there are always some strata with several generations of experience in higher schooling, while the newest strata to be recruited are sending their first generation into secondary and higher education. The educationally privileged are both able and motivated to maintain their privilege by self-segregation into élite schools. Thus a new source of educational inequality is generated, illustrating John Vaizey's thesis that ". . . even if a wholly egalitarian ethic prevailed in the public sector . . . , the provision of private facilities would always tend to restore the inequality prevailing in the economy as a whole." [41]

Whether the inequality is fully restored in Vaizey's meaning—that the distribution of education can be no more egalitarian than the distribution of income—is an unanswered question. A slightly different question, also unanswered, is whether mass education societies, like the United States and Puerto Rico, actually show smaller differences in educational achievement between social strata than industrial societies with selective secondary and higher schooling. Martin Trow suggests that they do. ". . . this is a very different kind of link between social class and educational opportunity than that provided by an élite university system which simply excludes the bulk of the lower classes from exposure to any kind of higher education."[42] Trow may be correct. Yet, it also seems possible that mass higher education reflects the society's high standard of living without obliterating the differentials which persist within the general affluence.

NOTES

1. Lawrence A. Cremin, *The Genius of American Education,* New York: Vintage Books, 1965, chapter 1.

2. Stanley L. Friedlander, *Labor Migration and Economic Growth: A case study of Puerto Rico,* The MIT Press, 1965, estimated that but for this emigration, consisting heavily of adults in child-bearing ages, Puerto Rico would have had 52% more people in 1962 than she actually had, p. 49.

3. Gordon Lewis, *Puerto Rico, Freedom and Power in the Caribbean,* New York: MR Press, 1963, p. 183.

4. Leila Sussmann, "Summary Review by the Rapporteur," *Social Objectives in Educational Planning,* Paris: OECD, 1968, pp. 15–27.

5. On social class segregation of elementary schools, cf. Robert Herriott and Nancy St. John, *Social Class and the Urban School,* New York: Wiley, 1966; on the high schools, cf. Natalie Rogoff Ramsy, "The Clientele of Comprehensive Secondary Schools in the United States," *Social Objectives in Educational Planning,* pp. 67–83; on the colleges and universities, cf. Martin Trow, "The Democratization of Higher Education in America," *The European Journal of Sociology,* 3 (no. 2, 1962), 249–257; and Peter Rose, "The Myth of Unanimity," *Sociology of Education,* 37 (no. 2), 129–149.

6. *A Survey of the Public Educational System of Porto Rico (sic),* New York: Bureau of Publications, Teachers College, Columbia University, 1926, chapter VIII, "Financing Public Education in Porto Rico."

7. Frederick Harbison and Charles A. Myers, *Education, Manpower and Economic Growth,* New York: McGraw-Hill, 1964.

8. *A Survey of the Public Educational System of Porto Rico, op. cit.,* p. 406.

9. Puerto Rico spent $50 (in 1958 U.S. dollars) as compared with Bolivia: $6; Brazil: $10; Ecuador: $12; Guatemala: $17; Paraguay: $5; Peru: $14; for the Latin American data, cf. *Conference on the Financing of Education for Economic Growth,* Paris:OECD, 1960, "Financial Aspects of the Educational Expansion in Developing Regions," p. 13.

10. *A Survey of the Public Educational System of Porto Rico, op. cit.,* pp. 296–298.

11. *Ibid.,* chapter III, "Measurement of Results of Instruction."

12. The statistics come from the annual reports of the Commissioner of Education, published in Hato Rey, Puerto Rico.

13. The OECD data come from *Targets for Education in Europe in 1970: Policy Conference on Economic Growth and Investment in Education,* Paris: OECD, 1962. The UN data used by Harbison and Myers calculate school enrollment ratios by dividing the number enrolled in school *at a given level* by the total number in the age groups considered broadly eligible for that level. The OECD enrollment ratios divide the total number of children of an age group enrolled in school *at any level* by the total number in the age group. Since the UN includes ages 5 and 6 in its elementary (unadjusted) age group, Puerto Rico, where children tend not to enter school before age 7, is at a disadvantage in those comparisons. On the other hand, the general tendency toward overageness in the Puerto Rican school system gives it an advantage in the OECD 15–19 and 20–24 year comparisons, since in the Island many 15–19 year olds are in school at lower than the appropriate level and many more 20–24 year olds than in the more advanced countries are still in the process of obtaining their first degree in higher education.

14. Beresford Hayward, *The Future of Education in Puerto Rico, Its Planning,* Department of Education, Oct. 6, 1961, mimeographed.

15. Leila Sussmann, *High School to University in Puerto Rico,* final report of Cooperative Research Project No. 1018, U. S. Office of Education, pp. 64–73.

16. William H. Knowles, "Manpower and Education in Puerto Rico," in Harbison and Myers (eds.), *Manpower and Education: Country Studies in Economic Development*, New York: McGraw-Hill, 1965, p. 116. "Normalista training" refers to a two-year college course leading to a diploma in elementary school teaching.

17. Sussmann, *High School to University in Puerto Rico*, p. 9.

18. *Ibid.*, p. 97. The survey was based on a random sample of Puerto Rican high schools stratified by public or private control and by size. In the case of each of the 14 high schools in the sample, the entire senior class (with the exception of a few who could not be reached) filled out a paper and pencil questionnaire. The sample included 10 percent of Puerto Rico's 139 high schools and high school seniors. For a detailed description of its selection cf. *High School to University in Puerto Rico*, Appendix B.

19. The U.S. college plans data come from *Background Factors Relating to College Plans and College Enrollment among Public High School Students*, Princeton, New Jersey: Educational Testing Service, 1957. The Puerto Rican data come from Sussmann, *High School to University in Puerto Rico*, p. 97.

20. Martin Trow, "The Second Transformation of American Secondary Education," *The International Journal of Comparative Sociology*, Vol. II, 2 (Sept. 1961).

21. Hayward, *op. cit.*

22. Knowles, *op. cit.*, p. 118.

23. Frank Bowles, "Preliminary Report on Certain Aspects of the Study of Institutions of Higher Learning," Superior Council on Education, University of Puerto Rico, 1959, mimeo. Another reason there was virtually no upper college work was the serious lack of articulation within the University program. The first two years were spent in the College of General Studies where all students were presumably introduced to world culture. During the second year, students entered one of the five colleges in which they would major and there, because the work in General Studies was not trusted as a foundation, they were put through another battery of courses introductory to their major fields.

24. Sussmann, *High School to University in Puerto Rico*, pp. 22–24.

25. With the possible exception of the College of Engineering at Mayguez, a campus on the west coast of Puerto Rico, separate from the main campus at Rio Piedras. Although engineering students have the highest entrance examination scores on the average of any students at the university, this college requires five years for its B.S. degree.

26. As Frank Bowles has pointed out, the University has no statistics on this and other important topics. It was necessary to go back to individual records to tabulate these data. cf. Bowles, "The High Cost of Low Cost Education" in Seymour Harris (ed.), *Higher Education in the United States: The Economic Problems*, Cambridge: Harvard University Press, 1960, p. 200.

27. Ismael Rodriguez-Bou, "Evaluation: Results of the Examinations Administered in Several Areas to Several Grade Levels in the School System," Superior Council on Education, University of Puerto Rico, 1958, mimeo.

28. "The Educational System in Puerto Rico: Recommendations and Suggestions" by Christian Casselmann, Professor of Education, University of Heidelberg, Alberto Borghi, Professor of Education, University of Florence, Italy and Morten Bredsdorff, President, Teacher's College, Vordinborg, Denmark, May, 1959, mimeo.

29. In 1958, U.S. dollars.

30. Pablo Roca quoted in I. Rodriguez-Bou, *La Doble Matricula en las Escuelas de Puerto Rico*, Dec. 17, 1950, mimeo., pp. 11–12. The translation from the Spanish is mine.

31. Sussmann, *High School to University in Puerto Rico*, pp. 138–141.

32. Another possible reason for using high school grades as part of the basis for admission was that the College of Education would have had difficulty recruiting students if rural and working class girls had been excluded from the University of Puerto Rico. In the cities the most able *public* high school girls took the commercial curriculum and thus were siphoned off early from the pool of potential teachers. Girls who attended private high schools entered the College of Humanities at the University rather than the College of Education.

33. For detailed data on the diffusion of education aspirations in Puerto Rico, cf. Melvin Tumin and Arnold Feldman, *Social Class and Social Change in Puerto Rico,* New Jersey: Princeton University Press, 1961, especially chapters 3, 4 and 7.

34. Sussmann, "Summary Review by the Rapporteur," p. 21.

35. *Ibid.,* pp. 17 and 19.

36. Martin Trow, *op. cit.,* p. 239.

37. Sussmann, *High School to University in Puerto Rico,* p. 39.

38. Lewis, *op. cit.,* p. 464.

39. For a detailed discussion of how the index was constructed, see Sussmann, *High School to University in Puerto Rico,* Appendix C.

40. This factor was suggested by Phillip Foster, "Secondary Schooling and Social Mobility in a West African Nation," *Sociology of Education,* 37 (No. 2) 150–171.

41. John Vaizey, "Some Dynamic Aspects of Inequality," in *Social Objectives in Educational Planning, op. cit.,* p. 51.

42. Trow, *op. cit.,* p. 239.

Religion

55. A SOCIOLOGICAL THEORY OF RELIGION

J. MILTON YINGER

The sociological approach to the study of religion avoids metaphysical debates over what is "true." It begins, instead, with acknowledgment of the fact that religious beliefs and practices do exist in all societies and that they have significant consequences for human behavior and social life.

In this selection, J. Milton Yinger briefly reviews three principal theories of religious origins, all of which deal with some aspect of human "needs." The first theory is basically cognitive and concerned with explaining the mysteries of life; the second is emotional and concerned with the gratification of psychological needs; and the third is interactional and concerned with the problems of creating and maintaining social cohesion. Yinger then outlines the functional approach to the analysis of religious systems and discusses in detail the integrative function of religion in various societies.

J. Milton Yinger is Professor of Sociology and Anthropology at Oberlin College. He is the author of Religion in the Struggle for Power (*1946*), Religion, Society, and the Individual (*1957*), Sociology Looks at Religion (*1963*), Toward a Field Theory of Behavior (*1965*), *and* A Minority Group in American Society (*1965*). *With George E. Simpson, he is a coauthor of* Racial and Cultural Minorities (*1953; revised 1965*).

One need scarcely point out that no one theory of religion is adequate for all purposes. Every theory starts from certain basic assumptions, useful for the purposes of the theorist, which are not demonstrable or provable. A scientist starts from the point of view that something interesting and useful (for the tasks of science) can be said about religion if one assumes that it is part of the world of nature, subject to the laws of causation, capable of analysis according to the methods of science. The adequacy of his statement is to be judged by its contribution to the systematic analysis of observations of an empirical, objective sort, and by the degree to which it aids further such observations. Persons asking theological, aesthetic, or moral questions may find the scientific statements irrelevant (or perhaps impudent). This need not be the case, however, if they do not try to use those statements for purposes of non-scientific investigations. It is equally incumbent on the scientist to avoid "intellectual imperialism": he should not mistake his theories for a theology, a philosophy, an ethical or an aesthetic study of religion.

Scientific theories are most frequently confused with philosophies of religion, with which, indeed, they have much in common. Yet it is well to recognize the differences. Philosophies of religion are usually specific expressions of a general philosophy—attempts to study reality as a whole, as well as to isolate its basic categories or structure. Philosophical observations may derive from intuition, revelation, logic, observation, and other modes of cognitive response to experience, for philosophy is not sharply limited in methodology, as science is. These two facts— the tendency toward a theoretical synthesis (not abstraction) and methodological diversity—make the philosophical approach to religion different from the scientific. That does not mean, however, that the scientists can disregard the observations of the philosophers. Indeed to do so is to forego a great wealth of hypotheses, sharp observations, fruitful discussion of concepts, and theoretical insights. Awareness of the philosophical quest can also help prevent the scientist from forgetting the nature of his abstraction—and the fact that he has abstracted —from a more complicated total reality than his theory can encompass. We shall draw on the philosophers wherever their observations would seem to help us to develop a sociological theory of religion; but we shall not try to develop a philosophy of religion.

We have been using the term "theory" in a broad sense. It is far too much to say that what follows is a scientific theory in the sense of a group of interrelated propositions, fully tested by empirical study, pertaining to the interaction of religious behavior with other phases of social life. Our "theory," instead, will combine propositions on several different levels, in the hope that a systematic statement at this time may make some contribution to the extensive research necessary before a well-tested theory is possible. Propositions will range from what we may call pre-hypotheses (insightful guesses about the relationship of variables which have not yet been posed in a manner that permits empirical tests), to hypotheses (propositions capable of testing, but not yet sufficiently explored), to statements that have been quite adequately tested by research. Since it is not known how some of these may stand up under further observation, we do not know how well the whole theoretical structure which is built out of them will carry the weight of continuing research and theoretical elaboration. Its adequacy is partly tied to the adequacy of the more general theories in sociology, anthropology, and social psychology, of which it is a specific application. Since these more general theories of human behavior have received more adequate testing in their application to other specific questions, there are reasonable grounds for the belief that they will be substantiated as our knowledge of religious behavior grows.

This theory of religious behavior may help, on the other hand, to indicate the research necessary for further development of some of the major propositions in contemporary social science.

Theories of the Origin of Religion

We shall be primarily concerned with the development of a functional theory of religion. Our approach is systematic, not historical or biographical. Some attention to the history of theories, however, may help us to reach toward a systematic statement. Perhaps this can be done most effectively by stating briefly some of the theories of the origin of religion, for they indicate the way many social scientists first structured their questions about religion. These theories raised a number of fundamental problems, and some of them contained a great deal of implicit functional analysis from which valuable leads can be drawn.

It is now generally agreed that a scientific theory of the origin of religion is impossible. It seems clear that religious beliefs and practices reach back in the history of man tens of thousands of years; and the story of their origins has to be built out of the flimsiest of archeological, philological, and anthropological evidence, filled out with psychological and sociological guesses. These guesses have by no means been fruitless, however, for the development of a scientific theory of religion. As Herskovits says, commenting on various theories of religious origins:

Each of these scholars has provided more than enough evidence, on the face of it, to document his theory and to satisfy any who will read what he has written. Enough, that is, until the evidence for some other theory is studied, a cup equally filled to the brim and running over, and equally convincing. The contribution of these scholars, however, lies not in their having solved the riddle of how religion originated, or the steps by which it developed, or its social or psychological roots; but rather in the different phenomena of religion each emphasized and, by so doing, imprinted indelibly on all future discussions of the subject.[1]

The observations of the early scientific students of religion were based largely on data drawn from living preliterate societies. Although these data could scarcely support a theory of origins, since these societies had religions for thousands of years, and could not solve the problem of "how religion arose out of a life not religious at all," as T. H. Grafton puts it, they could, as a by-product of their search for origins, throw light on the nature and variety of religious behavior and on the functions it serves. It is possible that the functional approach of contemporary theory may repay the debt by furnishing interesting ideas concerning religious origins.

A further caution, not always observed by the students of the origin of religion, is necessary if we are to avoid the misuse of our data. Just as we need to withhold conclusions concerning religious origins that are drawn from the study of living societies, so too we need to be cautious not to assume that the study of preliterate societies is an adequate guide to the study of modern, complex, and literate societies. A general theory will be able to explain religion in the whole range of types of societies, but will indicate also the differences in religion and the variables related to those differences.

Three Types of Explanation of Religious Origins

In briefest outline, social scientific theories of the origin of religion may be classified into three types, each with some elements of functional analysis implicit within it or explicitly developed. We shall state them here, with a few comments on some of the major authors, and then pick up the functional aspects of their theories in our systematic statement below.

The first group emphasizes the cognitive aspects of religion, the need for an explanation of mysterious and awesome events. This theory can be characterized as basically intellectualistic, individualistic, and evolutionary. Religion, according to this interpretation, springs from the efforts of primitive men to explain the phenomena of dreams, echoes, visions, and above all of death. The key element in the explanation, in Tylor's famous formulation, is the concept of the soul. Such a concept gives to "the savage mind" an explanation of many puzzling bodily and mental conditions—they are the "effects of the departure of the soul." This animistic view of the world, the basis of religion in Tylor's view, represents a "fairly consistent and rational primitive philosophy."

This rationalistic conception of religion was easily related to the evolutionary doctrine. If animism is a primitive effort to explain the puzzling facts of a complicated world, it will undergo step by step modification as man's knowledge of the world increases. Presumably the final result will be the disappearance of religion when its basic function—explanation—is taken over by other elements of culture, particularly by science.

It is unnecessary for our purposes to undertake a lengthy critique of this conception of the origin of religion. It seems obviously inadequate as a total explanation, although the swing of the pendulum away from such rationalistic interpretations of human behavior may have carried too far. The failure to explore fully the deep-seated emotional qualities of religion makes the work of Spencer and Tylor seem strangely anachronistic today.

Let us recall how religion actually operates. Our reaction to the death of a deeply loved friend or relative is not simply one of cognition. We are not satisfied merely with knowing how he died. We want something more satisfying than this cold knowledge. Our emotional equilibrium has been upset, our hopes and desires frustrated. We need, in short, an interpretation in terms of sentiments and values.[2]

The animistic theory of religious origins is inadequate also in its disregard of the social and group elements in religious life. How can one account for the obligatory element in religious belief, and for its continuation in modern life despite the growth of knowledge of the naturalistic causes of the events on which animism presumably rested? An adequate theory must deal with the integrative, the social aspects of religion.[3]

The assumption of unilineal evolution has proved to be equally unsatisfactory. It was criticized both by those who, with Lang and Schmidt, believed that conceptions of "high-gods" can be found at very early stages in the development of religion, and by those who believed, with Codrington, Marett, and others, that belief in an impersonal supernatural force —mana—preceded the appearance of belief in spirits. These criticisms represent an increase in attention to the emotional and to the functional aspects of religion, but they accepted a great deal of the evolutionary approach. A sharper criticism, particularly of the assumption that religion was gradually being destroyed by the evolutionary increase in knowledge, stems from a fully developed functional theory.[4]

A second major approach to the question of the origin of religion places great emphasis on man's emotional needs. This view is readily translated into a concern for functions and an interest in the sources of the continuing influence of religion, as contrasted with efforts at historical reconstruction. Some of the writers . . . use this approach as the basis for a theory of the origin of religion as well. In *Totem and Taboo* and elsewhere, for example, Freud develops his version of "the elementary forms of the religious life," to use Durkheim's well-known title. It is a vastly different conception from that of Tylor. In Freud's interpretation, a primeval slaying of the father by the sons, primarily because the tyrannical father had monopolized the females of the horde, and the attendant guilt and repression, are the source of totemism. Out of this emerge the later forms of religion and the whole pattern of culture.

Paul Radin interprets the origin of religion in a way that ties it closely to a functional theory. He asks, "What is it that originally led man to postulate the supernatural?" To answer the question, we must try to visualize the conditions under which man lived at the dawn of civilization. With wholly inadequate technological preparation, he was helpless before the powerful and capricious forces of the environment.

His mentality was still overwhelmingly dominated by definitely animal characteristics although the life-values themselves—the desire for success, for happiness, and for long life —were naturally already present. . . . No economic security could have existed, and we cannot go far wrong in assuming that, where economic security does not exist, emotional insecurity and its correlates, the sense of powerlessness and the feeling of insignificance, are bound to develop. . . .

It is but natural for the psyche, under such circumstances, to take refuge in compensation fantasies. . . . the main goal and objective of all his strivings was the canalization of his fears and feelings and the validation of his compensation dreams.[5]

Thus religion springs primarily, according to Radin, from man's emotional responses to a threatening situation. The third line of argument concerning the origin of religion differs from the individualistic emphasis of the first two. It sees religion as primarily a product of social interaction and group life. Once again, since we have no direct interest in a complete survey of origin theories, we shall be content with a brief mention of only two writers who make social factors the focus of their attention. These ideas are also easily transposed into functional terms, without attention to the question of historical origins at all. Simmel, in fact, who emphasizes the human relations source of religion, indicates that he is not trying to describe the historical origin, but what he calls its "psychological origin," as one of

many sources. And Durkheim, the other writer whom we shall mention in this connection, is certainly important primarily, not for his speculations about origin, but for his functional analysis.

Simmel develops the thesis that one of the sources of religion is human relations which themselves are non-religious. "I do not believe that the religious feelings and impulses manifest themselves in religion only. . . ."[6] Religion is the heightening and abstracting from their particular content of certain human relations—of exaltation, devotion, fervency, and the like— that are found widely in social life. Faith, for example, is first of all a relation between individuals; we don't base our relations with others on what we conclusively know about them. "The social role of this faith has never been investigated; but this much is certain, that without it society would disintegrate. . . . In faith in a deity the highest development of faith has become incorporate, so to speak; has been relieved of its connection with its social counterpart."[7] Thus, in Simmel's view, religion is an outgrowth of human relations.

Durkheim's emphasis on the social origin of religion is more extreme than that of Simmel. For Durkheim, society is the object of religious veneration and the basic source of "the sacred." The primary function of religion is the preservation of social unity. "So everything leads us back to this same idea: before all, rites are means by which the social group reaffirms itself periodically."[8] Thus he calls attention to aspects of religion that had certainly been given inadequate attention— rite, cult organization, its relationship to the social structure. It is in such a context that he interprets totemic cults, which he considers "the elementary forms of the religious life."

From this, we may be able to reconstruct hypothetically the way in which the totemic cult should have arisen originally. Men who feel themselves united, partially by bonds of blood, but still more by a community of interest and tradition, assemble and become conscious of their moral unity. . . . they are led to represent this unity in the form of a very special kind of consubstantiality: they think of themselves as all participating in the nature of some determined animal. Under these circumstances, there is only one way for them to affirm their collective existence: this is to affirm that they are like the animals of this species, and to do so not only in the silence of their own thoughts, but also by material acts.[9]

As a theory of the origin of religion, Durkheim's interpretation is doubtless one-sided, and like all the others, quite beyond demonstration. Its importance rests primarily on the attention it focuses on the group aspects of religion. It is basically a functional interpretation, not a study of origins. From this brief commentary on his, and other essays on the origin of religion, we can profitably turn to an examination of the functional theory.

The Functional Approach to Religion

It is a fairly short step from the question, "How did religion originate?" to, "What does it do for human societies and individuals?" We have suggested that the second question was implicit in much of the earlier work devoted to the study of origins. It is the virtue of more recent studies, however, that they have made the functional question explicit, thus being able to use it more effectively while at the same time pointing up its limitations and its hidden assumptions. As Kingsley Davis has pointed out, social theory has often been inadequate to interpret religion, because it has asked the wrong, or the relatively less important, questions. Viewing religion primarily from a cognitive standpoint, it has asked, "Do religious ideas represent reality?" This leads to questions concerning the nature of reality and the reasons for any errors that religious beliefs may be said to contain. There is value in this approach, but also a great weakness, for it tends to reduce religion to a system of beliefs or statements of pur-

ported facts. Whether religious ideas are "true" hinges on one's definition of the truth, and hence becomes a metaphysical, not a scientific problem. The virtue of functional analysis is that it avoids the metaphysical debate (which, for problems other than those of empirical study, may be an important debate), and states, instead: Religious beliefs and practices do exist; they have consequences for human behavior. How are they used?

Since every society seems to have something called religion, its presence can hardly be dismissed as a sociological accident. If, given the major conditions of human social life as known up to now, religion made no contribution to societal survival or was not inextricably attached to something that did contribute to survival, one would expect that social systems and cultures would long since have evolved without it. There need be no assumption that religion is entirely adaptive, that its role is identical in all types of societies, or that in some distant future its functions might not be instrumented by some other kind of cultural structure. There is simply a good *prima facie* case for asking a question about its functions and trying to answer the question scientifically.[10]

A functional interpretation rests upon several related ideas. Perhaps most important is the conception that societies are systems of interdependent parts. The religious patterns, therefore, cannot be understood in isolation from the whole structure in which they are embedded. For example, Fortes and Evans-Pritchard, in their discussion of *African Political Systems*, describe the ways in which religious symbols, rites, dogmas, and sacred places unify the social systems of which they are a part. They give the whole system a mystical value that promotes acceptance far beyond the obedience that the secular sanctions could bring.

The social system is, as it were, removed to a mystical plane, where it figures as a system of social values beyond criticism or revision. . . . The African sees these ritual observances as the supreme safeguard of the basic needs of his existence and of the basic relations that make up his social order—land, cattle, rain, bodily health, the family, the clan, the state. . . . Periodical ceremonies are necessary to affirm and consolidate these values because, in the ordinary course of events, people are preoccupied with sectional and private interests and are apt to lose sight of the common interest and of their political interdependence.[11]

An idea that is closely linked to the concept of system is the proposition that there are some "invariant points of reference," in the nature of man as a biological type, in his psychology, in the structure of social systems, etc., which pose certain necessary conditions for the existence of any society. These are perhaps best stated in the form of questions, to indicate the tentative quality of many of the propositions: What is the significance of man's biological patterns—the long infancy, the length of the life span, the relative lack of "instinctual" responses, and the like—for human interaction? Are there pan-human responses to extreme stress and frustration that are manifest in every social system? Do groups as such have basic isolable properties that set limits to the kinds of developments possible in a society? Do these lead to certain "functional prerequisites" in all societies, to patterns essential for the very existence of a society? [12]

To some degree, these concepts are in opposition to the extreme relativism that characterized an earlier sociology. They do not deny the relativism in specific cultural content, but regard many of the specific forms as alternative ways of meeting functionally similar requirements of social life. Religion is thought, by most functional theorists, to be among the necessary patterns.

Difficulties in the Functional Approach

Functional analysis, to be sure, is not without weaknesses and difficulties. It is sometimes used to "prove" the ultimate validity, or inevitability, or changelessness

of some specific practice or belief. These non-empirical propositions are unwarranted. Durkheim's famous proposition that social facts cannot be explained by psychological theories might be matched here by the formulation: do not try to support non-empirical statements (this religious practice is good and true because it is universal) by empirical generalizations (religion is universal). Some people have used Heisenberg's principle of indeterminacy in physics to support theological ideas. Others have jumped, reluctantly or enthusiastically, from "the mores can make anything right," (an overly simple empirical generalization) to the moral— or if you prefer, immoral—conclusion that the culture of one society is as good as that of any other.

Perhaps more unfortunate than the floating back and forth between value judgments and statements of fact on the part of "laymen" has been the tendency on the part of some of the functionalists themselves to go beyond their evidence and to disregard the problem of dysfunctions. Robert Merton has shown that three interconnected postulates are often used, by the more extreme functionalists, that are not necessary to functional analysis and tend to make of it an ideology:

1. The postulate of the functional unity of a society—that every standardized activity or belief is functional, that is, necessary and useful, for the whole social system.

2. The postulate that every social form has a positive function—universal functionalism. ". . . no culture forms survive unless they constitute responses which are adjustive or adaptive, in some sense . . ." (quoting Clyde Kluckhohn).

3. The postulate of indispensability—that certain functions are necessary to the survival of a society and/or that particular cultural or social forms are indispensable in carrying out these functions.[13]

So long as these postulates are assumptions, rather than propositions to be tested by empirical study, functional analysis will be inadequate. In the contrast that he draws between manifest and latent functions, in the attention to functional alternatives, and in his emphasis on the need to study dysfunctions and functionally irrelevant patterns of behavior, Merton develops concepts that help us to avoid these assumptions. It is particularly the study of latent functions (and dysfunctions) that is likely to add significantly to our knowledge of a social process, for these, by definition, are not common knowledge; their consequences are unintended and unrecognized.

. . . research which uncovers latent functions very often produces "paradoxical" results. The seeming paradox arises from the sharp modification of a familiar popular preconception which regards a standardized practice or belief *only* in terms of its manifest functions by indicating some of its subsidiary or collateral latent functions.[14]

This is particularly true, perhaps, of the study of religion, in which the analysis is very likely to be carried on in terms of what religion "does" for society or the individual only as expressed in the prevailing ideology. Or, on the other hand, in various "debunking" studies, attention is paid only to manifest and latent dysfunctions, with little or no attention to possible latent functions. Preconceptions of either sort will block our ability to explore religion fully.

Goode summarizes the situation well by indicating the six questions that need to be raised if one is to develop an adequate functional analysis:

Positive Function		Negative Function	
Manifest	Latent	Manifest	Latent
	Irrelevant		
	Manifest	Latent	

Functional anthropologists have concentrated upon those *positive functions* which are *not usually known* to the members of the society, i.e., the positive, latent functions. The rebels and debunkers among modern economists and historians have concentrated upon the *negative latent functions*. It is clear that much exploration remains to be done among the remaining cells.[15]

One seldom noticed, and not altogether happy, consequence of the shift, in theoretical interest, from the question of the origin of religion to the problem of functions, has been a concomitant shift in emphasis in the study of the interaction of religion and society. The student of the origin of religion tended to ask: How does a society (or, as Durkheim might say, the very fact of society) influence the development of religion? Or, how do individual intellectual and emotional needs affect religious origins? Religion was treated primarily as a dependent variable. The "functionalist," taking religion as an established fact, is more likely to ask: What does religion do for societies and individuals? He tends to deal with religion as the independent variable. A theory that maintains a continuous and systematic interest in the *interaction* of religion and society seems to be difficult to develop. Just as questions concerning origins *tend toward* an ideology that religion is an archaic survival, destined gradually to be outgrown (Spencer and Tylor, for example), so questions concerning functions *tend toward* a conservative ideology. An objective science of religion can accept neither ideology, although it is perfectly willing to move toward one or the other proposition if the evidence points in that direction. A broad enough functional theory, one that includes latent and dysfunctional processes, can encompass the questions raised by the concept of interaction. To do this, however, requires that we avoid the assumption that society, or personality, or religion is always to be treated as the independent variable, with the others as dependent.

Religion as an Integrator of Society

It is difficult to find a neutral vocabulary by means of which one can express the "function-dysfunction" of religion in its relationship to social integration. (The lack of an objective vocabulary doubtless indicates the absence of objective study of these phenomena.) To most people it is probably assumed that to integrate a society is good, purely and simply. No distinction is raised in their minds between integration as a general fact and a specific pattern of integration. Religion, in this view, as the primary source of integration, is good and necessary; and the particular religious beliefs and practices of the moment are therefore defended. To others, religion is a necessary ingredient of a well-integrated society because of the passions and lack of intelligence of the "masses," who must be protected from their own inadequacies. This is an ancient view, expressed, for example, by Polybius, the Greek historian. Commenting on the honesty of the Romans, because they feared their gods, he admits that his own countrymen:

. . . if entrusted with a single talent, though protected by ten checking-clerks, as many seals and twice as many witnesses, yet cannot be induced to keep faith. However, the Romans have managed to forge the main bond of social order out of something which the rest of the world execrates: I mean, out of Superstition. . . . In my opinion, however, the Romans have done it with an eye to the masses. If it were possible to have an electorate that was composed exclusively of sages, this chicanery might perhaps be unnecessary; but, as a matter of fact, the masses are always unstable and always full of lawless passions, irrational temper and violent rage; and so there is nothing but to control them by "the fear of the unknown" and play-acting of that sort.[16]

E. A. Ross gives a modern version of the same thesis:

The genius who is to impress the mind of coming generations as the hand impresses the waxen tablet, does not commend his ideal on the ground that it is good for society. He does not advertise it as a means of securing order. He knows that men will not do as they would be done by, or forgive injuries, or subject their impulses to reason, for mere utility's sake. The genius that succeeds takes high ground from the first. His way is not merely a better way of getting along together. He declares it the one possible path of life. It is the God-ordained type of living. It is prescribed by man's nature. It is the goal of history. It is the destiny of the race. So it comes to pass that the inventors of right and wrong, the authors of ideals, not only disguise their sociology as ethics, but often go farther and disguise their ethics as religion.[17]

Many others would agree with this doctrine that religion gives support to social order, but would not see it as a matter of conscious manipulation by an elite and would treat religion, as with Plato, somewhat more piously.

Other writers, starting from different value premises, while agreeing that religion may hold a society together, would call this, not integration, but rigidity. According to this view, the explosive tensions of a society are kept in check by the religious beliefs and practices, but this is done for the benefit of the dominant few, while the creative energies of the great majority are bottled up. This, of course, is the interpretation given by Marx in his proposition that "religion is the opiate of the people," but a similar critical view of traditional religion may be taken by others who strongly disagree with him in their judgment of how to meet the situation. Thus a wide diversity of proposals for new ways to achieve the integration of society, ranging from "scientific" humanism to "scientific" Marxism, has been developed. It is paradoxical that Marxism, despite the vigor of its attack on religion, can itself readily be interpreted as a religious movement. Far from destroying the idea of the need for an integrating system of values, it simply offers itself as a substitute.

In studying these various approaches to the question of the integrating effects of religion, the functionalist makes a necessary distinction. He does not equate the concept that *some* integrating system of beliefs and practices is necessary to the survival of society, a proposition with strong empirical support (whether society ought to survive is itself, of course, a value judgment, but one which few care to deny), with the idea that a particular system, as it is operating, contributes to social integration. It is now coming widely to be observed that the "spaceless and timeless generalizations about the 'integrative functions of religion' are largely, although not of course entirely, derived from observations in non-literate societies."[18] But what, Merton asks, are the consequences when different religions coexist in the same society? This need not always produce disharmony, as Merton seems to imply, but it often does. And how does religion make for integration in the larger, more complex societies if it defends values that contradict other values of those societies? Can Hindu defense of caste-purity help to integrate a society in which value is gradually coming to be attached to efficient industrial production, with the accompanying demand for rational organization of the work situation? Whether one of these values is "better" than another need not concern us here. We are simply asking whether Hinduism can integrate a society into which the other value is intruding.

THE PROBLEM OF ORDER Before we explore in more detail this question of relationship between religion and social integration, we need to take a brief look at a more general question concerning social "order." One need not agree entirely with Hobbes that human life, before the establishment of strong governments, was "solitary, poor, nasty, brutish, and short," to realize that man's egocentric tendencies place strong difficulties in the way of smoothly running social groups. Even the smallest and most stable of human societies faces the problem of distributing scarce values. The economic means of livelihood, power (the ability to influence others in directions one desires more than they can influence him), and prestige (comparative by its very nature, so that if one has more, another has less) are all, by definition, in scarce supply. How can a society prevent individual and sub-group pursuit of these values from disrupting the network of agreements and accommodations that social life requires? And how do social groups prevent the hostility that is generated by frustration, by a sense of injustice, by guilt, from constantly tearing the fabric of society? Pushed back further, the question becomes: How can we account for the fact that societies manage to exist at all, when the tendencies toward self-aggrandizement are so strong and hostile feelings so abundant?

Aristotle raised this question, and gave us the answer: "Man is by nature social" (political), a theory picked up in the twentieth century in the McDougallian idea of "gregarious instincts." In a day when man's anti-social potentialities loom so large, however, we are not much impressed by these doctrines, nor by the whole attempt to explain behavior by putting something "in" man, which is then pointed to as a simple "explanation" when questions arise. We are perhaps more likely to be persuaded by Hobbes' doleful belief in an ever-threatening "war of all against all," and its twentieth century variant, the Freudian doctrine that every individual has a reservoir of hostility, partly (and here we leave Hobbes) because of the very fact of society.

An adequate view, it would seem, must recognize that man has potentialities both for social life and for hostility and self-centered pursuit of values. How do societies manage to keep the latter at a minimum (or at least aimed in directions not likely to injure the social order) while strengthening the potentialities for social life? One may guess that those societies that did not learn to do this were simply torn apart and disappeared (and that this process continues). This does not tell us, however, what they learned.

There are doubtless several related social processes, some of them a long way from our conception of religion, which can be understood in this context: The hostility may be directed toward other societies. It may be focused on socially approved scapegoats within a society (it is interesting here that the term scapegoat, originally with a religious meaning, has now acquired a broader referent). There may be processes whereby the hostility and egocentricity are sublimated into activities that are not socially disruptive. (Sublimation is a slippery concept, capable of about as many nonscientific distortions as "instinct." We cannot discuss its weaknesses here, but use it in the minimal sense of accepting a substitute activity for a blocked one.) And finally, coming to the function of religion in these processes, intragroup hostility and egocentricism may be prevented from reaching destructive force by the organized system of rites and beliefs. This last requires more careful explanation.

If a society is to exist at all, it must find some means for distributing its scarce goods and values in such a way that the great majority accept the outcome or protest against it only by means approved by the social system itself. And it must find a way to control the expression of hostility generated by frustration, pain, and guilt. That even complex and mobile societies succeed in these tasks is a matter of daily observation. Although the violations get the headlines, the more important fact is the number of times we count on, and receive, normatively prescribed behavior, even from strangers. Most of us, most of the time, use means that are approved by our society, and do not use other means which, although perhaps more technically efficient in helping us acquire scarce values, are forbidden. We do not steal money, but work for it at a socially approved task; we do not destroy our competitor or spread malicious gossip about him, but compete against him. Even when we buy goods and services from strangers —a much more common occurrence in urban societies—we generally get full measure and quality. We accept the "strait-jacket of culture" (as Freud might

call it), at least on the conscious level, despite our tensions and fears. No strictly egocentric theory of man can explain these facts. How can we account for this order?

Certainly one level of explanation is the fear of punishment: fear of ridicule, isolation, and public censure in the simpler societies, and, added to those, the power of explicit political authorities to coerce and punish in "civil" societies. We abide by the normatively approved means for acquiring scarce values, we express our hostility only in socially designated ways, because violations threaten greater loss than gain. Obviously this fear of punishment or loss is only partially successful. In the larger, more mobile societies the amount of effort necessary to enforce the norms must be increased. Moreover, the problem of integration and social order is not thus solved, because there is the continuing danger that the enforcement authorities themselves—those who have been assigned the task of upholding the normative system of the society—may use the coercive means given them for their own advantage. This is the eternal political problem. Every society must have a pattern of control "beyond politics" that will reduce the necessity for coercion and keep the authorities themselves within bounds. This final basis of social order rests on what Davis calls the "common-ultimate ends," socialized into the individual members of that society as their basic values. These values are shared, noncompetitive values, against which all other derivative goals are judged.

. . . these ends can refer not so much to a future state of the individual himself as to the future state of other individuals and, in the last analysis, to the group itself. . . . As between two different groups holding an entirely different set of common-ultimate ends, there is no recourse. But within the same community this type of ends constitutes the integrating feature.[19]

How does religion come into this picture? The answer is much clearer for static and isolated societies than for changing ones: Insofar as it is accepted, religion, by rite and symbol, gives emotional support to the fundamental values of a society; it softens the hardness of the struggle for scarce values by emphasizing values than can be achieved by all (e.g., salvation); and it lessens the tensions of those who have failed to achieve a desired level of a society's values by approved means by emphasizing supra-mundane values. Beyond the integration that comes from socialization and social control in their secular aspects, beyond economic and political integration, beyond the focusing of disruptive hostilities onto socially designated scapegoats within the society or enemies without, every society has a transcendent system of unifying values, beyond politics and, indeed, in most cases, beyond history.

This is not to say that any particular religion is, therefore, good. The statement above is empirical, not valuational. The support it gives may be to a society based on principles one considers bad, e.g., slavery; the rites it uses may, from the value stand of the outsider, seem barbarous, e.g., human sacrifice; the lowering of the sense of frustration may, in some circumstances, cut the nerve of effort that many would regard as essential. On another level, in connection with the relations between societies which have a different kind of religious integration, strong barriers to inter-society cooperation and accommodation may be erected. One's value judgment concerning the integrative function of religion, therefore, can most profitably be based on the analysis of *all* the consequences, manifest and latent.

The concept of religion as an integrator of society is, as we have seen, an ancient one. It is at least as old as Confucius, who declared that rites bind the multitudes together and "serve as dikes against excesses to which the people are prone." Leaping across the centuries, one finds integration to be an important function of what Henri Bergson calls the static religion of the closed society. In his view, ". . . religion is then a defensive reaction of nature against the dissolvent power of intelligence." Individual intelligence, unregulated, would lead primarily, Bergson says, to egocentric behavior. "Primitive religion, taken from our first standpoint, is a precaution against the danger man runs, as soon as he thinks at all, of thinking of himself alone." [20]

Bergson also stresses, as we shall see, the function of religion in countering the fact of death. Some writers, however, have placed almost the whole emphasis on the role of religion as social integrator. Benjamin Kidd builds this idea into his very definition when he writes that a religion ". . . is a form of belief, providing an ultra-rational sanction for that large class of conduct in the individual where his interests and the interests of the social organism are antagonistic, and by which the former are rendered subordinate to the latter in the general interests of the evolution which the race is undergoing." [21] This statement is inadequate both as definition and as a theory of the functions of religion. Like other writers of the same period, Kidd placed too much emphasis on the "belief" aspects of religion; and as a theory of functions, the statement is a great over-simplification.

DIFFICULTIES IN THE EMPHASIS ON INTEGRATION How can this approach to religion be brought into an adequate theory? Several problems need to be solved before this long-established insight into the role of religion as "integrator of society" can take its place in a scientific theory of religion:

1) A great deal of empirical observation, in different types of societies, is still needed to discover how generally the proposition applies, to discover where, if at all, it does not apply (religion as disintegrator of society, or as unimportant in this regard), and to specify the *conditions under which* these various possibilities occur. Did religion "integrate" Russian society, 1915–1917? Would Taoism and

Buddhism, independent of Confucianism, have held Chinese society together? Although this insight is perhaps three thousand years old and has taken its place in dozens of philosophies of religion, the task of isolating the conditions under which it applies has not yet adequately been carried out.

2) A statement of the integrative function must be united with statements of religion's other functions and dysfunctions, and this broader statement tested by widespread empirical observation. Is there a changeless core of functions without which one should not speak of "religion"; or are some of these functions performed primarily by other kinds of social structures in certain kinds of societies? (Here again, the problem of definition is not easily solved.) Is there an "inherently" inter-related group of functions that one finds always embodied together in religion because one cannot be carried out effectively in the absence of the other? It is a plausible hypothesis that the functions for the individual are better served by a religious system that also integrates society, and that the group function is more adequately performed by a religion which also satisfies various individual needs. Oppositely, societal integration is less likely to be accomplished, according to this hypothesis, by a pattern of beliefs and practices which fails to satisfy important needs in the lives of individual adherents (remembering how exceedingly various these needs, many of them defined by the religion itself, may be). And finally, in this regard, a religious system that for the moment satisfies individual needs but fails to hold together the society within which those satisfactions are achieved is unlikely to be able to continue to carry out even the individual functions. Before the observation that religion contributes to social integration can become part of an adequate scientific theory of religion, this hypothesis needs further exploration.

3) The proposition also needs to be related to broader theories of society and personality. If it is true that a system of religious beliefs and practices supports, under stated conditions, social integration, what is there about the nature of society and of personality that makes this true? Is this proposition congruent with other statements about society and personality? Can it be reduced to a more general theory of human behavior, following the principle of parsimony, thus bringing it more solidly into the framework of sociology?

We are slowly making headway in answering these questions; and it is our hope that this essay, drawing on the increasingly rich resources, can contribute to the process of bringing such ancient insights as we are discussing into the framework of an adequate theory.

VARIABLES INFLUENCING THE INTEGRATIVE FUNCTION OF RELIGION The growth of the comparative study of religions, both of preliterate and literate societies, and the study of how a religion changes as the society in which it is embedded changes are our primary sources of information. On the basis of that material the following propositions concerning religion and social integration seem justified. These propositions are not mutually exclusive, because each one deals with part of an interacting group of forces—where one is present, several others are also likely to be found. The statements are put negatively, reversing the usual emphasis, to point up the need for indicating the conditions under which religion will tend to produce social cohesion. The integrative function of religion is at a minimum—other things being equal:

1) In societies where more than one religion is practiced.

2) When the "established expectancies" of the members of a society are frustrated. This refers, not to some absolute level of need, but to the satisfactions that the members of a society have come to expect. When these are denied, those who feel frustrated may become "more reli-

gious," in the manner of the "Old Believers" in Russia, and as it is seen in the explosive Kitiwala movement in the Belgian Congo—a politico-religious sect built around Christian symbols—but not in the sense of embracing more strongly a unifying religious tradition. They are more likely to use religion to express their sense of separation and even as a weapon to fight for the reestablishment of their "rights." This is illustrated by the way in which nominally Christian Indians used the Ghost Dance against white Americans.

3) When social change reduces the appeal of the ritual and belief systems. What will give one generation a sense of a unifying tradition may alienate parts of another generation who have been subjected to different social and cultural influences.

4) When mobility from society to society is greatest; and the corollary, when a society is composed of members who were socialized to different patterns of behavior. Even when the mobility is among societies sharing the same basic religious system, there are bound to be local variations in the religious tradition, and the heterogeneous society will have a wider range of personality system to integrate.

5) When a society is sharply divided into classes, or other hierarchical divisions, and this is strongly felt as an oppressive fact. Religion itself may help to *prevent* a stratification system from being felt as an oppressive fact, as in the case of classic Hinduism or medieval Christianity, but it may not be able to do so in the face of competing value systems derived from nonreligious sources or from some aspects of the religion itself. If a religion cannot "explain away" the differences in income, power, and prestige on the basis of its own principles, it is less able to serve the function of integrating a society. Those who are most disadvantaged are particularly likely, under these circumstances, to desert the dominant religion and to accept some new religion or proto-religion as the way to solve their problems. In such a situation, the religious forces are as likely to express and even to accentuate the internal tensions of a society as they are to integrate that society. Thus the lower classes were those most likely to desert the emperor worship of Rome in favor of Christianity. In the nineteenth and twentieth centuries, the lower classes and alienated members of the middle and upper classes have been the most likely to leave Christianity for the secular salvation of communism. And in India today, most converts to Christianity from Hinduism are drawn from the highly disadvantaged groups. The proponents of a religious system are likely to argue that "true" Christianity or "true" Hinduism could not thus be involved in social conflict instead of social integration. Only "corrupt" versions could do that. This is a point on which debate is likely to be fruitless. Let us say simply that, whatever may be the basic ideology, religion as it is lived and used becomes, under certain circumstances, an important factor, as symbol and cause, of social conflict.

6) When outside pressures split a society. Perhaps this is only to say that when outside forces are strong enough or of a particular kind, the cohesive effects of religion may be inadequate to maintain the unity of a society. Thus many American Indian tribes are divided into "reactionaries" (those who want to reaffirm the validity of their original culture) and "liberals" (who would prefer recognition simply as individual Americans), with many positions in between. Religious differences usually match these differences and perhaps intensify them. We must state, of course, that under other circumstances outside pressure may have the opposite effect: It may revivify a religious system and greatly increase the internal solidarity of a society. Judaism is often cited as the classic illustration of this process. It is well to recognize that often both tendencies—the unifying and the disrupting—may be present in an ambivalent relationship. Thus there have been continual splits

among Jews, showing that religion is unable to resolve all the differences that may occur as a result of the outside situation. And, oppositely, some of the religious movements among American Indians served to express their unity, as against the white man. (It is in such a situation, where opposite tendencies are found, that analysis is most complicated and where overly simple theories are most likely to prevail. Only more intensive search for the many variables involved can reduce this difficulty.)

These are among the conditions which, when present, reduce the integrative effects of religion. This discussion perhaps serves to make clear why we cannot accept the simple assertion that "religion produces social integration." When the tendencies that we have discussed run in the opposite direction, of course, they will serve to strengthen the integrative aspects of religion. It should also be noted that we have used a "society" as our unit. When one is concerned with some subdivision of a society—a class or minority-group, for example—some of the limitations on the power of social cohesion through religion do not apply, although several of them are relevant even to the question of integration of such groups.

Many students of religion might accept these qualifications with respect to the integrative function of religion, but then ask: Is it not true that there is a *tendency* in a society, in the face of these disintegrative influences, to recover or discover a unifying religious theme? If we define religion broadly enough, the answer would seem to be yes. These tendencies, however, may not have time to work themselves out before new disintegrative influences enter the scene—thus maintaining a continuously mixed situation. Here we are in the realm of pre-hypothesis, but the speculation may be worthwhile. When religious integration is weakened, other types of integration for subdivisions of a society or the whole society tend to emerge, because of the functional necessity of a unifying system of values. Nationalism is an outstanding example in our time. (The causal sequence may, of course, be the other way around: Nationalism, as a unifying system of values, may have come about as a result of causes independent of the presence or absence of a unifying religious tradition and then *caused* the weakening of the religious view. More likely, the various influences continuously interacted.)

It may be true, however, that sub-societal religions or secular systems of value integration *tend toward* a full-fledged religious pattern, because such a pattern serves the individual and group functions more successfully. Religion may tend to spread to the boundaries of a society (and in our time, beyond), because the existence of conflicting systems weakens these functions. Most secular systems of value integration, moreover—what we may call incipient or proto-religions—tend to prove inadequate because of their inability to achieve their proclaimed goals. Religion, by making extra-empirical goals (salvation) most important (not necessarily all-important), by trans-valuing the meaning of human failure and suffering, by dealing in shared, not scarce and therefore competitive, values, may reduce this difficulty.

These propositions are to some degree illustrated by Warner's description of the half-patriotic, half-religious ceremonies of Memorial Day in the United States. In this description, one sees a complex and heterogeneous society struggling toward a group of cohering, unifying beliefs and practices, building the unifying theme out of materials from the society's own experience—the widely shared and emotionally significant experiences of death in war.

It is the thesis of this chapter that the Memorial Day ceremonies and subsidiary rites (such as those of Armistice Day) of today, yesterday, and tomorrow are rituals of a sacred symbol system which functions periodically to unify the whole community, with its conflicting symbols and its opposing, autonomous churches and associations. It is contended here that in the Memorial Day ceremonies the anxieties which man has about death are confronted with a system of sacred beliefs about death which gives the individuals involved and the collectivity of individuals a feeling of well-being. Further, the feeling of triumph over death by collective action in the Memorial Day parade is made possible by re-creating the feeling of well-being and the sense of group strength and individual strength in the group power, which is felt so intensely during the wars when the veterans' associations are created and when the feeling so necessary for the Memorial Day's symbol is originally experienced.

Memorial Day is a cult of the dead which organizes and integrates the various faiths and national and class groups into a sacred unity. It is a cult of the dead organized around the community cemeteries. Its principal themes are those of the sacrifice of the soldier dead for the living and the obligation of the living to sacrifice their individual purposes for the good of the group, so that they, too, can perform their spiritual obligations.[22]

Summary of Social Integrative Function of Religion

Our discussion of this aspect of a sociological theory of religion, and its relationship to a general theory of society, may be summarized in the following propositions:

1) Social order requires a unifying value scheme, specifying approved means and ends, to hold in check the conflict involved in the individual pursuit of scarce values and the hostility generated by the frustrations and disappointments of life.

2) This value scheme must be largely "self-enforcing"—built into the personalities of the members of the society—if it is to withstand the strains imposed by man's egocentric pursuit of his own interests.

3) Political enforcement—designation of legitimate authorities who may use force, taxation, and other coercive measures (widely variant from society to society)—becomes more and more important as societies become larger and mobility more common. This source of order, however, continues to rely on the self-enforcing source of order; and it raises the new problem of the use of political authority for individual gain.

4) Religion may, under some circumstances, help to solve the problem of order, both as a designator of goals (with particular emphasis on shared goals), and as an enforcer of means. By ritual, by symbol, by its system of beliefs, its doctrines of rewards and punishments, religion may help to produce the socialized individuals who accept the dominant values as to legitimate means and ends. This aids the political authorities, but also applies to them.

5) None of these points implies a value judgment concerning the desirability or undesirability of any *particular* system of social order. Religion may help to preserve a social order which, from stated value premises, is bad.

6) Certain conditions weaken, or even reverse, the place of religion in social integration. In some times and places it becomes involved, as symbol and cause, in social conflict and the reduction of order. Again, whether this is desirable or undesirable can be stated only with reference to certain stated values and cannot be determined "in general."

NOTES

1. M. J. Herskovits, *Man and His Works,* New York: A. A. Knopf, 1948, pp. 349–350.

2. Kingsley Davis, *Human Society,* New York: Macmillan Co., 1949, p. 517.

3. See W. J. Goode, *Religion Among the Primitives,* Glencoe, Ill.: Free Press, 1951, pp. 243–246.

4. On this whole approach to a theory of the origins of religion and some of the controversy which it generated, see Sir James G. Frazer, *The Golden Bough,* New York: The Macmillan

Co., 1922; Irving King, *The Development of Religion,* New York: The Macmillan Co., 1910; Andrew Lang, *The Making of Religion* and *Magic and Religion,* New York: Longmans, Green & Co., 1900; R. R. Marett, *The Threshold of Religion;* P. W. Schmidt, *The Origin and Growth of Religion;* Herbert Spencer, *The Principles of Sociology,* Vol. I; Edward B. Tylor, *Primitive Culture.*

5. Paul Radin, *Primitive Religion, Its Nature and Origin,* New York: The Viking Press, 1937, pp. 6–9.

6. Georg Simmel, "A Contribution to the Sociology of Religion," *American Journal of Sociology,* 11 (1905), p. 360.

7. *Ibid.,* pp. 366–367.

8. Emile Durkheim, *The Elementary Forms of the Religious Life,* Glencoe, Ill.: Free Press, 1954, p. 387.

9. *Ibid.*

10. Kingsley Davis in Introduction to Goode, *op. cit.,* p. 15.

11. M. J. Fortes and E. Evans-Pritchard, *African Political Systems,* London: Oxford University Press, 1948, p. 16 ff.

12. See the excellent discussion by Clyde Kluckhohn in *Anthropology Today,* edited by A. L. Kroeber, New York: Harcourt, Brace, 1948, pp. 507–523. This whole question is treated with greatest care by Talcott Parsons in several works. See also David Aberle *et al.,* "The Functional Prerequisites of Society," *Ethics,* 60 (1950), 100–111.

13. See Robert Merton, *Social Theory and Social Structure,* Glencoe, Ill.: Free Press, 1951, pp. 27–38.

14. *Ibid.,* p. 68.

15. Goode, *op. cit.,* p. 33. See also Harry C. Bredemeier, "The Methodology of Functionalism," *American Sociological Review,* 20 (1955), 173–180.

16. Quoted by Homer Smith, *Man and His Gods,* Boston: Little, Brown, 1952, pp. 166–167.

17. E. A. Ross, *Social Control,* New York: The Macmillan Co., 1901, pp. 358–359.

18. Merton, *op. cit.,* p. 30.

19. Kingsley Davis, *Human Society,* pp. 141–143.

20. Henri Bergson, *The Two Sources of Morality and Religion,* New York: Henry Holt, 1935, pp. 112–113.

21. Benjamin Kidd, *Social Evolution,* New York: The Macmillan Co., 1894, p. 111.

22. W. Lloyd Warner, *American Life: Dream and Reality,* Chicago: University of Chicago Press, 1953, pp. 2–3.

56. AN ANALYSIS OF SECT DEVELOPMENT

BRYAN R. WILSON

In addition to the study of the functions of religion, the analysis of religious organization has been subject to extensive sociological inquiry. For many years sociologists conventionally have divided religious forms in advanced societies into four "ideal type" categories: ecclesia, denominations (or churches), sects, and cults. These, in turn, are frequently subdivided according to their intrinsic characteristics.

In "An Analysis of Sect Development," Bryan R. Wilson questions this typology and discusses the problem of maintaining original value orientations faced by religious groups experiencing changing social circumstances. The tensions, he suggests, are clearly evident in sects because members have explicit value commitments that often run counter to those of the wider society, have clearly delineated organizational patterns, and are peculiarly self-conscious in their relations with outsiders. Some sects are markedly successful in the preservations of undiluted values of protest; others. notably those that gradually become denominationalized, are much less successful in preserving traditional values. Wilson's paper seeks to distinguish and characterize distinctive kinds of sects, and to use such characterizations to determine specific elements, and combinations of elements, that promote or retard such development.

Bryan R. Wilson is Oxford University's Senior Appointment in Sociology. He is the author of Sects and Society *(1961) and* Religion in Secular Society *(1968), and editor of* Patterns of Sectarianism *(1967).*

The tendency for sects to become denominations has frequently been noted, and on the basis of this tendency the generalization has sometimes been made that a sect-type organization can exist for only one generation, that in the second generation the sect (and the cult in Becker's use of the term) becomes a church or a denomination.[1] Yet, if one surveys existing religious organizations, it is evident that, in both the sociological and the everyday use of the term, some sects persist as such over several generations. In view of the fact that some sects have undeniably gravitated towards a denominational structure, however, we need to know just what factors in the organization and circumstances of sects promote or retard this develop-ment.[2] Since sects are not all of a piece, we need to distinguish and delineate certain sub-types which should prove of greater predictive utility than does the grosser concept of the sect, and with which we may pass from crude hypothesis to more fully developed theory. Once these sub-types have been identified we may turn to the elements in sect organizations which are focal points of tension. It is here hypothesized that sects experience different types of tension which vary according to their own constellation of values, as well as the circumstances of their origin. In response to such tensions, in the attempt at their management, we may expect to find the genesis of processes which cause some sects to develop into denomi-

Reprinted from the *American Sociological Review,* **24** (1959), 3–15, by permission of the author and the American Sociological Association.

nations, others to wither, some to be exterminated, some to fragment, and some to remain, over several generations, as sects.[3] This paper considers the following elements: the circumstances of sect emergence, the internal structure of sect organization, the degree of separateness from the external world, the coherence of sect values, and group commitments and relationships.

Characterization of Sect and Denomination

Typically a *sect* may be identified by the following characteristics: it is a voluntary association; membership is by proof to sect authorities of some claim to personal merit—such as knowledge of doctrine, affirmation of a conversion experience, or recommendation of members in good standing; exclusiveness is emphasized, and expulsion exercised against those who contravene doctrinal, moral, or organizational precepts; its self-conception is of an elect, a gathered remnant, possessing special enlightenment; personal perfection is the expected standard of aspiration, in whatever terms this is judged; it accepts, at least as an ideal, the priesthood of all believers; there is a high level of lay participation; there is opportunity for the member spontaneously to express his commitment; the sect is hostile or indifferent to the secular society and to the state.[4]

In elaboration of this general identification of the sect, it might be added that although sects differ among themselves in their characteristic social relationships, the commitment of the sectarian is always more total and more defined than that of the member of other religious organizations. The ideology of the sect is much more clearly crystallized, and the member is much more distinctly characterized than is the adherent of the larger denomination or church. The behavioral correlates of his ideological commitment also serve to set him and keep him apart from "the world." Sects have a totalitarian rather than a segmental hold over their members: they dictate the member's ideological orientation to secular society; or they rigorously specify the necessary standards of moral rectitude; or they compel the member's involvement in group activity. Ideological conformity may be achieved by compulsory participation, but the system of control varies widely.[5] Not only does the sect discipline or expel the member who entertains heretical opinions, or commits a moral misdemeanor, but it regards such defection as betrayal of the cause, unless confession of fault and appeal for forgiveness is forthcoming.

The *denomination,* in contrast, shows the following features: it is formally a voluntary association; it accepts adherents without imposition of traditional prerequisites of entry, and employs purely formalized procedures of admission; breadth and tolerance are emphasized; since membership is laxly enrolled, expulsion is not a common device for dealing with the apathetic and the wayward; its self-conception is unclear and its doctrinal position unstressed; it is content to be one movement among others, all of which are thought to be acceptable in the sight of God; it accepts the standards and values of the prevailing culture and conventional morality; there is a trained professional ministry; lay participation occurs but is typically restricted to particular sections of the laity and to particular areas of activity; services are formalized and spontaneity is absent; education of the young is of greater concern than the evangelism of the outsider; additional activities are largely non-religious in character; individual commitment is not very intense; the denomination accepts the values of the secular society and the state; members are drawn from any section of the community, but within one church, or any one region, membership will tend to limit itself to those who are socially compatible.[6]

Characterization of Types of Sect

Given these general types of organization, we need to distinguish the sub-types of sects.[7] The basis of the present classification is the characterization of types of mission which might be discerned among sects. Generally these types of mission rest on the ideological and doctrinal character of sects, and serve as useful indicators of the clusters of other characteristics to be found in each type. For our purposes, within the framework of Protestant Christianity, four broad types may be discerned. Such a classification is not necessarily exhaustive, nor necessarily exclusive of alternative types. It rests essentially on the response of the sect to the values and relationships prevailing in society. This response, in the nature of sectarianism as we have already described it, is necessarily one of greater or lesser rejection. The *Conversionist* sects seek to alter men, and thereby to alter the world; the response is free-will optimism. The *Adventist* sects predict drastic alteration of the world, and seek to prepare for the new dispensation —a pessimistic determinism. The *Introversionists* reject the world's values and replace them with higher inner values, for the realization of which inner resources are cultivated. The *Gnostic* sects accept in large measure the world's goals but seek a new and esoteric means to achieve these ends—a wishful mysticism. This classification is sociological rather than psychological; the responses are built into particular institutions. The implications of these four depictions are elaborated in the following characterizations, and although the empirical correlates of each type are not explored, the implications themselves are not simply logical extensions of the hypothesized types of response. What is here suggested is that, given particular responses *within the context of Christianity,* these further corollaries may be expected.[8]

1) The Conversionist sect is one whose teaching and activity centers on evangelism; in contemporary Christianity it is typically the orthodox fundamentalist or pentecostal sect. It is typified by extreme bibliolatry: the Bible is taken as the only guide to salvation, and is accepted as literally true. Conversion experience and the acceptance of Jesus as a personal saviour are the test of admission to the fellowship; extreme emphasis is given to individual guilt for sin and the need to obtain redemption through Christ. Despite the theoretical limit on the number who can gain salvation, the sect precludes no one and revivalist techniques are employed in evangelism. It is distrustful of, or indifferent toward, the denominations and churches which at best have diluted, and at worst betrayed, Christianity; it is hostile to clerical learning and especially to modernism; it is opposed to modern science, particularly to geology and to evolutionary theories; it disdains culture and the artistic values accepted in the wider society. Examples are to be found in the Salvation Army and the Pentecostal sects.

2) The Adventist—or revolutionist— sect focuses attention on the coming overturn of the present world order: in contemporary Christianity it is the adventist movement. It is typified by its emphasis on the Bible, and particularly of its exegesis of the allegorical and prophetic books from which the time and circumstances of the second advent of Christ are discerned. The conventional eschatological ideas of heaven and hell are regarded as false, and the resurrection of the dead for judgment is accepted as the principal eschatological event. Christ is regarded as a divine commander, not only as a saviour, and a high moral standard is based on the moral precepts of Jesus. Participation in the new kingdom will be limited and only those who have maintained doctrinal and moral rectitude will be eligible; admission to the fellowship is by thorough understanding of necessary doctrine, and not by affirmation of conversion. Evangelism is undertaken by way of preaching

the word but quick conversions are not sought and revivalism is despised as emotional and misguided. The established church is regarded as fulfilling the role of the anti-Christ: clerical learning is despised (but science is depreciated only in so far as its doctrines conflict with adventist biblical exegesis) and the professional ministry is vigorously opposed. Separation from the world is a more crucial interdiction than are restrictions placed upon certain worldly activities. The sect is hostile towards the wider society and looks forward to its overthrow.[9] Examples are Jehovah's Witnesses and the Christadelphians.

3) The Introversionist—or pietist—sect directs the attention of its followers away from the world and to the community and more particularly to the members' possession of the Spirit; in recent Christianity it is exemplified in the pietist sect. Such a sect is typified by reliance on inner illumination, whether this be regarded as the voice of conscience or the action of the Holy Ghost. The Bible is a source or stimulant of inner inspiration and ethical insight; doctrine is of lesser importance in that the letter has surrendered to the spirit, the deepening of which is a central preoccupation. The sect develops a particular *Weltanschauung* and considers itself an enlightened elect; inner values may be regarded as incommunicable and eschatological ideas are unarticulated or of little significance. No evangelism is undertaken and a strong ingroup morality is developed; the sect withdraws from the world, or allows its members to be active in the world only for human betterment at the behest of conscience and at the periphery of social concern. It is indifferent to other religious movements. It admits of no spiritual directors or ministers. Examples include some Holiness movements, Quakers, and the Society of the Truly Inspired (Amana Community).

4) The Gnostic sect emphasizes some special body of teaching of an esoteric kind. In contemporary Christianity it is a sect offering a new or revived interpretation of Christian teaching. It accepts the Bible as allegorical and complementary to its own gnosis; conventional Christian eschatology is replaced by a more optimistic and esoteric eschatology; Christ is a way-shower, an exemplar of truth, rather than a saviour. Christian mystical teachings, such as the Trinity, are replaced by other more exclusive mysticism, the significance of which the adherent can hope only gradually to penetrate; doctrine includes teachings which replace secular scientific explanations, and offer a cosmology, an anthropology, and a psychology of their own. The utility of the gnosis for everyday life is emphasized, particularly in the achievement of worldly success, self-realization, health, material well-being and happiness. Conversion is an alien concept to the Gnostic sect, but instruction and guidance are offered to the outsider or the neophyte; there are stages in understanding: enlightenment "unfolds." There is a charismatic leader (or a succession of such leaders) who pronounces wisdom; ministers are usually styled as teachers or guides, and ministerial functions are subdivided among laity with appropriate qualification. Other churches are regarded with indifference as ignorant or backward; secular knowledge is seen as valid and useful relatively, except where it contravenes sect teaching. The cultural standards of the society are accepted and even utilized: the Gnostic sectarian does not withdraw from the world but seeks to use his special knowledge for his own advancement, or that of the movement, in the world. These traits are found, for example, in Christian Science, New Thought sects, Koreshanity, and the Order of the Cross.[10]

Circumstances of Sect Emergence

The conditions under which sects emerge may, for analytical purposes, be divided into three elements: the method by which the sect comes into being, the specific factors of stimulus, and the external social conditions prevailing.

1) The principal methods of sect emergence are by spontaneous development around a local charismatic leader, by schism, and by organized revival. In the case of a sect emerging around a leader much will depend on his teaching and his organizational ability. Some such sects disappear when the leader dies or departs. Others, particularly those in which the leader offers a new gnosis which is consonant with the age, spread and retain their identity. The gnosis may be a new combination of ideas or the retailing of older ideas to a new audience.[11] Thus the optimism, feminism, and success-orientation of the New Thought sects and of Christian Science fitted well with American ideals at the end of the nineteenth century. If the leader offers a variant of traditional Christianity, however, then such a group is likely to remain local and, if persisting, eventually to make common cause with other fundamentalist movements or with the fundamentalist wing of one of the larger denominations, usually the Baptists. Many independent missions of this type joined with the pentecostal sects in England during the first three decades of this century. But if such sects spread they appear to be particularly likely to become denominationalized, as the distinctive needs of members change—assuming that there is no constant stream of new admissions to keep alive the pristine spirit of the movement.

The schismatic sect tends to be vigorous as long as its protest against the parent body remains significant, and as long as the rival group exists as a challenge; in this period it is likely to grow only by accretions from the parent body. Subsequently, as the issue of disagreement wanes in importance, such a schismatic group may adjust to continuance as a sect, may decay in the absence of opposition, or may partially and gradually rejoin the parent body. Illustrations of such processes are afforded in the history of the Plymouth Brethren in England, and of the Christadelphians in England, the United States, Canada, and Australia.

Organized revival is the method of development most usual to fundamentalist sects, and may well begin in a non-denominational spirit. Success, however, tends to impose organizational responsibilities and, if there are distinctive teachings, sects tend to emerge. The Full Gospel Testimony and the Elim Foursquare Gospel Church in England are examples of this development, the teachings being pentecostal. Such groups usually experience rapid growth and high turnover of personnel; since they rely on revivalists for stability and permanence there is, in the nature of the case, an acceptance of trained functionaries, and in this respect a tendency towards denominational development.

2) The specific factors of stimulus of sect emergence are usually found in the stresses and tensions differentially experienced within the total society. Change in the economic position of a particular group (which may be a change only in relative position); disturbance of normal social relations, for instance in the circumstances of industrialization and urbanization; the failure of the social system to accommodate particular age, sex, and status groups—all of these are possible stimuli in the emergence of sects. These are the needs to which sects, to some extent, respond. Particular groups are rendered marginal by some process of social change; there is a sudden need for a new interpretation of their social position or for a transvaluation of their experience. Insecurity, differential status anxiety, cultural neglect, prompt a need for readjustment which sects may, for some, provide. The maladjusted may be communities, or occupational groups, or dispersed individuals in similar marginal positions. The former cases are more typical for the emergence of Conversionist, Adventist, and Introversionist groups, the latter for

the Gnostic sects. Sudden social disloca-
tion, as experienced in urbanization and
industrialization, appears to be a frequent
circumstance in which Conversionist sects
emerge, while Adventists and Introversionists have arisen in the midst of longer
persisting deprivation.

3) The external social conditions are
not easily distinguished from the stimulus
factors considered above, but taken in
their widest sense it is evident that there
are different consequences for sects according to the political and moral character of the society in which they emerge. In
feudal, authoritarian, or totalitarian societies, the sect is persecuted; if it persists it
will do so only as a clandestine organization. It will tend to be hostile to the world
(whether or not this was its original orientation) and may, in reality or in fantasy,
project this hostility upon society. The
very early Quakers, the Fifth Monarchy
Men, and the numerous pietist and millennial movements in Europe from the
thirteenth to the eighteenth centuries, illustrate this reaction.[12] An alternative development in the past has been for the sect
to migrate and seek an environment where
it could live according to its own standards. The achievement of such isolation
has, in itself, consequences for sect organization and promotes communistic arrangements. Examples here are the Rap-
pites, Amana Society, and other
movements flourishing in eighteenth and
nineteenth century America after migrat-
ing from Germany.[13] In such circumstances, to which more specific reference
is made below, the sect is unlikely to show
marked denominational tendencies.

In democratic or pluralist societies the
sect is not pushed into the search for
isolation, and although revolutionary type
movements (Adventist) may emerge, they
are likely to maintain their separation
from the world by other methods. Clearly,
during rapid social change the various
stimulus factors discussed above are more
likely to become operative, and it is empirically well established that sects prolif-
erate in periods of social unrest. In this
connection, some very general propositions have been offered on the basis of
data drawn from the United States in the
period from 1800 to the present time.
This was a society undergoing almost
uninterrupted expansion, rapid social
change, high mobility, intense urbanization, and successive waves of immigration
(from which its proletariat was continually re-recruited). In face of these developments the original social values were
undergoing constant modification through
differential acceptance by diverse ethnic
and religious groups. In short, this was a
highly atypical context from which to
make generalizations concerning the development of sects. The absence of tradition and of stable class differences, the
promotion of denominational competition,
and the expectation of growth and development resulted in extreme accommodation which helped sects rapidly to evolve
into denominations—almost as part of a
"success-pattern." In this situation even
the Quakers could develop a schism which
accepted ministry and became virtually a
denomination. The external social circumstances, rather than the intrinsic nature of
the sect as such, must here be invoked
to explain why sects become denominations.[14]

The Internal Structure of Sect Organization

A feature of sects in contemporary society
is that they tend to develop some sort of
centralized organization, however minimal. This development has been prompted
by the need for communication between
dispersed communities, the increase in
mobility, and the growing impact of legislation on sects, particularly in wartime.
Central organization in itself, however, is
not to be equated with a denominational
tendency, since central control may be

effectively employed to prevent such trends, as with Jehovah's Witnesses.[15] On the other hand, such agencies may be a departure from the original sect ideal—their development may be a response to some external threat to the sect's values, but they also imply the surrender of other values. The most significant question about this development would seem to be whether or not those who acquire responsibilities in the central agencies of the sect become professional *public* functionaries—where functions become institutionally differentiated and specialization of roles occurs.

The initial position of the sect, where there is no local charismatic leader, is the occupation of officers by members in rotation, by lot, or by seniority, and subsequently to institute the lay leader, usually chosen by the group for his particular abilities. Once the concept of special training of such leaders is admitted, then a step to denominationalism has been taken. Training implies lack of parity between leaders and members, it compromises the radical democracy of the sect and the ideal of the priesthood of all believers. Spontaneity disappears, and leaders employ the status symbols of their profession, seeking equal esteem with the pastors of other movements.[16]

Such a radical departure from sect values does not normally occur abruptly, nor does denominational character rest on this one factor alone. Obviously, different types of sects show a different proclivity to this development. We can fully expect sects highly concerned with evangelism and revivalism to be most prone to evolve in this way. If missionaries and revivalists are being supported by the group, the value of special training is likely to be accepted and will probably be provided within and by the organization itself. The economies of scale may well induce the movement to train more people than can readily be absorbed in the mission field, or than can be supported there, while there is also a limit to the number of active revivalists who can operate on behalf of a particular movement. The replacement of local lay pastors by trained ministers is then a likely consequence. Something like this sequence can be seen in the development of pentecostal sects in Britain. Of other groups, the sect known as the Church of God in the British Isles and Overseas has full-time itinerant revivalists who preach in the meeting houses in place of local lay leaders. This development may be regarded as a stage in the same general process, retarded in this instance by the sect's strong anti-ministerial ideology.

This type of development is most probable in the Conversionist sects. The orthodox fundamentalist sect stands nearest to traditional Christianity and may have had its own origins in some larger movement with a ministry, whose organization might be accepted even if its teachings are rejected. The Adventist sect resists organizational change in its confident expectation of an early end to the present dispensation and is, in any case, hostile to any institution associated with the established order. Similarly, the pietist (Introversionist) sect is ideologically resistant to the development of a ministry and, moreover, is not concerned with evangelism. In that the adventists evangelize they do so without the use of revivalist techniques. The Gnostic sect, while usually instituting a system of special instruction, does so for the private and personal benefit of the member and not as a qualification for any particular office in the movement, even though in practice the more highly taught are likely to gain easier admission to leadership positions. Worship is not usually of major importance to the Gnostic sect and when professional functionaries do arise they are more likely to be private counsellors than public ministers.

Elites emerge in sects both at the local level and, once centralized agencies have arisen, also at the center. They may be elected by the generality, but they tend to become self-recruiting both locally and at the center. Central control of local leaders may also occur, and when it does the local elite will be the group which interprets, explains, and rationalizes the activity of the central group. In such movements there is a distinct centripetal tendency of responsibility: allegiance is to "headquarters," "the central board," "the executive." Christian Science and Jehovah's Witnesses both typify this organizational structure. The existence of such elites has no specific implication for the development of the sect into a denomination for the crucial matters are whether the elite is specially trained and whether its function becomes that of a professional ministry. What may be noted, however, is that centralized movements appear to be better able to prevent schism than movements in which the central agencies are less well articulated and in which centripetal responsibility has not developed.

Schism is a feature of sects and of churches more than of denominations (except in the early period of denominational development). (This is partly because sects and churches tend to possess a much more clearly articulated structure of doctrine and organization than do denominations.) Otherwise, schism usually centers on the question of purity of doctrine, and successful schism usually finds its leader in the very inner elite of the movement.[17] Schism of this kind serves to preserve the distinctive sectarian character of the organization since the schismatic groups tend to become the keepers of each other's consciences in relation to the maintenance of traditional values. The two groups compete for the same public, and frequently appeal to the same sources and authorities in legitimation of their position, thus engendering a competitive struggle to prove the purity of their doctrine and social practice. The Plymouth Brethren, the Mennonites, and the Christadelphians provide illustrations of this development.

Degree of Separateness from the World

The relationship which a sect permits itself and its members to the external world is of vital importance to the nature of its continuance. In some measure, and by some methods, the sect is committed to keeping itself "unspotted from the world": its distinctness must be evident both to its own members and to others. To this end there are two principal types of mechanism, *isolation* and *insulation*. Isolation may be consciously designed, or unconsciously accepted. It may be vicinal isolation in which social isolation is necessarily implied, but this is readily achieved only by groups which accept a communistic type of organization; such organization, in turn, acts as a further isolating device. Sects which have aspired to be self-contained in this way, and have sought to avoid the "alien" even in those spheres where most sects are prepared to treat with him, have usually been of the Introversionist type. Clearly, such a radical mechanism for the achievement of self-maintenance would mean too profound a change in sect character for Conversionist sects, while the expectation of an early overturn of normal social relations makes such action premature for Adventists. Gnostic sects usually lack the community basis for such a venture and seek their separateness from the world in different ways. Isolation may also be linguistic, a condition illustrated by the various bodies of Mennonites, Hutterites, and Doukhobors. Finally, isolation may be simply the injunction to maintain social separateness from the alien; this is urged by most sects, even the evangelical.

Insulation consists of behavioral rules calculated to protect sect values by reducing the influence of the external world when contact necessarily occurs. Of course, insulation may be a latent function of the moral demands of sect teaching, the justification for which is biblical or revealed prescription; the sect leaders and the members themselves, however, often become aware of the real value of such precepts. Distinctive dress is such an insulating device, characteristic of some Mennonites, early Quakers, and Hutterites. Group endogamy is a more widely used method of insulation and is the rule for most Adventist and Introversionist sects, the expectation in many Conversionist sects, and the preferred form, if marriage is approved at all, in Gnostic sects.

The Coherence of Sect Values

Separateness from the world is clearly a part of the general constellation of values embraced by sects. The coherence of such values and the tensions which their acceptance involves are discussed below. However, it is analytically possible to distinguish between tensions arising from the conflict of this particular value and others embraced by the sect and the tensions resulting from the conflict between sect ideals and the ideals of the wider society, and ultimately with those of the state.

The principal tension between the demand for separateness and other sect values arises in the injunction, accepted by many sects, to go out and preach the gospel. Evangelism means exposure to the world and the risk of alienation of the evangelizing agents. It means also the willingness to accept into the sect new members. This throws a particular weight on the standards of admission if, through the impact of recruitment, the sect itself is not to feel the effect of members who are incompletely socialized from the sect's point of view. The more distinctive are sect doctrines and the more emphatic the insistence on strict standards of doctrinal understanding, the less likely it is that the sect will suffer from its evangelism. The Introversionist and Gnostic sects do not experience this type of tension since they do not evangelize the alien, or seek to do so only by formalized procedures. The Adventist sect regards it as one of its responsibilities to preach the kingdom, to

forewarn the world of events portending, and to gather a remnant, but it sends its evangelizing agents into the world only after their doctrinal understanding has been thoroughly tested and their allegiance well tried. Equally it does not expect rapid returns, but subjects those who wish to join the movement to examination of their doctrinal knowledge. The Conversionist sects, which are fundamentalists, experience this tension most fully and have evolved least protection for themselves on these vulnerable points. Their agents are young, their doctrine often less sharply distinguished from that of the denominations, and their tests of good faith inadequate, subordinate to conversionist enthusiasm, and easily, if unwittingly, counterfeited by the emotionally overwrought in the revivalist situation.

The recruitment of the second generation is also an aspect of evangelism. There are similar problems of the tests of admission and the process of socializing the in-comers. Niebuhr, and subsequently Pope, pin-pointed a key tension for sect organization in recognizing the significance of accepting the second generation.[18] It is an oversimplification to say, however, that the second generation makes the sect into a denomination. As indicated above, such development depends on the standards of admission imposed by the sect, the previous rigor with which children have been kept separate from the world, and on the point at which a balance is struck between the natural desire of parents to have their children included in salvation and their awareness of the community view that any sort of salvation depends on the maintenance of doctrinal and moral standards. Obviously, whether the sect tends to embrace whole families or simply individuals is a significant matter. In general, Gnostic sects, which tend to have an individualistic appeal and do not emphasize the normal type of separation from the world, have more difficulty in winning the allegiance of the second generation than have other sects. Pietistic and Adventist sects, enjoying both doctrinal distinctiveness and the allegiance of whole families (supported by endogamous injunctions) and also tending to have exacting standards for would-be joiners, are apt to hold their second generation without damage to sect identity. The fundamentalist Conversionist groups—who often appeal to individuals, have a less clearly articulated difference of doctrine from the denominations, and whose standards of admission are simply acceptance of a Saviour—are most likely to be affected by the degree of adherence of the second generation.[19]

The sect's desire to be separate from the world and its concerns—and the values which express that separateness—results in certain distinct tensions for the organization and for its members. For each sect there must be a position of optimal tension, where any greater degree of hostility against the world portends direct conflict, and any less suggests accommodation to worldly values. The typical issues of this conflict of values include: divergence of sect and external society on what constitutes true knowledge (which leads to conflict concerning education); the refusal of sects to recognize the legitimacy of society's legal arrangements and the refusal to accept conventionalized sacred practices such as oath-swearing; withdrawal of the sect from the political arrangements of society, refusal to vote, to salute national emblems, and the like; conscientious objection to participation in military activities of the state; the refusal to recognize the marital and familial regulations imposed by the state; objection to state medical regulations; disregard of economic institutions of society, as in the refusal to register land ownership or to join labor unions.

The means used by the sect to cope with these particular tensions is crucial for the persistence of sect organization. The sect may depart from the accepted moral rules of the wider society, but beyond a certain point the sect comes into conflict with even the democratic state in the pluralist society. The state does not always win in such conflicts, as the exemptions from oath-swearing, flag-saluting, military service, and medical regulation, all illustrate. But the sect itself, in pursuit of its values, in its search for exemption, may experience change of character. It must, for instance, develop agencies to treat with the state; to preserve its values it may be thrust into new types of social action, new contact with worldly organization—perhaps even fighting its case in the law courts of "the world," although this conflicts with the desire of most sects to be a law unto themselves. Action to reduce external tensions may in this way generate new internal tensions as the sect departs from older practices and values.

Thus when Christian Scientists joined with other unconventional healing movements to resist state legislation concerning medical care, they appeared, to some members, to compromise their stand that Christian Science alone could really heal. When, in Britain in the first World War, Christadelphians developed an organization to seek exemptions from military service, they allowed the activities of the state to induce them to establish committees at a national level, which conflicted with their ideal of minimal organization and prompted dissension and schism. When the Doukhobors, facing the demand of the state that it regulate its marriages and accept secular schooling, resort to arson and violence, they trespass on their own pacifist ideals.[20] Clearly in such cases of challenge and response there may readily be the beginnings of sect change in that the sect develops agencies more like those of denominations, and admits, by the back door, the values prevalent in the wider society.

If the sect is to persist as an organization it must not only separate its members from the world, but must also maintain the dissimilarity of its own values from those of the secular society. Its members must not normally be allowed to accept the values of the status system of the external world. The sect must see itself as marginal to the wider society, and even when the marginality of extreme poverty, for example, has objectively disappeared, the consciousness of the inapplicability of the standards of the outside world must be retained. Whatever the changes in their material circumstances, the group must persist in the feeling of being a people apart if it is to persist. Status must be status within the sect, and this should be the only group to which the status-conscious individual makes reference. Yet for the proselytizing sect this is often accomplished only with difficulty since the social status of its members may radically affect its prospect of winning recruits. Even the sect of the very poor is usually pleased when a prominent personage is converted and often accords him a place of honor because of his status in the wider society. The classic cases of sects developing into denominations (usually accompanied by schism from the parent body on the part of those poorer members who resist the growth of formality and other denominational characteristics) illustrate just such a conflict of sect values: between genuine separateness from the world and the desire for social respectability.[21]

As we have seen, the Adventist and Introversionist sects are more fully insulated against this type of value conflict. Nor does this type of tension occur in the Gnostic sects which insulate the two areas ideologically by teaching, in many cases, that the material world is less real. Although the member might gain status in the group if improvement in his material circumstances can be attributed to his special sect-inculcated knowledge, still the two levels of experience are clearly distinguished.

Finally, we may note the significance of exclusiveness in the development of sects. The more fully the sect sees itself as a chosen remnant, the more fully will it offer resistance to the broadening process which is implied in becoming a denomina-

tion. Such resistance is more likely to be successful, however, if the sect has an aristocratic ethic concerning salvation—if it sees itself as a chosen elect, limited in size by divine command. Sects which emphasize free-will and the availability of Christ to all (even if they accompany such a teaching with an expectation that not many will in fact avail themselves of the opportunity), and which thus accept a general Arminian position theologically, are much more likely to practice evangelism and to seek rapid growth than are the others.[22] The Conversionist sects inherit this theological position and accept this mission, whereas the Adventist sects, who accept the command to preach the truth, nonetheless make truth difficult to obtain. Both Introversionist and Gnostic sects emphasize a gradual unfolding of grace or truth to the individual; although, particularly in the Gnostic groups, there is no sense of absolute exclusiveness, in both types there is an emphasis on an elect.

Group Commitments and Relationships

At some level the individual member's commitment to the sect must be total. This may mean the acceptance of a leader's commands, or a general ideological commitment, or a more specific doctrinal commitment, or a commitment to regulate all social and moral affairs entirely as the sect directs. In the Gnostic sect commitment tends to be simply to the leader or to the general ideological position of the movement; the member must acquire the *Weltanschauung* of the sect if benefit of its special gnosis is to be gained. There are few moral correlates of this ideological position, and those which do exist are typically personal aids to self-fulfilment, for example, abstinence in matters of diet and in use of drugs, tobacco, and alcohol. The Introversionist sects (which may or may not have recognized leaders, and whose leaders may or may not claim distinctive charisma) add to the commitment of the member a distinct moral commitment: certain types of behavior are expected, and there is a strong commitment to the fellowship itself. The Adventist group demands commitment to specific doctrine and specific morality, which further implies commitment to the brethren themselves. The Conversionist sects, while expecting doctrinal and moral rectitude, are less sharply exclusive in demands toward the fellowship as such and are even prepared to extend their general ideal of community to embrace "all born-again believers."

Introversionist and Adventist sects are distinctly *Gemeinschaften*. Fellowship is an important value for all members: fellow-members are "brethren"; relationships as far as possible are primary; the local meeting is a face-to-face group. The individual is a sect-member before he is anything else, he is expected to find his friends within the group, group endogamy is the rule, and there is expulsion of the wayward and lax. The membership is a membership of families rather than of individuals and sect values are mediated by the kin-group. The Introversionists are sharers of an inner and unseen truth; the Adventists are participants in revolutionary intrigue. The Conversionist sect shares these general characteristics only partially: its concept of brotherhood extends beyond sect boundaries and its standards are less rigorous. It accepts individuals more lightly, socializes them less intensely, and loses them more easily—all of which disturbs the strong sense of community. Its appeal is to the individual seeking salvation, and consequently it is less typically composed of families. The Gnostic sect is much more frankly a *Gesellschaft*: the individual's relationships to other devotees are secondary to his commitment to the ideology and the leadership. Brotherhood is an alien concept. Discipline is for disloyalty, not for specific moral misdemeanor. The impersonality of relationships may even be regarded as ideal, since the gnosis, "the principle," is what mat-

ters. Since there are fewer behavioral correlates of sect affiliation, the member, socially, may hide his membership and so avoid the disapproval of the outside world.

Conclusions

Our analysis has brought out a number of items which are subject to variation as between different types of sect and which help to determine the likely development of such movements. Thus it is clear that sects with a general democratic ethic, which stress simple affirmation of intense subjective experience as a criterion for admission, which stand in the orthodox fundamentalist tradition, which emphasize evangelism and use revivalist techniques, and which seek to accommodate groups dislocated by rapid social change are particularly subject to denominationalizing tendencies. These same tendencies are likely to be intensified if the sect is unclear concerning the boundaries of the saved community and extends its rules of endogamy to include any saved person as an eligible spouse; if its moral injunctions are unclearly distinguished from conventional or traditional morality; and if it accepts simple assertion of remorse for sin as sufficient to re-admit or to retain a backslidden member. Denominationalization is all the more likely when such a sect inherits, or evolves, any type of preaching order, lay pastors, or itinerant ministers; when revivalism leads to special training for the revivalist themselves (and so leads to a class of professionals who cease to rely on "love-offerings" but are granted a fixed stipend); and when the members are ineffectively separated from the world, a condition enhanced by proselytizing activities.

It is clear that the types of sect which we described as Conversionist are most likely to fulfil the conditions which transform sects into denominations and are least likely to enjoy the circumstances preventing this process. The Adventist and the Introversionist types appear to be best protected from this development, although by different mechanisms: they fulfil few of the conditions supporting this evolution and often enjoy or create the factors which retard it. The Gnostic sect is in some ways less clearly protected, but its distinctive ideology performs in some measure the functions which social insulating mechanisms perform for other types.

In a broad way, we can see why certain earlier studies of sects fell into errors of prediction, since the conclusions rested on the experience of certain types of sects, sects which existed in very particular social circumstances, and accommodated people whose social marginality and sense of anomie were often temporary and a consequence of inadequate readjustment to rapidly changing social conditions. Of course, to predict the development of any given sect requires examination in close detail of its circumstances. Once these are known, however, the foregoing analysis should provide a guide for the interpretation of these facts.

NOTES

1. H. Richard Niebuhr, *The Social Sources of Denominationalism*, New York: Holt, 1929, p. 19; Howard Becker, *Systematic Sociology on the Basis of the Beziehungslehre and Gebildelehre of Leopold von Wiese*, New York: Wiley, 1932; Liston Pope, *Millhands and Preachers*, New Haven: Yale University Press, 1942, pp. 118 ff.

2. J. M. Yinger, *Religion in the Struggle for Power*, Durham, N.C.: Duke University Press, 1946, suggested an alternative development for the sect, into an "established sect." More recently Yinger has suggested that established sects develop because they emphasize the evil nature of society, while denominationalizing sects are those which stress the reduction of individual anxiety and guilt—a conclusion generally consistent with the analysis proposed here; see Yinger's *Religion, Society and the Individual*, New York: Macmillan, 1957, pp. 151–152. Recognition of the limitations of the Niebuhr hypothesis is offered in the context of a discussion somewhat different from the above by Benton Johnson, "A Critical Appraisal of Church-Sect Typology," *American Sociological Review*, 22 (1957), 88–92. For another approach to this process, see Harold W. Pfautz, "The Sociology of Secularization: Religious Groups," *American Journal of Sociology*, 61 (1955), 121–128.

3. The type of analysis to be followed owes much to the work and the suggestions of Philip Selznick; see especially his book, *The Organizational Weapon*, New York: McGraw-Hill, 1952.

4. The characterization of the sect here proposed is in many respects more general than the "type-constructs" offered by Becker, Yinger, and Pope in the works cited above, and by E. D. C. Brewer, "Sect and Church in Methodism," *Social Forces*, 30 (1952), 400–408. It omits such characteristics as subjectivism, informality, the expression of fervor, and poverty, since these characteristics appear to belong to certain subtypes only.

5. Thus in Christian Science, for example, doctrinal purity is maintained without members being compelled to participate in an intense round of group activity. Illustrative material is largely from the writer's own research into sects and sect literature in England; for these cases and for cases where the facts are widely known or well established, specific citations are omitted.

6. This characterization of the denomination stresses many points similar to those suggested by Pope, *op. cit.*, pp. 120 ff., but avoids making a direct comparison of sect traits and denominational traits, as well as the implication that sect characteristics automatically undergo mutation and become denominational traits.

7. An earlier categorization of sects is offered by E. T. Clark in *The Small Sects in America*, Nashville: Abingdon Press, 1937, which uses rather diverse criteria, including attitudinal, doctrinal, and organizational elements. In the classification offered here the distinction advanced by Howard Becker, *op. cit.*, between sects and cults, and more recently employed by W. E. Mann, *Sect, Cult and Church in Alberta*, Toronto: University of Toronto Press, 1955, is abandoned; movements styled as cults by Becker and Mann are here subsumed in a more

generalized typification of the sect, and as a subtype would figure principally among gnostic sects. For an extremely suggestive classification of sects, which has come to my notice since this paper was written, but which shares certain similarities with the categorization here proposed, see Peter L. Berger, "The Sociological Study of Sectarianism," *Social Research,* 21 (1954), 467–485.

8. The basic types of response here proposed may be compared to the typology of modes of individual adaptation in Robert K. Merton's "Social Structure and Anomie," *Social Theory and Social Structure,* Glencoe, Ill.: Free Press, 1957, pp. 131 ff. There is some correspondence between introversionist sects and the retreatist response, revolutionist sects and the rebellious response, and gnostic sects and the innovative type. Merton's conformist case is clearly not appropriate to sects, nor is the ritualist, unless one admits some schisms of the Catholic church, and even then the case is doubtful. See also, Karen Horney, *The Neurotic Personality of Our Time,* New York: Norton, 1937.

It is clear that a given sect may well shift in its response to the external society and, while remaining a protest group, alter the terms of its protest. Our analysis here is primarily concerned with the process of accommodation—the conditions under which sects become denominations or fail to do so. A development unexplored here is the sect which, whilst remaining a sect, changes character by changing its response; frequently the shift will be of emphasis rather than of complete transformation. There is some evidence to show that revolutionist sects, under circumstances of external duress, have altered their response to one of introversion. The processes here involved would require further analysis in the light of the sociological variables underlying such changes, both as internal and external factors.

9. The similarities of the adventist-type sect and the revolutionary political movement have been brought out by Donald G. MacRae in "The Bolshevik Ideology," *The Cambridge Journal,* 3 (1954), 164–177, and are also dealt with in Bryan R. Wilson, *Sects and Society,* London: Heinemann, 1961. See also Werner Cohn, "Jehovah's Witnessses as a Proletarian Movement," *The American Scholar,* 24 (1955), 281–298.

10. The types here hypothesized are primarily Christian, and each type finds some support within Christian scriptures. Whether such a classification could be usefully employed for other major religions is doubtful in that, although revolutionist and introversionist sects appear to be common to many religions, and the gnostic sects occur in some, conversionism is perhaps less widespread. The situation is sometimes confused with regard to the relative positions of orthodoxy and sectarianism, and by the difference between the relationship of religion and the state which prevails in many non-Christian countries and the pattern which has generally obtained in the West.

11. This syncretistic approach is typical of gnostic sects: many such movements have drawn on diverse sources for their teachings. See, for example, Bryan R. Wilson, "The Origins of Christian Science," *The Hibbert Journal,* 57 (1959), 161–170.

12. On European millennial movements see Norman Cohn, *The Pursuit of the Millennium,* London: Secker and Warburg, 1957.

13. For a recent brief account of such movements, see Henri Desroche, "Micromillenarismes et Communautorismes Utopique en Amérique du Nord du XVII° au XIX° Siécle," *Archives de Sociologie des Religions,* 4 (1957), 57–92.

14. For a discussion of internal and external factors in a clinical, as distinct from a typological, examination of sect development, see Bryan R. Wilson, "Apparition et Persistence des Sectes dans un Milieu Social en évolution," *Archives de Sociologie des Religions,* 5 (1958), 140–150.

15. See H. H. Stroup, *Jehovah's Witnesses,* New York: Columbia University Press, 1945; also E. Royston Pike, *Jehovah's Witnesses,* London: Watts, 1954; Werner Cohn, *op. cit.*

16. The equivocal position of the ministry emerging within a sect which is undergoing transformation to a denomination is discussed in Bryan R. Wilson, "Role Conflicts and Status Contradictions of the Pentecostal Minister," *American Journal of Sociology,* 64 (1959), 494–504.

17. For an excellent illustration of this point, see A. K. Swihart, *Since Mrs. Eddy,* New York: Holt, 1931; for further examples in Christian Science and other movements, see Wilson, *Sects and Society.*

18. Niebuhr, *op. cit.;* Pope, *op. cit.*

19. Both Niebuhr and Pope base their generalizations on the examination of what we have called Conversionist sects; the present classification has thus prevented or decreased errors in prediction.

20. On the Doukhobors, see H. B. Hawthorn (ed.), *The Doukhobors of British Columbia,* University of British Columbia Press, 1955.

21. The history of Methodism, the Church of the Nazarene, and some Pentecostal groups illustrate this process. See, for example, E. D. C. Brewer, *op. cit.;* W. R. Goldschmidt, "Class Denominationalism in Rural California Churches," *American Journal of Sociology,* 49 (1944), 348–355; Oliver R. Whitley, "The Sect to Denomination Process in an American Religious Movement: The Disciples of Christ," *Southwestern Social Science Quarterly,* 36 (1955), 275–282.

22. Arminian theology, as distinct from Calvinism, would appear to be a significant factor in promoting the growth of sect to denomination; Benton Johnson's statement in "A Critical Appraisal of Church: Sect Typology" (*op. cit.*), that this development is largely confined to voluntarist Calvinist sects, is in need of clarification. That some Calvinist groups could pass from sect to established church was made possible by the unusual circumstances of the settlement by sectarians of new territories. (It is doubtful whether the establishment of the Calvinist church at Geneva could be described as a sect-to-church process.) Elsewhere the Calvinist sects which developed into denominations did so only as their Calvinism gave way to a more Arminian and less exclusive teaching, as with the Baptists in England. Those groups which have retained Calvinistic teaching in anything like its pristine rigor have not fully experienced denominational development, e.g., the Strict and Particular Baptists, whose organization remains essentially sectarian in character.

57. THE DESIRE FOR SURVIVAL

MARSHALL SKLARE

According to such writers as Ruby Jo Reeves Kennedy and Will Herberg, the United States is becoming a "triple melting pot," a society divided less by ethnic distinctiveness than by religious identification as Protestant, Catholic, or Jewish. This view rests upon studies of assimilation that indicate that there has been a reduction in the resistance of those who share religious identity to marry across nationality lines.

While the overall trend is unquestionable, the "triple melting pot" thesis tends to oversimplify the fact of continuing differences within and between the three divisions. Unlike most Roman Catholics, Protestants vary considerably in their manner of worship and in religious commitment; so do Jews. Yet most Jews, unlike most Protestants, are bound by specific cultural as well as religious ties. Judaism in America is more than a religion, it constitutes "a fellowship whose members are differentiated from those belonging to other denominations by virtue of their special descent as well as by their doctrines or practices." It is an "ethnic church."

In this selection from his book, Conservative Judaism: An American Religious Movement, *Marshall Sklare discusses the institutionalized means for maintaining the social cohesion of the Jewish community while it adapts to American life. He sees the ethnic church as unique in its articulation of ethnicity and religiosity in pluralistic America where ethnic groups, like the Jews, are essentially minorities.*

The former Director of the Institute of Human Relations at the American Jewish Committee, Marshall Sklare is now Professor of Sociology at Yeshiva University. In addition to being the author of Conservative Judaism *(1955), Sklare is the editor of* The Jews: Social Patterns of an American Group *(1958), and coeditor, with J. Greenblum, of* Jewish Identity on the Suburban Frontier *(1967).*

It was once thought that each ethnic group would—in the space of a few decades—leave their "ghetto" and fuse into the melting pot. Sociologists conceded that groups which came here fairly late, against whom discrimination was practiced, or whose original culture was strikingly different from the dominant one, might be more cohesive than others. But assimilation was considered inevitable. At present it is becoming increasingly evident that ethnicity still remains a significant basis of social stratification. For example, an investigation in New Haven, Connecti-cut, discloses that Swedes and Danes—who came here earlier than many other groups and whose culture was not strikingly deviant—still constitute recognizable entities in that city.[1] Does this result from prejudice, from rejection by the dominant group?[2] Is it traceable to the influence of ethnic survivalists who are strongly attached to the old culture and who preserve the sub-community by influencing marginal individuals to remain loyal? Is it that the content of the original culture, once it is adapted to American conditions, retains a degree of attractiveness? Or is it because ethnic solidarity now serves a new purpose: protection from *anomie*—the atomization and disorganization characteristic of present-day society which results in a loss of the feeling of social solidarity?

This last suggestion is a particularly intriguing one since the problem of *anomie* exists for all peoples who live in a society characterized by mobility, by the segregation of kinship, occupation, and leisure-time roles, by shifting norms, and by clashing social systems. One of the structures which compensates for this characteristic feature of modern life is the voluntary association. These groups help to create for the individual additional primary and secondary relationships. Viewing such bonds as a "defense" against *anomie,* it is apparent that they can be elaborated on various levels: class ends, shared life experiences, similar play interests, or *common descent*. While the present-day ethnic is no longer in need of a therapeutic instrument to reduce the trauma resulting from encountering radically new norms and values (as was the case with his father or grandfather), he *is* in need of meaningful social relationships. Participation in the affairs of his ethnic group may be a convenient way of meeting this requirement. The "defense against *anomie*" theory may well help to explain why some of the sub-communities preserve a degree of integration in spite of the participants having shed many old-world culture patterns.[3]

Rejection, the influence of the survivalists, the adapted culture, and the *anomie* problem are undoubtedly all factors which operate to retard—although perhaps only temporarily—the assimilation of ethnics. With the amount of knowledge which we have at our disposal, it is difficult to decide just how much weight should be assigned to each of these forces, as well as to others detailed below. Whatever the situation in other groups, it will be conceded that Jews have shown themselves *particularly* desirous of retaining some

form of group identity.[4] Marden has gone so far as to state that "The prospects for Jews in American society appear different from those of any other minority . . ."[5] for he doubts whether the other groups will be able to persist indefinitely. Marden explains that while Jews have been subject to much acculturation, this process has not led to the further step of assimilation:

> The acculturation of Jews, however, presents some striking differences to that of other immigrant groups. In many ways the Jewish group became more rapidly and successfully adjusted to life in America than the other immigrant groups. This has been true with reference to economic success, participation in civic life, and educational achievement.

> . . . increasing acculturation has not led to complete assimilation, nor are there any indications . . . that it will ever do so. The Jewish community within the larger gentile community, modernized and adaptive as much of its cultural content is, still remains distinct.[6]

A full explanation of this almost unique desire for survival will not be attempted here. Some of the causes have already been cited. In addition there is the fact that Jews still possess a feeling of superiority, although more in the moral and intellectual realms now than in the area of spiritual affairs. While the feeling of superiority is a factor which has received comparatively little attention from students of the problem, it is of crucial importance because it operates to retard assimilation. Leaving the group becomes a psychological threat: such a move is viewed not as an advancement but as cutting oneself off from a claim to superiority.[7] However explained, the "will to live" serves to encourage the making of experiments, like Conservatism, which aim to discover a *modus vivendi* for the Jewish community.

Judaism constitutes an *ethnic church:*[8] a fellowship whose members are differentiated from those belonging to other denominations by virtue of their special *descent* as well as by their doctrines or practices.[9] In America the uniqueness of this type of church is its articulation of ethnicity and religiosity in a multi-ethnic society where ethnic groups are essentially minority groups, i.e., subordinate to a majority group presumed to be non-ethnic. In addition to Jews and others, this type of body is found in the three divisions of Christianity: the Protestant, Roman Catholic, and Eastern Orthodox Churches. To illustrate for the Protestant group, special Lutheran bodies and synods exist for the Danes, Finns, Germans, Hungarians, Icelanders, Norwegians, Slovaks, Swedes, and others. Special nationality parishes have been established in the United States for Roman Catholics who come from Armenia, Croatia, Italy, Poland, Portugal, the Ukraine, and many other places.[10]

These groups are first of all churches, for like all religious organizations they seek to provide ". . . a way of facing the problems of ultimate and unavoidable frustration, of 'evil,' and the generalized problem of meaning in some non-empirical sense, of finding some ultimate why." [11] But concurrently they have an additional task: the preservation of a particular sub-culture or ethnic group. Note that the language used in sermons, liturgy, or hymns may be the one spoken in the homeland; that certain rites and holidays are observed which are celebrated only by members of the special ethnic group; and that celebrations commemorate events unique to the history of the group.[12] The ethnic church commonly makes special educational arrangements designed to teach its youth those special loyalties necessary for group survival. This frequently includes some training in the language of the homeland. Understandably, the ethnic church appears to be a highly sectarian institution to those who do not possess loyalty to a sub-culture. H. Richard Niebuhr, for example, has complained that:

. . . many an immigrant church became more a racial and cultural than a religious institution in the New World. Its parochial schools were fostered not only that the children might receive instruction in religion but also that they might learn the mother-tongue and with it the attitudes and social ideals of the old homeland. In many a Sunday School German or Swedish readers were the only textbooks; in many a pulpit the duty of loyalty to the old language was almost as frequent a theme as the duty of loyalty to the old faith. So the churches of the immigrants often found a new and additional reason for their separate existence. They now represented racial sectarianism. . . . They became competitive conflict societies, intent upon maintaining their distinction from other groups, no matter how closely these might be akin to them in doctrine, polity and piety.[13]

Leaving aside consideration of the polemical tone of his statement, Niebuhr is correct in suggesting that these churches have become an important mechanism for the preservation of ethnicity. Religion easily recommended itself for this role. The church was one of the few institutions of the original culture capable of re-establishment in the new land. Also, since the ethnic church is the counterpart of non-ethnic institutions of the same order, it would automatically receive identical formal recognition, although of course its status position may not be on the same level. Furthermore, while ethnic separatism is not very highly valued in our culture, religious distinctiveness is allowable —even esteemed in a way because it is "American." Given the attraction of national culture patterns which have slowly but surely impressed themselves upon the ethnic, group distinctiveness could be preserved—even if emptied of much of its content—under the banner of religion. Thus, because of the challenge to group survival, ethnicity has tended to retreat and to reappear in a very different form.

In summary, the forces working toward the continuation of the special function of the ethnic church converge from the following two directions: 1) From the dynamic of the institution itself. Since the future of the church generally hinges on the persistence of the ethnic group, it must promote ethnic group solidarity in order to survive. 2) From ethnics who—whether consciously or not—realize that religion is an acceptable method of group differentiation, that church functions may include much more than the dissemination of the word of God. Such individuals see suprasocial differences as legitimating the perpetuation of divisions in the social structure. While it is true that in some cases group persistence has been in outright ethnic form, in other instances the main index to continuing ethnicity is to be found in the survival of churches whose membership is relatively homogeneous. Most of the group are still descended from individuals who come from the same homeland. American ethnic groups are tending to change their outward appearances. They can preserve themselves as religious groups.

On the whole, Jews in the United States choose to be regarded as members of a religious denomination. However, the various groups in the community who have arrived at this consensus are differently motivated. There are, of course, those who feel (as well as act) that religion is the prime expression of Judaism. The religious designation is, therefore, expressive of their true ideological preferences. Another segment of the community has wider Jewish interests than simply religion (or even possesses other Jewish interests which serve to replace religion), but they feel nonetheless that—given American traditions—religion must become the main expression of Jewish identification as well as the guarantor of Jewish ethnic survival. At the very least, they would contend that the designation of the Jewish group as constituting a denomination is a highly convenient fiction which it is wise to cultivate. Lastly, there are those whose feelings of Jewish identification are weak or conflicted, and whose survivalistic urges are consequently questionable. Nevertheless, because of public relations considerations, they feel that it is essential that Jews stress the religious designation. The middle group seems to be the predominant one at present. While few Jews —particularly those in the middle group —could succeed in verbalizing their feelings as we have set them down, there is ample evidence available pointing to the existence of these trends.[14]

It is significant that although overall Jewish identification has remained at a high level (and while synagogue affiliation appears to be greater than previously), Jews today hardly seem very observant of religious practices. Their day-to-day religious behavior is readily apparent from data gathered in a poll conducted by the National Opinion Research Center during 1945. This survey reveals that only 6% of those who identify themselves as Catholic state that they seldom or never attend religious services, 19% of the Protestants make this statement, but no less than 32% of the Jews are found in this category. Of the Catholics, 69% attend religious services once a week or more, 36% of the Protestants do likewise, but a mere 9% of the Jews attend. Worshipping at least once a month are 81% of the Catholics, 62% of the Protestants, and only 24% of the Jews.[15] It would seem then that many wish to identify themselves as being members of a religious group while at the same time they lack much religious interest. Because of such a trend, one student of Jewish problems speaks of the ". . . paradox of the concentration of Diaspora survivalism on religious channels in the face of increasing weakening of religion."[16] Although the fundamental tie in the Jewish community continues to be on the level of common ethnicity, many apparently share Mordecai M. Kaplan's viewpoint that ". . . [the synagogue] is the only institution that can define our aims to a world that will otherwise be at a loss to understand why we persist in retaining our corporate individuality."[17]

All of this results in the strengthening of the religious structure in spite of increasing secularization. As we noted, reinforcement comes from different directions. The ethnic survivalists concentrate upon religion as the most satisfactory means of Jewish identification, and the more marginal group seizes upon it as a protective device which will help to raise status, draw allies to the Jewish cause, and in the long run serve to decrease the virulence of anti-Semitism. Both are forced into "making good" on the stereotype by according some support to religious causes. Whatever their real feelings, their very desire to project the stereotype means that they have to concede a responsibility for supporting religious institutions. Additionally, the stereotype—once it is successfully established—reacts back on the Jew himself. Whether because of impressions conveyed by Jews, or because of factors which operate independently of minority-generated pressures, Gentiles may begin to convey that they consider the Jewish group as just another religious denomination. At this juncture, the Jew may find himself propelled into fulfilling the image projected by the Gentile. Although he himself may not actually believe the stereotype to be wholly valid, he feels that he must act like the type of "good Jew" which the Gentile imagines— the Jew who is loyal to his rabbi, interested in his synagogue.

Such developments do not prepare the ground for any kind of true religious revival. Attendance at services may not even grow very substantially. However, religious institutions will receive increasing financial support and community esteem, particularly if they offer a program which includes non-religious activities and is strongly oriented toward ethnic values. We can assume that Conservatism resulted in part from the feeling that the Orthodox synagogue was inadequate to meet the demands of the environment— that ethnic solidarity would have to be perpetuated chiefly under religious auspices and that consequently a new type of institution was required.

NOTES

1. See Mhyra S. Minnis, "Cleavage in Women's Organizations: A Reflection of the Social Structure of a City," *American Sociological Review*, 18 (1953), 47–53.

2. Note Arnold and Caroline Rose, *America Divided*, New York: Alfred A. Knopf, Inc., 1948, pp. 178–182. These writers stress rejection as the causative factor for minority group identification.

3. Earlier theorists had equated ethnic group identification with cultural deviation. As a consequence the tendency to discard old-world traits was taken as an index of assimilation: cultural assimilation meant group assimilation. The possibility that social differentiation might continue in spite of a high rate of acculturation was neglected. Robert E. Park, for example, considered the problem almost completely from the standpoint of the social processes working to destroy the integrity of immigrant communities. He and others saw ethnic persistence as an imbalance or temporary stage which would be righted as the operation of social processes inevitably leveled these groups. See Robert E. Park and Herbert A. Miller, *Old World Traits Transplanted*, New York: Harper & Brothers, 1921, pp. 303–308, as well as a more recent statement by Maurice R. Davie, "Our Vanishing Minorities," *One America*, ed. by F. J. Brown and J. S. Roucek (third ed.), New York: Prentice-Hall, Inc., 1952, pp. 545–557. For a contrasting view, see Peter A. Munch, "Social Adjustment among Wisconsin Norwegians," *American Sociological Review*, 14 (1949), 780–787.

4. *Cf.* Louis Wirth, "Education for Survival: The Jews," *American Journal of Sociology*, 48 (1942–43), 682–691. For the Yankee City Jewish community and the operation of the desire for survival, see W. L. Warner and Leo Srole, *Social Systems of American Ethnic Groups*, New Haven: Yale University Press, 1945, pp. 205–217.

5. Charles F. Marden, *Minorities in American Society*, New York: American Book Co., 1952, p. 427.

6. *Ibid.*, pp. 415–416. Note that our treatment of American Jewry as constituting an *ethnic* group follows that of many present-day sociologists. In addition to Marden, see R. A.

Schermerhorn, *These Our People*, Boston: D. C. Heath & Co., 1949, and Warner and Srole, *op. cit.* This designation should be taken as an approximation. We do not deny the possibility that Jews can also be studied with profit by the employment of a special category necessitated by the presence of certain features unique to the group, e.g., their intermarriage taboo and consequent endogamy.

7. I am grateful to Mark Zborowski for pointing up this factor in the course of discussions conducted about another piece of research. It is hoped that it will be fully documented and developed in a future publication.

8. In order that the Negroes may be included, some prefer the term "minority church" instead of "ethnic church." See Stanley H. Chapman, "New Haven Churches," unpublished Ph.D. dissertation, Dept. of Sociology, Yale University, 1942. Chyz and Lewis, on the other hand, use the term "nationality church." See Y. J. Chyz and Read Lewis, "Agencies Organized by Nationality Groups in the United States," *The Annals*, 262 (1949), 149–153. For an analysis of some of the main distinguishing marks of the ethnic church, see Ch. I of *CJSA*.

9. Of course in the broadest sense all denominations, in contrast with sects, are descent groups. Furthermore, by distinguishing between "ethnic" and "nonethnic" churches we mean only to imply that the nonethnic churches represent the dominant group. Thus ultimately they are also "ethnic," and possess ethnic functions.

The classic statement of the relationship between *religio* and *ethnos* is Émile Durkheim's, *The Elementary Forms of the Religious Life*, trans. Joseph Ward Swain, Glencoe, Ill.: The Free Press, 1947. Aside from the functionalists, interesting contemporary examples of the problem can be found in a historical treatment such as Salo W. Baron, *Modern Nationalism and Religion*, New York: Harper & Brothers, 1947. Another significant application is made by Werner Cahnman, "Religion and Nationality," *American Journal of Sociology*, 49 (1943–44), 524–529.

10. Some Lutheran churches, it should be noted, exhibit ambivalence about their ethnicity and would prefer to be identified as nonethnic churches. See Erich C. Knorr, "The Adjustment of the Lutheran Church to Social Change in the Modern World," unpublished Ph.D. dissertation, Dept. of Sociology, University of Washington, 1946. On the other hand, the Jewish group may well constitute the "ideal type" in the ethnic church category. If one wishes to remain a Jew, except in certain special cases the only church to which he may belong is the Jewish one. Thus in Judaism *religion* and *ethnicity* are perfectly articulated. The following case cited by Baron illustrates the process: "The first Czechoslovak census of 1921 [revealed] that eleven residents of Prague and hundreds more throughout the country registered as belonging to the Jewish 'nationality' and the Roman Catholic 'religion.' . . . Six other Prague Jewish 'nationals' stated that they professed Protestantism or Greek Orthodoxy. The Zionists [the group which tended to de-emphasize religion by their very stress on ethnicity and who, as nationalists, might be expected to welcome everyone who was of Jewish descent] had long received with open arms Jews having no religious affiliation, but they drew the line in the case of converts to another faith." (Baron, *op. cit.*, p. 241.) For a detailed analysis of Jewry as an "ideal type," see *CJSA*, pp. 27–34.

11. Robin M. Williams, Jr., *American Society*, New York: Alfred A. Knopf, Inc., 1951, p. 307. See also J. O. Hertzler, "Religious Institutions," *The Annals*, 256 (1948), 1–13.

12. See Chyz and Lewis, *op. cit.* When an international church is resistant to special ethnic purposes, or favors one ethnic group as over against another, schisms may result. This has been the case with the Catholic Church in the United States, and may be illustrated by the relationship between the Church and the Polish-American group. While the Catholic Church in Poland had been very sympathetic to nationalistic aspirations, the Poles found that here it was controlled by the Irish. This group favored a policy of de-Polonization and discriminated against Polish priests in the making of clerical appointments above the parish level. Hence starting in 1904 we find the growth of a secessionist movement under the name of the "Polish National Independent Catholic Church."

13. H. R. Niebuhr, *The Social Sources of Denominationalism*, New York: Henry Holt & Co., 1929, pp. 223–224. Cf. Robert M. MacIver and Charles H. Page, *Society*, New York: Rinehart & Co., 1949, p. 493.

14. They will be documented in a forthcoming publication by the author and others of a study of the attitudes of some two hundred Jewish families residing in a middle-sized Eastern city.

15. *Opinion News,* December 25, 1945. Cf. Havemann and West, *op. cit.,* pp. 105–107. Some would doubt whether attendance at services is a valid criterion of religiosity for the Jewish group. They would hold that the home is as important as the synagogue as a *locus* of religious observance. Even if this approach were a correct one, these figures would still be highly significant.

16. Abraham G. Duker, *Outline of Comprehensive Introductory Course for Adult Jewish Studies,* New York: American Jewish Congress, 1951, p. 25. Some significant interpretation of trends in Jewish communal life can be found in H. B. Grinstein, "Communal and Social Aspects of American Jewish History," *Publications of the American Jewish Historical Society,* 309 (1949–50), 267–282.

17. M. M. Kaplan in *Jewish Communal Register,* 1917–18, New York: Kehillah of New York City, 1918, p. 122. While Kaplan stresses the factor of Jewish ethnicity in his writings, at the same time he generally compares Jews to Catholics and Protestants (see, for example, *The Reconstructionist,* December 1, 1950, 29). In addition, note Samuel Margoshes in R. A., *Proceedings,* 10 (1947), 261–262.

That the synagogue-centered forces in the Jewish community appeal for support on the basis of their actual or potential contribution toward bettering group relations can be gathered from the documents quoted by Rabbi Ahron Opher in *American Jewish Year Book,* 48 (1946–47), 133–135. As a non-Jew, MacIver's general agreement with Opher's viewpoint is particularly significant (see MacIver, *op. cit., passim*).

58. AMERICAN RELIGION AND THE NEGRO

FR. JOSEPH H. FICHTER

There is at least one major segment of American society which does not fit into the "triple melting pot" model. Though predominantly Protestant, the vast majority of black Americans are not fully integrated with their white coreligionists. In fact, as the late Bishop James A. Pike once said, "Eleven o'clock on Sunday morning is the most segregated hour of the week." Sociologists studying religion in the United States tend to subdivide society into four major categories: Catholics, Jews, White Protestants, and black Protestants.

In the following essay Father Joseph Fichter, a sociologist of religion, examines the problem of racial segregation in America's churches and relates it to broader social issues. He describes both "white" and "Negro" religious organizations and measures—some feeble, others significant—taken (and being taken) to change the practice of acceding to culture patterns rather than attempting to reform them by various organized religious bodies.

Joseph H. Fichter, S. J., is Professor of Roman Catholic Studies at the Harvard Divinity School, Harvard University. His books on the sociology of religion include The Roots of Change *(1939),* Southern Parish *(1951),* Social Relations in the Urban Parish *(1954),* Parochial School: A Sociological Study *(1958),* Religion as an Occupation *(1961),* Priest and People *(1965), and* America's Forgotten Priests: What Are They Saying? *(1968). He is also the author of a basic textbook,* Sociology *(1957).*

The role of organized religion in the current Negro freedom movement is symbolized by the leadership of Martin Luther King, who is primarily concerned neither with an appointment to a "white pulpit" nor with the dissolution of Negro church denominations. In other words, neither the mixing of the races nor the mixing of the religions is the main objective of any churchman's participation in the movement for Negro rights. What is important is "freedom now" for both races, and "equality now" for all citizens, regardless of racial and religious affiliation. A free society can be pluralistic by the choice and decision of its citizens, but a pluralistic society can be free only if its major institutions support freedom for all.

Better than any other institution, organized religion ought to understand the terms of the struggle for racial freedom and equality. Religious-minded people ought to grasp more readily than others such concepts as reparation for wrongdoing, reconciliation of the estranged, resolution for improvement, commitment to values, firm purpose of amendment, fellowship and brotherhood, love and justice. The slogan of the rights movement, "freedom now," had great significance to the ancient Jews in bondage, to the early Christians in pagan Rome, to the Catholics in the English persecutions, to the Huguenots in the French persecutions. If

Reprinted from *Daedalus*, **94** (1965), *The Negro American*, 1085–1106, by permission of the author and the American Academy of Arts and Sciences, Brookline, Massachusetts.

the historical analogy between religious liberty and racial liberty is so close, one wonders why the churches delayed so long before entering the civil rights movement. But now that the commitment has been made and the struggle has been joined, one may speculate about further and fuller religious influence and participation in the movement.

Organized religion has certainly contributed to the moral awakening of Americans to the race problem, and the young generation of people now in the pulpits and pews of American churches and synagogues gives assurance that this will continue. These people do not accept the old caricature of religion as merely a personal and private affair. They have repudiated the peculiar notion that the race question is a political and legal matter, not a religious and moral concern. The "proper scope" of religious activity has been widened by them; we now frequently hear about the relevance of religion to modern life, to the crowded city, to business practices, to political organizations, to educational systems, and to racial and other minority problems.

Changes in religious activities are uneven, as they are in all institutionalized areas of society. There are major trends and minor counter-trends, but the main direction of religious influence in this regard is clear and ineluctable. There is criticism of white clergymen who have few Negroes in their own congregations, but who go South to engage in sit-ins at restaurants and to picket voting registrars. There is criticism of church leaders who use their moral influence more often for the desegregation of non-church institutions than they do for the desegregation of their own organizations. It is said, on the one hand, that "the present movement to do away with segregation as an ultimate ideal has stemmed mainly from the churches," [1] and, on the other hand, that "as long as churches remain segregated through subtle techniques, they give moral

sanction to segregation in other areas of social life." [2]

It has often been said, and by religious people themselves, that Sunday morning at church is the most segregated time in America; and it probably offers little consolation to insist that Saturday night at the country club is an even more segregated time. We do not expect the country club to set standards of moral principle and practice, but we do await guidance from the church in both respects. The church cannot afford to wait for the Congress, the President, and the Supreme Court to provide its moral standards and values. Yet, as Liston Pope has remarked, the church has "lagged behind the Supreme Court as the conscience of the nation on questions of race." [3]

White religionists have found this disconcerting, and Negro religionists have considered it a demonstration of white insincerity. As Embree wrote more than thirty years ago, "Segregation in Christian churches is an embarrassment. In a religion whose central teaching is brotherly love and the golden rule, preachers have to do a great deal of rationalizing as they expound their own gospel." [4] We are not limiting the present discussion to the extent to which the churches have remained internally conservative and segregated or have become internally progressive and integrated. We are interested also in the moral impact which the church has had on the larger society, the extent to which church people have promoted external, non-denominational integration and reconciliation of the races. Whatever their previous conservative stance has been, the churches have now become "spearheads of reform." [5]

The ways in which churches approach the problem of desegregation vary according to region and are the result both of the voluntary nature of church membership and of local cultural patterns. Thus, in the Southern states, where local customs—and often legal intimidation—prevent the races from associating voluntarily even in the churches, those interested in racial justice become involved in non-church desegregation, as of public facilities, schools, buses, libraries, parks, and voting. In the North and West, however, where Negroes and whites can associate more freely than in the South, the churches tend to promote the desegregation of their own congregations as well as of public and civic institutions.

–1–

What have the churches in America done about their own internal pattern of racial segregation? It must be said in all fairness that in the second half of the last century segregated patterns in religion came as a *consequence* of community practice and legislation.[6] In this sense, the church bowed to the culture instead of resisting and reforming it. The seeds of separation had been sown even before the Civil War, when large Southern Protestant denominations declared their independence. In the ensuing decades the separation of the Negro Protestant bodies came about either by expulsion from the white denominations or by the Negroes' own withdrawal to independent churches.

Negro religion in America is by definition segregated religion, but it embraces a wide range of structures, patterns, and attitudes. At one end are the completely separatist religious cults, the best known of which is now the Black Muslim Movement, which repudiates Christian and Caucasian civilization and turns to Asiatic culture and the religion of Islam.[7] An earlier Negro nationalist cult, now declining in influence, is the Moorish Temple of Science in America, which also repudiates the white man, his religion, and his culture.[8] These groups extol the black man as superior to the white and scoff at the notion of reconciliation or integration with white Christians. One of the most

spectacular anti-white movements was Marcus Garvey's Universal Mutual Improvement Association, which was both political and religious. It did not turn to Asia and Islam, but glorified Negritude with its black Christ and black God. It disparaged white culture and wanted to return to Africa for the fulfillment of a pure religion and a higher civilization.[9] The memory of Garvey as the "lost savior" of the race lingers among Negroes, and some of his former adherents are seeking the new savior among the Black Muslims.

These black religious and nationalist movements, because they are antagonistic to whites and fight against cultural assimilation, are opposed by most Negro leaders and feared by some whites. They speak boldly of the need for Negro courage and physical resistance to white discrimination and injustice. They are the most vocal protest of despair and frustration over the white man's failure to practice the ideals of Christianity and the principles of democracy in relation to American Negroes. They serve to dramatize the Negro's plight in America, and, while proclaiming the advantages of withdrawal from white America, they are also serving the latent function of arousing white America to the need for interracial justice and integration.[10]

The black nationalist groups make a direct appeal to the racial pride of the most disadvantaged Negroes and are effective in reforming the moral behavior of their members. They are puritanical in their rules on sexual behavior, smoking, drinking, dancing, and work habits. While repudiating Christianity they are emulating the Christian, Puritan, bourgeois way of life. The numerous Holiness sects also have great influence on the behavior of the lower classes of urban Negroes. These people seek personal sanctification and a sinless way of life. Their preachers concentrate on other-worldly sermons and the futility of worldly and material comforts, possessions, and status. They are seldom concerned about social justice, integration, and the civil rights movement. Instead of demanding separatism, as the Black Muslims do, they seem to accept it apathetically as a worldly evil, and for this they are chided by American Negro leadership.[11]

The positive segregation of the black nationalists and the negative segregation of the Holiness sects both are functions of their differing religious ideologies, and they both make their appeal to the poorest class of Negroes. The great majority of American Negroes belong to the large Protestant denominations, but they are also in a segregated church system. This must be said of the Baptist denomination, to which six out of ten Negro church members belong.[12] It must also be said of the Methodist denomination, which has the second largest Negro membership and which was reorganized in 1939 into five white geographical jurisdictions and one Negro Central Jurisdiction, embracing all Negro congregations regardless of their location.[13]

From the point of view of ultimate socio-religious integration, the large separate Negro Protestant churches present a double rationalization. The first is that their white fellow Protestants, especially in the Southeast, are not "ready" for integration and that if congregational integration were now to take place the Negro members would again be relegated to the fringes of church participation. The second is that Negroes have freer expression within their own congregations, enjoy a common meeting place and center of communication; they can discuss and promote the elimination of Negro disabilities. "The Negro church remains one of the few areas in which the Negro can retain his identity as an individual and yet have a vehicle for self-expression and the exercise of his own abilities."[14]

It can be argued that the *felix culpa* of the Negro Protestant denominations is that they have been a training ground for the most successful integrationist leaders. We must remember that Nat Turner, leader of the slave revolt in 1831, was a preacher, and many Negro political leaders during Reconstruction were recruited from the pulpit.[15] It was only when the Negro preacher advised patience and forbearance among his congregation that he came to earn "considerable good will among the whites," and religion was "assumed to be a force for good in all respects and, particularly, in race relations."[16] As Charles Johnson wrote a quarter of a century ago, "the indifference of the Negro church to current social issues and its emphasis on the values of a future life lent indirect but vital support to the race patterns."[17]

The relatively recent emergence of Negro preachers as outspoken proponents of civil rights has been accompanied by a loss of this "white good will." The burnings and bombings of Negro churches in the South by white racists clearly demonstrate that religion is no longer "good" for conservation of racial segregation. The anomaly, therefore, is that the segregated Negro Protestant church has been the most effective instrument in breaking down non-church segregation. If these people had been absorbed into the white Protestant denominations they may well have lost their leadership to whites, and would probably have lost the sense of solidarity that now characterizes their program of desegregation.[18]

Whatever the ambiguous position of the Negro clergy may have been before the 1950's, whether they had been a hindrance or a help to integration, whether they had been leaders or followers in the upsurge of Negro protest, there can be no doubt that they have contributed both techniques and ideology to the current civil rights movement.[19] They evolved a moral philosophy of non-violence, which draws upon the teachings of Gandhi and also presents a powerful example of Christian virtue. This effective weapon of passive resistance, Christian patience, and love must not be confused with the escapist philosophy that is still found among the Negro Holiness sects and is condemned by all prominent Negro leaders in the country.[20]

To what extent have the white Protestant denominations "cleaned their own house" of racial discrimination? At the national level every major Protestant Church body has gone on record in favor of desegregating its own congregations. Although preserving the Negro Central Jurisdiction, seventy-four Methodist bishops joined in a 1960 declaration on race relations, saying: "To discriminate against a person solely on the basis of his race is both unfair and un-Christian. There must be no place in the Methodist Church for racial discrimination or enforced segregation." [21]

The Baptists probably have a wider separation than do any of the other large denominations. The National Baptist Convention, USA, and the National Baptist Convention of America are the two largest Negro religious bodies in the country. Among the whites, the Southern Baptists differ quite sharply from the American Baptist Convention, for they continue to maintain and defend a formalized policy against internal integration. There is a similar problem of disagreement between the United Presbyterian Church and the Presbyterian Church of the United States, the latter being made up of Southern adherents who are reluctant to change segregated patterns.[22] The Protestant Episcopal Church does not have a "Southern Branch," and most of its bishops and lay leaders have spoken out clearly for racial unity, but some of its Southern officials have taken exception to this stand.[23]

The religious denomination is not the only social organization in which national and regional policies clash with local customs. The urban church congregation includes people who live mainly in racially separated residential areas. There have been genuine efforts to achieve desegregation in local Protestant churches, but these still tend to be exceptions to the pattern.[24]

Despite all efforts to the contrary, the membership of a congregation does change when the population of the neighborhood shifts. For example, one Methodist congregation in Los Angeles deliberately planned total integration, but "rather than racial inclusiveness, what the church really achieved was a relatively trouble-free transition from a Caucasian to a Negro membership." [25] The experience of this congregation is probably a paradigm for local urban churches elsewhere. "There were Negroes in the community long before there were Negroes in this church. Negroes did not come to worship until the Caucasians had largely left. The Caucasian exodus accelerated when Negroes did begin to come in significant numbers. The implication would seem to be clear: for the most part these Caucasian churchmen did not wish to live alongside or worship God together with Negro churchmen. A further implication is that for the most part Negro churchmen return this particular compliment of their white brethren." [26]

There are several reasons that white Protestantism, even with the best will of its ministers and leading lay people, has not succeeded widely in integrating its churches: a) Protestant denominations lack the coercive influence of ecclesiastical authority at the higher levels and therefore allow each local congregation to determine its own course of action and its own moral rationalization for not acting to desegregate. b) The different local congregations do not take a united position on the race issue.[27] c) The Protestant principle of face-to-face primary groupings and close fellowship is difficult to institute in the religious context when it does not exist between the races in other community activities. d) Protestant congregations are often willing to pay the high cost of moving their church to another location in order to remain segregated.[28]

Except for a few places in Maryland, Kentucky, and Louisiana, the Roman

Catholic Church has been almost exclusively a white church in America. It has had relatively little influence in the Southeastern states, where the majority of Negroes lived, and even with its high rate of urban conversions it can probably still claim only about five per cent of the Negro population. Although the Catholic Church followed local patterns in providing separate facilities for Negroes, there have always been Negroes who attended Mass in white parishes and whites who attended Mass in Negro parishes. Myrdal pointed out that, in the South, "the Roman Catholic Church is the only one where Negroes are allowed to attend white churches," and he says later that because the Church includes persons from all classes in the same congregation "there is a relatively greater feeling of equality among Catholic laymen." [29]

The Catholic Church in America is not subdivided into regional or racial denominations, and it is thus in a strategic position to implement internal integration. Even in those places where segregated parishes and schools are still maintained —as in some Southern dioceses—the Negroes, priests, and others involved in them are under the jurisdiction of the same bishop and chancery office as are their neighboring white Catholics. The continuation of separate Negro parishes remains the major obstacle to complete Catholic racial integration. On it depend separate parochial schools, parents' clubs, local organizations such as the Holy Name Society, the Sodality, Altar and Rosary societies, choirs, acolytes, youth clubs, study groups, and so forth.[30] Catholic colleges and universities, and in some instances high schools, which are under the authority of diocesan officials and religious orders, are generally desegregated. Practically all seminaries, as well as novitiates and houses of study for religious Sisters, have by this time opened their doors to Negro candidates. There are, however, still a few segregated Catholic hospitals in the Southeastern states.

Like the leaders of the Protestant churches, the bishops of the Catholic Church, individually and collectively, have condemned racism. The Popes have spoken on the subject as early as the sixteenth century. Bishop Waters of Raleigh, North Carolina, was the first of the Southern prelates to integrate the Churches of his diocese; and Archbishop Rummel, through the Catholic Committee of the South, preached about the immorality of segregation. Perhaps the most effective churchman in this regard was the late Father LaFarge, who founded the Catholic interracial Councils in various cities.[31]

It is probably true that the hierarchal structure of the Catholic Church, with its emphasis on episcopal authority in the realm of faith and morals, has an advantage in imposing integration "from above." [32] The threat of excommunication, though seldom employed, is also an effective instrument.[33] Perhaps of more importance is the fact that the typical urban parish tends to be a large, secondary association in which most parishioners are not expected to have the close social bonds of fellowship that one finds in Protestant congregations. In spite of the recent liturgical drive for communal awareness, the typical Catholic still tends to focus his attention on the altar more than on his fellow parishioners.[34]

In spite of the common religious commitment to the moral value of interracial brotherhood, there is an important difference between the *Gemeinschaftlich* and the *Gesellschaftlich* structure of a church congregation. This is roughly similar to the associational type of industrial labor union, which has indeed had greater success in assimilating Negro workers than has the more close-knit, primary, exclusive type of craft union. The "higher law" principle of human relations should be operative in both types, but internal, local, structural integration can be better achieved where there is more stress on the worship of God and less on the fellowship of human beings.

–2–

The ability of a religious denomination or local congregation to integrate its own membership is not the same as its capacity to influence race relations in the surrounding community. In this instance it appears that success in creating cooperation across racial lines, as it has been across creedal lines, is greatest when the moral issues are clearest and when the personal contacts are informal. There is a lesson here in the ecumenical experiences of the last decade. Ancient concepts of better or worse, of inferior or superior, had to be put aside. Respect for the dignity and worth of individuals of another religious persuasion underlay the whole approach to ecumenism. Taking the larger picture of the American society, we may ask in what ways religious bodies have affected the structure of race relations outside their own organizations. First, it must be mentioned that some of the most virulent propagandists for the preservation of racial segregation are fundamentalist preachers, that some Southern ministers have been members of the Ku Klux Klan, and that clergymen sometimes lend respectability to White Citizens' Councils by offering a prayer at their meetings.[35] These are, of course, a small and diminishing minority when compared to the vast number of American clergymen who stand in opposition to racial discrimination.

Since the end of the Second World War there has been an enormous increase in religious preachment about better race relations. One of the most widely publicized examples of this was "An Appeal to the Conscience of the American People," adopted at the close of the National Conference of Religion and Race in Chicago in 1963, in which more than seventy organizations representing the major religious denominations participated.[36] This appeal sought a reign of justice, love, courage, and prayer in the area of American race relations; and the closing plenary session accepted sixty-two practical program suggestions dealing with almost every conceivable aspect of the racial situation.[37] Subsequently, local councils on religion and race have been established throughout the country, including the deep South.

The day is long past when the pulpit was used to expound theological and Biblical arguments in favor of racial segregation. Only the racist extremists are attempting to revive these discredited arguments.[38] In fact, a flood of arguments favoring racial integration has come from the main religious representatives of the National Council of Churches, the National Catholic Welfare Conference, and the Synagogue Council of America. Perhaps no group has been so energetic in promoting the religious basis for civil rights and racial integration as the Anti-Defamation League of B'nai B'rith. Since there are very few Negro Jews, the temples and synagogues are not faced with the problem of integrating their congregations, but Jewish leaders have been very active in promoting better race relations.[39]

The great practical impact of the moral pronouncements of religious leaders about racial integration stems in part from the fact that they are so completely in accord with the democratic values of the American culture. Religious and political motivations are mutually supportive—the politician can use scripture to confirm constitutional arguments, and the religious spokesman can use the principles of democracy to confirm the need for brotherhood under God.[40] From a sociological point of view, one may debate, and perhaps never settle, whether in American society religion simply reflects the culture or whether cultural patterns are largely the consequence of religious values. The case of the Southeastern region must be considered in this regard since in the matter of racial beliefs and practices the regional differences are greater than the differences among the major religious denominations.

Compared to other sections of the nation, the Southeast was least influenced by the rational and religious reforms of the last century and by the social gospel movement at the beginning of this century.[41] In his most recent book, James Dabbs charges white Southern Protestants with failure. "The South tried to live, on the one hand, by a highly social cuture, on the other by a highly individualistic religion. The culture did not support the religion, the religion did not support the culture." [42] In spite of its high rate of church affiliation and attendance at religious services, the white Southeast is still generally reluctant to accept the modern American and religious interpretation of civil rights and race relations.

In spite of Will Herberg's protestation that an American "culture religion" is developing and President Johnson's assertions that race relations constitute a "national problem," the issue is joined in the Southeastern states, and Negro Protestant clergymen now provide the most effective influence there. It is somewhat surprising, then, to find that the Negro clergy is under attack for refusing to participate in the civil rights struggle,[43] or to read that "neither religious ideology nor religious leaders were in any important way responsible for the increased restiveness and mood of protest among Negroes during the mid-1950's." [44] Negro ministers, and especially Martin Luther King, must be given credit for this role in developing the non-violent techniques of protest.

The significant contribution of Negro preachers and Negro churches toward the elimination of racial discrimination has sometimes been misunderstood. In his small, posthumous book, E. Franklin Frazier wrote that the Negro church was "the most important cultural institution created by Negroes," but that it was also "the most important institutional barrier to integration and the assimilation of Negroes." He speaks also of the few Negro individuals who have been "able to escape from the stifling domination of the church." [45] In his review of this book,

Horace Cayton remarks that "Frazier did not live to witness the fervor of the continuing Negro rebellion and the position of leadership which the church and churchmen are taking in it. Perhaps, if he had, his final judgment on the importance and resilience of the Negro church might have been tempered." [46]

If religious organizations were not segregated, probably no other form of American organization would be segregated, and there would be no need for a springboard like the Negro churches from which an attack could be mounted against other forms of institutional segregation and discrimination. It seems true to say that, on the American scene, racial integration is resisted most in groups where the membership is voluntary, where the organizational status is private (that is, non-governmental), and where the relationships are personal and primary. These characteristics are present, at least conceptually, in the typical religious congregation, which is deliberately exempted from anti-segregation legislation and from official public pressure.

They are present too in the Negro church, and it seems symptomatic of their interpretation of different types of institutions that Negroes are more interested in integrating schools (70 per cent) than in going to church with whites (52 per cent).[47] Furthermore, the segregated congregation is a concomitant—if not always a consequence—of other social phenomena. For example, the cultural taboo against interracial marriage and the hard facts of residential segregation work against the kind of association that is ideally expected among members of the same religious congregation. The existence of integrated religious organizations would be a demonstration that these factors had been minimized, and that non-church types of segregation had decreased.

The organized church, the "most important Negro cultural institution," has provided continued protest against all forms of racial injustice and discrimination. The most famous slave insurrections were led by Negro preachers, Gabriel Prosser in 1800, Denmark Vesey in 1822, Nat Turner in 1831. Speaking from a historical perspective, Liston Pope has said that "the mounting spirit of revolt among Negroes, often robed in biblical teachings on release from bondage, revealed most especially in insurrections and revolts in the period between 1800 and 1831, was also related to the creation of separate Negro denominations." [48]

Anyone who has been observing developments on the racial front since the 1955 Montgomery bus boycott need not be reminded that "Negro ministers constitute the largest segment of the leadership class." Obviously, as Thompson points out, the clergy must spend most of their time on pastoral duties. This is their primary professional function. Nevertheless, "there are a few prominent Negro ministers who can always be found in the vanguard of the Negro's march toward full participation in community affairs. These ministers are generally well-trained, articulate and courageous. Their churches are made available for mass meetings, forums, and other types of programs designed to acquaint the Negro masses with major social issues facing them." [49]

It must be remembered, too, that white clergymen, Christian and Jewish, also have a primary obligation to pastoral duties and that one cannot expect the majority of them to be involved mainly in action programs for civil rights. Anyone who has participated in Southern demonstrations, marches, and other civil rights programs has heard the cry of white segregationists that preachers should stay in their pulpits and not "meddle" in these affairs. In fact, the three bishops of Alabama, Catholic, Episcopal, and Methodist, said as much about non-Southern clergymen (and Sisters) who participated in the Selma-Montgomery demonstrations of 1965. They felt that these "outsiders" should stay home and "clean up their own backyard."

It may be argued that neither churches nor churchmen should be "used" as an instrument to promote "extraneous" purposes. Major institutions, economic, political, and educational, are said to function well in the American culture because the means they employ are focused exclusively on definite objectives. This is only relatively true, however, because all cultural institutions intermesh in daily life and affect each other's means and ends—a fact which is becoming increasingly evident. Only those who argue for "complete" separation of the religious and political institutions, Church and State, continue to be blind to the fact that neither can divorce itself "completely" from the other.

The Negro clergyman typically does not "mind his own business" in the restricted sense of remaining apart from the large social problems of his people, while the white clergyman, priest, or rabbi, in his segregated church or synagogue, often stays aloof from the larger social problems of the day. This contrast is sharpened when we realize that racial segregation has been forced upon Negro churches, has been instituted and perpetuated by white churches.[50] It requires a special effort by white clergymen to look outside their own groups and to recognize the areas of discrimination and injustice in the larger community. The importance of the Protestant "witness" as a servant church to the society has been the theme of the writing of Gibson Winter and Peter Berger in recent years.[51]

If white clergymen maintain a personal, individual philosophy of religious behavior, they are likely to withdraw completely from the area of civic behavior or even, as some have done, oppose their colleagues who are socially concerned. If they are aware of the social problems of their communities, they may limit themselves to the level of preaching and prayer or may operate at the level of action and involvement. Since the end of the Second World War there has been a continuous increase in the number of ministers, priests, and rabbis who preach and pray about race relations, and an even more rapid growth in the number who have involved themselves in action programs.

Clergymen were instrumental in changing California's laws on miscegenation and in desegregating their own high schools, colleges, and seminaries; they participated in the Freedom Rides, in demonstrations and sit-ins all over the South, in the march on Washington, and in the march on Montgomery. The sympathy marches that occurred all over the country following the murder of Reverend James Reeb and of Mrs. Viola Liuzzo were often promoted and always participated in by clergymen. The reluctance and reticence noted by Thomas Pettigrew among the ministers of Little Rock have since been far outbalanced by the vocal and physical presence of clergymen in the struggle for racial justice.[52]

When discussing the march on Washington in 1963, James Reston felt that moral reaction would have to precede political reaction. "This whole movement for equality in American life will have to return to first principles before it will 'overcome' anything." [53] This is the familiar argument, used by moralists and clergymen and by some psychologists, that there must be a "change of heart" and reformed attitudes among the people before we can expect law and customs to improve. There is no doubt that genuine spiritual conversion has a marked effect on the external behavior of the convert; thus the more converts there are to love and brotherhood, the more quickly will America rid itself of racial discrimination.

The march on Washington in 1963 was indeed followed by continued interest and action by organized religious bodies, and was followed also by the Civil Rights Law of 1964. One cannot prove a causal sequence here—the political action perhaps would have occurred without the intervening religious action. A clearer sequence is

seen in the active religious leadership of the march on Montgomery in 1965, which was followed immediately by President Johnson's proposal for a voting rights law.[54] In this instance there can be no doubt that the "call to conscience" made by the moral and religious leaders of America led to practical results.

The involvement of organized religion in the race problems of America has sharpened the recognition of the logical connection between prayer, study, and personal virtue, on the one hand, and action, cooperation, and social virtue, on the other. These are mutually reinforcing elements in the whole complex approach to a better human relationship between the races. College students concerned with religion have shifted "from study-involvement to involvement-study," as Paul Zietlow has remarked.[55] They started the sit-ins in 1960, initiated demonstrations in Birmingham, Jackson, Greensboro, Nashville, and other places in 1963, and participated in marches wherever they have occurred. A National Student Leadership Conference on Religion and Race also had ecumenical overtones in the cooperation of the B'nai B'rith Hillel Foundations, National Club Foundation, National Federation of Catholic College Students, and the National Student Christian Federation.

While trying to ameliorate present conditions of discrimination, Negroes are probably more interested today in the removal of unjust external racial practices than they are in the growth of love and kindness in the hearts of prejudiced people. There is ample evidence that white attitudes toward racial integration have improved in accompaniment to the legal and actual removal of racial barriers.[56] This has occurred even though we cannot make a universal application of this principle. "It is certainly true," wrote Gordon Allport in 1964, "that prejudiced attitudes do not always lead to prejudiced behavior. It is equally true that a person with equalitarian attitudes may engage in unjust discrimination, especially if he lives in South Africa or in Mississippi." [57]

–3–

Cultural change has affected religious people and religious institutions, as it has other areas of American life, and it has been so rapid that any precise forecast of combined religious and racial trends would be senseless. Who could have foreseen the effective impact of religious people and organizations on Washington officialdom before the 1960's? To go back further, who could have foreseen that the conservative religious forces which influenced southern state legislatures even to the extent of textbook censorship, which urged the Congress to pass the Volstead Act, which intervened so strongly in the 1928 presidential campaign, would now have lost most of their influence?

Organized religion has had, and should have, a conservative and preservative role in the larger society, but in too many instances this role seems to function in a negative and reactionary fashion. What has come to the fore in the civil rights movement is the prophetic, creative, and positive role of religion, which has long been recognized almost exclusively in the area of personal piety and family morality. That the church has also a positive social function in the larger society has not always been clearly understood, perhaps because the society is much more morally complex than the individual human being. To be against sin, personal and social, is only one aspect of genuine religiosity. To be for virtue, personal and social, is a morally inalienable imperative of the church and its members.

Change and development have not led to an abandonment of the "old time" religion, or of the eternal truths, as some rigid racists would claim. We have not diluted or repudiated genuine religious truths, principles, and values. We have reviewed them in light of new knowledge about psychological and sociological phenomena. This creative social revolution, which churchmen now sponsor so vigorously, implies an expansion and fulfillment of divine precepts of behavior which we have always struggled to understand in an imperfect and human way.

Why are churchmen so deeply involved in the civil rights movement, and why are they impelled to continue this mission to the larger society? The principal motivation must always be that this is the right and moral thing to do. Store owners and factory managers may say that improved race relations are good for the economy. Mayors and governors may say that the racial solution must be found for the sake of peace and order in the community. National leaders may worry about the "world image" of American democracy that must offset Communist rivalries and meet the expectations of emerging nations. The religionist can certainly approve all of these reasons, but his most impelling motive is that the virtues of love and justice demand the removal of racism and all of its discriminatory effects and practices.

Aside from interim strategies and long-range programs, which may require the technical knowledge of social scientists more than the theological knowledge of churchmen, the church has had its greatest effect in the current drive for Negro freedom precisely because Americans are willing to listen to the moral argument. Whatever one may think of Myrdal's analysis of the American race problem, it is significant that he recognized the moral dilemma of the white man's conscience. As James Weldon Johnson has said, the solution of the race problem involves the salvation of the white man's soul and of the black man's body.[58] If the ordinary American has an uneasy conscience about the American record on race relations, he ought to be able to turn to his religion, the "keeper" of his conscience, for the grace and strength to do the right thing.

The much-discussed "failure" of church members and clergymen, of organized Protestants, Catholics, and Jews, has been so widely publicized that it has evoked wide-spread contrition. The current movement toward rectification of this failure and toward positive implementation of moral principles is basically a religious movement. It is probably true to say that the postwar American experience of race relations has been a major catalyst for both the organizational and doctrinal

perspectives of American religion. The self-analysis that has been forced upon religious-minded individuals, and upon the religious bodies to which they belong, has certainly clarified the American moral dilemma of race. Quite aside from these speculative considerations, this test of America's religious ideology has resulted in pragmatic decisions to reconstitute congregational membership; it has resulted, perhaps more significantly, in the deliberate moral impact of religious leaders on the extra-church institutions of the American culture.

NOTES

1. Anson Phelps Stokes *et al., Negro Status and Race Relations in the United States,* New York: Phelps-Stokes Fund, 1948, p. 50.

2. David Moberg. *The Church as a Social Institution,* Englewood Cliffs, N.J.: Prentice Hall, 1962, p. 453.

3. Liston Pope. *The Kingdom Beyond Caste,* New York: Friendship Press, 1957, p. 105.

4. Edwin R. Embree. *Brown America,* New York: The Viking Press, 1931, pp. 208–209.

5. It is Myrdal's theory that the church changes with the community. "Few Christian churches have ever been, whether in America or elsewhere, the spearheads of reform." Gunnar Myrdal, *An American Dilemma,* New York: Harper & Row, 1944, p. 877.

6. C. Vann Woodward. *The Strange Career of Jim Crow,* New York: Oxford University Press, 1955, has demonstrated that formal segregation of the races is a much more recent phenomenon than many people realized, especially in the Southeast.

7. See C. Eric Lincoln. *The Black Muslims in America,* Boston: Beacon Press, 1961, and E. U. Essien-Udom, *Black Nationalism,* Chicago: University of Chicago Press, 1962.

8. C. Eric Lincoln. *op. cit.,* p. 53.

9. Edmund D. Cronon. *Black Moses: The Story of Marcus Garvey and the Universal Negro Improvement Association,* Madison: University of Wisconsin Press, 1955.

10. For an analysis of various Negro religious cults, see Arthur H. Fauset, *Black Gods of the Metropolis,* Philadelphia: Philadelphia Anthropological Society, 1944.

11. See the views of Benton Johnson, "Do Holiness Sects Socialize in Dominant Values?" *Social Forces,* 39 (1961), 309–316. James Baldwin came out of this kind of religious environment. He has repudiated this philosophy, but has not embraced the ideology of the Black Muslims.

12. See Frank S. Loescher, *The Protestant Church and the Negro: A Pattern of Segregation,* New York: Association Press, 1948.

13. Dwight W. Culver. *Negro Segregation in the Methodist Church,* New Haven, Conn.: Yale University Press, 1953.

14. Lyle E. Schaller. *Planning for Protestantism in Urban America,* New York: Abingdon, 1965, p. 188.

15. Myrdal. *op. cit.,* p. 861.

16. *Ibid.,* p. 862.

17. Charles S. Johnson. *Growing Up in the Black Belt,* Washington: American Council on Education, 1941, pp. 135–136. See also the more recent analysis of Joseph R. Washington, "Are American Negro Churches Christian?" *Theology Today* (April 1963), 76–86.

18. Martin Luther King. *Stride Toward Freedom,* New York: Harper & Row, 1958. "The nonviolent movement in America has come not from secular forces but from the heart of the Negro church. This movement has done a great deal to revitalize the Negro church and to give its message a relevant and authentic ring." King, p. 165, in Mathew Ahmann (ed.), *Race: Challenge to Religion,* Chicago: H. Regnery Co., 1963.

19. Norval Glenn, "Negro Religion and Negro Status in the United States," in Louis Schneider (ed.), *Religion, Culture and Society,* New York: John Wiley & Sons, 1964, pp. 623–638, argues as though the Negro preachers were only reluctantly drawn into the civil rights struggle. "The middle-class ministers of the city could hardly have avoided involvement in the boycott: King and several of the others organized and led it." (p. 633) Yet, nearly half (47 per cent) of the Negroes told the *Newsweek* poll that their ministers are "helping a lot." See William Brink and Louis Harris, *The Negro Revolution in America,* New York: Simon and Schuster, 1964, Ch. 6, "The Role of the Negro Church," and the tables on pp. 220–223.

20. See James W. Vander Zanden, "The Non-Violent Resistance Movement Against Segregation," *American Journal of Sociology,* 68 (1963), 544–550.

21. Reported in *The New York Times,* April 28, 1960. For the attitudes of southern Methodist laymen on racial segregation, see Stotts and Deats, *Methodism and Society: Guidelines for Strategy,* Nashville, Tenn.: Abingdon, 1959, Vol. 4, Appendix A.

22. See David M. Reimers, "The Race Problem and Presbyterian Union," *Church History* (June 1962), 203–215; and also John L. Bell, "The Presbyterian Church and the Negro in North Carolina," *North Carolina Historical Review* (January 1963), 15–36.

23. See the summary on the Protestant churches by W. Seward Salisbury, *Religion in American Culture,* Homewood, Ill.: Dorsey Press, 1964, pp. 472–475. See also the penetrating analysis by Thomas F. Pettigrew, "Wherein the Church Has Failed in Race," *Religious Education,* 59 (1964), 64–73; and Walter B. Posey, "The Protestant Episcopal Church; An American Adaptation," *Journal of Southern History* (February 1959), 3–30.

24. For examples at the local church level see Robert W. Root, *Progress Against Prejudice,* New York, 1957.

25. Reported by Grover C. Bagby in Galen R. Weaver (ed.), *Religion's Role in Racial Crisis,* New York, 1964, p. 16.

26. *Ibid.,* p. 16; see also the research report by Henry Clark, "Churchmen and Residential Desegregation," *Review of Religious Research,* 5 (1964), 157–164.

27. The difficulty of getting interdenominational consensus on the race question seems to reflect the lack of moral and doctrinal consensus among the Protestant denominations. See Kyle Haselden, *The Racial Problem in Christian Perspective,* New York: Harper and Row, 1964.

28. These reasons are discussed by Lyle E. Schaller, *op. cit.,* pp. 187–190. He considers residential segregation an "excuse," but not a reason for the perpetuation of racial segregation in churches. See also the earlier article by Samuel S. Hill, "Southern Protestantism and Racial Integration," *Religion in Life,* 33 (1964), 421–429, where he discusses similar "factors" as operative in the South.

29. Myrdal, *op. cit.,* pp. 870, 1411. In the *Newsweek* poll, more Negroes (58 per cent) think that "Catholic priests" are helpful to the cause than say this about "white churches" (24 per cent). Brink and Harris, *op. cit.,* pp. 133, 233.

30. Joseph H. Fichter. "The Catholic South and Race," *Religious Education,* 59 (1964), 30–33; also Joseph H. Fichter and George L. Maddox, "Religion in the South, Old and New," in John McKinney and Edgar Thompson (eds.), *The South in Continuity and Change,* Durham, N.C.: Duke University Press, 1965.

31. John LaFarge. "Caste in the Church: The Roman Catholic Experience," *Survey Graphic,* 36 (1947), 61 ff., 104–106; also *The Catholic Viewpoint on Race Relations,* Garden City, N.Y.: Doubleday & Co., 1960.

32. Liston Pope, *op. cit.,* p. 140, feels that this is "in line with the findings of social scientists in the last few years as the most effective means of achieving desegregation and the diminution of prejudice."

33. The excommunication of three Louisiana Catholics by Archbishop Rummel did not seem to diminish their racist activities in the White Citizens' Council, although it probably acted as a deterrent to others.

34. The difference between "objective and subjective worship" of Catholicism and Protestantism was analyzed by James B. Pratt, *The Religious Consciousness*, New York: The Macmillan Company, 1927, pp. 290–309, reprinted in Schneider, *op. cit.*, pp. 143–156. The way in which this applies to race relations among Catholics is indicated by Elizabeth M. Eddy, "Student Perspectives on the Southern Church," *Phylon*, 25 (1964), 369–381.

35. There seems to be a "pattern" in clergymen's attitudes. "The small-sect minister is typically segregationist and vocal, whereas the denomination minister is typically integrationist and silent." Ernest Q. Campbell, "Moral Discomfort and Racial Segregation—An Examination of the Myrdal Hypothesis," *Social Forces* (1961), 229.

36. Mathew Ahmann, *op. cit.*, pp. 171–173, contains the original essays of the prominent speakers at the Conference.

37. Galen R. Weaver (ed.), *Religion's Role in Racial Conflict*, New York, 1963, Ch. 7, "Programmatic Recommendations."

38. The propaganda of the White Citizens' Councils in several southeastern states abounds with these "Biblical proofs" that God was the First Segregationist, and with charges that integrationists, especially white clergymen, are the dupes of atheistic communism. What Negroes think of communism is shown in the fact that about the same minority (6 per cent) approve of the Black Muslim movement as believe (5 per cent) the communist claim of no discrimination under their system. Brink and Harris, *op. cit.*, pp. 201, 225.

39. See, for example, the speeches of Rabbi Morris Adler, Dr. Julius Mark, and Dr. Abraham J. Heschel, in Mathew Ahmann (ed.), *op. cit.*, at the National Conference on Race and Religion.

40. For a few examples of this trend see William S. Nelson (ed.), *The Christian Way in Race Relations*, New York: Harper & Row, 1948; Will Campbell, *Race and Renewal of the Church*, Philadelphia: Westminster Press, 1962; and Benjamin E. Mays, *Seeking to Be a Christian in Race Relations*, New York: Friendship Press, 1946.

41. See Kenneth K. Bailey, *Southern White Protestantism in the Twentieth Century*, New York: Harper & Row, 1964; also James Sellers, *The South and Christian Ethics*, New York: Association Press, 1962; and Robert M. Miller, *American Protestantism and Social Issues*, Chapel Hill: University of North Carolina Press, 1958.

42. James McBride Dabbs, *Who Speaks for the South?*, New York: Funk & Wagnalls Company, 1964. That the Southerner, even in his religion, is not just another American, was also held by W. J. Cash, *The Mind of the South*, New York: Alfred A. Knopf, 1941; C. Vann Woodward, *The Burden of Southern History*, Baton Rouge: Louisiana State University Press, 1960; and Francis B. Simkins, *The Everlasting South*, Baton Rouge: Louisiana State University Press, 1963. Others have seen the Southerner as American; for example, Harry Ashmore, *An Epitaph for Dixie*, New York: W. W. Norton & Company, 1958; Charles Sellers, *The Southerner as American*, Chapel Hill: University of North Carolina Press, 1960; Thomas D. Clark, *The Emerging South*, New York: Oxford University Press, 1961; and Howard Zinn, *The Southern Mystique*, New York: Alfred A. Knopf, 1964.

43. This is the contention of Simeon Booker, *Black Man's America*, Englewood Cliffs, N.J.: Prentice Hall, 1964.

44. See Norval Glenn, *op. cit.*, p. 632; also James W. Vander Zanden, "The Non-Violent Resistance Movement against Segregation," *American Journal of Sociology*, 68 (1963), 544–550.

45. E. Franklin Frazier. *The Negro Church in America*, New York: Schocken Books, 1963, pp. 70, 86.

46. Horace Cayton. "E. Franklin Frazier: A Tribute and a Review," *Review of Religious Research*, 5 (1964), 137–142 (p. 141).

47. Brink and Harris, *op. cit.*, pp. 223, 236.

48. Liston Pope. "The Negro and Religion in America," *Review of Religious Research*, 5 (1964), 142–152 (p. 144). He adds that "the Negro ministry is on the ascendancy in the eyes

of all Americans" (p. 147). In the same issue of the *Review,* Walter Muelder, "Recruitment of Negroes for Theological Studies," pp. 152–156, says that "the ministry, once the chief outlet for Negro ambition, is declining significantly in relative importance among professionals. It should be noted that Negro enrollments in medicine and law have also been dropping" (p. 155).

49. Daniel C. Thompson. *The Negro Leadership Class,* Englewood Cliffs, N.J.: Prentice Hall, 1963, p. 36.

50. The oft-repeated expression of white Southerners that "Negroes prefer to be by themselves" has validity only if it means that they prefer this to unjust and discriminatory treatment in churches, schools, parks, buses, restaurants, and elsewhere.

51. See Gibson Winter, *The Suburban Captivity of the Churches,* Garden City, N.Y.: Doubleday & Co., 1962; and *The New Creation as Metropolis,* 1963; and Peter Berger, *The Noise of Solemn Assemblies,* 1961; and *The Precarious Vision,* Garden City, N.Y.: Doubleday & Co., 1963.

52. Ernest Q. Campbell and Thomas Pettigrew, *Christians in Racial Crisis,* Washington, D.C.: Public Affairs Press, 1959, and their article, "Racial and Moral Crisis: The Role of Little Rock Ministers," *American Journal of Sociology,* 64 (1959), 509–516.

53. James Reston. "The Churches, the Synagogues, and the March on Washington," *Religious Education,* 59 (1964), 5 ff., reprinted from *The New York Times,* August 30, 1963.

54. It may be argued that the shocking brutality, official and unofficial, of the die-hard segregationists in Alabama was the main galvanizing force for reform.

55. Carl P. Zietlow, "Race, Students, and Non-Violence," *Religious Education,* 59 (1964), 116–120.

56. See William Brink and Louis Harris, *op. cit.;* also the changes noted by Herbert Hyman and Paul Sheatsley, "How Whites View Negroes, 1942–1963," *New York Herald Tribune,* November 19, 1963; and "Attitudes Toward Desegregation—Seven Years Later," *Scientific American,* 211 (1964).

57. Gordon W. Allport, "Prejudice: Is It Societal or Personal?" *Religious Education,* 59 (1964), 20–29.

58. James Weldon Johnson, *Along This Way,* New York: The Viking Press, 1933, p. 318, quoted by Myrdal, *op. cit.,* p. 43.

SUGGESTIONS FOR FURTHER READING
on *Selected Social Institutions*

The Family

FRIEDAN, BETTY. *The Feminine Mystique*. New York: Norton, 1963. A controversial appraisal of the status of American females and the roles they have learned to play.

GOODE, WILLIAM J. *World Revolution and Family Patterns*. New York: Free Press, 1963. A prize-winning analysis of family structures in a changing world.

LEWIS, OSCAR. *Five Families*. New York: Basic Books, 1959. A description of five Mexican families in different social and economic settings.

MACE, DAVID, and VERA MACE. *Marriage: East and West*. Garden City, N.Y.: Doubleday, 1960. A comparison of marriage practices in Europe and Asia.

The Negro Family. Washington, D.C.: Office of Policy Planning and Research, United States Department of Labor, 1965. The controversial report on some aspects of the background and current status of Negro families in the United States.

NIMKOFF, M. F., ed. *Comparative Family Systems*. Boston: Houghton Mifflin, 1965. A collection of articles on the family in various cultures.

RAINWATER, LEE, and WILLIAM L. YANCEY. *The Moynihan Report and the Politics of Controversy*. Cambridge, Mass.: M.I.T. Press, 1967. Essays discussing the government's report on *The Negro Family* and related subjects.

The Economic System

BELL, DANIEL. *Work and Its Discontents*. Boston: Beacon Press, 1956. A sociologist looks at the meaning of work in modern society.

HARRINGTON, MICHAEL. *The Other American*. New York: Macmillan, 1962. The book that examined the under side of "the affluent society."

HEILBRONER, ROBERT. *The Making of Economic Society*. Englewood Cliffs, N.J.: Prentice-Hall, 1962. An economic history of capitalism in the Western world.

JONES, PETER D'A. *The Consumer Society*. Baltimore: Penguin Books, 1965. A history of American capitalism.

MARX, KARL, and FREDERICK ENGELS. *The Communist Manifesto*. Originally published in 1848 and available in many editions. The famous statement of the Communist program.

MOORE, WILBERT E. *Economy and Society*. New York: Random House, 1955. An introduction to the sociological study of economic systems.

NOSOW, SIGMUND, and WILLIAM H. FORM, eds. *Man, Work and Society*. New York: Basic Books, 1962. A reader on the sociology of occupations.

PHILIPSON, MORRIS. *Automation*. New York: Random House, 1962. Essays on the implications of automation for the future.

SHONFIELD, ANDREW. *Modern Capitalism*. New York: Oxford University Press, 1966. An analysis of the changing balance of public and private power in the economy.

The Polity

BELL, DANIEL. *The End of Ideology*. New York: Collier Books, 1961. Part of this book is an examination of political ideologies—or their lack—in the 1950s.

BERELSON, BERNARD R., PAUL K. LAZARSFELD, and WILLIAM N. MCPHEE. *Voting*. Chicago:

University of Chicago Press, 1954. A study of opinion formation in one community during the 1948 presidential election.

DAHL, ROBERT. *Who Governs?* New Haven, Conn.: Yale University Press, 1961. Democracy and power in an American city.

KELLER, SUZANNE. *Beyond the Ruling Class.* New York: Random House, 1963. A study of strategic elites in modern society.

KEY, V. O. *Southern Politics.* New York: Alfred A. Knopf, 1950. Traditional party politics in the southern United States.

LIPSET, SEYMOUR MARTIN. *Political Man.* New York: Doubleday, 1963. The social bases of politics.

MILLS, C. WRIGHT. *The Power Elite.* New York: Oxford University Press, 1956. An attempt to define the loci of power in the United States.

PORTER, JOHN. *The Vertical Mosaic.* Toronto: University of Toronto Press, 1965. An analysis of social class and political power in Canada.

WHITE, T. H. *The Making of the President 1968.* New York: Atheneum, 1969. A penetrating account of the year in which Richard M. Nixon was elected President of the United States.

Education

CLARK, BURTON R. *Educating the Expert Society.* San Francisco: Chandler, 1962. A systematic study of the sociology of American education.

COLEMAN, JAMES S. *The Adolescent Society.* New York: Free Press, 1961. The social life of the teenager and its impact on education.

JENCKS, CHRISTOPHER, and DAVID RIESMAN. *The Academic Revolution.* Garden City: Doubleday, 1968. Views of the backgrounds and characteristics of American colleges and universities.

HALSEY, A. H., JEAN FLOUD, and C. ARNOLD ANDERSON, eds. *Education, Economy, and Society.* New York: Free Press, 1961. A reader on the sociology of education, with particular emphasis on the relation between economic changes and educational practices.

MAYER, MARTIN. *The Schools.* New York: Harper, 1961. A report on schooling in the United States in comparison with several other societies.

MICHAEL, DONALD N. *The Next Generation.* New York: Random House, 1965. The prospects for youth today and tomorrow.

PAGE, CHARLES HUNT, ed. *Sociology and Contemporary Education.* New York: Random House, 1964. Five essays on sociology as an educational enterprise.

RIESMAN, DAVID. *Constraint and Variety in American Education.* Lincoln: University of Nebraska Press, 1956. Three lectures on education in America.

SANFORD, NEVITT, ed. *The American College.* New York: John Wiley, 1962. A compendium of articles on the structure, character, and effect of higher education.

Religion

BERGER, PETER L. *The Sacred Canopy.* New York: Doubleday, 1967. Elements of a sociological theory of religion.

BIRNBAUM, NORMAN, and GERTRUD LENZER, eds. *Sociology and Religion.* Englewood Cliffs, N.J.: Prentice-Hall, 1969. An excellent collection of readings.

BROTZ, HOWARD. *The Black Jews of Harlem.* New York: Free Press, 1964. An analysis of a syncretist religious group and a general commentary on Negro nationalism.

DEMERATH, N. J., III. *Social Class in American Protestantism.* Chicago: Rand McNally, 1965. The results of a survey of the attitudes, activities, and socioeconomic status of representatives of five Protestant denominations.

HERBERG, WILL. *Protestant, Catholic, Jew.* Garden City, N.Y.: Doubleday, 1955. An examination of religion in America and a discussion of the theory of the "triple melting pot."

LENSKI, GERHARD. *The Religious Factor.* Garden City, N.Y.: Doubleday, 1961. A study of the role of religious affiliation in social attitudes and behavior in a major American city.

MALINOWSKI, BRONISLAW. *Magic, Science, and Religion.* Garden City, N.Y.: Doubleday, 1954. Essays on the differences between the three phenomena by a distinguished anthropologist; see especially the title essay.

SKLARE, MARSHALL. *Conservative Judaism.* Glencoe, Ill.: Free Press, 1955. A sociological analysis of an American religious movement.

WILSON, BRYAN R. *Sects and Societies.* Berkeley: University of California Press, 1961. A study of three religious movements; the Elim Tabernacle, Christian Science, and the Christadelphians.

YINGER, J. MILTON. *Religion, Society, and the Individual.* New York: Macmillan, 1957. A textbook and reader on the sociology of religion.

PART SIX
CONFORMITY AND
DEVIANCE

Varying perspectives on
the maintenance of
order and the nature
of deviance

This mission of the sociologist is manifold. One part of it, as Everett C. Hughes says, is "to catch the goings-on of people and institutions." He means all sorts of people and all kinds of institutions. This involves seeing not only the dominant (and the dominating) themes and patterns but those of people who, for various reasons, do not accept the legitimacy of particular societal or communal standards of thought or behavior. Here one must consider the codes and manners of disaffected members of society, including those who have been on the inside and have opted out; those who are disadvantaged or displaced or disenfranchised; and also those who are not only deviants from the general norms but are so labeled and come to define themselves as such.

In point of fact, deviations from the norms (and those who deviate) are defined differently in different parts of the social world. "Aberrant behavior" in one locale may be "conformity" in another. The generation gap offers a good example. To increasing numbers of young people in this country, the "all-American boy" is somehow an atavistic reflection of an earlier time. The swinger is in. To others, the long-haired youth is an anathema. (Norman Vincent Peale, for example, in talking about today's disheveled young intellectuals, said "I'd rather be dumb and clean than smart and dirty, any time.")

Still, it is true that when most people speak or write of conformity, they tend to mean conformity to the rules and practices laid down or upheld by the "established authorities." They start from one set of assumptions about the importance of tradition and the maintenance of the social order. Sociologists of deviance, by contrast, often begin with another point of view. They recognize the conventional wisdom (as they must) and study patterns of social control, problems in the enforcement of norms, and the salience of certain standards and values for various segments of the population. But they also examine the functions of conformity and deviance as well. And, going a step further, they frequently attempt to relate life on the "outside" of society to that within.

The essays in Part Six deal with sociological interpretations of the enforcement and violation of norms, and with deviant behavior itself. In the first set of papers, A. L. Clark and Jack P. Gibbs introduce the subject in their essay, "Social Control." James Q. Wilson, a political scientist, then discusses some dilemmas confronting those assigned the task of maintaining order and enforcing the law. In "Is Punishment Necessary?" Jackson Toby examines the various arguments used to justify the use of punishment.

Bridging the first and second set of papers, Lewis A. Coser discusses "Some Functions of Deviant Behavior."

The first part of Kai T. Erikson's book, *Wayward Puritan,* offers a review of the sociology of deviance. His observations are reprinted here; so, too, is the famous paper, "Illegitimate Means, Anomie, and Deviant Behavior," by Richard Cloward. The last two papers deal with contracultures and subcultures. The authors are J. Milton Yinger and David J. Bordua.

Norms: Enforcement and Violation

59. SOCIAL CONTROL

A. L. CLARK *and* JACK P. GIBBS

In this essay the authors suggest that social control should be viewed as social reaction to behavior defined as deviant, including over-conformity to, as well as violation of, norms. Unlike many others who have written on the subject, Alexander L. Clark and Jack B. Gibbs shift attention away from the study of the sort of disembodied societal reaction to that of people themselves.

They indicate that the following variable normative reactions are essential for any comprehension of social control: generality, specificity, contingency, consensus, and consistency. The applicability of the approach is illustrated when the authors describe and discuss actual reactions to behavior considered deviant.

A. L. Clark is a Staff Associate, Division of Behavioral Sciences at the National Academy of Sciences, and a frequent contributor to social science journals.

Jack P. Gibbs, Professor of Sociology at the University of Texas, is the author of Urban Research Methods (*1961*), Suicide (*1968*), *and co-author of* Status Integration and Suicide (*1968*).

While the term social control remains in common usage, systematic attention to the field has long since withered away, a de-velopment which we attribute primarily to inadequate delimitations of the field. Ac-cordingly, this paper suggests a distinctive

Reprinted from *Social Problems,* **12** (Spring 1965), 398–415, by permission of the authors and The Society for the Study of Social Problems. This article was originally entitled "Social Control: A Reformulation."

subject matter for social control in the hope that a reformulation will lend new life to this sociological specialty.

. . .

Reaction to Deviant Behavior

We propose here to wed the languishing concept of social control to a relatively long-neglected area of social behavior. With few exceptions, sociologists have been preoccupied with the sources of deviant behavior rather than *reactions to deviant behavior*.[1] Specifically, current theories on mental illness, crime, juvenile delinquency, alcoholism, prostitution, etc., focus on the developmental or situational determinants of deviants far more than on reaction to deviation. To the extent that attention is devoted to reactions, it is centered characteristically on the relative effectiveness of various reactions for the deviant's rehabilitation. Concomitantly, concern with rehabilitation seems to have led to the premature rejection of the possibility that the character of reaction may influence the rate of deviation. To the extent that this is true, the relative neglect of reaction suggests that sociologists have been seduced by the gross non-sequitur that since formal mechanisms of control are ineffective they are, therefore, unimportant. Apart from the fact that the influence of reaction on the volume of deviant behavior has not really been determined, all societies have more or less institutionalized reaction patterns, and variations in these patterns require explanation in their own right. As a case in point, why is reaction in some societies oriented toward the principle of rehabilitation?

In recent years, sociologists have become somewhat more concerned with the study of reactions to deviant behavior. Lemert, for example, not only sees reactions as an important element in the study of deviant behavior, but links reactions to the concept of social control.[2] However, in Lemert's view, reactions to deviant behavior constitute social control only when such reactions have been organized into public or private agencies.[3] Further, Lemert has not systematized the study of social control in terms of formulating central questions or identifying major variables.

Some investigators of reaction to deviant behavior make no explicit attempt to link their studies to social control. These studies appear to fall into one of three general types. The first type is distinguished by a common concern with the labelling of persons or groups as deviant. The works of Becker[4] and Kitsuse[5] illustrate a primary attention to the kinds of behavior that are likely to be judged deviant and a partial consideration of the reactions that a "deviant" is likely to experience as a result of having been so labelled. Similarly, Scheff argues that identification of bizarre ("residual") conduct as "mental illness" not only serves to isolate individuals so defined, but also is instrumental in promoting and maintaining the behavior appropriate to the deviant label.[6] These writers make it explicit that labelling is but the first step in a reaction process; but, in the main, they are more concerned with accounting for the determinants of labelling than with an explanation of societal variations in the consequences of persons or groups being defined as deviant. In any event, they have not identified the major analytical properties of reaction, nor have they sought to explain variation in these properties.

A second class of studies seems to be written more for the purpose of exhortation than for the cumulative contribution of research to the development of social theory. For example, studies of official reactions to adult crime and delinquency often seem more concerned with documenting and judging these practices as discriminatory or ineffective, than with attempting to explain through a comparative design why the character of reaction varies among societies or other social units.[7]

A third class of studies considers the association between characteristics of the deviant and reaction to his deviation. For example, several investigations have been concerned with variations in the reactions to mental illness as they may be related to social class.[8] Similarly, the sex status of deviants conditions reaction, as evidenced by the fact that an illegitimate child reflects more on the esteem of the mother than on the father.[9] While studies in this class do focus attention on reaction, each, for the most part, is concerned with only one aspect of reaction and not in a comparative context.

Social Control as Reaction to Deviant Behavior

We define social control as: *social reactions to behavior defined as deviant, including over-conformity to, as well as violations of, norms.* This definition excludes from consideration that vast range of crescive and unwitting social processes that may in some way contribute to social order. On the other hand, all reactions to deviant behavior, regardless of the intent of the reactors, are included.

The reformulation is preferable to existing definitions in that the latter typically not only give the field of social control an impossibly broad subject matter but also make it difficult to formulate questions for theory and research. For example, if social control is defined as all phenomena that induce conformity to norms, such a definition not only fails to distinguish social control from sociology generally but also is virtually impossible to apply. To apply it, one must show that a given event or class of events does in fact induce conformity before he can justifiably treat it as social control. The definition thus assumes that we know what in fact actually remains to be demonstrated. The reformulation proposed here makes no such assumption.

In addition to reactions to the fact of deviant behavior, the subject matter of social control also encompasses deliberate anticipatory reactions; otherwise, organizations such as prisons and mental hospitals, which exist in anticipation of deviant behavior and not as reactions to *particular* deviant acts, would be excluded. However, such behavior patterns as neo-local residence and the symbolization of marital status by rings are not included. Although these practices may decrease the probability of incest and marital infidelity, they are crescively developed practices rather than witting and deliberate reactions to the anticipation of deviant conduct. However, to make our position clear, formal and informal, legal and non-legal reactions to instances of incest and marital infidelity are definitely viewed as aspects of social control.

Social control, as reformulated here, is clearly intended as the study of *social* reactions to deviant behavior rather than *societal* reactions. The distinction is important in two respects. First, a concern with reaction to deviant behavior at only the societal level leads to a preoccupation with formal sanctions. And, second, while the term social reactions includes formal sanctions, it also encompasses informal and non-legal reactions as they occur both in societies and in smaller social units.

The present delimitation of social control represents first and foremost an attempt to give the field an independent and meaningful subject matter. We are not concerned with why the norms are what they are, or why persons commit deviant acts, or even with why persons come to be defined as deviants. Such questions are the proper subject matter of criminology, the sociology of deviant behavior, and social organization generally. In contrast, it is the focus on reaction to deviant behavior (i.e., behavior socially defined as deviant) that distinguishes the study of social control.

The dearth of sociological attempts to explain variations in social reactions to deviance has left unfulfilled the need for an adequate conceptualization in terms of which the immense detail of variation may be classified, investigated, and, subsequently, explained. Unlike most earlier studies,[10] we do not favor conceptualizing reactions in terms of punitiveness. Judgments of reactions as more or less punitive rest on subjective and ethnocentric standards and ignore a number of other properties of reaction as well. For example, on what basis do we decide whether the enforcement of public copulation is more or less punitive than imprisonment? And how do we describe the social organization of reaction in terms of punitiveness?

Inasmuch as an adequate conceptual scheme for the analysis of reactions to deviation does not exist, the first step toward substantive research and theory must be the definition of concepts in terms of which variations in reactions may be examined universally. Accordingly, no articulation of substantive theory is attempted; rather, our primary concern is with the formulation of the central concepts and major questions in the study of social control. Further, although some data are presented, a systematic investigation of variation in all of the properties of reaction to deviant behavior among societies and other social units remains to be accomplished.

The central concepts in this delimitation of social control are those which are necessary for analyzing the organization of reaction to deviant behavior. As a working assumption, we submit that such reactions cannot be viewed as organized without the presence of: (1) norms which specify what the reaction to deviation should be, (2) normative identification of the persons who should react, (3) patterns in actual reactions to deviation, (4) differentiation in the characteristics of actual reactors, and (5) a correspondence between the normative and the actual. Accordingly, the universally applicable concepts set forth here represent the minimal components of the organization of reaction to deviant behavior, and thereby provide the basis for strategic comparisons of social units. It must be emphasized that while reaction to deviation is organized in all social units, the study of social control seeks to explain variation in the form and degree of such organization.

Normative Reactions

For every norm there is a corresponding belief as to what should and/or what will happen in instances of behavior contrary to the norm.[11] We refer to such beliefs as normative reactions or reactive norms to distinguish them from what in fact happens, i.e., the actual reactions.

There are three distinct types of normative reactions. The first, which may be termed *evaluative,* refers to popular conceptions of what should happen given the occurrence of deviant behavior. An example of this type of normative reaction is the belief shared by many Americans that the mentally ill should be treated rather than punished. A second type of normative reaction, the *legal,* can best be described as the legitimate reaction alternatives of agents with the official responsibility for reacting to deviant conduct. An example is provided in the statement of a law of Colonial Massachusetts: "And every person Drunken, *viz.* so as he be thereby bereaved or disabled in the use of his understanding, appearing in his speech or gesture, in any of the said Houses or elsewhere, shall forfeit *ten shillings,* and for excessive Drinking *three shillings four pence,* and for continueing above half an hour Tipling *two shillings six pence,* and for Tipling at unseasonable times, or after nine of the Clock at night *five shillings* for every Offence in those particulars, being lawfully convicted thereof, and for want of payment, they shall be imprisoned till they pay, or be set in the Stocks one hour or more (in some open place) as the Weather will permit not exceeding three hours." [12] The third class of normative reactions, the *expecta-*

tional, refers to popular conceptions of what *will happen* given the occurrence of deviance. Expectational reactions are illustrated by the belief among the Kapauku Papuans that a husband will die if his wife should break certain food taboos.[13]

Early writers have documented the range of variation in normative reactions by compiling encyclopedic lists of reactions in various societies; but on the whole they chose to characterize the observed differences along the single dimension of punitiveness.[14] As a first step toward a more adequate conceptualization, we propose that variation in normative reactions be examined in terms of generality, specificity, contingency, consensus, and consistency.

GENERALITY   All social units are faced with a fundamental decision in the organization of reaction to deviant behavior—whether the same normative reaction should apply to all deviant acts or whether different reactions should be normatively prescribed for each type of deviation. To illustrate the contrast that may be observed in normative legal reactions, in early 19th century England capital punishment applied to at least 200 different offenses,[15] while in three of the United States (as of about 1955) it applied to only one type of crime.[16] Thus, capital punishment as a normative reaction is far more general in the former case than the latter.

SPECIFICITY   As is the case for any social activity, the organization of reaction to deviation varies from one social unit to the next in terms of the degree of discretion which is permitted the actors in the system. Discretion in this context is largely a matter of the specificity of normative reactions. A normative reaction may be specific in that one and only one particular reaction is prescribed for an act defined as deviant. A perfectly specific legal reaction is illustrated by the mandatory death penalty for first degree murder, while the least specific is illustrated by the specification that the reaction is to be left to the discretion of the reactor (e.g., a juvenile court judge).

Evaluative reactive norms also vary with regard to specificity. The Comanche, for example, believed that a male offended by his wife's adultery should either kill her, cut off her nose, beat her, divorce her, or collect damages from her lover. Among the Kapauku Papuans, on the other hand, it was felt that the only just punishment for an adulteress is death.

The specificity of expectational norms refers to the number of reactions which may or will occur given a particular deviant act. For example, it is expected that failure to stop for a stop sign will result (if detected by a police officer) in a fine for the offending motorist. A much less specific expectational reaction on the other hand applies to the detection of a married man's act of homosexuality. Given this case, the expectation may be that he is likely to lose his job, his family, his reputation, and/or suffer the legal consequences of his act as well. However, the specificity of an expectational norm should not be confused with its certainty of application. The expectation that a specific traffic offense may result in a fine is highly specific, but it is by no means certain that the offense will be detected or the fine imposed if it is detected. That is to say, one would expect to be fined or not to be fined, but he would not expect to be exiled, beaten, publicly humiliated, etc.

CONTINGENCY   Discretion as an element in reactions to deviation may be organized by norms which prescribe that reactions *should* depend on specified characteristics of the deviant, the victim, the normative reactor, and/or situational circumstances; and to the extent this is so the reactive norm is *contingent.*

Contingency is actually one of the pleas of modern correctional reformers. However, the idea that the legal reactive norm should be contingent is by no means novel or recent. Among the Aztecs there were evidently at least four different normative reactions for drunkenness: for the plebeian, shaving the head in public; for priests, death by unspecified means; for dignitaries, loss of office and titles; and for the nobility, strangulation in private.[17] Thus, the only novelty in modern correctional reform is the emphasis on the personal (mostly psychological) characteristics of offenders rather than their formal statuses.

Reactive norms also may be contingent on factors other than the characteristics of the deviant. Among the early Norwegians (*circa* 1150) the legal reaction for wounding a man depended not only on the statuses of the deviant but also on the statuses of the victim. The early Norwegians also incorporated situational factors in their legal reactive norms, as witness the following: "If a man slays the king's bailiff, he shall pay an atonement of fifteen marks, unless he slays him at the king's table while he is serving the king; in that case he shall be outlawed."[18]

Finally, it is probably true that in all societies the normative reaction is contingent on the reactor (e.g., Americans probably expect, in the evaluational or expectational sense, a different reaction from parents than from school teachers for a scholastically recalcitrant child).

CONSENSUS Observations on the subject tend to suggest that in any population there is one and only one reactive norm for any particular kind of deviation. However, when one attempts to identify reactive norms in a population it becomes obvious that they are not evident. The difficulty lies in the discrepancies between the qualities ascribed to norms at the purely conceptual level and the means that are used to identify them empirically. Typically, a norm is described as "superorganic," meaning existing independent of any particular individual. In a certain sense this is true—no living person invented the proscription of incest and the consequences of defying the proscription are not dictated by the actor. However, with the possible exception of laws, there

is no empirical basis for identifying norms other than analysis of the opinions of individuals, and the same is true of reactive norms. By definition, both evaluative and expectational reactive norms represent what the members of a social unit think should or will happen to a deviant; but the members typically do not agree completely as to what will or what should be the consequences of a norm violation. Thus, theoretically, there may be as many opinions as there are persons in a social unit. The fact that in no society does this condition appear to hold is indicative of the superorganic quality of norms, but the lack of agreement is still a conceptual problem. One can argue that a reactive norm is what the greatest number or majority of the members think should happen or will happen to a deviant, but this criterion is obviously arbitrary. Further, what is the reactive norm when the members are equally divided in the way of opposing opinions?

As we see it, the conclusion with regard to the dilemma of identifying reactive norms is inescapable—there are as many reactive norms as there are different opinions as to what should or what will happen to a deviant. However, not all opinions are norms to the same degree, because opinions are norms only to the extent they are prevalent in the social unit. Consequently, the *degree of consensus* is another characteristic of both evaluative and expectational reactions.

The characteristic of consensus does not apply to laws, because typically there are no opposing or conflicting laws, as witness the fact that in any one of the United States there is one and only one law concerning the penalty for armed robbery. True, in a society with a federated system of government (such as the United States), the laws of the various political subdivisions of the society may not be the same; but, if such is the case, the proper unit for the analysis of legal reactions to crime would be the individual political division and not the society as a whole.

Further, while some laws may not have popular support, this pertains to the consistency between legal and evaluative reactions, a characteristic distinct from consensus.

CONSISTENCY   The concept of consistency refers to the degree of correspondence among evaluational, legal, and expectational reactions. For example, if the death penalty is the legal reactive norm to a particular crime, but all of the members of the social unit think that imprisonment for life should be the reaction, and yet none of the members expect that persons so sentenced will actually remain in prison for life, then consistency is at a minimum.[19]

Certainly sociologists are familiar with the notion that laws may be impotent if contrary to evaluational norms and that a disparity between evaluational and expectational norms is symptomatic of social change; but truly *comparative* studies of the extent, conditions, and consequences of discrepancy among types of normative reactions have yet to be attempted.[20]

Actual Reactions

While the aforementioned variable properties pose major questions in the study of social control, we do not regard normative reactions to deviant behavior as any more important than actual reactions. Indeed, quite apart from reactive norms, the organization of reaction to deviant behavior implies that actual reactions are more or less patterned. If we attempt to discover patterns in all kinds of specific actual reactions, our inventory would undoubtedly be as long as the imaginative capabilities of the human mind. To illustrate, Comanche males often cut off the nose of their faithless wife, while in certain New Guinea tribes a wife's indiscretion was sometimes reacted to by a group of men copulating with the adulteress in public.[21] While psychiatric observation characteristically is the contemporary American re-

action to attempted suicide, if a Kapauku Papuan woman attempted suicide she was punished by a beating administered by the person or persons who had a claim to her brideprice.

The point is that an analysis in terms of such specific reactions simply is not feasible. Moreover, a problem is posed by the fact that conventionally recognized categories of reactions are not mutually exclusive. Consider, for example, death, loss of property, deprivation of status, physical punishment, social exclusion, redemption, and reward. While these categories reduce the number of units in the analysis of actual reactions, they are not exhaustive and certainly not mutually exclusive. Imprisonment, for example, clearly involves, at least, social exclusion, deprivation of status, and loss of property. These observations point to the need for a logical, rigorous taxonomy of actual reactions to deviant behavior.[22] While presently we are unable to offer such a taxonomy, patterns in actual reactions can be sought in terms of the properties of association and contingency.

ASSOCIATION   Since actual reactions to deviant behavior may be unrelated to legal, evaluative, and expectational norms, there may be no association whatever between how people actually react and what they are reacting to (i.e., the type of deviant behavior). However, when one studies the association between actual reaction and types of deviation, patterns typically emerge. These patterns are described in terms of generality, variation, distinctiveness, and differentiation.

"Generality" refers to the extent to which a particular kind of actual reaction applies to all types of deviant acts. The degree of generality is expressed as follows: $1-[\sum X^2/(\sum X)^2]$, where X is the number of actual reactions of a particular kind to a given class of deviant acts.[23] For purposes of illustration, statistics on sentences imposed by the California Superior Courts in 1962 on 27,084 persons convicted of a felony [24] have been used to compute the degree of generality for nine types of actual legal reactions: death sentence, .15; prison sentence, .87; commitment to the California Rehabilitation Center, .42; commitment to the Youth Authority, .83; probation without a jail sentence, .91; probation with a jail sentence, .88; jail sentence, .87; fine, .86; and commitment to the Department of Mental Hygiene, .59. Thus, the death sentence as an actual legal reaction has the least generality, while probation without a jail sentence has the most.

It is probably true that in no society is there one and only one type of actual reaction to all instances of a particular kind of deviation; but the "degree of variation" in actual reactions is by no means constant for all types of deviant acts. This is illustrated again by the California statistics on actual legal reactions, in this case a measure of the degree of variation by offense:[25] murder, .13; manslaughter, .64; manslaughter with vehicle, .69; robbery, .59; assault, .77; burglary, .79; theft, other than auto, .76; auto theft, .79; receiving stolen property, .76; forgery and other check offenses, .76; rape, .75; lewd and lascivious conduct, .69; other sex offenses, .65; narcotics violations, .79; violations concerning deadly weapons, .74; drunk driving, .67; failure to render aid, .67; escape, .60; bookmaking, .34; contributing to the delinquency of a minor, .60; all other, .73.

Types of actual reactions differ not only with regard to generality but also with regard to "distinctiveness," meaning the degree to which a given type of reaction differs from all other types in terms of the kinds of deviant acts to which it is applied. Measures of distinctiveness[26] for the actual legal reactions in California vary from a high of 83.4 for the death penalty to a low of 27.3 for probation with a jail sentence.

Contrary to the classical theory of justice, actual reactions to deviant acts are not always highly "differentiated," meaning that the actual reactions to one particular type of deviant act may be very much like the reactions to other kinds of deviant acts. Measures of the "degree of differentiation"[27] for the 21 offense categories in California vary from a high of 75.9 for murder to a low of 9.2 for forgery and other check offenses.

While we are concerned with variation in the associational properties of particular kinds of reactions and different types of deviant acts, the overall degree of generality, variation, differentiation, and distinctiveness is the primary concern. To date, our findings reveal considerable variation in composite measures of actual legal reactions, even among counties within the same state. Variation within the same state is particularly important because it is indicative of a lack of specificity in legal reactive norms. Where this is the case actual legal reactions cannot be explained wholly in terms of norms. Thus, some of the differences in the above associational measures are undoubtedly due to varying degrees of specificity, but by no means all. Indeed, the extent to which actual reactions can be explained in terms of the normative is a central question in the study of social control.

CONTINGENCY Measures of generality and variation reveal that actual reactions to deviant conduct, even acts of the same kind, are not the same. However, this does not mean that the differences are random. On the contrary, actual reactions are *contingent* on at least five factors: the characteristics of the normative reactor, the deviant, the victim, the actual reactor, and the situational circumstances of the deviant act. Variations occasioned by these circumstances are termed the contingency of actual reactions. Some research has been accomplished on the contingency of actual reactions to deviant behavior. We know, for example, that the social class characteristics of juvenile offenders affect the probability of their being defined officially as delinquent,[28] and that "Characteristically psychotherapy is prescribed for upper-class (mental) patients and shock treatment for those of the lower class." [29] Also, the fact that actual reaction is in some measure contingent on the status of the reactor is evidenced by at least one research that indicates that individuals exhibiting similar symptoms of mental illness are more sympathetically dealt with by the community if they seek help from clergymen and physicians than from psychiatrists or mental hospitals.[30] While numerous studies have documented what is here designated as contingency, an explanation of variation in the bases (statuses of deviants, statuses of victims, etc.) and the degree of contingency, particularly *among* societies, is still wanting.

Normative Versus the Actual

Current debates on the relative merits of alternative reactions to crime and juvenile delinquency focus almost exclusively on the issue of effectiveness, i.e., whether or not a particular type of reaction results in rehabilitation and/or deterrence. Social scientists have participated in these debates by offering what purports to be relevant empirical evidence. However, both the debates and the related research tend to consider only normative reactions. As a case in point, numerous studies have compared the homicide rates of political units that differ with regard to statutory provision for the death penalty. Whatever the merits of these studies, insofar as they ignore the correspondence between normative and actual reactions, the results are inconclusive. One could argue that the effectiveness of any kind of legal reactive norm is partially a function of the correspondence between the normative and the actual. In the present reformulation this correspondence is considered in terms of two properties—certainty and relativity.

CERTAINTY In London and Middlesex, England, the ratio of the number of persons convicted of a capital crime to the number actually executed (the legal reactive norm) increased from 1.8 during the years 1756–1758 to 10.6 during the years 1802–1804.[31] This change illustrates a decrease in the certainty of the legal reactive norm. Note, however, that the element of certainty characterizes each step in the reaction process. Thus, while we can speak of the certainty of the imposition of a penalty, we can also inquire as to the certainty of detection, being tried, or being convicted if tried. As an illustration of differences in certainty at various steps in the reaction process, of all cases of rape known to the police in 14 districts of England and Wales (*circa* 1950), 80.8 per cent resulted in the offender being identified, and 90.5 per cent of the identified offenders were tried, but only 52.6 per cent of the offenders tried were convicted.[32] The corresponding figures for sexual offenses designated as "gross indecency" are 99.2, 99.2 and 94.5.

RELATIVITY Whereas certainty refers to the correspondence between the normative and the actual reaction to any particular kind of deviation, relativity refers to variation in the correspondence from one condition to the next. A tentative list of the conditions that are associated with the relativity of certainty includes the characteristics of the deviant, the victim, and the actual reactors, and situational circumstances.[33] A comparison of convicted murderers in Pennsylvania (1914–1958) who were executed with those who had their death sentence commuted illustrates two conditions of relativity.[34] It was found that a statistically significant greater proportion of whites had their sentence commuted than did Negroes. Moreover, private counsels (one of the actual reactors in the reaction process) secured more commuted sentences than did court-appointed counsels. On the other hand, no statistically significant differences were found in the per cent executed by nativity, occupation, or marital status.

Insofar as the discrepancy between the normative and the actual is revealed in a high degree of relativity, it may be indicative of a disjunction between the substance of reactive norms and the prevailing ideologies among such reactors as judges, psychiatrists and probation workers. In organizational terms, such discrepancy is indicative of opposition between the manifest and latent principles of social control.

Normative Reactors

The celebrated trial of Jack Ruby illustrates the point that in some instances only persons in a particular status are expected to react in a certain way to suspicion of deviant conduct. Such persons are designated as normative reactors, and represent organization of the allocation of rights and duties with regard to reaction. As in the case of reactive norms, there are three types of normative reactors—(1) the legal, (2) the evaluative, and (3) the expectational. With the possible exception of the legal reactor, all three types are found in any society; but social units differ as to the characteristics of normative reactors, and this variation poses another major question in the study of social control.

ROLE EXCLUSIVENESS Regardless of the social unit, the positions of normative reactors in the organization of reaction to deviation are identified in terms of statuses; but social units differ in the extent to which such statuses are defined exclusively in terms of the responsibility for reacting to deviant behavior. To illustrate, a husband among the Comanches was expected to demand damages from a warrior who had absconded with his wife, but this was only one of many roles of a husband; therefore, the status is not defined exclusively in terms of reaction.

The greater the proportion of the roles of a given status that are defined in terms of the responsibility for reacting to deviant behavior the more exclusive that status as a normative reactor. Presently, we have neither the data nor the methods for a systematic inventory of the roles of statuses in different societies. Nevertheless,

statuses can be roughly classified as to whether they represent maximum role exclusiveness, and such a classification reveals a tremendous difference among societies. For example, there was not one single status among the Eskimo [35] or the Comanche which is defined largely in terms of reaction to deviant behavior, while in the United States there are at least four reactor statuses that approach the maximum in role exclusiveness—detectives, district attorneys, criminal court judges, and prison wardens.

OCCUPATIONAL EXCLUSIVENESS Normative reactor stauses differ not only in the degree of role exclusiveness but also in the extent to which the status represents a full-time occupation. Societies differ sharply with regard to this characteristic of reactors. Among the Eskimo, for example, there was apparently no status that even remotely resembles that of the police officer, district attorney, or judge, all of which are typically full-time occupations in urban societies.

At first glance it might appear that role exclusiveness and occupational exclusiveness are essentially the same, but such is not the case. Logically, a status may be defined exclusively in terms of reaction to deviant behavior, even though all of the persons in the status have other occupational pursuits. We suspect that there is a close empirical relation among social units between the degree of role exclusiveness and the degree of occupational exclusiveness, but this is only one of several questions posed in the study of normative reactors.

CONSISTENCY While there may be one and only one legal designation of reactors, these reactors may not be identical to those defined by expectational or evaluative norms and, if so, there may be a conflict in the allocation of rights and duties in the organization of reaction. The correspondence between the three types of normative reactors is referred to here as the *degree of consistency*.

A survey of the attitudes of the adult

residents of Nebraska toward the law reveals an instance of a low degree of consistency between legal reactors and evaluative reactors. As one of a series of questions the residents were asked whether a child should be allowed to recover damages from a man if the man disrupts the child's family relationships by courting the affection of the child's mother.[36] Sixty per cent of the residents answered "yes" to the question. In essence, the majority of the residents have granted the status of a normative reactor to the child, but the law denies the child that status.

Stated generally, the degree of consistency between the legal and the evaluative designations of reactors is the proportion of the members of a social unit who hold opinions as to who should react which corresponds to the legal designation as to who should react. The same meaning of consistency applies to the degree of correspondence between the legal and the expectational conceptions of normative reactors and between expectational and evaluational.

CONSENSUS   Consensus with regard to normative reactors refers to the extent to which members of a social unit agree as to either who should react to a particular kind of deviance (evaluational) or who will react (expectational). The opinions of the Nebraska residents as described above also illustrate consensus as to normative reactors (in this case the evaluative type). Had all of the residents agreed that the child should recover damages, rather than only 60 per cent, consensus with regard to the evaluative reactor would have been at the maximum.

CONTINGENCY   Normative reactors may vary as a consequence of the characteristics of the deviant, the victim, and/or the situational circumstances surrounding the deviant act. For example, the legal reactor to unlawful acts in the United States is contingent at some stage in the reaction process on the age status of the deviant. Similarly, the concept of proper

jurisdiction in American jurisprudence reflects the fact that legal reactors are highly contingent on the purely locational circumstance of deviation, a characteristic of the organization of reaction which appears much more prevalent among literate than nonliterate societies.

A maximum degree of contingency would obtain in a society if for each type of norm violation there was a different normative reactor for each of all possible combinations of statuses of deviants, statuses of victims, and situations.[37] No society examined to date remotely approaches maximum contingency, but general observations suggest sharp differences among societies in degree.

GENERALITY   Whereas the contingency of normative reactors refers to the factors that condition a reactor's authority to react to a particular kind of deviant behavior, generality refers to the extent to which a reactor has the authority to react to all kinds of deviation. In Comanche war parties, the war chief had the right to react to all kinds of deviation and his reaction authority might therefore be described as highly general. Lesser degrees of generality describe reaction statuses that are restricted by the nature of deviant acts. For example, the reaction authority of members of the FBI appears far less general than was the authority of the members of the Gestapo in Nazi Germany.

Actual Reactors

When a judge in his capacity as normative reactor sentences a felon to a term in prison, we often may observe that other actual reactors include the felon's wife who divorces him, his colleagues who ostracize him, and his children who disown him. This illustration introduces another central concept in the study of social control—actual reactors.

Sociological interest in other than official reactions to deviant behavior characteristically has lumped nonofficial reactions in the category of informal reactions. However, the notion that reactions to deviant behavior should be viewed as a sequence of various reactions employed by a variety of reactors, some normative and others not, necessitates that the characteristics of actual reactors be more precisely defined.[38] We propose that actual reactors be investigated in terms of status differentiation, association, and contingency.

STATUS DIFFERENTIATION Status differentiation refers to the extent to which the statuses of actual reactors differ from the statuses of persons who do not react to instances of deviance. As far as actual legal reactors in the United States are concerned, there is a high degree of status differentiation in terms of age, sex, and race, as witness the age composition of judges, the small number of women in any of the legal reaction statuses, and, particularly in the South, the underrepresentation of Negroes in police personnel.[39]

The status differentiation of actual reactors is particularly important for an understanding of the social organization of normative phenomena. When actual reactors are highly differentiated from nonreactors in terms of such statuses as social class, caste, age, and sex, it is indicative of a close relation between the organization of reaction and the larger social structure. This relationship could not be revealed from an analysis of normative reaction statuses alone (e.g., detectives, judges, etc.) since these are but positions in the social structure and consequently by definition lack further identifying status characteristics.

ASSOCIATION As with actual reactions, association in the case of actual reactors refers to the properties of generality, variation, differentiation, and distinctiveness,[40] all of which represent a dimension of the organization of reaction.

"Variation" refers to the degree of heterogeneity in the statuses of the actual reactors to a particular kind of deviation.

For example, in cases of adultery among the Comanche, in most instances the husband and only the husband is the actual reactor, whereas for wife-absconding a "champion at law" often reacted in cohort with or instead of the husband. Thus, in cases of adultery we can predict with fair degree of certainty who the reactor would be, while such is not the case with wife-absconding, meaning that in the latter case the statuses of actual reactors are more heterogeneous.

The Comanche case also illustrates the variable property of "generality" in actual reactors. Persons in the status of husband are more general actual reactors because they react to both adultery and wife-absconding, while "champions at law" are less general actual reactors, being called upon for the most part only in instances of wife-absconding.

"Distinctiveness" is the degree of difference among the various status configurations of actual reactors in terms of the types of deviant conduct to which they react. Thus, to illustrate, if only males of a certain age react to certain kinds of deviant conduct, the actual reactors are to that extent distinctive.

"Differentiation" refers to the differences among types of deviant conduct in terms of the statuses of the actual reactors. For example, if a given type of deviant act results in reaction by persons in statuses that are different from the actual reactors to all other types of deviant conduct, then to that extent the different types of deviant acts are highly differentiated in terms of actual reactors.

Since legal norms typically do not identify reactors in terms of marital status, sex, race, etc., distinctiveness and differentiation probably reflect the degree to which expectational and evaluative reactions incorporate status distinctions. Note, however, that this in turn probably depends on the extent to which status distinctions are emphasized in the society. Thus, assuming some degree of correspondence between normative and actual reactors, in a society where race is not emphasized, the prediction would be a low degree of racial distinctiveness and differentiation for actual reactors to deviation.

CONTINGENCY Who actually reacts to a particular kind of deviation may be, and in fact typically is, contingent on the characteristics of the deviant, the victim, and/or situation. For example, of 120 cases of "indecent sexual assaults" on males in England, in 91.7 per cent of the cases someone other than the victim reported the act to the police, while the corresponding per cent for 456 assaults on females is only 73.5.[41] In this instance, the status of the victim is related to who becomes involved in the actual reactions that lead to a police investigation.

Normative Versus Actual Reactors

In all societies examined to date there are instances of a discrepancy between normative and actual reactors, but the magnitude of the discrepancy (i.e., the *certainty* that the normative and the actual reactor are the same) appears to vary from one society to the next. Further, in all societies examined to date, there is evidence of *relativity* in the correspondence between normative and actual reactors. As a case in point, among the Kapauku Papuans the husband is the normative reactor to the violation of any norm by a married woman. But, as Pospisil observes, some married women dominate their husbands and thereby create a condition wherein someone other than the husband must react to a norm violation by a dominant married woman if a sanction is to be applied.

The limitation of space precludes an articulation of the broader theoretical issues implicit in the study of the degree of certainty and relativity in the relation between normative and actual reactors. However, it should be apparent that these relationships are dependent on varying degrees of consensus and consistency in the three types of reactors and thereby reflect some conditions of variations in political order.

More broadly, the correspondence between normative and actual reactors is a crucial factor in the social organization of normative phenomena. Norms alone are not sufficient for social order; in addition, there must be the recognition of authority to enforce the norms. Whether official or unofficial, formal or informal, the granting of authority appears in the form of normative reactors. But whether or not the authority of normative reactors is actually accepted is largely reflected by the degree of correspondence between normative and actual reactors to deviant conduct.

The Question of Effectiveness

One perennial social problem is summed up in a question which confronts all societies: How should we react to deviation? Since this is a question which calls for a value judgment, it is of no direct concern to the study of social control. However, insofar as one holds that reaction to deviant behavior should be such as to maximize deterrence and rehabilitation, the question is not unrelated to the concepts of the field. As we see it, all ideologies concerning crime and criminals can be described in terms of the formal properties of reaction as described herein. Thus, the classical theory of justice is essentially a plea for minimizing contingency, generality, variation, and relativity, and in so doing to maximize specificity, and differentiation, distinctiveness, and certainty. Exactly the opposite is true for the positivist school, which is now clearly dominant in modern correctional reform.

We do not pass judgment on the merits of either school, but the issue is related to a secondary question in the study of social control: What is the relationship between each of the various properties of reaction to deviant behavior and rehabilitation or deterrence? Stated otherwise and in the terms employed here to analyze social control: What is the reaction of deviants to reaction and what is the reaction of the public to reaction? Needless to say, we do not have the data necessary to provide answers to such questions, and it may well be that they can never be answered satisfactorily. Indeed, we freely entertain the possibility that reaction to deviant behavior is not closely related to the incidence of deviant acts or recidivism. Nonetheless, the conceptual scheme set forth here offers a basis for structuring empirical inquiry on the question.

NOTES

1. Current conceptions for the study of conformity and deviance favor at least two exclusive views of the relation of deviance to reactions. Merton and his elaborators, who view deviant behavior as falling into one of several classes of adaptation, describe deviance in terms of the acts themselves rather than the social reactions to the acts. Consequently, reactions to deviant behavior provide a subject matter independent of the study of the origins and character of deviance. In this regard, Merton states ". . . we can now see the need for a typology of community response *to* deviant behavior comparable to the typology *of* deviant behavior." Robert K. Merton, "Social Conformity, Deviation, and Opportunity-Structures: A Comment on the Contributions of Dubin and Cloward," *American Sociological Review,* 24 (April, 1959), 186. Another view of the relationship between deviance and reaction sees the latter as the criterion of the former. In this regard, Erikson writes: "Deviance is not a property *inherent in* certain forms of behavior; it is a property *conferred upon* these forms by the audiences which directly or indirectly witness them. Sociologically, then, the critical variable in the study of deviance is the social *audience* rather than the individual *person,* since it is the audience which eventually decides whether or not any given action or actions will become a visible case of deviation." Kai T. Erikson, "Notes on the Sociology of Deviance," *Social Problems,* 9 (Spring, 1962), 308. Similarly, Becker believes that ". . . deviance is *not* a quality of the act the person commits, but rather a consequence of the application by others of rules and sanctions to an offender." Howard S. Becker, *Outsiders: Studies in the Sociology of Deviance,* New York: Free Press, 1963, p. 9. A concern for the implications of these differing conceptions is worthy of further elaboration, but for our purposes it is sufficient to point out that the relative merits of these viewpoints are more crucial for the study of deviance than for the study of reactions. Whether deviant behavior can be identified and investigated in terms independent of behavior being labeled as deviant and/or subsequent reactions does not affect the argument that reactions to deviant behavior provide an independent subject matter for the study of social control, which is the primary contention of this article.

2. Edwin M. Lemert, *Social Pathology,* New York: McGraw-Hill, 1951.

3. *Ibid.,* pp. 68–71.

4. *Op. cit.*

5. John I. Kitsuse, "Societal Reaction to Deviant Behavior: Problems of Theory and Method," *Social Problems,* 9 (Winter, 1962), 247–256.

6. Thomas J. Scheff, "The Role of the Mentally Ill and the Dynamics of Mental Disorder: A Research Framework," *Sociometry,* 26 (December, 1963), 436–453.

7. See, e.g., Alfred R. Lindesmith, "Federal Law and Drug Addiction," *Social Problems,* 7 (Summer, 1959), 48–57.

8. See, e.g., August B. Hollingshead and Fredrick C. Redlich, *Social Class and Mental Illness,* New York: Wiley, 1958, and Howard E. Freeman and Ozzie G. Simmons, "Social Class and Post-Hospital Performance Levels," *American Sociological Review,* 24 (June, 1959), 345–351.

9. Clark E. Vincent, "Unmarried Fathers and the Mores: 'Sexual Exploiter' as an Ex Post Facto Label," *American Sociological Review,* 25 (February, 1960), 40–46.

10. As an illustration of predominant concern with the punitiveness of reaction, see Edwin H. Sutherland and Donald R. Cressey, *Principles of Criminology,* 6th ed., Chicago: Lippincott, 1960, chaps. 14–15.

11. There is a tendency to think and write of reaction to deviant behavior as though it is one particular act. Nothing could be more erroneous. Typically, both normative and actual reactions take the form of a sequence of acts and reactors. Thus, to illustrate, the legal reaction (normative or actual) to armed robbery is not just imprisonment. It also involves detection, arrest, trial, conviction, and sentencing, all of which are just as much reactions as imprisonment itself. Concomitantly, there is a series of reactors (police officers, district attorneys, judges, etc.). Indeed, the sequence of reactors and the hierarchy of authority among them is recognized as a property of social control, though not one treated here. Space limitations preclude an adequate treatment of reaction as a process, but it must be understood that we do not view reaction to deviant behavior as an isolated act, even though some of the illustrations may suggest this conception. For an example of an empirical concern with reaction as a process see Elliot G. Mishler and Nancy E. Waxler, "Decision Processes in Psychiatric Hospitalization: Patients Referred, Accepted, and Admitted to a Psychiatric Hospital," *American Sociological Review*, 28 (August, 1963), 576–587.

12. City Council of Boston, *The Colonial Laws of Massachusetts*, Boston: 1887, pp. 80–81. All subsequent references to Colonial Massachusetts are based on this source.

13. Leopold Pospisil, *Kapauku Papuans and Their Law*, Yale University Publications in Anthropology, No. 54, New Haven: Yale University, 1958, pp. 33–34. This illustration indicates that supernatural as well as secular phenomena are included in the concept of reaction. Whether or not the husband actually dies is beside the point, because the reaction is the belief that he will die. Subsequent references to the Kapauku Papuans are based on this source.

14. See, e.g., Harry Elmer Barnes, *The Story of Punishment*, Boston: The Stratford Co., 1930; and William Andrews, *Bygone Punishments*, London: William Andrews and Co., 1899. The most recent systematic attempt to explain variation in reaction to crime is found in Georg Rusche and Otto Kirchheimer, *Punishment and Social Structure*, New York: Columbia University Press, 1939. For a succinct summary of other theories see Sutherland and Cressey, *op. cit.* Durkheim's assertion of an inverse relation between the division of labor and punitive reaction is the best known theory on the subject. However, to date, our research suggests little empirical support for any of the theories, including Durkheim's. For example, by virtually any standard, the reaction to crime or deviant behavior was apparently much milder among the Cheyenne, Kiowa, and Comanche than in medieval Nuremberg. [See K. N. Llewellyn and E. Adamson Hoebel, *The Cheyenne Way*, Norman: University of Oklahoma Press, 1941; Jane Richardson, *Law and Status Among the Kiowa Indians*, New York: J. J. Augustin, 1940; Theodor Hampe, *Crime and Punishment in Germany*, trans. by Malcolm Letts, London: George Routledge, 1929; and Albrecht Keller (ed.), *A Hangman's Diary*, London: Philip Allan, 1928. All subsequent references to the Cheyenne, Kiowa, and to Nuremburg are based on these sources.] For a similar evaluation of Durkheim's observations on punitiveness, see Richard D. Schwartz and James C. Miller, "Legal-Evolution and Societal Complexity," *American Journal of Sociology*, 70 (September, 1964), 166–167.

15. Leon Radzinowicz, *A History of English Criminal Law and Its Administration from 1750*, Vol. I, London: Stevens and Sons, 1948, pp. 4–5. The exact number of capital offenses cannot be stated with certainty because of the composite character of some of the capital statutes.

16. Richard Reifsnyder, "Capital Crimes in the States," *Journal of Criminal Law, Criminology, and Police Science*, 45 (March–April, 1955), 690–693.

17. Jacques Soustelle, *The Daily Life of the Aztecs*, New York: Macmillan, 1962, pp. 156–157.

18. Laurence M. Larson (transl.), *The Earliest Norwegian Laws*, New York: Columbia University Press, 1935, p. 135. The importance of situational factors in differential official reactions to violations of legal norms is investigated in Arthur L. Stinchcombe, "Institutions of Privacy in the Determination of Police Administrative Practice," *American Journal of Sociology*, 69 (September, 1963), 150–160.

19. As a concrete illustration of a lack of consistency between the legal and the evaluative and variation in the degree of consistency, a Gallup poll survey found 51 per cent of a 1960 sample of Americans in favor of the death penalty for murder (the legal norm in the vast majority of the United States), as compared to 68 per cent in 1953 and 62 per cent in 1936. See Grant S. McClellan (ed.), *Capital Punishment*, New York: H. W. Wilson, 1961, pp. 93–96.

20. As one of the very few studies reported in sociological literature see Arnold M. Rose and

Arthur E. Prell, "Does the Punishment Fit the Crime? A Study in Social Valuation," *American Journal of Sociology*, 61 (November, 1955), 247–259.

21. Ronald M. Berndt, *Excess and Restraint*, Chicago: University of Chicago Press, 1962, chap. 9.

22. Comments on the classificatory problem apply to the content of normative as well as actual reactions.

23. The minimum value for the measure of generality is always .00, and the maximum value is 1–1/N, where N is the number of classes of deviant acts.

24. Bureau of Criminal Statistics, State of California, *Crime in California, 1962* (place of publication, publisher, and date of publication not shown), p. 131.

25. Formula for the degree of variation: $1-[\Sigma X^2/(\Sigma X)^2]$, where X is the number of actual reactions of a particular type to the offense in question. See footnote 31. The minimum value in this instance is .00 and the maximum value is .89.

26. Formula: $\Sigma|X\text{-}Y|/2$, where X is the per cent of actual reactions of a certain type in a given offense category, and Y is the corresponding per cent for *all* reactions. The formula yields the minimum per cent of the cases that would have had to have received a different sentence to realize a condition of no difference from one reaction category to the next in the distribution of cases among offense categories. Measures reported here are standardized in that the percentages are based on 1,000 cases in each reaction category distributed in proportion to the actual number of cases. This standardization eliminates numerical differences from one reaction category to the next.

27. The measure for the degree of differentiation is exactly like the measure of distinctiveness, except it applies to the distribution of cases among reaction categories.

28. For a brief summary of studies on the subject see James F. Short, Jr., and F. Ivan Nye, "Extent of Unrecorded Juvenile Delinquency: Tentative Conclusions," *Journal of Criminal Law, Criminology, and Police Science*, 49 (November–December, 1958), 296–302.

29. Freeman and Simmons, *op. cit.*, p. 350. For observations on the sex of deviants and reaction to symptoms of mental illness, see Derek L. Phillips, "Rejection of the Mentally Ill: The Influence of Behavior and Sex," *American Sociological Review*, 29 (October, 1964), 679–687.

30. Derek L. Phillips, "Rejection: A Possible Consequence of Seeking Help for Mental Disorders," *American Sociological Review*, 28 (December, 1963), 963–972.

31. Radzinowicz, *op. cit.*, pp. 158–159.

32. Cambridge Department of Criminal Science, *Sexual Offenses*, London: Macmillan, 1957, chaps. 2–4. For evidence that situational factors affect variations in arrests and convictions in the U.S. see Stinchcombe, *op. cit.*

33. For an example of an instance in which the certainty of non-normative reactions is relative to characterisitcs of the normative reactors, see Thomas J. Scheff, "The Societal Reaction to Deviance: Ascriptive Elements in the Psychiatric Screening of Mental Patients in a Midwestern State," *Social Problems*, 11 (Spring, 1964), 401–413.

34. Marvin E. Wolfgang, *et al.*, "Comparison of the Executed and the Commuted Among Admissions to Death Row," *Journal of Criminal Law, Criminology, and Police Science*, 53 (September, 1962), 301–311.

35. E. Adamson Hoebel, *The Law of Primitive Man*, Cambridge: Harvard University Press, 1954, chap. 5. All subsequent references to the Eskimo are based on this source.

36. Julius Cohen, *et al.*, *Parental Authority: The Community and the Law*, New Brunswick, New Jersey: Rutgers University Press, 1958, pp. 81–82.

37. The establishment of juvenile courts is actually a step toward greater contingency in the organization of normative reactors.

38. Several recent investigations of actual reactors in the reaction process are: Howard E. Freeman and Ozzie G. Simmons, "Feelings of Stigma Among Relatives of Former Mental Patients," *Social Problems*, 8 (Spring, 1961), 312–321; Edwin M. Lemert, "Paranoia and the Dynamics of Exclusion," *Sociometry*, 25 (March, 1962), 2–20; Harold Sampson, *et al.*, "The

Mental Hospital and Marital Family Ties," *Social Problems,* 3 (Fall, 1961), 141–155; and Richard D. Schwartz and Jerome H. Skolnick, "Two Studies of Legal Stigma," *Social Problems,* 10 (Fall, 1962), 133–142.

39. See, e.g., Elliott M. Rudwick, "The Negro Policeman in the South," *Journal of Criminal Law, Criminology, and Police Science,* 51 (July–August, 1960), 273–276.

40. Measures for these properties as they apply to actual reactors are identical to those previously described for actual reactions.

41. Cambridge Department of Criminal Science, *op. cit.,* p. 29.

60. DILEMMAS OF POLICE ADMINISTRATION

JAMES Q. WILSON

Policemen are the agents of formalized social control. They are given a variety of tasks to perform but underlying them all are the maintenance of order and the enforcement of the law. While the latter is fairly clear cut, the former is not. What constitutes order, and (if one follows the arguments presented in the previous article by Clark and Gibbs) whose order is to be followed?

James Q. Wilson discusses these matters in terms of dilemmas faced by police administrators and differential views of the police functions by varying segments of the community.

The author is Professor of Political Science at Harvard University. A specialist in the field of urban government, his books include Negro Politics: Search for Leadership *(1960),* Amateur Democrat *(1962), and* Varieties of Police Behavior *(1968). He is also editor of the anthology,* Urban Renewal: The Record and the Controversy *(1966),* The Metropolitan Enigma *(1968), and coeditor, with Edward C. Banfield, of* City Politics *(1963).*

Policy making for the police is complicated by the fact that, at least in large cities, the police department is an organization with at least two objectives, one of which produces conflict and the other of which cannot be attained.[1] The dilemmas facing police administrators arise out of their inability to obtain agreement on what constitutes satisfactory performance of the first objective, and their difficulty in finding a strategy which would permit the realization of the (agreed-upon) second objective. (There are, of course, additional objectives which a police department serves—providing certain nonpolice services and handling large-scale disorders, for example. . . .)

Objectives

The first objective I call *order maintenance*—the handling of disputes, or behavior which threatens to produce disputes, among persons who disagree over what ought to be right or seemly conduct or over the assignment of blame for what is agreed to be wrong or unseemly conduct. A family quarrel, a noisy drunk, a tavern brawl, a street disturbance by teenagers, the congregation on the sidewalk of idle young men (especially in eccentric clothes or displaying an unconventional demeanor)—all these are cases in which citizens disagree as whether or how the police should intervene. If the police do intervene, one party or another is likely to feel harassed, outraged, or neglected. Though a law may have been broken, as with an assault inflicted by a husband on his wife, the police do not perceive their responsibilities as involving simply the comparing of a particular behavior to a clear legal standard and making an arrest if the standard has been violated. For one thing, the legal rule is, in many order-

Reprinted from *Public Administration Review,* bimonthly journal of the American Society for Public Administration, **28,** 5 (September/October 1968), 407–417, by permission of the author and publisher.

maintenance cases, ambiguous. A "breach of the peace" implies a prior definition of "peace," and this is a matter on which persons commonly disagree. For another thing, even when the legal standard is clear enough—as with an assault—the "victim" is often not innocent (indeed, he may have called for the police because he was losing a fight he started) and thus the question of *blame* may be to the participants more important than the question of "guilt" and they will expect the officer to take this into account. Finally, most order-maintenance situations do not result in an arrest—the parties involved wish the officer to "do something" that will "settle things," but they often do not wish to see that settlement entail on arrest. And in any case the infraction is likely to be a misdemeanor and thus, in many states, the officer cannot make a valid arrest unless the illegality was committed in his presence or unless the victim is willing to sign a complaint. As a result, the officer cannot expect a judge to dispose of the case; the former must devise a substantive solution for a disorderly event which the latter will never hear of.

The second objective is *law enforcement*—the application of legal sanctions, usually by means of an arrest, to persons who injure or deprive innocent victims. A burglary, purse snatch, mugging, robbery, or auto theft are usually crimes committed by strangers on persons who did not provoke the attack. Though there is, in these matters, a problem of finding the guilty party, once guilt is established there is no question of blame. For almost all such law-enforcement situations, the officer is expected to either make an arrest or act so as to prevent the violation from occurring in the first place. His task is the seemingly ministerial and technical act of either apprehending or deterring the criminal. The difficulty is that the officer lacks the means —the information, primarily—to apprehend or deter more than a very small fraction of all criminals. Leaving aside murder, rape, and aggravated assault—in

which a high proportion of suspects are known or even related to their victims— few major crimes such as burglary and robbery that are of primary concern to the citizen are "cleared by arrest." In 1965 only 38 per cent of all *known* robberies and 25 per cent of all *known* burglaries were cleared by arrest, and even that figure is artificially high. The household victimization study done by the National Opinion Research Center for the President's Commission on Law Enforcement and Administration of Justice [2] showed that in 1965 there were over three times as many burglaries and 50 per cent more robberies than were reported to and recorded by the police; thus, the adjusted clearance rates are only about 8 per cent for burglary and 24 per cent for robbery. But even those figures may be too high, for, as Skolnick points out, there are often strong organizational pressures leading detectives to induce arrested burglars and robbers to "cop out" to as many offenses as possible in order to boost the clearance rate.[3]

There is, of course, no way to measure the number of crimes prevented by police activity, but the number is not likely to be large. Crimes of passion that occur in private places (many, if not most, murders, rapes, and serious assaults are in this category) probably happen at a rate independent of the nature or intensity of police activity. Crimes of stealth, such as burglary and many forms of larceny, may in unknown ways be affected by police activity, but the effect is probably not great—no city, whatever its police strategy, has been able to show any dramatic reversal in the rising rates of reported thefts. There is some evidence that certain kinds of street crimes—muggings, purse snatches, holdups of taxi and bus drivers, and the like—can be reduced by very intensive police patrol, the use of officers disguised as cabbies or lady shoppers, the formation of citizen auxiliaries, and the like. But even with these crimes, which surely are the ones most disturbing to the average person, two problems exist. First, no one is confident that what appears to be a reduction is not in fact a displacement of crime (to other places or to other forms of crime), or that if a reduction genuinely occurs it will persist over time.[4] And second, the kinds of police activities apparently best adapted to suppressing street crime—intensive patrols, close surveillance of "suspicious" persons, frequent street stops of pedestrians and motorists, and so on—are precisely those most likely to place the police in conflict with important segments of the community—primarily with persons who because of their age, race, or social class are regarded (and, as far as the evidence goes, correctly regarded) as most likely to commit criminal acts. In short, in the one aspect of law enforcement where there may be opportunities for substantial deterrence, the police are obliged to act in a way which, like their actions in order-maintenance situations, is most likely to bring them into conflict with the citizen.

The dilemmas of police administration arise out of the difficulty confronting a chief who seeks policies which can guide his men in performing the order-maintenance function and a technique which will prove efficacious in serving the law-enforcement function. The conflict over how the police should behave in order-maintenance cases results from differing expectations as to the appropriate level of public or private order and differing judgments over what constitutes a just resolution of a given dispute. In a homogeneous community, where widely shared norms define both the meaning of order and the standards of justice (who is equal to whom and in what sense), the police role is comparatively simple. But where the community, usually because of differences of class or race, has no common normative framework, the police have no reliable guides to action and efforts to devise such guides will either be half-hearted or sources of important public controversy. The conflict that arises over the perform-

ance of the law-enforcement function, on the other hand, arises out of the lack of any technique by which crime can be reduced significantly and without incurring high costs in terms of other values—privacy, freedom, and so forth. The dispute about the law-enforcement function is, unlike the dispute over order maintenance, not over ends but over means.

Criticisms

Organizations to which society gives tasks that cannot be performed to the satisfaction of society suffer not only certain frustrations but some fundamental administrative problems as well. The criticisms directed at the police are well known and often sound, but conditions giving rise to these criticisms are frequently not well understood by the critic. For example, police departments are frequently charged with hiring unqualified personnel, suppressing or manipulating crime reports, condoning the use of improper or illegal procedures, using patrol techniques that create tensions and irritation among the citizens, and either over-reacting (using too much force too quickly) or under-reacting (ignoring dangerous situations until it is too late) in the face of incipient disorder. All of these criticisms are true to some extent, though the extent of the deficiencies is often exaggerated. But let us concede for the moment that they are all true. Why are they true?

Explanations vary, but commonly they are some variation on the "bad men" theme. Unqualified, unintelligent, rude, brutal, intolerant, or insensitive men, so this theory goes, find their way (or are selectively recruited into) police work where they express their prejudices and crudeness under color of the law. Though a few of the commanding officers of the department may try to improve matters, on the whole they are ineffective. At best they invent paper palliatives—empty departmental directives, superficial community relations program, one-sided internal disciplinary units—which do little more than offer a chance for issuing favorable, but misleading, publicity statements about the "new look." And at worst, the theory continues, such administrators exacerbate tensions by encouraging, in the name of efficiency or anti-crime strategies, various techniques, such as aggressive preventive patrol, that lead to the harassment of innocent citizens. The solution for these problems is, clearly, to hire "better men" —college graduates, Negroes, men who can pass tests that weed out "authoritarian" personalities, and the like. And those on the force should attend universities, go through sensitivity training, and apply for grants to develop "meaningful" community relations programs.[5]

Some critics go even further. Not only do the police fail to do the right thing, they systematically do the wrong thing. Not only do the police fail to prevent crime, *the police actually cause crime.* Not only do the police fail to handle riots properly, *the police cause riots.* Presumably, things might improve if we had no police at all, but since even the strongest critics usually recognize the need for the police under some circumstances, they are willing to permit the police to function provided that they are under "community control"—controlled, that is, by the neighborhoods (especially Negro neighborhoods) where they operate. If police departments are at best a necessary evil, filled with inept or intolerant men exploiting the fact that they are necessary, then the solution to the problem of abuse is to put the police under the strictest and closest control of those whose activities they are supposed to regulate.

The view taken in this paper is quite different from at least the more extreme of these arguments. If all big-city police departments were filled tomorrow with Negro college graduates and placed under the control of the neighborhoods they are supposed to control, most of the problems that exist today would continue to exist

and some in fact might get worse. The crime rate would not go down; indeed, owing to police timidity about making arrests among people who have a voice in their management, it might go up marginally. Police involvement in conflict and disorder would have no happier outcomes, because most disorder—family or neighbor quarrels—does not involve the community nor would the community necessarily have any better idea how to resolve it than do the police now. Perceived police abuse and harassment might decline in the neighborhood, but since each neighborhood would have its own police, the amount of abuse and harassment perceived by a person from one neighborhood entering a different neighborhood (say a Negro entering a white area, or vice versa) might increase. The conflict between neighborhood residents who want more police protection (small businessmen, home-owners, older people) and those who want less (teenagers, transients, young men hanging on street corners) would remain and the police would tend, in the eyes of one group, to serve the standards of the other.

There would, of course, be some improvements. The police might have better information about the neighborhood if they were controlled by it and thus, in the event of largescale disorders, be able to distinguish more accurately between solid citizens and troublemakers. They might also be more alert to the customs of the area and thus prepared to tolerate behavior (street-corner gatherings, loud noises) which the neighborhood tolerates, even though in other places such behavior might be regarded as breaches of the peace. And college-educated men might display more civility in routine encounters, handling incidents more impersonally and people more politely.

But it is difficult to say that such gains would be more than marginal. Some police departments (such as those on the West Coast) already have large numbers of men with some college training, but these departments (Oakland and Los Angeles, for example) are frequently criticized by Negroes for being "too tough," "too impersonal," "gung ho," and the like. (There may be no causal relation between police education and Negro criticism, but it is possible that while college men are more civil, they also have a stronger sense of duty.) It is not clear that departments with large numbers of Negroes patrolling Negro areas have experienced less community tension than departments with few Negroes, or that in any given encounter a Negro officer behaves much differently from a white one. This is not an argument against hiring Negro police officers; on the contrary, there are in my view compelling reasons for having as many as possible patrolling Negro areas. But their value would, in my opinion, be primarily symbolic (no less important for that!) and their presence would not make substantially easier the policy-making or administrative problems of the police. Nor are the consequences of different patrol and community relations policies clear. Some departments (San Francisco, Chicago) have made a major community relations effort, but they seem to fare no better than those (such as Philadelphia or Albany) with a "get tough" policy. Departments which use aggressive preventive patrol and have strict traffic enforcement policies (such as Los Angeles) produce criticism and experience disorders, but so do departments (such as Boston) which are less aggressive or strict. Though there are these differences in police practices,[6] it is not clear how they affect the management of order, the enforcement of laws, or the maintenance of good community relations.

Nature of Police Function

The difficulty in managing the police arises, in my view, less from the quality of men recruited or the level at which authority is exercised and more from the nature of the police function. Mental hospitals provide a useful comparison to the police in this regard. Like the police, they are regarded as essential; like the police, they are routinely and repeatedly condemned for failures and inadequacies. The indictment of such institutions found, for example, in Ivan Belknap's book, has become commonplace.[7] The appalling conditions to be found in hospital wards, the apparent callousness and brutality of the staff, the denial of rights and privileges, the shortage of qualified psychiatric and medical staff, and (equally important) the inability of such professional staff as exists to control the practices of the hospital— all these circumstances have been described, and the accounts are no doubt in large measure correct. Repeated efforts at reform have been made. Budgets have been increased, hospitals have been reorganized, better-qualified personnel have been sought, staff services have been increased, and volumes of research have been published. And yet each decade sees essentially the same lamentable conditions exposed and the same indignation unleashed. With the failure of successive reform efforts, the prescriptions have become more radical. At first the need was thought to be for "better men" and "more money." Then the attack shifted to the professional staff itself—doctors and others were charged with "causing" mental illness, or at least retarding its elimination. The hospital was administration-centered; it should become patient-centered.[8]

In an incisive review of the literature on mental hospitals, Perrow concludes that the reason for the failure of reform has not been bad men or low budgets or improper organization or incompetent management (though all of those things may exist); the central problem is that we do not know how to cure mental illness. The problem is not one of ideology, but of technology. The hospitals are given a task they cannot perform, yet they must try to perform it, for the alternative (doing nothing) seems even worse.[9] The most important recent improvement in mental hospital care was the result of an advance in medical technology—the development of tranquilizer drugs. Changes in organization, leadership, and in the men recruited to hospital tasks have rarely produced significant or lasting results from the patient's point of view. To be sure, some hospitals manage to treat the inmates humanely— these are often small, heavily staffed hospitals with patients who can afford the high costs of such facilities. Bestial practices can be eliminated, but it costs a lot of money and requires large concentrations of scarce talent. But even in these circumstances, the improvement in the mental health of the patient does not seem to be much greater than whatever improvement occurs in less intensive (and less expensive) programs.[10]

The parallel with the police is striking. Abusive practices or indifference to citizen needs can be eliminated, but it typically requires a community that (like the intensive-treatment hospital) is small, expensive, and cooperative. In short, it requires a middle- or upper-middle class suburb. Some advocates of community control over the police argue that it is the close supervision of the police by the suburban community that accounts for the good relations between police and citizens to be found there; if one duplicates those political conditions in the central city—if one, in short, "suburbanizes" the central-city neighborhoods—comparable improvements in police-citizen relations will occur. My research suggests that it is not the degree or kind of control that produces this effect in the suburbs, it is the class composition of the community. In a homogeneous, middle-class suburb there is relatively little public disorder; consequently the police rarely need intervene in situations of high conflict, and thus rarely need become parties to conflict. When the chief law enforcement problem involves crimes of stealth (burglary and larceny) rather than street crimes (assaults, robberies, muggings), the police need not practice aggressive preventive patrol or otherwise keep persons on the streets under close surveillance; accordingly, it is rare for a suburban resident walking the streets at night to feel he is being "harassed." Finally, a socially homogeneous middle-class area provides the police with relative unambiguous cues as to who should be regarded as a "suspicious person" and thus who should be made the object of police attention. Teenagers hanging around a suburban ice-cream parlor late at night or a Negro in the back alley of an all-white residential community would be viewed suspiciously by the police and citizenry alike. Though this suspicion may be, in the particular case, unjust to the teenagers or the Negro, acting on the basis of it does not bring the police into conflict with the community. (But though an affluent suburb may provide the conditions that reduce the likelihood of police-citizen conflict or of police abuses of their authority, it does not provide the conditions that make the management of such disorder as exists or the prevention of such crimes as occur any easier. In short, high-status communities permit the police to solve their ideological but not their technological problems.)

The policy implications of this argument are clear, though gloomy. Substantial and lasting improvements in police-community relations are not likely until and unless there is a substantial and lasting change in the class composition of the central city population—i.e., until the street-crime rate and the incidence of public disorder in the central cities becomes closer to that in the middle-class suburbs. Only then will it be possible to reduce substantially the police-community tension generated by practices like aggressive preventive patrol and the use of gross indicators such as race and apparent class as clues to criminal potential.

Racial Complication

Race complicates the issue, of course, and renders it more explosive. A black person is more likely to be regarded as lower-class or otherwise suspicious than a white person, and thus a law-abiding and peaceful Negro is more likely to be treated as if he were potentially lawless and disorderly than an equivalent white person. Innocent Negroes so treated will naturally feel a deep sense of injustice. It is sometimes argued that this would not happen if police officers were not prejudiced. No doubt many officers are prejudiced (indeed, one study indicates that the vast majority are) and this prejudice may make matters worse.[11] But the crucial point is that large numbers of innocent Negroes would still be treated in (to them) unjust ways even if all policemen were entirely free of race prejudice so long as a disproportionate number of Negroes are lower class. Violent crime and disorder are predominantly (though not exclusively) lower-class phenomena;[12] Negroes are disproportionally (though far from exclusively) lower class; a black skin, therefore, will continue to be a statistically defensible (though individually unjust) cue that triggers an officer's suspicion. Among the consequences of this generalization will be continued police suspicion of blacks and continued Negro antagonism toward the police.

The point is perhaps more easily understood if we examine other cues to which police respond and other forms of prejudice which they may have. Young people commit a disproportionate share of many kinds of crime, especially crimes against property. Being young is therefore a statistically useful cue to an officer who is scanning a population in search of persons more likely than others to commit, or to have committed, a crime. In addition, it is quite possible that the police have "youth prejudice"—that is, they may impute to young people even more criminality than in fact they possess, just as officers having race prejudice impute to Negroes more criminality than in fact they display. But if all officers were cured of "youth prejudice," young people would still be singled out for special attention and suspicion. The difference, of course, is that young people outgrow their youth, while Negroes cannot outgrow their blackness.

The best evidence that race prejudice is not the crucial factor can be found in the behavior of Negro police officers. There has been no systematic study of such men, but my observations suggest that black policemen are as suspicious and tough in black neighborhoods as white officers. Indeed, in the long run Negroes have an advantage over youth. It may be possible to improve the class position of Negroes so that the crime rates found among them will be no higher (and perhaps even lower) than the rates found among whites. Then there will be no reason, other than prejudice, why an officer would treat a Negro differently from a white. By contrast, there is probably no way even in principle to reduce greatly the crimogenic properties of youth and therefore no way even in principle to make the police less suspicious of young people.

If the fundamental problem is one of class (admittedly greatly complicated by the problem of race), what can a police administrator do in the short run while he waits for society somehow to solve the class problem? If the point of view presented here is correct, not a great deal. But since even marginal gains are desirable when conditions are (or are widely thought to be) deplorable, it is worth considering palliatives however slight may be their benefits.

First, the police should recognize clearly that order maintenance is their central function—central both in the demands it makes on time and resources and in the opportunities it affords for making a difference in the lives of the citizens. Hunting criminals both occupies less time (at least for the patrolmen) and provides fewer chances for decisive action. How well disputes are settled may depend crucially on how competent, knowledgeable, and sensitive the police are; how fast the crime rate mounts is much less dependent on the level and nature of police activity. (As will be argued below, other than by reducing the size of the lower class the best way society can affect the crime rate may be through the court and correctional systems rather than through the police.)

Order-Maintenance Function

A police department that places order maintenance uppermost in its priorities will judge patrolmen less by their arrest records and more by their ability to keep the peace on their beat. This will require, in turn, that sergeants and other supervisory personnel concern themselves more with how the patrolmen function in family fights, teenage disturbances, street corner brawls, and civil disorders, and less with how well they take reports at the scene of burglary or how many traffic tickets they issue during a tour of duty. Order maintenance also requires that the police have available a wider range of options for handling disorder than is afforded by the choice between making an arrest and doing nothing. Detoxification centers should be available as an alternative to jail for drunks. Family-service units should be formed which can immediately assist patrolmen handling domestic quarrels. Community-service officers should be available to provide information, answer complaints, and deal with neighborhood tensions and rumors.

Patrolmen who are given the order-maintenance function will obviously require a great deal of information about their beats—more than can be obtained by riding around in a patrol car or rotating frequently among several beats. Obtaining this knowledge will be made easier by the decentralization of the patrol function so that local commanders deal with local conditions subject to general policy guidelines from the police administrator. This decentralization need not always take the form of proliferating precinct station houses—these facilities, as traditionally

used for mustering the watch, jailing prisoners, and keeping records, are expensive. Many of them, indeed, were built in a period when patrolmen, like firemen, slept in when they had night duty. Smaller, less elaborate, and more numerous "storefront" police offices scattered throughout central-city neighborhoods might prove more effective and less expensive. Officers assigned to a particular neighborhood ought to remain in that area for long periods of time, rather than experience frequent rotation among neighborhoods. An even more radical experiment might be to assess the value of having patrolmen actually live in certain key areas. For example, some officers might be encouraged, on a volunteer basis, to live in public housing projects. To make such an assignment more attractive and to increase the pay of the officer, he could be given the apartment rent-free or at a substantial discount.

Such decentralization of function requires the strengthening of the command system if it is not to produce inconsistent behavior, political intervention, and corruption. Supervisory officers, especially watch commanders, ought to have more authority to assign, direct, and evaluate their officers. Mechanical, fixed assignments and evaluation solely by written examinations decrease the possibility of inducing patrolmen to take seriously their order-maintenance function and lead them instead to emphasize following the safe routine, memorizing the penal code and departmental rule book, and "pushing paper"—filing reports, writing tickets, and so forth.

At the same time, if patrolmen are expected to devote themselves primarily to the most conflict-laden, unpleasant parts of their task, there must be rewards available that are commensurate with the burdens. At present, the major rewards open to the patrolman—promotion, higher pay, specialized duty—all take him out of the patrol force and place him in supervisory posts, criminal investigation, or headquarters staff units. If the patrol function is the most important and difficult job in the department, the best men ought to be rewarded for doing it well in ways that leave them *in* the patrol force and on the street. It should be possible to obtain substantial pay increases while remaining a patrolman, just as it is now possible to win higher salaries in the Federal Bureau of Investigation while remaining a special agent.

Getting good men to serve, not only in the police department, but in those police roles that are the most demanding, may produce only a marginal gain, but we are largely ignorant of how to achieve even that. Almost no systematic research has been done to define and measure those qualities characteristic of officers best able to keep the peace. Entrance examination in many states and cities may not measure any relevant quality other than (perhaps) general literacy, familiarity with a police handbook, or some knowledge of current events. Indeed, there is hardly any evidence that they measure even these traits very accurately. How—or indeed, whether—such tests can be more useful is a matter on which we know very little, and perhaps a modest amount of research would be in order (though I would not be surprised if such research turned out to be inconclusive).

Policy Statements

If able men are found and assigned to neighborhood patrol forces under conditions that will facilitate their understanding of neighborhood conditions and personalities and if they are rewarded for successful performance of the peace-keeping function, what in concrete terms will these men actually do? How, in short, does one keep the peace? Some have argued that police departments ought to develop and issue policy statements that will give some guidance to officers who must necessarily exercise wide discretion

with respect to matters where legal codes contain few applicable rules.[13] To the extent this is possible, of course it should be done, and it is not being done at all in many departments. But it would be a mistake to assume that policies can be found that will provide meaningful guides to action in most situations of real or potential disorder. The most feasible rules perhaps are those which tell the patrolman what *not* to do—don't use racial epithets, don't hit a man except in self-defense, don't grasp a man's arm or shoulder unless it is necessary to complete an arrest or prevent violence, and so forth. But relatively few rules can be devised that tell a patrolman what he *should* do with quarrelling lovers, angry neighbors, or disputatious drunks. This is not because the police have had little experience with such matters (on the contrary!) or even because they do know in a given case what to do (they may), but because so much depends on the particular circumstances of time, place, event, and personality. No psychiatrist would attempt to produce, much less use, a "how-to-do-it" manual for these cases, and he has the advantage of dealing with people at his leisure, over long periods of time, and in moments of relative calm. The best that can be done is to list "factors to be taken into account," but in the concrete case everything depends on *how* they are taken into account.

In the broadest terms, the patrolman in performing his order-maintenance function is neither a bureaucrat nor a professional, and thus neither increased bureaucratization nor increased professionalism will be of much value. He is not a bureaucrat in that he does not and cannot apply general rules to specific cases—there are no general rules, and thus his discretion is wide. (In performing his law-enforcement function, by contrast, he can act more nearly like a bureaucrat—the legal rules defining a crime are relatively unambiguous and the officer's discretion, especially if it is a serious crime, is narrow.) On the other hand, the patrolman is not a professional—there is no organized group of practitioners (as there is with doctors or physicists) who can impart to him by education certain information and equip him by apprenticeship with certain arts and skills that will make him competent to serve a "client" when the latter cannot be the sole judge of the quality of the service he receives. Nor do such external reference groups (professional societies) exist to certify that the patrolman is competent or to make him subject to a code of ethics and a sense of duty.

The patrolman is neither a bureaucrat nor a professional, but a member of a *craft*. As with most crafts, there is no generalized, written body of special knowledge; learning is by apprenticeship, but the apprenticeship takes place on the job rather than in an academy; the primary reference group from which the apprentice wins (or fails to win) respect are his colleagues on the job, not fellow members of his discipline wherever they may be; and the members, conscious of having a special skill or task, think of themselves as set apart from society and in need of restrictions on entry. But unlike other members of a craft—carpenters, for example, or journalists—the police work in an environment that is usually apprehensive and often hostile, and they produce no product (like a finished house or a well-written newspaper) the value of which is evident and easily judged.

An attempt to change a craft into a bureaucracy will be perceived by the members as a failure of confidence and a withdrawal of support and thus strongly resisted; efforts to change them into a profession will be seen as irrelevant and thus in great part ignored. Such gains as can be made in the way the police handle citizens are not likely to come primarily from either proliferating rules (i.e., bureaucratizing the police) or sending officers to colleges, special training programs, or human relations institutes (i.e., "professionalizing" the police). Instead, the most significant changes will be in organization

and leadership in order to increase the officer's familiarity with and sensitivity to the neighborhod he patrols and rewarding him for doing what is judged (necessarily after the fact) to be the right thing rather than simply the "efficient" thing.

Law-Enforcement Function

These recommendations leave out of account the law-enforcement function of the police. This has been deliberate, partly because the crook-catching, crime-stopping function is so often exaggerated. But obviously there is a law-enforcement function, and it is in any given case hard to separate from the order-maintenance function. Law enforcement ideally should be organized differently from order maintenance, however. It is, for example, more suitably managed through centralized command structures, the issuance of explicit rules, and the specialization of tasks (burglary details, homicide details, traffic enforcement divisions, and so forth). Perhaps a police department should make the two functions even more separate than they are now. For example, there is some impressionistic evidence that such tactics worsen police-community relations.[14] Perhaps the roving patrol force should be composed of men different from those in the neighborhood patrol force, so that the tensions created by the former could be directed away from the role performed by the latter. Or perhaps intensive street patrol in a particular area could be done under the guidance of and on the basis of tactical intelligence furnished by neighborhood patrol officers who are best able to distinguish between innocent and suspicious behavior and between decent citizens and "bad actors."

But in crime prevention not too much should be expected of the police. I doubt that any deployment, any strategy, or any organizational principles will permit the police to make more than a slight or temporary reduction in the rate of most common crimes. As the police themselves are fond of saying, "we don't cause crime," and, as I would like to see them add, "we can't stop crime." They can and should make arrests and they can and should investigate suspicious circumstances. But I know of no police administrator who is optimistic that they can make more than marginal gains, however they behave. It would be well, therefore, not to "oversell" proposed improvements in police manpower, organization, training, equipment, or tactics. Already too many citizens share the rather dangerous view that if only we "unleashed" the police we could "stop crime"—dangerous because if we act on that assumption we are likely to produce only frustrated expectations and deeper passions.

Indeed, it might be well if we shifted the focus of our legitimate concern to the behavior of those institutions that dispose of criminals once arrested—the courts and the correctional and probation systems. For all offenses other than the most trivial, the vast majority of the persons processed by these institutions are repeaters. According to one estimate, 87.5 per cent of all persons arrested for nontraffic offenses have been arrested before.[15] The average person arrested will be arrested 7.6 times in his lifetime.[16] The problem of recidivism is obviously of the greatest importance—if we fail to induce a person after his first arrest to avoid crime, there is a strong chance we will have to arrest him six or seven more times; how many more times we *should* arrest him for crimes we do not learn of is anyone's

guess. In the simplest cost-effective terms, a dollar invested in the right correctional program is likely to have a higher marginal product than a dollar invested in the right police program.

But what is the "right program"? Do we have a correctional technology capable of significantly reducing the recidivism rate? I am not sure we do, or that we ever will, but I suspect that we have not tried very hard to find out. There have been some promising experiments with community-based, heavily staffed programs in California, Utah, and New Jersey, but there appears to be little organized effort to repeat these experiments elsewhere, or if they are repeated to evaluate them rigorously, or if they are evaluated to institutionalize what we learn from them.[17] In our preoccupation with the crime problem, we have come to identify it either as wholly a "social" problem (which can only be solved in three or four generations by programs which might—no one quite seems to be sure how—eliminate the lower classes) or as a "police" problem which can be solved only by taking the "handcuffs" off the police and "cracking down." I am certainly not opposed to ameliorating social problems or to increasing public support for the police, but I would like to see at least an equivalent amount of attention given to improving the way existing institutions now manage the offenders who have already shown by their actions that antipoverty programs are yet to have a therapeutic effect, and by their appearance in court that they have not managed to escape the police.

NOTES

1. This article is in part adapted from material that will appear in my book-length study of the police, *Varieties of Police Behavior,* Cambridge: Harvard University Press, forthcoming.

2. Philip H. Ennis, *Criminal Victimization in the United States,* a report to the President's Commission on Law Enforcement and Administration of Justice, Washington, D.C.: U.S. Government Printing Office, 1967, p. 13.

3. See Jerome H. Skolnick, *Justice Without Trial,* New York: Wiley, 1966, pp. 167–181.

4. A "get-tough" policy by the police in Miami was reported to have led to a drop in street crimes, at least in one area of the city (*The New York Times,* February 19, 1968). When off-duty police officers began to work as taxi drivers in New York City, there was a drop in the number of robberies and assaults against cabbies (*The New York Times,* February 20, 1968).

After the stories appeared, however, it was reported that these street crimes had begun to show an increase, though they had not yet risen to the level they attained before the counter-measures were adopted. We know very little about how great a reduction in crime is the result of criminal perceptions of police intent and how much the result of the direct consequences of police actions, nor have we tried (except in a very few cases) to measure the persistence of such improvement as does occur.

5. Various proposals for changing police practices are reported in the President's Commission on Law Enforcement and Administration of Justice *Task Force Report: The Police,* Washington, D.C.: U.S. Government Printing Office, 1967, p. xi, and the National Advisory Commission on Civil Disorders *Report,* Washington, D.C.: U.S. Government Printing Office, 1968, chapter XI.

6. Differences in patrol styles or strategies are described and to some degree explained in Wilson, *op. cit.,* chapters IV–VII.

7. Ivan Belknap, *Human Problems of a State Mental Hospital,* New York: McGraw-Hill, 1956. It is striking to note the similarities between Belknap's description of mental hospital attendants and my description of patrolmen in large cities—see especially Belknap, pp. 115, 116, 138, 152, 154, and 170.

8. See the excellent analysis in Charles Perrow's "Hospitals: Technology, Structure, and Goals," in James G. March's (ed.) *Handbook of Organizations,* Chicago: Rand McNally, 1965, pp. 916–946; and the accounts of certain "elite" hospitals practicing "milieu therapy" in W. Caudill's *The Psychiatric Hospital as a Small Society,* Cambridge: Harvard University Press, 1958; R. N. Rapoport, et al., *Community as Doctor,* London: Tavistock, 1960; and A. H. Stanton and M. S. Schwartz's *The Mental Hospital,* New York: Basic Books, 1954.

9. See Perrow, *op. cit.,* pp. 925, 926, 930, 934.

10. Rapoport, et al., *op. cit.,* p. 208.

11. Donald J. Black and Albert J. Reiss, Jr., "Patterns in Police and Citizen Transactions," in *Studies of Crime and Law Enforcement in Major Metropolitan Areas,* a report to the President's Commission on Law Enforcement and Administration of Justice, Washington, D.C.: U.S. Government Printing Office, 1967, Vol. II, Section I, 132–139. Observers working under the direction of Black and Reiss in Boston, Chicago, and Washington, D.C. reported that 72 per cent of all white officers and 28 per cent of all Negro officers volunteered "highly prejudiced" or "prejudiced" comments about Negroes. There was, however, no clear relationship between attitude and behavior: "A recurring theme in the observer's reports was the great disparity between the verbalized attitudes of officers in the privacy of the patrol car, and the public conduct of officers in encounters with Negroes and members of other minority groups" (p. 138). After observing police behavior, Black and Reiss conclude that "Policemen generally do not disproportionately behave aggressively or negatively toward Negroes," though they do "disproportionately behave amiably or positively toward white citizens" (p. 56).

12. A good summary of the evidence on the disproportionately lower-class origin of assaultive crime is Marvin E. Wolfgang's *Crimes of Violence,* a report to the President's Commission on Law Enforcement and Administration of Justice (1967), pp. 166–169. Additional evidence based on direct observation can be found in Walter B. Miller's "Violent Crimes in City Gangs," *Annals,* Vol. 364 (March 1966), 96–112, and "Theft Behavior in City Gangs," in Malcolm W. Klein's *Juvenile Gangs in Context,* Englewood Cliffs, N.J.: Prentice-Hall, 1967, p. 34.

13. See President's Commission on Law Enforcement and Administration of Justice, *Task Force Report: The Police,* Washington, D.C.: U.S. Government Printing Office, 1967, pp. 21–27.

14. *Report* of the National Advisory Commission on Civil Disorders (1968), chapter 11.

15. Ronald Christensen, "Projected Percentage of U.S. Population With Criminal Arrest and Conviction Records," in President's Commission on Law Enforcement and Administration of Justice, *Task Force Report: Science and Technology,* Washington, D.C.: U.S. Government Printing Office, 1967, Appendix J, p. 220.

16. *Ibid.,* p. 227.

17. President's Commission on Law Enforcement and Administration of Justice, *Task Force Report: Corrections,* Washington, D.C.: U.S. Government Printing Office, 1967, chapter 4, especially pp. 38–39, 41–42.

61. IS PUNISHMENT NECESSARY?

JACKSON TOBY

*Many traditional criminologists have contended that conformity to prevailing mores
is enforced by the exercise of heavy sanctions for violations. One (or more) of three
arguments is usually presented to justify the use of punishment. First, punishment is
viewed as a means of preventing crime; the mere anticipation of sanctions is
believed to be an effective deterrent. Second, punishment is seen as a means of sustaining
the morale of the conformist, that is, it is used to prevent demoralization of law-
abiding citizens in the face of defiance by an offender. Finally, punishment is considered a means of reforming the violator.*

*In "Is Punishment Necessary?," Jackson Toby examines each of these views in
the light of contemporary sociological theory. He distinguishes between those who state
their case in terms of identification with the victim and those who identify (albeit
unconsciously) with the offender. Toby argues that "from the viewpoint of social
control, the alternative outcomes of the punishment or treatment processes, rehabilitation
or recidivism, are less important than the deviant's neutralization as a possible role
model." Whether punishment is or is not necessary ultimately rests on the extent to
which identification with the victim occurs, the extent to which nonconformity is prevented by the anticipation of punishment, the consequences for the morale of conformists
of punishing the deviant or treating his imputed pathologies, and the compatibility
of punishment and rehabilitation.*

Jackson Toby is Professor of Sociology at Rutgers University. He is the author of
Contemporary Society: Social Process and Social Structure in Urban Industrial Society
(*1964*), *and coauthor, with Harry C. Bredemeier, of* Social Problems in America:
Costs and Casualties in an Acquisitive Society (*1960*).

Of eleven contemporary textbooks in criminology written by sociologists, ten have
one or more chapters devoted to the punishment of offenders.[1] All ten include a
history of methods of punishment in
Western society and, more specifically, a
discussion of capital punishment. Seven
discuss punishment in pre-literate societies. Seven include theoretical or philosophical discussions of the "justification"
of punishment—usually in terms of "retribution," "deterrence," and "reformation."

These theoretical analyses are at least as
much indebted to law and philosophy as
to sociology. Thus, in considering the
basis for punishment, three textbooks
refer both to Jeremy Bentham and to
Emile Durkheim; three textbooks refer to
Bentham but not to Durkheim; and one
textbook refers to Durkheim but not to
Bentham. Several textbook writers express
their opposition to punishment, especially
to cruel punishment. This opposition is
alleged to be based on an incompatibility

Reprinted from the *Journal of Criminal Law, Criminology, and Police Science*, **55** (1964),
332–337, by permission of the author and the publisher. Copyright © 1964, The Williams and
Wilkins Company.
This article is a revised version of a paper presented to the 1959 meeting of the Eastern
Sociological Society.

of punishment with scientific considerations. The following quotation is a case in point:

We still punish primarily for vengeance, or to deter, or in the interest of a "just" balance of accounts between "deliberate" evildoers on the one hand and an injured and enraged society on the other. We do not yet generally punish or treat as scientific criminology would imply, namely, in order to change antisocial attitudes into social attitudes." [2]

Most of the textbook writers note with satisfaction that "the trend in modern countries has been toward humanizing punishment and toward the reduction of brutalities." [3] They point to the decreased use of capital punishment, the introduction of amenities into the modern prison by enlightened penology, and the increasing emphasis on nonpunitive and individualized methods of dealing with offenders, e.g., probation, parole, psychotherapy. In short, students reading these textbooks might infer that punishment is a vestigial carry-over of a barbaric past and will disappear as humanitarianism and rationality spread. Let us examine this inference in terms of the motives underlying punishment and the necessities of social control.

The Urge to Punish

Many crimes have identifiable victims. In the case of crimes against the person, physical or psychic injuries have been visited upon the victim. In the case of crimes against property, someone's property has been stolen or destroyed. In pressing charges against the offender, the victim may express hostility against the person who injured him in a socially acceptable way. Those who identify with the victim —not only his friends and family but those who can imagine the same injury being done to them—may join with him in clamoring for the punishment of the offender. If, as has been argued, the norm of reciprocity is fundamental to human

interaction, this hostility of the victim constituency toward offenders is an obstacle to the elimination of punishment from social life. [4] Of course, the size of the group constituted by victims and those who identify with victims may be small. Empirical study would probably show that it varies by offense. Thus, it is possible that nearly everyone identifies with the victim of a murderer but relatively few people with the victim of a blackmailer. The greater the size of the victim constituency, the greater the opposition to a nonpunitive reaction to the offender.

It would be interesting indeed to measure the size and the composition of the victim constituencies for various crimes. Take rape as an illustration. Since the victims of rape are females, we might hypothesize that *women* would express greater punitiveness toward rapists than *men* and that degrees of hostility would correspond to real or imaginary exposure to rape. Thus, pretty young girls might express more punitiveness toward rapists than homely women. Among males, we might predict that greater punitiveness would be expressed by those with more reason to identify with the victims. Thus, males having sisters or daughters in the late teens or early twenties might express more punitiveness toward rapists than males lacking vulnerable "hostages to fortune."

Such a study might throw considerable light on the wellsprings of punitive motivation, particularly if victimization reactions were distinguished from other reasons for punitiveness. One way to explore such motivation would be to ask the same respondents to express their punitive predispositions toward offenses which do not involve victims at all, e.g., gambling, or which involve victims of a quite different kind. Thus, rape might be balanced by an offense the victims of which are largely male. Survey research of this type is capable of ascertaining the opposition to milder penalties for various offenses. It would incidentally throw light on the comparatively gentle societal reaction to white-collar crime. Perhaps the explanation lies in the difficulty of identifying with the victims of patent infringement or watered hams.[5]

The Social Control Functions of Punishment

Conformists who identify with the *victim* are motivated to punish the offender out of some combination of rage and fear. Conformists who identify with the *offender*, albeit unconsciously, may wish to punish him for quite different reasons. Whatever the basis for the motivation to punish, the existence of punitive reactions to deviance is an obstacle to the abolition of punishment. However, it is by no means the sole obstacle. Even though a negligible segment of society felt punitive toward offenders, it might still not be feasible to eliminate punishment if the social control of deviance depended on it. Let us consider, therefore, the consequences of punishing offenders for a) preventing crime, b) sustaining the morale of conformists, and c) rehabilitating offenders.

Punishment as a means of crime prevention

Durkheim defined punishment as an act of vengeance. "What we avenge, what the criminal expiates, is the outrage to morality."[6] But why is vengeance necessary? Not because of the need to deter the bulk of the population from doing likewise. The socialization process prevents most deviant behavior. Those who have introjected the moral norms of their society cannot commit crimes because their self-concepts will not permit them to do so. Only the unsocialized (and therefore amoral) individual fits the model of classical criminology and is deterred from expressing deviant impulses by a nice calculation of pleasures and punishments.[7] Other things being equal, the anticipation of punishment would seem to have more

deterrent value for inadequately socialized members of the group. It is difficult to investigate this proposition empirically because other motivationally relevant factors are usually varying simultaneously, e.g., the situational temptations confronting various individuals, their optimism about the chances of escaping detection, and the differential impact of the same punishment on individuals of different status.[8] Clearly, though, the deterent effect of anticipated punishments is a complex empirical problem, and Durkheim was not interested in it. Feeling as he did that *some* crime is normal in every society, he apparently decided that the crime prevention function of punishment is not crucial. He pointed out that minute gradation in punishment would not be necessary if punishment were simply a means of deterring the potential offender (crime prevention). "Robbers are as strongly inclined to rob as murderers are to murder; the resistance offered by the former is not less than that of the latter, and consequently, to control it, we would have recourse to the same means."[9] Durkheim was factually correct; the offenses punished most severely are not necessarily the ones which present the greatest problem of social defense. Thus, quantitatively speaking, murder is an unimportant cause of death; in the United States it claims only half as many lives annually as does suicide and only one-fifth the toll of automobile accidents. Furthermore, criminologists have been unable to demonstrate a relationship between the murder rate of a community and its use or lack of use of capital punishment.

Most contemporary sociologists would agree with Durkheim that the anticipation of punishment is not the first line of defense against crime. The socialization process keeps most people law abiding, not the police—if for no other reason than the police are not able to catch every offender. This does not mean, however, that the police could be disbanded. During World War II, the Nazis deported all of Denmark's police force, thus providing a natural experiment testing the deterrent efficacy of formal sanctions.[10] Crime increased greatly. Even though punishment is uncertain, especially under contemporary urban conditions, the possibility of punishment keeps some conformists law-abiding. The empirical question is: *How many* conformists would become deviants if they did not fear punishment?

Punishment as a means of sustaining the morale of conformists

Durkheim considered punishment indispensable as a means of containing the demoralizing consequences of the crimes that could not be prevented. Punishment was not for Durkheim mere vindictiveness. Without punishment Durkheim anticipated the demoralization of "upright people" in the face of defiance of the collective conscience. He believed that unpunished deviance tends to demoralize the conformist and therefore he talked about punishment as a means of repairing "the wounds made upon collective sentiments." [11] Durkheim was not entirely clear; he expressed his ideas in metaphorical language. Nonetheless, we can identify the hypothesis that the punishment of offenders promotes the solidarity of conformists.

Durkheim anticipated psychoanalytic thinking as the following reformulation of his argument shows: One who resists the temptation to do what the group prohibits, to drive his car at 80 miles per hour, to beat up an enemy, to take what he wants without paying for it, would like to feel that these self-imposed abnegations have some meaning. When he sees others defy rules without untoward consequences, he needs some reassurance that his sacrifices were made in a good cause. If "the good die young and the wicked flourish as the green bay tree," the moral scruples which enable conformists to restrain their own deviant inclinations lack social validation. The social significance of punishing offenders is that deviance is thereby defined

as unsuccessful in the eyes of conformists, thus making the inhibition or repression of their own deviant impulses seem worthwhile. Righteous indignation is collectively sanctioned reaction formation. The law-abiding person who unconsciously resents restraining his desire to steal and murder has an opportunity, by identifying with the police and the courts, to affect the precarious balance within his own personality between internal controls and the temptation to deviate. A bizarre example of this psychological mechanism is the man who seeks out homosexuals and beats them up mercilessly. Such pathological hostility toward homosexuals is due to the sadist's anxiety over his own sex-role identification. By "punishing" the homosexual, he denies the latent homosexuality in his own psyche. No doubt, some of the persons involved in the administration of punishment are sadistically motivated. But Durkheim hypothesized that the psychic equilibrium of the *ordinary* members of the group may be threatened by violation of norms; Durkheim was not concerned about psychopathological punitiveness.

Whatever the practical difficulties, Durkheim's hypothesis is, in principle, testable. It should be possible to estimate the demoralizing impact of nonconformity on conformists. Clearly, though, this is no simple matter. The extent of demoralization resulting from the failure to punish may vary with type of crime. The unpunished traffic violator may cause more demoralization than the unpunished exhibitionist—depending on whether or not outwardly conforming members of society are more tempted to exceed the speed limit than to expose themselves. The extent of demoralization may also vary with position in the social structure occupied by the conformist. Thus, Ranulf suggested that the middle class was especially vulnerable:

> [The] disinterested tendency to inflict punishment is a distinctive characteristic of the lower middle class, that is, of a social class living under conditions which force its mem-

bers to an extraordinarily high degree of self-restraint and subject them to much frustration of natural desires. If a psychological interpretation is to be put on this correlation of facts, it can hardly be to any other effect than that moral indignation is a kind of resentment caused by the repression of instincts.[12]

Once the facts on the rate and the incidence of moral indignation are known, it will become possible to determine whether something must be done to the offender in order to prevent the demoralization of conformists. Suppose that research revealed that a very large proportion of conformists react with moral indignation to *most* violations of the criminal laws. Does this imply that punishment is a functional necessity? Durkheim apparently thought so, but he might have been less dogmatic in his approach to punishment had he specified the functional problem more clearly: making the nonconformist unattractive as a role model. If the norm violation can be defined as unenviable through some other process than by inflicting suffering upon him, punishment is not required by the exigencies of social control.

Punishment can be discussed on three distinct levels: a) in terms of the motivations of the societal agents administering it, b) in terms of the definition of the situation on the part of the person being punished, and c) in terms of its impact on conformists. At this point I am chiefly concerned with the third level, the impact on conformists. Note that punishment of offenders sustains the morale of conformists only under certain conditions. The first has already been discussed, namely that conformists unconsciously wish to violate the rules themselves. The second is that conformists implicitly assume that the nonconformity is a result of *deliberate defiance* of society's norms. For some conformists, this second condition is not met. Under the guidance of psychiatric thinking, some conformists assume that norm violation is the result of illness rather than

wickedness.[13] For such conformists, punishment of the offender does not contribute to their morale. Since they assume that the nonconformity is an involuntary symptom of a disordered personality, the offender is automatically unenviable because illness is (by definition) undesirable. Of course, it is an empirical question as to the relative proportions of the conforming members of society who make the "wicked" or the "sick" assumption about the motivation of the offender, but this can be discovered by investigation.

In Western industrial societies, there is increasing tendency to call contemporary methods of dealing with offenders "treatment" rather than "punishment." Perhaps this means that increasing proportions of the population are willing to accept the "sick" theory of nonconformity. Note, however, that the emphasis on "treatment" may be more a matter of symbolism than of substance. Although the definition of the situation as treatment rather than punishment tends to be humanizing —both to the offender and to the persons who must deal with him—there are still kind guards and cruel nurses. Furthermore, it would be an error to suppose that punishment is invariably experienced as painful by the criminal whereas treatment is always experienced as pleasant by the psychopathological offender. Some gang delinquents consider a reformatory sentence an opportunity to renew old acquaintances and to learn new delinquent skills; they resist fiercely the degrading suggestion that they need the services of the "nut doctor." Some mental patients are terrified by shock treatment and embarrassed by group therapy.

What then is the significance of the increasing emphasis on "treatment"? Why call an institution for the criminally insane a "hospital" although it bears a closer resemblance to a prison than to a hospital for the physically ill? In my opinion, the increased emphasis on treatment in penological thinking and practice reflects the existence of a large group of conformists who are undecided as between the "wicked" and the "sick" theories of nonconformity. When they observe that the offender is placed in "treatment," their provisional diagnosis of illness is confirmed, and therefore they do not feel that he has "gotten away with it." Note that "treatment" has the capacity to make the offender unenviable to conformists whether or not it is effective in rehabilitating him and whether or not he experiences it as pleasant. Those old-fashioned conformists who are not persuaded by official diagnoses of illness will not be satisfied by "treatment"; they will prefer to see an attempt made to visit physical suffering or mental anguish on the offender. For them, punishment is necessary to prevent demoralization.

Punishment as a means of reforming the offender

Rehabilitation of offenders swells the number of conformists and therefore is regarded both by humanitarians and by scientifically minded penologists as more constructive than punishment. Most of the arguments against imprisonment and other forms of punishment in the correctional literature boil down to the assertion that punishment is incompatible with rehabilitation. The high rate of recidivism for prisons and reformatories is cited as evidence of the irrationality of punishment.[14] What sense is there in subjecting offenders to the frustrations of incarceration? If rehabilitative programs are designed to help the offender cope with frustrations in his life situation, which presumably were responsible for his nonconformity, imprisoning him hardly seems a good way to begin. To generalize the argument, the status degradation inherent in punishment makes it more difficult to induce the offender to play a legitimate role instead of a nonconforming one. Whatever the offender's original motivations for nonconformity, punishment adds to them by neutralizing his fear of losing

the respect of the community; he has already lost it.

Plausible though this argument is, empirical research has not yet verified it. The superior rehabilitative efficacy of "enlightened" prisons is a humanitarian assumption, but brutal correctional systems have, so far as is known, comparable recidivism rates to "enlightened" systems. True, the recidivism rate of offenders who are fined or placed on probation is less than the recidivism rate of offenders who are incarcerated, but this comparison is not merely one of varying degrees of punishment. Presumably, more severe punishment is meted out to criminals who are more deeply committed to a deviant way of life. Until it is demonstrated that the recidivism rates of strictly comparable populations of deviants differ depending on the degree of punitiveness with which they are treated, the empirical incompatibility of punishment and rehabilitation will remain an open question.

Even on theoretical grounds, however, the incompatibility of punishment and rehabilitation can be questioned once it is recognized that one may precede the other. Perhaps, as Lloyd McCorkle and Richard Korn think, some types of deviants become willing to change only if the bankruptcy of their way of life is conclusively demonstrated to them.[15] On this assumption, punishment may be a necessary preliminary to a rehabilitative program in much the same way that shock treatment makes certain types of psychotics accessible to psychotherapy.

It seems to me that the compatibility of punishment and rehabilitation could be clarified (although not settled) if it were considered from the point of view of the *meaning* of punishment to the offender. Those offenders who regard punishment as a deserved deprivation resulting from their own misbehavior are qualitatively different from offenders who regard punishment as a misfortune bearing no relationship to morality. Thus, a child who is spanked by his father and the member of a bopping gang who is jailed for carrying concealed weapons are both "punished." But one accepts the deprivation as legitimate, and the other bows before superior force. I would hypothesize that punishment has rehabilitative significance only for the former. If this is so, correctional officials must convince the prisoner that his punishment is just before they can motivate him to change. This is no simple task. It is difficult for several reasons:

1) It is obvious to convicted offenders, if not to correctional officials, that *some* so-called "criminals" are being punished disproportionately for trifling offenses whereas *some* predatory business men and politicians enjoy prosperity and freedom. To deny that injustices occur confirms the cynical in their belief that "legitimate" people are not only as predatory as criminals but hypocritical to boot. When correctional officials act as though there were no intermediate position between asserting that perfect justice characterizes our society and that it is a jungle, they make it more difficult to persuade persons undergoing punishment that the best approximation of justice is available that imperfect human beings can manage.[16]

2) Of course, the more cases of injustice known to offenders, the harder it is to argue that the contemporary approximation of justice is the best that can be managed. It is difficult to persuade Negro inmates that their incarceration has moral significance if their life experience has demonstrated to them that the police and the courts are less scrupulous of *their* rights than of the rights of white persons. It is difficult to persuade an indigent inmate that his incarceration has moral significance if his poverty resulted in inadequate legal representation.[17]

3) Finally, the major form of punishment for serious offenders (imprisonment) tends to generate a contraculture which denies that justice has anything to do with legal penalties.[18] That is to say, it is too costly to confine large numbers of people in isolation from one another, yet

congregate confinement results in the mutual reinforcement of self-justifications. Even those who enter prison feeling contrite are influenced by the self-righteous inmate climate; this may be part of the reason recidivism rates rise with each successive commitment.[19]

In view of the foregoing considerations, I hypothesize that punishment—as it is now practiced in Western societies—is usually an obstacle to rehabilitation. Some exceptions to this generalization should be noted. A few small treatment institutions have not only prevented the development of a self-righteous contraculture but have managed to establish an inmate climate supportive of changed values.[20] In such institutions punishment has rehabilitative significance for the same reason it has educational significance in the normal family: it is legitimate.

To sum up: The social control functions of punishment include crime prevention, sustaining the morale of conformists, and the rehabilitation of offenders. All of the empirical evidence is not in, but it is quite possible that punishment contributes to some of these and interferes with others. Suppose, for example, that punishment is necessary for crime prevention and to maintain the morale of conformists but is generally an obstacle to the rehabilitation of offenders. Since the proportion of deviants is small in any viable system as compared with the proportion of conformists, the failure to rehabilitate them will not jeopardize the social order. Therefore, under these assumptions, sociological counsel would favor the continued employment of punishment.

Conclusion

A member of a social system who violates its cherished rules threatens the stability of that system. Conformists who identify with the victim are motivated to punish the criminal in order to feel safe. Conformists who unconsciously identify with the criminal fear their own ambivalence.

If norm violation is defined by conformists as willful, visiting upon the offender some injury or degradation will make him unenviable. If his behavior is defined by conformists as a symptom of pathology they are delighted not to share, putting him into treatment validates their diagnosis of undesirable illness. Whether he is "punished" or "treated," however, the disruptive consequence of his deviance is contained. Thus, from the viewpoint of social control, the alternative outcomes of the punishment or treatment processes, rehabilitation or recidivism, are less important than the deviant's neutralization as a possible role model. Whether punishment is or is not necessary rests ultimately on empirical questions: 1) the extent to which identification with the victim occurs, 2) the extent to which nonconformity is prevented by the anticipation of punishment, 3) what the consequences are for the morale of conformists of punishing the deviant or of treating his imputed pathology, and 4) the compatibility between punishment and rehabilitation.

NOTES

1. Harry E. Barnes and Negley K. Teeters, *New Horizons in Criminology*, 3rd ed., Englewood Cliffs, N.J.: Prentice-Hall, 1959; Robert G. Caldwell, *Criminology*, New York: Ronald Press, 1956; Ruth Cavan, *Criminology*, New York: Crowell, 1955; Mabel A. Elliot, *Crime in Modern Society*, New York: Harper, 1952; Richard Korn and Lloyd W. McCorkle, *Criminology and Penology*, New York: Holt, Rinehart and Winston, 1959; Edwin H. Sutherland and Donald R. Cressey, *The Principles of Criminology*, 5th ed., Philadelphia: Lippincott, 1955; Donald C. Taft, *Criminology*, 3rd ed., New York: Macmillan, 1956; Paul Tappan, *Crime, Justice and Correction*, New York: McGraw-Hill, 1960; Hans von Hentig, *Crime: Causes and Conditions*, New York: McGraw-Hill, 1947; Arthur E. Wood and John B. Waite, *Crime and Its Treatment*, New York: American Book Company, 1941.

2. Taft, *op. cit.*, p. 359.

3. Reckless, *Crime Problem*, New York: Appleton, p. 450.

4. Alvin W. Gouldner, "The Norm of Reciprocity," *American Sociological Review*, 25 (1960), 161–178.

5. In this connection, it is well to recall that there is less reluctance to steal from corporations than from humans. See A. W. Jones, *Life, Liberty, and Property*, New York: Lippincott, 1941.

6. Émile Durkheim, *The Division of Labor in Society*, Glencoe, Ill.: The Free Press, 1949, p. 89.

7. Talcott Parsons, *The Structure of Social Action*, Glencoe, Ill.: The Free Press, 1949, pp. 402–403.

8. Jackson Toby, "Social Disorganization and Stake in Conformity: Complementary Factors in the Predatory Behavior of Young Hoodlums," *Journal of Criminal Law, Criminology, and Police Science*, 48 (1957), 12.

9. *Op. cit.*, p. 88.

10. Trolle, *Syv Måneder Uten Politi* (*Seven Months without Police*), Copenhagen, 1945. Quoted in Christie, "Scandinavian Criminology," *Sociological Inquiry*, 31 (1961), 101.

11. Durkheim, *op. cit.*, p. 108.

12. Ranulf, *Moral Indignation and Middle Class Psychology*, Copenhagen, 1938, p. 198.

13. Talcott Parsons has repeatedly suggested the analogy between illness and criminality. See also Aubert and Messinger, "The Criminal and the Sick," *Inquiry*, 1 (1958), 137, and Wootton, *Social Science and Social Pathology*, New York: Macmillan, 1959, pp. 203–267.

14. Vold, "Does the Prison Reform?" *The Annals*, 293 (1954), 42–51.

15. Lloyd W. McCorkle and Richard Korn, "Resocialization within Walls," *The Annals*, 293 (1954), 88–91.

16. See the interesting discussions of human fallibility in the works of Reinhold Niebuhr—eg., *The Children of Light and the Children of Darkness*, New York: Charles Scribner's, 1944.

17. Trebach, "The Indigent Defendant," *Rutgers Law Review,* 11 (1957), 625.

18. For a discussion of the concept of contraculture, see J. Milton Yinger, *American Sociological Review,* 25 (1960), 625–635.

19. T. Bellin, "Recidivism and Maturation," *National Probation and Parole Academy Journal,* LI (1948), 241.

20. Lloyd W. McCorkle, Albert Elias, and F. Lovell Bixby, *The Highfields Story,* New York: Holt, 1958, and Empey and Rabow, "The Provo Experiment in Delinquency Rehabilitation," *American Sociological Review,* 26 (1961), 679–696.

62. SOME FUNCTIONS OF DEVIANT BEHAVIOR [1]

LEWIS A. COSER

Paradoxical though it may seem, deviant behavior may have latent consequences for maintaining the continuity of social structures and enhancing group cohesion. Deviation frequently serves to arouse the community to the consequences of a breach of its norms. It may, in some cases, be considered as the very basis for "normalcy."

Lewis A. Coser examines various structural and situational circumstances which lead groups to tolerate or even foster deviance. He analyzes the functions and dysfunctions of deviant behavior relating two variables—"strengthening of the group" and "rejection of the deviant"—as expressed in a typology consisting of the following hypothetical situations: 1) the deviant is opposed and the group is strengthened; 2) the deviant is tolerated or accepted and the group is strengthened; 3) the deviant is rejected and the group is weakened; and 4) the deviant is not rejected and the group is weakened. Suggesting that the last type is unproblematic, Coser discusses the first three situations in detail.

He then turns to the consequences of deviation for relations outside the community. Distinguishing criminal deviance from innovating nonconformity, Coser's article concludes with an analysis of various expressions of innovative departures from normalcy in terms of both motivation and impact upon group structure.

Lewis A. Coser is Distinguished Professor of Sociology at the State University of New York, Stony Brook. His published works include The Functions of Social Conflict *(1956),* The American Communist Party: A Critical History 1919–1957 *(with Irving Howe) (1957),* Men of Ideas *(1965), and* Continuities in the Study of Social Conflict *(1967). He is also the editor of* Sociology Through Literature *(1963),* Political Sociology: Selected Essays *(1966), and coeditor of* Sociological Theory: A Book of Readings *(1957).*

Most contemporary sociological theorizing about deviant behavior has tended to focus on mechanisms of social control. The analysis of instances in which behavior that violates institutional expectations may be considered functional for an ongoing social system has been largely neglected. This paper tries to highlight some functions of deviance for social structures. This does not deny, of course, the dysfunctions of deviance, but only suggests that an exclusive emphasis on these may result in inadequate and distorted analysis.

Consequences of Deviance for Internal Group Relations

We have known ever since Durkheim that crime alerts the common conscience and contributes to the revival and maintenance of common sentiments by arousing the community to the consequences of in-

Reprinted from the *American Journal of Sociology,* **68** (1962), 172–182, by permission of the author and The University of Chicago Press. Copyright © 1962 by The University of Chicago Press. This article was originally entitled "The Functions of Deviant Behavior and Normative Flexibility."

fringements of rules. "Crime," he wrote, "brings together upright consciences and concentrates them." [2] It will also be remembered that Mead wrote in a similar vein: "The criminal . . . is responsible for a sense of solidarity, aroused among those whose attitude would otherwise be centered upon interests quite divergent from each other. The attitude of hostility toward the lawbreaker has the unique advantage of uniting all members of the community." [3] Durkheim and Mead both state that, though an individual criminal act elicits negative sanctions, crime also has positive consequences for the society or group since the breach of a norm calls attention to its importance for the common weal. Like bodily pain serves as a danger signal, calling for the mobilization of energies against the source of disease, so crime, these writers argue, alerts the body social and leads to the mobilization of otherwise inactive defense mechanisms.

Durkheim and Mead are often quoted in current theorizing, yet their pertinent insight on the functions of crime has been somewhat neglected. Thus Parsons focuses attention on mechanisms of social control which serve to check deviant behavior but fails to consider possible contributions that deviance may make to the system in which it occurs. He distinguishes types of deviance that "fall within the range of permissiveness which should be considered normal to people under certain strains" and "a vicious circle of gratification of deviant wishes [leading to the] undermining of the main value system." [4] But he does not consider those deviant acts which, though not considered "normal to people under strain," reinforce rather than undermine the social system. We shall see in a later part of this paper that different types of deviant behavior must be discussed in terms of their differential impact. Even if we should agree, for the purpose of discussion, that deviants are always motivated to defy the group's norms, nothing requires us to assume that

such acts may not have the unanticipated consequence of strengthening those norms.

Durkheim and Mead see the functional consequences of deviance in the strengthening of the group which results from the collective rejection of the deviant. This assumption is indeed born out by much of small-group research. An article summarizing much of the research findings in this field states, for example: "When a member deviates markedly from a group standard, the remaining members of the group bring pressures to bear on the deviate to bring him back to conformity. If pressure is of no avail, the deviate is rejected and cast out of the group." [5] Statements such as these seem to imply, though the authors do not explicitly say so, that deviations from group standards lead to the mobilization of the group's energies. But small-group research has not adequately considered the possibility that the repression of deviance may not in all cases be functional for the group. Moreover, it has not been shown that all types of groups will reject deviance under all circumstances. These two variables—"strengthening of the group" and "rejection of the deviant"—call attention to four possible cases: 1) the deviant is opposed and the group is strengthened—the situation discussed by Durkheim and Mead; 2) the deviant is tolerated or even accepted and the group is strengthened; 3) the deviant is rejected and the group is weakened; and 4) the deviant is not rejected and the group is weakened. The last case is relatively unproblematical, but the other three have not been given sufficient systematic attention in sociological theorizing, although empirical evidence about them is available.

1) *The deviant is opposed and the group is strengthened.* In the process of uniting itself against deviance, the community not only revives and maintains common sentiments but creatively establishes moral rules and redefines "normal" behavior. "Each time the community

brings sanctions against a detail of behavior . . . it sharpens the authority of the violated norm and redefines the boundaries within which the norm exercises its special jurisdiction." [6] Thus the criminal, the scapegoat, the mentally ill, in their diverse ways, allow the group to reaffirm not only its social but also its moral identity, for they establish signposts which serve as normative yardsticks.[7] Deviance "establishes the point beyond which behavior is no longer within acceptable reach of the norm, and in this way gives substance and authority to the norm itself." [8]

Thus, definition of what is considered normal in the group takes place with reference to what is considered deviant, and morality is given its content through the contrast provided by that which is not moral. We touch here upon a dialectical relation which Gestalt psychology has discussed in detail with respect to perception. Figures cannot be perceived except in relation to grounds setting them off. In the same way, normalcy can hardly be perceived except against the ground of deviance; to be "good" makes sense only in relation to being "bad."

It is with the body social as it is with individuals: moral indignation against deviants serves to purge the righteous from a sense of their own sins and unworthiness and helps sustain their moral identity. Such indignation may well serve as a reaction-formation, securing the ego against the repressed impulse to identify with the criminal.[9] It is against the ground of their deviance that the righteous achieve the comforting affirmation of their normality. Inasmuch as "our" innocence is contingent upon "their" guilt, dereliction by others provides occasion for self-congratulations.

But dereliction by others also provides occasion for self-examination. Thus, when a crime is committed in the community, religious leaders use the occasion to exhort the congregation to re-examine themselves and "purify their souls." Deviance is taken as a warning that there is something foul in the state of Denmark that needs correction—correction not only on the individual level but in the social realm as well. Thus, Stewart and Helen Perry have shown that in the mental hospitals deviant patients may, by their acting out, "act as a fire alarm for the ward." By upsetting the social equilibrium of the ward, the "fire-alarm patient" may highlight such defects as understaffing, staff overwork, and the like and thus dramatize the need for remedial action.[10] Bureaucratic organizations are familiar with similar situations in which the failure effectively to control behavior in terms of official goals will be used by practitioners as a convincing means for appealing for increased resources. Thus many organizations (as well as many role incumbents) have a vested interest, though rarely acknowledged, in the very deviant behavior which they are set up to combat, for deviance provides the reason for their existence: Increases in deviance may help them to highlight the need for strengthening the organization (or the department in the organization) to cope more effectively with disturbing behavior.

2) What has been said so far about reactions to deviance—be it a spontaneous, that is, a non-deliberate "pulling together" of group members, or deliberate policy—refers to those instances in which deviant behavior leads to its rejection. The second case is that of *tolerance or acceptance of the deviant with concomitant strengthening of the group.* There are groups in which deviants provide the occasion for a reaffirmation of values without incurring rejection. Thus in a seminal paper, Dentler and Erikson gave illustrations from Quaker work camps and Army Basic Training Squads where deviants do indeed "become critical referents for establishing the end points (of the range of possibilities judged permissible within the group's boundaries)"—the figure-ground

effect discussed earlier—and where "the deviant is someone about whom something should be done, and the group, in expressing this concern, is able to affirm its essential cohesion and indicate what the group is and what it can do." [11] However, in these cases the occasion for affirmation of cohesion does not come from rejecting the deviant but rather from protecting him: he "becomes the ward of the group. . . . In a setting in which having buddies is highly valued, he is unlikely to receive any sociometric choices at all. But it would be quite unfortunate to assume that he is therefore isolated from the group or repudiated by it: an accurate sociogram would have the deviant individual encircled by the interlocking sociometric preferences, sheltered by the group structure." [12]

It would seem that in some groups tolerance of deviance is a function of a specific value system: among Quakers, "tolerance" is a salient component of the ideology. In tolerating or protecting a deviant, they practice what they publicly profess. (It may even be said that such groups do, in fact, need social objects upon whom "tolerance" can be exercised because they provide the occasion for testing and confirming their values.)

If it is objected that tolerance of deviance in army units is merely a manifestation of opposition to official army goals, that is, part of a collective effort to "get back" at army authority, this only confirms the analytical point: by setting itself off against an intolerant environment, the group exercises tolerance precisely with regard to those individuals who would otherwise be the victims of the very environment whose values the group rejects. In both cases—Quaker camps and army units—acceptance of deviance is contingent upon the value system of the group. What Kelley and Thibault say about the rejection of deviance applies to its tolerance as well: "Generally, the same factors responsible for the emergence of group

standards will also in large measure be responsible for the motivations to enforce conformity to them." [13] Thus in the groups discussed by Dentler and Erikson, the practice of tolerance—whether positively stated as a "way of life" as among Quakers, or stated in opposition to the intolerance of army authorities as in army units—would seem to be a basis for the emergence or strengthening of group standards and would therefore be the guiding principle that motivates the responses of group members to nonconformity among them.

3) So far, the assertion has been made that deviants offer to group members the opportunity to reaffirm common values, be it by providing an occasion to oppose them collectively (case 1), or by bringing about a situation in which their acceptance or tolerance serves as an affirmation of beliefs held in common (case 2). In these cases, the groups were strengthened. There are groups, however, for whom *rigid and repeated rejection of deviants has serious dysfunctional consequences* (case 3). Rigidly structured sects or radical political organizations of the sectarian type provide examples in point. Even a cursory perusal of the history of the Trotskyist movement leaves no doubt about the fact that the lack of ability to tolerate deviance led to further and further fragmentation of the movement. Religious sects provide similar examples.

To be sure, in such groups each single case of negative sanctions against deviant behavior led, at the moment the act of sanctioning occurred, to a reaffirmation of values among those who remained faithful. Yet, rejection of nonconformity as an ongoing organizational activity was disruptive as a *process* in that in the long run it weakened the group in relation to its external environment.

This calls attention to the need to consider the relation between the group within which deviance occurs and the external context.

Consequences of Deviance for Group Relations with the Outside

In the first two situations discussed—one of rejection and the other of tolerance of the deviant—our concern was with relationships within the group. It now turns out that what may be functional for the group in one respect—that is, the reaffirmation of its norms—may turn out to be detrimental in another respect, namely, in its relation to the outside. To consider only the internal consequences of deviance and of responses to it, that is, to limit analysis to the group processes within given subsystems without paying attention to the group's relations with the outside, is a common pitfall in sociological theorizing, especially in small-group research. In contrast to much of such research, Kelley and Shapiro set up an experimental group in a situation in which the group's norms were discordant with outside reality.[14] In this situation conformity to these norms tended to be detrimental to the success of the group. (Situations similar to those contrived in the laboratory are likely to occur when disparate rates of change impinge on a group and lead to cultural lags and dysfunctional resistances of vested interests.)

It turned out that in these experimental groups deviation from the norms did not call forth rejection. This case is, in this respect, more similar to case 2 discussed above, for here also deviance is accepted. While in the Quaker camps deviance may be *implicitly* welcomed as an occasion for group members to live up to professed values, in these experimental groups deviant behavior seems to have been *explicitly* welcomed as an occasion for better adaptability to outside reality. Indeed, it turned out that in these groups persons who deviated from the group's norms were also those who were judged to be highly acceptable as co-workers.

A consideration of the external environment for the understanding of internal dynamics of deviance and responses to it makes it possible to throw more light on the behavior of the Quaker camps and army units discussed earlier. There also the relation with the outside would seem to be one important determinant of inside responses: in Quaker groups and army camps alike, the norms that guide the behavior of members toward deviants seemed to consist in *countervalues* to patterns prevailing on the outside. Thus in Kelley and Thibault's groups, as in the groups studied by Dentler and Erikson, outside reality was an important determinant—whether as a spur for adaptation or for opposition to it—of the responses to deviant behavior within.

The evidence so far indicates that the widely accepted notion that groups always reject deviance is, at the least, open to question. To be sure, deviance may be *proscribed* as in the examples of criminal behavior used by Durkheim and Mead. Yet, a deviant redefinition of norms may be *permitted*, as when the value system of the group prescribes tolerance. It may be *preferred*, as when it is accepted as a means for better adaptability of the group.[15]

Deviant behavior may also be *prescribed*, as during periodic feasts when the participants are expected to infringe the norms of ordinary behavior.[16] These, however, are instances where it would be deviant not to deviate; that is, they are special instances of conformity which do not concern us here.

The recognition that departure from the norms may be preferred, permitted, or proscribed raises two related problems: 1) The license to deviate is differentially distributed among members of a group. For example, there is tolerance of deviance for special role incumbents such as the "star," the "stranger," or the "fool"; [17] or there is some expectation of deviance for some group leaders who are supposed to be flexible and to depart from the norms to further the tasks of the group. 2) Another important problem raised by the differential response to deviance is the need to distinguish between different types of deviant behavior.

Deviance and Innovation

So far the concept of deviance has been used here in accordance with its definition in most contemporary sociological work.[18] An overarching concept of this kind has the distinct merit of drawing attention to the structural similarities of a variety of behaviors which might otherwise seem but little related. Yet at the same time, it has the disadvantage of obscuring distinctions which might be crucial in certain contexts.[19] Thus Merton distinguishes nonconformity from such other kinds of deviant behavior as crime or juvenile delinquency. Criminal behavior is impelled by private and self-centered motives which are by definition antisocial. Innovating dissent of a nonconforming minority, on the other hand, may be manifestly intended to serve group interests in a more effective manner than the conforming majority. "These kinds of 'deviant behavior' differ structurally, culturally and functionally." [20]

While both the nonconformist and the criminal defy normative expectations, they are profoundly dissimilar: the nonconformist's dissent "is not a private dereliction, but a thrust toward a new morality (or a restoration of an old and almost forgotten morality). . . ." [21] I have argued elsewhere in a similar vein that "When all forms of dissent are [considered] criminal by definition, we are in the presence of a system which is ill-equipped to reveal fully the extent to which nonconformity, as distinct from crime, involves the striving forward on alternative moral basis rather than moral deviation." [22]

To be sure, the behavior of the nonconformist may bring forth community reactions similar to those occasioned by criminal violations of the norms, yet the innovations he proposes allegedly in the interest of the group's welfare are likely to be evaluated in their own right, if only by a minority. This is why, as distinct from the case of the criminal, there is likely to be buried under layers of hostility a certain measure of respect for the disinterested dissenter. Being oriented toward the collectivity, he is led to seek and to find an audience within it. The innovator sends a message intended to be picked up and diffused. His behavior proceeds, so to speak, in broad daylight in order to attract a maximum audience. While the criminal seeks to minimize the chances of detection, the innovator seeks maximum publicity for his message. One may argue with an innovator but hardly with a criminal.[23]

Just as with various types of deviance, the innovations which the nonconformist proposes for the consideration of the group may be prescribed or proscribed with various degrees of tolerance, depending on the structured and normative context. Moreover, they may be wittingly favored by the group or the group may unwittingly be favored by them.

When innovation is highly valued, as, for example, in scientific societies, innovating behavior must be considered a special type of conformity rather than deviation. In the context of the institution of science, innovations and discoveries, provided they satisfy the criteria of evidence, are highly valued variants that permit the goals of the group to be more adequately met—though even here the innovator may at first encounter the resistance of vested interests.[24]

On the other hand, in groups which place no value on innovation, an innovating response will be considered truly nonconformist. In contrast to the case of the criminal, however, at least some of the group's members might perceive that the innovator intends to perform a positive task for the group. This might then lead to a conflict within the group over the issue raised. If this happens, the innovator has transformed individual nonconformity into group conflict and has raised it from the idiosyncratic to the collective level.

Thus, pressures for innovation are likely to result in the emergence of social conflicts within a system. Such conflicts, as I have shown elsewhere, may be highly functional for that system.[25] Dewey has noted that "conflict shocks us out of sheeplike passivity, and sets us at noting and contriving . . . it is a *sine qua non* of reflection and ingenuity."[26] The innovator's behavior may serve to reduce the chances that adherence to the routines of yesterday render the group unable to meet the challenges of today. The innovator may thus be a pace-setter and a setter of new standards. By attacking vested interests in the habitual, the innovator helps insure that the group does not stifle in the deadening routines of ritualism.

What is said here of group process indeed applies to every fruitful interaction as well. Interaction does not merely consist of mutual filling of expectations but in ever renewed innovating contributions. In much current theorizing it is assumed that the equilibrium of a group is a function of the extent to which group members habitually conform to each other's expectations. The maintenance of complementarity between the interaction orientations of alter and ego is said to be the mark of a stable social system.[27] "This model seems to assume," Gouldner has noted, "that each of a sequence of identical conforming acts will yield either the same or an increasing degree of appreciation and satisfaction and will thus elicit the same or increasing amounts of reward."[28] Yet, "later conforming actions are worth less than earlier ones, in terms of the rewards or propensity to reciprocate which they elicit." When conformity is taken for granted, the propensity to reciprocate is weakened in the long run. Homans also states this principle of satiation, a version of marginal utility: "The more often a man has in the recent past received a rewarding activity from an-

other, the less valuable any further unit of that activity becomes to him."[29]

The Finnish sociologist Yrjö Littunen has formulated an "optimal frustration" hypothesis: "Persons who have to maintain a monotonous interaction pattern for a long period of time tend to become bored with each other. This phenomenon of *social fatigue* may be understood as a situation where there is no excitement in the interaction to maintain the cohesiveness, to increase liking."[30] Although sustained conformity may bring the reward of smooth adjustment to expectations, it also brings the penalty of boredom. That is why apathy and monotony may lead a person to "seek a frustration which his energy potential can adequately balance and overcome."[31] This hypothesis, which Littunen developed on the basis of the psychological research of Hebb and Thompson,[32] gains added theoretical relevance with Gouldner's recognition that a system built upon the habituation of conforming responses may be said to contain built-in tendencies toward a high level of entropy. It is high social entropy that the innovator, as an agent of change, helps to prevent.

Normative Flexibility and Innovating Roles

In monolithic structures role requirements may be so rigidly defined that only fully conforming role performance will be tolerated; in less rigid structures, on the other hand, a measure of diversity may be tolerated at various levels in the system.[33] For example, low-ranking deviants may perform important functions for the group. This was the case in the groups discussed earlier, about which Dentler and Erikson have argued that low-ranking members who deviate from the group's norms "become critical referents for establishing the end points" of the range of possibilities judged permissible within the group's boundaries.[34]

Such considerations direct attention to

the relation between status, group structure, and the acceptance of innovation by the group.

Deviant behavior as well as innovation varies within different social structures. Furthermore, the social structure puts pressure on some of its status-occupants to engage in innovating rather than in conforming behavior.[35] For example, as Veblen and Simmel,[36] among others, have pointed out, marginal individuals are likely to be highly motivated to engage in innovating behavior because they are structurally induced to depart from prevailing social norms. "With the least opportunity for full participation in the most valued activities of their own society," [37] they may be stimulated to make new responses which depart from the habitually required. Being less tied to the system of wont and use which regulates the lives of insiders, they may see alternatives of action that escape the latter's attention. The structural circumstance of their exclusion from some of the prized values of the group may make the marginal man more sensitive to the lacunae which may well remain hidden from "well-adjusted" members of the group. If he wishes to gain acceptance among insiders, he will be motivated to propose innovating means designed to allow the group to reach its goals more effectively than before.

There are also other positions in a group than those of marginal men that motivate innovating departures from the norms. For example, the status of leader requires the ability to adjust to new circumstances. The rank and file may take the customary for granted, but a break of wont and use may enhance the reputation of the leader. The flexibility required in leadership roles may entail greater or lesser departures from otherwise expected behavior so that a certain amount of license to deviate and to violate norms is built into the very definition of leadership.

Homans, who had argued in an earlier work that "the higher the rank (or status) of a person within a group, the more

nearly his activities conform to the norms of the group," [38] stated more recently, after discussing, among others, the above-quoted study by Kelley and Shapiro, that "we now have experimental evidence that it is not just the members of low status, but members of high status as well, who are prone at times to nonconformity." [39] It will be remembered that in these groups deviant behavior helped the group to adapt to the outside. This suggests that the pressure on the leader to engage in innovating behavior may derive from the structural circumstance that he is the group's representative to the outside. He stands at the point of interchange between in-group and out-group. A leader may be considered a special case of the marginal man: having the task to relate his group to the demands of the environment, he is oriented, at the same time as he is the group's representative, toward extra-group values.

In view of these requirements of leadership, it is not always clear whether the leader's innovation can be called "deviant" at all. Though it involves adoption of new procedures, innovation in this case still takes place within normative limits. Just as with groups in which innovation is highly prized, so in situations in which the leader's departure from institutionalized procedures is part of the system of expectations, what may be considered deviation from one point of view may well be considered conforming behavior from another.

Yet leaders are often also permitted some deviant behavior that neither increases the group's adaptation to the outside nor otherwise directly benefits the group in any way. Simply by virtue of otherwise showing prized qualities, a leader accumulates what Hollander has called "idiosyncrasy credit." [40]

One would assume that the more task-oriented a group, the less its tolerance of deviant behavior that interferes with the attainment of the group's goal. This may well be so, but if a leader is seen as important for the attainment of these goals, or even for their partial attainment, the group may tolerate individual deviation when it is seen as balanced by positive contributions. A man may lose credit for deviations, but only when his credit balance is exhausted will he be removed. If he continues to amass credit in the eyes of the members through group-approved activities, he attains a threshold permitting deviations from common expectations. This may explain, at least in part, why a leader may be given greater leeway for deviating behavior than his followers: his having accumulated highly visible merit gives him a leeway in behavior not granted to less meritorious members; the group will take from "him" what it will not take from "them." Task orientation and tolerance of deviance are therefore not necessarily mutually exclusive.

The term "idiosyncrasy credit" readily brings to mind the image of a "would-be" innovator, who is tolerated because of other contributions, yet whose innovating message is largely ignored by the group. This is not necessarily so. "Idiosyncrasy credit" because of high achievement does not merely imply tolerance of otherwise unacceptable behavior; it also implies that members of the group will listen more readily.

The Time Dimension of Innovation

Innovations must not only be analyzed in terms of the structural circumstances under which they occur but also in terms of their impact over time. They must be located in social time as well as in social space.

A type of behavior which might at first be perceived by the group as an attack on its norms and values might at a later time be considered in a different light. If this happens during the lifetime of the innovator he is likely to experience a sharp change in status; he will then reap the rewards of an action which was at first negatively sanctioned. The innovator is then co-opted, perhaps even against his will, into the ranks of the upholders of conformity. If, on the other hand, he obtains recognition only after his death, the lifelong heretic becomes, in effect, a posthumous saint. The Catholic church, with its amazing flexibility, has been especially adept at this process of social transmutation in which, through a remarkable alchemy, its victims have been transformed into patron saints so that Joan of Arc in due time became Saint Joan. As Merton has observed: "In the history of every society . . . some of its cultural heroes have been regarded as heroic precisely because they have had the courage and the vision to depart from norms then obtaining in the group. As we all know, the rebel, revolutionary, nonconformist, individualist, heretic and renegade of an earlier time is often the culture hero of today." [41] The Jewish prophets, those holy demagogues, were feared, despised, and outcast by the religious and secular powers of their day. Yet, as Max Weber has noted, "it is completely inconceivable that without a profound experience of a confirmation of the prophetic words of doom . . . the belief of the people was not only unbroken by the fearful political fate, but in a unique and quite unheard of historical paradox was definitely confirmed. The entire inner construction of the Old Testament is inconceivable without its orientation in terms of the oracles of the prophets. These giants cast their shadows through the millennia into the present." [42]

NOTES

1. This paper was substantially completed during the author's stay at the Institute for Social Research, Oslo, Norway, under a Fulbright Senior Research Scholarship. I wish to express my appreciation to a number of European colleagues, too numerous to mention, whose critical reading of an earlier draft of this paper was most helpful. I owe a special debt to Johan

Galtung, of the University of Oslo and the Institute for Social Research, Oslo, to Yrjö Littunen, School of Social Sciences, Tampere, Finland, and to Robert K. Merton, of Columbia University, who made a number of very valuable suggestions. Several propositions of this paper were adumbrated in the author's *The Functions of Social Conflict,* Glencoe, Ill.: Free Press, 1956.

2. Émile Durkheim, *Division of Labor in Society,* Glencoe, Ill.: Free Press, 1947, p. 102.

3. George Herbert Mead, "The Psychology of Punitive Justice," *American Journal of Sociology,* 23 (1928), 557–602, esp. 591. *Cf.* also Marx's parallel formulation: "The criminal produces an impression now moral, now tragic, and renders a 'service' by arousing the moral and aesthetic sentiments of the public." Quoted in Bottomore and Rubel, eds., *Karl Marx,* London: Watts & Co., 1956, p. 159.

4. Talcott Parsons, *The Social System,* Glencoe, Ill.: Free Press, 1951, p. 512.

5. Harold H. Kelley and John W. Thibault, "Experimental Studies of Group Problem Solving and Process," in Gardner Lindzey (ed.), *Handbook of Social Psychology,* Cambridge, Mass.: Addison Wesley Publishing Co., 1954, II, 768.

6. Kai T. Erikson, "Social Margins: Some Notes on the Sociology of Deviance" (paper read at the fifty-fifth meeting of the American Sociological Association, New York, 1960).

7. W. E. H. Lecky wrote about the prostitute: "herself the supreme type of vice, she is ultimately the most efficient guardian of virtue" (quoted by Kingsley Davis, "Prostitution" in Robert K. Merton and Robert A. Nisbet [eds.], *Contemporary Social Problems,* New York: Harcourt, Brace & World, Inc., 1961, pp. 262–288). Davis shows the close connection between prostitution and the maintenance of traditional family patterns.

8. Erikson, *op. cit. Cf.* also V. W. Turner's parallel formulation: "The norm derives strength and definition from condemnation of its breach in the public situations of ritual and law. The deviant, the haphazard and the contingent can only be recognized to be such where consensus to what is typical, orthodox, regular exists. And vice versa." (*Schism and Continuity in an African Society,* Manchester: Manchester University Press, 1957, p. 329.) This is of course what Hegel meant when he asserted that "no step in philosophy was possible" unless it was recognized that the positive and the negative gain their "truth only in their relation to each other so that each contains the other within it" (*Wissenschaft der Logik,* Lasson [ed.], Leipzig: Felix Meiner, 1923, II, 54–56).

9. *Cf.* Anna Freud, *The Ego and the Mechanisms of Defense,* New York: International Universities Press, 1946, pp. 117 ff.

10. Stewart E. Perry and Helen Swick Perry, "Deviant Behavior, Function and Dysfunction on the Psychiatric Ward" (paper read at the Eastern Sociological Society meetings, April 23–24, 1960, Boston, Mass.).

11. Robert A. Dentler and Kai T. Erikson, "The Functions of Deviance in Groups," *Social Problems,* 7 (1959), 98–107.

12. *Ibid.,* p. 105.

13. Kelley and Thibault, *op. cit.,* p. 766.

14. Harold H. Kelley and Martin M. Shapiro, "An Experiment on Conformity to Group Norms Where Conformity Is Detrimental to Group Achievement," *American Sociological Review,* 19 (1954), 667–677.

15. These variations in social control have been identified and discussed by Robert K. Merton in his "Social Structure and Anomie," *Social Theory and Social Structure,* rev. ed., Glencoe, Ill.: Free Press, 1957, esp. p. 133.

16. Roger Caillois, "Theory of the Festival," in *Man and the Sacred,* Glencoe, Ill.: Free Press, 1959.

17. Georg Simmel, "The Stranger," in Kurt H. Wolff (ed. and tr.), *The Sociology of Georg Simmel,* Glencoe, Ill.: Free Press, 1950; and Orrin E. Klapp, "The Fool as a Social Type," *American Journal of Sociology,* 55 (1949), 157–162.

18. *Cf.* Albert K. Cohen, "The Study of Social Organization and Deviant Behavior," in Merton *et al.* (eds.), *Sociology Today,* New York: Basic Books, 1959, pp. 461–484.

19. It was a distinct step forward to conceptualize the sick and the criminal as deviants from the institutionalized norms on the ground that both roles called forth social control mechanisms designed to restore "health." Nevertheless, as Vilhelm Aubert and Sheldon Messinger argued ("The Criminal and the Sick," *Inquiry* [Oslo], 1 (1958), 137–160), these roles are also crucially dissimilar insofar as, among other things, the sick is conceived as one who cannot be held responsible for his failure to perform previously assumed roles, while the criminal is not perceived in terms of inability but rather as having been able to act differently had he chosen to do so.

20. Merton, *op. cit.,* p. 360. *Cf.* also his "Social Problems and Sociological Theory" in Merton and Nisbet (eds.), *op. cit.,* pp. 697–737.

21. Merton, *op. cit.,* p. 363 *et passim.*

22. Lewis A. Coser, "Durkheim's Conservatism and Its Implications for Sociological Theory," in Kurt H. Wolff (ed.), *Émile Durkheim,* Columbus: Ohio State University Press, 1961, pp. 211–232. *Cf.* also Roger Nett, "Conformity-Deviation and the Social Control Concept," *Ethics,* 44 (1953), 38–45.

23. Gandhi distinguished between criminal and civil disobedience in terms of the concept of publicity. Civil disobedience, to him, was by definition public action.

24. Cf. Robert K. Merton, "Social Conformity, Deviation and Opportunity-Structures," *American Sociological Review,* 24 (1959), 177–189, esp. p. 181. *Cf.* also Herbert Menzel, "Innovation, Integration, and Marginality," *American Sociological Review,* 25 (1960), 704–713.

25. Lewis A. Coser, "Social Conflict and the Theory of Social Change," *British Journal of Sociology,* 8 (1957), 197–207.

26. John Dewey, *Human Nature and Conduct,* New York: Modern Library, 1930, p. 300.

27. Talcott Parsons, *op. cit.,* pp. 204–205 *et passim.*

28. Alvin M. Gouldner, "Organizational Analysis," in *Sociology Today,* pp. 423 ff.

29. George Homans, *Social Behavior,* New York: Harcourt, Brace & World, Inc., 1961, p. 55.

30. *Income-Security Values at Different Levels of Frustration,* Transactions of the Westermarck Society, Copenhagen: Ejnar Munksgaard, 1959, IV, 234–235 ff. *Cf.* also Goethe's "Nichts ist schwerer zu ertragen als eine Reihe von schoenen Tagen."

31. Littunen, *op. cit.,* p. 224. *Cf.* also Marx's statement: "The criminal interrupts the monotony and security of bourgeois life. Thus he protects it from stagnation" (*op. cit.,* p. 159).

32. D. O. Hebb and W. R. Thompson, "The Social Significance of Animal Studies," in *Handbook of Social Psychology,* 1, 532–561.

33. Daniel J. Levinson, "Role, Personality, and Social Structure in the Organizational Setting," *Journal of Abnormal and Social Psychology,* 58 (1959), 170–180. *Cf.* also Erving Goffman's discussion of "Role Distance" in his *Encounters,* Indianapolis: Bobbs-Merrill Co., 1961.

34. *Op. cit. Cf.* also E. Paul Torrance, "Function of Expressed Disagreement in Small Group Processes" in A. Rubenstein and C. Haberstroh (eds.), *Some Theories of Organization,* Homewood, Ill.: Dorsey Press, 1960, pp. 250–257.

35. Robert K. Merton, "Social Structure and Anomie," *op. cit.,* pp. 131–160.

36. Georg Simmel, "The Stranger," *op. cit.;* and Thorstein Veblen, "The Intellectual Preeminence of the Jews," in his *Essays in Our Changing Order,* East Orange, N.J.: Thomas Kelly, 1934, pp. 219–231.

37. H. G. Barnett, *Innovation—the Basis of Cultural Change,* New York: McGraw-Hill, 1953, p. 404. *Cf.* also Karl Mannheim, *Man and Society in an Age of Reconstruction,* London: Routledge & Kegan Paul, 1940, esp. pp. 56–57, as well as Robert Park's "Introduction" to E. V. Stonequist, *The Marginal Man,* New York: Charles Scribner's Sons, 1937.

38. George C. Homans, *The Human Group,* New York: Harcourt, Brace & Co., 1950, p. 141.

39. *Social Behavior,* p. 346. Recent experimental work throws doubt on the idea that the relation between status and conformity is ever a simple one. J. E. Dittes and H. H. Kelley showed, e.g., that individuals who felt acceptable in a group felt freer to express disagreements publicly, while those with a low sense of acceptance were much higher in their *public* than in

their *private* conformity. See "Effects of Different Conditions of Acceptance upon Conformity to Group Norms," *Journal of Abnormal and Social Psychology,* 53 (1956), 100–107. *Cf.* also Herbert Menzel, "Public and Private Conformity under Different Conditions of Acceptance in the Group," *Journal of Abnormal and Social Psychology,* 55 (1957), 398–402.

40. E. P. Hollander, "Conformity, Status and Idiosyncrasy Credit," *Psychological Review,* 65 (1958), 117–127.

41. Merton, *Social Theory,* p. 183.

42. Max Weber, *Ancient Judaism,* Hans H. Gerth and Don Martindale (tr. and ed.), Glencoe, Ill.: Free Press, 1952, p. 334.

On Deviance

63. NOTES ON THE SOCIOLOGY OF DEVIANCE

KAI T. ERIKSON

Kai T. Erikson suggests that "two separate yet often competing currents are found in any society: those forces which promote a high degree of conformity among the people of the community so that they know what to expect from one another, and those forces which encourage a certain degree of diversity so that people can be deployed across the range of group space to survey its potential, measure its capacity, and, in the case of those we call deviant, patrol its boundaries." His thesis is based upon the work of sociologists such as Emile Durkheim and George Herbert Mead and his own research on the "Wayward Puritans."

Kai T. Erikson is Professor of Sociology and Master of Trumbull College at Yale University. He has written a number of essays on the sociology of deviance and on sociology and history. His combined interests are best illustrated in the award-winning The Wayward Puritan *(1966), from which this selection was borrowed.*

In 1895 Émile Durkheim wrote a book called *The Rules of Sociological Method* which was intended as a working manual for persons interested in the systematic study of society. One of the most impor- tant themes of Durkheim's work was that sociologists should formulate a new set of criteria for distinguishing between "nor- mal" and "pathological" elements in the life of a society. Behavior which looks abnormal to the psychiatrist or the judge, he suggested, does not always look abnormal when viewed through the special lens of the sociologist; and thus students of the new science should be careful to understand that even the most aberrant forms of individual behavior may still be considered normal from this broader point of view. To illustrate his argument, Durkheim made the surprising observation that crime was really a natural kind of social activity, "an integral part of all healthy societies." [1]

Durkheim's interest in this subject had been expressed several years before when *The Division of Labor in Society* was first published.[2] In that important book, he had suggested that crime (and by extension other forms of deviation) may actually perform a needed service to society by drawing people together in a common posture of anger and indignation. The deviant individual violates rules of conduct which the rest of the community holds in high respect; and when these people come together to express their outrage over the offense and to bear witness against the offender, they develop a tighter bond of solidarity than existed earlier. The excitement generated by the crime, in other words, quickens the tempo of interaction in the group and creates a climate in which the private sentiments of many separate persons are fused together into a common sense of morality.

Crime brings together upright consciences and concentrates them. We have only to notice what happens, particularly in a small town, when some moral scandal has just been committed. They stop each other on the street, they visit each other, they seek to come together to talk of the event and to wax indignant in common. From all the similar impressions which are exchanged, for all the temper that gets itself expressed, there emerges a unique temper . . . which is everybody's without being anybody's in particular. That is the public temper.[3]

The deviant act, then, creates a sense of mutuality among the people of a community by supplying a focus for group feeling. Like a war, a flood, or some other emergency, deviance makes people more alert to the interests they share in common and draws attention to those values which constitute the "collective conscience" of the community. Unless the rhythm of group life is punctuated by occasional moments of deviant behavior, presumably, social organization would be impossible.[4]

This brief argument has been regarded a classic of sociological thinking ever since it was first presented, even though it has not inspired much in the way of empirical work. The purpose of the present chapter is to consider Durkheim's suggestion in terms more congenial to modern social theory and to see if these insights can be translated into useful research hypotheses. The pages to follow may range far afield from the starting point recommended by Durkheim, but they are addressed to the question he originally posed: does it make any sense to assert that deviant forms of behavior are a natural and even beneficial part of social life?

–1–

One of the earliest problems the sociologist encounters in his search for a meaningful approach to deviant behavior is that the subject itself does not seem to have any natural boundaries. Like people in any field, sociologists find it convenient to assume that the deviant person is somehow "different" from those of his fellows who manage to conform, but years of research into the problem have not yielded any important evidence as to what, if anything, this difference might be. Investigators have studied the character of the deviant's background, the content of his dreams, the shape of his skull, the substance of his thoughts—yet none of this information has enabled us to draw a clear line between the kind of person who commits deviant acts and the kind of person who does not. Nor can we gain a better perspective on the matter by shift-in our attention away from the individual deviant and looking instead at the behavior he enacts. Definitions of deviance vary widely as we range over the various classes found in a single society or across the various cultures into which mankind is divided, and it soon becomes apparent that there are no objective properties which all deviant acts can be said to share in common—even within the confines of a given group. Behavior which qualifies one man for prison may qualify another for sainthood, since the quality of the act itself depends so much on the circumstances under which it was performed and the temper of the audience which witnessed it.

This being the case, many sociologists employ a far simpler tactic in their approach to the problem—namely, to let each social group in question provide its own definitions of deviant behavior. In this study, as in others dealing with the same general subject,[5] the term "deviance" refers to conduct which the people of a group consider so dangerous or embarrassing or irritating that they bring special sanctions to bear against the persons who exhibit it. Deviance is not a property *inherent in* any particular kind of behavior; it is a property *conferred upon* that behavior by the people who come into direct or indirect contact with it. The only way an observer can tell whether or not a given style of behavior is deviant, then, is to learn something about the standards of the audience which responds to it.

This definition may seem a little awkward in practice, but it has the advantage of bringing a neglected issue into proper focus. When the people of a community decide that it is time to "do something" about the conduct of one of their number, they are involved in a highly intricate process. After all, even the worst miscreant in society conforms most of the time, if only in the sense that he uses the correct silver at dinner, stops obediently at traffic lights, or in a hundred other ways respects the ordinary conventions of his group. And if his fellows elect to bring sanctions against him for the occasions when he does misbehave, they are responding to a few deviant details scattered among a vast array of entirely acceptable conduct. The person who appears in a criminal court and is stamped a "thief" may have spent no more than a passing moment engaged in that activity, and the same can be said for many of the people who pass in review before some agency of control and return from the experience with a deviant label of one sort or another. When the community nominates someone to the deviant class, then, it is sifting a few important details out of the stream of behavior he has emitted and is in effect declaring that these details reflect the kind of person he "really" is. In law as well as in public opinion, the fact that someone has committed a felony or has been known to use narcotics can become the major identifying badge of his person: the very expression "he is a thief" or "he is an addict" seems to provide at once a description of his position in society and a profile of his character.

The manner in which a community sifts these telling details out of a person's overall performance, then, is an important part of its social control apparatus. And it is important to notice that the people of a community take a number of factors into account when they pass judgment on one another which are not immediately related to the deviant act itself: whether or not a person will be considered deviant, for instance, has something to do with his social class, his past record as an offender, the amount of remorse he manages to convey, and many similar concerns which take hold in the shifting mood of the community. Perhaps this is not so apparent in cases of serious crime or desperate illness, where the offending act looms so darkly that it obscures most of the other details of the person's life; but in the day-by-day sifting processes which take place throughout society this feature is always present. Some men who drink heavily are called alcoholics and others are not, some men who behave oddly are committed to hospitals and others are not, some men with no visible means of support are charged with vagrancy and others are not —and the difference between those who earn a deviant title in society and those who go their own way in peace is largely determined by the way in which the community filters out and codes the many details of behavior which come to its attention.

Once the problem is phrased in this manner we can ask: how does a community decide which of these behavioral details are important enough to merit special attention? And why, having made this decision, does it build institutions like prisons and asylums to detain the persons who perform them? The conventional answer to that question, of course, is that a society creates the machinery of control in order to protect itself against the "harmful" effects of deviation, in much the same way that an organism mobilizes its resources to combat an invasion of germs. Yet this simple view of the matter is apt to pose many more problems than it actually settles. As both Émile Durkheim and George Herbert Mead pointed out long ago, it is by no means evident that all acts considered deviant in society are in fact (or even in principle) harmful to group life. It is undoubtedly true that no culture would last long if its members engaged in murder or arson among themselves on any large scale, but there is no real evidence that many other of the activities considered deviant throughout the world (certain dietary prohibitions are a prominent example) have any relationship to the group's survival. In our own day, for instance, we might well ask why prostitution or marihuana smoking or homosexuality are thought to endanger the health of the social order. Perhaps these activities *are* dangerous, but to accept this conclusion without a thoughtful review of the situa-

tion is apt to blind us to the important fact that people in every corner of the world manage to survive handsomely while engaged in practices which their neighbors regard as extremely abhorrent. In the absence of any surer footing, then, it is quite reasonable for sociologists to return to the most innocent and yet the most basic question which can be asked about deviation: why does a community assign one form of behavior rather than another to the deviant class?

The following paragraphs will sugest one possible answer to that question.

–2–

Human actors are sorted into various kinds of collectivity, ranging from relatively small units such as the nuclear family to relatively large ones such as a nation or culture. One of the most stubborn difficulties in the study of deviation is that the problem is defined differently at each one of these levels: behavior that is considered unseemly within the context of a single family may be entirely acceptable to the community in general, while behavior that attracts severe censure from the members of the community may go altogether unnoticed elsewhere in the culture. People in society, then, must learn to deal separately with deviance at each one of these levels and to distinguish among them in his own daily activity. A man may disinherit his son for conduct that violates old family traditions or ostracize a neighbor for conduct that violates some local custom, but he is not expected to employ either of these standards when he serves as a juror in a court of law. In each of the three situations he is required to use a different set of criteria to decide whether or not the behavior in question exceeds tolerable limits.

In the next few pages we shall be talking about deviant behavior in social units called "communities," but the use of this term does not mean that the argument applies only at that level of organization. In theory, at least, the argument being made here should fit all kinds of human collectivity—families as well as whole cultures, small groups as well as nations— and the term "community" is only being used in this context because it seems particularly convenient.[6]

The people of a community spend most of their lives in close contact with one another, sharing a common sphere of experience which makes them feel that they belong to a special "kind" and live in a special "place." In the formal language of sociology, this means that communities are boundary maintaining: each has a specific territory in the world as a whole, not only in the sense that it occupies a defined region of geographical space but also in the sense that it takes over a particular niche in what might be called cultural space and develops its own "ethos" or "way" within that compass. Both of these dimensions of group space, the geographical and the cultural, set the community apart as a special place and provide an important point of reference for its members.

When one describes any system as boundary maintaining, one is saying that it controls the fluctuation of its constituent parts so that the whole retains a limited range of activity, a given pattern of constancy and stability, within the larger environment. A human community can be said to maintain boundaries, then, in the sense that its members tend to confine themselves to a particular radius of activity and to regard any conduct which drifts outside that radius as somehow inappropriate or immoral. Thus the group retains a kind of cultural integrity, a voluntary restriction on its own potential for expansion, beyond that which is strictly required for accommodation to the environment. Human behavior can vary over an enormous range, but each community draws a symbolic set of parentheses around a certain segment of that range and limits its own activities within that narrower zone.

These parentheses, so to speak, are the community's boundaries.

Now people who live together in communities cannot relate to one another in any coherent way or even acquire a sense of their own stature as group members unless they learn something about the boundaries of the territory they occupy in social space, if only because they need to sense what lies beyond the margins of the group before they can appreciate the special quality of the experience which takes place within it. Yet how do people learn about the boundaries of their community? And how do they convey this information to the generations which replace them?

To begin with, the only material found in a society for marking boundaries is the behavior of its members—or rather, the networks of interaction which link these members together in regular social relations. And the interactions which do the most effective job of locating and publicizing the group's outer edges would seem to be those which take place between deviant persons on the one side and official agents of the community on the other. The deviant is a person whose activities have moved outside the margins of the group, and when the community calls him to account for that vagrancy it is making a statement about the nature and placement of its boundaries. It is declaring how much variability and diversity can be tolerated within the group before it begins to lose its distinctive shape, its unique identity. Now there may be other moments in the life of the group which perform a similar service: wars, for instance, can publicize a group's boundaries by drawing attention to the line separating the group from an adversary, and certain kinds of religious ritual, dance ceremony, and other traditional pageantry can dramatize the difference between "we" and "they" by portraying a symbolic encounter between the two. But on the whole, members of a community inform one another about the placement of their boundaries by participating in the confrontations which occur when persons who venture out to the edges of the group are met by policing agents whose special business it is to guard the cultural integrity of the community. Whether these confrontations take the form of criminal trials, excommunication hearings, courts-martial, or even psychiatric case conferences, they act as boundary-maintaining devices in the sense that they demonstrate to whatever audience is concerned where the line is drawn between behavior that belongs in the special universe of the group and behavior that does not. In general, this kind of information is not easily relayed by the straightforward use of language. Most readers of this paragraph, for instance, have a fairly clear idea of the line separating theft from more legitimate forms of commerce, but few of them have ever seen a published statute describing these differences. More likely than not, our information on the subject has been drawn from publicized instances in which the relevant laws were applied—and for that matter, the law itself is largely a collection of past cases and decisions, a synthesis of the various confrontations which have occurred in the life of the legal order.

It may be important to note in this connection that confrontations between deviant offenders and the agents of control have always attracted a good deal of public attention. In our own past, the trial and punishment of offenders were staged in the market place and afforded the crowd a chance to participate in a direct, active way. Today, of course, we no longer parade deviants in the town square or expose them to the carnival atmosphere of a Tyburn, but it is interesting that the "reform" which brought about this change in penal practice coincided almost exactly with the development of newspapers as a medium of mass information. Perhaps this is no more than an accident of history, but it is nonetheless true that newspapers (and now radio and television) offer much the same kind of entertainment as public

hangings or a Sunday visit to the local gaol. A considerable portion of what we call "news" is devoted to reports about deviant behavior and its consequences, and it is no simple matter to explain why these items should be considered newsworthy or why they should command the extraordinary attention they do. Perhaps they appeal to a number of psychological perversities among the mass audience, as commentators have suggested, but at the same time they constitute one of our main sources of information about the normative outlines of society. In a figurative sense, at least, morality and immorality meet at the public scaffold, and it is during this meeting that the line between them is drawn.

Boundaries are never a fixed property of any community. They are always shifting as the people of the group find new ways to define the outer limits of their universe, new ways to position themselves on the larger cultural map. Sometimes changes occur within the structure of the group which require its members to make a new survey of their territory—a change of leadership, a shift of mood. Sometimes changes occur in the surrounding environment, altering the background against which the people of the group have measured their own uniqueness. And always, new generations are moving in to take their turn guarding old institutions and need to be informed about the contours of the world they are inheriting. Thus single encounters between the deviant and his community are only fragments of an ongoing social process. Like an article of common law, boundaries remain a meaningful point of reference only so long as they are repeatedly tested by persons on the fringes of the group and repeatedly defended by persons chosen to represent the group's inner morality. Each time the community moves to censure some act of deviation, then, and convenes a formal ceremony to deal with the responsible offender, it sharpens the authority of the violated norm and restates where the boundaries of the group are located.

For these reasons, deviant behavior is not a simple kind of leakage which occurs when the machinery of society is in poor working order, but may be, in controlled quantities, an important condition for preserving the stability of social life. Deviant forms of behavior, by marking the outer edges of group life, give the inner structure its special character and thus supply the framework within which the people of the group develop an orderly sense of their own cultural identity. Perhaps this is what Aldous Huxley had in mind when he wrote:

Now tidiness is undeniably good—but a good of which it is easily possible to have too much and at too high a price. . . . The good life can only be lived in a society in which tidiness is preached and practised, but not too fanatically, and where efficiency is always haloed, as it were, by a tolerated margin of mess.[7]

This raises a delicate theoretical issue. If we grant that human groups often derive benefit from deviant behavior, can we then assume that they are organized in such a way as to promote this resource? Can we assume, in other words, that forces operate in the social structure to recruit offenders and to commit them to long periods of service in the deviant ranks? This is not a question which can be answered with our present store of empirical data, but one observation can be made which gives the question an interesting perspective—namely, that deviant forms of conduct often seem to derive nourishment from the very agencies devised to inhibit them. Indeed, the agencies built by society for preventing deviance are often so poorly equipped for the task that we might well ask why this is regarded as their "real" function in the first place.

It is by now a thoroughly familiar argument that many of the institutions designed to discourage deviant behavior actually operate in such a way as to perpetuate it. For one thing, prisons, hospitals, and other similar agencies provide aid and shelter to large numbers of deviant persons, sometimes giving them a certain advantage in the competition for social resources. But beyond this, such institutions gather marginal people into tightly segregated groups, give them an opportunity to teach one another the skills and attitudes of a deviant career, and even provoke them into using these skills by reinforcing their sense of alienation from the rest of society.[8] Nor is this observation a modern one:

The misery suffered in gaols is not half their evil; they are filled with every sort of corruption that poverty and wickedness can generate; with all the shameless and profligate enormities that can be produced by the impudence of ignominy, the rage of want, and the malignity of dispair. In a prison the check of the public eye is removed; and the power of the law is spent. There are few fears, there are no blushes. The lewd inflame the more modest; the audacious harden the timid. Everyone fortifies himself as he can against his own remaining sensibility; endeavoring to practise on others the arts that are practised on himself; and to gain the applause of his worst associates by imitating their manners.[9]

These lines, written almost two centuries ago, are a harsh indictment of prisons, but many of the conditions they describe continue to be reported in even the most modern studies of prison life. Looking at the matter from a long-range historical perspective, it is fair to conclude that prisons have done a conspicuously poor job of reforming the convicts placed in their custody; but the very consistency of this failure may have a peculiar logic of its own. Perhaps we find it difficult to change the worst of our penal practices because we *expect* the prison to harden the inmate's commitment to deviant forms of behavior and draw him more deeply into the deviant ranks. On the whole, we are a people who do not really expect deviants to change very much as they are processed through the control agencies we provide for them, and we are often reluctant to devote much of the community's resources to the job of rehabilitation. In this sense, the prison which graduates long rows of accomplished criminals (or, for that matter, the state asylum which stores its most severe cases away in some back ward) may do serious violence to the aims of its founders, but it does very little violence to the expectations of the population it serves.

These expectations, moreover, are found in every corner of society and constitute an important part of the climate in which we deal with deviant forms of behavior.

To begin with, the community's decision to bring deviant sanctions against one of its members is not a simple act of censure. It is an intricate rite of transition, at once moving the individual out of his ordinary place in society and transferring him into a special deviant position.[10] The ceremonies which mark this change of status, generally, have a number of related phases. They supply a formal stage on which the deviant and his community can confront one another (as in the criminal trial); they make an announcement about the nature of his deviancy (a verdict or diagnosis, for example); and they place him in a particular role which is thought to neutralize the harmful effects of his misconduct (like the role of prisoner or patient). These commitment ceremonies tend to be occasions of wide public interest and ordinarily take place in a highly dramatic setting.[11] Perhaps the most obvious example of a commitment ceremony is the criminal trial, with its elaborate formality and exaggerated ritual, but more modest equivalents can be found wherever procedures are set up to judge whether or not someone is legitimately deviant.

Now an important feature of these ceremonies in our own culture is that they are almost irreversible. Most provisional roles conferred by society—those of the student or conscripted soldier, for exam-

ple—include some kind of terminal ceremony to mark the individual's movement back out of the role once its temporary advantages have been exhausted. But the roles allotted the deviant seldom make allowance for this type of passage. He is ushered into the deviant position by a decisive and often dramatic ceremony, yet is retired from it with scarcely a word of public notice. And as a result, the deviant often returns home with no proper license to resume a normal life in the community. Nothing has happened to cancel out the stigmas imposed upon him by earlier commitment ceremonies; nothing has happened to revoke the verdict or diagnosis pronounced upon him at that time. It should not be surprising, then, that the people of the community are apt to greet the returning deviant with a considerable degree of apprehension and distrust, for in a very real sense they are not at all sure who he is.

A circularity is thus set into motion which has all the earmarks of a "self-fulfilling prophecy," to use Merton's fine phrase. On the one hand, it seems quite obvious that the community's apprehensions help reduce whatever chances the deviant might otherwise have had for a successful return home. Yet at the same time, everyday experience seems to show that these suspicions are wholly reasonable, for it is a well-known and highly publicized fact that many if not most ex-convicts return to crime after leaving prison and that large numbers of mental patients require further treatment after an initial hospitalization. The common feeling that deviant persons never really change, then, may derive from a faulty premise; but the feeling is expressed so frequently and with such conviction that it eventually creates the facts which later "prove" it to be correct. If the returning deviant encounters this circularity often enough, it is quite understandable that he, too, may begin to wonder whether he has fully graduated from the deviant role, and he may respond to the uncertainty by resuming some kind of deviant activity. In many respects, this may be the only way for the individual and his community to agree what kind of person he is.

Moreover this prophecy is found in the official policies of even the most responsible agencies of control. Police departments could not operate with any real effectiveness if they did not regard ex-convicts as a ready pool of suspects to be tapped in the event of trouble, and psychiatric clinics could not do a successful job in the community if they were not always alert to the possibility of former patients suffering relapses. Thus the prophecy gains currency at many levels within the social order, not only in the poorly informed attitudes of the community at large, but in the best informed theories of most control agencies as well.

In one form or another this problem has been recognized in the West for many hundreds of years, and this simple fact has a curious implication. For if our culture has supported a steady flow of deviation throughout long periods of historical change, the rules which apply to any kind of evolutionary thinking would suggest that strong forces must be at work to keep the flow intact—and this because it contributes in some important way to the survival of the culture as a whole. This does not furnish us with sufficient warrant to declare that deviance is "functional" (in any of the many senses of that term), but it should certainly make us wary of the assumption so often made in sociological circles that any well-structured society is somehow designed to prevent deviant behavior from occurring.[12]

It might be then argued that we need new metaphors to carry our thinking about deviance onto a different plane. On the whole, American sociologists have devoted most of their attention to those forces in society which seem to assert a centralizing influence on human behavior, gathering people together into tight clusters called "groups" and bringing them under the jurisdiction of governing principles called "norms" or "standards." The questions which sociologists have traditionally asked of their data, then, are addressed to the uniformities rather than the divergencies of social life: how is it that people learn to think in similar ways, to accept the same group moralities, to move by the same rhythms of behavior, to see life with the same eyes? How is it, in short, that cultures accomplish the incredible alchemy of making unity out of diversity, harmony out of conflict, order out of confusion? Somehow we often act as if the differences between people can be taken for granted, being too natural to require comment, but that the symmetry which human groups manage to achieve must be explained by referring to the molding influence of the social structure.

But variety, too, is a product of the social structure. It is certainly remarkable that members of a culture come to look so much alike; but it is also remarkable that out of all this sameness a people can develop a complex division of labor, move off into diverging career lines, scatter across the surface of the territory they share in common, and create so many differences of temper, ideology, fashion, and mood. Perhaps we can conclude, then, that two separate yet often competing currents are found in any society: those forces which promote a high degree of conformity among the people of the community so that they know what to expect from one another, and those forces which encourage a certain degree of diversity so that people can be deployed across the range of group space to survey its potential, measure its capacity, and, in the case of those we call deviants, patrol its boundaries. In such a scheme, the deviant would appear as a natural product of group differentiation. He is not a bit of debris spun out by faulty social machinery, but a relevant figure in the community's overall division of labor.

NOTES

1. Émile Durkheim, *The Rules of Sociological Method,* S. A. Solovay and J. H. Mueller (trs.), Glencoe, Ill.: The Free Press, 1958, p. 67.

2. Émile Durkheim, *The Division of Labor in Society,* George Simpson (tr.), Glencoe, Ill.: The Free Press, 1960.

3. *Ibid.,* p. 102.

4. A similar point was later made by George Herbert Mead in his very important paper "The Psychology of Punitive Justice," *American Journal of Sociology,* XXIII (March 1918), 577–602.

5. See particularly the works of Edwin M. Lemert, Howard S. Becker, and John I. Kitsuse.

6. In fact, the first statement of the general notion presented here was concerned with the study of small groups. See Robert A. Dentler and Kai T. Erikson, "The Functions of Deviance in Groups," *Social Problems,* VII (Fall 1959), 98–107.

7. Aldous Huxley, *Prisons: The "Carceri" Etchings by Piranesi,* London: The Trianon Press, 1949, p. 13.

8. For a good description of this process in the modern prison, see Gresham Sykes, *The Society of Captives,* Princeton, N.J.: Princeton University Press, 1958. For discussions of similar problems in two different kinds of mental hospital, see Erving Goffman, *Asylums,* New York: Bobbs-Merrill, 1962, and Kai T. Erikson, "Patient Role and Social Uncertainty: A Dilemma of the Mentally Ill," *Psychiatry,* XX (August 1957), 263–274.

9. Written by "a celebrated" but not otherwise identified author (perhaps Henry Fielding) and quoted in John Howard, *The State of the Prisons,* London, 1777, London: J. M. Dent and Sons, 1929, p. 10.

10. The classic description of this process as it applies to the medical patient is found in Talcott Parsons, *The Social System,* Glencoe, Ill.: The Free Press, 1951.

11. See Harold Garfinkel, "Successful Degradation Ceremonies," *American Journal of Sociology,* LXI (January 1956), 420–424.

12. Albert K. Cohen, for example, speaking for a dominant strain in sociological thinking, takes the question quite for granted: "It would seem that the control of deviant behavior is, by definition, a culture goal." See "The Study of Social Disorganization and Deviant Behavior" in Merton, *et al.* (eds.), *Sociology Today,* New York: Basic Books, 1959, p. 465.

64. ILLEGITIMATE MEANS, ANOMIE, AND DEVIANT BEHAVIOR

RICHARD A. CLOWARD

The theory of anomie as an approach to the study of the causes and manifestations of deviant behavior has undergone three major phases of development. The first was marked by Émile Durkheim's analysis of the breakdown of regulatory norms (the situation he called "anomie") under intensive social pressure for personal achievement. The second was reflected in Robert K. Merton's systematic paradigm for investigating the relationship between culturally defined success-goals and accessibility of legitimate means to achieve them.

In the third phase, represented by Richard A. Cloward's work, an additional variable is added to the examination of anomie. Cloward introduces the concept of differential access to success-goals by illegitimate means in certain social situations. This latter emphasis is based upon two theoretical axes, one represented by Durkheim and Merton, the other by Clifford Shaw, Henry D. McKay, Edwin H. Sutherland, and others concerned with the processes of "cultural transmission" and "differential association." Cloward extends the theory of anomie to include seemingly unrelated theories of deviant behavior now contained in the traditional literature of criminology.

Richard A. Cloward is Professor of Social Work at Columbia University's School of Social Work. With Lloyd E. Ohlin, he is the author of Delinquency and Opportunity: A Theory of Delinquent Gangs (1959). *In addition, Professor Cloward is coeditor of* Social Perspectives on Behavior (1958) *and* Theoretical Studies in the Social Organization of the Prison (1960).

This paper [1] represents an attempt to consolidate two major sociological traditions of thought about the problem of deviant behavior. The first, exemplified by the work of Émile Durkheim and Robert K. Merton, may be called the anomie tradition.[2] The second, illustrated principally by the studies of Clifford R. Shaw, Henry D. McKay, and Edwin H. Sutherland, may be called the "cultural transmission" and "differential association" tradition.[3] Despite some reciprocal borrowing of ideas, these intellectual traditions developed more or less independently. By seeking to consolidate them, a more adequate theory of deviant behavior may be constructed.

Differentials in Availability of Legitimate Means: The Theory of Anomie

The theory of anomie has undergone two major phases of development. Durkheim first used the concept to explain deviant behavior. He focused on the way in which various social conditions lead to "overweening ambition," and how, in turn, unlimited aspirations ultimately produce a breakdown in regulatory norms. Robert

Reprinted from the *American Sociological Review*, **24** (1959), 164–176, by permission of the author and the American Sociological Association.

K. Merton has systematized and extended the theory, directing attention to patterns of disjunction between culturally prescribed goals and socially organized access to them by *legitimate* means. In this paper, a third phase is outlined. An additional variable is incorporated in the developing scheme of anomie, namely, the concept of differentials in access to success-goals by illegitimate means.[4]

Phase I: unlimited aspirations and the breakdown of regulatory norms

In Durkheim's work, a basic distinction is made between "physical needs" and "moral needs." The importance of this distinction was heightened for Durkheim because he viewed physical needs as being regulated automatically by features of man's organic structure. Nothing in the organic structure, however, is capable of regulating social desires; as Durkheim put it, man's "capacity for feeling is in itself an insatiable and bottomless abyss."[5] If man is to function without "friction," "the passions must first be limited. . . . But since the individual has no way of limiting them, this must be done by some force exterior to him." Durkheim viewed the collective order as the external regulating force which defined and ordered the goals to which men should orient their behavior. If the collective order is disrupted or disturbed, however, men's aspirations may then rise, exceeding all possibilities of fulfillment. Under these conditions, "de-regulation or anomy" ensues: "At the very moment when traditional rules have lost their authority, the richer prize offered these appetites stimulates them and makes them more exigent and impatient of control. The state of de-regulation or anomy is thus further heightened by passions being less disciplined precisely when they need more disciplining." Finally, pressures toward deviant behavior were said to develop when man's aspirations no longer matched the possibilities of fulfillment.

Durkheim therefore turned to the question of when the regulatory functions of the collective order break down. Several such states were identified, including sudden depression, sudden prosperity, and rapid technological change. His object was to show how, under these conditions, men are led to aspire to goals extremely difficult if not impossible to attain. As Durkheim saw it, sudden depression results in deviant behavior because "something like a declassification occurs which suddenly casts certain individuals into a lower state than their previous one. Then they must reduce their requirements, restrain their needs, learn greater self-control. . . . But society cannot adjust them instantaneously to this new life and teach them to practice the increased self-repression to which they are unaccustomed. So they are not adjusted to the condition forced on them, and its very prospect is intolerable; hence the suffering which detaches them from a reduced existence even before they have made trial of it." Prosperity, according to Durkheim, could have much the same effect as depression, particularly if upward changes in economic conditions are abrupt. The very abruptness of these changes presumably heightens aspirations beyond possibility of fulfillment, and this too puts a strain on the regulatory apparatus of the society.

According to Durkheim, "the sphere of trade and industry . . . is actually in a chronic state [of anomie]." Rapid technological developments and the existence of vast, unexploited markets excite the imagination with the seemingly limitless possibilities for the accumulation of wealth. As Durkheim said of the producer of goods, "now that he may assume to have almost the entire world as his customer, how could passions accept their former confinement in the face of such limitless prospects?" Continuing, Durkheim states that "such is the source of excitement predominating in this part of society. . . . Here the state of crisis and anomie [are] constant and, so to speak, normal. From top to bottom of the ladder, greed is aroused without knowing where to find ultimate foothold. Nothing can calm it, since its goal is far beyond all it can attain."

In developing the theory, Durkheim characterized goals in the industrial society, and specified the way in which unlimited aspirations are induced. He spoke of "dispositions . . . so inbred that society has grown to accept them and is accustomed to think them normal," and he portrayed these "inbred dispositions": "It is everlastingly repeated that it is man's nature to be eternally dissatisfied, constantly to advance, without relief or rest, toward an indefinite goal. The longing for infinity is daily represented as a mark of moral distinction. . . ." And it was precisely these pressures to strive for "infinite" or "receding" goals, in Durkheim's view, that generate a breakdown in regulatory norms, for "when there is no other aim but to outstrip constantly the point arrived at, how painful to be thrown back!"

Phase II: disjunction between cultural goals and socially structured opportunity

Durkheim's description of the emergence of "overweening ambition" and the subsequent breakdown of regulatory norms constitutes one of the links between his work and the later development of the theory by Robert K. Merton. In his classic essay, "Social Structure and Anomie," Merton suggests that goals and norms may vary independently of each other, and that this sometimes leads to malintegrated states. In his view, two polar types of disjunction may occur: "There may develop a very heavy, at times a virtually exclusive, stress upon the value of particular goals, involving comparatively little concern with the institutionally prescribed means of striving toward these goals. . . . This constitutes one type of malintegrated culture." [6] On the other hand, "A second polar type is found where activities originally conceived as instrumental are transmuted into self-contained practices, lacking further objectives. . . . Sheer conformity becomes a central value." Merton notes that "between these extreme types are societies which maintain a rough balance between emphases upon cultural goals and institutionalized practices, and these constitute the integrated and relatively stable, though changing societies."

Having identified patterns of disjunction between goals and norms, Merton is enabled to define anomie more precisely: "Anomie [may be] conceived as a breakdown in the cultural structure, occurring particularly when there is an acute disjunction between cultural norms and goals and the socially structured capacities of members of the group to act in accord with them."

Of the two kinds of malintegrated societies, Merton is primarily interested in the one in which "there is an exceptionally strong emphasis upon specific goals without a corresponding emphasis upon institutional procedures." He states that attenuation between goals and norms, leading to anomie or "normlessness," comes about because men in such societies internalize an emphasis on common success-goals under conditions of varying access to them. The essence of this hypothesis is captured in the following excerpt: "It is only when a system of cultural values extols, virtually above all else, certain *common* success-goals for the population at large while the social structure rigorously restricts or completely closes access to approved modes of reaching these goals *for a considerable part of the same population,* that deviant behavior ensues on a large scale." The focus, in short, is on the way in which the social structure puts a strain upon the cultural structure. Here one may point to diverse structural differentials in access to culturally approved goals by legitimate means, for example, differentials of age, sex, ethnic status, and social class. Pressures for anomie or normlessness vary from one social position to another, depending on the nature of these differentials.

In summary, Merton extends the theory of anomie in two principal ways. He explicitly identifies types of anomic or mal-integrated societies by focusing upon the relationship between cultural goals and norms. And, by directing attention to patterned differentials in the access to success-goals by legitimate means, he shows how the social structure exerts a strain upon the cultural structure, leading in turn to anomie or normlessness.

Phase III: the concept of illegitimate means

Once processes generating differentials in pressures are identified, there is then the question of how these pressures are resolved, or how men respond to them. In this connection, Merton enumerates five basic categories of behavior or role adaptations which are likely to emerge: conformity, innovation, ritualism, retreatism, and rebellion. These adaptations differ depending on the individual's acceptance or rejection of cultural goals, and depending on his adherence to or violation of institutional norms. Furthermore, Merton sees the distribution of these adaptations principally as the consequence of two variables: the relative extent of pressure, and values, particularly "internalized prohibitions," governing the use of various illegitimate means.

It is a familiar sociological idea that values serve to order the choices of deviant (as well as conforming) adaptations which develop under conditions of stress. Comparative studies of ethnic groups, for example, have shown that some tend to engage in distinctive forms of deviance; thus Jews exhibit low rates of alcoholism and alcoholic psychoses.[7] Various investigators have suggested that the emphasis on rationality, fear of expressing aggression, and other alleged components of the "Jewish" value system constrain modes of deviance which involve "loss of control"

over behavior.[8] In contrast, the Irish show a much higher rate of alcoholic deviance because, it has been argued, their cultural emphasis on masculinity encourages the excessive use of alcohol under conditions of strain.[9]

Merton suggests that differing rates of ritualistic and innovating behavior in the middle and lower classes result from differential emphases in socialization. The "rule-oriented" accent in middle-class socialization presumably disposes persons to handle stress by engaging in ritualistic rather than innovating behavior. The lower-class person, contrastingly, having internalized less stringent norms, can violate conventions with less guilt and anxiety.[10] Values, in other words, exercise a canalizing influence, limiting the choice of deviant adaptations for persons variously distributed throughout the social system.

Apart from both socially patterned pressures, which give rise to deviance, and from values, which determine choices of adaptations, a further variable should be taken into account: namely, *differentials in availability of illegitimate means*. For example, the notion that innovating behavior may result from unfulfilled aspirations and imperfect socialization with respect to conventional norms implies that illegitimate means are freely available—as if the individual, having decided that "you can't make it legitimately," then simply turns to illegitimate means which are readily at hand whatever his position in the social structure. However, these means may not be available. As noted above, the anomie theory assumes that conventional means are differentially distributed, that some individuals, because of their social position, enjoy certain advantages which are denied to others. Note, for example, variations in the degree to which members of various classes are fully exposed to and thus acquire the values, education, and skills which facilitate upward mobility. It should not be startling, therefore, to find similar variations in the availability of illegitimate means.

Several sociologists have alluded to such variations without explicitly incorporating this variable in a theory of deviant behavior. Sutherland, for example, writes that "an inclination to steal is not a sufficient explanation of the genesis of the professional thief." [11] Moreover, "the person must be appreciated by the professional thieves. He must be appraised as having an adequate equipment of wits, front, talking-ability, honesty, reliability, nerve and determination." In short, "a person can be a professional thief only if he is recognized and received as such by other professional thieves." But recognition is not freely accorded: "Selection and tutelage are the two necessary elements in the process of acquiring recognition as a professional thief. . . . A person cannot acquire recognition as a professional thief until he has had tutelage in professional theft, and tutelage is given only to a few persons selected from the total population." Furthermore, the aspirant is judged by high standards of performance, for only "a very small percentage of those who start on this process ever reach the stage of professional theft." The burden of these remarks—dealing with the processes of selection, induction, and assumption of full status in the criminal group—is that motivations or pressures toward deviance do not fully account for deviant behavior. The "self-made" thief—lacking knowledge of the ways of securing immunity from prosecution and similar techniques of defense—"would quickly land in prison." Sutherland is in effect pointing to differentials in access to the role of professional thief. Although the criteria of selection are not altogether clear from his analysis, definite evaluative standards do appear to exist; depending on their content, certain categories of individuals would be placed at a disadvantage and others would be favored.

The availability of illegitimate means, then, is controlled by various criteria in the same manner that has long been ascribed to conventional means. Both systems of opportunity are 1) limited, rather than infinitely available, and 2) differentially available depending on the location of persons in the social structure.

When we employ the term "means," whether legitimate or illegitimate, at least two things are implied: first, that there are appropriate learning environments for the acquisition of the values and skills associated with the performance of a particular role; and second, that the individual has opportunities to discharge the role once he has been prepared. The term subsumes, therefore, both *learning structures* and *opportunity structures*.

A case in point is recruitment and preparation for careers in the rackets. There are fertile criminal learning environments for the young in neighborhoods where the rackets flourish as stable, indigenous institutions. Because these environments afford integration of offenders of different ages, the young are exposed to "differential associations" which facilitate the acquisition of criminal values and skills. Yet preparation for the role may not insure that the individual will ever discharge it. For one thing, more youngsters may be recruited into these patterns of differential association than can possibly be absorbed, following their "training," by the adult criminal structure. There may be a surplus of contenders for these elite positions, leading in turn to the necessity for criteria and mechanisms of selection. Hence a certain proportion of those who aspire may not be permitted to engage in the behavior for which they have been prepared.

This illustration is similar in every respect, save for the route followed, to the case of those who seek careers in the sphere of legitimate business. Here, again, is the initial problem of securing access to appropriate learning environments, such as colleges and post-graduate schools of business. Having acquired the values and skills needed for a business career, graduates then face the problem of whether or not they can successfully discharge the roles for which they have been prepared.

Formal training itself is not sufficient for occupational success, for many forces intervene to determine who shall succeed and fail in the competitive world of business and industry—as throughout the entire conventional occupational structure.

This distinction between learning structures and opportunity structures was suggested some years ago by Sutherland. In 1944, he circulated an unpublished paper which briefly discusses the proposition that "criminal behavior is partially a function of opportunities to commit specific classes of crimes, such as embezzlement, bank burglary, or illicit heterosexual intercourse." [12] He did not, however, take up the problem of differentials in opportunity as a concept to be systematically incorporated in a theory of deviant behavior. Instead, he held that "opportunity" is a necessary but not sufficient explanation of the commission of criminal acts, "since some persons who have opportunities to embezzle, become intoxicated, engage in illicit heterosexual intercourse or to commit other crimes do not do so." He also noted that the differential association theory did not constitute a full explanation of criminal activity, for, notwithstanding differential association, "it is axiomatic that persons who commit a specific crime must have the opportunity to commit that crime." He therefore concluded that "while opportunity may be partially a function of association with criminal patterns and of the specialized techniques thus acquired, *it is not determined entirely in that manner,* and consequently differential association is not the sufficient cause of criminal behavior." (emphasis not in original)

In Sutherland's statements, two meanings are attributed to the term "opportunity." As suggested above, it may be useful to separate these for analytical purposes. In the first sense, Sutherland appears to be saying that opportunity consists in part of learning structures. The principal components of his theory of differential association are that "criminal behavior is learned," and, furthermore, that "criminal behavior is learned in interaction with other persons in a process of communication." But he also uses the term to describe situations conducive to carrying out criminal roles. Thus, for Sutherland, the commission of a criminal act would seem to depend upon the existence of two conditions: differential associations favoring the acquisition of criminal values and skills, and conditions encouraging participation in criminal activity.

This distinction heightens the importance of identifying and questioning the common assumption that illegitimate means are freely available. We can now ask 1) whether there are socially structured differentials in access to illegitimate learning environments, and 2) whether there are differentials limiting the fulfillment of illegitimate roles. If differentials exist and can be identified, we may then inquire about their consequences for the behavior of persons in different parts of the social structure. Before pursuing this question, however, we turn to a fuller discussion of the theoretical tradition established by Shaw, McKay, and Sutherland.

Differentials in Availability of Illegitimate Means: The Subculture Tradition

The concept of differentials in availability of illegitimate means is implicit in one of the major streams of American criminological theory. In this tradition, attention is focused on the processes by which persons are recruited into criminal learning environments and ultimately inducted into criminal roles. The problems here are to account for the acquisition of criminal roles and to describe the social organization of criminal activities. When the theoretical propositions contained in this tradition are reanalyzed, it becomes clear that one underlying conception is that of variations in access to success-goals by illegitimate means. Furthermore, this implicit concept may be shown to be one of the bases upon which the tradition was constructed.

In their studies of the ecology of deviant behavior in the urban environment, Shaw and McKay found that delinquency and crime tended to be confined to delimited areas and, furthermore, that such behavior persisted despite demographic changes in these areas. Hence they came to speak of "criminal tradition," of the "cultural transmission" of criminal values.[13] As a result of their observations of slum life, they concluded that particular *importance must be assigned to the integration of different age-levels of offenders.* Thus:

Stealing in the neighborhood was a common practice among the children and approved by the parents. Whenever the boys got together they talked about robbing and made more plans for stealing. I hardly knew any boys who did not go robbing. The little fellows went in for petty stealing, breaking into freight cars, and stealing junk. The older guys did big jobs like stick-up, burglary, and stealing autos. The little fellows admired the "big shots" and longed for the day when they could get into the big racket. Fellows who had "done time" were the big shots and looked up to and gave the little fellow tips on how to get by and pull off big jobs.[14]

In other words, access to criminal roles depends upon stable associations with others from whom the necessary values and skills may be learned. Shaw and McKay were describing deviant learning structures—that is, alternative routes by which people seek access to the goals which society holds to be worthwhile. They might also have pointed out that, in areas where such learning structures are unavailable, it is probably difficult for many individuals to secure access to stable criminal careers, even though motivated to do so.[15]

The concept of illegitimate means and the socially structured conditions of access to them were not eplicitly recognized in the work of Shaw and McKay because,

probably, they were disposed to view slum areas as "disorganized." Although they consistently referred to illegitimate activities as being organized, they nevertheless often depicted high-rate delinquency areas as disorganized because the values transmitted were criminal rather than conventional. Hence their work includes statements which we now perceive to be internally inconsistent, such as the following:

This community situation [in which Sidney was reared] was not only disorganized and thus ineffective as a unit of control, but it was characterized by a high rate of juvenile delinquency and adult crime, not to mention the widespread political corruption which had long existed in the area. Various forms of stealing and many organized delinquent and criminal gangs were prevalent in the area. These groups exercised a powerful influence and tended to create a community spirit which not only tolerated but actually fostered delinquent and criminal practices.[16]

Sutherland was among the first to perceive that the concept of social disorganization tended to obscure the stable patterns of interaction among carriers of criminal values. Like Shaw and McKay, he had been influenced by the observation that lower-class areas were organized in terms of both conventional and criminal values, but he was also impressed that these alternative value systems were supported by patterned systems of social relations. He expressly recognized that crime, far from being a random, unorganized activity, was typically an intricate and stable system of human arrangements. He therefore rejected the concept of "social disorganization" and substituted the concept of "differential group organization."

The third concept, social disorganization, was borrowed from Shaw and McKay. I had used it but had not been satisfied with it because the organization of the delinquent group, which is often very complex, is social disorganization only from an ethical or some other particularistic point of view. At the suggestion of Albert K. Cohen, this concept has been changed to differential group organization, with organization for criminal activities on one side and organization against criminal activities on the other.[17]

Having freed observation of the urban slum from conventional evaluations, Sutherland was able to focus more clearly on the way in which its social structure constitutes a "learning environment" for the acquisition of deviant values and skills. In the development of the theory of "differential association" and "differential group organization," he came close to stating explicitly the concept of differentials in access to illegitimate means. But Sutherland was essentially interested in learning processes, and thus he did not ask how such access varies in different parts of the social structure, nor did he inquire about the consequences for behavior of variations in the accessibility of these means.[18]

William F. Whyte, in his classic study of an urban slum, advanced the empirical description of the structure and organization of illegitimate means a step beyond that of Sutherland. Like Sutherland, Whyte rejected the earlier view of the slum as disorganized:

It is customary for the sociologist to study the slum district in terms of "social disorganization" and to neglect to see that an area such as Cornerville has a complex and well-established organization of its own. . . . I found that in every group there was a hierarchical structure of social relations binding the individuals to one another and that the groups were also related hierarchically to one another. Where the group was formally organized into a political club, this was immediately apparent, but for informal groups it was no less true.[19]

Whyte's contribution to our understanding of the organization of illegitimate means in the slum consists primarily in showing that individuals who participate in stable illicit enterprise do not constitute a separate or isolated segment of the community. Rather, these persons are closely integrated with the occupants of conventional roles. In describing the relationship between racketeers and politicians, for ex-

ample, he notes that "the rackets and political organizations extend from the bottom to the top of Cornerville society, mesh with one another, and integrate a large part of the life of the district. They provide a general framework for the understanding of the actions of both 'little guys' and 'big shots.' "[20] Whyte's view of the slum differs somewhat from that conveyed by the term "differential group organization." He does not emphasize the idea that the slum is composed of two different systems, conventional and deviant, but rather the way in which the occupants of these various roles are integrated in a single, stable structure which organizes and patterns the life of the community.

The description of the organization of illegitimate means in slums is further developed by Solomon Kobrin in his article, "The Conflict of Values in Delinquency Areas."[21] Kobrin suggests that urban slum areas vary in the degree to which the carriers of deviant and conventional values are integrated with one another. Hence he points the way to the development of a "typology of delinquency areas based on variations in the relationship between these two systems," depicting the "polar types" on such a continuum. The first type resembles the integrated areas described in preceding paragraphs. Here, claims Kobrin, there is not merely structural integration between carriers of the two value systems, but reciprocal participation by each in the value system of the other. Thus:

Leaders of [illegal] enterprises frequently maintain membership in such conventional institutions of their local communities as churches, fraternal and mutual benefit societies and political parties. . . . Within this framework the influence of each of the two value systems is reciprocal, the leaders of illegal enterprise participating in the primary orientation of the conventional elements in the population, and the latter, through their participation in a local power structure sustained in large part by illicit activity, participating perforce in the alternate, criminal value system.

Kobrin also notes that in some urban slums there is a tendency for the relationships between carriers of deviant and conventional values to break down. Such areas constitute the second polar type. Because of disorganizing forces such as "drastic change in the class, ethnic, or racial characteristics of its population," Kobrin suggests that "the bearers of the conventional culture and its value system are without the customary institutional machinery and therefore in effect partially demobilized with reference to the diffusion of their value system." At the same time, the criminal "value system remains implicit" since this type of area is "characterized principally by the absence of systematic and organized adult activity in violation of the law, despite the fact that many adults in these areas commit violations." Since both value systems remain implicit, the possibilities for effective integration are precluded.

The importance of these observations may be seen if we ask how accessibility of illegal means varies with the relative integration of conventional and criminal values from one type of area to another. In this connection, Kobrin points out that the "integrated" area apparently constitutes a "training ground" for the acquisition of criminal values and skills.

> The stable position of illicit enterprise in the adult society of the community is reflected in the character of delinquent conduct on the part of children. While delinquency in all high rate areas is intrinsically disorderly in that it is unrelated to official programs for the education of the young, in the [integrated community] boys may more or less realistically recognize the potentialities for personal progress in local society through access to delinquency. In a general way, therefore, delinquent activity in these areas constitutes a training ground for the acquisition of skill in the use of violence, concealment of offense, evasion of detection and arrest, and the purchase of immunity from punishment. Those who come to excel in these respects are frequently noted and valued by adult leaders in the rackets who are confronted, as are the leaders of all income-producing enterprises,

with problems of the recruitment of competent personnel.

With respect to the contrasting or "unintegrated area," Kobrin makes no mention of the extent to which learning structures and opportunities for criminal careers are available. Yet his portrayal of such areas as lacking in the articulation of either conventional or criminal values suggests that the appropriate learning structures—principally the integration of offenders of different age levels—are not available. Furthermore, his depiction of adult violative activity as "unorganized" suggests that the illegal opportunity structure is severely limited. Even if youngsters were able to secure adequate preparation for criminal roles, the problem would appear to be that the social structure of such neighborhoods provides few opportunities for stable, criminal careers. For Kobrin's analysis—as well as those of Whyte and others before him—leads to the conclusion that illegal opportunity structures tend to emerge in lower-class areas only when stable patterns of accommodation and integration arise between the carriers of conventional and deviant values. Where these values remain unorganized and implicit, or where their carriers are in open conflict, opportunities for stable criminal role performance are more or less limited.[22]

Other factors may be cited which affect access to criminal roles. For example, there is a good deal of anecdotal evidence which reveals that access to the upper echelons of organized racketeering is controlled, at least in part, by ethnicity. Some ethnic groups are found disproportionately in the upper ranks and others disproportionately in the lower. From an historical perspective, as Bell has shown, this realm has been successively dominated by Irish, East-European Jews, and more recently, by Italians.[23] Various other ethnic groups have been virtually excluded or at least relegated to lower-echelon positions. Despite the fact that many rackets (especially "policy") have flourished in predominantly Negro neighborhoods, there have been but one or two Negroes who have been known to rise to the top in syndicated crime. As in the conventional world, Negroes are relegated to the more menial tasks. Moreover, access to elite positions in the rackets may be governed in part by kinship criteria, for various accounts of the blood relations among top racketeers indicate that nepotism is the general rule.[24] It has also been noted that kinship criteria sometimes govern access to stable criminal roles, as in the case of the pickpocket.[25] And there are, of course, deep-rooted sex differentials in access to illegal means. Although women are often employed in criminal vocations—for example, thievery, confidence games, and extortion—and must be employed in others—such as prostitution—nevertheless females are excluded from many criminal activities.[26]

Of the various criteria governing access to illegitimate means, class differentials may be among the most important. The differentials noted in the preceding paragraph—age, sex, ethnicity, kinship, and the like—all pertain to criminal activity historically associated with the lower class. Most middle- or upper-class persons—even when interested in following "lower-class" criminal careers—would no doubt have difficulty in fulfilling this ambition because of inappropriate preparation. The prerequisite attitudes and skills are more easily acquired if the individual is a member of the lower class; most middle- and upper-class persons could not easily unlearn their own class culture in order to learn a new one. By the same token, access to many "white-collar" criminal roles is closed to lower-class persons. Some occupations afford abundant opportunities to engage in illegitimate activity; others offer virtually none. The businessman, for example, not only has at his disposal the means to do so, but, as some studies have shown, he is under persistent pressure to employ illegitimate means, if

only to maintain a competitive advantage in the market place. But for those in many other occupations, white-collar modes of criminal activity are simply not an alternative.[27]

Some Implications of a Consolidated Approach to Deviant Behavior

It is now possible to consolidate the two sociological traditions described above. Our analysis makes it clear that these traditions are oriented to different aspects of the same problem: differentials in access to opportunity. One tradition focuses on legitimate opportunity, the other on illegitimate. By incorporating the concept of differentials in access to *illegitimate* means, the theory of anomie may be extended to include seemingly unrelated studies and theories of deviant behavior which form a part of the literature of American criminology. In this final section, we try to show how a consolidated approach might advance the understanding of both rates and types of deviant conduct. The discussion centers on the conditions of access to both systems of means, legitimate and illegitimate.

The distribution of criminal behavior

One problem which has plagued the criminologist is the absence of adequate data on social differentials in criminal activity. Many have held that the highest crime rates are to be found in the lower social strata. Others have suggested that rates in the middle and upper classes may be much higher than is ordinarily thought. The question of the social distribution of crime remains problematic.

In the absence of adequate data, the theorist has sometimes attacked this problem by assessing the extent of pressures toward normative departures in various parts of the social structure. For example, Merton remarks that his "primary aim is to discover how some social structures exert a definite pressure upon certain persons in the society to engage in nonconforming rather than conforming conduct." [28] Having identified structural features which might be expected to generate deviance, Merton suggests the presence of a correlation between "pressures toward deviation" and "rate of deviance."

But whatever the differential rates of deviant behavior in the several social strata, and we know from many sources that the official crime statistics uniformly showing higher rates in the lower strata are far from complete or reliable, *it appears from our analysis that the greater pressures toward deviation are exerted upon the lower strata.* . . . Of those located in the lower reaches of the social structure, the culture makes incompatible demands. On the one hand they are asked to orient their behavior toward the prospect of large wealth . . . and on the other, they are largely denied effective opportunities to do so institutionally. *The consequence of this structural inconsistency is a high rate of deviant behavior.*[29]

Because of the paucity and unreliability of existing criminal statistics, there is as yet no way of knowing whether or not Merton's hypothesis is correct. Until comparative studies of crime rates are available the hypothesized correlation cannot be tested.

From a theoretical perspective, however, questions may be raised about this correlation. Would we expect, to raise the principal query, the correlation to be fixed or to vary depending on the distribution of access to illegitimate means? The three possibilities are 1) that access is distributed uniformly throughout the class structure, 2) that access varies inversely with class position, and 3) that access varies directly with class position. Specification of these possibilities permits a more precise statement of the conditions under which crime rates would be expected to vary.

If access to illegitimate means is uniformly distributed throughout the class structure, then the proposed correlation would probably hold—higher rates of innovating behavior would be expected in

the lower class than elsewhere. Lower-class persons apparently experience greater pressures toward deviance and are less restrained by internalized prohibitions from employing illegitimate means. Assuming uniform access to such means, it would therefore be reasonable to predict higher rates of innovating behavior in the lower social strata.

If access to illegitimate means varies *inversely* with class position, then the correlation would not only hold, but might even be strengthened. For pressures toward deviance, including socialization that does not altogether discourage the use of illegitimate means, would coincide with the availability of such means.

Finally, if access varies directly with class position, comparative rates of illegitimate activity become difficult to forecast. The higher the class position, the less the pressure to employ illegitimate means; furthermore, internalized prohibitions are apparently more effective in higher positions. If, at the same time, opportunities to use illegitimate methods are more abundant, then these factors would be in opposition. Until the precise effects of these several variables can be more adequately measured, rates cannot be safely forecast.

The concept of differentials in availability of illegitimate means may also help to clarify questions about varying crime rates among ethnic, age, religious, and sex groups, and other social divisions. This concept, then, can be systematically employed in the effort to further our understanding of the distribution of illegitimate behavior in the social structure.

Modes of adaptation: the case of retreatism

By taking into account the conditions of access to legitimate *and* illegitimate means, we can further specify the circumstances under which various modes of deviant behavior arise. This may be illustrated by the case of retreatism.[30]

As defined by Merton, retreatist adaptations include such categories of behavior as alcoholism, drug addiction, and psychotic withdrawal. These adaptations entail "escape" from the frustrations of unfulfilled aspirations by withdrawal from conventional social relationships. The processes leading to retreatism are described by Merton as follows: "[Retreatism] arises from continued failure to near the goal by legitimate measures and from an inability to use the illegitimate route because of internalized prohibitions, *this process occurring while the supreme value of the success-goal has not yet been renounced.* The conflict is resolved by abandoning *both* precipitating elements, the goals and means. The escape is complete, the conflict is eliminated, and the individual is asocialized." [31]

In this view, a crucial element encouraging retreatism is internalized constraint concerning the use of illegitimate means. But this element need not be present. Merton apparently assumed that such prohibitions are essential because, in their absence, the logic of his scheme would compel him to predict that innovating behavior would result. But the assumption that the individual uninhibited in the use of illegitimate means becomes an innovator presupposes that successful innovation is only a matter of motivation. Once the concept of differentials in access to illegitimate means is introduced, however, it becomes clear that retreatism is possible even in the absence of internalized prohibitions. For we may now ask how individuals respond when they fail in the use of *both* legitimate and illegitimate means. If illegitimate means are unavailable, if efforts at innovation fail, then retreatist adaptations may still be the consequence, and the "escape" mechanisms chosen by the defeated individual may perhaps be all the more deviant because of his "double failure."

This does not mean that retreatist adaptations cannot arise precisely as Merton suggests: namely, that the conversion from conformity to retreatism takes place in one step, without intervening adaptations. But this is only one route to retreatism. The conversion may at times entail intervening stages and intervening adaptations, particularly of an innovating type. This possibility helps to account for the fact that certain categories of individuals cited as retreatists—for example, hobos —often show extensive histories of arrests and convictions for various illegal acts. It also helps to explain retreatist adaptations among individuals who have not necessarily internalized strong restraints on the use of illegitimate means. In short, retreatist adaptations may arise with considerable frequency among those who are failures in both worlds, conventional and illegitimate alike.[32]

Future research on retreatist behavior might well examine the interval between conformity and retreatism. To what extent does the individual entertain the possibility of resorting to illegitimate means, and to what extent does he actually seek to mobilize such means? If the individual turns to innovating devices, the question of whether or not he becomes a retreatist may then depend upon the relative accessibility of illegitimate means. For although the frustrated conformist seeks a solution to status discontent by adopting such methods, there is the further problem of whether or not he possesses appropriate skills and has opportunities for their use. We suggest therefore that data be gathered on preliminary responses to status discontent—and on the individual's perceptions of the efficacy of employing illegitimate means, the content of his skills, and the objective situation of illegitimate opportunity available to him.

Respecification of the processes leading to retreatism may also help to resolve difficulties entailed in ascertaining rates of retreatism in different parts of the social structure. Although Merton does not indicate explicitly where this adaptation might be expected to arise, he specifies some of the social conditions which encourage high rates of retreatism. Thus the latter is apt to mark the behavior of downwardly mobile persons, who experience a sudden breakdown in established social relations, and such individuals as the retired, who have lost major social roles.[33]

The long-standing difficulties in forecasting differential rates of retreatism may perhaps be attributed to the assumption that retreatists have fully internalized values prohibiting the use of illegitimate means. That this prohibition especially characterizes socialization in the middle and upper classes probably calls for the prediction that retreatism occurs primarily in those classes—and that the hobohemias, "drug cultures," and the ranks of the alcoholics are populated primarily by individuals from the upper reaches of society. It would appear from various accounts of hobohemia and skid row, however, that many of these persons are the products of slum life, and, furthermore, that their behavior is not necessarily controlled by values which preclude resort to illegitimate means. But once it is recognized that retreatism may arise in response to limitations on both systems of means, the difficulty of locating this adaptation is lessened, if not resolved. Thus retreatist behavior may vary with the particular process by which it is generated. The process described by Merton may be somewhat more characteristic of higher positions in the social structure where rule-oriented socialization is typical, while in the lower strata retreatism may tend more often to be the consequence of unsuccessful attempts at innovation.

Summary

This paper attempts to identify and to define the concept of differential opportunity structures. It has been suggested that this concept helps to extend the developing theory of social structure and anomie. Furthermore, by linking propositions regarding the accessibility of *both* legitimate and illegitimate opportunity structures, a basis is provided for consolidating various major traditions of sociological thought on nonconformity. The concept of differential systems of opportunity and of variations in access to them, it is hoped, will suggest new possibilities for research on the relationship between social structure and deviant behavior.

NOTES

1. This paper is based on research conducted in a penal setting. For a more detailed statement see Richard A. Cloward, "Social Control in the Prison," in *Theoretical Studies in Social Organization of the Prison,* New York: Social Science Research Council, 1960, pp. 20–48.

2. See especially Émile Durkheim, *Suicide,* translated by J. A. Spaulding and George Simpson, Glencoe, Ill.: Free Press, 1951; and Robert K. Merton, *Social Theory and Social Structure,* Glencoe, Ill.: Free Press, 1957, Chapters 4 and 5.

3. See especially the following: Clifford R. Shaw, *The Jack-Roller,* Chicago: The University of Chicago Press, 1930; Clifford R. Shaw, *The Natural History of a Delinquent Career,* Chicago: The University of Chicago Press, 1931; Clifford R. Shaw et al., *Delinquency Areas,* Chicago: The University of Chicago Press, 1940; Clifford R. Shaw and Henry D. McKay, *Juvenile Delinquency and Urban Areas,* Chicago: The University of Chicago Press, 1942; Edwin H. Sutherland (ed.), *The Professional Thief,* Chicago: The University of Chicago Press, 1937; Edwin H. Sutherland, *Principles of Criminology,* 4th edition, Philadelphia: Lippincott, 1947; Edwin H. Sutherland, *White Collar Crime,* New York: Dryden, 1949.

4. "Illegitimate means" are those proscribed by the mores. The concept therefore includes "illegal means" as a special case but is not coterminous with illegal behavior, which refers only to the violation of legal norms. In several parts of this paper, I refer to particular forms of deviant behavior which entail violation of the law and there use the more restricted term, "illegal means." But the more general concept of illegitimate means is needed to cover the wider gamut of deviant behavior and to relate the theories under review here to the evolving theory of "legitimacy" in sociology.

5. All of the excerpts in this section are from Durkheim, *op. cit.,* pp. 247–257.

6. For this excerpt and those which follow immediately, see Merton, *op. cit.,* pp. 131–194.

7. See, e.g., Seldon D. Bacon, "Social Settings Conducive to Alcoholism—A Sociological Approach to a Medical Problem," *Journal of the American Medical Association,* 16 (1957), 177–181; Robert F. Bales, "Cultural Differences in Rates of Alcoholism," *Quarterly Journal of Studies on Alcohol,* 16 (1946), 480–499; Jerome H. Skolnick, "A Study of the Relation of Ethnic Background to Arrests for Inebriety," *Quarterly Journal of Studies on Alcohol,* 15 (1954), 451–474.

8. See Isidor T. Thorner, "Ascetic Protestantism and Alcoholism," *Psychiatry,* 16 (1953), 167–176; and Nathan Glazer, "Why Jews Stay Sober," *Commentary,* 13 (1952), 181–186.

9. See Bales, *op. cit.*

10. Merton, *op. cit.,* p. 151.

11. For this excerpt and those which follow immediately, see Sutherland, *The Professional Thief,* pp. 211–213.

12. For this excerpt and those which follow immediately, see Albert Cohen, Alfred Lindesmith, and Karl Schuessler (eds.), *The Sutherland Papers,* Bloomington: Indiana University Press, 1956, pp. 31–35.

13. See especially *Delinquency Areas,* Chapter 16.

14. Shaw, *The Jack-Roller,* p. 54.

15. We are referring here, and throughout the paper, to stable criminal roles to which persons may orient themselves on a career basis, as in the case of racketeers, professional thieves, and the like. The point is that access to stable roles depends in the first instance upon the availability of learning structures. As Frank Tannenbaum says, "It must be insisted on that unless there were older criminals in the neighborhood who provided a moral judgement in favor of the delinquent and to whom the delinquents could look for commendation, the careers of the younger ones could not develop at all." *Crime and the Community,* New York: Ginn, 1938, p. 60.

16. Shaw, *The Natural History of a Delinquent Career,* p. 229.

17. Cohen, Lindesmith, and Schuessler, *op. cit.,* p. 21.

18. It is interesting to note that the concept of differentials in access to *legitimate* means did not attain explicit recognition in Sutherland's work, nor in the work of many others in the "subculture" tradition. This attests to the independent development of the two traditions being discussed. Thus the ninth proposition in the differential association theory is stated as follows:
   Though criminal behavior is an expression of general needs and values, it is not explained by those general needs and values since noncriminal behavior is an expression of the same needs and values. Thieves generally steal in order to secure money, but likewise honest laborers work in order to secure money. The attempts by many scholars to explain criminal behavior by general drives and values, such as the happiness principle, striving for social status, the money motive, or frustration, have been and must continue to be futile since they explain lawful behavior as completely as they explain criminal behavior.
Of course, it is perfectly true that "striving for status," the "money motive," and similar modes of socially approved goal-oriented behavior do not as such account for both deviant and conformist behavior. But if goal-oriented behavior occurs under conditions of socially structured obstacles to fulfillment by legitimate means, the resulting pressures might then lead to deviance. In other words, Sutherland appears to assume that the distribution of access to success-goals by legitimate means is uniform rather than variable, irrespective of location in the social structure. See his *Principles of Criminology,* 4th edition, pp. 7–8.

19. William F. Whyte, *Street Corner Society* (original edition, 1943), Chicago: The University of Chicago Press, 1955, p. viii.

20. *Ibid.,* p. xviii.

21. *American Sociological Review,* 16 (1951), 657–658, which includes the excerpts which follow immediately.

22. The excellent work by Albert K. Cohen has been omitted from this discussion because it is dealt with in a second article, "Types of Delinquent Subcultures," prepared jointly with Lloyd

E. Ohlin (mimeographed, December, 1958, New York School of Social Work, Columbia University). It may be noted that although Cohen does not explicitly affirm continuity with either the Durkheim-Merton or the Shaw-McKay-Sutherland traditions, we believe that he clearly belongs in the former. He does not deal with what appears to be the essence of the Shaw-McKay-Sutherland tradition, namely, the crucial social functions performed by the integration of offenders of differing age levels and the integration of adult carriers of criminal and conventional values. Rather, he is concerned primarily with the way in which discrepancies between status aspirations and possibilities for achievement generate pressures for delinquent behavior. The latter notion is a central feature in the anomie tradition.

23. Daniel Bell, "Crime as an American Way of Life," *The Antioch Review* (1953), 131–154.

24. For a discussion of kinship relationships among top racketeers, see Stanley Frank, "The Rap Gangsters Fear Most," *The Saturday Evening Post* (August 9, 1958), pp. 26 ff. This article is based on a review of the files of the United States Immigration and Naturalization Service.

25. See David W. Maurer, *Whiz Mob: A Correlation of the Technical Argot of Pickpockets with Their Behavior Pattern,* Publication of the American Dialect Society, No. 24, 1955.

26. For a discussion of racial, nationality, and sex differentials governing access to a stable criminal role, see *ibid.,* Chapter 6.

27. Training in conventional, specialized occupational skills is often a prerequisite for the commission of white-collar crimes, since the individual must have these skills in hand before he can secure a position entailing "trust." As Cressey says, "It may be observed that persons trained to carry on the routine duties of a position of trust have at the same time been trained in whatever skills are necessary for the violation of that position, and the technical skill necessary to trust violation is simply the technical skill necessary to holding the position in the first place." (Donald R. Cressey, *Other People's Money,* Glencoe, Ill.: Free Press, 1953, pp. 81–82.) Thus skills required in certain crimes need not be learned in association with criminals; they can be acquired through conventional learning.

28. Merton, *op. cit.,* p. 132.

29. *Ibid.,* pp. 144–145.

30. Retreatist behavior is but one of many types of deviant adaptations which might be re-analyzed in terms of this consolidated theoretical approach. In subsequent papers, being prepared jointly with Lloyd E. Ohlin, other cases of deviant behavior—e.g., collective disturbances in prisons and subcultural adaptations among juvenile delinquents—will be examined. In this connection, see footnote 22.

31. Merton, *op. cit.,* pp. 153–154.

32. The processes of "double failure" being specified here may be of value in reanalyzing the correlation between alcoholism and petty crime. Investigation of the *careers* of petty criminals who are alcoholic may reveal that after being actively oriented toward stable criminal careers they then lost out in the competitive struggle. See, e.g., Irwin Deutscher, "The Petty Offender: A Sociological Alien," *The Journal of Criminal Law, Criminology and Police Science,* 44 (1954), 592–595; Albert D. Ullman *et al.,* "Some Social Characteristics of Misdemeanants," *The Journal of Criminal Law, Criminology and Police Science,* 48 (1957), 44–53.

33. Merton, *op. cit.,* pp. 188–189.

65. CONTRACULTURE AND SUBCULTURE

J. MILTON YINGER

The concept of subculture is extensively used in both anthropological and sociological writing. A study of 100 sources indicates that there are at least three ways in which the concept has been defined. In some anthropological works subculture is used to refer to "precultural" pan-human phenomena, that is, the universal bases upon which various cultures are built. In sociology, the term has been used to describe normative systems of groups that are smaller than societies (as, for example, ethnic enclaves, regions and social classes). It has also been applied by sociologists to those deviant groups whose character is defined by norms and values that run counter to those of the dominant society (such as delinquent gangs and radical parties).

To clarify conceptualization of subcultures, J. Milton Yinger suggests that the term "contraculture" be used wherever the normative system of a group contains, as a primary element, a theme of conflict with the values of the total society; where personality variables are directly involved in the development and maintenance of the group's values; and where the group's norms can be understood only by reference to its relationship to the surrounding culture. The usefulness of this distinction is explored with reference to several substantive areas of research.

J. Milton Yinger is Professor of Sociology and Anthropology at Oberlin College. A list of his major publications appears on page 666 of this volume.

In recent years there has been widespread and fruitful employment of the concept of subculture in sociological and anthropological research. The term has been used to focus attention not only on the wide diversity of norms to be found in many societies but on the normative aspects of deviant behavior. The ease with which the term has been adopted, with little study of its exact meaning or its values and its difficulties, is indicative of its utility in emphasizing a sociological point of view in research that has been strongly influenced both by individualistic and moralistic interpretations. To describe the normative qualities of an occupation, to contrast the value systems of social classes, or to emphasize the controlling power of the code of a delinquent gang is to underline a

sociological aspect of these phenomena that is often disregarded.

In the early days of sociology and anthropology, a key task was to document the enormous variability of culture from society to society and to explore the significance of the overly simplified but useful idea that "the mores can make anything right." In recent years that task has been extended to the study of the enormous variability of culture *within* some societies. It is unfortunate that "subculture," a central concept in this process, has seldom been adequately defined.[1] It has been used as an *ad hoc* concept whenever a writer wished to emphasize the normative aspects of behavior that differed from some general standard. The result has been a blurring of the meaning

Reprinted from the *American Sociological Review*, **25** (1960), 625–635, by permission of the author and the American Sociological Association.

of the term, confusion with other terms, and a failure frequently to distinguish between two levels of social causation.

Three Usages of Subculture

Few concepts appear so often in current sociological writing. In the course of twelve months, I have noted over 100 books and articles that make some use, from incidental to elaborate, of the idea of "subculture." The usages vary so widely, however, that the value of the term is severely limited. If chemists had only one word to refer to all colorless liquids and this led them to pay attention to only the two characteristics shared in common, their analysis would be exceedingly primitive. Such an analogy overstates the diversity of ideas covered by "subculture," but the range is very wide. Nevertheless three distinct meanings can be described.

In some anthropological work, subculture refers to certain universal tendencies that seem to occur in all societies. They underlie culture, precede it, and set limits to the range of its variation. Thus Kroeber writes: "Indeed, such more or less recurrent near-regularities of form or process as have to date been formulated for culture are actually subcultural in nature. They are limits set to culture by physical or organic factors." [2] In *The Study of Man,* Linton uses subculture to refer to various pan-human phenomena that seem to occur everywhere. Thus good-natured and tyrannical parents may be found in societies that differ widely in their family patterns. [3] This use shades off into other concepts that are similar but not identical: Edward Sapir's "precultural" and Cooley's "human nature" refer to biological and social influences that underlie all cultures. [4] Since subculture is only rarely used today to refer to this series of ideas, I shall exclude them from further consideration, with the suggestion that the use of Sapir's term "precultural" might well clarify our thinking.

Two other usages of subculture represent a much more serious confusion. The term is often used to point to the normative systems of groups smaller than a society, to give emphasis to the ways these groups differ in such things as language, values, religion, diet, and style of life from the larger society of which they are a part. Perhaps the most common referent in this usage is an ethnic enclave (French Canadians in Maine) or a region (the subculture of the South), [5] but the distinctive norms of much smaller and more temporary groups (even a particular friendship group) may be described as a subculture. Kluckhohn, for example, refers to "the subculture of anthropologists" and Riesman to "subcultures among the faculty."

This second meaning, which itself contains some ambiguities, as we shall see, must be distinguished from a third meaning associated with it when the reference is to norms that arise specifically from a frustrating situation or from conflict between a group and the larger society. Thus the emergent norms of a delinquent gang or the standards of an adolescent peer group have often been designated "subcultural." In addition to a cultural dimension, this third usage introduces a social-psychological dimension, for there is direct reference to the personality factors involved in the development and maintenance of the norms. Specifically, such personality tendencies as frustration, anxiety, feelings of role ambiguity, and resentment are shown to be involved in the creation of the subculture. The mutual influence of personality and culture is not a distinctive characteristic of this type of subculture, of course, for they are everywhere interactive. Thus:

Tendencies for parents to respond harshly to their children's aggressive behavior, for instance, if common to the members of a society, are to be referred equally to the culture and to the modal personality of the parents. But the result in the developing child is not a foregone conclusion: present knowledge suggests that under specifiable conditions outcomes as different as rigid politeness or touchy latent hostility may follow. These consequences in turn may lead to cultural elaborations that seem superficially remote from the cultural starting point, yet are dynamically linked with it. . . .[6]

As this quotation suggests, culture and personality are always empirically tied together. Yet the nature of the relation is not the same in all cases. The term subculture, when used in the third way described here, raises to a position of prominence one particular kind of dynamic linkage between norms and personality: the creation of a series of inverse or counter values (opposed to those of the surrounding society) in face of serious frustration or conflict. To call attention to the special aspects of this kind of normative system, I suggest the term *contraculture*. Before exploring the relationship between subculture and contraculture, however, the range of meanings given subculture even when it is limited to the second usage requires comment.

Subculture and Role

The variety of referents for the term subculture is very wide because the normative systems of subsocieties can be differentiated on many grounds. The groups involved may range from a large regional subdivision to a religious sect with only one small congregation. The distinctive norms may involve many aspects of life —religion, language, diet, moral values— or, for example, only a few separate practices among the members of an occupational group. Further distinctions among subcultures might be made on the basis of time (has the subculture persisted through a number of generations?), origin (by migration, absorption by a dominant society, social or physical segregation, occupational specialization, and other sources), and by the mode of relationship to the surrounding culture (from indifference to conflict). Such wide variation in the phenomena covered by a term can be handled by careful specification of the several grounds for subclassification. Confusion has arisen not so much from the scope of the term subculture as from its use as a substitute for "role." Only with great effort is some degree of clarity being achieved in the use of the role concept and the related terms "position" and "role behavior."[7] Were this development retarded by confusion of role with subculture it would be unfortunate. All societies have differentiating roles, but only heterogeneous societies have subcultures. Role is *that part of* a full culture that is assigned, as the appropriate rights and duties, to those occupying a given position.[8] These rights and duties usually interlock into a system with those of persons who occupy other positions. They are known to and accepted by all those who share the culture. Thus the role of a physician is known, at least in vague outline, by most persons in a society and it is seen as part of the total culture. (This is not to prejudge the question of role consensus, for there may be many non-role aspects of being a physician.) But subculture is not tied in this way into the larger cultural complex: it refers to norms that set a group apart from, not those that integrate a group with, the total society. Subcultural norms, as contrasted with role norms, are unknown to, looked down upon, or thought of as separating forces by the other members of a society. There are doubtless subcultural aspects of being a physician—normative influences affecting his behavior that are not part of his role, not culturally designated rights and duties. But the empirical mixture should not obscure the need for this analytic distinction.

Along with confusion with the role concept, "subculture" carries many of the ambiguities associated with the parent concept of culture. In much social scientific writing it is not at all clear whether culture refers to norms, that is, to expected or valued behavior, or to behavior that is widely followed and therefore normal in a statistical sense only. This dual referent is particularly likely to be found in the work of anthropologists. Perhaps because their concepts are derived largely from the study of relatively more stable and homogeneous societies, they draw less sharply the distinction between the statistically normal and the normative. Sociologists are more apt to find it necessary to explore the tensions between the social order and culture, to be alert to deviations, and they are therefore more likely to define culture abstractly as a shared normative system. Yet much of the commentary on subculture refers to behavior. In my judgment this identification is unwise. Behavior is the result of the convergence of many forces. One should not assume, when the members of a group behave in similar ways, that cultural norms produce this result. Collective behavior theory and personality theory may also help to account for the similarities.

Contraculture

Failure to distinguish between role and subculture and vagueness in the concept of culture itself are not the only difficulties in the use of the idea of subculture. Perhaps more serious is the tendency to obscure, under this one term, two levels of explanation, one sociological and the other social-psychological, with a resulting failure to understand the causal forces at work. On few topics can one get wider agreement among sociologists than on the dangers of reductionism. If a psychologist attempts to explain social facts by psychological theories, we throw the book (probably Durkheim) at him; we emphasize the "fallacy of misplaced concreteness." In view of the widespread neglect of socio-cultural factors in the explanation of behavior, this is a necessary task. It makes vitally important, however, keen awareness by sociologists that they also deal with an abstract model. Perhaps we can reverse Durkheim's dictum to say: Do

not try to explain social psychological facts by sociological theories; or, more adequately, do not try to explain *behavior* (a product of the interaction of socio-cultural and personality influences) by a sociological theory alone. Yablonsky has recently reminded us that an excessively sociological theory of gangs can result in our seeing a definite group structure and a clear pattern of norms where in fact there is a "near-group," with an imprecise definition of boundaries and limited agreement on norms.[9] Carelessly used, our concepts can obscure the facts we seek to understand.

To see the cultural element in delinquency or in the domination of an individual by his adolescent group, phenomena that on the surface are non-cultural or even "anti-cultural," was a long step forward in their explanation. But it is also necessary to see the non-cultural aspects of some "norms"—phenomena that on the surface seem thoroughly cultural. Our vocabulary needs to be rich enough to help us to deal with these differences. The tendency to use the same term to refer to phenomena that share *some* elements in common, disregarding important differences, is to be content with phyla names when we need also to designate genus and species.

To sharpen our analysis, I suggest the use of the term contraculture wherever the normative system of a group contains, as a primary element, a theme of conflict with the values of the total society, where personality variables are directly involved in the development and maintenance of the group's values, and wherever its norms can be understood only by reference to the relationships of the group to a surrounding dominant culture.[10] None of these criteria definitely separates contraculture from subculture because each is a continuum. Subsocieties fall along a range with respect to each criterion. The values of most subcultures probably conflict in some measure with the larger culture. In a contraculture, however, the conflict element is central; many of the values, indeed, are specifically contradictions of the values of the dominant culture. Similarly, personality variables are involved in the development and maintenance of all cultures and subcultures, but usually the influence of personality is by way of variations around a theme that is part of the culture. In a contraculture, on the other hand, the theme itself expresses the tendencies of the persons who compose it. Finally, the norms of all subcultures are doubtless affected in some degree by the nature of the relationship with the larger culture. A subculture, as a pure type, however, does not require, for its understanding, intensive analysis of interaction with the larger culture; that is, its norms are not, to any significant degree, a product of that interaction. But a contraculture can be understood only by giving full attention to the interaction of the group which is its bearer with the larger society. It is one thing to say that the subculture of the rural, lower-class Negro encourages slow, inefficient work. It is another thing to say, with Charles S. Johnson, that such a norm represents "pseudo-ignorant malingering," a contracultural way of describing the same phenomenon. Johnson stressed the conflict element, the extent to which the norm was a product of interaction of white and Negro. There is certainly value in emphasizing the subcultural source of some of the values of southern Negroes. Against racist views or individual explanations, the sociologist opposes the subcultural: If they strive less, have different sexual mores, or otherwise vary from standards of the dominant society, it is in part because they have been socialized in accordance with different norms. But this is not enough, for their similar behavior may be interpreted in part as a shared response to a frustrating environment.

Empirically, subcultural and contracultural influences may be mixed, of course. Delinquency and adolescent behavior almost certainly manifest both influences.

The need, however, is to develop a clean analytic distinction between the two in order to interpret the wide variations in their mixture.

Adolescent Subculture and Contraculture

The utility of the distinction between contraculture and subculture can be tested by applying it to several research problems where the concept of subculture has been widely used. There is an extensive literature that interprets the behavior of adolescents substantially in these terms.[11] In the words of Havighurst and Taba: "Recent studies of adolescents have emphasized the fact that boys and girls in their teens have a culture of their own with moral standards and with moral pressures behind those standards. This culture has been called the 'adolescent peer culture.'"[12] Or Riesman: "All the morality is the group's. Indeed, even the fact that it is a morality is concealed by the confusing notion that the function of the group is to have fun, to play. . . ."[13] A close reading of the literature on adolescent culture reveals at least four different levels of interpretation, often only partially distinguished:

1) There is a cultural level, in which the roles of adolescent boys and girls are described, or the specialties (in Linton's sense) are designated. There is no reason to introduce concepts other than role or specialty to refer to norms that are generally accepted by elders and youths alike as appropriate to youth.

2) On the subcultural level, there are norms that manifest some separate system of values accepted within the adolescent group. These norms are not part of the role of youth. In part they are unknown to the elders; in part they conflict with standards accepted by the elders. They are learned, not by socialization in the total society, but by interaction within the sub-society of youth. Thus interests, games, speech patterns, and aesthetic tastes may

be communicated among an age-group with little reference to the larger culture.

3) There are currents of fashion or of other collective behavior that sweep through an adolescent group, strongly influencing the behavior of its members.[14] Although it is difficult to distinguish fashion from culture—many empirical phenomena have aspects of both—it is wise to keep them apart conceptually. This is not always done. The terminology of Riesman is closer to that of fashion than of culture, but the net impression of his analysis is that he is thinking of control by the peer group primarily as a cultural phenomenon.[15] And the sentence following the one quoted above from Havighurst and Taba reads "Boys and girls, desiring the approval of their age mates, follow the fashions of the peer culture in morals, dress, and speech. . . ." If the peer group influence stems from fashion, then strictly speaking it is not culture. The two differ to some degree in their origins, their functions, and their consequences.[16]

4) Many analyses of the control exercised by a youth group over its members employ the *concept* of contraculture, although the terminology and the assumptions are often those of subculture or culture. There is emphasis on the cross-pressures which young people feel: they want to be adults, yet fear to leave the securities of childhood; they experience contradictory adult treatment—a demand for grownup behavior here, the prevention of it there; ambiguity of self-image leads to efforts to prove oneself a full-fledged adult; there is sexual frustration. The peer group may help one to struggle with these cross-pressures, as described by Parsons: "Perhaps the best single point of reference for characterizing the youth culture lies in its contrast with the dominant pattern of the adult male role. By contrast with emphasis on responsibility in this role, the orientation of the youth culture is more or less specifically irresponsible."[17] This irresponsibility cannot be understood simply as another cul-

tural norm, as part of the "role" of youth, although these are Parsons' terms. It must be studied in the context of strain, of role ambiguity. Some sociologists explain this irresponsibility as merely a manifestation of the youth culture, thus obscuring the personality factors also involved. The description and analysis of an adolescent subculture, to be sure, are an important contribution to the sociology of youth. Many adolescents spend a great deal of time in groups that sustain norms different from those of the adult world; and adults often respond to the behavior that follows these norms in an "ethnocentric" way. To rely on a subcultural explanation alone, however, is to disregard the emergent quality of many of the standards and to minimize the fact that they are often in direct conflict with adult standards (which most adolescents themselves will soon accept).

This sharp conflict of values requires explanation. Parsons states the facts clearly: "Negatively, there is a strong tendency to repudiate interests in adult things, and to feel at least a certain recalcitrance to the pressure of adult expectations and disciplines. . . . Thus the youth culture is not only, as is true of the curricular aspects of formal education, a matter of age status as such but also shows signs of being a product of tensions in the relationship of younger people and adults."[18] At several other points Parsons develops the "reaction" theme and later uses the concept of "reaction-formation."[19] Should these various phenomena be subsumed under the concept of culture? It is one thing for a society to train its youth to certain ways of behaving. It is quite another for a youth group to develop inverse values in an effort to struggle with role ambiguities and strains. The adolescent may experience both as normative sanctions; but that should scarcely lead the social analyst to disregard their differences. I suggest the term contraculture in order to indicate the normative *and* the conflict aspects of this type of situation.

Delinquent Contraculture

The usefulness of separating subcultural and contracultural influences is seen particularly clearly in the analysis of delinquency and of criminality generally. Perhaps in no other field were there more substantial gains in understanding made possible by the introduction of a sociological point of view to supplement and to correct individualistic and moralistic interpretations. There is little need to review the extensive literature, from *Delinquent Gangs* to *Delinquent Boys,* to establish the importance of the normative element in criminal and delinquent behavior. It is a mistake, however, to try to stretch a useful concept into a total theory. A "complex-adequate" analysis [20] may seem less sharp and definitive than one based on one factor, but it is likely to be far more useful. Cohen's excellent work,[21] although labeled as a study of the culture of the gang, does not overlook the psychogenic sources of delinquency. In fact, his explanation of the origins of the subculture (contraculture) and its functions for the lower-class male makes clear that the norms of the gang are not learned, accepted, and taught in the same way that we learn what foods to eat, what clothes to wear, what language to speak. The very existence of the gang is a sign, in part, of blocked ambition. Because tensions set in motion by this blockage cannot be resolved by achievement of dominant values, such values are repressed, their importance denied, counter-values affirmed. The gang member is often ambivalent. Thwarted in his desire to achieve higher status by the criteria of the dominant society, he accepts criteria he can meet; but the reaction-formation in this response is indicated by the content of the delinquent norms—non-utilitarian, malicious, and negativistic, in Cohen's terms. This negative polarity represents the need to repress his own tendencies to accept the dominant cultural standards. This is not to say that the values of the gang cannot be explained

partially by cultural analysis, by some extension of the idea that "the mores can make anything right." But I suggest that Cohen's multiple-factor analysis might have been clearer, and less subject to misinterpretation, had he introduced the concept of contraculture alongside the concept of subculture. One reviewer, for example, completely disregards the "negative polarity" theme:

> In an overall summary, cultural delinquency is a phenomenon of culture, society, and socio-cultural experience. It is a positive thing: members of the several social classes are socialized, but there is a differential content in the socialization. Delinquency is not a negative thing; it is not a result of the breakdown of society, nor of the failure to curb criminal instincts, nor of the failure of the family, the church, or the school. The same set of concepts, the same social processes, and the same set of logical assumptions account for both delinquency and lawfulness. Since delinquency is of this character, it is unnecessary to invent any pathology to account for it.[22]

This statement neither adequately represents Cohen's thesis nor encourages us to explore a number of important questions: Why do only some of those who are exposed to the delinquent "subculture" learn it? [23] Why do those who follow the subculture often manifest ambivalence and guilt feelings? [24] Why do many of the same patterns of behavior occur in areas and among groups where the presence of the subculture is much less clear (middle-class delinquency)? [25] What is the significance of the fact that the delinquent subculture is not only different from but in part at least a reversal of the values of the dominant culture? The use of a purely subcultural model of analysis discourages or even prevents the raising of these questions and thus precludes adequate answers to them.

Cohen and Short have dealt with several of these issues by suggesting the need for a typology. Specifically for the study of delinquency, they propose five types of subcultures: the parent male (the central pattern described in *Delinquent Boys*), the conflict-oriented, the drug addict, the semi-professional thief, and the middle-class subcultures.[26] Although the criteria of classification are not entirely clear, these categories are primarily descriptive. The concept of contraculture might be added to this list as a type of subculture, if the one distinctive criterion used to designate a subculture is the presence in a subsociety of a normative system that separates it from the total society. Such a procedure does not seem, however, to produce an adequate taxonomy. If the shift is made from description to analysis, or from an interest in the content of norms to their etiology, an important difference emerges between subculture and contraculture: the one set of norms derives from standard socialization in a subsociety; the other stems from conflict and frustration in the experience of those who share many of the values of the whole society but are thwarted in their efforts to achieve those values.

It should be stressed once more that these are analytic concepts, no one of which is adequate to handle the empirical variations of delinquent behavior. Failure to recognize the abstract quality of our conceptual tools leads to unnecessary disagreements. When Miller describes the "Lower Class Culture as a Generating Milieu of Gang Delinquency," for example, he points to an important series of influences that derive from the value system of the lower-class community.[27] In his effort to emphasize this aspect of the etiology of delinquency, however, he tends to overlook the kind of evidence reported by Sykes and Matza, Cohen, Finestone, Yablonsky, the McCords, and others concerning collective behavior and personality variables.[28] Surely the evidence is now rich enough for us to state definitively that delinquency is a multi-variable product. The task ahead is not to prove that it stems largely from cultural or subcultural or contracultural influences, but to spell out the conditions under which these and other factors will be found in various empirical mixtures.[29]

Contracultural Aspects of Class and Occupation

The same admixture of the concepts of culture, subculture, and contraculture is found in the extensive literature on occupations and classes. Doubtless all three forces are found in many instances, and the research task is to untangle their various influences. It may stretch the meaning of the term too far to speak of the *position* of the "middle-class member," with its culturally designated role specifications; although in relatively stable societies the usage seems appropriate. In such societies, many of the rights and obligations of various status levels are culturally defined. In more mobile class systems, however, subcultural and contracultural norms become important. Our understanding of the American class system has certainly been deepened in the last twenty years by the descriptions of differences, among classes, in value perspectives, time orientations, levels aspiration, leisure-time styles, and child-rearing practices.[30]

The introduction of the concept of subculture has helped to avoid class-derived biases in the interpretation of the wide variations in these phenomena. In class analysis as in the study of deviations, however, there may be some over-compensation in the effort to eliminate the distortions of a middle-class and often rural perspective.[31] There is evidence to suggest that differences between classes are based less upon different values and norms than the subcultural approach suggests. The "innovations" of lower-class members, to use Merton's term, are not simply subcultural acts defined as innovative by middle-class persons. They are in part responses to a frustrating situation. They are efforts to deal with the disjunction of means and ends. When the disjunction is reduced, the variations in value and behavior are reduced. Thus Rosen found, "surprisingly," that Negroes in the Northeast made higher scores on an "achievement value" test than his description of Negro "culture" led him to expect. This may indicate that the low achievement response is less the result of a subcultural norm than a protest against a difficult situation. If the situation improves, the achievement value changes.[32] Stephenson's discovery that occupational plans of lower-class youth are considerably below those of higher-class youth, but that their aspirations are only slightly lower, bears on this same point. His data suggest that the classes differ not only in norms, but also in opportunity.[33] Differences in behavior, therefore, are only partly a result of subcultural contrasts. The lower educational aspirations of lower-class members are also found to be in part situationally induced, not simply normatively induced. When the situation changes, values and behavior change, as Mulligan found in his study of the response of the sons of blue-collar workers to the educational opportunities of the GI Bill, and as Wilson reports in his investigation of the aspirations of lower-class boys attending higher-class schools and upper-class boys attending lower-class schools.[34]

In short, our thinking about differences in behavior among social classes will be sharpened if we distinguish among those differences that derive from role influences, those based on subcultural variations, and those that express contracultural responses to deprivation. The proportions will vary from society to society; the research task is to specify the conditions under which various distributions occur. One would expect, to propose one hypothesis, to find more contracultural norms among lower-class members of an open society than in a similar group in a closed society.

The interpretation of differential behavior among the members of various occupational categories can also be strengthened by the distinctions made above. Here the contrast between role and subculture is especially useful. The role of a teacher consists of the rights and duties that *integrate* him into a system of expected and established relationships with others. The teaching subculture, on the other hand, insofar as it exists, *separates* teachers from the cultural world of others. It is either unknown to others or, if known, a source of disagreement and perhaps of conflict with others. There are also contracultural aspects of some occupational styles of life. In interpreting the differences between the values of jazz musicians and "squares," for example, Becker writes: "Their rejection of commercialism in music and squares in social life was part of the casting aside of the total American culture by men who could enjoy privileged status but who were unable to achieve a satisfactory personal adjustment within it."[35] Their style of life, in other words, can be understood only by supplementing the cultural and subcultural dimensions with the conflict theme. Cameron develops the same point. Although he makes no use of the term subculture, he describes the differentiating norms of the dance-band group, presumably a result of the "esoteric" aspects of their art, the differences in their time schedule, and the like. But he also describes the *contra* aspects of some of the norms, and suggests that they derive from the fact that early recruitment ties the jazz musician to the adolescence problem.[36]

Conclusion

Poorly defined terms plague research in many areas, particularly in the specification of relationships between sociological and social psychological levels of analysis. Thus "anomie" is still used to refer both to a social structural fact and to a personality fact, although this confusion is gradually being reduced. "Role" may refer, alternately, to rights and duties prescribed for the occupants of a position or to individual performance of that position. And subculture, I have suggested, is used to designate both the traditional norms of a subsociety and the emergent norms of a group caught in a frustrating and conflict-laden situation. This paper indicates that there are differences in the origin, function, and perpetuation of traditional and emergent norms, and suggests that the use of the concept contraculture for the latter might improve sociological analysis.

Hypotheses to guide the study of subculture can most profitably be derived from a general theory of culture. As an illustration, it may be hypothesized that a subculture will appear, in the first instance, as a result of mobility or an extension of communication that brings groups of different cultural background into membership in the same society, followed by physical or social isolation or both that prevents full assimilation.

Hypotheses concerning contracultures, on the other hand, can best be derived from social psychological theory—from the study of collective behavior, the frustration-aggression thesis, or the theory of group formation. One might hypothesize, for example, that under conditions of deprivation and frustration of major values (in a context where the deprivation is obvious because of extensive communication with the dominant group), and where value confusion and weak social controls obtain, contracultural norms will appear. One would expect to find, according to these propositions, many subcultural values among southern rural Negroes. Among first and second generation urban Negroes, however, one would expect an increase in contracultural norms. Both groups are deprived, but in the urban situation there is more "value leakage" from the dominant group, more value confusion, and weakened social controls.[37]

The subculture of the sociologist requires sophistication about the full range of human behavior. This desideratum has led to the proposition that the vast diversity of norms believed in and acted upon by the members of a modern society is not a sign of value confusion and breakdown but rather an indication that urban life brings into one system of interaction persons drawn from many cultural worlds. One unanticipated consequence of the sociological subculture may be that we exaggerate the normative insulation and solidarity of these various worlds. An important empirical question concerns the extent and results of their interaction.

NOTES

1. There are a few formal definitions. For example: "The term 'subculture' refers in this paper to 'cultural variants displayed by certain segments of the population.' Subcultures are distinguished not by one or two isolated traits—they constitute relatively cohesive cultural systems. They are worlds within the larger world of our national culture." (Mirra Komarovsky and S. S. Sargent, "Research into Subcultural Influences upon Personality," in S. S. Sargent and M. W. Smith (eds.), *Culture and Personality,* New York: The Viking Fund, 1949, p. 143.) These authors then refer to class, race, occupation, residence, and region. After referring to subgroup values and language, Kimball Young and Raymond W. Mack state: "Such shared learned behaviors which are common to a specific group or category are called *subcultures.*" (*Sociology and Social Life,* New York: American Book, 1959, p. 49.) They refer then to ethnic, occupational, and regional variations. Blaine Mercer writes: "A society contains numerous subgroups, each with its own characteristic ways of thinking and acting. These cultures within a culture are called *subcultures.*" (*The Study of Society,* New York: Harcourt, Brace, 1958, p. 34.) Thereafter he discusses Whyte's *Street Corner Society.* Although these definitions are helpful, they fail to make several distinctions which are developed below.

2. A. L. Kroeber, "The Concept of Culture in Science," *Journal of General Education,* 3 (1949), 187. See also Clyde Kluckhohn's reference to this idea in "Culture and Behavior," in Gardner Lindzey (ed.), *Handbook of Social Psychology,* Cambridge: Addison-Wesley, 1954, 2, 954; and A. L. Kroeber in "Problems of Process: Results," in Sol Tax *et al.* (eds.), *An Appraisal of Anthropology Today,* Chicago: University of Chicago Press, 1953, p. 119.

3. Ralph Linton, *The Study of Man,* New York: Appleton-Century, 1936, p. 486. See also his *The Cultural Background of Personality,* New York: Appleton-Century-Crofts, 1945, pp. 148–151. Elsewhere in *The Study of Man,* Linton uses subculture in a different sense, similar to the second usage described below.

4. Edward Sapir, "Personality," in *Encyclopedia of the Social Sciences,* New York: Macmillan, 1931, Vol. 12, p. 86; Charles H. Cooley, *Human Nature and the Social Order,* rev. ed., New York: Scribner, 1922.

5. See, e.g., John K. Morland, *Millways of Kent,* Chapel Hill: University of North Carolina Press, 1958; Julian Steward, *The People of Puerto Rico,* Champaign: University of Illinois Press, 1956; Charles Wagley and Marvin Harris, "A Typology of Latin American Subcultures," *American Anthropologist,* 57 (1955), 428–451; Evon Z. Vogt, "American Subcultural Continua as Exemplified by the Mormons and Texans," *American Anthropologist,* 57 (1955), 1163–1172; Murray Straus, "Subcultural Variations in Ceylonese Mental Ability: A Study in National Character," *Journal of Social Psychology,* 39 (1954), 129–141; Joel B. Montague and Edgar G. Epps, "Attitudes Toward Social Mobility as Revealed by Samples of Negro and White Boys," *Pacific Sociological Review,* 1 (1958), 81–84; Hylan Lewis, *Blackways of Kent,* Chapel Hill: University of North Carolina Press, 1955; Robin M. Williams, Jr., *American Society,* New York: Knopf, 1951, Chapter 10; T. S. Langner, "A Test of Intergroup Prejudice Which Takes Account of Individual and Group Differences in Values," *Journal of Abnormal and Social Psychology,* 48 (1953), 548–554.

6. Brewster Smith, "Anthropology and Psychology," in John Gillin (ed.), *For a Science of Social Man,* New York: Macmillan, 1954, p. 61. See also Talcott Parsons and Edward A. Shils (eds.), *Toward A General Theory of Action,* Cambridge: Harvard University Press, 1951, esp. the monograph by the editors; and Ralph Linton's preface to Abram Kardiner, *The Psychological Frontiers of Society,* New York: Columbia University Press, 1945.

7. See, e.g., Neal Gross, Ward S. Mason, and A. W. McEachern, *Explorations in Role Analysis,* New York: Wiley, 1958; F. L. Bates, "Position, Role, and Status: A Reformulation of Concepts," *Social Forces,* 34 (1956), 313–321; Robert K. Merton, "The Role Set: Problems in Sociological Theory," *British Journal of Sociology,* 8 (1957), 106–120; S. F. Nadel, *The Theory of Social Structure,* Glencoe, Ill.: Free Press, 1957; Theodore R. Sarbin, "Role Theory," in *Handbook of Social Psychology, op. cit.,* Vol. 1, Chapter 6.

8. It is possible, of course, for a subculture to specify roles within its own system.

9. Lewis Yablonsky, "The Delinquent Gang as a Near-Group," *Social Problems,* 7 (1959), 108–117.

10. By the noun in "contraculture" I seek to call attention to the normative aspects of the phenomena under study and by the qualifying prefix to call attention to the conflict aspects. Similar terms are occasionally found in the literature, but they are either defined only by their use in context or are used differently from the meaning assigned to contraculture in this paper. Harold D. Lasswell uses the term "countermores" to refer to "culture patterns which appeal mainly to the id . . ." (*World Politics and Personal Insecurity,* New York: McGraw-Hill, 1935, p. 64). He then designates "revolutionists, prostitutes, prisoners, obscene and subversive talk"—which scarcely suggest a clear analytic category. In *World Revolutionary Propaganda,* New York: Knopf, 1939, Lasswell and Dorothy Blumenstock discuss the use of inverse values as a revolutionary propaganda weapon and comment on the presumed vulnerability of deprived persons to the countermores stressed in this propaganda. In *Power and Society,* New Haven: Yale University Press, 1950, p. 49, Lasswell uses the term somewhat differently: "*Countermores* are culture traits symbolized by the group as deviations from the mores, and yet are expected to occur." A certain amount of bribery, for example, is "normal" "and must be included by the candid observer as part of culture."

At various points, Talcott Parsons more nearly approaches the meaning of the concept contraculture as used here, although more by implication than by direct definition, and without distinguishing it from the concept of subculture. Referring to the ideological aspects of a subculture, he writes: "In such cases of an open break with the value-system and ideology of the wider society we may speak of a 'counter-ideology.'" (*The Social System,* Glencoe, Ill.: Free Press, 1951, p. 355.) And later: "If, however, the culture of the deviant group, like that of the delinquent gang, remains a 'counter-culture' it is difficult to find the bridges by which it can acquire influence over wider circles" (p. 522). It is not clear from these uses how counter-ideology and counter-culture are to be defined; but the important place Parsons gives to the element of ambivalence in his use of the concept subculture suggests that he has in mind something similar to our concept of contraculture in his use of these various terms. (See *ibid.*, p. 286.)

11. See Talcott Parsons, *Essays in Sociological Theory Pure and Applied*, Glencoe, Ill.: Free Press, 1949, Chapter 5; Howard Becker, *German Youth: Bond or Free*, New York: Oxford, 1946; S. N. Eisenstadt, *From Generation to Generation. Age Groups and the Social Structure*, Glencoe, Ill.: Free Press, 1956; David Riesman *et al., The Lonely Crowd*, New Haven: Yale University Press, 1950; R. J. Havighurst and Hilda Taba, *Adolescent Character and Personality*, New York: Wiley, 1949; Kingsley Davis, "The Sociology of Parent-Youth Conflict," *American Sociological Review*, 5 (1940), 523–534; Ralph Linton, "Age and Sex Categories," *American Sociological Review*, 7 (1942), 589–603; Joseph R. Gusfield, "The Problem of Generations in an Organizational Structure," *Social Forces*, 35 (1957), 323–330. For some contradictory evidence, see W. A. Westley and Frederick Elkin, "The Protective Environment and Adolescent Socialization," *Social Forces*, 35 (1957), 243–249; and Elkin and Westley, "The Myth of Adolescent Culture," *American Sociological Review*, 20 (1955), 680–684.

12. *Op. cit.*, p. 35.

13. *Op. cit.*, p. 72.

14. See Harold Finestone, "Cats, Kicks, and Color," *Social Problems*, 5 (1957), 3–13. Here the "cat" among some Negroes is seen as "the personal counterpart of an expressive social movement."

15. See Riesman, *op. cit.*, esp. Chapter 3, "A Jury of Their Peers."

16. The desirability of keeping distinct the analytic concepts of culture and collective behavior, including fashion, cannot be elaborated here. See Herbert Blumer, "Collective Behavior," in A. M. Lee (ed.), *Principles of Sociology*, New York: Barnes and Noble, 1951; Ralph H. Turner and Lewis M. Killian, *Collective Behavior*, Englewood Cliffs, N.J.: Prentice-Hall, 1957; Edward Sapir, "Fashion," *Encyclopedia of the Social Sciences*, New York: Macmillan, 1931, Vol. 6, pp. 139–144; Georg Simmel, "Fashion," *American Journal of Sociology*, 62 (1957), 541–558.

17. Parsons, *op. cit. Essays . . .* , p. 92.

18. *Ibid.*, pp. 92–93.

19. See *ibid.*, pp. 101–102, 189–190, 342–345, 355.

20. See Robin M. Williams, Jr., "Continuity and Change in Sociological Study," *American Sociological Review*, 23 (1958), 619–633.

21. Albert K. Cohen, *Delinquent Boys*, Glencoe, Ill.: Free Press, 1955.

22. Frank Hartung, in a review of *Delinquent Boys, American Sociological Review*, 20 (1955), 752.

23. See Solomon Kobrin, "The Conflict of Values in Delinquency Areas," *American Sociological Review*, 16 (1951), pp. 653–661; Alex Inkeles, "Personality and Social Structure," in Robert K. Merton *et al.* (eds.), *Sociology Today*, New York: Basic Books, 1959, p. 254.

24. See Gresham M. Sykes and David Matza, "Techniques of Neutralization: A Theory of Delinquency," *American Sociological Review*, 22 (1957), 664–670.

25. John I. Kitsuse and David C. Dietrick, *"Delinquent Boys:* A Critique," *American Sociological Review*, 24 (1959), 208–215.

26. See Albert Cohen and James Short, "Research in Delinquent Subcultures," *The Journal of Social Issues*, 14, 3 (1958), 20–37.

27. Walter B. Miller, "Lower Class Culture as a Generating Milieu of Gang Delinquency," *The Journal of Social Issues*, 14, 3 (1958), 5–19.

28. In addition to the studies of Sykes and Matza, Cohen, Finestone, and Yablonsky cited above, see William McCord and Joan McCord, *Origins of Crime: A New Evaluation of the Cambridge-Somerville Youth Study*, New York: Columbia University Press, 1959.

29. In a recent manuscript, Sykes and Matza suggest that delinquent behavior can profitably be studied as an exaggerated expression of certain "subterranean values" of the dominant society

(the search for excitement, the use of "pull" to get by without too much work, and aggression). This idea deserves careful study. The main research task is to discover the conditions which promote selective and exaggerated attention to these values at the cost of neglect of the more prominent "public" values. It seems likely that this task will lead to the incorporation of the "subterranean values" thesis into the larger complex of theories of delinquency. The thesis raises a question of terminology in connection with the present paper: At what point does exaggerated emphasis on a value become a counter-value by virtue of the exaggeration? *Some* cultural support can be found in a complex society for many patterns of behavior that are not fully valued. A society may accept or even applaud a pattern that is used to a limited degree while condemning its extravagant use. And the meaning of the pattern in the life of the individual when found in culturally approved degree differs from what it is when the pattern becomes a dominant theme. To discover why some subterranean values are raised into a style of life, therefore, requires more than cultural analysis. (See Gresham M. Sykes and David Matza, "Juvenile Delinquency and Subterranean Values," unpublished manuscript, 1960.)

30. Of the many studies in this area, see Charles McArthur, "Personality Differences Between Middle and Upper Classes," *Journal of Abnormal and Social Psychology,* 50 (1955), 247–254; Melvin L. Kohn, "Social Class and Parental Values," *American Journal of Sociology,* 64 (1959), 337–351; A. B. Hollingshead and Frederick C. Redlich, *Social Class and Mental Illness,* New York: Wiley, 1958; Clyde R. White, "Social Class Differences in the Uses of Leisure," *American Journal of Sociology,* 61 (1955), 145–151; John A. Clausen and Melvin L. Kohn, "The Ecological Approach in Social Psychiatry," *American Journal of Sociology,* 60 (1954), 140–151; A. B. Hollingshead, *Elmtown's Youth,* New York: Wiley, 1949; Louis Schneider and Sverre Lysgaard, "The Deferred Gratification Pattern: A Preliminary Study," *American Sociological Review,* 18 (1953), 142–149; Urie Bronfenbrenner, "Socialization and Social Class Through Time and Space," in Eleanor E. Maccoby *et al.* (eds.), *Readings in Social Psychology,* New York: Holt, 1958, 400–425.

31. C. Wright Mills, "The Professional Ideology of Social Pathologists," *American Journal of Sociology,* 49 (1943), 165–180.

32. Bernard C. Rosen, "Race, Ethnicity, and the Achievement Syndrome," *American Sociological Review,* 24 (1959), 47–60. It is highly important, in aspiration studies, to compare, not absolute levels, but the extent of aspiration above the existing level of individuals or their families. A low absolute target for lower-class members may require a larger *reach* than a higher target for middle-class persons. See Leonard Reissman, "Levels of Aspiration and Social Class," *American Sociological Review,* 18 (1953), 233–242.

33. Richard M. Stephenson, "Mobility Orientation and Stratification of 1,000 Ninth Graders," *American Sociological Review,* 22 (1957), 204–212.

34. Raymond A. Mulligan, "Socio-Economic Background and College Enrollment," *American Sociological Review,* 16 (1951), 188–196; Alan B. Wilson, "Residential Segregation of Social Classes and Aspirations of High School Boys," *American Sociological Review,* 24 (1959), 836–845.

35. Howard S. Becker, "The Professional Dance Musician and His Audience," *American Journal of Sociology,* 57 (1951), 136–144.

36. W. B. Cameron, "Sociological Notes on the Jam Session," *Social Forces,* 33 (1954), 177–182.

37. There are numerous alternative ways in which the protest against deprivation can be expressed. Delinquency and drug addiction often have a contracultural aspect; but somewhat less clearly, political and religious movements among disprivileged groups may also invert the values of the influential but inaccessible dominant group. Thus the concept of contraculture may help us to understand, for example, the Garveyite movement, the Ras Tafari cult, and some aspects of the value schemes of lower-class sects. (See, e.g., Liston Pope, *Millhands and Preachers,* New Haven: Yale University Press, 1942; and George E. Simpson, "The Ras Tafari Movement in Jamaica: A Study of Race and Class Conflict," *Social Forces,* 34 (1955), 167–170.)

66. DELINQUENT SUBCULTURES: SOCIOLOGICAL INTERPRETATIONS

DAVID J. BORDUA

Since the turn of the century four major interpretations of the origins of gang delinquency and delinquent subcultures have emerged. First there is Frederick Thrasher's view of spontaneous groups arising out of conditions of social disorganization. There is Albert K. Cohen's notion of response to status deprivation, and Richard Cloward and Lloyd Ohlin's idea of alienation where means to achieve in conventional ways are frustrated. Finally, there is Walter Miller's view that delinquent boys represent an adolescent variant on the more general life style of their lower-class world. To David J. Bordua, such theories, while useful, tend to ignore certain critical aspects of gang delinquency. His essay offers both a review and a critique of the four themes and their variations.

David J. Bordua teaches sociology at the University of Illinois, Urbana. He is the author of many essays on social deviance and the book, The Police: Six Sociological Essays *(1967).*

The problem of group delinquency has been a subject of theoretical interest for American sociologists and other social observers for well over a half century. In the course of that period, the group nature of delinquency has come to be a central starting point for many theories of delinquency, and delinquency causation has been seen by some sociologists as pre-eminently a process whereby the individual becomes associated with a group which devotes some or all of its time to planning, committing, or celebrating delinquencies and which has elaborated a set of lifeways —a subculture—which encourages and justifies behavior defined as delinquent by the larger society.

In addition to the processes whereby an individual takes on the beliefs and norms of a pre-existing group and thereby becomes delinquent—a process mysterious enough in itself in many cases—there is the more basic, and in many respects more complex, problem of how such groups begin in the first place. What are the social conditions that facilitate or cause the rise of delinquency-carrying groups? What are the varying needs and motives satisfied in individuals by such groups? What processes of planned social control might be useable in preventing the rise of such groups or in redirecting the behavior and moral systems of groups already in existence? All these questions and many others have been asked for at least two generations. Within the limits of this brief paper, it is impossible to present and analyze in detail the many answers to these questions which have been put forward by social scientists. What I can do is single out a few of the major viewpoints and concentrate on them.

Reprinted from *The Annals,* **338** (November 1961), 119–136, by permission of the author and The American Academy of Political and Social Sciences. This article was originally entitled "Delinquent Subcultures: Sociological Interpretations of Gang Delinquency."

In its more well-developed and extreme forms, gang or subcultural delinquency has been heavily concentrated in the low status areas of our large cities. The theoretical interpretations I will discuss all confine themselves to gang delinquency of this sort.

The Classical View

Still the best book on gangs, gang delinquency, and—though he did not use the term—delinquent subcultures is *The Gang* by Frederick M. Thrasher, and his formulations are the ones that I have labeled "the classical view." Not that he originated the basic interpretative framework, far from it, but his application of the theoretical materials available at the time plus his sensitivity to the effects of social environment and his willingness to consider processes at all behavioral levels from the basic needs of the child to the significance of the saloon, from the nature of city government to the crucial importance of the junk dealer, from the consequences of poverty to the nature of leadership in the gang still distinguish his book.[1]

Briefly, Thrasher's analysis may be characterized as operating on the following levels. The ecological processes which determine the structure of the city create the interstitial area characterized by a variety of indices of conflict, disorganization, weak family and neighborhood controls, and so on. In these interstitial areas, in response to universal childhood needs, spontaneous play groups develop. Because of the relatively uncontrolled nature of these groups—or of many of them at least —and because of the presence of many attractive and exciting opportunities for fun and adventure, these groups engage in a variety of activities, legal and illegal, which are determined, defined, and directed by the play group itself rather than by conventional adult supervision.

The crowded, exciting slum streets teem with such groups. Inevitably, in a situation of high population density, limited resources, and weak social control, they come into conflict with each other for space, playground facilities, reputation. Since many of their activities, even at an early age, are illegal, although often not feloniously so—they swipe fruit from peddlers, turn over garbage cans, stay away from home all night and steal milk and cakes for breakfast, play truant from school—they also come into conflict with adult authority. Parents, teachers, merchants, police, and others become the natural enemies of this kind of group and attempt to control it or to convert it to more conventional activities. With some groups they succeed, with some they do not.

If the group continues, it becomes part of a network of similar groups, increasingly freed from adult restraint, increasingly involved in intergroup conflict and fighting, increasingly engaged in illegal activities to support itself and to continue to receive the satisfactions of the "free" life of the streets. Conflict, especially with other groups, transforms the play group into the gang. Its illegal activities become more serious, its values hardened, its structure more determined by the necessity to maintain eternal vigilance in a hostile environment.

By middle adolescence, the group is a gang, often with a name, usually identified with a particular ethnic or racial group, and usually with an elaborate technology of theft and other means of self-support. Gradually, the gang may move in the direction of adult crime, armed robbery, perhaps, or other serious crimes.

Prior to that time, however, it is likely to have engaged in much stealing from stores, railroad cars, empty houses, parents, drunks, almost anywhere money or goods are available. The ready access to outlets for stolen goods is of major importance here. The junk dealer, especially the junk wagon peddler, the convenient no-questions-asked attitudes of large numbers of local adults who buy "hot" merchandise, and the early knowledge that customers are available all help to make theft easy and profitable as well as morally acceptable.[2]

Nonutilitarian?

It is appropriate at this point to deal with a matter that has become important in the discussion of more recent theories of group delinquency. This is Albert K. Cohen's famous characterization of the delinquent subculture as nonutilitarian, by which he seems to mean that activities, especially theft, are not oriented to calculated economic ends.[3]

Thrasher makes a great point of the play and adventure quality of many illegal acts, especially in the pregang stages of a group's development, but he also describes many cases where theft has a quite rational and instrumental nature, even at a fairly early age.

The theft activities and the disposition of the loot make instrumental sense in the context of Thrasher's description of the nature of the group or gang. Much theft is essentially for the purpose of maintaining the group in a state of freedom from adult authority. If a group of boys lives days or even weeks away from home, then the theft of food or of things which are sold to buy food is hardly nonutilitarian. If such a group steals from freight cars, peddles the merchandise to the neighbors for movie money, and so on, this can hardly be considered nonutilitarian. The behavior makes sense as instrumental behavior, however, only after one has a picture of the general life led by the group. Boys who feed themselves by duplicating keys to bakery delivery boxes, creep out of their club rooms right after delivery, steal the pastry, pick up a quart of milk from a doorstep, and then have breakfast may not have a highly developed sense of nutritional values, but this is not nonutilitarian.

Such youngsters may, of course, spend the two dollars gained from selling stolen goods entirely on doughnuts and gorge themselves and throw much of the food away. I think this largely indicates that they are children, not that they are nonutilitarian.[4]

Let us look a little more systematically at the Thrasher formulations, however, since such an examination can be instructive in dealing with the more recent theories. The analysis proceeds at several levels, as I have mentioned.

Levels of analysis

At the level of the local adult community, we may say that the social structure is permissive, attractive, facilitative, morally supportive of the gang development process.

It is permissive because control over children is weak; attractive because many enjoyable activities are available, some of which are illegal, like stealing fruit, but all of which can be enjoyed only if the child manages to evade whatever conventional controls do exist.

In another sense, the local environment is attractive because of the presence of adult crime of a variety of kinds ranging from organized vice to older adolescents and adults making a living by theft. The attraction lies, of course, in the fact that these adults may have a lot of money and live the carefree life and have high status in the neighborhood.

The local environment is facilitative in a number of ways. There are things readily available to steal, people to buy them, and places to hide without adult supervision.

The environment is morally supportive because of the presence of adult crime, as previously mentioned, but also for several additional reasons. One is the readiness of conventional adults to buy stolen goods. Even parents were discovered at this occasionally. The prevalence of political pull, which not only objectively protected adult crime but tended to undercut the norms against crime, must be mentioned then as now. The often bitter poverty which turned many situations into matters of desperate competition also contributed.

Additionally, many gang activities, especially in the protogang stage, are not seriously delinquent and receive adult approval. These activities include such things as playing baseball for "side money" and much minor gambling such as penny pitching. Within limits, fighting lies well within the local community's zone of tolerance, especially when it is directed against members of another ethnic group.

At the level of the adolescent and preadolescent groups themselves, the environment is essentially coercive of gang formation. The presence of large numbers of groups competing for limited resources leads to conflict, and the full-fledged adolescent gang is pre-eminently a conflict group with a high valuation of fighting skill, courage, and similar qualities. Thus, the transition from spontaneous group to gang is largely a matter of participating in the struggle for life of the adolescent world under the peculiar conditions of the slum.

At the level of the individual, Thrasher assumes a set of basic needs common to all children. He leans heavily on the famous four wishes of W. I. Thomas, security, response, recognition, and new experience, especially the last two. Gang boys and boys in gang areas are, in this sense, no different from other boys. They come to choose different ways of satisfying these needs. What determines which boys form gangs is the differential success of the agencies of socialization and social control in channeling these needs into conventional paths. Thus, due to family inadequacy or breakdown or school difficulties, coupled with the ever present temptations of the exciting, adventurous street as compared to the drab, dull, and unsatisfying family and school, some boys are more available for street life than others.

Finally, it should be pointed out that the gang engages in many activities of a quite ordinary sort. Athletics are very common and highly regarded at all age levels. Much time is spent simply talking and being with the gang. The gang's repertory is diverse—baseball, football, dice, poker, holding dances, shooting the breeze, shoplifting, rolling drunks, stealing cars.

This is more than enough to give the tenor of Thrasher's formulations. I have purposely attempted to convey the distinctive flavor of essentially healthy boys satisfying universal needs in a weakly controlled and highly seductive environment. Compared to the deprived and driven boys of more recent formulations with their status problems, blocked opportunities (or psychopathologies if one takes a more psychiatric view), Thrasher describes an age of innocence indeed.

This is, perhaps, the most important single difference between Thrasher and some—not all—of the recent views. Delinquency and crime were attractive, being a "good boy" was dull. They were attractive because they were fun and were profitable and because one could be a hero in a fight. Fun, profit, glory, and freedom is a combination hard to beat, particularly for the inadequate conventional institutions that formed the competition.

Working Class Boy and Middle Class Measuring Rod

If Thrasher saw the gang as being formed over time through the attractiveness of the free street life and the unattractiveness and moral weakness of the agencies of social control, Albert K. Cohen sees many working class boys as being driven to develop the delinquent subculture as a way of recouping the self-esteem destroyed by middle-class-dominated institutions.

Rather than focusing on the gang and its development over time, Cohen's theory focuses on the way of life of the gang—

the delinquent subculture. A collective way of life, a subculture, develops when a number of people with a common problem of adjustment are in effective interaction, according to Cohen. The bulk of his basic viewpoint is the attempted demonstration that the common problem of adjustment of the lower class gang boys who are the carriers of the delinquent subculture derives from their socialization in lower class families and their consequent lack of preparation to function successfully in middle class institutions such as the school.

The institutions within which the working class boy must function reward and punish him for acceptable or unacceptable performance according to the child-assessing version of middle class values. The middle class value pattern places great emphasis on ambition as a cardinal virtue, individual responsibility (as opposed to extreme emphasis on shared kin obligations, for example), the cultivation and possession of skills, the ability to postpone gratification, rationality, the rational cultivation of manners, the control of physical aggression and violence, the wholesome and constructive use of leisure, and respect for property (especially respect for the abstract rules defining rights of access to material things).[5]

The application of these values adapted to the judgment of children constitutes the "middle class measuring rod" by which all children are judged in institutions run by middle class personnel—the school, the settlement house, and the like. The fact that working class children must compete according to these standards is a consequence of what Cohen, in a most felicitous phrase, refers to as the "democratic status universe" characteristic of American society. Everyone is expected to strive, and everyone is measured against the same standard. Not everyone is equally prepared, however, and the working class boy is, with greater statistical frequency than the middle class boy, ill prepared through previous socialization.

Cultural setting

Social class for Cohen is not simply economic position but, much more importantly, a set of more or less vertically layered cultural settings which differ in the likelihood that boys will be taught the aspirations, ambitions, and psychological skills necessary to adjust to the demands of the larger institutions.

Cohen goes on to describe this predominantly lower working class cultural setting as more likely to show restricted aspirations, a live-for-today orientation toward consumption, a moral view which emphasizes reciprocity within the kin and other primary groups and correlatively less concern with abstract rules which apply across or outside of such particularistic circumstances. In addition, the working class child is less likely to be surrounded with educational toys, less likely to be trained in a family regimen of order, neatness, and punctuality. Of particular importance is the fact that physical aggression is more prevalent and more valued in the working class milieu.

When a working class boy thus equipped for life's struggle begins to function in the school, the settlement, and other middle-class-controlled institutions and encounters the middle class measuring rod, he inevitably receives a great deal of disapproval, rejection, and punishment. In short, in the eyes of the middle class evaluator, he does not measure up. This is what Cohen refers to as the problem of status deprivation which constitutes the fundamental problem of adjustment to which the delinquent subculture is a solution.

Self-derogation

But this deprivation derives not only from the negative evaluations of others but also from self-derogation. The working class boy shares in this evaluation of himself to some degree for a variety of reasons.[6] The first of these is the previously mentioned democratic status universe wherein the dominant culture requires everyone to compete against all comers. Second, the parents of working class boys, no matter how adjusted they seem to be to their low status position, are likely to project their frustrated aspirations onto their children. They may do little effective socialization to aid the child, but they are, nevertheless, likely at least to want their children to be better off than they are. Third, there is the effect of the mass media which spread the middle class life-style. And, of course, there is the effect of the fact of upward mobility as visible evidence that at least some people can make the grade.

In short, the working class boy is subjected to many social influences which emphasize the fact that the way to respect, status, and success lies in conforming to the demands of middle class society. Even more importantly, he very likely has partly accepted the middle class measuring rod as a legitimate, even superior, set of values. The profound ambivalence that this may lead to in the individual is simply a reflection of the fact that the larger culture penetrates the lower working class world in many ways.

Thus, to the external status problem posed by devaluations by middle class functionaries is added the internal status problem of low self-esteem.

This, then, is the common problem of adjustment. Given the availability of many boys similarly situated, a collective solution evolves, the delinquent subculture. This subculture is characterized by Cohen as nonutilitarian, malicious, and negativistic, characterized by versatility, short-run hedonism, and an emphasis on group autonomy, that is, freedom from adult restraint.

These are, of course, the direct antitheses of the components of the middle class measuring rod. The delinquent subculture functions simultaneously to combat the enemy without and the enemy within, both the hated agents of the middle class and the gnawing internal sense of inadequacy and low self-esteem. It does so by erecting a counterculture, an alternative set of status criteria.

Guilt

This subculture must do more than deal with the middle-class-dominated institutions on the one hand and the feelings of low self-esteem on the other. It must also deal with the feelings of guilt over aggression, theft, and the like that will inevitably arise. It must deal with the fact that the collective solution to the common problem of adjustment is an illicit one in the eyes of the larger society and, certainly, also in the eyes of the law-abiding elements of the local area.

It must deal, also, with the increasing opposition which the solution arouses in the police and other agencies of the conventional order. Over time, the subculture comes to contain a variety of definitions of these agents of conventionality which see them as the aggressors, thus legitimating the group's deviant activities.

Because of this requirement that the delinquent subculture constitute a solution to internal, psychological problems of self-esteem and guilt, Cohen sees the group behavior pattern as being over-determined in the psychological sense and as linking up with the mechanism of reaction formation.

Thus, the reason for the seeming irrationality of the delinquent subculture lies in the deeply rooted fears and anxieties of the status deprived boy. I have already discussed the shift from Thrasher's view of delinquency as attractive in a situation of weak social control to the views of it as more reactive held by some modern theorists. Cohen, of course, is prominent among these latter, the irrationalists. It is extremely difficult to bring these viewpoints together at all well except to point out that Cohen's position accords well with much research on school failure and its consequences in damaged self-esteem. It does seem unlikely, as I will point out later in another connection, that the failure of family, school, and neighborhood to control the behavior of Thrasher's boys would result in their simple withdrawal from such conventional contexts without hostility and loss of self-regard.

Cohen emphasizes that not all members of an ongoing delinquent group are motivated by this same problem of adjustment. Like any other protest movement, the motives which draw new members at different phases of its development will vary. It is sufficient that a core of members share the problem.

The analysis of the delinquent subculture of urban working class boys set forth in *Delinquent Boys* has been elaborated and supplemented in a later article by Cohen and James F. Short.[7]

Other delinquent subcultures

Responding to the criticism that there seemed a variety of kinds of delinquent subcultures, even among lower class urban youth, Cohen and Short distinguish the parent-male subculture, the conflict-oriented subculture, the drug addict subculture, and a subculture focused around semiprofessional theft.[8]

The parent subculture is the now familiar subculture described in *Delinquent Boys*. Cohen and Short describe it as the most common form.[9]

We refer to it as the parent sub-culture because it is probably the most common variety in this country—indeed, it might be called the "garden variety" of delinquent sub-culture—and because the characteristics listed above seem to constitute a common core shared by other important variants.

In discussing the conditions under which these different subcultures arise, Cohen and Short rely on a pivotal paper published in 1951 by Solomon Kobrin.[10] Dealing with the differential location of the conflict-oriented versus the semi-professional theft subculture, Kobrin pointed out that delinquency areas vary in the degree to which conventional and criminal

value systems are mutually integrated. In the integrated area, adult criminal activity is stable and organized, and adult criminals are integral parts of the local social structure—active in politics, fraternal orders, providers of employment. Here delinquency can form a kind of apprenticeship for adult criminal careers with such careers being relatively indistinct from conventional careers. More importantly, the interests of organized criminal groups in order and a lack of police attention would lead to attempts to prevent the wilder and more untrammeled forms of juvenile violence. This would mean, of course, that crime in these areas was largely of the stable, profitable sort ordinarily associated with the rackets.

Lower Class Boy and Lower Class Culture

The interpretation of the delinquent subculture associated with Albert Cohen that I have just described contrasts sharply in its main features with what has come to be called the lower class culture view associated with Walter B. Miller.[11] Miller disagrees with the Cohen position concerning the reactive nature of lower class gang culture.[12]

In the case of "gang" delinquency, the cultural system which exerts the most direct influences on behavior is that of the lower class community itself—a long-established, distinctively patterned tradition with an integrity of its own—rather than a so-called "delinquent sub-culture" which has arisen through conflict with middle class culture and is oriented to the deliberate violation of middle class norms.

What, then, is the lower class culture Miller speaks of and where is it located? Essentially, Miller describes a culture which he sees as emerging from the shaking-down processes of immigration, internal migration, and vertical mobility. Several population and cultural streams feed this process, but, primarily, lower class culture presents the emerging common adaptation of unsuccessful immigrants and Negroes.

It is the thesis of this paper that from these extremely diverse and heterogeneous origins (with, however, certain common features), there is emerging a relatively homogeneous and stabilized native-American lower class culture; however, in many communities the process of fusion is as yet in its earlier phases, and evidences of the original ethnic or locality culture are still strong.[13]

In his analysis, Miller is primarily concerned with what he calls the hard core group in the lower class—the same very bottom group referred to by Cohen as the lower-lower class. The properties of this emerging lower class culture as described by Miller may be divided into a series of social structural elements and a complex pattern of what Miller calls focal concerns.

Focal concerns

The first of the structural elements is what Miller calls the female-based household, that is, a family form wherein the key relationships are those among mature females (especially those of different generations but, perhaps, also sisters or cousins) and between these females and their children. The children may be by different men, and the biological fathers may play a very inconsistent and unpredictable role in the family. Most essentially, the family is not organized around the expectation of stable economic support provided by an adult male.

The relationship between adult females and males is characterized as one of serial mating, with the female finding it necessary repeatedly to go through a cycle of roles of mate-seeker, mother, and employee.

Closely related to and supportive of this form of household is the elaboration of a system of one-sex peer groups which, according to Miller, become emotional ha-

vens and major sources of psychic investment and support for both sexes and for both adolescents and adults. The family, then, is not the central focus of primary, intimate ties that it is in middle class circles.

In what is surely a masterpiece of cogent description, Miller presents the focal concerns of lower class culture as trouble, toughness, smartness, excitement, fate, and autonomy. His description of the complexly interwoven patterns assumed by these focal concerns cannot be repeated here, but a brief discussion seems appropriate.[14]

Trouble is what life gets you into—especially trouble with the agents of the larger society. The central aspect of this focal concern is the distinction between law-abiding and law-violating behavior, and where an individual stands along the implied dimension either by behavior, reputation, or commitment is crucial in the evaluation of him by others. Toughness refers to physical prowess, skill, masculinity, fearlessness, bravery, daring. It includes an almost compulsive opposition to things seen as soft and feminine, including much middle class behavior, and is related, on the one hand, to sex-role identification problems which flow from the young boy's growing up in the female-based household and, on the other hand, to the occupational demands of the lower class world. Toughness, along with the emphasis on excitement and autonomy, is one of the ways one gets into trouble.

Smartness refers to the ability to "con," outwit, dupe, that is, to manipulate things and people to one's own advantage with a minimum of conventional work. Excitement, both as an activity and as an ambivalently held goal, is best manifested in the patterned cycle of the week end night-on-the-town complete with much drink and sexual escapades, thereby creating the risk of fighting and trouble. Between week ends, life is dull and passive. Fate refers to the perception by many lower class individuals that their lives are determined by events and forces over which they have little or no control. It manifests itself in widespread gambling and fantasies of "when things break for me." Gambling serves multiple functions in the areas of fate, toughness, smartness, and excitement.

The last focal concern described by Miller is that of autonomy—concern over the amount, source, and severity of control by others. Miller describes the carrier of lower class culture as being highly ambivalent about such control by others. Overtly, he may protest bitterly about restraint and arbitrary interference while, covertly, he tends to equate coercion with care and unconsciously to seek situations where strong controls will satisfy nurturance needs.

Growing up

What is it like to grow up in lower class culture? A boy spends the major part of the first twelve years in the company of and under the domination of women. He learns during that time that women are the people who count, that men are despicable, dangerous, and desirable. He also learns that a "real man" is hated for his irresponsibility and considered very attractive on Saturday night. He learns, too, that, if he really loves his mother, he will not grow up to be "just like all men" but that, despite her best efforts, his mother's pride and joy will very likely turn out to be as much a "rogue male" as the rest. In short, he has sex-role problems.

The adolescent street group is the social mechanism which enables the maturing boy to cope with a basic problem of feminine identification coupled with the necessity of somehow growing up to be an appropriately hated and admired male in a culture which maximizes the necessity to fit into all male society as an adult. The seeking of adult status during adolescence, then, has a particular intensity, so that manifestations of the adult culture's focal concerns tend to be overdone. In addition,

the street group displays an exaggerated concern with status and belongingness which is common in all adolescent groups but becomes unusually severe for the lower class boy.

The street group, then, is an essential transition mechanism and training ground for the lower class boy. Some of the behavior involved is delinquent, but the degree to which the group engages in specifically delinquent acts, that is, constructs its internal status criteria around the law-violating end of the trouble continuum, may vary greatly depending on local circumstances. These include such things as the presence and salience of police, professional criminals, clergy, functioning recreational and settlement programs, and the like.

Like Thrasher, Miller emphasizes the wide range of activities of a nondelinquent nature that the gang members engage in, although, unlike Thrasher's boys, they do not do so because of poor social control, but because of the desire to be "real men."

Participation in the lower class street group may produce delinquency in several ways: [15]

1. Following cultural practices which comprise essential elements of the total pattern of lower class culture automatically violates certain legal norms.
2. In instances where alternative avenues to similar objectives are available, the non-law-abiding avenue frequently provides a greater and more immediate return for a relatively smaller investment of energy.
3. The "demanded" response to certain situations recurrently engendered within lower class culture involves the commission of illegal acts.

Impact of middle class values

Miller's approach, like the approaches of Thrasher and Cohen, has its strengths and weaknesses. Miller has not been very successful in refuting Cohen's insistence on the clash between middle class and lower class standards as it affects the sources of self-esteem. To be sure, Cohen's own presentation of just what the lower class boy has or has not internalized is considerably confused. As I have remarked elsewhere, Cohen seems to be saying that a little internalization is a dangerous thing.[16] Miller seems to be saying that the involvements in lower class culture are so deep and exclusive that contacts with agents of middle class dominated institutions, especially the schools, have no impact.

Actually, resolution of this problem does not seem so terribly difficult. In handling Cohen's formulations, I would suggest that previous internalization of middle class values is not particularly necessary, because the lower class boys will be told about them at the very time they are being status-deprived by their teachers and others. They will likely hate it and them (teachers and values), and the process is started. On the other hand, it seems unlikely that Miller's lower class boys can spend ten years in school without some serious outcomes. They should either come to accept middle class values or become even more antagonistic or both, and this should drive them further into the arms of lower class culture.

This would be especially the case because of the prevailing definition of school work as girlish, an attitude not at all limited to Miller's lower class culture. With the sex-role identification problems Miller quite reasonably poses for his boys, the demands of the middle class school teacher that he be neat and clean and well-behaved must be especially galling.[17] In short, it seems to me inconceivable that the objective conflict between the boys and the school, as the most crucial example, could end in a simple turning away.

Miller also seems to be weak when he insists upon seeing what he calls the hard core of lower class culture as a distinctive form and, at the same time, must posit varieties of lower class culture to account for variations in behavior and values. This is not necessarily a factually untrue position, but it would seem to underemphasize the fluidity and variability of American urban life. It is necessary for him to point out that objectively low status urban groups vary in the degree to which they display the core features of lower class culture, with Negroes and Irish groups among those he has studied displaying it more and Italians less.

Validity of female base

Miller seems so concerned that the features of lower class culture, especially the female-based household, not be seen as the disorganization of the more conventional system or as signs of social pathology that he seems to overdo it rather drastically. He is very concerned to show that lower class culture is of ancient lineage and is or was functional in American society. Yet, at the same time, he says that lower class culture is only now emerging at the bottom of the urban heap. He also forgets that none of the low status groups in the society, with the possible exception of low status Negroes, has any history of his female-based household, at least not in the extreme form that he describes.[18]

A closely related problem is posed by Miller's citation of cross-cultural evidence, for example, "The female-based household is a stabilized form in many societies —frequently associated with polygamy— and is found in 21 per cent of world societies." [19] I do not doubt the figure, but I question the implication that the female-based household as the household form, legitimated and normatively supported in societies practicing polygamy, can be very directly equated with a superficially similar system existing on the margins of a larger society and clearly seen as deviant by that larger society. Surely, in primitive societies, the household can count on the stable economic and judicial base provided by an adult male. The very fact that such a household in the United States is under continuous and heavy pressure from the law, the Aid to Dependent Children worker, and nearly all other agents of the conventional order must make for a very different situation than in societies where it is the accepted form. In such societies, would mothers generally regard men as "unreliable and untrustworthy" and would the statement "all men are no good" be common? [20] Surely, such an attitude implies some awareness that things should be otherwise.

All this is not to argue that tendencies of the sort Miller describes are not present nor to underestimate the value of his insistence that we look at this way of life in its own terms—a valuable contribution indeed—but only to ask for somewhat greater awareness of the larger social dynamics that produce his lower class culture.

Danger of tautology

Finally, a last criticism of Miller's formulations aims at the use of the focal concerns material. There seems more than a little danger of tautology here if the focal concerns are derived from observing behavior and then used to explain the same behavior. One would be on much safer ground to deal in much greater detail with the structural roots and reality situations to which lower class culture may be a response. Thus, for example, Miller makes no real use of the vast literature on the consequences of prolonged instability of employment, which seems to me the root of the matter.

These criticisms should not blind us to very real contributions in Miller's position. Most importantly, he tells us what the lower class street boys are for, rather than just what they are against. In addition, he deals provocatively and originally with the nature of the adult culture which serves as the context for adolescent behavior. Finally, he alerts us to a possible historical development that has received relatively little attention—the emergence of something like a stable American lower class. This possibility seems to have been largely neglected in studies of our increasingly middle class society.

Success Goals and Opportunity Structures

The last of the major approaches to the problem of lower class group delinquency to be considered here is associated with Richard A. Cloward and Lloyd E. Ohlin.[21] Stated in its briefest form, the theory is as follows: American culture makes morally mandatory the seeking of success goals but differentially distributes the morally acceptable means to these success goals, the legitimate opportunities that loom so large in the approach.[22]

This gap between culturally universalized goals and structurally limited means creates strain among lower class youths who aspire to economic advancement. Such strain and alienation leads to the formation of delinquent subcultures, that is, normative and belief systems that specifically support and legitimate delinquency, among those boys who blame the system rather than themselves for their impending or actual failure. The particular form of delinquent subculture—conflict, criminal, or retreatist (drug-using) —which results depends on the nature of the local neighborhood and, especially, on the availability of illegitimate opportunities, such as stable crime careers as models and training grounds.

The criminal subculture develops in stable neighborhoods with much regularized crime present; the conflict form develops in really disorganized neighborhoods where not even illegitimate opportunities are available; the retreatist, or drug-use, subculture develops among persons who are double failures due either to internalized prohibitions against violence or theft or to the objective unavailability of these solutions.

Intervening between the stress due to blocked aspirations and the creation of the full-fledged subculture of whatever type is a process of collectively supported "withdrawal of attributions of legitimacy from established social norms."

This process, coupled with the collective development of the relevant delinquent norms, serves to allay whatever guilt might have been felt over the illegal acts involved in following the delinquent norms.

Since the argument in *Delinquency and Opportunity* is, in many ways, even more complicated than those associated with Cohen, Short, and Miller, I will discuss only a few highlights.[23]

Potential delinquents

On the question of who aspires to what, which is so involved in the disagreements between Cohen and Miller, Cloward and Ohlin take the position that it is not the boys who aspire to middle class status— and, therefore, have presumably partially internalized the middle class measuring rod—who form the raw material for delinquent subculture, but those who wish only to improve their economic status without any change in class membership. Thus, it is appropriate in their argument to say that the genitors of the delinquent subcultures are not dealing so much with an internal problem of self-esteem as with an external problem of injustice. Cohen says, in effect, that the delinquent subculture prevents self-blame for failure from breaking through, the reaction formation function of the delinquent subculture. Cloward and Ohlin say that the delinquent norm systems are generated by boys who have already determined that their failures, actual or impending, are the fault of the larger social order.[24]

This insistence that it is the "system blamers" who form the grist for the subcultural mill leads Cloward and Ohlin into something of an impasse, it seems to me. They must, of course, then deal with the determinants of the two types of blame and choose to say that two factors are primarily relevant. First, the larger culture engenders expectations, not just aspirations, of success which are not met, and, second, there exist highly visible barriers to the fulfillment of these expectations, such as racial prejudice, which are defined as unjust.

These do not seem unreasonable, and, in fact, in the case of Negro youth, perhaps, largely fit the case. Cloward and Ohlin, however, are forced for what seems overwhelmingly polemical reasons into a position that the feeling of injustice must be objectively correct. Therefore, they say (1) that it is among those actually fitted for success where the sense of injustice will flourish and (2) that delinquent subcultures are formed by boys who do not essentially differ in their capacity to cope with the larger institutions from other boys. This point deserves some attention since it is so diametrically opposed to the Cohen position which states that some working class boys, especially lower working class boys, are unable to meet the demands of middle-class-dominated institutions.

It is our impression that a sense of being unjustly deprived of access to opportunities to which one is entitled is common among those who become participants in delinquent subcultures. Delinquents tend to be persons who have been led to expect opportunities because of their potential ability to meet the formal, institutionally-established criteria of evaluation. Their sense of injustice arises from the failure of the system to fulfill these expectations. Their criticism is not directed inward since they regard themselves in comparison with their fellows as capable of meeting the formal requirements of the system. It has frequently been noted that delinquents take special delight in discovering hypocrisy in the operation of the established social order. They like to point out that it's "who you know, not what you know" that enables one to advance or gain coveted social rewards. They become convinced that bribery, blackmail, fear-inspiring pressure, special influence, and similar factors are more important than the publicly avowed criteria of merit.[25]

Delinquents and nondelinquent peers

On the same page in a footnote, the authors go on to say that the research evidence indicates "the basic endowments of delinquents, such as intelligence, physical strength, and agility, are the equal of or greater than those of their non-delinquent peers."

The material in these quotations is so riddled with ambiguities it is difficult to know where to begin criticism, but we can at least point out the following. First, Cloward and Ohlin seem to be confusing the justificatory function of delinquent subcultures with their causation. All of these beliefs on the part of gang delinquents have been repeatedly reported in the literature, but, by the very argument of *Delinquency and Opportunity,* it is impossible to tell whether they constitute compensatory ideology or descriptions of objective reality.

Second, Cloward and Ohlin seem to be victims of their very general tendency to ignore the life histories of their delinquents.[26] Thus, there is no way of knowing really what these subcultural beliefs may reflect in the experience of the boys. Third, and closely related to the ignoring of life history material, is the problem of assessing the degree to which these gang boys are in fact prepared to meet the formal criteria for success. To say that they are intelligent, strong, and agile is to parody the criteria for advancement. Perhaps Cohen would point out that intelligent, agile, strong boys who begin the first grade using foul language, fighting among themselves, and using the school property as arts and crafts materials do not meet the criteria for advancement.

It is quite true that members of highly sophisticated delinquent gangs often find themselves blocked from whatever occupational opportunities there are, but this seems, often, the end product of a long history of their progressively cutting off opportunity and destroying their own capacities which may begin in the lower class family, as described by either Cohen or Miller, and continue through school failure and similar events. By the age of eighteen, many gang boys are, for all practical purposes, unemployable or need the support, instruction, and sponsorship of trained street-gang workers. Participation in gang delinquency in itself diminishes the fitness of many boys for effective functioning in the conventional world.[27]

If, indeed, Cloward and Ohlin mean to include the more attitudinal and characterological criteria for advancement, then it seems highly unlikely that any large number of boys trained and prepared to meet these demands of the occupational world could interpret failure exclusively in terms which blame the system. They would have been too well socialized, and, if they did form a delinquent subculture, it would have to perform the psychological function of mitigating the sense of internal blame. This, of course, would make them look much like Cohen's boys.

In short, Cloward and Ohlin run the risk of confusing justification and causation and of equating the end with the beginning.

All of this is not to deny that there are real obstacles to opportunity for lower class boys. There are. These blocks on both the performance and learning sides, are a major structural feature in accounting for much of the adaptation of lower class populations. But they do not operate solely or even primarily on the level of the adolescent. They create a social world in which he comes of age, and, by the time he reaches adolescence, he may find himself cut off from the larger society. Much of the Cloward and Ohlin approach seems better as a theory of the origins of Miller's lower class culture. Each generation does not meet and solve anew the problems of class structure barriers to opportunity but begins with the solution of its forebears.[28] This is why reform efforts can be so slow to succeed.

Some insights

The positive contributions of the Cloward-Ohlin approach seem to me to lie less on the side of the motivational sources of subcultural delinquency, where I feel their attempts to clarify the ambiguities in Cohen have merely led to new ambiguities, but more on the side of the factors in local social structure that determine the type of subcultural delinquency.

The major innovation here is the concept of illegitimate opportunities which serves to augment Kobrin's almost exclusive emphasis on the differentially controlling impact of different slum environments. I do think that Cloward and Ohlin may make too much of the necessity for systematic, organized criminal careers in order for the illegitimate opportunity structure to have an effect, but the general argument has great merit.

In addition to the concept of illegitimate opportunities and closely related to it is the description, or speculation, concerning historical changes in the social organization of slums. Changes in urban life in the United States may have truly produced the disorganized slum devoid of the social links between young and old, between children and older adolescents which characterized the slums described by Thrasher. Certainly, the new conditions of life seem to have created new problems of growing up, though our knowledge of their precise impact leaves much to be desired.

Conclusion

This paper should not, I hope, give the impression that current theoretical interpretations of lower class, urban, male subcultural delinquency are without value. Such is far from the case. Many of my comments have been negative since each of the theorists quite ably presents his own defense, which should be read in any case. In fact, I think that this problem has led to some of the most exciting and provocative intellectual interchange in all of sociology in recent years. I do believe, however, that this interchange has often been marred by unnecessary polemic and, even more, by a lack of relevant data.

As I have indicated, there have been some profound changes in the way social theorists view the processes of gang formation and persistence. These, I believe, derive only partially, perhaps even unimportantly, from changes in the facts to be explained. Indeed, we must wait for a study of gangs which will approach Thrasher's in thoroughness before we can know if there are new facts to be explained. Nor do I believe that the changes in viewpoint have come about entirely because old theories were shown to be inadequate to old facts. Both Cohen and Cloward and Ohlin feel that older theorists did not deal with the problem of the origins of delinquent subcultures, but only with the transmission of the subculture once developed.[29] A careful reading of Thrasher indicates that such is not the case.

All in all, though, it does not seem like much fun any more to be a gang delinquent. Thrasher's boys enjoyed themselves being chased by the police, shooting dice, skipping school, rolling drunks. It was fun. Miller's boys do have a little fun, with their excitement focal concern, but it seems so desperate somehow. Cohen's boys and Cloward and Ohlin's boys are driven by grim economic and psychic necessity into rebellion. It seems peculiar that modern analysts have stopped assuming that "evil" can be fun and see gang delinquency as arising only when boys are driven away from "good."[30]

NOTES

1. Frederick M. Thrasher, *The Gang,* Chicago: University of Chicago Press, 1927.

2. One of the charms of Thrasher's old-time sociology is the fashion in which fact intrudes itself upon the theorizing. For example, he tells us that there were an estimated 1,700 to 1,800 junk wagon men in Chicago, most of whom were suspected of being less than rigid in inquiring about the source of "junk." *Ibid.,* p. 148. He also does some other things that seem to have gone out of style, such as presenting information on the age and ethnic composition of as many of the 1,313 gangs as possible. *Ibid.,* pp. 73, 74, 191–193.

3. Albert K. Cohen, *Delinquent Boys: The Culture of the Gang,* Glencoe, Ill.: The Free Press, 1955, pp. 25, 26.

4. The examples cited above are all in Thrasher along with many others of a similar nature. In general, views of the nature of gang activity have shifted quite fundamentally toward a more irrationalist position. Thus, the gang's behavior seems to make no sense. Underlying this shift is a tendency to deal almost entirely with the gang's subculture, its values, beliefs, and the like, to deal with the relationships between this subculture and presumed motivational states which exist in the potential gang members before the gang or protogang is formed, and to deal very little with the developmental processes involved in the formation of gangs. Things which make no sense without consideration of the motivational consequences of gang membership are not necessarily so mysterious given Thrasher's highly sensitive analysis of the ways in which the nature of the gang as a group led to the development—in relation to the local environment—of the gang culture. Current theory focuses so heavily on motive and culture to the exclusion of group process that some essential points are underemphasized. It would not be too much of a distortion to say that Thrasher saw the delinquent subculture as the way of life that would be developed by a group becoming a gang and that some recent theorists look at the gang as the kind of group that would develop if boys set about creating a delinquent subculture.

5. Albert K. Cohen, *op. cit.,* pp. 88–93.

6. In presenting the theoretical work of someone else, it is often the case that the views of the original author are simplified to his disadvantage. I have tried to guard against this. At this point in Cohen's formulation, however, I may be oversimplifying to his benefit. In view of the considerable struggle over the matter of just what the working class boy is sensitive to, I should point out that Cohen is less than absolutely clear. He is not as unclear, however, as some of his critics have maintained. For the best statement in Cohen's work, see *Delinquent Boys,* pp. 121–128.

7. Albert K. Cohen and James F. Short, Jr., "Research in Delinquent Sub-Cultures," *Journal of Social Issues,* 14, 3 (1958), 20–36.

8. For criticism in this vein as well as for the most searching general analysis of material from *Delinquent Boys,* see Harold L. Wilensky and Charles N. Lebeaux, *Industrial Society and Social Welfare,* New York: Russell Sage Foundation, 1958, Chap. 9.

9. Cohen and Short, *op. cit.,* p. 24. The characteristics are those of maliciousness and so on that I have listed previously.

10. Solomon Kobrin, "The Conflict of Values in Delinquency Areas," *American Sociological Review,* 16, 5 (October 1951), 653–661.

11. See the following papers, all by Walter B. Miller: "Lower Class Culture as a Generating Milieu of Gang Delinquency," *Journal of Social Issues,* 14, 3 (1958), 5–19; "Preventive Work with Street Corner Groups: Boston Delinquency Project," *The Annals of the American Academy of Political and Social Science,* 322 (March 1959), 97–106; "Implications of Urban Lower Class Culture for Social Work," *The Social Service Review,* 33, 3 (September 1959), 219–236.

12. Walter B. Miller, "Lower Class Culture as a Generating Milieu of Gang Delinquency," *op. cit.,* pp. 5, 6.

13. Walter B. Miller, "Implications of Urban Lower Class Culture for Social Work," *op. cit.,* p. 225. Miller seems to be saying that the processes of sorting and segregating which characterized American industrial cities in the period referred to by Thrasher are beginning to show a product at the lower end of the status order. In this, as in several other ways, Miller is much more the inheritor of the classical view, as I have called it, than are Cohen or Cloward and Ohlin. Miller shows much the same concern for relatively wholistic description of the local community setting and much the same sensitivity to group process over time. Whether his tendency to see lower class culture in terms of a relatively closed system derives from differences in fact due to historical change or primarily to differences in theoretical perspective is hard to say.

14. This description of the focal concern is taken from Walter B. Miller, "Lower Class Culture as a Generating Milieu of Gang Delinquency," *op. cit.,* especially Chart 1, p. 7. In this case especially, the original should be read.

15. Walter B. Miller, "Lower Class Culture as a Generating Milieu of Gang Delinquency," *op. cit.*, p. 18.

16. David J. Bordua, *Sociological Theories and Their Implications for Juvenile Delinquency,* Children's Bureau, Juvenile Delinquency: Facts and Facets, No. 2; Washington, D.C.: U. S. Government Printing Office, 1960, pp. 9–11.

17. For evidence that lower class Negro girls seem to do much better than boys in adjusting to at least one middle class institution, see Martin Deutsch, *Minority Group and Class Status as Related to Social and Personality Factors in School Achievement,* Monograph No. 2, The Society for Applied Anthropology; Ithaca, New York: The Society, 1960.

18. E. Franklin Frazier, *The Negro Family in the United States,* Chicago: University of Chicago Press, 1939.

19. Walter B. Miller, "Implications of Urban Lower Class Culture for Social Work," *op. cit.,* p. 225 fn.

20. *Ibid.,* p. 226.

21. The full statement of the approach is in Richard A. Cloward and Lloyd E. Ohlin, *Delinquency and Opportunity,* Glencoe, Ill.: The Free Press, 1960; see also Richard A. Cloward "Illegitimate Means, Anomie and Deviant Behavior," *American Sociological Review,* 24, (April 1959), 164–176.

22. For the original version of this formulation, see Robert K. Merton, *Social Theory and Social Structure,* rev. and enl.; Glencoe, Ill.: The Free Press, 1951, Chaps. 4, 5.

23. Large segments of *Delinquency and Opportunity* are devoted to refutations of other positions, especially those of Cohen and Miller. I felt that, at least for the present paper, criticizing in detail other people's refutations of third parties might be carrying the matter too far. It should be pointed out, however, that the tendency to take extreme positions as a consequence of involvement in a polemic which is apparent in Miller's work seems even more apparent in the Cloward and Ohlin book.

24. Richard A. Cloward and Lloyd E. Ohlin, *Delinquency and Opportunity, op. cit.* For the problem of types of aspiration and their consequences, see, especially, pp. 86–97. For the matter of self-blame and their system blame for failure, see pp. 110–126.

25. *Ibid.,* p. 117.

26. This is the most fundamental weakness in the book. The delinquents in Thrasher, Cohen, and Miller were, in varying degrees, once recognizably children. Cloward and Ohlin's delinquents seem suddenly to appear on the scene sometime in adolescence, to look at the world, and to discover, "Man, there's no opportunity in my structure." It is instructive in this connection to note that the index to *Delinquency and Opportunity* contains only two references to the family. One says that the family no longer conducts occupational training; the other criticizes Miller's ideas on the female-based household.

27. Here, again, Thrasher seems superior to some of the modern theorists. He stressed the fact that long-term involvement in the "free, undisciplined" street life with money at hand from petty theft and with the days devoted to play was not exactly ideal preparation for the humdrum life of the job. Again, Thrasher's sensitivity to the attitudinal and subcultural consequences of the gang formation and maintenance process truly needs reintroduction.

28. Parenthetically, the Cloward and Ohlin position has great difficulty in accounting for the fact that lower class delinquent subculture carriers do not avail themselves of opportunities that do exist. The mixed success of vocational school training, for example, indicates that some fairly clear avenues of opportunity are foregone by many delinquent boys. For Negro boys, where avenues to the skilled trades may indeed be blocked, their argument seems reasonable. For white boys, I have serious question. In fact, the only really convincing case they make on the aspiration-blockage, system-blame side is for Negroes.

29. Albert K. Cohen, *Delinquent Boys, op. cit.,* p. 18; Richard A. Cloward and Lloyd E. Ohlin, *Delinquency and Opportunity, op. cit.,* p. 42.

30. For a more thorough commentary on changes in the view of human nature which, I think, partly underlie the decline of fun in theories of the gang, see Dennis Wrong, "The Oversocialized View of Man," *American Sociological Review,* 26, 3 (April 1961), 183–193.

SUGGESTIONS FOR FURTHER READING
on *Conformity and Deviance*

BECKER, HOWARD S. *The Other Side*. New York: Free Press, 1964. Various perspectives on deviant behavior.

BECKER, HOWARD S. ed. *Social Problems*. New York: Wiley, 1966. A text with chapters written by experts in a variety of "problem" areas.

BREDEMEIER, HARRY C., and JACKSON TOBY, eds. *Social Problems in America*. New York: John Wiley, 1960. Essays on the costs and casualties of striving to conform to the norms of an acquisitive society.

CLINARD, MARSHALL. *Anomie and Deviant Behavior*. New York: Free Press, 1964. A review of the literature and an explication of the theory of "anomie."

CLOWARD, RICHARD A., and LLOYD E. OHLIN. *Delinquency and Opportunity*. Glencoe, Ill.: Free Press, 1960. A theory of delinquent gangs.

COSER, LEWIS A. *The Functions of Social Conflict*. Glencoe, Ill.: Free Press, 1956. An examination of the positive values of conflict for all societies.

DURKHEIM, ÉMILE. *Suicide* (translated and edited by George Simpson). Glencoe, Ill.: Free Press, 1951. The classic study in which suicide is seen as conformity or deviation to social norms depending on social conditions.

KENISTON, KENNETH. *Young Radicals*. New York: Harcourt, Brace and World, 1968. Described by the author as "notes on committed youth."

KENISTON, KENNETH. *The Uncommitted*. New York: Harcourt, Brace and World, 1965. A study of "alienated" youth in contemporary American society.

MATZA, DAVID. *Delinquency and Drift*. New York: John Wiley, 1964. An essay on the relationship between the legal order and those who must subscribe to its prescriptions.

MERTON, ROBERT K., and ROBERT A. NISBET, eds. *Contemporary Social Problems*. New York: Harcourt, Brace and World, 1961, revised 1966. A collection of articles serving as an introduction to the sociology of deviant behavior and social disorganization.

SYKES, GRESHAM. *The Society of Captives*. Princeton: Princeton University Press, 1958. A study of a maximum security prison.

PART SEVEN
SOCIAL CHANGE

Backgrounds and analyses
of population problems,
social movements and
the contemporary scene

As Wilbert Moore has written: "Many of the significant components of man's social existence are persistent even if examined over considerable periods of time. The daily, weekly, and annual schedule of man's activities shows a remarkable consistency, as do the forms and patterns that deal with life's major events, such as birth, marriage, and death. The persistence of patterns gives order and constancy to recurrent events." There is strong evidence to suggest that, without some coherent patterning, social life would be utterly chaotic—and intolerable.

Yet, although persisting patterns do provide stability, no society is absolutely static. Population shifts, internal tensions, clamor against inequities, competition for power, and other dynamic factors always threaten to subvert or to redefine established ways. For certain elements, any change which is deemed as threatening to the status quo may generate a reactionary movement to maintain or to reestablish the old order. For others, even the remote possibility of another way of life may provoke revolutionary fervor and attempt to remake society.

While, as Neil Smelser has suggested, certain social and political movements are geared primarily toward altering the norms of society in order, for example, to give greater access to opportunity to those barred from full participation (as in the case of the struggle for women's rights in the United States during the nineteenth and early twentieth centuries); at other times basic values are called into question, leading to widespread attempts to overturn the existing regime or, at the least, to alter its social structure and change its political course.

In recent years we have been witness to dramatic expressions of change, not only in those areas collectively designated as "the third world" but in the United States as well. The portrait of a secure and tranquil democracy has been shattered by the frustrations of those dissatisfied with and, more often, disaffected from, the "American Way of Life." While, to be sure, there are millions who would argue that they never had it so good (and probably never did), who want to preserve the social world as they have come to appreciate it, there are others (especially the young and poor and black) seeking an alternative. As the voices grow more raucous and the demands more threatening to upholders of the status quo, American society will be tested as never before. For the sociologist (whether involved in the movement or detached from it), the years ahead will be challenging. He will be forced to question his own ideas about society, culture, and human institutions, including many considered in this volume.

This last part of *The Study of Society* is divided into three sections. In the first, Kurt B. Mayer reviews the developments in the field of demography. Ronald Freedman, Pascal Whelpton and John M. Smit consider social class, religion and fertility in the United States. Philip M. Hauser describes what he sees as our "chaotic society."

The second section deals with cultural moods and social movements. Included here are three papers: a general statement by Joseph R. Gusfield on "Mass Societies and Extremist Politics"; an insider's view of the social and political climate of Los Angeles by James Q. Wilson, and a historical survey of riots by Gary T. Marx.

The last section of Part Seven, and of this volume, is called "Today . . . and Tomorrow." One theme dominates: Protest. Each essay is, in a sense, a period piece. Each describes the present—but the implications for the future are unmistakable. Included is an essay by Robert A. Rosenstone on the music of protest, a review of the movement for black nationalism by J. Herman Blake, and a study of the student movement by Richard Flacks.

Demographic Trends

67. DEVELOPMENTS IN THE STUDY OF POPULATION

KURT B. MAYER

Those who study rates of birth and death and patterns of human migration are known as demographers. In this first essay in the section on social change, Kurt Mayer traces the development of the field of demography and outlines various theories about the growth and control of population. It is fitting to begin with such an overview for, today, the accelerating rate of population growth is affecting every sphere of life. In fact, many argue that this *is man's most critical problem.*

Kurt B. Mayer is Professor of Sociology at the University of Bern, Switzerland. He is author of the Population of Switzerland (*1952*), Economic Development and Population Growth in Rhode Island (*1953*), *and* Class and Society (*1964; revised 1969*).

In recent years there has been widespread concern with population questions. Stagnation and impending population decline, the popular cliches of the thirties, have been replaced by population explosion and urban sprawl as slogans of the fifties and sixties. Unfortunately, the bewildered layman finds little relief by turning to the demographers, because the professional students of population problems have been notoriously unsuccessful not only in predicting future population growth but

Reprinted from *Social Research,* **29**, 3 (Autumn 1962), 293–320 by permission of the author and publisher.

* AUTHOR'S NOTE—This is a revised and abbreviated version of an article contributed to a German symposium, edited by René König, *Handbuch der empirischen Sozialforschung,* **1** (Stuttgart 1962) 453–79, under the title "Bevölkerungslehre und Demographie."

even in explaining past population changes. These shortcomings of a discipline that ostensibly deals with hard, quantifiable data may seem surprising at first glance, but an examination of the development of population studies may reveal some of the reasons for their predicaments and permit some assessment of their future progress. For this purpose it is useful first to distinguish between two aspects of population studies, demography and population theory, which, though equally indispensable, have often traveled along different roads.[1]

Demography is concerned with three main tasks: ascertaining the numbers, the characteristics, and the distribution of people in a given area; determining changes in numbers, characteristics, and distribution over time; and explaining the major factors accounting for these changes. The explanation of population changes relies on three basic variables— fertility, mortality, and migration (the latter will not be discussed in this article)— for any factors affecting the numbers and distribution of people must operate through one or more of these variables; a population cannot change in any other way. The statistical measurement of fertility, mortality, and migration forms the core of formal demographic analysis. Formal demography stands out among the social sciences in its strong emphasis on quantification and its persistent use of precise mathematical models and various statistical techniques.

However, the study of population is not confined to measuring, counting, collecting, and analyzing statistical data. For it is evident that fertility, mortality, and migration are not independent variables; they are to a large extent socially and biologically determined. The numbers of births, deaths, and migrants are affected by a whole host of physical, biological, social, and psychological factors. In turn, population changes have far-reaching effects on the social organization and the economic system of the societies in which they

occur. Any meaningful interpretation of the causes and effects of population changes must therefore extend beyond formal statistical measurement of the components of change, and draw on the theoretical framework of several other disciplines for assistance. This analysis of the causal determinants and consequences of population changes forms the subject matter of population theory. Demography thus deals with the inner or formal variables in the population system, while population theory is concerned with the outer or ultimate variables, which are biological, economic, and sociological.

Despite their logical interdependence, formal demography and population theory have not developed at an even pace historically. The progress of demographic measurement has depended partly on the evolution of mathematical statistics, and to a large extent on the supply of basic demographic statistics, which are collected at great public expense, often primarily for administrative rather than for scientific purposes. The development of population theory, on the other hand, has been conditioned not only by the availability of demographic data but also by the growth of other sciences, some of which are of fairly recent origin, like sociology and psychology. Moreover, determining which of the sciences could provide the most suitable frame of reference for the causal analysis of demographic events posed a thorny question, which has found varying answers in the course of time. As a result of their uneven rates of progress, the relations between demography and population theory have often been tenuous. At times the formal analysis of demographic variables developed along strictly empirical lines, with little reference to causal interpretations. The development of population theory, however, was influenced by shifting interests and by preoccupations with the changing economic, social, and political problems of the day. Its progress has been marked by constant controversy, often taking a purely speculative and deductive turn, with only slight and casual references to empirical demographic phenomena. The study of population phenomena has thus been retarded by the disjointed way in which population theory and demography have often developed. Fortunately, there is some evidence of the emergence at long last of a modern population science in which formal demographic analysis and causal interpretation appear better integrated and more closely interrelated. However, we cannot properly understand recent developments in this complex field—the main concern of this paper—without a brief survey of historical origins.

Early Developments

The origins of formal demography antedate the development of a systematic population theory by a full century. The latter did not develop until late in the eighteenth century, when lively controversies about national population trends broke out both in England and in France. The first empirical investigations of demographic data, on the other hand, date back to the seventeenth-century mercantilist and cameralist writers, who called their studies "political arithmetic." In 1662 John Graunt published his *Natural and Political Observations . . . Made upon the Bills of Mortality.* These "bills of mortality" were weekly reports of buryings and christenings occurring in the London area. Analyzing these materials, Graunt observed the numerical regularity of deaths and births; calculated mortality rates, fertility ratios, sex ratios; classified deaths and death rates by cause; and constructed a London lifetable in skeleton form. His work greatly influenced Sir William Petty, who published similar *Observations* on the Dublin mortality bills in 1676 and 1683; the astronomer Halley, who in 1693 calculated a much more detailed life-table; and Johann Peter Suessmilch, who in 1742 wrote the first complete treatise on population, *Die Göttliche Ordnung in den Verände-*

rungen des menschlichen Geschlechts aus der Geburt, dem Tode und der Fortpflanzung desselben erwiesen. Yet, as the title of Suessmilch's volume so clearly indicates, while the demographic measurements of these writers were scientific, their causal interpretations were not. They interpreted the uniformity and the predictability of demographic phenomena as manifestations of the divine ordering of human events. This naive theological approach inhibited the further development of the new discipline. The discovery of previously unknown quantitative relations in the processes of life and death was considered an end in itself; since they represented the will of God, it was superfluous to search for causal interpretations.

Lacking an adequate theory, political arithmetic could not burgeon into a fullfledged science. Its methods of empirical inquiry were further developed only along one fairly narrow line: the analysis of mortality and the formulation of life expectancies, both propelled by the demand of insurance companies for more accurate actuarial values and by the increasingly scientific approach of public-health authorities in the control of diseases.

Systematic causal interpretations of population change began to develop when the Enlightenment replaced Christian metaphysics, and when theological explanations of demographic phenomena no longer appeared satisfactory in an age of rationality. Instead, population processes were now interpreted as determined by natural laws that rest on biological factors. Population dynamics were explained as the result of fixed universal relationships between man's biological nature and the physical environment. Although he was not the first proponent of this doctrine, Malthus, in his *Essay on the Principle of Population,* first published in 1798, became the most famous and the most influential expositor of the biological thesis. Postulating that man's powers of procreation are always and everywhere greater than nature's ability to produce food, Malthus asserted that man can increase means of subsistence only in arithmetic progression, whereas population tends to grow in a geometric ratio. Therefore population always tends to outgrow the limit of subsistence, but is contained within the limit by the operation of positive checks like famine, war, and disease, which raise the death rate, and by preventive checks operating through deferment of marriage and abstinence within marriage, which lower the birth rate.

Malthus' *Essay* aroused a storm of controversy that dominated the literature throughout the nineteenth century and has not yet completely diminished. Actually many, though by no means all, of Malthus' opponents shared the biological point of view. Although they violently attacked his pessimistic conclusions, they substituted other biological explanations, claiming that advancing civilization leads to a reduction of natural fecundity. The argument varied, but the different writers —like Spencer, Doubleday, and Sadler— shared the underlying causal assumption that population changes are determined by the relation of the human species to its physical environment.

Although the biological approach predominated in nineteenth-century population writings, the Malthusian debate also brought forth other theories, which drew on sociological and economic frames of reference rather than biological ones. One of the first to categorically reject the existence of any universal laws of population was Marx, who stated that every historic mode of production has its own laws of population, historically valid only within that period. Marx and his followers acknowledged the existence of population pressure on resources, but attributed its causes to the characteristics of the capitalistic mode of population, not to man's biological proclivities.

It is remarkable that the Malthusian controversy, which produced an abundance of theoretical writings, had comparatively little direct influence on the development of formal demography. The bulk of the many books, pamphlets, and articles on "the population question" which were published during the middle decades of the nineteenth century contained only slight and casual references to any empirical demographic data. Only a few of the scholars who engaged in the theoretical discussions undertook any serious empirical studies.

This does not mean, of course, that formal demography made no headway at all during this period. Indeed, a large measure of progress was made during the nineteenth century in developing population censuses and vital statistics. But the development of these basic sources of demographic data was stimulated only very indirectly by the debate on the population question. It was caused primarily by the administrative requirements of national governments that needed increasingly detailed information for the fulfillment of their rapidly expanding functions. The first reliable, periodic census count continuing into present days was instituted in Sweden in 1749, in the United States in 1790, and in both England and France in 1801. Thereafter the practice of taking regular national census counts was adopted by a steadily increasing number of nations. At the same time, the scope of the enumerations expanded and their accuracy increased. But even today there are large underdeveloped areas where reliable counts have never been made and where we must still rely on very rough estimates.

Systematic records of births, deaths, and marriages date back to the fifteenth and sixteenth centuries, when clergymen in most European countries were required to keep registers of all weddings, baptisms, and burials at which they officiated. In England and Ireland the ecclesiastical records were supplemented by the independently collected and published "bills of mortality." As pointed out before, these bills provided the basic sources for the "political arithmetic" of the seventeenth and early eighteenth centuries. The church registers laid the foundation for the subsequent development of national civil registration systems, although this transformation took considerable time. It was achieved first in Sweden, where a continuous series of national vital statistics has been available since 1748. In England and Wales a national system of civil registration was established in 1837; other European countries followed suit somewhat later in the nineteenth century. In general, the development of vital statistics had advanced in step with the development of census enumerations, with the notable exception of the United States, where more than a century elapsed between the inauguration of a periodic census program and the establishment of a nationwide vital-statistics system.

Developments Since 1870

Beginning with the 1870s, a combination of factual events and scientific developments opened up a new era of progress for both population theory and formal demography. First, a rapid expansion of economic production in manufacturing and extractive industries greatly improved conditions in Western countries. In the West, therefore, Malthus' positive checks lost their significance and the previous preoccupation of theorists with the relation of population to the means of support no longer seemed relevant. Second, in some of the economically most advanced countries the birth rate began to decline in the 1870s; in other countries a precipitate drop began around the turn of the century. This was brought about through the spreading use of birth control after marriage, a factor that neither Malthus nor Marx had taken into consideration. Third, the great improvement and extension of census and registration statistics had made available a vast body of appropriate and relatively accurate data, which now per-

mitted new refinements in the methods of analyzing demographic statistics.

Social and cultural theories of declining fertility

The events and discoveries that rendered the Malthusian fears obsolete, at any rate for the West, led many contemporary students of population to concentrate their attention on the decline of the birth rate. The causes of this decline became the subject of considerable conjecture and controversy, while its effects were viewed with a good deal of alarm. Interest centered particularly on the phenomenon of differential fertility. Differences in the fertility of social classes had long existed in the Western world, but these differences had been relatively small and quite stable. The general decline in the birth rate, however, greatly increased the existing group differentials. While all occupational and economic groups were eventually affected by the general fertility decline, it was evident that the groups of the highest socioeconomic status were the leaders. Numerous statistical investigations undertaken from the 1890s onward came to essentially similar conclusions, an almost universal inverse relationship between social status and fertility: the more fortunate and favorable the social and economic circumstances of a group or class, the lower was its fertility.

Most of the various theories that attempted to provide a causal explanation of the general decline of the birth rate and the widening fertility differentials advanced some sort of sociological interpretation, although their proponents were often economists by profession rather than sociologists or demographers. Among the most prominent explanations for a time was the theory of increasing prosperity, which attracted much attention, first in France, the classical country of declining fertility, and later on also in Germany. In the late nineteenth century

French scholars like Leroy-Beaulieu, Bertillon, Levasseru, and others advanced the thesis that the desire for a high standard of living or wealth motivates couples to limit the number of their offspring: the greater the family's prosperity the smaller its size. A more sophisticated attempt to explain fertility differentials also originated in France. In 1890 Dumont pointed out that there is no direct causal relationship between declining fertility and increasing prosperity; instead, both must be viewed as products of an underlying common cause, the striving of individuals to move up in the prestige hierarchy of their society. Dumont compared the individual's drive for social recognition to the capillarity of fluids: wherever there is a social hierarchy, the individual aspires to move up. Social capillarity is most effective in the open-class societies, where obstacles to movement from class to class are comparatively few. Here the acquisition of wealth tends to be the most important avenue of social mobility. At the same time children are encumbrances that retard or prevent the individual's struggle for advance. Therefore, Dumont concludes, prosperity varies directly, whereas fertility varies inversely, with social capillarity.

Along with social mobility and increasing wealth, urbanization has often been considered a major factor influencing the attitude of individuals toward parenthood. The decline in fertility was preceded and accompanied in all Western countries by a massive shift of the population from the country to the cities. Leroy-Beaulieu, Dumont, and many others suggested, therefore, that the rapid increase in the proportion of the population living in the cities is causally connected with the decline in fertility. It had long been known that urban populations are generally less fertile than rural populations. Urban-rural fertility differentials existed in many countries long before the onset of the decline in the birth rate. But as in the case of class differentials, the general decline of the birth rate increased the existing fertility

differences between town and country, because fertility declined more rapidly at first in the urban areas. This evidence was cited by many observers who analyzed various aspects of urban life which they believed to be particularly favorable to family limitation. First, the upbringing of children is more expensive in the city. Second, family life is less cohesive and plays a smaller role in the city. The urban adult tends to be involved in a broad range of outside interests and activities that draw him away from home; a large family would interfere with these varied urban pursuits. Third, as Dumont pointed out in his discussion of social capillarity, opportunities to gratify status aspirations are more plentiful in the cities, but those who wish to take advantage of them find children a liability in their upward struggles.

As time went on, it became increasingly evident that the decline in fertility was not confined to the upper classes and the urban population. By the second and third decades of the twentieth century, family limitation had spread widely among the working classes and the farm population in many Western countries. It appeared obvious, therefore, that theories that had sought to attribute the decline exclusively or primarily to such factors as urban residence, increasing wealth, or competition from social advancement could not adequately explain a phenomenon that was affecting very different population groups. A workable theory needed to explain not only the low fertility of the upper classes but also the recent fertility decline among the proletariat and the farmers. Hence some authors developed theories attributing the cause of the overall fertility decrease to the spread of a rationalistic mentality, a specific product of capitalism, inherent in the spirit of striving which started with the urban bourgeoisie but eventually permeated all classes of society: the proletariat now imitates the behavior of the upper classes, adopting their rationalistic attitude toward life and a correspondingly rationalistic reproductive-behavior pattern. Others, however, have warned against exaggerating the connection between capitalism and the motives in the minds of modern couples which guide their reproductive behavior, and some writers have rejected altogether the invocation of any unquantifiable "spirit" to explain historical changes in fertility patterns.

Despite considerable differences in emphasis, the various theories reviewed above generally agree that the explanation of the fertility decline must be sought in an interplay of various social and economic factors and their effects on the attitudes of individual couples. As to the causal connection between social factors and individual attitudes, most theories could offer no more than plausible inferences. There was no lack of empirical investigations that discovered and confirmed statistical relationships between fertility and socio-economic factors. Usually, however, the data of these studies were primary population statistics of the census type. That is, these data had been collected for other purposes, and the theories advanced to explain the statistical relationships discovered were developed ex post facto.

In the early 1930s a series of studies was undertaken in which data were especially collected to investigate the role of contraception in bringing about class differences in fertility. These studies furnished strong evidence that class fertility differentials can be accounted for almost entirely by differences in the prevalence and effectiveness of contraceptive practices; but they did not inquire into the causes underlying these differences. Obviously, contraception is the immediate means of family limitation; the causes are the factors that encourage or discourage its practice. In 1938, however, a committee of demographers, sociologists, and psychologists was organized in the United States for the specific purpose of undertaking a field study of the social and psy-

chological factors underlying reproductive behavior. This research, popularly known as the Indianapolis Study, was the first major empirical investigation designed to test causal hypotheses, by inquiring directly into the motivations and attitudes of married couples regarding the planning and having of children, and the factors responsible for differences in fertility. For various reasons the committee decided to restrict the study to native-white, urban, Protestant couples, married from twelve to fifteen years, living in the city of Indianapolis.

The Indianapolis Study clearly confirmed both the importance of contraception in the general reduction of fertility and the key role of socio-economic status in the effectiveness of contraceptive practices. Some form of contraception was practiced by virtually every couple in the sample; nevertheless, slightly over half of all the pregnancies occurred while birth control was being practiced. As expected, the effectiveness of contraceptive practices varied inversely with socio-economic status: the higher the income, occupational status, education, and the like, the greater was the proportion of couples practicing contraception effectively. Of special significance, however, was the finding that among those couples who had exercised complete and effective fertility control and therefore had no unplanned pregnancies, there obtained a *direct* relationship between fertility and socio-economic status: the higher the income, occupation, and education, the larger the size of the planned families.

Although the Indianapolis Study was a pioneer attempt to go beyond the collection of primary population statistics in order to investigate some of the complex causal factors underlying reproductive behavior, its success was limited. Because of a variety of weaknesses in conceptualization, limitations in the sample, and deficiencies in the data, most of the hypotheses that attempted to unravel the social and psychological variables underlying fertility differences were neither adequately confirmed nor decisively refuted. The Indianapolis Study thus adds comparatively little to the various theories that have attempted to explain the general decline in fertility. The same is true of another major study of family limitation undertaken in Great Britain in 1946, on behalf of the Royal Commission on Population. This investigation was based on interviews with 10,297 female patients in general hospitals, widely distributed throughout the country. The findings clearly demonstrate the continuously increasing use of birth control in Britain since the early years of this century. They also show the familiar inverse relationship of birth-control practice and social class, but give some indication that these differences are narrowing as knowledge and practice of contraception are increasing in all social classes. Although particularly valuable for international comparative purposes, the research was sheerly empirical and adds nothing new to the existing theories of declining fertility.

Most of these theories suffer from the same major limitation: they are all ad hoc theories, dealing only with one specific historical phenomenon, the decline of the birth rate and of family size in the Western world during the nineteenth and twentieth centuries. Limited in time and space, these theories do not meet the exacting qualifications of a comprehensive theory of population change, which must provide causal explanations also of the population dynamics of other societies and of different historical epochs. But though only small progress has been made to date toward the elaboration of a truly comprehensive sociological theory of population change, there has been no dearth of attempts to find universally valid laws of population growth outside the sociological frame of reference. While sociologically oriented theorists have focused their attention mainly on the phenomenon of overall decreasing fertility and fertility differentials, biologists and economic theorists have developed some ambitious theories of considerably wider scope. At the same time considerable progress has been made in the development and further refinement of formal demographic models.

Biological theories of population change

The search for biological laws of population growth, which had dominated the early Malthusian controversy, had a vigorous though fairly brief revival during the present century. In the 1920s the biometrician Raymond Pearl stirred up considerable excitement by reasserting the hypothesis of biological determinism and advancing a mathematical formula of population growth. Like other biological theorist, Pearl contended that the law of human population growth is fundamentally the same as that which regulates the growth of plants and animals: all living organisms increase in size in cyclical fashion, growing rapidly at first, slowly thereafter, until the organism finally dies. Arguing by analogy, Pearl assumed that the growth of collectivities like entire populations resembles that of individual organisms. Population growth, too, occurs in cycles consistent with the observed rhythm of growth characteristic of all living matter. Since populations always grow in a finite area they must have an upper limit, but in the case of human populations several successive growth cycles can occur in the same area, which reflect changes in the economic organization of society. Thus the transition from an agricultural to an industrial society, for example, creates the possibility of additional population growth in a new cycle. In the early stages of each growth cycle, population increases at an accelerating rate, until the mid-point is reached; thereafter the growth rate decreases. Represented graphically, population growth cycles form an elongated S-shaped curve, which in mathematical terminology is known as the logistic curve discovered in 1838 by Verhulst.

Comparison of the calculated values of the curve with the actual census data of several countries resulted in a remarkably good fit. Pearl therefore assumed that future population growth could be predicted with some confidence. He was not satisfied, however, with the purely empirical nature of the logistic formula, and attempted to explain the causal mechanism underlying it: the reason why population increases logistically in a spatially limited area is that fertility correlates inversely with population density, that is, as density increases, fertility declines. Pearl proclaimed this to be a biological principle that universally regulates the growth of all living matter throughout nature, adducing experimental evidence from the behavior of yeast cells and fruit flies in a bottle. However, this altogether too simple analogy was clearly refuted by Pearl's own later empirical investigations of contraceptive practices, which he had undertaken with the expectation of proving that variations in social conditions other than density have only a negligible influence on human fertility. As a result, the excitement about the logistic formula has subsided; it is now generally recognized that with respect to human populations the logistic curve is a purely empirical formula, which sometimes accurately describes the past course of population growth of a given area but does not necessarily predict its future development.

The evidence provided by Pearl's study, as well as by other investigations of the prevalence and nature of contraceptive practices, also contradicts the theories of those contemporary writers who have argued on various grounds that increasing prosperity tends to decrease the reproductive capacity of human beings. First advanced during the Malthusian controversy, such ideas were revived by some twentieth-century authors, especially Gini, who attributed the fertility decline and the widening of group fertility differentials to decreases in reproductive capacity, allegedly induced by the strains and stresses of

social mobility, which lead to the physical exhaustion of the upper classes. However, the accumulating evidence about the extent of contraception has documented rather decisively the lack of class differences in physiological capacity to reproduce. The Indianapolis Study, for example, found approximately the same proportion of sterile couples in each socio-economic status group, and among the fecund couples the fertility rates during periods of noncontraceptive exposure were strikingly similar, regardless of social class. In view of such evidence, Gini partly shifted his ground. Accepting the fact that the major part of the fertility decline is the result of contraception, he held that the spread of contraceptive practices is itself the result of biological decadence, an assertion that neither he nor anyone else has ever been able to prove.

The concept of the optimum population

In contrast to the exponents of the biological approach, many of the professional economists who have contributed to population theory have been less concerned with finding and expounding the *causes* of population change than with assessing its *results*. They have been interested in the economic and social effects of population growth or decline on natural resources, labor supply, levels of consumption and production, and so forth, rather than in the mode or rate at which population changes. In attempting to analyze the complex and intricate interrelationships between population and the economy, certain economists have raised the intriguing question: "What size of population is economically most advantageous in given circumstances?"

The theory of an optimum population size is the outgrowth of the synthesis of two different bodies of generally accepted economic theory. On the one hand there is the notion that a growing population results in an enlarged market and a greater division of labor, and consequently brings about an increase in productivity per capita. On the other hand there is the doctrine of diminishing returns, which holds that if other factors are held constant, productivity per capita will diminish if the number of people working given resources increases beyond a certain point. From a combination of these two doctrines, it logically follows that there must be a point at which the two opposing tendencies are in equilibrium: an optimum point at which a given (optimum) size of population results in maximum productivity per capita. Two further concepts follow from this premise: if the size of the population exceeds the (optimum) point that provides the highest possible level of per capita output, the area is overpopulated; and conversely, if population size is below the optimum, the area is underpopulated.

It has also been pointed out that the optimum point is never static but continually shifts, because the quantity and quality of resources and technology are constantly changing. It is clear, therefore, that empirical measurement of the optimum population presents enormous difficulties, and it is not surprising that to date no satisfactory statistical indicators of overpopulation or underpopulation have been devised, in spite of frequent attempts to do so. The theory of the optimum population is an ideal-typical construct that enables us to understand hypothetically the influence of population size on economic productivity. At the present state of knowledge, however, the optimum concept cannot be translated into empirical terms of any precision, and therefore it does not lend itself as instrument of practical population policy, despite the tempting policy implications inherent in its very terminology.

Formal demography

During the last thirty years considerable progress has been made in the development of a different body of abstract and logically interrelated principles which ap-pears to be more fruitful as a guide in the examination and interpretation of empirical population data. The theory concerns the universal relationships that always obtain between the basic components of population change—fertility, mortality, and migration. It has variously been called analytical theory, pure demography, or formal demography. The fact that a population consists of organisms that are subject to the inescapable biological processes of birth, maturation, and death makes it possible to view any human population as a sex and age structure that is determined by the vital processes and migration. Leaving migration out of account, the age and sex structure of a "closed" population at any given time is the result of the operation of specific mortality and fertility frequencies in the past. In turn, this structure influences and sets limits for future variations in fertility and mortality. It is therefore possible to establish deductively a series of mathematical theorems, much like geometrical axioms, which define the relationships between sex and age composition and the vital rates.

Pure demographic theory involves as a central core the concept of the "stable population," a hypothetical model of a particular age and sex structure that would ultimately develop in any population subject to age-specific fertility and mortality rates continuing unvaried for an extended period of time, if there were meanwhile no migration or other disturbing influences. The population that would eventually result from the long-time operation of constant vital rates is called "stable" because the proportion of the population in each age group will not vary in time, even though the size of the population as a whole might increase or decrease. In a stable population, the birth rate, death rate, and rate of natural increase remain constant and can be computed mathematically.

Although the basic principle of a stable population dates back to the development of Halley's life-table in 1693, the theory was not fully developed until 1925, when Lotka and Dublin introduced the idea of the reproduction of generations into the analysis of the stable population. They proved that the stable age distribution and the net reproduction rate are both the result of the same conditions, that is, of a long-time regime of constant age-specific fertility and mortality rates. A net reproduction rate is a measure of the number of daughters that one cohort of newborn girls would bear *if* the age-specific fertility rates and mortality rates of the current life-table were to continue unchanged to the end of their childbearing period. A net reproduction rate is thus an estimate of the extent to which a cohort of women of an actual population will replace itself, *provided* current fertility and mortality conditions continue unchanged. Therefore the net reproduction rate represents not only a replacement index of an actual population but also the ultimate rate of increase of the stable population. If now this rate of increase is expressed per annum instead of per generation, it corresponds to the intrinsic or "true" rate of natural increase of an actual population. The corresponding intrinsic or "true" birth and death rates of the actual population (which are also at the same time the crude death and birth rates of the stable population) can be calculated easily. Since in all three of the intrinsic rates the effect of age is controlled, these rates can be used for comparing the reproductive activities of actual populations regardless of differences in their age and sex composition. Intrinsic rates, like the net reproduction rate, measure correctly the current reproductive activity of an actual population, but since current conditions rarely remain unchanged, they have no predictive power and should not be used to forecast future population change, as has frequently been done with disastrous results.

The stable-population model, the net reproduction index, and the intrinsic vital rates are used in demographic research to discover relationships underlying actual vital processes but not visible in the observed crude rates of birth, death, and natural increase—just as geometrical models are used in engineering to measure concrete relations. Major interest attached to the indexes of reproductivity, especially during the 1920s and 1930s. It appeared at that time that the decline in the birth rate had temporarily inflated the proportion of persons in the childbearing ages. Consequently the crude rate of natural increase seemed to be spuriously high in Western nations, presenting a picture of continued population growth. At the same time, however, calculations of the intrinsic rates showed the "true" death rate exceeding the "true" birth rate, and the net reproduction rate well below unity in many countries, thus indicating that the current cohorts of women were not then giving birth to enough daughters to replace their numbers. Demographers therefore concluded that the observed vital rates were actually concealing a trend toward incipient decline, and did not hesitate to forecast the end of population growth and even population decline in the foreseeable future.

However, the unanticipated postwar upsurge of the birth rate brought massive population growth to most of the countries that had been labeled as those of "incipient decline," especially the United States and Canada. This made it painfully clear that net reproduction and intrinsic rates cannot serve as predictive instruments, because fertility and mortality are assumed constant in their computation. A further difficulty lies in the fact that the net reproduction rate is computed by the summation of age-specific fertility rates of all women in the childbearing ages during a *single year*. The net reproduction rate thus gives a cross-sectional view of the reproductive activity of a hypothetical generation, an artificial cohort. It cannot, therefore, measure the basic changes in the fertility behavior of real cohorts over time. This limitation very clearly indicates the need for longitudinal analysis of re-production, in terms of real cohorts of women, for example all women in the population born in the same year or mar-ried in the same year. The reproductive behavior of any given cohort is deter-mined not only by conditions of the mo-ment but also by past circumstances and by anticipation of future conditions. The fertility history of every real cohort is thus shaped by many factors, which do not necessarily operate the same way on dif-ferent cohorts. It is imperative, therefore, to study fertility behavior over time if one wants to detect genuine trends.

Intensive efforts to study fertility and reproduction from the real cohort or lon-gitudinal point of view were first begun in the 1940s, and this type of work continues prominently in the forefront of formal demographic endeavors at the present time. The substantive findings of these studies indicate, first, that most of the sharp fluctuations of the crude birth rate in the 1930s and 1940s reflect changes in the timing of family-building behavior of different cohorts; depression, war, and postwar prosperity caused a great deal of postponing, making-up, and moving ahead of births. The findings show, second, that over and above such changes in the timing of births, a definite change in the long-time downward trend of fertility is evi-dent. For example, in the United States the total number of children per 1,000 women born to each cohort of native white women declined continuously from the 1875 to the 1909 cohort, the total drop amounting to one-third. However, the cohorts of women born in 1910 and later give definite indications of having reversed the trend. It is too early as yet to gauge the extent of the change in fertility trends with any precision, but it does ap-pear that the long-term trend toward smaller family sizes has been halted in practically all countries of "incipient de-cline." In the countries of northwestern Europe, fertility seems to be stabilized for the time being at slightly above prewar

levels, while in the United States and in the British Dominions a trend toward larger families is unmistakable.

Current fertility research

In the United States the unanticipated up-turn in fertility, which clearly demon-strated the urgent need for improved measures of replacement and forecasting, has stimulated two major new field re-searches of fertility behavior and the so-cial and psychological factors that affect it. The first of these studies, undertaken jointly, in 1955, by the Scripps Founda-tion for Research in Population and the Survey Research Center of the University of Michigan, involved interviews with 2,713 married white women, aged 18–39 years, selected through a national area probability sample, including all religious groups.[2] The women were questioned about the following topics: socio-economic status, marital history, preg-nancy history, physical impairment of fer-tility, birth-control practices and attitudes toward birth control, expectations about the number and birth dates of additional children and the reasons for these expec-tations, attitudes toward children, and be-liefs about what constitutes the "ideal" family size.

The results indicate three main conclu-sions. First, family limitation is now al-most universally approved in the United States, and is practiced widely and effec-tively by white couples. Second, women of all social classes are largely agreed on the number of children wanted and expected. The average number of expected children is approximately three and, with the ex-ception of religion, the traditional fertility differentials appear sharply reduced if not eliminated. Catholics desire and expect more children than Protestants and Jews, but the difference lies within the range of two to four children generally accepted as the norm. Third, if the present family growth plans are continued and actually realized, the American population will

continue to grow rapidly. Although fecundity impairments are widespread, they
will not materially reduce the rate of population growth. Since all conclusions were
based on expectations only, the study was
repeated in 1960, albeit with a different
sample, in order to ascertain how expectations reported in 1955 compare with actual performance during the ensuing five-
year period. Preliminary indications are
that although there were numerous differences between expectations and performance, these differences canceled out, so
that the aggregated number of children
born by 1960 approximated closely the
number expected in 1955.[3]

The other project, a successor to the
Indianapolis Study, was undertaken by the
Office of Population Research of Princeton University, and is designed in longitudinal form. It is based on interviews and
questionnaires obtained in 1957 from a
sample of 1,165 native-born couples, selected at random in seven large metropolitan areas and including all religions. All
of these couples had a second child in
September 1956. The data gathered initially relate to the pregnancy and contraceptive histories, socioeconomic status and
related attitudes, personality characteristics and marital adjustment, aspirations
with respect to having a third child, and
the total size of family desired. The couples were reinterviewed after about thirty
months to ascertain how the actual fertility situation had developed. This study is
therefore a prediction study of a metropolitan sample of couples with two children, which attempts to isolate factors associated with future childbearing,
especially with respect to the timing of a
third child. Inherent in the research design
are provisions for testing the correctness
of the prediction.

To date only the findings of the first
round of interviews have been published.[4]
They strongly corroborate the conclusions
of the Michigan-Scripps study. Only 11
percent of the couples were not using contraception after a second birth. Family

sizes of two, three, and four children were
equally popular, and accounted for 90
percent of the reported preferences. While
class differentials were negligible, religion
exerted a strong influence on fertility, with
Catholics desiring larger families than
Protestants, and Jews wanting the smallest
number of children. Preliminary reports
from the second phase of the survey show
that the religious differences were clearly
manifested in actual fertility behavior.
Three-fifths of the Catholic, one-half of
the Protestant, but barely more than one-
fourth of the Jewish couples actually had
additional pregnancies in the two-and-
one-half-year interval between the first
and second interviews.[5]

Perhaps the most interesting aspect of
current American fertility research is the
virtual disappearance of the traditional
class differences in the number of children
American couples desire and expect.
Moreover, the remarkable convergence on
an average of three children means that
fertility will be high enough to maintain a
rapid rate of population increase in the
foreseeable future. This represents a definite change from the prewar situation.
However, the basic causes that have
brought about this change cannot possibly
be ascertained by interviewing methods.
Field research in fertility behavior has
definite limitations. It may reveal the
shifts in attitudes and motivations which
directly result in fertility "fashion
changes." Yet shifts in motivations and
corresponding changes in fertility behavior are themselves but reflections and symbols of underlying long-term changes in
social structure and economic systems of
human societies. Such basic factors cannot
be studied by means of attitude and opinion surveys; they require comprehensive
analysis of social structure and cultural
norms in historical depth.

*Comprehensive structural population
theories*

The lack of an adequate frame of reference that would permit us to understand

the fundamental social changes behind major shifts in reproductive behavior, not only in Western but also in many other societies, has recently prompted renewed attempts to formulate comprehensive sociological theories of population change. One such theory, which has been developed during the last thirty years, especially by American and British demographers, is known in the literature as the theory of the demographic transition. Briefly described, this theory explains the rapid growth of the world's population during the last three hundred years as the result of a transition from high to low birth and death rates which societies undergo in the process of industrialization and modernization. This growth began with reductions in mortality in Europe, caused by increases in food supply brought about by agricultural innovations and improved transportation, followed later by spectacular sanitary and medical advances. Fertility, less responsive to the processes of modernization, declined less rapidly at first. The widening gap between the two rates provided the tremendous growth of the European population and caused its swarming overseas. Eventually, however, the new urban-industrial conditions of life provided strong incentives to couples to limit their fertility through birth control, until finally a new demographic balance of low mortality plus low fertility was achieved, resulting in approaching population stability and possible decline.

Different countries reach different stages of the demographic cycle at different times. It is therefore possible to divide the world's population into three categories, according to the stages reached in the transition cycle. First, there are the countries of "incipient population decline," which have nearly completed the transition. This category includes the populations of northwestern and central Europe, North America, Australia, and New Zealand. Second are the countries in the stage of "transitional growth," where mortality is declining sharply and fertility has begun to decline but is still lagging behind, with the result that these populations are now experiencing very rapid growth. The nations in this stage include Eastern Europe, the Soviet Union, Japan, and parts of Latin America. Finally, we have the countries of "high growth potential," which have not yet begun the transition or are only on the verge of it. Here births and deaths are still high and growth is slow, but it could become explosive if and when the characteristic gap between mortality and fertility decline develops. Most of Africa, Asia, the Middle East, and much of Latin America belong in this category.

Although widely acclaimed for a time, the validity of the transition theory has been severely questioned in recent years. Examination of the demographic experience of several Western countries shows considerable variations in their history of population growth which do not fit the postulated three stages. Thus in France and in North America the decline in the birth rate began early, preceding modernization, while in England and the Netherlands fertility increases preceded the decline in mortality and accounted for the population growth in the eighteenth and through most of the nineteenth century. The accuracy of the theory as a description of past demographic history in the Western world is therefore in doubt. Moreover, major questions have been raised about its predictions of future population growth and the assumed sequences on which they are based. Analysis of recent population trends in underdeveloped countries leads to serious question whether the countries now assumed to be in the "transitional growth" stage will actually recapitulate either the demographic or the industrial experiences of the West. Furthermore, the strong postwar fertility upsurge in some of the countries in "incipient decline" casts doubt about the predictive aspects of the theory even if it is limited to the West. Some critics have therefore suggested that further stages should be added to the transition theory or that the United States and the British Dominions represent a special case where low mortality and moderately high fertility have resulted in a substantial rate of population increase.

Such modification and revisions reduce the status of the demographic transition concept to that of yet another ad hoc theory, limited in time and space, valid only for specific historical situations. Thus it would appear reasonable for population theorists and demographers to be finally willing to learn the lesson taught by two centuries of continued failures: there simply is no universal law of population change; therefore attempts to develop general theories designed to explain population changes occurring under widely differing social and cultural conditions by the same set of causal factors must necessarily be futile. This does not mean, however, that population theory must be confined to purely empirical generalizations or ad hoc hypotheses. On the contrary, there is urgent need for comprehensive sociological analyses of population dynamics, but such theories must clearly recognize the cultural relativity of demographic phenomena. Sociologically adequate theories must show how variations in the social structure and the cultural context produce differences in population structure. They will not imply a single or uniform factor as the cause for varying rates of population change. Instead, they will identify distinctive types of causal factors which operate differently in different social contexts.

Although an adequate conceptual framework for an acceptable structural population theory is still lacking, it is encouraging to note that real progress is now being made. Some preliminary steps in this direction have recently been taken in the United States by Lorimer and by Kingsley Davis, who have employed a structural-functional approach in analyzing specific aspects of social organization and cultural norms that are functionally related to fertility and mortality controls in different societies.[6] Their work illustrates what may be called a cross-cultural approach leading to a comparative sociology of population dynamics. It lacks, however, the historical depth that some recent European theories attempt to supply.

A sociologically and historically sophisticated theory has been advanced in Germany by Mackenroth, and his work has inspired a brief but excellent analysis by the Swiss economist and demographer Bickel.[7] Departing from the insight originally provided by Marx, that every historical epoch has its own laws of population, Mackenroth proceeds to trace the historical development of different European populations from mediaeval days to the present, relating in each instance the specific features of the changing social structure to the reproductive-behavior pattern typical of the particular historical context. Extending this analysis also to European settlements overseas and to non-Western societies, Mackenroth distinguishes typical demographic patterns, or population dynamics, as Bickel calls them, each of which is historically unique, depending on the reciprocal relationship between social structure, culture, and reproductive behavior.

As Mackenroth points out, however, the analysis of this relationship is complicated by two factors. Since every society is socially differentiated and stratified, its demographic pattern is not uniform; rather, every major social group has its own patterns of reproductive behavior, which must be identified separately. Moreover, since neither social structures nor population patterns are static, there is rarely a perfect synchronization between them. On the contrary, the reproductive behavior of a given group or of a society as a whole frequently overlaps different historical epochs, causing time lags and survivals to arise. For example, time lags tend to develop between changes in the social structure and the fertility behavior of different social groups whose population dynamics can often be understood only by reference to past rather than present conditions. At the same time the presence of group differences facilitates both statistical analysis and causal interpretation. Mackenroth interprets as lag phenomena not only class fertility differences but also the rapid population growth of Western nations during the nineteenth century. He attributes the latter to the overlapping of fertility mores and ethics typical of pre-industrial conditions into the epoch of urbanization and industrialization, where they were no longer appropriate. The subsequent decline in fertility can then be understood as an adaptation of reproductive behavior to changed social conditions.

Although neither Mackenroth nor Bickel offers an analysis of the postwar changes in fertility trends, this mode of analysis can be extended to include the most recent developments. For example,

analyzing the American experience, this writer has recently argued that basic changes in the social structure cause large swings in reproductive-behavior patterns.[8] The decline of American fertility below the replacement level in the 1930s represents the extreme point in a long swing that occurred as a reaction to the fundamental transformation from an agricultural to an urban-industrial society. Once the structural transformation was completed, the pendulum swung back, and the current convergence of fertility differentials marks the adaptation of the reproductive behavior of different population groups to an increasingly homogeneous social structure. To be sure, such hypotheses require rigorous testing, but it would seem that only systematic historic-structural analyses can ultimately lead to adequate interpretations.

NOTES

1. Two recent works present extensive accounts of the historical development of population theories and of the current status of demography: *The Determinants and Consequences of Population Trends*, published by the Population Division of the United Nations, New York: 1953; and Philip M. Hauser and Otis Dudley Duncan (eds.), *The Study of Population: An Inventory and Appraisal*, Chicago: University of Chicago Press, 1959. Instead of presenting a copious apparatus of footnotes, I refer the reader to the extensive bibliographies contained in these works. Only a few recent publications will be cited here.

2. Ronald Freedman, Pascal K. Whelpton, Arthur A. Campbell, *Family Planning, Sterility and Population Growth*, New York: McGraw-Hill, 1959.

3. P. K. Whelpton, Arthur Campbell, Richard Tomasson, "Preliminary Results from the 1960 Study of Growth of American Families," unpublished paper presented at the annual meeting of the Population Association of America, New York, May 5, 1961.

4. Charles F. Westoff, Robert G. Potter, Jr., Philip C. Sagi, and Elliot G. Mishler, *Family Growth in Metropolitan America*, Princeton: Princeton University Press, 1961.

5. Charles F. Westoff, Robert G. Potter, Jr., and Philip C. Sagi, "Preliminary Results from the Study of Family Growth in Metropolitan America," unpublished paper presented at the annual meeting of the Population Association of America, New York, May 5, 1961.

6. Frank Lorimer et al., *Culture and Human Fertility*, Unesco, Paris, 1954; Kingsley Davis and Judith Blake, "Social Structure and Fertility: An Analytical Framework," in *Economic Development and Cultural Change*, 4 (April 1956), 211–35; see also Kingsley Davis, *Human Society*, New York: Macmillan, 1949. Chapters 20–21.

7. Gerhard Mackenroth, *Bevölkerungslehre: Theorie, Soziologie und Statistik der Bevölkerung*, Berlin 1953; Wilhelm Bickel, "Bevölkerungsdynamik und Gesellschaftsstruktur," in *Schweizerische Zeitschrift für Volkswirtschaft und Statistik*, 92 (September 1956), 317–28. The interesting recent publication by Andreas Miller, *Kultur und menschliche Fruchtbarkeit*, Stuttgart 1962, which presents a sophisticated equilibrium theory of population developments, was received too late to be considered in this article.

8. Kurt Mayer, "Fertility Changes and Population Forecasts in the United States," in *Social Research*, 26 (Autumn 1959), 347–66.

68. SOCIAL CLASS, RELIGION, AND FERTILITY

RONALD FREEDMAN, PASCAL K. WHELPTON, *and*
J. WILLIAM SMIT

The recent controversy over the dissemination of birth control information has brought to public awareness the persistence of ethnic, religious, and class differences regarding fertility and family planning. Using precision matching to test whether religious differences in fertility behavior result from socioeconomic differences or religious norms, Ronald Freedman, Pascal K. Whelpton, and J. William Smit compared Jewish to Catholic and Protestant couples. This study was discussed in the previous article. They found that socioeconomic controls eliminated most Protestant-Jewish differences but not Catholic-Jewish ones. Their report follows.

   Ronald Freedman is Professor of Sociology and Associate Director of the Populations Studies Center, University of Michigan. His books include Principles of Sociology *(1956),* Population: The Vital Revolution *(1964), and the reader,* Population *(1965). The late Pascal K. Whelpton was also a demographer. He was director of the Scripps Foundation in Miami, Ohio. His many published works include* Cohort Fertility *(1954) and* Fertility and Family Planning in the United States *(1966). J. William Smit is Professor of Sociology at Calvin College, Grand Rapids, Michigan.*

Jews, Protestants, and Catholics in the United States are known to differ in their behavior and values in the area of fertility and fertility planning. Several recent studies [1] have provided systematic descriptions of the nature of these differences. The recent data show that Jews: (1) have the lowest current fertility, (2) expect to have the fewest children, (3) want the smallest families, (4) approve the use of contraception most strongly, (5) are most likely to have used contraception, (6) are most likely to plan the number and spacing of all their children, and (7) are most likely to use the effective appliance methods of contraception. On all of these aspects of the fertility complex, Catholics differ most from the Jews, and Protestants have an intermediate position.

The fertility norms and behavior of the Jews appear to be consistent with their distinctive social and economic characteristics. They have the fertility characteristics we would expect to be associated with their high educational, occupational, and income status, their high concentration in white-collar occupations, their high concentration in metropolitan areas, and the small amount of farm background in their recent history. These social and economic characteristics have been associated generally in both theoretical discussions and in empirical work with low fertility, low fertility values, and high rationality in family planning. These social and economic characteristics of the Jews are those toward which the whole American population is moving as it becomes more completely urbanized, although we cannot expect such a concentration in the higher occupational and income positions to become typical of the whole population. But it has

Reprinted from the *American Sociological Review,* **26** (August 1961), 608–614, by permission of the authors and the American Sociological Association. This article was originally entitled "Socio-Economic Factors in Religious Differentials in Fertility."

seemed reasonable in the past to speculate that the fertility behavior of the total population might develop in the future toward the present Jewish model, if the decisive factors in the present religious differences are related to differences in social and economic characteristics which will diminish. In earlier writing about higher Catholic fertility and associated behavior, the assumption has frequently been made that these differences would vanish as Catholics became similar to the general population in social and economic status.

Is it true that the fertility complex for Protestants and Catholics is different from that of Jews when they have similar social and economic characteristics, or is there a residual difference associated with religion even when these social and economic characteristics are taken into account? To provide some basis for answering this question a comparison is made below between the Jewish couples in a national sample and groups of Protestant and Catholic couples from the same sample who match the Jews on a set of relevant social and economic characteristics.

The 66 Jewish couples in the comparison include all the couples with both husband and wife Jewish in a national probability sample of white American couples with the wife 18 to 39 years old.[2] From the same national sample, 66 Protestant and 66 Catholic couples were selected to match the Jewish couples as closely as possible on six characteristics: occupation of husband, education of wife, income of husband, duration of marriage, metropolitan character of present residence, and farm background.[3] Cases where husband and wife did not have the same religious affiliation were excluded. The procedure was to find all the Protestant couples in the sample who had the same combination of characteristics as a particular Jewish couple and then to select randomly one of the Protestant couples as a match. The same procedure was followed in matching 66 Catholic couples with the Jewish sample. The cluster of characteristics of the

Jews was sufficiently distinctive so that the number of cases of multiple possibilities for matching was not great, despite the relatively large size of the Protestant and Catholic panels. In fact, in many cases it was not possible to match exactly in terms of the combined categories for all characteristics, and it was sometimes necessary to allow one and in a few cases two of the characteristics to be matched from the closest available category. When this was necessary the closest possible match was made. In some cases the match in an adjacent category was actually closer than possible within the category. Each of the Protestant and Catholic couples match the appropriate Jewish couple on occupation of husband, duration of marriage, and farm background. For Protestants, 45 of the 66 cases match exactly on all of the characteristics, 65 on at least five of the six characteristics, and all on at least four of the six. For Catholics, 35 of the 66 cases match exactly on all characteristics, 61 on at least five of the six, and all on at least four of the six. In carrying through the matching, income was the last criterion used and therefore most of the matching failures are with reference to income.

Since Catholics and Jews marry later than Protestants,[4] and since duration of marriage is significantly related to all of the variables of the fertility complex, it was considered important to match all the cases on number of years married. It was not possible with the number of cases available to match also on the wife's age. However, it seems quite unlikely that the fact that the matched Catholics are one year older than the Protestants and Jews could significantly affect the general results obtained. Leaving age uncontrolled while controlling on duration of marriage means that age at marriage has been permitted to vary. Within the controls imposed, there is some justification for permitting age at marriage to vary, since it is an important variable in the fertility complex being examined.

Table 1.   *Fertility Behavior of All Protestant, Catholic, and Jewish Couples in National Sample and of Protestant and Catholic Couples Who Match the Jewish Couples on Duration of Marriage and Selected Socio-Economic Characteristics*

Fertility and Demographic Characteristics	Total National Sample			Matched Groups		
	Protes-tants	Cath-olics	Jews	Protes-tants	Cath-olics	Jews
Number of Cases	1684	628	66	66	66	66
Mean expected number of births, when family completed	2.9	3.4	2.4	2.4	3.4	2.4
Mean number of births to date	2.1	2.1	1.7	1.4	2.0	1.7
Mean number of children wanted when interviewed	3.0	3.5	2.6	2.8	3.7	2.6
Mean number of children wanted if could start life over	3.4	3.8	3.2	3.2	4.2	3.2
Mean number of children considered ideal for Americans	3.4	3.6	3.1	3.2	3.2	3.1
Mean duration of marriage in years	10.1	8.8	8.5	8.6	8.6	8.5
Mean age in years of wife	29.8	30.0	30.3	30.0	31.1	30.3
Mean age at marriage of wife	19.7	21.2	21.8	21.4	22.5	21.8
Attitude towards use of family limitation methods						
Percentage expressing:						
Unqualified approval	73%	32%	89%	92%	18%	89%
Qualified approval	13	12	5	4	12	5
Pro-con	3	6	3	—	3	3
Qualified disapproval	9	35	3	2	58	3
Unqualified disapproval	1	13	—	2	9	—
Not ascertained	1	2	—	—	—	—
Total	100	100	100	100	100	100
Percentage who have already used contraception (including rhythm)	75	57	86	83	59	86
Percentage who planned number and spacing of all pregnancies	22	9	47	33	14	47
Methods of contraception						
Percentage of all couples (including nonusers) who have:						
Ever used an appliance or chemical method	67%	26%	83%	78%	15%	83%
Ever used a method unacceptable under Catholic church doctrine	69	29	84	80	15	84
Only used rhythm	5	29	1	3	44	1

Comparisons between the matched groups can be summarized as indicating that the fertility complex for Protestants is very much like that for Jews when they have similar social and economic characteristics, but that this is not true for Catholics. On almost all of the comparisons, the difference between Jews and Catholics is as great or greater when the social and economic characteristics are controlled as when they are not. Apparently, the dis-tinctiveness of Catholic fertility behavior as compared with that of Jews and Protestants cannot be explained by differences in the background characteristics considered here—at least not at the level set by taking the combination of characteristics of the Jews as a model. This broad summary of the results can be checked by comparing the results for the three religious groups in the original total sample and among the matched couples in Table 1.[5]

Several measures of fertility can be considered. The completed family size expected by wives in the total sample is significantly lower for Jews than for Catholics, and Protestants are in an intermediate position. In contrast among the matched couples, the Protestants expect the same low figure as the Jews, but the Catholic figure remains unchanged at the high level. In the total sample, actual mean number of births to date is lowest for the Jews and higher at the same level for Catholics and Protestants. (Fertility to date is the same for Catholics and Protestants in spite of the fact that the Catholics married later. They had the same number of children as the Protestants in a shorter period of time. There is reason to believe that Catholics will have more children than the Protestants by the end of the child-bearing period.[6]) In the matched groups, Protestant fertility to date is even lower than that for Jews, but Catholic fertility is high—considerably above that for either Protestants or Jews.

Each wife was asked several questions to ascertain how many children she wanted at the time of the interview in 1955. After matching, the mean value for Protestants is closer to the low Jewish figure, but the mean value for matched Catholics is even higher than that for all Catholics. Wives were also asked: "How many children would you choose to have if you could start your married life all over again and have just the number of children you would want by the time you are 45"? This was intended to give some indication of the respondents' personal ideals for family size in situations not too closely limited by their actual family history. Again here, the mean value for Protestants is identical with the lower figure for Jews after matching, while the Catholic mean value is even higher than it was before.

The measure for Catholics is close to that for Protestants and Jews for only one of the fertility values: the attitude on what is considered the ideal size of family for Americans in general. In this case, the mean values are very similar for the three matched groups, although they vary in the expected manner in the total sample.

Attitudes toward the use of family limitation by the general population are rather similar as between all Protestant and Jewish wives but Jews indicate the strongest approval. Catholics are much more likely to express disapproval or to qualify their approval. After matching, the attitude distribution of Protestants is even more similar to that for the Jews, but the Catholics are even more different, a larger proportion expressing disapproval.

With respect to the proportion who have used contraception to date,[7] matching brings the Protestant figure much closer to the high Jewish figure but increases the Catholic figure very little.

In the total sample, the Jewish couples are much more likely than couples of either of the two other groups to have planned the spacing and number of all their children by means of contraception.[8] After matching, the proportion of such planned families rises sharply among the Protestants toward the Jewish figure but the Catholic proportion rises only slightly.

The types of contraception used also are more similar for the Jews and matched Protestants after controls, while the practices of matched Catholics are even more distinctive. Thus the matched Protestant and Jewish groups are much more similar in the proportions who have ever used an appliance or chemical method of contraception. These methods, forbidden to observant Catholics under church doctrine,[9] are even less frequently used in the matched Catholic group than in the original sample. The proportion of Catholics using any method forbidden under church doctrine is less than half as large in the matched group as in the total sample. This is certainly not consistent with the view that Catholic adherence to church doctrine on these issues results from their distinctive distribution in respect to the social and economic characteristics considered in this analysis.

The general results of this analysis appear to be consistent with the hypothesis that Protestant-Jewish differences in the variables of the fertility complex are a function of differences in a few strategic social and economic background variables. When these background differences are controlled, the differences in the fertility complex are greatly diminished, disappear, or are even reversed.

However, the unique values of the fertility complex of Catholics cannot be explained in this simple way. Not only do their characteristics persist, but the differences are more likely to be increased than decreased when the effect of the specific social and economic characteristics in this analysis is controlled.

We have not controlled for the degree of involvement in the religious community in the matched comparisons shown in Table 1. In this analysis the respondents are classified as Catholics, Protestants, or Jews simply on the basis of their self-identification with one of these major religious divisions in response to a rather simple question about religious preference. Strictly speaking, then, we have not examined the effect of the religious communities on their close adherents, because many more Catholics than Protestants or Jews are closely attached to the formal rites and institutions of their religion. We have been examining the effect of the religious groupings as they now operate in the United States on their broad constituencies—whether weakly or strongly identified. This seems to us to be a more significant approach than one which would center on a comparison of the large group of Catholics closely identified with their church and the much smaller groups of Jews and Protestants who are closely attached by comparable criteria.

Nevertheless, it is quite unlikely that the differences between Catholics, on the

one hand, and Protestants and Jews, on the other, would disappear even if they were matched on such a criterion as frequency of church attendance. Neither the Princeton Study nor the Growth of American Families Study (GAF) found any significant variation in fertility behavior in relation to church attendance or indices of religous interest for non-Catholics. Among Protestants, major denominational differences are not related to major differentials in family planning practices. Catholic fertility and family planning do vary in relation to church attendance in the GAF study, but even the Catholics who report attending church "seldom or never" are markedly different (in "Catholic" directions) from non-Catholics for the major fertility variables considered in the GAF study.

The matching procedure used in our analysis does select Catholics more committed to the church; 86 per cent of the Catholic wives in the matched group reported regular attendance at church compared with 68 per cent in the original sample of Catholics. However, if we consider only the nine matched pairs for which the Catholics report less than regular church attendance, there are still very marked differences between Catholics and Jews: (1) the average expected number of children is 3.0 for Catholics and 1.9 for Jews, (2) live births to date average 2.3 for Catholics and 1.2 for Jews, and (3) 67 per cent of the Catholics and 88 per cent of the Jews approve the practice of family limitation without qualification.

Philip Sagi has pointed out,[10] on the basis of the findings of the Princeton Study that matching Catholics with the relatively well-educated Jewish group selects those Catholics who are most likely to be conforming to Catholic values about fertility, because: (1) Catholics who are well-educated are most likely to have most of their education in Catholic schools, and (2) Catholics who have extensive religious education are most likely to adhere to Catholic religious values about fertility.

Thus, Catholic religious education may be the factor which immediately explains the persistence of distinctive Catholic fertility patterns even under the impact of greater urbanization and higher status. While this explanation clarifies the problem, it does not eliminate it. We must still explain the strength of Catholic religious education. In the theory predicting elimination of Catholic-Protestant differentials, urbanization and increasing status for Catholics were expected to reduce their loyalty to distinctive Catholic values and institutions in general—not simply in the area of fertility. It may be that an explanation of the distinctiveness of Catholics with respect to fertility can be found only in a more general explanation of the continuing strength of American Catholic institutions and ideology.

The Catholic sub-culture involves an explicit and distinctive ideology about the fertility complex. In general, Jewish and Protestant groups have no special religious ideology on these issues. It may be that with more precise measurements of the variables for a larger sample,[11] or with the addition of other variables the distinctive Catholic position could be "explained away." The results obtained conceivably may depend on the particular weighting of the controls used for matching—those characterizing the Jewish group. This particular model was selected because it is the direction in which the general population appears to be moving with respect to urbanization and socio-economic status. Matching on the model of the Protestant or Catholic combination of background characteristics might produce different results. This will be explored in later work. But assuming that further work supports the results presented here, we are left with the question of why the specific Catholic ideology has arisen and has been maintained. Presumably it has an origin and a function which are not to be explained in any simple way by the variables treated here.

These results for the fertility complex are consistent with those for Catholic-Protestant differences in behavior and ideology obtained by Gerhard Lenski in a study in the Detroit area.[12] For a rather wide range of behavioral and attitudinal variables the Catholic-Protestant differences persist even when groups of similar social and economic status are compared.

Lenski finds that members of each major religious group tend to associate in primary groups mainly with people of their own faith. The existence of these partly closed religious communities within the larger community perpetuates and reinforces whatever unique values and ideologies the religion carries with it. In the case of the Catholics this no doubt includes distinctive values about family planning and fertility.

The Growth of American Families study calls attention to one subgroup in which Catholic-Protestant fertility and family planning differences are very small —the families in which the wife had worked a long time (at least five years) since marriage. In this subgroup, Protestants and Catholics tend to converge with respect to expected family size, attitude toward the use of family limitation methods, and the type of methods used.[13] If we interpret long work experience as facilitating the involvement of Catholic wives in groups outside the closed Catholic sub-community, this result is consistent with the hypothesis that distinctive Catholic fertility behavior tends to disappear when the barriers between the religious subcommunities are reduced. However, this relationship may also be a matter of selection, at least in part, i.e., Catholic wives who previously have acquired non-Catholic fertility values will be most likely to work. The selection hypothesis is supported by the findings of the Princeton Fertility Study that Catholic wives who have had little or none of their education in religious schools are most likely to work after marriage and resemble Protestants in their fertility behavior. Since only a small proportion of either Catholic or Protestant wives aged 18 to 39 years had worked five or more years since marriage, adding the wife's work history to the list of controls in the matching process would not have changed significantly the comparisons between the matched groups that are presented above.

We found earlier that controlling simultaneously on five socio-economic characteristics virtually eliminated the Protestant-Jewish differences on the fertility measures. To assess the extent to which each of the characteristics contributes to this result will require a different kind of analysis which we plan to carry out and report in a later paper. However, we can report some exploratory work in which matching procedures were used to test the hypothesis that one or a few of the characteristics could produce the observed results. This did not prove to be the case. When each of the socio-economic characteristics was controlled alone by matching, the Protestant values moved toward the Jewish values in a rather similar way, with income taken alone having the least effect and education and occupation taken alone having the most. However, when we matched simultaneously on all the characteristics except income we found that the Protestant values were not moved as closely to the Jewish as in our complete matching procedure. Apparently, income

does have an effect not covered completely by the other variables. All of the characteristics appear to have some effect on the final result of close similarity but the independent effect of each cannot be assessed adequately by matching.

The emphasis in this analysis on the differences between Catholics and non-Catholics should not lead to an exaggeration of religious differentials in fertility and family planning. From some points of view the similarities are more striking than the differences. For example, none of the major religious groupings can be characterized as having very large or very small families. Like the other major strata of our population, they place a high value on moderate size families (two to four children). A large majority of Catholics as well as of Protestants and Jews use some form of conception control sometime during the child-bearing period, and many Catholics are using methods of contraception forbidden under Catholic church doctrine. Nevertheless, significant differences remain, and statements that Catholics are fully adopting the Protestant family planning practices are not correct. Moreover, the present analysis seems to indicate that the persistent differences are unlikely to disappear simply as a result of movement to higher socio-economic status among the Catholic population.[14]

NOTES

1. The general characterization of religious differentials and the data used in this paper are taken from the Growth of American Families study. The design and major findings from this study are reported in Ronald Freedman, Pascal K. Whelpton, and Arthur A. Campbell, *Family Planning, Sterility, and Population Growth*, New York: McGraw-Hill, 1959. The United States Census Bureau report on actual fertility differences between religious groups is consistent with the results of the Growth of American Families study. (See U. S. Bureau of the Census, *Statistical Abstract of the United States, 1958*, p. 41.) The original differences between religious groups reported here are consistent with those found in the Princeton Fertility study, although the measures used are not always the same. The Princeton study is limited to residents of the ten largest metropolitan areas who had a recent second birth. See Charles F. Westoff, "Religion and Fertility in Metropolitan America," in *Thirty Years of Research in Human Fertility*, New York: Milbank Memorial Fund, 1959, pp. 117–134. A major book-length report on the Princeton study will be published soon by Charles Westoff, Robert Potter, Philip Sagi, and Elliot Mishler.

2. The sample for the larger study consisted of 2713 white, married women 18 to 39 years old, living with their husbands or temporarily separated because of his military service.

3. The categories used for matching were as follows: *occupation*—upper white collar, lower white collar, upper manual, lower manual, farm owner or worker; *education*—grade school only, one to three years of high school, four years of high school, college; *income of husband* —over $6000, $4000 to $6000, under $4000; *duration of marriage*—under five years, five to nine years, ten years or more; *present residence*—inside or outside of metropolitan area; *farm background*—either husband or wife has ever lived on a farm, neither has.

4. There is direct evidence on this point from the national sample under study.

5. See footnote 14.

6. For a fuller discussion of this point, see Freedman, Whelpton, and Campbell, *op. cit.,* p. 275.

7. Many of the couples who have not yet used contraception will do so in the future if we judge either on the basis of their own reported intentions or on the basis of the experience of the older women in the sample. A significant number of the couples in all three religious groups have not used contraception because fecundity impairments made such control unnecessary. The term, contraception, is used here interchangeably with the term, "family limitation," to refer to any method of avoiding conception, including mechanical or chemical methods, coitus interruptus, or "rhythm." It does not include abortion.

8. Here we are referring to couples who only conceived when they discontinued the use of contraception in order to have a child.

9. Roman Catholic doctrine forbids the use of mechanical or chemical contraceptives or coitus interruptus. The "rhythm" method is permitted under certain conditions. For a fuller statement of the Catholic position, see Freedman, Whelpton, and Campbell, *op. cit.,* Appendix A, pp. 415–419.

10. This interpretation was suggested by Philip Sagi in discussing this paper at the annual meetings of the Population Association of America in May, 1960, in Washington, D.C.

11. The consistent results obtained in this study make this seem unlikely. As a check on the possible effect of matching more exactly on all the variables simultaneously, we considered only the 35 Catholics who matched the Jewish group on all the characteristics. The differences between Catholics and Jews were substantially the same for these 35 cases as for the larger group of 66 cases less completely matched. It is conceivable that the concentration of the Jewish population in New York City may influence the results.

12. The results of Lenski's research, part of the continuing program of the Detroit Area Study of the University of Michigan, appear in Gerhard Lenski, *The Religious Factor: A Sociological Study of Religion's Impact on Politics, Economics, and Family Life,* Garden City, N.Y.: Doubleday & Co., 1961.

13. Similar results were obtained in a study in West Germany. See R. Freedman, G. Baumert, and M. Bolte, "Expected Family Size and Family Size Values in West Germany," *Population Studies,* 13 (November, 1959), 136–150.

14. A final note on tests of significance may be in order. In both the total original national sample and the matched panels the differences between Protestants and Catholics, on the one hand, and Jews, on the other, were tested to determine whether they were statistically significant. In the initial sample the mean values for both Catholics and Protestants were significantly higher than for the Jews on all the fertility measures listed and the distribution of Jews was significantly different from that of Catholics and Protestants on the measures involving percentage distributions.

In testing the differences between the matched groups in Table 1 for sampling variability, the correlation between matched pairs was taken into account. In this instance the clustering in the original national sample was ignored since the selection procedure for matching eliminated the clustering effect. All the differences between Catholics and Jews remain significant at the .05 level, except for two cases. (The difference in number of births to date is significant at the .10 level and the difference for ideal family size is negligible.) *None* of the differences between Jews and Protestants is significant after matching, except the difference in the proportion who planned the number and spacing of all their pregnancies. In the matched groups all the differences between Protestants and Catholics are significant at the .05 level except the two already noted for Jews.

69. THE CHAOTIC SOCIETY

PHILIP M. HAUSER

In his Presidential Address to the American Sociological Association in 1968, Philip Hauser described the social morphological revolution that is now occurring. He defined this in terms of "the changes in the size, the density and the heterogeneity of population and . . . the impact of these changes on man and society." Focusing attention upon demographic trends in the United States, Hauser described the consequences of what he calls "population implosion"—and other trends—as leading to "The Chaotic Society."

Philip M. Hauser is Professor of Sociology and Director of the Population Research Center at the University of Chicago. He is the author of many books and articles on urban sociology including Housing A Metropolis *(1960),* Urbanization in Latin America *(1961), and* The Population Dilemma *(1963). He is coauthor of* Study of Urbanization *(1965) and editor of the* Handbook for Social Research in Urban Areas *(1965).*

Society as a whole has been viewed historically from many perspectives. It has been envisaged among other ways as "the great society" (Wallas, 1916), "the acquisitive society" (Tawney, 1920), and "the affluent society" (Galbraith, 1958). Contemporary society, whether observed globally, nationally, or locally, is realistically characterized as "the chaotic society" and best understood as "the anachronistic society."

Contemporary society is realistically characterized as chaotic because of its manifest confusion and disorder—the essential elements of chaos. On the international scene, to draw upon a few examples, consider the situation in Vietnam, Czechoslovakia, the Middle East, and Nigeria. On the national level consider the United States, France, the United Kingdom, China, and almost any country in Asia, Latin America, or Africa. On the local level, in the United States, consider New York, Chicago, Los Angeles, Detroit, Cleveland, Memphis, Miami, and over 100 other cities which have been wracked by violence.

Contemporary society can be best understood when it is viewed as an anachronistic society. To be sure, society at any time, at least during the period of recorded history, has been an anachronistic society. For throughout the millennia of the historical era, society, at any instant in time, comprised layers of culture which, like geological strata, reflected the passage and deposits of time. Confusion and disorder, or chaos, may be viewed in large part as the resultant of the dissonance and discord among the various cultural strata, each of which tends to persist beyond the set of conditions, physical and social, which generated it.

In some ways chaos in contemporary society differs from that in earlier societies only in degree. But there are a number of unique factors in contemporary chaos which make it more a difference in kind. First, contemporary society, as the most recent, contains the greatest number of

Reprinted from the *American Sociological Review,* **34,** 1 (February 1969), 1–19, by permission of the author and the American Sociological Association. This article was originally entitled "The Chaotic Society: Product of the Social Morphological Revolution."

cultural layers, and, therefore, the greatest potential for confusion and disorder. Second, contemporary society, by reason of the social morphological revolution, possesses cultural layers much more diverse than any predecessor society and, therefore, much greater dissonance. Third, contemporary society, unlike any predecessor, contains the means of its own destruction, the ultimate weapon, the explosive power of nuclear fusion. Fourth, fortunately, contemporary society possesses the knowledge, embodied in the emerging social sciences, including sociology, that affords some hope for the dissipation of confusion and the restoration of order before the advent of collective suicide. It is a moot question, however, as to whether society yet possesses the will and the organization to utilize available knowledge to this end.

By reason of these considerations, the theme of this annual meeting of the American Sociological Association is most appropriate—"On the Gap Between Sociology and Social Policy." For sociology, as well as the other social sciences, provides knowledge, even though limited, permitting an understanding of society, contemporary and historical, and, in consequence, offers some hope for rational action towards the resolution of the chaos which afflicts us (Hauser, 1946).

It is my central thesis that contemporary society, the chaotic and anachronistic society, is experiencing unprecedented tensions and strains by reason of the social morphological revolution. The key to the understanding of contemporary society lies, therefore, in an understanding of the social morphological revolution. Moreover, it is a corollary thesis that comprehension of the social morphological revolution points to the directions social engineering must take for the reduction or elimination of the chaos that threatens the viability of contemporary society.

I am mindful of the fact that "the social morphological revolution" is not a familiar rubric to the sociological fraternity—nor to anyone else. It is a neologism, albeit with a legitimate and honorable ancestry, for which I must plead guilty. I offer two justifications for injecting this abominable rhetoric into the literature. First, I am convinced that it contains useful explanatory power that has not yet been fully exploited in macro-social considerations, or in empirical research, or in social engineering activities. Second, it is appropriate that the discipline of sociology possess a revolution of its own. After all, the agronomists have the "agricultural revolution"; economists, the "commercial" and "industrial" revolutions; natural scientists, the "scientific revolution"; engineers, the "technological revolution"; and demographers, the "vital revolution." Each of these revolutions is obviously the invention of scholars seeking a short and snappy chapter for a book title to connote complex and highly significant patterns of events. Sociologists, even if they have not formally recognized it, have the "social morphological revolution," and perhaps it is in order formally to acknowledge and to christen it.

The Social Morphological Revolution

What is this social morphological revolution and what are its antecedents?

To answer the second of these questions first, I must repeat that its ancestry is legitimate and honorable. Durkheim (1897–1898), encapsulating earlier literature, provided in a focused way insight into the implications of the most abstract way of viewing a society, namely, by size and density of its population. In his consideration of the structure of the social order Durkheim (1938:81) used the term "social morphology." Wirth (1956) in his classical article "Urbanism as a Way of Life," drawing on Aristotle, Durkheim, Toënnies, Sumner, Willcox, Park, Burgess, and others, explicitly dealt with the impact of size, density, and heterogeneity of population on human behavior and on the social order.

The social morphological revolution refers to the changes in the size, density, and heterogeneity of population and to the impact of these changes on man and society. As far as I know, the term was first published in my Presidential Address to the American Statistical Association (Hauser, 1963). It was used in conjunction with my explication of the "size-density model." This model provides a simplistic demonstration of the multiplier effect on potential human interaction of increased population density in a fixed land area and, therefore, can appropriately be described as an index of the size and density aspects of the social morphological revolution.

The essence of the size-density model, drawing on my earlier writing, is briefly given as follows: (Hauser, 1965:11–12)

Let us consider the implications of variation in size and density of population, confining our attention to a fixed land area. For purposes of convenience, consider a circle with a radius of 10 miles. Such a circle would have a total area of approximately 314 square miles. The size of the total population in such a circle under different density conditions is shown below:

areas of the United States in 1960. The density figure 17,000 is approximately that of Chicago, the figure of 25,000 approximately the density of New York, and the figure of 75,000 approximately the density of Manhattan Island.

In aboriginal America a person moving within the ten-mile circle could potentially make only 313 different contacts with other human beings. In contrast, the density of the United States as a whole today would make possible 15,699 contacts in the same land area. The density of the average central city in the United States would permit over 2.5 million contacts, the density of Chicago over 5.3 million contacts, the density of New York City over 7.0 million contacts, and the density of Manhattan over 23.5 million contacts in the same land area. The potential number of contacts, when considered as a measure of potential human interaction, provides, in a simplistic way to be sure, a basis for understanding the difference that city living makes.

This explication is not only simplistic but greatly curtailed, for it does not consider the effects on potential human interaction of contacts in diads, triads, and other size groupings which, obviously, would generate high orders in exponentials. Nor does the size-density model en-

Assumed Population Density (Persons Per Square Mile)	Area with Approximate Density Assumed	Number of Persons in Circle of 10-Mile Radius
1	U.S. in 1500	314
50	World in 1960	15,700
8,000	Average central city in metropolitan area in U.S.	2,512,000
17,000	Chicago	5,338,000
25,000	New York	7,850,000
75,000	Manhattan	23,550,000

The population densities shown are not unrealistic ones. The population density of 1 may be taken as an approximation of the density of the United States prior to European occupancy. Actually, the Indian population was approximately one-third as dense as this, but 1 is a convenient figure with which to work. The density of 50 is approximately that of the United States in 1960, and approximately the population density of the world as a whole. The density of 8,000 in round numbers is not too far from the density of the average central city in metropolitan

compass the impact of heterogeneity, which is affected by population size and density as well as human migration.

Elements

The social morphological revolution is the product of three developments, energized by, and in interaction with, a fourth. The three developments may be described in dramatic terms as the "population explosion," the "population implosion," and "population diversification." The fourth, and interrelated development, is the acceleration in the tempo of technological and social change.

The "population explosion" refers to the remarkable increase in the rate of world population growth, especially during the three centuries of the modern era. In the long view world population growth rates have increased from perhaps 2 percent per millennium during the Paleolithic Period to 2 percent per annum at the present time—a thousand-fold increase (Wellemeyer and Lorimer, 1962).

Since mid-seventeenth-century world population has increased over sixfold, from about one-half billion to 3.4 billion at the present time. In quick summary, it took most of the two to 2½ million years man, or a close relative, has occupied the earth to generate a world population of one billion persons—a number not achieved until about 1825. It required only 105 years more to reach a population of 2 billion, by 1930; and only 30 years more to reach a total population of 3 billion, by 1960 (United Nations, 1953:11 and 1966:15).

The population explosion is still under way and, in fact, has achieved a greater magnitude since the end of World War II with its extension to the two-thirds of mankind in the developing areas of the world—in Asia, Africa and Latin America. Despite growing efforts to dampen rates of population growth, and contrary to the wishful thinking of some family planners, the facts indicate continuing acceleration of world population. Certainly, short of the catastrophic, there is little prospect of significant reduction in world population growth between now and the end of this century. Present fertility and mortality trends would beget a world population of 7.5 billion by the year 2000, and even the relatively optimistic preferred projection of the United Nations gives a world total of 6.1 billion by the

century's end (United Nations, 1966:15). Despite efforts to reduce fertility, then, the realistic prospect is that continuing mortality declines, as well as stubbornly high birth rates, will continue to produce explosive world population growth for at least the next two human generations.

The "population implosion" refers to the increasing concentration of the world's peoples on a small proportion of the earth's surface—the phenomenon of urbanization and metropolitanization. Again, in the long view, this is a relatively recent development. Permanent human settlement was not achieved until the Neolithic Period. Such permanent settlement had to await the great inventions, technological and social organizational, of the Neolithic Revolution—including domesticated plants and animals, the proliferation of the crafts, and forms of collective behavior and social organization (Turner, 1941; Childe, 1941; Braidwood and Willey, 1962; Mumford, 1961). Clumpings of population large enough to be called towns or cities did not emerge until after about 3500 B.C., and mankind did not achieve the technological and social organizational development to permit cities of 100,000 or more until as recently as Greco-Roman civilization. With the collapse of the Roman Empire, the relatively large urban agglomerations in the Roman sphere of influence diminished in size to small towns providing services to rural hinterlands together with which they constituted almost autonomous subsistence economies.

With the emergence of Europe from the Dark Ages and the series of "revolutions" —the Agricultural Revolution, the Commercial Revolution, the Industrial Revolution, the Scientific Revolution, and the Technological Revolution—man achieved levels both of technological and social organizational development that permitted ever larger agglomerations of people and economic activities. In consequence, the proliferation of cities of 1,000,000 or more inhabitants became possible during the nineteenth century, and the emergence of metropolitan areas and megalopolis, the coalescence of metropolitan areas, during the second half of the twentieth century. In 1800 only 2.4 percent of the world's people resided in places of 20,000 or more; and only 1.7 percent in places of 100,000 or more. By 1960, 27.1 percent were located in places of 20,000 or more, and 19.9 percent in places of 100,000 or more (Davis, 1955; Breese, 1966).

The trend towards increased urban and metropolitan concentration of population is likely to continue. The reasons for this are to be found in the advantages of clumpings of population and economic activities. As Adam Smith noted, the greater the agglomeration, the greater is the division of labor possible; and this permits increased specialization, easier application of technology and the use of non-human energy, economies of scale, external economies, and the minimization of the frictions of space and communication. In brief, the population implosion is likely to continue because clumpings of people and economic activities constitute the most efficient producer and consumer units yet devised. Moreover, such population agglomerations generate a social milieu of excitement and lure which add to the forces making for larger aggregations. Projections of world urban population indicate that by the end of the century 42 percent of the world's peoples may be resident in places of 100,000 or more, as contrasted with 20 percent in 1960, 5.5 percent in 1900, and 1.7 percent in 1800 (Davis, 1955; Breese, 1966).

"Population diversification" alludes to the increasing heterogeneity of populations not only sharing the same geographic area but also, increasingly, the same life space—economic, social and political activity. And the "same geographic area" and "the same life space," with accelerating technological and social organizational developments, have expanded during the twentieth century virtually to embrace the entire world. Population heterogeneity involves diversity in culture, language, religion, values, behavior, ethnicity and race. These characteristics are obviously not mutually exclusive categories, but they constitute foci of problems of communication, conflicts of interest, and frictions of interaction. Population diversification connotes not only the physical presence of a heterogeneous human aggregation but also social interaction among the diverse elements. It involves not only physical density but also "moral density," as used by Durkheim—social contact and social interaction (Durkheim, 1933, Book II, Ch. 2).

Finally, the accelerated tempo of technological and social change requires little elaboration. Suffice it to say that technological change has, in general, preceded and necessitated social change, and that the difference between rates of technological and social change and differential rates of social change have originated great cultural strains and dissonance (Ogburn, 1922).

The four developments discussed are, needless to say, highly interrelated and constitute the important elements of the social morphological revolution. The population explosion has fed the population implosion. Both have fed population diversification. And the accelerated tempo of technological and social change has operated as both antecedents to, and consequences of, the other three developments. Each in its own way, and all four in concert, have precipitated severe problems: chronic and acute; physical, economic, social and political; domestic and international.

The social morphological revolution incorporates the vital revolution and is closely interrelated with the other revolutions—agricultural, commercial, scientific, technological, and industrial. It is both antecedent to, and consequent of, the other revolutions and, as such, should be, on the one hand, better understood when considered in relation to them and, on the other hand, should be helpful in explaining them.

The Social Morphological Revolution in the United States

The United States constitutes the world's most dramatic examples of all four of the developments described. These developments are reaching climactic proportions, have precipitated major crises, and constitute a framework for comprehending and dealing with America's urban difficulties. Virtually all of the urban problems which are increasingly and urgently requiring national attention, whether they be physical, personal, social, ethnic and racial, economic or governmental problems, may be viewed as frictions of the social morphological revolution which is still under way —frictions in the transition from an agrarian to an urban and metropolitan order.

THE POPULATION EXPLOSION In 1790, when the first Decennial Census of the United States was taken, the United States had a total population of less than 4 million persons. By 1960 the population of the nation numbered more than 180 million; during 1967 it reached 200 million.

The U. S. Bureau of the Census has from time to time made projections of United States population on varying assumptions about the future course of fertility and mortality. Such projections made in 1967 indicate that, despite the declining crude birth rate, the United States will continue to experience large absolute population increase in the decades which lie ahead. These projections show that by 1990, only 22 years hence, the population of the United States may reach a level of from 256 to 300 million. One of these projections, based on a fertility assumption that takes the current slump in the birth rate into account, would produce a population of 206 million by 1970, 232 million by 1980, and 267 million by 1990. The same projection gives a population of 308 million by the year 2000 and 374 million by 2015 (U. S. Bureau of the Census, 1957, 1962, 1967).

THE POPULATION IMPLOSION In 1790,

95 percent of the population of the United States lived in rural areas, on farms, or in places having fewer than 2500 persons. The 5 percent of the population which lived in cities were concentrated in 24 such places, only two of which (New York and Philadelphia) had populations of 25,000 or more. By 1850, population in urban places was still as low as 15 percent. By 1900, however, almost two-fifths of the population lived in cities. But it was not until as recently as 1920 that the United States became an urban nation in the sense that more than half of the population (51 percent) lived in cities. That many critical problems affect cities and urban populations should not be too surprising in light of the fact that it will not be until the next Census of Population is taken, in 1970, that the United States will have completed her first half century as an urban nation, a period shorter than a lifetime.

The speed of the population implosion becomes clear in an examination of developments since the turn of the century. In the first sixty years of this century the increase in urban population absorbed 92 percent of the total population growth in the nation. In the decade 1950 to 1960, the increase in urban population absorbed more than 100 percent of total national growth; that is, total rural population, including nonfarm as well as farm, actually diminished for the first time.

The increase in the population of metropolitan areas is equally dramatic. The increase in the population of the Standard Metropolitan Statistical Areas (SMSA's) absorbed 79 percent of total national growth between 1900 and 1960; and the 24 largest SMSA's, those with 1,000,000 or more, absorbed 43 percent in the first sixty years of this century.

The population implosion in this nation is still under way. Recent projections I have made with a colleague indicate that if present trends continue the metropolital population, between 1960 and 1985, will increase by some 58˙ percent, while the non-metropolitan population increases by less than 12 percent (Hodge and Hauser, 1968). By 1985, then, 71 percent of the people in this nation would reside in metropolitan areas as compared with 63 percent in 1960.

POPULATION DIVERSIFICATION The United States has been one of history's most dramatic examples of population diversification as well as of the population explosion and the population implosion. Although the original European settlers were predominantly from the United Kingdom, the infusion of African Negro population began during the seventeenth century and was followed by waves of diverse European stocks during the nineteenth and early twentieth centuries.

The Census of Population first counted "foreign born" whites in 1850. At that time they constituted 9.7 percent of the total population. Although successive waves of immigration were heavy, the foreign-born whites never exceeded 14.5 percent of the total, a level reached in 1890 and again in 1910; they have been a dwindling proportion of the total ever since. By reason of restrictions on immigration, the foreign-born will become a decreasing proportion of the population of the nation in the decades which lie ahead.

In 1850, native whites made up 74.6 percent of the population of the nation, and "nonwhites," mainly Negroes, 15.7 percent. By 1900, the proportion had changed little, 75.5 percent being native white and 12.1 percent nonwhite. As recently as 1900, however, little more than half the American people were native whites of native parentage. That is, about one-fifth of the population was "second generation" white, or native whites born of foreign or mixed parentage.

By 1960, native whites constituted 83 percent, foreign whites 5.2 percent, and Negroes 10.6 percent of the total. Native whites of native parentage made up 70 percent of the total, the remaining 13 percent of native whites being second generation. Thus, in 1960 "foreign white stock," foreign born plus second generation, still made up over 18 percent of the total population.

Although the foreign white stock will become a dwindling part of the population in the decades which lie ahead, the proportion of nonwhites, mainly Negroes, is likely to increase. In 1960, there were 20.7 million nonwhites in the United States, or 11.4 percent of the total. By 1990 it is estimated by the U. S. Bureau of the Census that nonwhites will double, increasing to 41.5 million. By 1990, nonwhites may, therefore, make up some 14.5 percent of the American people.

By reason of the "Negro Revolt," the most acute present manifestation of chaos in the United States, a closer examination of Negro population trends is required. In 1790, as recorded in the first census of the United States, there were fewer than 800,000 Negroes in the nation, but they made up about 20 percent of the total population. By that date they had already been resident in the colonies for 175 years, mainly as the property or indentured servants of their white masters.

Negro Americans remained about one-fifth of the total population until 1810. From then to 1930 they were an ever declining proportion of the total, as slave traffic ceased and white immigration continued. By 1930 the proportion of Negroes had diminished to less than one-tenth of the total. Since 1940, however, the Negro growth rate has been greater than that of the white population, and their proportion had risen to 11 percent by 1967.

In 1790, 91 percent of all Negroes lived in the South. The first large migratory flow of Negroes out of the South began during World War I, prompted by the need for wartime labor and the freeing of the Negro from the soil, with the diversification of agriculture and the onset of the delayed industrial revolution in the South. This migration of Negroes from the South was greatly increased during and after World War II. As a result, the proportion of total Negroes located in the North and West almost quadrupled between 1910 and 1960, increasing from 11 to 40 percent.

The migratory movement of Negroes from the South to the North and West effected not only a regional redistribution but also, significantly, an urban-rural redistribution. In 1910, before the out-migration of the Negro from the South began, 73 percent lived in rural areas. By 1960, within fifty years, the Negro had been transformed from 73 percent rural to 73 percent urban, and had become more urbanized than the white population.

The great urban concentration of Negro Americans is also revealed by their location in metropolitan areas. By 1910, only 29 percent of Negroes lived in the Standard Metropolitan Statistical Areas. By 1960, this concentration had increased to 65 percent. By 1960, 51 percent of all Negroes lived in the central cities of the SMSA's. Moreover, the 24 SMSA's with one million or more inhabitants contained 38 percent, and their central cities 31 percent, of all Negro Americans.

Again I draw on my recent projections estimating nonwhite population in metropolitan areas (SMSA's) by residence in central cities (as defined in 1960) would 1968). They show that present trends may well take the nation farther down the road toward a *de facto* "apartheid society." By 1985 the concentration of nonwhites in central cities (as defined in 1960) would increase to 58 percent from the level of 51 percent in 1960, while the concentration of white population in central cities would diminish by almost a third to 21 percent in 1985 from 30 percent in 1960. In consequence, by 1985, 75 percent of all nonwhites within metropolitan areas would be resident in central cities and only 25 percent in the suburbs. In contrast, by 1985, 70 percent of the whites would inhabit the suburbs and only 30 percent live in central cities. Thus, of the total population in SMSA's, the proportion of nonwhite would increase from 11.7 percent in 1960

to 15.1 percent by 1985. But the proportion of population in central cities which would be nonwhite would increase by about 73 percent, rising from 17.8 percent in 1960 to 30.7 percent in 1985.

Negro population changes, past and in prospect, have resulted in greatly increased sharing with whites of the same geographical local areas, accompanied by increased pressure for social contact and social interaction. The acute tensions which characterize white-black relationships in the United States today represent a compounding of the impact of the social morphological revolution. For within the framework of the general population explosion and implosion in the entire nation, there has occurred an even more dramatic population explosion and implosion among Afro-Americans. These developments have greatly exacerbated the problems of inter-group relations. The large increase in the population of Afro-Americans in urban and metropolitan areas over a relatively short period of time, and the contrast in background and life-styles between blacks and whites by reason of the disadvantaged position of blacks over the years, have combined to produce tensions that may well constitute the most serious domestic problem in the United States for some time to come (Hauser, 1966; Hauser, 1967a; Hauser, 1968a).

Consequences of the Social Morphological Revolution

The combined effects of the population explosion, the population implosion, and population diversification have produced in the realm of the social the equivalent of a mutation in the realm of the genetic. The social morphological revolution has profoundly altered human nature and the social order. In broad overview the social morphological revolution has modified the human aggregation as a physical construct and as an economic mechanism; it has transformed human behavior and social organization, including the nature of government; it has generated and aggravated a host of problems—physical, personal, social, institutional, and governmental.

Examples of the physical problems are given by the problems relating to housing supply and quality, circulation of persons and goods, solid and human waste removal, air and water pollution, recreational facilities, urban design, and the management of natural resources.

Examples of personal, social, and organizational problems are given by the incidence of delinquency and crime, alcoholism, drug addiction, and mental disorder. It is evident in the current revolt of youth, which at the extremes include the "hippie," who resolves his problems by retreat, and the "activist," who resolves his problems by beating his head against the doors of the Pentagon, or police clubs at the University of California at Berkeley and at other universities. It is revealed also in unemployment, poverty, racism, bigotry, inter-group conflict, family disorganization, differential morbidity and mortality, labor-management conflict, the conservative-liberal debate, the maladministration of criminal justice; and in corruption, malaportionment, and inertia in government, and the fragmentation and paralysis of local government. It is further revealed by continuing resort to physical force as a means for the resolution of conflicts of interest. No matter how laudable the goals, when force is employed by labor and management, by students, by advocates of peace, by minority groups, or in most extreme form by nations at war, it is a mechanism incompatible with the continued viability of contemporary society. In fact, if society is to remain viable, when there is disorder, it has no alternative to the use of overwhelming collective force for restoration of order. Of course, upon the restoration of order, the causes of disorder must be investigated and removed, or tensions may mount and produce even greater disorder. The point

is that contemporary society, by reason of unprecedented interdependence, is highly vulnerable and easily disrupted—a fact which is increasingly perceived and exploited by dissident persons and groups.

These types of problems may be viewed sociologically as consequences of the social morphological revolution which generated secondary group, as distinguished from primary group association; interpersonal relations based on utility from emotion and sentiment; the conjugal or nuclear, from the extended family; formal from informal social control; rational from traditional behavior; enacted from crescive institutions; and bureaucracy from small-scale and informal organization. Especially significant have been the changes in the elements and processes of the socialization of the child—the transformation of the helpless biological specimen, the infant, into a human being or member of society. In brief, the social morphological revolution transformed the "little community" (Redfield, 1955), which has characterized predecessor societies, into the "mass society" (Mannheim, 1940:61).

It is my contention that the confusion and disorder of contemporary life may be better understood and dealt with as frictions in the transition still under way from the little community to the mass society; and that the chaos of contemporary society, in large part, is the product of dissonance and conflict among the strata of culture which make up our social heritage. The problems or frictions are often visible manifestations of what my former teacher and colleague, William Fielding Ogburn, termed "cultural lag" (Ogburn, 1922: 200 ff).

Permit me to provide a few concrete examples of cultural lag in contemporary society—examples of special significance and impact. I do so, as a sociologist, to illustrate the use of the analytical framework provided by the social morphological revolution in the consideration of specific social problems.

GOVERNANCE   Focusing on the United States, consider the example of cultural lag in our system of governance. Needless to say, confusion and disorder in government has a multiplier impact on other realms of chaos.

Consider some of the elements involved in the raging "conservative-liberal" debate. In the ongoing political context, the polemic centers on the role of government in the social and economic order. It is evident in the attitudes toward "big government," and, in general, in anachronistic political ideology (Hauser, 1967c). Three illustrations of "cultural lag" in ideology help to explain the paralysis which afflicts this nation in efforts to deal with the acute problems which beset us.

One is the inherited shibboleth that "that government is best which governs least." The doctrine made considerable sense when our first census was taken in 1790. At that time, 95 percent of the American people lived on farms or in towns having fewer than 2500 persons. What was there for government to do, compared with the situation in 1960, in which 70 percent of the American people lived in urban places and about 63 percent were residents of metropolitan areas? Can you visualize a United States today without a Social Security System, without a Public Health Service, without a Federal Reserve Board, without the Interstate Commerce Commission, and without the Civil Aeronautics Administration? The slogan "that government is best which governs least" is a good example of a cultural survival which has persisted beyond its time.

Or contemplate next the shibboleth each man in pursuing his own interest, "as if guided by an invisible hand," promotes the interest of the entire society. This also made sense in the United States in 1790. Each person pursuing his own interest and supporting his family on a farm or in a small town was, to be sure, automatically acting in the interest of society. But can you imagine a United States today without

a Food and Drug Administration, a Securities and Exchange Commission, a Federal Trade Commission, and a Federal Communications Commission? The recent Federal intervention into automobile safety is a timely reminder of the fact that what is in the best interest of the Detroit automotive manufacturer is not necessarily in the best interest of the American people. The chasm between reality in economic behavior and extreme forms of classical and neo-classical economics grows broader and deeper with each passing year as the social morphological revolution continues in its inexorable course.

Consider, also, the shibboleths that taxes are what governments take away from the people and that government expenditures must be kept to a minimum. The Ways and Means Committee of the 90th House of Representatives and the majority in both Houses afford an excellent example of cultural lag and its consequences in their vestigial behavior in respect to the income tax surcharge. The critical question that the Congress should have asked is, "What are the essential needs of the United States to maintain this nation as a viable society?" And the next step should have been to arrange to finance the necessary programs. Taxes in a mass society are not what the government takes away from people, but rather what the people pay for essential services required for collective living in an interdependent society which, among other things, generates needs which cannot be met by the free market. Congress, exemplifying cultural lag, cut deeply into essential programs already pathetically inadequate to provide desperately needed services to many millions of Americans. Perhaps the highlight in the insensitivity and anachronistic character of the 90th House of Representatives was given by its Marie Antoinette type of performance which, in respect to the Afro-American urban slum residents, in effect said "Let them have rats."

Furthermore, apart from these examples of ideological atavisms, consider the irony in the national political situation, in which by reason of seniority provisions for committee memberships and chairmanships in the Congress and the one-party system in the post-bellum South, this most underdeveloped region of the United States, which is still in the early stages of the social morphological revolution, maintains a vise-like grip on the national legislative process—a grip bolstered by the filibuster which permits tyranny by a minority.

There are many other evidences of cultural lag in the Federal government and on the state and local levels of government. The rapidity with which this nation has become urbanized has produced serious malapportionment in the House of Representatives in the Congress, in state assemblies, and in municipal councils. For example, in 1960, there were 39 states with an urban population majority, but not a single state in the Union where the urban population controlled the state legislature (David and Eisenberg, 1961). This condition accelerated Federal interventionism. For it was the insensitivity to urban problems, the problems of the mass society, by the malapportioned rural-dominated legislatures that drew the Federal government into such realms as public housing, urban renewal, highways and expressways, civil rights, mass transportation, and education. To the addicts of the outmoded slogans discussed above, these programs are viewed as the violation of "states rights." But it is an ironic thing that the most vociferous advocates of states rights have played a major role, by their ignoring of twentieth-century mass society needs, in bringing about the increased centralization of governmental functions.

A final example of cultural lag in the American system of governance is given by the chaos in local government (Hauser, 1961). The framework for the structure of local government in the United States is the local governmental structure of eighteenth-century England. The Constitutional fathers did not, and could not have been expected to, anticipate the emergence of population agglomerations of great size, density, and heterogeneity, which transcended not only municipal and township lines but also county and state boundaries. In consequence, our metropolitan clumpings of people and economic activities are characterized by governmental fragmentation which paralyzes local efforts to deal with metropolitan area-wide problems, such as those relating to air and water pollution, traffic congestion, crime, employment, housing, and education.

By reason of its implications for the socialization of the child, the consequences of governmental fragmentation for public education at the primary and secondary levels are especially worthy of attention. It may be argued that public school education is today converting this nation into a caste society, stratified by race and by economic status. I illustrate this with another neologism for which I apologize. I refer to the "pre-conception IQ," the IQ of the child before he is conceived (Hauser, 1968a). The child with a very high pre-conception IQ, high enough to select white-skinned parents who live in the suburbs, has by this astute act guaranteed unto himself an input for public school education two to ten times that of the child with a miserably low pre-conception IQ, stupid enough to select black-skinned parents in the inner-city slums. The child with an intermediate pre-conception IQ, bright enough to select white-skinned parents but too stupid to pick parents living in the suburbs, gets an intermediate education. This is a way of saying that the child in the suburbs gets a first-class education, the white child living toward the periphery gets a second-class education, and the child in the inner city, black or white, gets a third- or fourth-rate education. As a result, education is no longer performing its historic mission in this nation in contributing to national unity and to the maintenance of an open society. On the contrary, the kind of education we now have in our slums and ghettos is recycling the present chaotic situation into perpetuity. Our metropolitan areas today have blacks who were born in the city, reared in the city, educated in the city, and who have not acquired the basic, the saleable or the citizenship skills prerequisite to their assuming the responsibilities and obligations as well as the rights of American citizenship. Quite apart from other factors operating, it is clear that the failure of local governmental structure to keep up with the social morphological revolution is a major element in this disastrous situation.

RACISM Without question, the most serious domestic problem which haunts the United States today is the Negro Revolt. There are only three considerations necessary to understand the "why" of this situation. First, the Afro-American has been on this continent for three and a half centuries. He involuntarily spent two and a half centuries in slavery; he spent a half century in the rural slum South under the unfulfilled promises of the Emancipation Proclamation; and he has spent an additional half century in the slum ghettos of metropolitan America, in the North and South.

Second, since World War II the entire world has been swept by what has felicitously been called "the revolution of rising expectations." This is the first generation in the history of man in which no peoples are left on the face of this earth who are willing to settle for second place in level of living and who do not insist on freedom and independence if not already achieved. This revolution of rising expectations has not bypassed Afro-Americans. In a fundamental sense the Negro Revolt is simply America's local manifestation of the revolution of rising expectations.

Third, there is a shorter-run and a more immediate consideration. With the Johnson administration and the success of previous Congresses in the passage of civil rights legislation, new vistas of opportunity and new expectations were aroused in the black community. It is an ironic thing that the Negro Revolt and the riots are not in spite of these advances but in a sense because of them. Blacks were led to believe that they were finally achieving full equality in the American scene. But what happened in reality? There was little to match the Federal leadership on the state front in terms of gubernatorial leadership, or on the local front in terms of mayoralty leadership, or in leadership in the private sector. Nothing substantial happened to change the reality of living in rat-infested slums and of unemployment rates two to three times that of whites. Little was done to change the character of the segregated communities in which the Negro lived, and little was done to change the character of the woefully deficient educational opportunities for the black child. As the gap between expectation and reality increased, so did frustration, alienation, and bitterness which have led to violence.

Underlying all three of these factors which account for the present restiveness, hostility, and violence of Afro-Americans is "white racism," the major cause of the present crisis, the term appropriately designated as such by the Kerner Commission (National Advisory Commission on Civil Disorders, 1968:91). Although immigrant newcomers to the United States have, on the whole, also been greeted with prejudice and discriminatory practices, the Negro, since his involuntary importation as a slave, has been the victim of a much more widespread, persistent, and virulent racist theory and practice.

Racist doctrine may be understood as a negative and extreme form of ethnocentrism, the product of the isolated little community of relatively small size, density, and cultural homogeneity. The persistence of racist attitudes and behavior constitutes another example of cultural lag —the survival of a little community into the mass society. A prejudicial attitude towards other human beings, whether in the positive form of ethnocentrism or its negative counterpart as hostility towards others on a categoric basis, is a cultural atavism—an anachronistic set of attitudes incompatible with the requirements of co-operative association in a mass society. In the context of large, dense, and heterogeneous population agglomerations, racism necessarily spells trouble and conflict. It should not be too surprising that white racism is now breeding or exacerbating black racism, and, therefore, intensifying hostility and conflict. Furthermore, the paralysis of government in the United States, as described above, further compounds the crisis and offers little hope of any short-run resolution of tension and conflict. This nation, on its present course, may well be in for an indefinite period of guerilla warfare on the domestic as well as on the international front (Hauser, 1968a:4–10).

OTHER EXAMPLES OF CULTURAL LAG There are many other examples of cultural lag in American society ranging from the trivial to the significant. In the trivial category is the persistence of the string, designed before the advent of the pin and the button to keep collars closed against inclement weather. This string has become the necktie, a relatively harmless, if not always esthetic vestige which has acquired a new function, i.e. decoration. But other vestiges are not as harmless. They include the constitutional right to bear arms—admittedly necessary in eighteenth-century America but a dangerous anachronism in the last third of twentieth-century America. They include also the inalienable rights of labor to strike and of management to shut down and employ the lockout, often through trial by ordeal of the public. In twentieth-century mass society, labor's right to strike and management's right to lockout may be described as the rights of labor and management to revert to the laws of the jungle—to resolve their conflicts of interest by means of brute force. The same can be said of

the so-called right of the students to impose their views through the employment of force, or of any person or group who fails to resolve conflicts of interest in a mass society by an adjudicative or democratic procedure.

Cultural atavisms are replete, also, in the administration of criminal justice, for many of the governing codes and procedures are of pre-social morphological revolution origin and constitute a menace to mass society.

Finally, and by no means to exhaust the universe of cultural lags, mention should be made of organized religion as a living museum of cultural atavisms adding to the confusion and disorder of contemporary life. Sunday morning Christians have learned to honor and revere the messenger, his mother, and his colleagues; they have learned to observe the ritual and practices of their churches which have endured for two millennia; but they have not received, or certainly they have not heeded, the message. For the message of the Judeo-Christian tradition is found in the concept of the Fatherhood of God—which implies the brotherhood of man. And comparable things can be said of the adherents of the other religions, the Jews, the Moslems, the Hindus, the Buddhists, etc.

Interestingly enough, the concept of the brotherhood of man, apart from its supernatural context, is an excellent example of an ancient ethical principle which has great applicability to contemporary as well as to previous societies. Although I have pointed to cultural survivals which create confusion and disorder, this is not to be interpreted to mean that all that is the product of the past is incompatible with the present. In fact, it may be argued that the increased interdependence and vulnerability of the mass society place a greater premium on this moral principle than any earlier society ever did. This is an example of a principle of mass living that has not yet taken hold despite its longevity, yet the adoption of which in deed, as well as in word, may be prerequisite to the continued existence of mankind.

Before departing from the subject of religion, I cannot, as a demographer, refrain from calling attention to the cultural dissonance represented by Pope Paul VI's recent encyclical "Of Human Life," which ignores the findings of empirical demography (*The New York Times*, 1968:20–21). This example of cultural lag closely parallels that afforded by the Roman Catholic Church during the reign of Pope Paul V, which, some three centuries ago, similarly ignored the findings of empirical astronomy and produced the Galileo incident.

Among the most serious consequences of the failure of contemporary American society to keep pace with the social morphological revolution are the deficiencies in the process of socialization. Bronfenbrenner (1968, forthcoming) illuminates this problem in his comparative study of education in the United States and the Soviet Union. In the USSR the child is so inbred with a sense of belonging and obligation to the society of which he is an infinitesimal part that he tends to lack initiative and creativity. In the United States, in contrast, the child is so little the recipient of a sense of membership in, and responsibility to, the social order that, although he develops great initiative and creativity, his attitude is essentially one of concern with how he gets his and unconcern with others. We have yet to achieve the golden mean in order to produce a harmonious mass society consisting of people with a balance of initiative, creativity and social responsibility.

On the international front, there is similar evidence of cultural lag. Most grave in its consequences, obviously, is the failure to achieve the resolution of national conflicts of interest by means other than physical force. Vietnam, the Middle East, and Nigeria are but a few timely reminders of this fact. The social morphological revolution has generated a highly interdependent, vulnerable, and shrunken world, increasing the probability and intensifying the nature of conflicts of interest. But the traditional means of resolving international tensions and hostilities, namely, war, in a society which possesses the hydrogen bomb, carries with it the threat of the ultimate disaster, even the extinction of mankind. Nevertheless, contemporary diplomatic policies and contemporary military postures are more the product of societies of the past than of the present.

To be sure, some progress has been made in the evolving of machinery for the peaceful resolution of international disputes as exemplified by the League of Nations, the World Court, the United Nations and the Specialized Agencies. But it is not yet certain that the United Nations will not follow the League of Nations into oblivion as is actually desired by some of our most anachronistic organizations, such as the Daughters of the American Revolution and the John Birch Society. If the plague of deleterious cultural survivals which afflicts contemporary society cannot be effectively dealt with, it may well be that nuclear holocaust will be the means to undo both the process and the products of the social morphological revolution.

Finally, again on the international front, mention must be made of the cleavages between the have and have-not nations, between the socialist and communist nations, and between the factions within these blocs. The great disparities in levels of living among the nations of the world and the great international ideological differences, in part products of the differential impact of the social morphological revolution, constitute the most serious threats to peace and are harbingers of potential disaster. It remains to be seen whether contemporary society can muster the will to utilize available knowledge in a manner to override ideological, structural, and procedural atavisms to cope with these problems. In this year, officially proclaimed by the United Nations as the International Human Rights Year, it is a sad commentary on the role of this nation that the Congress has reduced foreign aid appropriations to an all-time low. And it is an even sadder commentary on the state of international affairs that the world spends well over 100 billion dollars annually for the military, while the developing nations, after a disastrous "Development Decade," still starve for capital and other resources to achieve their economic development goals.

The Role of the Social Sciences Including Sociology

In contemporary society the approach to the solution of our problems, whether on the international or on the national front, is characteristically bifurcated, reflecting deep ideological cleavage. The approach to problem solution tends to be "conservative" or "liberal," or variations from "reactionary" to "revolutionary." It is my contention, again utilizing the social morphological framework, that the conservative and the liberal reflect the ideology of the social morphological conditions in which they were reared or to which they were exposed. It is not an accident, for example, that Barry Goldwater comes from a state which as recently as 1940 had a population density about the same as that of the United States in 1790—4.4 persons per square mile, and only 6.6 in 1950 and 11.5 in 1960. Nor is it a mere coincidence that Senator Jacob Javits, in contrast, comes from a state with population densities of 281.2 in 1940, 309.3 in 1950, and 350.1 in 1960 (Hauser, 1967c).

Needless to say, in a society such as that of the United States, in which the State of Alabama and the State of New York are simultaneously present, there is an extreme range in social morphological conditions. Furthermore, "urbanism as a way of life" is neither confined to the boundaries of a city nor ubiquitous and pervasive within it. That is, rural residents in a complex mass society may, by reason of their own life paths, take on urban patterns of thought and action and *vice versa*.

The conservative, including the reactionary, is the person socialized in a milieu, which although contemporary by the calendar, is essentially that of eighteenth- and nineteenth-century America. The liberal, including the revolutionary, in contrast, is the person who has been reared in a milieu more the product of the social morphological revolution. The conservative is essentially the representative of the past in the present; the liberal is more clearly the representative of the present.

This does not necessarily mean that the liberal has the answers for the solution of contemporary problems. The liberal, who is sure that he has the right answers because they are non-traditional or different from that of the conservative, is subject to the same basic blindness as is the conservative. The basic point is that the "right" answer is neither to be found in the "old," as old, nor the "new," as new. It is to be found rather in the specific analysis of a specific problem situation to which the application of knowledge and wisdom finds possible solutions quite independently of whether they are "old" or "new," or "conservative" or "liberal," or any variation of these postures.

Both the conservative and liberal approaches *per se* are as inconsistent with the contemporary urban and metropolitan order as the horse and buggy or any other outmoded artifact. The unprecedented problems arising as frictions of social change can be resolved by neither the conservative nor the liberal approach.

If the approach to the resolution of contemporary social problems is neither to be conservative nor liberal, what is it to be? The answer is the "social engineering" approach. The social engineering position, as distinguished from the conservative or liberal one, represents an utterly new approach to contemporary problems. It is an approach born of the social morphological revolution to cope with the problems engendered by it.

It is not possible here fully to trace the emergence of the social engineering approach. It may be briefly stated that it is a recent product of the whole series of developments which distinguishes the post-Newtonian from the pre-Newtonian world. The more recent of these developments has led to the application of the method of science to social, as well as to physical and biological phenomena; and to the emergence of social-engineering activities to parallel the engineering activities based on the physical and biological sciences. That is, the social engineer, as yet represented by a pathetically few professions—e.g., the public administrator, the city manager, the social worker, the educator, the criminologist, the planner, the professional businessman—is emerging to apply the knowledge of social-science to the solution of social problems, in the same manner as the electronics engineer applies the knowledge of physics to electronics problems, or the biological engineer, the physician, applies the knowledge of the life sciences to problems of ill health.

Only by the adoption of the social-engineering approach can we get beyond the conservative-liberal approach. Only in this manner can we avoid the blindness of both the conservative and the liberal—the one convinced that the past contains the answers to the present; the other that the past does not. That both the conservative and liberal approaches are blind may be argued on the basis of two generalizations, validated by the evidence produced by social science. The first is that if you find what is right and stick to it, you are bound to be wrong. For the world does not stay put; it changes. The second is that no degree of disillusionment with the past, no level of good intentions, and no amount of zeal by themselves necessarily provide an appropriate answer to anything.

The social-engineering approach is an approach as independent as possible of existent stereotyped postures or attitudes. It is neither conservative nor liberal, Republican nor Democratic, any more than is an electronic engineer's approach, or the approach of any expert, confronted with a problem which requires an effective and efficient solution. It is a twentieth-century approach consonant with twentieth-century metropolitan life and adapted to the resolution of twentieth-century problems.

The social-engineering approach is dependent on knowledge, drawn from social science, and wisdom, based on experience in problem solution. It is the role of the social sciences, in general, as well as sociology in particular, to provide the necessary knowledge. That is the object of research, data collection, data processing and analysis.

The practical purpose of social data is to permit social accounting (Hauser, 1967b). Accounting first was a set of principles and practices for collecting, collating, and reporting information relating to the activities of an organization, so that they could be evaluated in relation to the organization's objectives. In contemporary language, accounting is an information-control system, designed to serve the needs of administrators of an organization or a program.

Accounting procedures evolved in the development of private business and have only relatively recently been applied to the evaluation and control of an entire economy. The Employment Act of 1946 in the United States, which created the President's Council of Economic Advisors and requires an annual Economic Report to the nation, represents a major institutional invention to cope with the economic problems of the twentieth-century American economy.

A hopeful indication that the social morphological revolution is producing mechanisms for the resolution of the social problems it has precipitated lies in the bill introduced in the 90th Congress, calling for the establishment of a parallel Council of Social Advisors and an annual Social Report to the nation (Subcommittee on Government Research, 1968). Furthermore, the Department of Health, Education and Welfare, through its Advisory Panel on Social Indicators, and upon instruction from the President of the United States, has been engaged in the preparation of a prototype Social Report.

The unprecedented period of high level economic activity, uninterrupted by depression or recession, that this nation has recently experienced is certainly related to the existence and activities of the Council of Economic Advisors. We are now experiencing a costly inflation, and we are now threatened by a possible recession mainly because the Congress, a repository of cultural lag, has not heeded, or tardily heeded, the recommendations of the Administration based on the findings of the Council of Economic Advisors.

It is my judgment that had this nation possessed a Council of Social Advisors since 1947, along with the Council of Economic Advisors, and had the recommendations of such a Council been heeded by the Administration and the Congress, the "urban crisis" which sorely affects us would not have reached its present acute stage.

It is the role of the social sciences, including sociology, to generate the knowledge on the basis of which social policy and social action may be directed to the solution of our problems. The primary function of the social scientist is research, the production of knowledge. It is not the function of the social scientist, *qua* scientist, to be a social engineer (Hauser, 1949). To be sure, many of us social scientists have been called upon to perform both roles in the early stage of the development of the social sciences, but there can be no question about the fact that the two roles are distinct and that each, in the long run, will be better performed as separate and specialized activities.

More specifically, it is the role of the social scientist, including the sociologist, to develop and produce the "social indica-

tors" which will permit effective social accounting. Fortunately, the social morphological revolution has generated much in the way of social statistics and other types of knowledge, which are already quite impressive even if still deficient and in relatively early stages of evolution (Raymond M. Bauer, 1967; Hauser, 1967b; Hauser, 1963).

Social accounting will become possible only after consensus is achieved on social goals. The development of social goals is neither a scientific function nor a social engineering function. It is a function that must be performed by society as a whole, acting through its political and other leaders. In a democratic society it presumably reflects the desires of the majority of the people.

Although a majority of the people must fix the goals of a society, the social scientist and the social engineer are in a strategic position to participate in goal formation. They must work closely with political and other leaders to help develop a broad spectrum of choices, which will reflect, insofar as possible, the requirements and consequences of specific goals. I have elsewhere proposed one set of social goals for consideration—published in a recent report of the Joint Economic Committee of the Congress (Hauser, 1968b).

Concluding Observations

Man is the only significant culture-building animal on earth. He not only adapts to environment, he creates it as well. He has created a world in which mankind itself is the crucial environment—a mankind characterized by large numbers, high densities, and great heterogeneity. He is still learning how to live in this new world he has created. The product of the chief components of the social morphological revolution—the population explosion, the population implosion, and population diversification—together with rapid technological and social change—is contemporary society, a chaotic society, an anachronistic society. It is a society characterized by dissonant cultural strata—by confusion and disorder. It is also a society which for the first time in human history possesses the capacity to destroy itself—globally as well as nation by nation.

In addition to the acceleration in the rate of technological and social change, and partly in response to it, society has acquired a greater capacity for social change. Virtually instantaneous worldwide social interaction is possible with modern means of communication; and the mass media, bolstered by communication satellites and new educational hardware, create new opportunities for the modification and creation of attitudes and behaviorisms consistent with the realities of the contemporary world. But, although the capability for social change has undoubtedly increased, adequate and effective mechanisms for the control of social change, for accommodation and adaptation to the changing social milieu, as well as to the changing material world, have yet to be evolved. Planning as a mechanism for rational decision-making is still in its infancy and has yet to develop an integrated approach with apposite administrative, economic and social planning, along with physical planning. Progress is being made in this respect, however. In this nation, for example, planning has become a respectable word now if modified by the term "city"; but when modified by such terms as "metropolitan," "regional," or "national," it is still considered a dangerous thought in some quarters. But planning, in ever broader contexts, will undoubtedly be a first step in the dissipation of confusion and the restoration of order.

That we live in a chaotic world should not be too surprising in view of the perspective provided by calendar considerations. Only twelve human generations have elapsed since the "modern era" began. Only seven human generations

have elapsed since this nation was founded. Only six generations have elapsed since mankind acquired the means to permit the proliferation of cities of a million or more inhabitants. Only two generations have elapsed since the onset of significant internal migratory flows of Afro-Americans. Fewer than two generations have elapsed since the United States became an urban nation. Less than one generation has elapsed since the advent of the explosive power of the atom. Little more than a decade has elapsed since the Supreme Court decision outlawing *de jure* segregation in schools—and a clear-cut judicial decision on *de facto* segregation is yet to come.

Furthermore, only two human generations have elapsed since Durkheim and Weber and, to confine my attention to my own teachers and colleagues, less than one since Burgess, Ogburn, Redfield, and Wirth. The social sciences, in general, and sociology in particular, are still emergent sciences. It was only during the century roughly from about 1750 to 1850 that the physical sciences achieved the respectability and acceptance that paved the way, through engineering, for the transformation of the physical and material world. It was only during the century roughly from 1850 to 1950 that the bio-medical sciences achieved a similar status that paved the way, by means of bio-medical engineering, for the remarkable increase in longevity and health. It is to be hoped that the century from 1950 to 2050 will be the period during which the social sciences, including sociology, will achieve a level of respectability and acceptance that will pave the way for social engineering to eliminate the chaos that characterizes contemporary society. The question is whether mankind can muddle through without collective suicide before rational decision-making overtakes the confusion and disorder of our tottering transitional society.

It is to be emphasized that a modern Armageddon is not mankind's only alternative to continuing national or international chaos. For the social morphological revolution has also produced a material world, a social milieu, and an emancipated and reflective man who has the capacity to dissipate confusion and restore order. The social morphological revolution has initiated and nurtured the social sciences, including sociology; it has required the collection and funding of social knowledge in various forms, including social statistics; it has evolved a number of social engineering professions which are still proliferating, including planning; and it has opened up the new vistas of social accounting.

With the stress I have placed on the need for the restoration of order, I should make it clear that I recognize that disorder cannot, and should not, be entirely eliminated. For disorder betokens the need for change, often desirable, as well as necessary. Order as such is not by itself a discrete goal of high priority. Hitler, for example, achieved a high degree of order in his Third Reich; and Stalin, in his version of a communist society. The task is rather to welcome disorder, both in Durkheim's sense of helping to define the limits of order and as a symptom of needed change, but to control the levels of disorder, while effecting change, so that it does not threaten the viability of society.

In the United States, at the present time, "law and order" has become a political slogan with many overtones. But the disorder which afflicts American society by reason of the Negro Revolt and that of other minority groups, including the poor, points to the inadequacies of the slogan. The slogan is but a half-truth; and as Oliver Wendell Holmes once observed, "A half-truth is like a half-brick—it can be thrown a lot farther." The entire slogan, to meet the needs of our society, should be "law, justice, and order." For until justice is achieved by our minorities, we will not have order, unless we choose to make ourselves over into a repressive society.

I am aware that I have tread perilously on the border between social science and social engineering. I may be accused of polluting the science of sociology with the stigmata of social policy and implied, if not explicit, proposals for social action. I am sensitive, as well as open, to such criticism because I firmly believe in maintaining a sharp boundary between science and engineering, as I have indicated above. But the theme of this annual meeting, I repeat, is "On the Gap Between Sociology and Social Policy," and it is in an effort to close this gap that I have chosen to take the course I have followed. I may have failed, but I have tried to diagnose rather than to prescribe, to illuminate rather than to exhort, to point to the hiatus between sociology and social policy, rather than to persuade the scientific members of this Association, as scientists, to fill the gap.

At the annual meetings of this Association in March, 1946, after the shock of the first atomic bomb and the first radar contact with the moon, I delivered a paper entitled, "Are the Social Sciences Ready?" It was a question raised by the then only prospect for the creation of a National Science Foundation, which might include provisions for the support of the social sciences as well as the natural sciences.

I stated at that time (Hauser, 1946):

Much has been said or written by social scientists, philosophers of science and others to explain the disparities in the roles of the natural and the social sciences in human affairs. Whatever the reasons may be, we might well at this juncture be impressed with the two outstanding facts: First, that the social sciences have provided more knowledge and understanding about our social, political and economic life than society has actually used; second, that the social sciences have not produced enough. . . .

My purpose in dealing with policy matters as social facts in this paper is now, as it was 22 years ago, not to persuade sociologists or other social scientists to enter the realm of policy formation and social action *qua* scientists. It is rather my two-fold purpose to stress what you already know: one, that sociology has accumulated more knowledge than is yet being utilized by society; and two, that there is a great and increasing need for more knowledge—and for more solid knowledge of the type outlined in my 1946 paper.

I conclude with a variation on my major theme. The chaotic society when understood as an anachronistic society can be transformed into a coeval or synchro-nous society. The first step in this direction lies, necessarily, in the comprehension of the nature and consequences of the social morphological revolution—which will be the product of research. More knowledge than we now possess is needed. But we have sufficient knowledge, even now, to state that the remediation of our chaotic society can be accomplished by bridging the gap between the social sciences, including sociology, and social policy and action.

REFERENCES

Annals of the American Academy of Political and Social Science.
  1967   *Social Goals and Indicators for American Society.* Volume I, May 1967 and Volume II, September 1967.

BAUER, RAYMOND M. (ed.)
  1967   *Social Indicators.* Cambridge, Mass.: M.I.T. Press.

BRAIDWOOD, ROBERT J. and GORDON R. WILLEY (eds.)
  1962   *Courses Toward Urban Life.* Chicago: Aldine.

BREESE, GERALD.
  1966   *Urbanization in Newly Developing Countries.* Englewood Cliffs: Prentice-Hall.

BRONFENBRENNER, URIE.
  1968   *On the Making of New Men* (manuscript to be published by Russell Sage Foundation).

CHILDE, V. GORDON.
  1941   *Man Makes Himself.* London: Watts.
  1946   *What Happened in History.* London: Penguin Books.

DAVID, PAUL T. and RALPH EISENBERG.
  1961   *Devaluation of the Urban and Suburban Vote,* Volume I. Charlotteville: University of Virginia Press.

DAVIS, KINGSLEY.
  1955   "The origin and growth of urbanization in the world." *American Journal of Sociology,* 60(March),433.

DURKHEIM, ÉMILE.
  1897–98 *L'année Sociologique.* Volume II.
  1933   *On the Division of Labor in Sociology.* New York: Macmillan.
  1938   *The Rules of Sociological Method.* Glencoe, Ill.: The Free Press.

GALBRAITH, JOHN KENNETH.
  1958   *The Affluent Society.* Boston: Houghton Mifflin.

GRAS, N. S. B.
  1922   *An Introduction to Economic History.* New York: Harper & Row.

HAUSER, PHILIP M.
  1946   "Are the social sciences ready?" *American Sociological Review,* 11(August), 379–384.
  1949   "Social science and social engineering." *Philosophy of Science,* 16(July).
  1961   *On the Impact of Population and Community Changes on Local Government.* (Seventh Annual Wherrett Lecture on Local Government). Pittsburgh: Institute of Local Government, University of Pittsburgh.
  1963   "Statistics and Society." *Journal of the American Statistical Association,* 58(March), 1–12.
  1965   and Leo F. Schnore (eds). *The Study of Urbanization.* New York: Wiley, Chapter 1.

1966   "Demographic factors in the integration of the Negro," pp. 71–101 in Talcott Parsons and Kenneth B. Clark (eds.), *The Negro American*. Boston: Houghton Mifflin.

1967a "Environmental forces shaping our cities," pp. 31–45 in The National Conference on Social Welfare (ed.), *The Social Welfare Forum*. New York: Columbia University Press.

1967b "Social accounting," pp. 839–876 in Paul F. Lazarsfeld, William H. Sewell and Harold L. Wilensky (eds.), *The Uses of Sociology*. New York: Basic Books.

1967c "Lao-Tze, Confucius and the conservative-liberal debate." *Proceedings of the American Philosophical Society*, 3(October),259–267.

1968a "After the riots, what?" *The University of Chicago Magazine*, 60(May), 4–10.

1968b "Twentieth-century national goals in the development of human resources," pp. 38–51 in *Federal Programs for the Development of Human Resources* (90th Congress, 2nd Session, Joint Committee Print, Subcommittee on Economic Progress, Joint Economic Committee, Congress of the United States). Washington, D.C.: U.S. Government Printing Office.

HODGE, PATRICIA LEAVEY and PHILIP M. HAUSER.
1968   *The Challenge of America's Metropolitan Population Outlook—1960 to 1985*, Chapter I (Research Report Number 3). Washington, D.C.: The National Commission on Urban Problems.

MANNHEIM, KARL.
1940   *Man and Society in an Age of Reconstruction: Studies in Modern Social Structure* (trans. Edward Shils). London: K. Paul, Trench, Trubner, Ltd.

MUMFORD, LEWIS.
1961   *The City in History*. New York: Harcourt, Brace & World.

National Advisory Commission on Civil Disorders.
1968   *Report of the National Advisory Commission on Civil Disorders*. Washington, D.C.: U.S. Government Printing Office.

The New York Times.
1968   July 30:20–21.

OGBURN, WILLIAM F.
1922   *Social Change*. New York: The Viking Press, Inc.

REDFIELD, ROBERT.
1955   *The Little Community: Viewpoints for the Study of a Human Whole*. Chicago: University of Chicago Press.

Subcommittee on Government Research of the Committee on Government Operations.
1968   "Full Opportunity and Social Accounting Act," (S843). Introduced by Senator Walter F. Mondale and ten other Senators. See *Hearings Before The Subcommittee on Government Research of the Committee on Government Operations*, First Session on S843, Parts I, II, III, Washington, D.C.: U.S. Government Printing Office.

TAWNEY, RICHARD HENRY.
1920   *The Acquisitive Society*. New York: Harcourt, Brace & World.

TURNER, RALPH.
1941   *The Great Cultural Traditions*, Volume I, *The Ancient Cities*. New York: McGraw-Hill.

United Nations.
1953   *The Determinants and Consequences of Population Trends*. New York: United Nations.
1966   *World Population Prospects*. New York: United Nations.

U.S. Bureau of the Census.
1960   *Historical Statistics of the United States, Colonial Times to 1967*, Washington, D.C.: U.S. Government Printing Office.
1962   *Historical Statistics of the United States, Colonial Times to 1957: Continuation to 1962 and Revisions*, Washington, D.C.: U.S. Government Printing Office.
1967   *Statistical Abstract of the United States, 1967*, Washington, D.C.: U.S. Government Printing Office (annual).

WALLAS, GRAHAM.
  1916 *The Great Society: A Psychological Analysis.* New York: Macmillan (latest edition in 1967 by the University of Nebraska Press, Lincoln, Nebraska).

WELLEMEYER, FLETCHER and FRANK LORIMER.
  1962 "How many people have ever lived on earth." *Population Bulletin,* 18(February).

WIRTH, LOUIS.
  1956 *Community Life and Social Policy.* Chicago: University of Chicago Press.

Cultural Moods and Social Movements

70. MASS SOCIETY AND EXTREMIST POLITICS

JOSEPH R. GUSFIELD

This paper offers a critical view of those writers whom Joseph R. Gusfield describes as the advocates of the idealized theory of "mass politics," a theory which assumes adherence to democratic norms even when such norms frustrate certain basic values. According to Gusfield, "isolation from mass culture accentuates local sources of extremist response"—and there are many people in this country who are so isolated.

Joseph R. Gusfield is Professor and Chairman of the Department of Sociology at the University of California, San Diego. His books include Occupational Roles and Forms of Enterprise *(1961) and* Symbolic Crusade: State Politics and the American Temperance Movement *(1963).*

A dominant stream of thought in current political sociology explains many contemporary anti-democratic movements as products of a distinctive social organization—Mass Society. Writers who utilize this approach have maintained that modern, Western societies increasingly show characteristics of mass organization which sharply differ from the features of such societies in the nineteenth and earlier centuries. Mass societies, in this view, demonstrate a form of politics in which traditional sociological concepts, such as class or culture, are not relevant to an understanding of the sources, genesis, or careers of extremist, anti-democratic political

Reprinted from the *American Sociological Review,* **27** (February 1962), 19–30, by permission of the author and the American Sociological Association.

movements. Mass politics is the form of political action unique to mass societies. As modern democratic societies become mass societies, we may then anticipate that political crises are likely to generate extremist, anti-democratic responses. Leading advocates of this theory of "mass politics," in whole or part, are Hannah Arendt, Erich Fromm, Karl Mannheim, William Kornhauser, Robert Nisbet, and Philip Selznick.[1] This paper is a critical analysis of this approach and a reformulation of some of the relations between mass societies and political action.

There are two major contentions in this paper. The first is a criticism of the assumptions about democratic politics underlying the theory of mass politics. The second is a reformulated theory of the relation between mass society and political extremism in contemporary, democratic societies.

It is our first contention that implicit in the theory of mass politics is an idealized conception of the pluralistic social and political system held necessary for the maintenance of democratic institutions. This conception is idealized in that it fails to give adequate weight to barriers which conflicts of interest offer to political harmony and compromise under any political structure.

Our second contention is that the elements of mass societies viewed with alarm by mass politics theorists in actuality contain positive connotations for the maintenance of democratic political institutions. Mass communications, bureaucratic institutions, and equalitarianism have implications which strengthen pluralistic political structures. Extremist politics may be expected in modern societies as a response of those adversely affected by the changes towards a mass society and most insulated from mass institutions. Contrary to the theory of mass politics traditional concepts of political sociology *are* adequate to the analysis of extremism.

It must be made clear that our major interest in this paper is in the explanation of anti-democratic movements as they develop within historically democratic societies. This excludes consideration of authoritarian regimes in traditional societies or the development of anti-democratic movements in developing economies under the impact of intensive social and economic change.[2] Our interest is confined to those writers who explain such modern extremist movements as Fascism, Communism, or McCarthyism by reference to characteristics of mass society. These represent one variant of mass society theory, but an influential one.[3]

Mass Society and the Theory of Mass Politics

Mass Society analysts view modern social systems as significantly different from nonindustrial and earlier societies. Whatever the differences among individual writers, there is a common core of description in the term "mass society" which suggests the attenuation of primary and local associations and groups. Impersonal, bureaucratized relationships in large-scale organizations have replaced the informal systems of loyalty in small groups and local affiliations. Equalitarian conditions and ideologies have weakened systems of political and social authority characteristic of stratified communities. Technological innovations have made possible a high degree of standardization, both of products and ideas. The elongation of the chain of organizational command has enhanced the possibilities of oligarchic control as local groups are less viable, hence less resistant to control. The emphasis is upon the breakdown of immediate relationships and differentiations so that the population is now more homogeneous but also less sharply identified and affiliated with distinctive social groups. It is in this sense that the theorist of mass society views the traditional categories fo sociological analysis—family, class, community, ethnic identity, etc.—as having lost significance in mass societies. The mass is mass-like: shapeless, structureless, undifferentiated. Mass politics trace the implications of this loss of differentiation for the bonds of loyalty to democratic political institutions.

Exponents of mass politics viewpoints have described modern Western, industrial societies as ones in which persons lack attachment to primary and secondary associations. "The chief characteristic of the mass-man," Hannah Arendt has written, "is not brutality and backwardness, but his isolation and lack of normal social relationships." [4] Political extremism, manifested in anti-democratic movements, is seen as a result of the *structural* and *psychological* consequences for political loyalty or disattachment to democratic procedures and aims.

Supporters of this view hold that structural characteristics of bureaucratization and equality undermine the functions of secondary and primary associations in inculcating values and in transmitting political norms. In mass society, such theories maintain, secondary associations of school, church, community or union, operate in a large-scale fashion. Rank-and-file identification with the organizational elite is diminished as the member's associational life is peripheral and tangential. The high mobility rates and standardized life styles destroy economic class as an important source of motivation and interest in political events. Institutions functioning under conditions of mass society do not touch the character and the personal values of those exposed to them. Being solely instrumental means, the major associations and institutions of the society cannot act as agencies through which values are inculcated. Because of this, the political elites of the society cannot mediate political decisions to the acceptance of the rank-and-file. Such political "untouchables" are described by Selznick when he writes, "He has lost the meaning provided by the articulated social structure to which he belonged." [5]

In previous centuries the lack of integration of rank-and-file members of the society into political institutions was a matter of little political consequence. Mass societies, however, are politically equalitarian. The development of large aggregates of persons unattached to democratic political structures and norms is significant because such groups are capable of spontaneous development unguided by the norms of democratic society. The diminished role of intermediate structures—both institutions and specific political associations—leaves the person unattached and capable of being reunited into a new group. "A strong intermediate structure consists of stable and independent groups which represent diverse and frequently conflicting interests." [6] In mass society, however, the representative nature of these groups (classes, ethnic groups, regions, etc.) is undermined. Both because participation is peripheral and because political elites are limited in authority, mass societies are less able to control the values and political aspirations of citizens.

To the structural disintegration of society there is added the personal disorganization of the individual. The psychological consequences of mass society are described in terms of the feeling of detachment. The key word here is alienation, "a mode of experience in which the person experiences himself as an alien." [7] Whether the emphasis of the writer is on estrangement from work, the normlessness of contemporary culture or the powerless feeling of the individual in large-scale organizations, mass conditions are described as producing feelings of *malaise* and insecurity.

The alienation of the individual in modern societies is the psychological statement of detachment. It describes a condition in which the person is not involved in or committed to primary or secondary groups. It adds to this the description of the person as someone with positive, unfulfilled needs for identity, affection, and assurance.

In both its structural and psychological elements the theory of mass politics states that political alienation—the disattachment of the person from political institutions—is a function of the disintegrating influences of mass society on the ties of sentiment and loyalty to specific groups which characterized the social structure of democracies in an earlier historical period. Without attachment to primary or to intermediate structures, the individual has no bond to national political institutions which commands his loyalty to its political norms.

Pluralistic and Extremist Politics

In the emphasis on a transition from an earlier historical period to a modern, mass society the theories here considered have suggested that political democracy functioned relatively unimpeded under non-mass conditions. It is imperative then that we examine the type of political structure from which mass politics is seen as differing. Political extremism is so defined in contradistinction to pluralistic politics. The mass theorist sees pluralistic politics as impaired under current social conditions. As a corollary pluralistic structure is implicitly posited as an essential condition for democratic politics.

The theory of a balance of power among a plurality of groups has been the dominant analytical tool of American political scientists.[8] Its classic defense has been presented in Hamilton and Madison's *The Federalist Papers*. The theory presupposes a society of many and diverse social groups. The political institutions force each group to moderate and compromise their interests in the interplay of party, secondary association, and locality. In the pluralist conception of the citizen, each person is integrated into politics in his capacity as member of some segment of the society—worker or manager, city or country dweller, Southerner or Northerner, immigrant or native, white or black. The units of politics are thus organized groups built upon the sentiments and interests of persons in their affiliations with specific primary associations which occupy positions and perform specific functions within the major institutions.

Pluralistic politics involves certain "rules of the game" by which political conflict is carried on. These "rules of the game," part of the definition of politics as an institution, are adhered to by the participants. Chief among tenets of democratic politics is acceptance of opposing forces into the political process on the same terms as those binding on one's own group. This acceptance supplies the necessity for political compromise and conciliation. If all groups possess some political power and are admitted into the political process, bargaining and negotiation are the chief modes of political conflict. Violence is ruled out as a possible way of solving social or economic conflicts.

It is essential to this process that each group be willing to accept the total or partial defeat of its aims and accept the total or partial achievement of the aims of its opponents. Compromise includes the ability to settle for less than full victory. This "realistic" orientation is achieved in an atmosphere governed by rational calculation of interests. It is most negated when objectives have become correlated with considerations of honor and when compromise, negotiation, and defeat are suffused with connotations of dishonor.

Political extremism occurs when movements advocate violation of the democratic, pluralist "rules of the game." Shils suggests a distinction between pluralistic and ideological politics which emphasizes the disattachment of the extremist from self-limiting and rationally calculative aspects of pluralism:

Extremism consists in going to an extreme in zealous attachment to a particular value, e.g., private property, ethnic homogeneity, or status equality. . . . The extremist must be deeply alienated from the complex of rules which keep the strivings for various values in restraint and balance. An extremist group is an alienated group. . . . Its hostility is incompatible with that freedom from intense emotion which pluralistic politics needs for its prosperity. . . . The focus of the extremist's attention on one or a few completely fulfilled values and his impatience with compromise when a plurality of values, never internally consistent, have to be reconciled with each other makes the extremist feel that he is worlds apart from the compromising moderates.[9]

This distinction between pluralist and extremist politics differs, as others have pointed out,[10] from traditional distinctions between Right and Left, Conservative, Liberal and Radical, and reform and revolution. It is a distinction between styles and not between contents. It is in this sense that extremism is alienated from the institutions of democratic politics. It denies the legitimacy of democratic political institutions as devices for mediating conflict. Extremist style refuses to accept the possible or probable outcomes of whole or partial defeat. Total victory is too important in the hierarchy of values to permit of compromise.

In several ways, then, the extremist breaks with the normative patterns of pluralist political behavior: (1) *He attempts to close the political process to opposing forces:* Politics is held to be the legitimate area of conflict for some, but not for all groups. Both Fascism and Communism have made this a cornerstone of the political structure as well as a tenet of their movements.

(2) *He attempts to carry on social and economic conflicts outside of political institutions:* The confinement of conflict to politics marks a cardinal principle of democratic politics. Violence, intimidation and fraud are excluded as means of achieving group ends.

(3) *He impairs the culture of democratic discussion:* An emphasis is placed on the value of uniform opinions and behavior. The criteria of rational calculation of interests is replaced by intensive appeals to sentiment and symbolism. This strain in McCarthyism captured the attention of those concerned with extremism in politics. It is only in this sense that membership and participation in extremist movements seems authoritarian. The extremist style has little appreciation of dissent and schism in the total society.

The extremist movement is marked by the low degree of commitment to the values of procedure in democratic institutions. Pluralist norms enforce tolerance, barter, and the inclusion of opponents as joint members of the same social system. Extremist resentment against democratic politics is not that of indifference but that of intensive conviction. It is the thoroughly moralistic attitude which marks the extremist and distinguishes him from the slightly cynical pluralist.

As we have sketched it so far, political extremism is found in one or both forms: an increased attachment to a single, overriding value or a weakened attachment to the norms of pluralist politics. In either case, the extremist is alienated from the *existing* democratic order.[11]

The theorists of mass politics visualize extremist movements as consequences of weakened attachments to political institutions and persons resulting from the break-down in functioning of primary and secondary associations in mass societies. Without a sense of affiliation to specific interest groups, the citizen has no way to develop a frame of reference for political events. Intermediate secondary associations cannot touch him sufficiently to act as forces limiting intensity of opposition and resentment of rival political claims. Political figures become distrusted and democratic institutions no longer legitimate sources of social control. In Kornhauser's words:

. . . intermediate groups help to protect elites by functioning as channels through which popular participation in the larger society (especially in the national elites) may be directed and restrained.[12]

The mass theorist goes a step further and suggests that such detachment from democratic political institutions leaves the individual susceptible to political participation in extremist channels. The socially alienated individual is not only politically alienated; he is also more likely to become the extremist activist than is the member of a structured interest group. He is no longer limited in his attack on rivals by the controls of a structured pluralistic society. His resentments against opposing groups and against the existing institutions themselves need not be confined to the calculative, instrumental style of democratic politics. The mass man is a passionate supporter of ideology.

Lack of control mechanisms regulating the political attitudes and behavior of mass citizenry furthers the extremist character of participation in politics. It enables the person to project destructive impulses into the political arena. Mannheim, for example, maintained that in traditional societies collective impulses and wishes are absorbed by smaller groups and directed toward group aims. The social disintegration of modern society, he felt, set such impulses free to seek integration around some new object, often a symbol or a leader.[13]

The attenuation of local and primary associations and mediating secondary interest groups and associations, is, in the theory of mass politics, the source of the extremism frequent in contemporary mass societies. As a system of analysis this view finds that traditional concepts of class and status aims are limited ways of characterizing political movements. As a philosophy of politics, the theory adds up to a defense of the virtues of a pluralistic political system. The transition from a pluralistic society to a mass society is implicitly and explicitly bemoaned. For this reason, the analysis of pluralist assumptions is central to our discussion.

Pluralistic Sources of Political Extremism

The theory of mass politics assumes that a pluralistic social structure diminishes the possibilities that political action will take extremist directions. Conflicts and demands for change will occur but will be moderated by adherence to the style of democratic institutions. An analysis of this assumption, however, shows that extremism both *can* and often *does* occur within pluralistic structures. There are at least four situations in which pluralism either invites or fails to forestall behavior outside the range of democratic norms for the mediation of conflicts:

(1) *Disenfranchised classes:* Change often brings new groups into formation or increases the demands of old ones. In any case, at any given time, some groups are excluded from the political process. Often it is not in the interest of some or most of the included groups to accept new political forces. Excluded groups must either function outside of the political "game" or force their way into it. The militancy of the American Negro in the South today is of this nature. Compromise and legality are not relevant political alternatives unless a group is within the political structures in the first place.

(2) *Doomed and defeated classes:* The theory of democratic politics has never developed a satisfactory answer to the problem: When is compromise to be rejected? When is political defeat not an acceptable alternative to violence and other breaks with pluralist procedure? The facts of the American Civil War and of the Algerian crisis in contemporary France illustrate the thesis that well-structured groups, with channels of representation in parliamentary bodies, are far from willing to accept defeat of important aims through parliamentary procedures. Robert Dahl sees this as a serious impediment in democratic theory. Referring to the election of Abraham Lincoln in 1860, Dahl writes:

Thus any election interpreted as a clear-cut victory for one side was almost certain to be so intolerable to the other that it would refuse to accept the outcome. . . . Where each side is large and regards the victory of the other as a fundamental threat to some very highly ranked values, it is reasonable to expect serious difficulties in the continued operation of a (pluralistic) system.[14]

This is apt to be the case under conditions of social or economic change which gravely threaten a previous position of power and supremacy. To such "doomed classes," [15] the future looks far less inviting than the past. A radical reorganization of society might be a solution to their problem but such a reorganization against politically ascendent forces is precisely what the moderating elements in the structure of political balance operate against. Recent discussions of the plight of the "old middle classes" in American life have stressed the indignation of these groups at their loss of power and status.[16] It is not a failure to "belong" that lies at the source of their alienation and possible "right-wing radicalism." Their response is touched off by the contents of the social changes to which they react.

(3) *Public opinion and the imbalance of competing interests:* The theory of democratic politics as a balance between competing interests often ignores the important role played by the neutral, non-competing elements in the political process. A great many groups without specific interests in a particular issue nevertheless have power to effect governmental decisions. Such decisions are made with a concern for the general climate of opinion toward an issue. Whether the "public" is friendly or hostile is an important element in an interest group's decision to pursue its aims within or without the political process. As Murray Edelman has pointed out, labor will pursue its goals through economic processes (strikes, bargaining, etc.) when the political climate is hostile.[17] Recourse to non-political means is not ruled out by the existence of pluralistic machinery.

(4) *Development of periodic crisis:* Mass politics theory generally recognizes economic and military crisis as an essential "trigger" to extremist movements. Be-

cause pluralistic politics is oriented toward compromises between groups, it is less open to long-run considerations. This is especially the case in issues of foreign policy. Unless there is some consensual basis other than group interest, elites must "sell" policy in terms communicable to specific classes and interests. Even assuming a diffusion of power in the form of what Riesman calls "veto groups," [18] a hiatus develops between long-run perspectives of governmental leaders and the short-run perspectives of intermediate associations and their constituencies. The result is often a stalemate and an immobilism which enables problems to develop into major crises. One instance of this is contained in LaPalombara's analysis of French and Italian politics in the post-war years.[19] He explains greater cohesion and agreement within the Italian moderate parties than among the French as a consequence of differences in the power of the Communist Party in each of the countries. Italian moderates were forced into agreement by fear.

While there has not been any serious fear in France that PCF could come peacefully to power, this reassuring assessment has been denied the democratic party leaders in Italy. . . . They have not been able to permit themselves the capricious inaction in which the French Center Party Leaders have indulged over the last decade.[20]

Inability of political elites to deal with crisis is itself one strong source of mass alienation from a political institution. Third parties have fared better at the polls in the United States during periods of economic depression than during periods of prosperity.[21] As Lipset has pointed out, there is a direct correlation between levels of economic well-being and the existence of democratic political systems.[22] Prosperous countries may avoid problems which threaten political stability in less affluent nations.

In each of these four situations, extremist politics is developed and conducted by well-structured groups, representing discrete and organized parts of the social structure, acting to secure goals related to group needs. While such groups are alienated from the existing political institutions they are not socially disintegrated or unrelated to the society and its political system. They function within a pluralist framework in which their values receive short shrift. Failure to recognize that pluralist assumptions cannot alone sustain political institutions is at the root of the implicit ideology of the theorist of mass politics.

The Pluralist Ideology

The sanguine view of political balance at the base of mass politics theory reveals a repetition of the ideological bias of nineteenth-century liberalism—the assumption that there is a natural harmony of interests which sustains the social and political system. Occurrences of sharp conflict are therefore indicative of disruptions in the *form* of social arrangements. There is nothing in the *content* of interests and beliefs which makes compromise improbable. Mannheim reflects this ideology in a passage in *Man and Society* in which he suggests that experience in trade unions and in other associations trains participants for planning on a societal basis: "He is gradually realizing that by resigning partial advantages he helps to save the social and economic system and thereby also his own interests." [23]

The belief that participation in the primary and secondary associations of the society will moderate conflict arises from this ideological commitment to pluralist politics. It leads the mass politics theorist to identify political defeat with social alienation, to view extremist movements as actions of disattached persons, unrelated to specific social bases or pursuing interests of a discrete social base. Because of this tendency, the mass politics approach has felt traditional political analysis to be deficient.

It is *not* true that attachment to intermediate structures insures attachment to the larger national institutions and structures. As a society undergoes change, it is likely that specific groups will be adversely affected by economic or social change. Similarly, some groups may develop new aspirations and objectives. In both cases they may come to feel that the existent political order is insufficient to command their allegiance. A shifting balance of forces is, however, not the same phenomenon as the breakup of an associational structure, the shattering of a class, or the decline of primary group support. It is even reasonable to maintain that an external threat to a group promotes its sense of solidarity and aids in the development of group identity and organization. [24] Attachment to intermediate structures may indeed promote a shared sense of alienation of the group from the total political order. The more informal organization the group possesses the more likely is it that politically extremist sentiments can be communicated and legitimated. In playing the game of politics, it is not only important whether or not one is permitted to play, but also whether one is winning or not. This problem is not solved by the degree of access which the group has to political association.

The point can be made through an analysis of a frequently used study of McCarthyist attitudes, which mass politics theorists have used as support for their position. Trow's study of Bennington, Vermont found a disproportionate amount of support for Senator McCarthy among small businessmen, especially those holding the nineteenth-century liberal hostility to both big business and labor unions. [25] In explaining his findings, Trow maintains that not only are small businessmen "resentful of a world that continually offends their deepest values" but equally important is the fact that they have little voice or representation in political institutions, such as the major parties. Granting the rather dubious assumption that small business has little place in the current constellation of political and ideological forces in the United States, the picture of disaffection portrayed in Trow's study is a classic picture of a well-organized economic group losing out in the process of social and economic change. This type of disaffection is readily analyzed in terms of class and status conflict. If mass movements are not to be understood in traditional forms of political analysis, they must be shown to be unrelated to analysis in terms of group interests and discrete social bases. This would involve more than the traditional view that social change produces disaffection among groups adversely exposed to it.

The assumption of a natural harmony of interests gives rise to another failing of the mass politics approach. This is the lack of concern for the development of consensus around the norms of democratic politics. If it is assumed that representation of interests assures harmony, then the problem of achieving moral sentiments supportive of the political institution becomes meaningless. However, such moral sentiments *are* essential; otherwise, the source of moderate politics, of commitment to the political process *per se* is missing. When the values at stake are intensely held and the constellation of political forces is adverse to a group, there is nothing in pluralistic theory which suggests a source of loyalty to moderateness. Oscar Gass has expressed this in excellent fashion:

I know that Democracy is a technique for reaching agreement, but it in turn rests upon a measure of agreement. It is, of course, formally true that, if only you agree on the technique of getting decisions, you don't have to agree on the outcome. But that is merely like saying that people can ride on the same bus even if they wish to get off at different places. The places must not be *too* different —or else they have to set a value on riding beyond that of getting to their destinations.[26]

A pluralistic system can be maintained only if the conflict of interest groups is balanced to some extent by cohesive elements in the cultural and social system which moderate the intensity of conflicts and which provide loyalties to maintenance of a defined area in which politics is conducted under pluralistic rules.[27] The ideology of pluralism has become a defense of moderateness, and an attack on political activism. Yet pluralist structure enhances activist sentiments.

Mass Culture and Political Cohesion

Contrary to mass politics theory, conditions of mass societies are not necessarily detrimental to sentiments supporting pluralistic politics. In fact the opposite appears to be the case. Certain conditions of modern, mass societies function to increase cohesion and consensus around norms of pluralist politics.

Mass politics approaches have emphasized bureaucratization, equalitarianism, and technological integration as forces weakening past mediating structures. It must also be pointed out that the same forces operate to incorporate persons into a larger national culture and social system. While mediating structures and local units may be weakened, direct attachment to the total society is enhanced. In Shils' phrase, "The new society is a mass society precisely in the sense that the mass of the population has become incorporated into *society*."[28]

Conditions of mass society develop a homogeneous set of cultural experiences for members. Technological forces have led to an economy and a means of communication which can absorb all the citizens in common. As this has occurred, the autonomy of the local community has given way to a national politics, a national economy and a national culture. In an era of high mass consumption, the equalization of incomes and the style-setting influence of a national market have promoted a more homogeneous standard of living. In the use of commodities and of leisure, as well as in high rates of social mobility, class lines are becoming blurred. In this society, major social institutions operate in similar fashion upon all communities and within most classes. School, church, medicine, family, and politics are increasingly open to the influence and control of centrally-trained professionals and their organizations. The consequences of such homogenizing forces are the development of a national mass culture and a national society. In this society, common sentiments increasingly cut across the social segments of class, region, and other sub-cultural units. In this sense mass society is a new social system.

These features of mass society, of course, are recognized in the theories considered above. Where we differ, however, is in stressing these as positive agencies of social integration, rather than only as devices which weaken earlier units of social life. The theories of mass politics suggest only one possible relationship between mass societies and political extremism. In the remainder of this paper we wish to suggest another relationship, one in which the trend toward mass society provides opportunities for strengthening the attachments of the individuals to institutions which accept diversity and support political balance. The conditions of mass society, we suggest, mitigate against political extremism because they operate against the isolation of differentiated sub-cultures from which strong ideological attachments can develop. At the same time, they provide conditions which promote acceptance of innovations.

(1) *They provide sources of direct attachment to supra-local institutions.* It has become something of an axiom in electoral behavior studies that interest and participation is at its highest in national rather than local elections. In a mass society, the individual is oriented toward a national culture and stratification system. Mass culture is carried through national systems of communications and education which may be, and often are, in conflict with local groups. Lack of attachment to local agencies, kinship units, and secondary associations by no means implies a lack of attachment to standards, tastes, and values of the mass culture. The same is true in respect to political participation. As the range of areas affected by local decisions grows smaller, the orientation of the individual to national political units grows more significant. Studies of cosmopolitan and local types indicate that the individual may be marginal within his local environment but very much committed to structures of occupational, educational, and political organization at levels above that of the local community.[29]

(2) *Mass culture enhances the possibilities of substantive consensus.* We have argued above that although cultural and class diversity provides a resistant force against oligarchic controls, it may also develop intensive attachments to particular aims which prevent the compromise and toleration presupposed by political pluralism. Indeed, pluralistic politics is hard to reconcile with intensity of conviction and a moralistic approach to politics. Insofar as mass societies create homogeneous experience for a population, there is an increased possibility of consensus on substantive issues. Will Herberg's[30] thesis of a growing uniformity in American religions is a case in point. Similarity of education, consumer products, income, and communications is also associated with similarity in morals and, to some extent, interests. The issues open to political conflict are then limited and less apt to arouse intense opposition. While this may mean a diminution in ideological commitments and controversy, it is hardly the same thing as production of extremist activism. Indeed, those who are critical of contemporary American society for its presumed conformist tendencies are often dismayed at the disappearance of activism, utopian thought, and radical attitudes, all of which are also forms of extremism, alienation, and discontent.

(3) *Mass culture can, and often does,*

shore up the support for consensus on procedural norms of pluralistic politics. Because they include multiple sub-cultures, mass institutions are open to the influence of numerous social segments in ways in which local and class institutions are not. Further, mass culture is more apt to be influenced by norms of cosmopolitan and nationalized groups than local and sub-cultural units. Within American society today, the norms of pluralist styles in politics find more response at the national than at the local levels. Efforts to censor artistic and educational experiments and dissent are more frequent at the local than at the national levels of education and communications. The development of a mass educational system, with a high degree of equalitarian recruitment, has been a distinctive aid to the acceptance of civil liberties sentiment.[31]

(4) *Mass culture diminishes the intensity of social conflicts by evening out the impact of major social and cultural changes.* Major social changes are frequently disruptive and focus on dimensions which involve clashes between attackers and defenders of tradition. This is particularly true in areas of cultural conflict—religion, morality, or race relations are examples. The appearance of mass communications and educational agencies diminishes the degree to which the population is differentially exposed to a new set of norms. This is seen in the current desegregation crisis in the South. Opposition to a national culture of race relations is found most intensively among those most localistic, least educated, least urban, least exposed to mass media, and least integrated into the national economy.[32] Mass media, the extension of education and professionalization tend to equate the rates at which different classes and regions are exposed to changing standards.

(5) *Mass society increases the linkages between groups and minimizes the possibilities of "superimposition."* The concept of a pluralistic social system often fails to differentiate between two types of segmen-tation.[33] In one, which we will call "linked pluralism," there are multiple groups but membership in one often cuts across membership in others. A situation of linked pluralism, for example, would be one in which many Catholics are lower class and many are middle class while Protestants are similarly represented in each class. Both Catholics and Protestants are 'linked' as members of the same social class. "Superimposed" segmentation occurs when membership in one group also implies membership in another. If most Catholics were lower class and most Protestants were middle class, then class and religion would be superimposed. It is fairly evident that intense social conflicts are maximized under conditions of superimposition and minimized under conditions of linked pluralism. In the example used, superimposition would mean that religious conflicts tended to be class conflicts as well.

The conditions of mass society tend to increase linked forms of pluralism and to minimize superimposed forms of pluralism. Perhaps the most salient aspect of this is a result of equalitarianism and mobility. When groups are not frozen by rigid stratification into a specific occupational and class position, such social categories as religion, race, residence, and community play less of a role as devices isolating one part of society from another.

It follows from this analysis that there are two major ways in which extremist movements may develop within the framework of contemporary mass societies. In one case, we are dealing with the general problem of reactions to social and economic change already discussed above in reference to "doomed classes" and to groups previously excluded from the political process. The transition from pluralistic structure to mass society is most keenly felt as loss and deprivation by those whose social and economic position is threatened by the development of bureaucratic organization, equalitarian social structure, and mass culture. The attention given to the status loss and economic hardship of the "old middle classes" as the society becomes more consumption-oriented, more organizationally structured and more technically professionalized provides one strand of evidence in what Lipset has called the "extremism of the Center." [34] Riesman has expressed the same idea of reaction to change in characterological terms in saying:

. . . his own life experience is often disappointing; he is deprived of a feeling of competence and place. Even this would not be so bad if the world made sense, if he could apply to what goes on his internalized standards of judgment, but as it is, neither his character nor his work is rewarded. In that situation he tends to turn both on himself . . . and on the world. [35]

The other case exists when groups are isolated from the major institutions and cultural streams of mass society. Localized groups are less open to the impact of the mass agencies. The less educated, the lowest income levels, the least protected minorities, the most fundamentalist in religion are least oriented to the rhythm of modernity with which so much of mass influence is carried. In this case, it is those least "caught up" in the historical currents of transition that are most likely to be immune from the moderating influences of mass culture. To cite such groups as products *of* mass society is misleading.

Carried to a logical extreme, the mass society becomes a political community in which bland tolerance and uniform ideas are the rule. Carried to its logical extreme, pluralistic societies are likely to generate either disintegrating conflict or stalemate. It is fruitless, however, to push typologies to their logical extremes. An empirical sociology must be concerned with the interaction between mass and pluralistic conditions. Elements of one model interact with elements of the other, sometimes as figure, sometimes as ground. De Tocqueville pointed out that one of the characteristics of American political institutions was the moderation of popular government by a leaven of aristocratic rule. He viewed the Supreme Court power of review as one such instance of balance. [36]

Mass conditions are thus likely to present many features which are not only consistent with a pluralistic theory of politics but even enhance such features. Rather than providing a source of extremist movements they are just as likely to mitigate the development of opposition and to increase the degree of toleration for dissent. Whether variety and controversy are likely to develop under the dominance of mass conditions is another question. However, those who seek to understand the conditions of stable, democratic institutions are mistaken in dispensing with traditional concepts and in emphasizing mass society as a demonic villain.

NOTES

1. The following relevant writings embody the theory of mass politics: Hannah Arendt, *The Origins of Totalitarianism,* New York: Harcourt, Brace and Co., 1954; Erich Fromm, *Escape From Freedom,* New York: Rinehart, 1945; Karl Mannheim, *Man and Society in an Age of Reconstruction,* London: Routledge and Kegan Paul, 1940; William Kornhauser, *The Politics of Mass Society,* Glencoe, Ill.: The Free Press, 1959; Robert Nisbet, *The Quest for Community,* New York: Oxford University Press, 1953; Philip Selznick, *The Organizational Weapon,* New York: McGraw-Hill, 1952.

2. See the discussion of the political effects of social and economic change in Western and non-Western societies in Kornhauser, *op. cit.,* Chaps. 7, 8.

3. We have confined our analysis here to theorists who find mass societies an explanatory tool in analyzing the rise of contemporary anti-democratic movements. Other writers have also described modern society as mass-like and have evaluated it in negative terms. This latter group, however, has not viewed political extremism as a likely consequence of mass conditions.

Writers such as David Riesman, in *The Lonely Crowd,* New Haven: Yale University Press, 1950, and C. Wright Mills, in *The Power Elite,* New York: Oxford University Press, 1957. have emphasized developing trends toward conformity and passivity rather than toward militance and activism. Still another stream in mass society writings is represented by E. A. Shils. He agrees that modern society is, by reason of mass conditions, best described as qualitatively different from earlier Western societies. This stream of writings, however, denies the disorganizing and overconforming consequences stressed by the other views. See the positive acceptance of mass society in Edward A. Shils, "Mass Society and Its Culture," *Daedalus,* 89 (Spring, 1960), 288–314.

4. Hannah Arendt, *op. cit.,* p. 310.

5. Philip Selznick, *op. cit.,* p. 283.

6. William Kornhauser, *op. cit.,* p. 78.

7. Erich Fromm, *The Sane Society,* New York: Rinehart, 1955, p. 120.

8. The best descriptions of this process in contemporary political science are probably David Truman, *The Governmental Process,* New York: A. A. Knopf, 1951, and V. O. Key, *Parties, Politics and Pressure Groups,* New York: Thomas Y. Crowley, 1947.

9. Edward A. Shils, *The Torment of Secrecy,* Glencoe, Ill.: The Free Press, 1955, p. 231. In similar vein, Nathan Leites introduces his study of French politics by a statement exempting the Communists and the "extreme right" from his discussion. He reasons that their style in politics is distinctly different from the "national" groups of the Center. In the period of post-war politics which he studied, "the extremes entered but little in 'the game' so that the patterns of political calculation used in parliament had little reference to their behavior." Nathan Leites, *On the Game of Politics in France,* Stanford, Calif.: Stanford University Press, 1959, p. 1.

10. Milton Rokeach, *The Open and Closed Mind,* New York: Basic Books, 1960, Ch. 3; Edward A. Shils, "Authoritarianism—Right and Left," in R. Christie and M. Jahoda (eds.), *Studies in the Scope and Method of 'The Authoritarian Personality,'* Glencoe, Ill.: The Free Press, 1954.

11. It should be emphasized that the degree of commitment of democratic populations to its political institutions is a relative matter. Many studies of attitudes toward civil liberties show a great lap between the acceptance of civil liberties among a minority of educated and participating citizens and the rank and file, especially among the lower-income and lesser educated. In this case, political extremism represents less an alienation *from* political institutions than it does the advent of increased political democracy. For studies of civil liberties see Samuel Stouffer, *Communism, Conformity and Civil Liberties,* Garden City, N.Y.: Doubleday, 1955; Seymour Lipset, "Democracy and Working-Class Authoritarianism," in *Political Man,* Garden City, N.Y.: Doubleday, 1960, pp. 97–130, and Raymond Mack, "Do We Really Believe in the Bill of Rights?," *Social Problems,* 3 (April, 1956), 264–269.

12. Kornhauser, *op. cit.,* p. 77.

13. Mannheim, *op. cit.,* p. 62.

14. Robert Dahl, *A Preface to Democratic Theory,* Chicago: The University of Chicago Press, 1956, pp. 97–98.

15. The term is used by Franz Neumann in "Notes on the Theory of Dictatorship," in *The Democratic and the Authoritarian State,* Glencoe, Ill.: The Free Press, 1957, p. 251.

16. See the articles by Richard Hofstadter and by Seymour Lipset in Daniel Bell (ed.), *The New American Right,* New York: Criterion Books, 1955. For a fuller treatment of this theme see Seymour M. Lipset, "Social Stratification and Right-Wing Extremism," *British Journal of Sociology,* 10 (December, 1959), 1–32.

17. Murray Edelman, "Government's Balance of Power in Labor-Management Relations," *Labor Law Journal,* 2 (January, 1951), 31–35. This point is also discussed in C. Wright Mills, *The Power Elite, op. cit.,* pp. 246–248.

18. David Riesman, *The Lonely Crowd, op. cit.,* pp. 242–255.

19. Joseph LaPalombara, "Political Party Systems and Crisis Government: French and Italian Contrasts," *Midwest Journal of Political Science,* 11 (May, 1958), 117–139.

20. *Ibid.,* p. 133.

21. Murray and Susan Stedman, *Discontent at the Polls,* New York: Columbia University Press, 1950, Ch. 8.

22. Seymour M. Lipset, "Economic Development and Democracy," in *Political Man, op. cit.,* pp. 45–76.

23. Mannheim, *op. cit.,* p. 70. For discussions of the assumption of a natural harmony of interests see the analysis of sociological thought in C. Wright Mills, *op. cit.,* Chap. 11; Werner Stark, "Christian Thought in Social Theory" in *Social Theory and Christian Thought,* London: Routledge and Kegan Paul, 1959. Ralf Dahrendorf, *Class and Class Conflict in Industrial Society,* Stanford, Calif.: Stanford University Press, 1958.

24. See the discussions of this factor in the history of labor movements in Sidney and Beatrice Webb, *History of Trade Unionism,* New York: Longmans, Green and Co., 1920, Chap. 1, and in Selig Perlman, *Theory of the Labor Movement,* New York: Augustus M. Kelly, 1928, Chap. 5.

25. Martin Trow, "Small Business, Political Tolerance, and Support For McCarthy," *American Journal of Sociology,* 64 (November, 1958), 270–281.

26. Oscar Gass, "Socialism and Democracy," *Commentary,* 29 (June, 1960), 574.

27. For an especially illuminating statement of this view, see Adolf Lowe, *The Price of Liberty,* Day-to-Day Pamphlets, No. 36, London: Hogarth Press, 1937. Also see Edward A. Shils and M. Young, "The Meaning of the Coronation," *Sociological Review,* series 1, 1953, pp. 63–81. Political consensus as a focus of sociological study is a central theme in Seymour M. Lipset, "Political Sociology" in Robert K. Merton, Leonard Broom, and Leonard S. Cottrell, Jr. (eds.), *Sociology Today,* New York: Basic Books, 1959.

28. Edward A. Shils, "Mass Society and Its Culture," *op. cit.,* p. 288.

29. Robert K. Merton, "Patterns of Influence" in Paul Lazarsfeld and Frank Stanton (eds.), *Communications Research,* 1948–49, New York: Harper and Bros., 1949, pp. 180–219; Alvin W. Gouldner, "Cosmopolitans and Locals," *Administrative Science Quarterly,* 2 (December, 1957 and March, 1958), 281–306, 444–480.

30. Will Herberg, *Protestant, Catholic, Jew,* New York: Doubleday Anchor Books, 1955.

31. Studies of tolerance and authoritarianism have repeatedly shown a direct relation between amount of education and tolerance for political diversity. See Martin Trow, *op. cit.,* and the summarization of many studies in Seymour Lipset, "Working-Class Authoritarianism," *Political Man, op. cit.*

32. Melvin Tumin, *Desegregation,* Princeton, N.J.: Princeton University Press, 1958.

33. This distinction and the terms "pluralistic" and "superimposed" are used in Ralf Dahrendorf, *op. cit.,* pp. 213–218.

34. Seymour M. Lipset, *Political Man, op. cit.,* pp. 131–134, 173–176.

35. David Riesman, *op. cit.,* also see Joseph Gusfield, "Social Structure and Moral Reform," *American Journal of Sociology,* 61 (November, 1955), 221–232.

36. Alexis de Tocqueville, *Democracy in America,* New York and London: Oxford University Press, 1947, pp. 493–499.

71. THE POLITICAL CULTURE OF SOUTHERN CALIFORNIA

JAMES Q. WILSON

Everyone seems to have a picture of Brooklyn, of Texas, and of Southern California. The latter is usually viewed as the land of alienation, the source of the "plastic society," and the incubator of extremist politics. Those who live (or have lived) in such places have a different idea.

Here, in an article written shortly before the 1968 national political conventions, political scientist James Q. Wilson describes what it was like growing up in "Reagan Country"—and what it is like there today. He does not deny the existence of regional differences but puts them in their proper perspective (while dispelling several widely held myths).

James Q. Wilson is Professor of Political Science at Harvard University. A list of his publication is presented on page 742 of this volume.

A person like myself, who grew up in Southern California, finds it increasingly difficult to understand people who say they understand California. "Explaining California," especially Southern California, has always been a favorite pastime for New Yorkers and Bostonians who have changed planes in Los Angeles, or made a two-day trip to the RAND Corporation, or just speculated on what kind of state could be responsible for Hollywood. Nor need one be an Eastern to play the game; living in San Francisco carries with it a permanent license not only to explain but to explain away (*far* away) Los Angeles.

This game might have been regarded as an amusing (though to me, irritating) diversion so long as what was being explained or "understood" was Hollywood and Vine, or orange-juice stands shaped like oranges, or Aimee Semple McPherson, or the Great I Am, or traffic on the Los Angeles freeways. It became a little less amusing when the same "explanations" thought appropriate for Aimee and the poor orange-juice vendors (most of whom, by the way, have disappeared) were applied to the John Birch Society and other manifestations of the Far Right. Anybody crazy enough to buy orange juice at such places or to drive on those freeways must be crazy enough to be a Bircher. Let two Birchite loud-mouths pop off anywhere else in the country and we rush to our sociology texts to see whether it is alienation or the decline of the small entrepreneur that is the cause; let two of them say the same thing in Los Angeles, and we just smile knowingly and murmur, "It figures."

Even this systematic application of the double standard was harmless enough before Ronald Reagan. Now a striking conservative personality has become governor of the largest state in the union by an election plurality of over a million votes, most of which he picked up in Southern California. This Hollywood-actor-turned-politician ("it figures") has, to the amazement of many, made a rather considerable

Reprinted from *Commentary,* by permission; Copyright © 1967 by the American Jewish Committee. This article was originally entitled "A Guide to Reagan Country. The Political Culture of Southern California."

impression, not only on the voters of his state but on Republicans around the country including, apparently, a group of presumably toughminded fellow governors. From now at least through the 1968 convention we have to take Reagan quite seriously, and even if he fails to go the distance we must, I think, take Reaganism seriously. It will be with us for a long time under one guise or another. We will not take it seriously by trying to explain it away as if it were something sold at one of those orange-juice stands or preached from the pulpit at some cultist church.

I grew up in Reagan country—not Hollywood, but the lower-middle-class suburbs of Los Angeles. It was a distinctive way of life. I think I could still recognize another person who grew up there no matter where I should meet him, just as surely as an Italian can spot a person from his village or region even though they are both now in Queens. I am under no illusion that anyone has the slightest interest in my boyhood (I have next to no interest in it myself), but I do suspect that it may be useful to try to explain what it was like at least in general terms, and how what it was like is relevant to what is happening there today. Though I grew up and went to school there, I left a long time ago in order to acquire some expensive Eastern postgraduate degrees and a political outlook that would now make me vote against Reagan if I had the chance. I do not intend here to write an apology for Reagan; even if I thought like that, which I don't, I would never write it down anywhere my colleagues at Harvard might read it.

–1–

The important thing to know about Southern California is that the people who live there, who grew up there, love it. Not just the way one has an attachment to a hometown, any hometown, but the way people love the realization that they have found the right mode of life. People who live in Southern California are not richer or better educated than those who live in New York; the significant point about them is that they don't live in New York, and don't want to. If they did, they—the average Los Angeleno (my family, for example)—would have lived most of their lives in a walkup flat in, say, the Yorkville section of Manhattan or not far off Flatbush Avenue in Brooklyn. Given their income in 1930, life would have been crowded, noisy, cold, threatening—in short, *urban*. In Long Beach or Inglewood or Huntington Park or Bellflower, by contrast, life was carried on in a detached house with a lawn in front and a car in the garage, part of a quiet neighborhood, with no crime (except kids racing noisy cars), no cold, no smells, no congestion. The monthly payments on that bungalow —one or two bedrooms, one bath, a minuscule dining room, and never enough closets—would have been no more than the rent on the walkup flat in Brooklyn or Yorkville. In 1940, with the Depression still in force, *over half the population* of Los Angeles lived in single-family homes. Only about half of these were owner-occupied, but even to rent a house was such a vast improvement over renting an apartment that nobody looked back; they only looked ahead to the time they could pick up their own mortgage. San Francisco in the same year was another matter. Only a third of the population lived in single-family homes there, the reason being that there were almost no *houses* to rent; if you wanted a house, you had to buy it, and not many people in 1940 could afford to buy.

There has been a good deal of loose talk about "radical" politics (which I suppose means anything to the Right of Earl Warren) developing out of a rootless, highly mobile population with no sense of *place*, of continuity, of stability. That may explain radical politics somewhere, but not in Los Angeles. The people who voted for Reagan have lived for years, in many cases decades, in Southern California. And they have lived in houses, not anonymous, impersonal apartment buildings.

Indeed, it was during the period of Los Angeles's greatest population growth that it voted, over and over again, .for Earl Warren—the very embodiment (then) of moderation. The explanation, I believe, is quite simple: truly rootless, mobile people are more likely to vote the way established institutions—newspapers, churches, labor unions, business firms—tell them to vote. Revolutions are never made by the last man to get off the train; they are made by those who got off a long time ago and, having put down roots and formed their own assessment of matters, have the confidence, the long-nurtured discontent, and the knowledge of how to get things done sufficient to support independent political action. (Radical politics, I suspect, follows the same pattern as Negro riots: contrary to what the McCone Commission asserted but did not prove, the Negroes who rioted in Watts—or at least those who rioted violently enough to get themselves arrested—were Negroes who had been in Watts for a long time. Over half the teenage Negroes arrested had been *born* in California; over three-fourths had lived there for more than five years.)

In any case, it is a mistake to try to explain a particular election by underlying social trends. Elections, after all, are choices, and how they come out depends on who the voters have to choose between. That Reagan won last year does not mean that *last year* some ineluctable social force finally surfaced and carried the day. A vote for Reaganism was always possible in Southern California (and had revealed itself in countless congressional and local elections). The point I wish to make is that there has for a long time been a "Reagan point of view" in the Southern California electorate, that this point of view was powerfully shaped by the kinds of people who went to California and the conditions of life there.

The people who in 1940 lived in those hundreds of thousands of detached and semi-detached homes came from all over the country, but primarily they came from the Midwest, the border states, and the "near South." Almost none came from Europe: about 6 per cent, to be exact, had been born in Italy, Ireland, England, Germany, France, Sweden, or Russia; another 2½ per cent had been born in Mexico. (In San Francisco, the proportion of foreign-born was twice as large.) But 28 per cent had been born in the American heartland—the dustbowl states (Texas, Oklahoma, Arkansas, Louisiana, Kansas, Nebraska), or the border states (Indiana, Missouri, Tennessee, Kentucky) and the upper plains (Iowa, Wisconsin, Minnesota, the Dakotas). If you add in the nearby mountain and Southwestern states (Colorado, Utah, Arizona, New Mexico, Nevada), the total proportion rises to over a third. And if you add in the persons whose parents had been born in these states, the proportion no doubt (there are no figures) exceeds a half. Again, San Francisco is a contrast—only about a tenth of its people in 1940 were from the heartland states. Between 1920 and 1940, during the Depression, over 400,000 persons born in the heartland moved to Los Angeles. *Less than a tenth* as many moved to San Francisco.

Except for Arkansas, Louisiana, and Texas, no Southern states are included in these migration figures. This is important to bear in mind—such conservatism as Southern California displays was not imported from the Deep South. In fact, even those who came from Southern states were likely to be from places like West Texas, where Confederate sentiment was never very strong.

These migrants were rural and small-town people. And here, of course, another popular explanation of Southern California politics takes the stage. These voters are supposed to yearn for the simpler life and the small-town virtues that they left behind. They are reactionary, it is claimed, in the precise sense: seeking to turn back the clock to a day when life was easier, virtues less complicated, and the Ten Commandments a sufficient guide. Perhaps so—there is no doubt some truth in this. But it flies in the face of the fact that these are people who *left* small-town and rural America (millions more stayed behind, after all)—and left it for jobs in big defense plants and large office buildings. I was never aware of any effort to re-create small-town America in Southern California, unless you put in that category the Victory Gardens people planted to raise vegetables during the war. On the contrary, they adopted rather quickly a suburban style of life, with its attendant devotion to the growing of a decent lawn (how many farms have you ever seen with a good lawn?). Furthermore, it is not the migrants themselves who on the whole have voted for Reaganism, but their children. The migrants voted for Roosevelt and Upton Sinclair and looked on disapprovingly as their children began to adopt the hedonistic mores of Southern California teenage life. There was as much intergenerational conflict among the Okies and Arkies in California as among the Italians and the Irish in Boston or New York. And yet it was these youngsters who grew up, married, moved out to Orange County or to Lakewood, and voted for Reagan and castigated Pat Brown, the last of the New Deal-Fair Deal Democrats. (To be completely accurate, a lot of the older people voted for Reagan, too, but they, I imagine, found it much harder to let go of their traditional attachment to Franklin Roosevelt and Earl Warren; the young people had no trouble at all.)

This is not to say that the migrants brought nothing with them. On the contrary, they brought an essential ingredient of Southern California life—fundamentalist Protestant individualism. We like to think of the store-front church as being a Negro invention; not so. I remember scores of white store-front churches— mostly of small Pentecostal and Adventist sects—lining the main streets of Long Beach. Most people, of course, went to established churches, but these were only bigger and slightly more orthodox versions of the same thing—Baptists, Methodists, Mormons, Brethren, Church of God, and so on. Church was a very important part of life, but hardly any two people belonged to the same one. We were Catholics, and we had to drive out into the dairy forming country (I will never forget the way Sunday morning smelled —incense and cow manure, in equal portions) where there were enough Mexican farmhands and Dutch Catholic dairymen to make up a parish. All my friends sang hymns and listened to "preachin'." And the preaching was evangelical, fundamentalist, and preoccupied with the obligation of the *individual* to find and enter into a right relationship with God, with no sacraments, rituals, covenants, or grace to make it easy.

The religious character of San Francisco was strikingly different. In 1936 (the last time the government took a census of church organizations), 70 per cent of the reported church membership of San Francisco, but only 40 per cent of that in Los Angeles, was Catholic. And of the claimed members of Protestant sects, 40 per cent in San Francisco, but only 26 per cent in Los Angeles, belonged to the high-status, non-fundamentalist churches—Congregational, Episcopalian, Unitarian, and Universalist. Both cities had about the same proportion of Jews, but, as will be argued in a moment, the leadership, at least, of the two Jewish communities was rather different. Los Angeles, and even more its middle-class suburbs, was Protestant and fundamentalist Protestant at that.

The social structure did nothing to change the individualistic orientation of life. People had no identities except their personal identities, no obvious group affiliations to make possible any reference to them by collective nouns. I never heard the phrase "ethnic group" until I was in graduate school. I never knew there were Irishmen (I was amazed many years later to learn that, at least on my mother's side, I had been one all along) or Italians (except funny organ grinders in the movies, all of whom looked like Chico Marx). We knew there were Negroes (but none within miles of where we lived) and Jews (they ran Hollywood and New York, we knew, but not many of us had ever met one). Nobody ever even pointed out to me that I was a Catholic (except once, when a friend explained that that was probably the reason I wouldn't join the Order of De Molay, a young people's Masonic group).

The absence of such group identities and of neighborhoods associated with those identities may be one reason for the enormous emphasis on "personality." Teen-agers everywhere, of course, place great stock in this, mostly, I suppose, because they feel such an urgent need to establish an identity and to be liked by others. But in Southern California, it went far beyond that—there was a cult of personality that dominated every aspect of life. Everybody was compared in terms of his or her personality; contests for student-body office were based on it. To be "popular" and "sincere" was vital. In a New York high school, by contrast, personality would have to share importance in such contests with a certain amount of bloc voting among the Irish, Italians, and Jews, or between "project" people and brownstone people, or even between leftists and far leftists.

Perhaps because of the absence of ethnic and religious blocs which in turn are associated with certain political positions, perhaps because Southern California (then) was very remote from those urban centers where "The Future of Socialism" was being earnestly debated, student life in and around Los Angeles was remarkably apolitical. Most people were vaguely for Roosevelt, though there was a substantial (and growing) group that announced defiantly that while their parents had voted for FDR in '32, and perhaps even in '36, they weren't going to do *that* anymore. Registered Democrats who voted Republican were commonplace, but after noting that fact there wasn't, politically, much left to be said. (It was different in downtown Los Angeles where the Jews lived; L.A. High, and later Los Angeles State College, were very political. A considerable Wallace movement flourished in 1948. Many of those people are now in the Democratic club movement.)

Politics for these people came to mean, in later years, expressing directly one's individual political preferences and expecting them to be added up by a kind of political algebra into a general statement of the public interest. "Bloc voting" and group preferences were unheard of and, when heard of, unthinkable. And the idea that political parties ought to do anything besides help add up preferences was most heterodox—the worst thing that could be said about it was that it was "Eastern." The well-known institutional features of California's political system—weak parties, the extensive use of the referendum to decide policy issues, nonpartisanship— were perfectly matched to the political mentality that was nurtured in Southern California.

That nurturing was distinctive but hard to describe. Rural Anglo-Saxon Protestants have lived in lots of states, but they haven't produced the Southern California style of politics anywhere else. One reason is to be found in what it was like, and to a considerable extent is still like, to grow up in Southern California. Everybody, as I have already noted, lived in a single-family house. There was no public transportation to speak of, so that the movement of people within the city followed no set corridors. People moved about freely and in so doing saw how everybody lived. That movement was institutionalized in the Sunday Afternoon Drive—not to the beach or an amusement park, but just "around" to look at homes, call on friends, or visit distant relatives. A house was, as a Catholic might put it, the outward and visible sign of inward grace. There was no anonymity provided by apartment buildings or tenements or projects. Each family had a house; there it was, for all to see and inspect. With a practiced glance, one could tell how much it cost, how well it was cared for, how good a lawn had been coaxed into uncertain life, and how tastefully plants and shrubs had been set out.

A strong, socially reinforced commitment to property was thus developed, evident in how people treat those homes today. An enormous amount of energy and money is devoted to repairing, improving, remodeling, extending, and landscaping. Even in areas with fairly low incomes, such as those where the elderly and the retired live, houses are not on the whole allowed to deteriorate. A family might buy a house for six or seven thousand dollars with, for the period, a big mortgage, and then spend several times that over a generation or two in home improvements. Those who could not afford it substituted labor for capital. People were practicing do-it-yourself in Southern California long before anybody in the advertising business thought to give it a name. Year-round warm weather made year-round outdoor labor possible —and, of course, year-round outdoor inspection by one's critical neighbors.

Much of this labor was cooperative. The Southern California equivalent of the Eastern uncle who could "get it for you wholesale" was the Los Angeles brother-in-law who would help you put on a new roof, or paint the garage, or lend you (and show you how to use) his power saw. A vast, informally organized labor exchange permeated the region, with occasional trades of great complexity running through several intermediaries—the friend who would ask his brother, the plumber, to help you if you would ask

your uncle with the mixer to lay the concrete in front of somebody's sister's home. Saturday saw people driving all over the county carrying out these assignments.

Driving. Driving everywhere, over great distances, with scarcely any thought to the enormous mileages they were logging. A car was the absolutely essential piece of social overhead capital. With it, you could get a job, meet a girl, hang around with the boys, go to a drive-in, see football games away from home, take in the beach parties at Laguna or Corona del Mar, or go to the Palladium ballroom in Hollywood. To have a car meant being somebody; to have to borrow a car meant knowing somebody; to have no car at all, owned or borrowed, was to be left out— way out.

Those cars led parents and professional moralists to speak of "teen-agers and their jalopies." They were not jalopies—not to us, anyway. The oldest, most careworn Ford Model A was a thing of beauty. To be sure, the beauty often had to be coaxed out; yet what was life for but to do the coaxing and take credit for the beauty? Beauty, of course, meant different things to different boys. For some, it was speed and power; and so they would drop a V-8 block into the "A" chassis and then carefully, lovingly, bore it out, stroke it, port it, and put two barrels or four barrels on it. For others, beauty was in the body, not the engine, and their energies would go into customizing the car—dropping the rear end, chopping down the top, leading the fenders, stripping off the chrome (it took Detroit decades to recognize the merits of these changes and then to mass-produce them), and above all painting, sanding, rubbing, painting, sanding, rubbing—for ten or fifteen or twenty coats, usually of metallic paint. Again, warm weather made it easier—you could work outside year round and if you ran out of money before the job was finished (which was most of the time), you could drive around in the unfinished product with no top, primed but not painted, and no hood over the engine. Of late, Mr. Tom Wolfe of *New York* magazine has discovered car customizing and decided it is a folk art. It wasn't folk art in the 40's; it was life.

The sense of property developed by this activity has never been measured and perhaps never can be; I am convinced it was enormous and fundamental. After marriage, devoting energy to the improvement of a house was simply a grown-up extension of what, as a juvenile, one had done with cars. There is, of course, a paradox here: the car was used in great part to get girls. It was a hand-polished, custom-made rolling bedroom, or so its creators hoped. (In this they were as often disappointed as a Harvard man taking a Radcliffe girl into his house rooms during parietal hours; every girl likes to be *seen* in such places, but a distressingly small proportion are inclined to *do* anything there.) But the hedonistic purposes to which the car might be put did not detract from its power to create and sustain a very conventional and bourgeois sense of property and responsibility, for in the last analysis the car was not a means to an end but an end in itself. Shocked parents never got that point: they saw the excess that the car permitted, they did not see the intensely middle-class values that it instilled.

Low-density, single-family homes, a lack of public transportation, the absence of ethnic neighborhoods, and the use of cars combined to prevent the formation of streetcorner gangs, except in very central portions of Los Angeles and one or two older cities. The principal after-school occupation of a teen-ager Eastern boy from a working-class family is to "hang out" at the corner candy-store, the ice-cream parlor, or in front of the drugstore with class and ethnic compatriots. Having a "corner" of your own—or having "turf," in the case of the ambitious and imperialistic —would have made no sense to an equivalent group of young men in Southern California. The Eastern life-style produced a feeling of *territory,* the Western

life-style a feeling of *property*. Teen-agers in Southern California hung out together, to be sure, but not in any fixed spot, and where they did hang out tended to be a place reached by a car, with lots of free parking for other cars. The drive-in restaurant was the premier institution catering to this need. But it was also a very democratic institution, since it was not (and because of its location some distance from one's home, could not become) the "turf" of any particular gang. Rich and poor, Protestant and Catholic, anybody with a car could get there and, barring a losing fight over a girl, stay there. There were rivalries, but like modern warfare they tended to be between large, heterogeneous, and impersonal rivals—one high school against another, not one ethnic group against another.

Can all this explain why Southern California is so different, politically, from Northern California—why it, so much more than the Bay Area, supported Goldwater and Reagan? Perhaps not entirely. And yet I believe the kind of people living there and their life-styles are very important, much more important than, say, the presumed influence of the conservative Los Angeles *Times*. The Oakland *Tribune* is even more conservative, but the East Bay region it serves is more "liberal" in its voting than L.A. And the very liberal McClatchey newspapers in the Central Valley do not seem to have turned back the Reagan tide. On the other hand, San Francisco has Southern-California-style suburbs as well, with bungalows and cars and the like, and the people there are not as conservative as their counterparts in the South. But as we have seen, the people who migrated to San Francisco in the 30's and 40's were different from those who settled in Los Angeles. And once the different life-styles of the two cities became apparent, non-Californians must have begun deciding to move to the Bay Area or to Los Angeles on the basis, in part, of what they had heard about those styles. A small but visible difference in the beginning thus became a very large difference in the end.

–2–

The political institutions and economic character of Southern California reinforced the life style and gave it expression. Politics, as I have said, was nonpartisan, free-swinging, slightly populistic—a direct appeal to the people was to be made on all issues. The major parties for decades were virtually moribund and therefore never performed their customary (and to my thinking, desirable) task of aggregating interests, blurring issues, strengthening party loyalties, and finding moderate candidates. Not that the people wanted immoderate candidates. So long, at least, as the issues were not very grave—before civil rights, and welfare, and Berkeley, and crime—they wanted honest, competent administrators who favored change but in an orderly manner. In Earl Warren they got such a man and he made sure the regular Republican party, whose fat cats were on the whole considerably to his Right, would not have a chance to replace him. He built a personal following outside the regular, and cumbersome, party apparatus. Like most personal followings, however, it made no provision for a transfer of power. The obvious Warren protégé—Thomas Kuchel—was in the Senate, Warren's personal following in the state could not be handed to another man, and the party was in no shape to find a candidate of its own. Any man with money and a good smile could take a crack at capturing the nomination on his own, and many did.

Such organization as existed tended to be in the North, rather than the South. San Francisco and Alameda County across the bay had more in the way of party machinery, financed on a steady basis, than the South had, at least until the emergence of the California Democratic clubs. A little organization goes a long way in an organizational vaccuum, and

the North exercised a disproportionate influence in California politics for some time. The Northern Democrats had some old families—many Jewish—who helped pay the party's bills during the long, lean years.

The South had few such persons—or more accurately, it had some very rich, self-made men from the oil business and from the vast agricultural enterprises of the Imperial Valley who were conservative Democrats in the (by now) well-documented tradition of the American Southwest. They may be more visible in Texas today, but twenty years ago they were more influential in California.

Why? There were Jews in Southern California, tens of thousands of them in and around Los Angeles. (Yet looking back on my high-school days, I can think of only one Jew I was personally acquainted with, and he went to another high school across town. Jews were Hollywood, we all knew.) Many of them were in the movie industry and in command of wealth and great resources for publicity. Why didn't they help to finance and lead the Southern California Democratic party? Some did—or tried—at least for a while. A high point of that influence was the 1950 senatorial campaign of the liberal Helen Gahagan Douglas, the movie actress. It wasn't George Murphy or Ronald Reagan who put Hollywood into politics, it was Mrs. Douglas, who lost to Richard Nixon. Two years before, many of her supporters had turned, in frustration, to third-party politics and become important figures in the 1948 campaign of Henry Wallace. It was a disaster. Bolting the party nationally was a far more serious thing than bolting it locally, where it could hardly be said to exist. The Truman Democrats took control in California and, when Communist party influence in the Wallace movement became too obvious to be denied (Wallace himself was to admit it later), they were in a position to treat the Douglas and Wallace Democrats as thoroughly discredited in the eyes of the voters. Shortly thereafter, the era of McCarthyism descended upon the country, and in Hollywood involvement in politics was for the time being finished. What Mrs. Douglas had begun, Henry Wallace and Joe McCarthy succeeded in ending.

But it was not only that Hollywood Jews had lost power, it was also that Hollywood Jews were different from those in other urban centers. The social and economic heights of Hollywood were commanded, not by German Jews, but by East Europeans; not by old families but by immigrants; not by Wall Street smoothness but by *nouveau riche* entrepreneurship. Such Hollywood money as went into politics was used much as money was then used in the movie industry—impulsively, by dictatorial men used to having their own way, and on behalf of "stars." If the star system worked on the movie lots, why couldn't it work in politics? Thus, a glamorous figure, a big name, and occasionally a conspicuous nut could get *personal* backing for a campaign, but there was little or no money for organization, for routine affairs, or for professional (and necessarily bureaucratic) leadership.

Anyway, the voter wasn't much interested in liberalism even if it could be financed. Los Angeles was prosperous, and even greater prosperity seemed just around the corner. The aircraft plants and shipyards had taken tens of thousands of families and given every member, including the mother, a job, thereby putting them, in four years' time, in a wholly different and higher economic bracket. A generation of slow gain was compressed into a few years; progress wasn't around the corner, or something you hoped for for your kids, it was right here and now. War prosperity affected the whole country, but it had a special effect on Southern California—there was more of it, because there was more war industry located there, and it benefited people who only a few years before had been fighting for survival on a dust-swept farm in the Texas panhandle. John Steinbeck has told us how those farmers and sharecroppers saw California as the Promised Land. But they had only been promised relief checks from the Farm Security Administration; instead, they found overtime checks from Lockheed.

Next to the kind of people who live there, the rate of economic growth of Southern California—and today, of the whole Southwest—is the main key to its political life. Visiting scholars make much of the business domination of Dallas, or the presumed influence of the Los Angeles *Times* in Southern California, or the "Chamber of Commerce mentality" of San Diego. The important thing to understand is that these have not been alien influences imposed from above on the populace—they are merely the more obvious indicators of the fact that business values are widely shared. (Not business *control;* voters are as quick to resent that, when it is pointed out to them, in Los Angeles as anywhere. Sam Yorty became mayor by running against the *Times* and other "downtown interests," and he is still very popular in his city, however much ridicule he may take from Robert Kennedy in Washington.) Business values are here meant in the widest sense—a desire for expansion and growth, a high rate of increase in property values, finding and developing mass markets, and keeping capital moving and labor productive.

No one was immune from this psychology. How could he be? Everyone was buying, or intended to buy, his own home. Many factory workers and salesmen speculated in real estate on the side. A favorite topic of conversation at our dinner table, and I am sure at thousands of dinner tables just like it, was the latest story about the fantastic price a certain parcel had just been sold for and what a shame it was that we passed up the chance to buy it two years ago for peanuts. (We never seemed to have enough peanuts around at the right time.) The purpose of government was to facilitate this growth—open up new land, bring in water, make credit easy, keep the defense plants rolling. Government was not there to keep painfully-acquired positions secure by paying out benefits or legislating new regulations. Government was there to help bring in the future, not protect the past.

Not everyone felt this way, of course. Elderly people who came to California to retire had a different view. They wanted pensions, benefits, regulations. They were numerous and visible, but though they come quickly to mind when one thinks back on the shuffleboard and croquet courts at Lincoln Park in Long Beach or on the soapbox orators and bench-sitters in Pershing Square in Los Angeles, they were never representative of the local political ethos. They were the butt of countless jokes and the target for much political criticism: they wanted to hold back tomorrow (it was believed), cash their relief checks, and lie in the sun. That was *wrong,* most working families thought. The Negro, who today is the victim of the anti-welfare sentiment, was actually the second victim; the first was the old folks. They were attacked for moving to California "just to get a pension," told to "go back where they came from," and fought against in countless welfare issues. (About the only thing they were spared were allegations that they constituted a sexual threat. I cannot recall my father, no paragon of tolerance, ever trying to clinch an argument against a liberal by asking him how he would like it if his daughter grew up and married an old man.)

The old folks fought back, but in California it was a *protest* movement. George McLain organized the old folks (nobody ever called them "senior citizens"; they didn't even call themselves that) and made them a potent force in state politics, but it was a force directed *against* the two major parties and their candidates. He won concessions for his followers and now they may be so secure as to be accepted as a political fact of life; what they wanted, however, was never accepted.

Southern California's political culture, including but not limited to what might be called Reaganism, is one which I suspect is characteristic of areas experiencing rapid economic growth and general prosperity, especially if there are few institutions—political parties, churches, labor unions—to frame the issues and blunt popular instincts. People there are concerned about the growth in the size of the economic pie, not (except for the elderly) in preserving the size of their present slice. The attributes in a person to be admired are those which indicate his ability to enhance his position and expand his resources, not conserve his position and maintain his resources. If I had to cite only one way in which Southwestern politics differ from Northeastern politics, it would be this: the former region is developmental, future-oriented, and growth-conscious; the latter is conserving, past- or present-oriented, and security-conscious. Note that I say "conserving," not conservative; there is a difference. The Northeast by some measures is less "conservative" than the Southwest, though it is easy to exaggerate the difference. A conserv*ative* is usually thought of as a person who favors limited government, minimized administrative involvement in private affairs, maximum free choice. A conserv*er,* on the other hand, needs *more* government in order to protect present stakes from change, from threats posed by other groups, and from competition.

Before we get carried away with the difference, some qualifications are in order. There are conserving forces at work in Southern California. One is the elderly. Another is the slowly emerging labor movement. For years Lost Angeles was a tough city in which to be a trade unionist. There are still people who remember with horror the bombing of the Los Angeles *Times.* But unions are making headway. One is the Retail Clerks, which is organizing in the supermarkets and dime stores; another is the Machinists, active in aircraft and auto assembly plants. And the region's economic growth has not unleashed anything like the hysteria of the Florida land boom.

Even more important as a challenge to the general political culture of the region, with its concern for property, propriety, individual responsibility, economic growth, and limited government, is ideological liberalism. By the time McCarthyism was ending and the blacklists were beginning to lose their grip on Hollywood (perhaps because faced with the competition from television and European producers, Hollywood could no longer afford the luxury of a blacklist), Adlai Stevenson was making his appearance as a force in the Democratic party. The enormous outpouring of support for him in Southern California has been oft remarked upon, as has the vigorous club movement that grew up in the aftermath of his 1952 and 1956 Presidential campaigns. The movement activated a wholly new generation of political enthusiasts and provided a new base of operations for some of the leftovers from older forms of liberal and radical politics.

These clubs did not recruit the people I have been describing in earlier pages, nor have they taken hold in the areas in which these people live. The clubs grew up on the northern and eastern periphery of the region—the Hollywood hills, Santa Monica, Beverly Hills, Pacific Palisades, and out into the college towns, such as Pomona, in the interior. Young Jews, young intellectuals, persons transplanted to Los Angeles from the East (by 1940, about 10 per cent of the population had been born in New England, New Jersey, or Pennsylvania), and older California radicals flocked into the clubs. But the clubs never really took root among the working-class and middle-class bungalows of Long Beach, Inglewood, or Redondo Beach, to say nothing of Orange County to the Southeast. The Democratic clubs initially had little interest in Southern California; they were interested in national and international issues. (The civil-rights movement has changed that; the clubs are now deeply involved in such matters locally.) They had, at the outset, no real program for California (though they had one for just about everything else), and thus there was no necessary conflict between what they wanted and what those who later voted for Reagan wanted—no necessary conflict, perhaps, but conflict nonetheless. And the most intense kind of conflict, for what was at stake were large and symbolic issues—Red China, capital punishment, world peace, and civil liberties. The Southern California electorate quickly became deeply polarized.

The polarization is not immediately evident in voting statistics. In the aggregate, Southern California elects a mixture of liberals and conservatives much like any other region, and on many of its famous referenda votes for and against public expenditures about like other areas. But these aggregate figures conceal the real symptoms of polarization—several Democrats (not all) are as far to the Left of their party as is possible; several Republicans (not all) are as far to the Right of their party as possible. And on referenda issues—especially those involving such matters as open occupancy in housing—the returns and the polls suggest that Southern California has both the most intense proponents and the most intense opponents (the latter outnumbering the former: the region as a whole was against fair housing by a considerable margin; in San Francisco, the vote was both less lopsided and, I suspect, based on less intensely polarized views). This is *not* the same thing as saying that Southern California is more "bigoted" than the Bay Area. Because of the way the issue was framed, people were asked to vote *for* the *right* to sell their property to whomever they chose. In Southern California, property rights are vital and freedom in their exercise staunchly defended. There have been, I would guess, fewer attacks on Negro families seeking homes in white neighborhoods in Southern California than in, say, Pennsylvania, Ohio, or Illinois. The housing issue was fought out at a more general level—not over whether one was for or against Negroes, but over alternative conceptions of what freedom requires. And the polarization of opinion on this issue, as on most, was most intense among persons of higher status. The educated, affluent Easterners and intellectuals (who work in law firms or the communications media or the universities) are more inclined than their less well-off fellows to support the Democratic clubs and liberalism; the educated, affluent sons and daughters of the Midwestern migrants (who now work as engineers and accountants in aerospace and petroleum industries) are more inclined than their less well-off fellows to support Goldwater and Reagan.

–3–

Is Southern California's political culture unique? Not really—it is but the earliest, most publicized, and most heavily populated example of a pattern now to be found throughout much of the Southwest. It appeared first in Southern California because more people went there and because California's political institutions gave almost immediate expression to it. In other states, the party structure constrained its free expression for a time; the ambitions of rival politicians and factions in Texas and Arizona made the ideology less evident, at least for a while. Goldwater's easy victory at the 1964 Republican convention indicates how widespread are certain aspects of that culture—in fact, it overstates it, because Goldwater himself overstated many features of that culture. The Southern Californians about whom I have written want limited government, personal responsibility, "basic" education, a resurgence of patriotism, an end to "chiseling," and a more restrained Supreme Court. They are not quite so cer-

tain that they want an adventurous foreign policy or a high-risk international confrontation with Communism. No doubt the militant Goldwater enthusiasts wanted such a policy, but they must have mistaken what the rank-and-file would support. Reagan has not yet made the same mistake—he took Goldwater's views, stripped away the foreign policy (except for very general statements) and references to turning back the clock on Social Security (after all, he wanted a coalition between the elderly and the young).

But Goldwater, however badly-managed his campaign, won the convention and won it by methods and with supporters which, in whatever state they were found, could very easily have been found in Southern California. Amateur political clubs, impassioned volunteers, appeals to highly moral and symbolic issues—the Republican party professionals had, to their profound irritation, to put up with all of it, just as party professionals in California, Democrats and Republicans alike, have been putting up with it since the early 1950's.

The Southern California political style is spreading; it seems to be, at least in the Western part of the United States, the concomitant of the American success story. There, millions of people are realizing their ambitions. They are not "rootless" or yearning for "small-town simplicity" or profoundly irritated by all the hustle and bustle; they are acquiring security, education, living space, and a lifestyle that is based in its day-to-day routine on gentility, courtesy, hospitality, virtue. Why, then, are they so discontent? It is not with their lot that they are discontent, it is with the lot of the nation. *The very virtues they have and practice are, in their eyes, conspicuously absent from society as a whole.* Politics is corrupt—not in the petty sense, though there is that—but in the large sense; to these people, it consists of "deals," of the catering to selfish interests, of cynical manipulation and double-talk. The universities are corrupt—children don't act as if they appreciate what is being given them, they don't work hard, and they are lectured to by devious and wrongheaded professors. And above all, everywhere they look, somebody is trying to get "something for nothing," and succeeding.

These views may not be confined only to the political culture in which they are now articulated. Surveys I have taken, and others I have read, indicate that the single most widespread concern of middle-class Americans is over the "decay of values" —evidenced by "crime in the streets," juvenile delinquency, public lewdness, and the like, but going much beyond these manifestations to include everything that suggests that people no longer act in accordance with decent values and right reason. In many places, especially in the Northeast, our political institutions (happily) do not allow such views to play much part in elections. Parties, led by professionals, instinctively shun such issues, feeling somehow that public debate over virtue is irrelevant (what can government do about it?) and dangerous (nobody can agree on what virtue is or that your party has more of it). Powerful non-political institutions tend, also, to keep such issues out of politics or to insist that they be matters of private conscience. For one, the Catholic Church, which draws the religious and moral interests of its followers inward, toward the sacraments and the educational and religious facilities of the Church which must be maintained and served. For another, large labor unions which have never mistaken a "stamp out smut" campaign for a fifty-cent increase in the minimum wage. And a self-conscious intelligentsia with common ties to prestigious centers of liberal-arts education has, in many regions, especially the East and the Bay Area, an important role to play among local elites. They use their access to the mass media and to officialdom to make certain that other, non-moral issues predominate— after all, the major function of the schools they went to was to induce them to rebel against the "middle-class morality" which, in the modern parlance, is a hangup.

Regional differences will never disappear entirely, and thus the political culture of Southern California will never be *the* political culture of our society. But the strength of all those institutions which resist it is waning, and thus we are likely to have more of it in more places in the future. I happen to think that morality is important and that those concerned about it are decent people (after all, I'm related to a sizable number of them). But I fear for the time when politics is seized with the issue. Our system of government cannot handle matters of that sort (can any democratic system?) and it may be torn apart by the effort.

72. RIOTS

GARY T. MARX

As Gary T. Marx states in this essay, "a riot may share many social and psychological factors with other forms of mass behavior . . . , it differs from them in the outwardly hostile and aggressive action taken." Marx goes beyond the explication of the concept and describes riots in Europe and the United States and analyzes their causes and consequences.

Gary T. Marx teaches sociology at Harvard University. He has been a Research Associate on several studies of intergroup relations sponsored by the Anti-Defamation League and is author of Protest and Prejudice *(1967).*

The July 1863 New York City riots, the largest in American history, were triggered by fear of economic displacement by newly freed slaves and by resentment against a new conscription law that seemed to favor the rich. On the second day of a lottery to choose Civil War recruits, thousands of protestors milled around the draft office. The exact precipitating incident is unclear; however, the predominantly Irish crowd turned into a tumultuous, raging mob that at times numbered as many as 50,000 people. They took possession of the streets, and burned, looted, and murdered for several days until the appearance of the National Guard. Blacks were savagely attacked, tortured, and lynched, or thrown into rivers to drown. Police and soldiers found themselves in pitched battles with rioters. Estimates of the number killed ranged up to 2000 and perhaps as many as 10,000 were injured. The equivalent of about $60 million in damage was done. Like riots also occurred in Newark, Jersey City, Troy and Boston.

Though bloodier and somewhat larger in scope than most disorders, this outbreak contains the basic features of a riot: relatively spontaneous and temporary illegitimate group violence. These factors can be seen on a continuum, and are present in any given riot to varying degrees.

While a riot may share many social and psychological factors with (and indeed grow out of, or give rise to) other forms of mass behavior, such as panic, craze, or an expressive crowd, it differs from them in the outwardly hostile and aggressive action taken. Unlike a rebellion or an insurrection, a riot usually does not involve an intent to overthrow the government. It differs from peaceful protest demonstrations and civil disobedience because it involves violence.

Riots throughout the ages have been disproportionately urban phenomena. In modern times, the social contexts in which they have occurred most frequently are factories, governmental centers, ghettos, universities, prisons, recreation centers, and colonized or occupied areas. Perhaps the most important general statement to be made about riots is that they can both reflect and cause social change and cannot be understood apart from the main sources of cleavage and social conflict in a society. Among the most important kinds of riots have been those involving political, economic, racial, religious, and nationality issues. Of lesser historical significance are revelrous crowds and the large

Reprinted from the *Encyclopaedia Britannica,* by permission of the author and publisher.

number of instances where a specific incident such as overselling seats at a performance or inappropriate police handling of parade spectators or demonstrators leads to a riot.

As a legal concept, riot is a criminal offense against public order involving a group, however small, and the use of violence, however slight.

Riots in Europe

Europe since the 17th century has seen much collective violence in the form of brawls between rival guilds and communes, food riots, tax rebellions, mass forest and field trespassing, attacks on châteaus, machine breaking, programs, political rebellions, and strikes. Some periods have been more violent than others, such as the late 17th, the latter part of the 18th, and the first half of the 19th century in Great Britain and from the middle of the 18th to the middle of the 19th century in France.

Among some of the better known riots in Great Britain were the Wilkite Riots (1760s and 1770s), against the British government's treatment of John Wilkes; Gordon Riots (1780), against Catholics; Luddite Riots (1811–12); Rebecca Riots (1839; 1842–44); and the Plug Pot Riots of 1842. Among important mass disturbances in France were the Grain Riots of 1775, and the violence associated with the revolutions of 1789, 1830, 1848, 1851, and 1871.

The right of resistance, or right to riot, was a part of national tradition in England, and it touched those active in the American Revolution. European riots in the 17th, 18th, and well into the 19th century were rather conservative. Rulers were seen to have obligations to their people; among the most important was providing them with a livelihood. If the ruler met his obligations, the populace was prepared to defend him. If he failed to do his duty, the populace rioted, not to over-

throw him as would be the case later but to compel him to do his duty. Riots thus because quasi-institutionalized and perhaps as a result were rather patterned and restricted in their destruction. They represented a means, understood by the people as well as their rulers, by which those with few political or economic rights might gain concessions.

The traditional rural and urban food riots illustrate this. The main thrust of food riots was a demand to buy food at a "just price." Food riots tended to be associated with periodic famines, and increases in prices and unemployment. Demonstrations would be mounted against those presumed to be profiteering through the shipment or hoarding of grain. If the authorities failed to act and impose a just price on merchants, millers, farmers, or bakers, grain and its products would be seized and sold at a lower price with the proceeds going to the owner. With technical improvements in the production and distribution of grain in the 19th century, food riots disappeared.

Artisans, as well as peasants, participated in food riots, and the artisans also were engaged in industrial disputes. Workers' demands—pursued through attacks on industrial property, workshops, mines, mills, machinery, and "pulling down" the employers' houses—were common in the 18th and 19th centuries. E. J. Hobsbawm has called this "collective bargaining by riot." Violence was used by workers as a means of dealing with wage cuts and price increases or to protect their livelihood against the threat of new machinery.

Among the best known of the machine breakers were the British Luddites. Luddism occurred in a context in which war, bad harvests, and the collapse of the export trade raised prices to famine heights and seriously hurt the textile trade. Parliament had repealed paternalistic codes and imposed a laissez-faire economy on the workers. New machines and the factory system disrupted traditional ways of life. Independent artisans were displaced by unskilled factory workers operating new machines for much lower wages. Luddism of the early 19th century moved from a seemingly spontaneous demonstration of stocking workers "clamouring for work and a more liberal price" to a well-organized movement whose small disciplined bands moved swiftly at night. Attacks were selective and restrained, and frequently preceded by a letter warning the employer to change his ways or face the consequences. Machines rather than people were attacked until the authorities began attacking the Luddites. Luddism was short-lived because of increased efforts at social control.

In the mid-19th century, as the modern labour movement emerged and workers gained rights, the classical city mob tended to disappear. In its place emerged more organized demonstrations, strikes, and more sophisticated revolutionary efforts. Violence became more ideological, more associated with the political left, and concentrated more on institutions than on particular individuals. Instead of protesting some change or action that seemed to deprive them of rights they had once enjoyed, rioters came to protest the absence of new rights they felt entitled to. Workers' organizations, however, also meant greater control over potential rioters. To an important extent the amount of violence that occurred came to depend on how violent the authorities were in responding to large demonstrations.

The tolerance for, and amount of, public disorder declined as the nation-state increasingly gained a monopoly on the means of violence. This was related to new value patterns stressing national integration, new bureaucratic forms of police organization, and technical advances, such as the railway and telegraph, that greatly aided efforts at control.

Riots in the United States

In the United States, with its diverse population, riots have involved issues of race and ethnicity to a much greater extent than in Europe, taking the form of pogroms, communal riots, and the type of uprisings characteristic of colonized or occupied countries. Lynching, a form of mob violence somewhat restricted to the United States, originated in the middle of the 18th century.

Among prominent examples of ethnic violence were early attacks on Indians and Quakers; anti-Mormon and anti-Catholic riots in the 1840s; occasional slave uprisings; the New York City 1863 anti-draft, anti-Negro riots; the 1871 anti-Chinese riot in California; major race riots involving whites and blacks at East St. Louis in 1917, Chicago in 1919, and Detroit in 1943; the anti-Mexican riot in Los Angeles in 1943; and anti-Negro riots at the University of Mississippi, the burning of freedom buses, and attacks on Negroes participating in nonviolent demonstrations in the 1950s and 1960s.

Starting in 1964, racially inspired violence appeared in new form and on a scale unprecedented in American history. More than 200 American cities experienced black ghetto riots, with the largest disturbances occurring in the Watts area of Los Angeles in 1965 and in Newark, N.J., and Detroit, Mich., in 1967. By the late 1960s, approximately 200 persons, mostly Negro, were killed, 8,000 injured, and 50,000 arrested.

These riots followed a period in which black aspirations had been raised and promises to end racism and inequality went unfulfilled. A decade of nonviolent protest demonstrations had been relatively unsuccessful in changing the life situation of the average black. Earlier racial violence, such as that in East St. Louis, Chicago, and Detroit, was not restricted to ghetto areas, tended to be initiated by whites and involved white civilians attacking blacks (pogroms) or battles between white and black civilians (communal riots), with authorities often playing a passive role. In contrast, black riots of the 1960s, often growing out of a police incident, were restricted to ghetto areas and involved blacks striking out at the authorities, property, and symbols of white society, rather than at whites as individuals.

Other kinds of riots have not been lacking. During and after the Revolutionary War, riots such as those over the Stamp Act (1765–66), and accompanying Shays's Rebellion (1786) and the Whisky Insurrection tended to be political. As the country industrialized in the period from the Civil War to World War I, economic conflicts involving efforts at unionization and strikes were an important source of riots.

The 1960s saw the emergence of widespread student demonstrations, starting with the Free Speech Movement at the University of California at Berkeley in 1964. Many demonstrations ended in violence because of police provocation or a strategy of confrontation. The issues involved in student protest have been highly diverse, depending on the place and the country. A theme often present has been the demand for (or a reaction against encroachment upon) greater student power and participation in the affairs of the university or the larger society. The impersonality of the mass bureaucratic university and university traditionalism and imperviousness to change are factors conducive to student disorders.

In many universities there are long traditions of student activism. Historically, students have played important roles in movements of political change as in the French Revolution of 1848; the Russian Revolution; the fascist movements in Italy, Germany, and Spain; and nationalist struggles for independence in the colonized countries of Africa and Asia. Youthful idealism, ambiguities and frustrations in the student role, lesser commitments to familial and occupational roles, and the setting of the university which gathers together large numbers of people in a common situation, help explain the ease with which students can be mobilized for demonstrations. Some of these causes

also explain why youth in general seem to participate disproportionately in riots.

Communal Riots in Asia and Africa

Outbreaks of communal rioting in countries such as India-Pakistan (1947), Ceylon (1958), and Nigeria (1966–67) followed the demise of European colonial empires. New countries were often artifacts of arbitrary colonial boundaries and did not correspond to traditional group divisions. The fragile unity that had often been present in a common anti-colonial struggle gave way to bitter conflicts. Various racial, ethnic, tribal, religious, and linguistic groups, often with long histories of hostility, fought among themselves for autonomy. The weaker group feared domination by the stronger.

The most violent examples of such communal rioting involved Hindus and Muslims during the partition of India in 1947. Approximately a half-million people died, many in hideous massacres while trying to reach safety in their new country (Pakistan for Muslims and India for Hindus). Fighting was most pronounced in areas of mixed population such as Bengal and the Punjab. Communal riots such as these, in which the lines of cleavage flow out of racial, religious, or ethnic differences and where the essential humanity of the opponent can be denied, seem to have a much more violent and macabre potential than riots involving strictly political or economic issues.

ANALYSIS OF RIOTS can usefully be divided into factors in the pre-, actual, and post-riot situations. The first deals with the causes that increase the likelihood of the occurrence of a riot. The second deals with the precipitating incident, the role of ideas and rumour, leadership, the nature of participants, the interaction between rioters and authorities, and the patterning of the riot. Analysis of the post-riot situation considers the consequences of the violence.

The pre-riot situation

A riot can potentially occur anytime people are together in a group. Riots, however, do not occur randomly in time, place, or social setting. For example, 20th-century American race-linked riots have occurred when whites felt the segregatory status quo was threatened or when Negroes developed new equalitarian aspirations. Such riots have occurred especially during war periods, in urban areas, in summer, on weekends, and on main transportation routes. Certain conditions greatly increase the likelihood of rioting.

A group's predisposition to riot may be analyzed in light of the intensity of its grievances, the extent of opportunities to gain redress through normal channels, its cultural traditions regarding the use of violence, the extent to which its members are available for mass action, and the coercive power of the authorities to control outbreaks. To an important extent a riot is a function of these five factors. A riot is most likely to occur when a group has an intensely felt grievance, when it believes normal channels of protest are closed or ineffective, when its traditions favour violence, when it can easily come together for mass action, and when authorities are perceived as unable or unwilling to exercise strong control over violence.

An important impetus to many riots is some disruption, particularly if abrupt, of a group's traditional or anticipated way of life. When the expectations that previously guided action are no longer relevant, instrumental as well as expressive mass behaviour is made more likely. Riots have occurred disproportionately in periods of economic crisis, war, mass migration, catastrophe, and technical change, when normal routines of living are upset. When such changes are widespread they may not only engender dissatisfaction but also weaken traditional external and internal sources of control. The likelihood of violence from traditional as well as new strains may thus be increased.

Epidemics of plague in the Middle Ages greatly disrupted the European social order and gave rise to pogroms as well as dancing manias. Economic crises have been closely associated with a wide array of violent outbursts including European food and machine-breaking riots, American nativism, and Japanese peasant uprisings. The two periods in which American race riots against blacks were most prevalent were associated with large wartime northward migration and black entry into new areas of employment. The American prison riots of the early 1950s were associated with new administrative techniques that destroyed the informal inmate system of social control and reward distribution.

Riots are more likely not only when groups feel deprived of rights they once enjoyed but also when they come to feel that new rights are due them. Here the role of ideas, or what Neil Smelser (see *Bibliography*) has called a "generalized belief system," is particularly important. Such a belief system prepares people for action. It redefines an unstructured situation and fixes blame for the existing order which is considered intolerable. A better world seems possible if only some person or group of persons is destroyed, injured, removed, or restricted. Examples of well-developed generalized belief systems that have figured in riots include anticlericalism, anti-Semitism, Marxism, anarchism, fascism, and various nationalisms. Scholars disagree as to whether riots are more likely when people have a sense of despair or hope, and when things are getting worse or improving. Each of these factors, under not very well understood conditions, has been linked to outbursts. Disorders seem especially likely when periods of gain are interrupted by periods of decline. The important cause is not so much the amount of objective deprivation but how a group evaluates its position relative to other groups and the kinds of expectations it has.

Not all riots, however, involve a generalized belief. Recreational riots or expressive rampages tend to be relatively issue-less with respect to the larger society. The Saturday night brawls frequent in some lower status communities, ritualized disorders following school athletic events, Easter vacation riots of American students, and motorcycle riots have more of a playful tension-release character, with slight implications for social change. They are not much affected by the predisposing factors considered above. A pronounced weakening of authorities may also lead to relatively issueless rioting as was the case in the 1919 Boston police strike and some European riots as World War II came to an end.

Given a generalized belief that calls forth and explains dissatisfaction, it becomes important to ask what alternative means to violence are available. In colonized, occupied, or totalitarian countries, or highly authoritarian situations such as the American slave system, the early factory system, prisons, and many schools and universities—where there are no effective channels for the redress of grievances—violence may be seen as the only way of pressing a claim. In other situations the formal democratic process may be inoperative, either because a group is denied participation, or because its leaders are not seen as effectively representing the group. In many American cities that experienced riots in 1967, black political underrepresentation was pronounced and a feeling existed that all legitimate channels had been exhausted. Riots may also appear as a result of the closing off of previously accepted channels of protest, and disappear as new channels become available.

The likelihood of a riot is also increased to the extent that various social cleavages (*e.g.,* racial, national, linguistic, religious, tribal, regional, generational, economic, and political status) overlap rather than cut across each other. Where this is the case, as in many colonized countries, mutually reinforcing grievances on the part of the subordinate group are likely. In the United States race and class overlap. New dissatisfactions may be buttressed by traditional hostilities. In this context riots are likely to involve group conflict over power, income, and prestige.

THE RIOT is usually foreshadowed by a series of events that arouse the relevant public and focus attention on the source of dissatisfaction. In this context of heightened concern, a given incident, often innocuous, may confirm previous fears, expectations, and beliefs and come to be symbolic of all a group feels is wrong. Rumours, which reflect tension more than cause it, may selectively focus the group's attention and help create a polarized and oversimplified conception of the situation. Intense feelings of self-righteousness may develop. As with other kinds of mass behaviour, some crowd members may feel a sense of solidarity and heightened emotional ties to each other. As collective excitement builds up, an agitated member of the crowd may take some violent action, setting a pattern that others then follow.

Sometimes a single event can precipitate like disorders in many places. Following the assassination of Tsar Alexander II in 1881, Russian mobs in more than 200 cities attacked Jews, although the assassin was not Jewish. Following the killing of Martin Luther King, Jr., in 1968, more than 100 American cities experienced racial disorders. Food, prison, and university riots have tended to cluster together in time, often radiating outward. Some observers see in this a pattern of conspiracy; perhaps it is more likely that it represents a response to similar conditions and the provision of a role model. There are parallels to the spread of behaviour in fads, crazes, and panics that clearly do not involve an organized system of control by a leadership group. The mass media, particularly television, have greatly facilitated this communication process.

Early conservative theorists such as G. LeBon, E. D. Martin, and E. A. Ross emphasized the emotional character of crowd behaviour. For them the crowd evoked lurid images of destruction where the basest of human impulses were expressed. They wrote of "herd instincts," the "group mind," the "atavistic vulnerability of civilized men," "dirty people without name," and the "dangerous classes." The crowd was thought to be like-minded, destructive, irrational, fickle, and suggestible, and made up of social misfits, criminals, and riffraff.

In extreme form such ideas are now generally rejected. There is great variation both within and between crowds. There are types and degrees of participation. These may change as the riot develops. Individuals may engage in the same activity for different reasons. In many riots, a small active nucleus, often made up of younger men, can be differentiated from a large body of spectators. The characteristics of rioters, the degree of selectivity in their activities, and the amount of violence depend on the specific issues and the period of history. Yet much research suggests the classical image of the crowd to be incorrect.

G. Rudé, using police and judicial records in his studies of the crowd in France and England between 1730–1848, finds that criminal and lumpen proletariat participation was slight. Riot participants were not those at the margins of society; rather they tended to be well integrated into local settings and had specific grievances. The mob consisted of the ordinary urban poor, the *menu peuple*—small workshop masters, shopkeepers, apprentices, craftsmen, and labourers: employed people with settled abode and without criminal conviction. Similarly, research on black riot participants in the 1960s suggests that in many ways rioters were broadly representative of Negro youth. They were not disproportionately unemployed, criminal, or recent migrants, and had a strong sense of indignation over the place of Negroes in American society.

The personally disorganized, those with pronounced antisocial tendencies, criminals, and individualistic looters may take advantage of the general confusion in a riot to further their own ends. There are many historical examples of such people being drawn into a riot, unconcerned and perhaps even unaware of the broader issues. Riots clearly offer a cover for normally prohibited behaviour. Yet such people are always present, while riots occur infrequently and are very much related to broader social, political, economic, religious, and racial issues. An explanation that seeks the source of riots in the nature of man, or of certain men such as those of the lower social classes, cannot explain their variation in place and time.

The mechanisms by which people come to act differently in a crowd are not well understood. One relevant cause is interaction that leads to the emergence of new norms redefining the situation and justifying previously forbidden behaviour (*e.g.,* "Merchants have been exploiting and stealing from the people for years so we are not looting, but taking what is rightfully ours"). An individual may feel group pressure to conform to the new norm since not to do so may label him as a coward, a fool, or an enemy. Another cause is the weakening of external control that may permit the expression of deviant tendencies present in most people. The failure of authorities to act (either because they are undermanned, in sympathy with the crowd, or afraid of provoking it further) leads people to think they will escape punishment. The crowd offers anonymity. The possible rewards may seem to greatly outweigh the negative consequences.

The importance of the leader or agitator has long been a subject of dispute and clearly depends on the particular situation. In some countries, such as those of the Middle East, street rioting has been a recognized means of conflict that leaders effectively use. It is doubtful, however, that large numbers of people can be made to riot without grievances.

Where speech-making and planned demonstrations are involved, leaders may play important early roles. Where the crowd has a clearly defined end, and co-operative action is required as in a lynching or forcing entrance into a building, a clear leadership structure may be present and even restraining. The leader may lose all control, however, as the specific purpose is carried out, and the crowd may even turn on him if he tries to restrain them. This situation led early observers to characterize the crowd as vacillating and immoral. In other, more diffuse riots involving small congeries of people behaving in roughly parallel ways, such leadership will be lacking, though some men out of extreme ideological commitment or personal disorganization may set daring examples that others follow. To the extent that a crowd is open to the suggestions of leaders, this is limited to suggestions consistent with its mood; suggestions that the crowd disperse are often ineffective.

A riot, as with any kind of collective behaviour, has an emergent quality to it and over time may change greatly. Its norms are more spontaneous, and this fact gives it an important element of unpredictability. Important to the course of a riot is the interaction between control officials and rioters. Authorities face the dilemma of under- or overreaction. To underreact may permit the riot to spread as people see they are not being censured. To overreact may create martyrs and lead to the involvement of many who had been passive spectators.

A pattern that has sometimes emerged involves the escalation of the riot to include new and more general issues or the triggering of traditional hostilities unrelated to the original issues as new participants with other concerns become involved. Hostility may move from being focused on a single object or class of objects to a wide array of objects. It may move from involving the crowd as a unit to individual or small group actions that are roughly parallel. An early period of milling and chaotic violence may give rise to more planned and focused attacks. The level of violence may escalate from verbal insults to rock throwing to gunfire as au-thorities increase their efforts at control.

The riot may end when the crowd obtains its objective or realizes it is impossible to obtain it, when some shocking event occurs, when the crowd becomes fatigued, or when superior force is brought against it.

Post-riot consequences

Whatever the varied personal motives and characteristics of rioters, and the degree of instrumentality and spontaneity involved in their behaviour, the event they collectively help create often comes to have a meaning that far transcends their individual psychology and actions. The consequences of riots have been varied. Some have resulted only in brutal repression; others have been merely tolerated and had no important effects; while still others have been instrumental in directly or indirectly bringing about change.

Riots themselves often do not directly involve action rationally calculated to solve the issues which arouse the crowd. Indeed, the crowd's inability to deal with the issues it is concerned with can be an important stimulus to riotous action. Riots can heighten political consciousness and solidarity, however, and can serve as catalysts for more organized protest efforts carried out illegally or legally. They have often served as a prelude to broader movements of social upheaval.

Though he was unsympathetic, Gustave LeBon noted that crowds serve to destroy the old order in preparation for the emergence of a new one. An initial outburst may take on a symbolic meaning and give rise to new groups, heroes, and leaders. In ancient Greece and Rome the mob frequently led to the fall of governments and had important effects on the course of world history. The American, French, and Russian revolutions were preceded by riots. In the 1960s, student uprisings toppled governments in a number of countries. Where a riot does produce change, at a more general level, it may often be analyzed as part of a broader series of historical and social events conducive to both riots and the given change.

Riots can have a communications function and sensitize those with power to problems they previously were unaware of or had neglected. Grain riots often produced a reduction in prices and new efforts by local officials to assure an adequate grain supply at a just price. Negro riots in the 1960s visibly and forcefully brought racial problems to the forefront of domestic issues. American student disorders have triggered reanalysis of the nature of higher education. Where other means are lacking, riots can serve as a bargaining device by which powerless groups put forth their claims. This negative power to disrupt society and the threat of rioting has tempered the actions of many rulers.

In some riots a life cycle model—breakdown, chaotic violence and mass unrest, organized protest, social change, and the disappearance of violence—may be noted. U.S. labour violence and various nationalistic movements have undergone this cycle. Probably a majority of riots, however, do not show this pattern. Sporadic violence may accompany, or never lead to, more organized efforts at change. Rioting may also inhibit social change by offering leaders an excuse for bloody repression or by channeling mass anger onto a scapegoat, such as Jews or Negroes, and away from the basic source of discontent.

Other effects may be more limited or subtle. Fear of riot generated by the Chartist disorders was an important factor in the creation of a national police force in England. Fear of revolution influenced the planning of Paris, Vienna, and Washington, D.C. Following American ghetto riots some new buildings have been constructed without street-level windows. Some psychiatrists have theorized that through striking out, individuals who feel oppressed obtain a sense of dignity and catharsis.

BIBLIOGRAPHY

HISTORICAL G. Rudé, *The Crowd in History* (1964); E. J. Hobsbawm, *Primitive Rebels* (1959); J. W. Heaton, "Mob Violence in the Late Roman Republic," *Illinois University Studies in the Social Sciences,* vol. 23 (1938–39); M. Beloff, *Public Order and Popular Disturbances 1660–1714* (1938); F. O. Darvall, *Popular Disturbances and Public Order in Regency England* (1934); F. C. Mather, *Public Order in the Age of the Chartists* (1959); E. P. Thompson, *The Making of the English Working Class* (1964); R. S. Longley, "Mob Activities in Revolutionary Massachusetts," *New England Quarterly,* vol. vi (1933); C. Tilly, "The Changing Place of Collective Violence" in M. Richter (ed.), *Social Theory and Social History* (1969); J. McCague, *The Second Rebellion: the Story of the New York City Draft Riots of 1863* (1968); G. Meyers, *History of Bigotry in the United States,* rev. by H. M. Christman (1960); W. Heaps, *Riots, U.S.A. 1765–1965* (1966).

SOCIAL AND PSYCHOLOGICAL ANALYSIS G. LeBon, *The Crowd* (1947); E. D. Martin, *The Behavior of Crowds* (1920); S. Freud, *Group Psychology and the Analysis of the Ego* (1955); H. Cantril, *The Psychology of Social Movements* (1941); R. Brown, "Mass Phenomena" in G. Lindzey (ed.), *Handbook of Social Psychology,* vol. ii (1954); R. Turner and L. Killian, *Collective Behavior* (1957); K. Lang and G. E. Lang, *Collective Dynamics* (1961); N. Smelser, *Theory of Collective Behavior* (1963); C. Couch, "Collective Behavior: an Examination of Some Stereotypes," *Social Problems,* vol. 15, no. 3, 310–322 (1968); E. Canetti, *Crowds and Power* (1966); F. Fanon, *The Wretched of the Earth* (1965); G. Marx, "Civil Disorder and the Agents of Social Control," *Journal of Social Issues* (October 1969).

RACIAL RIOTS Chicago Commission on Race Relations, *The Negro in Chicago* (1922); E. Rudwick, *Race Riot at East St. Louis, July 2, 1919* (1966); A. M. Lee and N. D. Humphrey, *Race Riot* (1943); A. F. Raper, *The Tragedy of Lynching* (1933); T. Vittachi, *Emergency '58: the Story of the Ceylon Race Riots* (1958); R. Conot, *Rivers of Blood, Years of Darkness* (1967); *Report* of the National Advisory Commission on Civil Disorders (Kerner Commission Report) (1968); *Supplemental Studies* for the National Advisory Commission on Civil Disorders (1968); J. Hersey, *The Algiers Motel Incident* (1968); L. Masotti and D. Bowen (ed.), *Riots and Rebellion: Civil Violence in the Urban Community* (1968).

Today . . . and Tomorrow

73. "THE TIMES THEY ARE A-CHANGIN' "

ROBERT A. ROSENSTONE

In the early 1960s, Bob Dylan sang "The Times They are A-Changin'," words which symbolized the new mood among American youth. The cacophony of new lyrics and even newer sounds that Dylan and others offered have taken over the charts—and the hearts of the young. But, unlike early trends in popular music, the new songs and sounds cry out in protest against what concerns many young people most: war and injustice and the search for meaning in an increasingly complex and tension-ridden society.

In the following pages, Robert Rosenstone reviews the changing character of popular music and its meaning.

Robert A. Rosenstone is Associate Professor of History at the California Institute of Technology. He is editor of Protest from the Right *(1968) and is the author of a forthcoming book on the Abraham Lincoln Brigade, the Americans who fought in the Spanish Civil War.*

At the beginning of the 1960's, nobody took popular music very seriously. Adults only knew that rock n' roll, which had flooded the airwaves in the 1950's, had a strong beat and was terribly loud; it was generally believed that teen-agers alone

Reprinted from *The Annals,* **382** (March 1969), 131–144, by permission of the author and The American Academy of Political and Social Science. This article was originally entitled "The Times They Are A-Changin' ": The Music of Protest."

had thick enough eardrums, or insensitive enough souls, to enjoy it. Certainly, no critics thought of a popular star like the writhing Elvis Presley as being in any way a serious artist. Such a teen-age idol was simply considered a manifestation of a subculture that the young happily and inevitably outgrew—and, any parent would have added, the sooner the better.

Today, the view of popular music has drastically changed. Some parents may still wonder about the "noise" that their children listen to, but important segments of American society have come to recognize popular musicians as real artists saying serious things.[1] An indication of this change can be seen in magazine attitudes. In 1964, the *Saturday Evening Post* derided the Beatles—recognized giants of modern popular music—as "corny," and *Reporter* claimed: "They have debased Rock 'n Roll to its ultimate absurdity." Three years later the *Saturday Review* solemnly discussed a new Beatles record as a "highly ironic declaration of disaffection" with modern society, while in 1968 *Life* devoted a whole, laudatory section to "The New Rock," calling it music "that challenges the joys and ills of the . . . world."[2] Even in the intellectual community, popular music has found warm friends. Such sober journals as *The Listener, Columbia University Forum, New American Review,* and *Commentary* have sympathetically surveyed aspects of the "pop" scene, while in *The New York Review of Books*—a kind of house organ for American academia—composer Ned Rorem has declared that, at their best, the Beatles "compare with those composers from great eras of song: "Monteverdi, Schumann, Poulenc."[3]

The reasons for such changes in attitude are not difficult to find: there is no doubt that popular music has become more complex, and at the same time more serious, than it ever was before. Musically, it has broken down some of the old forms in which it was for a long time straight-jacketed. With a wide-ranging eclecticism, popular music has adapted to itself a bewildering variety of musical traditions and instruments, from the classic Indian sitar to the most recent electronic synthesizers favored by composers of "serious" concert music.

As the music has been revolutionized, so has the subject matter of the songs. In preceding decades, popular music was almost exclusively about love, and, in the words of poet Thomas Gunn, "a very limited kind [of love], constituting a sort of fag-end of the Petrarchan tradition."[4] The stories told in song were largely about lovers yearning for one another in some vaguely unreal world where nobody ever seemed to work or get married. All this changed in the 1960's. Suddenly, popular music began to deal with civil rights demonstrations and drug experiences, with interracial dating and war and explicit sexual encounters, with, in short, the real world in which people live. For perhaps the first time, popular songs became relevant to the lives of the teen-age audience that largely constitutes the record-buying public. The success of some of these works prompted others to be written, and the second half of the decade saw a full efflorescence of such topical songs, witten by young people for their peers. It is these works which should be grouped under the label of "protest" songs of the 1960's, for, taken together, they provide a wide-ranging critique of American life. Listening to them, one can get a full-blown picture of the antipathy that the young song writers have toward many American institutions.

Serious concerns entered popular music early in the 1960's, when a great revival of folk singing spread out from college campuses, engulfed the mass media, and created a wave of new "pop" stars, the best known of whom was Joan Baez. Yet, though the concerns of these folk songs were often serious, they were hardly contemporary. Popular were numbers about organizing unions, which might date from the 1930's or the late nineteenth century, or about the trials of escaping Negro slaves, or celebrating the cause of the defeated Republicans in the Spanish Civil War. Occasionally, there was something like "Talking A-Bomb Blues," but this was the rare exception rather than the rule.[5]

A change of focus came when performers began to write their own songs, rather than relying on the traditional folk repertoire. Chief among them, and destined to become the best known, was Bob Dylan. Consciously modeling himself on that wandering minstrel of the 1930's, Woody Guthrie, Dylan began by writing songs that often had little to do with the contemporary environment. Rather, his early ballads like "Masters of War" echoed the leftist concerns and rhetoric of an earlier era. Yet, simultaneously, Dylan was beginning to write songs like "Blowin' In the Wind," "A Hard Rain's A-Gonna Fall," and "The Times They Are A-Changin'," which dealt with civil rights, nuclear war, and the changing world of youth that parents and educators were not prepared to understand. Acclaimed as the best of protest-song-writers, Dylan in mid-decade shifted gears, and in the song "My Back Pages," he denounced his former moral fervor. In an ironic chorus claiming that he was much younger than he had been, Dylan specifically made social problems the worry of sober, serious, older men; presumably, youths had more important things than injustice to think about. After that, any social comment by Dylan came encapsulated in a series of surrealistic images; for the most part, he escaped into worlds of aestheticism, psychedelic drugs, and personal love relationships. Apparently attempting to come to grips in art with his own personality, Dylan was content to forget about the problems of other men.[6]

The development of Dylan is important not only because he is the leading song writer, but also because it parallels the concerns of popular music in the 1960's. Starting out with traditional liberal positions on war, discrimination, segregation, and exploitation, song writers of the decade turned increasingly to descriptions of the private worlds of drugs, sexual experience, and personal freedom. Though social concerns have never entirely faded, the private realm has been increasingly seen as the only one in which people can lead meaningful lives. Now, at the end of the decade, the realms of social protest and private indulgence exist side by side in the popular music, with the latter perceived as the only viable alternative to the world described in the former songs.[7]

The Negro in Song

In turning to the protest songs of the 1960's, one finds many of the traditional characters and concerns of such music missing. Gone are exploited, impoverished people, labor leaders, "finks," and company spies. This seems natural in the affluent 1960's, with youths from middle-class backgrounds writing songs. Of course, there has been one increasingly visible victim of exploitation in this decade, the Negro; and the songsters have not been blind to his plight. But, egalitarian as they are, the white musicians have not been able to describe the reality of the black man's situation.[8] Rather, they have chronicled Northern liberal attitudes towards the problem. Thus, composer-performer Phil Ochs penned works criticizing Southern attitudes towards Negroes, and containing stock portraits of corrupt politicians, law officials, and churchmen trembling before the Ku Klux Klan, while Paul Simon wrote a lament for a freedom rider killed by an angry Southern mob.[9] Similarly white-oriented was Janis Ian's very popular "Society's Child," concerned with the problem of interracial dating. Here a white girl capitulates to society's bigotry and breaks off a relationship with a Negro boy with the vague hope, "When we're older things may change/But for now this is the way they must remain." [10] Increasingly central to white-Negro relationships have been the ghetto and urban riots, and a taste of this entered the popular music. Phil Ochs, always on top of current events, produced "In the Heat of the Summer" shortly after the first major riot in Harlem in 1964. Partially sympathetic to the ghetto-dwellers' actions, he still misjudged their attitudes by ascribing to them feelings of shame—rather than satisfaction—in the aftermath of the destruction.[11] A later attempt, by Country Joe and the Fish, to describe Harlem ironically as a colorful vacation spot, verged on patronizing blacks, even while it poked fun at white stereotypes. Only the closing lines, "But if you can't go to Harlem . . .Maybe you'll be lucky and Harlem will come to you," followed by sounds of explosion, thrust home what indifference to the ghetto is doing to America.[12] The most successful song depicting the situation of the Negro was "Trouble Coming Everyday," written by Frank Zappa during the Watts uprising in 1965. Though the song does not go so far as to approve of rioting, it paints a brutal picture of exploitation by merchants, bad schooling, miserable housing, and police brutality—all of which affect ghetto-dwellers. Its most significant lines are Zappa's cry, "You know something people, I ain't black, but there's a whole lots of times I wish I could say I'm not white." No song writer showed more empathy with the black struggle for liberation than that.[13]

Politicians

While the downtrodden are heroes of many traditional protest songs, the villains are often politicians. Yet, politics rarely enters the songs of the 1960's. Ochs, an unreconstructed voice from the 1930's, depicts vacillating politicians in some works, and Dylan mentions corrupt ones early in the decade. But the typical attitude is to ignore politics, or, perhaps, to describe it in passing as "A yardstick for

lunatics, one point of view."[14] It is true that the death of President Kennedy inspired more than one song, but these were tributes to a martyr, not a politician.[15] If Kennedy in death could inspire music, Lyndon Johnson in life has seemed incapable of inspiring anything, except perhaps contempt. In a portrait of him, Country Joe and the Fish pictured the, then, President as flying through the sky like Superman ("It's a bird, it's a plane, it's a man insane/It's my President L. B. J."). Then they fantasized a Western setting:

Come out Lyndon with your hands
  held high
Drop your guns, baby, and reach for
  the sky
I've got you surrounded and you ain't
  got a chance
Send you back to Texas, make you
  work on your ranch.[16]

One traditional area, antiwar protest, does figure significantly in the music of the 1960's. With America's involvement in Vietnam and mounting draft-calls, this seems natural enough. Unlike many songs of this genre, however, the current ones rarely assess the causes of war, but dwell almost exclusively with the effect which war has on the individual. Thus, both Love and the Byrds sing about what nuclear war does to children, while the Peanut Butter Conspiracy pictures the effect of nuclear testing on everyone: "Firecracker sky filled with roots of fusion . . . /We're so far ahead we're losing."[17] Most popular of the antiwar songs was P. F. Sloan's "Eve of Destruction," which, for a time in 1965, was the best-selling record in the country (and which was banned by some patriotic radio-station directors). The title obviously gives the author's view of the world situation; the content deals mostly with its relationship to young men like himself: "You don't believe in war, but what's that gun you're totin'?"[18] There are alternatives to carrying a gun, and defiance of the draft enters some songs, subtly in Buffy St. Marie's "Universal Soldier" and stridently in Ochs' "I Ain't Marching Any More." [19] Perhaps more realistic in its reflection of youthful moods is the Byrds' "Draft Morning," a haunting portrait of a young man reluctantly leaving a warm bed to take up arms and kill "unknown faces." It ends with the poignant and unanswerable question, "Why should it happen?" [20]

If many songs criticize war in general, some have referred to Vietnam in particular. The Fugs give gory details of death and destruction being wreaked on the North by American bombers, which unleash napalm "rotisseries" upon the world.[21] In a similar song, Country Joe and the Fish describe children crying helplessly beneath the bombs, and then comment ironically, "Super heroes fill the skies, tally sheets in hand/Yes, keeping score in times of war takes a superman." [22] No doubt, it is difficult to make music out of the horrors of war, and a kind of black humor is a common response. In a rollicking number, the Fugs, with irony, worry that people may come to "love the Russians" and scream out a method often advocated for avoiding this: "Kill, kill, kill for peace." [23] And one of Country Joe's most popular numbers contains the following:

Well come on generals let's move fast
Your big chance has come at last
We gotta go out and get those reds
The only good Commie is one that's dead
And you know that peace can only be
   won
When we blow 'em all to kingdom come.[24]

The injustice and absurdity of America's Asian ventures, perceived by the song writers, does not surprise them, for they feel that life at home is much the same. The songs of the 1960's show the United States as a repressive society, where people who deviate from the norm are forced into conformity—sometimes at gunpoint; where those who do fit in lead empty,

frustrated lives; and where meaningful human experience is ignored in a search for artificial pleasures. Such a picture is hardly attractive, and one might argue that it is not fair. But it is so pervasive in popular music that it must be examined at some length. Indeed, it is the most important part of the protest music of the decade. Here are criticisms, not of exploitation, but of the quality of life in an affluent society: not only of physical oppression, but also of the far more subtle mental oppression that a mass society can produce.

Youth as Victim

Throughout the decade, young people have often been at odds with established authority, and, repeatedly, songs picture youth in the role of victim. Sometimes the victimization is mental, as when the Mothers of Invention complain of outworn thought patterns and say "All your children are poor/Unfortunate victims of lies /You believe." [25] On a much simpler level, Sonny Bono voices his annoyance that older people laugh at the clothes he wears, and he wonders why they enjoy "makin' fun" of him.[26] Now, Bono could musically shrug off the laughs as the price of freedom, but other songs document occasions when Establishment disapproval turned into physical oppression. Thus, Canned Heat tells of being arrested in Denver because the police did not want any "long hairs around." [27] The Buffalo Springfield, in a hit record, describe gun-bearing police rounding up teenagers on the Sunset Strip, and draw the moral, "Step out of line the men come and take you away." [28] On the same theme, Dylan ironically shows that adults arbitrarily oppose just about all activities of youths, saying that they should "look out" no matter what they are doing.[29] More bitter is the Mothers' description of police killing large numbers of hippies, which is then justified on the grounds "They looked too weird

. . . it served them right." [30] Though the incident is fictional, the Mothers clearly believe Americans capable of shooting down those who engage in deviant behavior.

Though the songs echo the oppression that youngsters have felt, they do not ignore the problems that all humans face in a mass society. Writer Tom Paxton knows that it is not easy to keep one's life from being forced into a predetermined mold. In "Mr. Blue" he has a Big-Brother-like narrator telling the title character, a kind of Everyman, that he is always under surveillance, and that he will never be able to indulge himself in his precious dreams of freedom from society. This is because society needs him to fill a slot, no matter what his personal desires. Of that slot, the narrator says, "You'll learn to love it/Or we'll break you." And then comes the chilling chorus:

What will it take to whip you into line
A broken heart?
A broken head?
It can be arranged.[31]

Though no other writer made the message so explicit, a similar fear of being forced into an unwelcome slot underlies many songs of the period.

The society of slotted people is an empty one, partly described as "TV dinner by the pool,/I'm so glad I finished school." [32] It is one in which people have been robbed of their humanity, receiving in return the "transient treasures" of wealth and the useless gadgets of a technological age. One of these is television, referred to simply as "that rotten box," or, in a more sinister image, as an "electronic shrine." This image of men worshipping gadgets recurs. In the nightmare vision of a McLuhanesque world—where the medium is the message—Simon and Garfunkel sing of men so busy bowing and praying to a "neon god" that they cannot understand or touch one another. Indeed, here electronics seem to hinder the process of communication rather than facilitate it. People talk and hear but never understand, as the "sounds of silence" fill the world.[33] Such lack of communication contributes to the indifference with which men can view the life and death of a neighbor, as in Simon's "A Most Peculiar Man." [34] It also creates the climate of fear which causes people to kill a stranger for no reason other than his unknown origins in Strawberry Alarm Clock's "They Saw the Fat One Coming." [35]

Alienated from his fellows, fearful and alone, modern man has also despoiled the natural world in which he lives. With anguish in his voice, Jim Morrison of the Doors asks:

What have they done to the earth?
What have they done to our fair sister?
Ravished and plundered and ripped
her and bit her
Stuck her with knives in the side of
the dawn
And tied her with fences and dragged
her down.[36]

In a lighter tone but with no less serious an intent, the Lewis and Clark Expedition describe the way man has cut himself off from nature.

There's a chain around the flowers
There's a fence around the trees
This is freedom's country
Do anything you please.

With a final thrust they add, "You don't need to touch the flowers/They're plastic anyway." [37]

This brings up a fear that haunts a number of recent songs, the worry that the technological age has created so many artificial things that nothing natural remains. Concerned with authenticity, the songsters are afraid that man himself is becoming an artifact, or, in their favorite word, "plastic." Thus, the Jefferson Airplane sing about a "Plastic Fantastic Lover," while the Iron Butterfly warn a girl to stay away from people "made of plastics." [38] The image recurs most frequently in the works of the Mothers of Invention. In one song, they depict the country as being run by a plastic Congress and President.[39] Then, in "Plastic People," they start with complaints about a girlfriend who uses "plastic goo" on her face, go on to a picture of teen-agers on the Sunset Strip—who are probably their fans—as being "plastic," too, and finally turn on their listeners and say "Go home and check yourself/You think we're talking about someone else." [40] Such a vision is frightening, for if the audience is plastic, perhaps the Mothers, themselves, are made of the same phony material. And if the whole world is plastic, who can be sure of his own authenticity?

Love Relationships

Toward the end of "Plastic People," the Mothers say, "I know true love can never be/A product of plasticity." [41] This brings up the greatest horror, that in a "plastic" society like the United States, love relationships are impossible. For the young song writers, American love is viewed as warped and twisted. Nothing about Establishment society frightens them more than its attitudes towards sex. Tim Buckley is typical in singing that older Americans are "Afraid to trust in their bodies," and in describing them as "Faking love on a bed made of knives." [42] Others give graphic portraits of deviant behavior. The Fugs tell of a "Dirty Old Man" hanging around high school playgrounds; the Velvet Underground portray a masochist; and the Mothers depict a middle-aged man lusting after his own thirteen-year-old daughter.[43] The fullest indictment of modern love is made by the United States of America, who devote almost an entire album to the subject. Here, in a twisted portrait of "pleasure and pain," is a world of loveless marriages, homosexual relationships in men's rooms, venomous attractions, and overt sadism—all masked by a middle-class, suburban world in which people consider "morality" important. To show that natural relationships are possible elsewhere, the group sings one tender love lyric; interestingly, it is the lament of a Cuban girl for the dead Ché Guevara.[44]

The fact that bourgeois America has warped attitudes towards sex and love is bad enough; the songsters are more worried that such attitudes will infect their own generation. Thus, the Collectors decry the fact that man-woman relationships are too often seen as some kind of contest, with a victor and vanquished, and in which violence is more acceptable than tenderness.[45] Perhaps because most of the singers are men, criticisms of female sexual attitudes abound. The Mothers say disgustedly to the American woman, "You lie in bed and grit your teeth," while the Sopwith Camel object to the traditional kind of purity by singing, "I don't want no woman wrapped up in cellophane." [46] This is because such a woman "will do you in/Bending your mind with her talking about sin." [47] All the musicians would prefer the girl about whom Moby Grape sings who is "super-powered, deflowered," and over eighteen.[48]

Living in a "plastic" world where honest human relationships are impossible, the song writers might be expected to wrap themselves in a mood of musical despair. But they are young—and often making plenty of money—and such an attitude is foreign to them. Musically, they are hopeful because, as the title of the Dylan song indicates, "The Times They Are A-Changin'." Without describing the changes, Dylan clearly threatens the older generation, as he tells critics, parents, and presumably anyone over thirty, to start swimming or they will drown in the rising floodwaters of social change.[49]

In another work, Dylan exploits the same theme. Here is a portrait of a presumably normal, educated man, faced with a series of bizarre situations, who is made to feel like a freak because he does not understand what is going on. The chorus is the young generation's comment to all adults, as it mocks "Mr. Jones" for not understanding what is happening all around him.[50]

The changes going on are, not surprisingly, associated with the carefree, joyful experiences of youth. As Jefferson Airplane sings, "It's a wild time/I see people all around me changing faces/It's a wild time/I'm doing things that haven't got a name yet."[51] The most full-blown description of the changing world is Tim Buckley's "Goodbye and Hello," a lengthy and explicit portrait of what the youth hope is happening. Throughout the song the author contrasts two kinds of people and their environments. On the one hand are the "antique people"—godless and sexless —of an industrial civilization, living in dark dungeons, working hard, worshipping technology and money, sacrificing their sons to placate "vaudeville" generals, and blinding themselves to the fact that their "masquerade towers" are "riddled by widening cracks." Opposed to them are the "new children," interested in flowers, streams, and the beauty of the sky, who wish to take off their clothes to dance and sing and love one another. What's more, the "antique people are fading away"; in fact, they are already wearing "death masks." As the son says, "The new children will live because their elders have died."[52]

Buckley's vision of the new world that is coming is obviously that of a kind of idyllic Eden before the fall, a world in which men will be free to romp and play and indulge their natural desires for love. It is a pagan world, the antithesis of the Christian ideal that would postpone fulfillment to some afterlife. Elsewhere, Buckley explicitly condemns Christianity, saying "I can't hesitate and I can't wait for pleasant street."[53] Similarly, the Doors' Jim Morrison states, "Cancel my subscription to the resurrection," and in the same song literally shrieks, "We want the world and want it now."[54] Here is the impatient demand of youth that all problems be swept aside and the world be made into paradise without delay.

How to Live

Though the times may be changing, the songsters are well aware that—despite their brave words and demands—there is plenty of strength left in the old social order. Obviously, they can see the war continuing, Negro demands not being met, and the continuing hostility of society toward their long hair, music, sexual behavior, and experimentation with drugs. Faced with these facts, the musicians must deal with the problem of how to live decently within the framework of the old society. Here they tend toward the world of private experience mentioned earlier in this article in connection with Dylan. Many of their songs are almost programs for youth's behavior in a world perceived as being unlivable.

The first element is to forget about the repressive society out there. As Sopwith Camel says, "Stamp out reality . . ./Before reality stamps out you."[55] Then it is imperative to forget about trying to understand the outside world rationally. In a typical anti-intellectual stance, the Byrds describe such attempts as "scientific delirium madness."[56] Others combine a similar attitude with a strong measure of *carpe diem*. Spirit deride people who are "always asking" for "the reason" when they should be enjoying life, while H. P. Lovecraft admits that the bird is on the wing and states, "You need not know why."[57] What is important is that the moment be seized and life lived to the fullest. As Simon and Garfunkel say, one has to make the "moment last," and this is done best by those who open themselves fully to the pleasures of the world.[58]

The most frequent theme of the song writers is the call to freedom, the total freedom of the individual to "do his own thing." Peanut Butter Conspiracy carry this so far as to hope for a life that can be lived "free of time." [59] Circus Maximus and the Byrds—despite the fact that they are young men—long to recapture some lost freedom that they knew as children. [60] Such freedom can be almost solipsistic; Jimi Hendrix claims that even if the sun did not rise and the mountains fell into the sea, he would not care because he has his "own world to live through." [61] But for others, it can lead to brotherhood. As H. P. Lovecraft says, "C'mon people now, let's get together/Smile on your brother,/Try and love one another right now." [62]

A desire for freedom is certainly nothing new. What is different in the songs of the 1960's is the conviction that this freedom should be used by the individual in an extensive exploration of his own internal world. Central to the vision of the song writers is the idea that the mind must be opened and expanded if the truths of life are to be perceived. Thus, the importance of external reality is subordinated to that of a psychological, even a metaphysical, realm. The most extensive treatment of this subject is by the Amboy Dukes, who devote half of a long-playing record to it. Their theme is stated quite simply: "How happy life would be/If all mankind /Would take the time to journey to the center of the mind." [63] Like any mystical trip, what happens when one reaches the center of the mind is not easy to describe. Perhaps the best attempt is by the Iron Butterfly, who claim that an unconscious power will be released, flooding the individual with sensations and fusing him with a freedom of thought that will allow him to "see every thing." At this point, man will be blessed with the almost supernatural power of knowing "all." [64]

Such a journey is, of course, difficult to make. But youth has discovered a short cut to the mind's center, through the use of hallucinogenic drugs. Indeed, such journeys are almost inconceivable without hallucinogens, and the so-called "head songs" about drug experiences are the

most prevalent of works that can be classified as "protest." [65] In this area, the songs carefully distinguish between "mind-expanding," nonaddictive marijuana and LSD, and hard, addictive drugs which destroy the body. Thus, the Velvet Underground and Love both tell of the dangers of heroin, while Canned Heat warn of methedrine use and the Fugs describe the problems of cocaine. [66] But none of the groups hesitate to recommend "grass" and "acid" trips as a prime way of opening oneself to the pleasures and beauties of the universe. As the Byrds claim in a typical "head song," drugs can free the individual from the narrow boundaries of the mundane world, allowing him to open his heart to the quiet joy and eternal love which pervade the whole universe. [67] Others find the reality of the drug experience more real than the day-to-day world, and some even hope for the possibility of staying "high" permanently. More frequent is the claim that "trips" are of lasting benefit because they improve the quality of life of an individual even after he "comes down." [68] The Peanut Butter Conspiracy, claiming that "everyone has a bomb" in his mind, even dream of some day turning the whole world on with drugs, thus solving mankind's plaguing problems by making the earth a loving place. [69] An extreme desire, perhaps, but one that would find much support among other musicians.

A Repressive Society

This, then is the portrait of America that emerges in the popular songs of the 1960's which can be labelled as "protest." It is, in the eyes of the song writers, a society which makes war on peoples abroad and acts repressively toward helpless minorities like Negroes, youth, and hippies at home. It is a land of people whose lives are devoid of feeling, love, and sexual pleasure. It is a country whose institutions are crumbling away, one which can presumably only be saved by a sort of cultural and spiritual revolution which the young themselves will lead.

Whether one agrees wholly, partly, or not at all with such a picture of the United States, the major elements of such a critical portrait are familiar enough. It is only in realizing that all this is being said in popular music, on records that sometimes sell a million copies to teen-agers, in songs that youngsters often dance to, that one comes to feel that something strange is happening today. Indeed, if parents fully understand what the youth are saying musically to one another, they must long for the simpler days of Elvis Presley and his blue suede shoes.

If the lyrics of the songs would disturb older people, the musical sound would do so even more. In fact, a good case could be made that the music itself expresses as much protest against the status quo as do the words. Performed in concert with electronic amplification on all instruments —or listened to at home at top volume— the music drowns the individual in waves of sound; sometimes it seems to be pulsating inside the listener. When coupled with a typical light show, where colors flash and swirl on huge screens, the music helps to provide an assault on the senses, creating an overwhelming personal experience of the kind that the songs advise people to seek. This sort of total experience is certainly a protest against the tepid, partial pleasures which other songs describe as the lot of bourgeois America.

Another aspect of the music which might be considered a kind of protest is the attempt of many groups to capture in sound the quality of a drug "trip," to try through melody, rhythm, and volume to —in the vernacular—"blow the mind" of the audience. Of course, youngsters often listen to such music while under the influence of hallucinogens. In such a state, the perceptive experience supposedly can have the quality of putting one in touch with regions of the mind and manifestations of the universe that can be felt in no other way. Such mysticism, such transcendental attitudes, are certainly a protest against a society in which reality is always pragmatic and truth instrumental.

To try to explain why the jingles and vapid love lyrics of popular music in the 1950's evolved into the social criticism and mystical vision of the 1960's is certainly not easy. Part of it is the fact that performers, who have always been young, started writing their own songs, out of their own life experiences, rather than accepting the commercial output of the older members of tin pan alley. But this does not explain the popularity of the new songs. Here one must look to the youthful audience, which decided it preferred buying works of the newer kind. For it was the commercial success of some of the new groups which opened the doors of the record companies to the many that flourish today.

The Function of Music

Though one cannot make definitive judgments about this record-buying audience, some things seem clear. Certainly, it is true that with increasingly rapid social change, parents—and adults in general— have less and less that they can tell their children about the ways of the world, for adult life experiences are not very relevant to current social conditions. Similarly, institutions like the school and the press suffer from a kind of cultural lag that makes their viewpoints valueless for youth. Into the place of these traditional sources of information have stepped the youth themselves, and through such things as the "underground" press and popular music they are telling each other exactly what is happening. In this way, the music has achieved popularity—at least in part —because it telegraphs important messages to young people and helps to define and codify the mores and standards of their own subculture. A youngster may personally feel that there is no difference between his parents' drinking and his use of marijuana. Certainly, it is comforting to him when his friends feel the same way, and when popular songs selling millions of copies deliver the same message, there are even stronger sanctions for his "turning on." Thus, the lyrics of the music serve a functional role in the world of youth.

It is interesting to note that the popular music also puts youth in touch with serious, intellectual critiques of American life. Perhaps it starts only as a gut reaction in the song writers, but they have put into music the ideas of many American social critics. Without reading Paul Goodman, David Riesman, C. Wright Mills, or Mary McCarthy, youngsters will know that life is a "rat race," that Americans are a "lonely crowd," that "white-collar" lives contain much frustration, and that the war in Vietnam is far from just. And they will have learned this from popular music, as well as from their own observation.

The other side of the coin from criticism of contemporary life is the search for personal experience, primarily of the "mind-expanding" sort. As is obvious by now, such expansion has nothing to do with the intellect, but is a spiritual phenomenon. Here a final critique is definitely implicit. Throughout the music—as in youth culture—there is the search for a kind of mystical unity, an ability to feel a oneness with the universe. This is what drugs are used for; this is what the total environment of the light and music shows is about; and this is what is sought in the sexual experience—often explicitly evident in the orgasmic grunts and moans of performers. Through the search for this unity, the music is implicitly condemning the fragmentation of the individual's life which is endemic in the modern world. The songsters are saying that it is wrong

to compartmentalize work and play, wrong to cut men off from the natural rhythms of nature, wrong to stifle sex and love and play in favor of greater productivity, wrong to say man's spiritual needs can be filled by providing him with more material possessions.

This is obviously a criticism that can only be made by an affluent people, but these youth do represent the most affluent of all countries. And rather than wallow in their affluence, they have sensed and expressed much of the malaise that plagues our technological society. The charge may be made against them that they are really utopians, but the feeling increases today that we are in need of more utopian thinking and feeling. And while one might not wish to follow their prescriptions for the good life, they have caught something of the desire for freedom that all men feel. What could be more utopian and yet more inviting in its freedom than the hopeful picture which the Mothers of Invention paint of the future:

There will come a time when everybody
Who is lonely will be free . . .
TO SING AND DANCE AND LOVE
There will come a time when every evil
That we know will be an evil
WE CAN RISE ABOVE
Who cares if hair is long or short
Or sprayed or partly grayed . . .
WE KNOW THAT HAIR
AINT WHERE IT'S AT
(There will come a time when you
won't even be ashamed if you are fat!)

Who cares if you're so poor
You can't afford to buy a pair
Of mod a-go go stretch elastic pants
THERE WILL COME A TIME
WHEN YOU CAN EVEN
TAKE   YOUR   CLOTHES   OFF
WHEN
YOU DANCE [70]

NOTES

1. The definition of "popular music" being used in this article is a broad one. It encompasses a multitude of styles, including folk, folk-rock, acid-rock, hard-rock, and blues, to give just a few names being used in the musical world today. It does so because the old musical classifications have been totally smashed and the forms now overlap in a way that makes meaningful distinction between them impossible. Though not every group or song referred to will have been popular in the sense of selling a million records, all of them are part of a broad, variegated scene termed "pop." Some of the groups, like Buffalo Springfield, Strawberry Alarm Clock, or the Byrds, have sold millions of records. Others, like the Fugs or Mothers of Invention, have never had a real hit, though they are played on radio stations allied to the "underground." Still, such groups do sell respectable numbers of records and do perform regularly at teen-age concerts, and thus must be considered part of the "pop" scene.

2. *Saturday Evening Post,* 237 (March 21, 1964), 30; *Reporter,* 30 (Feb. 27, 1964), 18; *Saturday Review,* 50 (August 19, 1967), 18; *Life,* 64 (June 28, 1968), 51.

3. "The Music of the Beatles," *New York Review of Books,* Jan. 15, 1968, pp. 23–27. See also "The New Music," *The Listener,* 78 (August 3, 1967), 129–130; *Columbia University Forum* (Fall 1967), 16–22; *New American Review,* 1 (April 1968), 118–139; Ellen Willis, "The Sound of Bob Dylan," *Commentary,* 44 (November 1967), 71–80. Many of these articles deal with English as well as American popular groups, and, in fact, the music of the two countries cannot, in any meaningful sense, be separated. This article will only survey American musical groups, though a look at English music would reveal the prevalence of most of the themes explored here.

4. "The New Music," *loc. cit.,* p. 129.

5. *Time,* 80 (Nov. 23, 1962), 54–60, gives a brief survey of the folk revival.

6. Wills, *op. cit.,* gives a good analysis of his work. Though he is very quotable, there will, unfortunately, be no quotations from Dylan in this article because the author cannot afford the enormous fees required by Dylan's publisher for even the briefest of quotations.

7. It must be pointed out that, in spite of the large amount of social criticism, most songs today are still about love, even those by groups such as Country Joe and the Fish, best known for their social satire.

8. This article is concerned almost exclusively with music written and performed by white musicians. While popular music by Negroes does contain social criticism, the current forms—loosely termed "soul music"—make comments about oppression similar to those which Negroes have always made. The real change in content has come largely in white music in the 1960's.

9. Phil Ochs, "Talking Birmingham Jam" and "Here's to the State of Mississippi," *I Ain't Marching Any More* (Elektra, 7237); Simon and Garfunkel, "He Was My Brother," *Wednesday Morning 3 A.M.* (Columbia, CS 9049). (Songs from records will be noted by performer, song title in quotation marks, and album title in italics, followed by record company and number in parentheses.)

10. Copyright 1966 by Dialogue Music, Inc. Used by permission.

11. Ochs, *I Ain't Marching Any More.*

12. "The Harlem Song," *Together* (Vanguard, VSD 79277). Copyright by Joyful Wisdom Music, Inc.

13. Mothers of Invention, *Freak Out* (Verve, 65005). Copyright 1968 by Frank Zappa Music, Inc. All rights reserved.

14. Strawberry Alarm Clock, "Incense and Peppermints," written by John Carter and Tim Gilbert, *Strawberry Alarm Clock* (Uni., 73014). Copyright by Claridge Music, Inc.

15. Phil Ochs, "That Was the President," *"I Ain't Marching Any More;* the Byrds, "He Was A Friend of Mine," *Turn! Turn!* (Columbia, CS 9254).

16. "Superbird," *Electric Music for the Mind and Body* (Vanguard, 79244). Copyright by Tradition Music Company.

17. Love, "Mushroom Clouds," *Love* (Elektra, EKL 4001); the Byrds, "I Come and Stand at Every Door," *Fifth Dimension* (Columbia, CS 9349); Peanut Butter Conspiracy, "Wonderment," written by John Merrill, *Great Conspiracy* (Columbia, CS 9590). Copyright by 4-Star Music Company, Inc.

18. Copyright 1965 by Trousdale Music Publishers, Inc.

19. Buffy St. Marie, "Universal Soldier," Southern Publishing, ASCAP; Ochs, *I Ain't Marching Any More.*

20. *The Notorious Byrd Brothers* (Columbia, CS 9575).

21. "War Song," *Tenderness Junction* (Reprise, S 6280).

22. "An Untitled Protest," *Together.* Copyright by Joyful Wisdom Music.

23. "Kill for Peace," *The Fugs* (Esp. 1028).

24. "I Feel Like I'm Fixin' to Die," *I Feel Like I'm Fixin' to Die* (Vanguard, 9266). Copyright by Tradition Music Company.

25. *We're Only in It for the Money* (Verve, 65045). Copyright by Frank Zappa Music, Inc. All rights reserved.

26. "Laugh at Me," *Five West Cotillion,* BMI.

27. "My Crime," *Boogie* (Liberty, 7541).

28. "For What It's Worth." Copyright 1966 by Cotillion Music, Inc.—Ten East Music—Springaloo Toones. Reprinted by permission.

29. "Subterranean Homesick Blues," *Bob Dylan's Greatest Hits* (Columbia, KCS 9463).

30. *We're Only in It for the Money.* Copyright 1968 by Frank Zappa Music, Inc. All rights reserved.

31. "Mr. Blue," written by Tom Paxton, *Clear Light* (Elektra, 74011). Copyright 1966 by Deep Fork Music, Inc. All rights reserved. Used with permission.

32. Mothers of Invention, "Brown Shoes Don't Make It," *Absolutely Free* (Verve, 65013). Copyright 1968 by Frank Zappa Music, Inc. All rights reserved.

33. "Sounds of Silence," *Sounds of Silence* (Columbia, CS 9269).

34. *Sounds of Silence.*

35. *Wake Up . . . It's Tomorrow* (Uni., 73025).

36. "When the Music's Over," *Strange Days* (Elektra, 74014). Copyright 1967 by Nipper Music, Inc. All rights reserved.

37. "Chain Around the Flowers," *The Lewis and Clark Expedition* (Colgems, COS 105). Words and music by John Vandiver. Copyright 1967 by Screen Gems—Columbia Music, Inc. Used by permission. Reproduction prohibited.

38. *Surrealistic Pillow* (Victor, LSP 3766); "Stamped Ideas," *Heavy* (Atco, S 33–227).

39. Uncle Bernie's Farm," *Absolutely Free.*

40. "Plastic People," *Absolutely Free.* Copyright 1968 by Frank Zappa Music, Inc. All rights reserved.

41. *Ibid.*

42. "Goodbye and Hello," written by Tim Buckley, *Goodbye and Hello* (Elektra, 7318). Copyright 1968 by Third Story Music, Inc. All rights reserved.

43. *The Fugs;* "Venus in Furs," *The Velvet Underground and Nico* (Verve, V6–5008); "Brown Shoes Don't Make It," *Absolutely Free.*

44. *The United States of America* (Columbia, CS 9614).

45. "What Love," *The Collectors* (Warner Bros.-Seven Arts, WS 1746).

46. *We're Only in It for the Money;* "Cellophane Woman," *The Sopwith Camel* (Kama Sutra, KLPS 8060). Copyright by Great Honesty Music, Inc.

47. "Cellophane Woman." Copyright by Great Honesty Music, Inc.

48. "Motorcycle Irene," *Wow* (Columbia, CS 9613).

49. *Bob Dylan's Greatest Hits.*

50. "Ballad of a Thin Man/Mr. Jones," *Highway 61 Revisited* (Columbia, CS 9189). Though this song has obvious homosexual overtones, it also stands as youth's criticism of the older generation.

51. "Wild Tyme (H)," *After Bathing at Baxter's* (Victor, LSO-1511). Copyright by Ice Bag Corporation.

52. "Goodbye and Hello," written by Tim Buckley, *Goodbye and Hello.* Copyright 1968 by Third Story Music, Inc. All rights reserved.

53. "Pleasant Street," written by Tim Buckley. Copyright 1968 by Third Story Music, Inc. All rights reserved.

54. "When the Music's Over," *Strange Days.* Copyright 1967 by Nipper Music Company, Inc. All rights reserved.

55. "Saga of the Low Down Let Down," *The Sopwith Camel.* Copyright by Great Honesty Music, Inc.

56. "Fifth Dimension," *Fifth Dimension.*

57. "Topanga Window," *Spirit* (Ode, 212 44004); "Let's Get Together," *H. P. Lovecraft* (Phillips, 600–252).

58. "Feeling Groovy," *Sounds of Silence.*

59. "Time Is After You," *West Coast Love-In* (Vault, LP 113).

60. "Lost Sea Shanty," *Circus Maximus* (Vanguard, 79260); "Going Back," *The Notorious Byrd Brothers.*

61. "If 6 Was 9," *Axis* (Reprise, S 6281).

62. H. P. Lovecraft, "Let's Get Together," written by Chester Powers, *H. P. Lovecraft.* Copyright by Irving Music, Inc.

63. "Journey to the Center of the Mind," *Journey to the Center of the Mind* (Mainstream, S 6112). Copyright 1968 by Brent Music Corporation.

64. "Unconscious Power," *Heavy.*

65. There are so many "head songs" that listing them would be an impossibly long task. Some of the most popular protest songs of the decade have been such works. They include Jefferson Airplane, "White Rabbit," *Surrealistic Pillow;* the Doors, "Light My Fire," *The Doors* (Elektra EKS 74007); Strawberry Alarm Clock, "Incense and Peppermints," *Incense and Peppermints;* and the Byrds, "Eight Miles High," *Fifth Dimension.*

66. "Heroin," *Velvet Underground;* "Signed D. C.," *Love* (Elektra, 74001); "Amphetamine Annie," *Boogie;* "Coming Down," *The Fugs.*

67. "Fifth Dimension," *Fifth Dimension.*

68. See Country Joe and the Fish, "Bass Strings, *Electric Music for the Mind and Body;* or United States of America, "Coming Down," *United States of America.*

69. "Living, Loving Life," *Great Conspiracy.*

70. "Take Your Clothes Off When You Dance," *We're Only in It for the Money.* Copyright 1968 by Frank Zappa Music, Inc. All rights reserved.

74. BLACK NATIONALISM

J. HERMAN BLAKE

For black people as well as whites, "the times they are a-changin'." Nowhere is this more apparent than in the growing cultural nationalism that has taken place in black communities during the past several years.

Here, J. Herman Blake traces the origins and describes the meaning of Black Nationalism and points out the fact that, at the present at least, most black people see themselves as a part of American society even while recognizing and feeling that they are apart from it. Their separateness is manifest in a variety of ways. But one thing seems fairly clear: pulling the communities together is seen as a means of both enhancing leverage and increasing pride.

J. Herman Blake is a Lecturer in Sociology and a Fellow of Cowell College of the University of California at Santa Cruz.

The price the immigrants paid to get into America was that they had to become Americans. The black man *cannot* become an American (unless we get a different set of *rules*) because he is black.

LeRoi Jones

It is one of the bitter ironies of American history that the seeds of the contradiction which created black nationalism were sown in the colony of Jamestown in 1619. When the settlers accepted twenty captured Africans as servants—an act which eventually led to slavery—the reality of black inequality in America was established at the same time that the rhetoric of democracy was articulated.[1] Black nationalism has been a major form of protest against this contradiction since the early nineteenth century. Early nationalist protest followed several different emphases, but in the twentieth century these different strands were incorporated into a unified form of protest. The most recent trends in black nationalism reveal some unique features which have significant implications for future developments.

Black nationalist thought is a consequence of the duality of the experience of Afro-Americans, a people who are identified by racial characteristics as different from the "typical" American and denied full participation in this society for that reason, while, at the same time, they are expected to meet all the responsibilities of citizenship. It reflects the negative self-image which many black people have unconsciously developed, and the sense of hopelessness that has persisted in the Afro-American community as a consequence of being treated as inferiors.

Early Trends

The first distinctive form of black nationalism was the desire to separate from America expressed by some free blacks in the early part of the nineteenth century.[2] The proponents of this form of *political nationalism* argued for the establishment of a black nation in Africa or some other territory. Their views were based on a conviction that Afro-Americans would never receive justice in America and that

Reprinted from *The Annals,* **382** (March 1969), 15–25, by permission of the author and The American Academy of Political and Social Science.

the only hope was to leave the country and establish a political entity for black people. The apex of this development came at the Emigration Convention of 1854, when three men were commissioned to investigate the possibilities of emigration of blacks to Central America, the Black Republic of Haiti, or the Niger Valley in West Africa.

The apparent permanence of American slavery and the racial barriers set up against freed blacks led these men to the conviction that true justice and equality for black people would never be reached in this country, and there were other territories to which they might emigrate. Thus, those in favor of emigration argued that the only hope for the black man was to leave this country and establish a black nation in which the emigrants could live free from fear, racial prejudice, and discrimination. The Civil War and emancipation of the slaves brought black agitation for emigration to a halt, and black people devoted themselves to the task of becoming a part of the American society.

Though emancipation increased the hopes of blacks that full participation in the society was forthcoming, post-Reconstruction developments made it increasingly clear that such was not to be the case. The depressing conditions which followed the Hayes compromise led to the development of philosophies of self-help, particularly as expressed in *economic nationalism*. This emphasis called for racial solidarity and economic co-operation as the solution to the problems of the Afro-American. The growing influx of Europeans into Northern cities and factories increased the pessimism of some influential Afro-Americans and led them to look for salvation within the race. Booker T. Washington, a major proponent of economic nationalism, felt that industrial education and the perfection of agricultural skills in the rural South would lead whites to the realization that black people were worthy of equal treatment. In his famous Atlanta Exposition Address of 1895,

Washington revealed that he was aware of the impact of European immigration upon American industry, and evidently felt that this trend closed the doors of opportunity in the North to blacks. Therefore, he pursued a policy of racial solidarity and economic self-sufficiency, establishing the National Negro Business League in 1900 for the purpose of stimulating business enterprise. At the 1904 convention of the League, Washington viewed the developments of black businesses through the support of black people as crucial to the removal of racial prejudice in America.[3] Unlike political nationalism, economic nationalism revealed a desire for participation in the society, but in the face of rejection by Americans, the economic emphasis worked on strengthening the internal community as part of an attack upon the racial barriers.

Cultural nationalism was another response to the denial of equality to Afro-Americans. Like economic nationalism, the emphasis was upon racial solidarity, with added attraction given to the development of racial pride and dignity. These goals were sought through the study of the history of the black man and his contribution to mankind. The essential belief of the cultural nationalists was that a scholarly analysis and study of the history of black people throughout the world, particularly in America, would show blacks and whites that Afro-Americans are descended from a proud heritage and have made outstanding contributions to human progress. It was thought that such an understanding would have two consequences: (1) It would give blacks a positive self-image and further the development of racial pride and solidarity; and (2) it would show whites that blacks were no better nor worse than any other race and that because of their contributions, they should be fully accepted into the society.

Although there were attempts to develop the study of Afro-American history before the Civil War, cultural nationalism received its greatest impetus during the latter part of the nineteenth century. The desire to give scholarly attention to the historical past of the black man resulted in the organization of the Association for the Study of Negro Life and History in 1915, and to the establishment of the *Journal of Negro History*.[4]

Political, economic, and cultural forms of black nationalism all had their roots in the social conditions confronting Afro-Americans. During the days of slavery, the desire for emigration and separation increased with the growing conviction that slavery would never be eliminated. It is noteworthy that the emigration movement among blacks reached its most significant point during the 1850's and that such interest declined with the onset of the Civil War. In the latter part of the nineteenth century, economic and cultural nationalism developed as a consequence of continued hostility and repression. The end of Reconstruction, the rise of Jim Crow, the lack of economic opportunity, and similar conditions led to the development of economic and cultural attempts to foster individual and collective strength within the black community while pursuing an attack upon the prejudiced and discriminatory behavior of the larger society. The major proponents of these various emphases came from the upper levels of the Afro-American community. Martin R. Delany, a supporter of emigration, was a physician and Harvard graduate; Booker T. Washington was the undisputed leader of black people from 1895 until his death in 1915; and Arthur A. Schomburg, Carter G. Woodson, and W. E. B. DuBois were all highly educated and literate men. Black nationalist movements did not develop a foundation among the masses until after World War I.

Twentieth-Century Patterns

Black nationalism as a mass movement followed the creation of a ready audience and the combination of the various strands of nationalistic thought into an integral whole. When Marcus Garvey, a native of Jamaica, established the Universal Negro Improvement Association and African Communities League (UNIA) in New York City in 1917, he brought *integral nationalism* to a people who were looking for hope in what appeared to be a hopeless situation.[5]

Garvey made his strongest appeal to the many blacks who had migrated out of the South shortly before his arrival in the country, seeking employment in the industrial centers of the North. Agricultural depression and the appearance of the boll weevil in Southern cotton had made living conditions extremely difficult. At the same time, the European war had placed heavy demands on Northern industry, and the supply of European immigrant labor had been cut off. Therefore, Northern industrialists began a campaign to induce blacks to leave the South and work in Northern factories. It is estimated that in one two-year period a half-million black people moved to the North.[6]

The many blacks who made this journey found that though they were often openly recruited, they were seldom welcomed, for they were crowded into urban slums and faced a continual round of unemployment, depression, and indigence. Furthermore, they met the massive hostility of whites—many of them newly arrived in this country—who saw the black in-migrants as threats to their economic security and reacted against them with devastating riots. The continued hardships of the blacks and the intense hostility of the whites created a situation in which Garvey's appeal seemed eminently rational. They were the same conditions which led to earlier forms of nationalism, except that the blacks perceived them in a much more intensified manner than previously. Garvey's integral form of black nationalism flourished in this situation, and its significance was not only that it was the first major social movement among the black masses; it also indicated the extent to which they "entertained doubts concerning the hope for first-class citizenship in the only fatherland of which they knew." [7]

The UNIA program combined previous emphases in black nationalism. Drawing upon the Booker T. Washington philosophy of economic independence, Garvey established various commercial enterprises, among them the Black Star Line, a steamship company designed to link the black peoples of the world through trade, and the Negro Factories Corporation, designed to build and operate factories in the industrial centers of the United States, Central America, the West Indies, and Africa. In the tradition of the political nationalists, Garvey sought to have all whites expelled from Africa so that it could become a territory for black people only. He told Afro-Americans that race prejudice was such an inherent part of white civilization that it was futile to appeal to the white man's sense of justice. The only hope was to leave America and return to Africa. His vigorous promotion of racial solidarity and black consciousness was one of his most lasting successes. Exalting everything black, he renewed the assertions that Africa had a noble history and urged Afro-Americans to be proud of their ancestry. Coming when it did, his program had a profound impact upon the black masses, and even his severest critics admit that in the early 1920's, his followers numbered perhaps half a million. [8]

The Garvey movement did not show the dualism found in earlier nationalist sentiment. It was a philosophy that fully embraced blackness and vigorously rejected white America. Although the movement declined after his imprisonment in 1925, the integral form of black nationalism was to continue. In the early 1930's the Lost Found Nation of Islam in the Wilderness of North America was established in Detroit, and began to grow under the leadership of Elijah Muhammad.

After two decades of relative obscurity, the Nation of Islam experienced rapid growth during the 1950's, particularly when the brilliant and articulate ex-convict, Malcolm X, began speaking around the country in the name of the organization. Like the UNIA, the Nation of Islam is an unequivocal rejection of white America and a turn inward to the black man and the black community as the only source of hope for resolving racial problems. Unlike the UNIA, the Nation of Islam contains a strong religious component which is a major binding force in the organization. There is the Holy Koran which provides scriptural guidance, Elijah Muhammad (The Messenger) who provides everyday leadership, an eschatology, and a set of rituals which give the members a valuable shared experience. [9] The rejection of white America involves a rejection of Christianity as the religion of the black man, English as the mother tongue of the black man, and the Stars and Stripes as the flag of the black man. Muslims also refuse to use the term "Negro," their family names, and traditional Southern foods, which are all taken as remnants of the slave condition and a reaffirmation of that condition so long as they are used.

The Nation of Islam places great emphasis upon black consciousness and racial pride, claiming that a man cannot know another man until he knows himself. This search for black identity is conducted through the study of the religious teachings of Islam, as interpreted by Elijah Muhammad, and through the study of Afro-American and African history.

Muslims also follow a strong program of economic nationalism, with their emphasis upon independent black businesses. Muslim enterprises, mostly of the service variety, have been established across the country and have been quite successful. They are now opening supermarkets and supplying them with produce from Muslim-owned farms. There is also some movement now into light manufacturing.

The Muslim emphasis upon a separate territory for black people gave new emphasis to political nationalism. They have never specified whether that land should be on this continent or another, but they have consistently argued that since blacks and whites cannot live together in peace in this country, it would be better if the blacks were to leave the country and set up an independent nation. In the Muslim view, such a nation would be an Islamic theocracy. This new element of political nationalism, emphasizing land rather than Africa, emigration, or colonization, has become a significant element of contemporary black nationalist protest.

The Nation of Islam had a profound effect upon the development of contemporary trends in black nationalism. There are very few ardent black nationalists today who have not had some close contact with the Nation of Islam either through membership or through having come under the influence of one of its eloquent ministers. Even though the Nation of Islam grew rapidly there were many black people who were deeply influenced but were not persuaded by the doctrine of total separation from America or by the religious emphasis. This was particularly true of college-educated blacks. The break between Malcolm X and the Nation of Islam in early 1964 had a profound impact on current trends by spurring the development of black nationalism among countless numbers of blacks who supported the Muslim emphasis upon black consciousness and racial solidarity.

The Universal Negro Improvement Association and African Communities League under Marcus Garvey and the Lost Found Nation of Islam in the Wilderness of North America under Elijah Muhammad have been very successful and influential forms of integral nationalism. Both the leaders and the followers came primarily from among the black masses of the urban North, whose lives had not seen the steady progress toward perfection which characterizes the myth of the American dream of success. These two movements brought the various threads of nineteenth-century black nationalism together, and wove them into a matrix out of which the more recent trends in black nationalist thought have developed. Contemporary trends, however, add some distinctive elements of their own which are shaping black nationalism and the current pattern of race relations in America.

Contemporary Developments

The development of black-nationalist-protest thought in recent years is related to the same conditions which produced such sentiment in earlier periods, as well as to some new and unique conditions. In recent years, the urbanization of the black man has proceeded at a very rapid pace. In 1960, a higher proportion of the black population (73 per cent) were residents of the cities than ever before, and this proportion exceeded that of the white population (70 per cent). Not only are blacks moving into the cities; whites are moving out, so that more of the central cities are becoming all-black enclaves. Between 1960 and 1965, the proportion of blacks in central cities increased by 23 per cent while the proportion of whites declined by 9 per cent.[10]

It is not simply that black people are now predominantly urban; in recent years, black urban residents have become new urbanites for two major reasons. Not a small proportion of the in-migrants to central cities are younger blacks who are generally better educated than those whites who remain in the cities.[11] Furthermore, a new generation of black people is coming to maturity, young people who were born and raised in the urban black communities. They do not use a previous Southern pattern of living as the framework through which they assess their current situation, but use an urban, mainstream-America framework, usually learned from the mass media rather than experienced. These youth comprise a very large proportion of the urban residents and are less enchanted by the view that, although things are bad, they are better than they used to be.[12] As such, they are very critical of attitudes of those blacks who see the situation of the black man as improving. A small but significant proportion of the new urbanites are young people who have graduated from first-rate colleges and hold white-collar positions in integrated firms. The subtle prejudices which they have encountered, along with the empty lives of the many middle-class whites whom they have met, have increased their awareness that there is a style and tone of life in the black community which gives much more satisfaction than that of the white middle class.[13] The heightened interaction of black youth as a result of urban living, the coming-of-age of a generation of post-World War II youth, and the rejection of some white middle-class values in the attempt to articulate values which grow out of the black experience [14] are some of the internal dynamics of black communities in the 1960's which are producing a new upsurge in nationalism.

The postwar independence movements around the world have also affected the thinking of black people. Earlier generations of black nationalists predicted the rise of Africa as part of the world community. They had preached about the day when "princes would come out of Ethiopia," but the present generation has witnessed that rise. Black urbanites, seeing African diplomats welcomed by American presidents and taking leading roles in the United Nations, became increasingly bitter about the limited freedom and opportunity of Afro-Americans.

While Africans and Asians were gaining independence and taking seats in the halls of world council, the gap between black and white Americans was not changing perceptibly. Since 1960, black males have not made appreciable gains on white males in income and occupation, black communities are more separated from white communities than ever before, and the education of black youth is still woefully inadequate. Even for those middle-class blacks who appear to have made many strides during the 1960's, the evidence indicates that they have made large relative gains over lower-class blacks, but have not reduced the gap between themselves and middle-class whites.[15]

There is one major positive change that has taken place in the past few years, however; a higher proportion of black youth are completing high school and college. Such youth are not following past patterns of individualistic escape from the black community—with their heightened awareness and knowledge, they are becoming more involved in black communities as residents and as activists. An important and new element in black nationalism in this union of black intellectuals and the black masses. While nationalism in the nineteenth century was notable for its lack of mass support, and for its lack of intellectual backing, in the mass movements of the twentieth century in recent years, intellectuals and the masses have combined their skills to give new impetus to nationalist movements. An excellent example is the development of the Mississippi Freedom Democratic Party.[16]

The key figure in the development of the recent trends was the late El-Hajj Malik El-Shabazz. After his break with the Nation of Islam, he began to link the struggle of Afro-Americans with the struggle of oppressed peoples throughout the world, and particularly in Africa. He also emphasized *human rights* rather than *civil rights,* thereby increasing the hope that the Afro-American struggle might come before the United Nations. In this way, he internationalized the conditions of Afro-Americans and increased their awareness of the value of links with the non-Western world.[17]

Malik El-Shabazz gave new emphasis to the possibility of reform in America, an idea which was not contained in the view of either Marcus Garvey or Elijah Muhammad. In his "The Ballot or the Bullet" speech, he expressed the view that it was possible to produce a bloodless revolution in this country. His views were close to those of earlier nationalists who saw the development of the inner strengths of the black community as a first step in attacking racial barriers.

Another key contribution was his ability to appeal to both intellectuals and the masses and bring them together. El-Shabazz was very widely read, and a brilliant and articulate spokesman. His knowledge and logic impressed black intellectuals deeply. He was also an ex-convict and a man of the streets. Consequently, those who were the most deprived could identify as strongly with him as could the intellectual. His dual appeal to intellectuals and the masses, along with his emphasis upon racial solidarity, helped to bring these two elements of the black community into greater harmony.

In addition, Malik El-Shabazz spurred the development of black consciousness and black dignity. He was a living example of the positive effect of black consciousness, and there were few black people who met him who were not profoundly moved by what he was. Said one writer: "The concept of Blackness, the concept of National Consciousness, the proposal of a political (and diplomatic) form for this aggregate of Black Spirit, these are the things given to us by Garvey, through Elijah Muhammad, and finally given motion into still another area of Black Response by Malcolm X." [18] Another captures the nature of the appeal of El-Shabazz:

It was not the Black Muslim movement itself that was so irresistibly appealing to the true believers. It was the awakening into self-consciousness of twenty million Negroes which was so compelling. Malcolm X articulated their aspirations better than any other man of our time. When he spoke under the banner of Elijah Muhammad, he was irresistible. When he spoke under his own banner, he was still irresistible. If he had become a Quaker, . . . and if he had continued to give

voice to the mute ambitions in the black man's soul, his message would still have been triumphant: because what was great was not Malcolm X but the truth he uttered. [19]

In the minds of present-day nationalists, El-Hajj Malik El-Shabazz was the greatest prince to come out of Ethiopia, and he is now the martyred saint of the movement. [20]

The articulation and development of the concept of Black Power continues the emphasis on an integral form of black nationalism, [21] yet with new elements. The political emphasis of Black Power renews the hope for reform in America, but with attention given to a reform of *values* as well as *behavior*. As such, it strikes more deeply at the basis of the problems separating blacks and whites. Black Power advocates also add a strong community orientation to black nationalism. They have not sought to build a unified mass movement around the country, but rather to develop programs and policies relating to the particular needs, conditions, and expressed desires of specific communities. The articulation of Black Power by a student-based organization, along with its community orientation, continued the unified approach of the intellectuals and the masses.

The development of black nationalist thought since the rise of El-Hajj Malik El-Shabazz has brought new emphasis to old issues, particularly the political and cultural forms of nationalism. The political emphasis is developing around the issues of colonization of black people, land, independence, self-determination for black communities, and the accountability of black leaders. When Malik El-Shabazz began to link black people with the Third World—a trend continued by Black Power advocates—black people became more aware that their situation in this country was very similar to that of colonized peoples throughout the world.

The large numbers of blacks in central cities, along with the presence of agencies of social control directed by forces outside of the black communities, bears a strong resemblance to a colonial situation.[22] This awareness has brought many blacks to the realization that such aggregations are similar to nations in the same way that Indian tribes saw themselves as nations, and they now occupy a territory which can be viewed as their own. LeRoi Jones puts it thus:

What the Black Man must do now is to look down at the ground upon which he stands, and claim it as his own. It is not abstract. Look down! Pick up the earth, or jab your fingernails into the concrete. It is real and it is yours, if you want it.

All the large concentrations of Black People in the West are already nations. All that is missing is the consciousness of this state of affairs.[23]

This awareness and consciousness is growing rapidly, and the emphasis upon self-determination for black communities is evidence of this fact. Indeed, if one understands this intense desire of black people to control their own communities and to determine their destinies, the urban insurrections of recent years take on another facet. If the community is seen as a colony and the social control agencies as colonial agents, then spontaneous outbursts may also be interpreted as attempts to reaffirm local rather than foreign control of the community. An altercation between a police officer and a black man is an assertion of colonial control, and the ensuing outburst, however destructive, is a reaffirmation of the view that such control does not lie exclusively with the colonial agencies.[24] Related to self-determination is the emphasis upon accountability being developed by nationalists. This view holds that those who hold positions of power which affect the black community must answer exclusively to the black community.

Colonization, land, self-determination, and accountability are the basic elements in recent developments in black nationalism, particularly the expansion of its political emphasis. Such views led one group of black militants, the Federation for Self-Determination in Detroit, to reject a grant of $100,000 from the New Detroit Committee in early 1968 on the grounds that there were too many controls attached to the grant. Such views led the militant Black Panther party, based in Oakland, California, to begin to develop a political program on the grounds that black men who represent either of the major political parties cannot be held wholly accountable by the black community. Similar examples can be found in black communities across the nation, for these views are crucial aspects of the present framework of action of black nationalists today.

In recent years, black consciousness has received added impetus in terms of racial solidarity and a positive self-image. Thus, there is the new emphasis upon black as beautiful, and black youth are adopting African-style clothing and wearing African or natural hair styles.[25] They are seeking to establish black studies and black curricula on college campuses. These courses of study, however, are to have a strong community and service orientation, rather than to become wholly intellectual pursuits. It is unquestionably the development of black consciousness and racial solidarity, along with the attitude of self-determination and black accountability, which has spurred the revolt of black athletes in many colleges and the attempt to obtain a black boycott of the 1968 Olympic Games. This is a new and revolutionary black consciousness, exemplified by El-Hajj Malik El-Shabazz and activated among black communities across the land.

Summary and Conclusion

Black nationalism has been one of the most militant and strident forms of Afro-American protest. It has grown out of the social conditions which have repeatedly indicated to black people that, though they are in this country, they are not a part of this country. The most recent emphases in nationalist thought are clearly developing the inner strengths of the black community through cultural nationalism, and expanding the concept of political nationalism. It may well be that black people will find that after all other barriers between the races have been eliminated, the barrier of color will prove to be ineradicable. Such a realization will give new and revolutionary impetus to black nationalism.

. . .

Some of us have been, and some still are, interested in learning whether it is *ultimately* possible to live in the same territory with people who seem so disagreeable to live with; still others want to get as far away from ofays as possible.

ELDRIDGE CLEAVER

NOTES

1. Vincent Harding, "The Uses of the Afro-American Past," *Negro Digest,* 17 (February 1968), 5.

2. E. U. Essien-Udom, *Black Nationalism: A Search for an Identity in America,* Chicago: University of Chicago Press, 1962, chap. ii; and August Meier, "The Emergence of Negro Nationalism," *The Midwest Journal,* 4 (Winter 1951), 96–104, and *ibid.* (Summer 1952), 95–111.

3. Meier, *op. cit.*

4. *Ibid.*

5. Edmund David Cronon, *Black Moses: The Story of Marcus Garvey and the Universal Negro Improvement Association,* Madison: University of Wisconsin Press, 1955. The UNIA was actually organized in Jamaica in 1914 by Garvey, but he experienced his greatest success in the United States.

6. Cronon, *op. cit.,* pp. 22–27.

7. John Hope Franklin, *From Slavery to Freedom,* New York: Alfred A. Knopf, 1963, p. 483.

8. Cronon, *op. cit.,* chap. iii; Franklin, *op. cit.,* pp. 481–483.

9. Essien-Udom, *op. cit.;* and C. Eric Lincoln, *The Black Muslims in America,* Boston: Beacon Press, 1961.

10. U. S. Department of Commerce, Bureau of the Census, *Current Population Reports,* Series P-20, No. 157, December 16, 1966.

11. Karl E. Taeuber and Alma F. Taeuber, "The Changing Character of Negro Migration," *American Journal of Sociology,* 70 (January 1965), 429–441.

12. Claude Brown states this issue well by raising the question: "Where does one run to when he's already in the promised land?"—*Manchild in the Promised Land,* New York: The Macmillan Company, 1965, p. 8.

13. This fact has been discovered by white middle-class youth as well, and they now seek to experience the authentic feeling-tone of Afro-American existence. Among black people, this new form of rejection of white America is authenticated by one's possession of that ethereal quality "soul," and is expressed in the "funky" music of black artists.

14. For a particularly profound and moving articulation of such issues, see Vincent Harding, "The Gift of Blackness," *Kattallagete* (Summer 1967), pp. 17–22.

15. J. Herman Blake, "The Black University and Its Community: Social Change in the Sixties," *Negro Digest,* 17 (March 1968), 87–90.

16. Stokely Carmichael and Charles V. Hamilton, *Black Power: The Politics of Liberation in America,* New York: Random House, 1967.

17. Malcolm X, *Autobiography,* New York: Grove Press, 1966; also, the brief movie *Malcolm X: Struggle for Freedom* gives important insights into his post-Nation of Islam ideas, including his expansion of the concept "Afro-American."

18. LeRoi Jones, *Home,* New York: Morrow, 1966, p. 243.

19. Eldridge Cleaver, *Soul on Ice,* New York: McGraw-Hill, 1968, p. 59.

20. See the moving eulogy of El-Hajj Malik El-Shabazz by Ossie Davis in *Liberator,* 5 (April 1965), 7.

21. Stokely Carmichael, "What We Want," *New York Review of Books,* 7 (September 22, 1966), 5.

22. For two excellent articulations of this view, see: Carmichael and Hamilton, *op. cit.,* chap. i; and Cleaver, *op. cit.,* pp. 112–137.

23. Jones, *op. cit.,* pp. 244 and 249.

24. See Anthony Oberschall, "The Los Angeles Riot of August 1965," *Social Problems,* 15 (Winter 1968), 322–341.

25. I received an excellent personal view of the impact of the new black consciousness on youth while teaching Afro-American history to junior high school youth each summer in a black community near San Francisco. In 1966, I showed the youths a picture of Crispus Attucks, and some of them exclaimed, "He's sure got a nappy head." In 1967 this same picture was greeted with the comment, "He's got a boss natural." This was the same community and some of the same youth. The only thing that had changed was their consciousness of themselves.

75. THE LIBERATED GENERATION: AN EXPLORATION OF THE ROOTS OF STUDENT PROTEST

RICHARD FLACKS

The Student Protest Movement is, as Richard Flacks points out, a social phenomenon of considerable significance. In his paper, Flacks offers an interpretation of the background and character of the Movement and summarizes the results of a study he conducted at the University of Chicago in the spring of 1966.

Flacks' essay is more than a report on "the liberated generation." It is a sociological statement which touches on the many areas of concern described in the preceding sections of this book—cultural norms and values, the process of socialization and its effects, ethnic and class factors in the determination of attitudes, familial and other influences, the issue of conformity and the strain toward deviance, and many more. The paper raises many questions, too. All told it is an appropriate ending for this volume— and a fitting beginning for further work on the study of society.

Richard Flacks was one of the founders of the Students for a Democratic Society. He now teaches sociology at the University of California at Santa Barbara.

As all of us are by now aware, there has emerged, during the past five years, an increasingly self-conscious student movement in the United States. This movement began primarily as a response to the efforts by southern Negro students to break the barriers of legal segregation in public accommodations—scores of northern white students engaged in sympathy demonstrations and related activities as early as 1960. But as we all know, the scope of the student concern expanded rapidly to include such issues as nuclear testing and the arms race, attacks on civil liberties, the problems of the poor in urban slum ghettoes, democracy and educational quality in universities, the war in Vietnam, conscription.

This movement represents a social phenomenon of considerable significance. In the first place, it is having an important direct and indirect impact on the larger society. But secondly it is significant because it is a phenomenon which was unexpected—unexpected, in particular, by those social scientists who are professionally responsible for locating and understanding such phenomena. Because it is an unanticipated event, the attempt to understand and explain the sources of the student movement may lead to fresh interpretations of some important trends in our society.

Radicalism and the Young Intelligentsia

In one sense, the existence of a radical student movement should not be unexpected. After all, the young intelligentsia seem almost always to be in revolt. Yet if we examine the case a bit more closely I think we will find that movements of active disaffection among intellectuals and

Reprinted from the *Journal of Social Issues,* **23,** 3(1967), 52–75, by permission of the author and The Society for the Psychological Study of Social Issues.

students tend to be concentrated at particular moments in history. Not every generation produces an organized oppositional movement.

In particular, students and young intellectuals seem to have become active agents of opposition and change under two sets of inter-related conditions:

When they have been marginal in the labor market because their numbers exceed the opportunities for employment commensurate with their abilities and training. This has most typically been the case in colonial or underdeveloped societies; it also seems to account, in part, for the radicalization of European Jewish intellectuals and American college-educated women at the turn of the century (Coser, 1965; Shils, 1960; Veblen, 1963).

When they found that the values with which they were closely connected by virtue of their upbringing no longer were appropriate to the developing social reality. This has been the case most typically at the point where traditional authority has broken down due to the impact of Westernization, industrialization, modernization. Under these conditions, the intellectuals, and particularly the youth, felt called upon to assert new values, new modes of legitimation, new styles of life. Although the case of breakdown of traditional authority is most typically the point at which youth movements have emerged, there seems, historically, to have been a second point in time—in Western Europe and the United States—when intellectuals were radicalized. This was, roughly, at the turn of the century, when values such as gentility, laissez faire, naive optimism, naive rationalism and naive nationalism seemed increasingly inappropriate due to the impact of large scale industrial organization, intensifying class conflict, economic crisis and the emergence of total war. Variants of radicalism waxed and waned in their influence among American intellectuals and students during the first four decades of the twentieth century (Aaron, 1965; Eisenstadt, 1956; Lasch, 1965).

If these conditions have historically been those which produced revolts among the young intelligentsia, then I think it is easy to understand why a relatively superficial observer would find the new wave of radicalism on the campus fairly mysterious.

In the first place, the current student generation can look forward, not to occupational insecurity or marginality, but to an unexampled opening up to opportunity for occupational advance in situations in which their skills will be maximally demanded and the prestige of their roles unprecedentedly high.

In the second place, there is no evident erosion of the legitimacy of established authority; we do not seem, at least on the surface, to be in a period of rapid disintegration of traditional values—at least no more so than a decade ago when sociologists were observing the *exhaustion* of opportunity for radical social movements in America (Bell, 1962; Lipset, 1960).

In fact, during the Fifties sociologists and social psychologists emphasized the decline in political commitment, particularly among the young, and the rise of a bland, security-oriented conformism throughout the population, but most particularly among college students. The variety of studies conducted then reported students as overwhelmingly unconcerned with value questions, highly complacent, status-oriented, privatized, uncommitted (Jacob, 1957; Goldsen, *et al.,* 1960). Most of us interpreted this situation as one to be expected given the opportunities newly opened to educated youth, and given the emergence of liberal pluralism and affluence as the characteristic features of postwar America. Several observers predicted an intensification of the pattern of middle-class conformism, declining individualism, and growing "other-directedness" based on the changing styles of child-rearing prevalent in the middle class. The democratic and "permissive" family would produce young men who knew how to cooperate in bureaucratic settings, but who lacked a strongly rooted ego-ideal and inner control (Miller and Swanson, 1958; Bronfenbrenner, 1961; Erickson, 1963). Although some observers reported that some students were searching for "meaning" and "self-expression," and others reported the existence of "subcultures" of alienation and bohemianism on some campuses (Keniston, 1965a; Trow, 1962; Newcomb and Flacks, 1963), not a single observer of the campus scene as late as 1959 anticipated the emergence of the organized disaffection, protest and activism which was to take shape early in the Sixties.

In short, the very occurrence of a student movement in the present American context is surprising because it seems to contradict our prior understanding of the determinants of disaffection among the young intelligentsia.

A Revolt of the Advantaged

The student movement is, I think, surprising for another set of reasons. These have to do with its social composition and the kinds of ideological themes which characterize it.

The current group of student activists is predominantly upper middle class, and frequently these students are of elite origins. This fact is evident as soon as one begins to learn the personal histories of activist leaders. Consider the following scene at a convention of Students for a Democratic Society a few years ago. Toward the end of several days of deliberation, someone decided that a quick way of raising funds for the organization would be to appeal to the several hundred students assembled at the convention to dig down deep into their pockets on the spot. To this end, one of the leadership, skilled at mimicry, stood on a chair, and in the style of a Southern Baptist preacher, appealed to the students to come forward, confess their sins and be saved by contributing to SDS. The students did come forward, and in each case, the sin confessed was the social class or occupation of their fathers. "My father is the editor of a Hearst newspaper, I give $25!" My father is Assistant Director of the _____ Bureau, I give $40." "My father is dean of a law school, here's $50!"

These impressions of the social composition of the student movement are supported and refined by more systematic sources of data. For example, when a random sample of students who participated in the anti-Selective Service sit-in at the University of Chicago Administration Building was compared with a sample composed of nonprotesters and students hostile to the protest, the protesters disproportionately reported their social class to be "upper middle," their family incomes to be disproportionately high, their parents' education to be disproportionately advanced. In addition, the protesters' fathers' occupations were primarily upper professional (doctors, college faculty, lawyers) rather than business, white collar, or working class. These findings parallel those of other investigators (Braungart, 1966). Thus, the student movement represents the disaffection not of an underprivileged stratum of the student population but of *the most advantaged* sector of the students.

One hypothesis to explain disaffection among socially advantaged youth would suggest that, although such students come from advantaged backgrounds, their academic performance leads them to anticipate downward mobility or failure. Stinchcombe, for example, found high rates of quasi-delinquent rebelliousness among middle-class high school youth with poor academic records (Stinchcombe, 1964). This hypothesis is not tenable with respect to college student protest, however. Our own data with respect to the anti-draft protest at Chicago indicate that the grade point average of the protesters average around B–B+ (with 75% of them reporting a B– or better average). This was slightly higher than the grade point average of our sample of nonprotesters. Other data from our own research indicate that student activists tend to be at the top of their high school class; in general, data from our own and other studies support the view that many activists are academically superior, and that very few activists are recruited from among low academic achievers. Thus, in terms of *both* the status of their families of origins *and* their own scholastic performance, student protest movements are predominantly composed of students who have been born to high social advantage and who are in a position to experience the career and status opportunities of the society without significant limitations.

Themes of the Protest

The positive correlation between disaffection and status among college students suggested by these observations is, I think, made even more paradoxical when one examines closely the main value themes which characterize the student movement. I want to describe these in an impressionistic way here; a more systematic depiction awaits further analysis of our data.

ROMANTICISM There is a strong stress among many movement participants on a quest for self-expression, often articulated in terms of leading a "free" life—i.e., one not bound by conventional restraints on feeling, experience, communication, expression. This is often coupled with aesthetic interests and a strong rejection of scientific and other highly rational pursuits. Students often express the classic romantic aspiration of "knowing" or "experiencing" "everything."

ANTI-AUTHORITARIANISM A strong antipathy toward arbitrary rule, centralized decision-making, "manipulation." The anti-authoritarian sentiment is fundamental to the widespread campus protests during the past few years; in most cases, the protests were precipitated by an administrative act which was interpreted as arbitrary, and received impetus when college administrators continued to act unilaterally, coercively or secretively. Anti-authoritarianism is manifested further by the styles and internal processes within activist organizations; for example, both SDS and SNCC have attempted to decentralize their operations quite radically and members are strongly critical of leadership within the organization when it is too assertive.

EGALITARIANISM, POPULISM A belief that all men are capable of political participation, that political power should be widely dispersed, that the locus of value in society lies with the people and not elites. This is a stress on something more than equality of opportunity or equal legal treatment; the students stress instead the notion of "participatory democracy"—direct participation in the making of decisions by those affected by them. Two common slogans—"One man, one vote"; "Let the people decide."

ANTI-DOGMATISM A strong reaction against doctrinaire ideological interpretations of events. Many of the students are quite restless when presented with formulated models of the social order, and specific programs for social change. This underlies much of their antagonism to the varieties of "old left" politics, and is one meaning of the oft-quoted (if not seriously used) phrase: "you can't trust anyone over thirty."

MORAL PURITY A strong antipathy to self-interested behavior, particularly when overlaid by claims of disinterestedness. A major criticism of the society is that it is "hypocritical." Another meaning of the criticism of the older generation has to do with the perception that (a) the older generation "sold out" the values it espouses; (b) to assume conventional adult roles usually leads to increasing self-interestedness, hence selling-out, or "phoniness." A particularly important criticism students make of the university is that it fails to live up to its professed ideals; there is an expectation that the institution ought to be *moral*—that is, not compromise its official values for the sake of institutional survival or aggrandizement.

COMMUNITY A strong emphasis on a desire for "human" relationships, for a full expression of emotions, for the breaking down of interpersonal barriers and the refusal to accept conventional norms concerning interpersonal contact (e.g., norms respecting sex, status, race, age, etc.). A central positive theme in the campus revolts has been the expression of the desire for a campus "community," for the breaking down of aspects of impersonality on the campus, for more direct contact between students and faculty. There is a frequent counterposing of bureaucratic norms to communal norms; a testing of the former against the latter. Many of the students involved in slum projects have experimented with attempts to achieve a "kibbutz"-like community amongst themselves entailing communal living and a strong stress on achieving intimacy and resolving tensions within the group.

ANTI-INSTITUTIONALISM A strong distrust of involvement with conventional institutional roles. This is most importantly expressed in the almost universal desire among the highly involved to avoid institutionalized careers. Our data suggest that few student activists look toward careers in the professions, the sciences, industry, or politics. Many of the most committed expect to continue to work full-time in the "movement" or, alternatively, to become free-lance writers, artists, intellectuals. A high proportion are oriented toward academic careers—at least so far the academic career seems still to have a reputation among many student activists for permitting "freedom."

Several of these themes, it should be noted, are not unique to student activists. In particular, the value we have described as "romanticism"—a quest for self-expression—has been found by observers, for example Kenneth Keniston (1965b), to be a central feature of the ideology of "alienated" or "bohemian" students (see also Keinston's article in this issue). Perhaps more important, the disaffection of student activists with conventional careers, their low valuation of careers as important in their personal aspirations, their quest for careers outside the institutionalized sphere—these attitudes toward

careers seem to be characteristic of other groups of students as well. It is certainly typical of youth involved in "bohemian" and aesthetic subcultures; it also characterizes students who volunteer for participation in such programs as the Peace Corps, Vista and other full-time commitments oriented toward service. In fact, it is our view that the dissatisfaction of socially advantaged youth with conventional career opportunities is a significant social trend, the most important single indicator of restlessness among sectors of the youth population. One expression of this restlessness is the student movement, but it is not the only one. One reason why it seems important to investigate the student movement in detail, despite the fact that it represents a small minority of the student population, is that it is a symptom of social and psychological strains experienced by a larger segment of the youth— strains not well understood or anticipated heretofore by social science.

If some of the themes listed above are not unique to student activists, several of them may characterize only a portion of the activist group itself. In particular, some of the more explicitly political values are likely to be articulated mainly by activists who are involved in radical organizations, particularly Students for a Democratic Society, and the Student Non-violent Coordinating Committee. This would be true particularly for such notions as "participatory democracy" and deep commitments to populist-like orientations. These orientations have been formulated within SDS and SNCC as these organizations have sought to develop a coherent strategy and a framework for establishing priorities. It is an empirical question whether students not directly involved in such organizations articulate similar attitudes. The impressions we have from a preliminary examination of our data suggest that they frequently do not. It is more likely that the student movement is very heterogeneous politically at this point. Most participants share a set of broad orientations, but differ greatly in the degree to which they are oriented toward ideology in general or to particular political positions. The degree of politicization of student activists is probably very much a function of the kinds of peer group and organizational relationships they have had; the underlying disaffection and tendency toward activism, however, is perhaps best understood as being based on more enduring, pre-established values, attitudes and needs.

Social-Psychological Roots of Student Protest: Some Hypotheses

How, then, can we account for the emergence of an obviously dynamic and attractive radical movement among American students in this period? Why should this movement be particularly appealing to youth from upper-status, highly educated families? Why should such youth be particularly concerned with problems of authority, of vocation, of equality, of moral consistency? Why should students in the most advantaged sector of the youth population be disaffected with their own privilege?

It should be stressed that the privileged status of the student protesters and the themes they express in their protest are not *in themselves* unique or surprising. Student movements in developing nations —e.g., Russia, Japan, and Latin America —typically recruit people of elite background; moreover, many of the themes of the "new left" are reminiscent of similar expressions in other student movements (Lipset, 1966). What is unexpected is that these should emerge in the American context at this time.

Earlier theoretical formulations about the social and psychological sources of strain for youth, for example the work of Parsons (1965), Eisenstadt (1956), and Erikson (1959), are important for understanding the emergence of self-conscious oppositional youth cultures and movements. At first glance, these theorists, who tend to see American youth as relatively well-integrated into the larger society, would seem to be unhelpful in providing a framework for explaining the emergence of a radical student movement at the present moment. Nevertheless, in developing our own hypotheses we have drawn freely on their work. What I want to do here is to sketch the notions which have guided our research.

What we have done is to accept the main lines of the argument made by Parsons and Eisenstadt about the social functions of youth cultures and movements. The kernel of their argument is that self-conscious subcultures and movements among adolescents tend to develop when there is a sharp disjunction between the values and expectations embodied in the traditional families in a society and the values and expectations prevailing in the occupational sphere. The greater the disjunction, the more self-conscious and oppositional will be the youth culture (as for example in the situation of rapid transition from a traditional-ascriptive to a bureaucratic-achievement social system).

In modern industrial society, such a disjunction exists as a matter of course, since families are, by definition, particularistic, ascriptive, diffuse, and the occupational sphere is universalistic, impersonal, achievement-oriented, functionally specific. But Parsons, and many others, have suggested that over time the American middle-class family has developed a structure and style which tends to articulate with the occupational sphere; thus, whatever youth culture does emerge in American society is likely to be fairly well-integrated with conventional values, not particularly self-conscious, not rebellious (Parsons, 1965).

The emergence of the student movement, and other expressions of estrangement among youth, leads us to ask whether, in fact, there may be families in the middle class which embody values and expectations which do *not* articulate with those prevailing in the occupational sphere, to look for previously unremarked incompatibilities between trends in the larger social system and trends in family life and early socialization.

The argument we have developed may be sketched as follows:

First, on the macro-structural level we assume that two related trends are of importance: one, the increasing rationalization of student life in high schools and universities, symbolized by the "multiversity," which entails a high degree of impersonality, competitiveness and an increasingly explicit and direct relationship between the university and corporate and governmental bureaucracies; two, the increasing unavailability of coherent careers independent of bureaucratic organizations.

Second, these trends converge, in time, with a particular trend in the development of the family; namely, the emergence of a pattern of familial relations, located most typically in upper middle class, professional homes, having the following elements:

a. a strong emphasis on democratic, egalitarian interpersonal relations
b. a high degree of permissiveness with respect to self-regulation
c. an emphasis on values *other than achievement;* in particular, a stress on the intrinsic worth of living up to intellectual, aesthetic, political, or religious ideals.

Third, young people raised in this kind of family setting, contrary to the expectations of some observers, find it difficult to accommodate to institutional expectations requiring submissiveness to adult authority, respect for established status distinctions, a high degree of competition, and firm regulation of sexual and expressive impulses. They are likely to be particularly sensitized to acts of arbitrary authority, to unexamined expressions of allegiance to conventional values, to instances of institutional practices which conflict with professed ideals. Further, the values embodied in their families are likely to be reinforced by other socializing experiences —for example, summer vacations at progressive children's camps, attendance at experimental private schools, growing up in a community with a high proportion of friends from similar backgrounds. Paralleling these experiences of positive reinforcement, there are likely to be experiences which reinforce a sense of estrangement from peers or conventional society. For instance, many of these young people experience a strong sense of being "different" or "isolated" in school; this sense of distance is often based on the relative uniqueness of their interests and values, their inability to accept conventional norms about appropriate sex-role behavior, and the like. An additional source of strain is generated when these young people perceive a fundamental discrepancy between the values espoused by their parents and the style of life actually practiced by them. This discrepancy is experienced as a feeling of "guilt" over "being middle class" and a perception of "hypocrisy" on the part of parents who express liberal or intellectual values while appearing to their children as acquisitive or self-interested.

Fourth, the incentives operative in the occupational sphere are of limited efficacy for these young people—achievement of status or material advantage is relatively ineffective for an individual who already has high status and affluence by virtue of his family origins. This means, on the one hand, that these students are less oriented toward occupational achievement; on the other hand, the operative sanctions within the school and the larger society are less effective in enforcing conformity.

It seems plausible that this is the first generation in which a substantial number of youth have both the impulse to free themselves from conventional status concerns *and can afford to do so.* In this sense they are a "liberated" generation; affluence has freed them, at least for a period of time, from some of the anxieties and preoccupations which have been the defining features of American middle-class social character.

Fifth, the emergence of the student movement is to be understood in large part as a consequence of opportunities for prolonged interaction available in the university environment. The kinds of personality structures produced by the socializing experiences outlined above need not necessarily have generated a collective response. In fact, Kenneth Keniston's recently published work on alienated students at Harvard suggests that students with similar characteristics to those described here were identifiable on college campuses in the Fifties. But Keniston makes clear that his highly alienated subjects were rarely involved in extensive peer-relationships, and that few opportunities for collective expressions of alienation were then available. The result was that each of his subjects attempted to work out a value-system and a mode of operation on his own (Keniston, 1965b; and this issue).

What seems to have happened was that during the Fifties, there began to emerge an "alienated" student culture, as students with alienated predispositions became visible to each other and began to interact. There was some tendency for these students to identify with the "Beat" style and related forms of bohemianism. Since this involved a high degree of disaffiliation, "cool" non-commitment and social withdrawal, observers tended to interpret this subculture as but a variant of the prevailing privatism of the Fifties. However, a series of precipitating events, most particularly the southern student sit-ins, the revolutionary successes of students in Cuba, Korea, and Turkey, and the suppression of student demonstrations against the House Un-American Activities Committee in San Francisco, suggested to groups of students that direct action was a plausible means for expressing their grievances.

These first stirrings out of apathy were soon enmeshed in a variety of organizations and publicized in several student-organized underground journals—thus enabling the movement to grow and become increasingly institutionalized. The story of the emergence and growth of the movement cannot be developed here; my main point now is that many of its characteristics cannot be understood solely as consequences of the structural and personality variables outlined earlier—in addition, a full understanding of the dynamics of the movement requires a "collective behavior" perspective.

Sixth, organized expressions of youth disaffection are likely to be an increasingly visible and established feature of our society. In important ways, the "new radicalism" is *not* new, but rather a more widespread version of certain subcultural phenomena with a considerable history. During the late 19th and early 20th century a considerable number of young people began to move out of their provincial environments as a consequence of university education; many of these people gathered in such locales as Greenwich Village and created the first visible bohemian subculture in the United States. The Village bohemians and associated young intellectuals shared a common concern with radical politics and, influenced by Freud, Dewey, etc., with the reform of the process of socialization in America— i.e., a restructuring of family and educational institutions (Lash, 1965; Coser, 1965). Although many of the reforms advocated by this group were only partially realized in a formal sense, it seems to be the case that the values and style of life which they advocated have become strongly rooted in American life. This has occurred in at least two ways: first, the subcultures created by the early intellectuals took root, have grown and been emulated in various parts of the country. Second, many of the *ideas* of the early twentieth-century intellectuals, particularly their critique of the bourgeois family and Victorian sensibility, spread rapidly; it now seems that an important defining characteristic of the college-educated mother is her willingness to adopt child-centered techniques of rearing, and of the college-educated couple that they create a family which is democratic and egalitarian in style. In this way, the values that an earlier generation espoused in an abstract way have become embodied as *personality traits* in the new generation—the rootedness of the bohemian and quasi-bohemian subcultures, and the spread of their ideas with the rapid increase in the number of families raising their children with considerable ambivalence about dominant values, incentives and expectations in the society. In this sense, the students who engage in protest or who participate in "alienated" styles of life are often not "converts" to a "deviant" adaptation, but people who have been socialized into a developing cultural tradition. Rising levels of affluence and education are drying up the traditional sources of alienation and radical politics; what we are now becoming aware of, however, is that this same situation is creating new sources of alienation and idealism, and new constituencies for radicalism.

The Youth and Social Change Project

These hypotheses have been the basis for two studies we have undertaken. Study One, begun in the Summer of 1965, involved extensive interviews with samples of student activists and nonactivists and their parents. Study Two, conducted in the Spring of 1966, involved interviews with samples of participants, nonparticipants and opponents of the tumultuous "anti-ranking" sit-in at the University of Chicago.

STUDY ONE—THE SOCIALIZATION OF STUDENT ACTIVISTS   For Study One, fifty students were selected from mailing lists of various peace, civil rights, and student movement organizations in the Chicago

area. An additional fifty students, matched for sex, neighborhood of parents' residence, and type of college attended, were drawn from student directories of Chicago-area colleges. In each case, an attempt was made to interview both parents of the student respondent, as well as the student himself. We were able to interview both parents of 82 of the students; there were two cases in which no parents were available for the interview, in the remaining 16 cases, one parent was interviewed. The interviews with both students and parents averaged about three hours in length, were closely parallel in content, and covered such matters as: political attitudes and participation; attitudes toward the student movement and "youth"; "values," broadly defined; family life, child-rearing, family conflict and other aspects of socialization. Rating scales and "projective" questions were used to assess family members' perceptions of parent-child relationships.

It was clear to us that our sampling procedures were prone to a certain degree of error in the classification of students as "activists" and "nonactivists." Some students who appeared on mailing lists of activist organizations had no substantial involvement in the student movement, while some of our "control" students had a considerable history of such involvement. Thus the data to be reported here are based on an index of activism constructed from interview responses to questions about participation in seven kinds of activity: attendance at rallies, picketing, canvassing, working on a project to help the disadvantaged, being jailed for civil disobedience, working full-time for a social action organization, serving as an officer in such organizations.

STUDY TWO—THE "ANTI-RANKING" SIT-IN   In May, 1966, about five hundred students sat-in at the Administration Building on the campus of the University of Chicago, barring the building to official use for two and a half days. The focal issue of the protest, emulated on a number of other campuses in the succeeding days, was the demand by the students that the University not cooperate with the Selective Service System in supplying class standings for the purpose of assigning student deferments. The students who sat-in formed an organization called "Students Against the Rank" (SAR). During the sit-in, another group of students, calling themselves "Students for a Free Choice" (SFC) circulated a petition opposing the sit-in and supporting the University Administration's view that each student had a right to submit (or withhold) his class standings—the University could not withhold the "rank" of students who requested it. This petition was signed by several hundred students.

Beginning about 10 days after the end of the sit-in, we undertook to interview three samples of students: a random sample of 65 supporters of SAR (the protesters); a random sample of 35 signers of the SFC petition (the anti-protesters); approximately 60 students who constituted the total population of two randomly selected floors in the student dormitories. Of about 160 students thus selected, 117 were finally either interviewed or returned mailed questionnaires. The interview schedule was based largely on items used in the original study; it also included some additional items relevant to the sit-in and the "ranking" controversy.

SOME PRELIMINARY FINDINGS At this writing, our data analysis is at an early stage. In general, however, it is clear that the framework of hypotheses with which we began is substantially supported, and in interesting ways, refined, by the data. Our principal findings thus far include the following:

ACTIVISTS TEND TO COME FROM UPPER-STATUS FAMILIES As indicated earlier, our study of the Chicago sit-in suggests that such actions attract students predominantly from upper-status backgrounds. When compared with students who did not sit-in, and with students who signed the anti-sit-in petition, the sit-in participants reported higher family incomes, higher levels of education for both fathers and mothers, and overwhelmingly perceived themselves to be "upper middle class." One illustrative finding: in our dormitory sample, of 24 students reporting family incomes of above $15,000, half participated in the sit-in. Of 23 students reporting family incomes below $15,000, only two sat-in.

Certain kinds of occupations are particularly characteristic of the parents of sit-in participants. In particular, their fathers tend to be professionals (college faculty, lawyers, doctors) rather than businessmen, white-collar employees or blue-collar workers. Moreover, somewhat unexpectedly, activists' mothers are likely to be employed, and are more likely to have "career" types of employment, than are the mothers of nonactivists.

Also of significance, although not particularly surprising, is the fact that activists are more likely to be Jewish than are nonactivists. (For example, 45% of our SAR sample reported that they were Jewish; only about one-fourth of the nonparticipants were Jewish). Furthermore, a very high proportion of both Jewish and non-Jewish activists report no religious preference for themselves and their parents. Associated with the Jewish ethnicity of a large proportion of our activist samples is the fact the great majority of activists' grandparents were foreign-born. Yet, despite this, data from Study One show that the grandparents of activists tend to be relatively highly educated as compared to the grandparents of nonactivists. Most of the grandparents of nonactivists had not completed high school; nearly half of the grandparents of activists had at least a high school education and fully one-fourth of their maternal grandmothers had attended college. These data suggest that relatively high status characterized the families of activists over several generations; this conclusion is supported by data showing that, unlike nonactivist grandfathers, the grandfathers of activists tended to have white-collar, professional and entrepreneurial occupations rather than blue-collar jobs.

In sum, our data suggest that, at least at major Northern colleges, students involved in protest activity are characteristically from families which are urban, highly educated, Jewish or irreligious, professional and affluent. It is perhaps particularly interesting that many of their mothers are uniquely well-educated and involved in careers, and that high status and education has characterized these families over at least two generations.

Activists are more "radical" than their parents; but activists' parents are decidedly more liberal than others of their status. The demographic data reported above suggests that activists come from high status families, but the occupational, religious and educational characteristics of these families are unique in several important ways. The distinctiveness of these families is especially clear when we examine data from Study One on the political attitudes of students and their parents. In this study, it should be remembered, activist and nonactivist families were roughly equivalent in status, income and education because of our sampling procedures. Our data quite clearly demonstrate that the fathers of activists are disproportionately liberal. For example, whereas forty per cent of the nonactivists' fathers said that they were Republican, only thirteen per cent of the activists' fathers were Republicans. Only six per cent of nonactivists' fathers were willing to describe themselves as "highly liberal" or "socialist," whereas sixty per cent of the activists' fathers accepted such designations. Forty per cent of the nonactivists' fathers described themselves as conservative; none of the activists' fathers endorsed that position.*

In general, differences in the political preferences of the students paralleled these parental differences. The nonactivist sample is only slightly less conservative and Republican than their fathers; all of the activist students with Republican fathers report their own party preferences as either Democrat or independent. Thirty-two per cent of the activists regard themselves as "socialist" as compared with sixteen per cent of their fathers. In general, both nonactivists and their fathers are typically "moderate" in their politics; activists and their fathers tend to be at least "liberal," but a substantial proportion of the activists prefer a more "radical" designation.

A somewhat more detailed picture of comparative political positions emerges when we examine responses of students and their fathers to a series of 6-point scales on which respondents rated their attitudes on such issues as: US bombing of North Vietnam, US troops in the Dominican Republic, student participation in protest demonstrations, civil rights protests involving civil disobedience, Lyndon Johnson, Barry Goldwater, congressional investigations of "un-American activities," full socialization of all industries, socialization of the medical profession.

Table 1 presents data on activists and nonactivists and their fathers with respect to these items. This table suggests, first, wide divergence between the two groups of fathers on most issues, with activists' fathers typically critical of current policies. Although activists' fathers are overwhelmingly "liberal" in their responses, for the most part, activist students tend to endorse "left-wing" positions more strongly and consistently than do their fathers. The items showing strongest divergence between activists and their

---

* For the purposes of this report, "activists" are those students who were in the top third of our activism index; "nonactivists" are those students who were in the bottom third—this latter group reported virtually no participation in any activity associated with the student movement. The "activists" on the other hand had taken part in at least one activity indicating high commitment to the movement (e.g., going to jail, working full-time, serving in a leadership capacity).

Table 1. *Students' and Fathers' Attitudes on Current Issues*

	Activists		Nonactivists	
Issue	*Students*	*Fathers*	*Students*	*Fathers*
Per cent who approve:				
Bombing of North Vietnam	9	27	73	80
American troops in Dominican Republic	6	33	65	50
Student participation in protest demonstrations	100	80	61	37
Civil disobedience in civil rights protests	97	57	28	23
Congressional investigations of "un-American activities"	3	7	73	57
Lyndon Johnson	35	77	81	83
Barry Goldwater	0	7	35	20
Full socialization of industry	62	23	5	10
Socialization of the medical profession	94	43	30	27
N	34	30	37	30

fathers are interesting. Whereas activists overwhelmingly endorse civil disobedience, nearly half of their fathers do not. Whereas fathers of both activists and nonactivists tend to approve of Lyndon Johnson, activist students tend to disapprove of him. Whereas activists' fathers tend to disapprove of "full socialization of industry," this item is endorsed by the majority of activists (although fewer gave an extremely radical response on this item than any other); whereas the vast majority of activists approve of socialized medicine, the majority of their fathers do not. This table provides further support for the view that activists, though more "radical" than their fathers, come predominantly from very liberal homes. The attitudes of nonactivists and their fathers are conventional and supportive of current policies; there is a slight tendency on some items for nonactivist students to endorse more conservative positions than their fathers.

It seems fair to conclude, then, that most students who are involved in the movement (at least those one finds in a city like Chicago) are involved in neither "conversion" from nor "rebellion" against the political perspectives of their fathers. A more supportable view suggests that the great majority of these students are attempting to fulfill and renew the political traditions of their families. However, data from our research which have not yet been analyzed as of this writing, will permit a more systematic analysis of the political orientations of the two generations.

Activism is related to a complex of values, not ostensibly political, shared by both the students and their parents. Data which we have just begun to analyze suggest that the political perspectives which differentiate the families of activists from other families at the same socioeconomic level are part of a more general clustering of values and orientations. Our findings and impressions on this point may be briefly summarized by saying that, whereas nonactivists and their parents tend to express conventional orientations toward achievement, material success, sexual morality and religion, the activists and their parents tend to place greater stress on involvement in intellectual and esthetic pursuits, humanitarian concerns, opportunity for self-expression, and tend to deemphasize or positively disvalue personal achievement, conventional morality and conventional religiosity.

When asked to rank order a list of "areas of life," nonactivist students and their parents typically indicate that marriage, career, and religion are most important. Activists, on the other hand, typically rank these lower than the "world of ideas, art, and music" and "work for national and international betterment"—and so, on the whole, do their parents (see also the relevant data presented by Trent and Craise in this issue).

When asked to indicate their vocational aspirations, nonactivist students are typically firmly decided on a career and typically mention orientations toward the professions, science, and business. Activists, on the other hand, are very frequently undecided on a career; and most typically those who have decided mention college teaching, the arts or social work as aspirations.

These kinds of responses suggest, somewhat crudely, that student activists identify with life goals which are intellectual and "humanitarian" and that they reject conventional and "privatized" goals more frequently than do nonactivist students.

Four Value Patterns

More detailed analyses which we are just beginning to undertake support the view that the value-patterns expressed by activists are highly correlated with those of their parents. This analysis has involved the isolation of a number of value-patterns which emerged in the interview material, the development of systems of code categories related to each of these patterns, and the blind coding of all the interviews with respect to these categories. The kinds of data we are obtaining in this way may be illustrated by describing four of the value patterns we have observed:

ROMANTICISM: ESTHETIC AND EMOTIONAL SENSITIVITY This variable is defined as: "sensitivity to beauty and art—appreciation of painting, literature and music, creativity in art forms—concern with esthetic experience and the development of capacities for esthetic expression—concern with emotions deriving from perception of beauty—attachment of great significance to esthetic experience. More broadly, it can be conceived of as involving explicit concern with experience as such, with feeling and passion, with immediate and inner experience; a concern for the realm of feeling rather than the rational, technological or instrumental side of life; preference for the realm of experience as against that of activity, doing or achieving." Thirteen items were coded in these terms: for each item a score of zero signified no mention of "romanticist" concerns, a score of one signified that such a concern appeared. Table 2 indicates the relationship between "romanticism" and activism. Very few activists received scores on romanticism which placed them as "low"; conversely, there were very few high "romantics" among the nonactivists.

INTELLECTUALISM This variable is defined as: "concern with ideas—desire to realize intellectual capacities—high valuation of intellectual creativities—appreciation of theory and knowledge—participation in intellectual activity (e.g., reading, studying, teaching, writing)—broad intellectual concerns." Ten items were scored for "intellectualism." Almost no activists are low on this variable; almost no nonactivists received a high score.

HUMANITARIANISM This variable is defined as: "concern with plight of others in society; desire to help others—value on compassion and sympathy—desire to alleviate suffering; value on egalitarianism in the sense of opposing privilege based on social and economic distinction; particular sensitivity to the deprived position of the disadvantaged." This variable was coded for ten items; an attempt was made to exclude from this index all items referring directly to participation in social action. As might be expected, "humanitarianism" is strongly related to activism, as evidenced in Table 2.

MORALISM AND SELF-CONTROL This variable is defined as: "concern about the importance of strictly controlling personal impulses—opposition to impulsive or spontaneous behavior —value on keeping tight control over emotions—adherence to conventional authority; adherence to conventional morality—a high degree of moralism about sex, drugs, alcohol, etc.—reliance on a set of external and inflexible rules to govern moral behavior; emphasis on importance of hard work; concern with determination, "stick-to-itiveness"; antagonism toward idleness—value on diligence, entrepreneurship, task orientation, ambition." Twelve items were scored for this variable. As Table 2 suggests, "moralism" is also strongly related to activism; very few activists score high on this variable, while the majority of nonactivists are high scorers.

These values are strongly related to activism. They are also highly intercorrelated, and, most importantly, parent and student scores on these variables are strongly correlated.

These and other value patterns will be used as the basis for studying value transmission in families, generational similarities and differences and several other problems. Our data with respect to them

Table 2. *Scores on Selected Values by Activism (Percentages)*

		Activists	Nonactivists
(a)	*Romanticism*		
	High	35	11
	Medium	47	49
	Low	18	40
(b)	*Intellectualism*		
	High	32	3
	Medium	65	57
	Low	3	40
(c)	*Humanitarianism*		
	High	35	0
	Medium	47	22
	Low	18	78
(d)	*Moralism*		
	High	6	54
	Medium	53	35
	Low	41	11
	N	34	37

Table 3. *Sons and Daughters' Ratings of Parents by Activism (Percentages)*

	Males		Females	
Trait of Parent	Hi Act	Lo Act	Hi Act	Lo Act
mild-stern				
per cent rating mother "mild"	63	44	59	47
per cent rating father "mild"	48	33	48	32
soft-hard				
per cent rating mother "soft"	69	61	60	57
per cent rating father "soft"	50	50	62	51
lenient-severe				
per cent rating mother "lenient"	94	61	66	63
per cent rating father "lenient"	60	44	47	42
easy-strict				
per cent rating mother "easy"	75	50	77	52
per cent rating father "easy"	69	44	47	37
N	23	24	27	26

Table 4.   *Father's Intervention—"If Child Dropped Out of School" (Percentages)*

Degree of Intervention	Activism of Child	
	High	Low
Low	56	37
High	44	63
N	30	30

Table 5.   *Father's Intervention—"If Child Were Living With Member of Opposite Sex" (Percentages)*

Degree of Intervention	Activism of Child	
	High	Low
None	20	14
Mild	50	28
Strong	30	58
N	30	30

provide further support for the view that the unconventionality of activists flows out of and is supported by their family traditions.

Activists' parents are more "permissive" than parents of nonactivists. We have just begun to get some findings bearing on our hypothesis that parents of activists will tend to have been more "permissive" in their child-rearing practices than parents of equivalent status whose children are not oriented toward activism.

One measure of parental permissiveness we have been using is a series of rating scales completed by each member of the family. A series of seven-point bipolar scales was presented in a format similar to that of the "Semantic Differential." Students were asked to indicate "how my mother (father) treated me as a child" on such scales as "warm-cold"; "stern-mild"; "hard-soft"—10 scales in all. Each parent, using the same scales, rated "how my child thinks I treated him."

Table 3 presents data on how sons and daughters rated each of their parents on each of four scales: "mild-stern"; "soft-hard"; "lenient-severe"; and "easy-strict." In general, this table shows that activist

sons and daughters tend to rate their parents as "milder," "more lenient," and "less severe" than do nonactivists. Similar data were obtained using the parents' ratings of themselves.

A different measure of permissiveness is based on the parents' response to a series of "hypothetical situations." Parents were asked, for example, what they would do if their son (daughter) "decided to drop out of school and doesn't know what he really wants to do." Responses to this open-ended question were coded as indicating "high intervention" or "low intervention." Data for fathers on this item are reported in Table 4. Another hypothetical situation presented to the parents was that their child was living with a member of the opposite sex. Responses to this item were coded as "strongly intervene, mildly intervene, not intervene." Data for this item for fathers appears in Table 5. Both tables show that fathers of activists report themselves to be much less interventionist than fathers of nonactivists. Similar results were obtained with mothers, and for other hypothetical situations.

Clearly both types of measures just reported provide support for our hypothesis about the relationship between parental permissiveness and activism. We expect these relationships to be strengthened if "activism" is combined with certain of the value-patterns described earlier.

A Concluding Note

The data reported here constitute a small but representative sampling of the material we have collected in our studies of the student movement. In general, they provide support for the impressions and expectations we had when we undertook this work. Our view of the student movement as an expression of deep discontent felt by certain types of high-status youth as they confront the incongruities between the values represented by the authority and occupational structure of the larger society and the values inculcated by their families and peer culture seems to fit well with the data we have obtained.

A variety of questions remain which, we hope, can be answered, at least in part, by further analyses of our data. Although it is clear that value differences between parents of activists and nonactivists are centrally relevant for understanding value, attitudinal and behavioral cleavages among types of students on the campus, it remains to be determined whether differences in family status, on the one hand, and child-rearing practices, on the other, make an independent contribution to the variance. A second issue has to do with political ideology. First impressions of our data suggest that activists vary considerably with respect to their degree of politicization and their concern with ideological issues. The problem of isolating the key determinants of this variation is one we will be paying close attention to in further analysis of our interview material. Two factors are likely to be of importance here —first, the degree to which the student participates in radical student organizations; second, the political history of his parents.

At least two major issues are not confronted by the research we have been doing. First, we have not examined in any detail the role of campus conditions as a determinant of student discontent. The research reported here emphasizes family socialization and other antecedent experiences as determinants of student protest, and leads to the prediction that students experiencing other patterns of early socialization will be unlikely to be in revolt. This view needs to be counterbalanced by recalling instances of active student unrest on campuses where very few students are likely to have the backgrounds suggested here as critical. Is it possible that there are two components to the student protest movement—one generated to a great extent by early socialization; the second by grievances indigenous to the campus? At any rate, the inter-relationships between personal dispositions and campus conditions need further detailed elucidation.

A second set of questions unanswerable by our research has to do with the future —what lies ahead for the movement as a whole and for the individual young people who participate in it? One direction for the student movement is toward institutionalization as an expression of youth discontent. This outcome, very typical of student movements in many countries, would represent a narrowing of the movement's political and social impact, a way of functionally integrating it into an otherwise stable society. Individual participants would be expected to pass through the movement on their way to eventual absorption, often at an elite level, into the established institutional order. An alternative direction would be toward the development of a full-fledged political "left," with the student movement serving, at least initially, as a nucleus. The potential for this latter development is apparent in recent events. It was the student movement which catalyzed professors and other adults into protest with respect to the Vietnam war. Students for a Democratic Society, the main organizational expression of the student movement, has had, for several years, a program for "community organizing," in which students and ex-students work full-time at the mobilization of constituencies for independent radical political and social action. This SDS program began in poverty areas; it is now beginning to spread to "middle-class" communities. These efforts and others like them, from Berkeley to New Haven, became particularly visible during the 1966 congressional elections, as a wave of "new left" candidates emerged across the country, often supported by large and sophisticated political organizations. Moreover, in addition to attempts at political organizations, SDS, through its "Radical Education Project" has begun to seek the involvement of faculty members, professionals, and other intellectuals for a program of research and education designed to lay the foundations for an intellectually substantial and ideologically developed "new left."

At its convention in September, 1966, SDS approached, but did not finally decide, the question of whether to continue to maintain its character as a campus-based, student organization or to transform itself into a "Movement for a Democratic Society." Characteristically, the young people there assembled amended the organization's constitution so that anyone regardless of status or age could join, while simultaneously they affirmed the student character of the group by projecting a more vigorous program to organize uncommitted students.

The historical significance of the student movement of the Sixties remains to be determined. Its impact on the campus and on the larger society has already been substantial. It is clearly a product of deep discontent in certain significant and rapidly growing segments of the youth population. Whether it becomes an expression of generational discontent, or the forerunner of major political realignments—or simply disintegrates—cannot really be predicted by detached social scientists. The ultimate personal and political meaning of the student movement remains a matter to be determined by those who are involved with it—as participants, as allies, as critics, as enemies.

REFERENCES

AARON, DANIEL. *Writers on the Left.* New York: Avon, 1965.

BELL, DANIEL. *The End of Ideology.* New York: The Free Press, 1962.

BRAUNGART, R. G. "Social Stratification and Political Attitudes." Pennsylvania State University, 1966 (unpublished ms.).

BRONFENBRENNER, U. "The Changing American Child: A Speculative Analysis." *Merrill-Palmer Quarterly,* 7(1961), 73–85.

COSER, LEWIS. *Men of Ideas.* New York: The Free Press, 1965.

ERIKSON, ERIK. "Identity and the Life-Cycle." *Psychological Issues,* 1(1959), 1–171.

ERIKSON, ERIK. *Childhood and Society.* New York: Norton, 1963, pp. 306–325.

EISENSTADT, SHMUEL N. *From Generation to Generation.* Glencoe, Ill.: The Free Press, 1956.

FLACKS, R. "The Liberated Generation." Chicago: University of Chicago, 1966. (mimeo)

GOLDSEN, ROSE; ROSENBERG, MORRIS; WILLIAMS, ROBIN; AND SUCHMAN, EDWARD. *What College Students Think,* Princeton: Van Nostrand, 1960.

JACOB, PHILIP. *Changing Values in College.* New York: Harper, 1957.

KENISTON, KENNETH. *The Uncommitted.* New York: Harcourt Brace, 1965a.

KENISTON, KENNETH. "Social Change and Youth in America," in E. Erikson (ed.), *The Challenge of Youth.* Garden City: Doubleday Anchor, 1965b.

LASCH, CHRISTOPHER. *The New Radicalism in America.* New York: Knopf, 1965.

LIPSET, SEYMOUR. *Political Man, the Social Bases of Politics.* Garden City, N.Y.: Doubleday Anchor, 1960.

LIPSET, SEYMOUR. "University Students and Politics in Underdeveloped Countries." *Comparative Education Review,* 10(1966), 132–162.

LIPSET, SEYMOUR AND ALTBACH, P. "Student Politics and Higher Education in the United States." *Comparative Education Review,* 1966, 10, 320–349.

MILLER, DANIEL AND SWANSON, G. E. *The Changing American Parent.* New York: Wiley, 1958.

NEWCOMB, THEODORE AND FLACKS, R. *Deviant Subcultures on a College Campus.* US Office of Education, 1963.

PARSONS, TALCOTT. "Youth in the Context of American Society," in E. Erikson (ed.), *The Challenge of Youth.* Garden City, N.Y.: Doubleday Anchor, 1965.

SHILS, EDWARD, "The Intellectuals in the Political Development of New States." *World Politics,* 12(1960), 329–368.

STINCHCOMBE, ARTHUR. *Rebellion in a High School.* Chicago: Quadrangle, 1964.

TROW, MARTIN. "Student Cultures and Administrative Action," in Sutherland, R. *et al.* (eds.), *Personality Factors on the College Campus.* Austin: Hogg Foundation for Mental Health, 1962.

VEBLEN, THORNSTEIN. "The Intellectual Pre-eminence of Jews in Modern Europe," in B. Rosenberg (ed.), *Thorstein Veblen.* New York: Crowell, 1963.

SUGGESTIONS FOR FURTHER READING
on *Social Change*

Demographic Trends

BOGUE, DONALD J. *The Population of the United States*. New York: Free Press, 1969. A reference book with interpretations of demographic patterns.

DAY, LINCOLN, and ALICE DAY. *Too Many Americans*. Boston: Riverside, 1964. An examination of population pressures in the United States.

FREEDMAN, RONALD, ed. *Population: The Vital Revolution*. Garden City: Doubleday, 1964. Essays on contemporary demographic problems.

THOMLINSON, RALPH. *Population Dynamics*. New York: Random House, 1965: An introduction to the study of population.

WRONG, DENNIS. *Population and Society*. New York: Random House, revised and enlarged, 1967. Key concepts and problems in demographic analysis are outlined and discussed.

Cultural Moods and Social Movements

Daedalus, "Students and Politics," Winter, 1968. A special issue.

FESTINGER, LEON, H. W. RIECKEN, and S. SCHACHTER. *When Prophecy Fails*. Minneapolis: University of Minnesota Press, 1956. An empirical study of a group who awaited a prophetic flood and the aftermath of their experience.

HOFFER, ERIC. *The True Believer*. New York: New American Library, 1958. Essays on the nature of mass movements.

KING, C. WENDELL. *Social Movements in the United States*. New York: Random House, 1956. An introduction to the study of social movements.

LIPSET, SEYMOUR MARTIN, and SHELDON S. WOLIN, eds. *The Berkeley Student Revolt*. Garden City, N.Y.: Doubleday, 1965. A collection of articles on the many sides of the "Free Speech Movement" at the University of California in 1964–1965.

MASCHMANN, MELITA. *Account Rendered* (translated by G. Strachan). New York: Abelard-Schuman, 1965. An autobiographical account by a young woman who became a Nazi youth leader during World War II.

SMELSER, NEIL J. *Theory of Collective Behavior*. New York: Free Press, 1963. A systematic approach to the study of social movements.

Today . . . And Tomorrow

DEUTSCH, STEVEN, and J. HOWARD. *Where It's At*. New York: Harper and Row, 1970. A collection of readings on the radical perspective on modern society.

EISEN, JONATHAN. *The Age of Rock*. New York: Vintage, 1969. Essays on the new music; the people who make it and the ones who listen.

GOODMAN, PAUL. *Growing Up Absurd*. New York: Random House, 1960. An early statement by one who suggested alternatives to most modern American lifeways.

KATOPE, CHRISTOPHER G., and PAUL G. ZOLBROD. *Beyond Berkeley*. New York: Harper and Row, 1970. A source book on student values and politics.

KEIL, CHARLES. *Urban Blues*. New York: William Morrow, 1963. A study of Negro music in white America.

KILLIAN, LEWIS M. *The Impossible Revolution?* New York: Random House, 1968. A highly informative study of the civil rights movement and some thoughts on the future.

OPPENHIMER, MARTIN. *The Urban Guerilla.* New York: Qaudrangle Books, 1969. A study of violent political protest.

WOLFE, TOM. *The Kandy-Kolored, Tangerine-Flake Streamline Baby.* New York: Farrar, Straus and Giroux, 1965. Essays on America in the 1960s.

INDEX